State Rankings 2020

State Rankings 2020

A Statistical View of America

Editors

Kathleen O'Leary Morgan
and
Scott Morgan

FOR INFORMATION:

CQ Press
An Imprint of SAGE Publications, Inc.
2455 Teller Road
Thousand Oaks, California 91320
E-mail: order@sagepub.com

SAGE Publications Ltd.
1 Oliver's Yard
55 City Road
London EC1Y 1SP
United Kingdom

SAGE Publications India Pvt. Ltd.
B 1/I 1 Mohan Cooperative Industrial Area
Mathura Road, New Delhi 110 044
India

SAGE Publications Asia-Pacific Pte. Ltd.
18 Cross Street #10-10/11/12
China Square Central
Singapore 048423

ISBN 978-1-5443-9129-8 (hardcover)
ISBN 978-1-5443-9130-4 (paper)
ISSN 1057-3623

Senior Acquisitions Editor:	Andrew Boney
Associate Editor:	Diana Aleman
Editorial Assistant:	Tamara Tanso
Production Editor:	Natasha Tiwari
Proofreader:	Tricia Currie-Knight
Cover Designer:	Candice Harman

20 21 22 23 24 10 9 8 7 6 5 4 3 2 1

Contents

Detailed Table of Contents

XIV. SOCIAL WELFARE   517

XV. TRANSPORTATION   557

Introduction and Methodology

State Rankings 2020 provides an easily accessible collection of data in a broad range of quality of life factors in the United States. In this latest 2020 edition, *State Rankings* compares data from the fifty states and the District of Columbia in 566 tables in the following fifteen different livability categories: agriculture, crime and law enforcement, defense, economy, education, employment and labor, energy and environment, geography, federal government finances, state and local government finances, health, households and housing, population, social welfare, and transportation.

Purpose of This Book

State Rankings 2020 translates complicated and often convoluted statistics into meaningful, easy-to-understand information. Too often there is an abundance of data but far too little information putting those data into context. This book allows researchers, legislators, policy analysts, journalists, and the general public to access information in a manner that not only provides basic facts about a state's quality of life but also gives a meaningful framework by comparing individual states against the rest of the country.

These data and rankings can be used in a variety of ways, by a variety of audiences, including the following examples:

- Policy makers can use the data to help identify areas warranting further study.

- Journalists can easily find impartial state information that puts stories into context.

- The general public can see how a particular state is faring compared to other states.

- Librarians can use the data as a quick reference to assist patrons in research and offer the sources and websites included as a starting point for finding other related data.

The comparison rankings in *State Rankings 2020* provide an annual snapshot of how the states are doing in the fifteen livability categories mentioned above. There are two principle approaches to using these rankings. The first is to examine how a state is doing compared to all other states via the comparison rankings in this book. The second approach is to compare a state to itself over a given period of time. Both approaches are important to achieving a good understanding of how and whether a state is making progress. It is important to keep in mind that the rankings are not a definitive determination of which state is the "best." However, since so many issues are surrounded by emotions, tracking them by the numbers can help bring the discussion back to a more balanced, unbiased review that in the end leads to better decisions.

Data and Limitations

The data featured in *State Rankings 2020* were chosen specifically by the editors from a variety of government and private sector sources. The statistics presented are intended to cover a broad array of quality-of-life subject areas, giving users of the book a solid collection of state information.

Nonetheless, the statistics are not inclusive of all the possible data that might be available. The statistics in the book are the latest available from the sources. In a few cases, we have retained tables that have not been updated for several years because we believe our readers will find the data relevant, even if updates are not available. In other cases, we replaced obsolete data with new tables. Longtime users should note in particular that we have updated Government Finances: Federal with new government spending data from the OMB's USASpending.gov, but differences in methodology make those data difficult to compare with past editions.

Previous editions of the book have used the term *most livable* when describing states with the highest livability ranking. This term is no longer being used because it is purely descriptive—at no time do we attempt to explain *why* a particular state is ranking higher or lower in livability factors than others or against the national average. This explanation—currently sought by social science researchers—is beyond the scope of this book. While our selection of factors clearly affects the rankings, we believe the rankings provide a solid measurement of how the fifty states and Washington, D.C., are faring with regard to quality of life in the United States. Researchers, practitioners, and others can confidently use the data to understand livability issues and guide policy decisions.

Methodology

The comparison rankings for *State Rankings 2020* are determined using the same methodology as we have used for the past twenty-plus years. The editors used the previously mentioned fifteen livability categories to select forty-three quality-of-life factors from a broad range of economic, educational, health-oriented, public safety, and environmental statistics. Overall comparison rankings were determined by averaging each state's ranking for each category. The scale is 1 to 50; the higher the number, the higher the state is in the rankings (i.e., 50 is the best score to receive). Data used are for the most recent year for which comparable numbers are available from most states. All factors are given equal weight.

While the 566 tables provided in *State Rankings 2020* are ranked highest to lowest without any subjective determination as to whether a subject is "positive" or "negative," for the state comparison rankings, the editors do make a subjective determination as to whether something is "positive" or "negative." Twenty-five of the forty-three factors were determined to be negative, and the remaining eighteen were viewed as positive.

The reason for this division between positive and negative is that if a state ranks first in crime rate (i.e., it has the highest crime rate), its comparison ranking is reduced. Whereas if a state ranks first in per-capita personal income (i.e., it has the highest income), its comparison ranking is increased. To account for this, we subtract the rankings for the positive factors from 51 so that a state with the highest ranking in a positive factor ends up with a 50 for that factor (remember, high numbers are best).

Once we have chosen the factors and divided them into positive and negative groupings, we simply average the ranking for each state in all forty-three factors. If a state is missing data for a given factor, its standing is based on the average ranking for the remaining factors. The book uses the latest available data for each livability factor.

As an example, Maine ranks 48th in crime rate (negative factor), 47th in personal bankruptcy rate (negative factor), and ranks 7th in percent of population graduated from high school (positive factor). The 48th and 47th rankings go straight into the comparison formula, whereas the number 7 ranking in percent of population graduated from high school is first subtracted from 51 with the resulting 44 going into the ranking. For these three factors for Maine, we would average 48, 47, and 44 with the result being 46.33. If these three factors were the only ones we used, then the resulting average of 46.33 would be the figure we would use to compare Maine to the other forty-nine states. However, for the *State Rankings* comparison rankings, an additional forty factors are added into the calculations before the final results are determined.

Designed with the researcher in mind, the numbers shown in *State Rankings* require no additional calculations to convert them from millions, thousands, etc. All states are ranked on a high-to-low basis, with any ties among the states listed alphabetically for a given ranking. Negative numbers are shown in parentheses. For tables displaying national totals (as opposed to rates, per capita, etc.), a separate column is included that shows what percent of the national total each individual state's total represents. This column is headed by "% of USA." This percentage figure is particularly interesting when compared with a state's population in a given year. Rates may be per 10,000 persons, per 100,000 persons, or per some other denominator; these are clearly explained by the text following the national rate and, if necessary, the footnotes.

To further assist readers, source information and footnotes clearly are shown at the bottom of each page, while national totals, rates, and percentages are prominently displayed at the top of each table. Every other line is shaded in gray for easier reading. Numerous information-finding tools are provided: a thorough table of contents, table listings at the beginning of each chapter, and a detailed index. In addition, a roster of sources with addresses, phone numbers, and websites is found in the back of the book.

About the Editors

Kathleen O'Leary Morgan and **Scott Morgan** founded Morgan Quitno Press in 1990. They edited more than 2,700 annual state and city statistical reference publications before selling the titles to CQ Press in 2007. They also edited a monthly journal, State Statistical Trends, for six years. They have continued to edit a number of the publications continued by CQ Press, as well as an ever-growing online database.

Kathleen received a BS and a master's in public administration from the University of Kansas. She served in a number of media and legislative positions within the U.S. Department of Transportation, where she also served as deputy director of congressional affairs.

Scott received both a BS and a law degree from the University of Kansas. He previously worked on the staffs of two U.S. senators as well as the Senate Judiciary Committee. He represented the Senate on the Federal Election Commission and served as Chief Counsel for Senator Bob Dole's presidential campaign in 1988. He was Chief Counsel for Governor Mike Hayden in Kansas until 1990.

The 2020 State Rankings

ALPHA ORDER

ALPHA ORDER

RANK	STATE	AVG	19 RANK	CHANGE
44	Alabama	20.26	45	1
36	Alaska	22.49	37	1
38	Arizona	22.40	41	3
48	Arkansas	17.98	44	-4
19	California	26.21	25	6
11	Colorado	29.98	7	-4
8	Connecticut	30.86	11	3
22	Delaware	25.51	23	1
26	Florida	25.07	33	7
34	Georgia	23.12	38	4
23	Hawaii	25.30	20	-3
21	Idaho	26.05	22	1
25	Illinois	25.09	31	6
37	Indiana	22.44	30	-7
7	Iowa	30.93	11	4
16	Kansas	27.93	19	3
46	Kentucky	18.77	47	1
50	Louisiana	15.16	50	0
12	Maine	29.88	9	-3
15	Maryland	28.16	17	2
3	Massachusetts	32.58	4	1
32	Michigan	23.98	29	-3
4	Minnesota	32.37	3	-1
49	Mississippi	15.60	49	0
33	Missouri	23.84	36	3
27	Montana	25.02	27	0
9	Nebraska	30.47	13	4
39	Nevada	22.05	39	0
1	New Hampshire	35.21	1	0
6	New Jersey	31.93	6	0
47	New Mexico	18.49	48	1
30	New York	24.63	21	-9
41	North Carolina	21.55	34	-7
10	North Dakota	30.30	16	6
35	Ohio	22.58	34	-1
45	Oklahoma	19.65	40	-5
28	Oregon	24.95	28	0
24	Pennsylvania	25.23	26	2
31	Rhode Island	24.21	24	-7
40	South Carolina	21.79	43	3
20	South Dakota	26.07	18	-2
42	Tennessee	20.93	42	0
29	Texas	24.74	32	3
2	Utah	34.86	2	0
5	Vermont	32.00	5	0
18	Virginia	27.51	15	-3
14	Washington	29.51	10	-4
43	West Virginia	20.37	46	3
17	Wisconsin	27.79	14	-3
13	Wyoming	29.53	8	-5

RANK ORDER

RANK	STATE	AVG	19 RANK	CHANGE
1	New Hampshire	35.21	1	0
2	Utah	34.86	2	0
3	Massachusetts	32.58	4	1
4	Minnesota	32.37	3	-1
5	Vermont	32.00	5	0
6	New Jersey	31.93	6	0
7	Iowa	30.93	11	4
8	Connecticut	30.86	11	3
9	Nebraska	30.47	13	4
10	North Dakota	30.30	16	6
11	Colorado	29.98	7	-4
12	Maine	29.88	9	-3
13	Wyoming	29.53	8	-5
14	Washington	29.51	10	-4
15	Maryland	28.16	17	2
16	Kansas	27.93	19	3
17	Wisconsin	27.79	14	-3
18	Virginia	27.51	15	-3
19	California	26.21	25	6
20	South Dakota	26.07	18	-2
21	Idaho	26.05	22	1
22	Delaware	25.51	23	1
23	Hawaii	25.30	20	-3
24	Pennsylvania	25.23	26	2
25	Illinois	25.09	31	6
26	Florida	25.07	33	7
27	Montana	25.02	27	0
28	Oregon	24.95	28	0
29	Texas	24.74	32	3
30	New York	24.63	21	-9
31	Rhode Island	24.21	24	-7
32	Michigan	23.98	29	-3
33	Missouri	23.84	36	3
34	Georgia	23.12	38	4
35	Ohio	22.58	34	-1
36	Alaska	22.49	37	1
37	Indiana	22.44	30	-7
38	Arizona	22.40	41	3
39	Nevada	22.05	39	0
40	South Carolina	21.79	43	3
41	North Carolina	21.55	34	-7
42	Tennessee	20.93	42	0
43	West Virginia	20.37	46	3
44	Alabama	20.26	45	1
45	Oklahoma	19.65	40	-5
46	Kentucky	18.77	47	1
47	New Mexico	18.49	48	1
48	Arkansas	17.98	44	-4
49	Mississippi	15.60	49	0
50	Louisiana	15.16	50	0

Date Each State Admitted to Statehood*

ALPHA ORDER

RANK	STATE	DATE OF ADMISSION
22	Alabama	December 14, 1819
49	Alaska	January 3, 1959
48	Arizona	February 14, 1912
25	Arkansas	June 15, 1836
31	California	September 9, 1850
38	Colorado	August 1, 1876
5	Connecticut	January 9, 1788
1	Delaware	December 7, 1787
27	Florida	March 3, 1845
4	Georgia	January 2, 1788
50	Hawaii	August 21, 1959
43	Idaho	July 3, 1890
21	Illinois	December 3, 1818
19	Indiana	December 11, 1816
29	Iowa	December 28, 1846
34	Kansas	January 29, 1861
15	Kentucky	June 1, 1792
18	Louisiana	April 30, 1812
23	Maine	March 15, 1820
7	Maryland	April 28, 1788
6	Massachusetts	February 6, 1788
26	Michigan	January 26, 1837
32	Minnesota	May 11, 1858
20	Mississippi	December 10, 1817
24	Missouri	August 10, 1821
41	Montana	November 8, 1889
37	Nebraska	March 1, 1867
36	Nevada	October 31, 1864
9	New Hampshire	June 21, 1788
3	New Jersey	December 18, 1787
47	New Mexico	January 6, 1912
11	New York	July 26, 1788
12	North Carolina	November 21, 1789
39	North Dakota	November 2, 1889
17	Ohio	March 1, 1803
46	Oklahoma	November 16, 1907
33	Oregon	February 14, 1859
2	Pennsylvania	December 12, 1787
13	Rhode Island	May 29, 1790
8	South Carolina	May 23, 1788
39	South Dakota	November 2, 1889
16	Tennessee	June 1, 1796
28	Texas	December 29, 1845
45	Utah	January 4, 1896
14	Vermont	March 4, 1791
10	Virginia	June 26, 1788
42	Washington	November 11, 1889
35	West Virginia	June 20, 1863
30	Wisconsin	May 29, 1848
44	Wyoming	July 10, 1890

RANK ORDER

RANK	STATE	DATE OF ADMISSION
1	Delaware	December 7, 1787
2	Pennsylvania	December 12, 1787
3	New Jersey	December 18, 1787
4	Georgia	January 2, 1788
5	Connecticut	January 9, 1788
6	Massachusetts	February 6, 1788
7	Maryland	April 28, 1788
8	South Carolina	May 23, 1788
9	New Hampshire	June 21, 1788
10	Virginia	June 26, 1788
11	New York	July 26, 1788
12	North Carolina	November 21, 1789
13	Rhode Island	May 29, 1790
14	Vermont	March 4, 1791
15	Kentucky	June 1, 1792
16	Tennessee	June 1, 1796
17	Ohio	March 1, 1803
18	Louisiana	April 30, 1812
19	Indiana	December 11, 1816
20	Mississippi	December 10, 1817
21	Illinois	December 3, 1818
22	Alabama	December 14, 1819
23	Maine	March 15, 1820
24	Missouri	August 10, 1821
25	Arkansas	June 15, 1836
26	Michigan	January 26, 1837
27	Florida	March 3, 1845
28	Texas	December 29, 1845
29	Iowa	December 28, 1846
30	Wisconsin	May 29, 1848
31	California	September 9, 1850
32	Minnesota	May 11, 1858
33	Oregon	February 14, 1859
34	Kansas	January 29, 1861
35	West Virginia	June 20, 1863
36	Nevada	October 31, 1864
37	Nebraska	March 1, 1867
38	Colorado	August 1, 1876
39	North Dakota	November 2, 1889
39	South Dakota	November 2, 1889
41	Montana	November 8, 1889
42	Washington	November 11, 1889
43	Idaho	July 3, 1890
44	Wyoming	July 10, 1890
45	Utah	January 4, 1896
46	Oklahoma	November 16, 1907
47	New Mexico	January 6, 1912
48	Arizona	February 14, 1912
49	Alaska	January 3, 1959
50	Hawaii	August 21, 1959

Source: U.S. Bureau of the Census
"1980 Census of Population" (vol. 1, part A, PC80-1-A)
*First thirteen states show date of ratification of Constitution.

STATE FAST FACTS

STATE	NICKNAME	CAPITAL	POPULATION*	AREA**
Alabama	Heart of Dixie	Montgomery	4,903,185	52,420
Alaska	The Last Frontier	Juneau	731,545	665,384
Arizona	Grand Canyon State	Phoenix	7,278,717	113,990
Arkansas	The Natural State	Little Rock	3,017,804	53,179
California	Golden State	Sacramento	39,512,223	163,695
Colorado	Centennial State	Denver	5,758,736	104,094
Connecticut	Constitution State	Hartford	3,565,287	5,543
Delaware	First State	Dover	973,764	2,489
Florida	Sunshine State	Tallahassee	21,477,737	65,758
Georgia	Peach State	Atlanta	10,617,423	59,425
Hawaii	Aloha State	Honolulu	1,415,872	10,932
Idaho	Gem State	Boise	1,787,065	83,569
Illinois	Land of Lincoln	Springfield	12,671,821	57,914
Indiana	Hoosier State	Indianapolis	6,732,219	36,420
Iowa	Hawkeye State	Des Moines	3,155,070	56,273
Kansas	Sunflower State	Topeka	2,913,314	82,278
Kentucky	Bluegrass State	Frankfort	4,467,673	40,408
Louisiana	Pelican State	Baton Rouge	4,648,794	52,378
Maine	Pine Tree State	Augusta	1,344,212	35,380
Maryland	Free State	Annapolis	6,045,680	12,406
Massachusetts	Bay State	Boston	6,892,503	10,554
Michigan	Great Lake State	Lansing	9,986,857	96,714
Minnesota	North Star State	St. Paul	5,639,632	86,936
Mississippi	Magnolia State	Jackson	2,976,149	48,432
Missouri	Show Me State	Jefferson City	6,137,428	69,707
Montana	Treasure State	Helena	1,068,778	147,040
Nebraska	Cornhusker State	Lincoln	1,934,408	77,348
Nevada	Silver State	Carson City	3,080,156	110,572
New Hampshire	Granite State	Concord	1,359,711	9,349
New Jersey	Garden State	Trenton	8,882,190	8,723
New Mexico	Land of Enchantment	Santa Fe	2,096,829	121,590
New York	Empire State	Albany	19,453,561	54,555
North Carolina	Tar Heel State	Raleigh	10,488,084	53,819
North Dakota	Peace Garden State	Bismarck	762,062	70,698
Ohio	Buckeye State	Columbus	11,689,100	44,826
Oklahoma	Sooner State	Oklahoma City	3,956,971	69,899
Oregon	Beaver State	Salem	4,217,737	98,379
Pennsylvania	Keystone State	Harrisburg	12,801,989	46,054
Rhode Island	Ocean State	Providence	1,059,361	1,545
South Carolina	Palmetto State	Columbia	5,148,714	32,020
South Dakota	Mount Rushmore State	Pierre	884,659	77,116
Tennessee	Volunteer State	Nashville	6,829,174	42,144
Texas	Lone Star State	Austin	28,995,881	268,596
Utah	Beehive State	Salt Lake City	3,205,958	84,897
Vermont	Green Mountain State	Montpelier	623,989	9,616
Virginia	Old Dominion	Richmond	8,535,519	42,775
Washington	Evergreen State	Olympia	7,614,893	71,298
West Virginia	Mountain State	Charleston	1,792,147	24,230
Wisconsin	Badger State	Madison	5,822,434	65,496
Wyoming	Equality State	Cheyenne	578,759	97,813

*U.S. Bureau of the Census, "Population Estimates" (December 2019, https://www.census.gov/programs-surveys/popest.html)
**Total of land and water area in square miles.

STATE SONG	STATE FLOWER	STATE TREE	STATE BIRD
Alabama	Camellia	Southern Pine	Yellowhammer
Alaska's Flag	Forget-Me-Not	Sitka Spruce	Willow Ptarmigan
Arizona	Saguaro Cactus Blossom	Palo Verde	Cactus Wren
Arkansas	Apple Blossom	Pine	Mockingbird
I Love You, California	Golden Poppy	California Redwood	California Valley Quail
Where the Columbines Grow	Rocky Mountain Columbine	Colorado Blue Spruce	Lark Bunting
Yankee Doodle Dandy	Mountain Laurel	White Oak	American Robin
Our Delaware	Peach Blossom	American Holly	Blue Hen Chicken
Swanee River	Orange Blossom	Sabal Palmetto Palm	Mockingbird
Georgia On My Mind	Cherokee Rose	Live Oak	Brown Thrasher
Hawaii Ponoi	Yellow Hibiscus	Candlenut	Nene
Here We Have Idaho	Syringa	White Pine	Mountain Bluebird
Illinois	Purple Violet	White Oak	Cardinal
On the Banks of the Wabash, Far Away	Peony	Tulip Poplar	Cardinal
The Song of Iowa	Wild Rose	Oak	Eastern Goldfinch
Home on the Range	Sunflower	Cottonwood	Western Meadowlark
My Old Kentucky Home	Goldenrod	Tulip Tree	Cardinal
Give Me Louisiana	Magnolia	Cypress	Eastern Brown Pelican
State of Maine Song	White Pine Cone and Tassel	Eastern White Pine	Chickadee
Maryland, My Maryland	Black-eyed Susan	White Oak	Baltimore Oriole
All Hail to Massachusetts	Mayflower	American Elm	Chickadee
Michigan, My Michigan	Apple Blossom	White Pine	Robin
Hail! Minnesota	Pink and White Lady's Slipper	Red Pine	Common Loon
Go, Mississippi!	Magnolia	Magnolia	Mockingbird
Missouri Waltz	Hawthorn	Dogwood	Bluebird
Montana	Bitterroot	Ponderosa Pine	Western Meadowlark
Beautiful Nebraska	Goldenrod	Cottonwood	Western Meadowlark
Home Means Nevada	Sagebrush	Single-Leaf Pinon	Mountain Bluebird
Old New Hampshire	Purple Lilac	White Birch	Purple Finch
Ode to New Jersey	Purple Violet	Red Oak	Eastern Goldfinch
O Fair New Mexico	Yucca	Pinon	Roadrunner
I Love New York	Rose	Sugar Maple	Bluebird
The Old North State	Dogwood	Pine	Cardinal
North Dakota Hymn	Wild Prairie Rose	American Elm	Western Meadowlark
Beautiful Ohio	Scarlet Carnation	Buckeye	Cardinal
Oklahoma!	Mistletoe	Redbud	Scissortailed Flycatcher
Oregon, My Oregon	Oregon Grape	Douglas Fir	Western Meadowlark
Hail! Pennsylvania	Mountain Laurel	Hemlock	Ruffed Grouse
Rhode Island	Violet	Red Maple	Rhode Island Red
Carolina	Yellow Jessamine	Palmetto	Carolina Wren
Hail, South Dakota	Pasque Flower	Black Hills Spruce	Ringnecked Pheasant
The Tennessee Waltz	Iris	Tulip Poplar	Mockingbird
Texas, Our Texas	Bluebonnet	Pecan	Mockingbird
Utah, We Love Thee	Sego Lily	Blue Spruce	Seagull
Hail, Vermont	Red Clover	Sugar Maple	Hermit Thrush
Carry Me Back to Old Virginia	Dogwood	Dogwood	Cardinal
Washington, My Home	Western Rhododendron	Western Hemlock	Willow Goldfinch
The West Virginia Hills; This Is My West Virginia; and West Virginia, My Home, Sweet Home	Big Rhododendron	Sugar Maple	Cardinal
On Wisconsin!	Wood Violet	Sugar Maple	Robin
Wyoming	Indian Paintbrush	Cottonwood	Meadowlark

I. Agriculture

Number of Farms in 2018

National Total = 2,029,200 Farms*

ALPHA ORDER

RANK	STATE	FARMS	% of USA
22	Alabama	39,700	2.0%
50	Alaska	1,000	0.0%
36	Arizona	19,200	0.9%
19	Arkansas	42,500	2.1%
9	California	69,400	3.4%
23	Colorado	38,900	1.9%
45	Connecticut	5,500	0.3%
48	Delaware	2,300	0.1%
15	Florida	47,500	2.3%
21	Georgia	41,600	2.1%
42	Hawaii	7,300	0.4%
32	Idaho	24,800	1.2%
7	Illinois	72,000	3.5%
13	Indiana	56,100	2.8%
3	Iowa	86,000	4.2%
12	Kansas	58,900	2.9%
6	Kentucky	75,100	3.7%
29	Louisiana	27,400	1.4%
41	Maine	7,600	0.4%
38	Maryland	12,400	0.6%
43	Massachusetts	7,200	0.4%
16	Michigan	47,000	2.3%
10	Minnesota	68,500	3.4%
26	Mississippi	34,700	1.7%
2	Missouri	95,000	4.7%
30	Montana	26,900	1.3%
18	Nebraska	45,900	2.3%
47	Nevada	3,400	0.2%
46	New Hampshire	4,100	0.2%
40	New Jersey	9,900	0.5%
33	New Mexico	24,700	1.2%
27	New York	33,400	1.6%
17	North Carolina	46,400	2.3%
31	North Dakota	26,100	1.3%
4	Ohio	77,800	3.8%
5	Oklahoma	77,300	3.8%
24	Oregon	37,200	1.8%
14	Pennsylvania	53,000	2.6%
49	Rhode Island	1,100	0.1%
34	South Carolina	24,600	1.2%
28	South Dakota	29,600	1.5%
8	Tennessee	70,000	3.4%
1	Texas	247,000	12.2%
37	Utah	18,100	0.9%
44	Vermont	6,800	0.3%
19	Virginia	42,500	2.1%
25	Washington	35,700	1.8%
35	West Virginia	23,400	1.2%
11	Wisconsin	64,800	3.2%
39	Wyoming	11,900	0.6%

RANK ORDER

RANK	STATE	FARMS	% of USA
1	Texas	247,000	12.2%
2	Missouri	95,000	4.7%
3	Iowa	86,000	4.2%
4	Ohio	77,800	3.8%
5	Oklahoma	77,300	3.8%
6	Kentucky	75,100	3.7%
7	Illinois	72,000	3.5%
8	Tennessee	70,000	3.4%
9	California	69,400	3.4%
10	Minnesota	68,500	3.4%
11	Wisconsin	64,800	3.2%
12	Kansas	58,900	2.9%
13	Indiana	56,100	2.8%
14	Pennsylvania	53,000	2.6%
15	Florida	47,500	2.3%
16	Michigan	47,000	2.3%
17	North Carolina	46,400	2.3%
18	Nebraska	45,900	2.3%
19	Arkansas	42,500	2.1%
19	Virginia	42,500	2.1%
21	Georgia	41,600	2.1%
22	Alabama	39,700	2.0%
23	Colorado	38,900	1.9%
24	Oregon	37,200	1.8%
25	Washington	35,700	1.8%
26	Mississippi	34,700	1.7%
27	New York	33,400	1.6%
28	South Dakota	29,600	1.5%
29	Louisiana	27,400	1.4%
30	Montana	26,900	1.3%
31	North Dakota	26,100	1.3%
32	Idaho	24,800	1.2%
33	New Mexico	24,700	1.2%
34	South Carolina	24,600	1.2%
35	West Virginia	23,400	1.2%
36	Arizona	19,200	0.9%
37	Utah	18,100	0.9%
38	Maryland	12,400	0.6%
39	Wyoming	11,900	0.6%
40	New Jersey	9,900	0.5%
41	Maine	7,600	0.4%
42	Hawaii	7,300	0.4%
43	Massachusetts	7,200	0.4%
44	Vermont	6,800	0.3%
45	Connecticut	5,500	0.3%
46	New Hampshire	4,100	0.2%
47	Nevada	3,400	0.2%
48	Delaware	2,300	0.1%
49	Rhode Island	1,100	0.1%
50	Alaska	1,000	0.0%
	District of Columbia	0	0.0%

Source: U.S. Department of Agriculture, National Agricultural Statistics Service
"Farms and Land in Farms" (https://usda.library.cornell.edu/concern/publications/5712m6524)
*A farm is any establishment from which $1,000 or more of agricultural products were sold or would normally be sold during the year. This includes places with five or more horses, except horses in boarding stables or racetracks.

Land in Farms in 2018

National Total = 899,500,000 Acres*

	ALPHA ORDER					RANK ORDER		
RANK	STATE	ACRES	% of USA		RANK	STATE	ACRES	% of USA
31	Alabama	8,500,000	0.9%		1	Texas	127,000,000	14.1%
44	Alaska	850,000	0.1%		2	Montana	58,000,000	6.4%
14	Arizona	26,200,000	2.9%		3	Kansas	45,800,000	5.1%
21	Arkansas	13,900,000	1.5%		4	Nebraska	45,000,000	5.0%
16	California	24,300,000	2.7%		5	South Dakota	43,200,000	4.8%
9	Colorado	31,800,000	3.5%		6	New Mexico	40,500,000	4.5%
49	Connecticut	380,000	0.0%		7	North Dakota	39,300,000	4.4%
46	Delaware	530,000	0.1%		8	Oklahoma	34,200,000	3.8%
30	Florida	9,700,000	1.1%		9	Colorado	31,800,000	3.5%
28	Georgia	10,100,000	1.1%		10	Iowa	30,600,000	3.4%
43	Hawaii	1,100,000	0.1%		11	Wyoming	29,000,000	3.2%
24	Idaho	11,600,000	1.3%		12	Missouri	27,700,000	3.1%
13	Illinois	27,000,000	3.0%		13	Illinois	27,000,000	3.0%
18	Indiana	15,000,000	1.7%		14	Arizona	26,200,000	2.9%
10	Iowa	30,600,000	3.4%		15	Minnesota	25,500,000	2.8%
3	Kansas	45,800,000	5.1%		16	California	24,300,000	2.7%
23	Kentucky	12,900,000	1.4%		17	Oregon	16,000,000	1.8%
33	Louisiana	8,000,000	0.9%		18	Indiana	15,000,000	1.7%
41	Maine	1,300,000	0.1%		19	Washington	14,700,000	1.6%
40	Maryland	2,000,000	0.2%		20	Wisconsin	14,300,000	1.6%
47	Massachusetts	500,000	0.1%		21	Arkansas	13,900,000	1.5%
29	Michigan	9,800,000	1.1%		21	Ohio	13,900,000	1.5%
15	Minnesota	25,500,000	2.8%		23	Kentucky	12,900,000	1.4%
27	Mississippi	10,400,000	1.2%		24	Idaho	11,600,000	1.3%
12	Missouri	27,700,000	3.1%		25	Tennessee	10,900,000	1.2%
2	Montana	58,000,000	6.4%		26	Utah	10,700,000	1.2%
4	Nebraska	45,000,000	5.0%		27	Mississippi	10,400,000	1.2%
37	Nevada	6,100,000	0.7%		28	Georgia	10,100,000	1.1%
48	New Hampshire	430,000	0.0%		29	Michigan	9,800,000	1.1%
45	New Jersey	750,000	0.1%		30	Florida	9,700,000	1.1%
6	New Mexico	40,500,000	4.5%		31	Alabama	8,500,000	0.9%
36	New York	6,900,000	0.8%		32	North Carolina	8,400,000	0.9%
32	North Carolina	8,400,000	0.9%		33	Louisiana	8,000,000	0.9%
7	North Dakota	39,300,000	4.4%		34	Virginia	7,800,000	0.9%
21	Ohio	13,900,000	1.5%		35	Pennsylvania	7,300,000	0.8%
8	Oklahoma	34,200,000	3.8%		36	New York	6,900,000	0.8%
17	Oregon	16,000,000	1.8%		37	Nevada	6,100,000	0.7%
35	Pennsylvania	7,300,000	0.8%		38	South Carolina	4,800,000	0.5%
50	Rhode Island	60,000	0.0%		39	West Virginia	3,600,000	0.4%
38	South Carolina	4,800,000	0.5%		40	Maryland	2,000,000	0.2%
5	South Dakota	43,200,000	4.8%		41	Maine	1,300,000	0.1%
25	Tennessee	10,900,000	1.2%		42	Vermont	1,200,000	0.1%
1	Texas	127,000,000	14.1%		43	Hawaii	1,100,000	0.1%
26	Utah	10,700,000	1.2%		44	Alaska	850,000	0.1%
42	Vermont	1,200,000	0.1%		45	New Jersey	750,000	0.1%
34	Virginia	7,800,000	0.9%		46	Delaware	530,000	0.1%
19	Washington	14,700,000	1.6%		47	Massachusetts	500,000	0.1%
39	West Virginia	3,600,000	0.4%		48	New Hampshire	430,000	0.0%
20	Wisconsin	14,300,000	1.6%		49	Connecticut	380,000	0.0%
11	Wyoming	29,000,000	3.2%		50	Rhode Island	60,000	0.0%
						District of Columbia	0	0.0%

Source: U.S. Department of Agriculture, National Agricultural Statistics Service
  "Farms and Land in Farms" (https://usda.library.cornell.edu/concern/publications/5712m6524)
*A farm is any establishment from which $1,000 or more of agricultural products were sold or would normally be sold during the
year. This includes places with five or more horses, except horses in boarding stables or racetracks.

Average Number of Acres per Farm in 2018

National Average = 443 Acres*

RANK	STATE (ALPHA ORDER)	ACRES		RANK	STATE (RANK ORDER)	ACRES
30	Alabama	214		1	Wyoming	2,437
9	Alaska	850		2	Montana	2,156
7	Arizona	1,365		3	Nevada	1,794
22	Arkansas	327		4	New Mexico	1,640
21	California	350		5	North Dakota	1,506
10	Colorado	817		6	South Dakota	1,459
48	Connecticut	69		7	Arizona	1,365
28	Delaware	230		8	Nebraska	980
33	Florida	204		9	Alaska	850
27	Georgia	243		10	Colorado	817
44	Hawaii	151		11	Kansas	778
14	Idaho	468		12	Utah	591
18	Illinois	375		13	Texas	514
26	Indiana	267		14	Idaho	468
20	Iowa	356		15	Oklahoma	442
11	Kansas	778		16	Oregon	430
39	Kentucky	172		17	Washington	412
24	Louisiana	292		18	Illinois	375
40	Maine	171		19	Minnesota	372
41	Maryland	161		20	Iowa	356
48	Massachusetts	69		21	California	350
31	Michigan	209		22	Arkansas	327
19	Minnesota	372		23	Mississippi	300
23	Mississippi	300		24	Louisiana	292
24	Missouri	292		24	Missouri	292
2	Montana	2,156		26	Indiana	267
8	Nebraska	980		27	Georgia	243
3	Nevada	1,794		28	Delaware	230
46	New Hampshire	105		29	Wisconsin	221
47	New Jersey	76		30	Alabama	214
4	New Mexico	1,640		31	Michigan	209
32	New York	207		32	New York	207
36	North Carolina	181		33	Florida	204
5	North Dakota	1,506		34	South Carolina	195
37	Ohio	179		35	Virginia	184
15	Oklahoma	442		36	North Carolina	181
16	Oregon	430		37	Ohio	179
45	Pennsylvania	138		38	Vermont	176
50	Rhode Island	55		39	Kentucky	172
34	South Carolina	195		40	Maine	171
6	South Dakota	1,459		41	Maryland	161
42	Tennessee	156		42	Tennessee	156
13	Texas	514		43	West Virginia	154
12	Utah	591		44	Hawaii	151
38	Vermont	176		45	Pennsylvania	138
35	Virginia	184		46	New Hampshire	105
17	Washington	412		47	New Jersey	76
43	West Virginia	154		48	Connecticut	69
29	Wisconsin	221		48	Massachusetts	69
1	Wyoming	2,437		50	Rhode Island	55
					District of Columbia	0

Source: U.S. Department of Agriculture, National Agricultural Statistics Service
   "Farms and Land in Farms" (https://usda.library.cornell.edu/concern/publications/5712m6524)
*A farm is any establishment from which $1,000 or more of agricultural products were sold or would normally be sold during the year. This includes places with five or more horses, except horses in boarding stables or racetracks.

Average per-Acre Value of Farmland in 2019

National Average = $3,160 per Acre*

ALPHA ORDER				RANK ORDER		
RANK	STATE	PER-ACRE VALUE		RANK	STATE	PER-ACRE VALUE
30	Alabama	$3,100		1	Rhode Island	$15,600
NA	Alaska**	NA		2	New Jersey	13,500
22	Arizona	3,800		3	Connecticut	12,200
27	Arkansas	3,320		4	Massachusetts	11,100
5	California	10,000		5	California	10,000
44	Colorado	1,570		6	Delaware	8,950
3	Connecticut	12,200		7	Maryland	8,060
6	Delaware	8,950		8	Illinois	7,280
13	Florida	5,950		9	Iowa	7,190
24	Georgia	3,470		10	Indiana	6,580
NA	Hawaii**	NA		11	Pennsylvania	6,470
31	Idaho	3,000		12	Ohio	6,290
8	Illinois	7,280		13	Florida	5,950
10	Indiana	6,580		14	New Hampshire	4,980
9	Iowa	7,190		15	Michigan	4,960
41	Kansas	1,960		16	Wisconsin	4,950
21	Kentucky	3,820		17	Minnesota	4,840
29	Louisiana	3,120		18	North Carolina	4,680
38	Maine	2,410		19	Virginia	4,650
7	Maryland	8,060		20	Tennessee	3,990
4	Massachusetts	11,100		21	Kentucky	3,820
15	Michigan	4,960		22	Arizona	3,800
17	Minnesota	4,840		23	Vermont	3,630
34	Mississippi	2,800		24	Georgia	3,470
25	Missouri	3,400		25	Missouri	3,400
46	Montana	915		25	South Carolina	3,400
32	Nebraska	2,850		27	Arkansas	3,320
45	Nevada	1,020		28	New York	3,250
14	New Hampshire	4,980		29	Louisiana	3,120
2	New Jersey	13,500		30	Alabama	3,100
48	New Mexico	570		31	Idaho	3,000
28	New York	3,250		32	Nebraska	2,850
18	North Carolina	4,680		33	Washington	2,820
43	North Dakota	1,740		34	Mississippi	2,800
12	Ohio	6,290		35	West Virginia	2,680
42	Oklahoma	1,870		36	Oregon	2,500
36	Oregon	2,500		37	Utah	2,420
11	Pennsylvania	6,470		38	Maine	2,410
1	Rhode Island	15,600		39	Texas	2,120
25	South Carolina	3,400		40	South Dakota	2,070
40	South Dakota	2,070		41	Kansas	1,960
20	Tennessee	3,990		42	Oklahoma	1,870
39	Texas	2,120		43	North Dakota	1,740
37	Utah	2,420		44	Colorado	1,570
23	Vermont	3,630		45	Nevada	1,020
19	Virginia	4,650		46	Montana	915
33	Washington	2,820		47	Wyoming	740
35	West Virginia	2,680		48	New Mexico	570
16	Wisconsin	4,950		NA	Alaska**	NA
47	Wyoming	740		NA	Hawaii**	NA
					District of Columbia**	NA

Source: U.S. Department of Agriculture, National Agricultural Statistics Service
  "Land Values and Cash Rents" (https://usda.library.cornell.edu/concern/publications/pn89d6567)
*Value of farmland and buildings in nominal dollars.
**Not applicable or available.

Percent Change in Average per-Acre Value of Farmland: 2018 to 2019

National Percent Change = 1.9% Increase*

ALPHA ORDER

RANK	STATE	PERCENT CHANGE
7	Alabama	4.0
NA	Alaska**	NA
36	Arizona	0.5
4	Arkansas	5.1
1	California	7.0
32	Colorado	0.6
46	Connecticut	(0.8)
2	Delaware	6.4
31	Florida	0.8
47	Georgia	(1.1)
NA	Hawaii**	NA
6	Idaho	4.5
37	Illinois	0.0
37	Indiana	0.0
47	Iowa	(1.1)
3	Kansas	5.9
26	Kentucky	1.3
14	Louisiana	2.6
23	Maine	1.7
16	Maryland	2.5
20	Massachusetts	1.8
37	Michigan	0.0
44	Minnesota	(0.2)
18	Mississippi	2.2
32	Missouri	0.6
43	Montana	(0.1)
9	Nebraska	3.6
37	Nevada	0.0
24	New Hampshire	1.6
37	New Jersey	0.0
29	New Mexico	0.9
32	New York	0.6
29	North Carolina	0.9
20	North Dakota	1.8
25	Ohio	1.5
8	Oklahoma	3.9
12	Oregon	2.9
10	Pennsylvania	3.5
14	Rhode Island	2.6
13	South Carolina	2.7
37	South Dakota	0.0
20	Tennessee	1.8
11	Texas	3.4
5	Utah	4.8
16	Vermont	2.5
32	Virginia	0.6
45	Washington	(0.7)
27	West Virginia	1.1
28	Wisconsin	1.0
19	Wyoming	1.9

RANK ORDER

RANK	STATE	PERCENT CHANGE
1	California	7.0
2	Delaware	6.4
3	Kansas	5.9
4	Arkansas	5.1
5	Utah	4.8
6	Idaho	4.5
7	Alabama	4.0
8	Oklahoma	3.9
9	Nebraska	3.6
10	Pennsylvania	3.5
11	Texas	3.4
12	Oregon	2.9
13	South Carolina	2.7
14	Louisiana	2.6
14	Rhode Island	2.6
16	Maryland	2.5
16	Vermont	2.5
18	Mississippi	2.2
19	Wyoming	1.9
20	Massachusetts	1.8
20	North Dakota	1.8
20	Tennessee	1.8
23	Maine	1.7
24	New Hampshire	1.6
25	Ohio	1.5
26	Kentucky	1.3
27	West Virginia	1.1
28	Wisconsin	1.0
29	New Mexico	0.9
29	North Carolina	0.9
31	Florida	0.8
32	Colorado	0.6
32	Missouri	0.6
32	New York	0.6
32	Virginia	0.6
36	Arizona	0.5
37	Illinois	0.0
37	Indiana	0.0
37	Michigan	0.0
37	Nevada	0.0
37	New Jersey	0.0
37	South Dakota	0.0
43	Montana	(0.1)
44	Minnesota	(0.2)
45	Washington	(0.7)
46	Connecticut	(0.8)
47	Georgia	(1.1)
47	Iowa	(1.1)
NA	Alaska**	NA
NA	Hawaii**	NA

| District of Columbia** | NA |

Source: U.S. Department of Agriculture, National Agricultural Statistics Service
   "Land Values and Cash Rents" (https://usda.library.cornell.edu/concern/publications/pn89d6567)
*Value of farmland and buildings in nominal dollars.
**Not applicable or available.

Net Farm Income in 2018

National Total = $83,995,681,000*

ALPHA ORDER

ALPHA ORDER

RANK ORDER

RANK	STATE	FARM INCOME	% of USA
24	Alabama	$1,412,720,000	1.7%
50	Alaska	(5,778,000)	0.0%
29	Arizona	933,004,000	1.1%
16	Arkansas	1,807,049,000	2.2%
1	California	15,627,251,000	18.6%
25	Colorado	1,260,992,000	1.5%
41	Connecticut	164,579,000	0.2%
34	Delaware	602,555,000	0.7%
5	Florida	3,052,803,000	3.6%
10	Georgia	2,309,391,000	2.7%
44	Hawaii	141,718,000	0.2%
17	Idaho	1,789,466,000	2.1%
4	Illinois	3,889,986,000	4.6%
13	Indiana	2,144,715,000	2.6%
2	Iowa	5,631,102,000	6.7%
7	Kansas	2,770,434,000	3.3%
19	Kentucky	1,722,718,000	2.1%
30	Louisiana	910,053,000	1.1%
43	Maine	144,409,000	0.2%
35	Maryland	539,229,000	0.6%
47	Massachusetts	72,001,000	0.1%
27	Michigan	1,115,389,000	1.3%
6	Minnesota	2,903,300,000	3.5%
22	Mississippi	1,589,895,000	1.9%
21	Missouri	1,612,265,000	1.9%
26	Montana	1,120,287,000	1.3%
8	Nebraska	2,586,632,000	3.1%
46	Nevada	84,945,000	0.1%
48	New Hampshire	57,286,000	0.1%
39	New Jersey	296,175,000	0.4%
31	New Mexico	860,928,000	1.0%
28	New York	1,073,220,000	1.3%
20	North Carolina	1,655,498,000	2.0%
15	North Dakota	1,927,350,000	2.3%
12	Ohio	2,189,250,000	2.6%
18	Oklahoma	1,788,644,000	2.1%
32	Oregon	844,577,000	1.0%
23	Pennsylvania	1,441,623,000	1.7%
49	Rhode Island	30,395,000	0.0%
40	South Carolina	274,499,000	0.3%
9	South Dakota	2,571,273,000	3.1%
38	Tennessee	325,261,000	0.4%
3	Texas	4,624,950,000	5.5%
36	Utah	473,999,000	0.6%
42	Vermont	148,476,000	0.2%
33	Virginia	656,644,000	0.8%
11	Washington	2,271,553,000	2.7%
45	West Virginia	86,300,000	0.1%
14	Wisconsin	2,133,145,000	2.5%
37	Wyoming	332,568,000	0.4%

RANK	STATE	FARM INCOME	% of USA
1	California	$15,627,251,000	18.6%
2	Iowa	5,631,102,000	6.7%
3	Texas	4,624,950,000	5.5%
4	Illinois	3,889,986,000	4.6%
5	Florida	3,052,803,000	3.6%
6	Minnesota	2,903,300,000	3.5%
7	Kansas	2,770,434,000	3.3%
8	Nebraska	2,586,632,000	3.1%
9	South Dakota	2,571,273,000	3.1%
10	Georgia	2,309,391,000	2.7%
11	Washington	2,271,553,000	2.7%
12	Ohio	2,189,250,000	2.6%
13	Indiana	2,144,715,000	2.6%
14	Wisconsin	2,133,145,000	2.5%
15	North Dakota	1,927,350,000	2.3%
16	Arkansas	1,807,049,000	2.2%
17	Idaho	1,789,466,000	2.1%
18	Oklahoma	1,788,644,000	2.1%
19	Kentucky	1,722,718,000	2.1%
20	North Carolina	1,655,498,000	2.0%
21	Missouri	1,612,265,000	1.9%
22	Mississippi	1,589,895,000	1.9%
23	Pennsylvania	1,441,623,000	1.7%
24	Alabama	1,412,720,000	1.7%
25	Colorado	1,260,992,000	1.5%
26	Montana	1,120,287,000	1.3%
27	Michigan	1,115,389,000	1.3%
28	New York	1,073,220,000	1.3%
29	Arizona	933,004,000	1.1%
30	Louisiana	910,053,000	1.1%
31	New Mexico	860,928,000	1.0%
32	Oregon	844,577,000	1.0%
33	Virginia	656,644,000	0.8%
34	Delaware	602,555,000	0.7%
35	Maryland	539,229,000	0.6%
36	Utah	473,999,000	0.6%
37	Wyoming	332,568,000	0.4%
38	Tennessee	325,261,000	0.4%
39	New Jersey	296,175,000	0.4%
40	South Carolina	274,499,000	0.3%
41	Connecticut	164,579,000	0.2%
42	Vermont	148,476,000	0.2%
43	Maine	144,409,000	0.2%
44	Hawaii	141,718,000	0.2%
45	West Virginia	86,300,000	0.1%
46	Nevada	84,945,000	0.1%
47	Massachusetts	72,001,000	0.1%
48	New Hampshire	57,286,000	0.1%
49	Rhode Island	30,395,000	0.0%
50	Alaska	(5,778,000)	0.0%
	District of Columbia	0	0.0%

Source: U.S. Department of Agriculture, Economic Research Service
   "Farm Sector Financial Indicators, State Rankings"
   (https://www.ers.usda.gov/data-products/farm-income-and-wealth-statistics.aspx)
*Net farm income is a measure of the net value of production in a given year. It is determined by subtracting total production expenses from gross farm income.

Net Farm Income per Operation in 2018

National Average = $41,199 per Operation*

ALPHA ORDER

RANK	STATE	PER OPERATION
21	Alabama	$35,524
50	Alaska	(5,950)
12	Arizona	49,140
16	Arkansas	42,510
2	California	225,050
25	Colorado	32,680
28	Connecticut	29,877
1	Delaware	261,510
7	Florida	64,260
10	Georgia	55,647
40	Hawaii	19,479
5	Idaho	72,072
11	Illinois	54,000
19	Indiana	38,181
6	Iowa	65,504
13	Kansas	46,680
36	Kentucky	23,048
23	Louisiana	33,288
41	Maine	18,981
15	Maryland	43,470
47	Massachusetts	9,936
35	Michigan	23,826
17	Minnesota	42,408
14	Mississippi	45,900
43	Missouri	16,936
18	Montana	40,964
9	Nebraska	55,860
34	Nevada	25,116
45	New Hampshire	13,965
27	New Jersey	30,020
22	New Mexico	34,440
26	New York	32,292
20	North Carolina	35,657
4	North Dakota	73,794
29	Ohio	28,282
37	Oklahoma	22,984
38	Oregon	22,790
31	Pennsylvania	27,186
30	Rhode Island	27,885
46	South Carolina	11,115
3	South Dakota	87,540
48	Tennessee	4,680
42	Texas	18,504
33	Utah	26,004
39	Vermont	21,824
44	Virginia	15,456
8	Washington	63,860
49	West Virginia	3,696
24	Wisconsin	32,929
32	Wyoming	26,807

RANK ORDER

RANK	STATE	PER OPERATION
1	Delaware	$261,510
2	California	225,050
3	South Dakota	87,540
4	North Dakota	73,794
5	Idaho	72,072
6	Iowa	65,504
7	Florida	64,260
8	Washington	63,860
9	Nebraska	55,860
10	Georgia	55,647
11	Illinois	54,000
12	Arizona	49,140
13	Kansas	46,680
14	Mississippi	45,900
15	Maryland	43,470
16	Arkansas	42,510
17	Minnesota	42,408
18	Montana	40,964
19	Indiana	38,181
20	North Carolina	35,657
21	Alabama	35,524
22	New Mexico	34,440
23	Louisiana	33,288
24	Wisconsin	32,929
25	Colorado	32,680
26	New York	32,292
27	New Jersey	30,020
28	Connecticut	29,877
29	Ohio	28,282
30	Rhode Island	27,885
31	Pennsylvania	27,186
32	Wyoming	26,807
33	Utah	26,004
34	Nevada	25,116
35	Michigan	23,826
36	Kentucky	23,048
37	Oklahoma	22,984
38	Oregon	22,790
39	Vermont	21,824
40	Hawaii	19,479
41	Maine	18,981
42	Texas	18,504
43	Missouri	16,936
44	Virginia	15,456
45	New Hampshire	13,965
46	South Carolina	11,115
47	Massachusetts	9,936
48	Tennessee	4,680
49	West Virginia	3,696
50	Alaska	(5,950)

District of Columbia**   NA

Source: CQ Press using data from U.S. Department of Agriculture, Economic Research Service
"Farm Sector Financial Indicators, State Rankings"
(https://www.ers.usda.gov/data-products/farm-income-and-wealth-statistics.aspx)
*Calculated by multiplying average acres per farm by average net farm income per acre.
**Not applicable.

Net Farm Income per Acre in 2018

National Average = $93 per Acre*

ALPHA ORDER

RANK	STATE	PER ACRE
12	Alabama	$166
50	Alaska	(7)
42	Arizona	36
24	Arkansas	130
2	California	643
41	Colorado	40
4	Connecticut	433
1	Delaware	1,137
6	Florida	315
8	Georgia	229
25	Hawaii	129
16	Idaho	154
19	Illinois	144
21	Indiana	143
11	Iowa	184
32	Kansas	60
22	Kentucky	134
27	Louisiana	114
30	Maine	111
7	Maryland	270
19	Massachusetts	144
27	Michigan	114
27	Minnesota	114
17	Mississippi	153
34	Missouri	58
47	Montana	19
35	Nebraska	57
48	Nevada	14
23	New Hampshire	133
5	New Jersey	395
46	New Mexico	21
14	New York	156
9	North Carolina	197
39	North Dakota	49
13	Ohio	158
38	Oklahoma	52
37	Oregon	53
9	Pennsylvania	197
3	Rhode Island	507
35	South Carolina	57
32	South Dakota	60
44	Tennessee	30
42	Texas	36
40	Utah	44
26	Vermont	124
31	Virginia	84
15	Washington	155
45	West Virginia	24
18	Wisconsin	149
49	Wyoming	11

RANK ORDER

RANK	STATE	PER ACRE
1	Delaware	$1,137
2	California	643
3	Rhode Island	507
4	Connecticut	433
5	New Jersey	395
6	Florida	315
7	Maryland	270
8	Georgia	229
9	North Carolina	197
9	Pennsylvania	197
11	Iowa	184
12	Alabama	166
13	Ohio	158
14	New York	156
15	Washington	155
16	Idaho	154
17	Mississippi	153
18	Wisconsin	149
19	Illinois	144
19	Massachusetts	144
21	Indiana	143
22	Kentucky	134
23	New Hampshire	133
24	Arkansas	130
25	Hawaii	129
26	Vermont	124
27	Louisiana	114
27	Michigan	114
27	Minnesota	114
30	Maine	111
31	Virginia	84
32	Kansas	60
32	South Dakota	60
34	Missouri	58
35	Nebraska	57
35	South Carolina	57
37	Oregon	53
38	Oklahoma	52
39	North Dakota	49
40	Utah	44
41	Colorado	40
42	Arizona	36
42	Texas	36
44	Tennessee	30
45	West Virginia	24
46	New Mexico	21
47	Montana	19
48	Nevada	14
49	Wyoming	11
50	Alaska	(7)

District of Columbia** NA

Source: CQ Press using data from U.S. Department of Agriculture, Economic Research Service
"Farm Sector Financial Indicators, State Rankings"
(https://www.ers.usda.gov/data-products/farm-income-and-wealth-statistics.aspx)
*Net farm income is a measure of the net value of production in a given year. It is determined by subtracting total production expenses from gross farm income.
**Not applicable.

Farm Income: Cash Receipts from Commodities in 2018

National Total = $372,016,365,000*

ALPHA ORDER

RANK	STATE	FARM INCOME	% of USA
25	Alabama	$5,801,665,000	1.6%
50	Alaska	38,653,000	0.0%
29	Arizona	4,158,639,000	1.1%
14	Arkansas	9,030,173,000	2.4%
1	California	49,866,201,000	13.4%
21	Colorado	7,086,467,000	1.9%
45	Connecticut	596,795,000	0.2%
39	Delaware	1,405,793,000	0.4%
20	Florida	7,315,011,000	2.0%
13	Georgia	9,189,878,000	2.5%
46	Hawaii	593,336,000	0.2%
19	Idaho	7,488,722,000	2.0%
6	Illinois	16,696,292,000	4.5%
10	Indiana	10,500,290,000	2.8%
2	Iowa	27,374,057,000	7.4%
7	Kansas	15,941,891,000	4.3%
24	Kentucky	5,888,997,000	1.6%
33	Louisiana	3,113,006,000	0.8%
43	Maine	665,594,000	0.2%
36	Maryland	2,237,072,000	0.6%
47	Massachusetts	432,518,000	0.1%
18	Michigan	7,530,049,000	2.0%
5	Minnesota	17,102,569,000	4.6%
26	Mississippi	5,476,087,000	1.5%
11	Missouri	10,070,792,000	2.7%
30	Montana	3,583,073,000	1.0%
4	Nebraska	21,117,971,000	5.7%
44	Nevada	654,588,000	0.2%
48	New Hampshire	222,562,000	0.1%
40	New Jersey	1,112,147,000	0.3%
34	New Mexico	2,931,216,000	0.8%
27	New York	5,018,596,000	1.3%
8	North Carolina	11,047,317,000	3.0%
17	North Dakota	7,727,899,000	2.1%
16	Ohio	8,924,513,000	2.4%
22	Oklahoma	6,766,107,000	1.8%
28	Oregon	4,921,874,000	1.3%
23	Pennsylvania	6,748,727,000	1.8%
49	Rhode Island	72,973,000	0.0%
35	South Carolina	2,512,749,000	0.7%
15	South Dakota	9,004,173,000	2.4%
32	Tennessee	3,515,107,000	0.9%
3	Texas	22,011,548,000	5.9%
37	Utah	1,685,479,000	0.5%
41	Vermont	733,169,000	0.2%
31	Virginia	3,520,658,000	0.9%
12	Washington	9,464,028,000	2.5%
42	West Virginia	684,274,000	0.2%
9	Wisconsin	10,884,455,000	2.9%
38	Wyoming	1,550,613,000	0.4%

RANK ORDER

RANK	STATE	FARM INCOME	% of USA
1	California	$49,866,201,000	13.4%
2	Iowa	27,374,057,000	7.4%
3	Texas	22,011,548,000	5.9%
4	Nebraska	21,117,971,000	5.7%
5	Minnesota	17,102,569,000	4.6%
6	Illinois	16,696,292,000	4.5%
7	Kansas	15,941,891,000	4.3%
8	North Carolina	11,047,317,000	3.0%
9	Wisconsin	10,884,455,000	2.9%
10	Indiana	10,500,290,000	2.8%
11	Missouri	10,070,792,000	2.7%
12	Washington	9,464,028,000	2.5%
13	Georgia	9,189,878,000	2.5%
14	Arkansas	9,030,173,000	2.4%
15	South Dakota	9,004,173,000	2.4%
16	Ohio	8,924,513,000	2.4%
17	North Dakota	7,727,899,000	2.1%
18	Michigan	7,530,049,000	2.0%
19	Idaho	7,488,722,000	2.0%
20	Florida	7,315,011,000	2.0%
21	Colorado	7,086,467,000	1.9%
22	Oklahoma	6,766,107,000	1.8%
23	Pennsylvania	6,748,727,000	1.8%
24	Kentucky	5,888,997,000	1.6%
25	Alabama	5,801,665,000	1.6%
26	Mississippi	5,476,087,000	1.5%
27	New York	5,018,596,000	1.3%
28	Oregon	4,921,874,000	1.3%
29	Arizona	4,158,639,000	1.1%
30	Montana	3,583,073,000	1.0%
31	Virginia	3,520,658,000	0.9%
32	Tennessee	3,515,107,000	0.9%
33	Louisiana	3,113,006,000	0.8%
34	New Mexico	2,931,216,000	0.8%
35	South Carolina	2,512,749,000	0.7%
36	Maryland	2,237,072,000	0.6%
37	Utah	1,685,479,000	0.5%
38	Wyoming	1,550,613,000	0.4%
39	Delaware	1,405,793,000	0.4%
40	New Jersey	1,112,147,000	0.3%
41	Vermont	733,169,000	0.2%
42	West Virginia	684,274,000	0.2%
43	Maine	665,594,000	0.2%
44	Nevada	654,588,000	0.2%
45	Connecticut	596,795,000	0.2%
46	Hawaii	593,336,000	0.2%
47	Massachusetts	432,518,000	0.1%
48	New Hampshire	222,562,000	0.1%
49	Rhode Island	72,973,000	0.0%
50	Alaska	38,653,000	0.0%
	District of Columbia	0	0.0%

Source: U.S. Department of Agriculture, Economic Research Service
"Farm Sector Financial Indicators, State Rankings" (www.ers.usda.gov/data-products/farm-income-and-wealth-statistics.aspx)
*Commodities include crops and livestock.

Farm Income: Crops in 2018

National Total = $195,486,640,000

<table>
<tr><td colspan="4">ALPHA ORDER</td><td colspan="4">RANK ORDER</td></tr>
<tr><td>RANK</td><td>STATE</td><td>FARM INCOME</td><td>% of USA</td><td>RANK</td><td>STATE</td><td>FARM INCOME</td><td>% of USA</td></tr>
<tr><td>33</td><td>Alabama</td><td>$1,257,562,000</td><td>0.6%</td><td>1</td><td>California</td><td>$38,128,281,000</td><td>19.5%</td></tr>
<tr><td>50</td><td>Alaska</td><td>30,618,000</td><td>0.0%</td><td>2</td><td>Illinois</td><td>14,366,585,000</td><td>7.3%</td></tr>
<tr><td>24</td><td>Arizona</td><td>2,423,881,000</td><td>1.2%</td><td>3</td><td>Iowa</td><td>13,083,420,000</td><td>6.7%</td></tr>
<tr><td>18</td><td>Arkansas</td><td>3,460,195,000</td><td>1.8%</td><td>4</td><td>Minnesota</td><td>9,629,900,000</td><td>4.9%</td></tr>
<tr><td>1</td><td>California</td><td>38,128,281,000</td><td>19.5%</td><td>5</td><td>Nebraska</td><td>9,203,503,000</td><td>4.7%</td></tr>
<tr><td>25</td><td>Colorado</td><td>2,384,421,000</td><td>1.2%</td><td>6</td><td>Texas</td><td>7,574,615,000</td><td>3.9%</td></tr>
<tr><td>40</td><td>Connecticut</td><td>416,664,000</td><td>0.2%</td><td>7</td><td>Washington</td><td>6,985,291,000</td><td>3.6%</td></tr>
<tr><td>44</td><td>Delaware</td><td>273,522,000</td><td>0.1%</td><td>8</td><td>Indiana</td><td>6,702,177,000</td><td>3.4%</td></tr>
<tr><td>11</td><td>Florida</td><td>5,716,556,000</td><td>2.9%</td><td>9</td><td>North Dakota</td><td>6,465,897,000</td><td>3.3%</td></tr>
<tr><td>21</td><td>Georgia</td><td>3,152,325,000</td><td>1.6%</td><td>10</td><td>Kansas</td><td>6,430,117,000</td><td>3.3%</td></tr>
<tr><td>39</td><td>Hawaii</td><td>427,521,000</td><td>0.2%</td><td>11</td><td>Florida</td><td>5,716,556,000</td><td>2.9%</td></tr>
<tr><td>20</td><td>Idaho</td><td>3,155,504,000</td><td>1.6%</td><td>12</td><td>Ohio</td><td>5,406,132,000</td><td>2.8%</td></tr>
<tr><td>2</td><td>Illinois</td><td>14,366,585,000</td><td>7.3%</td><td>13</td><td>Missouri</td><td>5,361,960,000</td><td>2.7%</td></tr>
<tr><td>8</td><td>Indiana</td><td>6,702,177,000</td><td>3.4%</td><td>14</td><td>South Dakota</td><td>4,932,488,000</td><td>2.5%</td></tr>
<tr><td>3</td><td>Iowa</td><td>13,083,420,000</td><td>6.7%</td><td>15</td><td>Michigan</td><td>4,233,229,000</td><td>2.2%</td></tr>
<tr><td>10</td><td>Kansas</td><td>6,430,117,000</td><td>3.3%</td><td>16</td><td>Wisconsin</td><td>3,542,816,000</td><td>1.8%</td></tr>
<tr><td>23</td><td>Kentucky</td><td>2,521,236,000</td><td>1.3%</td><td>17</td><td>Oregon</td><td>3,482,725,000</td><td>1.8%</td></tr>
<tr><td>29</td><td>Louisiana</td><td>1,975,263,000</td><td>1.0%</td><td>18</td><td>Arkansas</td><td>3,460,195,000</td><td>1.8%</td></tr>
<tr><td>42</td><td>Maine</td><td>378,977,000</td><td>0.2%</td><td>19</td><td>North Carolina</td><td>3,413,071,000</td><td>1.7%</td></tr>
<tr><td>36</td><td>Maryland</td><td>881,443,000</td><td>0.5%</td><td>20</td><td>Idaho</td><td>3,155,504,000</td><td>1.6%</td></tr>
<tr><td>43</td><td>Massachusetts</td><td>330,930,000</td><td>0.2%</td><td>21</td><td>Georgia</td><td>3,152,325,000</td><td>1.6%</td></tr>
<tr><td>15</td><td>Michigan</td><td>4,233,229,000</td><td>2.2%</td><td>22</td><td>Pennsylvania</td><td>2,523,868,000</td><td>1.3%</td></tr>
<tr><td>4</td><td>Minnesota</td><td>9,629,900,000</td><td>4.9%</td><td>23</td><td>Kentucky</td><td>2,521,236,000</td><td>1.3%</td></tr>
<tr><td>27</td><td>Mississippi</td><td>2,074,731,000</td><td>1.1%</td><td>24</td><td>Arizona</td><td>2,423,881,000</td><td>1.2%</td></tr>
<tr><td>13</td><td>Missouri</td><td>5,361,960,000</td><td>2.7%</td><td>25</td><td>Colorado</td><td>2,384,421,000</td><td>1.2%</td></tr>
<tr><td>28</td><td>Montana</td><td>1,976,841,000</td><td>1.0%</td><td>26</td><td>Tennessee</td><td>2,103,850,000</td><td>1.1%</td></tr>
<tr><td>5</td><td>Nebraska</td><td>9,203,503,000</td><td>4.7%</td><td>27</td><td>Mississippi</td><td>2,074,731,000</td><td>1.1%</td></tr>
<tr><td>46</td><td>Nevada</td><td>176,069,000</td><td>0.1%</td><td>28</td><td>Montana</td><td>1,976,841,000</td><td>1.0%</td></tr>
<tr><td>48</td><td>New Hampshire</td><td>115,578,000</td><td>0.1%</td><td>29</td><td>Louisiana</td><td>1,975,263,000</td><td>1.0%</td></tr>
<tr><td>35</td><td>New Jersey</td><td>981,074,000</td><td>0.5%</td><td>30</td><td>New York</td><td>1,940,351,000</td><td>1.0%</td></tr>
<tr><td>37</td><td>New Mexico</td><td>708,891,000</td><td>0.4%</td><td>31</td><td>Oklahoma</td><td>1,472,536,000</td><td>0.8%</td></tr>
<tr><td>30</td><td>New York</td><td>1,940,351,000</td><td>1.0%</td><td>32</td><td>Virginia</td><td>1,288,274,000</td><td>0.7%</td></tr>
<tr><td>19</td><td>North Carolina</td><td>3,413,071,000</td><td>1.7%</td><td>33</td><td>Alabama</td><td>1,257,562,000</td><td>0.6%</td></tr>
<tr><td>9</td><td>North Dakota</td><td>6,465,897,000</td><td>3.3%</td><td>34</td><td>South Carolina</td><td>1,123,106,000</td><td>0.6%</td></tr>
<tr><td>12</td><td>Ohio</td><td>5,406,132,000</td><td>2.8%</td><td>35</td><td>New Jersey</td><td>981,074,000</td><td>0.5%</td></tr>
<tr><td>31</td><td>Oklahoma</td><td>1,472,536,000</td><td>0.8%</td><td>36</td><td>Maryland</td><td>881,443,000</td><td>0.5%</td></tr>
<tr><td>17</td><td>Oregon</td><td>3,482,725,000</td><td>1.8%</td><td>37</td><td>New Mexico</td><td>708,891,000</td><td>0.4%</td></tr>
<tr><td>22</td><td>Pennsylvania</td><td>2,523,868,000</td><td>1.3%</td><td>38</td><td>Utah</td><td>485,771,000</td><td>0.2%</td></tr>
<tr><td>49</td><td>Rhode Island</td><td>43,593,000</td><td>0.0%</td><td>39</td><td>Hawaii</td><td>427,521,000</td><td>0.2%</td></tr>
<tr><td>34</td><td>South Carolina</td><td>1,123,106,000</td><td>0.6%</td><td>40</td><td>Connecticut</td><td>416,664,000</td><td>0.2%</td></tr>
<tr><td>14</td><td>South Dakota</td><td>4,932,488,000</td><td>2.5%</td><td>41</td><td>Wyoming</td><td>399,284,000</td><td>0.2%</td></tr>
<tr><td>26</td><td>Tennessee</td><td>2,103,850,000</td><td>1.1%</td><td>42</td><td>Maine</td><td>378,977,000</td><td>0.2%</td></tr>
<tr><td>6</td><td>Texas</td><td>7,574,615,000</td><td>3.9%</td><td>43</td><td>Massachusetts</td><td>330,930,000</td><td>0.2%</td></tr>
<tr><td>38</td><td>Utah</td><td>485,771,000</td><td>0.2%</td><td>44</td><td>Delaware</td><td>273,522,000</td><td>0.1%</td></tr>
<tr><td>45</td><td>Vermont</td><td>183,215,000</td><td>0.1%</td><td>45</td><td>Vermont</td><td>183,215,000</td><td>0.1%</td></tr>
<tr><td>32</td><td>Virginia</td><td>1,288,274,000</td><td>0.7%</td><td>46</td><td>Nevada</td><td>176,069,000</td><td>0.1%</td></tr>
<tr><td>7</td><td>Washington</td><td>6,985,291,000</td><td>3.6%</td><td>47</td><td>West Virginia</td><td>160,780,000</td><td>0.1%</td></tr>
<tr><td>47</td><td>West Virginia</td><td>160,780,000</td><td>0.1%</td><td>48</td><td>New Hampshire</td><td>115,578,000</td><td>0.1%</td></tr>
<tr><td>16</td><td>Wisconsin</td><td>3,542,816,000</td><td>1.8%</td><td>49</td><td>Rhode Island</td><td>43,593,000</td><td>0.0%</td></tr>
<tr><td>41</td><td>Wyoming</td><td>399,284,000</td><td>0.2%</td><td>50</td><td>Alaska</td><td>30,618,000</td><td>0.0%</td></tr>
<tr><td></td><td></td><td></td><td></td><td></td><td>District of Columbia</td><td>0</td><td>0.0%</td></tr>
</table>

Source: U.S. Department of Agriculture, Economic Research Service
"Farm Sector Financial Indicators, State Rankings" (www.ers.usda.gov/data-products/farm-income-and-wealth-statistics.aspx)

Farm Income: Livestock in 2018

National Total = $176,529,725,000*

<table>
<thead>
<tr><th colspan="4">ALPHA ORDER</th><th colspan="4">RANK ORDER</th></tr>
<tr><th>RANK</th><th>STATE</th><th>FARM INCOME</th><th>% of USA</th><th>RANK</th><th>STATE</th><th>FARM INCOME</th><th>% of USA</th></tr>
</thead>
<tbody>
<tr><td>14</td><td>Alabama</td><td>$4,544,103,000</td><td>2.6%</td><td>1</td><td>Texas</td><td>$14,436,933,000</td><td>8.2%</td></tr>
<tr><td>50</td><td>Alaska</td><td>8,035,000</td><td>0.0%</td><td>2</td><td>Iowa</td><td>14,290,637,000</td><td>8.1%</td></tr>
<tr><td>28</td><td>Arizona</td><td>1,734,758,000</td><td>1.0%</td><td>3</td><td>Nebraska</td><td>11,914,468,000</td><td>6.7%</td></tr>
<tr><td>10</td><td>Arkansas</td><td>5,569,978,000</td><td>3.2%</td><td>4</td><td>California</td><td>11,737,920,000</td><td>6.6%</td></tr>
<tr><td>4</td><td>California</td><td>11,737,920,000</td><td>6.6%</td><td>5</td><td>Kansas</td><td>9,511,774,000</td><td>5.4%</td></tr>
<tr><td>13</td><td>Colorado</td><td>4,702,046,000</td><td>2.7%</td><td>6</td><td>North Carolina</td><td>7,634,246,000</td><td>4.3%</td></tr>
<tr><td>44</td><td>Connecticut</td><td>180,131,000</td><td>0.1%</td><td>7</td><td>Minnesota</td><td>7,472,669,000</td><td>4.2%</td></tr>
<tr><td>39</td><td>Delaware</td><td>1,132,271,000</td><td>0.6%</td><td>8</td><td>Wisconsin</td><td>7,341,639,000</td><td>4.2%</td></tr>
<tr><td>30</td><td>Florida</td><td>1,598,455,000</td><td>0.9%</td><td>9</td><td>Georgia</td><td>6,037,553,000</td><td>3.4%</td></tr>
<tr><td>9</td><td>Georgia</td><td>6,037,553,000</td><td>3.4%</td><td>10</td><td>Arkansas</td><td>5,569,978,000</td><td>3.2%</td></tr>
<tr><td>45</td><td>Hawaii</td><td>165,815,000</td><td>0.1%</td><td>11</td><td>Oklahoma</td><td>5,293,571,000</td><td>3.0%</td></tr>
<tr><td>15</td><td>Idaho</td><td>4,333,218,000</td><td>2.5%</td><td>12</td><td>Missouri</td><td>4,708,832,000</td><td>2.7%</td></tr>
<tr><td>25</td><td>Illinois</td><td>2,329,707,000</td><td>1.3%</td><td>13</td><td>Colorado</td><td>4,702,046,000</td><td>2.7%</td></tr>
<tr><td>18</td><td>Indiana</td><td>3,798,113,000</td><td>2.2%</td><td>14</td><td>Alabama</td><td>4,544,103,000</td><td>2.6%</td></tr>
<tr><td>2</td><td>Iowa</td><td>14,290,637,000</td><td>8.1%</td><td>15</td><td>Idaho</td><td>4,333,218,000</td><td>2.5%</td></tr>
<tr><td>5</td><td>Kansas</td><td>9,511,774,000</td><td>5.4%</td><td>16</td><td>Pennsylvania</td><td>4,224,859,000</td><td>2.4%</td></tr>
<tr><td>21</td><td>Kentucky</td><td>3,367,761,000</td><td>1.9%</td><td>17</td><td>South Dakota</td><td>4,071,685,000</td><td>2.3%</td></tr>
<tr><td>38</td><td>Louisiana</td><td>1,137,743,000</td><td>0.6%</td><td>18</td><td>Indiana</td><td>3,798,113,000</td><td>2.2%</td></tr>
<tr><td>43</td><td>Maine</td><td>286,617,000</td><td>0.2%</td><td>19</td><td>Ohio</td><td>3,518,381,000</td><td>2.0%</td></tr>
<tr><td>34</td><td>Maryland</td><td>1,355,629,000</td><td>0.8%</td><td>20</td><td>Mississippi</td><td>3,401,356,000</td><td>1.9%</td></tr>
<tr><td>48</td><td>Massachusetts</td><td>101,588,000</td><td>0.1%</td><td>21</td><td>Kentucky</td><td>3,367,761,000</td><td>1.9%</td></tr>
<tr><td>22</td><td>Michigan</td><td>3,296,820,000</td><td>1.9%</td><td>22</td><td>Michigan</td><td>3,296,820,000</td><td>1.9%</td></tr>
<tr><td>7</td><td>Minnesota</td><td>7,472,669,000</td><td>4.2%</td><td>23</td><td>New York</td><td>3,078,245,000</td><td>1.7%</td></tr>
<tr><td>20</td><td>Mississippi</td><td>3,401,356,000</td><td>1.9%</td><td>24</td><td>Washington</td><td>2,478,737,000</td><td>1.4%</td></tr>
<tr><td>12</td><td>Missouri</td><td>4,708,832,000</td><td>2.7%</td><td>25</td><td>Illinois</td><td>2,329,707,000</td><td>1.3%</td></tr>
<tr><td>29</td><td>Montana</td><td>1,606,232,000</td><td>0.9%</td><td>26</td><td>Virginia</td><td>2,232,384,000</td><td>1.3%</td></tr>
<tr><td>3</td><td>Nebraska</td><td>11,914,468,000</td><td>6.7%</td><td>27</td><td>New Mexico</td><td>2,222,325,000</td><td>1.3%</td></tr>
<tr><td>42</td><td>Nevada</td><td>478,519,000</td><td>0.3%</td><td>28</td><td>Arizona</td><td>1,734,758,000</td><td>1.0%</td></tr>
<tr><td>47</td><td>New Hampshire</td><td>106,984,000</td><td>0.1%</td><td>29</td><td>Montana</td><td>1,606,232,000</td><td>0.9%</td></tr>
<tr><td>46</td><td>New Jersey</td><td>131,073,000</td><td>0.1%</td><td>30</td><td>Florida</td><td>1,598,455,000</td><td>0.9%</td></tr>
<tr><td>27</td><td>New Mexico</td><td>2,222,325,000</td><td>1.3%</td><td>31</td><td>Oregon</td><td>1,439,149,000</td><td>0.8%</td></tr>
<tr><td>23</td><td>New York</td><td>3,078,245,000</td><td>1.7%</td><td>32</td><td>Tennessee</td><td>1,411,257,000</td><td>0.8%</td></tr>
<tr><td>6</td><td>North Carolina</td><td>7,634,246,000</td><td>4.3%</td><td>33</td><td>South Carolina</td><td>1,389,643,000</td><td>0.8%</td></tr>
<tr><td>35</td><td>North Dakota</td><td>1,262,002,000</td><td>0.7%</td><td>34</td><td>Maryland</td><td>1,355,629,000</td><td>0.8%</td></tr>
<tr><td>19</td><td>Ohio</td><td>3,518,381,000</td><td>2.0%</td><td>35</td><td>North Dakota</td><td>1,262,002,000</td><td>0.7%</td></tr>
<tr><td>11</td><td>Oklahoma</td><td>5,293,571,000</td><td>3.0%</td><td>36</td><td>Utah</td><td>1,199,708,000</td><td>0.7%</td></tr>
<tr><td>31</td><td>Oregon</td><td>1,439,149,000</td><td>0.8%</td><td>37</td><td>Wyoming</td><td>1,151,329,000</td><td>0.7%</td></tr>
<tr><td>16</td><td>Pennsylvania</td><td>4,224,859,000</td><td>2.4%</td><td>38</td><td>Louisiana</td><td>1,137,743,000</td><td>0.6%</td></tr>
<tr><td>49</td><td>Rhode Island</td><td>29,380,000</td><td>0.0%</td><td>39</td><td>Delaware</td><td>1,132,271,000</td><td>0.6%</td></tr>
<tr><td>33</td><td>South Carolina</td><td>1,389,643,000</td><td>0.8%</td><td>40</td><td>Vermont</td><td>549,954,000</td><td>0.3%</td></tr>
<tr><td>17</td><td>South Dakota</td><td>4,071,685,000</td><td>2.3%</td><td>41</td><td>West Virginia</td><td>523,494,000</td><td>0.3%</td></tr>
<tr><td>32</td><td>Tennessee</td><td>1,411,257,000</td><td>0.8%</td><td>42</td><td>Nevada</td><td>478,519,000</td><td>0.3%</td></tr>
<tr><td>1</td><td>Texas</td><td>14,436,933,000</td><td>8.2%</td><td>43</td><td>Maine</td><td>286,617,000</td><td>0.2%</td></tr>
<tr><td>36</td><td>Utah</td><td>1,199,708,000</td><td>0.7%</td><td>44</td><td>Connecticut</td><td>180,131,000</td><td>0.1%</td></tr>
<tr><td>40</td><td>Vermont</td><td>549,954,000</td><td>0.3%</td><td>45</td><td>Hawaii</td><td>165,815,000</td><td>0.1%</td></tr>
<tr><td>26</td><td>Virginia</td><td>2,232,384,000</td><td>1.3%</td><td>46</td><td>New Jersey</td><td>131,073,000</td><td>0.1%</td></tr>
<tr><td>24</td><td>Washington</td><td>2,478,737,000</td><td>1.4%</td><td>47</td><td>New Hampshire</td><td>106,984,000</td><td>0.1%</td></tr>
<tr><td>41</td><td>West Virginia</td><td>523,494,000</td><td>0.3%</td><td>48</td><td>Massachusetts</td><td>101,588,000</td><td>0.1%</td></tr>
<tr><td>8</td><td>Wisconsin</td><td>7,341,639,000</td><td>4.2%</td><td>49</td><td>Rhode Island</td><td>29,380,000</td><td>0.0%</td></tr>
<tr><td>37</td><td>Wyoming</td><td>1,151,329,000</td><td>0.7%</td><td>50</td><td>Alaska</td><td>8,035,000</td><td>0.0%</td></tr>
<tr><td></td><td></td><td></td><td></td><td></td><td>District of Columbia</td><td>0</td><td>0.0%</td></tr>
</tbody>
</table>

Source: U.S. Department of Agriculture, Economic Research Service
   "Farm Sector Financial Indicators, State Rankings" (www.ers.usda.gov/data-products/farm-income-and-wealth-statistics.aspx)
*Includes livestock products.

Farm Income: Government Payments in 2018

National Total = $13,669,010,000*

ALPHA ORDER

RANK ORDER

RANK	STATE	FARM INCOME	% of USA		RANK	STATE	FARM INCOME	% of USA
30	Alabama	$104,958,000	0.8%		1	Iowa	$1,183,601,000	8.7%
45	Alaska	12,158,000	0.1%		2	Illinois	1,050,927,000	7.7%
35	Arizona	58,683,000	0.4%		3	Texas	850,290,000	6.2%
9	Arkansas	628,869,000	4.6%		4	Minnesota	826,925,000	6.0%
19	California	275,474,000	2.0%		5	South Dakota	802,929,000	5.9%
21	Colorado	229,920,000	1.7%		6	Kansas	795,346,000	5.8%
49	Connecticut	5,666,000	0.0%		7	North Dakota	738,975,000	5.4%
40	Delaware	17,152,000	0.1%		8	Nebraska	686,692,000	5.0%
26	Florida	137,238,000	1.0%		9	Arkansas	628,869,000	4.6%
16	Georgia	325,523,000	2.4%		10	Missouri	580,255,000	4.2%
43	Hawaii	13,802,000	0.1%		11	Indiana	516,224,000	3.8%
24	Idaho	157,284,000	1.2%		12	Ohio	446,206,000	3.3%
2	Illinois	1,050,927,000	7.7%		13	Mississippi	366,164,000	2.7%
11	Indiana	516,224,000	3.8%		14	Montana	340,924,000	2.5%
1	Iowa	1,183,601,000	8.7%		15	Oklahoma	333,553,000	2.4%
6	Kansas	795,346,000	5.8%		16	Georgia	325,523,000	2.4%
23	Kentucky	161,992,000	1.2%		17	Wisconsin	300,846,000	2.2%
18	Louisiana	282,117,000	2.1%		18	Louisiana	282,117,000	2.1%
41	Maine	16,187,000	0.1%		19	California	275,474,000	2.0%
37	Maryland	39,230,000	0.3%		20	Michigan	232,258,000	1.7%
47	Massachusetts	7,774,000	0.1%		21	Colorado	229,920,000	1.7%
20	Michigan	232,258,000	1.7%		22	Washington	196,925,000	1.4%
4	Minnesota	826,925,000	6.0%		23	Kentucky	161,992,000	1.2%
13	Mississippi	366,164,000	2.7%		24	Idaho	157,284,000	1.2%
10	Missouri	580,255,000	4.2%		25	Tennessee	138,968,000	1.0%
14	Montana	340,924,000	2.5%		26	Florida	137,238,000	1.0%
8	Nebraska	686,692,000	5.0%		27	Oregon	117,571,000	0.9%
42	Nevada	14,667,000	0.1%		28	New Mexico	111,866,000	0.8%
48	New Hampshire	7,526,000	0.1%		29	North Carolina	105,916,000	0.8%
46	New Jersey	9,942,000	0.1%		30	Alabama	104,958,000	0.8%
28	New Mexico	111,866,000	0.8%		31	Pennsylvania	90,960,000	0.7%
32	New York	81,203,000	0.6%		32	New York	81,203,000	0.6%
29	North Carolina	105,916,000	0.8%		33	Virginia	76,055,000	0.6%
7	North Dakota	738,975,000	5.4%		34	Utah	63,477,000	0.5%
12	Ohio	446,206,000	3.3%		35	Arizona	58,683,000	0.4%
15	Oklahoma	333,553,000	2.4%		36	South Carolina	56,522,000	0.4%
27	Oregon	117,571,000	0.9%		37	Maryland	39,230,000	0.3%
31	Pennsylvania	90,960,000	0.7%		38	Wyoming	33,860,000	0.2%
50	Rhode Island	2,192,000	0.0%		39	Vermont	22,810,000	0.2%
36	South Carolina	56,522,000	0.4%		40	Delaware	17,152,000	0.1%
5	South Dakota	802,929,000	5.9%		41	Maine	16,187,000	0.1%
25	Tennessee	138,968,000	1.0%		42	Nevada	14,667,000	0.1%
3	Texas	850,290,000	6.2%		43	Hawaii	13,802,000	0.1%
34	Utah	63,477,000	0.5%		44	West Virginia	12,406,000	0.1%
39	Vermont	22,810,000	0.2%		45	Alaska	12,158,000	0.1%
33	Virginia	76,055,000	0.6%		46	New Jersey	9,942,000	0.1%
22	Washington	196,925,000	1.4%		47	Massachusetts	7,774,000	0.1%
44	West Virginia	12,406,000	0.1%		48	New Hampshire	7,526,000	0.1%
17	Wisconsin	300,846,000	2.2%		49	Connecticut	5,666,000	0.0%
38	Wyoming	33,860,000	0.2%		50	Rhode Island	2,192,000	0.0%
						District of Columbia	0	0.0%

Source: U.S. Department of Agriculture, Economic Research Service
   "Farm Sector Financial Indicators, State Rankings" (www.ers.usda.gov/data-products/farm-income-and-wealth-statistics.aspx)
*Government payments made directly to farmers in cash.

Acres Planted in 2019

National Total = 302,635,000 Acres*

ALPHA ORDER

RANK	STATE	ACRES	% of USA
30	Alabama	2,115,000	0.7%
48	Alaska	28,000	0.0%
38	Arizona	634,000	0.2%
15	Arkansas	6,598,000	2.2%
27	California	2,941,000	1.0%
16	Colorado	6,091,000	2.0%
45	Connecticut	70,000	0.0%
41	Delaware	435,000	0.1%
35	Florida	1,072,000	0.4%
25	Georgia	3,354,000	1.1%
NA	Hawaii**	NA	NA
21	Idaho	4,107,000	1.4%
4	Illinois	21,590,000	7.1%
10	Indiana	11,250,000	3.7%
1	Iowa	23,935,000	7.9%
3	Kansas	23,113,000	7.6%
17	Kentucky	5,712,000	1.9%
26	Louisiana	3,025,000	1.0%
44	Maine	229,000	0.1%
32	Maryland	1,556,000	0.5%
46	Massachusetts	65,000	0.0%
18	Michigan	5,541,000	1.8%
7	Minnesota	18,349,000	6.1%
22	Mississippi	3,822,000	1.3%
9	Missouri	12,827,000	4.2%
11	Montana	9,946,000	3.3%
6	Nebraska	19,176,000	6.3%
40	Nevada	450,000	0.1%
47	New Hampshire	61,000	0.0%
42	New Jersey	282,000	0.1%
37	New Mexico	823,000	0.3%
29	New York	2,591,000	0.9%
20	North Carolina	4,400,000	1.5%
2	North Dakota	23,221,000	7.7%
13	Ohio	8,595,000	2.8%
12	Oklahoma	9,390,000	3.1%
31	Oregon	1,905,000	0.6%
23	Pennsylvania	3,686,000	1.2%
49	Rhode Island	7,000	0.0%
34	South Carolina	1,428,000	0.5%
8	South Dakota	13,816,000	4.6%
19	Tennessee	4,836,000	1.6%
5	Texas	21,418,000	7.1%
36	Utah	907,000	0.3%
43	Vermont	241,000	0.1%
28	Virginia	2,609,000	0.9%
24	Washington	3,542,000	1.2%
39	West Virginia	567,000	0.2%
14	Wisconsin	7,624,000	2.5%
33	Wyoming	1,504,000	0.5%

RANK ORDER

RANK	STATE	ACRES	% of USA
1	Iowa	23,935,000	7.9%
2	North Dakota	23,221,000	7.7%
3	Kansas	23,113,000	7.6%
4	Illinois	21,590,000	7.1%
5	Texas	21,418,000	7.1%
6	Nebraska	19,176,000	6.3%
7	Minnesota	18,349,000	6.1%
8	South Dakota	13,816,000	4.6%
9	Missouri	12,827,000	4.2%
10	Indiana	11,250,000	3.7%
11	Montana	9,946,000	3.3%
12	Oklahoma	9,390,000	3.1%
13	Ohio	8,595,000	2.8%
14	Wisconsin	7,624,000	2.5%
15	Arkansas	6,598,000	2.2%
16	Colorado	6,091,000	2.0%
17	Kentucky	5,712,000	1.9%
18	Michigan	5,541,000	1.8%
19	Tennessee	4,836,000	1.6%
20	North Carolina	4,400,000	1.5%
21	Idaho	4,107,000	1.4%
22	Mississippi	3,822,000	1.3%
23	Pennsylvania	3,686,000	1.2%
24	Washington	3,542,000	1.2%
25	Georgia	3,354,000	1.1%
26	Louisiana	3,025,000	1.0%
27	California	2,941,000	1.0%
28	Virginia	2,609,000	0.9%
29	New York	2,591,000	0.9%
30	Alabama	2,115,000	0.7%
31	Oregon	1,905,000	0.6%
32	Maryland	1,556,000	0.5%
33	Wyoming	1,504,000	0.5%
34	South Carolina	1,428,000	0.5%
35	Florida	1,072,000	0.4%
36	Utah	907,000	0.3%
37	New Mexico	823,000	0.3%
38	Arizona	634,000	0.2%
39	West Virginia	567,000	0.2%
40	Nevada	450,000	0.1%
41	Delaware	435,000	0.1%
42	New Jersey	282,000	0.1%
43	Vermont	241,000	0.1%
44	Maine	229,000	0.1%
45	Connecticut	70,000	0.0%
46	Massachusetts	65,000	0.0%
47	New Hampshire	61,000	0.0%
48	Alaska	28,000	0.0%
49	Rhode Island	7,000	0.0%
NA	Hawaii**	NA	NA
	District of Columbia**	NA	NA

Source: U.S. Department of Agriculture, National Agricultural Statistics Service
   "Crop Production: 2019 Summary" (January 2020, https://usda.library.cornell.edu/concern/publications/k3569432s)
*Estimated totals.
**No acreage or not available.

Acres Harvested in 2019

National Total = 284,949,000 Acres*

<table>
<tr><td colspan="4">ALPHA ORDER</td><td colspan="4">RANK ORDER</td></tr>
<tr><td>RANK</td><td>STATE</td><td>ACRES</td><td>% of USA</td><td>RANK</td><td>STATE</td><td>ACRES</td><td>% of USA</td></tr>
<tr><td>30</td><td>Alabama</td><td>2,050,000</td><td>0.7%</td><td>1</td><td>Iowa</td><td>23,619,000</td><td>8.3%</td></tr>
<tr><td>48</td><td>Alaska</td><td>27,000</td><td>0.0%</td><td>2</td><td>Kansas</td><td>22,268,000</td><td>7.8%</td></tr>
<tr><td>37</td><td>Arizona</td><td>625,000</td><td>0.2%</td><td>3</td><td>North Dakota</td><td>21,372,000</td><td>7.5%</td></tr>
<tr><td>15</td><td>Arkansas</td><td>6,417,000</td><td>2.3%</td><td>4</td><td>Illinois</td><td>21,210,000</td><td>7.4%</td></tr>
<tr><td>27</td><td>California</td><td>2,542,000</td><td>0.9%</td><td>5</td><td>Nebraska</td><td>18,777,000</td><td>6.6%</td></tr>
<tr><td>16</td><td>Colorado</td><td>5,799,000</td><td>2.0%</td><td>6</td><td>Minnesota</td><td>17,849,000</td><td>6.3%</td></tr>
<tr><td>45</td><td>Connecticut</td><td>68,000</td><td>0.0%</td><td>7</td><td>Texas</td><td>16,799,000</td><td>5.9%</td></tr>
<tr><td>41</td><td>Delaware</td><td>415,000</td><td>0.1%</td><td>8</td><td>South Dakota</td><td>13,269,000</td><td>4.7%</td></tr>
<tr><td>34</td><td>Florida</td><td>1,059,000</td><td>0.4%</td><td>9</td><td>Missouri</td><td>12,367,000</td><td>4.3%</td></tr>
<tr><td>25</td><td>Georgia</td><td>3,152,000</td><td>1.1%</td><td>10</td><td>Indiana</td><td>11,070,000</td><td>3.9%</td></tr>
<tr><td>NA</td><td>Hawaii**</td><td>NA</td><td>NA</td><td>11</td><td>Montana</td><td>9,403,000</td><td>3.3%</td></tr>
<tr><td>21</td><td>Idaho</td><td>3,956,000</td><td>1.4%</td><td>12</td><td>Ohio</td><td>8,340,000</td><td>2.9%</td></tr>
<tr><td>4</td><td>Illinois</td><td>21,210,000</td><td>7.4%</td><td>13</td><td>Oklahoma</td><td>7,416,000</td><td>2.6%</td></tr>
<tr><td>10</td><td>Indiana</td><td>11,070,000</td><td>3.9%</td><td>14</td><td>Wisconsin</td><td>7,086,000</td><td>2.5%</td></tr>
<tr><td>1</td><td>Iowa</td><td>23,619,000</td><td>8.3%</td><td>15</td><td>Arkansas</td><td>6,417,000</td><td>2.3%</td></tr>
<tr><td>2</td><td>Kansas</td><td>22,268,000</td><td>7.8%</td><td>16</td><td>Colorado</td><td>5,799,000</td><td>2.0%</td></tr>
<tr><td>17</td><td>Kentucky</td><td>5,552,000</td><td>1.9%</td><td>17</td><td>Kentucky</td><td>5,552,000</td><td>1.9%</td></tr>
<tr><td>26</td><td>Louisiana</td><td>2,952,000</td><td>1.0%</td><td>18</td><td>Michigan</td><td>5,345,000</td><td>1.9%</td></tr>
<tr><td>44</td><td>Maine</td><td>222,000</td><td>0.1%</td><td>19</td><td>Tennessee</td><td>4,716,000</td><td>1.7%</td></tr>
<tr><td>33</td><td>Maryland</td><td>1,346,000</td><td>0.5%</td><td>20</td><td>North Carolina</td><td>4,273,000</td><td>1.5%</td></tr>
<tr><td>46</td><td>Massachusetts</td><td>62,000</td><td>0.0%</td><td>21</td><td>Idaho</td><td>3,956,000</td><td>1.4%</td></tr>
<tr><td>18</td><td>Michigan</td><td>5,345,000</td><td>1.9%</td><td>22</td><td>Mississippi</td><td>3,720,000</td><td>1.3%</td></tr>
<tr><td>6</td><td>Minnesota</td><td>17,849,000</td><td>6.3%</td><td>23</td><td>Pennsylvania</td><td>3,495,000</td><td>1.2%</td></tr>
<tr><td>22</td><td>Mississippi</td><td>3,720,000</td><td>1.3%</td><td>24</td><td>Washington</td><td>3,471,000</td><td>1.2%</td></tr>
<tr><td>9</td><td>Missouri</td><td>12,367,000</td><td>4.3%</td><td>25</td><td>Georgia</td><td>3,152,000</td><td>1.1%</td></tr>
<tr><td>11</td><td>Montana</td><td>9,403,000</td><td>3.3%</td><td>26</td><td>Louisiana</td><td>2,952,000</td><td>1.0%</td></tr>
<tr><td>5</td><td>Nebraska</td><td>18,777,000</td><td>6.6%</td><td>27</td><td>California</td><td>2,542,000</td><td>0.9%</td></tr>
<tr><td>40</td><td>Nevada</td><td>447,000</td><td>0.2%</td><td>28</td><td>New York</td><td>2,504,000</td><td>0.9%</td></tr>
<tr><td>47</td><td>New Hampshire</td><td>60,000</td><td>0.0%</td><td>29</td><td>Virginia</td><td>2,474,000</td><td>0.9%</td></tr>
<tr><td>42</td><td>New Jersey</td><td>272,000</td><td>0.1%</td><td>30</td><td>Alabama</td><td>2,050,000</td><td>0.7%</td></tr>
<tr><td>39</td><td>New Mexico</td><td>543,000</td><td>0.2%</td><td>31</td><td>Oregon</td><td>1,878,000</td><td>0.7%</td></tr>
<tr><td>28</td><td>New York</td><td>2,504,000</td><td>0.9%</td><td>32</td><td>Wyoming</td><td>1,456,000</td><td>0.5%</td></tr>
<tr><td>20</td><td>North Carolina</td><td>4,273,000</td><td>1.5%</td><td>33</td><td>Maryland</td><td>1,346,000</td><td>0.5%</td></tr>
<tr><td>3</td><td>North Dakota</td><td>21,372,000</td><td>7.5%</td><td>34</td><td>Florida</td><td>1,059,000</td><td>0.4%</td></tr>
<tr><td>12</td><td>Ohio</td><td>8,340,000</td><td>2.9%</td><td>35</td><td>South Carolina</td><td>1,015,000</td><td>0.4%</td></tr>
<tr><td>13</td><td>Oklahoma</td><td>7,416,000</td><td>2.6%</td><td>36</td><td>Utah</td><td>887,000</td><td>0.3%</td></tr>
<tr><td>31</td><td>Oregon</td><td>1,878,000</td><td>0.7%</td><td>37</td><td>Arizona</td><td>625,000</td><td>0.2%</td></tr>
<tr><td>23</td><td>Pennsylvania</td><td>3,495,000</td><td>1.2%</td><td>38</td><td>West Virginia</td><td>565,000</td><td>0.2%</td></tr>
<tr><td>49</td><td>Rhode Island</td><td>7,000</td><td>0.0%</td><td>39</td><td>New Mexico</td><td>543,000</td><td>0.2%</td></tr>
<tr><td>35</td><td>South Carolina</td><td>1,015,000</td><td>0.4%</td><td>40</td><td>Nevada</td><td>447,000</td><td>0.2%</td></tr>
<tr><td>8</td><td>South Dakota</td><td>13,269,000</td><td>4.7%</td><td>41</td><td>Delaware</td><td>415,000</td><td>0.1%</td></tr>
<tr><td>19</td><td>Tennessee</td><td>4,716,000</td><td>1.7%</td><td>42</td><td>New Jersey</td><td>272,000</td><td>0.1%</td></tr>
<tr><td>7</td><td>Texas</td><td>16,799,000</td><td>5.9%</td><td>43</td><td>Vermont</td><td>237,000</td><td>0.1%</td></tr>
<tr><td>36</td><td>Utah</td><td>887,000</td><td>0.3%</td><td>44</td><td>Maine</td><td>222,000</td><td>0.1%</td></tr>
<tr><td>43</td><td>Vermont</td><td>237,000</td><td>0.1%</td><td>45</td><td>Connecticut</td><td>68,000</td><td>0.0%</td></tr>
<tr><td>29</td><td>Virginia</td><td>2,474,000</td><td>0.9%</td><td>46</td><td>Massachusetts</td><td>62,000</td><td>0.0%</td></tr>
<tr><td>24</td><td>Washington</td><td>3,471,000</td><td>1.2%</td><td>47</td><td>New Hampshire</td><td>60,000</td><td>0.0%</td></tr>
<tr><td>38</td><td>West Virginia</td><td>565,000</td><td>0.2%</td><td>48</td><td>Alaska</td><td>27,000</td><td>0.0%</td></tr>
<tr><td>14</td><td>Wisconsin</td><td>7,086,000</td><td>2.5%</td><td>49</td><td>Rhode Island</td><td>7,000</td><td>0.0%</td></tr>
<tr><td>32</td><td>Wyoming</td><td>1,456,000</td><td>0.5%</td><td>NA</td><td>Hawaii**</td><td>NA</td><td>NA</td></tr>
<tr><td></td><td></td><td></td><td></td><td></td><td>District of Columbia**</td><td>NA</td><td>NA</td></tr>
</table>

Source: U.S. Department of Agriculture, National Agricultural Statistics Service
    "Crop Production: 2019 Summary" (January 2020, https://usda.library.cornell.edu/concern/publications/k3569432s)
*Estimated totals.
**No acreage or not available.

Acres Harvested: Corn in 2019

National Total = 81,482,000 Acres*

ALPHA ORDER

RANK	STATE	ACRES	% of USA
28	Alabama	305,000	0.4%
NA	Alaska**	NA	NA
40	Arizona	37,000	0.0%
19	Arkansas	725,000	0.9%
34	California	60,000	0.1%
15	Colorado	1,300,000	1.6%
NA	Connecticut**	NA	NA
29	Delaware	180,000	0.2%
36	Florida	54,000	0.1%
25	Georgia	350,000	0.4%
NA	Hawaii**	NA	NA
30	Idaho	148,000	0.2%
2	Illinois	10,200,000	12.5%
6	Indiana	4,820,000	5.9%
1	Iowa	13,050,000	16.0%
5	Kansas	6,020,000	7.4%
14	Kentucky	1,450,000	1.8%
21	Louisiana	545,000	0.7%
NA	Maine**	NA	NA
23	Maryland	460,000	0.6%
NA	Massachusetts**	NA	NA
13	Michigan	1,610,000	2.0%
4	Minnesota	7,260,000	8.9%
20	Mississippi	620,000	0.8%
9	Missouri	2,990,000	3.7%
34	Montana	60,000	0.1%
3	Nebraska	9,810,000	12.0%
NA	Nevada**	NA	NA
NA	New Hampshire**	NA	NA
32	New Jersey	68,000	0.1%
38	New Mexico	46,000	0.1%
21	New York	545,000	0.7%
17	North Carolina	930,000	1.1%
8	North Dakota	3,230,000	4.0%
11	Ohio	2,570,000	3.2%
27	Oklahoma	330,000	0.4%
37	Oregon	48,000	0.1%
16	Pennsylvania	1,060,000	1.3%
NA	Rhode Island**	NA	NA
25	South Carolina	350,000	0.4%
7	South Dakota	3,910,000	4.8%
18	Tennessee	910,000	1.1%
12	Texas	2,150,000	2.6%
41	Utah	26,000	0.0%
NA	Vermont**	NA	NA
24	Virginia	380,000	0.5%
31	Washington	90,000	0.1%
39	West Virginia	38,000	0.0%
10	Wisconsin	2,680,000	3.3%
33	Wyoming	67,000	0.1%

RANK ORDER

RANK	STATE	ACRES	% of USA
1	Iowa	13,050,000	16.0%
2	Illinois	10,200,000	12.5%
3	Nebraska	9,810,000	12.0%
4	Minnesota	7,260,000	8.9%
5	Kansas	6,020,000	7.4%
6	Indiana	4,820,000	5.9%
7	South Dakota	3,910,000	4.8%
8	North Dakota	3,230,000	4.0%
9	Missouri	2,990,000	3.7%
10	Wisconsin	2,680,000	3.3%
11	Ohio	2,570,000	3.2%
12	Texas	2,150,000	2.6%
13	Michigan	1,610,000	2.0%
14	Kentucky	1,450,000	1.8%
15	Colorado	1,300,000	1.6%
16	Pennsylvania	1,060,000	1.3%
17	North Carolina	930,000	1.1%
18	Tennessee	910,000	1.1%
19	Arkansas	725,000	0.9%
20	Mississippi	620,000	0.8%
21	Louisiana	545,000	0.7%
21	New York	545,000	0.7%
23	Maryland	460,000	0.6%
24	Virginia	380,000	0.5%
25	Georgia	350,000	0.4%
25	South Carolina	350,000	0.4%
27	Oklahoma	330,000	0.4%
28	Alabama	305,000	0.4%
29	Delaware	180,000	0.2%
30	Idaho	148,000	0.2%
31	Washington	90,000	0.1%
32	New Jersey	68,000	0.1%
33	Wyoming	67,000	0.1%
34	California	60,000	0.1%
34	Montana	60,000	0.1%
36	Florida	54,000	0.1%
37	Oregon	48,000	0.1%
38	New Mexico	46,000	0.1%
39	West Virginia	38,000	0.0%
40	Arizona	37,000	0.0%
41	Utah	26,000	0.0%
NA	Alaska**	NA	NA
NA	Connecticut**	NA	NA
NA	Hawaii**	NA	NA
NA	Maine**	NA	NA
NA	Massachusetts**	NA	NA
NA	Nevada**	NA	NA
NA	New Hampshire**	NA	NA
NA	Rhode Island**	NA	NA
NA	Vermont**	NA	NA
	District of Columbia**	NA	NA

Source: U.S. Department of Agriculture, National Agricultural Statistics Service
   "Crop Production: 2019 Summary" (January 2020, https://usda.library.cornell.edu/concern/publications/k3569432s)
*Estimated totals. Acres harvested for grain.
**No acreage or not available.

Acres Harvested: Soybeans in 2019

National Total = 75,021,000 Acres*

Source: U.S. Department of Agriculture, National Agricultural Statistics Service
"Crop Production: 2019 Summary" (January 2020, https://usda.library.cornell.edu/concern/publications/k3569432s)
*Estimated totals.
**No acreage or not available.

Acres Harvested: Wheat in 2019

National Total = 37,162,000 Acres*

RANK	STATE	ACRES	% of USA
29	Alabama	85,000	0.2%
NA	Alaska**	NA	NA
35	Arizona	33,000	0.1%
31	Arkansas	50,000	0.1%
24	California	122,000	0.3%
7	Colorado	2,000,000	5.4%
NA	Connecticut**	NA	NA
31	Delaware	50,000	0.1%
NA	Florida**	NA	NA
31	Georgia	50,000	0.1%
NA	Hawaii**	NA	NA
10	Idaho	1,125,000	3.0%
13	Illinois	550,000	1.5%
18	Indiana	260,000	0.7%
NA	Iowa**	NA	NA
2	Kansas	6,500,000	17.5%
17	Kentucky	330,000	0.9%
NA	Louisiana**	NA	NA
NA	Maine**	NA	NA
21	Maryland	165,000	0.4%
NA	Massachusetts**	NA	NA
14	Michigan	480,000	1.3%
8	Minnesota	1,400,000	3.8%
36	Mississippi	21,000	0.1%
15	Missouri	390,000	1.0%
3	Montana	5,175,000	13.9%
11	Nebraska	970,000	2.6%
NA	Nevada**	NA	NA
NA	New Hampshire**	NA	NA
37	New Jersey	14,000	0.0%
27	New Mexico	105,000	0.3%
30	New York	66,000	0.2%
19	North Carolina	225,000	0.6%
1	North Dakota	6,620,000	17.8%
16	Ohio	385,000	1.0%
4	Oklahoma	2,750,000	7.4%
12	Oregon	730,000	2.0%
23	Pennsylvania	140,000	0.4%
NA	Rhode Island**	NA	NA
34	South Carolina	45,000	0.1%
9	South Dakota	1,375,000	3.7%
20	Tennessee	215,000	0.6%
6	Texas	2,050,000	5.5%
25	Utah	116,000	0.3%
NA	Vermont**	NA	NA
27	Virginia	105,000	0.3%
5	Washington	2,205,000	5.9%
NA	West Virginia**	NA	NA
22	Wisconsin	150,000	0.4%
26	Wyoming	110,000	0.3%

RANK	STATE	ACRES	% of USA
1	North Dakota	6,620,000	17.8%
2	Kansas	6,500,000	17.5%
3	Montana	5,175,000	13.9%
4	Oklahoma	2,750,000	7.4%
5	Washington	2,205,000	5.9%
6	Texas	2,050,000	5.5%
7	Colorado	2,000,000	5.4%
8	Minnesota	1,400,000	3.8%
9	South Dakota	1,375,000	3.7%
10	Idaho	1,125,000	3.0%
11	Nebraska	970,000	2.6%
12	Oregon	730,000	2.0%
13	Illinois	550,000	1.5%
14	Michigan	480,000	1.3%
15	Missouri	390,000	1.0%
16	Ohio	385,000	1.0%
17	Kentucky	330,000	0.9%
18	Indiana	260,000	0.7%
19	North Carolina	225,000	0.6%
20	Tennessee	215,000	0.6%
21	Maryland	165,000	0.4%
22	Wisconsin	150,000	0.4%
23	Pennsylvania	140,000	0.4%
24	California	122,000	0.3%
25	Utah	116,000	0.3%
26	Wyoming	110,000	0.3%
27	New Mexico	105,000	0.3%
27	Virginia	105,000	0.3%
29	Alabama	85,000	0.2%
30	New York	66,000	0.2%
31	Arkansas	50,000	0.1%
31	Delaware	50,000	0.1%
31	Georgia	50,000	0.1%
34	South Carolina	45,000	0.1%
35	Arizona	33,000	0.1%
36	Mississippi	21,000	0.1%
37	New Jersey	14,000	0.0%
NA	Alaska**	NA	NA
NA	Connecticut**	NA	NA
NA	Florida**	NA	NA
NA	Hawaii**	NA	NA
NA	Iowa**	NA	NA
NA	Louisiana**	NA	NA
NA	Maine**	NA	NA
NA	Massachusetts**	NA	NA
NA	Nevada**	NA	NA
NA	New Hampshire**	NA	NA
NA	Rhode Island**	NA	NA
NA	Vermont**	NA	NA
NA	West Virginia**	NA	NA
	District of Columbia**	NA	NA

Source: U.S. Department of Agriculture, National Agricultural Statistics Service
   "Crop Production: 2019 Summary" (January 2020, https://usda.library.cornell.edu/concern/publications/k3569432s)
*Estimated totals.
**No acreage or not available.

Cattle on Farms in 2020

National Total = 94,413,300 Cattle*

ALPHA ORDER

RANK	STATE	CATTLE	% of USA
24	Alabama	1,310,000	1.4%
48	Alaska	17,000	0.0%
31	Arizona	970,000	1.0%
17	Arkansas	1,740,000	1.8%
4	California	5,200,000	5.5%
10	Colorado	2,800,000	3.0%
44	Connecticut	49,000	0.1%
49	Delaware	15,000	0.0%
18	Florida	1,680,000	1.8%
29	Georgia	1,100,000	1.2%
42	Hawaii	140,000	0.1%
12	Idaho	2,490,000	2.6%
29	Illinois	1,100,000	1.2%
33	Indiana	840,000	0.9%
7	Iowa	3,900,000	4.1%
3	Kansas	6,450,000	6.8%
14	Kentucky	2,130,000	2.3%
36	Louisiana	780,000	0.8%
43	Maine	80,000	0.1%
41	Maryland	179,000	0.2%
45	Massachusetts	34,000	0.0%
28	Michigan	1,150,000	1.2%
13	Minnesota	2,280,000	2.4%
32	Mississippi	920,000	1.0%
6	Missouri	4,350,000	4.6%
11	Montana	2,500,000	2.6%
2	Nebraska	6,800,000	7.2%
37	Nevada	480,000	0.5%
46	New Hampshire	32,000	0.0%
47	New Jersey	28,000	0.0%
21	New Mexico	1,450,000	1.5%
20	New York	1,470,000	1.6%
35	North Carolina	810,000	0.9%
15	North Dakota	1,900,000	2.0%
25	Ohio	1,290,000	1.4%
4	Oklahoma	5,200,000	5.5%
26	Oregon	1,280,000	1.4%
19	Pennsylvania	1,530,000	1.6%
50	Rhode Island	4,300	0.0%
39	South Carolina	340,000	0.4%
7	South Dakota	3,900,000	4.1%
16	Tennessee	1,810,000	1.9%
1	Texas	13,000,000	13.8%
34	Utah	820,000	0.9%
40	Vermont	250,000	0.3%
21	Virginia	1,450,000	1.5%
27	Washington	1,200,000	1.3%
38	West Virginia	395,000	0.4%
9	Wisconsin	3,450,000	3.7%
23	Wyoming	1,320,000	1.4%

RANK ORDER

RANK	STATE	CATTLE	% of USA
1	Texas	13,000,000	13.8%
2	Nebraska	6,800,000	7.2%
3	Kansas	6,450,000	6.8%
4	California	5,200,000	5.5%
4	Oklahoma	5,200,000	5.5%
6	Missouri	4,350,000	4.6%
7	Iowa	3,900,000	4.1%
7	South Dakota	3,900,000	4.1%
9	Wisconsin	3,450,000	3.7%
10	Colorado	2,800,000	3.0%
11	Montana	2,500,000	2.6%
12	Idaho	2,490,000	2.6%
13	Minnesota	2,280,000	2.4%
14	Kentucky	2,130,000	2.3%
15	North Dakota	1,900,000	2.0%
16	Tennessee	1,810,000	1.9%
17	Arkansas	1,740,000	1.8%
18	Florida	1,680,000	1.8%
19	Pennsylvania	1,530,000	1.6%
20	New York	1,470,000	1.6%
21	New Mexico	1,450,000	1.5%
21	Virginia	1,450,000	1.5%
23	Wyoming	1,320,000	1.4%
24	Alabama	1,310,000	1.4%
25	Ohio	1,290,000	1.4%
26	Oregon	1,280,000	1.4%
27	Washington	1,200,000	1.3%
28	Michigan	1,150,000	1.2%
29	Georgia	1,100,000	1.2%
29	Illinois	1,100,000	1.2%
31	Arizona	970,000	1.0%
32	Mississippi	920,000	1.0%
33	Indiana	840,000	0.9%
34	Utah	820,000	0.9%
35	North Carolina	810,000	0.9%
36	Louisiana	780,000	0.8%
37	Nevada	480,000	0.5%
38	West Virginia	395,000	0.4%
39	South Carolina	340,000	0.4%
40	Vermont	250,000	0.3%
41	Maryland	179,000	0.2%
42	Hawaii	140,000	0.1%
43	Maine	80,000	0.1%
44	Connecticut	49,000	0.1%
45	Massachusetts	34,000	0.0%
46	New Hampshire	32,000	0.0%
47	New Jersey	28,000	0.0%
48	Alaska	17,000	0.0%
49	Delaware	15,000	0.0%
50	Rhode Island	4,300	0.0%
	District of Columbia	0	0.0%

Source: U.S. Department of Agriculture, National Agricultural Statistics Service
"Cattle" (https://usda.library.cornell.edu/concern/publications/h702q636h?locale=en)
*As of January 1, 2020.

Milk Cows on Farms in 2018

National Total = 9,399,000 Milk Cows*

ALPHA ORDER

RANK	STATE	MILK COWS	% of USA
46	Alabama	5,000	0.1%
50	Alaska	300	0.0%
13	Arizona	208,000	2.2%
43	Arkansas	6,000	0.1%
1	California	1,734,000	18.4%
15	Colorado	176,000	1.9%
34	Connecticut	19,000	0.2%
47	Delaware	4,800	0.1%
20	Florida	120,000	1.3%
25	Georgia	82,000	0.9%
48	Hawaii	2,000	0.0%
4	Idaho	609,000	6.5%
22	Illinois	90,000	1.0%
14	Indiana	184,000	2.0%
12	Iowa	220,000	2.3%
16	Kansas	159,000	1.7%
27	Kentucky	55,000	0.6%
39	Louisiana	11,000	0.1%
33	Maine	30,000	0.3%
28	Maryland	45,000	0.5%
39	Massachusetts	11,000	0.1%
8	Michigan	424,000	4.5%
7	Minnesota	453,000	4.8%
41	Mississippi	9,000	0.1%
23	Missouri	83,000	0.9%
37	Montana	12,000	0.1%
26	Nebraska	60,000	0.6%
32	Nevada	32,000	0.3%
37	New Hampshire	12,000	0.1%
43	New Jersey	6,000	0.1%
9	New Mexico	330,000	3.5%
3	New York	623,000	6.6%
29	North Carolina	44,000	0.5%
35	North Dakota	15,000	0.2%
11	Ohio	259,000	2.8%
30	Oklahoma	40,000	0.4%
18	Oregon	123,000	1.3%
6	Pennsylvania	519,000	5.5%
49	Rhode Island	700	0.0%
36	South Carolina	14,000	0.1%
19	South Dakota	121,000	1.3%
31	Tennessee	37,000	0.4%
5	Texas	537,000	5.7%
21	Utah	100,000	1.1%
17	Vermont	127,000	1.4%
23	Virginia	83,000	0.9%
10	Washington	277,000	2.9%
42	West Virginia	7,000	0.1%
2	Wisconsin	1,274,000	13.6%
43	Wyoming	6,000	0.1%

RANK ORDER

RANK	STATE	MILK COWS	% of USA
1	California	1,734,000	18.4%
2	Wisconsin	1,274,000	13.6%
3	New York	623,000	6.6%
4	Idaho	609,000	6.5%
5	Texas	537,000	5.7%
6	Pennsylvania	519,000	5.5%
7	Minnesota	453,000	4.8%
8	Michigan	424,000	4.5%
9	New Mexico	330,000	3.5%
10	Washington	277,000	2.9%
11	Ohio	259,000	2.8%
12	Iowa	220,000	2.3%
13	Arizona	208,000	2.2%
14	Indiana	184,000	2.0%
15	Colorado	176,000	1.9%
16	Kansas	159,000	1.7%
17	Vermont	127,000	1.4%
18	Oregon	123,000	1.3%
19	South Dakota	121,000	1.3%
20	Florida	120,000	1.3%
21	Utah	100,000	1.1%
22	Illinois	90,000	1.0%
23	Missouri	83,000	0.9%
23	Virginia	83,000	0.9%
25	Georgia	82,000	0.9%
26	Nebraska	60,000	0.6%
27	Kentucky	55,000	0.6%
28	Maryland	45,000	0.5%
29	North Carolina	44,000	0.5%
30	Oklahoma	40,000	0.4%
31	Tennessee	37,000	0.4%
32	Nevada	32,000	0.3%
33	Maine	30,000	0.3%
34	Connecticut	19,000	0.2%
35	North Dakota	15,000	0.2%
36	South Carolina	14,000	0.1%
37	Montana	12,000	0.1%
37	New Hampshire	12,000	0.1%
39	Louisiana	11,000	0.1%
39	Massachusetts	11,000	0.1%
41	Mississippi	9,000	0.1%
42	West Virginia	7,000	0.1%
43	Arkansas	6,000	0.1%
43	New Jersey	6,000	0.1%
43	Wyoming	6,000	0.1%
46	Alabama	5,000	0.1%
47	Delaware	4,800	0.1%
48	Hawaii	2,000	0.0%
49	Rhode Island	700	0.0%
50	Alaska	300	0.0%
	District of Columbia	0	0.0%

Source: U.S. Department of Agriculture, National Agricultural Statistics Service
"Milk Production, Disposition and Income: 2018 Summary" (May 2019)
(https://usda.library.cornell.edu/concern/publications/4b29b5974)
*Average number during year. Excludes heifers not yet fresh.

Milk Production in 2018

National Total = 217,575,000,000 Pounds of Milk*

ALPHA ORDER

RANK	STATE	POUNDS	% of USA
47	Alabama	73,000,000	0.0%
50	Alaska	2,800,000	0.0%
13	Arizona	4,978,000,000	2.3%
46	Arkansas	74,000,000	0.0%
1	California	40,413,000,000	18.6%
14	Colorado	4,557,000,000	2.1%
34	Connecticut	427,000,000	0.2%
45	Delaware	91,500,000	0.0%
20	Florida	2,381,000,000	1.1%
23	Georgia	1,766,000,000	0.8%
48	Hawaii	34,000,000	0.0%
3	Idaho	15,149,000,000	7.0%
22	Illinois	1,878,000,000	0.9%
15	Indiana	4,161,000,000	1.9%
12	Iowa	5,268,000,000	2.4%
16	Kansas	3,708,000,000	1.7%
27	Kentucky	1,009,000,000	0.5%
40	Louisiana	152,000,000	0.1%
33	Maine	618,000,000	0.3%
29	Maryland	925,000,000	0.4%
39	Massachusetts	202,000,000	0.1%
6	Michigan	11,168,000,000	5.1%
8	Minnesota	9,868,000,000	4.5%
42	Mississippi	129,000,000	0.1%
26	Missouri	1,194,000,000	0.5%
36	Montana	274,000,000	0.1%
25	Nebraska	1,440,000,000	0.7%
30	Nevada	734,000,000	0.3%
37	New Hampshire	249,000,000	0.1%
44	New Jersey	110,000,000	0.1%
9	New Mexico	8,285,000,000	3.8%
4	New York	14,882,000,000	6.8%
28	North Carolina	937,000,000	0.4%
35	North Dakota	334,000,000	0.2%
11	Ohio	5,532,000,000	2.5%
31	Oklahoma	725,000,000	0.3%
19	Oregon	2,531,000,000	1.2%
7	Pennsylvania	10,665,000,000	4.9%
49	Rhode Island	11,700,000	0.0%
38	South Carolina	242,000,000	0.1%
17	South Dakota	2,705,000,000	1.2%
32	Tennessee	634,000,000	0.3%
5	Texas	12,852,000,000	5.9%
21	Utah	2,322,000,000	1.1%
18	Vermont	2,680,000,000	1.2%
24	Virginia	1,635,000,000	0.8%
10	Washington	6,736,000,000	3.1%
43	West Virginia	111,000,000	0.1%
2	Wisconsin	30,579,000,000	14.1%
41	Wyoming	142,200,000	0.1%

RANK ORDER

RANK	STATE	POUNDS	% of USA
1	California	40,413,000,000	18.6%
2	Wisconsin	30,579,000,000	14.1%
3	Idaho	15,149,000,000	7.0%
4	New York	14,882,000,000	6.8%
5	Texas	12,852,000,000	5.9%
6	Michigan	11,168,000,000	5.1%
7	Pennsylvania	10,665,000,000	4.9%
8	Minnesota	9,868,000,000	4.5%
9	New Mexico	8,285,000,000	3.8%
10	Washington	6,736,000,000	3.1%
11	Ohio	5,532,000,000	2.5%
12	Iowa	5,268,000,000	2.4%
13	Arizona	4,978,000,000	2.3%
14	Colorado	4,557,000,000	2.1%
15	Indiana	4,161,000,000	1.9%
16	Kansas	3,708,000,000	1.7%
17	South Dakota	2,705,000,000	1.2%
18	Vermont	2,680,000,000	1.2%
19	Oregon	2,531,000,000	1.2%
20	Florida	2,381,000,000	1.1%
21	Utah	2,322,000,000	1.1%
22	Illinois	1,878,000,000	0.9%
23	Georgia	1,766,000,000	0.8%
24	Virginia	1,635,000,000	0.8%
25	Nebraska	1,440,000,000	0.7%
26	Missouri	1,194,000,000	0.5%
27	Kentucky	1,009,000,000	0.5%
28	North Carolina	937,000,000	0.4%
29	Maryland	925,000,000	0.4%
30	Nevada	734,000,000	0.3%
31	Oklahoma	725,000,000	0.3%
32	Tennessee	634,000,000	0.3%
33	Maine	618,000,000	0.3%
34	Connecticut	427,000,000	0.2%
35	North Dakota	334,000,000	0.2%
36	Montana	274,000,000	0.1%
37	New Hampshire	249,000,000	0.1%
38	South Carolina	242,000,000	0.1%
39	Massachusetts	202,000,000	0.1%
40	Louisiana	152,000,000	0.1%
41	Wyoming	142,200,000	0.1%
42	Mississippi	129,000,000	0.1%
43	West Virginia	111,000,000	0.1%
44	New Jersey	110,000,000	0.1%
45	Delaware	91,500,000	0.0%
46	Arkansas	74,000,000	0.0%
47	Alabama	73,000,000	0.0%
48	Hawaii	34,000,000	0.0%
49	Rhode Island	11,700,000	0.0%
50	Alaska	2,800,000	0.0%
	District of Columbia	0	0.0%

Source: U.S. Department of Agriculture, National Agricultural Statistics Service
  "Milk Production, Disposition and Income: 2018 Summary" (May 2019)
  (https://usda.library.cornell.edu/concern/publications/4b29b5974)
*Excludes milk suckled by calves.

Milk Production per Milk Cow in 2018

National Average = 23,149 Pounds of Milk per Cow*

ALPHA ORDER

RANK	STATE	POUNDS
45	Alabama	14,600
50	Alaska	9,333
9	Arizona	23,933
49	Arkansas	12,333
14	California	23,306
2	Colorado	25,892
19	Connecticut	22,474
35	Delaware	19,063
33	Florida	19,842
23	Georgia	21,537
42	Hawaii	17,000
4	Idaho	24,875
27	Illinois	20,867
18	Indiana	22,614
8	Iowa	23,945
13	Kansas	23,321
37	Kentucky	18,345
48	Louisiana	13,818
29	Maine	20,600
31	Maryland	20,556
36	Massachusetts	18,364
1	Michigan	26,340
22	Minnesota	21,784
47	Mississippi	14,333
46	Missouri	14,386
17	Montana	22,833
7	Nebraska	24,000
16	Nevada	22,938
28	New Hampshire	20,750
38	New Jersey	18,333
3	New Mexico	25,106
11	New York	23,888
25	North Carolina	21,295
21	North Dakota	22,267
24	Ohio	21,359
39	Oklahoma	18,125
30	Oregon	20,577
32	Pennsylvania	20,549
43	Rhode Island	16,714
40	South Carolina	17,286
20	South Dakota	22,355
41	Tennessee	17,135
9	Texas	23,933
15	Utah	23,220
26	Vermont	21,102
34	Virginia	19,699
5	Washington	24,318
44	West Virginia	15,857
6	Wisconsin	24,002
12	Wyoming	23,700

RANK ORDER

RANK	STATE	POUNDS
1	Michigan	26,340
2	Colorado	25,892
3	New Mexico	25,106
4	Idaho	24,875
5	Washington	24,318
6	Wisconsin	24,002
7	Nebraska	24,000
8	Iowa	23,945
9	Arizona	23,933
9	Texas	23,933
11	New York	23,888
12	Wyoming	23,700
13	Kansas	23,321
14	California	23,306
15	Utah	23,220
16	Nevada	22,938
17	Montana	22,833
18	Indiana	22,614
19	Connecticut	22,474
20	South Dakota	22,355
21	North Dakota	22,267
22	Minnesota	21,784
23	Georgia	21,537
24	Ohio	21,359
25	North Carolina	21,295
26	Vermont	21,102
27	Illinois	20,867
28	New Hampshire	20,750
29	Maine	20,600
30	Oregon	20,577
31	Maryland	20,556
32	Pennsylvania	20,549
33	Florida	19,842
34	Virginia	19,699
35	Delaware	19,063
36	Massachusetts	18,364
37	Kentucky	18,345
38	New Jersey	18,333
39	Oklahoma	18,125
40	South Carolina	17,286
41	Tennessee	17,135
42	Hawaii	17,000
43	Rhode Island	16,714
44	West Virginia	15,857
45	Alabama	14,600
46	Missouri	14,386
47	Mississippi	14,333
48	Louisiana	13,818
49	Arkansas	12,333
50	Alaska	9,333
	District of Columbia**	NA

Source: U.S. Department of Agriculture, National Agricultural Statistics Service
"Milk Production, Disposition and Income: 2018 Summary" (May 2019)
(https://usda.library.cornell.edu/concern/publications/4b29b5974)
*Excludes milk suckled by calves.
**Not applicable.

Hogs and Pigs on Farms in 2019

National Total = 77,337,600 Hogs and Pigs*

	ALPHA ORDER					RANK ORDER		
RANK	STATE	HOGS AND PIGS	% of USA		RANK	STATE	HOGS AND PIGS	% of USA
31	Alabama	36,000	0.0%		1	Iowa	24,800,000	32.1%
49	Alaska	1,900	0.0%		2	Minnesota	9,200,000	11.9%
24	Arizona	161,000	0.2%		2	North Carolina	9,200,000	11.9%
26	Arkansas	117,000	0.2%		4	Illinois	5,350,000	6.9%
27	California	106,000	0.1%		5	Indiana	4,300,000	5.6%
16	Colorado	750,000	1.0%		6	Nebraska	3,750,000	4.8%
44	Connecticut	4,000	0.0%		7	Missouri	3,250,000	4.2%
40	Delaware	7,000	0.0%		8	Ohio	2,800,000	3.6%
37	Florida	10,000	0.0%		9	Oklahoma	2,270,000	2.9%
29	Georgia	62,000	0.1%		10	Kansas	2,140,000	2.8%
35	Hawaii	11,000	0.0%		11	South Dakota	1,990,000	2.6%
32	Idaho	35,000	0.0%		12	Pennsylvania	1,310,000	1.7%
4	Illinois	5,350,000	6.9%		13	Michigan	1,220,000	1.6%
5	Indiana	4,300,000	5.6%		14	Texas	1,130,000	1.5%
1	Iowa	24,800,000	32.1%		15	Utah	960,000	1.2%
10	Kansas	2,140,000	2.8%		16	Colorado	750,000	1.0%
17	Kentucky	435,000	0.6%		17	Kentucky	435,000	0.6%
41	Louisiana	6,000	0.0%		18	Wisconsin	365,000	0.5%
43	Maine	4,600	0.0%		19	Virginia	340,000	0.4%
33	Maryland	20,000	0.0%		20	Tennessee	250,000	0.3%
38	Massachusetts	8,000	0.0%		21	Montana	210,000	0.3%
13	Michigan	1,220,000	1.6%		22	South Carolina	195,000	0.3%
2	Minnesota	9,200,000	11.9%		23	Mississippi	190,000	0.2%
23	Mississippi	190,000	0.2%		24	Arizona	161,000	0.2%
7	Missouri	3,250,000	4.2%		25	North Dakota	142,000	0.2%
21	Montana	210,000	0.3%		26	Arkansas	117,000	0.2%
6	Nebraska	3,750,000	4.8%		27	California	106,000	0.1%
42	Nevada	5,000	0.0%		28	Wyoming	94,000	0.1%
46	New Hampshire	3,400	0.0%		29	Georgia	62,000	0.1%
39	New Jersey	7,500	0.0%		30	New York	53,000	0.1%
48	New Mexico	2,000	0.0%		31	Alabama	36,000	0.0%
30	New York	53,000	0.1%		32	Idaho	35,000	0.0%
2	North Carolina	9,200,000	11.9%		33	Maryland	20,000	0.0%
25	North Dakota	142,000	0.2%		34	Washington	17,000	0.0%
8	Ohio	2,800,000	3.6%		35	Hawaii	11,000	0.0%
9	Oklahoma	2,270,000	2.9%		35	Oregon	11,000	0.0%
35	Oregon	11,000	0.0%		37	Florida	10,000	0.0%
12	Pennsylvania	1,310,000	1.7%		38	Massachusetts	8,000	0.0%
50	Rhode Island	1,600	0.0%		39	New Jersey	7,500	0.0%
22	South Carolina	195,000	0.3%		40	Delaware	7,000	0.0%
11	South Dakota	1,990,000	2.6%		41	Louisiana	6,000	0.0%
20	Tennessee	250,000	0.3%		42	Nevada	5,000	0.0%
14	Texas	1,130,000	1.5%		43	Maine	4,600	0.0%
15	Utah	960,000	1.2%		44	Connecticut	4,000	0.0%
45	Vermont	3,600	0.0%		45	Vermont	3,600	0.0%
19	Virginia	340,000	0.4%		46	New Hampshire	3,400	0.0%
34	Washington	17,000	0.0%		47	West Virginia	3,000	0.0%
47	West Virginia	3,000	0.0%		48	New Mexico	2,000	0.0%
18	Wisconsin	365,000	0.5%		49	Alaska	1,900	0.0%
28	Wyoming	94,000	0.1%		50	Rhode Island	1,600	0.0%
						District of Columbia	0	0.0%

Source: U.S. Department of Agriculture, National Agricultural Statistics Service
 "Quarterly Hogs and Pigs" (https://usda.library.cornell.edu/concern/publications/rj430453j)
*As of December 1, 2019.

Chickens in 2018

National Total = 9,037,100,000 Chickens*

ALPHA ORDER

RANK	STATE	CHICKENS	% of USA
2	Alabama	1,123,700,000	12.4%
NA	Alaska***	NA	NA
NA	Arizona***	NA	NA
3	Arkansas	1,092,000,000	12.1%
NA	California**	NA	NA
NA	Colorado***	NA	NA
NA	Connecticut***	NA	NA
11	Delaware	263,600,000	2.9%
18	Florida	65,400,000	0.7%
1	Georgia	1,361,400,000	15.1%
NA	Hawaii***	NA	NA
NA	Idaho***	NA	NA
NA	Illinois**	NA	NA
NA	Indiana**	NA	NA
NA	Iowa**	NA	NA
NA	Kansas***	NA	NA
7	Kentucky	303,300,000	3.4%
NA	Louisiana**	NA	NA
NA	Maine***	NA	NA
9	Maryland	289,400,000	3.2%
NA	Massachusetts***	NA	NA
NA	Michigan**	NA	NA
19	Minnesota	59,100,000	0.7%
5	Mississippi	747,800,000	8.3%
8	Missouri	293,100,000	3.2%
NA	Montana***	NA	NA
NA	Nebraska**	NA	NA
NA	Nevada***	NA	NA
NA	New Hampshire***	NA	NA
NA	New Jersey***	NA	NA
NA	New Mexico***	NA	NA
NA	New York**	NA	NA
4	North Carolina	873,600,000	9.7%
NA	North Dakota***	NA	NA
16	Ohio	107,900,000	1.2%
14	Oklahoma	196,800,000	2.2%
NA	Oregon**	NA	NA
13	Pennsylvania	200,100,000	2.2%
NA	Rhode Island***	NA	NA
12	South Carolina	237,800,000	2.6%
NA	South Dakota***	NA	NA
15	Tennessee	177,300,000	2.0%
6	Texas	653,500,000	7.2%
NA	Utah***	NA	NA
NA	Vermont***	NA	NA
10	Virginia	278,900,000	3.1%
NA	Washington**	NA	NA
17	West Virginia	83,300,000	0.9%
20	Wisconsin	55,800,000	0.6%
NA	Wyoming***	NA	NA

RANK ORDER

RANK	STATE	CHICKENS	% of USA
1	Georgia	1,361,400,000	15.1%
2	Alabama	1,123,700,000	12.4%
3	Arkansas	1,092,000,000	12.1%
4	North Carolina	873,600,000	9.7%
5	Mississippi	747,800,000	8.3%
6	Texas	653,500,000	7.2%
7	Kentucky	303,300,000	3.4%
8	Missouri	293,100,000	3.2%
9	Maryland	289,400,000	3.2%
10	Virginia	278,900,000	3.1%
11	Delaware	263,600,000	2.9%
12	South Carolina	237,800,000	2.6%
13	Pennsylvania	200,100,000	2.2%
14	Oklahoma	196,800,000	2.2%
15	Tennessee	177,300,000	2.0%
16	Ohio	107,900,000	1.2%
17	West Virginia	83,300,000	0.9%
18	Florida	65,400,000	0.7%
19	Minnesota	59,100,000	0.7%
20	Wisconsin	55,800,000	0.6%
NA	Alaska***	NA	NA
NA	Arizona***	NA	NA
NA	California**	NA	NA
NA	Colorado***	NA	NA
NA	Connecticut***	NA	NA
NA	Hawaii***	NA	NA
NA	Idaho***	NA	NA
NA	Illinois**	NA	NA
NA	Indiana**	NA	NA
NA	Iowa**	NA	NA
NA	Kansas***	NA	NA
NA	Louisiana**	NA	NA
NA	Maine***	NA	NA
NA	Massachusetts***	NA	NA
NA	Michigan**	NA	NA
NA	Montana***	NA	NA
NA	Nebraska**	NA	NA
NA	Nevada***	NA	NA
NA	New Hampshire***	NA	NA
NA	New Jersey***	NA	NA
NA	New Mexico***	NA	NA
NA	New York**	NA	NA
NA	North Dakota***	NA	NA
NA	Oregon**	NA	NA
NA	Rhode Island***	NA	NA
NA	South Dakota***	NA	NA
NA	Utah***	NA	NA
NA	Vermont***	NA	NA
NA	Washington**	NA	NA
NA	Wyoming***	NA	NA
	District of Columbia***	NA	NA

Source: U.S. Department of Agriculture, National Agricultural Statistics Service
"Poultry - Production and Value: 2018 Summary" (May 2019, https://usda.library.cornell.edu/concern/publications/m039k491c)
*Broilers. Total includes numbers for states not shown separately but excludes states producing less than 500,000 birds. **These states produced a combined total of 573,300,000 chickens. They are combined to avoid disclosing individual operations.
National total does not include chickens used for egg production. ***Produces fewer than 500,000 chickens or are not available.

Eggs Produced in 2018

National Total = 109,192,100,000 Eggs*

ALPHA ORDER

RANK	STATE	EGGS	% of USA
14	Alabama	2,133,300,000	2.0%
NA	Alaska**	NA	NA
NA	Arizona**	NA	NA
10	Arkansas	3,534,700,000	3.2%
8	California	4,294,600,000	3.9%
20	Colorado	1,482,900,000	1.4%
NA	Connecticut**	NA	NA
NA	Delaware**	NA	NA
17	Florida	2,005,400,000	1.8%
6	Georgia	4,871,100,000	4.5%
NA	Hawaii**	NA	NA
NA	Idaho**	NA	NA
18	Illinois	1,764,100,000	1.6%
2	Indiana	9,658,600,000	8.8%
1	Iowa	16,273,800,000	14.9%
NA	Kansas**	NA	NA
21	Kentucky	1,434,400,000	1.3%
30	Louisiana	517,500,000	0.5%
NA	Maine**	NA	NA
26	Maryland	780,600,000	0.7%
35	Massachusetts	43,100,000	0.0%
7	Michigan	4,548,100,000	4.2%
12	Minnesota	3,131,800,000	2.9%
22	Mississippi	1,418,600,000	1.3%
11	Missouri	3,473,900,000	3.2%
33	Montana	292,500,000	0.3%
13	Nebraska	2,388,800,000	2.2%
NA	Nevada**	NA	NA
NA	New Hampshire**	NA	NA
NA	New Jersey**	NA	NA
NA	New Mexico**	NA	NA
19	New York	1,656,500,000	1.5%
9	North Carolina	3,705,400,000	3.4%
NA	North Dakota**	NA	NA
3	Ohio	9,364,900,000	8.6%
29	Oklahoma	697,100,000	0.6%
27	Oregon	732,400,000	0.7%
4	Pennsylvania	8,423,100,000	7.7%
NA	Rhode Island**	NA	NA
24	South Carolina	1,156,200,000	1.1%
25	South Dakota	797,900,000	0.7%
31	Tennessee	388,800,000	0.4%
5	Texas	6,108,500,000	5.6%
23	Utah	1,403,400,000	1.3%
34	Vermont	61,700,000	0.1%
28	Virginia	716,700,000	0.7%
15	Washington	2,102,100,000	1.9%
32	West Virginia	295,900,000	0.3%
16	Wisconsin	2,077,800,000	1.9%
NA	Wyoming**	NA	NA

RANK ORDER

RANK	STATE	EGGS	% of USA
1	Iowa	16,273,800,000	14.9%
2	Indiana	9,658,600,000	8.8%
3	Ohio	9,364,900,000	8.6%
4	Pennsylvania	8,423,100,000	7.7%
5	Texas	6,108,500,000	5.6%
6	Georgia	4,871,100,000	4.5%
7	Michigan	4,548,100,000	4.2%
8	California	4,294,600,000	3.9%
9	North Carolina	3,705,400,000	3.4%
10	Arkansas	3,534,700,000	3.2%
11	Missouri	3,473,900,000	3.2%
12	Minnesota	3,131,800,000	2.9%
13	Nebraska	2,388,800,000	2.2%
14	Alabama	2,133,300,000	2.0%
15	Washington	2,102,100,000	1.9%
16	Wisconsin	2,077,800,000	1.9%
17	Florida	2,005,400,000	1.8%
18	Illinois	1,764,100,000	1.6%
19	New York	1,656,500,000	1.5%
20	Colorado	1,482,900,000	1.4%
21	Kentucky	1,434,400,000	1.3%
22	Mississippi	1,418,600,000	1.3%
23	Utah	1,403,400,000	1.3%
24	South Carolina	1,156,200,000	1.1%
25	South Dakota	797,900,000	0.7%
26	Maryland	780,600,000	0.7%
27	Oregon	732,400,000	0.7%
28	Virginia	716,700,000	0.7%
29	Oklahoma	697,100,000	0.6%
30	Louisiana	517,500,000	0.5%
31	Tennessee	388,800,000	0.4%
32	West Virginia	295,900,000	0.3%
33	Montana	292,500,000	0.3%
34	Vermont	61,700,000	0.1%
35	Massachusetts	43,100,000	0.0%
NA	Alaska**	NA	NA
NA	Arizona**	NA	NA
NA	Connecticut**	NA	NA
NA	Delaware**	NA	NA
NA	Hawaii**	NA	NA
NA	Idaho**	NA	NA
NA	Kansas**	NA	NA
NA	Maine**	NA	NA
NA	Nevada**	NA	NA
NA	New Hampshire**	NA	NA
NA	New Jersey**	NA	NA
NA	New Mexico**	NA	NA
NA	North Dakota**	NA	NA
NA	Rhode Island**	NA	NA
NA	Wyoming**	NA	NA
	District of Columbia	0	0.0%

Source: U.S. Department of Agriculture, National Agricultural Statistics Service
   "Poultry - Production and Value: 2018 Summary" (May 2019, https://usda.library.cornell.edu/concern/publications/m039k491c)
*Includes hatching and market (table) eggs. **These states produced a combined 5,455,900,000 eggs. They are combined to avoid disclosing individual operations.

II. Crime and Law Enforcement

Arrests:

Important Note Regarding Arrest Numbers

The state arrest numbers reported by the FBI and shown on page 55 are only from those law enforcement agencies that submitted complete arrests reports for twelve months in 2018. The arrest rates were calculated by the editors using population totals provided by the FBI for those jurisdictions reporting. Reports from law enforcement agencies in Illinois, Iowa, Mississippi, and the District of Columbia were insufficient to calculate rates. Reports from Kansas, New York, North Carolina, and West Virginia represented less than 60 percent of their state population. Rates for these states should be interpreted with caution.

Juveniles:

Important Note Regarding Juvenile Arrest Rates

The juvenile arrest rates shown on page 56 were calculated by the editors as follows:

The state arrest numbers reported by the FBI are only from those law enforcement agencies that submitted complete arrest reports for twelve months in 2018. Included in the FBI report are population totals of these reporting jurisdictions by state. Using these FBI population figures, we first determined what percentage the FBI numbers represented of each state's total resident population. Next, using 2018 Census state estimates for ten- to seventeen-year-olds, we multiplied the percentages derived from the FBI population figures into the Census Bureau's total juvenile population counts. The resulting juvenile population is the base that was used to determine juvenile arrests per 100,000 juvenile population. The national rate was calculated in the same manner.

Reports from law enforcement agencies in Illinois, Iowa, Mississippi, and the District of Columbia were insufficient to calculate rates. Reports from Kansas, New York, North Carolina, and West Virginia represented less than 60 percent of their state population. Rates for these states should be interpreted with caution.

Crimes (Revised Definition) in 2018

National Total = 8,441,110 Crimes*

ALPHA ORDER

RANK	STATE	CRIMES	% of USA
19	Alabama	163,099	1.9%
40	Alaska	30,865	0.4%
12	Arizona	226,032	2.7%
28	Arkansas	104,177	1.2%
1	California	1,118,600	13.3%
17	Colorado	174,787	2.1%
35	Connecticut	67,466	0.8%
43	Delaware	26,578	0.3%
3	Florida	567,997	6.7%
5	Georgia	305,093	3.6%
38	Hawaii	44,304	0.5%
42	Idaho	29,619	0.4%
7	Illinois	297,754	3.5%
18	Indiana	171,419	2.0%
36	Iowa	61,278	0.7%
32	Kansas	89,468	1.1%
29	Kentucky	97,162	1.2%
16	Louisiana	177,710	2.1%
45	Maine	19,674	0.2%
21	Maryland	151,184	1.8%
26	Massachusetts	110,533	1.3%
13	Michigan	210,198	2.5%
25	Minnesota	124,243	1.5%
34	Mississippi	78,765	0.9%
14	Missouri	192,931	2.3%
41	Montana	30,492	0.4%
37	Nebraska	45,620	0.5%
30	Nevada	90,405	1.1%
46	New Hampshire	19,284	0.2%
22	New Jersey	143,693	1.7%
31	New Mexico	89,606	1.1%
4	New York	350,002	4.1%
6	North Carolina	298,189	3.5%
48	North Dakota	17,640	0.2%
8	Ohio	287,219	3.4%
24	Oklahoma	131,744	1.6%
23	Oregon	133,244	1.6%
11	Pennsylvania	230,008	2.7%
44	Rhode Island	19,878	0.2%
15	South Carolina	178,246	2.1%
47	South Dakota	18,821	0.2%
10	Tennessee	233,505	2.8%
2	Texas	797,357	9.4%
33	Utah	82,524	1.0%
50	Vermont	9,113	0.1%
20	Virginia	158,917	1.9%
9	Washington	245,483	2.9%
39	West Virginia	32,063	0.4%
27	Wisconsin	107,862	1.3%
49	Wyoming	11,539	0.1%

RANK ORDER

RANK	STATE	CRIMES	% of USA
1	California	1,118,600	13.3%
2	Texas	797,357	9.4%
3	Florida	567,997	6.7%
4	New York	350,002	4.1%
5	Georgia	305,093	3.6%
6	North Carolina	298,189	3.5%
7	Illinois	297,754	3.5%
8	Ohio	287,219	3.4%
9	Washington	245,483	2.9%
10	Tennessee	233,505	2.8%
11	Pennsylvania	230,008	2.7%
12	Arizona	226,032	2.7%
13	Michigan	210,198	2.5%
14	Missouri	192,931	2.3%
15	South Carolina	178,246	2.1%
16	Louisiana	177,710	2.1%
17	Colorado	174,787	2.1%
18	Indiana	171,419	2.0%
19	Alabama	163,099	1.9%
20	Virginia	158,917	1.9%
21	Maryland	151,184	1.8%
22	New Jersey	143,693	1.7%
23	Oregon	133,244	1.6%
24	Oklahoma	131,744	1.6%
25	Minnesota	124,243	1.5%
26	Massachusetts	110,533	1.3%
27	Wisconsin	107,862	1.3%
28	Arkansas	104,177	1.2%
29	Kentucky	97,162	1.2%
30	Nevada	90,405	1.1%
31	New Mexico	89,606	1.1%
32	Kansas	89,468	1.1%
33	Utah	82,524	1.0%
34	Mississippi	78,765	0.9%
35	Connecticut	67,466	0.8%
36	Iowa	61,278	0.7%
37	Nebraska	45,620	0.5%
38	Hawaii	44,304	0.5%
39	West Virginia	32,063	0.4%
40	Alaska	30,865	0.4%
41	Montana	30,492	0.4%
42	Idaho	29,619	0.4%
43	Delaware	26,578	0.3%
44	Rhode Island	19,878	0.2%
45	Maine	19,674	0.2%
46	New Hampshire	19,284	0.2%
47	South Dakota	18,821	0.2%
48	North Dakota	17,640	0.2%
49	Wyoming	11,539	0.1%
50	Vermont	9,113	0.1%
	District of Columbia	37,720	0.4%

Source: CQ Press using reported data from the Federal Bureau of Investigation
   "Crime in the United States 2018" (Uniform Crime Reports, September 30, 2019, https://ucr.fbi.gov/)
*Includes murder, rape (revised definition), robbery, aggravated assault, burglary, larceny-theft, and motor vehicle theft.

Crime Rate (Revised Definition) in 2018

National Rate = 2,580.1 Crimes per 100,000 Population*

ALPHA ORDER

RANK	STATE	RATE
8	Alabama	3,336.8
2	Alaska	4,185.5
11	Arizona	3,151.7
5	Arkansas	3,456.6
20	California	2,827.8
15	Colorado	3,068.8
38	Connecticut	1,888.4
22	Delaware	2,748.0
23	Florida	2,666.7
17	Georgia	2,900.3
13	Hawaii	3,118.9
45	Idaho	1,688.5
30	Illinois	2,336.9
26	Indiana	2,561.6
37	Iowa	1,941.6
14	Kansas	3,072.9
33	Kentucky	2,174.5
3	Louisiana	3,813.5
48	Maine	1,469.9
27	Maryland	2,502.0
47	Massachusetts	1,601.4
35	Michigan	2,102.9
32	Minnesota	2,214.2
24	Mississippi	2,637.4
12	Missouri	3,149.2
19	Montana	2,870.4
29	Nebraska	2,364.7
16	Nevada	2,979.3
50	New Hampshire	1,421.7
46	New Jersey	1,613.0
1	New Mexico	4,276.3
43	New York	1,791.0
18	North Carolina	2,871.7
31	North Dakota	2,320.8
28	Ohio	2,457.0
7	Oklahoma	3,341.1
10	Oregon	3,179.5
42	Pennsylvania	1,795.9
39	Rhode Island	1,880.0
4	South Carolina	3,505.9
34	South Dakota	2,133.4
6	Tennessee	3,449.1
21	Texas	2,778.1
25	Utah	2,610.6
49	Vermont	1,455.1
40	Virginia	1,865.8
9	Washington	3,257.7
44	West Virginia	1,775.5
41	Wisconsin	1,855.3
36	Wyoming	1,997.3

RANK ORDER

RANK	STATE	RATE
1	New Mexico	4,276.3
2	Alaska	4,185.5
3	Louisiana	3,813.5
4	South Carolina	3,505.9
5	Arkansas	3,456.6
6	Tennessee	3,449.1
7	Oklahoma	3,341.1
8	Alabama	3,336.8
9	Washington	3,257.7
10	Oregon	3,179.5
11	Arizona	3,151.7
12	Missouri	3,149.2
13	Hawaii	3,118.9
14	Kansas	3,072.9
15	Colorado	3,068.8
16	Nevada	2,979.3
17	Georgia	2,900.3
18	North Carolina	2,871.7
19	Montana	2,870.4
20	California	2,827.8
21	Texas	2,778.1
22	Delaware	2,748.0
23	Florida	2,666.7
24	Mississippi	2,637.4
25	Utah	2,610.6
26	Indiana	2,561.6
27	Maryland	2,502.0
28	Ohio	2,457.0
29	Nebraska	2,364.7
30	Illinois	2,336.9
31	North Dakota	2,320.8
32	Minnesota	2,214.2
33	Kentucky	2,174.5
34	South Dakota	2,133.4
35	Michigan	2,102.9
36	Wyoming	1,997.3
37	Iowa	1,941.6
38	Connecticut	1,888.4
39	Rhode Island	1,880.0
40	Virginia	1,865.8
41	Wisconsin	1,855.3
42	Pennsylvania	1,795.9
43	New York	1,791.0
44	West Virginia	1,775.5
45	Idaho	1,688.5
46	New Jersey	1,613.0
47	Massachusetts	1,601.4
48	Maine	1,469.9
49	Vermont	1,455.1
50	New Hampshire	1,421.7

District of Columbia 5,369.7

Source: CQ Press using reported data from the Federal Bureau of Investigation
   "Crime in the United States 2018" (Uniform Crime Reports, September 30, 2019, https://ucr.fbi.gov/)
*Includes murder, rape (revised definition), robbery, aggravated assault, burglary, larceny-theft, and motor vehicle theft.

Percent Change in Crime Rate (Revised Definition): 2017 to 2018

National Percent Change = 6.4% Decrease*

ALPHA ORDER			RANK ORDER		
RANK	STATE	PERCENT CHANGE	RANK	STATE	PERCENT CHANGE
11	Alabama	(3.9)	1	Hawaii	1.0
15	Alaska	(4.8)	2	Oklahoma	(0.2)
28	Arizona	(7.7)	3	Colorado	(0.3)
24	Arkansas	(6.8)	4	Oregon	(1.7)
13	California	(4.4)	5	Kansas	(1.8)
3	Colorado	(0.3)	6	Wyoming	(2.7)
19	Connecticut	(6.1)	7	Louisiana	(2.8)
17	Delaware	(5.4)	7	North Carolina	(2.8)
32	Florida	(8.7)	9	Montana	(3.2)
40	Georgia	(9.8)	10	New York	(3.6)
1	Hawaii	1.0	11	Alabama	(3.9)
44	Idaho	(11.2)	11	Illinois	(3.9)
11	Illinois	(3.9)	13	California	(4.4)
29	Indiana	(7.9)	13	Tennessee	(4.4)
50	Iowa	(18.3)	15	Alaska	(4.8)
5	Kansas	(1.8)	16	South Carolina	(5.2)
34	Kentucky	(8.8)	17	Delaware	(5.4)
7	Louisiana	(2.8)	18	Rhode Island	(5.7)
40	Maine	(9.8)	19	Connecticut	(6.1)
32	Maryland	(8.7)	19	Washington	(6.1)
42	Massachusetts	(10.1)	21	Missouri	(6.5)
22	Michigan	(6.6)	22	Michigan	(6.6)
38	Minnesota	(9.2)	23	North Dakota	(6.7)
45	Mississippi	(12.8)	24	Arkansas	(6.8)
21	Missouri	(6.5)	24	Nevada	(6.8)
9	Montana	(3.2)	26	Texas	(7.1)
36	Nebraska	(9.0)	27	Virginia	(7.3)
24	Nevada	(6.8)	28	Arizona	(7.7)
39	New Hampshire	(9.4)	29	Indiana	(7.9)
43	New Jersey	(10.8)	30	Pennsylvania	(8.2)
34	New Mexico	(8.8)	31	South Dakota	(8.4)
10	New York	(3.6)	32	Florida	(8.7)
7	North Carolina	(2.8)	32	Maryland	(8.7)
23	North Dakota	(6.7)	34	Kentucky	(8.8)
37	Ohio	(9.1)	34	New Mexico	(8.8)
2	Oklahoma	(0.2)	36	Nebraska	(9.0)
4	Oregon	(1.7)	37	Ohio	(9.1)
30	Pennsylvania	(8.2)	38	Minnesota	(9.2)
18	Rhode Island	(5.7)	39	New Hampshire	(9.4)
16	South Carolina	(5.2)	40	Georgia	(9.8)
31	South Dakota	(8.4)	40	Maine	(9.8)
13	Tennessee	(4.4)	42	Massachusetts	(10.1)
26	Texas	(7.1)	43	New Jersey	(10.8)
48	Utah	(13.6)	44	Idaho	(11.2)
45	Vermont	(12.8)	45	Mississippi	(12.8)
27	Virginia	(7.3)	45	Vermont	(12.8)
19	Washington	(6.1)	47	Wisconsin	(13.0)
49	West Virginia	(17.5)	48	Utah	(13.6)
47	Wisconsin	(13.0)	49	West Virginia	(17.5)
6	Wyoming	(2.7)	50	Iowa	(18.3)

District of Columbia   1.8

Source: CQ Press using reported data from the Federal Bureau of Investigation
   "Crime in the United States 2018" (Uniform Crime Reports, September 30, 2019, https://ucr.fbi.gov/)
*Includes murder, rape (revised definition), robbery, aggravated assault, burglary, larceny-theft, and motor vehicle theft.

Violent Crimes (Revised Definition) in 2018

National Total = 1,245,065 Violent Crimes*

ALPHA ORDER

RANK ORDER

RANK	STATE	CRIMES	% of USA
16	Alabama	25,399	2.0%
37	Alaska	6,526	0.5%
11	Arizona	34,058	2.7%
28	Arkansas	16,384	1.3%
1	California	176,982	14.2%
21	Colorado	22,624	1.8%
34	Connecticut	7,411	0.6%
40	Delaware	4,097	0.3%
3	Florida	81,980	6.6%
10	Georgia	34,355	2.8%
44	Hawaii	3,532	0.3%
41	Idaho	3,983	0.3%
5	Illinois	51,490	4.1%
15	Indiana	25,581	2.1%
33	Iowa	7,893	0.6%
29	Kansas	12,782	1.0%
32	Kentucky	9,467	0.8%
17	Louisiana	25,049	2.0%
48	Maine	1,501	0.1%
14	Maryland	28,320	2.3%
20	Massachusetts	23,337	1.9%
6	Michigan	44,918	3.6%
30	Minnesota	12,369	1.0%
36	Mississippi	6,999	0.6%
13	Missouri	30,758	2.5%
42	Montana	3,974	0.3%
38	Nebraska	5,494	0.4%
27	Nevada	16,420	1.3%
45	New Hampshire	2,349	0.2%
22	New Jersey	18,537	1.5%
24	New Mexico	17,949	1.4%
4	New York	68,495	5.5%
8	North Carolina	39,210	3.1%
47	North Dakota	2,133	0.2%
12	Ohio	32,723	2.6%
23	Oklahoma	18,380	1.5%
31	Oregon	11,966	1.0%
9	Pennsylvania	39,192	3.1%
46	Rhode Island	2,317	0.2%
18	South Carolina	24,825	2.0%
43	South Dakota	3,570	0.3%
7	Tennessee	42,226	3.4%
2	Texas	117,927	9.5%
35	Utah	7,368	0.6%
50	Vermont	1,077	0.1%
26	Virginia	17,032	1.4%
19	Washington	23,472	1.9%
39	West Virginia	5,236	0.4%
25	Wisconsin	17,176	1.4%
49	Wyoming	1,226	0.1%

RANK	STATE	CRIMES	% of USA
1	California	176,982	14.2%
2	Texas	117,927	9.5%
3	Florida	81,980	6.6%
4	New York	68,495	5.5%
5	Illinois	51,490	4.1%
6	Michigan	44,918	3.6%
7	Tennessee	42,226	3.4%
8	North Carolina	39,210	3.1%
9	Pennsylvania	39,192	3.1%
10	Georgia	34,355	2.8%
11	Arizona	34,058	2.7%
12	Ohio	32,723	2.6%
13	Missouri	30,758	2.5%
14	Maryland	28,320	2.3%
15	Indiana	25,581	2.1%
16	Alabama	25,399	2.0%
17	Louisiana	25,049	2.0%
18	South Carolina	24,825	2.0%
19	Washington	23,472	1.9%
20	Massachusetts	23,337	1.9%
21	Colorado	22,624	1.8%
22	New Jersey	18,537	1.5%
23	Oklahoma	18,380	1.5%
24	New Mexico	17,949	1.4%
25	Wisconsin	17,176	1.4%
26	Virginia	17,032	1.4%
27	Nevada	16,420	1.3%
28	Arkansas	16,384	1.3%
29	Kansas	12,782	1.0%
30	Minnesota	12,369	1.0%
31	Oregon	11,966	1.0%
32	Kentucky	9,467	0.8%
33	Iowa	7,893	0.6%
34	Connecticut	7,411	0.6%
35	Utah	7,368	0.6%
36	Mississippi	6,999	0.6%
37	Alaska	6,526	0.5%
38	Nebraska	5,494	0.4%
39	West Virginia	5,236	0.4%
40	Delaware	4,097	0.3%
41	Idaho	3,983	0.3%
42	Montana	3,974	0.3%
43	South Dakota	3,570	0.3%
44	Hawaii	3,532	0.3%
45	New Hampshire	2,349	0.2%
46	Rhode Island	2,317	0.2%
47	North Dakota	2,133	0.2%
48	Maine	1,501	0.1%
49	Wyoming	1,226	0.1%
50	Vermont	1,077	0.1%
	District of Columbia	6,996	0.6%

Source: Reported data from the Federal Bureau of Investigation
"Crime in the United States 2018" (Uniform Crime Reports, September 30, 2019, https://ucr.fbi.gov/)
*Violent crimes are offenses of murder, rape (revised definition), robbery, and aggravated assault.

Violent Crime Rate (Revised Definition) in 2018

National Rate = 380.6 Violent Crimes per 100,000 Population*

ALPHA ORDER

RANK	STATE	RATE
7	Alabama	519.6
1	Alaska	885.0
10	Arizona	474.9
4	Arkansas	543.6
14	California	447.4
20	Colorado	397.2
46	Connecticut	207.4
16	Delaware	423.6
21	Florida	384.9
27	Georgia	326.6
37	Hawaii	248.6
40	Idaho	227.1
19	Illinois	404.1
22	Indiana	382.3
36	Iowa	250.1
15	Kansas	439.0
44	Kentucky	211.9
6	Louisiana	537.5
50	Maine	112.1
11	Maryland	468.7
26	Massachusetts	338.1
13	Michigan	449.4
41	Minnesota	220.4
38	Mississippi	234.4
8	Missouri	502.1
24	Montana	374.1
33	Nebraska	284.8
5	Nevada	541.1
48	New Hampshire	173.2
45	New Jersey	208.1
2	New Mexico	856.6
25	New York	350.5
23	North Carolina	377.6
34	North Dakota	280.6
35	Ohio	279.9
12	Oklahoma	466.1
32	Oregon	285.5
29	Pennsylvania	306.0
42	Rhode Island	219.1
9	South Carolina	488.3
18	South Dakota	404.7
3	Tennessee	623.7
17	Texas	410.9
39	Utah	233.1
49	Vermont	172.0
47	Virginia	200.0
28	Washington	311.5
31	West Virginia	289.9
30	Wisconsin	295.4
43	Wyoming	212.2

RANK ORDER

RANK	STATE	RATE
1	Alaska	885.0
2	New Mexico	856.6
3	Tennessee	623.7
4	Arkansas	543.6
5	Nevada	541.1
6	Louisiana	537.5
7	Alabama	519.6
8	Missouri	502.1
9	South Carolina	488.3
10	Arizona	474.9
11	Maryland	468.7
12	Oklahoma	466.1
13	Michigan	449.4
14	California	447.4
15	Kansas	439.0
16	Delaware	423.6
17	Texas	410.9
18	South Dakota	404.7
19	Illinois	404.1
20	Colorado	397.2
21	Florida	384.9
22	Indiana	382.3
23	North Carolina	377.6
24	Montana	374.1
25	New York	350.5
26	Massachusetts	338.1
27	Georgia	326.6
28	Washington	311.5
29	Pennsylvania	306.0
30	Wisconsin	295.4
31	West Virginia	289.9
32	Oregon	285.5
33	Nebraska	284.8
34	North Dakota	280.6
35	Ohio	279.9
36	Iowa	250.1
37	Hawaii	248.6
38	Mississippi	234.4
39	Utah	233.1
40	Idaho	227.1
41	Minnesota	220.4
42	Rhode Island	219.1
43	Wyoming	212.2
44	Kentucky	211.9
45	New Jersey	208.1
46	Connecticut	207.4
47	Virginia	200.0
48	New Hampshire	173.2
49	Vermont	172.0
50	Maine	112.1
	District of Columbia	995.9

Source: Reported data from the Federal Bureau of Investigation
"Crime in the United States 2018" (Uniform Crime Reports, September 30, 2019, https://ucr.fbi.gov/)
*Violent crimes are offenses of murder, rape (revised definition), robbery, and aggravated assault.

Percent Change in Violent Crime Rate (Revised Definition): 2017 to 2018

National Percent Change = 3.6% Decrease*

RANK	STATE	PERCENT CHANGE
11	Alabama	(0.5)
4	Alaska	3.3
32	Arizona	(6.1)
23	Arkansas	(3.9)
15	California	(1.3)
3	Colorado	6.7
45	Connecticut	(9.5)
37	Delaware	(7.4)
29	Florida	(5.7)
42	Georgia	(8.4)
14	Hawaii	(1.0)
27	Idaho	(5.1)
37	Illinois	(7.4)
18	Indiana	(3.2)
49	Iowa	(13.0)
2	Kansas	9.6
41	Kentucky	(8.3)
19	Louisiana	(3.4)
36	Maine	(7.0)
35	Maryland	(6.9)
24	Massachusetts	(4.6)
10	Michigan	(0.1)
39	Minnesota	(8.0)
43	Mississippi	(8.5)
28	Missouri	(5.5)
9	Montana	0.1
44	Nebraska	(8.7)
20	Nevada	(3.5)
48	New Hampshire	(11.5)
47	New Jersey	(10.2)
1	New Mexico	10.0
17	New York	(2.9)
6	North Carolina	1.9
12	North Dakota	(0.6)
29	Ohio	(5.7)
6	Oklahoma	1.9
8	Oregon	1.8
16	Pennsylvania	(2.2)
34	Rhode Island	(6.4)
20	South Carolina	(3.5)
31	South Dakota	(5.8)
25	Tennessee	(4.8)
32	Texas	(6.1)
22	Utah	(3.8)
13	Vermont	(0.7)
26	Virginia	(5.0)
5	Washington	2.9
50	West Virginia	(19.7)
40	Wisconsin	(8.2)
45	Wyoming	(9.5)

RANK	STATE	PERCENT CHANGE
1	New Mexico	10.0
2	Kansas	9.6
3	Colorado	6.7
4	Alaska	3.3
5	Washington	2.9
6	North Carolina	1.9
6	Oklahoma	1.9
8	Oregon	1.8
9	Montana	0.1
10	Michigan	(0.1)
11	Alabama	(0.5)
12	North Dakota	(0.6)
13	Vermont	(0.7)
14	Hawaii	(1.0)
15	California	(1.3)
16	Pennsylvania	(2.2)
17	New York	(2.9)
18	Indiana	(3.2)
19	Louisiana	(3.4)
20	Nevada	(3.5)
20	South Carolina	(3.5)
22	Utah	(3.8)
23	Arkansas	(3.9)
24	Massachusetts	(4.6)
25	Tennessee	(4.8)
26	Virginia	(5.0)
27	Idaho	(5.1)
28	Missouri	(5.5)
29	Florida	(5.7)
29	Ohio	(5.7)
31	South Dakota	(5.8)
32	Arizona	(6.1)
32	Texas	(6.1)
34	Rhode Island	(6.4)
35	Maryland	(6.9)
36	Maine	(7.0)
37	Delaware	(7.4)
37	Illinois	(7.4)
39	Minnesota	(8.0)
40	Wisconsin	(8.2)
41	Kentucky	(8.3)
42	Georgia	(8.4)
43	Mississippi	(8.5)
44	Nebraska	(8.7)
45	Connecticut	(9.5)
45	Wyoming	(9.5)
47	New Jersey	(10.2)
48	New Hampshire	(11.5)
49	Iowa	(13.0)
50	West Virginia	(19.7)

	District of Columbia	(0.7)

Source: Reported data from the Federal Bureau of Investigation
   "Crime in the United States 2018" (Uniform Crime Reports, September 30, 2019, https://ucr.fbi.gov/)
*Violent crimes are offenses of murder, rape (revised definition), robbery, and aggravated assault.

Murders in 2018

National Total = 16,214 Murders*

ALPHA ORDER					RANK ORDER			
RANK	STATE		MURDERS	% of USA	RANK	STATE	MURDERS	% of USA
18	Alabama		383	2.4%	1	California	1,739	10.7%
39	Alaska		47	0.3%	2	Texas	1,322	8.2%
19	Arizona		369	2.3%	3	Florida	1,107	6.8%
23	Arkansas		216	1.3%	4	Illinois	884	5.5%
1	California		1,739	10.7%	5	Pennsylvania	784	4.8%
24	Colorado		210	1.3%	6	Georgia	642	4.0%
33	Connecticut		83	0.5%	7	North Carolina	628	3.9%
38	Delaware		48	0.3%	8	Missouri	607	3.7%
3	Florida		1,107	6.8%	9	Ohio	564	3.5%
6	Georgia		642	4.0%	10	New York	562	3.5%
41	Hawaii		36	0.2%	11	Michigan	551	3.4%
42	Idaho		35	0.2%	12	Louisiana	530	3.3%
4	Illinois		884	5.5%	13	Tennessee	498	3.1%
15	Indiana		438	2.7%	14	Maryland	490	3.0%
37	Iowa		54	0.3%	15	Indiana	438	2.7%
31	Kansas		113	0.7%	16	South Carolina	392	2.4%
21	Kentucky		244	1.5%	17	Virginia	391	2.4%
12	Louisiana		530	3.3%	18	Alabama	383	2.4%
44	Maine		24	0.1%	19	Arizona	369	2.3%
14	Maryland		490	3.0%	20	New Jersey	286	1.8%
30	Massachusetts		136	0.8%	21	Kentucky	244	1.5%
11	Michigan		551	3.4%	22	Washington	236	1.5%
32	Minnesota		106	0.7%	23	Arkansas	216	1.3%
28	Mississippi		171	1.1%	24	Colorado	210	1.3%
8	Missouri		607	3.7%	25	Oklahoma	206	1.3%
43	Montana		34	0.2%	26	Nevada	202	1.2%
40	Nebraska		44	0.3%	27	Wisconsin	176	1.1%
26	Nevada		202	1.2%	28	Mississippi	171	1.1%
45	New Hampshire		21	0.1%	29	New Mexico	167	1.0%
20	New Jersey		286	1.8%	30	Massachusetts	136	0.8%
29	New Mexico		167	1.0%	31	Kansas	113	0.7%
10	New York		562	3.5%	32	Minnesota	106	0.7%
7	North Carolina		628	3.9%	33	Connecticut	83	0.5%
46	North Dakota		18	0.1%	34	Oregon	82	0.5%
9	Ohio		564	3.5%	35	West Virginia	67	0.4%
25	Oklahoma		206	1.3%	36	Utah	60	0.4%
34	Oregon		82	0.5%	37	Iowa	54	0.3%
5	Pennsylvania		784	4.8%	38	Delaware	48	0.3%
47	Rhode Island		16	0.1%	39	Alaska	47	0.3%
16	South Carolina		392	2.4%	40	Nebraska	44	0.3%
49	South Dakota		12	0.1%	41	Hawaii	36	0.2%
13	Tennessee		498	3.1%	42	Idaho	35	0.2%
2	Texas		1,322	8.2%	43	Montana	34	0.2%
36	Utah		60	0.4%	44	Maine	24	0.1%
50	Vermont		10	0.1%	45	New Hampshire	21	0.1%
17	Virginia		391	2.4%	46	North Dakota	18	0.1%
22	Washington		236	1.5%	47	Rhode Island	16	0.1%
35	West Virginia		67	0.4%	48	Wyoming	13	0.1%
27	Wisconsin		176	1.1%	49	South Dakota	12	0.1%
48	Wyoming		13	0.1%	50	Vermont	10	0.1%
						District of Columbia	160	1.0%

Source: Reported data from the Federal Bureau of Investigation
    "Crime in the United States 2018" (Uniform Crime Reports, September 30, 2019, https://ucr.fbi.gov/)
*Includes nonnegligent manslaughter.

Murder Rate in 2018

National Rate = 5.0 Murders per 100,000 Population*

ALPHA ORDER

RANK	STATE	RATE
5	Alabama	7.8
12	Alaska	6.4
21	Arizona	5.1
8	Arkansas	7.2
26	California	4.4
28	Colorado	3.7
37	Connecticut	2.3
22	Delaware	5.0
19	Florida	5.2
13	Georgia	6.1
35	Hawaii	2.5
40	Idaho	2.0
9	Illinois	6.9
11	Indiana	6.5
46	Iowa	1.7
27	Kansas	3.9
17	Kentucky	5.5
1	Louisiana	11.4
45	Maine	1.8
3	Maryland	8.1
40	Massachusetts	2.0
17	Michigan	5.5
43	Minnesota	1.9
16	Mississippi	5.7
2	Missouri	9.9
30	Montana	3.2
37	Nebraska	2.3
10	Nevada	6.7
48	New Hampshire	1.5
30	New Jersey	3.2
4	New Mexico	8.0
34	New York	2.9
15	North Carolina	6.0
36	North Dakota	2.4
23	Ohio	4.8
19	Oklahoma	5.2
40	Oregon	2.0
13	Pennsylvania	6.1
48	Rhode Island	1.5
6	South Carolina	7.7
50	South Dakota	1.4
7	Tennessee	7.4
24	Texas	4.6
43	Utah	1.9
47	Vermont	1.6
24	Virginia	4.6
32	Washington	3.1
28	West Virginia	3.7
33	Wisconsin	3.0
37	Wyoming	2.3

RANK ORDER

RANK	STATE	RATE
1	Louisiana	11.4
2	Missouri	9.9
3	Maryland	8.1
4	New Mexico	8.0
5	Alabama	7.8
6	South Carolina	7.7
7	Tennessee	7.4
8	Arkansas	7.2
9	Illinois	6.9
10	Nevada	6.7
11	Indiana	6.5
12	Alaska	6.4
13	Georgia	6.1
13	Pennsylvania	6.1
15	North Carolina	6.0
16	Mississippi	5.7
17	Kentucky	5.5
17	Michigan	5.5
19	Florida	5.2
19	Oklahoma	5.2
21	Arizona	5.1
22	Delaware	5.0
23	Ohio	4.8
24	Texas	4.6
24	Virginia	4.6
26	California	4.4
27	Kansas	3.9
28	Colorado	3.7
28	West Virginia	3.7
30	Montana	3.2
30	New Jersey	3.2
32	Washington	3.1
33	Wisconsin	3.0
34	New York	2.9
35	Hawaii	2.5
36	North Dakota	2.4
37	Connecticut	2.3
37	Nebraska	2.3
37	Wyoming	2.3
40	Idaho	2.0
40	Massachusetts	2.0
40	Oregon	2.0
43	Minnesota	1.9
43	Utah	1.9
45	Maine	1.8
46	Iowa	1.7
47	Vermont	1.6
48	New Hampshire	1.5
48	Rhode Island	1.5
50	South Dakota	1.4
	District of Columbia	22.8

Source: Reported data from the Federal Bureau of Investigation
  "Crime in the United States 2018" (Uniform Crime Reports, September 30, 2019, https://ucr.fbi.gov/)
*Includes nonnegligent manslaughter.

Percent of Murders Involving Firearms in 2018

National Percent = 72.7% of Murders*

ALPHA ORDER				RANK ORDER		
RANK	STATE	PERCENT		RANK	STATE	PERCENT
NA	Alabama**	NA		1	Missouri	85.2
29	Alaska	66.0		2	Louisiana	83.7
34	Arizona	59.9		3	Delaware	83.3
18	Arkansas	71.6		4	Mississippi	83.1
25	California	67.7		5	Maryland	82.6
20	Colorado	71.0		6	Illinois	81.9
30	Connecticut	65.1		7	Georgia	81.0
3	Delaware	83.3		8	Tennessee	80.0
NA	Florida**	NA		9	Indiana	79.2
7	Georgia	81.0		10	South Carolina	76.7
47	Hawaii	33.3		11	Wisconsin	76.4
37	Idaho	59.4		12	Virginia	76.0
6	Illinois	81.9		13	Kentucky	75.5
9	Indiana	79.2		14	Rhode Island	75.0
46	Iowa	46.5		15	Pennsylvania	73.7
21	Kansas	70.9		16	Texas	73.5
13	Kentucky	75.5		17	North Carolina	72.2
2	Louisiana	83.7		18	Arkansas	71.6
43	Maine	47.8		18	Michigan	71.6
5	Maryland	82.6		20	Colorado	71.0
24	Massachusetts	68.4		21	Kansas	70.9
18	Michigan	71.6		22	New Jersey	70.6
45	Minnesota	47.1		23	Ohio	70.1
4	Mississippi	83.1		24	Massachusetts	68.4
1	Missouri	85.2		25	California	67.7
42	Montana	50.0		26	Nevada	66.7
33	Nebraska	60.5		26	Wyoming	66.7
26	Nevada	66.7		28	Oklahoma	66.3
40	New Hampshire	57.1		29	Alaska	66.0
22	New Jersey	70.6		30	Connecticut	65.1
31	New Mexico	63.5		31	New Mexico	63.5
39	New York	57.3		32	South Dakota	61.5
17	North Carolina	72.2		33	Nebraska	60.5
41	North Dakota	56.3		34	Arizona	59.9
23	Ohio	70.1		35	West Virginia	59.6
28	Oklahoma	66.3		36	Washington	59.5
38	Oregon	59.3		37	Idaho	59.4
15	Pennsylvania	73.7		38	Oregon	59.3
14	Rhode Island	75.0		39	New York	57.3
10	South Carolina	76.7		40	New Hampshire	57.1
32	South Dakota	61.5		41	North Dakota	56.3
8	Tennessee	80.0		42	Montana	50.0
16	Texas	73.5		43	Maine	47.8
44	Utah	47.5		44	Utah	47.5
48	Vermont	30.0		45	Minnesota	47.1
12	Virginia	76.0		46	Iowa	46.5
36	Washington	59.5		47	Hawaii	33.3
35	West Virginia	59.6		48	Vermont	30.0
11	Wisconsin	76.4		NA	Alabama**	NA
26	Wyoming	66.7		NA	Florida**	NA
					District of Columbia	79.5

Source: CQ Press using reported data from the Federal Bureau of Investigation
    "Crime in the United States 2018" (Uniform Crime Reports, September 30, 2019, https://ucr.fbi.gov/)
*Of the 14,123 murders in 2018 for which supplemental data were received by the FBI. There were an additional 2,091 murders for which the type of murder weapon was not reported to the FBI. Includes nonnegligent manslaughter. National and state percents based on reporting jurisdictions only.
**Not available.

Rapes (Revised Definition) in 2018

National Total = 139,380 Rapes*

ALPHA ORDER

RANK	STATE	RAPES	% of USA
26	Alabama	1,996	1.4%
35	Alaska	1,192	0.9%
10	Arizona	3,638	2.6%
24	Arkansas	2,196	1.6%
1	California	15,505	11.1%
9	Colorado	4,070	2.9%
37	Connecticut	840	0.6%
48	Delaware	338	0.2%
3	Florida	8,438	6.1%
15	Georgia	2,651	1.9%
40	Hawaii	625	0.4%
38	Idaho	791	0.6%
6	Illinois	5,859	4.2%
20	Indiana	2,370	1.7%
36	Iowa	976	0.7%
31	Kansas	1,567	1.1%
30	Kentucky	1,707	1.2%
25	Louisiana	2,085	1.5%
46	Maine	446	0.3%
27	Maryland	1,979	1.4%
19	Massachusetts	2,410	1.7%
4	Michigan	7,690	5.5%
17	Minnesota	2,462	1.8%
43	Mississippi	537	0.4%
13	Missouri	2,912	2.1%
42	Montana	551	0.4%
34	Nebraska	1,233	0.9%
21	Nevada	2,329	1.7%
44	New Hampshire	534	0.4%
32	New Jersey	1,424	1.0%
33	New Mexico	1,354	1.0%
5	New York	6,575	4.7%
16	North Carolina	2,633	1.9%
47	North Dakota	397	0.3%
7	Ohio	5,300	3.8%
22	Oklahoma	2,299	1.6%
28	Oregon	1,975	1.4%
8	Pennsylvania	4,483	3.2%
45	Rhode Island	481	0.3%
18	South Carolina	2,434	1.7%
41	South Dakota	614	0.4%
14	Tennessee	2,821	2.0%
2	Texas	14,693	10.5%
29	Utah	1,753	1.3%
49	Vermont	287	0.2%
12	Virginia	2,924	2.1%
11	Washington	3,413	2.4%
39	West Virginia	652	0.5%
23	Wisconsin	2,248	1.6%
50	Wyoming	243	0.2%

RANK ORDER

RANK	STATE	RAPES	% of USA
1	California	15,505	11.1%
2	Texas	14,693	10.5%
3	Florida	8,438	6.1%
4	Michigan	7,690	5.5%
5	New York	6,575	4.7%
6	Illinois	5,859	4.2%
7	Ohio	5,300	3.8%
8	Pennsylvania	4,483	3.2%
9	Colorado	4,070	2.9%
10	Arizona	3,638	2.6%
11	Washington	3,413	2.4%
12	Virginia	2,924	2.1%
13	Missouri	2,912	2.1%
14	Tennessee	2,821	2.0%
15	Georgia	2,651	1.9%
16	North Carolina	2,633	1.9%
17	Minnesota	2,462	1.8%
18	South Carolina	2,434	1.7%
19	Massachusetts	2,410	1.7%
20	Indiana	2,370	1.7%
21	Nevada	2,329	1.7%
22	Oklahoma	2,299	1.6%
23	Wisconsin	2,248	1.6%
24	Arkansas	2,196	1.6%
25	Louisiana	2,085	1.5%
26	Alabama	1,996	1.4%
27	Maryland	1,979	1.4%
28	Oregon	1,975	1.4%
29	Utah	1,753	1.3%
30	Kentucky	1,707	1.2%
31	Kansas	1,567	1.1%
32	New Jersey	1,424	1.0%
33	New Mexico	1,354	1.0%
34	Nebraska	1,233	0.9%
35	Alaska	1,192	0.9%
36	Iowa	976	0.7%
37	Connecticut	840	0.6%
38	Idaho	791	0.6%
39	West Virginia	652	0.5%
40	Hawaii	625	0.4%
41	South Dakota	614	0.4%
42	Montana	551	0.4%
43	Mississippi	537	0.4%
44	New Hampshire	534	0.4%
45	Rhode Island	481	0.3%
46	Maine	446	0.3%
47	North Dakota	397	0.3%
48	Delaware	338	0.2%
49	Vermont	287	0.2%
50	Wyoming	243	0.2%
	District of Columbia	450	0.3%

Source: Reported data from the Federal Bureau of Investigation
"Crime in the United States 2018" (Uniform Crime Reports, September 30, 2019, https://ucr.fbi.gov/)
*The definition of rape was revised in 2013 to "Penetration, no matter how slight, of the vagina or anus with any body part or object, or oral penetration by a sex organ of another person, without the consent of the victim. Attempts or assaults to commit rape are also included; however, statutory rape and incest are excluded." This revised definition includes both male and female victims and drops "forcible" from the title.

Rape Rate (Revised Definition) in 2018

National Rate = 42.6 Rapes per 100,000 Population*

ALPHA ORDER

RANK	STATE	RATE
30	Alabama	40.8
1	Alaska	161.6
15	Arizona	50.7
4	Arkansas	72.9
33	California	39.2
5	Colorado	71.5
48	Connecticut	23.5
39	Delaware	34.9
31	Florida	39.6
47	Georgia	25.2
26	Hawaii	44.0
24	Idaho	45.1
19	Illinois	46.0
37	Indiana	35.4
45	Iowa	30.9
11	Kansas	53.8
35	Kentucky	38.2
25	Louisiana	44.7
43	Maine	33.3
44	Maryland	32.8
39	Massachusetts	34.9
2	Michigan	76.9
27	Minnesota	43.9
49	Mississippi	18.0
17	Missouri	47.5
13	Montana	51.9
8	Nebraska	63.9
3	Nevada	76.8
32	New Hampshire	39.4
50	New Jersey	16.0
7	New Mexico	64.6
42	New York	33.6
46	North Carolina	25.4
12	North Dakota	52.2
22	Ohio	45.3
9	Oklahoma	58.3
18	Oregon	47.1
38	Pennsylvania	35.0
21	Rhode Island	45.5
16	South Carolina	47.9
6	South Dakota	69.6
29	Tennessee	41.7
14	Texas	51.2
10	Utah	55.5
20	Vermont	45.8
41	Virginia	34.3
22	Washington	45.3
36	West Virginia	36.1
34	Wisconsin	38.7
28	Wyoming	42.1

RANK ORDER

RANK	STATE	RATE
1	Alaska	161.6
2	Michigan	76.9
3	Nevada	76.8
4	Arkansas	72.9
5	Colorado	71.5
6	South Dakota	69.6
7	New Mexico	64.6
8	Nebraska	63.9
9	Oklahoma	58.3
10	Utah	55.5
11	Kansas	53.8
12	North Dakota	52.2
13	Montana	51.9
14	Texas	51.2
15	Arizona	50.7
16	South Carolina	47.9
17	Missouri	47.5
18	Oregon	47.1
19	Illinois	46.0
20	Vermont	45.8
21	Rhode Island	45.5
22	Ohio	45.3
22	Washington	45.3
24	Idaho	45.1
25	Louisiana	44.7
26	Hawaii	44.0
27	Minnesota	43.9
28	Wyoming	42.1
29	Tennessee	41.7
30	Alabama	40.8
31	Florida	39.6
32	New Hampshire	39.4
33	California	39.2
34	Wisconsin	38.7
35	Kentucky	38.2
36	West Virginia	36.1
37	Indiana	35.4
38	Pennsylvania	35.0
39	Delaware	34.9
39	Massachusetts	34.9
41	Virginia	34.3
42	New York	33.6
43	Maine	33.3
44	Maryland	32.8
45	Iowa	30.9
46	North Carolina	25.4
47	Georgia	25.2
48	Connecticut	23.5
49	Mississippi	18.0
50	New Jersey	16.0
	District of Columbia	64.1

Source: Reported data from the Federal Bureau of Investigation
  "Crime in the United States 2018" (Uniform Crime Reports, September 30, 2019, https://ucr.fbi.gov/)
*The definition of rape was revised in 2013 to "Penetration, no matter how slight, of the vagina or anus with any body part or object, or oral penetration by a sex organ of another person, without the consent of the victim. Attempts or assaults to commit rape are also included; however, statutory rape and incest are excluded." This revised definition includes both male and female victims and drops "forcible" from the title.

Robberies in 2018

National Total = 282,061 Robberies*

ALPHA ORDER					RANK ORDER			
RANK	STATE	ROBBERIES	% of USA		RANK	STATE	ROBBERIES	% of USA
20	Alabama	4,076	1.4%		1	California	54,326	19.3%
38	Alaska	896	0.3%		2	Texas	28,256	10.0%
12	Arizona	6,523	2.3%		3	New York	18,187	6.4%
33	Arkansas	1,594	0.6%		4	Florida	16,884	6.0%
1	California	54,326	19.3%		5	Illinois	14,208	5.0%
22	Colorado	3,797	1.3%		6	Pennsylvania	9,848	3.5%
31	Connecticut	2,194	0.8%		7	Maryland	9,716	3.4%
39	Delaware	866	0.3%		8	Ohio	9,185	3.3%
4	Florida	16,884	6.0%		9	North Carolina	8,423	3.0%
10	Georgia	8,279	2.9%		10	Georgia	8,279	2.9%
36	Hawaii	946	0.3%		11	Tennessee	7,190	2.5%
47	Idaho	200	0.1%		12	Arizona	6,523	2.3%
5	Illinois	14,208	5.0%		13	New Jersey	6,364	2.3%
14	Indiana	5,939	2.1%		14	Indiana	5,939	2.1%
37	Iowa	932	0.3%		15	Michigan	5,656	2.0%
34	Kansas	1,543	0.5%		16	Washington	5,572	2.0%
30	Kentucky	2,457	0.9%		17	Missouri	5,197	1.8%
18	Louisiana	4,568	1.6%		18	Louisiana	4,568	1.6%
46	Maine	228	0.1%		19	Massachusetts	4,143	1.5%
7	Maryland	9,716	3.4%		20	Alabama	4,076	1.4%
19	Massachusetts	4,143	1.5%		21	Nevada	3,862	1.4%
15	Michigan	5,656	2.0%		22	Colorado	3,797	1.3%
26	Minnesota	2,944	1.0%		23	Virginia	3,604	1.3%
32	Mississippi	1,595	0.6%		24	South Carolina	3,553	1.3%
17	Missouri	5,197	1.8%		25	Wisconsin	3,489	1.2%
44	Montana	269	0.1%		26	Minnesota	2,944	1.0%
40	Nebraska	756	0.3%		27	New Mexico	2,830	1.0%
21	Nevada	3,862	1.4%		28	Oklahoma	2,791	1.0%
43	New Hampshire	359	0.1%		29	Oregon	2,549	0.9%
13	New Jersey	6,364	2.3%		30	Kentucky	2,457	0.9%
27	New Mexico	2,830	1.0%		31	Connecticut	2,194	0.8%
3	New York	18,187	6.4%		32	Mississippi	1,595	0.6%
9	North Carolina	8,423	3.0%		33	Arkansas	1,594	0.6%
48	North Dakota	158	0.1%		34	Kansas	1,543	0.5%
8	Ohio	9,185	3.3%		35	Utah	1,236	0.4%
28	Oklahoma	2,791	1.0%		36	Hawaii	946	0.3%
29	Oregon	2,549	0.9%		37	Iowa	932	0.3%
6	Pennsylvania	9,848	3.5%		38	Alaska	896	0.3%
42	Rhode Island	454	0.2%		39	Delaware	866	0.3%
24	South Carolina	3,553	1.3%		40	Nebraska	756	0.3%
45	South Dakota	262	0.1%		41	West Virginia	572	0.2%
11	Tennessee	7,190	2.5%		42	Rhode Island	454	0.2%
2	Texas	28,256	10.0%		43	New Hampshire	359	0.1%
35	Utah	1,236	0.4%		44	Montana	269	0.1%
50	Vermont	70	0.0%		45	South Dakota	262	0.1%
23	Virginia	3,604	1.3%		46	Maine	228	0.1%
16	Washington	5,572	2.0%		47	Idaho	200	0.1%
41	West Virginia	572	0.2%		48	North Dakota	158	0.1%
25	Wisconsin	3,489	1.2%		49	Wyoming	100	0.0%
49	Wyoming	100	0.0%		50	Vermont	70	0.0%
						District of Columbia	2,415	0.9%

Source: Reported data from the Federal Bureau of Investigation
"Crime in the United States 2018" (Uniform Crime Reports, September 30, 2019, https://ucr.fbi.gov/)
*Robbery is the taking or attempting to take anything of value by force or threat of force.

Robbery Rate in 2018

National Rate = 86.2 Robberies per 100,000 Population*

ALPHA ORDER

RANK	STATE	RATE
15	Alabama	83.4
5	Alaska	121.5
11	Arizona	91.0
35	Arkansas	52.9
2	California	137.3
25	Colorado	66.7
27	Connecticut	61.4
12	Delaware	89.5
17	Florida	79.3
18	Georgia	78.7
26	Hawaii	66.6
49	Idaho	11.4
6	Illinois	111.5
13	Indiana	88.7
43	Iowa	29.5
34	Kansas	53.0
32	Kentucky	55.0
9	Louisiana	98.0
48	Maine	17.0
1	Maryland	160.8
29	Massachusetts	60.0
31	Michigan	56.6
36	Minnesota	52.5
33	Mississippi	53.4
14	Missouri	84.8
45	Montana	25.3
39	Nebraska	39.2
4	Nevada	127.3
44	New Hampshire	26.5
22	New Jersey	71.4
3	New Mexico	135.1
10	New York	93.1
16	North Carolina	81.1
46	North Dakota	20.8
19	Ohio	78.6
23	Oklahoma	70.8
28	Oregon	60.8
20	Pennsylvania	76.9
37	Rhode Island	42.9
24	South Carolina	69.9
42	South Dakota	29.7
7	Tennessee	106.2
8	Texas	98.4
40	Utah	39.1
50	Vermont	11.2
38	Virginia	42.3
21	Washington	73.9
41	West Virginia	31.7
29	Wisconsin	60.0
47	Wyoming	17.3

RANK ORDER

RANK	STATE	RATE
1	Maryland	160.8
2	California	137.3
3	New Mexico	135.1
4	Nevada	127.3
5	Alaska	121.5
6	Illinois	111.5
7	Tennessee	106.2
8	Texas	98.4
9	Louisiana	98.0
10	New York	93.1
11	Arizona	91.0
12	Delaware	89.5
13	Indiana	88.7
14	Missouri	84.8
15	Alabama	83.4
16	North Carolina	81.1
17	Florida	79.3
18	Georgia	78.7
19	Ohio	78.6
20	Pennsylvania	76.9
21	Washington	73.9
22	New Jersey	71.4
23	Oklahoma	70.8
24	South Carolina	69.9
25	Colorado	66.7
26	Hawaii	66.6
27	Connecticut	61.4
28	Oregon	60.8
29	Massachusetts	60.0
29	Wisconsin	60.0
31	Michigan	56.6
32	Kentucky	55.0
33	Mississippi	53.4
34	Kansas	53.0
35	Arkansas	52.9
36	Minnesota	52.5
37	Rhode Island	42.9
38	Virginia	42.3
39	Nebraska	39.2
40	Utah	39.1
41	West Virginia	31.7
42	South Dakota	29.7
43	Iowa	29.5
44	New Hampshire	26.5
45	Montana	25.3
46	North Dakota	20.8
47	Wyoming	17.3
48	Maine	17.0
49	Idaho	11.4
50	Vermont	11.2
	District of Columbia	343.8

Source: Reported data from the Federal Bureau of Investigation
"Crime in the United States 2018" (Uniform Crime Reports, September 30, 2019, https://ucr.fbi.gov/)
*Robbery is the taking or attempting to take anything of value by force or threat of force.

Aggravated Assaults in 2018

National Total = 807,410 Aggravated Assaults*

ALPHA ORDER

RANK	STATE	ASSAULTS	% of USA
13	Alabama	18,944	2.3%
35	Alaska	4,391	0.5%
10	Arizona	23,528	2.9%
24	Arkansas	12,378	1.5%
1	California	105,412	13.1%
20	Colorado	14,547	1.8%
37	Connecticut	4,294	0.5%
42	Delaware	2,845	0.4%
3	Florida	55,551	6.9%
11	Georgia	22,783	2.8%
44	Hawaii	1,925	0.2%
41	Idaho	2,957	0.4%
7	Illinois	30,539	3.8%
17	Indiana	16,834	2.1%
32	Iowa	5,931	0.7%
29	Kansas	9,559	1.2%
33	Kentucky	5,059	0.6%
15	Louisiana	17,866	2.2%
49	Maine	803	0.1%
19	Maryland	16,135	2.0%
18	Massachusetts	16,648	2.1%
6	Michigan	31,021	3.8%
31	Minnesota	6,857	0.8%
34	Mississippi	4,696	0.6%
12	Missouri	22,042	2.7%
40	Montana	3,120	0.4%
39	Nebraska	3,461	0.4%
28	Nevada	10,027	1.2%
46	New Hampshire	1,435	0.2%
26	New Jersey	10,463	1.3%
22	New Mexico	13,598	1.7%
4	New York	43,171	5.3%
8	North Carolina	27,526	3.4%
45	North Dakota	1,560	0.2%
16	Ohio	17,674	2.2%
23	Oklahoma	13,084	1.6%
30	Oregon	7,360	0.9%
9	Pennsylvania	24,077	3.0%
47	Rhode Island	1,366	0.2%
14	South Carolina	18,446	2.3%
43	South Dakota	2,682	0.3%
5	Tennessee	31,717	3.9%
2	Texas	73,656	9.1%
36	Utah	4,319	0.5%
50	Vermont	710	0.1%
27	Virginia	10,113	1.3%
21	Washington	14,251	1.8%
38	West Virginia	3,945	0.5%
25	Wisconsin	11,263	1.4%
48	Wyoming	870	0.1%

RANK ORDER

RANK	STATE	ASSAULTS	% of USA
1	California	105,412	13.1%
2	Texas	73,656	9.1%
3	Florida	55,551	6.9%
4	New York	43,171	5.3%
5	Tennessee	31,717	3.9%
6	Michigan	31,021	3.8%
7	Illinois	30,539	3.8%
8	North Carolina	27,526	3.4%
9	Pennsylvania	24,077	3.0%
10	Arizona	23,528	2.9%
11	Georgia	22,783	2.8%
12	Missouri	22,042	2.7%
13	Alabama	18,944	2.3%
14	South Carolina	18,446	2.3%
15	Louisiana	17,866	2.2%
16	Ohio	17,674	2.2%
17	Indiana	16,834	2.1%
18	Massachusetts	16,648	2.1%
19	Maryland	16,135	2.0%
20	Colorado	14,547	1.8%
21	Washington	14,251	1.8%
22	New Mexico	13,598	1.7%
23	Oklahoma	13,084	1.6%
24	Arkansas	12,378	1.5%
25	Wisconsin	11,263	1.4%
26	New Jersey	10,463	1.3%
27	Virginia	10,113	1.3%
28	Nevada	10,027	1.2%
29	Kansas	9,559	1.2%
30	Oregon	7,360	0.9%
31	Minnesota	6,857	0.8%
32	Iowa	5,931	0.7%
33	Kentucky	5,059	0.6%
34	Mississippi	4,696	0.6%
35	Alaska	4,391	0.5%
36	Utah	4,319	0.5%
37	Connecticut	4,294	0.5%
38	West Virginia	3,945	0.5%
39	Nebraska	3,461	0.4%
40	Montana	3,120	0.4%
41	Idaho	2,957	0.4%
42	Delaware	2,845	0.4%
43	South Dakota	2,682	0.3%
44	Hawaii	1,925	0.2%
45	North Dakota	1,560	0.2%
46	New Hampshire	1,435	0.2%
47	Rhode Island	1,366	0.2%
48	Wyoming	870	0.1%
49	Maine	803	0.1%
50	Vermont	710	0.1%
	District of Columbia	3,971	0.5%

Source: Reported data from the Federal Bureau of Investigation
   "Crime in the United States 2018" (Uniform Crime Reports, September 30, 2019, https://ucr.fbi.gov/)
*Aggravated assault is an attack for the purpose of inflicting severe bodily injury.

Aggravated Assault Rate in 2018

National Rate = 246.8 Aggravated Assaults per 100,000 Population*

ALPHA ORDER

RANK	STATE	RATE
5	Alabama	387.6
2	Alaska	595.4
12	Arizona	328.1
4	Arkansas	410.7
18	California	266.5
22	Colorado	255.4
44	Connecticut	120.2
15	Delaware	294.2
20	Florida	260.8
28	Georgia	216.6
41	Hawaii	135.5
36	Idaho	168.6
25	Illinois	239.7
23	Indiana	251.6
33	Iowa	187.9
11	Kansas	328.3
48	Kentucky	113.2
6	Louisiana	383.4
50	Maine	60.0
17	Maryland	267.0
24	Massachusetts	241.2
13	Michigan	310.3
43	Minnesota	122.2
37	Mississippi	157.2
8	Missouri	359.8
16	Montana	293.7
34	Nebraska	179.4
10	Nevada	330.4
49	New Hampshire	105.8
46	New Jersey	117.4
1	New Mexico	648.9
26	New York	220.9
19	North Carolina	265.1
29	North Dakota	205.2
38	Ohio	151.2
9	Oklahoma	331.8
35	Oregon	175.6
32	Pennsylvania	188.0
42	Rhode Island	129.2
7	South Carolina	362.8
14	South Dakota	304.0
3	Tennessee	468.5
21	Texas	256.6
40	Utah	136.6
47	Vermont	113.4
45	Virginia	118.7
31	Washington	189.1
27	West Virginia	218.5
30	Wisconsin	193.7
39	Wyoming	150.6

RANK ORDER

RANK	STATE	RATE
1	New Mexico	648.9
2	Alaska	595.4
3	Tennessee	468.5
4	Arkansas	410.7
5	Alabama	387.6
6	Louisiana	383.4
7	South Carolina	362.8
8	Missouri	359.8
9	Oklahoma	331.8
10	Nevada	330.4
11	Kansas	328.3
12	Arizona	328.1
13	Michigan	310.3
14	South Dakota	304.0
15	Delaware	294.2
16	Montana	293.7
17	Maryland	267.0
18	California	266.5
19	North Carolina	265.1
20	Florida	260.8
21	Texas	256.6
22	Colorado	255.4
23	Indiana	251.6
24	Massachusetts	241.2
25	Illinois	239.7
26	New York	220.9
27	West Virginia	218.5
28	Georgia	216.6
29	North Dakota	205.2
30	Wisconsin	193.7
31	Washington	189.1
32	Pennsylvania	188.0
33	Iowa	187.9
34	Nebraska	179.4
35	Oregon	175.6
36	Idaho	168.6
37	Mississippi	157.2
38	Ohio	151.2
39	Wyoming	150.6
40	Utah	136.6
41	Hawaii	135.5
42	Rhode Island	129.2
43	Minnesota	122.2
44	Connecticut	120.2
45	Virginia	118.7
46	New Jersey	117.4
47	Vermont	113.4
48	Kentucky	113.2
49	New Hampshire	105.8
50	Maine	60.0

| | District of Columbia | 565.3 |

Source: Reported data from the Federal Bureau of Investigation
"Crime in the United States 2018" (Uniform Crime Reports, September 30, 2019, https://ucr.fbi.gov/)
*Aggravated assault is an attack for the purpose of inflicting severe bodily injury.

Property Crimes in 2018

National Total = 7,196,045 Property Crimes*

<table>
<tr><td colspan="4">ALPHA ORDER</td><td colspan="4">RANK ORDER</td></tr>
<tr><td>RANK</td><td>STATE</td><td>CRIMES</td><td>% of USA</td><td>RANK</td><td>STATE</td><td>CRIMES</td><td>% of USA</td></tr>
<tr><td>20</td><td>Alabama</td><td>137,700</td><td>1.9%</td><td>1</td><td>California</td><td>941,618</td><td>13.1%</td></tr>
<tr><td>42</td><td>Alaska</td><td>24,339</td><td>0.3%</td><td>2</td><td>Texas</td><td>679,430</td><td>9.4%</td></tr>
<tr><td>10</td><td>Arizona</td><td>191,974</td><td>2.7%</td><td>3</td><td>Florida</td><td>486,017</td><td>6.8%</td></tr>
<tr><td>27</td><td>Arkansas</td><td>87,793</td><td>1.2%</td><td>4</td><td>New York</td><td>281,507</td><td>3.9%</td></tr>
<tr><td>1</td><td>California</td><td>941,618</td><td>13.1%</td><td>5</td><td>Georgia</td><td>270,738</td><td>3.8%</td></tr>
<tr><td>17</td><td>Colorado</td><td>152,163</td><td>2.1%</td><td>6</td><td>North Carolina</td><td>258,979</td><td>3.6%</td></tr>
<tr><td>35</td><td>Connecticut</td><td>60,055</td><td>0.8%</td><td>7</td><td>Ohio</td><td>254,496</td><td>3.5%</td></tr>
<tr><td>43</td><td>Delaware</td><td>22,481</td><td>0.3%</td><td>8</td><td>Illinois</td><td>246,264</td><td>3.4%</td></tr>
<tr><td>3</td><td>Florida</td><td>486,017</td><td>6.8%</td><td>9</td><td>Washington</td><td>222,011</td><td>3.1%</td></tr>
<tr><td>5</td><td>Georgia</td><td>270,738</td><td>3.8%</td><td>10</td><td>Arizona</td><td>191,974</td><td>2.7%</td></tr>
<tr><td>37</td><td>Hawaii</td><td>40,772</td><td>0.6%</td><td>11</td><td>Tennessee</td><td>191,279</td><td>2.7%</td></tr>
<tr><td>41</td><td>Idaho</td><td>25,636</td><td>0.4%</td><td>12</td><td>Pennsylvania</td><td>190,816</td><td>2.7%</td></tr>
<tr><td>8</td><td>Illinois</td><td>246,264</td><td>3.4%</td><td>13</td><td>Michigan</td><td>165,280</td><td>2.3%</td></tr>
<tr><td>18</td><td>Indiana</td><td>145,838</td><td>2.0%</td><td>14</td><td>Missouri</td><td>162,173</td><td>2.3%</td></tr>
<tr><td>36</td><td>Iowa</td><td>53,385</td><td>0.7%</td><td>15</td><td>South Carolina</td><td>153,421</td><td>2.1%</td></tr>
<tr><td>30</td><td>Kansas</td><td>76,686</td><td>1.1%</td><td>16</td><td>Louisiana</td><td>152,661</td><td>2.1%</td></tr>
<tr><td>28</td><td>Kentucky</td><td>87,695</td><td>1.2%</td><td>17</td><td>Colorado</td><td>152,163</td><td>2.1%</td></tr>
<tr><td>16</td><td>Louisiana</td><td>152,661</td><td>2.1%</td><td>18</td><td>Indiana</td><td>145,838</td><td>2.0%</td></tr>
<tr><td>44</td><td>Maine</td><td>18,173</td><td>0.3%</td><td>19</td><td>Virginia</td><td>141,885</td><td>2.0%</td></tr>
<tr><td>22</td><td>Maryland</td><td>122,864</td><td>1.7%</td><td>20</td><td>Alabama</td><td>137,700</td><td>1.9%</td></tr>
<tr><td>29</td><td>Massachusetts</td><td>87,196</td><td>1.2%</td><td>21</td><td>New Jersey</td><td>125,156</td><td>1.7%</td></tr>
<tr><td>13</td><td>Michigan</td><td>165,280</td><td>2.3%</td><td>22</td><td>Maryland</td><td>122,864</td><td>1.7%</td></tr>
<tr><td>25</td><td>Minnesota</td><td>111,874</td><td>1.6%</td><td>23</td><td>Oregon</td><td>121,278</td><td>1.7%</td></tr>
<tr><td>33</td><td>Mississippi</td><td>71,766</td><td>1.0%</td><td>24</td><td>Oklahoma</td><td>113,364</td><td>1.6%</td></tr>
<tr><td>14</td><td>Missouri</td><td>162,173</td><td>2.3%</td><td>25</td><td>Minnesota</td><td>111,874</td><td>1.6%</td></tr>
<tr><td>40</td><td>Montana</td><td>26,518</td><td>0.4%</td><td>26</td><td>Wisconsin</td><td>90,686</td><td>1.3%</td></tr>
<tr><td>38</td><td>Nebraska</td><td>40,126</td><td>0.6%</td><td>27</td><td>Arkansas</td><td>87,793</td><td>1.2%</td></tr>
<tr><td>32</td><td>Nevada</td><td>73,985</td><td>1.0%</td><td>28</td><td>Kentucky</td><td>87,695</td><td>1.2%</td></tr>
<tr><td>46</td><td>New Hampshire</td><td>16,935</td><td>0.2%</td><td>29</td><td>Massachusetts</td><td>87,196</td><td>1.2%</td></tr>
<tr><td>21</td><td>New Jersey</td><td>125,156</td><td>1.7%</td><td>30</td><td>Kansas</td><td>76,686</td><td>1.1%</td></tr>
<tr><td>34</td><td>New Mexico</td><td>71,657</td><td>1.0%</td><td>31</td><td>Utah</td><td>75,156</td><td>1.0%</td></tr>
<tr><td>4</td><td>New York</td><td>281,507</td><td>3.9%</td><td>32</td><td>Nevada</td><td>73,985</td><td>1.0%</td></tr>
<tr><td>6</td><td>North Carolina</td><td>258,979</td><td>3.6%</td><td>33</td><td>Mississippi</td><td>71,766</td><td>1.0%</td></tr>
<tr><td>47</td><td>North Dakota</td><td>15,507</td><td>0.2%</td><td>34</td><td>New Mexico</td><td>71,657</td><td>1.0%</td></tr>
<tr><td>7</td><td>Ohio</td><td>254,496</td><td>3.5%</td><td>35</td><td>Connecticut</td><td>60,055</td><td>0.8%</td></tr>
<tr><td>24</td><td>Oklahoma</td><td>113,364</td><td>1.6%</td><td>36</td><td>Iowa</td><td>53,385</td><td>0.7%</td></tr>
<tr><td>23</td><td>Oregon</td><td>121,278</td><td>1.7%</td><td>37</td><td>Hawaii</td><td>40,772</td><td>0.6%</td></tr>
<tr><td>12</td><td>Pennsylvania</td><td>190,816</td><td>2.7%</td><td>38</td><td>Nebraska</td><td>40,126</td><td>0.6%</td></tr>
<tr><td>45</td><td>Rhode Island</td><td>17,561</td><td>0.2%</td><td>39</td><td>West Virginia</td><td>26,827</td><td>0.4%</td></tr>
<tr><td>15</td><td>South Carolina</td><td>153,421</td><td>2.1%</td><td>40</td><td>Montana</td><td>26,518</td><td>0.4%</td></tr>
<tr><td>48</td><td>South Dakota</td><td>15,251</td><td>0.2%</td><td>41</td><td>Idaho</td><td>25,636</td><td>0.4%</td></tr>
<tr><td>11</td><td>Tennessee</td><td>191,279</td><td>2.7%</td><td>42</td><td>Alaska</td><td>24,339</td><td>0.3%</td></tr>
<tr><td>2</td><td>Texas</td><td>679,430</td><td>9.4%</td><td>43</td><td>Delaware</td><td>22,481</td><td>0.3%</td></tr>
<tr><td>31</td><td>Utah</td><td>75,156</td><td>1.0%</td><td>44</td><td>Maine</td><td>18,173</td><td>0.3%</td></tr>
<tr><td>50</td><td>Vermont</td><td>8,036</td><td>0.1%</td><td>45</td><td>Rhode Island</td><td>17,561</td><td>0.2%</td></tr>
<tr><td>19</td><td>Virginia</td><td>141,885</td><td>2.0%</td><td>46</td><td>New Hampshire</td><td>16,935</td><td>0.2%</td></tr>
<tr><td>9</td><td>Washington</td><td>222,011</td><td>3.1%</td><td>47</td><td>North Dakota</td><td>15,507</td><td>0.2%</td></tr>
<tr><td>39</td><td>West Virginia</td><td>26,827</td><td>0.4%</td><td>48</td><td>South Dakota</td><td>15,251</td><td>0.2%</td></tr>
<tr><td>26</td><td>Wisconsin</td><td>90,686</td><td>1.3%</td><td>49</td><td>Wyoming</td><td>10,313</td><td>0.1%</td></tr>
<tr><td>49</td><td>Wyoming</td><td>10,313</td><td>0.1%</td><td>50</td><td>Vermont</td><td>8,036</td><td>0.1%</td></tr>
<tr><td></td><td></td><td></td><td></td><td></td><td>District of Columbia</td><td>30,724</td><td>0.4%</td></tr>
</table>

Source: Reported data from the Federal Bureau of Investigation
"Crime in the United States 2018" (Uniform Crime Reports, September 30, 2019, https://ucr.fbi.gov/)
*Property crimes are offenses of burglary, larceny-theft, and motor vehicle theft.

Property Crime Rate in 2018

National Rate = 2,199.5 Property Crimes per 100,000 Population*

ALPHA ORDER

RANK ORDER

RANK	STATE	RATE
11	Alabama	2,817.2
2	Alaska	3,300.5
12	Arizona	2,676.8
6	Arkansas	2,913.0
21	California	2,380.4
13	Colorado	2,671.6
37	Connecticut	1,681.0
24	Delaware	2,324.4
25	Florida	2,281.8
16	Georgia	2,573.7
9	Hawaii	2,870.3
44	Idaho	1,461.4
33	Illinois	1,932.8
26	Indiana	2,179.3
36	Iowa	1,691.5
15	Kansas	2,633.9
32	Kentucky	1,962.6
3	Louisiana	3,276.0
47	Maine	1,357.8
30	Maryland	2,033.3
49	Massachusetts	1,263.3
40	Michigan	1,653.5
31	Minnesota	1,993.8
20	Mississippi	2,403.0
14	Missouri	2,647.1
17	Montana	2,496.3
28	Nebraska	2,079.9
19	Nevada	2,438.2
50	New Hampshire	1,248.5
46	New Jersey	1,404.9
1	New Mexico	3,419.7
45	New York	1,440.5
18	North Carolina	2,494.1
29	North Dakota	2,040.2
27	Ohio	2,177.1
8	Oklahoma	2,875.0
7	Oregon	2,894.0
42	Pennsylvania	1,489.9
39	Rhode Island	1,660.9
4	South Carolina	3,017.6
35	South Dakota	1,728.7
10	Tennessee	2,825.4
23	Texas	2,367.2
22	Utah	2,377.5
48	Vermont	1,283.1
38	Virginia	1,665.8
5	Washington	2,946.2
43	West Virginia	1,485.6
41	Wisconsin	1,559.9
34	Wyoming	1,785.1

RANK	STATE	RATE
1	New Mexico	3,419.7
2	Alaska	3,300.5
3	Louisiana	3,276.0
4	South Carolina	3,017.6
5	Washington	2,946.2
6	Arkansas	2,913.0
7	Oregon	2,894.0
8	Oklahoma	2,875.0
9	Hawaii	2,870.3
10	Tennessee	2,825.4
11	Alabama	2,817.2
12	Arizona	2,676.8
13	Colorado	2,671.6
14	Missouri	2,647.1
15	Kansas	2,633.9
16	Georgia	2,573.7
17	Montana	2,496.3
18	North Carolina	2,494.1
19	Nevada	2,438.2
20	Mississippi	2,403.0
21	California	2,380.4
22	Utah	2,377.5
23	Texas	2,367.2
24	Delaware	2,324.4
25	Florida	2,281.8
26	Indiana	2,179.3
27	Ohio	2,177.1
28	Nebraska	2,079.9
29	North Dakota	2,040.2
30	Maryland	2,033.3
31	Minnesota	1,993.8
32	Kentucky	1,962.6
33	Illinois	1,932.8
34	Wyoming	1,785.1
35	South Dakota	1,728.7
36	Iowa	1,691.5
37	Connecticut	1,681.0
38	Virginia	1,665.8
39	Rhode Island	1,660.9
40	Michigan	1,653.5
41	Wisconsin	1,559.9
42	Pennsylvania	1,489.9
43	West Virginia	1,485.6
44	Idaho	1,461.4
45	New York	1,440.5
46	New Jersey	1,404.9
47	Maine	1,357.8
48	Vermont	1,283.1
49	Massachusetts	1,263.3
50	New Hampshire	1,248.5

	District of Columbia	4,373.8

Source: Reported data from the Federal Bureau of Investigation
"Crime in the United States 2018" (Uniform Crime Reports, September 30, 2019, https://ucr.fbi.gov/)
*Property crimes are offenses of burglary, larceny-theft, and motor vehicle theft.

Percent Change in Property Crime Rate: 2017 to 2018

National Percent Change = 6.9% Decrease*

ALPHA ORDER				RANK ORDER		
RANK	STATE	PERCENT CHANGE		RANK	STATE	PERCENT CHANGE
13	Alabama	(4.5)		1	Hawaii	1.2
20	Alaska	(6.8)		2	Oklahoma	(0.5)
27	Arizona	(8.0)		3	Colorado	(1.3)
23	Arkansas	(7.4)		4	Wyoming	(1.8)
14	California	(5.0)		5	Oregon	(2.1)
3	Colorado	(1.3)		6	Louisiana	(2.7)
17	Connecticut	(5.6)		7	Illinois	(3.1)
15	Delaware	(5.1)		8	Kansas	(3.4)
34	Florida	(9.2)		9	North Carolina	(3.5)
39	Georgia	(10.0)		10	Montana	(3.7)
1	Hawaii	1.2		11	New York	(3.8)
43	Idaho	(12.0)		12	Tennessee	(4.3)
7	Illinois	(3.1)		13	Alabama	(4.5)
29	Indiana	(8.7)		14	California	(5.0)
50	Iowa	(19.0)		15	Delaware	(5.1)
8	Kansas	(3.4)		16	South Carolina	(5.5)
30	Kentucky	(8.9)		17	Connecticut	(5.6)
6	Louisiana	(2.7)		17	Rhode Island	(5.6)
39	Maine	(10.0)		19	Missouri	(6.7)
32	Maryland	(9.1)		20	Alaska	(6.8)
42	Massachusetts	(11.5)		21	Washington	(7.0)
28	Michigan	(8.3)		22	Texas	(7.3)
36	Minnesota	(9.3)		23	Arkansas	(7.4)
45	Mississippi	(13.2)		24	Nevada	(7.5)
19	Missouri	(6.7)		24	North Dakota	(7.5)
10	Montana	(3.7)		24	Virginia	(7.5)
32	Nebraska	(9.1)		27	Arizona	(8.0)
24	Nevada	(7.5)		28	Michigan	(8.3)
34	New Hampshire	(9.2)		29	Indiana	(8.7)
41	New Jersey	(10.9)		30	Kentucky	(8.9)
44	New Mexico	(12.6)		31	South Dakota	(9.0)
11	New York	(3.8)		32	Maryland	(9.1)
9	North Carolina	(3.5)		32	Nebraska	(9.1)
24	North Dakota	(7.5)		34	Florida	(9.2)
38	Ohio	(9.5)		34	New Hampshire	(9.2)
2	Oklahoma	(0.5)		36	Minnesota	(9.3)
5	Oregon	(2.1)		37	Pennsylvania	(9.4)
37	Pennsylvania	(9.4)		38	Ohio	(9.5)
17	Rhode Island	(5.6)		39	Georgia	(10.0)
16	South Carolina	(5.5)		39	Maine	(10.0)
31	South Dakota	(9.0)		41	New Jersey	(10.9)
12	Tennessee	(4.3)		42	Massachusetts	(11.5)
22	Texas	(7.3)		43	Idaho	(12.0)
48	Utah	(14.4)		44	New Mexico	(12.6)
47	Vermont	(14.2)		45	Mississippi	(13.2)
24	Virginia	(7.5)		46	Wisconsin	(13.9)
21	Washington	(7.0)		47	Vermont	(14.2)
49	West Virginia	(17.1)		48	Utah	(14.4)
46	Wisconsin	(13.9)		49	West Virginia	(17.1)
4	Wyoming	(1.8)		50	Iowa	(19.0)
					District of Columbia	2.3

Source: Reported data from the Federal Bureau of Investigation
   "Crime in the United States 2018" (Uniform Crime Reports, September 30, 2019, https://ucr.fbi.gov/)
*Property crimes are offenses of burglary, larceny-theft, and motor vehicle theft.

Burglaries in 2018

National Total = 1,230,149 Burglaries*

ALPHA ORDER

RANK	STATE	BURGLARIES	% of USA
15	Alabama	28,841	2.3%
41	Alaska	3,979	0.3%
11	Arizona	31,532	2.6%
23	Arkansas	19,193	1.6%
1	California	164,632	13.4%
20	Colorado	21,371	1.7%
36	Connecticut	7,948	0.6%
43	Delaware	3,158	0.3%
3	Florida	71,933	5.8%
6	Georgia	45,369	3.7%
37	Hawaii	5,631	0.5%
40	Idaho	4,940	0.4%
8	Illinois	39,080	3.2%
19	Indiana	25,268	2.1%
34	Iowa	11,127	0.9%
33	Kansas	12,537	1.0%
26	Kentucky	17,190	1.4%
13	Louisiana	31,132	2.5%
46	Maine	2,713	0.2%
24	Maryland	18,892	1.5%
32	Massachusetts	13,862	1.1%
10	Michigan	31,651	2.6%
28	Minnesota	16,185	1.3%
21	Mississippi	20,839	1.7%
16	Missouri	27,257	2.2%
42	Montana	3,257	0.3%
39	Nebraska	5,246	0.4%
25	Nevada	17,743	1.4%
48	New Hampshire	1,847	0.2%
22	New Jersey	19,232	1.6%
29	New Mexico	16,088	1.3%
12	New York	31,137	2.5%
4	North Carolina	62,290	5.1%
45	North Dakota	2,724	0.2%
5	Ohio	48,186	3.9%
18	Oklahoma	26,858	2.2%
27	Oregon	16,304	1.3%
17	Pennsylvania	27,104	2.2%
44	Rhode Island	2,810	0.2%
14	South Carolina	29,473	2.4%
47	South Dakota	2,571	0.2%
9	Tennessee	33,132	2.7%
2	Texas	117,911	9.6%
35	Utah	9,968	0.8%
50	Vermont	1,467	0.1%
30	Virginia	15,574	1.3%
7	Washington	40,201	3.3%
38	West Virginia	5,354	0.4%
31	Wisconsin	14,099	1.1%
49	Wyoming	1,525	0.1%

RANK ORDER

RANK	STATE	BURGLARIES	% of USA
1	California	164,632	13.4%
2	Texas	117,911	9.6%
3	Florida	71,933	5.8%
4	North Carolina	62,290	5.1%
5	Ohio	48,186	3.9%
6	Georgia	45,369	3.7%
7	Washington	40,201	3.3%
8	Illinois	39,080	3.2%
9	Tennessee	33,132	2.7%
10	Michigan	31,651	2.6%
11	Arizona	31,532	2.6%
12	New York	31,137	2.5%
13	Louisiana	31,132	2.5%
14	South Carolina	29,473	2.4%
15	Alabama	28,841	2.3%
16	Missouri	27,257	2.2%
17	Pennsylvania	27,104	2.2%
18	Oklahoma	26,858	2.2%
19	Indiana	25,268	2.1%
20	Colorado	21,371	1.7%
21	Mississippi	20,839	1.7%
22	New Jersey	19,232	1.6%
23	Arkansas	19,193	1.6%
24	Maryland	18,892	1.5%
25	Nevada	17,743	1.4%
26	Kentucky	17,190	1.4%
27	Oregon	16,304	1.3%
28	Minnesota	16,185	1.3%
29	New Mexico	16,088	1.3%
30	Virginia	15,574	1.3%
31	Wisconsin	14,099	1.1%
32	Massachusetts	13,862	1.1%
33	Kansas	12,537	1.0%
34	Iowa	11,127	0.9%
35	Utah	9,968	0.8%
36	Connecticut	7,948	0.6%
37	Hawaii	5,631	0.5%
38	West Virginia	5,354	0.4%
39	Nebraska	5,246	0.4%
40	Idaho	4,940	0.4%
41	Alaska	3,979	0.3%
42	Montana	3,257	0.3%
43	Delaware	3,158	0.3%
44	Rhode Island	2,810	0.2%
45	North Dakota	2,724	0.2%
46	Maine	2,713	0.2%
47	South Dakota	2,571	0.2%
48	New Hampshire	1,847	0.2%
49	Wyoming	1,525	0.1%
50	Vermont	1,467	0.1%
	District of Columbia	1,788	0.1%

Source: Reported data from the Federal Bureau of Investigation
   "Crime in the United States 2018" (Uniform Crime Reports, September 30, 2019, https://ucr.fbi.gov/)
*Burglary is the unlawful entry of a structure to commit a felony or theft. Attempts are included.

Burglary Rate in 2018

National Rate = 376.0 Burglaries per 100,000 Population*

ALPHA ORDER			RANK ORDER		
RANK	**STATE**	**RATE**	**RANK**	**STATE**	**RATE**
7	Alabama	590.1	1	New Mexico	767.8
10	Alaska	539.6	2	Mississippi	697.8
14	Arizona	439.7	3	Oklahoma	681.1
5	Arkansas	636.8	4	Louisiana	668.1
17	California	416.2	5	Arkansas	636.8
24	Colorado	375.2	6	North Carolina	599.9
43	Connecticut	222.5	7	Alabama	590.1
28	Delaware	326.5	8	Nevada	584.7
27	Florida	337.7	9	South Carolina	579.7
15	Georgia	431.3	10	Alaska	539.6
20	Hawaii	396.4	11	Washington	533.5
37	Idaho	281.6	12	Tennessee	489.4
32	Illinois	306.7	13	Missouri	444.9
23	Indiana	377.6	14	Arizona	439.7
26	Iowa	352.6	15	Georgia	431.3
16	Kansas	430.6	16	Kansas	430.6
22	Kentucky	384.7	17	California	416.2
4	Louisiana	668.1	18	Ohio	412.2
46	Maine	202.7	19	Texas	410.8
31	Maryland	312.6	20	Hawaii	396.4
47	Massachusetts	200.8	21	Oregon	389.1
29	Michigan	316.6	22	Kentucky	384.7
36	Minnesota	288.4	23	Indiana	377.6
2	Mississippi	697.8	24	Colorado	375.2
13	Missouri	444.9	25	North Dakota	358.4
33	Montana	306.6	26	Iowa	352.6
38	Nebraska	271.9	27	Florida	337.7
8	Nevada	584.7	28	Delaware	326.5
50	New Hampshire	136.2	29	Michigan	316.6
44	New Jersey	215.9	30	Utah	315.3
1	New Mexico	767.8	31	Maryland	312.6
49	New York	159.3	32	Illinois	306.7
6	North Carolina	599.9	33	Montana	306.6
25	North Dakota	358.4	34	West Virginia	296.5
18	Ohio	412.2	35	South Dakota	291.4
3	Oklahoma	681.1	36	Minnesota	288.4
21	Oregon	389.1	37	Idaho	281.6
45	Pennsylvania	211.6	38	Nebraska	271.9
39	Rhode Island	265.8	39	Rhode Island	265.8
9	South Carolina	579.7	40	Wyoming	264.0
35	South Dakota	291.4	41	Wisconsin	242.5
12	Tennessee	489.4	42	Vermont	234.2
19	Texas	410.8	43	Connecticut	222.5
30	Utah	315.3	44	New Jersey	215.9
42	Vermont	234.2	45	Pennsylvania	211.6
48	Virginia	182.8	46	Maine	202.7
11	Washington	533.5	47	Massachusetts	200.8
34	West Virginia	296.5	48	Virginia	182.8
41	Wisconsin	242.5	49	New York	159.3
40	Wyoming	264.0	50	New Hampshire	136.2
				District of Columbia	254.5

Source: Reported data from the Federal Bureau of Investigation
    "Crime in the United States 2018" (Uniform Crime Reports, September 30, 2019, https://ucr.fbi.gov/)
*Burglary is the unlawful entry of a structure to commit a felony or theft. Attempts are included.

Larceny-Thefts in 2018

National Total = 5,217,055 Larceny-Thefts*

ALPHA ORDER

RANK	STATE	THEFTS	% of USA
20	Alabama	95,747	1.8%
43	Alaska	16,364	0.3%
11	Arizona	141,303	2.7%
28	Arkansas	61,487	1.2%
1	California	621,775	11.9%
18	Colorado	109,119	2.1%
34	Connecticut	44,724	0.9%
42	Delaware	17,847	0.3%
3	Florida	372,919	7.1%
5	Georgia	200,609	3.8%
38	Hawaii	29,492	0.6%
41	Idaho	18,732	0.4%
6	Illinois	187,591	3.6%
19	Indiana	105,242	2.0%
36	Iowa	37,571	0.7%
31	Kansas	56,305	1.1%
29	Kentucky	60,244	1.2%
16	Louisiana	109,993	2.1%
44	Maine	14,683	0.3%
22	Maryland	91,835	1.8%
27	Massachusetts	66,728	1.3%
13	Michigan	116,178	2.2%
24	Minnesota	85,561	1.6%
32	Mississippi	46,627	0.9%
15	Missouri	115,101	2.2%
39	Montana	20,465	0.4%
37	Nebraska	30,006	0.6%
35	Nevada	44,338	0.8%
45	New Hampshire	14,219	0.3%
21	New Jersey	94,887	1.8%
33	New Mexico	45,390	0.9%
4	New York	237,233	4.5%
8	North Carolina	179,057	3.4%
48	North Dakota	11,008	0.2%
7	Ohio	186,401	3.6%
25	Oklahoma	73,217	1.4%
23	Oregon	88,418	1.7%
10	Pennsylvania	150,596	2.9%
46	Rhode Island	13,220	0.3%
17	South Carolina	109,616	2.1%
47	South Dakota	11,156	0.2%
12	Tennessee	137,708	2.6%
2	Texas	491,702	9.4%
30	Utah	57,460	1.1%
50	Vermont	6,316	0.1%
14	Virginia	115,533	2.2%
9	Washington	154,133	3.0%
40	West Virginia	18,954	0.4%
26	Wisconsin	67,953	1.3%
49	Wyoming	7,949	0.2%

RANK ORDER

RANK	STATE	THEFTS	% of USA
1	California	621,775	11.9%
2	Texas	491,702	9.4%
3	Florida	372,919	7.1%
4	New York	237,233	4.5%
5	Georgia	200,609	3.8%
6	Illinois	187,591	3.6%
7	Ohio	186,401	3.6%
8	North Carolina	179,057	3.4%
9	Washington	154,133	3.0%
10	Pennsylvania	150,596	2.9%
11	Arizona	141,303	2.7%
12	Tennessee	137,708	2.6%
13	Michigan	116,178	2.2%
14	Virginia	115,533	2.2%
15	Missouri	115,101	2.2%
16	Louisiana	109,993	2.1%
17	South Carolina	109,616	2.1%
18	Colorado	109,119	2.1%
19	Indiana	105,242	2.0%
20	Alabama	95,747	1.8%
21	New Jersey	94,887	1.8%
22	Maryland	91,835	1.8%
23	Oregon	88,418	1.7%
24	Minnesota	85,561	1.6%
25	Oklahoma	73,217	1.4%
26	Wisconsin	67,953	1.3%
27	Massachusetts	66,728	1.3%
28	Arkansas	61,487	1.2%
29	Kentucky	60,244	1.2%
30	Utah	57,460	1.1%
31	Kansas	56,305	1.1%
32	Mississippi	46,627	0.9%
33	New Mexico	45,390	0.9%
34	Connecticut	44,724	0.9%
35	Nevada	44,338	0.8%
36	Iowa	37,571	0.7%
37	Nebraska	30,006	0.6%
38	Hawaii	29,492	0.6%
39	Montana	20,465	0.4%
40	West Virginia	18,954	0.4%
41	Idaho	18,732	0.4%
42	Delaware	17,847	0.3%
43	Alaska	16,364	0.3%
44	Maine	14,683	0.3%
45	New Hampshire	14,219	0.3%
46	Rhode Island	13,220	0.3%
47	South Dakota	11,156	0.2%
48	North Dakota	11,008	0.2%
49	Wyoming	7,949	0.2%
50	Vermont	6,316	0.1%
	District of Columbia	26,343	0.5%

Source: Reported data from the Federal Bureau of Investigation
"Crime in the United States 2018" (Uniform Crime Reports, September 30, 2019, https://ucr.fbi.gov/)
*Larceny-theft is the unlawful taking of property without use of force, violence, or fraud. Attempts are included. Motor vehicle thefts are excluded.

Larceny-Theft Rate in 2018

National Rate = 1,594.6 Larceny-Thefts per 100,000 Population*

ALPHA ORDER

RANK	STATE	RATE
11	Alabama	1,958.9
2	Alaska	2,219.0
10	Arizona	1,970.3
8	Arkansas	2,040.2
25	California	1,571.8
14	Colorado	1,915.9
37	Connecticut	1,251.8
18	Delaware	1,845.3
20	Florida	1,750.8
15	Georgia	1,907.0
6	Hawaii	2,076.2
45	Idaho	1,067.8
30	Illinois	1,472.3
24	Indiana	1,572.7
40	Iowa	1,190.4
12	Kansas	1,933.9
35	Kentucky	1,348.2
1	Louisiana	2,360.4
44	Maine	1,097.1
29	Maryland	1,519.8
50	Massachusetts	966.8
43	Michigan	1,162.3
28	Minnesota	1,524.8
26	Mississippi	1,561.2
16	Missouri	1,878.8
13	Montana	1,926.5
27	Nebraska	1,555.3
31	Nevada	1,461.2
48	New Hampshire	1,048.2
46	New Jersey	1,065.1
3	New Mexico	2,166.1
39	New York	1,214.0
21	North Carolina	1,724.4
32	North Dakota	1,448.3
23	Ohio	1,594.6
17	Oklahoma	1,856.8
5	Oregon	2,109.9
41	Pennsylvania	1,175.9
38	Rhode Island	1,250.3
4	South Carolina	2,156.0
36	South Dakota	1,264.5
9	Tennessee	2,034.1
22	Texas	1,713.1
19	Utah	1,817.7
49	Vermont	1,008.5
34	Virginia	1,356.4
7	Washington	2,045.4
47	West Virginia	1,049.6
42	Wisconsin	1,168.9
33	Wyoming	1,375.9

RANK ORDER

RANK	STATE	RATE
1	Louisiana	2,360.4
2	Alaska	2,219.0
3	New Mexico	2,166.1
4	South Carolina	2,156.0
5	Oregon	2,109.9
6	Hawaii	2,076.2
7	Washington	2,045.4
8	Arkansas	2,040.2
9	Tennessee	2,034.1
10	Arizona	1,970.3
11	Alabama	1,958.9
12	Kansas	1,933.9
13	Montana	1,926.5
14	Colorado	1,915.9
15	Georgia	1,907.0
16	Missouri	1,878.8
17	Oklahoma	1,856.8
18	Delaware	1,845.3
19	Utah	1,817.7
20	Florida	1,750.8
21	North Carolina	1,724.4
22	Texas	1,713.1
23	Ohio	1,594.6
24	Indiana	1,572.7
25	California	1,571.8
26	Mississippi	1,561.2
27	Nebraska	1,555.3
28	Minnesota	1,524.8
29	Maryland	1,519.8
30	Illinois	1,472.3
31	Nevada	1,461.2
32	North Dakota	1,448.3
33	Wyoming	1,375.9
34	Virginia	1,356.4
35	Kentucky	1,348.2
36	South Dakota	1,264.5
37	Connecticut	1,251.8
38	Rhode Island	1,250.3
39	New York	1,214.0
40	Iowa	1,190.4
41	Pennsylvania	1,175.9
42	Wisconsin	1,168.9
43	Michigan	1,162.3
44	Maine	1,097.1
45	Idaho	1,067.8
46	New Jersey	1,065.1
47	West Virginia	1,049.6
48	New Hampshire	1,048.2
49	Vermont	1,008.5
50	Massachusetts	966.8

District of Columbia	3,750.1

Source: Reported data from the Federal Bureau of Investigation
   "Crime in the United States 2018" (Uniform Crime Reports, September 30, 2019, https://ucr.fbi.gov/)
*Larceny-theft is the unlawful taking of property without use of force, violence, or fraud. Attempts are included. Motor vehicle thefts are excluded.

Motor Vehicle Thefts in 2018

National Total = 748,841 Motor Vehicle Thefts*

ALPHA ORDER

RANK	STATE	THEFTS	% of USA
20	Alabama	13,112	1.8%
39	Alaska	3,996	0.5%
11	Arizona	19,139	2.6%
33	Arkansas	7,113	0.9%
1	California	155,211	20.7%
6	Colorado	21,673	2.9%
32	Connecticut	7,383	1.0%
46	Delaware	1,476	0.2%
3	Florida	41,165	5.5%
5	Georgia	24,760	3.3%
35	Hawaii	5,649	0.8%
42	Idaho	1,964	0.3%
10	Illinois	19,593	2.6%
15	Indiana	15,328	2.0%
37	Iowa	4,687	0.6%
30	Kansas	7,844	1.0%
26	Kentucky	10,261	1.4%
23	Louisiana	11,536	1.5%
49	Maine	777	0.1%
21	Maryland	12,137	1.6%
34	Massachusetts	6,606	0.9%
13	Michigan	17,451	2.3%
28	Minnesota	10,128	1.4%
38	Mississippi	4,300	0.6%
9	Missouri	19,815	2.6%
40	Montana	2,796	0.4%
36	Nebraska	4,874	0.7%
22	Nevada	11,904	1.6%
47	New Hampshire	869	0.1%
24	New Jersey	11,037	1.5%
27	New Mexico	10,179	1.4%
18	New York	13,137	1.8%
12	North Carolina	17,632	2.4%
43	North Dakota	1,775	0.2%
8	Ohio	19,909	2.7%
17	Oklahoma	13,289	1.8%
14	Oregon	16,556	2.2%
19	Pennsylvania	13,116	1.8%
44	Rhode Island	1,531	0.2%
16	South Carolina	14,332	1.9%
45	South Dakota	1,524	0.2%
7	Tennessee	20,439	2.7%
2	Texas	69,817	9.3%
31	Utah	7,728	1.0%
50	Vermont	253	0.0%
25	Virginia	10,778	1.4%
4	Washington	27,677	3.7%
41	West Virginia	2,519	0.3%
29	Wisconsin	8,634	1.2%
48	Wyoming	839	0.1%

RANK ORDER

RANK	STATE	THEFTS	% of USA
1	California	155,211	20.7%
2	Texas	69,817	9.3%
3	Florida	41,165	5.5%
4	Washington	27,677	3.7%
5	Georgia	24,760	3.3%
6	Colorado	21,673	2.9%
7	Tennessee	20,439	2.7%
8	Ohio	19,909	2.7%
9	Missouri	19,815	2.6%
10	Illinois	19,593	2.6%
11	Arizona	19,139	2.6%
12	North Carolina	17,632	2.4%
13	Michigan	17,451	2.3%
14	Oregon	16,556	2.2%
15	Indiana	15,328	2.0%
16	South Carolina	14,332	1.9%
17	Oklahoma	13,289	1.8%
18	New York	13,137	1.8%
19	Pennsylvania	13,116	1.8%
20	Alabama	13,112	1.8%
21	Maryland	12,137	1.6%
22	Nevada	11,904	1.6%
23	Louisiana	11,536	1.5%
24	New Jersey	11,037	1.5%
25	Virginia	10,778	1.4%
26	Kentucky	10,261	1.4%
27	New Mexico	10,179	1.4%
28	Minnesota	10,128	1.4%
29	Wisconsin	8,634	1.2%
30	Kansas	7,844	1.0%
31	Utah	7,728	1.0%
32	Connecticut	7,383	1.0%
33	Arkansas	7,113	0.9%
34	Massachusetts	6,606	0.9%
35	Hawaii	5,649	0.8%
36	Nebraska	4,874	0.7%
37	Iowa	4,687	0.6%
38	Mississippi	4,300	0.6%
39	Alaska	3,990	0.5%
40	Montana	2,796	0.4%
41	West Virginia	2,519	0.3%
42	Idaho	1,964	0.3%
43	North Dakota	1,775	0.2%
44	Rhode Island	1,531	0.2%
45	South Dakota	1,524	0.2%
46	Delaware	1,476	0.2%
47	New Hampshire	869	0.1%
48	Wyoming	839	0.1%
49	Maine	777	0.1%
50	Vermont	253	0.0%
	District of Columbia	2,593	0.3%

Source: Reported data from the Federal Bureau of Investigation
    "Crime in the United States 2018" (Uniform Crime Reports, September 30, 2019, https://ucr.fbi.gov/)
*Includes the theft or attempted theft of a self-propelled vehicle. Excludes motorboats, construction equipment, airplanes, and farming equipment.

Motor Vehicle Theft Rate in 2018

National Rate = 228.9 Motor Vehicle Thefts per 100,000 Population*

ALPHA ORDER				RANK ORDER		
RANK	STATE	RATE		RANK	STATE	RATE
14	Alabama	268.3		1	Alaska	541.9
1	Alaska	541.9		2	New Mexico	485.8
15	Arizona	266.9		3	Hawaii	397.7
21	Arkansas	236.0		4	Oregon	395.1
5	California	392.4		5	California	392.4
7	Colorado	380.5		6	Nevada	392.3
26	Connecticut	206.7		7	Colorado	380.5
35	Delaware	152.6		8	Washington	367.3
28	Florida	193.3		9	Oklahoma	337.0
22	Georgia	235.4		10	Missouri	323.4
3	Hawaii	397.7		11	Tennessee	301.9
44	Idaho	112.0		12	South Carolina	281.9
34	Illinois	153.8		13	Kansas	269.4
25	Indiana	229.1		14	Alabama	268.3
36	Iowa	148.5		15	Arizona	266.9
13	Kansas	269.4		16	Montana	263.2
24	Kentucky	229.6		17	Nebraska	252.6
18	Louisiana	247.6		18	Louisiana	247.6
49	Maine	58.1		19	Utah	244.5
27	Maryland	200.9		20	Texas	243.2
46	Massachusetts	95.7		21	Arkansas	236.0
30	Michigan	174.6		22	Georgia	235.4
29	Minnesota	180.5		23	North Dakota	233.5
40	Mississippi	144.0		24	Kentucky	229.6
10	Missouri	323.4		25	Indiana	229.1
16	Montana	263.2		26	Connecticut	206.7
17	Nebraska	252.6		27	Maryland	200.9
6	Nevada	392.3		28	Florida	193.3
48	New Hampshire	64.1		29	Minnesota	180.5
43	New Jersey	123.9		30	Michigan	174.6
2	New Mexico	485.8		31	South Dakota	172.7
47	New York	67.2		32	Ohio	170.3
33	North Carolina	169.8		33	North Carolina	169.8
23	North Dakota	233.5		34	Illinois	153.8
32	Ohio	170.3		35	Delaware	152.6
9	Oklahoma	337.0		36	Iowa	148.5
4	Oregon	395.1		36	Wisconsin	148.5
45	Pennsylvania	102.4		38	Wyoming	145.2
39	Rhode Island	144.8		39	Rhode Island	144.8
12	South Carolina	281.9		40	Mississippi	144.0
31	South Dakota	172.7		41	West Virginia	139.5
11	Tennessee	301.9		42	Virginia	126.5
20	Texas	243.2		43	New Jersey	123.9
19	Utah	244.5		44	Idaho	112.0
50	Vermont	40.4		45	Pennsylvania	102.4
42	Virginia	126.5		46	Massachusetts	95.7
8	Washington	367.3		47	New York	67.2
41	West Virginia	139.5		48	New Hampshire	64.1
36	Wisconsin	148.5		49	Maine	58.1
38	Wyoming	145.2		50	Vermont	40.4
					District of Columbia	369.1

Source: Reported data from the Federal Bureau of Investigation
"Crime in the United States 2018" (Uniform Crime Reports, September 30, 2019, https://ucr.fbi.gov/)
*Includes the theft or attempted theft of a self-propelled vehicle. Excludes motorboats, construction equipment, airplanes, and farming equipment.

Rate of Consumer Fraud Complaints in 2018

National Rate = 780 Complaints per 100,000 Population*

ALPHA ORDER

RANK	STATE	RATE
11	Alabama	688
42	Alaska	477
7	Arizona	739
37	Arkansas	522
17	California	634
12	Colorado	672
23	Connecticut	586
4	Delaware	805
1	Florida	1,002
2	Georgia	894
45	Hawaii	456
31	Idaho	557
27	Illinois	570
34	Indiana	530
48	Iowa	424
32	Kansas	549
33	Kentucky	532
26	Louisiana	581
43	Maine	475
6	Maryland	748
36	Massachusetts	523
10	Michigan	716
38	Minnesota	511
35	Mississippi	529
14	Missouri	657
29	Montana	566
46	Nebraska	438
3	Nevada	870
28	New Hampshire	569
19	New Jersey	627
15	New Mexico	650
22	New York	592
16	North Carolina	647
50	North Dakota	337
18	Ohio	628
41	Oklahoma	492
21	Oregon	606
20	Pennsylvania	607
23	Rhode Island	586
9	South Carolina	718
49	South Dakota	353
5	Tennessee	789
8	Texas	723
40	Utah	495
47	Vermont	431
13	Virginia	663
25	Washington	582
30	West Virginia	558
39	Wisconsin	500
44	Wyoming	457

RANK ORDER

RANK	STATE	RATE
1	Florida	1,002
2	Georgia	894
3	Nevada	870
4	Delaware	805
5	Tennessee	789
6	Maryland	748
7	Arizona	739
8	Texas	723
9	South Carolina	718
10	Michigan	716
11	Alabama	688
12	Colorado	672
13	Virginia	663
14	Missouri	657
15	New Mexico	650
16	North Carolina	647
17	California	634
18	Ohio	628
19	New Jersey	627
20	Pennsylvania	607
21	Oregon	606
22	New York	592
23	Connecticut	586
23	Rhode Island	586
25	Washington	582
26	Louisiana	581
27	Illinois	570
28	New Hampshire	569
29	Montana	566
30	West Virginia	558
31	Idaho	557
32	Kansas	549
33	Kentucky	532
34	Indiana	530
35	Mississippi	529
36	Massachusetts	523
37	Arkansas	522
38	Minnesota	511
39	Wisconsin	500
40	Utah	495
41	Oklahoma	492
42	Alaska	477
43	Maine	475
44	Wyoming	457
45	Hawaii	456
46	Nebraska	438
47	Vermont	431
48	Iowa	424
49	South Dakota	353
50	North Dakota	337
	District of Columbia	1,179

Source: Federal Trade Commission, Consumer Sentinel
"Consumer Sentinel Network Data Book for January - December 2018" (February 2019, https://www.ftc.gov/sentinel/)
*National rate includes complaints not shown by state. Rates include "other" complaints but do not include identity theft or "Do Not Call" registry complaints.

Rate of Identity Theft Complaints in 2018

National Rate = 136 Complaints per 100,000 Population*

<table>
<tr><td colspan="3">ALPHA ORDER</td><td colspan="3">RANK ORDER</td></tr>
<tr><td>RANK</td><td>STATE</td><td>RATE</td><td>RANK</td><td>STATE</td><td>RATE</td></tr>
<tr><td>18</td><td>Alabama</td><td>108</td><td>1</td><td>Georgia</td><td>229</td></tr>
<tr><td>40</td><td>Alaska</td><td>69</td><td>2</td><td>Nevada</td><td>194</td></tr>
<tr><td>10</td><td>Arizona</td><td>126</td><td>3</td><td>California</td><td>186</td></tr>
<tr><td>37</td><td>Arkansas</td><td>73</td><td>4</td><td>Florida</td><td>180</td></tr>
<tr><td>3</td><td>California</td><td>186</td><td>5</td><td>Texas</td><td>159</td></tr>
<tr><td>17</td><td>Colorado</td><td>110</td><td>6</td><td>Delaware</td><td>158</td></tr>
<tr><td>18</td><td>Connecticut</td><td>108</td><td>7</td><td>Maryland</td><td>145</td></tr>
<tr><td>6</td><td>Delaware</td><td>158</td><td>8</td><td>Michigan</td><td>140</td></tr>
<tr><td>4</td><td>Florida</td><td>180</td><td>9</td><td>Illinois</td><td>127</td></tr>
<tr><td>1</td><td>Georgia</td><td>229</td><td>10</td><td>Arizona</td><td>126</td></tr>
<tr><td>39</td><td>Hawaii</td><td>72</td><td>10</td><td>South Carolina</td><td>126</td></tr>
<tr><td>32</td><td>Idaho</td><td>80</td><td>12</td><td>New Jersey</td><td>125</td></tr>
<tr><td>9</td><td>Illinois</td><td>127</td><td>13</td><td>New York</td><td>122</td></tr>
<tr><td>35</td><td>Indiana</td><td>74</td><td>14</td><td>New Hampshire</td><td>117</td></tr>
<tr><td>49</td><td>Iowa</td><td>53</td><td>15</td><td>North Carolina</td><td>112</td></tr>
<tr><td>35</td><td>Kansas</td><td>74</td><td>16</td><td>Louisiana</td><td>111</td></tr>
<tr><td>46</td><td>Kentucky</td><td>57</td><td>17</td><td>Colorado</td><td>110</td></tr>
<tr><td>16</td><td>Louisiana</td><td>111</td><td>18</td><td>Alabama</td><td>108</td></tr>
<tr><td>47</td><td>Maine</td><td>56</td><td>18</td><td>Connecticut</td><td>108</td></tr>
<tr><td>7</td><td>Maryland</td><td>145</td><td>20</td><td>Pennsylvania</td><td>107</td></tr>
<tr><td>28</td><td>Massachusetts</td><td>93</td><td>21</td><td>Oregon</td><td>101</td></tr>
<tr><td>8</td><td>Michigan</td><td>140</td><td>21</td><td>Tennessee</td><td>101</td></tr>
<tr><td>37</td><td>Minnesota</td><td>73</td><td>23</td><td>Washington</td><td>100</td></tr>
<tr><td>24</td><td>Mississippi</td><td>97</td><td>24</td><td>Mississippi</td><td>97</td></tr>
<tr><td>31</td><td>Missouri</td><td>85</td><td>24</td><td>Virginia</td><td>97</td></tr>
<tr><td>34</td><td>Montana</td><td>76</td><td>26</td><td>New Mexico</td><td>96</td></tr>
<tr><td>41</td><td>Nebraska</td><td>67</td><td>27</td><td>Utah</td><td>94</td></tr>
<tr><td>2</td><td>Nevada</td><td>194</td><td>28</td><td>Massachusetts</td><td>93</td></tr>
<tr><td>14</td><td>New Hampshire</td><td>117</td><td>28</td><td>Rhode Island</td><td>93</td></tr>
<tr><td>12</td><td>New Jersey</td><td>125</td><td>30</td><td>Ohio</td><td>88</td></tr>
<tr><td>26</td><td>New Mexico</td><td>96</td><td>31</td><td>Missouri</td><td>85</td></tr>
<tr><td>13</td><td>New York</td><td>122</td><td>32</td><td>Idaho</td><td>80</td></tr>
<tr><td>15</td><td>North Carolina</td><td>112</td><td>33</td><td>Oklahoma</td><td>79</td></tr>
<tr><td>43</td><td>North Dakota</td><td>63</td><td>34</td><td>Montana</td><td>76</td></tr>
<tr><td>30</td><td>Ohio</td><td>88</td><td>35</td><td>Indiana</td><td>74</td></tr>
<tr><td>33</td><td>Oklahoma</td><td>79</td><td>35</td><td>Kansas</td><td>74</td></tr>
<tr><td>21</td><td>Oregon</td><td>101</td><td>37</td><td>Arkansas</td><td>73</td></tr>
<tr><td>20</td><td>Pennsylvania</td><td>107</td><td>37</td><td>Minnesota</td><td>73</td></tr>
<tr><td>28</td><td>Rhode Island</td><td>93</td><td>39</td><td>Hawaii</td><td>72</td></tr>
<tr><td>10</td><td>South Carolina</td><td>126</td><td>40</td><td>Alaska</td><td>69</td></tr>
<tr><td>47</td><td>South Dakota</td><td>56</td><td>41</td><td>Nebraska</td><td>67</td></tr>
<tr><td>21</td><td>Tennessee</td><td>101</td><td>42</td><td>Wisconsin</td><td>64</td></tr>
<tr><td>5</td><td>Texas</td><td>159</td><td>43</td><td>North Dakota</td><td>63</td></tr>
<tr><td>27</td><td>Utah</td><td>94</td><td>44</td><td>West Virginia</td><td>58</td></tr>
<tr><td>50</td><td>Vermont</td><td>51</td><td>44</td><td>Wyoming</td><td>58</td></tr>
<tr><td>24</td><td>Virginia</td><td>97</td><td>46</td><td>Kentucky</td><td>57</td></tr>
<tr><td>23</td><td>Washington</td><td>100</td><td>47</td><td>Maine</td><td>56</td></tr>
<tr><td>44</td><td>West Virginia</td><td>58</td><td>47</td><td>South Dakota</td><td>56</td></tr>
<tr><td>42</td><td>Wisconsin</td><td>64</td><td>49</td><td>Iowa</td><td>53</td></tr>
<tr><td>44</td><td>Wyoming</td><td>58</td><td>50</td><td>Vermont</td><td>51</td></tr>
<tr><td></td><td></td><td></td><td></td><td>District of Columbia</td><td>167</td></tr>
</table>

Source: Federal Trade Commission, Consumer Sentinel
"Consumer Sentinel Network Data Book for January - December 2018" (February 2019, https://www.ftc.gov/sentinel/)
*National rate includes complaints not shown by state. Rates do not include consumer fraud or "Do Not Call" registry complaints.

Reported Arrest Rate in 2018

National Rate = 3,169.3 Reported Arrests per 100,000 Population*

ALPHA ORDER				RANK ORDER		
RANK	STATE	RATE		RANK	STATE	RATE
12	Alabama	4,116.3		1	Kentucky	5,858.3
11	Alaska	4,173.1		2	Wyoming	5,602.1
15	Arizona	3,898.8		3	South Dakota	5,424.9
7	Arkansas	4,554.3		4	New Mexico	5,318.3
32	California	2,772.1		5	Tennessee	5,201.4
14	Colorado	3,901.4		6	Nevada	4,678.0
33	Connecticut	2,768.0		7	Arkansas	4,554.3
28	Delaware	2,981.2		8	Louisiana	4,464.0
23	Florida	3,362.2		9	North Dakota	4,386.3
29	Georgia	2,975.9		10	Wisconsin	4,275.9
46	Hawaii	2,132.8		11	Alaska	4,173.1
22	Idaho	3,362.9		12	Alabama	4,116.3
NA	Illinois**	NA		13	Utah	3,926.9
25	Indiana	3,118.6		14	Colorado	3,901.4
NA	Iowa**	NA		15	Arizona	3,898.8
41	Kansas	2,508.8		16	North Carolina	3,724.8
1	Kentucky	5,858.3		17	Missouri	3,659.6
8	Louisiana	4,464.0		18	New Hampshire	3,523.5
27	Maine	3,052.2		19	Nebraska	3,496.1
26	Maryland	3,086.0		20	South Carolina	3,462.6
47	Massachusetts	1,728.0		21	Oregon	3,375.5
44	Michigan	2,391.6		22	Idaho	3,362.9
38	Minnesota	2,645.3		23	Florida	3,362.2
NA	Mississippi**	NA		24	Virginia	3,253.4
17	Missouri	3,659.6		25	Indiana	3,118.6
34	Montana	2,748.9		26	Maryland	3,086.0
19	Nebraska	3,496.1		27	Maine	3,052.2
6	Nevada	4,678.0		28	Delaware	2,981.2
18	New Hampshire	3,523.5		29	Georgia	2,975.9
30	New Jersey	2,886.4		30	New Jersey	2,886.4
4	New Mexico	5,318.3		31	West Virginia	2,775.6
40	New York***	2,549.7		32	California	2,772.1
16	North Carolina	3,724.8		33	Connecticut	2,768.0
9	North Dakota	4,386.3		34	Montana	2,748.9
43	Ohio	2,423.8		35	Pennsylvania	2,738.2
39	Oklahoma	2,626.3		36	Texas	2,720.6
21	Oregon	3,375.5		37	Washington	2,669.5
35	Pennsylvania	2,738.2		38	Minnesota	2,645.3
42	Rhode Island	2,458.7		39	Oklahoma	2,626.3
20	South Carolina	3,462.6		40	New York***	2,549.7
3	South Dakota	5,424.9		41	Kansas	2,508.8
5	Tennessee	5,201.4		42	Rhode Island	2,458.7
36	Texas	2,720.6		43	Ohio	2,423.8
13	Utah	3,926.9		44	Michigan	2,391.6
45	Vermont	2,328.0		45	Vermont	2,328.0
24	Virginia	3,253.4		46	Hawaii	2,132.8
37	Washington	2,669.5		47	Massachusetts	1,728.0
31	West Virginia	2,775.6		NA	Illinois**	NA
10	Wisconsin	4,275.9		NA	Iowa**	NA
2	Wyoming	5,602.1		NA	Mississippi**	NA
					District of Columbia**	NA

Source: CQ Press using reported data from the Federal Bureau of Investigation
   "Crime in the United States 2018" (Uniform Crime Reports, September 30, 2019, https://ucr.fbi.gov/)
*By law enforcement agencies submitting complete reports to the FBI for 12 months in 2018. These rates based on population estimates for areas under the jurisdiction of those agencies reporting. Arrest rate based on the FBI estimate of total arrests is 3,151.6 reported and unreported arrests per 100,000 population.
**Not available. ***New York's figure does not include New York City.

Reported Juvenile Arrest Rate in 2018

National Rate = 2,130.5 Reported Arrests per 100,000 Juvenile Population*

ALPHA ORDER

RANK	STATE	RATE
42	Alabama	1,120.4
27	Alaska	2,148.7
17	Arizona	2,905.8
19	Arkansas	2,724.7
44	California	1,037.5
8	Colorado	3,544.6
30	Connecticut	2,034.8
15	Delaware	2,957.1
22	Florida	2,462.9
29	Georgia	2,039.4
37	Hawaii	1,668.1
11	Idaho	3,266.2
NA	Illinois**	NA
28	Indiana	2,050.3
NA	Iowa**	NA
43	Kansas	1,108.2
45	Kentucky	836.0
6	Louisiana	3,907.5
24	Maine	2,415.5
14	Maryland	3,001.8
46	Massachusetts	823.8
40	Michigan	1,332.5
10	Minnesota	3,315.0
NA	Mississippi**	NA
18	Missouri	2,794.0
7	Montana	3,740.0
5	Nebraska	4,150.5
12	Nevada	3,199.2
20	New Hampshire	2,679.9
39	New Jersey	1,424.9
31	New Mexico	2,033.7
38	New York***	1,604.3
32	North Carolina	1,981.5
3	North Dakota	5,633.0
26	Ohio	2,155.0
34	Oklahoma	1,803.1
25	Oregon	2,394.7
16	Pennsylvania	2,941.4
21	Rhode Island	2,550.4
23	South Carolina	2,450.2
4	South Dakota	5,544.1
13	Tennessee	3,033.9
36	Texas	1,737.0
9	Utah	3,438.6
41	Vermont	1,310.5
33	Virginia	1,925.2
35	Washington	1,746.8
47	West Virginia	496.2
1	Wisconsin	5,948.6
2	Wyoming	5,767.2

RANK ORDER

RANK	STATE	RATE
1	Wisconsin	5,948.6
2	Wyoming	5,767.2
3	North Dakota	5,633.0
4	South Dakota	5,544.1
5	Nebraska	4,150.5
6	Louisiana	3,907.5
7	Montana	3,740.0
8	Colorado	3,544.6
9	Utah	3,438.6
10	Minnesota	3,315.0
11	Idaho	3,266.2
12	Nevada	3,199.2
13	Tennessee	3,033.9
14	Maryland	3,001.8
15	Delaware	2,957.1
16	Pennsylvania	2,941.4
17	Arizona	2,905.8
18	Missouri	2,794.0
19	Arkansas	2,724.7
20	New Hampshire	2,679.9
21	Rhode Island	2,550.4
22	Florida	2,462.9
23	South Carolina	2,450.2
24	Maine	2,415.5
25	Oregon	2,394.7
26	Ohio	2,155.0
27	Alaska	2,148.7
28	Indiana	2,050.3
29	Georgia	2,039.4
30	Connecticut	2,034.8
31	New Mexico	2,033.7
32	North Carolina	1,981.5
33	Virginia	1,925.2
34	Oklahoma	1,803.1
35	Washington	1,746.8
36	Texas	1,737.0
37	Hawaii	1,668.1
38	New York***	1,604.3
39	New Jersey	1,424.9
40	Michigan	1,332.5
41	Vermont	1,310.5
42	Alabama	1,120.4
43	Kansas	1,108.2
44	California	1,037.5
45	Kentucky	836.0
46	Massachusetts	823.8
47	West Virginia	496.2
NA	Illinois**	NA
NA	Iowa**	NA
NA	Mississippi**	NA
	District of Columbia**	NA

Source: CQ Press using reported data from the Federal Bureau of Investigation
   "Crime in the United States 2018" (Uniform Crime Reports, September 30, 2019, https://ucr.fbi.gov/)
*By law enforcement agencies submitting complete reports to the FBI for twelve months in 2018. Arrests of youths seventeen years and younger divided into population of ten to seventeen-year-olds.
**Not available.
***New York's figure does not include New York City.

Prisoners in State Correctional Institutions: Year End 2017

National Total = 1,306,305 State Prisoners*

ALPHA ORDER					RANK ORDER			
RANK	STATE	PRISONERS	% of USA		RANK	STATE	PRISONERS	% of USA
17	Alabama	27,608	2.1%		1	Texas	162,523	12.4%
42	Alaska	4,399	0.3%		2	California	131,039	10.0%
8	Arizona	42,030	3.2%		3	Florida	98,504	7.5%
27	Arkansas	18,070	1.4%		4	Georgia	53,667	4.1%
2	California	131,039	10.0%		5	Ohio	51,478	3.9%
21	Colorado	19,946	1.5%		6	New York	49,461	3.8%
29	Connecticut	14,040	1.1%		7	Pennsylvania	48,333	3.7%
38	Delaware	6,443	0.5%		8	Arizona	42,030	3.2%
3	Florida	98,504	7.5%		9	Illinois	41,471	3.2%
4	Georgia	53,667	4.1%		10	Michigan	39,666	3.0%
40	Hawaii	5,630	0.4%		11	Virginia	37,158	2.8%
35	Idaho	8,579	0.7%		12	North Carolina	36,394	2.8%
9	Illinois	41,471	3.2%		13	Louisiana	33,739	2.6%
18	Indiana	26,024	2.0%		14	Missouri	32,601	2.5%
34	Iowa	9,024	0.7%		15	Tennessee	28,980	2.2%
32	Kansas	9,971	0.8%		16	Oklahoma	28,143	2.2%
20	Kentucky	23,543	1.8%		17	Alabama	27,608	2.1%
13	Louisiana	33,739	2.6%		18	Indiana	26,024	2.0%
48	Maine	2,404	0.2%		19	Wisconsin	23,945	1.8%
25	Maryland	19,367	1.5%		20	Kentucky	23,543	1.8%
33	Massachusetts	9,133	0.7%		21	Colorado	19,946	1.5%
10	Michigan	39,666	3.0%		22	South Carolina	19,906	1.5%
31	Minnesota	10,708	0.8%		23	Washington	19,656	1.5%
26	Mississippi	19,103	1.5%		24	New Jersey	19,585	1.5%
14	Missouri	32,601	2.5%		25	Maryland	19,367	1.5%
44	Montana	3,698	0.3%		26	Mississippi	19,103	1.5%
41	Nebraska	5,313	0.4%		27	Arkansas	18,070	1.4%
30	Nevada	13,671	1.0%		28	Oregon	15,218	1.2%
46	New Hampshire	2,750	0.2%		29	Connecticut	14,040	1.1%
24	New Jersey	19,585	1.5%		30	Nevada	13,671	1.0%
36	New Mexico	7,276	0.6%		31	Minnesota	10,708	0.8%
6	New York	49,461	3.8%		32	Kansas	9,971	0.8%
12	North Carolina	36,394	2.8%		33	Massachusetts	9,133	0.7%
49	North Dakota	1,723	0.1%		34	Iowa	9,024	0.7%
5	Ohio	51,478	3.9%		35	Idaho	8,579	0.7%
16	Oklahoma	28,143	2.2%		36	New Mexico	7,276	0.6%
28	Oregon	15,218	1.2%		37	West Virginia	7,092	0.5%
7	Pennsylvania	48,333	3.7%		38	Delaware	6,443	0.5%
45	Rhode Island	2,861	0.2%		38	Utah	6,443	0.5%
22	South Carolina	19,906	1.5%		40	Hawaii	5,630	0.4%
43	South Dakota	3,970	0.3%		41	Nebraska	5,313	0.4%
15	Tennessee	28,980	2.2%		42	Alaska	4,399	0.3%
1	Texas	162,523	12.4%		43	South Dakota	3,970	0.3%
38	Utah	6,443	0.5%		44	Montana	3,698	0.3%
50	Vermont	1,546	0.1%		45	Rhode Island	2,861	0.2%
11	Virginia	37,158	2.8%		46	New Hampshire	2,750	0.2%
23	Washington	19,656	1.5%		47	Wyoming	2,473	0.2%
37	West Virginia	7,092	0.5%		48	Maine	2,404	0.2%
19	Wisconsin	23,945	1.8%		49	North Dakota	1,723	0.1%
47	Wyoming	2,473	0.2%		50	Vermont	1,546	0.1%
					District of Columbia**		NA	NA

Source: U.S. Department of Justice, Bureau of Justice Statistics
"Prisoners in 2017" (April 2019, NCJ 252156, https://www.bjs.gov/)
*As of December 31, 2017. Totals reflect all prisoners, including those sentenced to a year or less and those unsentenced.
National total does not include 183,058 prisoners under federal jurisdiction. State and federal prisoners combined total 1,489,363.
**Responsibility for sentenced felons in D.C. was transferred to the Federal Bureau of Prisons in 2001.

State Prisoner Imprisonment Rate in 2017

National Rate = 390 State Prisoners per 100,000 Population*

ALPHA ORDER

RANK	STATE	RATE
10	Alabama	486
39	Alaska	258
5	Arizona	569
4	Arkansas	598
32	California	328
27	Colorado	351
37	Connecticut	268
19	Delaware	420
11	Florida	466
9	Georgia	506
41	Hawaii	240
14	Idaho	447
33	Illinois	324
23	Indiana	389
35	Iowa	285
31	Kansas	332
8	Kentucky	527
1	Louisiana	719
49	Maine	134
34	Maryland	317
50	Massachusetts	120
20	Michigan	397
46	Minnesota	191
3	Mississippi	619
7	Missouri	532
28	Montana	350
36	Nebraska	273
13	Nevada	451
45	New Hampshire	204
43	New Jersey	217
29	New Mexico	344
40	New York	249
30	North Carolina	341
42	North Dakota	226
15	Ohio	441
2	Oklahoma	704
26	Oregon	364
25	Pennsylvania	375
48	Rhode Island	170
24	South Carolina	386
12	South Dakota	453
17	Tennessee	429
6	Texas	553
44	Utah	206
47	Vermont	180
16	Virginia	437
38	Washington	262
21	West Virginia	392
22	Wisconsin	391
17	Wyoming	429

RANK ORDER

RANK	STATE	RATE
1	Louisiana	719
2	Oklahoma	704
3	Mississippi	619
4	Arkansas	598
5	Arizona	569
6	Texas	553
7	Missouri	532
8	Kentucky	527
9	Georgia	506
10	Alabama	486
11	Florida	466
12	South Dakota	453
13	Nevada	451
14	Idaho	447
15	Ohio	441
16	Virginia	437
17	Tennessee	429
17	Wyoming	429
19	Delaware	420
20	Michigan	397
21	West Virginia	392
22	Wisconsin	391
23	Indiana	389
24	South Carolina	386
25	Pennsylvania	375
26	Oregon	364
27	Colorado	351
28	Montana	350
29	New Mexico	344
30	North Carolina	341
31	Kansas	332
32	California	328
33	Illinois	324
34	Maryland	317
35	Iowa	285
36	Nebraska	273
37	Connecticut	268
38	Washington	262
39	Alaska	258
40	New York	249
41	Hawaii	240
42	North Dakota	226
43	New Jersey	217
44	Utah	206
45	New Hampshire	204
46	Minnesota	191
47	Vermont	180
48	Rhode Island	170
49	Maine	134
50	Massachusetts	120

District of Columbia**   NA

Source: U.S. Department of Justice, Bureau of Justice Statistics
"Prisoners in 2017" (April 2019, NCJ 252156, https://www.bjs.gov/)

*Figures as of December 31, 2017. Includes only inmates sentenced to more than one year. Does not include federal imprisonment rate of 51 prisoners per 100,000 population. State and federal combined imprisonment rate is 440 prisoners per 100,000 population.

**Responsibility for sentenced felons in D.C. was transferred to the Federal Bureau of Prisons in 2001.

Percent Change in Number of State Prisoners: 2016 to 2017

National Percent Change = 1.0% Decrease*

ALPHA ORDER				RANK ORDER		
RANK	STATE	PERCENT CHANGE		RANK	STATE	PERCENT CHANGE
NA	Alabama**	NA		1	Utah	4.3
27	Alaska	(0.8)		2	Wyoming	4.2
25	Arizona	(0.7)		3	Idaho	4.0
5	Arkansas	3.0		4	South Dakota	3.6
13	California	0.7		5	Arkansas	3.0
22	Colorado	(0.2)		6	Washington	2.9
45	Connecticut	(6.1)		7	Tennessee	2.8
34	Delaware	(2.2)		8	Wisconsin	2.4
31	Florida	(1.5)		9	Kentucky	2.3
19	Georgia	0.1		10	North Carolina	2.0
14	Hawaii	0.5		11	Indiana	1.9
3	Idaho	4.0		12	Minnesota	1.1
42	Illinois	(5.0)		13	California	0.7
11	Indiana	1.9		14	Hawaii	0.5
21	Iowa	(0.1)		14	Kansas	0.5
14	Kansas	0.5		16	Missouri	0.4
9	Kentucky	2.3		17	Oregon	0.3
43	Louisiana	(5.4)		18	Nebraska	0.2
20	Maine	0.0		19	Georgia	0.1
39	Maryland	(3.1)		20	Maine	0.0
37	Massachusetts	(2.9)		21	Iowa	(0.1)
40	Michigan	(3.5)		22	Colorado	(0.2)
12	Minnesota	1.1		23	Mississippi	(0.5)
23	Mississippi	(0.5)		24	Nevada	(0.6)
16	Missouri	0.4		25	Arizona	(0.7)
38	Montana	(3.0)		25	Texas	(0.7)
18	Nebraska	0.2		27	Alaska	(0.8)
24	Nevada	(0.6)		28	New Jersey	(1.0)
35	New Hampshire	(2.4)		28	West Virginia	(1.0)
28	New Jersey	(1.0)		30	Ohio	(1.3)
NA	New Mexico**	NA		31	Florida	(1.5)
36	New York	(2.5)		32	Virginia	(1.7)
10	North Carolina	2.0		33	Pennsylvania	(1.8)
NA	North Dakota**	NA		34	Delaware	(2.2)
30	Ohio	(1.3)		35	New Hampshire	(2.4)
44	Oklahoma	(5.9)		36	New York	(2.5)
17	Oregon	0.3		37	Massachusetts	(2.9)
33	Pennsylvania	(1.8)		38	Montana	(3.0)
46	Rhode Island	(7.8)		39	Maryland	(3.1)
41	South Carolina	(4.6)		40	Michigan	(3.5)
4	South Dakota	3.6		41	South Carolina	(4.6)
7	Tennessee	2.8		42	Illinois	(5.0)
25	Texas	(0.7)		43	Louisiana	(5.4)
1	Utah	4.3		44	Oklahoma	(5.9)
47	Vermont	(10.9)		45	Connecticut	(6.1)
32	Virginia	(1.7)		46	Rhode Island	(7.8)
6	Washington	2.9		47	Vermont	(10.9)
28	West Virginia	(1.0)		NA	Alabama**	NA
8	Wisconsin	2.4		NA	New Mexico**	NA
2	Wyoming	4.2		NA	North Dakota**	NA
					District of Columbia***	NA

Source: U.S. Department of Justice, Bureau of Justice Statistics
"Prisoners in 2017" (April 2019, NCJ 252156, https://www.bjs.gov/)
*From December 31, 2016 to December 31, 2017. Includes inmates sentenced to more than one year and those sentenced to a year or less or with no sentence. The percent change in number of prisoners under federal jurisdiction during the same period was a 3.2% decrease. The combined state and federal decrease was 1.2%. **Not available.
***Responsibility for sentenced felons in D.C. was transferred to the Federal Bureau of Prisons in 2001.

Prisoners under Sentence of Death as of July 1, 2019 (NAACP)

National Total = 2,595 State Prisoners*

ALPHA ORDER

RANK	STATE	PRISONERS	% of USA
4	Alabama	177	6.8%
NA	Alaska**	NA	NA
8	Arizona	122	4.7%
16	Arkansas	32	1.2%
1	California	729	28.1%
25	Colorado	3	0.1%
NA	Connecticut**	NA	NA
NA	Delaware**	NA	NA
2	Florida	348	13.4%
12	Georgia	51	2.0%
NA	Hawaii**	NA	NA
23	Idaho	8	0.3%
NA	Illinois**	NA	NA
22	Indiana	9	0.3%
NA	Iowa**	NA	NA
21	Kansas	10	0.4%
18	Kentucky	30	1.2%
10	Louisiana	69	2.7%
NA	Maine**	NA	NA
NA	Maryland**	NA	NA
NA	Massachusetts**	NA	NA
NA	Michigan**	NA	NA
NA	Minnesota**	NA	NA
14	Mississippi	44	1.7%
19	Missouri	24	0.9%
27	Montana	2	0.1%
20	Nebraska	12	0.5%
9	Nevada	74	2.9%
29	New Hampshire	1	0.0%
NA	New Jersey**	NA	NA
NA	New Mexico**	NA	NA
NA	New York**	NA	NA
6	North Carolina	144	5.5%
NA	North Dakota**	NA	NA
7	Ohio	140	5.4%
13	Oklahoma	46	1.8%
16	Oregon	32	1.2%
5	Pennsylvania	154	5.9%
NA	Rhode Island**	NA	NA
15	South Carolina	40	1.5%
27	South Dakota	2	0.1%
11	Tennessee	56	2.2%
3	Texas	224	8.6%
23	Utah	8	0.3%
NA	Vermont**	NA	NA
25	Virginia	3	0.1%
NA	Washington**	NA	NA
NA	West Virginia**	NA	NA
NA	Wisconsin**	NA	NA
29	Wyoming	1	0.0%

RANK ORDER

RANK	STATE	PRISONERS	% of USA
1	California	729	28.1%
2	Florida	348	13.4%
3	Texas	224	8.6%
4	Alabama	177	6.8%
5	Pennsylvania	154	5.9%
6	North Carolina	144	5.5%
7	Ohio	140	5.4%
8	Arizona	122	4.7%
9	Nevada	74	2.9%
10	Louisiana	69	2.7%
11	Tennessee	56	2.2%
12	Georgia	51	2.0%
13	Oklahoma	46	1.8%
14	Mississippi	44	1.7%
15	South Carolina	40	1.5%
16	Arkansas	32	1.2%
16	Oregon	32	1.2%
18	Kentucky	30	1.2%
19	Missouri	24	0.9%
20	Nebraska	12	0.5%
21	Kansas	10	0.4%
22	Indiana	9	0.3%
23	Idaho	8	0.3%
23	Utah	8	0.3%
25	Colorado	3	0.1%
25	Virginia	3	0.1%
27	Montana	2	0.1%
27	South Dakota	2	0.1%
29	New Hampshire	1	0.0%
29	Wyoming	1	0.0%
NA	Alaska**	NA	NA
NA	Connecticut**	NA	NA
NA	Delaware**	NA	NA
NA	Hawaii**	NA	NA
NA	Illinois**	NA	NA
NA	Iowa**	NA	NA
NA	Maine**	NA	NA
NA	Maryland**	NA	NA
NA	Massachusetts**	NA	NA
NA	Michigan**	NA	NA
NA	Minnesota**	NA	NA
NA	New Jersey**	NA	NA
NA	New Mexico**	NA	NA
NA	New York**	NA	NA
NA	North Dakota**	NA	NA
NA	Rhode Island**	NA	NA
NA	Vermont**	NA	NA
NA	Washington**	NA	NA
NA	West Virginia**	NA	NA
NA	Wisconsin**	NA	NA
	District of Columbia**	NA	NA

Source: NAACP Legal Defense and Educational Fund, Inc., Criminal Justice Project
"Death Row USA, Summer 2019" (https://www.naacpldf.org/our-thinking/death-row-usa/)
*Total does not include sixty-five federal prisoners or five military prisoners under sentence of death. Four prisoners are sentenced to death in more than one state and are counted twice.
**No death penalty as of July 1, 2019.

Rate of State and Local Police Officers in 2018

National Rate = 22 Officers per 10,000 Population*

ALPHA ORDER

RANK	STATE	RATE
9	Alabama	23
40	Alaska	17
29	Arizona	20
14	Arkansas	22
33	California	19
22	Colorado	21
14	Connecticut	22
14	Delaware	22
29	Florida	20
22	Georgia	21
14	Hawaii	22
47	Idaho	16
4	Illinois	26
33	Indiana	19
40	Iowa	17
9	Kansas	23
40	Kentucky	17
3	Louisiana	28
37	Maine	18
14	Maryland	22
8	Massachusetts	24
40	Michigan	17
40	Minnesota	17
9	Mississippi	23
9	Missouri	23
40	Montana	17
33	Nebraska	19
37	Nevada	18
14	New Hampshire	22
2	New Jersey	31
14	New Mexico	22
1	New York	40
4	North Carolina	26
22	North Dakota	21
29	Ohio	20
22	Oklahoma	21
48	Oregon	15
22	Pennsylvania	21
9	Rhode Island	23
14	South Carolina	22
33	South Dakota	19
4	Tennessee	26
29	Texas	20
49	Utah	14
40	Vermont	17
22	Virginia	21
49	Washington	14
37	West Virginia	18
22	Wisconsin	21
7	Wyoming	25

RANK ORDER

RANK	STATE	RATE
1	New York	40
2	New Jersey	31
3	Louisiana	28
4	Illinois	26
4	North Carolina	26
4	Tennessee	26
7	Wyoming	25
8	Massachusetts	24
9	Alabama	23
9	Kansas	23
9	Mississippi	23
9	Missouri	23
9	Rhode Island	23
14	Arkansas	22
14	Connecticut	22
14	Delaware	22
14	Hawaii	22
14	Maryland	22
14	New Hampshire	22
14	New Mexico	22
14	South Carolina	22
22	Colorado	21
22	Georgia	21
22	North Dakota	21
22	Oklahoma	21
22	Pennsylvania	21
22	Virginia	21
22	Wisconsin	21
29	Arizona	20
29	Florida	20
29	Ohio	20
29	Texas	20
33	California	19
33	Indiana	19
33	Nebraska	19
33	South Dakota	19
37	Maine	18
37	Nevada	18
37	West Virginia	18
40	Alaska	17
40	Iowa	17
40	Kentucky	17
40	Michigan	17
40	Minnesota	17
40	Montana	17
40	Vermont	17
47	Idaho	16
48	Oregon	15
49	Utah	14
49	Washington	14
	District of Columbia	54

Source: CQ Press using data from U.S. Bureau of the Census, Governments Division
"Annual Survey of Public Employment and Payroll" (https://www.census.gov/programs-surveys/apes.html)
*Full-time equivalent as of March 2018. Does not include employees of police departments who are not officers.

Per Capita State and Local Government Expenditures for Police Protection in 2017
National Per Capita = $354*

ALPHA ORDER

RANK	STATE	PER CAPITA
39	Alabama	$261
2	Alaska	493
14	Arizona	355
48	Arkansas	229
3	California	487
19	Colorado	335
22	Connecticut	329
9	Delaware	394
8	Florida	404
37	Georgia	268
18	Hawaii	338
36	Idaho	270
7	Illinois	413
45	Indiana	239
40	Iowa	260
31	Kansas	296
50	Kentucky	186
15	Louisiana	353
47	Maine	232
4	Maryland	442
11	Massachusetts	377
43	Michigan	255
13	Minnesota	357
42	Mississippi	257
32	Missouri	290
30	Montana	297
40	Nebraska	260
5	Nevada	428
25	New Hampshire	311
10	New Jersey	392
17	New Mexico	341
1	New York	529
20	North Carolina	332
27	North Dakota	301
23	Ohio	328
34	Oklahoma	279
21	Oregon	331
27	Pennsylvania	301
6	Rhode Island	424
38	South Carolina	263
44	South Dakota	241
26	Tennessee	302
33	Texas	288
45	Utah	239
16	Vermont	350
29	Virginia	298
35	Washington	275
49	West Virginia	217
24	Wisconsin	322
12	Wyoming	361

RANK ORDER

RANK	STATE	PER CAPITA
1	New York	$529
2	Alaska	493
3	California	487
4	Maryland	442
5	Nevada	428
6	Rhode Island	424
7	Illinois	413
8	Florida	404
9	Delaware	394
10	New Jersey	392
11	Massachusetts	377
12	Wyoming	361
13	Minnesota	357
14	Arizona	355
15	Louisiana	353
16	Vermont	350
17	New Mexico	341
18	Hawaii	338
19	Colorado	335
20	North Carolina	332
21	Oregon	331
22	Connecticut	329
23	Ohio	328
24	Wisconsin	322
25	New Hampshire	311
26	Tennessee	302
27	North Dakota	301
27	Pennsylvania	301
29	Virginia	298
30	Montana	297
31	Kansas	296
32	Missouri	290
33	Texas	288
34	Oklahoma	279
35	Washington	275
36	Idaho	270
37	Georgia	268
38	South Carolina	263
39	Alabama	261
40	Iowa	260
40	Nebraska	260
42	Mississippi	257
43	Michigan	255
44	South Dakota	241
45	Indiana	239
45	Utah	239
47	Maine	232
48	Arkansas	229
49	West Virginia	217
50	Kentucky	186
	District of Columbia	910

Source: CQ Press using data from U.S. Bureau of the Census, Governments Division
"2017 State and Local Government Finances" (https://www.census.gov/programs-surveys/gov-finances.html)
*Direct general expenditures.

Per Capita State and Local Government Expenditures for Corrections in 2017

National Per Capita = $242*

ALPHA ORDER				RANK ORDER		
RANK	STATE	PER CAPITA		RANK	STATE	PER CAPITA
48	Alabama	$150		1	Alaska	$436
1	Alaska	436		2	California	371
19	Arizona	235		3	New Mexico	345
31	Arkansas	198		4	New York	340
2	California	371		5	Delaware	339
18	Colorado	242		6	Maryland	318
39	Connecticut	174		6	Wyoming	318
5	Delaware	339		8	Oregon	316
28	Florida	207		9	Virginia	310
29	Georgia	204		10	North Dakota	300
45	Hawaii	161		11	Pennsylvania	290
19	Idaho	235		12	Wisconsin	263
44	Illinois	163		13	Nevada	260
46	Indiana	160		14	Nebraska	257
49	Iowa	139		15	Michigan	249
34	Kansas	186		16	Montana	245
24	Kentucky	213		17	Vermont	243
25	Louisiana	210		18	Colorado	242
32	Maine	195		19	Arizona	235
6	Maryland	318		19	Idaho	235
49	Massachusetts	139		21	Washington	233
15	Michigan	249		22	New Jersey	230
30	Minnesota	200		23	Texas	225
40	Mississippi	173		24	Kentucky	213
43	Missouri	164		25	Louisiana	210
16	Montana	245		25	Rhode Island	210
14	Nebraska	257		27	South Dakota	208
13	Nevada	260		28	Florida	207
42	New Hampshire	167		29	Georgia	204
22	New Jersey	230		30	Minnesota	200
3	New Mexico	345		31	Arkansas	198
4	New York	340		32	Maine	195
35	North Carolina	185		32	West Virginia	195
10	North Dakota	300		34	Kansas	186
37	Ohio	181		35	North Carolina	185
35	Oklahoma	185		35	Oklahoma	185
8	Oregon	316		37	Ohio	181
11	Pennsylvania	290		38	Utah	180
25	Rhode Island	210		39	Connecticut	174
47	South Carolina	156		40	Mississippi	173
27	South Dakota	208		41	Tennessee	171
41	Tennessee	171		42	New Hampshire	167
23	Texas	225		43	Missouri	164
38	Utah	180		44	Illinois	163
17	Vermont	243		45	Hawaii	161
9	Virginia	310		46	Indiana	160
21	Washington	233		47	South Carolina	156
32	West Virginia	195		48	Alabama	150
12	Wisconsin	263		49	Iowa	139
6	Wyoming	318		49	Massachusetts	139
					District of Columbia	226

Source: CQ Press using data from U.S. Bureau of the Census, Governments Division
"2017 State and Local Government Finances" (https://www.census.gov/programs-surveys/gov-finances.html)
*Direct general expenditures.

Per Capita State and Local Government Expenditures for Judicial and Legal Services in 2017
National Per Capita = $147*

ALPHA ORDER

RANK	STATE	PER CAPITA
49	Alabama	$75
1	Alaska	326
20	Arizona	147
50	Arkansas	73
2	California	228
24	Colorado	140
8	Connecticut	190
6	Delaware	209
38	Florida	112
26	Georgia	133
3	Hawaii	227
29	Idaho	122
36	Illinois	114
45	Indiana	91
34	Iowa	118
38	Kansas	112
23	Kentucky	145
20	Louisiana	147
46	Maine	84
15	Maryland	162
10	Massachusetts	178
30	Michigan	120
25	Minnesota	136
43	Mississippi	92
43	Missouri	92
7	Montana	202
41	Nebraska	98
12	Nevada	167
30	New Hampshire	120
11	New Jersey	171
17	New Mexico	156
5	New York	219
47	North Carolina	78
12	North Dakota	167
16	Ohio	157
42	Oklahoma	93
8	Oregon	190
17	Pennsylvania	156
19	Rhode Island	151
47	South Carolina	78
40	South Dakota	109
27	Tennessee	124
37	Texas	113
30	Utah	120
28	Vermont	123
30	Virginia	120
14	Washington	164
20	West Virginia	147
35	Wisconsin	115
4	Wyoming	226

RANK ORDER

RANK	STATE	PER CAPITA
1	Alaska	$326
2	California	228
3	Hawaii	227
4	Wyoming	226
5	New York	219
6	Delaware	209
7	Montana	202
8	Connecticut	190
8	Oregon	190
10	Massachusetts	178
11	New Jersey	171
12	Nevada	167
12	North Dakota	167
14	Washington	164
15	Maryland	162
16	Ohio	157
17	New Mexico	156
17	Pennsylvania	156
19	Rhode Island	151
20	Arizona	147
20	Louisiana	147
20	West Virginia	147
23	Kentucky	145
24	Colorado	140
25	Minnesota	136
26	Georgia	133
27	Tennessee	124
28	Vermont	123
29	Idaho	122
30	Michigan	120
30	New Hampshire	120
30	Utah	120
30	Virginia	120
34	Iowa	118
35	Wisconsin	115
36	Illinois	114
37	Texas	113
38	Florida	112
38	Kansas	112
40	South Dakota	109
41	Nebraska	98
42	Oklahoma	93
43	Mississippi	92
43	Missouri	92
45	Indiana	91
46	Maine	84
47	North Carolina	78
47	South Carolina	78
49	Alabama	75
50	Arkansas	73

District of Columbia — 213

Source: CQ Press using data from U.S. Bureau of the Census, Governments Division
"2017 State and Local Government Finances" (https://www.census.gov/programs-surveys/gov-finances.html)
*Direct general expenditures. Includes courts, prosecution and legal services, and public defense.

Base Salary for Justices of States' Highest Courts in 2019

National Average = $176,714*

ALPHA ORDER				RANK ORDER		
RANK	STATE	SALARY		RANK	STATE	SALARY
27	Alabama	$172,716		1	California	$253,189
7	Alaska	205,176		2	Illinois	234,391
35	Arizona	159,685		3	New York	230,200
25	Arkansas	174,925		4	Hawaii	227,664
1	California	253,189		5	Florida	220,600
17	Colorado	182,671		6	Pennsylvania	211,027
14	Connecticut	185,610		7	Alaska	205,176
11	Delaware	196,245		8	New Jersey	201,842
5	Florida	220,600		9	Massachusetts	200,984
24	Georgia	175,600		10	Virginia	197,827
4	Hawaii	227,664		11	Delaware	196,245
41	Idaho	151,400		12	Washington	190,415
2	Illinois	234,391		13	Tennessee	188,952
20	Indiana	177,244		14	Connecticut	185,610
26	Iowa	174,808		15	Rhode Island	183,872
45	Kansas	142,089		16	Utah	182,950
47	Kentucky	138,890		17	Colorado	182,671
29	Louisiana	170,325		18	Maryland	181,433
48	Maine	138,070		19	Minnesota	177,697
18	Maryland	181,433		20	Indiana	177,244
9	Massachusetts	200,984		21	Nebraska	176,299
33	Michigan	164,610		22	Missouri	176,157
19	Minnesota	177,697		23	New Hampshire	175,837
40	Mississippi	152,250		24	Georgia	175,600
22	Missouri	176,157		25	Arkansas	174,925
44	Montana	144,061		26	Iowa	174,808
21	Nebraska	176,299		27	Alabama	172,716
30	Nevada	170,000		28	Ohio	172,200
23	New Hampshire	175,837		29	Louisiana	170,325
8	New Jersey	201,842		30	Nevada	170,000
46	New Mexico	139,819		31	Texas	168,000
3	New York	230,200		32	Wyoming	165,000
42	North Carolina	149,115		33	Michigan	164,610
37	North Dakota	157,009		34	Vermont	163,757
28	Ohio	172,200		35	Arizona	159,685
38	Oklahoma	154,174		36	Wisconsin	159,297
39	Oregon	154,040		37	North Dakota	157,009
6	Pennsylvania	211,027		38	Oklahoma	154,174
15	Rhode Island	183,872		39	Oregon	154,040
43	South Carolina	148,794		40	Mississippi	152,250
49	South Dakota	136,893		41	Idaho	151,400
13	Tennessee	188,952		42	North Carolina	149,115
31	Texas	168,000		43	South Carolina	148,794
16	Utah	182,950		44	Montana	144,061
34	Vermont	163,757		45	Kansas	142,089
10	Virginia	197,827		46	New Mexico	139,819
12	Washington	190,415		47	Kentucky	138,890
50	West Virginia	136,000		48	Maine	138,070
36	Wisconsin	159,297		49	South Dakota	136,893
32	Wyoming	165,000		50	West Virginia	136,000
					District of Columbia	220,600

Source: National Center for State Courts
  "Survey of Judicial Salaries" (Volume 44, Number 1, https://www.ncsc.org/salarytracker)
*As of January 2019.

Base Salary for Judges of General Trial Courts in 2019

National Average = $158,748*

ALPHA ORDER

RANK	STATE	SALARY
40	Alabama	$138,991
5	Alaska	189,720
29	Arizona	149,383
15	Arkansas	168,096
2	California	207,424
14	Colorado	168,202
16	Connecticut	167,634
7	Delaware	184,444
21	Florida	160,688
11	Georgia	173,714
3	Hawaii	205,080
42	Idaho	135,400
4	Illinois	202,433
33	Indiana	147,164
32	Iowa	147,494
50	Kansas	125,499
47	Kentucky	127,733
26	Louisiana	153,143
45	Maine	129,397
23	Maryland	159,433
6	Massachusetts	184,694
34	Michigan	146,721
24	Minnesota	157,179
41	Mississippi	136,000
27	Missouri	151,840
44	Montana	132,558
20	Nebraska	163,077
22	Nevada	160,000
19	New Hampshire	164,911
9	New Jersey	181,000
48	New Mexico	126,187
1	New York	208,000
43	North Carolina	135,236
35	North Dakota	143,869
31	Ohio	147,600
39	Oklahoma	139,298
36	Oregon	142,136
8	Pennsylvania	183,184
18	Rhode Island	165,545
38	South Carolina	141,354
46	South Dakota	127,862
10	Tennessee	176,364
30	Texas	149,000
17	Utah	166,300
25	Vermont	155,677
13	Virginia	171,120
12	Washington	172,571
49	West Virginia	126,000
37	Wisconsin	141,773
28	Wyoming	150,000

RANK ORDER

RANK	STATE	SALARY
1	New York	$208,000
2	California	207,424
3	Hawaii	205,080
4	Illinois	202,433
5	Alaska	189,720
6	Massachusetts	184,694
7	Delaware	184,444
8	Pennsylvania	183,184
9	New Jersey	181,000
10	Tennessee	176,364
11	Georgia	173,714
12	Washington	172,571
13	Virginia	171,120
14	Colorado	168,202
15	Arkansas	168,096
16	Connecticut	167,634
17	Utah	166,300
18	Rhode Island	165,545
19	New Hampshire	164,911
20	Nebraska	163,077
21	Florida	160,688
22	Nevada	160,000
23	Maryland	159,433
24	Minnesota	157,179
25	Vermont	155,677
26	Louisiana	153,143
27	Missouri	151,840
28	Wyoming	150,000
29	Arizona	149,383
30	Texas	149,000
31	Ohio	147,600
32	Iowa	147,494
33	Indiana	147,164
34	Michigan	146,721
35	North Dakota	143,869
36	Oregon	142,136
37	Wisconsin	141,773
38	South Carolina	141,354
39	Oklahoma	139,298
40	Alabama	138,991
41	Mississippi	136,000
42	Idaho	135,400
43	North Carolina	135,236
44	Montana	132,558
45	Maine	129,397
46	South Dakota	127,862
47	Kentucky	127,733
48	New Mexico	126,187
49	West Virginia	126,000
50	Kansas	125,499
	District of Columbia	208,000

Source: National Center for State Courts
"Survey of Judicial Salaries" (Volume 44, Number 1, https://www.ncsc.org/salarytracker)
*As of January 2019.

III. Defense

Homeland Security Grants in 2019

National Total = $1,005,000,000*

ALPHA ORDER					RANK ORDER			
RANK	STATE	GRANTS	% of USA		RANK	STATE	GRANTS	% of USA
23	Alabama	$4,077,500	0.4%		1	New York	$255,680,000	25.4%
23	Alaska	4,077,500	0.4%		2	California	185,911,000	18.5%
16	Arizona	8,077,500	0.8%		3	Illinois	83,712,000	8.3%
23	Arkansas	4,077,500	0.4%		4	Texas	65,341,000	6.5%
2	California	185,911,000	18.5%		5	Pennsylvania	29,350,000	2.9%
17	Colorado	7,327,500	0.7%		6	New Jersey	28,050,000	2.8%
23	Connecticut	4,077,500	0.4%		7	Florida	24,066,000	2.4%
23	Delaware	4,077,500	0.4%		8	Massachusetts	23,900,000	2.4%
7	Florida	24,066,000	2.4%		9	Washington	13,000,000	1.3%
12	Georgia	11,750,000	1.2%		10	Virginia	12,450,000	1.2%
17	Hawaii	7,327,500	0.7%		11	Maryland	12,000,000	1.2%
23	Idaho	4,077,500	0.4%		12	Georgia	11,750,000	1.2%
3	Illinois	83,712,000	8.3%		13	Michigan	10,750,000	1.1%
23	Indiana	4,077,500	0.4%		14	Minnesota	9,077,500	0.9%
23	Iowa	4,077,500	0.4%		14	Nevada	9,077,500	0.9%
23	Kansas	4,077,500	0.4%		16	Arizona	8,077,500	0.8%
23	Kentucky	4,077,500	0.4%		17	Colorado	7,327,500	0.7%
23	Louisiana	4,077,500	0.4%		17	Hawaii	7,327,500	0.7%
23	Maine	4,077,500	0.4%		17	Missouri	7,327,500	0.7%
11	Maryland	12,000,000	1.2%		17	Oregon	7,327,500	0.7%
8	Massachusetts	23,900,000	2.4%		21	Ohio	7,000,000	0.7%
13	Michigan	10,750,000	1.1%		22	North Carolina	5,750,000	0.6%
14	Minnesota	9,077,500	0.9%		23	Alabama	4,077,500	0.4%
23	Mississippi	4,077,500	0.4%		23	Alaska	4,077,500	0.4%
17	Missouri	7,327,500	0.7%		23	Arkansas	4,077,500	0.4%
23	Montana	4,077,500	0.4%		23	Connecticut	4,077,500	0.4%
23	Nebraska	4,077,500	0.4%		23	Delaware	4,077,500	0.4%
14	Nevada	9,077,500	0.9%		23	Idaho	4,077,500	0.4%
23	New Hampshire	4,077,500	0.4%		23	Indiana	4,077,500	0.4%
6	New Jersey	28,050,000	2.8%		23	Iowa	4,077,500	0.4%
23	New Mexico	4,077,500	0.4%		23	Kansas	4,077,500	0.4%
1	New York	255,680,000	25.4%		23	Kentucky	4,077,500	0.4%
22	North Carolina	5,750,000	0.6%		23	Louisiana	4,077,500	0.4%
23	North Dakota	4,077,500	0.4%		23	Maine	4,077,500	0.4%
21	Ohio	7,000,000	0.7%		23	Mississippi	4,077,500	0.4%
23	Oklahoma	4,077,500	0.4%		23	Montana	4,077,500	0.4%
17	Oregon	7,327,500	0.7%		23	Nebraska	4,077,500	0.4%
5	Pennsylvania	29,350,000	2.9%		23	New Hampshire	4,077,500	0.4%
23	Rhode Island	4,077,500	0.4%		23	New Mexico	4,077,500	0.4%
23	South Carolina	4,077,500	0.4%		23	North Dakota	4,077,500	0.4%
23	South Dakota	4,077,500	0.4%		23	Oklahoma	4,077,500	0.4%
23	Tennessee	4,077,500	0.4%		23	Rhode Island	4,077,500	0.4%
4	Texas	65,341,000	6.5%		23	South Carolina	4,077,500	0.4%
23	Utah	4,077,500	0.4%		23	South Dakota	4,077,500	0.4%
23	Vermont	4,077,500	0.4%		23	Tennessee	4,077,500	0.4%
10	Virginia	12,450,000	1.2%		23	Utah	4,077,500	0.4%
9	Washington	13,000,000	1.3%		23	Vermont	4,077,500	0.4%
23	West Virginia	4,077,500	0.4%		23	West Virginia	4,077,500	0.4%
23	Wisconsin	4,077,500	0.4%		23	Wisconsin	4,077,500	0.4%
23	Wyoming	4,077,500	0.4%		23	Wyoming	4,077,500	0.4%
						District of Columbia	58,500,000	5.8%

Source: CQ Press using data from U.S. Department of Homeland Security
   "FY 2019 Homeland Security Grant Program (HSGP)" (https://www.fema.gov/media-library/assets/documents/178515)
*For fiscal year 2019. National total includes $8,077,000 in grants to U.S. territories. The Homeland Security Grant Program (HSGP) includes three sub-grant programs: State Homeland Security Program (SHSP), Urban Area Security Initiative (UASI), and Operation Stonegarden (OPSG). Law Enforcement Terrorism Prevention Activities (LETPA) allocations are a 25 percent subset of the SHSP and UASI allocations.

Per Capita Homeland Security Grants in 2019

National Per Capita = $3.04*

ALPHA ORDER

ALPHA ORDER

RANK ORDER

RANK	STATE	PER CAPITA		RANK	STATE	PER CAPITA
44	Alabama	$0.83		1	New York	$13.14
5	Alaska	5.57		2	Wyoming	7.05
38	Arizona	1.11		3	Illinois	6.61
31	Arkansas	1.35		4	Vermont	6.53
8	California	4.71		5	Alaska	5.57
33	Colorado	1.27		6	North Dakota	5.35
36	Connecticut	1.14		7	Hawaii	5.18
10	Delaware	4.19		8	California	4.71
37	Florida	1.12		9	South Dakota	4.61
38	Georgia	1.11		10	Delaware	4.19
7	Hawaii	5.18		11	Rhode Island	3.85
19	Idaho	2.28		12	Montana	3.82
3	Illinois	6.61		13	Massachusetts	3.47
47	Indiana	0.61		14	New Jersey	3.16
32	Iowa	1.29		15	Maine	3.03
29	Kansas	1.40		16	New Hampshire	3.00
42	Kentucky	0.91		17	Nevada	2.95
43	Louisiana	0.88		18	Pennsylvania	2.29
15	Maine	3.03		19	Idaho	2.28
23	Maryland	1.98		19	West Virginia	2.28
13	Massachusetts	3.47		21	Texas	2.25
40	Michigan	1.08		22	Nebraska	2.11
27	Minnesota	1.61		23	Maryland	1.98
30	Mississippi	1.37		24	New Mexico	1.94
35	Missouri	1.19		25	Oregon	1.74
12	Montana	3.82		26	Washington	1.71
22	Nebraska	2.11		27	Minnesota	1.61
17	Nevada	2.95		28	Virginia	1.46
16	New Hampshire	3.00		29	Kansas	1.40
14	New Jersey	3.16		30	Mississippi	1.37
24	New Mexico	1.94		31	Arkansas	1.35
1	New York	13.14		32	Iowa	1.29
50	North Carolina	0.55		33	Colorado	1.27
6	North Dakota	5.35		33	Utah	1.27
48	Ohio	0.60		35	Missouri	1.19
41	Oklahoma	1.03		36	Connecticut	1.14
25	Oregon	1.74		37	Florida	1.12
18	Pennsylvania	2.29		38	Arizona	1.11
11	Rhode Island	3.85		38	Georgia	1.11
45	South Carolina	0.79		40	Michigan	1.08
9	South Dakota	4.61		41	Oklahoma	1.03
48	Tennessee	0.60		42	Kentucky	0.91
21	Texas	2.25		43	Louisiana	0.88
33	Utah	1.27		44	Alabama	0.83
4	Vermont	6.53		45	South Carolina	0.79
28	Virginia	1.46		46	Wisconsin	0.70
26	Washington	1.71		47	Indiana	0.61
19	West Virginia	2.28		48	Ohio	0.60
46	Wisconsin	0.70		48	Tennessee	0.60
2	Wyoming	7.05		50	North Carolina	0.55

District of Columbia   82.89

Source: CQ Press using data from CQ Press using data from U.S. Department of Homeland Security
"FY 2019 Homeland Security Grant Program (HSGP)" (https://www.fema.gov/media-library/assets/documents/178515)
*For fiscal year 2019. National per capita does not include grants to U.S. territories. The Homeland Security Grant Program (HSGP) includes three sub-grant programs: State Homeland Security Program (SHSP), Urban Area Security Initiative (UASI), and Operation Stonegarden (OPSG). Law Enforcement Terrorism Prevention Activities (LETPA) allocations are a 25 percent subset of the SHSP and UASI allocations.

U.S. Department of Defense Expenditures in 2018

National Total = $365,397,000,000*

ALPHA ORDER

RANK	STATE	EXPENDITURES	% of USA
11	Alabama	$10,832,000,000	3.0%
33	Alaska	1,769,000,000	0.5%
10	Arizona	12,736,000,000	3.5%
43	Arkansas	362,000,000	0.1%
2	California	36,808,000,000	10.1%
18	Colorado	5,771,000,000	1.6%
6	Connecticut	14,792,000,000	4.0%
50	Delaware	155,000,000	0.0%
5	Florida	15,585,000,000	4.3%
17	Georgia	6,794,000,000	1.9%
29	Hawaii	2,101,000,000	0.6%
45	Idaho	267,000,000	0.1%
14	Illinois	7,323,000,000	2.0%
25	Indiana	3,277,000,000	0.9%
34	Iowa	1,750,000,000	0.5%
38	Kansas	900,000,000	0.2%
13	Kentucky	8,295,000,000	2.3%
32	Louisiana	1,832,000,000	0.5%
37	Maine	1,230,000,000	0.3%
4	Maryland	15,906,000,000	4.4%
9	Massachusetts	12,821,000,000	3.5%
21	Michigan	4,682,000,000	1.3%
27	Minnesota	2,337,000,000	0.6%
15	Mississippi	7,098,000,000	1.9%
7	Missouri	13,886,000,000	3.8%
46	Montana	253,000,000	0.1%
40	Nebraska	660,000,000	0.2%
30	Nevada	1,998,000,000	0.5%
31	New Hampshire	1,989,000,000	0.5%
20	New Jersey	5,498,000,000	1.5%
36	New Mexico	1,558,000,000	0.4%
16	New York	6,946,000,000	1.9%
22	North Carolina	3,884,000,000	1.1%
48	North Dakota	172,000,000	0.0%
19	Ohio	5,500,000,000	1.5%
24	Oklahoma	3,337,000,000	0.9%
39	Oregon	783,000,000	0.2%
8	Pennsylvania	12,951,000,000	3.5%
41	Rhode Island	641,000,000	0.2%
23	South Carolina	3,453,000,000	0.9%
44	South Dakota	312,000,000	0.1%
28	Tennessee	2,126,000,000	0.6%
1	Texas	40,475,000,000	11.1%
35	Utah	1,659,000,000	0.5%
42	Vermont	485,000,000	0.1%
3	Virginia	36,467,000,000	10.0%
12	Washington	9,622,000,000	2.6%
47	West Virginia	189,000,000	0.1%
26	Wisconsin	2,806,000,000	0.8%
49	Wyoming	170,000,000	0.0%

RANK ORDER

RANK	STATE	EXPENDITURES	% of USA
1	Texas	$40,475,000,000	11.1%
2	California	36,808,000,000	10.1%
3	Virginia	36,467,000,000	10.0%
4	Maryland	15,906,000,000	4.4%
5	Florida	15,585,000,000	4.3%
6	Connecticut	14,792,000,000	4.0%
7	Missouri	13,886,000,000	3.8%
8	Pennsylvania	12,951,000,000	3.5%
9	Massachusetts	12,821,000,000	3.5%
10	Arizona	12,736,000,000	3.5%
11	Alabama	10,832,000,000	3.0%
12	Washington	9,622,000,000	2.6%
13	Kentucky	8,295,000,000	2.3%
14	Illinois	7,323,000,000	2.0%
15	Mississippi	7,098,000,000	1.9%
16	New York	6,946,000,000	1.9%
17	Georgia	6,794,000,000	1.9%
18	Colorado	5,771,000,000	1.6%
19	Ohio	5,500,000,000	1.5%
20	New Jersey	5,498,000,000	1.5%
21	Michigan	4,682,000,000	1.3%
22	North Carolina	3,884,000,000	1.1%
23	South Carolina	3,453,000,000	0.9%
24	Oklahoma	3,337,000,000	0.9%
25	Indiana	3,277,000,000	0.9%
26	Wisconsin	2,806,000,000	0.8%
27	Minnesota	2,337,000,000	0.6%
28	Tennessee	2,126,000,000	0.6%
29	Hawaii	2,101,000,000	0.6%
30	Nevada	1,998,000,000	0.5%
31	New Hampshire	1,989,000,000	0.5%
32	Louisiana	1,832,000,000	0.5%
33	Alaska	1,769,000,000	0.5%
34	Iowa	1,750,000,000	0.5%
35	Utah	1,659,000,000	0.5%
36	New Mexico	1,558,000,000	0.4%
37	Maine	1,230,000,000	0.3%
38	Kansas	900,000,000	0.2%
39	Oregon	783,000,000	0.2%
40	Nebraska	660,000,000	0.2%
41	Rhode Island	641,000,000	0.2%
42	Vermont	485,000,000	0.1%
43	Arkansas	362,000,000	0.1%
44	South Dakota	312,000,000	0.1%
45	Idaho	267,000,000	0.1%
46	Montana	253,000,000	0.1%
47	West Virginia	189,000,000	0.1%
48	North Dakota	172,000,000	0.0%
49	Wyoming	170,000,000	0.0%
50	Delaware	155,000,000	0.0%
	District of Columbia	4,773,000,000	1.3%

Source: U.S. Department of the Treasury, USAspending.gov
"Award Data Archive" (https://www.usaspending.gov/, as of January 10, 2020)
*For fiscal year 2018. Total includes $27,384,000,000 in U.S. territories and in expenditures not distributed by state. Expenditures allocated based on place of performance of a contract. Includes contracts, grants, direct payments, insurance, and "other."
Total Department of Defense expenditures are more than shown through USAspending.gov.

Per Capita U.S. Department of Defense Expenditures in 2018

National Per Capita = $1,035*

ALPHA ORDER

RANK	STATE	PER CAPITA
7	Alabama	$2,216
4	Alaska	2,407
10	Arizona	1,779
49	Arkansas	120
17	California	933
15	Colorado	1,014
2	Connecticut	4,142
47	Delaware	161
22	Florida	734
25	Georgia	646
11	Hawaii	1,479
48	Idaho	152
28	Illinois	576
31	Indiana	489
29	Iowa	556
42	Kansas	309
9	Kentucky	1,859
36	Louisiana	393
18	Maine	918
3	Maryland	2,635
8	Massachusetts	1,863
34	Michigan	469
35	Minnesota	417
5	Mississippi	2,381
6	Missouri	2,268
44	Montana	238
40	Nebraska	343
24	Nevada	660
12	New Hampshire	1,469
26	New Jersey	619
21	New Mexico	745
38	New York	356
37	North Carolina	374
45	North Dakota	227
33	Ohio	471
19	Oklahoma	847
46	Oregon	187
16	Pennsylvania	1,012
27	Rhode Island	606
23	South Carolina	679
39	South Dakota	355
41	Tennessee	314
13	Texas	1,414
30	Utah	526
20	Vermont	776
1	Virginia	4,290
14	Washington	1,279
50	West Virginia	105
32	Wisconsin	483
43	Wyoming	295

RANK ORDER

RANK	STATE	PER CAPITA
1	Virginia	$4,290
2	Connecticut	4,142
3	Maryland	2,635
4	Alaska	2,407
5	Mississippi	2,381
6	Missouri	2,268
7	Alabama	2,216
8	Massachusetts	1,863
9	Kentucky	1,859
10	Arizona	1,779
11	Hawaii	1,479
12	New Hampshire	1,469
13	Texas	1,414
14	Washington	1,279
15	Colorado	1,014
16	Pennsylvania	1,012
17	California	933
18	Maine	918
19	Oklahoma	847
20	Vermont	776
21	New Mexico	745
22	Florida	734
23	South Carolina	679
24	Nevada	660
25	Georgia	646
26	New Jersey	619
27	Rhode Island	606
28	Illinois	576
29	Iowa	556
30	Utah	526
31	Indiana	489
32	Wisconsin	483
33	Ohio	471
34	Michigan	469
35	Minnesota	417
36	Louisiana	393
37	North Carolina	374
38	New York	356
39	South Dakota	355
40	Nebraska	343
41	Tennessee	314
42	Kansas	309
43	Wyoming	295
44	Montana	238
45	North Dakota	227
46	Oregon	187
47	Delaware	161
48	Idaho	152
49	Arkansas	120
50	West Virginia	105

District of Columbia   6,803

Source: CQ Press using data from U.S. Department of the Treasury, USAspending.gov
"Award Data Archive" (https://www.usaspending.gov/, as of January 10, 2020)
*For fiscal year 2018. National per capita excludes expenditures and population for territories and undistributed amounts.
Expenditures allocated based on place of performance of a contract. Includes contracts, grants, direct payments, insurance, and "other." Total Department of Defense expenditures are more than shown through USAspending.gov.

U.S. Department of Defense Expenditures as a Percent of Total Federal Government Expenditures in 2018
National Percent = 10.3%*

ALPHA ORDER

RANK	STATE	PERCENT
7	Alabama	18.8
9	Alaska	17.9
12	Arizona	16.1
48	Arkansas	1.5
15	California	11.7
14	Colorado	13.8
5	Connecticut	21.5
46	Delaware	2.1
25	Florida	8.1
19	Georgia	9.9
11	Hawaii	16.6
46	Idaho	2.1
23	Illinois	8.2
43	Indiana	2.4
26	Iowa	7.2
34	Kansas	4.8
21	Kentucky	9.2
33	Louisiana	4.9
18	Maine	10.1
4	Maryland	21.8
8	Massachusetts	18.7
31	Michigan	5.7
44	Minnesota	2.3
2	Mississippi	23.6
3	Missouri	22.3
41	Montana	2.7
35	Nebraska	4.3
20	Nevada	9.8
10	New Hampshire	17.6
23	New Jersey	8.2
30	New Mexico	6.0
37	New York	4.0
32	North Carolina	5.4
50	North Dakota	0.3
28	Ohio	6.4
16	Oklahoma	11.0
45	Oregon	2.2
29	Pennsylvania	6.1
27	Rhode Island	6.5
39	South Carolina	3.5
35	South Dakota	4.3
42	Tennessee	2.6
6	Texas	19.3
17	Utah	10.2
22	Vermont	8.6
1	Virginia	33.1
13	Washington	15.7
49	West Virginia	1.1
40	Wisconsin	3.1
38	Wyoming	3.9

RANK ORDER

RANK	STATE	PERCENT
1	Virginia	33.1
2	Mississippi	23.6
3	Missouri	22.3
4	Maryland	21.8
5	Connecticut	21.5
6	Texas	19.3
7	Alabama	18.8
8	Massachusetts	18.7
9	Alaska	17.9
10	New Hampshire	17.6
11	Hawaii	16.6
12	Arizona	16.1
13	Washington	15.7
14	Colorado	13.8
15	California	11.7
16	Oklahoma	11.0
17	Utah	10.2
18	Maine	10.1
19	Georgia	9.9
20	Nevada	9.8
21	Kentucky	9.2
22	Vermont	8.6
23	Illinois	8.2
23	New Jersey	8.2
25	Florida	8.1
26	Iowa	7.2
27	Rhode Island	6.5
28	Ohio	6.4
29	Pennsylvania	6.1
30	New Mexico	6.0
31	Michigan	5.7
32	North Carolina	5.4
33	Louisiana	4.9
34	Kansas	4.8
35	Nebraska	4.3
35	South Dakota	4.3
37	New York	4.0
38	Wyoming	3.9
39	South Carolina	3.5
40	Wisconsin	3.1
41	Montana	2.7
42	Tennessee	2.6
43	Indiana	2.4
44	Minnesota	2.3
45	Oregon	2.2
46	Delaware	2.1
46	Idaho	2.1
48	Arkansas	1.5
49	West Virginia	1.1
50	North Dakota	0.3

District of Columbia	13.6

Source: CQ Press using data from U.S. Department of the Treasury, USAspending.gov
"Award Data Archive" (https://www.usaspending.gov/, as of January 10, 2020)
*For fiscal year 2018. National percent excludes expenditures and population for territories and undistributed amounts.
Expenditures allocated based on place of performance of a contract. Includes contracts, grants, direct payments, insurance, and "other." Total Department of Defense expenditures are more than shown through USAspending.gov.

U.S. Active Duty Military Personnel Stationed in the United States in 2018

National Total = 1,132,833 Personnel*

ALPHA ORDER				RANK ORDER			
RANK	STATE	PERSONNEL	% of USA	RANK	STATE	PERSONNEL	% of USA
24	Alabama	7,962	0.7%	1	California	153,505	13.6%
18	Alaska	17,732	1.6%	2	Virginia	122,314	10.8%
17	Arizona	18,850	1.7%	3	Texas	117,844	10.4%
31	Arkansas	3,531	0.3%	4	North Carolina	99,193	8.8%
1	California	153,505	13.6%	5	Georgia	65,371	5.8%
10	Colorado	35,012	3.1%	6	Florida	60,251	5.3%
29	Connecticut	5,547	0.5%	7	Washington	58,115	5.1%
32	Delaware	3,506	0.3%	8	Hawaii	41,803	3.7%
6	Florida	60,251	5.3%	9	South Carolina	39,237	3.5%
5	Georgia	65,371	5.8%	10	Colorado	35,012	3.1%
8	Hawaii	41,803	3.7%	11	Kentucky	32,247	2.8%
33	Idaho	3,477	0.3%	12	Maryland	28,259	2.5%
14	Illinois	20,955	1.8%	13	Kansas	21,507	1.9%
43	Indiana	947	0.1%	14	Illinois	20,955	1.8%
47	Iowa	215	0.0%	15	Oklahoma	20,807	1.8%
13	Kansas	21,507	1.9%	16	New York	19,710	1.7%
11	Kentucky	32,247	2.8%	17	Arizona	18,850	1.7%
20	Louisiana	14,419	1.3%	18	Alaska	17,732	1.6%
50	Maine	121	0.0%	19	Missouri	16,908	1.5%
12	Maryland	28,259	2.5%	20	Louisiana	14,419	1.3%
39	Massachusetts	2,123	0.2%	21	New Mexico	12,523	1.1%
42	Michigan	956	0.1%	22	Mississippi	12,076	1.1%
46	Minnesota	464	0.0%	23	Nevada	11,070	1.0%
22	Mississippi	12,076	1.1%	24	Alabama	7,962	0.7%
19	Missouri	16,908	1.5%	25	North Dakota	7,374	0.7%
35	Montana	3,303	0.3%	26	Ohio	6,558	0.6%
27	Nebraska	6,270	0.6%	27	Nebraska	6,270	0.6%
23	Nevada	11,070	1.0%	28	New Jersey	6,103	0.5%
41	New Hampshire	1,084	0.1%	29	Connecticut	5,547	0.5%
28	New Jersey	6,103	0.5%	30	Utah	4,277	0.4%
21	New Mexico	12,523	1.1%	31	Arkansas	3,531	0.3%
16	New York	19,710	1.7%	32	Delaware	3,506	0.3%
4	North Carolina	99,193	8.8%	33	Idaho	3,477	0.3%
25	North Dakota	7,374	0.7%	34	South Dakota	3,413	0.3%
26	Ohio	6,558	0.6%	35	Montana	3,303	0.3%
15	Oklahoma	20,807	1.8%	36	Wyoming	3,196	0.3%
45	Oregon	548	0.0%	37	Rhode Island	3,075	0.3%
38	Pennsylvania	2,230	0.2%	38	Pennsylvania	2,230	0.2%
37	Rhode Island	3,075	0.3%	39	Massachusetts	2,123	0.2%
9	South Carolina	39,237	3.5%	40	Tennessee	2,017	0.2%
34	South Dakota	3,413	0.3%	41	New Hampshire	1,084	0.1%
40	Tennessee	2,017	0.2%	42	Michigan	956	0.1%
3	Texas	117,844	10.4%	43	Indiana	947	0.1%
30	Utah	4,277	0.4%	44	Wisconsin	709	0.1%
48	Vermont	135	0.0%	45	Oregon	548	0.0%
2	Virginia	122,314	10.8%	46	Minnesota	464	0.0%
7	Washington	58,115	5.1%	47	Iowa	215	0.0%
48	West Virginia	135	0.0%	48	Vermont	135	0.0%
44	Wisconsin	709	0.1%	48	West Virginia	135	0.0%
36	Wyoming	3,196	0.3%	50	Maine	121	0.0%
					District of Columbia	8,108	0.7%

Source: U.S. Department of Defense
"Demographics 2018" (https://www.militaryonesource.mil/reports-and-surveys/demographic-profiles)
*Includes 5,741 not shown by state. Numbers reflect where the personnel are stationed.

U.S. Selected Reserve Personnel Stationed in the United States in 2018

National Total = 778,908 Personnel*

ALPHA ORDER					RANK ORDER			
RANK	STATE	PERSONNEL	% of USA		RANK	STATE	PERSONNEL	% of USA
11	Alabama	19,524	2.5%		1	California	56,085	7.2%
43	Alaska	4,631	0.6%		2	Texas	53,746	6.9%
24	Arizona	14,995	1.9%		3	Florida	36,615	4.7%
30	Arkansas	10,802	1.4%		4	Pennsylvania	29,896	3.8%
1	California	56,085	7.2%		5	New York	28,860	3.7%
26	Colorado	13,568	1.7%		6	Ohio	28,310	3.6%
37	Connecticut	6,691	0.9%		7	Georgia	26,824	3.4%
41	Delaware	4,998	0.6%		8	Virginia	26,411	3.4%
3	Florida	36,615	4.7%		9	Illinois	24,345	3.1%
7	Georgia	26,824	3.4%		10	North Carolina	21,667	2.8%
33	Hawaii	9,390	1.2%		11	Alabama	19,524	2.5%
39	Idaho	5,526	0.7%		12	Missouri	19,145	2.5%
9	Illinois	24,345	3.1%		13	Indiana	18,826	2.4%
13	Indiana	18,826	2.4%		14	Minnesota	18,502	2.4%
31	Iowa	10,711	1.4%		15	Maryland	18,429	2.4%
32	Kansas	10,072	1.3%		16	Washington	18,251	2.3%
28	Kentucky	12,502	1.6%		17	Tennessee	18,071	2.3%
19	Louisiana	17,213	2.2%		18	South Carolina	17,781	2.3%
48	Maine	3,757	0.5%		19	Louisiana	17,213	2.2%
15	Maryland	18,429	2.4%		20	New Jersey	17,178	2.2%
23	Massachusetts	15,100	1.9%		21	Mississippi	16,447	2.1%
22	Michigan	15,269	2.0%		22	Michigan	15,269	2.0%
14	Minnesota	18,502	2.4%		23	Massachusetts	15,100	1.9%
21	Mississippi	16,447	2.1%		24	Arizona	14,995	1.9%
12	Missouri	19,145	2.5%		25	Wisconsin	14,402	1.8%
46	Montana	4,303	0.6%		26	Colorado	13,568	1.7%
38	Nebraska	6,167	0.8%		27	Oklahoma	13,400	1.7%
36	Nevada	7,596	1.0%		28	Kentucky	12,502	1.6%
47	New Hampshire	4,131	0.5%		29	Utah	11,980	1.5%
20	New Jersey	17,178	2.2%		30	Arkansas	10,802	1.4%
40	New Mexico	5,026	0.6%		31	Iowa	10,711	1.4%
5	New York	28,860	3.7%		32	Kansas	10,072	1.3%
10	North Carolina	21,667	2.8%		33	Hawaii	9,390	1.2%
44	North Dakota	4,356	0.6%		34	Oregon	9,382	1.2%
6	Ohio	28,310	3.6%		35	West Virginia	8,341	1.1%
27	Oklahoma	13,400	1.7%		36	Nevada	7,596	1.0%
34	Oregon	9,382	1.2%		37	Connecticut	6,691	0.9%
4	Pennsylvania	29,896	3.8%		38	Nebraska	6,167	0.8%
45	Rhode Island	4,314	0.6%		39	Idaho	5,526	0.7%
18	South Carolina	17,781	2.3%		40	New Mexico	5,026	0.6%
42	South Dakota	4,698	0.6%		41	Delaware	4,998	0.6%
17	Tennessee	18,071	2.3%		42	South Dakota	4,698	0.6%
2	Texas	53,746	6.9%		43	Alaska	4,631	0.6%
29	Utah	11,980	1.5%		44	North Dakota	4,356	0.6%
49	Vermont	3,528	0.5%		45	Rhode Island	4,314	0.6%
8	Virginia	26,411	3.4%		46	Montana	4,303	0.6%
16	Washington	18,251	2.3%		47	New Hampshire	4,131	0.5%
35	West Virginia	8,341	1.1%		48	Maine	3,757	0.5%
25	Wisconsin	14,402	1.8%		49	Vermont	3,528	0.5%
50	Wyoming	2,902	0.4%		50	Wyoming	2,902	0.4%
						District of Columbia	4,244	0.5%

Source: U.S. Department of Defense
   "Demographics 2018" (https://www.militaryonesource.mil/reports-and-surveys/demographic-profiles)
*Numbers reflect where the personnel are stationed.

Veterans in 2019

National Total = 19,209,704 Veterans*

ALPHA ORDER

RANK	STATE	VETERANS	% of USA
20	Alabama	361,673	1.9%
45	Alaska	68,891	0.4%
13	Arizona	492,472	2.6%
29	Arkansas	216,323	1.1%
1	California	1,578,509	8.2%
17	Colorado	394,145	2.1%
34	Connecticut	170,454	0.9%
44	Delaware	69,715	0.4%
3	Florida	1,457,205	7.6%
9	Georgia	690,726	3.6%
40	Hawaii	110,524	0.6%
39	Idaho	119,696	0.6%
10	Illinois	591,989	3.1%
18	Indiana	392,388	2.0%
31	Iowa	196,376	1.0%
32	Kansas	188,503	1.0%
27	Kentucky	287,790	1.5%
28	Louisiana	276,931	1.4%
41	Maine	108,547	0.6%
19	Maryland	371,164	1.9%
24	Massachusetts	298,515	1.6%
11	Michigan	552,412	2.9%
23	Minnesota	308,725	1.6%
33	Mississippi	186,702	1.0%
15	Missouri	426,190	2.2%
43	Montana	89,096	0.5%
38	Nebraska	124,439	0.6%
30	Nevada	210,766	1.1%
42	New Hampshire	100,020	0.5%
22	New Jersey	325,981	1.7%
35	New Mexico	154,172	0.8%
7	New York	718,900	3.7%
6	North Carolina	725,313	3.8%
48	North Dakota	50,842	0.3%
5	Ohio	733,082	3.8%
25	Oklahoma	296,891	1.5%
26	Oregon	290,444	1.5%
4	Pennsylvania	768,094	4.0%
47	Rhode Island	58,976	0.3%
16	South Carolina	398,589	2.1%
46	South Dakota	64,119	0.3%
14	Tennessee	460,692	2.4%
2	Texas	1,562,722	8.1%
37	Utah	130,817	0.7%
50	Vermont	41,073	0.2%
8	Virginia	714,410	3.7%
12	Washington	544,290	2.8%
36	West Virginia	137,337	0.7%
21	Wisconsin	344,785	1.8%
49	Wyoming	46,613	0.2%

RANK ORDER

RANK	STATE	VETERANS	% of USA
1	California	1,578,509	8.2%
2	Texas	1,562,722	8.1%
3	Florida	1,457,205	7.6%
4	Pennsylvania	768,094	4.0%
5	Ohio	733,082	3.8%
6	North Carolina	725,313	3.8%
7	New York	718,900	3.7%
8	Virginia	714,410	3.7%
9	Georgia	690,726	3.6%
10	Illinois	591,989	3.1%
11	Michigan	552,412	2.9%
12	Washington	544,290	2.8%
13	Arizona	492,472	2.6%
14	Tennessee	460,692	2.4%
15	Missouri	426,190	2.2%
16	South Carolina	398,589	2.1%
17	Colorado	394,145	2.1%
18	Indiana	392,388	2.0%
19	Maryland	371,164	1.9%
20	Alabama	361,673	1.9%
21	Wisconsin	344,785	1.8%
22	New Jersey	325,981	1.7%
23	Minnesota	308,725	1.6%
24	Massachusetts	298,515	1.6%
25	Oklahoma	296,891	1.5%
26	Oregon	290,444	1.5%
27	Kentucky	287,790	1.5%
28	Louisiana	276,931	1.4%
29	Arkansas	216,323	1.1%
30	Nevada	210,766	1.1%
31	Iowa	196,376	1.0%
32	Kansas	188,503	1.0%
33	Mississippi	186,702	1.0%
34	Connecticut	170,454	0.9%
35	New Mexico	154,172	0.8%
36	West Virginia	137,337	0.7%
37	Utah	130,817	0.7%
38	Nebraska	124,439	0.6%
39	Idaho	119,696	0.6%
40	Hawaii	110,524	0.6%
41	Maine	108,547	0.6%
42	New Hampshire	100,020	0.5%
43	Montana	89,096	0.5%
44	Delaware	69,715	0.4%
45	Alaska	68,891	0.4%
46	South Dakota	64,119	0.3%
47	Rhode Island	58,976	0.3%
48	North Dakota	50,842	0.3%
49	Wyoming	46,613	0.2%
50	Vermont	41,073	0.2%
	District of Columbia	26,863	0.1%

Source: U.S. Department of Veteran Affairs
"Veteran Data and Information" (https://www.va.gov/vetdata/Veteran_Population.asp)
*Estimates based on 2016 data. Includes 173,811 veterans in U.S. territories or other countries.

Percent of Adult Population Who Are Veterans in 2019

National Percent = 7.5%*

ALPHA ORDER			RANK ORDER		
RANK	**STATE**	**PERCENT**	**RANK**	**STATE**	**PERCENT**
11	Alabama	9.5	1	Alaska	12.4
1	Alaska	12.4	2	Montana	10.7
21	Arizona	8.9	2	Virginia	10.7
13	Arkansas	9.4	4	Wyoming	10.5
48	California	5.2	5	Maine	10.0
21	Colorado	8.9	5	South Carolina	10.0
44	Connecticut	6.0	7	Hawaii	9.9
16	Delaware	9.1	7	Oklahoma	9.9
28	Florida	8.5	9	New Mexico	9.6
26	Georgia	8.6	9	South Dakota	9.6
7	Hawaii	9.9	11	Alabama	9.5
15	Idaho	9.2	11	West Virginia	9.5
44	Illinois	6.0	13	Arkansas	9.4
37	Indiana	7.7	14	Washington	9.3
32	Iowa	8.1	15	Idaho	9.2
28	Kansas	8.5	16	Delaware	9.1
30	Kentucky	8.3	16	New Hampshire	9.1
36	Louisiana	7.8	18	Missouri	9.0
5	Maine	10.0	18	Nevada	9.0
35	Maryland	7.9	18	North Carolina	9.0
47	Massachusetts	5.4	21	Arizona	8.9
42	Michigan	7.1	21	Colorado	8.9
41	Minnesota	7.2	23	Oregon	8.8
31	Mississippi	8.2	23	Tennessee	8.8
18	Missouri	9.0	25	North Dakota	8.7
2	Montana	10.7	26	Georgia	8.6
26	Nebraska	8.6	26	Nebraska	8.6
18	Nevada	9.0	28	Florida	8.5
16	New Hampshire	9.1	28	Kansas	8.5
49	New Jersey	4.7	30	Kentucky	8.3
9	New Mexico	9.6	31	Mississippi	8.2
50	New York	4.6	32	Iowa	8.1
18	North Carolina	9.0	32	Ohio	8.1
25	North Dakota	8.7	34	Vermont	8.0
32	Ohio	8.1	35	Maryland	7.9
7	Oklahoma	9.9	36	Louisiana	7.8
23	Oregon	8.8	37	Indiana	7.7
38	Pennsylvania	7.6	38	Pennsylvania	7.6
43	Rhode Island	6.9	38	Wisconsin	7.6
5	South Carolina	10.0	40	Texas	7.3
9	South Dakota	9.6	41	Minnesota	7.2
23	Tennessee	8.8	42	Michigan	7.1
40	Texas	7.3	43	Rhode Island	6.9
46	Utah	5.9	44	Connecticut	6.0
34	Vermont	8.0	44	Illinois	6.0
2	Virginia	10.7	46	Utah	5.9
14	Washington	9.3	47	Massachusetts	5.4
11	West Virginia	9.5	48	California	5.2
38	Wisconsin	7.6	49	New Jersey	4.7
4	Wyoming	10.5	50	New York	4.6
				District of Columbia	4.7

Source: CQ Press using data from U.S. Department of Veteran Affairs
  "Veteran Data and Information" (https://www.va.gov/vetdata/Veteran_Population.asp)
*Estimates based on 2016 data. National figures does not include veterans in U.S. territories or other countries. Percent calculated with population eighteen years old and older in 2018.

U.S. Military Fatalities in Iraq and Afghanistan as of January 24, 2020

National Total = 7,013 Fatalities*

ALPHA ORDER

RANK ORDER

RANK	STATE	FATALITIES	% of USA
26	Alabama	106	1.5%
45	Alaska	26	0.4%
13	Arizona	155	2.2%
29	Arkansas	89	1.3%
1	California	750	10.7%
25	Colorado	109	1.6%
38	Connecticut	50	0.7%
48	Delaware	20	0.3%
3	Florida	354	5.0%
9	Georgia	220	3.1%
43	Hawaii	40	0.6%
38	Idaho	50	0.7%
7	Illinois	261	3.7%
12	Indiana	157	2.2%
32	Iowa	73	1.0%
31	Kansas	78	1.1%
23	Kentucky	113	1.6%
19	Louisiana	127	1.8%
37	Maine	51	0.7%
22	Maryland	124	1.8%
17	Massachusetts	129	1.8%
8	Michigan	229	3.3%
28	Minnesota	97	1.4%
30	Mississippi	79	1.1%
15	Missouri	145	2.1%
41	Montana	41	0.6%
33	Nebraska	61	0.9%
35	Nevada	54	0.8%
41	New Hampshire	41	0.6%
19	New Jersey	127	1.8%
34	New Mexico	57	0.8%
4	New York	308	4.4%
11	North Carolina	191	2.7%
48	North Dakota	20	0.3%
6	Ohio	283	4.0%
18	Oklahoma	128	1.8%
24	Oregon	110	1.6%
5	Pennsylvania	300	4.3%
50	Rhode Island	17	0.2%
27	South Carolina	98	1.4%
46	South Dakota	24	0.3%
16	Tennessee	143	2.0%
2	Texas	619	8.8%
36	Utah	52	0.7%
44	Vermont	27	0.4%
10	Virginia	205	2.9%
13	Washington	155	2.2%
40	West Virginia	43	0.6%
19	Wisconsin	127	1.8%
47	Wyoming	22	0.3%

RANK	STATE	FATALITIES	% of USA
1	California	750	10.7%
2	Texas	619	8.8%
3	Florida	354	5.0%
4	New York	308	4.4%
5	Pennsylvania	300	4.3%
6	Ohio	283	4.0%
7	Illinois	261	3.7%
8	Michigan	229	3.3%
9	Georgia	220	3.1%
10	Virginia	205	2.9%
11	North Carolina	191	2.7%
12	Indiana	157	2.2%
13	Arizona	155	2.2%
13	Washington	155	2.2%
15	Missouri	145	2.1%
16	Tennessee	143	2.0%
17	Massachusetts	129	1.8%
18	Oklahoma	128	1.8%
19	Louisiana	127	1.8%
19	New Jersey	127	1.8%
19	Wisconsin	127	1.8%
22	Maryland	124	1.8%
23	Kentucky	113	1.6%
24	Oregon	110	1.6%
25	Colorado	109	1.6%
26	Alabama	106	1.5%
27	South Carolina	98	1.4%
28	Minnesota	97	1.4%
29	Arkansas	89	1.3%
30	Mississippi	79	1.1%
31	Kansas	78	1.1%
32	Iowa	73	1.0%
33	Nebraska	61	0.9%
34	New Mexico	57	0.8%
35	Nevada	54	0.8%
36	Utah	52	0.7%
37	Maine	51	0.7%
38	Connecticut	50	0.7%
38	Idaho	50	0.7%
40	West Virginia	43	0.6%
41	Montana	41	0.6%
41	New Hampshire	41	0.6%
43	Hawaii	40	0.6%
44	Vermont	27	0.4%
45	Alaska	26	0.4%
46	South Dakota	24	0.3%
47	Wyoming	22	0.3%
48	Delaware	20	0.3%
48	North Dakota	20	0.3%
50	Rhode Island	17	0.2%
	District of Columbia	10	0.1%

Source: U.S. Department of Defense, Defense Casualty Analysis System
   "U.S. Military Casualties" (https://dcas.dmdc.osd.mil/dcas/pages/report_sum_all.xhtml)
*Total includes 118 deaths of soldiers from U.S. territories. Total does not include deaths of United Kingdom soldiers or other coalition nations. Includes 5,443 combat and 1,570 noncombat deaths. Includes 4,493 deaths in Iraq, 2,433 deaths in Afghanistan, and 87 deaths fighting Islamic State in Syria and Iraq.

Rate of U.S. Military Fatalities in Iraq and Afghanistan as of January 24, 2020

National Rate = 2.1 Fatalities per 100,000 Population*

<table>
<tr><td colspan="3">ALPHA ORDER</td><td colspan="3">RANK ORDER</td></tr>
<tr><td>RANK</td><td>STATE</td><td>RATE</td><td>RANK</td><td>STATE</td><td>RATE</td></tr>
<tr><td>28</td><td>Alabama</td><td>2.2</td><td>1</td><td>Vermont</td><td>4.3</td></tr>
<tr><td>5</td><td>Alaska</td><td>3.6</td><td>2</td><td>Maine</td><td>3.8</td></tr>
<tr><td>30</td><td>Arizona</td><td>2.1</td><td>2</td><td>Montana</td><td>3.8</td></tr>
<tr><td>9</td><td>Arkansas</td><td>2.9</td><td>2</td><td>Wyoming</td><td>3.8</td></tr>
<tr><td>38</td><td>California</td><td>1.9</td><td>5</td><td>Alaska</td><td>3.6</td></tr>
<tr><td>38</td><td>Colorado</td><td>1.9</td><td>6</td><td>Nebraska</td><td>3.2</td></tr>
<tr><td>49</td><td>Connecticut</td><td>1.4</td><td>6</td><td>Oklahoma</td><td>3.2</td></tr>
<tr><td>30</td><td>Delaware</td><td>2.1</td><td>8</td><td>New Hampshire</td><td>3.0</td></tr>
<tr><td>45</td><td>Florida</td><td>1.6</td><td>9</td><td>Arkansas</td><td>2.9</td></tr>
<tr><td>30</td><td>Georgia</td><td>2.1</td><td>10</td><td>Hawaii</td><td>2.8</td></tr>
<tr><td>10</td><td>Hawaii</td><td>2.8</td><td>10</td><td>Idaho</td><td>2.8</td></tr>
<tr><td>10</td><td>Idaho</td><td>2.8</td><td>12</td><td>Kansas</td><td>2.7</td></tr>
<tr><td>30</td><td>Illinois</td><td>2.1</td><td>12</td><td>Louisiana</td><td>2.7</td></tr>
<tr><td>24</td><td>Indiana</td><td>2.3</td><td>12</td><td>Mississippi</td><td>2.7</td></tr>
<tr><td>24</td><td>Iowa</td><td>2.3</td><td>12</td><td>New Mexico</td><td>2.7</td></tr>
<tr><td>12</td><td>Kansas</td><td>2.7</td><td>12</td><td>South Dakota</td><td>2.7</td></tr>
<tr><td>19</td><td>Kentucky</td><td>2.5</td><td>17</td><td>North Dakota</td><td>2.6</td></tr>
<tr><td>12</td><td>Louisiana</td><td>2.7</td><td>17</td><td>Oregon</td><td>2.6</td></tr>
<tr><td>2</td><td>Maine</td><td>3.8</td><td>19</td><td>Kentucky</td><td>2.5</td></tr>
<tr><td>30</td><td>Maryland</td><td>2.1</td><td>20</td><td>Missouri</td><td>2.4</td></tr>
<tr><td>38</td><td>Massachusetts</td><td>1.9</td><td>20</td><td>Ohio</td><td>2.4</td></tr>
<tr><td>24</td><td>Michigan</td><td>2.3</td><td>20</td><td>Virginia</td><td>2.4</td></tr>
<tr><td>44</td><td>Minnesota</td><td>1.7</td><td>20</td><td>West Virginia</td><td>2.4</td></tr>
<tr><td>12</td><td>Mississippi</td><td>2.7</td><td>24</td><td>Indiana</td><td>2.3</td></tr>
<tr><td>20</td><td>Missouri</td><td>2.4</td><td>24</td><td>Iowa</td><td>2.3</td></tr>
<tr><td>2</td><td>Montana</td><td>3.8</td><td>24</td><td>Michigan</td><td>2.3</td></tr>
<tr><td>6</td><td>Nebraska</td><td>3.2</td><td>24</td><td>Pennsylvania</td><td>2.3</td></tr>
<tr><td>42</td><td>Nevada</td><td>1.8</td><td>28</td><td>Alabama</td><td>2.2</td></tr>
<tr><td>8</td><td>New Hampshire</td><td>3.0</td><td>28</td><td>Wisconsin</td><td>2.2</td></tr>
<tr><td>49</td><td>New Jersey</td><td>1.4</td><td>30</td><td>Arizona</td><td>2.1</td></tr>
<tr><td>12</td><td>New Mexico</td><td>2.7</td><td>30</td><td>Delaware</td><td>2.1</td></tr>
<tr><td>45</td><td>New York</td><td>1.6</td><td>30</td><td>Georgia</td><td>2.1</td></tr>
<tr><td>42</td><td>North Carolina</td><td>1.8</td><td>30</td><td>Illinois</td><td>2.1</td></tr>
<tr><td>17</td><td>North Dakota</td><td>2.6</td><td>30</td><td>Maryland</td><td>2.1</td></tr>
<tr><td>20</td><td>Ohio</td><td>2.4</td><td>30</td><td>Tennessee</td><td>2.1</td></tr>
<tr><td>6</td><td>Oklahoma</td><td>3.2</td><td>30</td><td>Texas</td><td>2.1</td></tr>
<tr><td>17</td><td>Oregon</td><td>2.6</td><td>37</td><td>Washington</td><td>2.0</td></tr>
<tr><td>24</td><td>Pennsylvania</td><td>2.3</td><td>38</td><td>California</td><td>1.9</td></tr>
<tr><td>45</td><td>Rhode Island</td><td>1.6</td><td>38</td><td>Colorado</td><td>1.9</td></tr>
<tr><td>38</td><td>South Carolina</td><td>1.9</td><td>38</td><td>Massachusetts</td><td>1.9</td></tr>
<tr><td>12</td><td>South Dakota</td><td>2.7</td><td>38</td><td>South Carolina</td><td>1.9</td></tr>
<tr><td>30</td><td>Tennessee</td><td>2.1</td><td>42</td><td>Nevada</td><td>1.8</td></tr>
<tr><td>30</td><td>Texas</td><td>2.1</td><td>42</td><td>North Carolina</td><td>1.8</td></tr>
<tr><td>45</td><td>Utah</td><td>1.6</td><td>44</td><td>Minnesota</td><td>1.7</td></tr>
<tr><td>1</td><td>Vermont</td><td>4.3</td><td>45</td><td>Florida</td><td>1.6</td></tr>
<tr><td>20</td><td>Virginia</td><td>2.4</td><td>45</td><td>New York</td><td>1.6</td></tr>
<tr><td>37</td><td>Washington</td><td>2.0</td><td>45</td><td>Rhode Island</td><td>1.6</td></tr>
<tr><td>20</td><td>West Virginia</td><td>2.4</td><td>45</td><td>Utah</td><td>1.6</td></tr>
<tr><td>28</td><td>Wisconsin</td><td>2.2</td><td>49</td><td>Connecticut</td><td>1.4</td></tr>
<tr><td>2</td><td>Wyoming</td><td>3.8</td><td>49</td><td>New Jersey</td><td>1.4</td></tr>
<tr><td></td><td></td><td></td><td></td><td>District of Columbia</td><td>1.4</td></tr>
</table>

Source: CQ Press using data from U.S. Department of Defense, Defense Casualty Analysis System
"U.S. Military Casualties" (https://dcas.dmdc.osd.mil/dcas/pages/report_sum_all.xhtml)
*National rate does not include deaths of soldiers from U.S. territories. Includes combat and noncombat deaths. Calculated with 2019 population estimates.

U.S. Military Wounded in Iraq and Afghanistan as of January 24, 2020

National Total = 60,190 Wounded*

ALPHA ORDER					RANK ORDER			
RANK	STATE	WOUNDED	% of USA		RANK	STATE	WOUNDED	% of USA
18	Alabama	868	1.6%		1	California	4,905	9.2%
46	Alaska	162	0.3%		2	Texas	4,405	8.3%
14	Arizona	1,173	2.2%		3	Florida	2,529	4.8%
29	Arkansas	653	1.2%		4	New York	2,344	4.4%
1	California	4,905	9.2%		5	Ohio	2,055	3.9%
22	Colorado	833	1.6%		6	Pennsylvania	2,019	3.8%
34	Connecticut	427	0.8%		7	Illinois	1,766	3.3%
50	Delaware	87	0.2%		8	Michigan	1,644	3.1%
3	Florida	2,529	4.8%		9	Georgia	1,524	2.9%
9	Georgia	1,524	2.9%		10	North Carolina	1,463	2.8%
43	Hawaii	210	0.4%		11	Washington	1,303	2.5%
36	Idaho	393	0.7%		12	Virginia	1,215	2.3%
7	Illinois	1,766	3.3%		13	Missouri	1,200	2.3%
15	Indiana	1,114	2.1%		14	Arizona	1,173	2.2%
31	Iowa	628	1.2%		15	Indiana	1,114	2.1%
30	Kansas	635	1.2%		16	Tennessee	1,029	1.9%
27	Kentucky	751	1.4%		17	Wisconsin	920	1.7%
21	Louisiana	835	1.6%		18	Alabama	868	1.6%
41	Maine	326	0.6%		19	Oklahoma	866	1.6%
28	Maryland	686	1.3%		20	Massachusetts	843	1.6%
20	Massachusetts	843	1.6%		21	Louisiana	835	1.6%
8	Michigan	1,644	3.1%		22	Colorado	833	1.6%
26	Minnesota	759	1.4%		23	Oregon	798	1.5%
33	Mississippi	446	0.8%		24	New Jersey	780	1.5%
13	Missouri	1,200	2.3%		25	South Carolina	766	1.4%
40	Montana	330	0.6%		26	Minnesota	759	1.4%
39	Nebraska	340	0.6%		27	Kentucky	751	1.4%
37	Nevada	384	0.7%		28	Maryland	686	1.3%
42	New Hampshire	300	0.6%		29	Arkansas	653	1.2%
24	New Jersey	780	1.5%		30	Kansas	635	1.2%
34	New Mexico	427	0.8%		31	Iowa	628	1.2%
4	New York	2,344	4.4%		32	Utah	462	0.9%
10	North Carolina	1,463	2.8%		33	Mississippi	446	0.8%
49	North Dakota	117	0.2%		34	Connecticut	427	0.8%
5	Ohio	2,055	3.9%		34	New Mexico	427	0.8%
19	Oklahoma	866	1.6%		36	Idaho	393	0.7%
23	Oregon	798	1.5%		37	Nevada	384	0.7%
6	Pennsylvania	2,019	3.8%		38	West Virginia	374	0.7%
45	Rhode Island	170	0.3%		39	Nebraska	340	0.6%
25	South Carolina	766	1.4%		40	Montana	330	0.6%
44	South Dakota	194	0.4%		41	Maine	326	0.6%
16	Tennessee	1,029	1.9%		42	New Hampshire	300	0.6%
2	Texas	4,405	8.3%		43	Hawaii	210	0.4%
32	Utah	462	0.9%		44	South Dakota	194	0.4%
47	Vermont	153	0.3%		45	Rhode Island	170	0.3%
12	Virginia	1,215	2.3%		46	Alaska	162	0.3%
11	Washington	1,303	2.5%		47	Vermont	153	0.3%
38	West Virginia	374	0.7%		48	Wyoming	150	0.3%
17	Wisconsin	920	1.7%		49	North Dakota	117	0.2%
48	Wyoming	150	0.3%		50	Delaware	87	0.2%
						District of Columbia	30	0.1%

Source: U.S. Department of Defense, Defense Casualty Analysis System
    "U.S. Military Casualties" (https://dcas.dmdc.osd.mil/dcas/pages/report_sum_all.xhtml)
*Total includes 4,386 wounded soldiers from U.S. territories. Total does not include wounded soldiers of United Kingdom or other coalition nations. Only includes wounded in action. Includes 32,292 wounded in Iraq, 20,711 wounded in Afghanistan, and 174 wounded fighting the Islamic State in Syria and Iraq.

IV. Economy

Gross Domestic Product in 2018

National Total = $20,580,223,000,000*

ALPHA ORDER

RANK	STATE	G.D.P.	% of USA
27	Alabama	$221,735,500,000	1.1%
46	Alaska	54,734,100,000	0.3%
20	Arizona	348,297,100,000	1.7%
34	Arkansas	128,418,900,000	0.6%
1	California	2,997,732,800,000	14.6%
16	Colorado	371,749,600,000	1.8%
23	Connecticut	275,726,900,000	1.3%
42	Delaware	73,481,300,000	0.4%
4	Florida	1,039,236,400,000	5.0%
9	Georgia	592,153,400,000	2.9%
38	Hawaii	93,797,900,000	0.5%
41	Idaho	77,052,000,000	0.4%
5	Illinois	865,310,400,000	4.2%
18	Indiana	366,800,500,000	1.8%
30	Iowa	189,701,600,000	0.9%
33	Kansas	168,318,000,000	0.8%
28	Kentucky	208,087,500,000	1.0%
24	Louisiana	257,287,800,000	1.3%
43	Maine	64,856,000,000	0.3%
15	Maryland	412,584,200,000	2.0%
10	Massachusetts	569,488,000,000	2.8%
14	Michigan	527,095,800,000	2.6%
17	Minnesota	368,852,400,000	1.8%
36	Mississippi	114,834,200,000	0.6%
22	Missouri	318,921,000,000	1.5%
48	Montana	50,326,600,000	0.2%
35	Nebraska	123,977,900,000	0.6%
32	Nevada	169,309,900,000	0.8%
39	New Hampshire	84,463,900,000	0.4%
8	New Jersey	622,002,800,000	3.0%
37	New Mexico	100,296,800,000	0.5%
3	New York	1,668,866,200,000	8.1%
12	North Carolina	563,690,500,000	2.7%
45	North Dakota	56,082,300,000	0.3%
7	Ohio	675,905,200,000	3.3%
29	Oklahoma	202,554,100,000	1.0%
25	Oregon	239,782,800,000	1.2%
6	Pennsylvania	783,167,800,000	3.8%
44	Rhode Island	60,587,600,000	0.3%
26	South Carolina	233,929,900,000	1.1%
47	South Dakota	52,014,900,000	0.3%
19	Tennessee	364,104,900,000	1.8%
2	Texas	1,802,511,200,000	8.8%
31	Utah	178,137,600,000	0.9%
50	Vermont	33,256,300,000	0.2%
13	Virginia	532,892,500,000	2.6%
11	Washington	565,831,000,000	2.7%
40	West Virginia	77,437,600,000	0.4%
21	Wisconsin	336,294,000,000	1.6%
49	Wyoming	39,118,500,000	0.2%

RANK ORDER

RANK	STATE	G.D.P.	% of USA
1	California	$2,997,732,800,000	14.6%
2	Texas	1,802,511,200,000	8.8%
3	New York	1,668,866,200,000	8.1%
4	Florida	1,039,236,400,000	5.0%
5	Illinois	865,310,400,000	4.2%
6	Pennsylvania	783,167,800,000	3.8%
7	Ohio	675,905,200,000	3.3%
8	New Jersey	622,002,800,000	3.0%
9	Georgia	592,153,400,000	2.9%
10	Massachusetts	569,488,000,000	2.8%
11	Washington	565,831,000,000	2.7%
12	North Carolina	563,690,500,000	2.7%
13	Virginia	532,892,500,000	2.6%
14	Michigan	527,095,800,000	2.6%
15	Maryland	412,584,200,000	2.0%
16	Colorado	371,749,600,000	1.8%
17	Minnesota	368,852,400,000	1.8%
18	Indiana	366,800,500,000	1.8%
19	Tennessee	364,104,900,000	1.8%
20	Arizona	348,297,100,000	1.7%
21	Wisconsin	336,294,000,000	1.6%
22	Missouri	318,921,000,000	1.5%
23	Connecticut	275,726,900,000	1.3%
24	Louisiana	257,287,800,000	1.3%
25	Oregon	239,782,800,000	1.2%
26	South Carolina	233,929,900,000	1.1%
27	Alabama	221,735,500,000	1.1%
28	Kentucky	208,087,500,000	1.0%
29	Oklahoma	202,554,100,000	1.0%
30	Iowa	189,701,600,000	0.9%
31	Utah	178,137,600,000	0.9%
32	Nevada	169,309,900,000	0.8%
33	Kansas	168,318,000,000	0.8%
34	Arkansas	128,418,900,000	0.6%
35	Nebraska	123,977,900,000	0.6%
36	Mississippi	114,834,200,000	0.6%
37	New Mexico	100,296,800,000	0.5%
38	Hawaii	93,797,900,000	0.5%
39	New Hampshire	84,463,900,000	0.4%
40	West Virginia	77,437,600,000	0.4%
41	Idaho	77,052,000,000	0.4%
42	Delaware	73,481,300,000	0.4%
43	Maine	64,856,000,000	0.3%
44	Rhode Island	60,587,600,000	0.3%
45	North Dakota	56,082,300,000	0.3%
46	Alaska	54,734,100,000	0.3%
47	South Dakota	52,014,900,000	0.3%
48	Montana	50,326,600,000	0.2%
49	Wyoming	39,118,500,000	0.2%
50	Vermont	33,256,300,000	0.2%
	District of Columbia	140,660,900,000	0.7%

Source: U.S. Department of Commerce, Bureau of Economic Analysis
"Gross Domestic Product Data" (https://apps.bea.gov/iTable/index_regional.cfm)
*G.D.P. is the market value of goods and services produced by the labor and property located in a state. It is the state counterpart to the nation's Gross Domestic Product. This was formerly known as Gross State Product (G.S.P.). The difference between the United States and sum-of-states reflects overseas activity, economic activity taking place outside the borders of the United States by the military and associated federal civilian support staff.

Percent Change in Gross Domestic Product: 2014 to 2018
(Adjusted to Constant 2012 Dollars)
National Percent Change = 10.2% Increase*

ALPHA ORDER

RANK	STATE	PERCENT CHANGE
29	Alabama	6.2
47	Alaska	(0.3)
9	Arizona	13.9
41	Arkansas	3.9
3	California	17.7
5	Colorado	15.3
42	Connecticut	3.0
48	Delaware	(1.2)
7	Florida	14.9
10	Georgia	13.6
15	Hawaii	10.9
8	Idaho	14.8
35	Illinois	4.7
33	Indiana	5.0
39	Iowa	4.2
21	Kansas	7.8
40	Kentucky	4.0
46	Louisiana	1.6
22	Maine	7.5
19	Maryland	8.9
13	Massachusetts	11.5
17	Michigan	9.0
20	Minnesota	8.0
44	Mississippi	2.7
37	Missouri	4.3
23	Montana	7.1
27	Nebraska	6.5
6	Nevada	15.2
17	New Hampshire	9.0
31	New Jersey	5.7
34	New Mexico	4.8
28	New York	6.4
16	North Carolina	9.3
50	North Dakota	(6.5)
30	Ohio	5.9
35	Oklahoma	4.7
2	Oregon	19.1
26	Pennsylvania	6.8
43	Rhode Island	2.9
11	South Carolina	12.9
32	South Dakota	5.3
14	Tennessee	11.0
12	Texas	12.5
4	Utah	16.7
37	Vermont	4.3
24	Virginia	7.0
1	Washington	20.2
45	West Virginia	2.3
25	Wisconsin	6.9
49	Wyoming	(1.8)

RANK ORDER

RANK	STATE	PERCENT CHANGE
1	Washington	20.2
2	Oregon	19.1
3	California	17.7
4	Utah	16.7
5	Colorado	15.3
6	Nevada	15.2
7	Florida	14.9
8	Idaho	14.8
9	Arizona	13.9
10	Georgia	13.6
11	South Carolina	12.9
12	Texas	12.5
13	Massachusetts	11.5
14	Tennessee	11.0
15	Hawaii	10.9
16	North Carolina	9.3
17	Michigan	9.0
17	New Hampshire	9.0
19	Maryland	8.9
20	Minnesota	8.0
21	Kansas	7.8
22	Maine	7.5
23	Montana	7.1
24	Virginia	7.0
25	Wisconsin	6.9
26	Pennsylvania	6.8
27	Nebraska	6.5
28	New York	6.4
29	Alabama	6.2
30	Ohio	5.9
31	New Jersey	5.7
32	South Dakota	5.3
33	Indiana	5.0
34	New Mexico	4.8
35	Illinois	4.7
35	Oklahoma	4.7
37	Missouri	4.3
37	Vermont	4.3
39	Iowa	4.2
40	Kentucky	4.0
41	Arkansas	3.9
42	Connecticut	3.0
43	Rhode Island	2.9
44	Mississippi	2.7
45	West Virginia	2.3
46	Louisiana	1.6
47	Alaska	(0.3)
48	Delaware	(1.2)
49	Wyoming	(1.8)
50	North Dakota	(6.5)

	District of Columbia	7.9

Source: CQ Press using data from U.S. Department of Commerce, Bureau of Economic Analysis
"Gross Domestic Product Data" (https://apps.bea.gov/iTable/index_regional.cfm)

*G.D.P. is the market value of goods and services produced by the labor and property located in a state. It is the state counterpart to the nation's Gross Domestic Product. This was formerly known as Gross State Product (G.S.P.). Adjusted for inflation using chained 2012 dollars.

Average Annual Change in Gross Domestic Product: 2014 to 2018
(Adjusted to Constant 2012 Dollars)
National Annual Percent Change = 2.0% Increase*

ALPHA ORDER

RANK	STATE	PERCENT CHANGE
28	Alabama	1.2
47	Alaska	(0.1)
9	Arizona	2.6
37	Arkansas	0.8
3	California	3.3
5	Colorado	2.9
42	Connecticut	0.6
48	Delaware	(0.2)
7	Florida	2.8
9	Georgia	2.6
14	Hawaii	2.1
7	Idaho	2.8
35	Illinois	0.9
32	Indiana	1.0
37	Iowa	0.8
20	Kansas	1.5
37	Kentucky	0.8
46	Louisiana	0.3
20	Maine	1.5
17	Maryland	1.7
13	Massachusetts	2.2
17	Michigan	1.7
20	Minnesota	1.5
44	Mississippi	0.5
37	Missouri	0.8
23	Montana	1.4
25	Nebraska	1.3
5	Nevada	2.9
17	New Hampshire	1.7
30	New Jersey	1.1
32	New Mexico	1.0
28	New York	1.2
16	North Carolina	1.8
50	North Dakota	(1.3)
30	Ohio	1.1
35	Oklahoma	0.9
2	Oregon	3.6
25	Pennsylvania	1.3
42	Rhode Island	0.6
11	South Carolina	2.5
32	South Dakota	1.0
14	Tennessee	2.1
12	Texas	2.4
4	Utah	3.1
37	Vermont	0.8
23	Virginia	1.4
1	Washington	3.7
44	West Virginia	0.5
25	Wisconsin	1.3
49	Wyoming	(0.4)

RANK ORDER

RANK	STATE	PERCENT CHANGE
1	Washington	3.7
2	Oregon	3.6
3	California	3.3
4	Utah	3.1
5	Colorado	2.9
5	Nevada	2.9
7	Florida	2.8
7	Idaho	2.8
9	Arizona	2.6
9	Georgia	2.6
11	South Carolina	2.5
12	Texas	2.4
13	Massachusetts	2.2
14	Hawaii	2.1
14	Tennessee	2.1
16	North Carolina	1.8
17	Maryland	1.7
17	Michigan	1.7
17	New Hampshire	1.7
20	Kansas	1.5
20	Maine	1.5
20	Minnesota	1.5
23	Montana	1.4
23	Virginia	1.4
25	Nebraska	1.3
25	Pennsylvania	1.3
25	Wisconsin	1.3
28	Alabama	1.2
28	New York	1.2
30	New Jersey	1.1
30	Ohio	1.1
32	Indiana	1.0
32	New Mexico	1.0
32	South Dakota	1.0
35	Illinois	0.9
35	Oklahoma	0.9
37	Arkansas	0.8
37	Iowa	0.8
37	Kentucky	0.8
37	Missouri	0.8
37	Vermont	0.8
42	Connecticut	0.6
42	Rhode Island	0.6
44	Mississippi	0.5
44	West Virginia	0.5
46	Louisiana	0.3
47	Alaska	(0.1)
48	Delaware	(0.2)
49	Wyoming	(0.4)
50	North Dakota	(1.3)

	District of Columbia	1.5

Source: CQ Press using data from U.S. Department of Commerce, Bureau of Economic Analysis
  "Gross Domestic Product Data" (https://apps.bea.gov/iTable/index_regional.cfm)
*G.D.P. is the market value of goods and services produced by the labor and property located in a state. It is the state counterpart to the nation's Gross Domestic Product. This was formerly known as Gross State Product (G.S.P.). Adjusted for inflation using chained 2012 dollars.

Per Capita Gross Domestic Product in 2018

National Per Capita = $62,997*

ALPHA ORDER				RANK ORDER		
RANK	STATE	PER CAPITA		RANK	STATE	PER CAPITA
46	Alabama	$45,366		1	New York	$85,450
7	Alaska	74,454		2	Massachusetts	82,743
40	Arizona	48,658		3	Connecticut	77,202
49	Arkansas	42,668		4	Delaware	76,109
5	California	75,966		5	California	75,966
15	Colorado	65,319		6	Washington	75,205
3	Connecticut	77,202		7	Alaska	74,454
4	Delaware	76,109		8	North Dakota	73,979
39	Florida	48,918		9	New Jersey	69,998
29	Georgia	56,336		10	Maryland	68,356
13	Hawaii	66,027		11	Illinois	68,011
47	Idaho	44,016		12	Wyoming	67,726
11	Illinois	68,011		13	Hawaii	66,027
32	Indiana	54,783		14	Minnesota	65,793
21	Iowa	60,249		15	Colorado	65,319
25	Kansas	57,814		16	Nebraska	64,384
44	Kentucky	46,644		17	Texas	62,962
31	Louisiana	55,216		18	Virginia	62,684
41	Maine	48,434		19	New Hampshire	62,406
10	Maryland	68,356		20	Pennsylvania	61,181
2	Massachusetts	82,743		21	Iowa	60,249
36	Michigan	52,794		22	South Dakota	59,195
14	Minnesota	65,793		23	Wisconsin	57,908
50	Mississippi	38,522		24	Ohio	57,887
37	Missouri	52,097		25	Kansas	57,814
43	Montana	47,448		26	Oregon	57,338
16	Nebraska	64,384		27	Rhode Island	57,251
30	Nevada	55,927		28	Utah	56,488
19	New Hampshire	62,406		29	Georgia	56,336
9	New Jersey	69,998		30	Nevada	55,927
42	New Mexico	47,926		31	Louisiana	55,216
1	New York	85,450		32	Indiana	54,783
33	North Carolina	54,297		33	North Carolina	54,297
8	North Dakota	73,979		34	Tennessee	53,769
24	Ohio	57,887		35	Vermont	53,265
38	Oklahoma	51,407		36	Michigan	52,794
26	Oregon	57,338		37	Missouri	52,097
20	Pennsylvania	61,181		38	Oklahoma	51,407
27	Rhode Island	57,251		39	Florida	48,918
45	South Carolina	46,012		40	Arizona	48,658
22	South Dakota	59,195		41	Maine	48,434
34	Tennessee	53,769		42	New Mexico	47,926
17	Texas	62,962		43	Montana	47,448
28	Utah	56,488		44	Kentucky	46,644
35	Vermont	53,265		45	South Carolina	46,012
18	Virginia	62,684		46	Alabama	45,366
6	Washington	75,205		47	Idaho	44,016
48	West Virginia	42,919		48	West Virginia	42,919
23	Wisconsin	57,908		49	Arkansas	42,668
12	Wyoming	67,726		50	Mississippi	38,522
					District of Columbia	200,501

Source: CQ Press using data from U.S. Department of Commerce, Bureau of Economic Analysis
"Gross Domestic Product Data" (https://apps.bea.gov/iTable/index_regional.cfm)
*G.D.P. is the market value of goods and services produced by the labor and property located in a state. It is the state counterpart to the nation's Gross Domestic Product. This was formerly known as Gross State Product (G.S.P.).

Percent Change in Per Capita Gross Domestic Product: 2014 to 2018
(Adjusted to Constant 2012 Dollars)
National Percent Change = 7.2% Increase*

ALPHA ORDER

RANK	STATE	PERCENT CHANGE
25	Alabama	5.2
47	Alaska	(0.5)
18	Arizona	6.9
44	Arkansas	2.3
1	California	14.9
7	Colorado	8.4
35	Connecticut	3.6
49	Delaware	(4.7)
14	Florida	7.1
6	Georgia	8.7
4	Hawaii	10.5
20	Idaho	6.8
22	Illinois	5.9
36	Indiana	3.4
42	Iowa	2.7
10	Kansas	7.4
41	Kentucky	2.8
46	Louisiana	1.2
18	Maine	6.9
10	Maryland	7.4
5	Massachusetts	9.3
9	Michigan	8.3
28	Minnesota	4.9
40	Mississippi	2.9
37	Missouri	3.1
38	Montana	3.0
34	Nebraska	3.8
16	Nevada	7.0
12	New Hampshire	7.2
25	New Jersey	5.2
30	New Mexico	4.6
16	New York	7.0
30	North Carolina	4.6
50	North Dakota	(9.3)
27	Ohio	5.1
38	Oklahoma	3.0
2	Oregon	12.6
21	Pennsylvania	6.7
42	Rhode Island	2.7
14	South Carolina	7.1
45	South Dakota	1.3
12	Tennessee	7.2
24	Texas	5.7
7	Utah	8.4
33	Vermont	4.1
32	Virginia	4.4
3	Washington	12.5
29	West Virginia	4.8
23	Wisconsin	5.8
48	Wyoming	(0.9)

RANK ORDER

RANK	STATE	PERCENT CHANGE
1	California	14.9
2	Oregon	12.6
3	Washington	12.5
4	Hawaii	10.5
5	Massachusetts	9.3
6	Georgia	8.7
7	Colorado	8.4
7	Utah	8.4
9	Michigan	8.3
10	Kansas	7.4
10	Maryland	7.4
12	New Hampshire	7.2
12	Tennessee	7.2
14	Florida	7.1
14	South Carolina	7.1
16	Nevada	7.0
16	New York	7.0
18	Arizona	6.9
18	Maine	6.9
20	Idaho	6.8
21	Pennsylvania	6.7
22	Illinois	5.9
23	Wisconsin	5.8
24	Texas	5.7
25	Alabama	5.2
25	New Jersey	5.2
27	Ohio	5.1
28	Minnesota	4.9
29	West Virginia	4.8
30	New Mexico	4.6
30	North Carolina	4.6
32	Virginia	4.4
33	Vermont	4.1
34	Nebraska	3.8
35	Connecticut	3.6
36	Indiana	3.4
37	Missouri	3.1
38	Montana	3.0
38	Oklahoma	3.0
40	Mississippi	2.9
41	Kentucky	2.8
42	Iowa	2.7
42	Rhode Island	2.7
44	Arkansas	2.3
45	South Dakota	1.3
46	Louisiana	1.2
47	Alaska	(0.5)
48	Wyoming	(0.9)
49	Delaware	(4.7)
50	North Dakota	(9.3)
	District of Columbia	1.8

Source: CQ Press using data from U.S. Department of Commerce, Bureau of Economic Analysis
"Gross Domestic Product Data" (https://apps.bea.gov/iTable/index_regional.cfm)
*G.D.P. is the market value of goods and services produced by the labor and property located in a state. It is the state counterpart to the nation's Gross Domestic Product. This was formerly known as Gross State Product (G.S.P.). Adjusted for inflation using chained 2012 dollars.

State Exports in 2018

National Total = $1,664,055,600,000*

ALPHA ORDER					RANK ORDER			
RANK	STATE	EXPORTS	% of USA		RANK	STATE	EXPORTS	% of USA
23	Alabama	$21,349,240,000	1.3%		1	Texas	$315,447,760,000	19.0%
40	Alaska	4,773,110,000	0.3%		2	California	178,404,770,000	10.7%
21	Arizona	22,388,340,000	1.3%		3	New York	81,487,260,000	4.9%
37	Arkansas	6,466,440,000	0.4%		4	Washington	77,700,210,000	4.7%
2	California	178,404,770,000	10.7%		5	Louisiana	66,236,860,000	4.0%
33	Colorado	8,317,250,000	0.5%		6	Illinois	65,415,150,000	3.9%
25	Connecticut	17,399,910,000	1.0%		7	Michigan	57,940,090,000	3.5%
41	Delaware	4,703,210,000	0.3%		8	Florida	57,240,940,000	3.4%
8	Florida	57,240,940,000	3.4%		9	Ohio	54,292,820,000	3.3%
11	Georgia	40,551,360,000	2.4%		10	Pennsylvania	41,049,630,000	2.5%
50	Hawaii	646,940,000	0.0%		11	Georgia	40,551,360,000	2.4%
42	Idaho	4,021,590,000	0.2%		12	Indiana	39,338,640,000	2.4%
6	Illinois	65,415,150,000	3.9%		13	New Jersey	35,662,510,000	2.1%
12	Indiana	39,338,640,000	2.4%		14	South Carolina	34,637,030,000	2.1%
28	Iowa	14,323,740,000	0.9%		15	North Carolina	32,729,770,000	2.0%
31	Kansas	11,603,590,000	0.7%		16	Tennessee	32,703,150,000	2.0%
17	Kentucky	31,757,170,000	1.9%		17	Kentucky	31,757,170,000	1.9%
5	Louisiana	66,236,860,000	4.0%		18	Massachusetts	27,139,830,000	1.6%
45	Maine	2,825,340,000	0.2%		19	Wisconsin	22,709,320,000	1.4%
29	Maryland	12,075,750,000	0.7%		20	Minnesota	22,684,570,000	1.4%
18	Massachusetts	27,139,830,000	1.6%		21	Arizona	22,388,340,000	1.3%
7	Michigan	57,940,090,000	3.5%		22	Oregon	22,292,680,000	1.3%
20	Minnesota	22,684,570,000	1.4%		23	Alabama	21,349,240,000	1.3%
30	Mississippi	11,808,270,000	0.7%		24	Virginia	18,357,710,000	1.1%
26	Missouri	14,499,770,000	0.9%		25	Connecticut	17,399,910,000	1.0%
47	Montana	1,653,540,000	0.1%		26	Missouri	14,499,770,000	0.9%
35	Nebraska	7,944,790,000	0.5%		27	Utah	14,373,260,000	0.9%
32	Nevada	11,084,530,000	0.7%		28	Iowa	14,323,740,000	0.9%
39	New Hampshire	5,285,590,000	0.3%		29	Maryland	12,075,750,000	0.7%
13	New Jersey	35,662,510,000	2.1%		30	Mississippi	11,808,270,000	0.7%
43	New Mexico	3,654,790,000	0.2%		31	Kansas	11,603,590,000	0.7%
3	New York	81,487,260,000	4.9%		32	Nevada	11,084,530,000	0.7%
15	North Carolina	32,729,770,000	2.0%		33	Colorado	8,317,250,000	0.5%
36	North Dakota	6,778,340,000	0.4%		34	West Virginia	8,124,170,000	0.5%
9	Ohio	54,292,820,000	3.3%		35	Nebraska	7,944,790,000	0.5%
38	Oklahoma	6,102,430,000	0.4%		36	North Dakota	6,778,340,000	0.4%
22	Oregon	22,292,680,000	1.3%		37	Arkansas	6,466,440,000	0.4%
10	Pennsylvania	41,049,630,000	2.5%		38	Oklahoma	6,102,430,000	0.4%
46	Rhode Island	2,399,760,000	0.1%		39	New Hampshire	5,285,590,000	0.3%
14	South Carolina	34,637,030,000	2.1%		40	Alaska	4,773,110,000	0.3%
48	South Dakota	1,437,230,000	0.1%		41	Delaware	4,703,210,000	0.3%
16	Tennessee	32,703,150,000	2.0%		42	Idaho	4,021,590,000	0.2%
1	Texas	315,447,760,000	19.0%		43	New Mexico	3,654,790,000	0.2%
27	Utah	14,373,260,000	0.9%		44	Vermont	2,919,610,000	0.2%
44	Vermont	2,919,610,000	0.2%		45	Maine	2,825,340,000	0.2%
24	Virginia	18,357,710,000	1.1%		46	Rhode Island	2,399,760,000	0.1%
4	Washington	77,700,210,000	4.7%		47	Montana	1,653,540,000	0.1%
34	West Virginia	8,124,170,000	0.5%		48	South Dakota	1,437,230,000	0.1%
19	Wisconsin	22,709,320,000	1.4%		49	Wyoming	1,356,050,000	0.1%
49	Wyoming	1,356,050,000	0.1%		50	Hawaii	646,940,000	0.0%
						District of Columbia	2,726,320,000	0.2%

Source: U.S. Bureau of the Census
"State Trade Data" (https://www.census.gov/foreign-trade/statistics/state/index.html)
*Based on the state from which the merchandise starts its journey to the port of export; that is, the data reflect the transportation origin of exports. Total includes exports from Puerto Rico, Virgin Islands, and exports with unidentified origin.

Per Capita State Exports in 2018

National Per Capita = $4,863*

ALPHA ORDER

RANK	STATE	PER CAPITA
21	Alabama	$4,368
7	Alaska	6,493
35	Arizona	3,128
42	Arkansas	2,149
19	California	4,521
49	Colorado	1,461
12	Connecticut	4,872
13	Delaware	4,871
36	Florida	2,694
31	Georgia	3,858
50	Hawaii	455
39	Idaho	2,297
11	Illinois	5,141
8	Indiana	5,875
18	Iowa	4,549
26	Kansas	3,986
5	Kentucky	7,119
1	Louisiana	14,215
43	Maine	2,110
44	Maryland	2,001
28	Massachusetts	3,943
9	Michigan	5,803
24	Minnesota	4,046
27	Mississippi	3,961
37	Missouri	2,369
47	Montana	1,559
23	Nebraska	4,126
32	Nevada	3,661
30	New Hampshire	3,905
25	New Jersey	4,013
45	New Mexico	1,746
22	New York	4,172
34	North Carolina	3,153
4	North Dakota	8,941
16	Ohio	4,650
48	Oklahoma	1,549
10	Oregon	5,331
33	Pennsylvania	3,207
40	Rhode Island	2,268
6	South Carolina	6,813
46	South Dakota	1,636
14	Tennessee	4,829
2	Texas	11,019
17	Utah	4,558
15	Vermont	4,676
41	Virginia	2,159
3	Washington	10,327
20	West Virginia	4,503
29	Wisconsin	3,910
38	Wyoming	2,348

RANK ORDER

RANK	STATE	PER CAPITA
1	Louisiana	$14,215
2	Texas	11,019
3	Washington	10,327
4	North Dakota	8,941
5	Kentucky	7,119
6	South Carolina	6,813
7	Alaska	6,493
8	Indiana	5,875
9	Michigan	5,803
10	Oregon	5,331
11	Illinois	5,141
12	Connecticut	4,872
13	Delaware	4,871
14	Tennessee	4,829
15	Vermont	4,676
16	Ohio	4,650
17	Utah	4,558
18	Iowa	4,549
19	California	4,521
20	West Virginia	4,503
21	Alabama	4,368
22	New York	4,172
23	Nebraska	4,126
24	Minnesota	4,046
25	New Jersey	4,013
26	Kansas	3,986
27	Mississippi	3,961
28	Massachusetts	3,943
29	Wisconsin	3,910
30	New Hampshire	3,905
31	Georgia	3,858
32	Nevada	3,661
33	Pennsylvania	3,207
34	North Carolina	3,153
35	Arizona	3,128
36	Florida	2,694
37	Missouri	2,369
38	Wyoming	2,348
39	Idaho	2,297
40	Rhode Island	2,268
41	Virginia	2,159
42	Arkansas	2,149
43	Maine	2,110
44	Maryland	2,001
45	New Mexico	1,746
46	South Dakota	1,636
47	Montana	1,559
48	Oklahoma	1,549
49	Colorado	1,461
50	Hawaii	455

| | District of Columbia | 3,886 |

Source: CQ Press using data from U.S. Bureau of the Census
  "State Trade Data" (https://www.census.gov/foreign-trade/statistics/state/index.html)
*Based on the state from which the merchandise starts its journey to the port of export; that is, the data reflect the transportation origin of exports. National figure does not include population or exports from Puerto Rico, Virgin Islands, and exports with unidentified origin.

State Imports in 2018

National Total = $2,542,733,260,000*

RANK	STATE	IMPORTS	% of USA
23	Alabama	$26,220,730,000	1.0%
48	Alaska	1,894,340,000	0.1%
24	Arizona	22,458,020,000	0.9%
34	Arkansas	11,523,540,000	0.5%
1	California	441,166,090,000	17.4%
30	Colorado	13,526,210,000	0.5%
27	Connecticut	19,874,430,000	0.8%
38	Delaware	8,890,050,000	0.3%
10	Florida	80,612,900,000	3.2%
7	Georgia	98,781,810,000	3.9%
41	Hawaii	4,526,000,000	0.2%
39	Idaho	6,880,540,000	0.3%
3	Illinois	157,402,430,000	6.2%
12	Indiana	61,751,990,000	2.4%
36	Iowa	10,695,360,000	0.4%
32	Kansas	12,326,490,000	0.5%
13	Kentucky	54,559,330,000	2.1%
17	Louisiana	40,007,740,000	1.6%
43	Maine	3,835,200,000	0.2%
19	Maryland	35,173,370,000	1.4%
18	Massachusetts	35,488,330,000	1.4%
4	Michigan	146,826,970,000	5.8%
20	Minnesota	32,807,490,000	1.3%
28	Mississippi	16,676,880,000	0.7%
25	Missouri	20,651,950,000	0.8%
40	Montana	4,699,270,000	0.2%
42	Nebraska	4,467,170,000	0.2%
33	Nevada	11,799,060,000	0.5%
31	New Hampshire	12,495,930,000	0.5%
6	New Jersey	127,991,960,000	5.0%
47	New Mexico	2,606,270,000	0.1%
5	New York	137,133,360,000	5.4%
15	North Carolina	53,429,740,000	2.1%
46	North Dakota	3,387,450,000	0.1%
11	Ohio	70,211,440,000	2.8%
35	Oklahoma	11,278,110,000	0.4%
26	Oregon	20,070,950,000	0.8%
8	Pennsylvania	88,575,840,000	3.5%
37	Rhode Island	10,525,290,000	0.4%
16	South Carolina	40,212,930,000	1.6%
49	South Dakota	1,114,810,000	0.0%
9	Tennessee	86,183,500,000	3.4%
2	Texas	304,623,270,000	12.0%
29	Utah	15,142,300,000	0.6%
45	Vermont	3,424,370,000	0.1%
22	Virginia	29,465,430,000	1.2%
14	Washington	54,394,860,000	2.1%
44	West Virginia	3,435,230,000	0.1%
21	Wisconsin	30,992,410,000	1.2%
50	Wyoming	1,085,490,000	0.0%

RANK	STATE	IMPORTS	% of USA
1	California	$441,166,090,000	17.4%
2	Texas	304,623,270,000	12.0%
3	Illinois	157,402,430,000	6.2%
4	Michigan	146,826,970,000	5.8%
5	New York	137,133,360,000	5.4%
6	New Jersey	127,991,960,000	5.0%
7	Georgia	98,781,810,000	3.9%
8	Pennsylvania	88,575,840,000	3.5%
9	Tennessee	86,183,500,000	3.4%
10	Florida	80,612,900,000	3.2%
11	Ohio	70,211,440,000	2.8%
12	Indiana	61,751,990,000	2.4%
13	Kentucky	54,559,330,000	2.1%
14	Washington	54,394,860,000	2.1%
15	North Carolina	53,429,740,000	2.1%
16	South Carolina	40,212,930,000	1.6%
17	Louisiana	40,007,740,000	1.6%
18	Massachusetts	35,488,330,000	1.4%
19	Maryland	35,173,370,000	1.4%
20	Minnesota	32,807,490,000	1.3%
21	Wisconsin	30,992,410,000	1.2%
22	Virginia	29,465,430,000	1.2%
23	Alabama	26,220,730,000	1.0%
24	Arizona	22,458,020,000	0.9%
25	Missouri	20,651,950,000	0.8%
26	Oregon	20,070,950,000	0.8%
27	Connecticut	19,874,430,000	0.8%
28	Mississippi	16,676,880,000	0.7%
29	Utah	15,142,300,000	0.6%
30	Colorado	13,526,210,000	0.5%
31	New Hampshire	12,495,930,000	0.5%
32	Kansas	12,326,490,000	0.5%
33	Nevada	11,799,060,000	0.5%
34	Arkansas	11,523,540,000	0.5%
35	Oklahoma	11,278,110,000	0.4%
36	Iowa	10,695,360,000	0.4%
37	Rhode Island	10,525,290,000	0.4%
38	Delaware	8,890,050,000	0.3%
39	Idaho	6,880,540,000	0.3%
40	Montana	4,699,270,000	0.2%
41	Hawaii	4,526,000,000	0.2%
42	Nebraska	4,467,170,000	0.2%
43	Maine	3,835,200,000	0.2%
44	West Virginia	3,435,230,000	0.1%
45	Vermont	3,424,370,000	0.1%
46	North Dakota	3,387,450,000	0.1%
47	New Mexico	2,606,270,000	0.1%
48	Alaska	1,894,340,000	0.1%
49	South Dakota	1,114,810,000	0.0%
50	Wyoming	1,085,490,000	0.0%
	District of Columbia	762,240,000	0.0%

Source: U.S. Bureau of the Census
   "State Trade Data" (https://www.census.gov/foreign-trade/statistics/state/index.html)
*Based on where the merchandise is destined, as known at the time of entry summary filing. If the contents of the shipment are destined to more than one state, territory, or possession, or if the entry summary represents a consolidated shipment, the state of destination is that with the greatest aggregate value.

Per Capita State Imports in 2018

National Per Capita = $7,634*

<table>
<tr><td colspan="3">ALPHA ORDER</td><td colspan="3">RANK ORDER</td></tr>
<tr><th>RANK</th><th>STATE</th><th>PER CAPITA</th><th>RANK</th><th>STATE</th><th>PER CAPITA</th></tr>
<tr><td>24</td><td>Alabama</td><td>$5,365</td><td>1</td><td>Michigan</td><td>$14,706</td></tr>
<tr><td>44</td><td>Alaska</td><td>2,577</td><td>2</td><td>New Jersey</td><td>14,404</td></tr>
<tr><td>41</td><td>Arizona</td><td>3,137</td><td>3</td><td>Tennessee</td><td>12,727</td></tr>
<tr><td>35</td><td>Arkansas</td><td>3,829</td><td>4</td><td>Illinois</td><td>12,371</td></tr>
<tr><td>6</td><td>California</td><td>11,180</td><td>5</td><td>Kentucky</td><td>12,230</td></tr>
<tr><td>45</td><td>Colorado</td><td>2,377</td><td>6</td><td>California</td><td>11,180</td></tr>
<tr><td>22</td><td>Connecticut</td><td>5,565</td><td>7</td><td>Texas</td><td>10,640</td></tr>
<tr><td>12</td><td>Delaware</td><td>9,208</td><td>8</td><td>Rhode Island</td><td>9,946</td></tr>
<tr><td>36</td><td>Florida</td><td>3,795</td><td>9</td><td>Georgia</td><td>9,398</td></tr>
<tr><td>9</td><td>Georgia</td><td>9,398</td><td>10</td><td>New Hampshire</td><td>9,233</td></tr>
<tr><td>40</td><td>Hawaii</td><td>3,186</td><td>11</td><td>Indiana</td><td>9,223</td></tr>
<tr><td>33</td><td>Idaho</td><td>3,931</td><td>12</td><td>Delaware</td><td>9,208</td></tr>
<tr><td>4</td><td>Illinois</td><td>12,371</td><td>13</td><td>Louisiana</td><td>8,586</td></tr>
<tr><td>11</td><td>Indiana</td><td>9,223</td><td>14</td><td>South Carolina</td><td>7,909</td></tr>
<tr><td>38</td><td>Iowa</td><td>3,397</td><td>15</td><td>Washington</td><td>7,230</td></tr>
<tr><td>32</td><td>Kansas</td><td>4,234</td><td>16</td><td>New York</td><td>7,022</td></tr>
<tr><td>5</td><td>Kentucky</td><td>12,230</td><td>17</td><td>Pennsylvania</td><td>6,919</td></tr>
<tr><td>13</td><td>Louisiana</td><td>8,586</td><td>18</td><td>Ohio</td><td>6,013</td></tr>
<tr><td>42</td><td>Maine</td><td>2,864</td><td>19</td><td>Minnesota</td><td>5,852</td></tr>
<tr><td>20</td><td>Maryland</td><td>5,827</td><td>20</td><td>Maryland</td><td>5,827</td></tr>
<tr><td>26</td><td>Massachusetts</td><td>5,156</td><td>21</td><td>Mississippi</td><td>5,594</td></tr>
<tr><td>1</td><td>Michigan</td><td>14,706</td><td>22</td><td>Connecticut</td><td>5,565</td></tr>
<tr><td>19</td><td>Minnesota</td><td>5,852</td><td>23</td><td>Vermont</td><td>5,485</td></tr>
<tr><td>21</td><td>Mississippi</td><td>5,594</td><td>24</td><td>Alabama</td><td>5,365</td></tr>
<tr><td>39</td><td>Missouri</td><td>3,374</td><td>25</td><td>Wisconsin</td><td>5,337</td></tr>
<tr><td>31</td><td>Montana</td><td>4,430</td><td>26</td><td>Massachusetts</td><td>5,156</td></tr>
<tr><td>46</td><td>Nebraska</td><td>2,320</td><td>27</td><td>North Carolina</td><td>5,147</td></tr>
<tr><td>34</td><td>Nevada</td><td>3,897</td><td>28</td><td>Utah</td><td>4,802</td></tr>
<tr><td>10</td><td>New Hampshire</td><td>9,233</td><td>29</td><td>Oregon</td><td>4,799</td></tr>
<tr><td>2</td><td>New Jersey</td><td>14,404</td><td>30</td><td>North Dakota</td><td>4,468</td></tr>
<tr><td>50</td><td>New Mexico</td><td>1,245</td><td>31</td><td>Montana</td><td>4,430</td></tr>
<tr><td>16</td><td>New York</td><td>7,022</td><td>32</td><td>Kansas</td><td>4,234</td></tr>
<tr><td>27</td><td>North Carolina</td><td>5,147</td><td>33</td><td>Idaho</td><td>3,931</td></tr>
<tr><td>30</td><td>North Dakota</td><td>4,468</td><td>34</td><td>Nevada</td><td>3,897</td></tr>
<tr><td>18</td><td>Ohio</td><td>6,013</td><td>35</td><td>Arkansas</td><td>3,829</td></tr>
<tr><td>43</td><td>Oklahoma</td><td>2,862</td><td>36</td><td>Florida</td><td>3,795</td></tr>
<tr><td>29</td><td>Oregon</td><td>4,799</td><td>37</td><td>Virginia</td><td>3,466</td></tr>
<tr><td>17</td><td>Pennsylvania</td><td>6,919</td><td>38</td><td>Iowa</td><td>3,397</td></tr>
<tr><td>8</td><td>Rhode Island</td><td>9,946</td><td>39</td><td>Missouri</td><td>3,374</td></tr>
<tr><td>14</td><td>South Carolina</td><td>7,909</td><td>40</td><td>Hawaii</td><td>3,186</td></tr>
<tr><td>49</td><td>South Dakota</td><td>1,269</td><td>41</td><td>Arizona</td><td>3,137</td></tr>
<tr><td>3</td><td>Tennessee</td><td>12,727</td><td>42</td><td>Maine</td><td>2,864</td></tr>
<tr><td>7</td><td>Texas</td><td>10,640</td><td>43</td><td>Oklahoma</td><td>2,862</td></tr>
<tr><td>28</td><td>Utah</td><td>4,802</td><td>44</td><td>Alaska</td><td>2,577</td></tr>
<tr><td>23</td><td>Vermont</td><td>5,485</td><td>45</td><td>Colorado</td><td>2,377</td></tr>
<tr><td>37</td><td>Virginia</td><td>3,466</td><td>46</td><td>Nebraska</td><td>2,320</td></tr>
<tr><td>15</td><td>Washington</td><td>7,230</td><td>47</td><td>West Virginia</td><td>1,904</td></tr>
<tr><td>47</td><td>West Virginia</td><td>1,904</td><td>48</td><td>Wyoming</td><td>1,879</td></tr>
<tr><td>25</td><td>Wisconsin</td><td>5,337</td><td>49</td><td>South Dakota</td><td>1,269</td></tr>
<tr><td>48</td><td>Wyoming</td><td>1,879</td><td>50</td><td>New Mexico</td><td>1,245</td></tr>
<tr><td></td><td></td><td></td><td></td><td>District of Columbia</td><td>1,087</td></tr>
</table>

Source: CQ Press using data from U.S. Bureau of the Census
   "State Trade Data" (https://www.census.gov/foreign-trade/statistics/state/index.html)
*Based on where the merchandise is destined, as known at the time of entry summary filing. If the contents of the shipment are destined to more than one state, territory, or possession, or if the entry summary represents a consolidated shipment, the state of destination is that with the greatest aggregate value. National figure does not include population or imports from Puerto Rico, Virgin Islands, and imports with unidentified origin.

Personal Income in 2018

National Total = $17,813,035,000,000*

RANK	STATE	INCOME	% of USA
27	Alabama	$206,455,000,000	1.2%
47	Alaska	43,818,200,000	0.2%
18	Arizona	317,912,900,000	1.8%
34	Arkansas	130,296,700,000	0.7%
1	California	2,514,129,300,000	14.1%
16	Colorado	332,942,600,000	1.9%
23	Connecticut	273,152,400,000	1.5%
44	Delaware	50,783,100,000	0.3%
4	Florida	1,066,446,900,000	6.0%
11	Georgia	488,964,100,000	2.7%
39	Hawaii	78,721,100,000	0.4%
40	Idaho	77,012,300,000	0.4%
5	Illinois	724,189,100,000	4.1%
20	Indiana	315,516,000,000	1.8%
30	Iowa	158,197,200,000	0.9%
31	Kansas	149,859,100,000	0.8%
28	Kentucky	189,717,400,000	1.1%
25	Louisiana	215,488,700,000	1.2%
42	Maine	65,454,100,000	0.4%
15	Maryland	382,828,900,000	2.1%
9	Massachusetts	494,764,600,000	2.8%
12	Michigan	484,029,800,000	2.7%
17	Minnesota	322,727,600,000	1.8%
35	Mississippi	112,991,700,000	0.6%
22	Missouri	292,512,800,000	1.6%
45	Montana	50,499,700,000	0.3%
36	Nebraska	102,759,300,000	0.6%
32	Nevada	149,218,600,000	0.8%
38	New Hampshire	83,142,600,000	0.5%
7	New Jersey	607,884,500,000	3.4%
37	New Mexico	87,188,800,000	0.5%
3	New York	1,341,932,000,000	7.5%
13	North Carolina	478,861,600,000	2.7%
48	North Dakota	42,147,700,000	0.2%
8	Ohio	569,726,700,000	3.2%
29	Oklahoma	182,301,900,000	1.0%
26	Oregon	213,070,100,000	1.2%
6	Pennsylvania	720,073,400,000	4.0%
43	Rhode Island	57,993,800,000	0.3%
24	South Carolina	222,188,800,000	1.2%
46	South Dakota	46,066,400,000	0.3%
19	Tennessee	317,514,900,000	1.8%
2	Texas	1,445,270,400,000	8.1%
33	Utah	146,422,500,000	0.8%
50	Vermont	33,928,600,000	0.2%
10	Virginia	492,312,700,000	2.8%
14	Washington	467,399,000,000	2.6%
41	West Virginia	73,808,900,000	0.4%
21	Wisconsin	299,932,700,000	1.7%
49	Wyoming	34,872,700,000	0.2%

RANK	STATE	INCOME	% of USA
1	California	$2,514,129,300,000	14.1%
2	Texas	1,445,270,400,000	8.1%
3	New York	1,341,932,000,000	7.5%
4	Florida	1,066,446,900,000	6.0%
5	Illinois	724,189,100,000	4.1%
6	Pennsylvania	720,073,400,000	4.0%
7	New Jersey	607,884,500,000	3.4%
8	Ohio	569,726,700,000	3.2%
9	Massachusetts	494,764,600,000	2.8%
10	Virginia	492,312,700,000	2.8%
11	Georgia	488,964,100,000	2.7%
12	Michigan	484,029,800,000	2.7%
13	North Carolina	478,861,600,000	2.7%
14	Washington	467,399,000,000	2.6%
15	Maryland	382,828,900,000	2.1%
16	Colorado	332,942,600,000	1.9%
17	Minnesota	322,727,600,000	1.8%
18	Arizona	317,912,900,000	1.8%
19	Tennessee	317,514,900,000	1.8%
20	Indiana	315,516,000,000	1.8%
21	Wisconsin	299,932,700,000	1.7%
22	Missouri	292,512,800,000	1.6%
23	Connecticut	273,152,400,000	1.5%
24	South Carolina	222,188,800,000	1.2%
25	Louisiana	215,488,700,000	1.2%
26	Oregon	213,070,100,000	1.2%
27	Alabama	206,455,000,000	1.2%
28	Kentucky	189,717,400,000	1.1%
29	Oklahoma	182,301,900,000	1.0%
30	Iowa	158,197,200,000	0.9%
31	Kansas	149,859,100,000	0.8%
32	Nevada	149,218,600,000	0.8%
33	Utah	146,422,500,000	0.8%
34	Arkansas	130,296,700,000	0.7%
35	Mississippi	112,991,700,000	0.6%
36	Nebraska	102,759,300,000	0.6%
37	New Mexico	87,188,800,000	0.5%
38	New Hampshire	83,142,600,000	0.5%
39	Hawaii	78,721,100,000	0.4%
40	Idaho	77,012,300,000	0.4%
41	West Virginia	73,808,900,000	0.4%
42	Maine	65,454,100,000	0.4%
43	Rhode Island	57,993,800,000	0.3%
44	Delaware	50,783,100,000	0.3%
45	Montana	50,499,700,000	0.3%
46	South Dakota	46,066,400,000	0.3%
47	Alaska	43,818,200,000	0.2%
48	North Dakota	42,147,700,000	0.2%
49	Wyoming	34,872,700,000	0.2%
50	Vermont	33,928,600,000	0.2%
	District of Columbia	57,604,800,000	0.3%

Source: U.S. Department of Commerce, Bureau of Economic Analysis
"Annual State Personal Income" (https://apps.bea.gov/iTable/index_regional.cfm)
*The national total shown here is the sum of the state estimates. It differs from the national income and product accounts (NIPA) estimate of personal income because it omits the earnings of federal civilian and military personnel stationed abroad and of U.S. residents employed abroad temporarily by private U.S. firms.

Percent Change in Personal Income: 2017 to 2018

National Percent Change = 5.6% Increase*

ALPHA ORDER				RANK ORDER		
RANK	STATE	PERCENT CHANGE		RANK	STATE	PERCENT CHANGE
43	Alabama	4.6		1	Washington	7.5
46	Alaska	4.3		2	Utah	7.2
12	Arizona	6.1		3	Colorado	7.1
44	Arkansas	4.5		4	Nevada	7.0
12	California	6.1		5	Wyoming	6.8
3	Colorado	7.1		6	South Dakota	6.5
17	Connecticut	5.8		6	Texas	6.5
24	Delaware	5.4		8	Idaho	6.4
9	Florida	6.2		9	Florida	6.2
24	Georgia	5.4		9	Oklahoma	6.2
48	Hawaii	4.0		9	Oregon	6.2
8	Idaho	6.4		12	Arizona	6.1
35	Illinois	5.0		12	California	6.1
39	Indiana	4.8		14	Iowa	6.0
14	Iowa	6.0		14	North Dakota	6.0
24	Kansas	5.4		16	Pennsylvania	5.9
49	Kentucky	3.9		17	Connecticut	5.8
35	Louisiana	5.0		17	Montana	5.8
28	Maine	5.3		17	Nebraska	5.8
35	Maryland	5.0		20	Massachusetts	5.7
20	Massachusetts	5.7		21	Minnesota	5.5
38	Michigan	4.9		21	New Hampshire	5.5
21	Minnesota	5.5		21	North Carolina	5.5
49	Mississippi	3.9		24	Delaware	5.4
41	Missouri	4.7		24	Georgia	5.4
17	Montana	5.8		24	Kansas	5.4
17	Nebraska	5.8		24	New Mexico	5.4
4	Nevada	7.0		28	Maine	5.3
21	New Hampshire	5.5		28	New Jersey	5.3
28	New Jersey	5.3		28	Tennessee	5.3
24	New Mexico	5.4		31	South Carolina	5.2
46	New York	4.3		31	Virginia	5.2
21	North Carolina	5.5		33	West Virginia	5.1
14	North Dakota	6.0		33	Wisconsin	5.1
41	Ohio	4.7		35	Illinois	5.0
9	Oklahoma	6.2		35	Louisiana	5.0
9	Oregon	6.2		35	Maryland	5.0
16	Pennsylvania	5.9		38	Michigan	4.9
39	Rhode Island	4.8		39	Indiana	4.8
31	South Carolina	5.2		39	Rhode Island	4.8
6	South Dakota	6.5		41	Missouri	4.7
28	Tennessee	5.3		41	Ohio	4.7
6	Texas	6.5		43	Alabama	4.6
2	Utah	7.2		44	Arkansas	4.5
44	Vermont	4.5		44	Vermont	4.5
31	Virginia	5.2		46	Alaska	4.3
1	Washington	7.5		46	New York	4.3
33	West Virginia	5.1		48	Hawaii	4.0
33	Wisconsin	5.1		49	Kentucky	3.9
5	Wyoming	6.8		49	Mississippi	3.9
					District of Columbia	4.9

Source: U.S. Department of Commerce, Bureau of Economic Analysis
"Annual State Personal Income" (https://apps.bea.gov/iTable/index_regional.cfm)
*Based on revised 2017 figures.

Per Capita Personal Income in 2018

National Per Capita = $54,446*

<table>
<tr><td colspan="3">ALPHA ORDER</td><td colspan="3">RANK ORDER</td></tr>
<tr><td>RANK</td><td>STATE</td><td>PER CAPITA</td><td>RANK</td><td>STATE</td><td>PER CAPITA</td></tr>
<tr><td>47</td><td>Alabama</td><td>$42,238</td><td>1</td><td>Connecticut</td><td>$76,456</td></tr>
<tr><td>10</td><td>Alaska</td><td>59,420</td><td>2</td><td>Massachusetts</td><td>71,683</td></tr>
<tr><td>42</td><td>Arizona</td><td>44,329</td><td>3</td><td>New York</td><td>68,668</td></tr>
<tr><td>45</td><td>Arkansas</td><td>43,233</td><td>4</td><td>New Jersey</td><td>68,236</td></tr>
<tr><td>5</td><td>California</td><td>63,557</td><td>5</td><td>California</td><td>63,557</td></tr>
<tr><td>11</td><td>Colorado</td><td>58,456</td><td>6</td><td>Maryland</td><td>63,354</td></tr>
<tr><td>1</td><td>Connecticut</td><td>76,456</td><td>7</td><td>Washington</td><td>62,026</td></tr>
<tr><td>21</td><td>Delaware</td><td>52,507</td><td>8</td><td>New Hampshire</td><td>61,294</td></tr>
<tr><td>28</td><td>Florida</td><td>50,070</td><td>9</td><td>Wyoming</td><td>60,361</td></tr>
<tr><td>37</td><td>Georgia</td><td>46,482</td><td>10</td><td>Alaska</td><td>59,420</td></tr>
<tr><td>17</td><td>Hawaii</td><td>55,418</td><td>11</td><td>Colorado</td><td>58,456</td></tr>
<tr><td>43</td><td>Idaho</td><td>43,901</td><td>12</td><td>Virginia</td><td>57,799</td></tr>
<tr><td>14</td><td>Illinois</td><td>56,839</td><td>13</td><td>Minnesota</td><td>57,515</td></tr>
<tr><td>35</td><td>Indiana</td><td>47,149</td><td>14</td><td>Illinois</td><td>56,839</td></tr>
<tr><td>27</td><td>Iowa</td><td>50,124</td><td>15</td><td>Pennsylvania</td><td>56,225</td></tr>
<tr><td>24</td><td>Kansas</td><td>51,471</td><td>16</td><td>North Dakota</td><td>55,452</td></tr>
<tr><td>46</td><td>Kentucky</td><td>42,458</td><td>17</td><td>Hawaii</td><td>55,418</td></tr>
<tr><td>39</td><td>Louisiana</td><td>46,242</td><td>18</td><td>Rhode Island</td><td>54,850</td></tr>
<tr><td>30</td><td>Maine</td><td>48,905</td><td>19</td><td>Vermont</td><td>54,173</td></tr>
<tr><td>6</td><td>Maryland</td><td>63,354</td><td>20</td><td>Nebraska</td><td>53,263</td></tr>
<tr><td>2</td><td>Massachusetts</td><td>71,683</td><td>21</td><td>Delaware</td><td>52,507</td></tr>
<tr><td>32</td><td>Michigan</td><td>48,423</td><td>22</td><td>South Dakota</td><td>52,216</td></tr>
<tr><td>13</td><td>Minnesota</td><td>57,515</td><td>23</td><td>Wisconsin</td><td>51,592</td></tr>
<tr><td>50</td><td>Mississippi</td><td>37,834</td><td>24</td><td>Kansas</td><td>51,471</td></tr>
<tr><td>33</td><td>Missouri</td><td>47,746</td><td>25</td><td>Oregon</td><td>50,843</td></tr>
<tr><td>34</td><td>Montana</td><td>47,538</td><td>26</td><td>Texas</td><td>50,355</td></tr>
<tr><td>20</td><td>Nebraska</td><td>53,263</td><td>27</td><td>Iowa</td><td>50,124</td></tr>
<tr><td>29</td><td>Nevada</td><td>49,176</td><td>28</td><td>Florida</td><td>50,070</td></tr>
<tr><td>8</td><td>New Hampshire</td><td>61,294</td><td>29</td><td>Nevada</td><td>49,176</td></tr>
<tr><td>4</td><td>New Jersey</td><td>68,236</td><td>30</td><td>Maine</td><td>48,905</td></tr>
<tr><td>48</td><td>New Mexico</td><td>41,609</td><td>31</td><td>Ohio</td><td>48,739</td></tr>
<tr><td>3</td><td>New York</td><td>68,668</td><td>32</td><td>Michigan</td><td>48,423</td></tr>
<tr><td>41</td><td>North Carolina</td><td>46,117</td><td>33</td><td>Missouri</td><td>47,746</td></tr>
<tr><td>16</td><td>North Dakota</td><td>55,452</td><td>34</td><td>Montana</td><td>47,538</td></tr>
<tr><td>31</td><td>Ohio</td><td>48,739</td><td>35</td><td>Indiana</td><td>47,149</td></tr>
<tr><td>40</td><td>Oklahoma</td><td>46,233</td><td>36</td><td>Tennessee</td><td>46,900</td></tr>
<tr><td>25</td><td>Oregon</td><td>50,843</td><td>37</td><td>Georgia</td><td>46,482</td></tr>
<tr><td>15</td><td>Pennsylvania</td><td>56,225</td><td>38</td><td>Utah</td><td>46,320</td></tr>
<tr><td>18</td><td>Rhode Island</td><td>54,850</td><td>39</td><td>Louisiana</td><td>46,242</td></tr>
<tr><td>44</td><td>South Carolina</td><td>43,702</td><td>40</td><td>Oklahoma</td><td>46,233</td></tr>
<tr><td>22</td><td>South Dakota</td><td>52,216</td><td>41</td><td>North Carolina</td><td>46,117</td></tr>
<tr><td>36</td><td>Tennessee</td><td>46,900</td><td>42</td><td>Arizona</td><td>44,329</td></tr>
<tr><td>26</td><td>Texas</td><td>50,355</td><td>43</td><td>Idaho</td><td>43,901</td></tr>
<tr><td>38</td><td>Utah</td><td>46,320</td><td>44</td><td>South Carolina</td><td>43,702</td></tr>
<tr><td>19</td><td>Vermont</td><td>54,173</td><td>45</td><td>Arkansas</td><td>43,233</td></tr>
<tr><td>12</td><td>Virginia</td><td>57,799</td><td>46</td><td>Kentucky</td><td>42,458</td></tr>
<tr><td>7</td><td>Washington</td><td>62,026</td><td>47</td><td>Alabama</td><td>42,238</td></tr>
<tr><td>49</td><td>West Virginia</td><td>40,873</td><td>48</td><td>New Mexico</td><td>41,609</td></tr>
<tr><td>23</td><td>Wisconsin</td><td>51,592</td><td>49</td><td>West Virginia</td><td>40,873</td></tr>
<tr><td>9</td><td>Wyoming</td><td>60,361</td><td>50</td><td>Mississippi</td><td>37,834</td></tr>
<tr><td></td><td></td><td></td><td></td><td>District of Columbia</td><td>82,005</td></tr>
</table>

Source: U.S. Department of Commerce, Bureau of Economic Analysis
   "Annual State Personal Income" (https://apps.bea.gov/iTable/index_regional.cfm)
*The national figure is based on the sum of the state estimates. It differs from the national income and product accounts
(NIPA) estimate of personal income because it omits the earnings of federal civilian and military personnel stationed abroad and
of U.S. residents employed abroad temporarily by private U.S. firms.

Percent Change in Per Capita Personal Income: 2017 to 2018

National Percent Change = 4.9% Increase*

RANK	STATE	PERCENT CHANGE
36	Alabama	4.4
31	Alaska	4.6
40	Arizona	4.3
47	Arkansas	4.1
7	California	5.7
8	Colorado	5.6
3	Connecticut	5.9
40	Delaware	4.3
31	Florida	4.6
36	Georgia	4.4
40	Hawaii	4.3
40	Idaho	4.3
10	Illinois	5.4
40	Indiana	4.3
8	Iowa	5.6
12	Kansas	5.3
50	Kentucky	3.6
16	Louisiana	5.2
22	Maine	5.0
26	Maryland	4.7
17	Massachusetts	5.1
26	Michigan	4.7
26	Minnesota	4.7
48	Mississippi	4.0
36	Missouri	4.4
24	Montana	4.9
17	Nebraska	5.1
25	Nevada	4.8
22	New Hampshire	5.0
17	New Jersey	5.1
12	New Mexico	5.3
31	New York	4.6
36	North Carolina	4.4
12	North Dakota	5.3
34	Ohio	4.5
2	Oklahoma	6.0
17	Oregon	5.1
5	Pennsylvania	5.8
26	Rhode Island	4.7
49	South Carolina	3.9
10	South Dakota	5.4
40	Tennessee	4.3
17	Texas	5.1
12	Utah	5.3
46	Vermont	4.2
34	Virginia	4.5
3	Washington	5.9
5	West Virginia	5.8
26	Wisconsin	4.7
1	Wyoming	7.1

RANK	STATE	PERCENT CHANGE
1	Wyoming	7.1
2	Oklahoma	6.0
3	Connecticut	5.9
3	Washington	5.9
5	Pennsylvania	5.8
5	West Virginia	5.8
7	California	5.7
8	Colorado	5.6
8	Iowa	5.6
10	Illinois	5.4
10	South Dakota	5.4
12	Kansas	5.3
12	New Mexico	5.3
12	North Dakota	5.3
12	Utah	5.3
16	Louisiana	5.2
17	Massachusetts	5.1
17	Nebraska	5.1
17	New Jersey	5.1
17	Oregon	5.1
17	Texas	5.1
22	Maine	5.0
22	New Hampshire	5.0
24	Montana	4.9
25	Nevada	4.8
26	Maryland	4.7
26	Michigan	4.7
26	Minnesota	4.7
26	Rhode Island	4.7
26	Wisconsin	4.7
31	Alaska	4.6
31	Florida	4.6
31	New York	4.6
34	Ohio	4.5
34	Virginia	4.5
36	Alabama	4.4
36	Georgia	4.4
36	Missouri	4.4
36	North Carolina	4.4
40	Arizona	4.3
40	Delaware	4.3
40	Hawaii	4.3
40	Idaho	4.3
40	Indiana	4.3
40	Tennessee	4.3
46	Vermont	4.2
47	Arkansas	4.1
48	Mississippi	4.0
49	South Carolina	3.9
50	Kentucky	3.6
	District of Columbia	3.8

Source: U.S. Department of Commerce, Bureau of Economic Analysis
    "Annual State Personal Income" (https://apps.bea.gov/iTable/index_regional.cfm)
*Based on revised 2017 figures.

Disposable Personal Income in 2018

National Total = $15,737,171,000,000*

ALPHA ORDER

RANK	STATE	INCOME	% of USA
26	Alabama	$186,791,100,000	1.2%
47	Alaska	40,139,000,000	0.3%
18	Arizona	286,540,400,000	1.8%
34	Arkansas	118,053,800,000	0.8%
1	California	2,167,721,000,000	13.8%
16	Colorado	292,780,100,000	1.9%
23	Connecticut	232,448,200,000	1.5%
45	Delaware	44,882,600,000	0.3%
4	Florida	964,278,500,000	6.1%
9	Georgia	437,374,200,000	2.8%
39	Hawaii	70,295,500,000	0.4%
40	Idaho	69,444,100,000	0.4%
6	Illinois	635,650,900,000	4.0%
19	Indiana	283,623,000,000	1.8%
30	Iowa	141,917,000,000	0.9%
31	Kansas	134,096,100,000	0.9%
28	Kentucky	170,135,900,000	1.1%
25	Louisiana	195,977,600,000	1.2%
42	Maine	58,767,600,000	0.4%
15	Maryland	333,124,800,000	2.1%
13	Massachusetts	422,043,200,000	2.7%
11	Michigan	429,619,300,000	2.7%
20	Minnesota	280,007,000,000	1.8%
35	Mississippi	103,789,200,000	0.7%
22	Missouri	261,274,900,000	1.7%
44	Montana	45,282,800,000	0.3%
36	Nebraska	92,471,800,000	0.6%
32	Nevada	133,652,200,000	0.8%
38	New Hampshire	74,592,800,000	0.5%
7	New Jersey	527,205,000,000	3.4%
37	New Mexico	79,769,600,000	0.5%
3	New York	1,133,548,500,000	7.2%
12	North Carolina	426,240,000,000	2.7%
48	North Dakota	38,032,100,000	0.2%
8	Ohio	509,416,300,000	3.2%
29	Oklahoma	165,639,200,000	1.1%
27	Oregon	186,053,500,000	1.2%
5	Pennsylvania	638,680,600,000	4.1%
43	Rhode Island	51,535,400,000	0.3%
24	South Carolina	200,319,300,000	1.3%
46	South Dakota	42,131,100,000	0.3%
17	Tennessee	290,582,000,000	1.8%
2	Texas	1,317,528,300,000	8.4%
33	Utah	130,484,700,000	0.8%
50	Vermont	30,450,400,000	0.2%
10	Virginia	431,224,300,000	2.7%
14	Washington	417,860,300,000	2.7%
41	West Virginia	66,925,300,000	0.4%
21	Wisconsin	265,871,300,000	1.7%
49	Wyoming	31,610,000,000	0.2%

RANK ORDER

RANK	STATE	INCOME	% of USA
1	California	$2,167,721,000,000	13.8%
2	Texas	1,317,528,300,000	8.4%
3	New York	1,133,548,500,000	7.2%
4	Florida	964,278,500,000	6.1%
5	Pennsylvania	638,680,600,000	4.1%
6	Illinois	635,650,900,000	4.0%
7	New Jersey	527,205,000,000	3.4%
8	Ohio	509,416,300,000	3.2%
9	Georgia	437,374,200,000	2.8%
10	Virginia	431,224,300,000	2.7%
11	Michigan	429,619,300,000	2.7%
12	North Carolina	426,240,000,000	2.7%
13	Massachusetts	422,043,200,000	2.7%
14	Washington	417,860,300,000	2.7%
15	Maryland	333,124,800,000	2.1%
16	Colorado	292,780,100,000	1.9%
17	Tennessee	290,582,000,000	1.8%
18	Arizona	286,540,400,000	1.8%
19	Indiana	283,623,000,000	1.8%
20	Minnesota	280,007,000,000	1.8%
21	Wisconsin	265,871,300,000	1.7%
22	Missouri	261,274,900,000	1.7%
23	Connecticut	232,448,200,000	1.5%
24	South Carolina	200,319,300,000	1.3%
25	Louisiana	195,977,600,000	1.2%
26	Alabama	186,791,100,000	1.2%
27	Oregon	186,053,500,000	1.2%
28	Kentucky	170,135,900,000	1.1%
29	Oklahoma	165,639,200,000	1.1%
30	Iowa	141,917,000,000	0.9%
31	Kansas	134,096,100,000	0.9%
32	Nevada	133,652,200,000	0.8%
33	Utah	130,484,700,000	0.8%
34	Arkansas	118,053,800,000	0.8%
35	Mississippi	103,789,200,000	0.7%
36	Nebraska	92,471,800,000	0.6%
37	New Mexico	79,769,600,000	0.5%
38	New Hampshire	74,592,800,000	0.5%
39	Hawaii	70,295,500,000	0.4%
40	Idaho	69,444,100,000	0.4%
41	West Virginia	66,925,300,000	0.4%
42	Maine	58,767,600,000	0.4%
43	Rhode Island	51,535,400,000	0.3%
44	Montana	45,282,800,000	0.3%
45	Delaware	44,882,600,000	0.3%
46	South Dakota	42,131,100,000	0.3%
47	Alaska	40,139,000,000	0.3%
48	North Dakota	38,032,100,000	0.2%
49	Wyoming	31,610,000,000	0.2%
50	Vermont	30,450,400,000	0.2%
	District of Columbia	49,289,200,000	0.3%

Source: U.S. Department of Commerce, Bureau of Economic Analysis
   "Annual State Personal Income" (https://apps.bea.gov/iTable/index_regional.cfm)
*Disposable personal income is personal income less personal tax and nontax payments. It is the income available to persons for spending or saving.

Per Capita Disposable Personal Income in 2018

National Per Capita = $48,101*

ALPHA ORDER				RANK ORDER		
RANK	STATE	PER CAPITA		RANK	STATE	PER CAPITA
46	Alabama	$38,215		1	Connecticut	$65,063
10	Alaska	54,430		2	Massachusetts	61,147
42	Arizona	39,955		3	New Jersey	59,180
45	Arkansas	39,171		4	New York	58,005
8	California	54,800		5	Washington	55,452
11	Colorado	51,405		6	Maryland	55,128
1	Connecticut	65,063		7	New Hampshire	54,991
22	Delaware	46,406		8	California	54,800
26	Florida	45,273		9	Wyoming	54,713
39	Georgia	41,578		10	Alaska	54,430
17	Hawaii	49,487		11	Colorado	51,405
43	Idaho	39,587		12	Virginia	50,627
15	Illinois	49,890		13	North Dakota	50,037
36	Indiana	42,383		14	Minnesota	49,902
27	Iowa	44,965		15	Illinois	49,890
23	Kansas	46,057		16	Pennsylvania	49,869
47	Kentucky	38,075		17	Hawaii	49,487
37	Louisiana	42,055		18	Rhode Island	48,742
30	Maine	43,909		19	Vermont	48,620
6	Maryland	55,128		20	Nebraska	47,931
2	Massachusetts	61,147		21	South Dakota	47,755
32	Michigan	42,979		22	Delaware	46,406
14	Minnesota	49,902		23	Kansas	46,057
50	Mississippi	34,752		24	Texas	45,904
34	Missouri	42,647		25	Wisconsin	45,733
35	Montana	42,627		26	Florida	45,273
20	Nebraska	47,931		27	Iowa	44,965
29	Nevada	44,046		28	Oregon	44,397
7	New Hampshire	54,991		29	Nevada	44,046
3	New Jersey	59,180		30	Maine	43,909
48	New Mexico	38,068		31	Ohio	43,579
4	New York	58,005		32	Michigan	42,979
41	North Carolina	41,049		33	Tennessee	42,922
13	North Dakota	50,037		34	Missouri	42,647
31	Ohio	43,579		35	Montana	42,627
38	Oklahoma	42,008		36	Indiana	42,383
28	Oregon	44,397		37	Louisiana	42,055
16	Pennsylvania	49,869		38	Oklahoma	42,008
18	Rhode Island	48,742		39	Georgia	41,578
44	South Carolina	39,401		40	Utah	41,278
21	South Dakota	47,755		41	North Carolina	41,049
33	Tennessee	42,922		42	Arizona	39,955
24	Texas	45,904		43	Idaho	39,587
40	Utah	41,278		44	South Carolina	39,401
19	Vermont	48,620		45	Arkansas	39,171
12	Virginia	50,627		46	Alabama	38,215
5	Washington	55,452		47	Kentucky	38,075
49	West Virginia	37,061		48	New Mexico	38,068
25	Wisconsin	45,733		49	West Virginia	37,061
9	Wyoming	54,713		50	Mississippi	34,752
					District of Columbia	70,167

Source: U.S. Department of Commerce, Bureau of Economic Analysis
   "Annual State Personal Income" (https://apps.bea.gov/iTable/index_regional.cfm)
*Disposable personal income is personal income less personal tax and nontax payments. It is the income available to persons for spending or saving.

Median Household Income in 2018

National Median = $62,589*

ALPHA ORDER

RANK	STATE	INCOME
45	Alabama	$49,965
4	Alaska	77,003
26	Arizona	61,128
46	Arkansas	49,430
13	California	70,891
8	Colorado	74,401
6	Connecticut	76,363
20	Delaware	64,144
41	Florida	54,232
39	Georgia	56,702
5	Hawaii	76,759
31	Idaho	59,910
14	Illinois	67,604
32	Indiana	59,608
18	Iowa	64,588
27	Kansas	60,812
44	Kentucky	51,385
49	Louisiana	46,916
38	Maine	56,782
1	Maryland	84,109
2	Massachusetts	80,816
33	Michigan	59,474
12	Minnesota	72,405
50	Mississippi	43,383
35	Missouri	59,196
36	Montana	58,318
23	Nebraska	63,541
28	Nevada	60,503
3	New Hampshire	80,292
11	New Jersey	72,484
48	New Mexico	47,308
17	New York	65,135
43	North Carolina	53,119
21	North Dakota	63,760
30	Ohio	60,330
42	Oklahoma	54,118
16	Oregon	65,346
22	Pennsylvania	63,679
19	Rhode Island	64,551
37	South Carolina	56,852
34	South Dakota	59,238
40	Tennessee	55,417
29	Texas	60,457
9	Utah	73,359
15	Vermont	65,996
10	Virginia	73,226
7	Washington	75,189
47	West Virginia	47,873
24	Wisconsin	62,658
25	Wyoming	61,452

RANK ORDER

RANK	STATE	INCOME
1	Maryland	$84,109
2	Massachusetts	80,816
3	New Hampshire	80,292
4	Alaska	77,003
5	Hawaii	76,759
6	Connecticut	76,363
7	Washington	75,189
8	Colorado	74,401
9	Utah	73,359
10	Virginia	73,226
11	New Jersey	72,484
12	Minnesota	72,405
13	California	70,891
14	Illinois	67,604
15	Vermont	65,996
16	Oregon	65,346
17	New York	65,135
18	Iowa	64,588
19	Rhode Island	64,551
20	Delaware	64,144
21	North Dakota	63,760
22	Pennsylvania	63,679
23	Nebraska	63,541
24	Wisconsin	62,658
25	Wyoming	61,452
26	Arizona	61,128
27	Kansas	60,812
28	Nevada	60,503
29	Texas	60,457
30	Ohio	60,330
31	Idaho	59,910
32	Indiana	59,608
33	Michigan	59,474
34	South Dakota	59,238
35	Missouri	59,196
36	Montana	58,318
37	South Carolina	56,852
38	Maine	56,782
39	Georgia	56,702
40	Tennessee	55,417
41	Florida	54,232
42	Oklahoma	54,118
43	North Carolina	53,119
44	Kentucky	51,385
45	Alabama	49,965
46	Arkansas	49,430
47	West Virginia	47,873
48	New Mexico	47,308
49	Louisiana	46,916
50	Mississippi	43,383
	District of Columbia	81,685

Source: U.S. Bureau of the Census
"Historical Income Tables" (www.census.gov/data/tables/time-series/demo/income-poverty/historical-income-households.html)
*This is a three-year-average of inflation-adjusted single-year medians for the years 2016 through 2018.

Regional Price Parities in 2017

National Index = 100.0*

ALPHA ORDER				RANK ORDER		
RANK	STATE	RATIO		RANK	STATE	RATIO
48	Alabama	86.7		1	Hawaii	118.5
10	Alaska	104.4		2	New York	115.8
25	Arizona	96.4		3	California	114.8
49	Arkansas	86.5		4	New Jersey	112.9
3	California	114.8		5	Maryland	109.4
11	Colorado	103.2		6	Connecticut	108.0
6	Connecticut	108.0		7	Massachusetts	107.9
14	Delaware	100.1		8	Washington	106.4
15	Florida	99.9		9	New Hampshire	105.8
31	Georgia	92.5		10	Alaska	104.4
1	Hawaii	118.5		11	Colorado	103.2
29	Idaho	93.0		12	Vermont	102.5
18	Illinois	98.5		13	Virginia	102.1
39	Indiana	89.8		14	Delaware	100.1
39	Iowa	89.8		15	Florida	99.9
38	Kansas	90.0		16	Oregon	99.5
46	Kentucky	87.9		17	Rhode Island	98.6
36	Louisiana	90.1		18	Illinois	98.5
19	Maine	98.4		19	Maine	98.4
5	Maryland	109.4		20	Pennsylvania	97.9
7	Massachusetts	107.9		21	Nevada	97.6
29	Michigan	93.0		22	Minnesota	97.5
22	Minnesota	97.5		23	Texas	97.0
50	Mississippi	85.7		23	Utah	97.0
42	Missouri	89.5		25	Arizona	96.4
27	Montana	94.6		26	Wyoming	95.2
41	Nebraska	89.6		27	Montana	94.6
21	Nevada	97.6		28	New Mexico	93.3
9	New Hampshire	105.8		29	Idaho	93.0
4	New Jersey	112.9		29	Michigan	93.0
28	New Mexico	93.3		31	Georgia	92.5
2	New York	115.8		32	Wisconsin	92.4
33	North Carolina	91.3		33	North Carolina	91.3
36	North Dakota	90.1		34	South Carolina	90.4
44	Ohio	88.9		34	Tennessee	90.4
43	Oklahoma	89.0		36	Louisiana	90.1
16	Oregon	99.5		36	North Dakota	90.1
20	Pennsylvania	97.9		38	Kansas	90.0
17	Rhode Island	98.6		39	Indiana	89.8
34	South Carolina	90.4		39	Iowa	89.8
45	South Dakota	88.2		41	Nebraska	89.6
34	Tennessee	90.4		42	Missouri	89.5
23	Texas	97.0		43	Oklahoma	89.0
23	Utah	97.0		44	Ohio	88.9
12	Vermont	102.5		45	South Dakota	88.2
13	Virginia	102.1		46	Kentucky	87.9
8	Washington	106.4		47	West Virginia	87.0
47	West Virginia	87.0		48	Alabama	86.7
32	Wisconsin	92.4		49	Arkansas	86.5
26	Wyoming	95.2		50	Mississippi	85.7
					District of Columbia	116.9

Source: U.S. Department of Commerce, Bureau of Economic Analysis
   "Annual State Personal Income" (https://apps.bea.gov/iTable/index_regional.cfm)
*Regional Price Parities (RPPs) are regional price levels expressed as a percentage of the overall national price level for a given year. The price levels are determined by the average prices paid by consumers for the mix of goods and services consumed in each region. Taking the ratio of RPPs shows the difference in price levels across regions.

Real Personal Income in 2017

National Total = $15,925,840,500,000*

ALPHA ORDER

RANK	STATE	INCOME	% of USA
26	Alabama	$215,669,800,000	1.4%
48	Alaska	38,119,900,000	0.2%
20	Arizona	294,575,600,000	1.8%
32	Arkansas	136,629,500,000	0.9%
1	California	1,955,659,600,000	12.3%
22	Colorado	285,343,000,000	1.8%
23	Connecticut	226,462,200,000	1.4%
46	Delaware	45,604,300,000	0.3%
4	Florida	952,254,700,000	6.0%
9	Georgia	475,057,900,000	3.0%
41	Hawaii	60,538,500,000	0.4%
39	Idaho	73,733,000,000	0.5%
5	Illinois	663,495,600,000	4.2%
15	Indiana	317,709,300,000	2.0%
30	Iowa	157,475,000,000	1.0%
31	Kansas	149,752,500,000	0.9%
27	Kentucky	196,801,600,000	1.2%
25	Louisiana	215,828,200,000	1.4%
42	Maine	59,852,200,000	0.4%
17	Maryland	315,780,100,000	2.0%
13	Massachusetts	411,236,000,000	2.6%
11	Michigan	470,290,200,000	3.0%
18	Minnesota	297,250,900,000	1.9%
35	Mississippi	120,168,100,000	0.8%
19	Missouri	295,937,000,000	1.9%
44	Montana	47,795,500,000	0.3%
36	Nebraska	102,684,000,000	0.6%
33	Nevada	135,398,900,000	0.9%
40	New Hampshire	70,567,800,000	0.4%
8	New Jersey	484,446,000,000	3.0%
37	New Mexico	83,983,000,000	0.5%
3	New York	1,052,014,900,000	6.6%
10	North Carolina	470,769,500,000	3.0%
47	North Dakota	41,813,400,000	0.3%
7	Ohio	579,989,000,000	3.6%
29	Oklahoma	182,675,300,000	1.1%
28	Oregon	191,045,100,000	1.2%
6	Pennsylvania	657,657,900,000	4.1%
43	Rhode Island	53,154,500,000	0.3%
24	South Carolina	221,332,700,000	1.4%
45	South Dakota	46,475,000,000	0.3%
16	Tennessee	315,891,100,000	2.0%
2	Texas	1,325,668,800,000	8.3%
34	Utah	133,378,300,000	0.8%
50	Vermont	29,993,200,000	0.2%
12	Virginia	434,480,000,000	2.7%
14	Washington	387,227,700,000	2.4%
38	West Virginia	76,464,200,000	0.5%
21	Wisconsin	292,707,600,000	1.8%
49	Wyoming	32,486,000,000	0.2%

RANK ORDER

RANK	STATE	INCOME	% of USA
1	California	$1,955,659,600,000	12.3%
2	Texas	1,325,668,800,000	8.3%
3	New York	1,052,014,900,000	6.6%
4	Florida	952,254,700,000	6.0%
5	Illinois	663,495,600,000	4.2%
6	Pennsylvania	657,657,900,000	4.1%
7	Ohio	579,989,000,000	3.6%
8	New Jersey	484,446,000,000	3.0%
9	Georgia	475,057,900,000	3.0%
10	North Carolina	470,769,500,000	3.0%
11	Michigan	470,290,200,000	3.0%
12	Virginia	434,480,000,000	2.7%
13	Massachusetts	411,236,000,000	2.6%
14	Washington	387,227,700,000	2.4%
15	Indiana	317,709,300,000	2.0%
16	Tennessee	315,891,100,000	2.0%
17	Maryland	315,780,100,000	2.0%
18	Minnesota	297,250,900,000	1.9%
19	Missouri	295,937,000,000	1.9%
20	Arizona	294,575,600,000	1.8%
21	Wisconsin	292,707,600,000	1.8%
22	Colorado	285,343,000,000	1.8%
23	Connecticut	226,462,200,000	1.4%
24	South Carolina	221,332,700,000	1.4%
25	Louisiana	215,828,200,000	1.4%
26	Alabama	215,669,800,000	1.4%
27	Kentucky	196,801,600,000	1.2%
28	Oregon	191,045,100,000	1.2%
29	Oklahoma	182,675,300,000	1.1%
30	Iowa	157,475,000,000	1.0%
31	Kansas	149,752,500,000	0.9%
32	Arkansas	136,629,500,000	0.9%
33	Nevada	135,398,900,000	0.9%
34	Utah	133,378,300,000	0.8%
35	Mississippi	120,168,100,000	0.8%
36	Nebraska	102,684,000,000	0.6%
37	New Mexico	83,983,000,000	0.5%
38	West Virginia	76,464,200,000	0.5%
39	Idaho	73,733,000,000	0.5%
40	New Hampshire	70,567,800,000	0.4%
41	Hawaii	60,538,500,000	0.4%
42	Maine	59,852,200,000	0.4%
43	Rhode Island	53,154,500,000	0.3%
44	Montana	47,795,500,000	0.3%
45	South Dakota	46,475,000,000	0.3%
46	Delaware	45,604,300,000	0.3%
47	North Dakota	41,813,400,000	0.3%
48	Alaska	38,119,900,000	0.2%
49	Wyoming	32,486,000,000	0.2%
50	Vermont	29,993,200,000	0.2%
	District of Columbia	44,516,300,000	0.3%

Source: U.S. Department of Commerce, Bureau of Economic Analysis
   "Annual State Personal Income" (https://apps.bea.gov/iTable/index_regional.cfm)
*Real personal income is personal income at Regional Price Parities (RPPs) divided by the national Personal Consumption Expenditure price index (a measure of U.S. inflation). RPPs are regional price levels expressed as a percentage of the overall national price level for a given year. The price levels are determined by the average prices paid by consumers for the mix of goods and services consumed in each region. Taking the ratio of RPPs shows the difference in price levels across regions.

Percent Change in Real Personal Income: 2016 to 2017

National Percent Change = 2.9% Increase*

ALPHA ORDER				RANK ORDER		
RANK	STATE	PERCENT CHANGE		RANK	STATE	PERCENT CHANGE
37	Alabama	1.6		1	New York	5.4
48	Alaska	0.1		2	Colorado	5.0
7	Arizona	3.9		3	Florida	4.6
16	Arkansas	2.7		4	Texas	4.5
20	California	2.6		5	Utah	4.2
2	Colorado	5.0		5	Washington	4.2
29	Connecticut	2.1		7	Arizona	3.9
15	Delaware	2.9		7	Idaho	3.9
3	Florida	4.6		7	Nevada	3.9
12	Georgia	3.5		10	South Carolina	3.7
27	Hawaii	2.2		11	Oregon	3.6
7	Idaho	3.9		12	Georgia	3.5
39	Illinois	1.3		13	Massachusetts	3.2
32	Indiana	2.0		13	Rhode Island	3.2
46	Iowa	0.8		15	Delaware	2.9
42	Kansas	1.2		16	Arkansas	2.7
32	Kentucky	2.0		16	Maine	2.7
39	Louisiana	1.3		16	Oklahoma	2.7
16	Maine	2.7		16	West Virginia	2.7
44	Maryland	1.1		20	California	2.6
13	Massachusetts	3.2		20	North Carolina	2.6
37	Michigan	1.6		22	Montana	2.5
29	Minnesota	2.1		23	New Hampshire	2.4
39	Mississippi	1.3		23	New Jersey	2.4
35	Missouri	1.8		23	Wisconsin	2.4
22	Montana	2.5		26	Ohio	2.3
42	Nebraska	1.2		27	Hawaii	2.2
7	Nevada	3.9		27	Virginia	2.2
23	New Hampshire	2.4		29	Connecticut	2.1
23	New Jersey	2.4		29	Minnesota	2.1
48	New Mexico	0.1		29	Wyoming	2.1
1	New York	5.4		32	Indiana	2.0
20	North Carolina	2.6		32	Kentucky	2.0
50	North Dakota	(0.3)		34	Tennessee	1.9
26	Ohio	2.3		35	Missouri	1.8
16	Oklahoma	2.7		35	Pennsylvania	1.8
11	Oregon	3.6		37	Alabama	1.6
35	Pennsylvania	1.8		37	Michigan	1.6
13	Rhode Island	3.2		39	Illinois	1.3
10	South Carolina	3.7		39	Louisiana	1.3
44	South Dakota	1.1		39	Mississippi	1.3
34	Tennessee	1.9		42	Kansas	1.2
4	Texas	4.5		42	Nebraska	1.2
5	Utah	4.2		44	Maryland	1.1
47	Vermont	0.2		44	South Dakota	1.1
27	Virginia	2.2		46	Iowa	0.8
5	Washington	4.2		47	Vermont	0.2
16	West Virginia	2.7		48	Alaska	0.1
23	Wisconsin	2.4		48	New Mexico	0.1
29	Wyoming	2.1		50	North Dakota	(0.3)
					District of Columbia	0.2

Source: U.S. Department of Commerce, Bureau of Economic Analysis
"Annual State Personal Income" (https://apps.bea.gov/iTable/index_regional.cfm)
*Real personal income is personal income at Regional Price Parities (RPPs) divided by the national Personal Consumption Expenditure price index (a measure of U.S. inflation). RPPs are regional price levels expressed as a percentage of the overall national price level for a given year. The price levels are determined by the average prices paid by consumers for the mix of goods and services consumed in each region. Taking the ratio of RPPs shows the difference in price levels across regions.

Per Capita Real Personal Income in 2017

National Per Capita = $48,980*

ALPHA ORDER				RANK ORDER		
RANK	STATE	PER CAPITA		RANK	STATE	PER CAPITA
41	Alabama	$44,239		1	Connecticut	$63,366
14	Alaska	51,528		2	Massachusetts	59,919
48	Arizona	41,790		3	Wyoming	56,114
37	Arkansas	45,498		4	North Dakota	55,369
23	California	49,637		5	New Jersey	54,502
18	Colorado	50,810		6	New York	53,700
1	Connecticut	63,366		7	Nebraska	53,549
27	Delaware	47,650		8	Minnesota	53,384
38	Florida	45,396		9	South Dakota	53,219
35	Georgia	45,621		10	Maryland	52,413
46	Hawaii	42,507		11	New Hampshire	52,281
45	Idaho	42,895		12	Washington	52,149
13	Illinois	51,892		13	Illinois	51,892
26	Indiana	47,704		14	Alaska	51,528
21	Iowa	50,093		15	Kansas	51,449
15	Kansas	51,449		16	Pennsylvania	51,418
42	Kentucky	44,187		17	Virginia	51,325
32	Louisiana	46,208		18	Colorado	50,810
40	Maine	44,831		19	Wisconsin	50,536
10	Maryland	52,413		20	Rhode Island	50,313
2	Massachusetts	59,919		21	Iowa	50,093
28	Michigan	47,140		22	Ohio	49,724
8	Minnesota	53,384		23	California	49,637
49	Mississippi	40,195		24	Missouri	48,446
24	Missouri	48,446		25	Vermont	48,026
39	Montana	45,386		26	Indiana	47,704
7	Nebraska	53,549		27	Delaware	47,650
36	Nevada	45,552		28	Michigan	47,140
11	New Hampshire	52,281		29	Tennessee	47,086
5	New Jersey	54,502		30	Texas	46,806
50	New Mexico	40,118		31	Oklahoma	46,451
6	New York	53,700		32	Louisiana	46,208
34	North Carolina	45,836		33	Oregon	46,073
4	North Dakota	55,369		34	North Carolina	45,836
22	Ohio	49,724		35	Georgia	45,621
31	Oklahoma	46,451		36	Nevada	45,552
33	Oregon	46,073		37	Arkansas	45,498
16	Pennsylvania	51,418		38	Florida	45,396
20	Rhode Island	50,313		39	Montana	45,386
43	South Carolina	44,079		40	Maine	44,831
9	South Dakota	53,219		41	Alabama	44,239
29	Tennessee	47,086		42	Kentucky	44,187
30	Texas	46,806		43	South Carolina	44,079
44	Utah	42,982		44	Utah	42,982
25	Vermont	48,026		45	Idaho	42,895
17	Virginia	51,325		46	Hawaii	42,507
12	Washington	52,149		47	West Virginia	42,082
47	West Virginia	42,082		48	Arizona	41,790
19	Wisconsin	50,536		49	Mississippi	40,195
3	Wyoming	56,114		50	New Mexico	40,118
					District of Columbia	63,989

Source: U.S. Department of Commerce, Bureau of Economic Analysis
"Annual State Personal Income" (https://apps.bea.gov/iTable/index_regional.cfm)
*Real personal income is personal income at Regional Price Parities (RPPs) divided by the national Personal Consumption Expenditure price index (a measure of U.S. inflation). RPPs are regional price levels expressed as a percentage of the overall national price level for a given year. The price levels are determined by the average prices paid by consumers for the mix of goods and services consumed in each region. Taking the ratio of RPPs shows the difference in price levels across regions.

Percent Change in Per Capita Real Personal Income: 2016 to 2017

National Percent Change = 2.2% Increase*

ALPHA ORDER			RANK ORDER		
RANK	STATE	PERCENT CHANGE	RANK	STATE	PERCENT CHANGE
34	Alabama	1.4	1	New York	5.7
46	Alaska	0.3	2	Colorado	3.5
11	Arizona	2.4	2	West Virginia	3.5
16	Arkansas	2.3	4	Rhode Island	3.3
21	California	2.1	5	Texas	3.1
2	Colorado	3.5	6	Wyoming	3.0
17	Connecticut	2.2	7	Florida	2.9
21	Delaware	2.1	8	Massachusetts	2.6
7	Florida	2.9	9	Maine	2.5
11	Georgia	2.4	9	Oklahoma	2.5
11	Hawaii	2.4	11	Arizona	2.4
28	Idaho	1.7	11	Georgia	2.4
30	Illinois	1.6	11	Hawaii	2.4
30	Indiana	1.6	11	South Carolina	2.4
45	Iowa	0.5	11	Washington	2.4
41	Kansas	1.2	16	Arkansas	2.3
28	Kentucky	1.7	17	Connecticut	2.2
34	Louisiana	1.4	17	New Jersey	2.2
9	Maine	2.5	17	Oregon	2.2
43	Maryland	0.8	17	Utah	2.2
8	Massachusetts	2.6	21	California	2.1
34	Michigan	1.4	21	Delaware	2.1
38	Minnesota	1.3	21	Ohio	2.1
38	Mississippi	1.3	24	Nevada	2.0
34	Missouri	1.4	24	Wisconsin	2.0
38	Montana	1.3	26	New Hampshire	1.9
44	Nebraska	0.6	27	Pennsylvania	1.8
24	Nevada	2.0	28	Idaho	1.7
26	New Hampshire	1.9	28	Kentucky	1.7
17	New Jersey	2.2	30	Illinois	1.6
48	New Mexico	0.0	30	Indiana	1.6
1	New York	5.7	30	Virginia	1.6
33	North Carolina	1.5	33	North Carolina	1.5
50	North Dakota	(0.4)	34	Alabama	1.4
21	Ohio	2.1	34	Louisiana	1.4
9	Oklahoma	2.5	34	Michigan	1.4
17	Oregon	2.2	34	Missouri	1.4
27	Pennsylvania	1.8	38	Minnesota	1.3
4	Rhode Island	3.3	38	Mississippi	1.3
11	South Carolina	2.4	38	Montana	1.3
49	South Dakota	(0.1)	41	Kansas	1.2
42	Tennessee	0.9	42	Tennessee	0.9
5	Texas	3.1	43	Maryland	0.8
17	Utah	2.2	44	Nebraska	0.6
47	Vermont	0.1	45	Iowa	0.5
30	Virginia	1.6	46	Alaska	0.3
11	Washington	2.4	47	Vermont	0.1
2	West Virginia	3.5	48	New Mexico	0.0
24	Wisconsin	2.0	49	South Dakota	(0.1)
6	Wyoming	3.0	50	North Dakota	(0.4)
				District of Columbia	(1.1)

Source: U.S. Department of Commerce, Bureau of Economic Analysis
"Annual State Personal Income" (https://apps.bea.gov/iTable/index_regional.cfm)
*Real personal income is personal income at Regional Price Parities (RPPs) divided by the national Personal Consumption Expenditure price index (a measure of U.S. inflation). RPPs are regional price levels expressed as a percentage of the overall national price level for a given year. The price levels are determined by the average prices paid by consumers for the mix of goods and services consumed in each region. Taking the ratio of RPPs shows the difference in price levels across regions.

Personal Consumption Expenditures in 2018

National Total = $13,988,761,900,000*

ALPHA ORDER

RANK	STATE	EXPENDITURES	% of USA
27	Alabama	$165,716,500,000	1.2%
47	Alaska	37,053,100,000	0.3%
17	Arizona	257,505,500,000	1.8%
34	Arkansas	102,754,900,000	0.7%
1	California	1,858,420,900,000	13.3%
19	Colorado	251,595,200,000	1.8%
23	Connecticut	189,140,800,000	1.4%
45	Delaware	42,654,900,000	0.3%
4	Florida	876,422,000,000	6.3%
11	Georgia	383,834,000,000	2.7%
39	Hawaii	69,262,300,000	0.5%
41	Idaho	64,514,100,000	0.5%
5	Illinois	574,428,900,000	4.1%
18	Indiana	252,150,300,000	1.8%
31	Iowa	122,913,700,000	0.9%
33	Kansas	110,338,600,000	0.8%
28	Kentucky	157,065,600,000	1.1%
26	Louisiana	168,245,400,000	1.2%
42	Maine	60,894,000,000	0.4%
15	Maryland	282,920,600,000	2.0%
12	Massachusetts	380,277,100,000	2.7%
9	Michigan	407,475,200,000	2.9%
16	Minnesota	266,160,500,000	1.9%
35	Mississippi	92,831,300,000	0.7%
22	Missouri	245,424,700,000	1.8%
44	Montana	45,358,700,000	0.3%
36	Nebraska	80,431,700,000	0.6%
30	Nevada	125,800,900,000	0.9%
38	New Hampshire	70,698,800,000	0.5%
8	New Jersey	469,735,400,000	3.4%
37	New Mexico	75,976,600,000	0.5%
3	New York	1,029,887,800,000	7.4%
13	North Carolina	370,882,500,000	2.7%
48	North Dakota	36,863,100,000	0.3%
7	Ohio	477,536,400,000	3.4%
29	Oklahoma	136,037,400,000	1.0%
24	Oregon	179,014,900,000	1.3%
6	Pennsylvania	573,815,400,000	4.1%
43	Rhode Island	47,731,300,000	0.3%
25	South Carolina	176,365,000,000	1.3%
46	South Dakota	38,949,600,000	0.3%
21	Tennessee	246,025,300,000	1.8%
2	Texas	1,120,664,500,000	8.0%
32	Utah	119,239,900,000	0.9%
49	Vermont	31,283,800,000	0.2%
10	Virginia	384,478,900,000	2.7%
14	Washington	350,959,400,000	2.5%
40	West Virginia	65,138,400,000	0.5%
20	Wisconsin	246,818,000,000	1.8%
50	Wyoming	24,707,400,000	0.2%

RANK ORDER

RANK	STATE	EXPENDITURES	% of USA
1	California	$1,858,420,900,000	13.3%
2	Texas	1,120,664,500,000	8.0%
3	New York	1,029,887,800,000	7.4%
4	Florida	876,422,000,000	6.3%
5	Illinois	574,428,900,000	4.1%
6	Pennsylvania	573,815,400,000	4.1%
7	Ohio	477,536,400,000	3.4%
8	New Jersey	469,735,400,000	3.4%
9	Michigan	407,475,200,000	2.9%
10	Virginia	384,478,900,000	2.7%
11	Georgia	383,834,000,000	2.7%
12	Massachusetts	380,277,100,000	2.7%
13	North Carolina	370,882,500,000	2.7%
14	Washington	350,959,400,000	2.5%
15	Maryland	282,920,600,000	2.0%
16	Minnesota	266,160,500,000	1.9%
17	Arizona	257,505,500,000	1.8%
18	Indiana	252,150,300,000	1.8%
19	Colorado	251,595,200,000	1.8%
20	Wisconsin	246,818,000,000	1.8%
21	Tennessee	246,025,300,000	1.8%
22	Missouri	245,424,700,000	1.8%
23	Connecticut	189,140,800,000	1.4%
24	Oregon	179,014,900,000	1.3%
25	South Carolina	176,365,000,000	1.3%
26	Louisiana	168,245,400,000	1.2%
27	Alabama	165,716,500,000	1.2%
28	Kentucky	157,065,600,000	1.1%
29	Oklahoma	136,037,400,000	1.0%
30	Nevada	125,800,900,000	0.9%
31	Iowa	122,913,700,000	0.9%
32	Utah	119,239,900,000	0.9%
33	Kansas	110,338,600,000	0.8%
34	Arkansas	102,754,900,000	0.7%
35	Mississippi	92,831,300,000	0.7%
36	Nebraska	80,431,700,000	0.6%
37	New Mexico	75,976,600,000	0.5%
38	New Hampshire	70,698,800,000	0.5%
39	Hawaii	69,262,300,000	0.5%
40	West Virginia	65,138,400,000	0.5%
41	Idaho	64,514,100,000	0.5%
42	Maine	60,894,000,000	0.4%
43	Rhode Island	47,731,300,000	0.3%
44	Montana	45,358,700,000	0.3%
45	Delaware	42,654,900,000	0.3%
46	South Dakota	38,949,600,000	0.3%
47	Alaska	37,053,100,000	0.3%
48	North Dakota	36,863,100,000	0.3%
49	Vermont	31,283,800,000	0.2%
50	Wyoming	24,707,400,000	0.2%
	District of Columbia	44,360,800,000	0.3%

Source: U.S. Department of Commerce, Bureau of Economic Analysis
    "Personal Consumption Expenditures by State" (https://apps.bea.gov/iTable/index_regional.cfm)
*PCE by state is the state counterpart of the Nation's personal consumption expenditures (PCE). PCE represents the goods and services purchased by or on behalf of households, plus the purchases of nonprofit institutions serving households. For each state and for the District of Columbia, personal consumption expenditures are those expenditures made by or on behalf of residents. These expenditures include expenditures on activities outside of the state.

Per Capita Personal Consumption Expenditures in 2018

National Per Capita = $42,757*

ALPHA ORDER

RANK	STATE	PER CAPITA
49	Alabama	$33,904
6	Alaska	50,246
43	Arizona	35,906
48	Arkansas	34,095
11	California	46,981
19	Colorado	44,174
2	Connecticut	52,941
21	Delaware	44,103
28	Florida	41,148
38	Georgia	36,488
8	Hawaii	48,759
37	Idaho	36,777
17	Illinois	45,085
36	Indiana	37,680
33	Iowa	38,944
34	Kansas	37,897
45	Kentucky	35,150
41	Louisiana	36,104
14	Maine	45,497
12	Maryland	46,820
1	Massachusetts	55,095
30	Michigan	40,764
10	Minnesota	47,434
50	Mississippi	31,083
31	Missouri	40,060
24	Montana	42,698
26	Nebraska	41,690
27	Nevada	41,458
5	New Hampshire	52,120
3	New Jersey	52,729
40	New Mexico	36,258
4	New York	52,701
44	North Carolina	35,718
9	North Dakota	48,499
29	Ohio	40,852
47	Oklahoma	34,500
23	Oregon	42,717
18	Pennsylvania	44,805
15	Rhode Island	45,144
46	South Carolina	34,689
20	South Dakota	44,149
39	Tennessee	36,340
32	Texas	39,045
35	Utah	37,721
7	Vermont	49,950
16	Virginia	45,139
13	Washington	46,574
42	West Virginia	36,071
25	Wisconsin	42,456
22	Wyoming	42,766

RANK ORDER

RANK	STATE	PER CAPITA
1	Massachusetts	$55,095
2	Connecticut	52,941
3	New Jersey	52,729
4	New York	52,701
5	New Hampshire	52,120
6	Alaska	50,246
7	Vermont	49,950
8	Hawaii	48,759
9	North Dakota	48,499
10	Minnesota	47,434
11	California	46,981
12	Maryland	46,820
13	Washington	46,574
14	Maine	45,497
15	Rhode Island	45,144
16	Virginia	45,139
17	Illinois	45,085
18	Pennsylvania	44,805
19	Colorado	44,174
20	South Dakota	44,149
21	Delaware	44,103
22	Wyoming	42,766
23	Oregon	42,717
24	Montana	42,698
25	Wisconsin	42,456
26	Nebraska	41,690
27	Nevada	41,458
28	Florida	41,148
29	Ohio	40,852
30	Michigan	40,764
31	Missouri	40,060
32	Texas	39,045
33	Iowa	38,944
34	Kansas	37,897
35	Utah	37,721
36	Indiana	37,680
37	Idaho	36,777
38	Georgia	36,488
39	Tennessee	36,340
40	New Mexico	36,258
41	Louisiana	36,104
42	West Virginia	36,071
43	Arizona	35,906
44	North Carolina	35,718
45	Kentucky	35,150
46	South Carolina	34,689
47	Oklahoma	34,500
48	Arkansas	34,095
49	Alabama	33,904
50	Mississippi	31,083
	District of Columbia	63,151

Source: U.S. Department of Commerce, Bureau of Economic Analysis
"Personal Consumption Expenditures by State" (https://apps.bea.gov/iTable/index_regional.cfm)
*PCE by state is the state counterpart of the Nation's personal consumption expenditures (PCE). PCE represents the goods and services purchased by or on behalf of households, plus the purchases of nonprofit institutions serving households. For each state and for the District of Columbia, personal consumption expenditures are those expenditures made by or on behalf of residents. These expenditures include expenditures on activities outside of the state.

Percent Change in Personal Consumption Expenditures: 2017 to 2018

National Percent Change = 5.1% Increase*

ALPHA ORDER

RANK	STATE	PERCENT CHANGE
28	Alabama	4.5
37	Alaska	4.2
5	Arizona	6.0
41	Arkansas	4.0
5	California	6.0
4	Colorado	6.1
41	Connecticut	4.0
23	Delaware	4.8
9	Florida	5.7
12	Georgia	5.4
16	Hawaii	5.1
3	Idaho	6.3
28	Illinois	4.5
39	Indiana	4.1
48	Iowa	3.7
45	Kansas	3.9
37	Kentucky	4.2
47	Louisiana	3.8
18	Maine	5.0
45	Maryland	3.9
41	Massachusetts	4.0
31	Michigan	4.4
14	Minnesota	5.2
48	Mississippi	3.7
41	Missouri	4.0
14	Montana	5.2
31	Nebraska	4.4
7	Nevada	5.8
24	New Hampshire	4.7
25	New Jersey	4.6
25	New Mexico	4.6
12	New York	5.4
9	North Carolina	5.7
35	North Dakota	4.3
39	Ohio	4.1
20	Oklahoma	4.9
11	Oregon	5.6
20	Pennsylvania	4.9
31	Rhode Island	4.4
31	South Carolina	4.4
18	South Dakota	5.0
16	Tennessee	5.1
7	Texas	5.8
1	Utah	7.3
25	Vermont	4.6
28	Virginia	4.5
2	Washington	6.8
50	West Virginia	3.6
20	Wisconsin	4.9
35	Wyoming	4.3

RANK ORDER

RANK	STATE	PERCENT CHANGE
1	Utah	7.3
2	Washington	6.8
3	Idaho	6.3
4	Colorado	6.1
5	Arizona	6.0
5	California	6.0
7	Nevada	5.8
7	Texas	5.8
9	Florida	5.7
9	North Carolina	5.7
11	Oregon	5.6
12	Georgia	5.4
12	New York	5.4
14	Minnesota	5.2
14	Montana	5.2
16	Hawaii	5.1
16	Tennessee	5.1
18	Maine	5.0
18	South Dakota	5.0
20	Oklahoma	4.9
20	Pennsylvania	4.9
20	Wisconsin	4.9
23	Delaware	4.8
24	New Hampshire	4.7
25	New Jersey	4.6
25	New Mexico	4.6
25	Vermont	4.6
28	Alabama	4.5
28	Illinois	4.5
28	Virginia	4.5
31	Michigan	4.4
31	Nebraska	4.4
31	Rhode Island	4.4
31	South Carolina	4.4
35	North Dakota	4.3
35	Wyoming	4.3
37	Alaska	4.2
37	Kentucky	4.2
39	Indiana	4.1
39	Ohio	4.1
41	Arkansas	4.0
41	Connecticut	4.0
41	Massachusetts	4.0
41	Missouri	4.0
45	Kansas	3.9
45	Maryland	3.9
47	Louisiana	3.8
48	Iowa	3.7
48	Mississippi	3.7
50	West Virginia	3.6
	District of Columbia	5.4

Source: U.S. Department of Commerce, Bureau of Economic Analysis
"Personal Consumption Expenditures by State" (https://apps.bea.gov/iTable/index_regional.cfm)
*PCE by state is the state counterpart of the Nation's personal consumption expenditures (PCE). PCE represents the goods and services purchased by or on behalf of households, plus the purchases of nonprofit institutions serving households. For each state and for the District of Columbia, personal consumption expenditures are those expenditures made by or on behalf of residents. These expenditures include expenditures on activities outside of the state.

Percent Change in Per Capita
Personal Consumption Expenditures: 2017 to 2018
National Percent Change = 4.5% Increase*

ALPHA ORDER

RANK	STATE	PERCENT CHANGE
24	Alabama	4.2
10	Alaska	4.6
24	Arizona	4.2
44	Arkansas	3.6
2	California	5.6
10	Colorado	4.6
33	Connecticut	4.0
40	Delaware	3.7
30	Florida	4.1
17	Georgia	4.4
3	Hawaii	5.4
30	Idaho	4.1
6	Illinois	4.9
44	Indiana	3.6
49	Iowa	3.3
34	Kansas	3.9
34	Kentucky	3.9
30	Louisiana	4.1
8	Maine	4.7
44	Maryland	3.6
48	Massachusetts	3.4
24	Michigan	4.2
17	Minnesota	4.4
38	Mississippi	3.8
40	Missouri	3.7
20	Montana	4.3
40	Nebraska	3.7
40	Nevada	3.7
24	New Hampshire	4.2
20	New Jersey	4.3
12	New Mexico	4.5
1	New York	5.7
12	North Carolina	4.5
44	North Dakota	3.6
38	Ohio	3.8
8	Oklahoma	4.7
12	Oregon	4.5
7	Pennsylvania	4.8
20	Rhode Island	4.3
50	South Carolina	3.1
34	South Dakota	3.9
24	Tennessee	4.2
17	Texas	4.4
3	Utah	5.4
20	Vermont	4.3
34	Virginia	3.9
5	Washington	5.3
24	West Virginia	4.2
12	Wisconsin	4.5
12	Wyoming	4.5

RANK ORDER

RANK	STATE	PERCENT CHANGE
1	New York	5.7
2	California	5.6
3	Hawaii	5.4
3	Utah	5.4
5	Washington	5.3
6	Illinois	4.9
7	Pennsylvania	4.8
8	Maine	4.7
8	Oklahoma	4.7
10	Alaska	4.6
10	Colorado	4.6
12	New Mexico	4.5
12	North Carolina	4.5
12	Oregon	4.5
12	Wisconsin	4.5
12	Wyoming	4.5
17	Georgia	4.4
17	Minnesota	4.4
17	Texas	4.4
20	Montana	4.3
20	New Jersey	4.3
20	Rhode Island	4.3
20	Vermont	4.3
24	Alabama	4.2
24	Arizona	4.2
24	Michigan	4.2
24	New Hampshire	4.2
24	Tennessee	4.2
24	West Virginia	4.2
30	Florida	4.1
30	Idaho	4.1
30	Louisiana	4.1
33	Connecticut	4.0
34	Kansas	3.9
34	Kentucky	3.9
34	South Dakota	3.9
34	Virginia	3.9
38	Mississippi	3.8
38	Ohio	3.8
40	Delaware	3.7
40	Missouri	3.7
40	Nebraska	3.7
40	Nevada	3.7
44	Arkansas	3.6
44	Indiana	3.6
44	Maryland	3.6
44	North Dakota	3.6
48	Massachusetts	3.4
49	Iowa	3.3
50	South Carolina	3.1

| | District of Columbia | 4.4 |

Source: U.S. Department of Commerce, Bureau of Economic Analysis
   "Personal Consumption Expenditures by State" (https://apps.bea.gov/iTable/index_regional.cfm)
*PCE by state is the state counterpart of the Nation's personal consumption expenditures (PCE). PCE represents the goods and services purchased by or on behalf of households, plus the purchases of nonprofit institutions serving households. For each state and for the District of Columbia, personal consumption expenditures are those expenditures made by or on behalf of residents. These expenditures include expenditures on activities outside of the state.

Bankruptcy Filings in 2019

National Total = 776,674 Bankruptcies*

ALPHA ORDER					RANK ORDER			
RANK	STATE	BANKRUPTCIES	% of USA		RANK	STATE	BANKRUPTCIES	% of USA
10	Alabama	26,783	3.6%		1	California	69,263	9.2%
50	Alaska	426	0.1%		2	Illinois	48,223	6.4%
17	Arizona	16,950	2.2%		3	Florida	46,317	6.1%
25	Arkansas	10,678	1.4%		4	Georgia	44,226	5.9%
1	California	69,263	9.2%		5	Ohio	37,449	5.0%
24	Colorado	11,409	1.5%		6	Texas	35,791	4.7%
34	Connecticut	6,228	0.8%		7	New York	35,606	4.7%
39	Delaware	2,936	0.4%		8	Tennessee	34,028	4.5%
3	Florida	46,317	6.1%		9	Michigan	30,424	4.0%
4	Georgia	44,226	5.9%		10	Alabama	26,783	3.6%
43	Hawaii	1,650	0.2%		11	New Jersey	25,399	3.4%
37	Idaho	3,746	0.5%		12	Virginia	23,318	3.1%
2	Illinois	48,223	6.4%		13	Indiana	23,156	3.1%
13	Indiana	23,156	3.1%		14	Pennsylvania	21,310	2.8%
35	Iowa	4,787	0.6%		15	Maryland	17,357	2.3%
32	Kansas	6,877	0.9%		16	Missouri	17,084	2.3%
19	Kentucky	15,341	2.0%		17	Arizona	16,950	2.2%
21	Louisiana	13,074	1.7%		18	Wisconsin	16,588	2.2%
44	Maine	1,362	0.2%		19	Kentucky	15,341	2.0%
15	Maryland	17,357	2.3%		20	North Carolina	13,451	1.8%
31	Massachusetts	7,883	1.0%		21	Louisiana	13,074	1.7%
9	Michigan	30,424	4.0%		22	Washington	12,843	1.7%
27	Minnesota	9,845	1.3%		23	Mississippi	12,655	1.7%
23	Mississippi	12,655	1.7%		24	Colorado	11,409	1.5%
16	Missouri	17,084	2.3%		25	Arkansas	10,678	1.4%
45	Montana	1,347	0.2%		26	Nevada	9,962	1.3%
36	Nebraska	4,146	0.6%		27	Minnesota	9,845	1.3%
26	Nevada	9,962	1.3%		28	Utah	9,758	1.3%
42	New Hampshire	1,836	0.2%		29	Oklahoma	9,527	1.3%
11	New Jersey	25,399	3.4%		30	Oregon	8,986	1.2%
38	New Mexico	3,064	0.4%		31	Massachusetts	7,883	1.0%
7	New York	35,606	4.7%		32	Kansas	6,877	0.9%
20	North Carolina	13,451	1.8%		33	South Carolina	6,730	0.9%
48	North Dakota	728	0.1%		34	Connecticut	6,228	0.8%
5	Ohio	37,449	5.0%		35	Iowa	4,787	0.6%
29	Oklahoma	9,527	1.3%		36	Nebraska	4,146	0.6%
30	Oregon	8,986	1.2%		37	Idaho	3,746	0.5%
14	Pennsylvania	21,310	2.8%		38	New Mexico	3,064	0.4%
41	Rhode Island	2,047	0.3%		39	Delaware	2,936	0.4%
33	South Carolina	6,730	0.9%		40	West Virginia	2,868	0.4%
46	South Dakota	1,008	0.1%		41	Rhode Island	2,047	0.3%
8	Tennessee	34,028	4.5%		42	New Hampshire	1,836	0.2%
6	Texas	35,791	4.7%		43	Hawaii	1,650	0.2%
28	Utah	9,758	1.3%		44	Maine	1,362	0.2%
49	Vermont	559	0.1%		45	Montana	1,347	0.2%
12	Virginia	23,318	3.1%		46	South Dakota	1,008	0.1%
22	Washington	12,843	1.7%		47	Wyoming	879	0.1%
40	West Virginia	2,868	0.4%		48	North Dakota	728	0.1%
18	Wisconsin	16,588	2.2%		49	Vermont	559	0.1%
47	Wyoming	879	0.1%		50	Alaska	426	0.1%
						District of Columbia	832	0.1%

Source: CQ Press using data from Administrative Office of the U.S. Courts
"Table F-2, U.S. Bankruptcy Courts" (https://www.uscourts.gov/statistics-reports/caseload-statistics-data-tables)
*For 12 months through September 2019. Includes business (22,910) and non-business (753,764) filings. Includes all chapters
of bankruptcy. National total includes 7,934 bankruptcies in U.S. territories.

Personal Bankruptcy Rate in 2019

National Rate = 227 Personal Bankruptcies per 100,000 Population*

ALPHA ORDER				RANK ORDER		
RANK	STATE	RATE		RANK	STATE	RATE
1	Alabama	541		1	Alabama	541
50	Alaska	53		2	Tennessee	492
22	Arizona	227		3	Mississippi	418
6	Arkansas	347		4	Georgia	409
32	California	168		5	Illinois	373
27	Colorado	192		6	Arkansas	347
30	Connecticut	169		7	Indiana	339
20	Delaware	229		8	Kentucky	337
24	Florida	207		9	Ohio	316
4	Georgia	409		10	Nevada	313
44	Hawaii	112		11	Utah	300
26	Idaho	205		12	Michigan	299
5	Illinois	373		13	Maryland	281
7	Indiana	339		14	Wisconsin	279
36	Iowa	146		15	New Jersey	278
21	Kansas	228		16	Louisiana	274
8	Kentucky	337		16	Missouri	274
16	Louisiana	274		18	Virginia	268
47	Maine	96		19	Oklahoma	233
13	Maryland	281		20	Delaware	229
45	Massachusetts	110		21	Kansas	228
12	Michigan	299		22	Arizona	227
30	Minnesota	169		23	Oregon	208
3	Mississippi	418		24	Florida	207
16	Missouri	274		24	Nebraska	207
42	Montana	122		26	Idaho	205
24	Nebraska	207		27	Colorado	192
10	Nevada	313		28	Rhode Island	187
39	New Hampshire	130		29	New York	171
15	New Jersey	278		30	Connecticut	169
38	New Mexico	142		30	Minnesota	169
29	New York	171		32	California	168
41	North Carolina	124		33	Washington	164
48	North Dakota	92		34	Pennsylvania	161
9	Ohio	316		35	West Virginia	155
19	Oklahoma	233		36	Iowa	146
23	Oregon	208		37	Wyoming	145
34	Pennsylvania	161		38	New Mexico	142
28	Rhode Island	187		39	New Hampshire	130
40	South Carolina	128		40	South Carolina	128
46	South Dakota	107		41	North Carolina	124
2	Tennessee	492		42	Montana	122
43	Texas	115		43	Texas	115
11	Utah	300		44	Hawaii	112
49	Vermont	84		45	Massachusetts	110
18	Virginia	268		46	South Dakota	107
33	Washington	164		47	Maine	96
35	West Virginia	155		48	North Dakota	92
14	Wisconsin	279		49	Vermont	84
37	Wyoming	145		50	Alaska	53
					District of Columbia	111

Source: CQ Press using data from Administrative Office of the U.S. Courts
"Table F-2, U.S. Bankruptcy Courts" (https://www.uscourts.gov/statistics-reports/caseload-statistics-data-tables)
*For 12 months through September 2019. National rate does not include bankruptcies or population in U.S. territories. Includes all nonbusiness bankruptcies.

Percent Change in Personal Bankruptcy Rate: 2018 to 2019

National Percent Change = 0.0% Change*

RANK	STATE	PERCENT CHANGE
20	Alabama	0.2
47	Alaska	(8.6)
10	Arizona	2.7
19	Arkansas	0.3
16	California	0.6
32	Colorado	(1.5)
6	Connecticut	5.0
27	Delaware	(0.9)
2	Florida	8.4
39	Georgia	(4.2)
1	Hawaii	10.9
26	Idaho	(0.5)
31	Illinois	(1.3)
21	Indiana	0.0
6	Iowa	5.0
24	Kansas	(0.4)
15	Kentucky	0.9
35	Louisiana	(2.8)
49	Maine	(9.4)
28	Maryland	(1.1)
44	Massachusetts	(7.6)
14	Michigan	1.4
29	Minnesota	(1.2)
17	Mississippi	0.5
35	Missouri	(2.8)
5	Montana	5.2
12	Nebraska	2.5
3	Nevada	5.7
13	New Hampshire	1.6
38	New Jersey	(4.1)
43	New Mexico	(7.2)
9	New York	3.0
40	North Carolina	(6.1)
40	North Dakota	(6.1)
21	Ohio	0.0
33	Oklahoma	(2.5)
17	Oregon	0.5
29	Pennsylvania	(1.2)
48	Rhode Island	(9.2)
21	South Carolina	0.0
46	South Dakota	(8.5)
35	Tennessee	(2.8)
4	Texas	5.5
34	Utah	(2.6)
6	Vermont	5.0
10	Virginia	2.7
42	Washington	(6.3)
45	West Virginia	(7.7)
24	Wisconsin	(0.4)
50	Wyoming	(17.6)

RANK	STATE	PERCENT CHANGE
1	Hawaii	10.9
2	Florida	8.4
3	Nevada	5.7
4	Texas	5.5
5	Montana	5.2
6	Connecticut	5.0
6	Iowa	5.0
6	Vermont	5.0
9	New York	3.0
10	Arizona	2.7
10	Virginia	2.7
12	Nebraska	2.5
13	New Hampshire	1.6
14	Michigan	1.4
15	Kentucky	0.9
16	California	0.6
17	Mississippi	0.5
17	Oregon	0.5
19	Arkansas	0.3
20	Alabama	0.2
21	Indiana	0.0
21	Ohio	0.0
21	South Carolina	0.0
24	Kansas	(0.4)
24	Wisconsin	(0.4)
26	Idaho	(0.5)
27	Delaware	(0.9)
28	Maryland	(1.1)
29	Minnesota	(1.2)
29	Pennsylvania	(1.2)
31	Illinois	(1.3)
32	Colorado	(1.5)
33	Oklahoma	(2.5)
34	Utah	(2.6)
35	Louisiana	(2.8)
35	Missouri	(2.8)
35	Tennessee	(2.8)
38	New Jersey	(4.1)
39	Georgia	(4.2)
40	North Carolina	(6.1)
40	North Dakota	(6.1)
42	Washington	(6.3)
43	New Mexico	(7.2)
44	Massachusetts	(7.6)
45	West Virginia	(7.7)
46	South Dakota	(8.5)
47	Alaska	(8.6)
48	Rhode Island	(9.2)
49	Maine	(9.4)
50	Wyoming	(17.6)

| | District of Columbia | (2.6) |

Source: CQ Press using data from Administrative Office of the U.S. Courts
"Table F-2, U.S. Bankruptcy Courts" (https://www.uscourts.gov/statistics-reports/caseload-statistics-data-tables)
*Twelve months ending in September 2018 to 12 months ending in September 2019. National rate does not include bankruptcies or population in U.S. territories. Includes all nonbusiness bankruptcies.

2020 State Business Tax Climate Index

National Average Score = 5.14*

ALPHA ORDER

RANK	STATE	SCORE
40	Alabama	4.53
3	Alaska	7.22
20	Arizona	5.26
46	Arkansas	4.34
48	California	4.02
17	Colorado	5.30
47	Connecticut	4.23
11	Delaware	5.57
4	Florida	6.80
32	Georgia	4.91
37	Hawaii	4.68
21	Idaho	5.23
35	Illinois	4.87
10	Indiana	5.59
42	Iowa	4.38
34	Kansas	4.88
24	Kentucky	5.10
41	Louisiana	4.41
33	Maine	4.90
43	Maryland	4.37
36	Massachusetts	4.81
12	Michigan	5.54
45	Minnesota	4.35
31	Mississippi	4.96
14	Missouri	5.43
5	Montana	6.16
28	Nebraska	5.01
7	Nevada	5.88
6	New Hampshire	6.01
50	New Jersey	3.24
22	New Mexico	5.13
49	New York	4.01
15	North Carolina	5.43
16	North Dakota	5.36
38	Ohio	4.67
27	Oklahoma	5.01
8	Oregon	5.74
29	Pennsylvania	4.97
39	Rhode Island	4.57
30	South Carolina	4.96
2	South Dakota	7.34
18	Tennessee	5.29
13	Texas	5.46
9	Utah	5.70
44	Vermont	4.35
25	Virginia	5.02
19	Washington	5.28
23	West Virginia	5.12
26	Wisconsin	5.01
1	Wyoming	7.62

RANK ORDER

RANK	STATE	SCORE
1	Wyoming	7.62
2	South Dakota	7.34
3	Alaska	7.22
4	Florida	6.80
5	Montana	6.16
6	New Hampshire	6.01
7	Nevada	5.88
8	Oregon	5.74
9	Utah	5.70
10	Indiana	5.59
11	Delaware	5.57
12	Michigan	5.54
13	Texas	5.46
14	Missouri	5.43
15	North Carolina	5.43
16	North Dakota	5.36
17	Colorado	5.30
18	Tennessee	5.29
19	Washington	5.28
20	Arizona	5.26
21	Idaho	5.23
22	New Mexico	5.13
23	West Virginia	5.12
24	Kentucky	5.10
25	Virginia	5.02
26	Wisconsin	5.01
27	Oklahoma	5.01
28	Nebraska	5.01
29	Pennsylvania	4.97
30	South Carolina	4.96
31	Mississippi	4.96
32	Georgia	4.91
33	Maine	4.90
34	Kansas	4.88
35	Illinois	4.87
36	Massachusetts	4.81
37	Hawaii	4.68
38	Ohio	4.67
39	Rhode Island	4.57
40	Alabama	4.53
41	Louisiana	4.41
42	Iowa	4.38
43	Maryland	4.37
44	Vermont	4.35
45	Minnesota	4.35
46	Arkansas	4.34
47	Connecticut	4.23
48	California	4.02
49	New York	4.01
50	New Jersey	3.24
	District of Columbia	4.24

Source: The Tax Foundation
"State Business Tax Climate Index" (October 2019, https://taxfoundation.org/publications/state-business-tax-climate-index/)
*This index looks at levels of taxation and complexity of compliance to compare the states on how "business friendly" each state is compared to the others. The scale for each factor considered is 1 to 10, with 10 being the "best." Rankings are based on unrounded scores and reflect those of The Tax Foundation.

Fortune 500 Companies in 2019

National Total = 500 Companies*

ALPHA ORDER

RANK	STATE	COMPANIES	% of USA
36	Alabama	1	0.2%
37	Alaska	0	0.0%
22	Arizona	6	1.2%
22	Arkansas	6	1.2%
2	California	54	10.8%
17	Colorado	10	2.0%
14	Connecticut	14	2.8%
28	Delaware	3	0.6%
9	Florida	19	3.8%
10	Georgia	18	3.6%
37	Hawaii	0	0.0%
30	Idaho	2	0.4%
4	Illinois	36	7.2%
21	Indiana	8	1.6%
30	Iowa	2	0.4%
30	Kansas	2	0.4%
30	Kentucky	2	0.4%
30	Louisiana	2	0.4%
37	Maine	0	0.0%
28	Maryland	3	0.6%
12	Massachusetts	16	3.2%
12	Michigan	16	3.2%
11	Minnesota	17	3.4%
37	Mississippi	0	0.0%
17	Missouri	10	2.0%
37	Montana	0	0.0%
25	Nebraska	4	0.8%
25	Nevada	4	0.8%
37	New Hampshire	0	0.0%
7	New Jersey	20	4.0%
37	New Mexico	0	0.0%
1	New York	56	11.2%
15	North Carolina	12	2.4%
37	North Dakota	0	0.0%
5	Ohio	24	4.8%
24	Oklahoma	5	1.0%
30	Oregon	2	0.4%
7	Pennsylvania	20	4.0%
25	Rhode Island	4	0.8%
37	South Carolina	0	0.0%
37	South Dakota	0	0.0%
17	Tennessee	10	2.0%
3	Texas	49	9.8%
37	Utah	0	0.0%
37	Vermont	0	0.0%
6	Virginia	21	4.2%
16	Washington	11	2.2%
37	West Virginia	0	0.0%
20	Wisconsin	9	1.8%
37	Wyoming	0	0.0%

RANK ORDER

RANK	STATE	COMPANIES	% of USA
1	New York	56	11.2%
2	California	54	10.8%
3	Texas	49	9.8%
4	Illinois	36	7.2%
5	Ohio	24	4.8%
6	Virginia	21	4.2%
7	New Jersey	20	4.0%
7	Pennsylvania	20	4.0%
9	Florida	19	3.8%
10	Georgia	18	3.6%
11	Minnesota	17	3.4%
12	Massachusetts	16	3.2%
12	Michigan	16	3.2%
14	Connecticut	14	2.8%
15	North Carolina	12	2.4%
16	Washington	11	2.2%
17	Colorado	10	2.0%
17	Missouri	10	2.0%
17	Tennessee	10	2.0%
20	Wisconsin	9	1.8%
21	Indiana	8	1.6%
22	Arizona	6	1.2%
22	Arkansas	6	1.2%
24	Oklahoma	5	1.0%
25	Nebraska	4	0.8%
25	Nevada	4	0.8%
25	Rhode Island	4	0.8%
28	Delaware	3	0.6%
28	Maryland	3	0.6%
30	Idaho	2	0.4%
30	Iowa	2	0.4%
30	Kansas	2	0.4%
30	Kentucky	2	0.4%
30	Louisiana	2	0.4%
30	Oregon	2	0.4%
36	Alabama	1	0.2%
37	Alaska	0	0.0%
37	Hawaii	0	0.0%
37	Maine	0	0.0%
37	Mississippi	0	0.0%
37	Montana	0	0.0%
37	New Hampshire	0	0.0%
37	New Mexico	0	0.0%
37	North Dakota	0	0.0%
37	South Carolina	0	0.0%
37	South Dakota	0	0.0%
37	Utah	0	0.0%
37	Vermont	0	0.0%
37	West Virginia	0	0.0%
37	Wyoming	0	0.0%
	District of Columbia	2	0.4%

Source: Fortune magazine
   "Fortune 500" (June 2019)
*By state where each company's headquarters is located.

V. Education

(Continued)

(Continued)

Estimated Percent of School-Age Population in Public Schools in 2018

National Percent = 94.6%*

ALPHA ORDER

RANK	STATE	PERCENT
28	Alabama	93.2
2	Alaska	101.7
33	Arizona	92.1
10	Arkansas	96.7
12	California	96.3
7	Colorado	98.1
13	Connecticut	96.2
38	Delaware	91.6
36	Florida	91.8
17	Georgia	95.7
50	Hawaii	83.8
42	Idaho	91.1
18	Illinois	95.6
37	Indiana	91.7
15	Iowa	96.1
13	Kansas	96.2
30	Kentucky	92.9
44	Louisiana	90.6
9	Maine	97.0
38	Maryland	91.6
16	Massachusetts	95.8
21	Michigan	95.2
26	Minnesota	93.4
34	Mississippi	91.9
41	Missouri	91.2
47	Montana	89.6
25	Nebraska	94.2
11	Nevada	96.6
32	New Hampshire	92.4
7	New Jersey	98.1
26	New Mexico	93.4
29	New York	93.1
34	North Carolina	91.9
45	North Dakota	90.3
46	Ohio	89.8
5	Oklahoma	99.9
22	Oregon	95.1
48	Pennsylvania	88.7
24	Rhode Island	94.8
18	South Carolina	95.6
49	South Dakota	88.6
42	Tennessee	91.1
4	Texas	100.5
6	Utah	98.4
1	Vermont	102.0
23	Virginia	95.0
31	Washington	92.5
3	West Virginia	101.3
40	Wisconsin	91.4
20	Wyoming	95.3

RANK ORDER

RANK	STATE	PERCENT
1	Vermont	102.0
2	Alaska	101.7
3	West Virginia	101.3
4	Texas	100.5
5	Oklahoma	99.9
6	Utah	98.4
7	Colorado	98.1
7	New Jersey	98.1
9	Maine	97.0
10	Arkansas	96.7
11	Nevada	96.6
12	California	96.3
13	Connecticut	96.2
13	Kansas	96.2
15	Iowa	96.1
16	Massachusetts	95.8
17	Georgia	95.7
18	Illinois	95.6
18	South Carolina	95.6
20	Wyoming	95.3
21	Michigan	95.2
22	Oregon	95.1
23	Virginia	95.0
24	Rhode Island	94.8
25	Nebraska	94.2
26	Minnesota	93.4
26	New Mexico	93.4
28	Alabama	93.2
29	New York	93.1
30	Kentucky	92.9
31	Washington	92.5
32	New Hampshire	92.4
33	Arizona	92.1
34	Mississippi	91.9
34	North Carolina	91.9
36	Florida	91.8
37	Indiana	91.7
38	Delaware	91.6
38	Maryland	91.6
40	Wisconsin	91.4
41	Missouri	91.2
42	Idaho	91.1
42	Tennessee	91.1
44	Louisiana	90.6
45	North Dakota	90.3
46	Ohio	89.8
47	Montana	89.6
48	Pennsylvania	88.7
49	South Dakota	88.6
50	Hawaii	83.8

District of Columbia — 106.6

Source: CQ Press using data from U.S. Department of Education, National Center for Education Statistics

"ElSi Table Generator" (https://nces.ed.gov/ccd/elsi/)

*Estimate based on 2018 Census population estimates for five to seventeen-year-olds compared to estimated 2017–2018 school year public school student membership. Student membership figures include counts for pre-kindergarten programs. Figures higher than 100 percent reflect using different sources for population and for student membership.

Regular Public Elementary and Secondary School Districts in 2017

National Total = 13,598 Districts*

ALPHA ORDER

RANK	STATE	DISTRICTS	% of USA
34	Alabama	134	1.0%
43	Alaska	53	0.4%
23	Arizona	226	1.7%
22	Arkansas	234	1.7%
1	California	1,057	7.8%
27	Colorado	178	1.3%
30	Connecticut	169	1.2%
48	Delaware	19	0.1%
41	Florida	67	0.5%
24	Georgia	180	1.3%
50	Hawaii	1	0.0%
36	Idaho	115	0.8%
3	Illinois	854	6.3%
18	Indiana	294	2.2%
13	Iowa	333	2.4%
16	Kansas	307	2.3%
29	Kentucky	173	1.3%
40	Louisiana	69	0.5%
20	Maine	249	1.8%
47	Maryland	24	0.2%
15	Massachusetts	326	2.4%
7	Michigan	540	4.0%
14	Minnesota	332	2.4%
33	Mississippi	144	1.1%
8	Missouri	518	3.8%
12	Montana	401	2.9%
21	Nebraska	245	1.8%
49	Nevada	18	0.1%
24	New Hampshire	180	1.3%
6	New Jersey	565	4.2%
38	New Mexico	89	0.7%
4	New York	689	5.1%
36	North Carolina	115	0.8%
27	North Dakota	178	1.3%
5	Ohio	620	4.6%
9	Oklahoma	513	3.8%
26	Oregon	179	1.3%
10	Pennsylvania	500	3.7%
46	Rhode Island	32	0.2%
39	South Carolina	84	0.6%
31	South Dakota	150	1.1%
32	Tennessee	146	1.1%
2	Texas	1,025	7.5%
45	Utah	41	0.3%
19	Vermont	278	2.0%
35	Virginia	130	1.0%
17	Washington	299	2.2%
42	West Virginia	55	0.4%
11	Wisconsin	421	3.1%
44	Wyoming	48	0.4%

RANK ORDER

RANK	STATE	DISTRICTS	% of USA
1	California	1,057	7.8%
2	Texas	1,025	7.5%
3	Illinois	854	6.3%
4	New York	689	5.1%
5	Ohio	620	4.6%
6	New Jersey	565	4.2%
7	Michigan	540	4.0%
8	Missouri	518	3.8%
9	Oklahoma	513	3.8%
10	Pennsylvania	500	3.7%
11	Wisconsin	421	3.1%
12	Montana	401	2.9%
13	Iowa	333	2.4%
14	Minnesota	332	2.4%
15	Massachusetts	326	2.4%
16	Kansas	307	2.3%
17	Washington	299	2.2%
18	Indiana	294	2.2%
19	Vermont	278	2.0%
20	Maine	249	1.8%
21	Nebraska	245	1.8%
22	Arkansas	234	1.7%
23	Arizona	226	1.7%
24	Georgia	180	1.3%
24	New Hampshire	180	1.3%
26	Oregon	179	1.3%
27	Colorado	178	1.3%
27	North Dakota	178	1.3%
29	Kentucky	173	1.3%
30	Connecticut	169	1.2%
31	South Dakota	150	1.1%
32	Tennessee	146	1.1%
33	Mississippi	144	1.1%
34	Alabama	134	1.0%
35	Virginia	130	1.0%
36	Idaho	115	0.8%
36	North Carolina	115	0.8%
38	New Mexico	89	0.7%
39	South Carolina	84	0.6%
40	Louisiana	69	0.5%
41	Florida	67	0.5%
42	West Virginia	55	0.4%
43	Alaska	53	0.4%
44	Wyoming	48	0.4%
45	Utah	41	0.3%
46	Rhode Island	32	0.2%
47	Maryland	24	0.2%
48	Delaware	19	0.1%
49	Nevada	18	0.1%
50	Hawaii	1	0.0%
	District of Columbia	1	0.0%

Source: U.S. Department of Education, National Center for Education Statistics
"Digest of Education Statistics 2018" (https://nces.ed.gov/programs/digest/)
*For school year 2016–2017. Regular school districts are agencies responsible for providing free public education for school-age children residing within their jurisdiction. Included in these figures are districts that reported having no students. This can occur when a small district has no pupils or contracts with another district to educate the students under its jurisdiction.

Private Elementary and Secondary Schools in 2018

National Total = 32,461 Schools*

ALPHA ORDER

RANK	STATE	SCHOOLS	% of USA
26	Alabama	370	1.1%
47	Alaska	54	0.2%
29	Arizona	333	1.0%
33	Arkansas	231	0.7%
1	California	3,339	10.3%
23	Colorado	406	1.3%
27	Connecticut	366	1.1%
36	Delaware	162	0.5%
2	Florida	2,869	8.8%
11	Georgia	841	2.6%
41	Hawaii	132	0.4%
31	Idaho	279	0.9%
7	Illinois	1,352	4.2%
10	Indiana	907	2.8%
30	Iowa	318	1.0%
34	Kansas	203	0.6%
22	Kentucky	425	1.3%
20	Louisiana	534	1.6%
39	Maine	139	0.4%
16	Maryland	754	2.3%
17	Massachusetts	661	2.0%
12	Michigan	837	2.6%
14	Minnesota	805	2.5%
35	Mississippi	201	0.6%
15	Missouri	778	2.4%
43	Montana	117	0.4%
32	Nebraska	272	0.8%
40	Nevada	138	0.4%
28	New Hampshire	351	1.1%
8	New Jersey	1,096	3.4%
NA	New Mexico**	NA	NA
5	New York	1,688	5.2%
18	North Carolina	644	2.0%
48	North Dakota	50	0.2%
6	Ohio	1,425	4.4%
37	Oklahoma	152	0.5%
24	Oregon	403	1.2%
3	Pennsylvania	2,502	7.7%
44	Rhode Island	105	0.3%
25	South Carolina	391	1.2%
46	South Dakota	76	0.2%
21	Tennessee	490	1.5%
4	Texas	2,090	6.4%
37	Utah	152	0.5%
45	Vermont	99	0.3%
13	Virginia	823	2.5%
19	Washington	622	1.9%
42	West Virginia	123	0.4%
9	Wisconsin	914	2.8%
49	Wyoming	35	0.1%

RANK ORDER

RANK	STATE	SCHOOLS	% of USA
1	California	3,339	10.3%
2	Florida	2,869	8.8%
3	Pennsylvania	2,502	7.7%
4	Texas	2,090	6.4%
5	New York	1,688	5.2%
6	Ohio	1,425	4.4%
7	Illinois	1,352	4.2%
8	New Jersey	1,096	3.4%
9	Wisconsin	914	2.8%
10	Indiana	907	2.8%
11	Georgia	841	2.6%
12	Michigan	837	2.6%
13	Virginia	823	2.5%
14	Minnesota	805	2.5%
15	Missouri	778	2.4%
16	Maryland	754	2.3%
17	Massachusetts	661	2.0%
18	North Carolina	644	2.0%
19	Washington	622	1.9%
20	Louisiana	534	1.6%
21	Tennessee	490	1.5%
22	Kentucky	425	1.3%
23	Colorado	406	1.3%
24	Oregon	403	1.2%
25	South Carolina	391	1.2%
26	Alabama	370	1.1%
27	Connecticut	366	1.1%
28	New Hampshire	351	1.1%
29	Arizona	333	1.0%
30	Iowa	318	1.0%
31	Idaho	279	0.9%
32	Nebraska	272	0.8%
33	Arkansas	231	0.7%
34	Kansas	203	0.6%
35	Mississippi	201	0.6%
36	Delaware	162	0.5%
37	Oklahoma	152	0.5%
37	Utah	152	0.5%
39	Maine	139	0.4%
40	Nevada	138	0.4%
41	Hawaii	132	0.4%
42	West Virginia	123	0.4%
43	Montana	117	0.4%
44	Rhode Island	105	0.3%
45	Vermont	99	0.3%
46	South Dakota	76	0.2%
47	Alaska	54	0.2%
48	North Dakota	50	0.2%
49	Wyoming	35	0.1%
NA	New Mexico**	NA	NA
	District of Columbia	58	0.2%

Source: U.S. Department of Education, National Center for Education Statistics
"Characteristics of Private Schools in the United States" (https://nces.ed.gov/pubsearch/pubsinfo.asp?pubid=2019071)
*For school year 2017–2018. Includes private schools that provide instruction for one or more grades kindergarten through 12 (or comparable ungraded levels).
**Not available.

Private Elementary and Secondary School Enrollment in 2018

National Total = 4,898,154 Students*

ALPHA ORDER

RANK	STATE	STUDENTS	% of USA
23	Alabama	60,554	1.2%
48	Alaska	3,422	0.1%
26	Arizona	48,039	1.0%
36	Arkansas	24,565	0.5%
1	California	559,217	11.4%
30	Colorado	42,562	0.9%
24	Connecticut	56,600	1.2%
37	Delaware	22,679	0.5%
3	Florida	401,068	8.2%
9	Georgia	136,174	2.8%
33	Hawaii	37,270	0.8%
41	Idaho	16,844	0.3%
6	Illinois	215,524	4.4%
13	Indiana	128,032	2.6%
28	Iowa	45,115	0.9%
32	Kansas	39,190	0.8%
22	Kentucky	74,925	1.5%
12	Louisiana	129,206	2.6%
40	Maine	16,977	0.3%
10	Maryland	133,796	2.7%
18	Massachusetts	107,482	2.2%
14	Michigan	126,967	2.6%
16	Minnesota	113,829	2.3%
31	Mississippi	41,492	0.8%
15	Missouri	116,760	2.4%
45	Montana	8,420	0.2%
27	Nebraska	46,301	0.9%
38	Nevada	20,723	0.4%
35	New Hampshire	25,482	0.5%
8	New Jersey	178,864	3.7%
NA	New Mexico**	NA	NA
2	New York	419,145	8.6%
17	North Carolina	109,461	2.2%
47	North Dakota	7,676	0.2%
7	Ohio	212,807	4.3%
34	Oklahoma	26,916	0.5%
29	Oregon	43,642	0.9%
5	Pennsylvania	246,773	5.0%
42	Rhode Island	16,666	0.3%
25	South Carolina	49,788	1.0%
44	South Dakota	10,166	0.2%
20	Tennessee	85,576	1.7%
4	Texas	278,641	5.7%
39	Utah	19,091	0.4%
46	Vermont	8,404	0.2%
19	Virginia	105,335	2.2%
21	Washington	82,486	1.7%
43	West Virginia	12,538	0.3%
11	Wisconsin	133,103	2.7%
49	Wyoming	1,608	0.0%

RANK ORDER

RANK	STATE	STUDENTS	% of USA
1	California	559,217	11.4%
2	New York	419,145	8.6%
3	Florida	401,068	8.2%
4	Texas	278,641	5.7%
5	Pennsylvania	246,773	5.0%
6	Illinois	215,524	4.4%
7	Ohio	212,807	4.3%
8	New Jersey	178,864	3.7%
9	Georgia	136,174	2.8%
10	Maryland	133,796	2.7%
11	Wisconsin	133,103	2.7%
12	Louisiana	129,206	2.6%
13	Indiana	128,032	2.6%
14	Michigan	126,967	2.6%
15	Missouri	116,760	2.4%
16	Minnesota	113,829	2.3%
17	North Carolina	109,461	2.2%
18	Massachusetts	107,482	2.2%
19	Virginia	105,335	2.2%
20	Tennessee	85,576	1.7%
21	Washington	82,486	1.7%
22	Kentucky	74,925	1.5%
23	Alabama	60,554	1.2%
24	Connecticut	56,600	1.2%
25	South Carolina	49,788	1.0%
26	Arizona	48,039	1.0%
27	Nebraska	46,301	0.9%
28	Iowa	45,115	0.9%
29	Oregon	43,642	0.9%
30	Colorado	42,562	0.9%
31	Mississippi	41,492	0.8%
32	Kansas	39,190	0.8%
33	Hawaii	37,270	0.8%
34	Oklahoma	26,916	0.5%
35	New Hampshire	25,482	0.5%
36	Arkansas	24,565	0.5%
37	Delaware	22,679	0.5%
38	Nevada	20,723	0.4%
39	Utah	19,091	0.4%
40	Maine	16,977	0.3%
41	Idaho	16,844	0.3%
42	Rhode Island	16,666	0.3%
43	West Virginia	12,538	0.3%
44	South Dakota	10,166	0.2%
45	Montana	8,420	0.2%
46	Vermont	8,404	0.2%
47	North Dakota	7,676	0.2%
48	Alaska	3,422	0.1%
49	Wyoming	1,608	0.0%
NA	New Mexico**	NA	NA
	District of Columbia	13,208	0.3%

Source: U.S. Department of Education, National Center for Education Statistics
"Characteristics of Private Schools in the United States" (https://nces.ed.gov/pubsearch/pubsinfo.asp?pubid=2019071)
*For school year 2017–2018. Includes private schools that provide instruction for one or more grades kindergarten through 12 (or comparable ungraded levels).
**Not available.

Public Elementary and Secondary Schools in 2018

National Total = 98,495 Schools*

ALPHA ORDER

RANK	STATE	SCHOOLS	% of USA
24	Alabama	1,474	1.5%
44	Alaska	509	0.5%
14	Arizona	2,330	2.4%
32	Arkansas	1,087	1.1%
1	California	10,323	10.5%
19	Colorado	1,900	1.9%
35	Connecticut	1,031	1.0%
50	Delaware	228	0.2%
4	Florida	4,322	4.4%
15	Georgia	2,307	2.3%
49	Hawaii	292	0.3%
38	Idaho	741	0.8%
5	Illinois	4,241	4.3%
18	Indiana	1,920	1.9%
27	Iowa	1,322	1.3%
28	Kansas	1,319	1.3%
23	Kentucky	1,533	1.6%
26	Louisiana	1,390	1.4%
42	Maine	599	0.6%
25	Maryland	1,420	1.4%
20	Massachusetts	1,854	1.9%
6	Michigan	3,730	3.8%
11	Minnesota	2,525	2.6%
33	Mississippi	1,060	1.1%
13	Missouri	2,414	2.5%
37	Montana	820	0.8%
31	Nebraska	1,095	1.1%
40	Nevada	708	0.7%
45	New Hampshire	490	0.5%
10	New Jersey	2,594	2.6%
36	New Mexico	881	0.9%
3	New York	4,795	4.9%
9	North Carolina	2,647	2.7%
43	North Dakota	515	0.5%
7	Ohio	3,604	3.7%
21	Oklahoma	1,800	1.8%
30	Oregon	1,249	1.3%
8	Pennsylvania	2,982	3.0%
47	Rhode Island	317	0.3%
29	South Carolina	1,255	1.3%
41	South Dakota	697	0.7%
22	Tennessee	1,782	1.8%
2	Texas	8,909	9.0%
34	Utah	1,051	1.1%
48	Vermont	311	0.3%
17	Virginia	2,113	2.1%
12	Washington	2,425	2.5%
39	West Virginia	730	0.7%
16	Wisconsin	2,261	2.3%
46	Wyoming	369	0.4%

RANK ORDER

RANK	STATE	SCHOOLS	% of USA
1	California	10,323	10.5%
2	Texas	8,909	9.0%
3	New York	4,795	4.9%
4	Florida	4,322	4.4%
5	Illinois	4,241	4.3%
6	Michigan	3,730	3.8%
7	Ohio	3,604	3.7%
8	Pennsylvania	2,982	3.0%
9	North Carolina	2,647	2.7%
10	New Jersey	2,594	2.6%
11	Minnesota	2,525	2.6%
12	Washington	2,425	2.5%
13	Missouri	2,414	2.5%
14	Arizona	2,330	2.4%
15	Georgia	2,307	2.3%
16	Wisconsin	2,261	2.3%
17	Virginia	2,113	2.1%
18	Indiana	1,920	1.9%
19	Colorado	1,900	1.9%
20	Massachusetts	1,854	1.9%
21	Oklahoma	1,800	1.8%
22	Tennessee	1,782	1.8%
23	Kentucky	1,533	1.6%
24	Alabama	1,474	1.5%
25	Maryland	1,420	1.4%
26	Louisiana	1,390	1.4%
27	Iowa	1,322	1.3%
28	Kansas	1,319	1.3%
29	South Carolina	1,255	1.3%
30	Oregon	1,249	1.3%
31	Nebraska	1,095	1.1%
32	Arkansas	1,087	1.1%
33	Mississippi	1,060	1.1%
34	Utah	1,051	1.1%
35	Connecticut	1,031	1.0%
36	New Mexico	881	0.9%
37	Montana	820	0.8%
38	Idaho	741	0.8%
39	West Virginia	730	0.7%
40	Nevada	708	0.7%
41	South Dakota	697	0.7%
42	Maine	599	0.6%
43	North Dakota	515	0.5%
44	Alaska	509	0.5%
45	New Hampshire	490	0.5%
46	Wyoming	369	0.4%
47	Rhode Island	317	0.3%
48	Vermont	311	0.3%
49	Hawaii	292	0.3%
50	Delaware	228	0.2%
	District of Columbia	224	0.2%

Source: U.S. Department of Education, National Center for Education Statistics
"ElSi Table Generator" (https://nces.ed.gov/ccd/elsi/)
*For school year 2017–2018.

Enrollment in Public Elementary and Secondary Schools in 2018

National Total = 50,685,567 Students*

ALPHA ORDER

RANK	STATE	STUDENTS	% of USA
24	Alabama	742,444	1.5%
47	Alaska	132,872	0.3%
13	Arizona	1,110,851	2.2%
33	Arkansas	496,085	1.0%
1	California	6,304,266	12.4%
19	Colorado	910,280	1.8%
30	Connecticut	531,288	1.0%
46	Delaware	136,293	0.3%
3	Florida	2,832,424	5.6%
6	Georgia	1,768,642	3.5%
40	Hawaii	180,837	0.4%
38	Idaho	301,186	0.6%
5	Illinois	2,005,153	4.0%
15	Indiana	1,054,187	2.1%
31	Iowa	511,850	1.0%
32	Kansas	497,088	1.0%
27	Kentucky	680,978	1.3%
25	Louisiana	715,135	1.4%
41	Maine	180,473	0.4%
20	Maryland	893,684	1.8%
17	Massachusetts	964,791	1.9%
10	Michigan	1,516,398	3.0%
21	Minnesota	884,944	1.7%
35	Mississippi	478,321	0.9%
18	Missouri	915,472	1.8%
43	Montana	149,474	0.3%
37	Nebraska	323,766	0.6%
34	Nevada	485,785	1.0%
42	New Hampshire	179,433	0.4%
11	New Jersey	1,408,102	2.8%
36	New Mexico	334,345	0.7%
4	New York	2,724,663	5.4%
9	North Carolina	1,553,513	3.1%
48	North Dakota	111,920	0.2%
8	Ohio	1,704,399	3.4%
26	Oklahoma	695,092	1.4%
29	Oregon	608,014	1.2%
7	Pennsylvania	1,726,809	3.4%
44	Rhode Island	142,949	0.3%
23	South Carolina	777,507	1.5%
45	South Dakota	137,823	0.3%
16	Tennessee	1,001,967	2.0%
2	Texas	5,401,341	10.7%
28	Utah	668,274	1.3%
50	Vermont	88,028	0.2%
12	Virginia	1,291,462	2.5%
14	Washington	1,110,367	2.2%
39	West Virginia	272,266	0.5%
22	Wisconsin	860,753	1.7%
49	Wyoming	94,258	0.2%

RANK ORDER

RANK	STATE	STUDENTS	% of USA
1	California	6,304,266	12.4%
2	Texas	5,401,341	10.7%
3	Florida	2,832,424	5.6%
4	New York	2,724,663	5.4%
5	Illinois	2,005,153	4.0%
6	Georgia	1,768,642	3.5%
7	Pennsylvania	1,726,809	3.4%
8	Ohio	1,704,399	3.4%
9	North Carolina	1,553,513	3.1%
10	Michigan	1,516,398	3.0%
11	New Jersey	1,408,102	2.8%
12	Virginia	1,291,462	2.5%
13	Arizona	1,110,851	2.2%
14	Washington	1,110,367	2.2%
15	Indiana	1,054,187	2.1%
16	Tennessee	1,001,967	2.0%
17	Massachusetts	964,791	1.9%
18	Missouri	915,472	1.8%
19	Colorado	910,280	1.8%
20	Maryland	893,684	1.8%
21	Minnesota	884,944	1.7%
22	Wisconsin	860,753	1.7%
23	South Carolina	777,507	1.5%
24	Alabama	742,444	1.5%
25	Louisiana	715,135	1.4%
26	Oklahoma	695,092	1.4%
27	Kentucky	680,978	1.3%
28	Utah	668,274	1.3%
29	Oregon	608,014	1.2%
30	Connecticut	531,288	1.0%
31	Iowa	511,850	1.0%
32	Kansas	497,088	1.0%
33	Arkansas	496,085	1.0%
34	Nevada	485,785	1.0%
35	Mississippi	478,321	0.9%
36	New Mexico	334,345	0.7%
37	Nebraska	323,766	0.6%
38	Idaho	301,186	0.6%
39	West Virginia	272,266	0.5%
40	Hawaii	180,837	0.4%
41	Maine	180,473	0.4%
42	New Hampshire	179,433	0.4%
43	Montana	149,474	0.3%
44	Rhode Island	142,949	0.3%
45	South Dakota	137,823	0.3%
46	Delaware	136,293	0.3%
47	Alaska	132,872	0.3%
48	North Dakota	111,920	0.2%
49	Wyoming	94,258	0.2%
50	Vermont	88,028	0.2%
	District of Columbia	87,315	0.2%

Source: U.S. Department of Education, National Center for Education Statistics
"ElSi Table Generator" (https://nces.ed.gov/ccd/elsi/)
*For school year 2017–2018.

Public Elementary and Secondary School Teachers in 2018

National Total = 3,169,750 Teachers*

ALPHA ORDER

RANK	STATE	TEACHERS	% of USA
26	Alabama	41,802	1.3%
49	Alaska	7,743	0.2%
23	Arizona	47,868	1.5%
30	Arkansas	35,800	1.1%
2	California	271,523	8.6%
22	Colorado	52,373	1.7%
24	Connecticut	45,081	1.4%
46	Delaware	9,399	0.3%
4	Florida	186,128	5.9%
7	Georgia	116,022	3.7%
42	Hawaii	12,033	0.4%
39	Idaho	16,592	0.5%
5	Illinois	128,204	4.0%
16	Indiana	61,018	1.9%
31	Iowa	35,553	1.1%
29	Kansas	36,387	1.1%
25	Kentucky	42,064	1.3%
28	Louisiana	40,281	1.3%
40	Maine	14,760	0.5%
18	Maryland	60,175	1.9%
13	Massachusetts	73,381	2.3%
12	Michigan	84,473	2.7%
20	Minnesota	57,260	1.8%
32	Mississippi	31,625	1.0%
14	Missouri	68,496	2.2%
44	Montana	10,515	0.3%
35	Nebraska	23,771	0.7%
36	Nevada	23,709	0.7%
41	New Hampshire	14,589	0.5%
8	New Jersey	115,496	3.6%
37	New Mexico	21,092	0.7%
3	New York	213,159	6.7%
9	North Carolina	100,401	3.2%
47	North Dakota	9,284	0.3%
10	Ohio	98,912	3.1%
27	Oklahoma	41,597	1.3%
33	Oregon	29,909	0.9%
6	Pennsylvania	121,918	3.8%
43	Rhode Island	10,687	0.3%
21	South Carolina	52,467	1.7%
45	South Dakota	9,833	0.3%
15	Tennessee	64,019	2.0%
1	Texas	356,877	11.3%
34	Utah	29,212	0.9%
48	Vermont	8,313	0.3%
11	Virginia	85,936	2.7%
17	Washington	60,183	1.9%
38	West Virginia	19,239	0.6%
19	Wisconsin	58,598	1.8%
50	Wyoming	7,335	0.2%

RANK ORDER

RANK	STATE	TEACHERS	% of USA
1	Texas	356,877	11.3%
2	California	271,523	8.6%
3	New York	213,159	6.7%
4	Florida	186,128	5.9%
5	Illinois	128,204	4.0%
6	Pennsylvania	121,918	3.8%
7	Georgia	116,022	3.7%
8	New Jersey	115,496	3.6%
9	North Carolina	100,401	3.2%
10	Ohio	98,912	3.1%
11	Virginia	85,936	2.7%
12	Michigan	84,473	2.7%
13	Massachusetts	73,381	2.3%
14	Missouri	68,496	2.2%
15	Tennessee	64,019	2.0%
16	Indiana	61,018	1.9%
17	Washington	60,183	1.9%
18	Maryland	60,175	1.9%
19	Wisconsin	58,598	1.8%
20	Minnesota	57,260	1.8%
21	South Carolina	52,467	1.7%
22	Colorado	52,373	1.7%
23	Arizona	47,868	1.5%
24	Connecticut	45,081	1.4%
25	Kentucky	42,064	1.3%
26	Alabama	41,802	1.3%
27	Oklahoma	41,597	1.3%
28	Louisiana	40,281	1.3%
29	Kansas	36,387	1.1%
30	Arkansas	35,800	1.1%
31	Iowa	35,553	1.1%
32	Mississippi	31,625	1.0%
33	Oregon	29,909	0.9%
34	Utah	29,212	0.9%
35	Nebraska	23,771	0.7%
36	Nevada	23,709	0.7%
37	New Mexico	21,092	0.7%
38	West Virginia	19,239	0.6%
39	Idaho	16,592	0.5%
40	Maine	14,760	0.5%
41	New Hampshire	14,589	0.5%
42	Hawaii	12,033	0.4%
43	Rhode Island	10,687	0.3%
44	Montana	10,515	0.3%
45	South Dakota	9,833	0.3%
46	Delaware	9,399	0.3%
47	North Dakota	9,284	0.3%
48	Vermont	8,313	0.3%
49	Alaska	7,743	0.2%
50	Wyoming	7,335	0.2%
	District of Columbia	6,659	0.2%

Source: U.S. Department of Education, National Center for Education Statistics
  "ElSi Table Generator" (https://nces.ed.gov/ccd/elsi/)
*For school year 2017–2018. Counts are full-time equivalent figures.

Pupil-Teacher Ratio in Public Elementary and Secondary Schools in 2018

National Ratio = 16.0 Pupils per Teacher*

ALPHA ORDER

RANK	STATE	RATIO
9	Alabama	17.8
13	Alaska	17.2
1	Arizona	23.2
37	Arkansas	13.9
1	California	23.2
11	Colorado	17.4
49	Connecticut	11.8
31	Delaware	14.5
22	Florida	15.2
22	Georgia	15.2
26	Hawaii	15.0
7	Idaho	18.2
19	Illinois	15.6
12	Indiana	17.3
32	Iowa	14.4
38	Kansas	13.7
16	Kentucky	16.2
9	Louisiana	17.8
46	Maine	12.2
28	Maryland	14.9
42	Massachusetts	13.2
8	Michigan	18.0
20	Minnesota	15.5
24	Mississippi	15.1
40	Missouri	13.4
33	Montana	14.2
39	Nebraska	13.6
4	Nevada	20.5
45	New Hampshire	12.3
46	New Jersey	12.2
17	New Mexico	15.9
44	New York	12.8
20	North Carolina	15.5
48	North Dakota	12.1
13	Ohio	17.2
15	Oklahoma	16.7
5	Oregon	20.3
33	Pennsylvania	14.2
40	Rhode Island	13.4
29	South Carolina	14.8
36	South Dakota	14.0
18	Tennessee	15.7
24	Texas	15.1
3	Utah	22.9
50	Vermont	10.6
26	Virginia	15.0
6	Washington	18.5
33	West Virginia	14.2
30	Wisconsin	14.7
43	Wyoming	12.9

RANK ORDER

RANK	STATE	RATIO
1	Arizona	23.2
1	California	23.2
3	Utah	22.9
4	Nevada	20.5
5	Oregon	20.3
6	Washington	18.5
7	Idaho	18.2
8	Michigan	18.0
9	Alabama	17.8
9	Louisiana	17.8
11	Colorado	17.4
12	Indiana	17.3
13	Alaska	17.2
13	Ohio	17.2
15	Oklahoma	16.7
16	Kentucky	16.2
17	New Mexico	15.9
18	Tennessee	15.7
19	Illinois	15.6
20	Minnesota	15.5
20	North Carolina	15.5
22	Florida	15.2
22	Georgia	15.2
24	Mississippi	15.1
24	Texas	15.1
26	Hawaii	15.0
26	Virginia	15.0
28	Maryland	14.9
29	South Carolina	14.8
30	Wisconsin	14.7
31	Delaware	14.5
32	Iowa	14.4
33	Montana	14.2
33	Pennsylvania	14.2
33	West Virginia	14.2
36	South Dakota	14.0
37	Arkansas	13.9
38	Kansas	13.7
39	Nebraska	13.6
40	Missouri	13.4
40	Rhode Island	13.4
42	Massachusetts	13.2
43	Wyoming	12.9
44	New York	12.8
45	New Hampshire	12.3
46	Maine	12.2
46	New Jersey	12.2
48	North Dakota	12.1
49	Connecticut	11.8
50	Vermont	10.6
	District of Columbia	13.1

Source: U.S. Department of Education, National Center for Education Statistics
"ElSi Table Generator" (https://nces.ed.gov/ccd/elsi/)
*For school year 2017–2018. Based on full-time equivalency counts of teachers.

Estimated Average Salary of Public School Teachers in 2019
(National Education Association)
National Average = $61,730*

ALPHA ORDER				RANK ORDER		
RANK	STATE	SALARY		RANK	STATE	SALARY
39	Alabama	$50,810		1	New York	$85,889
7	Alaska	70,277		2	California	82,282
44	Arizona	49,892		3	Massachusetts	82,042
36	Arkansas	51,019		4	Connecticut	76,465
2	California	82,282		5	Washington	72,965
31	Colorado	53,301		6	Maryland	70,463
4	Connecticut	76,465		7	Alaska	70,277
13	Delaware	62,308		8	New Jersey	70,212
47	Florida	48,395		9	Pennsylvania	68,141
22	Georgia	57,137		10	Rhode Island	67,040
16	Hawaii	59,757		11	Illinois	66,600
40	Idaho	50,757		12	Oregon	64,385
11	Illinois	66,600		13	Delaware	62,308
37	Indiana	50,937		14	Michigan	61,825
20	Iowa	58,140		15	Vermont	61,027
45	Kansas	49,800		16	Hawaii	59,757
29	Kentucky	53,434		17	Wyoming	58,618
38	Louisiana	50,923		18	Minnesota	58,221
23	Maine	54,974		19	New Hampshire	58,146
6	Maryland	70,463		20	Iowa	58,140
3	Massachusetts	82,042		21	Ohio	57,799
14	Michigan	61,825		22	Georgia	57,137
18	Minnesota	58,221		23	Maine	54,974
50	Mississippi	45,574		24	Nebraska	54,506
43	Missouri	50,064		25	Nevada	54,280
27	Montana	54,034		26	Texas	54,155
24	Nebraska	54,506		27	Montana	54,034
25	Nevada	54,280		28	North Carolina	53,975
19	New Hampshire	58,146		29	Kentucky	53,434
8	New Jersey	70,212		29	North Dakota	53,434
48	New Mexico	47,826		31	Colorado	53,301
1	New York	85,889		32	Virginia	52,466
28	North Carolina	53,975		33	Oklahoma	52,412
29	North Dakota	53,434		34	Tennessee	51,714
21	Ohio	57,799		35	Wisconsin	51,453
33	Oklahoma	52,412		36	Arkansas	51,019
12	Oregon	64,385		37	Indiana	50,937
9	Pennsylvania	68,141		38	Louisiana	50,923
10	Rhode Island	67,040		39	Alabama	50,810
41	South Carolina	50,395		40	Idaho	50,757
46	South Dakota	48,786		41	South Carolina	50,395
34	Tennessee	51,714		42	Utah	50,342
26	Texas	54,155		43	Missouri	50,064
42	Utah	50,342		44	Arizona	49,892
15	Vermont	61,027		45	Kansas	49,800
32	Virginia	52,466		46	South Dakota	48,786
5	Washington	72,965		47	Florida	48,395
49	West Virginia	47,681		48	New Mexico	47,826
35	Wisconsin	51,453		49	West Virginia	47,681
17	Wyoming	58,618		50	Mississippi	45,574
					District of Columbia	78,477

Source: National Education Association, Washington, D.C.
  "Rankings and Estimates" (Copyright © 2019, NEA, https://www.nea.org/home/44479.htm)
*Estimates for school year 2018–2019 for classroom teachers.

Average Teacher's Salary as a Percent of Average Annual Pay in 2018

National Average = 106.7% of Average Annual Pay*

ALPHA ORDER				RANK ORDER		
RANK	STATE	PERCENT		RANK	STATE	PERCENT
28	Alabama	106.9		1	Vermont	127.6
2	Alaska	125.7		2	Alaska	125.7
47	Arizona	95.1		3	Rhode Island	124.5
14	Arkansas	115.5		4	Montana	123.0
10	California	119.0		5	Pennsylvania	121.9
49	Colorado	89.9		6	Wyoming	121.7
23	Connecticut	111.4		7	Iowa	121.2
26	Delaware	109.2		8	Oregon	120.1
46	Florida	96.4		9	Maine	119.9
32	Georgia	106.1		10	California	119.0
15	Hawaii	115.4		11	Nebraska	117.5
13	Idaho	116.6		12	New York	116.7
24	Illinois	110.4		13	Idaho	116.6
30	Indiana	106.7		14	Arkansas	115.5
7	Iowa	121.2		15	Hawaii	115.4
29	Kansas	106.8		16	Michigan	115.0
17	Kentucky	114.9		17	Kentucky	114.9
35	Louisiana	105.2		18	Maryland	114.5
9	Maine	119.9		18	Ohio	114.5
18	Maryland	114.5		20	Mississippi	113.8
22	Massachusetts	111.8		21	South Carolina	112.4
16	Michigan	115.0		22	Massachusetts	111.8
44	Minnesota	100.0		23	Connecticut	111.4
20	Mississippi	113.8		24	Illinois	110.4
42	Missouri	101.3		25	South Dakota	110.3
4	Montana	123.0		26	Delaware	109.2
11	Nebraska	117.5		27	Nevada	108.5
27	Nevada	108.5		28	Alabama	106.9
39	New Hampshire	102.1		29	Kansas	106.8
31	New Jersey	106.6		30	Indiana	106.7
36	New Mexico	105.1		31	New Jersey	106.6
12	New York	116.7		32	Georgia	106.1
37	North Carolina	103.6		33	Oklahoma	105.6
41	North Dakota	101.5		34	Wisconsin	105.3
18	Ohio	114.5		35	Louisiana	105.2
33	Oklahoma	105.6		36	New Mexico	105.1
8	Oregon	120.1		37	North Carolina	103.6
5	Pennsylvania	121.9		38	Utah	103.1
3	Rhode Island	124.5		39	New Hampshire	102.1
21	South Carolina	112.4		40	Tennessee	101.7
25	South Dakota	110.3		41	North Dakota	101.5
40	Tennessee	101.7		42	Missouri	101.3
48	Texas	93.1		43	West Virginia	101.2
38	Utah	103.1		44	Minnesota	100.0
1	Vermont	127.6		45	Washington	97.3
50	Virginia	89.7		46	Florida	96.4
45	Washington	97.3		47	Arizona	95.1
43	West Virginia	101.2		48	Texas	93.1
34	Wisconsin	105.3		49	Colorado	89.9
6	Wyoming	121.7		50	Virginia	89.7
					District of Columbia	80.8

Source: CQ Press using data from National Education Association, Washington, D.C.
"Rankings and Estimates" (Copyright © 2019, NEA, https://www.nea.org/home/44479.htm) and
"Quarterly Census of Employment and Wages" (https://www.bls.gov/cew/data.htm)
*Average of public elementary and secondary teacher salary for school years 2017–2018 and 2018–2019 compared to each state's 2018 average annual pay for all workers covered by federal unemployment.

Percent of Public School Fourth Graders
Proficient or Better in Reading in 2019
National Percent = 34%*

	ALPHA ORDER			RANK ORDER	
RANK	STATE	PERCENT	RANK	STATE	PERCENT
47	Alabama	28	1	Massachusetts	45
49	Alaska	25	2	New Jersey	42
41	Arizona	31	3	Wyoming	41
41	Arkansas	31	4	Colorado	40
36	California	32	4	Connecticut	40
4	Colorado	40	4	Pennsylvania	40
4	Connecticut	40	4	Utah	40
35	Delaware	33	8	Florida	38
8	Florida	38	8	Minnesota	38
36	Georgia	32	8	New Hampshire	38
28	Hawaii	34	8	Virginia	38
12	Idaho	37	12	Idaho	37
28	Illinois	34	12	Indiana	37
12	Indiana	37	12	Nebraska	37
22	Iowa	35	12	Vermont	37
28	Kansas	34	16	Maine	36
22	Kentucky	35	16	Montana	36
48	Louisiana	26	16	North Carolina	36
16	Maine	36	16	Ohio	36
22	Maryland	35	16	South Dakota	36
1	Massachusetts	45	16	Wisconsin	36
36	Michigan	32	22	Iowa	35
8	Minnesota	38	22	Kentucky	35
36	Mississippi	32	22	Maryland	35
28	Missouri	34	22	Rhode Island	35
16	Montana	36	22	Tennessee	35
12	Nebraska	37	22	Washington	35
41	Nevada	31	28	Hawaii	34
8	New Hampshire	38	28	Illinois	34
2	New Jersey	42	28	Kansas	34
50	New Mexico	24	28	Missouri	34
28	New York	34	28	New York	34
16	North Carolina	36	28	North Dakota	34
28	North Dakota	34	28	Oregon	34
16	Ohio	36	35	Delaware	33
46	Oklahoma	29	36	California	32
28	Oregon	34	36	Georgia	32
4	Pennsylvania	40	36	Michigan	32
22	Rhode Island	35	36	Mississippi	32
36	South Carolina	32	36	South Carolina	32
16	South Dakota	36	41	Arizona	31
22	Tennessee	35	41	Arkansas	31
44	Texas	30	41	Nevada	31
4	Utah	40	44	Texas	30
12	Vermont	37	44	West Virginia	30
8	Virginia	38	46	Oklahoma	29
22	Washington	35	47	Alabama	28
44	West Virginia	30	48	Louisiana	26
16	Wisconsin	36	49	Alaska	25
3	Wyoming	41	50	New Mexico	24
				District of Columbia	30

Source: U.S. Department of Education, National Center for Education Statistics
"The Nation's Report Card: Reading 2019" (www.nationsreportcard.gov)
*There are four achievement levels: Below Basic, Basic, Proficient, and Advanced. Proficient represents solid academic mastery for fourth graders. Students reaching this level have demonstrated competency over challenging subject matter, including subject matter knowledge, application of such knowledge to real-world situations, and analytical skills appropriate to the subject matter.

Percent of Public School Eighth Graders
Proficient or Better in Reading in 2019
National Percent = 32%*

ALPHA ORDER				RANK ORDER		
RANK	STATE	PERCENT		RANK	STATE	PERCENT
48	Alabama	24		1	Massachusetts	45
49	Alaska	23		2	New Jersey	43
42	Arizona	28		3	Connecticut	41
37	Arkansas	30		4	Vermont	40
37	California	30		5	Wisconsin	39
6	Colorado	38		6	Colorado	38
3	Connecticut	41		6	New Hampshire	38
35	Delaware	31		6	Ohio	38
18	Florida	34		6	Utah	38
29	Georgia	32		6	Washington	38
39	Hawaii	29		11	Idaho	37
11	Idaho	37		11	Indiana	37
15	Illinois	35		13	Maine	36
11	Indiana	37		13	Maryland	36
24	Iowa	33		15	Illinois	35
29	Kansas	32		15	Pennsylvania	35
24	Kentucky	33		15	Rhode Island	35
43	Louisiana	27		18	Florida	34
13	Maine	36		18	Minnesota	34
13	Maryland	36		18	Montana	34
1	Massachusetts	45		18	Nebraska	34
35	Michigan	31		18	Oregon	34
18	Minnesota	34		18	Wyoming	34
45	Mississippi	25		24	Iowa	33
24	Missouri	33		24	Kentucky	33
18	Montana	34		24	Missouri	33
18	Nebraska	34		24	North Carolina	33
39	Nevada	29		24	Virginia	33
6	New Hampshire	38		29	Georgia	32
2	New Jersey	43		29	Kansas	32
49	New Mexico	23		29	New York	32
29	New York	32		29	North Dakota	32
24	North Carolina	33		29	South Dakota	32
29	North Dakota	32		29	Tennessee	32
6	Ohio	38		35	Delaware	31
44	Oklahoma	26		35	Michigan	31
18	Oregon	34		37	Arkansas	30
15	Pennsylvania	35		37	California	30
15	Rhode Island	35		39	Hawaii	29
39	South Carolina	29		39	Nevada	29
29	South Dakota	32		39	South Carolina	29
29	Tennessee	32		42	Arizona	28
45	Texas	25		43	Louisiana	27
6	Utah	38		44	Oklahoma	26
4	Vermont	40		45	Mississippi	25
24	Virginia	33		45	Texas	25
6	Washington	38		45	West Virginia	25
45	West Virginia	25		48	Alabama	24
5	Wisconsin	39		49	Alaska	23
18	Wyoming	34		49	New Mexico	23
					District of Columbia	23

Source: U.S. Department of Education, National Center for Education Statistics
    "The Nation's Report Card: Reading 2019" (www.nationsreportcard.gov)
*There are four achievement levels: Below Basic, Basic, Proficient, and Advanced. Proficient represents solid academic mastery for eighth graders. Students reaching this level have demonstrated competency over challenging subject matter, including subject matter knowledge, application of such knowledge to real-world situations, and analytical skills appropriate to the subject matter.

Percent of Public School Fourth Graders Proficient or Better in Mathematics in 2019
National Percent = 40%*

ALPHA ORDER

ALPHA ORDER

RANK	STATE	PERCENT
50	Alabama	28
45	Alaska	33
36	Arizona	37
45	Arkansas	33
43	California	34
14	Colorado	44
11	Connecticut	45
29	Delaware	39
3	Florida	48
39	Georgia	36
24	Hawaii	40
17	Idaho	43
35	Illinois	38
7	Indiana	47
20	Iowa	42
24	Kansas	40
24	Kentucky	40
48	Louisiana	29
20	Maine	42
29	Maryland	39
2	Massachusetts	50
39	Michigan	36
1	Minnesota	53
29	Mississippi	39
29	Missouri	39
17	Montana	43
11	Nebraska	45
43	Nevada	34
9	New Hampshire	46
3	New Jersey	48
48	New Mexico	29
36	New York	37
22	North Carolina	41
14	North Dakota	44
22	Ohio	41
42	Oklahoma	35
36	Oregon	37
7	Pennsylvania	47
24	Rhode Island	40
39	South Carolina	36
17	South Dakota	43
24	Tennessee	40
14	Texas	44
9	Utah	46
29	Vermont	39
3	Virginia	48
29	Washington	39
47	West Virginia	30
11	Wisconsin	45
3	Wyoming	48

RANK ORDER

RANK	STATE	PERCENT
1	Minnesota	53
2	Massachusetts	50
3	Florida	48
3	New Jersey	48
3	Virginia	48
3	Wyoming	48
7	Indiana	47
7	Pennsylvania	47
9	New Hampshire	46
9	Utah	46
11	Connecticut	45
11	Nebraska	45
11	Wisconsin	45
14	Colorado	44
14	North Dakota	44
14	Texas	44
17	Idaho	43
17	Montana	43
17	South Dakota	43
20	Iowa	42
20	Maine	42
22	North Carolina	41
22	Ohio	41
24	Hawaii	40
24	Kansas	40
24	Kentucky	40
24	Rhode Island	40
24	Tennessee	40
29	Delaware	39
29	Maryland	39
29	Mississippi	39
29	Missouri	39
29	Vermont	39
29	Washington	39
35	Illinois	38
36	Arizona	37
36	New York	37
36	Oregon	37
39	Georgia	36
39	Michigan	36
39	South Carolina	36
42	Oklahoma	35
43	California	34
43	Nevada	34
45	Alaska	33
45	Arkansas	33
47	West Virginia	30
48	Louisiana	29
48	New Mexico	29
50	Alabama	28

| | District of Columbia | 34 |

Source: U.S. Department of Education, National Center for Education Statistics
"The Nation's Report Card: Mathematics 2019" (www.nationsreportcard.gov)
*There are four achievement levels: Below Basic, Basic, Proficient, and Advanced. Proficient represents solid academic mastery for fourth graders. Students reaching this level have demonstrated competency over challenging subject matter, including subject matter knowledge, application of such knowledge to real-world situations, and analytical skills appropriate to the subject matter.

Percent of Public School Eighth Graders Proficient or Better in Mathematics in 2019
National Percent = 33%*

ALPHA ORDER

RANK	STATE	PERCENT
49	Alabama	21
36	Alaska	29
29	Arizona	31
43	Arkansas	27
36	California	29
13	Colorado	37
6	Connecticut	39
36	Delaware	29
29	Florida	31
29	Georgia	31
42	Hawaii	28
13	Idaho	37
22	Illinois	34
13	Indiana	37
25	Iowa	33
25	Kansas	33
36	Kentucky	29
48	Louisiana	23
22	Maine	34
25	Maryland	33
1	Massachusetts	47
29	Michigan	31
2	Minnesota	44
46	Mississippi	24
28	Missouri	32
21	Montana	36
13	Nebraska	37
44	Nevada	26
9	New Hampshire	38
2	New Jersey	44
49	New Mexico	21
22	New York	34
13	North Carolina	37
13	North Dakota	37
9	Ohio	38
44	Oklahoma	26
29	Oregon	31
6	Pennsylvania	39
36	Rhode Island	29
36	South Carolina	29
6	South Dakota	39
29	Tennessee	31
35	Texas	30
13	Utah	37
9	Vermont	38
9	Virginia	38
5	Washington	40
46	West Virginia	24
4	Wisconsin	41
13	Wyoming	37

RANK ORDER

RANK	STATE	PERCENT
1	Massachusetts	47
2	Minnesota	44
2	New Jersey	44
4	Wisconsin	41
5	Washington	40
6	Connecticut	39
6	Pennsylvania	39
6	South Dakota	39
9	New Hampshire	38
9	Ohio	38
9	Vermont	38
9	Virginia	38
13	Colorado	37
13	Idaho	37
13	Indiana	37
13	Nebraska	37
13	North Carolina	37
13	North Dakota	37
13	Utah	37
13	Wyoming	37
21	Montana	36
22	Illinois	34
22	Maine	34
22	New York	34
25	Iowa	33
25	Kansas	33
25	Maryland	33
28	Missouri	32
29	Arizona	31
29	Florida	31
29	Georgia	31
29	Michigan	31
29	Oregon	31
29	Tennessee	31
35	Texas	30
36	Alaska	29
36	California	29
36	Delaware	29
36	Kentucky	29
36	Rhode Island	29
36	South Carolina	29
42	Hawaii	28
43	Arkansas	27
44	Nevada	26
44	Oklahoma	26
46	Mississippi	24
46	West Virginia	24
48	Louisiana	23
49	Alabama	21
49	New Mexico	21
	District of Columbia	23

Source: U.S. Department of Education, National Center for Education Statistics
"The Nation's Report Card: Mathematics 2019" (www.nationsreportcard.gov)
*There are four achievement levels: Below Basic, Basic, Proficient, and Advanced. Proficient represents solid academic mastery for eighth graders. Students reaching this level have demonstrated competency over challenging subject matter, including subject matter knowledge, application of such knowledge to real-world situations, and analytical skills appropriate to the subject matter.

Percent of Population Graduated from High School in 2018

National Percent = 88.3%*

RANK	STATE	PERCENT
45	Alabama	86.6
4	Alaska	93.3
40	Arizona	87.5
41	Arkansas	87.2
50	California	83.8
14	Colorado	91.9
20	Connecticut	90.9
29	Delaware	89.8
33	Florida	88.5
39	Georgia	87.6
13	Hawaii	92.0
20	Idaho	90.9
30	Illinois	89.5
32	Indiana	89.0
9	Iowa	92.3
18	Kansas	91.0
44	Kentucky	86.8
46	Louisiana	85.8
7	Maine	93.0
24	Maryland	90.5
22	Massachusetts	90.8
17	Michigan	91.1
3	Minnesota	93.4
47	Mississippi	85.4
24	Missouri	90.5
1	Montana	93.9
16	Nebraska	91.4
43	Nevada	86.9
6	New Hampshire	93.1
27	New Jersey	90.2
47	New Mexico	85.4
42	New York	87.1
36	North Carolina	88.2
9	North Dakota	92.3
23	Ohio	90.7
34	Oklahoma	88.4
24	Oregon	90.5
18	Pennsylvania	91.0
31	Rhode Island	89.1
34	South Carolina	88.4
9	South Dakota	92.3
37	Tennessee	87.8
49	Texas	84.0
8	Utah	92.4
2	Vermont	93.5
28	Virginia	89.9
15	Washington	91.6
37	West Virginia	87.8
12	Wisconsin	92.1
4	Wyoming	93.3

RANK	STATE	PERCENT
1	Montana	93.9
2	Vermont	93.5
3	Minnesota	93.4
4	Alaska	93.3
4	Wyoming	93.3
6	New Hampshire	93.1
7	Maine	93.0
8	Utah	92.4
9	Iowa	92.3
9	North Dakota	92.3
9	South Dakota	92.3
12	Wisconsin	92.1
13	Hawaii	92.0
14	Colorado	91.9
15	Washington	91.6
16	Nebraska	91.4
17	Michigan	91.1
18	Kansas	91.0
18	Pennsylvania	91.0
20	Connecticut	90.9
20	Idaho	90.9
22	Massachusetts	90.8
23	Ohio	90.7
24	Maryland	90.5
24	Missouri	90.5
24	Oregon	90.5
27	New Jersey	90.2
28	Virginia	89.9
29	Delaware	89.8
30	Illinois	89.5
31	Rhode Island	89.1
32	Indiana	89.0
33	Florida	88.5
34	Oklahoma	88.4
34	South Carolina	88.4
36	North Carolina	88.2
37	Tennessee	87.8
37	West Virginia	87.8
39	Georgia	87.6
40	Arizona	87.5
41	Arkansas	87.2
42	New York	87.1
43	Nevada	86.9
44	Kentucky	86.8
45	Alabama	86.6
46	Louisiana	85.8
47	Mississippi	85.4
47	New Mexico	85.4
49	Texas	84.0
50	California	83.8
	District of Columbia	92.1

Source: U.S. Bureau of the Census
"2018 American Community Survey-Table CP02" (https://data.census.gov/cedsci/)
*Persons age 25 and older. Includes equivalency status.

Projected Public High School Graduates in 2020

National Total = 3,303,890 Graduates*

ALPHA ORDER

RANK	STATE	GRADUATES	% of USA
24	Alabama	44,070	1.3%
47	Alaska	7,840	0.2%
15	Arizona	69,610	2.1%
33	Arkansas	31,320	0.9%
1	California	421,890	12.8%
22	Colorado	57,760	1.7%
29	Connecticut	35,980	1.1%
45	Delaware	9,080	0.3%
4	Florida	175,370	5.3%
8	Georgia	105,660	3.2%
42	Hawaii	10,820	0.3%
38	Idaho	19,440	0.6%
5	Illinois	139,490	4.2%
16	Indiana	69,520	2.1%
31	Iowa	33,390	1.0%
32	Kansas	33,330	1.0%
25	Kentucky	43,760	1.3%
27	Louisiana	40,430	1.2%
41	Maine	12,100	0.4%
19	Maryland	60,180	1.8%
14	Massachusetts	69,790	2.1%
10	Michigan	98,170	3.0%
21	Minnesota	58,510	1.8%
34	Mississippi	26,680	0.8%
18	Missouri	60,750	1.8%
44	Montana	9,610	0.3%
36	Nebraska	22,750	0.7%
35	Nevada	25,150	0.8%
40	New Hampshire	12,960	0.4%
11	New Jersey	96,210	2.9%
37	New Mexico	20,780	0.6%
3	New York	179,160	5.4%
9	North Carolina	104,770	3.2%
48	North Dakota	6,850	0.2%
6	Ohio	121,250	3.7%
26	Oklahoma	41,640	1.3%
30	Oregon	35,190	1.1%
7	Pennsylvania	118,130	3.6%
43	Rhode Island	10,390	0.3%
23	South Carolina	46,620	1.4%
46	South Dakota	8,380	0.3%
17	Tennessee	64,430	2.0%
2	Texas	352,500	10.7%
28	Utah	39,140	1.2%
50	Vermont	5,750	0.2%
12	Virginia	87,800	2.7%
13	Washington	72,220	2.2%
39	West Virginia	17,230	0.5%
20	Wisconsin	60,040	1.8%
49	Wyoming	5,770	0.2%

RANK ORDER

RANK	STATE	GRADUATES	% of USA
1	California	421,890	12.8%
2	Texas	352,500	10.7%
3	New York	179,160	5.4%
4	Florida	175,370	5.3%
5	Illinois	139,490	4.2%
6	Ohio	121,250	3.7%
7	Pennsylvania	118,130	3.6%
8	Georgia	105,660	3.2%
9	North Carolina	104,770	3.2%
10	Michigan	98,170	3.0%
11	New Jersey	96,210	2.9%
12	Virginia	87,800	2.7%
13	Washington	72,220	2.2%
14	Massachusetts	69,790	2.1%
15	Arizona	69,610	2.1%
16	Indiana	69,520	2.1%
17	Tennessee	64,430	2.0%
18	Missouri	60,750	1.8%
19	Maryland	60,180	1.8%
20	Wisconsin	60,040	1.8%
21	Minnesota	58,510	1.8%
22	Colorado	57,760	1.7%
23	South Carolina	46,620	1.4%
24	Alabama	44,070	1.3%
25	Kentucky	43,760	1.3%
26	Oklahoma	41,640	1.3%
27	Louisiana	40,430	1.2%
28	Utah	39,140	1.2%
29	Connecticut	35,980	1.1%
30	Oregon	35,190	1.1%
31	Iowa	33,390	1.0%
32	Kansas	33,330	1.0%
33	Arkansas	31,320	0.9%
34	Mississippi	26,680	0.8%
35	Nevada	25,150	0.8%
36	Nebraska	22,750	0.7%
37	New Mexico	20,780	0.6%
38	Idaho	19,440	0.6%
39	West Virginia	17,230	0.5%
40	New Hampshire	12,960	0.4%
41	Maine	12,100	0.4%
42	Hawaii	10,820	0.3%
43	Rhode Island	10,390	0.3%
44	Montana	9,610	0.3%
45	Delaware	9,080	0.3%
46	South Dakota	8,380	0.3%
47	Alaska	7,840	0.2%
48	North Dakota	6,850	0.2%
49	Wyoming	5,770	0.2%
50	Vermont	5,750	0.2%
	District of Columbia	4,270	0.1%

Source: U.S. Department of Education, National Center for Education Statistics
   "Digest of Education Statistics" (https://nces.ed.gov/programs/digest/index.asp)
*Projected for school year 2019–2020. Excludes persons receiving high school equivalency
certificates.

Adjusted Cohort Graduation Rate for Public High Schools in 2017

National Average = 84.6%*

ALPHA ORDER				RANK ORDER		
RANK	STATE	PERCENT		RANK	STATE	PERCENT
7	Alabama	89.3		1	Iowa	91.0
46	Alaska	78.2		2	New Jersey	90.5
48	Arizona	78.0		3	Tennessee	89.8
14	Arkansas	88.0		4	Kentucky	89.7
34	California	82.7		4	Texas	89.7
45	Colorado	79.1		6	West Virginia	89.4
15	Connecticut	87.9		7	Alabama	89.3
19	Delaware	86.9		8	Nebraska	89.1
38	Florida	82.3		8	Vermont	89.1
41	Georgia	80.6		10	New Hampshire	88.9
34	Hawaii	82.7		11	Wisconsin	88.6
43	Idaho	79.7		12	Massachusetts	88.3
18	Illinois	87.0		12	Missouri	88.3
30	Indiana	83.8		14	Arkansas	88.0
1	Iowa	91.0		15	Connecticut	87.9
24	Kansas	86.5		16	Maryland	87.7
4	Kentucky	89.7		17	North Dakota	87.2
47	Louisiana	78.1		18	Illinois	87.0
19	Maine	86.9		19	Delaware	86.9
16	Maryland	87.7		19	Maine	86.9
12	Massachusetts	88.3		19	Virginia	86.9
42	Michigan	80.2		22	North Carolina	86.6
34	Minnesota	82.7		22	Pennsylvania	86.6
33	Mississippi	83.0		24	Kansas	86.5
12	Missouri	88.3		25	Wyoming	86.2
27	Montana	85.8		26	Utah	86.0
8	Nebraska	89.1		27	Montana	85.8
40	Nevada	80.9		28	Ohio	84.2
10	New Hampshire	88.9		29	Rhode Island	84.1
2	New Jersey	90.5		30	Indiana	83.8
50	New Mexico	71.1		31	South Dakota	83.7
39	New York	81.8		32	South Carolina	83.6
22	North Carolina	86.6		33	Mississippi	83.0
17	North Dakota	87.2		34	California	82.7
28	Ohio	84.2		34	Hawaii	82.7
37	Oklahoma	82.6		34	Minnesota	82.7
49	Oregon	76.7		37	Oklahoma	82.6
22	Pennsylvania	86.6		38	Florida	82.3
29	Rhode Island	84.1		39	New York	81.8
32	South Carolina	83.6		40	Nevada	80.9
31	South Dakota	83.7		41	Georgia	80.6
3	Tennessee	89.8		42	Michigan	80.2
4	Texas	89.7		43	Idaho	79.7
26	Utah	86.0		44	Washington	79.4
8	Vermont	89.1		45	Colorado	79.1
19	Virginia	86.9		46	Alaska	78.2
44	Washington	79.4		47	Louisiana	78.1
6	West Virginia	89.4		48	Arizona	78.0
11	Wisconsin	88.6		49	Oregon	76.7
25	Wyoming	86.2		50	New Mexico	71.1
					District of Columbia	73.2

Source: U.S. Department of Education, National Center for Education Statistics
   "Common Core of Data (CCD) Database"" (https://nces.ed.gov/ccd/data_tables.asp)
*The Adjusted Cohort Graduation Rate (ACGR) is the number of students who graduate in four years with a regular high school diploma divided by the number of students who form the adjusted cohort for the graduating class. From the beginning of ninth grade, students who are entering that grade for the first time form a cohort that is "adjusted" by adding any students who subsequently transfer into the cohort and subtracting any students who subsequently transfer out, immigrate to another country, or die.

Adjusted Cohort Graduation Rate for Public High School Economically Disadvantaged Students in 2017
National Average = 78.3%*

ALPHA ORDER

RANK	STATE	PERCENT
NA	Alabama**	NA
40	Alaska	72.1
39	Arizona	72.4
5	Arkansas	84.9
20	California	78.8
45	Colorado	68.5
22	Connecticut	78.1
23	Delaware	78.0
28	Florida	76.8
33	Georgia	76.4
24	Hawaii	77.9
41	Idaho	71.6
16	Illinois	79.4
12	Indiana	80.3
8	Iowa	83.7
21	Kansas	78.6
2	Kentucky	87.0
38	Louisiana	72.6
17	Maine	79.3
17	Maryland	79.3
19	Massachusetts	79.0
46	Michigan	67.9
44	Minnesota	69.0
14	Mississippi	79.9
13	Missouri	80.1
31	Montana	76.6
9	Nebraska	81.8
28	Nevada	76.8
26	New Hampshire	77.5
7	New Jersey	84.0
48	New Mexico	66.4
35	New York	75.3
9	North Carolina	81.8
36	North Dakota	74.0
37	Ohio	73.1
28	Oklahoma	76.8
42	Oregon	70.1
15	Pennsylvania	79.8
34	Rhode Island	76.0
4	South Carolina	85.1
47	South Dakota	67.0
6	Tennessee	84.5
3	Texas	86.9
31	Utah	76.6
11	Vermont	81.0
25	Virginia	77.8
43	Washington	70.0
1	West Virginia	87.3
27	Wisconsin	77.4
49	Wyoming	65.0

RANK ORDER

RANK	STATE	PERCENT
1	West Virginia	87.3
2	Kentucky	87.0
3	Texas	86.9
4	South Carolina	85.1
5	Arkansas	84.9
6	Tennessee	84.5
7	New Jersey	84.0
8	Iowa	83.7
9	Nebraska	81.8
9	North Carolina	81.8
11	Vermont	81.0
12	Indiana	80.3
13	Missouri	80.1
14	Mississippi	79.9
15	Pennsylvania	79.8
16	Illinois	79.4
17	Maine	79.3
17	Maryland	79.3
19	Massachusetts	79.0
20	California	78.8
21	Kansas	78.6
22	Connecticut	78.1
23	Delaware	78.0
24	Hawaii	77.9
25	Virginia	77.8
26	New Hampshire	77.5
27	Wisconsin	77.4
28	Florida	76.8
28	Nevada	76.8
28	Oklahoma	76.8
31	Montana	76.6
31	Utah	76.6
33	Georgia	76.4
34	Rhode Island	76.0
35	New York	75.3
36	North Dakota	74.0
37	Ohio	73.1
38	Louisiana	72.6
39	Arizona	72.4
40	Alaska	72.1
41	Idaho	71.6
42	Oregon	70.1
43	Washington	70.0
44	Minnesota	69.0
45	Colorado	68.5
46	Michigan	67.9
47	South Dakota	67.0
48	New Mexico	66.4
49	Wyoming	65.0
NA	Alabama**	NA
	District of Columbia	72.9

Source: U.S. Department of Education, National Center for Education Statistics
   "Common Core of Data (CCD) Database"" (https://nces.ed.gov/ccd/data_tables.asp)
*The Adjusted Cohort Graduation Rate (ACGR) is the number of students who graduate in four years with a regular high school diploma divided by the number of students who form the adjusted cohort for the graduating class. From the beginning of ninth grade, students who are entering that grade for the first time form a cohort that is "adjusted" by adding any students who subsequently transfer into the cohort and subtracting any students who subsequently transfer out, immigrate to another country, or die. **Not available.

Adjusted Cohort Graduation Rate for Public High School Students with Limited English Proficiency in 2017
National Average = 66.4%*

ALPHA ORDER

RANK	STATE	PERCENT
NA	Alabama**	NA
36	Alaska	58.0
48	Arizona	30.0
1	Arkansas	82.0
22	California	67.2
31	Colorado	64.6
20	Connecticut	68.0
16	Delaware	69.0
21	Florida	67.3
34	Georgia	59.0
16	Hawaii	69.0
11	Idaho	75.0
13	Illinois	73.6
43	Indiana	50.0
4	Iowa	80.0
5	Kansas	79.7
23	Kentucky	67.0
46	Louisiana	36.0
3	Maine	81.0
45	Maryland	45.0
32	Massachusetts	63.4
15	Michigan	69.4
30	Minnesota	64.7
23	Mississippi	67.0
23	Missouri	67.0
33	Montana	63.0
43	Nebraska	50.0
2	Nevada	81.7
6	New Hampshire	78.0
9	New Jersey	76.1
19	New Mexico	68.1
47	New York	30.8
36	North Carolina	58.0
16	North Dakota	69.0
41	Ohio	55.0
40	Oklahoma	57.0
41	Oregon	55.0
28	Pennsylvania	65.0
14	Rhode Island	72.0
7	South Carolina	77.0
34	South Dakota	59.0
12	Tennessee	74.0
10	Texas	75.5
23	Utah	67.0
27	Vermont	66.0
39	Virginia	57.3
38	Washington	57.8
NA	West Virginia**	NA
28	Wisconsin	65.0
7	Wyoming	77.0

RANK ORDER

RANK	STATE	PERCENT
1	Arkansas	82.0
2	Nevada	81.7
3	Maine	81.0
4	Iowa	80.0
5	Kansas	79.7
6	New Hampshire	78.0
7	South Carolina	77.0
7	Wyoming	77.0
9	New Jersey	76.1
10	Texas	75.5
11	Idaho	75.0
12	Tennessee	74.0
13	Illinois	73.6
14	Rhode Island	72.0
15	Michigan	69.4
16	Delaware	69.0
16	Hawaii	69.0
16	North Dakota	69.0
19	New Mexico	68.1
20	Connecticut	68.0
21	Florida	67.3
22	California	67.2
23	Kentucky	67.0
23	Mississippi	67.0
23	Missouri	67.0
23	Utah	67.0
27	Vermont	66.0
28	Pennsylvania	65.0
28	Wisconsin	65.0
30	Minnesota	64.7
31	Colorado	64.6
32	Massachusetts	63.4
33	Montana	63.0
34	Georgia	59.0
34	South Dakota	59.0
36	Alaska	58.0
36	North Carolina	58.0
38	Washington	57.8
39	Virginia	57.3
40	Oklahoma	57.0
41	Ohio	55.0
41	Oregon	55.0
43	Indiana	50.0
43	Nebraska	50.0
45	Maryland	45.0
46	Louisiana	36.0
47	New York	30.8
48	Arizona	30.0
NA	Alabama**	NA
NA	West Virginia**	NA
	District of Columbia	63.0

Source: U.S. Department of Education, National Center for Education Statistics
"Common Core of Data (CCD) Database"" (https://nces.ed.gov/ccd/data_tables.asp)
*The Adjusted Cohort Graduation Rate (ACGR) is the number of students who graduate in four years with a regular high school diploma divided by the number of students who form the adjusted cohort for the graduating class. From the beginning of ninth grade, students who are entering that grade for the first time form a cohort that is "adjusted" by adding any students who subsequently transfer into the cohort and subtracting any students who subsequently transfer out, immigrate to another country, or die. **Not available.

Adjusted Cohort Graduation Rate for Public High School Students with Disabilities in 2017
National Average = 67.1%*

<table>
<tr><td colspan="3">ALPHA ORDER</td><td colspan="3">RANK ORDER</td></tr>
<tr><td>RANK</td><td>STATE</td><td>PERCENT</td><td>RANK</td><td>STATE</td><td>PERCENT</td></tr>
<tr><td>NA</td><td>Alabama**</td><td>NA</td><td>1</td><td>Arkansas</td><td>83.8</td></tr>
<tr><td>41</td><td>Alaska</td><td>59.0</td><td>2</td><td>New Jersey</td><td>78.8</td></tr>
<tr><td>28</td><td>Arizona</td><td>66.4</td><td>3</td><td>Kansas</td><td>78.4</td></tr>
<tr><td>1</td><td>Arkansas</td><td>83.8</td><td>4</td><td>Texas</td><td>77.4</td></tr>
<tr><td>31</td><td>California</td><td>65.0</td><td>5</td><td>Montana</td><td>77.0</td></tr>
<tr><td>44</td><td>Colorado</td><td>56.8</td><td>5</td><td>Oklahoma</td><td>77.0</td></tr>
<tr><td>27</td><td>Connecticut</td><td>66.7</td><td>7</td><td>Missouri</td><td>76.9</td></tr>
<tr><td>23</td><td>Delaware</td><td>69.0</td><td>8</td><td>Vermont</td><td>76.0</td></tr>
<tr><td>29</td><td>Florida</td><td>66.0</td><td>8</td><td>West Virginia</td><td>76.0</td></tr>
<tr><td>42</td><td>Georgia</td><td>58.9</td><td>10</td><td>Kentucky</td><td>74.4</td></tr>
<tr><td>31</td><td>Hawaii</td><td>65.0</td><td>11</td><td>Iowa</td><td>74.3</td></tr>
<tr><td>37</td><td>Idaho</td><td>61.0</td><td>12</td><td>New Hampshire</td><td>74.0</td></tr>
<tr><td>17</td><td>Illinois</td><td>71.2</td><td>13</td><td>Pennsylvania</td><td>73.6</td></tr>
<tr><td>19</td><td>Indiana</td><td>70.9</td><td>14</td><td>Massachusetts</td><td>72.8</td></tr>
<tr><td>11</td><td>Iowa</td><td>74.3</td><td>15</td><td>Tennessee</td><td>72.7</td></tr>
<tr><td>3</td><td>Kansas</td><td>78.4</td><td>16</td><td>Maine</td><td>72.5</td></tr>
<tr><td>10</td><td>Kentucky</td><td>74.4</td><td>17</td><td>Illinois</td><td>71.2</td></tr>
<tr><td>48</td><td>Louisiana</td><td>52.5</td><td>18</td><td>Nebraska</td><td>71.0</td></tr>
<tr><td>16</td><td>Maine</td><td>72.5</td><td>19</td><td>Indiana</td><td>70.9</td></tr>
<tr><td>26</td><td>Maryland</td><td>67.5</td><td>20</td><td>Ohio</td><td>70.5</td></tr>
<tr><td>14</td><td>Massachusetts</td><td>72.8</td><td>21</td><td>North Carolina</td><td>70.3</td></tr>
<tr><td>45</td><td>Michigan</td><td>56.7</td><td>22</td><td>Utah</td><td>69.4</td></tr>
<tr><td>36</td><td>Minnesota</td><td>61.2</td><td>23</td><td>Delaware</td><td>69.0</td></tr>
<tr><td>49</td><td>Mississippi</td><td>36.4</td><td>24</td><td>Wisconsin</td><td>68.2</td></tr>
<tr><td>7</td><td>Missouri</td><td>76.9</td><td>25</td><td>Wyoming</td><td>68.0</td></tr>
<tr><td>5</td><td>Montana</td><td>77.0</td><td>26</td><td>Maryland</td><td>67.5</td></tr>
<tr><td>18</td><td>Nebraska</td><td>71.0</td><td>27</td><td>Connecticut</td><td>66.7</td></tr>
<tr><td>33</td><td>Nevada</td><td>64.7</td><td>28</td><td>Arizona</td><td>66.4</td></tr>
<tr><td>12</td><td>New Hampshire</td><td>74.0</td><td>29</td><td>Florida</td><td>66.0</td></tr>
<tr><td>2</td><td>New Jersey</td><td>78.8</td><td>29</td><td>North Dakota</td><td>66.0</td></tr>
<tr><td>35</td><td>New Mexico</td><td>61.5</td><td>31</td><td>California</td><td>65.0</td></tr>
<tr><td>46</td><td>New York</td><td>55.4</td><td>31</td><td>Hawaii</td><td>65.0</td></tr>
<tr><td>21</td><td>North Carolina</td><td>70.3</td><td>33</td><td>Nevada</td><td>64.7</td></tr>
<tr><td>29</td><td>North Dakota</td><td>66.0</td><td>34</td><td>Rhode Island</td><td>63.0</td></tr>
<tr><td>20</td><td>Ohio</td><td>70.5</td><td>35</td><td>New Mexico</td><td>61.5</td></tr>
<tr><td>5</td><td>Oklahoma</td><td>77.0</td><td>36</td><td>Minnesota</td><td>61.2</td></tr>
<tr><td>43</td><td>Oregon</td><td>58.8</td><td>37</td><td>Idaho</td><td>61.0</td></tr>
<tr><td>13</td><td>Pennsylvania</td><td>73.6</td><td>38</td><td>South Dakota</td><td>60.0</td></tr>
<tr><td>34</td><td>Rhode Island</td><td>63.0</td><td>39</td><td>Virginia</td><td>59.8</td></tr>
<tr><td>47</td><td>South Carolina</td><td>53.5</td><td>40</td><td>Washington</td><td>59.4</td></tr>
<tr><td>38</td><td>South Dakota</td><td>60.0</td><td>41</td><td>Alaska</td><td>59.0</td></tr>
<tr><td>15</td><td>Tennessee</td><td>72.7</td><td>42</td><td>Georgia</td><td>58.9</td></tr>
<tr><td>4</td><td>Texas</td><td>77.4</td><td>43</td><td>Oregon</td><td>58.8</td></tr>
<tr><td>22</td><td>Utah</td><td>69.4</td><td>44</td><td>Colorado</td><td>56.8</td></tr>
<tr><td>8</td><td>Vermont</td><td>76.0</td><td>45</td><td>Michigan</td><td>56.7</td></tr>
<tr><td>39</td><td>Virginia</td><td>59.8</td><td>46</td><td>New York</td><td>55.4</td></tr>
<tr><td>40</td><td>Washington</td><td>59.4</td><td>47</td><td>South Carolina</td><td>53.5</td></tr>
<tr><td>8</td><td>West Virginia</td><td>76.0</td><td>48</td><td>Louisiana</td><td>52.5</td></tr>
<tr><td>24</td><td>Wisconsin</td><td>68.2</td><td>49</td><td>Mississippi</td><td>36.4</td></tr>
<tr><td>25</td><td>Wyoming</td><td>68.0</td><td>NA</td><td>Alabama**</td><td>NA</td></tr>
<tr><td></td><td></td><td></td><td></td><td>District of Columbia</td><td>53.0</td></tr>
</table>

Source: U.S. Department of Education, National Center for Education Statistics
   "Common Core of Data (CCD) Database"" (https://nces.ed.gov/ccd/data_tables.asp)
*The Adjusted Cohort Graduation Rate (ACGR) is the number of students who graduate in four years with a regular high school diploma divided by the number of students who form the adjusted cohort for the graduating class. From the beginning of ninth grade, students who are entering that grade for the first time form a cohort that is "adjusted" by adding any students who subsequently transfer into the cohort and subtracting any students who subsequently transfer out, immigrate to another country, or die. **Not available.

ACT Average Composite Score in 2019

National Average = 20.7*

ALPHA ORDER

RANK	STATE	AVERAGE SCORE
45	Alabama	18.9
31	Alaska	20.1
42	Arizona	19.0
40	Arkansas	19.3
15	California	22.6
13	Colorado	23.8
1	Connecticut	25.5
11	Delaware	24.0
31	Florida	20.1
22	Georgia	21.4
42	Hawaii	19.0
16	Idaho	22.5
7	Illinois	24.3
16	Indiana	22.5
20	Iowa	21.6
24	Kansas	21.2
36	Kentucky	19.8
47	Louisiana	18.8
7	Maine	24.3
18	Maryland	22.3
1	Massachusetts	25.5
6	Michigan	24.4
22	Minnesota	21.4
49	Mississippi	18.4
26	Missouri	20.8
36	Montana	19.8
33	Nebraska	20.0
50	Nevada	17.9
3	New Hampshire	25.0
9	New Jersey	24.2
40	New Mexico	19.3
5	New York	24.5
42	North Carolina	19.0
35	North Dakota	19.9
33	Ohio	20.0
45	Oklahoma	18.9
25	Oregon	21.1
14	Pennsylvania	23.6
4	Rhode Island	24.7
47	South Carolina	18.8
20	South Dakota	21.6
39	Tennessee	19.4
28	Texas	20.5
29	Utah	20.3
10	Vermont	24.1
11	Virginia	24.0
19	Washington	22.1
26	West Virginia	20.8
29	Wisconsin	20.3
36	Wyoming	19.8

RANK ORDER

RANK	STATE	AVERAGE SCORE
1	Connecticut	25.5
1	Massachusetts	25.5
3	New Hampshire	25.0
4	Rhode Island	24.7
5	New York	24.5
6	Michigan	24.4
7	Illinois	24.3
7	Maine	24.3
9	New Jersey	24.2
10	Vermont	24.1
11	Delaware	24.0
11	Virginia	24.0
13	Colorado	23.8
14	Pennsylvania	23.6
15	California	22.6
16	Idaho	22.5
16	Indiana	22.5
18	Maryland	22.3
19	Washington	22.1
20	Iowa	21.6
20	South Dakota	21.6
22	Georgia	21.4
22	Minnesota	21.4
24	Kansas	21.2
25	Oregon	21.1
26	Missouri	20.8
26	West Virginia	20.8
28	Texas	20.5
29	Utah	20.3
29	Wisconsin	20.3
31	Alaska	20.1
31	Florida	20.1
33	Nebraska	20.0
33	Ohio	20.0
35	North Dakota	19.9
36	Kentucky	19.8
36	Montana	19.8
36	Wyoming	19.8
39	Tennessee	19.4
40	Arkansas	19.3
40	New Mexico	19.3
42	Arizona	19.0
42	Hawaii	19.0
42	North Carolina	19.0
45	Alabama	18.9
45	Oklahoma	18.9
47	Louisiana	18.8
47	South Carolina	18.8
49	Mississippi	18.4
50	Nevada	17.9

District of Columbia 23.5

Source: The American College Testing Program (Copyright © 2019)
"Average ACT Scores by State" (http://leadershipblog.act.org/)

*The ACT score range is 1 to 36. Slightly more than 1.7 million 2019 U.S. high school graduates took the test. Caution should be used in using ACT scores to compare states. The percentage of high graduates taking the test varies greatly from one state to another. For example, all graduates are required to take the test in many states but, in Maine, only 6 percent of graduates took the test.

Education Expenditures by State and Local Governments in 2017

National Total = $1,011,708,338,000*

ALPHA ORDER

RANK	STATE	EXPENDITURES	% of USA
24	Alabama	$14,067,061,000	1.4%
45	Alaska	3,279,234,000	0.3%
20	Arizona	16,596,683,000	1.6%
33	Arkansas	8,377,620,000	0.8%
1	California	131,235,701,000	13.0%
19	Colorado	17,098,280,000	1.7%
26	Connecticut	13,480,700,000	1.3%
40	Delaware	3,928,643,000	0.4%
5	Florida	42,677,790,000	4.2%
10	Georgia	28,063,419,000	2.8%
44	Hawaii	3,409,590,000	0.3%
41	Idaho	3,562,975,000	0.4%
6	Illinois	37,945,248,000	3.8%
18	Indiana	17,820,415,000	1.8%
29	Iowa	11,055,089,000	1.1%
32	Kansas	9,810,772,000	1.0%
27	Kentucky	12,876,347,000	1.3%
28	Louisiana	12,349,672,000	1.2%
42	Maine	3,549,154,000	0.4%
15	Maryland	20,748,730,000	2.1%
14	Massachusetts	23,157,690,000	2.3%
9	Michigan	30,736,448,000	3.0%
16	Minnesota	19,733,470,000	2.0%
34	Mississippi	8,179,810,000	0.8%
21	Missouri	15,414,753,000	1.5%
48	Montana	2,955,272,000	0.3%
35	Nebraska	7,324,943,000	0.7%
37	Nevada	6,676,468,000	0.7%
39	New Hampshire	4,131,259,000	0.4%
7	New Jersey	36,638,231,000	3.6%
36	New Mexico	6,814,945,000	0.7%
3	New York	85,174,344,000	8.4%
12	North Carolina	26,697,153,000	2.6%
47	North Dakota	3,011,815,000	0.3%
8	Ohio	36,105,618,000	3.6%
30	Oklahoma	10,544,576,000	1.0%
25	Oregon	13,631,379,000	1.3%
4	Pennsylvania	43,826,185,000	4.3%
43	Rhode Island	3,522,540,000	0.3%
22	South Carolina	15,074,653,000	1.5%
50	South Dakota	2,435,875,000	0.2%
23	Tennessee	14,634,538,000	1.4%
2	Texas	89,470,555,000	8.8%
31	Utah	9,948,798,000	1.0%
49	Vermont	2,839,485,000	0.3%
11	Virginia	26,958,715,000	2.7%
13	Washington	24,580,882,000	2.4%
38	West Virginia	5,393,805,000	0.5%
17	Wisconsin	18,189,701,000	1.8%
46	Wyoming	3,064,476,000	0.3%

RANK ORDER

RANK	STATE	EXPENDITURES	% of USA
1	California	$131,235,701,000	13.0%
2	Texas	89,470,555,000	8.8%
3	New York	85,174,344,000	8.4%
4	Pennsylvania	43,826,185,000	4.3%
5	Florida	42,677,790,000	4.2%
6	Illinois	37,945,248,000	3.8%
7	New Jersey	36,638,231,000	3.6%
8	Ohio	36,105,618,000	3.6%
9	Michigan	30,736,448,000	3.0%
10	Georgia	28,063,419,000	2.8%
11	Virginia	26,958,715,000	2.7%
12	North Carolina	26,697,153,000	2.6%
13	Washington	24,580,882,000	2.4%
14	Massachusetts	23,157,690,000	2.3%
15	Maryland	20,748,730,000	2.1%
16	Minnesota	19,733,470,000	2.0%
17	Wisconsin	18,189,701,000	1.8%
18	Indiana	17,820,415,000	1.8%
19	Colorado	17,098,280,000	1.7%
20	Arizona	16,596,683,000	1.6%
21	Missouri	15,414,753,000	1.5%
22	South Carolina	15,074,653,000	1.5%
23	Tennessee	14,634,538,000	1.4%
24	Alabama	14,067,061,000	1.4%
25	Oregon	13,631,379,000	1.3%
26	Connecticut	13,480,700,000	1.3%
27	Kentucky	12,876,347,000	1.3%
28	Louisiana	12,349,672,000	1.2%
29	Iowa	11,055,089,000	1.1%
30	Oklahoma	10,544,576,000	1.0%
31	Utah	9,948,798,000	1.0%
32	Kansas	9,810,772,000	1.0%
33	Arkansas	8,377,620,000	0.8%
34	Mississippi	8,179,810,000	0.8%
35	Nebraska	7,324,943,000	0.7%
36	New Mexico	6,814,945,000	0.7%
37	Nevada	6,676,468,000	0.7%
38	West Virginia	5,393,805,000	0.5%
39	New Hampshire	4,131,259,000	0.4%
40	Delaware	3,928,643,000	0.4%
41	Idaho	3,562,975,000	0.4%
42	Maine	3,549,154,000	0.4%
43	Rhode Island	3,522,540,000	0.3%
44	Hawaii	3,409,590,000	0.3%
45	Alaska	3,279,234,000	0.3%
46	Wyoming	3,064,476,000	0.3%
47	North Dakota	3,011,815,000	0.3%
48	Montana	2,955,272,000	0.3%
49	Vermont	2,839,485,000	0.3%
50	South Dakota	2,435,875,000	0.2%
	District of Columbia	2,906,833,000	0.3%

Source: U.S. Bureau of the Census, Governments Division
"2017 State and Local Government Finances" (https://www.census.gov/programs-surveys/gov-finances.html)
*Direct general expenditures for higher, secondary, elementary, and "other" education. Includes capital outlays.

Per Capita State and Local Government Expenditures for Education in 2017

National Per Capita = $3,112*

ALPHA ORDER

RANK	STATE	PER CAPITA
33	Alabama	$2,885
3	Alaska	4,433
46	Arizona	2,355
35	Arkansas	2,790
17	California	3,331
28	Colorado	3,045
9	Connecticut	3,772
6	Delaware	4,105
50	Florida	2,035
38	Georgia	2,695
45	Hawaii	2,394
49	Idaho	2,073
30	Illinois	2,968
40	Indiana	2,676
11	Iowa	3,517
15	Kansas	3,371
32	Kentucky	2,891
42	Louisiana	2,644
41	Maine	2,658
12	Maryland	3,444
14	Massachusetts	3,374
26	Michigan	3,081
10	Minnesota	3,544
37	Mississippi	2,736
44	Missouri	2,523
34	Montana	2,806
8	Nebraska	3,820
47	Nevada	2,246
27	New Hampshire	3,061
5	New Jersey	4,122
20	New Mexico	3,255
4	New York	4,348
43	North Carolina	2,599
7	North Dakota	3,988
25	Ohio	3,095
39	Oklahoma	2,681
19	Oregon	3,287
13	Pennsylvania	3,426
16	Rhode Island	3,334
29	South Carolina	3,002
36	South Dakota	2,789
48	Tennessee	2,181
23	Texas	3,159
21	Utah	3,206
2	Vermont	4,547
22	Virginia	3,185
18	Washington	3,310
30	West Virginia	2,968
24	Wisconsin	3,140
1	Wyoming	5,293

RANK ORDER

RANK	STATE	PER CAPITA
1	Wyoming	$5,293
2	Vermont	4,547
3	Alaska	4,433
4	New York	4,348
5	New Jersey	4,122
6	Delaware	4,105
7	North Dakota	3,988
8	Nebraska	3,820
9	Connecticut	3,772
10	Minnesota	3,544
11	Iowa	3,517
12	Maryland	3,444
13	Pennsylvania	3,426
14	Massachusetts	3,374
15	Kansas	3,371
16	Rhode Island	3,334
17	California	3,331
18	Washington	3,310
19	Oregon	3,287
20	New Mexico	3,255
21	Utah	3,206
22	Virginia	3,185
23	Texas	3,159
24	Wisconsin	3,140
25	Ohio	3,095
26	Michigan	3,081
27	New Hampshire	3,061
28	Colorado	3,045
29	South Carolina	3,002
30	Illinois	2,968
30	West Virginia	2,968
32	Kentucky	2,891
33	Alabama	2,885
34	Montana	2,806
35	Arkansas	2,790
36	South Dakota	2,789
37	Mississippi	2,736
38	Georgia	2,695
39	Oklahoma	2,681
40	Indiana	2,676
41	Maine	2,658
42	Louisiana	2,644
43	North Carolina	2,599
44	Missouri	2,523
45	Hawaii	2,394
46	Arizona	2,355
47	Nevada	2,246
48	Tennessee	2,181
49	Idaho	2,073
50	Florida	2,035
	District of Columbia	4,178

Source: CQ Press using data from U.S. Bureau of the Census, Governments Division
"2017 State and Local Government Finances" (https://www.census.gov/programs-surveys/gov-finances.html)
*Direct general expenditures for higher, secondary, elementary, and "other" education. Includes capital outlays.

Expenditures for Education as a Percent of
All State and Local Government Expenditures in 2017
National Percent = 32.9%*

ALPHA ORDER

RANK	STATE	PERCENT
20	Alabama	33.9
49	Alaska	25.8
29	Arizona	33.3
28	Arkansas	33.4
47	California	28.8
18	Colorado	34.2
3	Connecticut	39.7
11	Delaware	36.4
48	Florida	27.8
4	Georgia	39.3
50	Hawaii	24.3
40	Idaho	30.6
34	Illinois	32.4
25	Indiana	33.5
14	Iowa	35.3
10	Kansas	36.5
33	Kentucky	32.7
46	Louisiana	29.0
40	Maine	30.6
17	Maryland	34.3
45	Massachusetts	29.7
12	Michigan	36.3
29	Minnesota	33.3
37	Mississippi	31.2
32	Missouri	32.9
37	Montana	31.2
1	Nebraska	41.6
42	Nevada	30.4
8	New Hampshire	37.3
2	New Jersey	39.8
35	New Mexico	31.7
44	New York	30.1
19	North Carolina	34.0
37	North Dakota	31.2
25	Ohio	33.5
13	Oklahoma	36.0
42	Oregon	30.4
20	Pennsylvania	33.9
24	Rhode Island	33.6
15	South Carolina	34.8
20	South Dakota	33.9
36	Tennessee	31.4
4	Texas	39.3
7	Utah	38.2
6	Vermont	38.6
9	Virginia	36.6
31	Washington	33.0
25	West Virginia	33.5
20	Wisconsin	33.9
16	Wyoming	34.5

RANK ORDER

RANK	STATE	PERCENT
1	Nebraska	41.6
2	New Jersey	39.8
3	Connecticut	39.7
4	Georgia	39.3
4	Texas	39.3
6	Vermont	38.6
7	Utah	38.2
8	New Hampshire	37.3
9	Virginia	36.6
10	Kansas	36.5
11	Delaware	36.4
12	Michigan	36.3
13	Oklahoma	36.0
14	Iowa	35.3
15	South Carolina	34.8
16	Wyoming	34.5
17	Maryland	34.3
18	Colorado	34.2
19	North Carolina	34.0
20	Alabama	33.9
20	Pennsylvania	33.9
20	South Dakota	33.9
20	Wisconsin	33.9
24	Rhode Island	33.6
25	Indiana	33.5
25	Ohio	33.5
25	West Virginia	33.5
28	Arkansas	33.4
29	Arizona	33.3
29	Minnesota	33.3
31	Washington	33.0
32	Missouri	32.9
33	Kentucky	32.7
34	Illinois	32.4
35	New Mexico	31.7
36	Tennessee	31.4
37	Mississippi	31.2
37	Montana	31.2
37	North Dakota	31.2
40	Idaho	30.6
40	Maine	30.6
42	Nevada	30.4
42	Oregon	30.4
44	New York	30.1
45	Massachusetts	29.7
46	Louisiana	29.0
47	California	28.8
48	Florida	27.8
49	Alaska	25.8
50	Hawaii	24.3
	District of Columbia	21.9

Source: CQ Press using data from U.S. Bureau of the Census, Governments Division
"2017 State and Local Government Finances" (https://www.census.gov/programs-surveys/gov-finances.html)
*Direct general expenditures for higher, secondary, elementary, and "other" education as a percent of all direct general expenditures. Includes capital outlays.

State and Local Government Expenditures for Elementary and Secondary Education in 2017
National Total = $660,154,828,000*

ALPHA ORDER

RANK	STATE	EXPENDITURES	% of USA
26	Alabama	$7,854,223,000	1.2%
42	Alaska	2,346,857,000	0.4%
24	Arizona	8,243,834,000	1.2%
32	Arkansas	5,132,406,000	0.8%
1	California	83,376,774,000	12.6%
20	Colorado	9,949,680,000	1.5%
22	Connecticut	9,358,047,000	1.4%
45	Delaware	2,052,117,000	0.3%
5	Florida	28,349,858,000	4.3%
9	Georgia	19,868,901,000	3.0%
44	Hawaii	2,068,737,000	0.3%
43	Idaho	2,204,638,000	0.3%
7	Illinois	26,590,214,000	4.0%
19	Indiana	10,219,739,000	1.5%
29	Iowa	6,682,248,000	1.0%
30	Kansas	6,026,134,000	0.9%
28	Kentucky	7,322,005,000	1.1%
25	Louisiana	8,083,569,000	1.2%
40	Maine	2,560,962,000	0.4%
15	Maryland	13,697,743,000	2.1%
12	Massachusetts	16,239,532,000	2.5%
11	Michigan	17,433,881,000	2.6%
16	Minnesota	13,004,611,000	2.0%
36	Mississippi	4,621,112,000	0.7%
18	Missouri	10,433,667,000	1.6%
47	Montana	1,864,118,000	0.3%
34	Nebraska	4,708,010,000	0.7%
35	Nevada	4,631,745,000	0.7%
39	New Hampshire	2,971,769,000	0.5%
6	New Jersey	27,266,254,000	4.1%
37	New Mexico	3,708,851,000	0.6%
2	New York	68,902,105,000	10.4%
14	North Carolina	14,624,427,000	2.2%
48	North Dakota	1,807,396,000	0.3%
8	Ohio	24,341,095,000	3.7%
31	Oklahoma	5,766,457,000	0.9%
27	Oregon	7,581,818,000	1.1%
4	Pennsylvania	29,533,474,000	4.5%
41	Rhode Island	2,507,355,000	0.4%
23	South Carolina	9,145,389,000	1.4%
50	South Dakota	1,513,203,000	0.2%
21	Tennessee	9,787,910,000	1.5%
3	Texas	56,489,114,000	8.6%
33	Utah	5,122,667,000	0.8%
49	Vermont	1,650,954,000	0.3%
10	Virginia	17,618,250,000	2.7%
13	Washington	15,748,757,000	2.4%
38	West Virginia	3,100,226,000	0.5%
17	Wisconsin	11,350,610,000	1.7%
46	Wyoming	1,909,154,000	0.3%

RANK ORDER

RANK	STATE	EXPENDITURES	% of USA
1	California	$83,376,774,000	12.6%
2	New York	68,902,105,000	10.4%
3	Texas	56,489,114,000	8.6%
4	Pennsylvania	29,533,474,000	4.5%
5	Florida	28,349,858,000	4.3%
6	New Jersey	27,266,254,000	4.1%
7	Illinois	26,590,214,000	4.0%
8	Ohio	24,341,095,000	3.7%
9	Georgia	19,868,901,000	3.0%
10	Virginia	17,618,250,000	2.7%
11	Michigan	17,433,881,000	2.6%
12	Massachusetts	16,239,532,000	2.5%
13	Washington	15,748,757,000	2.4%
14	North Carolina	14,624,427,000	2.2%
15	Maryland	13,697,743,000	2.1%
16	Minnesota	13,004,611,000	2.0%
17	Wisconsin	11,350,610,000	1.7%
18	Missouri	10,433,667,000	1.6%
19	Indiana	10,219,739,000	1.5%
20	Colorado	9,949,680,000	1.5%
21	Tennessee	9,787,910,000	1.5%
22	Connecticut	9,358,047,000	1.4%
23	South Carolina	9,145,389,000	1.4%
24	Arizona	8,243,834,000	1.2%
25	Louisiana	8,083,569,000	1.2%
26	Alabama	7,854,223,000	1.2%
27	Oregon	7,581,818,000	1.1%
28	Kentucky	7,322,005,000	1.1%
29	Iowa	6,682,248,000	1.0%
30	Kansas	6,026,134,000	0.9%
31	Oklahoma	5,766,457,000	0.9%
32	Arkansas	5,132,406,000	0.8%
33	Utah	5,122,667,000	0.8%
34	Nebraska	4,708,010,000	0.7%
35	Nevada	4,631,745,000	0.7%
36	Mississippi	4,621,112,000	0.7%
37	New Mexico	3,708,851,000	0.6%
38	West Virginia	3,100,226,000	0.5%
39	New Hampshire	2,971,769,000	0.5%
40	Maine	2,560,962,000	0.4%
41	Rhode Island	2,507,355,000	0.4%
42	Alaska	2,346,857,000	0.4%
43	Idaho	2,204,638,000	0.3%
44	Hawaii	2,068,737,000	0.3%
45	Delaware	2,052,117,000	0.3%
46	Wyoming	1,909,154,000	0.3%
47	Montana	1,864,118,000	0.3%
48	North Dakota	1,807,396,000	0.3%
49	Vermont	1,650,954,000	0.3%
50	South Dakota	1,513,203,000	0.2%
	District of Columbia	2,782,231,000	0.4%

Source: U.S. Bureau of the Census, Governments Division
"2017 State and Local Government Finances" (https://www.census.gov/programs-surveys/gov-finances.html)
*Direct general expenditures. Includes capital outlays.

Per Capita State and Local Government Expenditures for Elementary and Secondary Education in 2017
National Per Capita = $2,030*

ALPHA ORDER

RANK	STATE	PER CAPITA
40	Alabama	$1,611
3	Alaska	3,172
50	Arizona	1,170
35	Arkansas	1,709
18	California	2,116
29	Colorado	1,772
6	Connecticut	2,618
15	Delaware	2,144
48	Florida	1,351
26	Georgia	1,908
46	Hawaii	1,453
49	Idaho	1,283
21	Illinois	2,080
43	Indiana	1,534
16	Iowa	2,126
22	Kansas	2,070
39	Kentucky	1,644
34	Louisiana	1,731
25	Maine	1,918
13	Maryland	2,274
10	Massachusetts	2,366
32	Michigan	1,748
11	Minnesota	2,336
42	Mississippi	1,546
36	Missouri	1,708
31	Montana	1,770
7	Nebraska	2,455
41	Nevada	1,558
14	New Hampshire	2,202
4	New Jersey	3,068
29	New Mexico	1,772
1	New York	3,517
47	North Carolina	1,424
8	North Dakota	2,393
19	Ohio	2,087
44	Oklahoma	1,466
27	Oregon	1,828
12	Pennsylvania	2,309
9	Rhode Island	2,373
28	South Carolina	1,821
33	South Dakota	1,733
45	Tennessee	1,459
23	Texas	1,994
38	Utah	1,651
5	Vermont	2,644
20	Virginia	2,081
17	Washington	2,121
37	West Virginia	1,706
24	Wisconsin	1,960
2	Wyoming	3,298

RANK ORDER

RANK	STATE	PER CAPITA
1	New York	$3,517
2	Wyoming	3,298
3	Alaska	3,172
4	New Jersey	3,068
5	Vermont	2,644
6	Connecticut	2,618
7	Nebraska	2,455
8	North Dakota	2,393
9	Rhode Island	2,373
10	Massachusetts	2,366
11	Minnesota	2,336
12	Pennsylvania	2,309
13	Maryland	2,274
14	New Hampshire	2,202
15	Delaware	2,144
16	Iowa	2,126
17	Washington	2,121
18	California	2,116
19	Ohio	2,087
20	Virginia	2,081
21	Illinois	2,080
22	Kansas	2,070
23	Texas	1,994
24	Wisconsin	1,960
25	Maine	1,918
26	Georgia	1,908
27	Oregon	1,828
28	South Carolina	1,821
29	Colorado	1,772
29	New Mexico	1,772
31	Montana	1,770
32	Michigan	1,748
33	South Dakota	1,733
34	Louisiana	1,731
35	Arkansas	1,709
36	Missouri	1,708
37	West Virginia	1,706
38	Utah	1,651
39	Kentucky	1,644
40	Alabama	1,611
41	Nevada	1,558
42	Mississippi	1,546
43	Indiana	1,534
44	Oklahoma	1,466
45	Tennessee	1,459
46	Hawaii	1,453
47	North Carolina	1,424
48	Florida	1,351
49	Idaho	1,283
50	Arizona	1,170
	District of Columbia	3,999

Source: CQ Press using data from U.S. Bureau of the Census, Governments Division
"2017 State and Local Government Finances" (https://www.census.gov/programs-surveys/gov-finances.html)
*Direct general expenditures. Includes capital outlays.

Expenditures for Elementary and Secondary Education as a Percent of All State and Local Government Expenditures in 2017
National Percent = 21.5%*

ALPHA ORDER

RANK	STATE	PERCENT
39	Alabama	18.9
44	Alaska	18.4
49	Arizona	16.5
29	Arkansas	20.5
45	California	18.3
30	Colorado	19.9
3	Connecticut	27.6
36	Delaware	19.0
43	Florida	18.5
2	Georgia	27.8
50	Hawaii	14.8
36	Idaho	19.0
11	Illinois	22.7
34	Indiana	19.2
20	Iowa	21.3
15	Kansas	22.4
41	Kentucky	18.6
36	Louisiana	19.0
17	Maine	22.1
11	Maryland	22.7
27	Massachusetts	20.8
28	Michigan	20.6
18	Minnesota	21.9
46	Mississippi	17.6
16	Missouri	22.3
31	Montana	19.7
4	Nebraska	26.8
21	Nevada	21.1
4	New Hampshire	26.8
1	New Jersey	29.7
47	New Mexico	17.2
7	New York	24.4
41	North Carolina	18.6
40	North Dakota	18.7
13	Ohio	22.6
31	Oklahoma	19.7
48	Oregon	16.9
10	Pennsylvania	22.9
8	Rhode Island	23.9
21	South Carolina	21.1
25	South Dakota	21.0
25	Tennessee	21.0
6	Texas	24.8
31	Utah	19.7
14	Vermont	22.5
8	Virginia	23.9
21	Washington	21.1
34	West Virginia	19.2
21	Wisconsin	21.1
19	Wyoming	21.5

RANK ORDER

RANK	STATE	PERCENT
1	New Jersey	29.7
2	Georgia	27.8
3	Connecticut	27.6
4	Nebraska	26.8
4	New Hampshire	26.8
6	Texas	24.8
7	New York	24.4
8	Rhode Island	23.9
8	Virginia	23.9
10	Pennsylvania	22.9
11	Illinois	22.7
11	Maryland	22.7
13	Ohio	22.6
14	Vermont	22.5
15	Kansas	22.4
16	Missouri	22.3
17	Maine	22.1
18	Minnesota	21.9
19	Wyoming	21.5
20	Iowa	21.3
21	Nevada	21.1
21	South Carolina	21.1
21	Washington	21.1
21	Wisconsin	21.1
25	South Dakota	21.0
25	Tennessee	21.0
27	Massachusetts	20.8
28	Michigan	20.6
29	Arkansas	20.5
30	Colorado	19.9
31	Montana	19.7
31	Oklahoma	19.7
31	Utah	19.7
34	Indiana	19.2
34	West Virginia	19.2
36	Delaware	19.0
36	Idaho	19.0
36	Louisiana	19.0
39	Alabama	18.9
40	North Dakota	18.7
41	Kentucky	18.6
41	North Carolina	18.6
43	Florida	18.5
44	Alaska	18.4
45	California	18.3
46	Mississippi	17.6
47	New Mexico	17.2
48	Oregon	16.9
49	Arizona	16.5
50	Hawaii	14.8

| | District of Columbia | 21.0 |

Source: CQ Press using data from U.S. Bureau of the Census, Governments Division
"2017 State and Local Government Finances" (https://www.census.gov/programs-surveys/gov-finances.html)
*Direct general expenditures as a percent of all direct general expenditures. Includes capital outlays.

Estimated Per Pupil Public Elementary and Secondary School Current Expenditures in 2019
National Per Pupil = $12,920*

ALPHA ORDER

RANK	STATE	PER PUPIL
40	Alabama	$9,967
2	Alaska	20,948
46	Arizona	8,519
39	Arkansas	10,082
17	California	13,783
30	Colorado	11,490
5	Connecticut	19,031
16	Delaware	13,995
42	Florida	9,901
34	Georgia	10,883
15	Hawaii	14,656
50	Idaho	6,861
11	Illinois	15,547
48	Indiana	8,289
32	Iowa	11,385
27	Kansas	11,705
35	Kentucky	10,791
26	Louisiana	11,791
18	Maine	13,744
13	Maryland	15,043
4	Massachusetts	19,394
37	Michigan	10,699
19	Minnesota	13,532
45	Mississippi	9,153
31	Missouri	11,434
28	Montana	11,662
22	Nebraska	12,324
43	Nevada	9,847
8	New Hampshire	17,343
3	New Jersey	20,465
33	New Mexico	11,012
1	New York	24,565
41	North Carolina	9,907
12	North Dakota	15,239
25	Ohio	11,960
47	Oklahoma	8,449
21	Oregon	12,601
7	Pennsylvania	17,360
10	Rhode Island	16,213
24	South Carolina	12,040
36	South Dakota	10,721
44	Tennessee	9,393
38	Texas	10,096
49	Utah	7,330
9	Vermont	17,320
23	Virginia	12,269
14	Washington	14,698
20	West Virginia	12,889
29	Wisconsin	11,644
6	Wyoming	17,412

RANK ORDER

RANK	STATE	PER PUPIL
1	New York	$24,565
2	Alaska	20,948
3	New Jersey	20,465
4	Massachusetts	19,394
5	Connecticut	19,031
6	Wyoming	17,412
7	Pennsylvania	17,360
8	New Hampshire	17,343
9	Vermont	17,320
10	Rhode Island	16,213
11	Illinois	15,547
12	North Dakota	15,239
13	Maryland	15,043
14	Washington	14,698
15	Hawaii	14,656
16	Delaware	13,995
17	California	13,783
18	Maine	13,744
19	Minnesota	13,532
20	West Virginia	12,889
21	Oregon	12,601
22	Nebraska	12,324
23	Virginia	12,269
24	South Carolina	12,040
25	Ohio	11,960
26	Louisiana	11,791
27	Kansas	11,705
28	Montana	11,662
29	Wisconsin	11,644
30	Colorado	11,490
31	Missouri	11,434
32	Iowa	11,385
33	New Mexico	11,012
34	Georgia	10,883
35	Kentucky	10,791
36	South Dakota	10,721
37	Michigan	10,699
38	Texas	10,096
39	Arkansas	10,082
40	Alabama	9,967
41	North Carolina	9,907
42	Florida	9,901
43	Nevada	9,847
44	Tennessee	9,393
45	Mississippi	9,153
46	Arizona	8,519
47	Oklahoma	8,449
48	Indiana	8,289
49	Utah	7,330
50	Idaho	6,861
	District of Columbia	21,139

Source: National Education Association, Washington, D.C.
"Rankings and Estimates" (Copyright © 2019, NEA, https://www.nea.org/home/44479.htm)
*Estimates for school year 2018–2019. Based on student membership.

Higher Education Expenditures by State and Local Governments in 2017

National Total = $297,258,709,000*

ALPHA ORDER					RANK ORDER			
RANK	STATE	EXPENDITURES	% of USA		RANK	STATE	EXPENDITURES	% of USA
21	Alabama	$5,111,951,000	1.7%		1	California	$41,476,361,000	14.0%
47	Alaska	847,344,000	0.3%		2	Texas	30,593,618,000	10.3%
17	Arizona	6,051,870,000	2.0%		3	New York	14,179,854,000	4.8%
35	Arkansas	2,634,939,000	0.9%		4	Michigan	11,861,290,000	4.0%
1	California	41,476,361,000	14.0%		5	Pennsylvania	11,691,350,000	3.9%
14	Colorado	6,393,971,000	2.2%		6	Florida	11,071,724,000	3.7%
32	Connecticut	3,399,363,000	1.1%		7	North Carolina	10,216,187,000	3.4%
39	Delaware	1,391,337,000	0.5%		8	Ohio	9,890,532,000	3.3%
6	Florida	11,071,724,000	3.7%		9	Illinois	9,232,771,000	3.1%
18	Georgia	6,013,401,000	2.0%		10	Virginia	8,199,004,000	2.8%
40	Hawaii	1,206,613,000	0.4%		11	Washington	7,464,698,000	2.5%
41	Idaho	1,126,817,000	0.4%		12	New Jersey	7,457,451,000	2.5%
9	Illinois	9,232,771,000	3.1%		13	Indiana	6,427,256,000	2.2%
13	Indiana	6,427,256,000	2.2%		14	Colorado	6,393,971,000	2.2%
28	Iowa	3,867,960,000	1.3%		15	Maryland	6,277,635,000	2.1%
30	Kansas	3,491,121,000	1.2%		16	Wisconsin	6,254,027,000	2.1%
24	Kentucky	4,479,553,000	1.5%		17	Arizona	6,051,870,000	2.0%
31	Louisiana	3,478,033,000	1.2%		18	Georgia	6,013,401,000	2.0%
48	Maine	782,344,000	0.3%		19	Minnesota	5,693,338,000	1.9%
15	Maryland	6,277,635,000	2.1%		20	Massachusetts	5,538,034,000	1.9%
20	Massachusetts	5,538,034,000	1.9%		21	Alabama	5,111,951,000	1.7%
4	Michigan	11,861,290,000	4.0%		22	Oregon	4,776,669,000	1.6%
19	Minnesota	5,693,338,000	1.9%		23	Utah	4,572,790,000	1.5%
33	Mississippi	3,020,360,000	1.0%		24	Kentucky	4,479,553,000	1.5%
27	Missouri	4,059,673,000	1.4%		25	South Carolina	4,445,277,000	1.5%
43	Montana	972,056,000	0.3%		26	Oklahoma	4,117,970,000	1.4%
36	Nebraska	2,364,593,000	0.8%		27	Missouri	4,059,673,000	1.4%
38	Nevada	1,498,413,000	0.5%		28	Iowa	3,867,960,000	1.3%
44	New Hampshire	940,165,000	0.3%		29	Tennessee	3,751,844,000	1.3%
12	New Jersey	7,457,451,000	2.5%		30	Kansas	3,491,121,000	1.2%
34	New Mexico	2,684,927,000	0.9%		31	Louisiana	3,478,033,000	1.2%
3	New York	14,179,854,000	4.8%		32	Connecticut	3,399,363,000	1.1%
7	North Carolina	10,216,187,000	3.4%		33	Mississippi	3,020,360,000	1.0%
42	North Dakota	1,112,925,000	0.4%		34	New Mexico	2,684,927,000	0.9%
8	Ohio	9,890,532,000	3.3%		35	Arkansas	2,634,939,000	0.9%
26	Oklahoma	4,117,970,000	1.4%		36	Nebraska	2,364,593,000	0.8%
22	Oregon	4,776,669,000	1.6%		37	West Virginia	1,769,466,000	0.6%
5	Pennsylvania	11,691,350,000	3.9%		38	Nevada	1,498,413,000	0.5%
50	Rhode Island	692,395,000	0.2%		39	Delaware	1,391,337,000	0.5%
25	South Carolina	4,445,277,000	1.5%		40	Hawaii	1,206,613,000	0.4%
49	South Dakota	748,879,000	0.3%		41	Idaho	1,126,817,000	0.4%
29	Tennessee	3,751,844,000	1.3%		42	North Dakota	1,112,925,000	0.4%
2	Texas	30,593,618,000	10.3%		43	Montana	972,056,000	0.3%
23	Utah	4,572,790,000	1.5%		44	New Hampshire	940,165,000	0.3%
46	Vermont	892,984,000	0.3%		45	Wyoming	910,974,000	0.3%
10	Virginia	8,199,004,000	2.8%		46	Vermont	892,984,000	0.3%
11	Washington	7,464,698,000	2.5%		47	Alaska	847,344,000	0.3%
37	West Virginia	1,769,466,000	0.6%		48	Maine	782,344,000	0.3%
16	Wisconsin	6,254,027,000	2.1%		49	South Dakota	748,879,000	0.3%
45	Wyoming	910,974,000	0.3%		50	Rhode Island	692,395,000	0.2%
						District of Columbia	124,602,000	0.0%

Source: U.S. Bureau of the Census, Governments Division
"2017 State and Local Government Finances" (https://www.census.gov/programs-surveys/gov-finances.html)
*Direct general expenditures. Includes capital outlays.

Per Capita State and Local Government Expenditures for Higher Education in 2017
National Per Capita = $914*

ALPHA ORDER

RANK	STATE	PER CAPITA
17	Alabama	$1,049
12	Alaska	1,145
33	Arizona	859
32	Arkansas	877
16	California	1,053
13	Colorado	1,139
28	Connecticut	951
4	Delaware	1,454
49	Florida	528
47	Georgia	577
36	Hawaii	847
44	Idaho	656
41	Illinois	722
27	Indiana	965
8	Iowa	1,230
9	Kansas	1,199
22	Kentucky	1,006
39	Louisiana	745
46	Maine	586
19	Maryland	1,042
38	Massachusetts	807
10	Michigan	1,189
20	Minnesota	1,022
21	Mississippi	1,010
43	Missouri	665
29	Montana	923
7	Nebraska	1,233
50	Nevada	504
42	New Hampshire	697
37	New Jersey	839
6	New Mexico	1,283
40	New York	724
24	North Carolina	995
2	North Dakota	1,474
35	Ohio	848
18	Oklahoma	1,047
11	Oregon	1,152
30	Pennsylvania	914
45	Rhode Island	655
31	South Carolina	885
34	South Dakota	858
48	Tennessee	559
14	Texas	1,080
2	Utah	1,474
5	Vermont	1,430
26	Virginia	969
23	Washington	1,005
25	West Virginia	974
14	Wisconsin	1,080
1	Wyoming	1,574

RANK ORDER

RANK	STATE	PER CAPITA
1	Wyoming	$1,574
2	North Dakota	1,474
2	Utah	1,474
4	Delaware	1,454
5	Vermont	1,430
6	New Mexico	1,283
7	Nebraska	1,233
8	Iowa	1,230
9	Kansas	1,199
10	Michigan	1,189
11	Oregon	1,152
12	Alaska	1,145
13	Colorado	1,139
14	Texas	1,080
14	Wisconsin	1,080
16	California	1,053
17	Alabama	1,049
18	Oklahoma	1,047
19	Maryland	1,042
20	Minnesota	1,022
21	Mississippi	1,010
22	Kentucky	1,006
23	Washington	1,005
24	North Carolina	995
25	West Virginia	974
26	Virginia	969
27	Indiana	965
28	Connecticut	951
29	Montana	923
30	Pennsylvania	914
31	South Carolina	885
32	Arkansas	877
33	Arizona	859
34	South Dakota	858
35	Ohio	848
36	Hawaii	847
37	New Jersey	839
38	Massachusetts	807
39	Louisiana	745
40	New York	724
41	Illinois	722
42	New Hampshire	697
43	Missouri	665
44	Idaho	656
45	Rhode Island	655
46	Maine	586
47	Georgia	577
48	Tennessee	559
49	Florida	528
50	Nevada	504
	District of Columbia	179

Source: CQ Press using data from U.S. Bureau of the Census, Governments Division
   "2017 State and Local Government Finances" (https://www.census.gov/programs-surveys/gov-finances.html)
*Direct general expenditures. Includes capital outlays.

Expenditures for Higher Education as a Percent
of All State and Local Government Expenditures in 2017
National Percent = 9.7%*

ALPHA ORDER

RANK	STATE	PERCENT
11	Alabama	12.3
47	Alaska	6.7
13	Arizona	12.1
23	Arkansas	10.5
34	California	9.1
9	Colorado	12.8
29	Connecticut	10.0
8	Delaware	12.9
44	Florida	7.2
39	Georgia	8.4
37	Hawaii	8.6
31	Idaho	9.7
43	Illinois	7.9
13	Indiana	12.1
11	Iowa	12.3
6	Kansas	13.0
19	Kentucky	11.4
40	Louisiana	8.2
47	Maine	6.7
24	Maryland	10.4
45	Massachusetts	7.1
3	Michigan	14.0
32	Minnesota	9.6
17	Mississippi	11.5
36	Missouri	8.7
26	Montana	10.3
5	Nebraska	13.4
46	Nevada	6.8
38	New Hampshire	8.5
41	New Jersey	8.1
10	New Mexico	12.5
50	New York	5.0
6	North Carolina	13.0
17	North Dakota	11.5
33	Ohio	9.2
2	Oklahoma	14.1
22	Oregon	10.6
35	Pennsylvania	9.0
49	Rhode Island	6.6
26	South Carolina	10.3
24	South Dakota	10.4
42	Tennessee	8.0
4	Texas	13.5
1	Utah	17.6
13	Vermont	12.1
20	Virginia	11.1
29	Washington	10.0
21	West Virginia	11.0
16	Wisconsin	11.7
26	Wyoming	10.3

RANK ORDER

RANK	STATE	PERCENT
1	Utah	17.6
2	Oklahoma	14.1
3	Michigan	14.0
4	Texas	13.5
5	Nebraska	13.4
6	Kansas	13.0
6	North Carolina	13.0
8	Delaware	12.9
9	Colorado	12.8
10	New Mexico	12.5
11	Alabama	12.3
11	Iowa	12.3
13	Arizona	12.1
13	Indiana	12.1
13	Vermont	12.1
16	Wisconsin	11.7
17	Mississippi	11.5
17	North Dakota	11.5
19	Kentucky	11.4
20	Virginia	11.1
21	West Virginia	11.0
22	Oregon	10.6
23	Arkansas	10.5
24	Maryland	10.4
24	South Dakota	10.4
26	Montana	10.3
26	South Carolina	10.3
26	Wyoming	10.3
29	Connecticut	10.0
29	Washington	10.0
31	Idaho	9.7
32	Minnesota	9.6
33	Ohio	9.2
34	California	9.1
35	Pennsylvania	9.0
36	Missouri	8.7
37	Hawaii	8.6
38	New Hampshire	8.5
39	Georgia	8.4
40	Louisiana	8.2
41	New Jersey	8.1
42	Tennessee	8.0
43	Illinois	7.9
44	Florida	7.2
45	Massachusetts	7.1
46	Nevada	6.8
47	Alaska	6.7
47	Maine	6.7
49	Rhode Island	6.6
50	New York	5.0
	District of Columbia	0.9

Source: CQ Press using data from U.S. Bureau of the Census, Governments Division
"2017 State and Local Government Finances" (https://www.census.gov/programs-surveys/gov-finances.html)
*Direct general expenditures for higher education as a percent of all direct general expenditures. Includes capital outlays.

Average Faculty Salary at Institutions of Higher Education in 2018

National Average = $86,701*

ALPHA ORDER

RANK	STATE	AVERAGE SALARY
37	Alabama	$72,167
18	Alaska	82,491
14	Arizona	84,944
49	Arkansas	63,044
3	California	105,504
27	Colorado	78,455
4	Connecticut	104,525
5	Delaware	103,108
20	Florida	81,273
31	Georgia	77,458
12	Hawaii	89,453
44	Idaho	67,824
11	Illinois	91,514
17	Indiana	83,119
29	Iowa	77,927
39	Kansas	69,327
43	Kentucky	68,190
41	Louisiana	68,635
35	Maine	75,806
16	Maryland	84,268
1	Massachusetts	109,773
9	Michigan	92,728
19	Minnesota	81,488
50	Mississippi	61,964
34	Missouri	75,869
45	Montana	67,375
32	Nebraska	77,331
13	Nevada	85,824
8	New Hampshire	97,902
2	New Jersey	107,662
46	New Mexico	67,168
7	New York	98,056
26	North Carolina	78,963
39	North Dakota	69,327
22	Ohio	81,193
42	Oklahoma	68,554
25	Oregon	79,014
10	Pennsylvania	92,443
6	Rhode Island	100,078
38	South Carolina	70,124
47	South Dakota	65,212
33	Tennessee	77,204
23	Texas	80,852
28	Utah	78,206
24	Vermont	80,432
15	Virginia	84,295
21	Washington	81,250
48	West Virginia	63,854
30	Wisconsin	77,722
36	Wyoming	73,473

RANK ORDER

RANK	STATE	AVERAGE SALARY
1	Massachusetts	$109,773
2	New Jersey	107,662
3	California	105,504
4	Connecticut	104,525
5	Delaware	103,108
6	Rhode Island	100,078
7	New York	98,056
8	New Hampshire	97,902
9	Michigan	92,728
10	Pennsylvania	92,443
11	Illinois	91,514
12	Hawaii	89,453
13	Nevada	85,824
14	Arizona	84,944
15	Virginia	84,295
16	Maryland	84,268
17	Indiana	83,119
18	Alaska	82,491
19	Minnesota	81,488
20	Florida	81,273
21	Washington	81,250
22	Ohio	81,193
23	Texas	80,852
24	Vermont	80,432
25	Oregon	79,014
26	North Carolina	78,963
27	Colorado	78,455
28	Utah	78,206
29	Iowa	77,927
30	Wisconsin	77,722
31	Georgia	77,458
32	Nebraska	77,331
33	Tennessee	77,204
34	Missouri	75,869
35	Maine	75,806
36	Wyoming	73,473
37	Alabama	72,167
38	South Carolina	70,124
39	Kansas	69,327
39	North Dakota	69,327
41	Louisiana	68,635
42	Oklahoma	68,554
43	Kentucky	68,190
44	Idaho	67,824
45	Montana	67,375
46	New Mexico	67,168
47	South Dakota	65,212
48	West Virginia	63,854
49	Arkansas	63,044
50	Mississippi	61,964
	District of Columbia	117,213

Source: U.S. Department of Education, National Center for Education Statistics
  "Digest of Education Statistics" (https://nces.ed.gov/programs/digest/index.asp)
*For 2017–2018 school year. For full-time instructional faculty on nine-month contracts at four-year and two-year public and private degree-granting institutions.

Average Student Costs at Public Institutions of Higher Education in 2018

National Average = $20,050*

ALPHA ORDER

RANK	STATE	AVERAGE COSTS
23	Alabama	$19,673
30	Alaska	18,373
12	Arizona	22,629
38	Arkansas	17,479
16	California	22,081
18	Colorado	21,514
6	Connecticut	25,182
13	Delaware	22,371
48	Florida	14,896
37	Georgia	17,705
19	Hawaii	21,201
47	Idaho	15,455
7	Illinois	25,089
25	Indiana	19,297
29	Iowa	18,426
34	Kansas	17,963
21	Kentucky	20,745
27	Louisiana	18,835
24	Maine	19,500
20	Maryland	21,177
5	Massachusetts	25,229
11	Michigan	22,665
22	Minnesota	20,420
36	Mississippi	17,718
33	Missouri	18,106
46	Montana	15,800
28	Nebraska	18,449
40	Nevada	16,810
2	New Hampshire	27,570
3	New Jersey	26,542
45	New Mexico	15,803
14	New York	22,343
39	North Carolina	17,343
44	North Dakota	15,998
17	Ohio	21,674
43	Oklahoma	16,263
10	Oregon	22,710
4	Pennsylvania	25,795
8	Rhode Island	24,280
15	South Carolina	22,132
42	South Dakota	16,421
26	Tennessee	18,951
32	Texas	18,271
50	Utah	14,174
1	Vermont	27,782
9	Virginia	23,427
31	Washington	18,323
35	West Virginia	17,803
41	Wisconsin	16,544
49	Wyoming	14,486

RANK ORDER

RANK	STATE	AVERAGE COSTS
1	Vermont	$27,782
2	New Hampshire	27,570
3	New Jersey	26,542
4	Pennsylvania	25,795
5	Massachusetts	25,229
6	Connecticut	25,182
7	Illinois	25,089
8	Rhode Island	24,280
9	Virginia	23,427
10	Oregon	22,710
11	Michigan	22,665
12	Arizona	22,629
13	Delaware	22,371
14	New York	22,343
15	South Carolina	22,132
16	California	22,081
17	Ohio	21,674
18	Colorado	21,514
19	Hawaii	21,201
20	Maryland	21,177
21	Kentucky	20,745
22	Minnesota	20,420
23	Alabama	19,673
24	Maine	19,500
25	Indiana	19,297
26	Tennessee	18,951
27	Louisiana	18,835
28	Nebraska	18,449
29	Iowa	18,426
30	Alaska	18,373
31	Washington	18,323
32	Texas	18,271
33	Missouri	18,106
34	Kansas	17,963
35	West Virginia	17,803
36	Mississippi	17,718
37	Georgia	17,705
38	Arkansas	17,479
39	North Carolina	17,343
40	Nevada	16,810
41	Wisconsin	16,544
42	South Dakota	16,421
43	Oklahoma	16,263
44	North Dakota	15,998
45	New Mexico	15,803
46	Montana	15,800
47	Idaho	15,455
48	Florida	14,896
49	Wyoming	14,486
50	Utah	14,174

District of Columbia**   NA

Source: U.S. Department of Education, National Center for Education Statistics
   "Digest of Education Statistics" (https://nces.ed.gov/programs/digest/index.asp)
*Data for 2017–2018 school year. Based on average in-state tuition, room and board, and fees for full-time students in public four-year institutions for an entire academic year.
**Not available.

Average Student Costs at Private Institutions of Higher Education in 2018

National Average = $43,139*

	ALPHA ORDER			RANK ORDER	
RANK	STATE	AVERAGE COSTS	RANK	STATE	AVERAGE COSTS
43	Alabama	$26,164	1	Massachusetts	$59,559
42	Alaska	26,887	2	Vermont	56,172
45	Arizona	22,939	3	Maryland	55,685
38	Arkansas	30,828	4	Rhode Island	54,877
13	California	47,410	5	Connecticut	54,819
30	Colorado	35,152	6	New York	53,659
5	Connecticut	54,819	7	Pennsylvania	53,239
41	Delaware	26,928	8	Oregon	50,617
24	Florida	37,336	9	New Jersey	50,321
22	Georgia	40,414	10	Maine	49,994
40	Hawaii	28,858	11	Louisiana	49,452
49	Idaho	13,488	12	Washington	48,518
15	Illinois	45,046	13	California	47,410
18	Indiana	43,764	14	New Hampshire	47,030
23	Iowa	37,380	15	Illinois	45,046
39	Kansas	30,240	16	North Carolina	44,050
28	Kentucky	35,948	17	Texas	43,866
11	Louisiana	49,452	18	Indiana	43,764
10	Maine	49,994	19	Wisconsin	43,332
3	Maryland	55,685	20	Minnesota	42,716
1	Massachusetts	59,559	21	Ohio	42,254
26	Michigan	36,664	22	Georgia	40,414
20	Minnesota	42,716	23	Iowa	37,380
44	Mississippi	25,774	24	Florida	37,336
31	Missouri	34,623	25	Tennessee	37,162
34	Montana	33,739	26	Michigan	36,664
32	Nebraska	34,598	27	Nevada	36,163
27	Nevada	36,163	28	Kentucky	35,948
14	New Hampshire	47,030	29	Oklahoma	35,542
9	New Jersey	50,321	30	Colorado	35,152
36	New Mexico	33,620	31	Missouri	34,623
6	New York	53,659	32	Nebraska	34,598
16	North Carolina	44,050	33	South Carolina	34,421
46	North Dakota	22,511	34	Montana	33,739
21	Ohio	42,254	35	Virginia	33,658
29	Oklahoma	35,542	36	New Mexico	33,620
8	Oregon	50,617	37	South Dakota	32,157
7	Pennsylvania	53,239	38	Arkansas	30,828
4	Rhode Island	54,877	39	Kansas	30,240
33	South Carolina	34,421	40	Hawaii	28,858
37	South Dakota	32,157	41	Delaware	26,928
25	Tennessee	37,162	42	Alaska	26,887
17	Texas	43,866	43	Alabama	26,164
48	Utah	15,389	44	Mississippi	25,774
2	Vermont	56,172	45	Arizona	22,939
35	Virginia	33,658	46	North Dakota	22,511
12	Washington	48,518	47	West Virginia	21,300
47	West Virginia	21,300	48	Utah	15,389
19	Wisconsin	43,332	49	Idaho	13,488
NA	Wyoming**	NA	NA	Wyoming**	NA
				District of Columbia	57,611

Source: U.S. Department of Education, National Center for Education Statistics
     "Digest of Education Statistics" (https://nces.ed.gov/programs/digest/index.asp)
*Data for 2017–2018 school year. Based on average in-state tuition, room and board, and fees for full-time students in private four-year institutions for an entire academic year.
**Not available.

Average College Graduate Debt: Class of 2018

National Average Debt = $29,200*

ALPHA ORDER

RANK	STATE	AVERAGE DEBT
22	Alabama	$29,469
NA	Alaska**	NA
NA	Arizona**	NA
36	Arkansas	26,579
45	California	22,585
39	Colorado	24,888
1	Connecticut	38,669
6	Delaware	34,144
41	Florida	24,428
26	Georgia	28,824
42	Hawaii	24,162
30	Idaho	27,682
21	Illinois	29,855
25	Indiana	29,064
19	Iowa	30,045
34	Kansas	26,764
28	Kentucky	28,435
32	Louisiana	27,151
7	Maine	32,676
24	Maryland	29,178
11	Massachusetts	31,882
9	Michigan	32,158
8	Minnesota	32,317
18	Mississippi	30,117
23	Missouri	29,224
29	Montana	28,032
37	Nebraska	26,422
44	Nevada	22,600
3	New Hampshire	36,776
5	New Jersey	34,387
46	New Mexico	21,858
14	New York	31,127
35	North Carolina	26,683
NA	North Dakota**	NA
17	Ohio	30,323
38	Oklahoma	25,221
27	Oregon	28,628
2	Pennsylvania	37,061
4	Rhode Island	36,036
15	South Carolina	30,838
10	South Dakota	31,895
33	Tennessee	26,838
31	Texas	27,293
47	Utah	19,728
13	Vermont	31,431
16	Virginia	30,363
43	Washington	23,524
20	West Virginia	30,014
12	Wisconsin	31,705
40	Wyoming	24,474

RANK ORDER

RANK	STATE	AVERAGE DEBT
1	Connecticut	$38,669
2	Pennsylvania	37,061
3	New Hampshire	36,776
4	Rhode Island	36,036
5	New Jersey	34,387
6	Delaware	34,144
7	Maine	32,676
8	Minnesota	32,317
9	Michigan	32,158
10	South Dakota	31,895
11	Massachusetts	31,882
12	Wisconsin	31,705
13	Vermont	31,431
14	New York	31,127
15	South Carolina	30,838
16	Virginia	30,363
17	Ohio	30,323
18	Mississippi	30,117
19	Iowa	30,045
20	West Virginia	30,014
21	Illinois	29,855
22	Alabama	29,469
23	Missouri	29,224
24	Maryland	29,178
25	Indiana	29,064
26	Georgia	28,824
27	Oregon	28,628
28	Kentucky	28,435
29	Montana	28,032
30	Idaho	27,682
31	Texas	27,293
32	Louisiana	27,151
33	Tennessee	26,838
34	Kansas	26,764
35	North Carolina	26,683
36	Arkansas	26,579
37	Nebraska	26,422
38	Oklahoma	25,221
39	Colorado	24,888
40	Wyoming	24,474
41	Florida	24,428
42	Hawaii	24,162
43	Washington	23,524
44	Nevada	22,600
45	California	22,585
46	New Mexico	21,858
47	Utah	19,728
NA	Alaska**	NA
NA	Arizona**	NA
NA	North Dakota**	NA
	District of Columbia	34,046

Source: The Project on Student Debt
"Student Debt and the Class of 2018" (September 2019, https://ticas.org/posd/map-state-data)
*For students receiving a bachelor's degree in 2018.
**Not available.

Percent of College Graduates with Debt: Class of 2018

National Percent = 65%*

ALPHA ORDER			RANK ORDER		
RANK	STATE	PERCENT	RANK	STATE	PERCENT
37	Alabama	51	1	New Hampshire	76
NA	Alaska**	NA	2	South Dakota	72
NA	Arizona**	NA	3	Minnesota	68
35	Arkansas	53	4	Illinois	66
39	California	49	5	Pennsylvania	65
36	Colorado	52	5	West Virginia	65
17	Connecticut	59	7	Kentucky	64
13	Delaware	62	7	New Jersey	64
46	Florida	44	7	Wisconsin	64
24	Georgia	57	10	Iowa	63
43	Hawaii	47	10	Rhode Island	63
13	Idaho	62	10	Vermont	63
4	Illinois	66	13	Delaware	62
24	Indiana	57	13	Idaho	62
10	Iowa	63	15	Maine	61
20	Kansas	58	16	Ohio	60
7	Kentucky	64	17	Connecticut	59
39	Louisiana	49	17	Michigan	59
15	Maine	61	17	New York	59
31	Maryland	55	20	Kansas	58
24	Massachusetts	57	20	Mississippi	58
17	Michigan	59	20	Missouri	58
3	Minnesota	68	20	South Carolina	58
20	Mississippi	58	24	Georgia	57
20	Missouri	58	24	Indiana	57
24	Montana	57	24	Massachusetts	57
31	Nebraska	55	24	Montana	57
37	Nevada	51	24	Virginia	57
1	New Hampshire	76	29	North Carolina	56
7	New Jersey	64	29	Texas	56
39	New Mexico	49	31	Maryland	55
17	New York	59	31	Nebraska	55
29	North Carolina	56	31	Oregon	55
NA	North Dakota**	NA	31	Tennessee	55
16	Ohio	60	35	Arkansas	53
43	Oklahoma	47	36	Colorado	52
31	Oregon	55	37	Alabama	51
5	Pennsylvania	65	37	Nevada	51
10	Rhode Island	63	39	California	49
20	South Carolina	58	39	Louisiana	49
2	South Dakota	72	39	New Mexico	49
31	Tennessee	55	42	Washington	48
29	Texas	56	43	Hawaii	47
47	Utah	36	43	Oklahoma	47
10	Vermont	63	45	Wyoming	46
24	Virginia	57	46	Florida	44
42	Washington	48	47	Utah	36
5	West Virginia	65	NA	Alaska**	NA
7	Wisconsin	64	NA	Arizona**	NA
45	Wyoming	46	NA	North Dakota**	NA
				District of Columbia	51

Source: The Project on Student Debt
"Student Debt and the Class of 2018" (September 2019, https://ticas.org/posd/map-state-data)
*For students receiving a bachelor's degree in 2018.
**Not available.

Institutions of Higher Education in 2018

National Total = 4,313 Institutions*

ALPHA ORDER

RANK	STATE	INSTITUTIONS	% of USA
23	Alabama	72	1.7%
49	Alaska	8	0.2%
19	Arizona	78	1.8%
31	Arkansas	53	1.2%
1	California	441	10.2%
18	Colorado	79	1.8%
33	Connecticut	43	1.0%
49	Delaware	8	0.2%
5	Florida	201	4.7%
9	Georgia	123	2.9%
44	Hawaii	20	0.5%
46	Idaho	17	0.4%
7	Illinois	171	4.0%
16	Indiana	80	1.9%
26	Iowa	62	1.4%
24	Kansas	69	1.6%
25	Kentucky	67	1.6%
27	Louisiana	60	1.4%
38	Maine	31	0.7%
30	Maryland	56	1.3%
11	Massachusetts	116	2.7%
15	Michigan	94	2.2%
14	Minnesota	95	2.2%
36	Mississippi	38	0.9%
12	Missouri	115	2.7%
41	Montana	23	0.5%
35	Nebraska	41	1.0%
40	Nevada	24	0.6%
39	New Hampshire	25	0.6%
21	New Jersey	75	1.7%
34	New Mexico	42	1.0%
2	New York	301	7.0%
8	North Carolina	144	3.3%
44	North Dakota	20	0.5%
6	Ohio	185	4.3%
28	Oklahoma	59	1.4%
29	Oregon	57	1.3%
4	Pennsylvania	239	5.5%
47	Rhode Island	13	0.3%
22	South Carolina	73	1.7%
41	South Dakota	23	0.5%
13	Tennessee	100	2.3%
3	Texas	261	6.1%
37	Utah	32	0.7%
41	Vermont	23	0.5%
10	Virginia	122	2.8%
16	Washington	80	1.9%
32	West Virginia	44	1.0%
20	Wisconsin	76	1.8%
48	Wyoming	10	0.2%

RANK ORDER

RANK	STATE	INSTITUTIONS	% of USA
1	California	441	10.2%
2	New York	301	7.0%
3	Texas	261	6.1%
4	Pennsylvania	239	5.5%
5	Florida	201	4.7%
6	Ohio	185	4.3%
7	Illinois	171	4.0%
8	North Carolina	144	3.3%
9	Georgia	123	2.9%
10	Virginia	122	2.8%
11	Massachusetts	116	2.7%
12	Missouri	115	2.7%
13	Tennessee	100	2.3%
14	Minnesota	95	2.2%
15	Michigan	94	2.2%
16	Indiana	80	1.9%
16	Washington	80	1.9%
18	Colorado	79	1.8%
19	Arizona	78	1.8%
20	Wisconsin	76	1.8%
21	New Jersey	75	1.7%
22	South Carolina	73	1.7%
23	Alabama	72	1.7%
24	Kansas	69	1.6%
25	Kentucky	67	1.6%
26	Iowa	62	1.4%
27	Louisiana	60	1.4%
28	Oklahoma	59	1.4%
29	Oregon	57	1.3%
30	Maryland	56	1.3%
31	Arkansas	53	1.2%
32	West Virginia	44	1.0%
33	Connecticut	43	1.0%
34	New Mexico	42	1.0%
35	Nebraska	41	1.0%
36	Mississippi	38	0.9%
37	Utah	32	0.7%
38	Maine	31	0.7%
39	New Hampshire	25	0.6%
40	Nevada	24	0.6%
41	Montana	23	0.5%
41	South Dakota	23	0.5%
41	Vermont	23	0.5%
44	Hawaii	20	0.5%
44	North Dakota	20	0.5%
46	Idaho	17	0.4%
47	Rhode Island	13	0.3%
48	Wyoming	10	0.2%
49	Alaska	8	0.2%
49	Delaware	8	0.2%
	District of Columbia	19	0.4%

Source: U.S. Department of Education, National Center for Education Statistics
   "Digest of Education Statistics" (https://nces.ed.gov/programs/digest/index.asp)
*For 2017–2018 school year. Consists of 2,828 four-year and 1,485 two-year public and private (profit and not-for-profit)
degree-granting institutions. Includes five U.S. Service Schools not shown by state.

Enrollment in Institutions of Higher Education in 2017

National Total = 19,765,598 Students*

RANK	STATE	STUDENTS	% of USA	RANK	STATE	STUDENTS	% of USA
24	Alabama	306,822	1.6%	1	California	2,714,051	13.7%
50	Alaska	26,905	0.1%	2	Texas	1,630,516	8.2%
8	Arizona	591,626	3.0%	3	New York	1,260,240	6.4%
34	Arkansas	164,082	0.8%	4	Florida	1,071,484	5.4%
1	California	2,714,051	13.7%	5	Illinois	757,002	3.8%
20	Colorado	360,236	1.8%	6	Pennsylvania	717,289	3.6%
32	Connecticut	197,534	1.0%	7	Ohio	649,687	3.3%
44	Delaware	60,338	0.3%	8	Arizona	591,626	3.0%
4	Florida	1,071,484	5.4%	9	North Carolina	563,831	2.9%
12	Georgia	538,124	2.7%	10	Michigan	558,053	2.8%
43	Hawaii	64,125	0.3%	11	Virginia	554,212	2.8%
38	Idaho	131,803	0.7%	12	Georgia	538,124	2.7%
5	Illinois	757,002	3.8%	13	Massachusetts	503,508	2.5%
16	Indiana	398,804	2.0%	14	New Jersey	419,037	2.1%
25	Iowa	260,954	1.3%	15	Minnesota	412,966	2.1%
30	Kansas	213,962	1.1%	16	Indiana	398,804	2.0%
26	Kentucky	258,498	1.3%	17	Missouri	383,489	1.9%
28	Louisiana	242,065	1.2%	18	Washington	367,944	1.9%
42	Maine	71,811	0.4%	19	Maryland	364,207	1.8%
19	Maryland	364,207	1.8%	20	Colorado	360,236	1.8%
13	Massachusetts	503,508	2.5%	21	Wisconsin	340,770	1.7%
10	Michigan	558,053	2.8%	22	Utah	332,334	1.7%
15	Minnesota	412,966	2.1%	23	Tennessee	323,157	1.6%
33	Mississippi	171,751	0.9%	24	Alabama	306,822	1.6%
17	Missouri	383,489	1.9%	25	Iowa	260,954	1.3%
47	Montana	50,642	0.3%	26	Kentucky	258,498	1.3%
37	Nebraska	135,864	0.7%	27	South Carolina	246,388	1.2%
40	Nevada	117,574	0.6%	28	Louisiana	242,065	1.2%
35	New Hampshire	149,184	0.8%	29	Oregon	229,936	1.2%
14	New Jersey	419,037	2.1%	30	Kansas	213,962	1.1%
39	New Mexico	129,494	0.7%	31	Oklahoma	202,051	1.0%
3	New York	1,260,240	6.4%	32	Connecticut	197,534	1.0%
9	North Carolina	563,831	2.9%	33	Mississippi	171,751	0.9%
45	North Dakota	53,749	0.3%	34	Arkansas	164,082	0.8%
7	Ohio	649,687	3.3%	35	New Hampshire	149,184	0.8%
31	Oklahoma	202,051	1.0%	36	West Virginia	142,963	0.7%
29	Oregon	229,936	1.2%	37	Nebraska	135,864	0.7%
6	Pennsylvania	717,289	3.6%	38	Idaho	131,803	0.7%
41	Rhode Island	82,766	0.4%	39	New Mexico	129,494	0.7%
27	South Carolina	246,388	1.2%	40	Nevada	117,574	0.6%
46	South Dakota	53,620	0.3%	41	Rhode Island	82,766	0.4%
23	Tennessee	323,157	1.6%	42	Maine	71,811	0.4%
2	Texas	1,630,516	8.2%	43	Hawaii	64,125	0.3%
22	Utah	332,334	1.7%	44	Delaware	60,338	0.3%
48	Vermont	43,855	0.2%	45	North Dakota	53,749	0.3%
11	Virginia	554,212	2.8%	46	South Dakota	53,620	0.3%
18	Washington	367,944	1.9%	47	Montana	50,642	0.3%
36	West Virginia	142,963	0.7%	48	Vermont	43,855	0.2%
21	Wisconsin	340,770	1.7%	49	Wyoming	33,015	0.2%
49	Wyoming	33,015	0.2%	50	Alaska	26,905	0.1%
					District of Columbia	95,999	0.5%

ALPHA ORDER — RANK ORDER

Source: U.S. Department of Education, National Center for Education Statistics
"Digest of Education Statistics" (https://nces.ed.gov/programs/digest/index.asp)
*Fall 2017 enrollment. Includes full-time and part-time students at Title IV eligible, degree-granting four-year and two-year institutions. National total includes 15,281 students at U.S. Service Schools not shown by state.

Enrollment Rate in Institutions of Higher Education in 2017

National Rate = 646 Students per 1,000 Population 18 to 24 Years Old*

ALPHA ORDER

RANK	STATE	RATE
17	Alabama	673
50	Alaska	373
4	Arizona	880
36	Arkansas	583
11	California	714
14	Colorado	691
40	Connecticut	561
13	Delaware	710
29	Florida	615
42	Georgia	536
47	Hawaii	516
5	Idaho	830
24	Illinois	633
32	Indiana	606
7	Iowa	814
9	Kansas	722
28	Kentucky	618
41	Louisiana	556
21	Maine	655
16	Maryland	674
10	Massachusetts	719
38	Michigan	575
6	Minnesota	817
35	Mississippi	587
19	Missouri	672
48	Montana	515
12	Nebraska	711
49	Nevada	472
1	New Hampshire	1,174
43	New Jersey	532
22	New Mexico	650
17	New York	673
37	North Carolina	580
27	North Dakota	622
33	Ohio	605
43	Oklahoma	532
24	Oregon	633
31	Pennsylvania	610
8	Rhode Island	728
45	South Carolina	527
23	South Dakota	648
45	Tennessee	527
34	Texas	589
2	Utah	961
20	Vermont	656
15	Virginia	689
39	Washington	564
3	West Virginia	901
30	Wisconsin	612
26	Wyoming	628

RANK ORDER

RANK	STATE	RATE
1	New Hampshire	1,174
2	Utah	961
3	West Virginia	901
4	Arizona	880
5	Idaho	830
6	Minnesota	817
7	Iowa	814
8	Rhode Island	728
9	Kansas	722
10	Massachusetts	719
11	California	714
12	Nebraska	711
13	Delaware	710
14	Colorado	691
15	Virginia	689
16	Maryland	674
17	Alabama	673
17	New York	673
19	Missouri	672
20	Vermont	656
21	Maine	655
22	New Mexico	650
23	South Dakota	648
24	Illinois	633
24	Oregon	633
26	Wyoming	628
27	North Dakota	622
28	Kentucky	618
29	Florida	615
30	Wisconsin	612
31	Pennsylvania	610
32	Indiana	606
33	Ohio	605
34	Texas	589
35	Mississippi	587
36	Arkansas	583
37	North Carolina	580
38	Michigan	575
39	Washington	564
40	Connecticut	561
41	Louisiana	556
42	Georgia	536
43	New Jersey	532
43	Oklahoma	532
45	South Carolina	527
45	Tennessee	527
47	Hawaii	516
48	Montana	515
49	Nevada	472
50	Alaska	373

District of Columbia — 1,284

Source: CQ Press using data from U.S. Department of Education, National Center for Education Statistics
"Digest of Education Statistics" (https://nces.ed.gov/programs/digest/index.asp)

*Based on fall 2017 enrollment and population. National rate includes U.S. Service Schools. Includes students at four-year and two-year public and private degree-granting institutions. Enrollment based on location of institution. Population based on residence.

Enrollment in Public Institutions of Higher Education in 2017

National Total = 14,560,155 Students*

ALPHA ORDER

RANK	STATE	STUDENTS	% of USA
19	Alabama	254,071	1.7%
49	Alaska	25,850	0.2%
12	Arizona	366,787	2.5%
33	Arkansas	146,697	1.0%
1	California	2,246,844	15.4%
18	Colorado	278,909	1.9%
35	Connecticut	116,090	0.8%
45	Delaware	42,321	0.3%
3	Florida	798,045	5.5%
9	Georgia	428,586	2.9%
40	Hawaii	51,674	0.4%
39	Idaho	75,792	0.5%
7	Illinois	478,042	3.3%
16	Indiana	301,562	2.1%
31	Iowa	170,427	1.2%
29	Kansas	179,856	1.2%
25	Kentucky	202,266	1.4%
24	Louisiana	210,691	1.4%
42	Maine	46,999	0.3%
15	Maryland	303,640	2.1%
23	Massachusetts	213,389	1.5%
6	Michigan	478,735	3.3%
20	Minnesota	249,385	1.7%
32	Mississippi	152,319	1.0%
21	Missouri	235,540	1.6%
43	Montana	46,002	0.3%
37	Nebraska	101,038	0.7%
36	Nevada	107,864	0.7%
47	New Hampshire	39,761	0.3%
13	New Jersey	334,597	2.3%
34	New Mexico	125,280	0.9%
4	New York	697,458	4.8%
8	North Carolina	454,632	3.1%
41	North Dakota	47,574	0.3%
5	Ohio	497,473	3.4%
30	Oklahoma	174,140	1.2%
27	Oregon	192,334	1.3%
10	Pennsylvania	400,943	2.8%
46	Rhode Island	41,018	0.3%
26	South Carolina	200,622	1.4%
44	South Dakota	44,630	0.3%
22	Tennessee	223,179	1.5%
2	Texas	1,448,385	9.9%
28	Utah	180,034	1.2%
50	Vermont	25,300	0.2%
11	Virginia	389,249	2.7%
14	Washington	318,336	2.2%
38	West Virginia	83,895	0.6%
17	Wisconsin	279,533	1.9%
48	Wyoming	32,551	0.2%

RANK ORDER

RANK	STATE	STUDENTS	% of USA
1	California	2,246,844	15.4%
2	Texas	1,448,385	9.9%
3	Florida	798,045	5.5%
4	New York	697,458	4.8%
5	Ohio	497,473	3.4%
6	Michigan	478,735	3.3%
7	Illinois	478,042	3.3%
8	North Carolina	454,632	3.1%
9	Georgia	428,586	2.9%
10	Pennsylvania	400,943	2.8%
11	Virginia	389,249	2.7%
12	Arizona	366,787	2.5%
13	New Jersey	334,597	2.3%
14	Washington	318,336	2.2%
15	Maryland	303,640	2.1%
16	Indiana	301,562	2.1%
17	Wisconsin	279,533	1.9%
18	Colorado	278,909	1.9%
19	Alabama	254,071	1.7%
20	Minnesota	249,385	1.7%
21	Missouri	235,540	1.6%
22	Tennessee	223,179	1.5%
23	Massachusetts	213,389	1.5%
24	Louisiana	210,691	1.4%
25	Kentucky	202,266	1.4%
26	South Carolina	200,622	1.4%
27	Oregon	192,334	1.3%
28	Utah	180,034	1.2%
29	Kansas	179,856	1.2%
30	Oklahoma	174,140	1.2%
31	Iowa	170,427	1.2%
32	Mississippi	152,319	1.0%
33	Arkansas	146,697	1.0%
34	New Mexico	125,280	0.9%
35	Connecticut	116,090	0.8%
36	Nevada	107,864	0.7%
37	Nebraska	101,038	0.7%
38	West Virginia	83,895	0.6%
39	Idaho	75,792	0.5%
40	Hawaii	51,674	0.4%
41	North Dakota	47,574	0.3%
42	Maine	46,999	0.3%
43	Montana	46,002	0.3%
44	South Dakota	44,630	0.3%
45	Delaware	42,321	0.3%
46	Rhode Island	41,018	0.3%
47	New Hampshire	39,761	0.3%
48	Wyoming	32,551	0.2%
49	Alaska	25,850	0.2%
50	Vermont	25,300	0.2%
	District of Columbia	4,529	0.0%

Source: U.S. Department of Education, National Center for Education Statistics
 "Digest of Education Statistics" (https://nces.ed.gov/programs/digest/index.asp)
*Fall 2017 enrollment. Includes full-time and part-time students at Title IV eligible, degree-granting four-year and two-year institutions. National total includes 15,281 students at U.S. Service Schools not shown by state.

Enrollment in Private Institutions of Higher Education in 2017

National Total = 5,205,443 Students*

ALPHA ORDER					RANK ORDER			
RANK	STATE	STUDENTS	% of USA		RANK	STATE	STUDENTS	% of USA
29	Alabama	52,751	1.0%		1	New York	562,782	10.8%
49	Alaska	1,055	0.0%		2	California	467,207	9.0%
7	Arizona	224,839	4.3%		3	Pennsylvania	316,346	6.1%
42	Arkansas	17,385	0.3%		4	Massachusetts	290,119	5.6%
2	California	467,207	9.0%		5	Illinois	278,960	5.4%
22	Colorado	81,327	1.6%		6	Florida	273,439	5.3%
21	Connecticut	81,444	1.6%		7	Arizona	224,839	4.3%
41	Delaware	18,017	0.3%		8	Texas	182,131	3.5%
6	Florida	273,439	5.3%		9	Virginia	164,963	3.2%
14	Georgia	109,538	2.1%		10	Minnesota	163,581	3.1%
43	Hawaii	12,451	0.2%		11	Utah	152,300	2.9%
28	Idaho	56,011	1.1%		12	Ohio	152,214	2.9%
5	Illinois	278,960	5.4%		13	Missouri	147,949	2.8%
18	Indiana	97,242	1.9%		14	Georgia	109,538	2.1%
19	Iowa	90,527	1.7%		15	New Hampshire	109,423	2.1%
35	Kansas	34,106	0.7%		16	North Carolina	109,199	2.1%
27	Kentucky	56,232	1.1%		17	Tennessee	99,978	1.9%
36	Louisiana	31,374	0.6%		18	Indiana	97,242	1.9%
38	Maine	24,812	0.5%		19	Iowa	90,527	1.7%
25	Maryland	60,567	1.2%		20	New Jersey	84,440	1.6%
4	Massachusetts	290,119	5.6%		21	Connecticut	81,444	1.6%
23	Michigan	79,318	1.5%		22	Colorado	81,327	1.6%
10	Minnesota	163,581	3.1%		23	Michigan	79,318	1.5%
39	Mississippi	19,432	0.4%		24	Wisconsin	61,237	1.2%
13	Missouri	147,949	2.8%		25	Maryland	60,567	1.2%
47	Montana	4,640	0.1%		26	West Virginia	59,068	1.1%
34	Nebraska	34,826	0.7%		27	Kentucky	56,232	1.1%
44	Nevada	9,710	0.2%		28	Idaho	56,011	1.1%
15	New Hampshire	109,423	2.1%		29	Alabama	52,751	1.0%
20	New Jersey	84,440	1.6%		30	Washington	49,608	1.0%
48	New Mexico	4,214	0.1%		31	South Carolina	45,766	0.9%
1	New York	562,782	10.8%		32	Rhode Island	41,748	0.8%
16	North Carolina	109,199	2.1%		33	Oregon	37,602	0.7%
46	North Dakota	6,175	0.1%		34	Nebraska	34,826	0.7%
12	Ohio	152,214	2.9%		35	Kansas	34,106	0.7%
37	Oklahoma	27,911	0.5%		36	Louisiana	31,374	0.6%
33	Oregon	37,602	0.7%		37	Oklahoma	27,911	0.5%
3	Pennsylvania	316,346	6.1%		38	Maine	24,812	0.5%
32	Rhode Island	41,748	0.8%		39	Mississippi	19,432	0.4%
31	South Carolina	45,766	0.9%		40	Vermont	18,555	0.4%
45	South Dakota	8,990	0.2%		41	Delaware	18,017	0.3%
17	Tennessee	99,978	1.9%		42	Arkansas	17,385	0.3%
8	Texas	182,131	3.5%		43	Hawaii	12,451	0.2%
11	Utah	152,300	2.9%		44	Nevada	9,710	0.2%
40	Vermont	18,555	0.4%		45	South Dakota	8,990	0.2%
9	Virginia	164,963	3.2%		46	North Dakota	6,175	0.1%
30	Washington	49,608	1.0%		47	Montana	4,640	0.1%
26	West Virginia	59,068	1.1%		48	New Mexico	4,214	0.1%
24	Wisconsin	61,237	1.2%		49	Alaska	1,055	0.0%
50	Wyoming	464	0.0%		50	Wyoming	464	0.0%
						District of Columbia	91,470	1.8%

Source: U.S. Department of Education, National Center for Education Statistics
   "Digest of Education Statistics" (https://nces.ed.gov/programs/digest/index.asp)
*Fall 2017 enrollment. Includes full-time and part-time students at Title IV eligible, degree-granting four-year and two-year institutions.

Percent of Population with a Bachelor's Degree or More in 2018

National Percent = 32.6%*

ALPHA ORDER

RANK	STATE	PERCENT
44	Alabama	25.5
28	Alaska	30.2
30	Arizona	29.7
48	Arkansas	23.3
15	California	34.2
2	Colorado	41.7
5	Connecticut	39.6
25	Delaware	31.3
26	Florida	30.4
20	Georgia	31.9
18	Hawaii	33.5
38	Idaho	27.7
12	Illinois	35.1
41	Indiana	27.1
35	Iowa	29.0
17	Kansas	33.8
46	Kentucky	24.8
47	Louisiana	24.3
24	Maine	31.5
3	Maryland	40.8
1	Massachusetts	44.5
32	Michigan	29.6
10	Minnesota	36.7
49	Mississippi	23.2
33	Missouri	29.5
23	Montana	31.7
19	Nebraska	32.4
45	Nevada	24.9
9	New Hampshire	36.8
3	New Jersey	40.8
38	New Mexico	27.7
8	New York	37.2
20	North Carolina	31.9
30	North Dakota	29.7
35	Ohio	29.0
43	Oklahoma	25.6
16	Oregon	34.0
22	Pennsylvania	31.8
14	Rhode Island	34.4
37	South Carolina	28.3
34	South Dakota	29.2
40	Tennessee	27.5
27	Texas	30.3
13	Utah	34.9
7	Vermont	38.7
6	Virginia	39.3
10	Washington	36.7
50	West Virginia	21.3
29	Wisconsin	30.0
42	Wyoming	26.9

RANK ORDER

RANK	STATE	PERCENT
1	Massachusetts	44.5
2	Colorado	41.7
3	Maryland	40.8
3	New Jersey	40.8
5	Connecticut	39.6
6	Virginia	39.3
7	Vermont	38.7
8	New York	37.2
9	New Hampshire	36.8
10	Minnesota	36.7
10	Washington	36.7
12	Illinois	35.1
13	Utah	34.9
14	Rhode Island	34.4
15	California	34.2
16	Oregon	34.0
17	Kansas	33.8
18	Hawaii	33.5
19	Nebraska	32.4
20	Georgia	31.9
20	North Carolina	31.9
22	Pennsylvania	31.8
23	Montana	31.7
24	Maine	31.5
25	Delaware	31.3
26	Florida	30.4
27	Texas	30.3
28	Alaska	30.2
29	Wisconsin	30.0
30	Arizona	29.7
30	North Dakota	29.7
32	Michigan	29.6
33	Missouri	29.5
34	South Dakota	29.2
35	Iowa	29.0
35	Ohio	29.0
37	South Carolina	28.3
38	Idaho	27.7
38	New Mexico	27.7
40	Tennessee	27.5
41	Indiana	27.1
42	Wyoming	26.9
43	Oklahoma	25.6
44	Alabama	25.5
45	Nevada	24.9
46	Kentucky	24.8
47	Louisiana	24.3
48	Arkansas	23.3
49	Mississippi	23.2
50	West Virginia	21.3

District of Columbia		60.4

Source: U.S. Bureau of the Census
   "2018 American Community Survey-Table CP02" (https://data.census.gov/cedsci/)
*Persons age 25 and older.

Percent of Population Who Have Completed an Advanced Degree in 2018

National Percent = 12.6%*

ALPHA ORDER				RANK ORDER		
RANK	STATE	PERCENT		RANK	STATE	PERCENT
40	Alabama	9.5		1	Massachusetts	20.1
22	Alaska	11.7		2	Maryland	18.9
29	Arizona	11.2		3	Connecticut	17.8
47	Arkansas	8.6		4	Virginia	17.1
14	California	12.9		5	New York	16.4
7	Colorado	15.7		6	New Jersey	16.0
3	Connecticut	17.8		7	Colorado	15.7
13	Delaware	13.1		8	Vermont	15.6
28	Florida	11.3		9	New Hampshire	14.5
19	Georgia	12.3		9	Rhode Island	14.5
23	Hawaii	11.5		11	Illinois	14.0
42	Idaho	9.0		12	Washington	13.9
11	Illinois	14.0		13	Delaware	13.1
39	Indiana	9.8		14	California	12.9
41	Iowa	9.4		14	Oregon	12.9
16	Kansas	12.8		16	Kansas	12.8
36	Kentucky	10.3		17	Pennsylvania	12.7
49	Louisiana	8.4		18	Minnesota	12.5
26	Maine	11.4		19	Georgia	12.3
2	Maryland	18.9		20	New Mexico	12.0
1	Massachusetts	20.1		20	Utah	12.0
23	Michigan	11.5		22	Alaska	11.7
18	Minnesota	12.5		23	Hawaii	11.5
45	Mississippi	8.8		23	Michigan	11.5
23	Missouri	11.5		23	Missouri	11.5
32	Montana	11.0		26	Maine	11.4
30	Nebraska	11.1		26	North Carolina	11.4
46	Nevada	8.7		28	Florida	11.3
9	New Hampshire	14.5		29	Arizona	11.2
6	New Jersey	16.0		30	Nebraska	11.1
20	New Mexico	12.0		30	Ohio	11.1
5	New York	16.4		32	Montana	11.0
26	North Carolina	11.4		33	Texas	10.7
50	North Dakota	7.6		34	Wisconsin	10.6
30	Ohio	11.1		35	South Carolina	10.4
42	Oklahoma	9.0		36	Kentucky	10.3
14	Oregon	12.9		37	Tennessee	10.2
17	Pennsylvania	12.7		38	Wyoming	10.0
9	Rhode Island	14.5		39	Indiana	9.8
35	South Carolina	10.4		40	Alabama	9.5
42	South Dakota	9.0		41	Iowa	9.4
37	Tennessee	10.2		42	Idaho	9.0
33	Texas	10.7		42	Oklahoma	9.0
20	Utah	12.0		42	South Dakota	9.0
8	Vermont	15.6		45	Mississippi	8.8
4	Virginia	17.1		46	Nevada	8.7
12	Washington	13.9		47	Arkansas	8.6
48	West Virginia	8.5		48	West Virginia	8.5
34	Wisconsin	10.6		49	Louisiana	8.4
38	Wyoming	10.0		50	North Dakota	7.6
					District of Columbia	34.5

Source: U.S. Bureau of the Census
"2018 American Community Survey-Table CP02" (https://data.census.gov/cedsci/)
*Persons age 25 and older who have earned a master's degree or higher.

Public Libraries and Branches in 2017

National Total = 16,557 Libraries and Branches*

ALPHA ORDER

RANK	STATE	LIBRARIES	% of USA
22	Alabama	290	1.8%
46	Alaska	77	0.5%
31	Arizona	221	1.3%
27	Arkansas	235	1.4%
1	California	1,124	6.8%
24	Colorado	261	1.6%
29	Connecticut	228	1.4%
50	Delaware	32	0.2%
9	Florida	533	3.2%
14	Georgia	396	2.4%
49	Hawaii	50	0.3%
39	Idaho	147	0.9%
4	Illinois	784	4.7%
13	Indiana	425	2.6%
8	Iowa	559	3.4%
16	Kansas	364	2.2%
34	Kentucky	203	1.2%
21	Louisiana	335	2.0%
28	Maine	232	1.4%
36	Maryland	190	1.1%
10	Massachusetts	459	2.8%
6	Michigan	643	3.9%
19	Minnesota	356	2.2%
26	Mississippi	236	1.4%
17	Missouri	363	2.2%
42	Montana	117	0.7%
25	Nebraska	254	1.5%
44	Nevada	84	0.5%
30	New Hampshire	227	1.4%
12	New Jersey	428	2.6%
43	New Mexico	115	0.7%
2	New York	1,067	6.4%
15	North Carolina	389	2.3%
45	North Dakota	81	0.5%
5	Ohio	716	4.3%
33	Oklahoma	214	1.3%
32	Oregon	218	1.3%
7	Pennsylvania	621	3.8%
48	Rhode Island	71	0.4%
35	South Carolina	194	1.2%
40	South Dakota	141	0.9%
23	Tennessee	284	1.7%
3	Texas	863	5.2%
41	Utah	126	0.8%
38	Vermont	164	1.0%
18	Virginia	359	2.2%
20	Washington	348	2.1%
37	West Virginia	172	1.0%
10	Wisconsin	459	2.8%
47	Wyoming	76	0.5%

RANK ORDER

RANK	STATE	LIBRARIES	% of USA
1	California	1,124	6.8%
2	New York	1,067	6.4%
3	Texas	863	5.2%
4	Illinois	784	4.7%
5	Ohio	716	4.3%
6	Michigan	643	3.9%
7	Pennsylvania	621	3.8%
8	Iowa	559	3.4%
9	Florida	533	3.2%
10	Massachusetts	459	2.8%
10	Wisconsin	459	2.8%
12	New Jersey	428	2.6%
13	Indiana	425	2.6%
14	Georgia	396	2.4%
15	North Carolina	389	2.3%
16	Kansas	364	2.2%
17	Missouri	363	2.2%
18	Virginia	359	2.2%
19	Minnesota	356	2.2%
20	Washington	348	2.1%
21	Louisiana	335	2.0%
22	Alabama	290	1.8%
23	Tennessee	284	1.7%
24	Colorado	261	1.6%
25	Nebraska	254	1.5%
26	Mississippi	236	1.4%
27	Arkansas	235	1.4%
28	Maine	232	1.4%
29	Connecticut	228	1.4%
30	New Hampshire	227	1.4%
31	Arizona	221	1.3%
32	Oregon	218	1.3%
33	Oklahoma	214	1.3%
34	Kentucky	203	1.2%
35	South Carolina	194	1.2%
36	Maryland	190	1.1%
37	West Virginia	172	1.0%
38	Vermont	164	1.0%
39	Idaho	147	0.9%
40	South Dakota	141	0.9%
41	Utah	126	0.8%
42	Montana	117	0.7%
43	New Mexico	115	0.7%
44	Nevada	84	0.5%
45	North Dakota	81	0.5%
46	Alaska	77	0.5%
47	Wyoming	76	0.5%
48	Rhode Island	71	0.4%
49	Hawaii	50	0.3%
50	Delaware	32	0.2%
	District of Columbia	26	0.2%

Source: Institute of Museum and Library Services
"Public Library Survey Fiscal Year 2017" (https://www.imls.gov/research-evaluation)
*For fiscal year 2017. Total of central and branch outlets. Does not include bookmobiles. There are 9,045 public libraries.

Rate of Public Libraries and Branches in 2017

National Average = 19,628 Population per Library*

ALPHA ORDER

RANK	STATE	RATE
25	Alabama	16,809
40	Alaska	9,606
5	Arizona	31,873
35	Arkansas	12,772
3	California	35,016
16	Colorado	21,501
28	Connecticut	15,672
7	Delaware	29,901
1	Florida	39,331
10	Georgia	26,289
8	Hawaii	28,488
38	Idaho	11,685
26	Illinois	16,300
29	Indiana	15,666
49	Iowa	5,620
43	Kansas	7,991
15	Kentucky	21,932
34	Louisiana	13,942
48	Maine	5,753
6	Maryland	31,705
32	Massachusetts	14,945
31	Michigan	15,510
30	Minnesota	15,635
36	Mississippi	12,663
24	Missouri	16,823
42	Montana	8,996
45	Nebraska	7,543
2	Nevada	35,356
47	New Hampshire	5,942
18	New Jersey	20,761
23	New Mexico	18,189
22	New York	18,359
9	North Carolina	26,396
41	North Dakota	9,320
27	Ohio	16,284
21	Oklahoma	18,371
20	Oregon	19,007
19	Pennsylvania	20,592
33	Rhode Island	14,869
11	South Carolina	25,883
46	South Dakota	6,191
13	Tennessee	23,623
4	Texas	32,787
12	Utah	24,611
50	Vermont	3,807
14	Virginia	23,575
17	Washington	21,332
39	West Virginia	10,564
37	Wisconsin	12,615
44	Wyoming	7,618

RANK ORDER

RANK	STATE	RATE
1	Florida	39,331
2	Nevada	35,356
3	California	35,016
4	Texas	32,787
5	Arizona	31,873
6	Maryland	31,705
7	Delaware	29,901
8	Hawaii	28,488
9	North Carolina	26,396
10	Georgia	26,289
11	South Carolina	25,883
12	Utah	24,611
13	Tennessee	23,623
14	Virginia	23,575
15	Kentucky	21,932
16	Colorado	21,501
17	Washington	21,332
18	New Jersey	20,761
19	Pennsylvania	20,592
20	Oregon	19,007
21	Oklahoma	18,371
22	New York	18,359
23	New Mexico	18,189
24	Missouri	16,823
25	Alabama	16,809
26	Illinois	16,300
27	Ohio	16,284
28	Connecticut	15,672
29	Indiana	15,666
30	Minnesota	15,635
31	Michigan	15,510
32	Massachusetts	14,945
33	Rhode Island	14,869
34	Louisiana	13,942
35	Arkansas	12,772
36	Mississippi	12,663
37	Wisconsin	12,615
38	Idaho	11,685
39	West Virginia	10,564
40	Alaska	9,606
41	North Dakota	9,320
42	Montana	8,996
43	Kansas	7,991
44	Wyoming	7,618
45	Nebraska	7,543
46	South Dakota	6,191
47	New Hampshire	5,942
48	Maine	5,753
49	Iowa	5,620
50	Vermont	3,807

District of Columbia   26,727

Source: CQ Press using data from Institute of Museum and Library Services
   "Public Library Survey Fiscal Year 2017" (https://www.imls.gov/research-evaluation)
*For fiscal year 2017. Based on total of central and branch outlets. Does not include bookmobiles.

Rate of Books in Public Libraries in 2017

National Rate = 2,200 Books per 1,000 Population*

ALPHA ORDER

RANK	STATE	RATE
36	Alabama	1,807
19	Alaska	2,816
50	Arizona	1,077
30	Arkansas	2,025
43	California	1,578
40	Colorado	1,696
7	Connecticut	3,622
46	Delaware	1,499
48	Florida	1,343
44	Georgia	1,558
29	Hawaii	2,051
25	Idaho	2,457
13	Illinois	3,126
11	Indiana	3,210
6	Iowa	3,724
15	Kansas	3,019
31	Kentucky	2,003
23	Louisiana	2,513
1	Maine	4,436
37	Maryland	1,781
2	Massachusetts	4,342
20	Michigan	2,802
24	Minnesota	2,474
35	Mississippi	1,835
22	Missouri	2,571
26	Montana	2,380
18	Nebraska	2,858
49	Nevada	1,318
3	New Hampshire	4,196
17	New Jersey	2,894
32	New Mexico	1,952
8	New York	3,478
45	North Carolina	1,512
16	North Dakota	2,898
9	Ohio	3,395
42	Oklahoma	1,634
27	Oregon	2,158
34	Pennsylvania	1,895
10	Rhode Island	3,278
38	South Carolina	1,720
12	South Dakota	3,153
41	Tennessee	1,679
47	Texas	1,354
28	Utah	2,065
4	Vermont	4,185
33	Virginia	1,927
39	Washington	1,710
21	West Virginia	2,723
14	Wisconsin	3,123
5	Wyoming	3,880

RANK ORDER

RANK	STATE	RATE
1	Maine	4,436
2	Massachusetts	4,342
3	New Hampshire	4,196
4	Vermont	4,185
5	Wyoming	3,880
6	Iowa	3,724
7	Connecticut	3,622
8	New York	3,478
9	Ohio	3,395
10	Rhode Island	3,278
11	Indiana	3,210
12	South Dakota	3,153
13	Illinois	3,126
14	Wisconsin	3,123
15	Kansas	3,019
16	North Dakota	2,898
17	New Jersey	2,894
18	Nebraska	2,858
19	Alaska	2,816
20	Michigan	2,802
21	West Virginia	2,723
22	Missouri	2,571
23	Louisiana	2,513
24	Minnesota	2,474
25	Idaho	2,457
26	Montana	2,380
27	Oregon	2,158
28	Utah	2,065
29	Hawaii	2,051
30	Arkansas	2,025
31	Kentucky	2,003
32	New Mexico	1,952
33	Virginia	1,927
34	Pennsylvania	1,895
35	Mississippi	1,835
36	Alabama	1,807
37	Maryland	1,781
38	South Carolina	1,720
39	Washington	1,710
40	Colorado	1,696
41	Tennessee	1,679
42	Oklahoma	1,634
43	California	1,578
44	Georgia	1,558
45	North Carolina	1,512
46	Delaware	1,499
47	Texas	1,354
48	Florida	1,343
49	Nevada	1,318
50	Arizona	1,077
	District of Columbia	1,510

Source: CQ Press using data from Institute of Museum and Library Services
   "Public Library Survey Fiscal Year 2017" (https://www.imls.gov/research-evaluation)
*For fiscal year 2017. Includes serial back files in print.

Rate of Electronic Books in Public Libraries in 2017

National Rate = 1,426 Electronic Books per 1,000 Population*

ALPHA ORDER

RANK	STATE	RATE
24	Alabama	915
17	Alaska	1,428
32	Arizona	622
38	Arkansas	475
41	California	345
37	Colorado	502
33	Connecticut	567
35	Delaware	519
46	Florida	248
49	Georgia	74
50	Hawaii	58
44	Idaho	300
13	Illinois	1,708
20	Indiana	1,297
4	Iowa	4,644
1	Kansas	11,305
7	Kentucky	2,910
29	Louisiana	677
15	Maine	1,567
45	Maryland	257
8	Massachusetts	2,690
26	Michigan	843
23	Minnesota	940
48	Mississippi	209
30	Missouri	675
19	Montana	1,361
10	Nebraska	2,309
47	Nevada	221
5	New Hampshire	3,539
28	New Jersey	703
43	New Mexico	327
16	New York	1,452
31	North Carolina	625
21	North Dakota	1,172
3	Ohio	6,984
25	Oklahoma	879
14	Oregon	1,706
12	Pennsylvania	2,069
9	Rhode Island	2,457
42	South Carolina	343
18	South Dakota	1,425
6	Tennessee	3,157
39	Texas	364
34	Utah	531
40	Vermont	362
22	Virginia	1,156
35	Washington	519
11	West Virginia	2,091
2	Wisconsin	10,862
27	Wyoming	833

RANK ORDER

RANK	STATE	RATE
1	Kansas	11,305
2	Wisconsin	10,862
3	Ohio	6,984
4	Iowa	4,644
5	New Hampshire	3,539
6	Tennessee	3,157
7	Kentucky	2,910
8	Massachusetts	2,690
9	Rhode Island	2,457
10	Nebraska	2,309
11	West Virginia	2,091
12	Pennsylvania	2,069
13	Illinois	1,708
14	Oregon	1,706
15	Maine	1,567
16	New York	1,452
17	Alaska	1,428
18	South Dakota	1,425
19	Montana	1,361
20	Indiana	1,297
21	North Dakota	1,172
22	Virginia	1,156
23	Minnesota	940
24	Alabama	915
25	Oklahoma	879
26	Michigan	843
27	Wyoming	833
28	New Jersey	703
29	Louisiana	677
30	Missouri	675
31	North Carolina	625
32	Arizona	622
33	Connecticut	567
34	Utah	531
35	Delaware	519
35	Washington	519
37	Colorado	502
38	Arkansas	475
39	Texas	364
40	Vermont	362
41	California	345
42	South Carolina	343
43	New Mexico	327
44	Idaho	300
45	Maryland	257
46	Florida	248
47	Nevada	221
48	Mississippi	209
49	Georgia	74
50	Hawaii	58
	District of Columbia	42

Source: CQ Press using data from Institute of Museum and Library Services
   "Public Library Survey Fiscal Year 2017" (https://www.imls.gov/research-evaluation)
*For fiscal year 2017.

Internet Terminals in Public Libraries in 2017

National Total = 300,199 Terminals*

ALPHA ORDER

RANK	STATE	TERMINALS	% of USA
24	Alabama	5,046	1.7%
48	Alaska	904	0.3%
14	Arizona	7,364	2.5%
33	Arkansas	2,811	0.9%
1	California	23,489	7.8%
17	Colorado	6,413	2.1%
28	Connecticut	4,270	1.4%
46	Delaware	1,046	0.3%
4	Florida	16,813	5.6%
8	Georgia	9,533	3.2%
50	Hawaii	564	0.2%
36	Idaho	1,976	0.7%
5	Illinois	15,834	5.3%
10	Indiana	8,389	2.8%
23	Iowa	5,061	1.7%
29	Kansas	3,657	1.2%
25	Kentucky	4,995	1.7%
20	Louisiana	5,677	1.9%
37	Maine	1,837	0.6%
22	Maryland	5,191	1.7%
16	Massachusetts	6,585	2.2%
7	Michigan	12,205	4.1%
19	Minnesota	5,707	1.9%
34	Mississippi	2,783	0.9%
26	Missouri	4,890	1.6%
43	Montana	1,295	0.4%
32	Nebraska	2,899	1.0%
42	Nevada	1,375	0.5%
39	New Hampshire	1,527	0.5%
9	New Jersey	8,398	2.8%
38	New Mexico	1,748	0.6%
3	New York	20,973	7.0%
13	North Carolina	7,611	2.5%
49	North Dakota	765	0.3%
6	Ohio	14,305	4.8%
30	Oklahoma	3,211	1.1%
31	Oregon	3,017	1.0%
11	Pennsylvania	8,127	2.7%
40	Rhode Island	1,480	0.5%
27	South Carolina	4,274	1.4%
44	South Dakota	1,118	0.4%
21	Tennessee	5,649	1.9%
2	Texas	21,710	7.2%
35	Utah	2,244	0.7%
45	Vermont	1,092	0.4%
12	Virginia	7,737	2.6%
15	Washington	6,996	2.3%
41	West Virginia	1,383	0.5%
18	Wisconsin	6,312	2.1%
47	Wyoming	913	0.3%

RANK ORDER

RANK	STATE	TERMINALS	% of USA
1	California	23,489	7.8%
2	Texas	21,710	7.2%
3	New York	20,973	7.0%
4	Florida	16,813	5.6%
5	Illinois	15,834	5.3%
6	Ohio	14,305	4.8%
7	Michigan	12,205	4.1%
8	Georgia	9,533	3.2%
9	New Jersey	8,398	2.8%
10	Indiana	8,389	2.8%
11	Pennsylvania	8,127	2.7%
12	Virginia	7,737	2.6%
13	North Carolina	7,611	2.5%
14	Arizona	7,364	2.5%
15	Washington	6,996	2.3%
16	Massachusetts	6,585	2.2%
17	Colorado	6,413	2.1%
18	Wisconsin	6,312	2.1%
19	Minnesota	5,707	1.9%
20	Louisiana	5,677	1.9%
21	Tennessee	5,649	1.9%
22	Maryland	5,191	1.7%
23	Iowa	5,061	1.7%
24	Alabama	5,046	1.7%
25	Kentucky	4,995	1.7%
26	Missouri	4,890	1.6%
27	South Carolina	4,274	1.4%
28	Connecticut	4,270	1.4%
29	Kansas	3,657	1.2%
30	Oklahoma	3,211	1.1%
31	Oregon	3,017	1.0%
32	Nebraska	2,899	1.0%
33	Arkansas	2,811	0.9%
34	Mississippi	2,783	0.9%
35	Utah	2,244	0.7%
36	Idaho	1,976	0.7%
37	Maine	1,837	0.6%
38	New Mexico	1,748	0.6%
39	New Hampshire	1,527	0.5%
40	Rhode Island	1,480	0.5%
41	West Virginia	1,383	0.5%
42	Nevada	1,375	0.5%
43	Montana	1,295	0.4%
44	South Dakota	1,118	0.4%
45	Vermont	1,092	0.4%
46	Delaware	1,046	0.3%
47	Wyoming	913	0.3%
48	Alaska	904	0.3%
49	North Dakota	765	0.3%
50	Hawaii	564	0.2%
	District of Columbia	1,000	0.3%

Source: Institute of Museum and Library Services
  "Public Library Survey Fiscal Year 2017" (https://www.imls.gov/research-evaluation)
*For fiscal year 2017. Total of public-use Internet terminals in central and branch outlets.

Rate of Internet Terminals in Public Libraries in 2017

National Rate = 18.1 Terminals per Library*

ALPHA ORDER

RANK	STATE	RATE
24	Alabama	17.4
39	Alaska	11.7
1	Arizona	33.3
36	Arkansas	12.0
11	California	20.9
6	Colorado	24.6
22	Connecticut	18.7
2	Delaware	32.7
3	Florida	31.5
8	Georgia	24.1
41	Hawaii	11.3
34	Idaho	13.4
13	Illinois	20.2
17	Indiana	19.7
45	Iowa	9.1
43	Kansas	10.1
6	Kentucky	24.6
25	Louisiana	17.0
47	Maine	7.9
4	Maryland	27.3
30	Massachusetts	14.4
21	Michigan	19.0
27	Minnesota	16.0
38	Mississippi	11.8
33	Missouri	13.5
42	Montana	11.1
40	Nebraska	11.4
26	Nevada	16.4
49	New Hampshire	6.7
19	New Jersey	19.6
28	New Mexico	15.2
17	New York	19.7
19	North Carolina	19.6
44	North Dakota	9.4
15	Ohio	20.0
29	Oklahoma	15.0
31	Oregon	13.8
35	Pennsylvania	13.1
11	Rhode Island	20.9
9	South Carolina	22.0
47	South Dakota	7.9
16	Tennessee	19.9
5	Texas	25.2
23	Utah	17.8
49	Vermont	6.7
10	Virginia	21.6
14	Washington	20.1
46	West Virginia	8.0
31	Wisconsin	13.8
36	Wyoming	12.0

RANK ORDER

RANK	STATE	RATE
1	Arizona	33.3
2	Delaware	32.7
3	Florida	31.5
4	Maryland	27.3
5	Texas	25.2
6	Colorado	24.6
6	Kentucky	24.6
8	Georgia	24.1
9	South Carolina	22.0
10	Virginia	21.6
11	California	20.9
11	Rhode Island	20.9
13	Illinois	20.2
14	Washington	20.1
15	Ohio	20.0
16	Tennessee	19.9
17	Indiana	19.7
17	New York	19.7
19	New Jersey	19.6
19	North Carolina	19.6
21	Michigan	19.0
22	Connecticut	18.7
23	Utah	17.8
24	Alabama	17.4
25	Louisiana	17.0
26	Nevada	16.4
27	Minnesota	16.0
28	New Mexico	15.2
29	Oklahoma	15.0
30	Massachusetts	14.4
31	Oregon	13.8
31	Wisconsin	13.8
33	Missouri	13.5
34	Idaho	13.4
35	Pennsylvania	13.1
36	Arkansas	12.0
36	Wyoming	12.0
38	Mississippi	11.8
39	Alaska	11.7
40	Nebraska	11.4
41	Hawaii	11.3
42	Montana	11.1
43	Kansas	10.1
44	North Dakota	9.4
45	Iowa	9.1
46	West Virginia	8.0
47	Maine	7.9
47	South Dakota	7.9
49	New Hampshire	6.7
49	Vermont	6.7
	District of Columbia	38.5

Source: Institute of Museum and Library Services
"Public Library Survey Fiscal Year 2017" (https://www.imls.gov/research-evaluation)
*For fiscal year 2017. Total of public-use Internet terminals in central and branch outlets divided by the number of outlets.

Per Capita State Art Agencies' Legislative Appropriations in 2020

National Per Capita = $1.39*

ALPHA ORDER

RANK	STATE	PER CAPITA
17	Alabama	$1.19
24	Alaska	0.96
46	Arizona	0.31
37	Arkansas	0.47
14	California	1.42
45	Colorado	0.35
13	Connecticut	1.46
4	Delaware	3.43
16	Florida	1.25
49	Georgia	0.14
2	Hawaii	4.92
35	Idaho	0.50
12	Illinois	1.80
31	Indiana	0.59
39	Iowa	0.46
48	Kansas	0.17
43	Kentucky	0.39
39	Louisiana	0.46
28	Maine	0.75
3	Maryland	3.92
5	Massachusetts	2.63
23	Michigan	1.00
1	Minnesota	7.26
43	Mississippi	0.39
21	Missouri	1.07
34	Montana	0.52
27	Nebraska	0.78
42	Nevada	0.44
31	New Hampshire	0.59
11	New Jersey	1.84
30	New Mexico	0.64
7	New York	2.25
25	North Carolina	0.85
22	North Dakota	1.06
15	Ohio	1.41
29	Oklahoma	0.74
37	Oregon	0.47
26	Pennsylvania	0.82
9	Rhode Island	1.97
8	South Carolina	2.23
20	South Dakota	1.13
18	Tennessee	1.18
33	Texas	0.53
6	Utah	2.44
19	Vermont	1.15
41	Virginia	0.45
47	Washington	0.29
36	West Virginia	0.48
49	Wisconsin	0.14
10	Wyoming	1.92

RANK ORDER

RANK	STATE	PER CAPITA
1	Minnesota	$7.26
2	Hawaii	4.92
3	Maryland	3.92
4	Delaware	3.43
5	Massachusetts	2.63
6	Utah	2.44
7	New York	2.25
8	South Carolina	2.23
9	Rhode Island	1.97
10	Wyoming	1.92
11	New Jersey	1.84
12	Illinois	1.80
13	Connecticut	1.46
14	California	1.42
15	Ohio	1.41
16	Florida	1.25
17	Alabama	1.19
18	Tennessee	1.18
19	Vermont	1.15
20	South Dakota	1.13
21	Missouri	1.07
22	North Dakota	1.06
23	Michigan	1.00
24	Alaska	0.96
25	North Carolina	0.85
26	Pennsylvania	0.82
27	Nebraska	0.78
28	Maine	0.75
29	Oklahoma	0.74
30	New Mexico	0.64
31	Indiana	0.59
31	New Hampshire	0.59
33	Texas	0.53
34	Montana	0.52
35	Idaho	0.50
36	West Virginia	0.48
37	Arkansas	0.47
37	Oregon	0.47
39	Iowa	0.46
39	Louisiana	0.46
41	Virginia	0.45
42	Nevada	0.44
43	Kentucky	0.39
43	Mississippi	0.39
45	Colorado	0.35
46	Arizona	0.31
47	Washington	0.29
48	Kansas	0.17
49	Georgia	0.14
49	Wisconsin	0.14
	District of Columbia	47.88

Source: National Assembly of State Arts Agencies
"State Arts Agency Legislative Appropriations Preview Fiscal Year 2020" (https://nasaa-arts.org/Research/Funding/)
*Projected figures for fiscal year 2020. Includes line item appropriations. Line items are legislative appropriations that are not controlled by the state art agencies but are passed through their budgets directly to another entity. Calculated using 2018 Census population estimates.

Federal Allocations for Head Start Program in 2018

National Total = $9,838,693,013*

ALPHA ORDER

RANK	STATE	EXPENDITURES	% of USA
20	Alabama	$143,506,782	1.5%
50	Alaska	16,990,529	0.2%
17	Arizona	151,261,832	1.5%
29	Arkansas	92,081,850	0.9%
1	California	1,173,973,635	11.9%
26	Colorado	103,819,522	1.1%
35	Connecticut	66,995,105	0.7%
47	Delaware	19,518,534	0.2%
4	Florida	376,991,324	3.8%
9	Georgia	236,460,419	2.4%
43	Hawaii	29,002,038	0.3%
41	Idaho	31,755,165	0.3%
5	Illinois	363,169,807	3.7%
21	Indiana	138,388,507	1.4%
33	Iowa	67,693,469	0.7%
31	Kansas	71,953,412	0.7%
16	Kentucky	156,020,771	1.6%
12	Louisiana	188,036,102	1.9%
39	Maine	37,487,962	0.4%
28	Maryland	102,761,089	1.0%
19	Massachusetts	143,821,413	1.5%
7	Michigan	322,772,191	3.3%
27	Minnesota	103,367,874	1.1%
11	Mississippi	206,565,616	2.1%
14	Missouri	167,211,107	1.7%
40	Montana	32,050,444	0.3%
37	Nebraska	50,953,745	0.5%
38	Nevada	38,247,816	0.4%
48	New Hampshire	18,834,273	0.2%
13	New Jersey	171,816,866	1.7%
32	New Mexico	69,904,056	0.7%
3	New York	564,745,959	5.7%
10	North Carolina	210,677,222	2.1%
45	North Dakota	22,656,981	0.2%
6	Ohio	341,431,136	3.5%
24	Oklahoma	119,170,464	1.2%
30	Oregon	89,625,254	0.9%
8	Pennsylvania	314,025,088	3.2%
42	Rhode Island	30,583,690	0.3%
25	South Carolina	116,934,865	1.2%
44	South Dakota	25,417,918	0.3%
15	Tennessee	161,868,221	1.6%
2	Texas	642,483,951	6.5%
36	Utah	61,625,674	0.6%
46	Vermont	19,665,325	0.2%
22	Virginia	137,254,439	1.4%
18	Washington	149,498,318	1.5%
34	West Virginia	67,330,645	0.7%
23	Wisconsin	130,869,509	1.3%
49	Wyoming	18,038,075	0.2%

RANK ORDER

RANK	STATE	EXPENDITURES	% of USA
1	California	$1,173,973,635	11.9%
2	Texas	642,483,951	6.5%
3	New York	564,745,959	5.7%
4	Florida	376,991,324	3.8%
5	Illinois	363,169,807	3.7%
6	Ohio	341,431,136	3.5%
7	Michigan	322,772,191	3.3%
8	Pennsylvania	314,025,088	3.2%
9	Georgia	236,460,419	2.4%
10	North Carolina	210,677,222	2.1%
11	Mississippi	206,565,616	2.1%
12	Louisiana	188,036,102	1.9%
13	New Jersey	171,816,866	1.7%
14	Missouri	167,211,107	1.7%
15	Tennessee	161,868,221	1.6%
16	Kentucky	156,020,771	1.6%
17	Arizona	151,261,832	1.5%
18	Washington	149,498,318	1.5%
19	Massachusetts	143,821,413	1.5%
20	Alabama	143,506,782	1.5%
21	Indiana	138,388,507	1.4%
22	Virginia	137,254,439	1.4%
23	Wisconsin	130,869,509	1.3%
24	Oklahoma	119,170,464	1.2%
25	South Carolina	116,934,865	1.2%
26	Colorado	103,819,522	1.1%
27	Minnesota	103,367,874	1.1%
28	Maryland	102,761,089	1.0%
29	Arkansas	92,081,850	0.9%
30	Oregon	89,625,254	0.9%
31	Kansas	71,953,412	0.7%
32	New Mexico	69,904,056	0.7%
33	Iowa	67,693,469	0.7%
34	West Virginia	67,330,645	0.7%
35	Connecticut	66,995,105	0.7%
36	Utah	61,625,674	0.6%
37	Nebraska	50,953,745	0.5%
38	Nevada	38,247,816	0.4%
39	Malne	37,487,962	0.4%
40	Montana	32,050,444	0.3%
41	Idaho	31,755,165	0.3%
42	Rhode Island	30,583,690	0.3%
43	Hawaii	29,002,038	0.3%
44	South Dakota	25,417,918	0.3%
45	North Dakota	22,656,981	0.2%
46	Vermont	19,665,325	0.2%
47	Delaware	19,518,534	0.2%
48	New Hampshire	18,834,273	0.2%
49	Wyoming	18,038,075	0.2%
50	Alaska	16,990,529	0.2%
	District of Columbia	31,913,607	0.3%

Source: U.S. Department of Health and Human Services, Administration for Children and Families
"Head Start Fact Sheet Fiscal Year 2018" (https://eclkc.ohs.acf.hhs.gov/about-us/article/head-start-program-facts)
*For fiscal year 2018. National total includes $653,907,162 to migrant and Native American programs not included in state totals, $324,104,925 to U.S. territories, and $365,746,673 in various research, monitoring, training, and support expenditures.

Head Start Program Enrollment in 2018

National Total = 887,125 Children*

ALPHA ORDER

RANK	STATE	ENROLLMENT	% of USA
16	Alabama	15,255	1.7%
49	Alaska	1,518	0.2%
21	Arizona	13,423	1.5%
28	Arkansas	9,967	1.1%
1	California	91,231	10.3%
30	Colorado	9,474	1.1%
35	Connecticut	5,875	0.7%
45	Delaware	2,147	0.2%
4	Florida	39,655	4.5%
9	Georgia	24,363	2.7%
40	Hawaii	2,959	0.3%
41	Idaho	2,956	0.3%
6	Illinois	34,904	3.9%
20	Indiana	14,119	1.6%
34	Iowa	7,202	0.8%
33	Kansas	7,406	0.8%
14	Kentucky	15,830	1.8%
12	Louisiana	21,049	2.4%
39	Maine	3,048	0.3%
29	Maryland	9,541	1.1%
25	Massachusetts	12,002	1.4%
8	Michigan	30,232	3.4%
27	Minnesota	11,202	1.3%
10	Mississippi	23,640	2.7%
17	Missouri	14,952	1.7%
38	Montana	3,061	0.3%
37	Nebraska	4,819	0.5%
42	Nevada	2,954	0.3%
48	New Hampshire	1,563	0.2%
15	New Jersey	15,775	1.8%
32	New Mexico	7,512	0.8%
3	New York	50,288	5.7%
11	North Carolina	21,309	2.4%
46	North Dakota	1,964	0.2%
7	Ohio	34,831	3.9%
18	Oklahoma	14,313	1.6%
23	Oregon	12,716	1.4%
5	Pennsylvania	35,678	4.0%
44	Rhode Island	2,696	0.3%
24	South Carolina	12,604	1.4%
43	South Dakota	2,759	0.3%
13	Tennessee	17,197	1.9%
2	Texas	72,053	8.1%
36	Utah	5,671	0.6%
50	Vermont	1,447	0.2%
19	Virginia	14,230	1.6%
26	Washington	11,985	1.4%
31	West Virginia	7,937	0.9%
22	Wisconsin	13,380	1.5%
47	Wyoming	1,590	0.2%

RANK ORDER

RANK	STATE	ENROLLMENT	% of USA
1	California	91,231	10.3%
2	Texas	72,053	8.1%
3	New York	50,288	5.7%
4	Florida	39,655	4.5%
5	Pennsylvania	35,678	4.0%
6	Illinois	34,904	3.9%
7	Ohio	34,831	3.9%
8	Michigan	30,232	3.4%
9	Georgia	24,363	2.7%
10	Mississippi	23,640	2.7%
11	North Carolina	21,309	2.4%
12	Louisiana	21,049	2.4%
13	Tennessee	17,197	1.9%
14	Kentucky	15,830	1.8%
15	New Jersey	15,775	1.8%
16	Alabama	15,255	1.7%
17	Missouri	14,952	1.7%
18	Oklahoma	14,313	1.6%
19	Virginia	14,230	1.6%
20	Indiana	14,119	1.6%
21	Arizona	13,423	1.5%
22	Wisconsin	13,380	1.5%
23	Oregon	12,716	1.4%
24	South Carolina	12,604	1.4%
25	Massachusetts	12,002	1.4%
26	Washington	11,985	1.4%
27	Minnesota	11,202	1.3%
28	Arkansas	9,967	1.1%
29	Maryland	9,541	1.1%
30	Colorado	9,474	1.1%
31	West Virginia	7,937	0.9%
32	New Mexico	7,512	0.8%
33	Kansas	7,406	0.8%
34	Iowa	7,202	0.8%
35	Connecticut	5,875	0.7%
36	Utah	5,671	0.6%
37	Nebraska	4,819	0.5%
38	Montana	3,061	0.3%
39	Maine	3,048	0.3%
40	Hawaii	2,959	0.3%
41	Idaho	2,956	0.3%
42	Nevada	2,954	0.3%
43	South Dakota	2,759	0.3%
44	Rhode Island	2,696	0.3%
45	Delaware	2,147	0.2%
46	North Dakota	1,964	0.2%
47	Wyoming	1,590	0.2%
48	New Hampshire	1,563	0.2%
49	Alaska	1,518	0.2%
50	Vermont	1,447	0.2%
	District of Columbia	3,509	0.4%

Source: U.S. Department of Health and Human Services, Administration for Children and Families
"Head Start Fact Sheet Fiscal Year 2018" (https://eclkc.ohs.acf.hhs.gov/about-us/article/head-start-program-facts)
*For fiscal year 2018. National total includes 53,421 enrollees not included in state totals enrolled in Migrant and Native American programs and 35,913 enrollees in U.S. territories.

VI. Employment and Labor

Average Annual Pay in 2018

National Average = $57,266*

ALPHA ORDER

RANK	STATE	ANNUAL PAY
37	Alabama	$47,414
15	Alaska	55,668
22	Arizona	51,865
46	Arkansas	43,950
3	California	68,478
9	Colorado	58,941
4	Connecticut	67,742
13	Delaware	56,814
27	Florida	50,094
19	Georgia	53,496
23	Hawaii	50,977
49	Idaho	42,882
8	Illinois	59,941
35	Indiana	47,590
36	Iowa	47,511
39	Kansas	46,607
40	Kentucky	46,302
32	Louisiana	48,116
43	Maine	45,370
7	Maryland	61,151
2	Massachusetts	72,606
17	Michigan	53,803
11	Minnesota	58,007
50	Mississippi	39,762
29	Missouri	49,053
48	Montana	43,407
41	Nebraska	46,262
28	Nevada	50,041
14	New Hampshire	56,782
6	New Jersey	65,727
44	New Mexico	45,167
1	New York	72,900
24	North Carolina	50,756
21	North Dakota	52,356
25	Ohio	50,573
38	Oklahoma	46,727
20	Oregon	53,053
16	Pennsylvania	55,628
18	Rhode Island	53,736
45	South Carolina	44,729
47	South Dakota	43,694
26	Tennessee	50,450
12	Texas	57,747
31	Utah	48,513
34	Vermont	47,640
10	Virginia	58,239
5	Washington	66,119
42	West Virginia	46,120
30	Wisconsin	48,872
33	Wyoming	48,059

RANK ORDER

RANK	STATE	ANNUAL PAY
1	New York	$72,900
2	Massachusetts	72,606
3	California	68,478
4	Connecticut	67,742
5	Washington	66,119
6	New Jersey	65,727
7	Maryland	61,151
8	Illinois	59,941
9	Colorado	58,941
10	Virginia	58,239
11	Minnesota	58,007
12	Texas	57,747
13	Delaware	56,814
14	New Hampshire	56,782
15	Alaska	55,668
16	Pennsylvania	55,628
17	Michigan	53,803
18	Rhode Island	53,736
19	Georgia	53,496
20	Oregon	53,053
21	North Dakota	52,356
22	Arizona	51,865
23	Hawaii	50,977
24	North Carolina	50,756
25	Ohio	50,573
26	Tennessee	50,450
27	Florida	50,094
28	Nevada	50,041
29	Missouri	49,053
30	Wisconsin	48,872
31	Utah	48,513
32	Louisiana	48,116
33	Wyoming	48,059
34	Vermont	47,640
35	Indiana	47,590
36	Iowa	47,511
37	Alabama	47,414
38	Oklahoma	46,727
39	Kansas	46,607
40	Kentucky	46,302
41	Nebraska	46,262
42	West Virginia	46,120
43	Maine	45,370
44	New Mexico	45,167
45	South Carolina	44,729
46	Arkansas	43,950
47	South Dakota	43,694
48	Montana	43,407
49	Idaho	42,882
50	Mississippi	39,762
	District of Columbia	95,909

Source: U.S. Department of Labor, Bureau of Labor Statistics
   "Quarterly Census of Employment and Wages" (https://www.bls.gov/cew/data.htm)
*Computed by dividing total annual wages of employees covered by unemployment insurance programs by the average monthly number of these employees. Includes bonuses, cash value of meals and lodging, tips, and, in many states, employer contributions to certain deferred compensation plans such as 401(k) plans.

Percent Change in Average Annual Pay: 2017 to 2018

National Percent Change = 3.4% Increase*

RANK	STATE	PERCENT CHANGE		RANK	STATE	PERCENT CHANGE
28	Alabama	3.1		1	Washington	6.6
13	Alaska	3.6		2	West Virginia	6.2
20	Arizona	3.4		3	Utah	4.2
46	Arkansas	2.3		4	North Dakota	4.1
5	California	4.0		5	California	4.0
13	Colorado	3.6		5	Nevada	4.0
48	Connecticut	1.7		7	Wyoming	3.9
47	Delaware	1.8		8	Massachusetts	3.8
20	Florida	3.4		8	North Carolina	3.8
42	Georgia	2.5		8	Oregon	3.8
39	Hawaii	2.6		11	Idaho	3.7
11	Idaho	3.7		11	New Mexico	3.7
20	Illinois	3.4		13	Alaska	3.6
34	Indiana	3.0		13	Colorado	3.6
28	Iowa	3.1		13	Missouri	3.6
23	Kansas	3.3		13	Oklahoma	3.6
42	Kentucky	2.5		17	Louisiana	3.5
17	Louisiana	3.5		17	Texas	3.5
23	Maine	3.3		17	Wisconsin	3.5
39	Maryland	2.6		20	Arizona	3.4
8	Massachusetts	3.8		20	Florida	3.4
42	Michigan	2.5		20	Illinois	3.4
23	Minnesota	3.3		23	Kansas	3.3
42	Mississippi	2.5		23	Maine	3.3
13	Missouri	3.6		23	Minnesota	3.3
27	Montana	3.2		23	Tennessee	3.3
28	Nebraska	3.1		27	Montana	3.2
5	Nevada	4.0		28	Alabama	3.1
34	New Hampshire	3.0		28	Iowa	3.1
39	New Jersey	2.6		28	Nebraska	3.1
11	New Mexico	3.7		28	New York	3.1
28	New York	3.1		28	Vermont	3.1
8	North Carolina	3.8		28	Virginia	3.1
4	North Dakota	4.1		34	Indiana	3.0
38	Ohio	2.9		34	New Hampshire	3.0
13	Oklahoma	3.6		34	Pennsylvania	3.0
8	Oregon	3.8		34	South Dakota	3.0
34	Pennsylvania	3.0		38	Ohio	2.9
48	Rhode Island	1.7		39	Hawaii	2.6
50	South Carolina	1.2		39	Maryland	2.6
34	South Dakota	3.0		39	New Jersey	2.6
23	Tennessee	3.3		42	Georgia	2.5
17	Texas	3.5		42	Kentucky	2.5
3	Utah	4.2		42	Michigan	2.5
28	Vermont	3.1		42	Mississippi	2.5
28	Virginia	3.1		46	Arkansas	2.3
1	Washington	6.6		47	Delaware	1.8
2	West Virginia	6.2		48	Connecticut	1.7
17	Wisconsin	3.5		48	Rhode Island	1.7
7	Wyoming	3.9		50	South Carolina	1.2
					District of Columbia	3.6

Source: CQ Press using data from U.S. Department of Labor, Bureau of Labor Statistics
   "Quarterly Census of Employment and Wages" (https://www.bls.gov/cew/data.htm)
*Includes bonuses, cash value of meals and lodging, tips, and, in many states, employer contributions to certain deferred compensation plans such as 401(k) plans.

Median Earnings of Male Full-Time Workers in 2018

National Median = $52,004

ALPHA ORDER

RANK	STATE	EARNINGS
33	Alabama	$49,210
6	Alaska	61,226
37	Arizona	47,854
50	Arkansas	42,364
14	California	55,646
13	Colorado	56,377
3	Connecticut	65,948
20	Delaware	51,923
47	Florida	44,520
32	Georgia	50,133
26	Hawaii	51,413
39	Idaho	47,182
11	Illinois	56,838
29	Indiana	50,774
24	Iowa	51,488
27	Kansas	50,872
38	Kentucky	47,370
25	Louisiana	51,453
35	Maine	48,522
4	Maryland	62,167
1	Massachusetts	67,147
19	Michigan	52,332
12	Minnesota	56,809
48	Mississippi	44,495
34	Missouri	49,109
36	Montana	48,037
31	Nebraska	50,286
43	Nevada	46,556
7	New Hampshire	61,046
2	New Jersey	66,532
49	New Mexico	42,673
9	New York	58,064
41	North Carolina	46,941
15	North Dakota	55,608
22	Ohio	51,681
40	Oklahoma	47,031
23	Oregon	51,627
18	Pennsylvania	53,269
10	Rhode Island	57,416
46	South Carolina	46,080
42	South Dakota	46,784
44	Tennessee	46,357
30	Texas	50,394
17	Utah	53,409
28	Vermont	50,828
8	Virginia	59,305
5	Washington	61,666
45	West Virginia	46,346
21	Wisconsin	51,766
16	Wyoming	54,834

RANK ORDER

RANK	STATE	EARNINGS
1	Massachusetts	$67,147
2	New Jersey	66,532
3	Connecticut	65,948
4	Maryland	62,167
5	Washington	61,666
6	Alaska	61,226
7	New Hampshire	61,046
8	Virginia	59,305
9	New York	58,064
10	Rhode Island	57,416
11	Illinois	56,838
12	Minnesota	56,809
13	Colorado	56,377
14	California	55,646
15	North Dakota	55,608
16	Wyoming	54,834
17	Utah	53,409
18	Pennsylvania	53,269
19	Michigan	52,332
20	Delaware	51,923
21	Wisconsin	51,766
22	Ohio	51,681
23	Oregon	51,627
24	Iowa	51,488
25	Louisiana	51,453
26	Hawaii	51,413
27	Kansas	50,872
28	Vermont	50,828
29	Indiana	50,774
30	Texas	50,394
31	Nebraska	50,286
32	Georgia	50,133
33	Alabama	49,210
34	Missouri	49,109
35	Maine	48,522
36	Montana	48,037
37	Arizona	47,854
38	Kentucky	47,370
39	Idaho	47,182
40	Oklahoma	47,031
41	North Carolina	46,941
42	South Dakota	46,784
43	Nevada	46,556
44	Tennessee	46,357
45	West Virginia	46,346
46	South Carolina	46,080
47	Florida	44,520
48	Mississippi	44,495
49	New Mexico	42,673
50	Arkansas	42,364
	District of Columbia	81,267

Source: U.S. Bureau of the Census
"2018 American Community Survey-Table DP03" (https://data.census.gov/cedsci/)

Median Earnings of Female Full-Time Workers in 2018

National Median = $42,238

ALPHA ORDER

RANK	STATE	EARNINGS
45	Alabama	$35,854
6	Alaska	49,020
27	Arizona	40,311
44	Arkansas	36,042
7	California	49,009
12	Colorado	46,498
2	Connecticut	55,155
15	Delaware	43,803
37	Florida	37,821
28	Georgia	40,254
19	Hawaii	42,584
40	Idaho	36,846
13	Illinois	45,910
36	Indiana	38,031
26	Iowa	40,353
30	Kansas	40,045
38	Kentucky	37,379
46	Louisiana	35,758
25	Maine	40,421
3	Maryland	53,421
1	Massachusetts	55,942
21	Michigan	41,205
11	Minnesota	46,861
49	Mississippi	33,530
35	Missouri	38,414
41	Montana	36,741
29	Nebraska	40,156
31	Nevada	40,004
14	New Hampshire	45,346
4	New Jersey	52,383
47	New Mexico	35,683
5	New York	50,921
33	North Carolina	39,126
23	North Dakota	40,582
22	Ohio	40,913
48	Oklahoma	35,556
16	Oregon	43,586
18	Pennsylvania	43,243
9	Rhode Island	47,356
42	South Carolina	36,720
43	South Dakota	36,467
39	Tennessee	37,210
24	Texas	40,499
32	Utah	39,342
17	Vermont	43,376
10	Virginia	47,002
8	Washington	48,706
50	West Virginia	32,778
20	Wisconsin	41,263
34	Wyoming	38,434

RANK ORDER

RANK	STATE	EARNINGS
1	Massachusetts	$55,942
2	Connecticut	55,155
3	Maryland	53,421
4	New Jersey	52,383
5	New York	50,921
6	Alaska	49,020
7	California	49,009
8	Washington	48,706
9	Rhode Island	47,356
10	Virginia	47,002
11	Minnesota	46,861
12	Colorado	46,498
13	Illinois	45,910
14	New Hampshire	45,346
15	Delaware	43,803
16	Oregon	43,586
17	Vermont	43,376
18	Pennsylvania	43,243
19	Hawaii	42,584
20	Wisconsin	41,263
21	Michigan	41,205
22	Ohio	40,913
23	North Dakota	40,582
24	Texas	40,499
25	Maine	40,421
26	Iowa	40,353
27	Arizona	40,311
28	Georgia	40,254
29	Nebraska	40,156
30	Kansas	40,045
31	Nevada	40,004
32	Utah	39,342
33	North Carolina	39,126
34	Wyoming	38,434
35	Missouri	38,414
36	Indiana	38,031
37	Florida	37,821
38	Kentucky	37,379
39	Tennessee	37,210
40	Idaho	36,846
41	Montana	36,741
42	South Carolina	36,720
43	South Dakota	36,467
44	Arkansas	36,042
45	Alabama	35,854
46	Louisiana	35,758
47	New Mexico	35,683
48	Oklahoma	35,556
49	Mississippi	33,530
50	West Virginia	32,778
	District of Columbia	70,911

Source: U.S. Bureau of the Census
"2018 American Community Survey-Table DP03" (https://data.census.gov/cedsci/)

State Minimum Wage Rates in 2020

National Rate = $7.25 per Hour*

ALPHA ORDER				RANK ORDER		
RANK	STATE	MINIMUM WAGE		RANK	STATE	MINIMUM WAGE
NA	Alabama**	NA		1	Washington	$13.50
14	Alaska	10.19		2	Massachusetts	12.75
4	Arizona	12.00		3	Colorado	12.10
16	Arkansas	10.00		4	Arizona	12.00
4	California	12.00		4	California	12.00
3	Colorado	12.10		4	Maine	12.00
9	Connecticut	11.00		7	New York	11.80
21	Delaware	9.25		8	Oregon	11.25
28	Florida	8.56		9	Connecticut	11.00
30	Georgia	7.25		9	Maryland	11.00
15	Hawaii	10.10		9	New Jersey	11.00
30	Idaho	7.25		12	Vermont	10.96
21	Illinois	9.25		13	Rhode Island	10.50
30	Indiana	7.25		14	Alaska	10.19
30	Iowa	7.25		15	Hawaii	10.10
30	Kansas	7.25		16	Arkansas	10.00
30	Kentucky	7.25		16	Minnesota	10.00
NA	Louisiana**	NA		18	Michigan	9.65
4	Maine	12.00		19	Missouri	9.45
9	Maryland	11.00		20	South Dakota	9.30
2	Massachusetts	12.75		21	Delaware	9.25
18	Michigan	9.65		21	Illinois	9.25
16	Minnesota	10.00		23	Nebraska	9.00
NA	Mississippi**	NA		23	New Mexico	9.00
19	Missouri	9.45		25	West Virginia	8.75
27	Montana	8.65		26	Ohio	8.70
23	Nebraska	9.00		27	Montana	8.65
29	Nevada	8.25		28	Florida	8.56
30	New Hampshire	7.25		29	Nevada	8.25
9	New Jersey	11.00		30	Georgia	7.25
23	New Mexico	9.00		30	Idaho	7.25
7	New York	11.80		30	Indiana	7.25
30	North Carolina	7.25		30	Iowa	7.25
30	North Dakota	7.25		30	Kansas	7.25
26	Ohio	8.70		30	Kentucky	7.25
30	Oklahoma	7.25		30	New Hampshire	7.25
8	Oregon	11.25		30	North Carolina	7.25
30	Pennsylvania	7.25		30	North Dakota	7.25
13	Rhode Island	10.50		30	Oklahoma	7.25
NA	South Carolina**	NA		30	Pennsylvania	7.25
20	South Dakota	9.30		30	Texas	7.25
NA	Tennessee**	NA		30	Utah	7.25
30	Texas	7.25		30	Virginia	7.25
30	Utah	7.25		30	Wisconsin	7.25
12	Vermont	10.96		30	Wyoming	7.25
30	Virginia	7.25		NA	Alabama**	NA
1	Washington	13.50		NA	Louisiana**	NA
25	West Virginia	8.75		NA	Mississippi**	NA
30	Wisconsin	7.25		NA	South Carolina**	NA
30	Wyoming	7.25		NA	Tennessee**	NA
					District of Columbia	14.00

Source: U.S. Department of Labor, Employment Standards Administration
   "Minimum Wage Laws in the States" (https://www.dol.gov/whd/minwage/america.htm)
*As of January 1, 2020. State minimum wage rates are for those employers and jobs not covered by the federal program.
**No separate state program.

Average Hourly Earnings of Production Workers
on Manufacturing Payrolls in 2019
National Average = $27.77*

ALPHA ORDER			RANK ORDER		
RANK	STATE	HOURLY EARNINGS	RANK	STATE	HOURLY EARNINGS
42	Alabama	$19.77	1	Washington	$29.36
34	Alaska	20.33	2	Colorado	27.58
36	Arizona	20.26	3	Connecticut	27.49
49	Arkansas	18.71	4	Wyoming	25.16
6	California	24.45	5	Massachusetts	24.75
2	Colorado	27.58	6	California	24.45
3	Connecticut	27.49	7	New Jersey	24.13
37	Delaware	20.18	8	Texas	23.65
9	Florida	23.37	9	Florida	23.37
45	Georgia	19.58	10	Minnesota	22.98
17	Hawaii	22.27	11	New York	22.94
47	Idaho	19.27	12	Louisiana	22.70
20	Illinois	21.77	13	Maine	22.68
26	Indiana	21.35	14	Oregon	22.66
31	Iowa	20.52	15	Michigan	22.58
31	Kansas	20.52	16	New Hampshire	22.46
29	Kentucky	20.67	17	Hawaii	22.27
12	Louisiana	22.70	18	Missouri	21.98
13	Maine	22.68	19	Utah	21.86
28	Maryland	20.97	20	Illinois	21.77
5	Massachusetts	24.75	21	Pennsylvania	21.64
15	Michigan	22.58	21	West Virginia	21.64
10	Minnesota	22.98	23	Wisconsin	21.59
30	Mississippi	20.66	24	Ohio	21.50
18	Missouri	21.98	25	North Dakota	21.42
33	Montana	20.46	26	Indiana	21.35
38	Nebraska	20.15	27	Vermont	21.03
40	Nevada	20.09	28	Maryland	20.97
16	New Hampshire	22.46	29	Kentucky	20.67
7	New Jersey	24.13	30	Mississippi	20.66
44	New Mexico	19.59	31	Iowa	20.52
11	New York	22.94	31	Kansas	20.52
50	North Carolina	18.39	33	Montana	20.46
25	North Dakota	21.42	34	Alaska	20.33
24	Ohio	21.50	35	South Carolina	20.28
48	Oklahoma	19.06	36	Arizona	20.26
14	Oregon	22.66	37	Delaware	20.18
21	Pennsylvania	21.64	38	Nebraska	20.15
39	Rhode Island	20.14	39	Rhode Island	20.14
35	South Carolina	20.28	40	Nevada	20.09
46	South Dakota	19.45	41	Tennessee	19.99
41	Tennessee	19.99	42	Alabama	19.77
8	Texas	23.65	43	Virginia	19.70
19	Utah	21.86	44	New Mexico	19.59
27	Vermont	21.03	45	Georgia	19.58
43	Virginia	19.70	46	South Dakota	19.45
1	Washington	29.36	47	Idaho	19.27
21	West Virginia	21.64	48	Oklahoma	19.06
23	Wisconsin	21.59	49	Arkansas	18.71
4	Wyoming	25.16	50	North Carolina	18.39
				District of Columbia**	NA

Source: U.S. Department of Labor, Bureau of Labor Statistics
    "State and Metro Area Employment, Hours and Earnings" (https://www.bls.gov/sae/home.htm)
*Preliminary data for July 2019. Not seasonally adjusted except for national figure.
**Not available.

Average Weekly Earnings of Production Workers on Manufacturing Payrolls in 2019
National Average = $1,121.91*

ALPHA ORDER

RANK	STATE	WEEKLY EARNINGS
28	Alabama	$850.11
42	Alaska	811.17
30	Arizona	846.87
47	Arkansas	759.63
9	California	970.67
3	Colorado	1,105.96
2	Connecticut	1,149.08
19	Delaware	887.92
7	Florida	993.23
36	Georgia	828.23
39	Hawaii	815.08
45	Idaho	768.87
16	Illinois	912.16
21	Indiana	881.76
34	Iowa	835.16
40	Kansas	814.64
23	Kentucky	876.41
10	Louisiana	964.75
12	Maine	945.76
25	Maryland	874.45
5	Massachusetts	1,022.18
15	Michigan	919.01
13	Minnesota	937.58
35	Mississippi	828.47
17	Missouri	909.97
48	Montana	748.84
33	Nebraska	838.24
31	Nevada	843.78
11	New Hampshire	963.53
8	New Jersey	984.50
49	New Mexico	748.34
14	New York	929.07
50	North Carolina	746.63
38	North Dakota	816.10
26	Ohio	872.90
32	Oklahoma	840.55
29	Oregon	847.48
22	Pennsylvania	880.75
43	Rhode Island	773.38
24	South Carolina	876.10
46	South Dakota	766.33
41	Tennessee	811.59
6	Texas	1,021.68
20	Utah	885.33
37	Vermont	824.38
44	Virginia	772.24
1	Washington	1,244.86
18	West Virginia	893.73
27	Wisconsin	857.12
4	Wyoming	1,074.33

RANK ORDER

RANK	STATE	WEEKLY EARNINGS
1	Washington	$1,244.86
2	Connecticut	1,149.08
3	Colorado	1,105.96
4	Wyoming	1,074.33
5	Massachusetts	1,022.18
6	Texas	1,021.68
7	Florida	993.23
8	New Jersey	984.50
9	California	970.67
10	Louisiana	964.75
11	New Hampshire	963.53
12	Maine	945.76
13	Minnesota	937.58
14	New York	929.07
15	Michigan	919.01
16	Illinois	912.16
17	Missouri	909.97
18	West Virginia	893.73
19	Delaware	887.92
20	Utah	885.33
21	Indiana	881.76
22	Pennsylvania	880.75
23	Kentucky	876.41
24	South Carolina	876.10
25	Maryland	874.45
26	Ohio	872.90
27	Wisconsin	857.12
28	Alabama	850.11
29	Oregon	847.48
30	Arizona	846.87
31	Nevada	843.78
32	Oklahoma	840.55
33	Nebraska	838.24
34	Iowa	835.16
35	Mississippi	828.47
36	Georgia	828.23
37	Vermont	824.38
38	North Dakota	816.10
39	Hawaii	815.08
40	Kansas	814.64
41	Tennessee	811.59
42	Alaska	811.17
43	Rhode Island	773.38
44	Virginia	772.24
45	Idaho	768.87
46	South Dakota	766.33
47	Arkansas	759.63
48	Montana	748.84
49	New Mexico	748.34
50	North Carolina	746.63

District of Columbia**   NA

Source: U.S. Department of Labor, Bureau of Labor Statistics
"State and Metro Area Employment, Hours and Earnings" (https://www.bls.gov/sae/home.htm)
*Preliminary data for July 2019. Not seasonally adjusted except for national figure.
**Not available.

Average Work Week of Production Workers
on Manufacturing Payrolls in 2019
National Average = 40.4 Hours per Week*

ALPHA ORDER				RANK ORDER		
RANK	STATE	WEEKLY HOURS		RANK	STATE	WEEKLY HOURS
5	Alabama	43.0		1	Oklahoma	44.1
37	Alaska	39.9		2	Delaware	44.0
15	Arizona	41.8		3	South Carolina	43.2
29	Arkansas	40.6		3	Texas	43.2
39	California	39.7		5	Alabama	43.0
35	Colorado	40.1		6	New Hampshire	42.9
15	Connecticut	41.8		7	Wyoming	42.7
2	Delaware	44.0		8	Florida	42.5
8	Florida	42.5		8	Louisiana	42.5
12	Georgia	42.3		10	Kentucky	42.4
49	Hawaii	36.6		10	Washington	42.4
37	Idaho	39.9		12	Georgia	42.3
14	Illinois	41.9		13	Nevada	42.0
21	Indiana	41.3		14	Illinois	41.9
26	Iowa	40.7		15	Arizona	41.8
39	Kansas	39.7		15	Connecticut	41.8
10	Kentucky	42.4		17	Maine	41.7
8	Louisiana	42.5		17	Maryland	41.7
17	Maine	41.7		19	Nebraska	41.6
17	Maryland	41.7		20	Missouri	41.4
21	Massachusetts	41.3		21	Indiana	41.3
26	Michigan	40.7		21	Massachusetts	41.3
24	Minnesota	40.8		21	West Virginia	41.3
35	Mississippi	40.1		24	Minnesota	40.8
20	Missouri	41.4		24	New Jersey	40.8
49	Montana	36.6		26	Iowa	40.7
19	Nebraska	41.6		26	Michigan	40.7
13	Nevada	42.0		26	Pennsylvania	40.7
6	New Hampshire	42.9		29	Arkansas	40.6
24	New Jersey	40.8		29	North Carolina	40.6
46	New Mexico	38.2		29	Ohio	40.6
33	New York	40.5		29	Tennessee	40.6
29	North Carolina	40.6		33	New York	40.5
47	North Dakota	38.1		33	Utah	40.5
29	Ohio	40.6		35	Colorado	40.1
1	Oklahoma	44.1		35	Mississippi	40.1
48	Oregon	37.4		37	Alaska	39.9
26	Pennsylvania	40.7		37	Idaho	39.9
45	Rhode Island	38.4		39	California	39.7
3	South Carolina	43.2		39	Kansas	39.7
42	South Dakota	39.4		39	Wisconsin	39.7
29	Tennessee	40.6		42	South Dakota	39.4
3	Texas	43.2		43	Vermont	39.2
33	Utah	40.5		43	Virginia	39.2
43	Vermont	39.2		45	Rhode Island	38.4
43	Virginia	39.2		46	New Mexico	38.2
10	Washington	42.4		47	North Dakota	38.1
21	West Virginia	41.3		48	Oregon	37.4
39	Wisconsin	39.7		49	Hawaii	36.6
7	Wyoming	42.7		49	Montana	36.6
					District of Columbia**	NA

Source: U.S. Department of Labor, Bureau of Labor Statistics
    "State and Metro Area Employment, Hours and Earnings" (https://www.bls.gov/sae/home.htm)
*Preliminary data for July 2019. Not seasonally adjusted except for national figure.
**Not available.

Average Weekly Unemployment Benefit in 2019

National Average = $368.79 a Week

ALPHA ORDER

ALPHA ORDER

RANK	STATE	BENEFIT
48	Alabama	$226.58
41	Alaska	266.79
47	Arizona	232.66
43	Arkansas	266.00
32	California	335.04
7	Colorado	449.70
12	Connecticut	398.75
39	Delaware	273.15
45	Florida	251.11
37	Georgia	303.29
2	Hawaii	528.98
30	Idaho	338.83
13	Illinois	397.45
38	Indiana	296.67
11	Iowa	408.27
17	Kansas	385.09
24	Kentucky	359.40
49	Louisiana	214.76
26	Maine	345.83
25	Maryland	352.17
1	Massachusetts	537.04
33	Michigan	323.18
4	Minnesota	469.34
50	Mississippi	211.49
42	Missouri	266.08
20	Montana	376.32
27	Nebraska	345.47
22	Nevada	364.08
31	New Hampshire	335.62
6	New Jersey	461.24
28	New Mexico	341.98
23	New York	363.81
40	North Carolina	267.73
5	North Dakota	462.27
19	Ohio	376.65
16	Oklahoma	385.36
10	Oregon	414.59
15	Pennsylvania	394.13
21	Rhode Island	368.09
44	South Carolina	262.83
29	South Dakota	341.21
46	Tennessee	240.29
9	Texas	417.64
8	Utah	425.41
18	Vermont	379.14
36	Virginia	315.83
3	Washington	478.28
35	West Virginia	322.88
34	Wisconsin	323.04
14	Wyoming	396.34

RANK ORDER

RANK	STATE	BENEFIT
1	Massachusetts	$537.04
2	Hawaii	528.98
3	Washington	478.28
4	Minnesota	469.34
5	North Dakota	462.27
6	New Jersey	461.24
7	Colorado	449.70
8	Utah	425.41
9	Texas	417.64
10	Oregon	414.59
11	Iowa	408.27
12	Connecticut	398.75
13	Illinois	397.45
14	Wyoming	396.34
15	Pennsylvania	394.13
16	Oklahoma	385.36
17	Kansas	385.09
18	Vermont	379.14
19	Ohio	376.65
20	Montana	376.32
21	Rhode Island	368.09
22	Nevada	364.08
23	New York	363.81
24	Kentucky	359.40
25	Maryland	352.17
26	Maine	345.83
27	Nebraska	345.47
28	New Mexico	341.98
29	South Dakota	341.21
30	Idaho	338.83
31	New Hampshire	335.62
32	California	335.04
33	Michigan	323.18
34	Wisconsin	323.04
35	West Virginia	322.88
36	Virginia	315.83
37	Georgia	303.29
38	Indiana	296.67
39	Delaware	273.15
40	North Carolina	267.73
41	Alaska	266.79
42	Missouri	266.08
43	Arkansas	266.00
44	South Carolina	262.83
45	Florida	251.11
46	Tennessee	240.29
47	Arizona	232.66
48	Alabama	226.58
49	Louisiana	214.76
50	Mississippi	211.49
	District of Columbia	359.01

Source: CQ Press using data from U.S. Department of Labor, Bureau of Labor Statistics
"Unemployment Insurance Data Summary" (https://workforcesecurity.doleta.gov/unemploy/DataDashboard.asp)

Workers' Compensation Benefit Payments in 2017

National Total = $62,016,029,000*

ALPHA ORDER

RANK	STATE	PAYMENTS	% of USA
27	Alabama	$600,358,000	1.0%
42	Alaska	226,159,000	0.4%
23	Arizona	744,135,000	1.2%
44	Arkansas	215,440,000	0.3%
1	California	12,134,198,000	19.6%
21	Colorado	811,174,000	1.3%
20	Connecticut	911,367,000	1.5%
43	Delaware	221,786,000	0.4%
3	Florida	3,431,599,000	5.5%
10	Georgia	1,372,084,000	2.2%
34	Hawaii	325,104,000	0.5%
38	Idaho	283,157,000	0.5%
7	Illinois	2,313,784,000	3.7%
29	Indiana	594,813,000	1.0%
26	Iowa	657,956,000	1.1%
31	Kansas	424,970,000	0.7%
28	Kentucky	598,584,000	1.0%
22	Louisiana	798,713,000	1.3%
40	Maine	255,267,000	0.4%
17	Maryland	933,154,000	1.5%
11	Massachusetts	1,205,421,000	1.9%
19	Michigan	919,749,000	1.5%
15	Minnesota	1,056,596,000	1.7%
35	Mississippi	318,053,000	0.5%
14	Missouri	1,070,824,000	1.7%
41	Montana	253,763,000	0.4%
36	Nebraska	309,910,000	0.5%
33	Nevada	352,792,000	0.6%
45	New Hampshire	206,628,000	0.3%
6	New Jersey	2,386,911,000	3.8%
37	New Mexico	296,730,000	0.5%
2	New York	6,191,035,000	10.0%
13	North Carolina	1,114,979,000	1.8%
47	North Dakota	157,209,000	0.3%
8	Ohio	1,757,283,000	2.8%
30	Oklahoma	566,680,000	0.9%
24	Oregon	688,626,000	1.1%
4	Pennsylvania	2,818,291,000	4.5%
48	Rhode Island	156,210,000	0.3%
18	South Carolina	925,874,000	1.5%
50	South Dakota	99,820,000	0.2%
25	Tennessee	661,846,000	1.1%
9	Texas	1,423,721,000	2.3%
39	Utah	274,275,000	0.4%
49	Vermont	143,985,000	0.2%
16	Virginia	968,342,000	1.6%
5	Washington	2,464,784,000	4.0%
32	West Virginia	412,633,000	0.7%
12	Wisconsin	1,169,773,000	1.9%
46	Wyoming	176,433,000	0.3%

RANK ORDER

RANK	STATE	PAYMENTS	% of USA
1	California	$12,134,198,000	19.6%
2	New York	6,191,035,000	10.0%
3	Florida	3,431,599,000	5.5%
4	Pennsylvania	2,818,291,000	4.5%
5	Washington	2,464,784,000	4.0%
6	New Jersey	2,386,911,000	3.8%
7	Illinois	2,313,784,000	3.7%
8	Ohio	1,757,283,000	2.8%
9	Texas	1,423,721,000	2.3%
10	Georgia	1,372,084,000	2.2%
11	Massachusetts	1,205,421,000	1.9%
12	Wisconsin	1,169,773,000	1.9%
13	North Carolina	1,114,979,000	1.8%
14	Missouri	1,070,824,000	1.7%
15	Minnesota	1,056,596,000	1.7%
16	Virginia	968,342,000	1.6%
17	Maryland	933,154,000	1.5%
18	South Carolina	925,874,000	1.5%
19	Michigan	919,749,000	1.5%
20	Connecticut	911,367,000	1.5%
21	Colorado	811,174,000	1.3%
22	Louisiana	798,713,000	1.3%
23	Arizona	744,135,000	1.2%
24	Oregon	688,626,000	1.1%
25	Tennessee	661,846,000	1.1%
26	Iowa	657,956,000	1.1%
27	Alabama	600,358,000	1.0%
28	Kentucky	598,584,000	1.0%
29	Indiana	594,813,000	1.0%
30	Oklahoma	566,680,000	0.9%
31	Kansas	424,970,000	0.7%
32	West Virginia	412,633,000	0.7%
33	Nevada	352,792,000	0.6%
34	Hawaii	325,104,000	0.5%
35	Mississippi	318,053,000	0.5%
36	Nebraska	309,910,000	0.5%
37	New Mexico	296,730,000	0.5%
38	Idaho	283,157,000	0.5%
39	Utah	274,275,000	0.4%
40	Maine	255,267,000	0.4%
41	Montana	253,763,000	0.4%
42	Alaska	226,159,000	0.4%
43	Delaware	221,786,000	0.4%
44	Arkansas	215,440,000	0.3%
45	New Hampshire	206,628,000	0.3%
46	Wyoming	176,433,000	0.3%
47	North Dakota	157,209,000	0.3%
48	Rhode Island	156,210,000	0.3%
49	Vermont	143,985,000	0.2%
50	South Dakota	99,820,000	0.2%
	District of Columbia	129,604,000	0.2%

Source: National Academy of Social Insurance (Washington, DC)
"Workers' Compensation: Benefits, Coverage, and Costs, 2017" (https://www.nasi.org/research/workers-compensation)
*Estimated payments from private insurance, state and federal funds, and self insurance. National total includes payments for federal civilian employee program, Black Lung Program, and other federal programs.

Workers' Compensation Benefit Payment per Covered Worker in 2017

National Average = $442*

<table>
<tr><td colspan="3">ALPHA ORDER</td><td colspan="3">RANK ORDER</td></tr>
<tr><th>RANK</th><th>STATE</th><th>PAYMENTS</th><th>RANK</th><th>STATE</th><th>PAYMENTS</th></tr>
<tr><td>31</td><td>Alabama</td><td>$332</td><td>1</td><td>Washington</td><td>$767</td></tr>
<tr><td>2</td><td>Alaska</td><td>737</td><td>2</td><td>Alaska</td><td>737</td></tr>
<tr><td>40</td><td>Arizona</td><td>276</td><td>3</td><td>California</td><td>723</td></tr>
<tr><td>49</td><td>Arkansas</td><td>187</td><td>4</td><td>New York</td><td>678</td></tr>
<tr><td>3</td><td>California</td><td>723</td><td>5</td><td>Wyoming</td><td>673</td></tr>
<tr><td>37</td><td>Colorado</td><td>319</td><td>6</td><td>West Virginia</td><td>626</td></tr>
<tr><td>9</td><td>Connecticut</td><td>552</td><td>7</td><td>New Jersey</td><td>603</td></tr>
<tr><td>11</td><td>Delaware</td><td>510</td><td>8</td><td>Montana</td><td>574</td></tr>
<tr><td>17</td><td>Florida</td><td>429</td><td>9</td><td>Connecticut</td><td>552</td></tr>
<tr><td>33</td><td>Georgia</td><td>330</td><td>10</td><td>Hawaii</td><td>524</td></tr>
<tr><td>10</td><td>Hawaii</td><td>524</td><td>11</td><td>Delaware</td><td>510</td></tr>
<tr><td>21</td><td>Idaho</td><td>408</td><td>12</td><td>Pennsylvania</td><td>496</td></tr>
<tr><td>22</td><td>Illinois</td><td>396</td><td>13</td><td>Vermont</td><td>480</td></tr>
<tr><td>47</td><td>Indiana</td><td>200</td><td>14</td><td>South Carolina</td><td>477</td></tr>
<tr><td>15</td><td>Iowa</td><td>437</td><td>15</td><td>Iowa</td><td>437</td></tr>
<tr><td>38</td><td>Kansas</td><td>318</td><td>16</td><td>Maine</td><td>432</td></tr>
<tr><td>35</td><td>Kentucky</td><td>327</td><td>17</td><td>Florida</td><td>429</td></tr>
<tr><td>18</td><td>Louisiana</td><td>427</td><td>18</td><td>Louisiana</td><td>427</td></tr>
<tr><td>16</td><td>Maine</td><td>432</td><td>19</td><td>Wisconsin</td><td>418</td></tr>
<tr><td>26</td><td>Maryland</td><td>373</td><td>20</td><td>Missouri</td><td>412</td></tr>
<tr><td>29</td><td>Massachusetts</td><td>345</td><td>21</td><td>Idaho</td><td>408</td></tr>
<tr><td>46</td><td>Michigan</td><td>218</td><td>22</td><td>Illinois</td><td>396</td></tr>
<tr><td>25</td><td>Minnesota</td><td>377</td><td>23</td><td>North Dakota</td><td>392</td></tr>
<tr><td>39</td><td>Mississippi</td><td>301</td><td>24</td><td>New Mexico</td><td>391</td></tr>
<tr><td>20</td><td>Missouri</td><td>412</td><td>25</td><td>Minnesota</td><td>377</td></tr>
<tr><td>8</td><td>Montana</td><td>574</td><td>26</td><td>Maryland</td><td>373</td></tr>
<tr><td>34</td><td>Nebraska</td><td>328</td><td>27</td><td>Oklahoma</td><td>372</td></tr>
<tr><td>41</td><td>Nevada</td><td>271</td><td>28</td><td>Oregon</td><td>371</td></tr>
<tr><td>36</td><td>New Hampshire</td><td>320</td><td>29</td><td>Massachusetts</td><td>345</td></tr>
<tr><td>7</td><td>New Jersey</td><td>603</td><td>30</td><td>Rhode Island</td><td>335</td></tr>
<tr><td>24</td><td>New Mexico</td><td>391</td><td>31</td><td>Alabama</td><td>332</td></tr>
<tr><td>4</td><td>New York</td><td>678</td><td>31</td><td>Ohio</td><td>332</td></tr>
<tr><td>43</td><td>North Carolina</td><td>268</td><td>33</td><td>Georgia</td><td>330</td></tr>
<tr><td>23</td><td>North Dakota</td><td>392</td><td>34</td><td>Nebraska</td><td>328</td></tr>
<tr><td>31</td><td>Ohio</td><td>332</td><td>35</td><td>Kentucky</td><td>327</td></tr>
<tr><td>27</td><td>Oklahoma</td><td>372</td><td>36</td><td>New Hampshire</td><td>320</td></tr>
<tr><td>28</td><td>Oregon</td><td>371</td><td>37</td><td>Colorado</td><td>319</td></tr>
<tr><td>12</td><td>Pennsylvania</td><td>496</td><td>38</td><td>Kansas</td><td>318</td></tr>
<tr><td>30</td><td>Rhode Island</td><td>335</td><td>39</td><td>Mississippi</td><td>301</td></tr>
<tr><td>14</td><td>South Carolina</td><td>477</td><td>40</td><td>Arizona</td><td>276</td></tr>
<tr><td>44</td><td>South Dakota</td><td>246</td><td>41</td><td>Nevada</td><td>271</td></tr>
<tr><td>45</td><td>Tennessee</td><td>237</td><td>42</td><td>Virginia</td><td>270</td></tr>
<tr><td>50</td><td>Texas</td><td>148</td><td>43</td><td>North Carolina</td><td>268</td></tr>
<tr><td>48</td><td>Utah</td><td>197</td><td>44</td><td>South Dakota</td><td>246</td></tr>
<tr><td>13</td><td>Vermont</td><td>480</td><td>45</td><td>Tennessee</td><td>237</td></tr>
<tr><td>42</td><td>Virginia</td><td>270</td><td>46</td><td>Michigan</td><td>218</td></tr>
<tr><td>1</td><td>Washington</td><td>767</td><td>47</td><td>Indiana</td><td>200</td></tr>
<tr><td>6</td><td>West Virginia</td><td>626</td><td>48</td><td>Utah</td><td>197</td></tr>
<tr><td>19</td><td>Wisconsin</td><td>418</td><td>49</td><td>Arkansas</td><td>187</td></tr>
<tr><td>5</td><td>Wyoming</td><td>673</td><td>50</td><td>Texas</td><td>148</td></tr>
<tr><td></td><td></td><td></td><td></td><td>District of Columbia</td><td>229</td></tr>
</table>

Source: CQ Press using data from National Academy of Social Insurance (Washington, DC)
"Workers' Compensation: Benefits, Coverage, and Costs, 2017" (https://www.nasi.org/research/workers-compensation)
*Estimated payments from private insurance, state and federal funds, and self insurance. National rate includes payments for federal civilian employee program, Black Lung Program, and other federal programs. Total divided by number of workers covered by workers' compensation.

Percent Change in Workers' Compensation Benefit Payments: 2016 to 2017

National Percent Change = 0.1% Decrease*

ALPHA ORDER

RANK	STATE	PERCENT CHANGE
28	Alabama	(0.2)
26	Alaska	(0.1)
33	Arizona	(1.0)
2	Arkansas	9.1
26	California	(0.1)
18	Colorado	1.5
17	Connecticut	1.9
36	Delaware	(1.4)
10	Florida	3.6
30	Georgia	(0.3)
3	Hawaii	6.2
6	Idaho	5.7
37	Illinois	(1.8)
11	Indiana	3.2
33	Iowa	(1.0)
23	Kansas	0.3
48	Kentucky	(6.5)
23	Louisiana	0.3
4	Maine	6.0
13	Maryland	2.7
5	Massachusetts	5.8
42	Michigan	(3.9)
13	Minnesota	2.7
8	Mississippi	4.0
7	Missouri	4.3
38	Montana	(2.8)
35	Nebraska	(1.2)
25	Nevada	0.0
22	New Hampshire	0.5
19	New Jersey	1.3
42	New Mexico	(3.9)
9	New York	3.9
49	North Carolina	(7.4)
46	North Dakota	(5.3)
44	Ohio	(4.6)
47	Oklahoma	(6.2)
1	Oregon	9.4
50	Pennsylvania	(9.8)
32	Rhode Island	(0.6)
16	South Carolina	2.3
45	South Dakota	(4.7)
40	Tennessee	(3.7)
39	Texas	(3.0)
30	Utah	(0.3)
12	Vermont	2.8
15	Virginia	2.4
20	Washington	1.1
41	West Virginia	(3.8)
28	Wisconsin	(0.2)
21	Wyoming	0.8

RANK ORDER

RANK	STATE	PERCENT CHANGE
1	Oregon	9.4
2	Arkansas	9.1
3	Hawaii	6.2
4	Maine	6.0
5	Massachusetts	5.8
6	Idaho	5.7
7	Missouri	4.3
8	Mississippi	4.0
9	New York	3.9
10	Florida	3.6
11	Indiana	3.2
12	Vermont	2.8
13	Maryland	2.7
13	Minnesota	2.7
15	Virginia	2.4
16	South Carolina	2.3
17	Connecticut	1.9
18	Colorado	1.5
19	New Jersey	1.3
20	Washington	1.1
21	Wyoming	0.8
22	New Hampshire	0.5
23	Kansas	0.3
23	Louisiana	0.3
25	Nevada	0.0
26	Alaska	(0.1)
26	California	(0.1)
28	Alabama	(0.2)
28	Wisconsin	(0.2)
30	Georgia	(0.3)
30	Utah	(0.3)
32	Rhode Island	(0.6)
33	Arizona	(1.0)
33	Iowa	(1.0)
35	Nebraska	(1.2)
36	Delaware	(1.4)
37	Illinois	(1.8)
38	Montana	(2.8)
39	Texas	(3.0)
40	Tennessee	(3.7)
41	West Virginia	(3.8)
42	Michigan	(3.9)
42	New Mexico	(3.9)
44	Ohio	(4.6)
45	South Dakota	(4.7)
46	North Dakota	(5.3)
47	Oklahoma	(6.2)
48	Kentucky	(6.5)
49	North Carolina	(7.4)
50	Pennsylvania	(9.8)

	District of Columbia	8.4

Source: CQ Press using data from National Academy of Social Insurance (Washington, DC)
    "Workers' Compensation: Benefits, Coverage, and Costs, 2017" (https://www.nasi.org/research/workers-compensation)
*Estimated payments from private insurance, state and federal funds, and self insurance. National rate includes payments for
federal civilian employee program, Black Lung Program, and other federal programs.

Civilian Labor Force in 2019

National Total = 164,556,000 Workers*

ALPHA ORDER

RANK	STATE	LABOR FORCE	% of USA
24	Alabama	2,266,198	1.4%
48	Alaska	347,109	0.2%
15	Arizona	3,600,776	2.2%
34	Arkansas	1,368,565	0.8%
1	California	19,544,474	11.9%
19	Colorado	3,176,599	1.9%
28	Connecticut	1,927,671	1.2%
45	Delaware	491,958	0.3%
3	Florida	10,511,038	6.4%
8	Georgia	5,133,559	3.1%
42	Hawaii	664,533	0.4%
38	Idaho	889,092	0.5%
6	Illinois	6,479,970	3.9%
16	Indiana	3,386,154	2.1%
30	Iowa	1,763,275	1.1%
33	Kansas	1,496,270	0.9%
27	Kentucky	2,087,383	1.3%
26	Louisiana	2,102,200	1.3%
41	Maine	691,998	0.4%
18	Maryland	3,288,322	2.0%
14	Massachusetts	3,856,457	2.3%
10	Michigan	4,956,384	3.0%
20	Minnesota	3,132,198	1.9%
35	Mississippi	1,288,294	0.8%
21	Missouri	3,128,928	1.9%
44	Montana	536,741	0.3%
36	Nebraska	1,046,290	0.6%
32	Nevada	1,562,408	0.9%
40	New Hampshire	777,801	0.5%
11	New Jersey	4,554,687	2.8%
37	New Mexico	966,624	0.6%
4	New York	9,549,675	5.8%
9	North Carolina	5,130,786	3.1%
47	North Dakota	405,273	0.2%
7	Ohio	5,838,717	3.5%
29	Oklahoma	1,846,283	1.1%
25	Oregon	2,114,935	1.3%
5	Pennsylvania	6,551,585	4.0%
43	Rhode Island	558,519	0.3%
23	South Carolina	2,384,934	1.4%
46	South Dakota	470,455	0.3%
17	Tennessee	3,368,072	2.0%
2	Texas	14,188,089	8.6%
31	Utah	1,622,735	1.0%
49	Vermont	342,146	0.2%
12	Virginia	4,454,888	2.7%
13	Washington	3,956,849	2.4%
39	West Virginia	805,706	0.5%
22	Wisconsin	3,120,013	1.9%
50	Wyoming	292,408	0.2%

RANK ORDER

RANK	STATE	LABOR FORCE	% of USA
1	California	19,544,474	11.9%
2	Texas	14,188,089	8.6%
3	Florida	10,511,038	6.4%
4	New York	9,549,675	5.8%
5	Pennsylvania	6,551,585	4.0%
6	Illinois	6,479,970	3.9%
7	Ohio	5,838,717	3.5%
8	Georgia	5,133,559	3.1%
9	North Carolina	5,130,786	3.1%
10	Michigan	4,956,384	3.0%
11	New Jersey	4,554,687	2.8%
12	Virginia	4,454,888	2.7%
13	Washington	3,956,849	2.4%
14	Massachusetts	3,856,457	2.3%
15	Arizona	3,600,776	2.2%
16	Indiana	3,386,154	2.1%
17	Tennessee	3,368,072	2.0%
18	Maryland	3,288,322	2.0%
19	Colorado	3,176,599	1.9%
20	Minnesota	3,132,198	1.9%
21	Missouri	3,128,928	1.9%
22	Wisconsin	3,120,013	1.9%
23	South Carolina	2,384,934	1.4%
24	Alabama	2,266,198	1.4%
25	Oregon	2,114,935	1.3%
26	Louisiana	2,102,200	1.3%
27	Kentucky	2,087,383	1.3%
28	Connecticut	1,927,671	1.2%
29	Oklahoma	1,846,283	1.1%
30	Iowa	1,763,275	1.1%
31	Utah	1,622,735	1.0%
32	Nevada	1,562,408	0.9%
33	Kansas	1,496,270	0.9%
34	Arkansas	1,368,565	0.8%
35	Mississippi	1,288,294	0.8%
36	Nebraska	1,046,290	0.6%
37	New Mexico	966,624	0.6%
38	Idaho	889,092	0.5%
39	West Virginia	805,706	0.5%
40	New Hampshire	777,801	0.5%
41	Maine	691,998	0.4%
42	Hawaii	664,533	0.4%
43	Rhode Island	558,519	0.3%
44	Montana	536,741	0.3%
45	Delaware	491,958	0.3%
46	South Dakota	470,455	0.3%
47	North Dakota	405,273	0.2%
48	Alaska	347,109	0.2%
49	Vermont	342,146	0.2%
50	Wyoming	292,408	0.2%
	District of Columbia	413,358	0.3%

Source: U.S. Department of Labor, Bureau of Labor Statistics
   "State Employment and Unemployment" (press release, January 24, 2020, www.bls.gov/bls/newsrels.htm)
*Seasonally adjusted preliminary data as of December 2019. National total calculated through a different formula.

Employed Civilian Labor Force in 2019

National Total = 158,803,000 Employed Workers*

ALPHA ORDER

RANK	STATE	EMPLOYED	% of USA
24	Alabama	2,204,740	1.4%
49	Alaska	325,923	0.2%
15	Arizona	3,434,621	2.2%
34	Arkansas	1,319,789	0.8%
1	California	18,786,757	11.8%
19	Colorado	3,096,379	1.9%
28	Connecticut	1,855,687	1.2%
45	Delaware	472,823	0.3%
3	Florida	10,199,732	6.4%
8	Georgia	4,971,026	3.1%
42	Hawaii	646,992	0.4%
38	Idaho	863,323	0.5%
6	Illinois	6,239,909	3.9%
16	Indiana	3,277,798	2.1%
30	Iowa	1,716,096	1.1%
33	Kansas	1,449,063	0.9%
27	Kentucky	1,996,905	1.3%
26	Louisiana	1,998,774	1.3%
41	Maine	672,252	0.4%
18	Maryland	3,174,515	2.0%
14	Massachusetts	3,746,980	2.4%
10	Michigan	4,764,989	3.0%
20	Minnesota	3,029,826	1.9%
35	Mississippi	1,215,402	0.8%
21	Missouri	3,027,015	1.9%
44	Montana	518,309	0.3%
36	Nebraska	1,014,018	0.6%
32	Nevada	1,502,934	0.9%
40	New Hampshire	757,714	0.5%
11	New Jersey	4,393,432	2.8%
37	New Mexico	920,787	0.6%
4	New York	9,172,280	5.8%
9	North Carolina	4,939,767	3.1%
47	North Dakota	395,437	0.2%
7	Ohio	5,596,108	3.5%
29	Oklahoma	1,783,293	1.1%
25	Oregon	2,035,663	1.3%
5	Pennsylvania	6,258,910	3.9%
43	Rhode Island	539,113	0.3%
23	South Carolina	2,329,639	1.5%
46	South Dakota	455,504	0.3%
17	Tennessee	3,256,382	2.1%
2	Texas	13,697,783	8.6%
31	Utah	1,584,814	1.0%
48	Vermont	334,265	0.2%
12	Virginia	4,338,521	2.7%
13	Washington	3,787,821	2.4%
39	West Virginia	765,516	0.5%
22	Wisconsin	3,014,552	1.9%
50	Wyoming	281,690	0.2%

RANK ORDER

RANK	STATE	EMPLOYED	% of USA
1	California	18,786,757	11.8%
2	Texas	13,697,783	8.6%
3	Florida	10,199,732	6.4%
4	New York	9,172,280	5.8%
5	Pennsylvania	6,258,910	3.9%
6	Illinois	6,239,909	3.9%
7	Ohio	5,596,108	3.5%
8	Georgia	4,971,026	3.1%
9	North Carolina	4,939,767	3.1%
10	Michigan	4,764,989	3.0%
11	New Jersey	4,393,432	2.8%
12	Virginia	4,338,521	2.7%
13	Washington	3,787,821	2.4%
14	Massachusetts	3,746,980	2.4%
15	Arizona	3,434,621	2.2%
16	Indiana	3,277,798	2.1%
17	Tennessee	3,256,382	2.1%
18	Maryland	3,174,515	2.0%
19	Colorado	3,096,379	1.9%
20	Minnesota	3,029,826	1.9%
21	Missouri	3,027,015	1.9%
22	Wisconsin	3,014,552	1.9%
23	South Carolina	2,329,639	1.5%
24	Alabama	2,204,740	1.4%
25	Oregon	2,035,663	1.3%
26	Louisiana	1,998,774	1.3%
27	Kentucky	1,996,905	1.3%
28	Connecticut	1,855,687	1.2%
29	Oklahoma	1,783,293	1.1%
30	Iowa	1,716,096	1.1%
31	Utah	1,584,814	1.0%
32	Nevada	1,502,934	0.9%
33	Kansas	1,449,063	0.9%
34	Arkansas	1,319,789	0.8%
35	Mississippi	1,215,402	0.8%
36	Nebraska	1,014,018	0.6%
37	New Mexico	920,787	0.6%
38	Idaho	863,323	0.5%
39	West Virginia	765,516	0.5%
40	New Hampshire	757,714	0.5%
41	Maine	672,252	0.4%
42	Hawaii	646,992	0.4%
43	Rhode Island	539,113	0.3%
44	Montana	518,309	0.3%
45	Delaware	472,823	0.3%
46	South Dakota	455,504	0.3%
47	North Dakota	395,437	0.2%
48	Vermont	334,265	0.2%
49	Alaska	325,923	0.2%
50	Wyoming	281,690	0.2%
	District of Columbia	391,352	0.2%

Source: CQ Press using data from U.S. Department of Labor, Bureau of Labor Statistics
"State Employment and Unemployment" (press release, January 24, 2020, www.bls.gov/bls/newsrels.htm)
*Seasonally adjusted preliminary data as of December 2019. National total calculated through a different formula.

Employment to Population Ratio in 2019

National Percent = 60.6% of Population 16 Years and Older Employed*

ALPHA ORDER

RANK	STATE	PERCENT
44	Alabama	56.2
41	Alaska	56.9
27	Arizona	60.1
46	Arkansas	55.2
34	California	59.5
4	Colorado	67.7
15	Connecticut	63.3
27	Delaware	60.1
38	Florida	58.1
30	Georgia	59.9
43	Hawaii	56.4
13	Idaho	63.6
25	Illinois	61.1
20	Indiana	61.8
1	Iowa	68.4
14	Kansas	63.4
45	Kentucky	55.9
48	Louisiana	54.2
27	Maine	60.1
10	Maryland	65.4
9	Massachusetts	65.7
37	Michigan	58.9
2	Minnesota	68.1
50	Mississippi	51.5
21	Missouri	61.7
26	Montana	60.4
5	Nebraska	67.4
18	Nevada	62.1
6	New Hampshire	67.0
24	New Jersey	61.2
46	New Mexico	55.2
40	New York	57.6
36	North Carolina	59.2
8	North Dakota	66.1
34	Ohio	59.5
39	Oklahoma	57.7
33	Oregon	59.6
32	Pennsylvania	59.8
23	Rhode Island	61.5
42	South Carolina	56.8
7	South Dakota	66.3
30	Tennessee	59.9
19	Texas	61.9
3	Utah	68.0
12	Vermont	63.7
15	Virginia	63.3
17	Washington	62.6
49	West Virginia	51.6
11	Wisconsin	64.3
22	Wyoming	61.6

RANK ORDER

RANK	STATE	PERCENT
1	Iowa	68.4
2	Minnesota	68.1
3	Utah	68.0
4	Colorado	67.7
5	Nebraska	67.4
6	New Hampshire	67.0
7	South Dakota	66.3
8	North Dakota	66.1
9	Massachusetts	65.7
10	Maryland	65.4
11	Wisconsin	64.3
12	Vermont	63.7
13	Idaho	63.6
14	Kansas	63.4
15	Connecticut	63.3
15	Virginia	63.3
17	Washington	62.6
18	Nevada	62.1
19	Texas	61.9
20	Indiana	61.8
21	Missouri	61.7
22	Wyoming	61.6
23	Rhode Island	61.5
24	New Jersey	61.2
25	Illinois	61.1
26	Montana	60.4
27	Arizona	60.1
27	Delaware	60.1
27	Maine	60.1
30	Georgia	59.9
30	Tennessee	59.9
32	Pennsylvania	59.8
33	Oregon	59.6
34	California	59.5
34	Ohio	59.5
36	North Carolina	59.2
37	Michigan	58.9
38	Florida	58.1
39	Oklahoma	57.7
40	New York	57.6
41	Alaska	56.9
42	South Carolina	56.8
43	Hawaii	56.4
44	Alabama	56.2
45	Kentucky	55.9
46	Arkansas	55.2
46	New Mexico	55.2
48	Louisiana	54.2
49	West Virginia	51.6
50	Mississippi	51.5

District of Columbia — 66.8

Source: CQ Press using data from U.S. Department of Labor, Bureau of Labor Statistics
"State Employment and Unemployment" (press release, January 24, 2020, www.bls.gov/bls/newsrels.htm)
*Seasonally adjusted preliminary data as of December 2019. Calculated with 2018 population data.

Unemployed Civilian Labor Force in 2019

National Total = 5,753,000 Unemployed Workers*

<table>
<tr><td colspan="4">ALPHA ORDER</td><td colspan="4">RANK ORDER</td></tr>
<tr><td>RANK</td><td>STATE</td><td>UNEMPLOYED</td><td>% of USA</td><td>RANK</td><td>STATE</td><td>UNEMPLOYED</td><td>% of USA</td></tr>
<tr><td>29</td><td>Alabama</td><td>61,458</td><td>1.1%</td><td>1</td><td>California</td><td>757,717</td><td>13.2%</td></tr>
<tr><td>40</td><td>Alaska</td><td>21,186</td><td>0.4%</td><td>2</td><td>Texas</td><td>490,306</td><td>8.5%</td></tr>
<tr><td>11</td><td>Arizona</td><td>166,155</td><td>2.9%</td><td>3</td><td>New York</td><td>377,395</td><td>6.6%</td></tr>
<tr><td>32</td><td>Arkansas</td><td>48,776</td><td>0.8%</td><td>4</td><td>Florida</td><td>311,306</td><td>5.4%</td></tr>
<tr><td>1</td><td>California</td><td>757,717</td><td>13.2%</td><td>5</td><td>Pennsylvania</td><td>292,675</td><td>5.1%</td></tr>
<tr><td>24</td><td>Colorado</td><td>80,220</td><td>1.4%</td><td>6</td><td>Ohio</td><td>242,609</td><td>4.2%</td></tr>
<tr><td>27</td><td>Connecticut</td><td>71,984</td><td>1.3%</td><td>7</td><td>Illinois</td><td>240,061</td><td>4.2%</td></tr>
<tr><td>44</td><td>Delaware</td><td>19,135</td><td>0.3%</td><td>8</td><td>Michigan</td><td>191,395</td><td>3.3%</td></tr>
<tr><td>4</td><td>Florida</td><td>311,306</td><td>5.4%</td><td>9</td><td>North Carolina</td><td>191,019</td><td>3.3%</td></tr>
<tr><td>12</td><td>Georgia</td><td>162,533</td><td>2.8%</td><td>10</td><td>Washington</td><td>169,028</td><td>2.9%</td></tr>
<tr><td>46</td><td>Hawaii</td><td>17,541</td><td>0.3%</td><td>11</td><td>Arizona</td><td>166,155</td><td>2.9%</td></tr>
<tr><td>39</td><td>Idaho</td><td>25,769</td><td>0.4%</td><td>12</td><td>Georgia</td><td>162,533</td><td>2.8%</td></tr>
<tr><td>7</td><td>Illinois</td><td>240,061</td><td>4.2%</td><td>13</td><td>New Jersey</td><td>161,255</td><td>2.8%</td></tr>
<tr><td>18</td><td>Indiana</td><td>108,356</td><td>1.9%</td><td>14</td><td>Virginia</td><td>116,367</td><td>2.0%</td></tr>
<tr><td>34</td><td>Iowa</td><td>47,179</td><td>0.8%</td><td>15</td><td>Maryland</td><td>113,807</td><td>2.0%</td></tr>
<tr><td>33</td><td>Kansas</td><td>47,207</td><td>0.8%</td><td>16</td><td>Tennessee</td><td>111,690</td><td>1.9%</td></tr>
<tr><td>23</td><td>Kentucky</td><td>90,478</td><td>1.6%</td><td>17</td><td>Massachusetts</td><td>109,477</td><td>1.9%</td></tr>
<tr><td>20</td><td>Louisiana</td><td>103,426</td><td>1.8%</td><td>18</td><td>Indiana</td><td>108,356</td><td>1.9%</td></tr>
<tr><td>42</td><td>Maine</td><td>19,746</td><td>0.3%</td><td>19</td><td>Wisconsin</td><td>105,461</td><td>1.8%</td></tr>
<tr><td>15</td><td>Maryland</td><td>113,807</td><td>2.0%</td><td>20</td><td>Louisiana</td><td>103,426</td><td>1.8%</td></tr>
<tr><td>17</td><td>Massachusetts</td><td>109,477</td><td>1.9%</td><td>21</td><td>Minnesota</td><td>102,372</td><td>1.8%</td></tr>
<tr><td>8</td><td>Michigan</td><td>191,395</td><td>3.3%</td><td>22</td><td>Missouri</td><td>101,913</td><td>1.8%</td></tr>
<tr><td>21</td><td>Minnesota</td><td>102,372</td><td>1.8%</td><td>23</td><td>Kentucky</td><td>90,478</td><td>1.6%</td></tr>
<tr><td>26</td><td>Mississippi</td><td>72,892</td><td>1.3%</td><td>24</td><td>Colorado</td><td>80,220</td><td>1.4%</td></tr>
<tr><td>22</td><td>Missouri</td><td>101,913</td><td>1.8%</td><td>25</td><td>Oregon</td><td>79,272</td><td>1.4%</td></tr>
<tr><td>45</td><td>Montana</td><td>18,432</td><td>0.3%</td><td>26</td><td>Mississippi</td><td>72,892</td><td>1.3%</td></tr>
<tr><td>38</td><td>Nebraska</td><td>32,272</td><td>0.6%</td><td>27</td><td>Connecticut</td><td>71,984</td><td>1.3%</td></tr>
<tr><td>30</td><td>Nevada</td><td>59,474</td><td>1.0%</td><td>28</td><td>Oklahoma</td><td>62,990</td><td>1.1%</td></tr>
<tr><td>41</td><td>New Hampshire</td><td>20,087</td><td>0.3%</td><td>29</td><td>Alabama</td><td>61,458</td><td>1.1%</td></tr>
<tr><td>13</td><td>New Jersey</td><td>161,255</td><td>2.8%</td><td>30</td><td>Nevada</td><td>59,474</td><td>1.0%</td></tr>
<tr><td>35</td><td>New Mexico</td><td>45,837</td><td>0.8%</td><td>31</td><td>South Carolina</td><td>55,295</td><td>1.0%</td></tr>
<tr><td>3</td><td>New York</td><td>377,395</td><td>6.6%</td><td>32</td><td>Arkansas</td><td>48,776</td><td>0.8%</td></tr>
<tr><td>9</td><td>North Carolina</td><td>191,019</td><td>3.3%</td><td>33</td><td>Kansas</td><td>47,207</td><td>0.8%</td></tr>
<tr><td>49</td><td>North Dakota</td><td>9,836</td><td>0.2%</td><td>34</td><td>Iowa</td><td>47,179</td><td>0.8%</td></tr>
<tr><td>6</td><td>Ohio</td><td>242,609</td><td>4.2%</td><td>35</td><td>New Mexico</td><td>45,837</td><td>0.8%</td></tr>
<tr><td>28</td><td>Oklahoma</td><td>62,990</td><td>1.1%</td><td>36</td><td>West Virginia</td><td>40,190</td><td>0.7%</td></tr>
<tr><td>25</td><td>Oregon</td><td>79,272</td><td>1.4%</td><td>37</td><td>Utah</td><td>37,921</td><td>0.7%</td></tr>
<tr><td>5</td><td>Pennsylvania</td><td>292,675</td><td>5.1%</td><td>38</td><td>Nebraska</td><td>32,272</td><td>0.6%</td></tr>
<tr><td>43</td><td>Rhode Island</td><td>19,406</td><td>0.3%</td><td>39</td><td>Idaho</td><td>25,769</td><td>0.4%</td></tr>
<tr><td>31</td><td>South Carolina</td><td>55,295</td><td>1.0%</td><td>40</td><td>Alaska</td><td>21,186</td><td>0.4%</td></tr>
<tr><td>47</td><td>South Dakota</td><td>14,951</td><td>0.3%</td><td>41</td><td>New Hampshire</td><td>20,087</td><td>0.3%</td></tr>
<tr><td>16</td><td>Tennessee</td><td>111,690</td><td>1.9%</td><td>42</td><td>Maine</td><td>19,746</td><td>0.3%</td></tr>
<tr><td>2</td><td>Texas</td><td>490,306</td><td>8.5%</td><td>43</td><td>Rhode Island</td><td>19,406</td><td>0.3%</td></tr>
<tr><td>37</td><td>Utah</td><td>37,921</td><td>0.7%</td><td>44</td><td>Delaware</td><td>19,135</td><td>0.3%</td></tr>
<tr><td>50</td><td>Vermont</td><td>7,881</td><td>0.1%</td><td>45</td><td>Montana</td><td>18,432</td><td>0.3%</td></tr>
<tr><td>14</td><td>Virginia</td><td>116,367</td><td>2.0%</td><td>46</td><td>Hawaii</td><td>17,541</td><td>0.3%</td></tr>
<tr><td>10</td><td>Washington</td><td>169,028</td><td>2.9%</td><td>47</td><td>South Dakota</td><td>14,951</td><td>0.3%</td></tr>
<tr><td>36</td><td>West Virginia</td><td>40,190</td><td>0.7%</td><td>48</td><td>Wyoming</td><td>10,718</td><td>0.2%</td></tr>
<tr><td>19</td><td>Wisconsin</td><td>105,461</td><td>1.8%</td><td>49</td><td>North Dakota</td><td>9,836</td><td>0.2%</td></tr>
<tr><td>48</td><td>Wyoming</td><td>10,718</td><td>0.2%</td><td>50</td><td>Vermont</td><td>7,881</td><td>0.1%</td></tr>
<tr><td></td><td></td><td></td><td></td><td></td><td>District of Columbia</td><td>22,006</td><td>0.4%</td></tr>
</table>

Source: U.S. Department of Labor, Bureau of Labor Statistics
"State Employment and Unemployment" (press release, January 24, 2020, www.bls.gov/bls/newsrels.htm)
*Seasonally adjusted preliminary data as of December 2019. National total calculated through a different formula.

Unemployment Rate in 2019

National Rate = 3.5% of Labor Force Unemployed*

ALPHA ORDER

RANK	STATE	PERCENT
41	Alabama	2.7
1	Alaska	6.1
6	Arizona	4.6
21	Arkansas	3.6
12	California	3.9
46	Colorado	2.5
16	Connecticut	3.7
12	Delaware	3.9
37	Florida	3.0
32	Georgia	3.2
43	Hawaii	2.6
38	Idaho	2.9
16	Illinois	3.7
32	Indiana	3.2
41	Iowa	2.7
32	Kansas	3.2
8	Kentucky	4.3
4	Louisiana	4.9
38	Maine	2.9
22	Maryland	3.5
40	Massachusetts	2.8
12	Michigan	3.9
29	Minnesota	3.3
2	Mississippi	5.7
29	Missouri	3.3
26	Montana	3.4
36	Nebraska	3.1
15	Nevada	3.8
43	New Hampshire	2.6
22	New Jersey	3.5
5	New Mexico	4.7
11	New York	4.0
16	North Carolina	3.7
47	North Dakota	2.4
10	Ohio	4.2
26	Oklahoma	3.4
16	Oregon	3.7
7	Pennsylvania	4.5
22	Rhode Island	3.5
48	South Carolina	2.3
32	South Dakota	3.2
29	Tennessee	3.3
22	Texas	3.5
48	Utah	2.3
48	Vermont	2.3
43	Virginia	2.6
8	Washington	4.3
3	West Virginia	5.0
26	Wisconsin	3.4
16	Wyoming	3.7

RANK ORDER

RANK	STATE	PERCENT
1	Alaska	6.1
2	Mississippi	5.7
3	West Virginia	5.0
4	Louisiana	4.9
5	New Mexico	4.7
6	Arizona	4.6
7	Pennsylvania	4.5
8	Kentucky	4.3
8	Washington	4.3
10	Ohio	4.2
11	New York	4.0
12	California	3.9
12	Delaware	3.9
12	Michigan	3.9
15	Nevada	3.8
16	Connecticut	3.7
16	Illinois	3.7
16	North Carolina	3.7
16	Oregon	3.7
16	Wyoming	3.7
21	Arkansas	3.6
22	Maryland	3.5
22	New Jersey	3.5
22	Rhode Island	3.5
22	Texas	3.5
26	Montana	3.4
26	Oklahoma	3.4
26	Wisconsin	3.4
29	Minnesota	3.3
29	Missouri	3.3
29	Tennessee	3.3
32	Georgia	3.2
32	Indiana	3.2
32	Kansas	3.2
32	South Dakota	3.2
36	Nebraska	3.1
37	Florida	3.0
38	Idaho	2.9
38	Maine	2.9
40	Massachusetts	2.8
41	Alabama	2.7
41	Iowa	2.7
43	Hawaii	2.6
43	New Hampshire	2.6
43	Virginia	2.6
46	Colorado	2.5
47	North Dakota	2.4
48	South Carolina	2.3
48	Utah	2.3
48	Vermont	2.3

	District of Columbia	5.3

Source: U.S. Department of Labor, Bureau of Labor Statistics
"State Employment and Unemployment" (press release, January 24, 2020, www.bls.gov/bls/newsrels.htm)
*Seasonally adjusted preliminary data as of December 2019. National figure calculated through a different formula.

Women in Civilian Labor Force in 2018

National Total = 75,978,000 Women*

<table>
<tr><td colspan="4">ALPHA ORDER</td><td colspan="4">RANK ORDER</td></tr>
<tr><td>RANK</td><td>STATE</td><td>WOMEN</td><td>% of USA</td><td>RANK</td><td>STATE</td><td>WOMEN</td><td>% of USA</td></tr>
<tr><td>24</td><td>Alabama</td><td>1,027,000</td><td>1.4%</td><td>1</td><td>California</td><td>8,798,000</td><td>11.6%</td></tr>
<tr><td>49</td><td>Alaska</td><td>164,000</td><td>0.2%</td><td>2</td><td>Texas</td><td>6,243,000</td><td>8.2%</td></tr>
<tr><td>15</td><td>Arizona</td><td>1,591,000</td><td>2.1%</td><td>3</td><td>Florida</td><td>4,865,000</td><td>6.4%</td></tr>
<tr><td>34</td><td>Arkansas</td><td>633,000</td><td>0.8%</td><td>4</td><td>New York</td><td>4,570,000</td><td>6.0%</td></tr>
<tr><td>1</td><td>California</td><td>8,798,000</td><td>11.6%</td><td>5</td><td>Illinois</td><td>3,065,000</td><td>4.0%</td></tr>
<tr><td>22</td><td>Colorado</td><td>1,417,000</td><td>1.9%</td><td>6</td><td>Pennsylvania</td><td>3,050,000</td><td>4.0%</td></tr>
<tr><td>28</td><td>Connecticut</td><td>915,000</td><td>1.2%</td><td>7</td><td>Ohio</td><td>2,730,000</td><td>3.6%</td></tr>
<tr><td>45</td><td>Delaware</td><td>236,000</td><td>0.3%</td><td>8</td><td>Georgia</td><td>2,448,000</td><td>3.2%</td></tr>
<tr><td>3</td><td>Florida</td><td>4,865,000</td><td>6.4%</td><td>9</td><td>North Carolina</td><td>2,408,000</td><td>3.2%</td></tr>
<tr><td>8</td><td>Georgia</td><td>2,448,000</td><td>3.2%</td><td>10</td><td>Michigan</td><td>2,307,000</td><td>3.0%</td></tr>
<tr><td>42</td><td>Hawaii</td><td>329,000</td><td>0.4%</td><td>11</td><td>New Jersey</td><td>2,096,000</td><td>2.8%</td></tr>
<tr><td>38</td><td>Idaho</td><td>385,000</td><td>0.5%</td><td>12</td><td>Virginia</td><td>2,060,000</td><td>2.7%</td></tr>
<tr><td>5</td><td>Illinois</td><td>3,065,000</td><td>4.0%</td><td>13</td><td>Massachusetts</td><td>1,866,000</td><td>2.5%</td></tr>
<tr><td>16</td><td>Indiana</td><td>1,573,000</td><td>2.1%</td><td>14</td><td>Washington</td><td>1,705,000</td><td>2.2%</td></tr>
<tr><td>30</td><td>Iowa</td><td>791,000</td><td>1.0%</td><td>15</td><td>Arizona</td><td>1,591,000</td><td>2.1%</td></tr>
<tr><td>32</td><td>Kansas</td><td>687,000</td><td>0.9%</td><td>16</td><td>Indiana</td><td>1,573,000</td><td>2.1%</td></tr>
<tr><td>27</td><td>Kentucky</td><td>974,000</td><td>1.3%</td><td>17</td><td>Maryland</td><td>1,535,000</td><td>2.0%</td></tr>
<tr><td>25</td><td>Louisiana</td><td>1,008,000</td><td>1.3%</td><td>18</td><td>Tennessee</td><td>1,515,000</td><td>2.0%</td></tr>
<tr><td>41</td><td>Maine</td><td>337,000</td><td>0.4%</td><td>19</td><td>Wisconsin</td><td>1,510,000</td><td>2.0%</td></tr>
<tr><td>17</td><td>Maryland</td><td>1,535,000</td><td>2.0%</td><td>20</td><td>Missouri</td><td>1,488,000</td><td>2.0%</td></tr>
<tr><td>13</td><td>Massachusetts</td><td>1,866,000</td><td>2.5%</td><td>21</td><td>Minnesota</td><td>1,473,000</td><td>1.9%</td></tr>
<tr><td>10</td><td>Michigan</td><td>2,307,000</td><td>3.0%</td><td>22</td><td>Colorado</td><td>1,417,000</td><td>1.9%</td></tr>
<tr><td>21</td><td>Minnesota</td><td>1,473,000</td><td>1.9%</td><td>23</td><td>South Carolina</td><td>1,094,000</td><td>1.4%</td></tr>
<tr><td>35</td><td>Mississippi</td><td>620,000</td><td>0.8%</td><td>24</td><td>Alabama</td><td>1,027,000</td><td>1.4%</td></tr>
<tr><td>20</td><td>Missouri</td><td>1,488,000</td><td>2.0%</td><td>25</td><td>Louisiana</td><td>1,008,000</td><td>1.3%</td></tr>
<tr><td>44</td><td>Montana</td><td>245,000</td><td>0.3%</td><td>26</td><td>Oregon</td><td>989,000</td><td>1.3%</td></tr>
<tr><td>36</td><td>Nebraska</td><td>484,000</td><td>0.6%</td><td>27</td><td>Kentucky</td><td>974,000</td><td>1.3%</td></tr>
<tr><td>31</td><td>Nevada</td><td>691,000</td><td>0.9%</td><td>28</td><td>Connecticut</td><td>915,000</td><td>1.2%</td></tr>
<tr><td>40</td><td>New Hampshire</td><td>360,000</td><td>0.5%</td><td>29</td><td>Oklahoma</td><td>828,000</td><td>1.1%</td></tr>
<tr><td>11</td><td>New Jersey</td><td>2,096,000</td><td>2.8%</td><td>30</td><td>Iowa</td><td>791,000</td><td>1.0%</td></tr>
<tr><td>37</td><td>New Mexico</td><td>448,000</td><td>0.6%</td><td>31</td><td>Nevada</td><td>691,000</td><td>0.9%</td></tr>
<tr><td>4</td><td>New York</td><td>4,570,000</td><td>6.0%</td><td>32</td><td>Kansas</td><td>687,000</td><td>0.9%</td></tr>
<tr><td>9</td><td>North Carolina</td><td>2,408,000</td><td>3.2%</td><td>33</td><td>Utah</td><td>684,000</td><td>0.9%</td></tr>
<tr><td>47</td><td>North Dakota</td><td>180,000</td><td>0.2%</td><td>34</td><td>Arkansas</td><td>633,000</td><td>0.8%</td></tr>
<tr><td>7</td><td>Ohio</td><td>2,730,000</td><td>3.6%</td><td>35</td><td>Mississippi</td><td>620,000</td><td>0.8%</td></tr>
<tr><td>29</td><td>Oklahoma</td><td>828,000</td><td>1.1%</td><td>36</td><td>Nebraska</td><td>484,000</td><td>0.6%</td></tr>
<tr><td>26</td><td>Oregon</td><td>989,000</td><td>1.3%</td><td>37</td><td>New Mexico</td><td>448,000</td><td>0.6%</td></tr>
<tr><td>6</td><td>Pennsylvania</td><td>3,050,000</td><td>4.0%</td><td>38</td><td>Idaho</td><td>385,000</td><td>0.5%</td></tr>
<tr><td>43</td><td>Rhode Island</td><td>268,000</td><td>0.4%</td><td>39</td><td>West Virginia</td><td>364,000</td><td>0.5%</td></tr>
<tr><td>23</td><td>South Carolina</td><td>1,094,000</td><td>1.4%</td><td>40</td><td>New Hampshire</td><td>360,000</td><td>0.5%</td></tr>
<tr><td>46</td><td>South Dakota</td><td>214,000</td><td>0.3%</td><td>41</td><td>Maine</td><td>337,000</td><td>0.4%</td></tr>
<tr><td>18</td><td>Tennessee</td><td>1,515,000</td><td>2.0%</td><td>42</td><td>Hawaii</td><td>329,000</td><td>0.4%</td></tr>
<tr><td>2</td><td>Texas</td><td>6,243,000</td><td>8.2%</td><td>43</td><td>Rhode Island</td><td>268,000</td><td>0.4%</td></tr>
<tr><td>33</td><td>Utah</td><td>684,000</td><td>0.9%</td><td>44</td><td>Montana</td><td>245,000</td><td>0.3%</td></tr>
<tr><td>48</td><td>Vermont</td><td>167,000</td><td>0.2%</td><td>45</td><td>Delaware</td><td>236,000</td><td>0.3%</td></tr>
<tr><td>12</td><td>Virginia</td><td>2,060,000</td><td>2.7%</td><td>46</td><td>South Dakota</td><td>214,000</td><td>0.3%</td></tr>
<tr><td>14</td><td>Washington</td><td>1,705,000</td><td>2.2%</td><td>47</td><td>North Dakota</td><td>180,000</td><td>0.2%</td></tr>
<tr><td>39</td><td>West Virginia</td><td>364,000</td><td>0.5%</td><td>48</td><td>Vermont</td><td>167,000</td><td>0.2%</td></tr>
<tr><td>19</td><td>Wisconsin</td><td>1,510,000</td><td>2.0%</td><td>49</td><td>Alaska</td><td>164,000</td><td>0.2%</td></tr>
<tr><td>50</td><td>Wyoming</td><td>131,000</td><td>0.2%</td><td>50</td><td>Wyoming</td><td>131,000</td><td>0.2%</td></tr>
<tr><td></td><td></td><td></td><td></td><td></td><td>District of Columbia</td><td>205,000</td><td>0.3%</td></tr>
</table>

Source: U.S. Department of Labor, Bureau of Labor Statistics
  "Geographic Profiles of Employment and Unemployment, 2018" (https://www.bls.gov/lau/ex14tables.htm)
*Annual averages.

Percent of Women in the Civilian Labor Force in 2018

National Percent = 57.1% of Women*

ALPHA ORDER

RANK ORDER

RANK	STATE	PERCENT	RANK	STATE	PERCENT
49	Alabama	50.7	1	Minnesota	66.3
13	Alaska	61.1	2	Nebraska	64.7
38	Arizona	55.4	3	Wisconsin	64.4
46	Arkansas	52.2	4	South Dakota	63.9
38	California	55.4	5	Massachusetts	63.7
10	Colorado	62.7	6	New Hampshire	63.5
11	Connecticut	61.3	7	Iowa	63.4
23	Delaware	58.3	8	Vermont	63.2
41	Florida	54.2	9	North Dakota	63.1
28	Georgia	57.3	10	Colorado	62.7
24	Hawaii	58.2	11	Connecticut	61.3
31	Idaho	57.1	11	Maryland	61.3
18	Illinois	59.2	13	Alaska	61.1
21	Indiana	58.8	14	Kansas	60.6
7	Iowa	63.4	15	Missouri	60.0
14	Kansas	60.6	16	Rhode Island	59.8
42	Kentucky	54.0	17	Virginia	59.6
43	Louisiana	53.6	18	Illinois	59.2
18	Maine	59.2	18	Maine	59.2
11	Maryland	61.3	20	Utah	59.1
5	Massachusetts	63.7	21	Indiana	58.8
34	Michigan	56.2	21	Wyoming	58.8
1	Minnesota	66.3	23	Delaware	58.3
48	Mississippi	51.0	24	Hawaii	58.2
15	Missouri	60.0	25	Montana	58.0
25	Montana	58.0	26	Nevada	57.4
2	Nebraska	64.7	26	Oregon	57.4
26	Nevada	57.4	28	Georgia	57.3
6	New Hampshire	63.5	28	Pennsylvania	57.3
32	New Jersey	57.0	30	Ohio	57.2
45	New Mexico	53.3	31	Idaho	57.1
37	New York	55.7	32	New Jersey	57.0
34	North Carolina	56.2	33	Washington	56.6
9	North Dakota	63.1	34	Michigan	56.2
30	Ohio	57.2	34	North Carolina	56.2
44	Oklahoma	53.5	34	Texas	56.2
26	Oregon	57.4	37	New York	55.7
28	Pennsylvania	57.3	38	Arizona	55.4
16	Rhode Island	59.8	38	California	55.4
47	South Carolina	51.7	40	Tennessee	54.5
4	South Dakota	63.9	41	Florida	54.2
40	Tennessee	54.5	42	Kentucky	54.0
34	Texas	56.2	43	Louisiana	53.6
20	Utah	59.1	44	Oklahoma	53.5
8	Vermont	63.2	45	New Mexico	53.3
17	Virginia	59.6	46	Arkansas	52.2
33	Washington	56.6	47	South Carolina	51.7
50	West Virginia	48.8	48	Mississippi	51.0
3	Wisconsin	64.4	49	Alabama	50.7
21	Wyoming	58.8	50	West Virginia	48.8
				District of Columbia	66.8

Source: U.S. Department of Labor, Bureau of Labor Statistics
"Geographic Profiles of Employment and Unemployment, 2018" (https://www.bls.gov/lau/ex14tables.htm)
*Annual averages. Women sixteen years and older.

Percent of Civilian Labor Force Comprised of Women in 2018

National Percent = 46.9% of Civilian Labor Force*

ALPHA ORDER

RANK	STATE	PERCENT
34	Alabama	46.5
40	Alaska	46.1
36	Arizona	46.4
23	Arkansas	47.3
43	California	45.4
41	Colorado	45.8
9	Connecticut	48.2
2	Delaware	48.7
17	Florida	47.5
14	Georgia	47.9
5	Hawaii	48.5
48	Idaho	44.9
18	Illinois	47.4
39	Indiana	46.2
31	Iowa	46.8
36	Kansas	46.4
25	Kentucky	47.2
14	Louisiana	47.9
6	Maine	48.4
9	Maryland	48.2
1	Massachusetts	48.8
29	Michigan	47.0
11	Minnesota	48.1
3	Mississippi	48.6
3	Missouri	48.6
32	Montana	46.7
29	Nebraska	47.0
41	Nevada	45.8
28	New Hampshire	47.1
18	New Jersey	47.4
25	New Mexico	47.2
14	New York	47.9
8	North Carolina	48.3
46	North Dakota	45.0
18	Ohio	47.4
48	Oklahoma	44.9
18	Oregon	47.4
18	Pennsylvania	47.4
11	Rhode Island	48.1
25	South Carolina	47.2
34	South Dakota	46.5
32	Tennessee	46.7
46	Texas	45.0
50	Utah	44.0
11	Vermont	48.1
23	Virginia	47.3
45	Washington	45.1
36	West Virginia	46.4
6	Wisconsin	48.4
44	Wyoming	45.3

RANK ORDER

RANK	STATE	PERCENT
1	Massachusetts	48.8
2	Delaware	48.7
3	Mississippi	48.6
3	Missouri	48.6
5	Hawaii	48.5
6	Maine	48.4
6	Wisconsin	48.4
8	North Carolina	48.3
9	Connecticut	48.2
9	Maryland	48.2
11	Minnesota	48.1
11	Rhode Island	48.1
11	Vermont	48.1
14	Georgia	47.9
14	Louisiana	47.9
14	New York	47.9
17	Florida	47.5
18	Illinois	47.4
18	New Jersey	47.4
18	Ohio	47.4
18	Oregon	47.4
18	Pennsylvania	47.4
23	Arkansas	47.3
23	Virginia	47.3
25	Kentucky	47.2
25	New Mexico	47.2
25	South Carolina	47.2
28	New Hampshire	47.1
29	Michigan	47.0
29	Nebraska	47.0
31	Iowa	46.8
32	Montana	46.7
32	Tennessee	46.7
34	Alabama	46.5
34	South Dakota	46.5
36	Arizona	46.4
36	Kansas	46.4
36	West Virginia	46.4
39	Indiana	46.2
40	Alaska	46.1
41	Colorado	45.8
41	Nevada	45.8
43	California	45.4
44	Wyoming	45.3
45	Washington	45.1
46	North Dakota	45.0
46	Texas	45.0
48	Idaho	44.9
48	Oklahoma	44.9
50	Utah	44.0

District of Columbia 50.6

Source: CQ Press using data from U.S. Department of Labor, Bureau of Labor Statistics
"Geographic Profiles of Employment and Unemployment, 2018" (https://www.bls.gov/lau/ex14tables.htm)
*Annual averages.

Job Growth: 2018 to 2019

National Percent Change = 1.4% Increase*

ALPHA ORDER			RANK ORDER		
RANK	STATE	PERCENT CHANGE	RANK	STATE	PERCENT CHANGE
7	Alabama	2.2	1	Utah	3.1
45	Alaska	0.0	2	Idaho	2.9
3	Arizona	2.8	3	Arizona	2.8
18	Arkansas	1.4	4	Texas	2.7
12	California	1.8	5	Florida	2.4
8	Colorado	2.1	5	Washington	2.4
41	Connecticut	0.2	7	Alabama	2.2
20	Delaware	1.3	8	Colorado	2.1
5	Florida	2.4	8	North Carolina	2.1
16	Georgia	1.5	10	Nevada	1.9
30	Hawaii	0.8	10	Oregon	1.9
2	Idaho	2.9	12	California	1.8
32	Illinois	0.7	12	New Mexico	1.8
44	Indiana	0.1	14	Rhode Island	1.7
46	Iowa	(0.2)	15	Tennessee	1.6
18	Kansas	1.4	16	Georgia	1.5
32	Kentucky	0.7	16	Nebraska	1.5
35	Louisiana	0.5	18	Arkansas	1.4
22	Maine	1.2	18	Kansas	1.4
24	Maryland	1.1	20	Delaware	1.3
22	Massachusetts	1.2	20	South Carolina	1.3
40	Michigan	0.4	22	Maine	1.2
41	Minnesota	0.2	22	Massachusetts	1.2
35	Mississippi	0.5	24	Maryland	1.1
32	Missouri	0.7	24	New York	1.1
30	Montana	0.8	24	Virginia	1.1
16	Nebraska	1.5	27	New Hampshire	0.9
10	Nevada	1.9	27	New Jersey	0.9
27	New Hampshire	0.9	27	South Dakota	0.9
27	New Jersey	0.9	30	Hawaii	0.8
12	New Mexico	1.8	30	Montana	0.8
24	New York	1.1	32	Illinois	0.7
8	North Carolina	2.1	32	Kentucky	0.7
35	North Dakota	0.5	32	Missouri	0.7
35	Ohio	0.5	35	Louisiana	0.5
47	Oklahoma	(0.3)	35	Mississippi	0.5
10	Oregon	1.9	35	North Dakota	0.5
35	Pennsylvania	0.5	35	Ohio	0.5
14	Rhode Island	1.7	35	Pennsylvania	0.5
20	South Carolina	1.3	40	Michigan	0.4
27	South Dakota	0.9	41	Connecticut	0.2
15	Tennessee	1.6	41	Minnesota	0.2
4	Texas	2.7	41	Wisconsin	0.2
1	Utah	3.1	44	Indiana	0.1
47	Vermont	(0.3)	45	Alaska	0.0
24	Virginia	1.1	46	Iowa	(0.2)
5	Washington	2.4	47	Oklahoma	(0.3)
49	West Virginia	(0.4)	47	Vermont	(0.3)
41	Wisconsin	0.2	49	West Virginia	(0.4)
50	Wyoming	(1.1)	50	Wyoming	(1.1)
				District of Columbia	1.4

Source: CQ Press using data from U.S. Department of Labor, Bureau of Labor Statistics
    "State Employment and Unemployment" (press release, January 24, 2020, www.bls.gov/bls/newsrels.htm)
*Nonfarm jobs. December 2018 to December 2019, seasonally adjusted. National figure based on nonfarm employment from a different survey.

Employees on Nonfarm Payrolls in 2019

National Total = 152,383,000 Employees*

ALPHA ORDER				RANK ORDER			
RANK	STATE	EMPLOYEES	% of USA	RANK	STATE	EMPLOYEES	% of USA
24	Alabama	2,103,300	1.4%	1	California	17,612,500	11.6%
48	Alaska	329,200	0.2%	2	Texas	12,976,700	8.5%
18	Arizona	2,971,800	2.0%	3	New York	9,821,800	6.4%
34	Arkansas	1,287,700	0.8%	4	Florida	9,104,000	6.0%
1	California	17,612,500	11.6%	5	Illinois	6,193,300	4.1%
21	Colorado	2,803,500	1.8%	6	Pennsylvania	6,063,400	4.0%
28	Connecticut	1,700,400	1.1%	7	Ohio	5,610,600	3.7%
45	Delaware	470,400	0.3%	8	Georgia	4,653,700	3.1%
4	Florida	9,104,000	6.0%	9	North Carolina	4,593,600	3.0%
8	Georgia	4,653,700	3.1%	10	Michigan	4,451,700	2.9%
41	Hawaii	664,200	0.4%	11	New Jersey	4,218,100	2.8%
38	Idaho	763,900	0.5%	12	Virginia	4,053,800	2.7%
5	Illinois	6,193,300	4.1%	13	Massachusetts	3,694,000	2.4%
15	Indiana	3,165,500	2.1%	14	Washington	3,528,400	2.3%
30	Iowa	1,591,000	1.0%	15	Indiana	3,165,500	2.1%
32	Kansas	1,443,400	0.9%	16	Tennessee	3,136,500	2.1%
27	Kentucky	1,953,600	1.3%	17	Wisconsin	2,991,500	2.0%
25	Louisiana	1,991,200	1.3%	18	Arizona	2,971,800	2.0%
42	Maine	635,300	0.4%	19	Minnesota	2,967,400	1.9%
22	Maryland	2,790,700	1.8%	20	Missouri	2,914,200	1.9%
13	Massachusetts	3,694,000	2.4%	21	Colorado	2,803,500	1.8%
10	Michigan	4,451,700	2.9%	22	Maryland	2,790,700	1.8%
19	Minnesota	2,967,400	1.9%	23	South Carolina	2,193,700	1.4%
35	Mississippi	1,168,700	0.8%	24	Alabama	2,103,300	1.4%
20	Missouri	2,914,200	1.9%	25	Louisiana	1,991,200	1.3%
44	Montana	485,000	0.3%	26	Oregon	1,957,700	1.3%
36	Nebraska	1,039,500	0.7%	27	Kentucky	1,953,600	1.3%
33	Nevada	1,440,100	0.9%	28	Connecticut	1,700,400	1.1%
40	New Hampshire	690,100	0.5%	29	Oklahoma	1,691,400	1.1%
11	New Jersey	4,218,100	2.8%	30	Iowa	1,591,000	1.0%
37	New Mexico	861,800	0.6%	31	Utah	1,588,200	1.0%
3	New York	9,821,800	6.4%	32	Kansas	1,443,400	0.9%
9	North Carolina	4,593,600	3.0%	33	Nevada	1,440,100	0.9%
47	North Dakota	436,900	0.3%	34	Arkansas	1,287,700	0.8%
7	Ohio	5,610,600	3.7%	35	Mississippi	1,168,700	0.8%
29	Oklahoma	1,691,400	1.1%	36	Nebraska	1,039,500	0.7%
26	Oregon	1,957,700	1.3%	37	New Mexico	861,800	0.6%
6	Pennsylvania	6,063,400	4.0%	38	Idaho	763,900	0.5%
43	Rhode Island	506,300	0.3%	39	West Virginia	727,500	0.5%
23	South Carolina	2,193,700	1.4%	40	New Hampshire	690,100	0.5%
46	South Dakota	449,500	0.3%	41	Hawaii	664,200	0.4%
16	Tennessee	3,136,500	2.1%	42	Maine	635,300	0.4%
2	Texas	12,976,700	8.5%	43	Rhode Island	506,300	0.3%
31	Utah	1,588,200	1.0%	44	Montana	485,000	0.3%
49	Vermont	315,500	0.2%	45	Delaware	470,400	0.3%
12	Virginia	4,053,800	2.7%	46	South Dakota	449,500	0.3%
14	Washington	3,528,400	2.3%	47	North Dakota	436,900	0.3%
39	West Virginia	727,500	0.5%	48	Alaska	329,200	0.2%
17	Wisconsin	2,991,500	2.0%	49	Vermont	315,500	0.2%
50	Wyoming	285,800	0.2%	50	Wyoming	285,800	0.2%
					District of Columbia	804,000	0.5%

Source: U.S. Department of Labor, Bureau of Labor Statistics
   "State Employment and Unemployment" (press release, January 24, 2020, www.bls.gov/bls/newsrels.htm)
*Seasonally adjusted preliminary data as of December 2019. National total calculated through a different formula.

Employees in Construction in 2019

National Total = 7,551,000 Employees*

ALPHA ORDER

RANK	STATE	EMPLOYEES	% of USA
28	Alabama	96,200	1.3%
49	Alaska	16,700	0.2%
12	Arizona	178,900	2.4%
35	Arkansas	52,800	0.7%
1	California	902,400	12.0%
13	Colorado	174,600	2.3%
33	Connecticut	58,000	0.8%
46	Delaware**	22,800	0.3%
3	Florida	575,000	7.6%
10	Georgia	207,800	2.8%
40	Hawaii**	37,800	0.5%
37	Idaho	52,100	0.7%
7	Illinois	223,000	3.0%
18	Indiana	153,900	2.0%
30	Iowa	81,400	1.1%
32	Kansas	63,100	0.8%
31	Kentucky	79,000	1.0%
19	Louisiana	139,500	1.8%
41	Maine	30,100	0.4%
15	Maryland**	166,800	2.2%
17	Massachusetts	156,300	2.1%
14	Michigan	172,900	2.3%
21	Minnesota	125,100	1.7%
39	Mississippi	43,400	0.6%
22	Missouri	124,300	1.6%
42	Montana	29,000	0.4%
34	Nebraska**	54,600	0.7%
27	Nevada	102,000	1.4%
43	New Hampshire	28,900	0.4%
16	New Jersey	162,600	2.2%
36	New Mexico	52,400	0.7%
4	New York	402,500	5.3%
8	North Carolina	219,800	2.9%
44	North Dakota	28,200	0.4%
9	Ohio	215,700	2.9%
29	Oklahoma	82,800	1.1%
25	Oregon	110,900	1.5%
5	Pennsylvania	256,800	3.4%
48	Rhode Island	19,200	0.3%
26	South Carolina	104,200	1.4%
45	South Dakota**	24,200	0.3%
23	Tennessee**	124,200	1.6%
2	Texas	809,500	10.7%
24	Utah	113,400	1.5%
50	Vermont	14,100	0.2%
11	Virginia	198,500	2.6%
6	Washington	227,900	3.0%
38	West Virginia	44,100	0.6%
20	Wisconsin	128,000	1.7%
47	Wyoming	20,000	0.3%

RANK ORDER

RANK	STATE	EMPLOYEES	% of USA
1	California	902,400	12.0%
2	Texas	809,500	10.7%
3	Florida	575,000	7.6%
4	New York	402,500	5.3%
5	Pennsylvania	256,800	3.4%
6	Washington	227,900	3.0%
7	Illinois	223,000	3.0%
8	North Carolina	219,800	2.9%
9	Ohio	215,700	2.9%
10	Georgia	207,800	2.8%
11	Virginia	198,500	2.6%
12	Arizona	178,900	2.4%
13	Colorado	174,600	2.3%
14	Michigan	172,900	2.3%
15	Maryland**	166,800	2.2%
16	New Jersey	162,600	2.2%
17	Massachusetts	156,300	2.1%
18	Indiana	153,900	2.0%
19	Louisiana	139,500	1.8%
20	Wisconsin	128,000	1.7%
21	Minnesota	125,100	1.7%
22	Missouri	124,300	1.6%
23	Tennessee**	124,200	1.6%
24	Utah	113,400	1.5%
25	Oregon	110,900	1.5%
26	South Carolina	104,200	1.4%
27	Nevada	102,000	1.4%
28	Alabama	96,200	1.3%
29	Oklahoma	82,800	1.1%
30	Iowa	81,400	1.1%
31	Kentucky	79,000	1.0%
32	Kansas	63,100	0.8%
33	Connecticut	58,000	0.8%
34	Nebraska**	54,600	0.7%
35	Arkansas	52,800	0.7%
36	New Mexico	52,400	0.7%
37	Idaho	52,100	0.7%
38	West Virginia	44,100	0.6%
39	Mississippi	43,400	0.6%
40	Hawaii**	37,800	0.5%
41	Maine	30,100	0.4%
42	Montana	29,000	0.4%
43	New Hampshire	28,900	0.4%
44	North Dakota	28,200	0.4%
45	South Dakota**	24,200	0.3%
46	Delaware**	22,800	0.3%
47	Wyoming	20,000	0.3%
48	Rhode Island	19,200	0.3%
49	Alaska	16,700	0.2%
50	Vermont	14,100	0.2%
	District of Columbia**	15,700	0.2%

Source: U.S. Department of Labor, Bureau of Labor Statistics
   "State Employment and Unemployment" (press release, January 24, 2020, www.bls.gov/bls/newsrels.htm)
*Seasonally adjusted preliminary data as of December 2019. National total calculated through a different formula.
**Figures for these states include employees in mining and logging.

Percent of Nonfarm Employees in Construction in 2019

National Percent = 5.0% of Employees*

ALPHA ORDER				RANK ORDER		
RANK	STATE	PERCENT		RANK	STATE	PERCENT
30	Alabama	4.6		1	Nevada	7.1
20	Alaska	5.1		1	Utah	7.1
13	Arizona	6.0		3	Louisiana	7.0
40	Arkansas	4.1		3	Wyoming	7.0
20	California	5.1		5	Idaho	6.8
9	Colorado	6.2		6	North Dakota	6.5
50	Connecticut	3.4		6	Washington	6.5
26	Delaware**	4.8		8	Florida	6.3
8	Florida	6.3		9	Colorado	6.2
31	Georgia	4.5		9	Texas	6.2
16	Hawaii**	5.7		11	New Mexico	6.1
5	Idaho	6.8		11	West Virginia	6.1
49	Illinois	3.6		13	Arizona	6.0
23	Indiana	4.9		13	Maryland**	6.0
20	Iowa	5.1		13	Montana	6.0
33	Kansas	4.4		16	Hawaii**	5.7
42	Kentucky	4.0		16	Oregon	5.7
3	Louisiana	7.0		18	South Dakota**	5.4
28	Maine	4.7		19	Nebraska**	5.3
13	Maryland**	6.0		20	Alaska	5.1
36	Massachusetts	4.2		20	California	5.1
44	Michigan	3.9		20	Iowa	5.1
36	Minnesota	4.2		23	Indiana	4.9
48	Mississippi	3.7		23	Oklahoma	4.9
34	Missouri	4.3		23	Virginia	4.9
13	Montana	6.0		26	Delaware**	4.8
19	Nebraska**	5.3		26	North Carolina	4.8
1	Nevada	7.1		28	Maine	4.7
36	New Hampshire	4.2		28	South Carolina	4.7
44	New Jersey	3.9		30	Alabama	4.6
11	New Mexico	6.1		31	Georgia	4.5
40	New York	4.1		31	Vermont	4.5
26	North Carolina	4.8		33	Kansas	4.4
6	North Dakota	6.5		34	Missouri	4.3
46	Ohio	3.8		34	Wisconsin	4.3
23	Oklahoma	4.9		36	Massachusetts	4.2
16	Oregon	5.7		36	Minnesota	4.2
36	Pennsylvania	4.2		36	New Hampshire	4.2
46	Rhode Island	3.8		36	Pennsylvania	4.2
28	South Carolina	4.7		40	Arkansas	4.1
18	South Dakota**	5.4		40	New York	4.1
42	Tennessee**	4.0		42	Kentucky	4.0
9	Texas	6.2		42	Tennessee**	4.0
1	Utah	7.1		44	Michigan	3.9
31	Vermont	4.5		44	New Jersey	3.9
23	Virginia	4.9		46	Ohio	3.8
6	Washington	6.5		46	Rhode Island	3.8
11	West Virginia	6.1		48	Mississippi	3.7
34	Wisconsin	4.3		49	Illinois	3.6
3	Wyoming	7.0		50	Connecticut	3.4
					District of Columbia**	2.0

Source: CQ Press using data from U.S. Department of Labor, Bureau of Labor Statistics
    "State Employment and Unemployment" (press release, January 24, 2020, www.bls.gov/bls/newsrels.htm)
*Seasonally adjusted preliminary data as of December 2019. National figure calculated through a different formula.
**Figures for these states include employees in mining and logging.

Employees in Education and Health Services in 2019

National Total = 24,559,000 Employees*

ALPHA ORDER

RANK	STATE	EMPLOYEES	% of USA
28	Alabama	250,500	1.0%
49	Alaska	49,800	0.2%
19	Arizona	474,800	1.9%
33	Arkansas	197,500	0.8%
1	California	2,855,300	11.6%
22	Colorado	355,600	1.4%
23	Connecticut	347,000	1.4%
44	Delaware	83,800	0.3%
4	Florida	1,382,600	5.6%
12	Georgia	616,400	2.5%
43	Hawaii	87,800	0.4%
42	Idaho	109,400	0.4%
6	Illinois	959,300	3.9%
17	Indiana	490,700	2.0%
30	Iowa	234,300	1.0%
32	Kansas	201,500	0.8%
26	Kentucky	293,400	1.2%
24	Louisiana	326,000	1.3%
40	Maine	126,300	0.5%
18	Maryland	483,400	2.0%
8	Massachusetts	825,800	3.4%
10	Michigan	672,900	2.7%
14	Minnesota	539,100	2.2%
35	Mississippi	147,100	0.6%
16	Missouri	491,000	2.0%
45	Montana	78,600	0.3%
34	Nebraska	158,100	0.6%
36	Nevada	145,000	0.6%
38	New Hampshire	130,600	0.5%
9	New Jersey	722,800	2.9%
37	New Mexico	142,800	0.6%
2	New York	2,146,200	8.7%
11	North Carolina	625,900	2.5%
48	North Dakota	66,300	0.3%
7	Ohio	954,800	3.9%
29	Oklahoma	241,000	1.0%
25	Oregon	307,300	1.3%
5	Pennsylvania	1,295,000	5.3%
41	Rhode Island	110,600	0.5%
27	South Carolina	258,800	1.1%
46	South Dakota	74,000	0.3%
21	Tennessee	441,200	1.8%
3	Texas	1,773,100	7.2%
31	Utah	218,100	0.9%
47	Vermont	66,700	0.3%
13	Virginia	560,200	2.3%
15	Washington	518,100	2.1%
39	West Virginia	129,300	0.5%
20	Wisconsin	461,000	1.9%
50	Wyoming	27,500	0.1%

RANK ORDER

RANK	STATE	EMPLOYEES	% of USA
1	California	2,855,300	11.6%
2	New York	2,146,200	8.7%
3	Texas	1,773,100	7.2%
4	Florida	1,382,600	5.6%
5	Pennsylvania	1,295,000	5.3%
6	Illinois	959,300	3.9%
7	Ohio	954,800	3.9%
8	Massachusetts	825,800	3.4%
9	New Jersey	722,800	2.9%
10	Michigan	672,900	2.7%
11	North Carolina	625,900	2.5%
12	Georgia	616,400	2.5%
13	Virginia	560,200	2.3%
14	Minnesota	539,100	2.2%
15	Washington	518,100	2.1%
16	Missouri	491,000	2.0%
17	Indiana	490,700	2.0%
18	Maryland	483,400	2.0%
19	Arizona	474,800	1.9%
20	Wisconsin	461,000	1.9%
21	Tennessee	441,200	1.8%
22	Colorado	355,600	1.4%
23	Connecticut	347,000	1.4%
24	Louisiana	326,000	1.3%
25	Oregon	307,300	1.3%
26	Kentucky	293,400	1.2%
27	South Carolina	258,800	1.1%
28	Alabama	250,500	1.0%
29	Oklahoma	241,000	1.0%
30	Iowa	234,300	1.0%
31	Utah	218,100	0.9%
32	Kansas	201,500	0.8%
33	Arkansas	197,500	0.8%
34	Nebraska	158,100	0.6%
35	Mississippi	147,100	0.6%
36	Nevada	145,000	0.6%
37	New Mexico	142,800	0.6%
38	New Hampshire	130,600	0.5%
39	West Virginia	129,300	0.5%
40	Maine	126,300	0.5%
41	Rhode Island	110,600	0.5%
42	Idaho	109,400	0.4%
43	Hawaii	87,800	0.4%
44	Delaware	83,800	0.3%
45	Montana	78,600	0.3%
46	South Dakota	74,000	0.3%
47	Vermont	66,700	0.3%
48	North Dakota	66,300	0.3%
49	Alaska	49,800	0.2%
50	Wyoming	27,500	0.1%
	District of Columbia	131,800	0.5%

Source: U.S. Department of Labor, Bureau of Labor Statistics
"State Employment and Unemployment" (press release, January 24, 2020, www.bls.gov/bls/newsrels.htm)
*Seasonally adjusted preliminary data as of December 2019. National total calculated through a different formula.

Percent of Nonfarm Employees in Education and Health Services in 2019

National Percent = 16.1% of Employees*

ALPHA ORDER				RANK ORDER		
RANK	STATE	PERCENT		RANK	STATE	PERCENT
47	Alabama	11.9		1	Massachusetts	22.4
30	Alaska	15.1		2	New York	21.9
21	Arizona	16.0		3	Rhode Island	21.8
26	Arkansas	15.3		4	Pennsylvania	21.4
19	California	16.2		5	Vermont	21.1
45	Colorado	12.7		6	Connecticut	20.4
6	Connecticut	20.4		7	Maine	19.9
10	Delaware	17.8		8	New Hampshire	18.9
27	Florida	15.2		9	Minnesota	18.2
43	Georgia	13.2		10	Delaware	17.8
43	Hawaii	13.2		10	West Virginia	17.8
35	Idaho	14.3		12	Maryland	17.3
23	Illinois	15.5		13	New Jersey	17.1
23	Indiana	15.5		14	Ohio	17.0
33	Iowa	14.7		15	Missouri	16.8
38	Kansas	14.0		16	New Mexico	16.6
32	Kentucky	15.0		17	South Dakota	16.5
18	Louisiana	16.4		18	Louisiana	16.4
7	Maine	19.9		19	California	16.2
12	Maryland	17.3		19	Montana	16.2
1	Massachusetts	22.4		21	Arizona	16.0
30	Michigan	15.1		22	Oregon	15.7
9	Minnesota	18.2		23	Illinois	15.5
46	Mississippi	12.6		23	Indiana	15.5
15	Missouri	16.8		25	Wisconsin	15.4
19	Montana	16.2		26	Arkansas	15.3
27	Nebraska	15.2		27	Florida	15.2
49	Nevada	10.1		27	Nebraska	15.2
8	New Hampshire	18.9		27	North Dakota	15.2
13	New Jersey	17.1		30	Alaska	15.1
16	New Mexico	16.6		30	Michigan	15.1
2	New York	21.9		32	Kentucky	15.0
42	North Carolina	13.6		33	Iowa	14.7
27	North Dakota	15.2		33	Washington	14.7
14	Ohio	17.0		35	Idaho	14.3
36	Oklahoma	14.2		36	Oklahoma	14.2
22	Oregon	15.7		37	Tennessee	14.1
4	Pennsylvania	21.4		38	Kansas	14.0
3	Rhode Island	21.8		39	Virginia	13.8
48	South Carolina	11.8		40	Texas	13.7
17	South Dakota	16.5		40	Utah	13.7
37	Tennessee	14.1		42	North Carolina	13.6
40	Texas	13.7		43	Georgia	13.2
40	Utah	13.7		43	Hawaii	13.2
5	Vermont	21.1		45	Colorado	12.7
39	Virginia	13.8		46	Mississippi	12.6
33	Washington	14.7		47	Alabama	11.9
10	West Virginia	17.8		48	South Carolina	11.8
25	Wisconsin	15.4		49	Nevada	10.1
50	Wyoming	9.6		50	Wyoming	9.6
					District of Columbia	16.4

Source: CQ Press using data from U.S. Department of Labor, Bureau of Labor Statistics
"State Employment and Unemployment" (press release, January 24, 2020, www.bls.gov/bls/newsrels.htm)
*Seasonally adjusted preliminary data as of December 2019. National figure calculated through a different formula.

Employees in Financial Activities in 2019

National Total = 8,737,000 Employees*

ALPHA ORDER

RANK	STATE	EMPLOYEES	% of USA
27	Alabama	97,600	1.1%
48	Alaska	11,800	0.1%
12	Arizona	224,800	2.6%
35	Arkansas	61,300	0.7%
1	California	847,000	9.7%
17	Colorado	170,500	2.0%
23	Connecticut	127,600	1.5%
36	Delaware	48,400	0.6%
4	Florida	597,600	6.8%
8	Georgia	251,600	2.9%
45	Hawaii	28,800	0.3%
38	Idaho	38,800	0.4%
5	Illinois	407,000	4.7%
22	Indiana	139,300	1.6%
24	Iowa	107,700	1.2%
32	Kansas	77,900	0.9%
28	Kentucky	94,900	1.1%
30	Louisiana	90,600	1.0%
42	Maine	32,400	0.4%
21	Maryland	143,700	1.6%
13	Massachusetts	223,200	2.6%
11	Michigan	226,400	2.6%
15	Minnesota	186,300	2.1%
37	Mississippi	45,400	0.5%
16	Missouri	177,000	2.0%
46	Montana	26,200	0.3%
33	Nebraska	75,600	0.9%
34	Nevada	73,000	0.8%
41	New Hampshire	33,400	0.4%
10	New Jersey	246,800	2.8%
40	New Mexico	35,600	0.4%
3	New York	712,100	8.2%
8	North Carolina	251,600	2.9%
47	North Dakota	24,400	0.3%
7	Ohio	309,900	3.5%
31	Oklahoma	79,100	0.9%
26	Oregon	103,500	1.2%
6	Pennsylvania	332,500	3.8%
39	Rhode Island	35,900	0.4%
25	South Carolina	104,800	1.2%
44	South Dakota	29,000	0.3%
18	Tennessee	168,200	1.9%
2	Texas	818,300	9.4%
29	Utah	91,200	1.0%
49	Vermont	11,400	0.1%
14	Virginia	212,500	2.4%
19	Washington	166,700	1.9%
43	West Virginia	29,100	0.3%
20	Wisconsin	153,200	1.8%
50	Wyoming	11,200	0.1%

RANK ORDER

RANK	STATE	EMPLOYEES	% of USA
1	California	847,000	9.7%
2	Texas	818,300	9.4%
3	New York	712,100	8.2%
4	Florida	597,600	6.8%
5	Illinois	407,000	4.7%
6	Pennsylvania	332,500	3.8%
7	Ohio	309,900	3.5%
8	Georgia	251,600	2.9%
8	North Carolina	251,600	2.9%
10	New Jersey	246,800	2.8%
11	Michigan	226,400	2.6%
12	Arizona	224,800	2.6%
13	Massachusetts	223,200	2.6%
14	Virginia	212,500	2.4%
15	Minnesota	186,300	2.1%
16	Missouri	177,000	2.0%
17	Colorado	170,500	2.0%
18	Tennessee	168,200	1.9%
19	Washington	166,700	1.9%
20	Wisconsin	153,200	1.8%
21	Maryland	143,700	1.6%
22	Indiana	139,300	1.6%
23	Connecticut	127,600	1.5%
24	Iowa	107,700	1.2%
25	South Carolina	104,800	1.2%
26	Oregon	103,500	1.2%
27	Alabama	97,600	1.1%
28	Kentucky	94,900	1.1%
29	Utah	91,200	1.0%
30	Louisiana	90,600	1.0%
31	Oklahoma	79,100	0.9%
32	Kansas	77,900	0.9%
33	Nebraska	75,600	0.9%
34	Nevada	73,000	0.8%
35	Arkansas	61,300	0.7%
36	Delaware	48,400	0.6%
37	Mississippi	45,400	0.5%
38	Idaho	38,800	0.4%
39	Rhode Island	35,900	0.4%
40	New Mexico	35,600	0.4%
41	New Hampshire	33,400	0.4%
42	Maine	32,400	0.4%
43	West Virginia	29,100	0.3%
44	South Dakota	29,000	0.3%
45	Hawaii	28,800	0.3%
46	Montana	26,200	0.3%
47	North Dakota	24,400	0.3%
48	Alaska	11,800	0.1%
49	Vermont	11,400	0.1%
50	Wyoming	11,200	0.1%
	District of Columbia	30,200	0.3%

Source: U.S. Department of Labor, Bureau of Labor Statistics
"State Employment and Unemployment" (press release, January 24, 2020, www.bls.gov/bls/newsrels.htm)
*Seasonally adjusted preliminary data as of December 2019. National total calculated through a different formula. Financial activities include insurance and real estate.

Percent of Nonfarm Employees in Financial Activities in 2019

National Percent = 5.7% of Employees*

ALPHA ORDER

RANK	STATE	PERCENT
41	Alabama	4.6
49	Alaska	3.6
2	Arizona	7.6
35	Arkansas	4.8
35	California	4.8
13	Colorado	6.1
3	Connecticut	7.5
1	Delaware	10.3
8	Florida	6.6
22	Georgia	5.4
44	Hawaii	4.3
28	Idaho	5.1
8	Illinois	6.6
43	Indiana	4.4
7	Iowa	6.8
22	Kansas	5.4
34	Kentucky	4.9
41	Louisiana	4.6
28	Maine	5.1
28	Maryland	5.1
15	Massachusetts	6.0
28	Michigan	5.1
11	Minnesota	6.3
47	Mississippi	3.9
13	Missouri	6.1
22	Montana	5.4
4	Nebraska	7.3
28	Nevada	5.1
35	New Hampshire	4.8
16	New Jersey	5.9
45	New Mexico	4.1
4	New York	7.3
19	North Carolina	5.5
18	North Dakota	5.6
19	Ohio	5.5
39	Oklahoma	4.7
26	Oregon	5.3
19	Pennsylvania	5.5
6	Rhode Island	7.1
35	South Carolina	4.8
10	South Dakota	6.5
22	Tennessee	5.4
11	Texas	6.3
17	Utah	5.7
49	Vermont	3.6
27	Virginia	5.2
39	Washington	4.7
46	West Virginia	4.0
28	Wisconsin	5.1
47	Wyoming	3.9

RANK ORDER

RANK	STATE	PERCENT
1	Delaware	10.3
2	Arizona	7.6
3	Connecticut	7.5
4	Nebraska	7.3
4	New York	7.3
6	Rhode Island	7.1
7	Iowa	6.8
8	Florida	6.6
8	Illinois	6.6
10	South Dakota	6.5
11	Minnesota	6.3
11	Texas	6.3
13	Colorado	6.1
13	Missouri	6.1
15	Massachusetts	6.0
16	New Jersey	5.9
17	Utah	5.7
18	North Dakota	5.6
19	North Carolina	5.5
19	Ohio	5.5
19	Pennsylvania	5.5
22	Georgia	5.4
22	Kansas	5.4
22	Montana	5.4
22	Tennessee	5.4
26	Oregon	5.3
27	Virginia	5.2
28	Idaho	5.1
28	Maine	5.1
28	Maryland	5.1
28	Michigan	5.1
28	Nevada	5.1
28	Wisconsin	5.1
34	Kentucky	4.9
35	Arkansas	4.8
35	California	4.8
35	New Hampshire	4.8
35	South Carolina	4.8
39	Oklahoma	4.7
39	Washington	4.7
41	Alabama	4.6
41	Louisiana	4.6
43	Indiana	4.4
44	Hawaii	4.3
45	New Mexico	4.1
46	West Virginia	4.0
47	Mississippi	3.9
47	Wyoming	3.9
49	Alaska	3.6
49	Vermont	3.6
	District of Columbia	3.8

Source: CQ Press using data from U.S. Department of Labor, Bureau of Labor Statistics
 "State Employment and Unemployment" (press release, January 24, 2020, www.bls.gov/bls/newsrels.htm)
*Seasonally adjusted preliminary data as of December 2019. National figure calculated through a different formula. Financial activities include insurance and real estate.

Employees in Government in 2019

National Total = 22,646,000 Employees*

ALPHA ORDER

RANK	STATE	EMPLOYEES	% of USA
23	Alabama	391,300	1.7%
45	Alaska	80,500	0.4%
21	Arizona	417,800	1.8%
34	Arkansas	212,800	0.9%
1	California	2,641,700	11.7%
16	Colorado	453,600	2.0%
33	Connecticut	235,100	1.0%
48	Delaware	68,300	0.3%
4	Florida	1,129,300	5.0%
10	Georgia	702,300	3.1%
40	Hawaii	126,700	0.6%
39	Idaho	127,500	0.6%
5	Illinois	839,800	3.7%
18	Indiana	433,900	1.9%
30	Iowa	262,300	1.2%
29	Kansas	262,900	1.2%
27	Kentucky	311,000	1.4%
26	Louisiana	325,200	1.4%
41	Maine	100,200	0.4%
14	Maryland	511,300	2.3%
15	Massachusetts	458,800	2.0%
11	Michigan	614,400	2.7%
20	Minnesota	426,800	1.9%
32	Mississippi	242,400	1.1%
19	Missouri	433,300	1.9%
42	Montana	91,100	0.4%
36	Nebraska	175,700	0.8%
37	Nevada	165,000	0.7%
43	New Hampshire	88,500	0.4%
12	New Jersey	601,000	2.7%
35	New Mexico	187,200	0.8%
3	New York	1,496,400	6.6%
7	North Carolina	733,700	3.2%
44	North Dakota	82,600	0.4%
6	Ohio	780,900	3.4%
25	Oklahoma	346,900	1.5%
28	Oregon	299,800	1.3%
9	Pennsylvania	709,400	3.1%
49	Rhode Island	61,500	0.3%
24	South Carolina	376,600	1.7%
46	South Dakota	80,300	0.4%
17	Tennessee	440,700	1.9%
2	Texas	1,971,300	8.7%
31	Utah	254,200	1.1%
50	Vermont	55,200	0.2%
8	Virginia	718,600	3.2%
13	Washington	586,200	2.6%
38	West Virginia	151,400	0.7%
22	Wisconsin	404,400	1.8%
47	Wyoming	68,800	0.3%

RANK ORDER

RANK	STATE	EMPLOYEES	% of USA
1	California	2,641,700	11.7%
2	Texas	1,971,300	8.7%
3	New York	1,496,400	6.6%
4	Florida	1,129,300	5.0%
5	Illinois	839,800	3.7%
6	Ohio	780,900	3.4%
7	North Carolina	733,700	3.2%
8	Virginia	718,600	3.2%
9	Pennsylvania	709,400	3.1%
10	Georgia	702,300	3.1%
11	Michigan	614,400	2.7%
12	New Jersey	601,000	2.7%
13	Washington	586,200	2.6%
14	Maryland	511,300	2.3%
15	Massachusetts	458,800	2.0%
16	Colorado	453,600	2.0%
17	Tennessee	440,700	1.9%
18	Indiana	433,900	1.9%
19	Missouri	433,300	1.9%
20	Minnesota	426,800	1.9%
21	Arizona	417,800	1.8%
22	Wisconsin	404,400	1.8%
23	Alabama	391,300	1.7%
24	South Carolina	376,600	1.7%
25	Oklahoma	346,900	1.5%
26	Louisiana	325,200	1.4%
27	Kentucky	311,000	1.4%
28	Oregon	299,800	1.3%
29	Kansas	262,900	1.2%
30	Iowa	262,300	1.2%
31	Utah	254,200	1.1%
32	Mississippi	242,400	1.1%
33	Connecticut	235,100	1.0%
34	Arkansas	212,800	0.9%
35	New Mexico	187,200	0.8%
36	Nebraska	175,700	0.8%
37	Nevada	165,000	0.7%
38	West Virginia	151,400	0.7%
39	Idaho	127,500	0.6%
40	Hawaii	126,700	0.6%
41	Maine	100,200	0.4%
42	Montana	91,100	0.4%
43	New Hampshire	88,500	0.4%
44	North Dakota	82,600	0.4%
45	Alaska	80,500	0.4%
46	South Dakota	80,300	0.4%
47	Wyoming	68,800	0.3%
48	Delaware	68,300	0.3%
49	Rhode Island	61,500	0.3%
50	Vermont	55,200	0.2%
	District of Columbia	238,700	1.1%

Source: U.S. Department of Labor, Bureau of Labor Statistics
   "State Employment and Unemployment" (press release, January 24, 2020, www.bls.gov/bls/newsrels.htm)
*Seasonally adjusted preliminary data as of December 2019. National total calculated through a different formula.

Percent of Nonfarm Employees in Government in 2019

National Percent = 14.9% of Employees*

ALPHA ORDER				RANK ORDER		
RANK	STATE	PERCENT		RANK	STATE	PERCENT
10	Alabama	18.6		1	Alaska	24.5
1	Alaska	24.5		2	Wyoming	24.1
37	Arizona	14.1		3	New Mexico	21.7
20	Arkansas	16.5		4	West Virginia	20.8
32	California	15.0		5	Mississippi	20.7
23	Colorado	16.2		6	Oklahoma	20.5
40	Connecticut	13.8		7	Hawaii	19.1
34	Delaware	14.5		8	North Dakota	18.9
46	Florida	12.4		9	Montana	18.8
31	Georgia	15.1		10	Alabama	18.6
7	Hawaii	19.1		11	Maryland	18.3
18	Idaho	16.7		12	Kansas	18.2
43	Illinois	13.6		13	South Dakota	17.9
42	Indiana	13.7		14	Virginia	17.7
20	Iowa	16.5		15	Vermont	17.5
12	Kansas	18.2		16	South Carolina	17.2
26	Kentucky	15.9		17	Nebraska	16.9
22	Louisiana	16.3		18	Idaho	16.7
27	Maine	15.8		19	Washington	16.6
11	Maryland	18.3		20	Arkansas	16.5
46	Massachusetts	12.4		20	Iowa	16.5
40	Michigan	13.8		22	Louisiana	16.3
35	Minnesota	14.4		23	Colorado	16.2
5	Mississippi	20.7		24	North Carolina	16.0
33	Missouri	14.9		24	Utah	16.0
9	Montana	18.8		26	Kentucky	15.9
17	Nebraska	16.9		27	Maine	15.8
50	Nevada	11.5		28	Oregon	15.3
45	New Hampshire	12.8		29	New York	15.2
36	New Jersey	14.2		29	Texas	15.2
3	New Mexico	21.7		31	Georgia	15.1
29	New York	15.2		32	California	15.0
24	North Carolina	16.0		33	Missouri	14.9
8	North Dakota	18.9		34	Delaware	14.5
39	Ohio	13.9		35	Minnesota	14.4
6	Oklahoma	20.5		36	New Jersey	14.2
28	Oregon	15.3		37	Arizona	14.1
49	Pennsylvania	11.7		37	Tennessee	14.1
48	Rhode Island	12.1		39	Ohio	13.9
16	South Carolina	17.2		40	Connecticut	13.8
13	South Dakota	17.9		40	Michigan	13.8
37	Tennessee	14.1		42	Indiana	13.7
29	Texas	15.2		43	Illinois	13.6
24	Utah	16.0		44	Wisconsin	13.5
15	Vermont	17.5		45	New Hampshire	12.8
14	Virginia	17.7		46	Florida	12.4
19	Washington	16.6		46	Massachusetts	12.4
4	West Virginia	20.8		48	Rhode Island	12.1
44	Wisconsin	13.5		49	Pennsylvania	11.7
2	Wyoming	24.1		50	Nevada	11.5
					District of Columbia	29.7

Source: CQ Press using data from U.S. Department of Labor, Bureau of Labor Statistics
"State Employment and Unemployment" (press release, January 24, 2020, www.bls.gov/bls/newsrels.htm)
*Seasonally adjusted preliminary data as of December 2019. National figure calculated through a different formula.

Employees in Leisure and Hospitality in 2019

National Total = 16,942,000 Employees*

<table>
<tr><td colspan="4">ALPHA ORDER</td><td colspan="4">RANK ORDER</td></tr>
<tr><th>RANK</th><th>STATE</th><th>EMPLOYEES</th><th>% of USA</th><th>RANK</th><th>STATE</th><th>EMPLOYEES</th><th>% of USA</th></tr>
<tr><td>27</td><td>Alabama</td><td>217,100</td><td>1.3%</td><td>1</td><td>California</td><td>2,032,700</td><td>12.0%</td></tr>
<tr><td>50</td><td>Alaska</td><td>35,900</td><td>0.2%</td><td>2</td><td>Texas</td><td>1,415,600</td><td>8.4%</td></tr>
<tr><td>18</td><td>Arizona</td><td>338,400</td><td>2.0%</td><td>3</td><td>Florida</td><td>1,288,000</td><td>7.6%</td></tr>
<tr><td>36</td><td>Arkansas</td><td>123,300</td><td>0.7%</td><td>4</td><td>New York</td><td>983,300</td><td>5.8%</td></tr>
<tr><td>1</td><td>California</td><td>2,032,700</td><td>12.0%</td><td>5</td><td>Illinois</td><td>640,600</td><td>3.8%</td></tr>
<tr><td>17</td><td>Colorado</td><td>347,000</td><td>2.0%</td><td>6</td><td>Ohio</td><td>587,800</td><td>3.5%</td></tr>
<tr><td>31</td><td>Connecticut</td><td>159,400</td><td>0.9%</td><td>7</td><td>Pennsylvania</td><td>577,800</td><td>3.4%</td></tr>
<tr><td>45</td><td>Delaware</td><td>54,300</td><td>0.3%</td><td>8</td><td>North Carolina</td><td>538,100</td><td>3.2%</td></tr>
<tr><td>3</td><td>Florida</td><td>1,288,000</td><td>7.6%</td><td>9</td><td>Georgia</td><td>514,400</td><td>3.0%</td></tr>
<tr><td>9</td><td>Georgia</td><td>514,400</td><td>3.0%</td><td>10</td><td>Michigan</td><td>445,300</td><td>2.6%</td></tr>
<tr><td>35</td><td>Hawaii</td><td>127,700</td><td>0.8%</td><td>11</td><td>Virginia</td><td>428,200</td><td>2.5%</td></tr>
<tr><td>39</td><td>Idaho</td><td>79,000</td><td>0.5%</td><td>12</td><td>New Jersey</td><td>417,400</td><td>2.5%</td></tr>
<tr><td>5</td><td>Illinois</td><td>640,600</td><td>3.8%</td><td>13</td><td>Massachusetts</td><td>378,000</td><td>2.2%</td></tr>
<tr><td>20</td><td>Indiana</td><td>304,000</td><td>1.8%</td><td>14</td><td>Tennessee</td><td>362,800</td><td>2.1%</td></tr>
<tr><td>32</td><td>Iowa</td><td>145,300</td><td>0.9%</td><td>15</td><td>Nevada</td><td>359,200</td><td>2.1%</td></tr>
<tr><td>34</td><td>Kansas</td><td>137,900</td><td>0.8%</td><td>16</td><td>Washington</td><td>355,900</td><td>2.1%</td></tr>
<tr><td>28</td><td>Kentucky</td><td>203,400</td><td>1.2%</td><td>17</td><td>Colorado</td><td>347,000</td><td>2.0%</td></tr>
<tr><td>25</td><td>Louisiana</td><td>241,800</td><td>1.4%</td><td>18</td><td>Arizona</td><td>338,400</td><td>2.0%</td></tr>
<tr><td>42</td><td>Maine</td><td>71,200</td><td>0.4%</td><td>19</td><td>Missouri</td><td>313,500</td><td>1.9%</td></tr>
<tr><td>22</td><td>Maryland</td><td>292,100</td><td>1.7%</td><td>20</td><td>Indiana</td><td>304,000</td><td>1.8%</td></tr>
<tr><td>13</td><td>Massachusetts</td><td>378,000</td><td>2.2%</td><td>21</td><td>Minnesota</td><td>292,500</td><td>1.7%</td></tr>
<tr><td>10</td><td>Michigan</td><td>445,300</td><td>2.6%</td><td>22</td><td>Maryland</td><td>292,100</td><td>1.7%</td></tr>
<tr><td>21</td><td>Minnesota</td><td>292,500</td><td>1.7%</td><td>23</td><td>Wisconsin</td><td>289,900</td><td>1.7%</td></tr>
<tr><td>33</td><td>Mississippi</td><td>140,500</td><td>0.8%</td><td>24</td><td>South Carolina</td><td>272,100</td><td>1.6%</td></tr>
<tr><td>19</td><td>Missouri</td><td>313,500</td><td>1.9%</td><td>25</td><td>Louisiana</td><td>241,800</td><td>1.4%</td></tr>
<tr><td>43</td><td>Montana</td><td>66,300</td><td>0.4%</td><td>26</td><td>Oregon</td><td>218,200</td><td>1.3%</td></tr>
<tr><td>38</td><td>Nebraska</td><td>96,600</td><td>0.6%</td><td>27</td><td>Alabama</td><td>217,100</td><td>1.3%</td></tr>
<tr><td>15</td><td>Nevada</td><td>359,200</td><td>2.1%</td><td>28</td><td>Kentucky</td><td>203,400</td><td>1.2%</td></tr>
<tr><td>41</td><td>New Hampshire</td><td>72,800</td><td>0.4%</td><td>29</td><td>Oklahoma</td><td>172,600</td><td>1.0%</td></tr>
<tr><td>12</td><td>New Jersey</td><td>417,400</td><td>2.5%</td><td>30</td><td>Utah</td><td>159,700</td><td>0.9%</td></tr>
<tr><td>37</td><td>New Mexico</td><td>101,400</td><td>0.6%</td><td>31</td><td>Connecticut</td><td>159,400</td><td>0.9%</td></tr>
<tr><td>4</td><td>New York</td><td>983,300</td><td>5.8%</td><td>32</td><td>Iowa</td><td>145,300</td><td>0.9%</td></tr>
<tr><td>8</td><td>North Carolina</td><td>538,100</td><td>3.2%</td><td>33</td><td>Mississippi</td><td>140,500</td><td>0.8%</td></tr>
<tr><td>47</td><td>North Dakota</td><td>40,000</td><td>0.2%</td><td>34</td><td>Kansas</td><td>137,900</td><td>0.8%</td></tr>
<tr><td>6</td><td>Ohio</td><td>587,800</td><td>3.5%</td><td>35</td><td>Hawaii</td><td>127,700</td><td>0.8%</td></tr>
<tr><td>29</td><td>Oklahoma</td><td>172,600</td><td>1.0%</td><td>36</td><td>Arkansas</td><td>123,300</td><td>0.7%</td></tr>
<tr><td>26</td><td>Oregon</td><td>218,200</td><td>1.3%</td><td>37</td><td>New Mexico</td><td>101,400</td><td>0.6%</td></tr>
<tr><td>7</td><td>Pennsylvania</td><td>577,800</td><td>3.4%</td><td>38</td><td>Nebraska</td><td>96,600</td><td>0.6%</td></tr>
<tr><td>44</td><td>Rhode Island</td><td>60,300</td><td>0.4%</td><td>39</td><td>Idaho</td><td>79,000</td><td>0.5%</td></tr>
<tr><td>24</td><td>South Carolina</td><td>272,100</td><td>1.6%</td><td>40</td><td>West Virginia</td><td>75,000</td><td>0.4%</td></tr>
<tr><td>46</td><td>South Dakota</td><td>48,800</td><td>0.3%</td><td>41</td><td>New Hampshire</td><td>72,800</td><td>0.4%</td></tr>
<tr><td>14</td><td>Tennessee</td><td>362,800</td><td>2.1%</td><td>42</td><td>Maine</td><td>71,200</td><td>0.4%</td></tr>
<tr><td>2</td><td>Texas</td><td>1,415,600</td><td>8.4%</td><td>43</td><td>Montana</td><td>66,300</td><td>0.4%</td></tr>
<tr><td>30</td><td>Utah</td><td>159,700</td><td>0.9%</td><td>44</td><td>Rhode Island</td><td>60,300</td><td>0.4%</td></tr>
<tr><td>48</td><td>Vermont</td><td>38,700</td><td>0.2%</td><td>45</td><td>Delaware</td><td>54,300</td><td>0.3%</td></tr>
<tr><td>11</td><td>Virginia</td><td>428,200</td><td>2.5%</td><td>46</td><td>South Dakota</td><td>48,800</td><td>0.3%</td></tr>
<tr><td>16</td><td>Washington</td><td>355,900</td><td>2.1%</td><td>47</td><td>North Dakota</td><td>40,000</td><td>0.2%</td></tr>
<tr><td>40</td><td>West Virginia</td><td>75,000</td><td>0.4%</td><td>48</td><td>Vermont</td><td>38,700</td><td>0.2%</td></tr>
<tr><td>23</td><td>Wisconsin</td><td>289,900</td><td>1.7%</td><td>49</td><td>Wyoming</td><td>37,200</td><td>0.2%</td></tr>
<tr><td>49</td><td>Wyoming</td><td>37,200</td><td>0.2%</td><td>50</td><td>Alaska</td><td>35,900</td><td>0.2%</td></tr>
<tr><td></td><td></td><td></td><td></td><td colspan="2">District of Columbia</td><td>81,900</td><td>0.5%</td></tr>
</table>

Source: U.S. Department of Labor, Bureau of Labor Statistics
"State Employment and Unemployment" (press release, January 24, 2020, www.bls.gov/bls/newsrels.htm)
*Seasonally adjusted preliminary data as of December 2019. National total calculated through a different formula.

Percent of Nonfarm Employees in Leisure and Hospitality in 2019

National Percent = 11.1% of Employees*

<table>
<tr><td colspan="3">ALPHA ORDER</td><td colspan="3">RANK ORDER</td></tr>
<tr><th>RANK</th><th>STATE</th><th>PERCENT</th><th>RANK</th><th>STATE</th><th>PERCENT</th></tr>
<tr><td>30</td><td>Alabama</td><td>10.3</td><td>1</td><td>Nevada</td><td>24.9</td></tr>
<tr><td>21</td><td>Alaska</td><td>10.9</td><td>2</td><td>Hawaii</td><td>19.2</td></tr>
<tr><td>17</td><td>Arizona</td><td>11.4</td><td>3</td><td>Florida</td><td>14.1</td></tr>
<tr><td>43</td><td>Arkansas</td><td>9.6</td><td>4</td><td>Montana</td><td>13.7</td></tr>
<tr><td>15</td><td>California</td><td>11.5</td><td>5</td><td>Wyoming</td><td>13.0</td></tr>
<tr><td>6</td><td>Colorado</td><td>12.4</td><td>6</td><td>Colorado</td><td>12.4</td></tr>
<tr><td>47</td><td>Connecticut</td><td>9.4</td><td>6</td><td>South Carolina</td><td>12.4</td></tr>
<tr><td>15</td><td>Delaware</td><td>11.5</td><td>8</td><td>Vermont</td><td>12.3</td></tr>
<tr><td>3</td><td>Florida</td><td>14.1</td><td>9</td><td>Louisiana</td><td>12.1</td></tr>
<tr><td>19</td><td>Georgia</td><td>11.1</td><td>10</td><td>Mississippi</td><td>12.0</td></tr>
<tr><td>2</td><td>Hawaii</td><td>19.2</td><td>11</td><td>Rhode Island</td><td>11.9</td></tr>
<tr><td>30</td><td>Idaho</td><td>10.3</td><td>12</td><td>New Mexico</td><td>11.8</td></tr>
<tr><td>30</td><td>Illinois</td><td>10.3</td><td>13</td><td>North Carolina</td><td>11.7</td></tr>
<tr><td>43</td><td>Indiana</td><td>9.6</td><td>14</td><td>Tennessee</td><td>11.6</td></tr>
<tr><td>50</td><td>Iowa</td><td>9.1</td><td>15</td><td>California</td><td>11.5</td></tr>
<tr><td>43</td><td>Kansas</td><td>9.6</td><td>15</td><td>Delaware</td><td>11.5</td></tr>
<tr><td>29</td><td>Kentucky</td><td>10.4</td><td>17</td><td>Arizona</td><td>11.4</td></tr>
<tr><td>9</td><td>Louisiana</td><td>12.1</td><td>18</td><td>Maine</td><td>11.2</td></tr>
<tr><td>18</td><td>Maine</td><td>11.2</td><td>19</td><td>Georgia</td><td>11.1</td></tr>
<tr><td>26</td><td>Maryland</td><td>10.5</td><td>19</td><td>Oregon</td><td>11.1</td></tr>
<tr><td>34</td><td>Massachusetts</td><td>10.2</td><td>21</td><td>Alaska</td><td>10.9</td></tr>
<tr><td>38</td><td>Michigan</td><td>10.0</td><td>21</td><td>South Dakota</td><td>10.9</td></tr>
<tr><td>40</td><td>Minnesota</td><td>9.9</td><td>21</td><td>Texas</td><td>10.9</td></tr>
<tr><td>10</td><td>Mississippi</td><td>12.0</td><td>24</td><td>Missouri</td><td>10.8</td></tr>
<tr><td>24</td><td>Missouri</td><td>10.8</td><td>25</td><td>Virginia</td><td>10.6</td></tr>
<tr><td>4</td><td>Montana</td><td>13.7</td><td>26</td><td>Maryland</td><td>10.5</td></tr>
<tr><td>48</td><td>Nebraska</td><td>9.3</td><td>26</td><td>New Hampshire</td><td>10.5</td></tr>
<tr><td>1</td><td>Nevada</td><td>24.9</td><td>26</td><td>Ohio</td><td>10.5</td></tr>
<tr><td>26</td><td>New Hampshire</td><td>10.5</td><td>29</td><td>Kentucky</td><td>10.4</td></tr>
<tr><td>40</td><td>New Jersey</td><td>9.9</td><td>30</td><td>Alabama</td><td>10.3</td></tr>
<tr><td>12</td><td>New Mexico</td><td>11.8</td><td>30</td><td>Idaho</td><td>10.3</td></tr>
<tr><td>38</td><td>New York</td><td>10.0</td><td>30</td><td>Illinois</td><td>10.3</td></tr>
<tr><td>13</td><td>North Carolina</td><td>11.7</td><td>30</td><td>West Virginia</td><td>10.3</td></tr>
<tr><td>49</td><td>North Dakota</td><td>9.2</td><td>34</td><td>Massachusetts</td><td>10.2</td></tr>
<tr><td>26</td><td>Ohio</td><td>10.5</td><td>34</td><td>Oklahoma</td><td>10.2</td></tr>
<tr><td>34</td><td>Oklahoma</td><td>10.2</td><td>36</td><td>Utah</td><td>10.1</td></tr>
<tr><td>19</td><td>Oregon</td><td>11.1</td><td>36</td><td>Washington</td><td>10.1</td></tr>
<tr><td>46</td><td>Pennsylvania</td><td>9.5</td><td>38</td><td>Michigan</td><td>10.0</td></tr>
<tr><td>11</td><td>Rhode Island</td><td>11.9</td><td>38</td><td>New York</td><td>10.0</td></tr>
<tr><td>6</td><td>South Carolina</td><td>12.4</td><td>40</td><td>Minnesota</td><td>9.9</td></tr>
<tr><td>21</td><td>South Dakota</td><td>10.9</td><td>40</td><td>New Jersey</td><td>9.9</td></tr>
<tr><td>14</td><td>Tennessee</td><td>11.6</td><td>42</td><td>Wisconsin</td><td>9.7</td></tr>
<tr><td>21</td><td>Texas</td><td>10.9</td><td>43</td><td>Arkansas</td><td>9.6</td></tr>
<tr><td>36</td><td>Utah</td><td>10.1</td><td>43</td><td>Indiana</td><td>9.6</td></tr>
<tr><td>8</td><td>Vermont</td><td>12.3</td><td>43</td><td>Kansas</td><td>9.6</td></tr>
<tr><td>25</td><td>Virginia</td><td>10.6</td><td>46</td><td>Pennsylvania</td><td>9.5</td></tr>
<tr><td>36</td><td>Washington</td><td>10.1</td><td>47</td><td>Connecticut</td><td>9.4</td></tr>
<tr><td>30</td><td>West Virginia</td><td>10.3</td><td>48</td><td>Nebraska</td><td>9.3</td></tr>
<tr><td>42</td><td>Wisconsin</td><td>9.7</td><td>49</td><td>North Dakota</td><td>9.2</td></tr>
<tr><td>5</td><td>Wyoming</td><td>13.0</td><td>50</td><td>Iowa</td><td>9.1</td></tr>
<tr><td></td><td></td><td></td><td></td><td>District of Columbia</td><td>10.2</td></tr>
</table>

Source: CQ Press using data from U.S. Department of Labor, Bureau of Labor Statistics
"State Employment and Unemployment" (press release, January 24, 2020, www.bls.gov/bls/newsrels.htm)
*Seasonally adjusted preliminary data as of December 2019. National figure calculated through a different formula.

Employees in Manufacturing in 2019

National Total = 12,855,000 Employees*

ALPHA ORDER

RANK	STATE	EMPLOYEES	% of USA
17	Alabama	271,800	2.1%
49	Alaska	12,100	0.1%
25	Arizona	179,600	1.4%
27	Arkansas	163,900	1.3%
1	California	1,344,200	10.5%
29	Colorado	150,300	1.2%
28	Connecticut	161,100	1.3%
45	Delaware	27,400	0.2%
12	Florida	383,600	3.0%
11	Georgia	409,900	3.2%
48	Hawaii	14,100	0.1%
36	Idaho	69,900	0.5%
5	Illinois	588,000	4.6%
7	Indiana	536,100	4.2%
23	Iowa	226,500	1.8%
26	Kansas	167,200	1.3%
18	Kentucky	256,600	2.0%
31	Louisiana	140,000	1.1%
39	Maine	53,700	0.4%
34	Maryland	108,300	0.8%
22	Massachusetts	241,500	1.9%
4	Michigan	628,900	4.9%
14	Minnesota	318,500	2.5%
30	Mississippi	148,000	1.2%
16	Missouri	276,200	2.1%
47	Montana	20,500	0.2%
35	Nebraska	100,300	0.8%
38	Nevada	61,200	0.5%
37	New Hampshire	69,600	0.5%
20	New Jersey	252,900	2.0%
44	New Mexico	27,800	0.2%
10	New York	437,200	3.4%
9	North Carolina	472,300	3.7%
46	North Dakota	25,900	0.2%
3	Ohio	701,500	5.5%
33	Oklahoma	134,400	1.0%
24	Oregon	203,100	1.6%
6	Pennsylvania	565,100	4.4%
42	Rhode Island	39,200	0.3%
19	South Carolina	255,900	2.0%
41	South Dakota	45,500	0.4%
13	Tennessee	359,300	2.8%
2	Texas	917,800	7.1%
32	Utah	138,400	1.1%
43	Vermont	30,100	0.2%
21	Virginia	247,400	1.9%
15	Washington	300,400	2.3%
40	West Virginia	47,500	0.4%
8	Wisconsin	473,400	3.7%
50	Wyoming	10,100	0.1%

RANK ORDER

RANK	STATE	EMPLOYEES	% of USA
1	California	1,344,200	10.5%
2	Texas	917,800	7.1%
3	Ohio	701,500	5.5%
4	Michigan	628,900	4.9%
5	Illinois	588,000	4.6%
6	Pennsylvania	565,100	4.4%
7	Indiana	536,100	4.2%
8	Wisconsin	473,400	3.7%
9	North Carolina	472,300	3.7%
10	New York	437,200	3.4%
11	Georgia	409,900	3.2%
12	Florida	383,600	3.0%
13	Tennessee	359,300	2.8%
14	Minnesota	318,500	2.5%
15	Washington	300,400	2.3%
16	Missouri	276,200	2.1%
17	Alabama	271,800	2.1%
18	Kentucky	256,600	2.0%
19	South Carolina	255,900	2.0%
20	New Jersey	252,900	2.0%
21	Virginia	247,400	1.9%
22	Massachusetts	241,500	1.9%
23	Iowa	226,500	1.8%
24	Oregon	203,100	1.6%
25	Arizona	179,600	1.4%
26	Kansas	167,200	1.3%
27	Arkansas	163,900	1.3%
28	Connecticut	161,100	1.3%
29	Colorado	150,300	1.2%
30	Mississippi	148,000	1.2%
31	Louisiana	140,000	1.1%
32	Utah	138,400	1.1%
33	Oklahoma	134,400	1.0%
34	Maryland	108,300	0.8%
35	Nebraska	100,300	0.8%
36	Idaho	69,900	0.5%
37	New Hampshire	69,600	0.5%
38	Nevada	61,200	0.5%
39	Maine	53,700	0.4%
40	West Virginia	47,500	0.4%
41	South Dakota	45,500	0.4%
42	Rhode Island	39,200	0.3%
43	Vermont	30,100	0.2%
44	New Mexico	27,800	0.2%
45	Delaware	27,400	0.2%
46	North Dakota	25,900	0.2%
47	Montana	20,500	0.2%
48	Hawaii	14,100	0.1%
49	Alaska	12,100	0.1%
50	Wyoming	10,100	0.1%
	District of Columbia	1,400	0.0%

Source: U.S. Department of Labor, Bureau of Labor Statistics
  "State Employment and Unemployment" (press release, January 24, 2020, www.bls.gov/bls/newsrels.htm)
*Seasonally adjusted preliminary data as of December 2019. National total calculated through a different formula.

Percent of Nonfarm Employees in Manufacturing in 2019

National Percent = 8.4% of Employees*

ALPHA ORDER				RANK ORDER		
RANK	STATE	PERCENT		RANK	STATE	PERCENT
6	Alabama	12.9		1	Indiana	16.9
47	Alaska	3.7		2	Wisconsin	15.8
37	Arizona	6.0		3	Iowa	14.2
7	Arkansas	12.7		4	Michigan	14.1
31	California	7.6		5	Kentucky	13.1
41	Colorado	5.4		6	Alabama	12.9
19	Connecticut	9.5		7	Arkansas	12.7
40	Delaware	5.8		7	Mississippi	12.7
43	Florida	4.2		9	Ohio	12.5
25	Georgia	8.8		10	South Carolina	11.7
50	Hawaii	2.1		11	Kansas	11.6
24	Idaho	9.2		12	Tennessee	11.5
19	Illinois	9.5		13	Minnesota	10.7
1	Indiana	16.9		14	Oregon	10.4
3	Iowa	14.2		15	North Carolina	10.3
11	Kansas	11.6		16	New Hampshire	10.1
5	Kentucky	13.1		16	South Dakota	10.1
33	Louisiana	7.0		18	Nebraska	9.6
27	Maine	8.5		19	Connecticut	9.5
46	Maryland	3.9		19	Illinois	9.5
34	Massachusetts	6.5		19	Missouri	9.5
4	Michigan	14.1		19	Vermont	9.5
13	Minnesota	10.7		23	Pennsylvania	9.3
7	Mississippi	12.7		24	Idaho	9.2
19	Missouri	9.5		25	Georgia	8.8
43	Montana	4.2		26	Utah	8.7
18	Nebraska	9.6		27	Maine	8.5
43	Nevada	4.2		27	Washington	8.5
16	New Hampshire	10.1		29	Oklahoma	7.9
37	New Jersey	6.0		30	Rhode Island	7.7
49	New Mexico	3.2		31	California	7.6
42	New York	4.5		32	Texas	7.1
15	North Carolina	10.3		33	Louisiana	7.0
39	North Dakota	5.9		34	Massachusetts	6.5
9	Ohio	12.5		34	West Virginia	6.5
29	Oklahoma	7.9		36	Virginia	6.1
14	Oregon	10.4		37	Arizona	6.0
23	Pennsylvania	9.3		37	New Jersey	6.0
30	Rhode Island	7.7		39	North Dakota	5.9
10	South Carolina	11.7		40	Delaware	5.8
16	South Dakota	10.1		41	Colorado	5.4
12	Tennessee	11.5		42	New York	4.5
32	Texas	7.1		43	Florida	4.2
26	Utah	8.7		43	Montana	4.2
19	Vermont	9.5		43	Nevada	4.2
36	Virginia	6.1		46	Maryland	3.9
27	Washington	8.5		47	Alaska	3.7
34	West Virginia	6.5		48	Wyoming	3.5
2	Wisconsin	15.8		49	New Mexico	3.2
48	Wyoming	3.5		50	Hawaii	2.1
					District of Columbia	0.2

Source: CQ Press using data from U.S. Department of Labor, Bureau of Labor Statistics
"State Employment and Unemployment" (press release, January 24, 2020, www.bls.gov/bls/newsrels.htm)
*Seasonally adjusted preliminary data as of December 2019. National figure calculated through a different formula.

Employees in Mining and Logging in 2019

National Total = 731,000 Employees*

ALPHA ORDER

RANK	STATE	EMPLOYEES	% of USA
16	Alabama	9,500	1.3%
13	Alaska	13,400	1.8%
11	Arizona	13,600	1.9%
30	Arkansas	5,600	0.8%
7	California	23,300	3.2%
5	Colorado	27,800	3.8%
47	Connecticut	500	0.1%
NA	Delaware**	NA	NA
29	Florida	5,900	0.8%
17	Georgia	9,300	1.3%
NA	Hawaii**	NA	NA
37	Idaho	3,300	0.5%
20	Illinois	7,100	1.0%
27	Indiana	6,100	0.8%
38	Iowa	2,300	0.3%
23	Kansas	7,000	1.0%
19	Kentucky	8,000	1.1%
3	Louisiana	36,900	5.0%
39	Maine	2,200	0.3%
41	Maryland	1,300	0.2%
42	Massachusetts	1,000	0.1%
24	Michigan	6,900	0.9%
26	Minnesota	6,200	0.8%
25	Mississippi	6,600	0.9%
36	Missouri	4,100	0.6%
20	Montana	7,100	1.0%
42	Nebraska	1,000	0.1%
11	Nevada	13,600	1.9%
42	New Hampshire	1,000	0.1%
40	New Jersey	1,400	0.2%
6	New Mexico	26,300	3.6%
32	New York	5,300	0.7%
31	North Carolina	5,500	0.8%
9	North Dakota	20,400	2.8%
14	Ohio	12,100	1.7%
2	Oklahoma	48,600	6.6%
20	Oregon	7,100	1.0%
4	Pennsylvania	29,200	4.0%
48	Rhode Island	200	0.0%
33	South Carolina	4,600	0.6%
45	South Dakota	900	0.1%
34	Tennessee	4,400	0.6%
1	Texas	247,000	33.8%
15	Utah	9,700	1.3%
46	Vermont	700	0.1%
18	Virginia	8,200	1.1%
27	Washington	6,100	0.8%
8	West Virginia	21,200	2.9%
34	Wisconsin	4,400	0.6%
10	Wyoming	19,800	2.7%

RANK ORDER

RANK	STATE	EMPLOYEES	% of USA
1	Texas	247,000	33.8%
2	Oklahoma	48,600	6.6%
3	Louisiana	36,900	5.0%
4	Pennsylvania	29,200	4.0%
5	Colorado	27,800	3.8%
6	New Mexico	26,300	3.6%
7	California	23,300	3.2%
8	West Virginia	21,200	2.9%
9	North Dakota	20,400	2.8%
10	Wyoming	19,800	2.7%
11	Arizona	13,600	1.9%
11	Nevada	13,600	1.9%
13	Alaska	13,400	1.8%
14	Ohio	12,100	1.7%
15	Utah	9,700	1.3%
16	Alabama	9,500	1.3%
17	Georgia	9,300	1.3%
18	Virginia	8,200	1.1%
19	Kentucky	8,000	1.1%
20	Illinois	7,100	1.0%
20	Montana	7,100	1.0%
20	Oregon	7,100	1.0%
23	Kansas	7,000	1.0%
24	Michigan	6,900	0.9%
25	Mississippi	6,600	0.9%
26	Minnesota	6,200	0.8%
27	Indiana	6,100	0.8%
27	Washington	6,100	0.8%
29	Florida	5,900	0.8%
30	Arkansas	5,600	0.8%
31	North Carolina	5,500	0.8%
32	New York	5,300	0.7%
33	South Carolina	4,600	0.6%
34	Tennessee	4,400	0.6%
34	Wisconsin	4,400	0.6%
36	Missouri	4,100	0.6%
37	Idaho	3,300	0.5%
38	Iowa	2,300	0.3%
39	Maine	2,200	0.3%
40	New Jersey	1,400	0.2%
41	Maryland	1,300	0.2%
42	Massachusetts	1,000	0.1%
42	Nebraska	1,000	0.1%
42	New Hampshire	1,000	0.1%
45	South Dakota	900	0.1%
46	Vermont	700	0.1%
47	Connecticut	500	0.1%
48	Rhode Island	200	0.0%
NA	Delaware**	NA	NA
NA	Hawaii**	NA	NA
	District of Columbia**	NA	NA

Source: U.S. Department of Labor, Bureau of Labor Statistics
   "State Employment and Unemployment" (press release, January 24, 2020, www.bls.gov/bls/newsrels.htm)
*Not seasonally adjusted preliminary data as of December 2019. National total calculated through a different formula.
**The Bureau of Labor Statistics does not publish figures in this category for these states.

Percent of Nonfarm Employees in Mining and Logging in 2019

National Percent = 0.5% of Employees*

ALPHA ORDER

RANK	STATE	PERCENT
17	Alabama	0.4
3	Alaska	4.3
14	Arizona	0.5
17	Arkansas	0.4
33	California	0.1
10	Colorado	1.0
44	Connecticut	0.0
NA	Delaware**	NA
33	Florida	0.1
23	Georgia	0.2
NA	Hawaii**	NA
17	Idaho	0.4
33	Illinois	0.1
23	Indiana	0.2
33	Iowa	0.1
14	Kansas	0.5
17	Kentucky	0.4
8	Louisiana	1.8
22	Maine	0.3
44	Maryland	0.0
44	Massachusetts	0.0
23	Michigan	0.2
23	Minnesota	0.2
12	Mississippi	0.6
33	Missouri	0.1
9	Montana	1.5
33	Nebraska	0.1
11	Nevada	0.9
33	New Hampshire	0.1
44	New Jersey	0.0
4	New Mexico	3.0
33	New York	0.1
33	North Carolina	0.1
2	North Dakota	4.7
23	Ohio	0.2
5	Oklahoma	2.9
17	Oregon	0.4
14	Pennsylvania	0.5
44	Rhode Island	0.0
23	South Carolina	0.2
23	South Dakota	0.2
33	Tennessee	0.1
7	Texas	1.9
12	Utah	0.6
23	Vermont	0.2
23	Virginia	0.2
23	Washington	0.2
5	West Virginia	2.9
33	Wisconsin	0.1
1	Wyoming	7.0

RANK ORDER

RANK	STATE	PERCENT
1	Wyoming	7.0
2	North Dakota	4.7
3	Alaska	4.3
4	New Mexico	3.0
5	Oklahoma	2.9
5	West Virginia	2.9
7	Texas	1.9
8	Louisiana	1.8
9	Montana	1.5
10	Colorado	1.0
11	Nevada	0.9
12	Mississippi	0.6
12	Utah	0.6
14	Arizona	0.5
14	Kansas	0.5
14	Pennsylvania	0.5
17	Alabama	0.4
17	Arkansas	0.4
17	Idaho	0.4
17	Kentucky	0.4
17	Oregon	0.4
22	Maine	0.3
23	Georgia	0.2
23	Indiana	0.2
23	Michigan	0.2
23	Minnesota	0.2
23	Ohio	0.2
23	South Carolina	0.2
23	South Dakota	0.2
23	Vermont	0.2
23	Virginia	0.2
23	Washington	0.2
33	California	0.1
33	Florida	0.1
33	Illinois	0.1
33	Iowa	0.1
33	Missouri	0.1
33	Nebraska	0.1
33	New Hampshire	0.1
33	New York	0.1
33	North Carolina	0.1
33	Tennessee	0.1
33	Wisconsin	0.1
44	Connecticut	0.0
44	Maryland	0.0
44	Massachusetts	0.0
44	New Jersey	0.0
44	Rhode Island	0.0
NA	Delaware**	NA
NA	Hawaii**	NA
	District of Columbia**	NA

Source: CQ Press using data from U.S. Department of Labor, Bureau of Labor Statistics
"State Employment and Unemployment" (press release, January 24, 2020, www.bls.gov/bls/newsrels.htm)
*Not seasonally adjusted preliminary data as of December 2019. National figure calculated through a different formula.
**The Bureau of Labor Statistics does not publish seasonally adjusted figures in this category for these states.

Employees in Professional and Business Services in 2019

National Total = 21,651,000 Employees*

RANK	STATE	EMPLOYEES	% of USA
24	Alabama	261,000	1.2%
49	Alaska	27,000	0.1%
17	Arizona	443,300	2.0%
33	Arkansas	150,400	0.7%
1	California	2,768,100	12.8%
15	Colorado	456,700	2.1%
27	Connecticut	222,800	1.0%
44	Delaware	62,000	0.3%
3	Florida	1,424,300	6.6%
9	Georgia	702,000	3.2%
40	Hawaii	84,100	0.4%
38	Idaho	103,100	0.5%
5	Illinois	957,000	4.4%
21	Indiana	348,100	1.6%
34	Iowa	140,100	0.6%
32	Kansas	186,300	0.9%
29	Kentucky	214,800	1.0%
28	Louisiana	214,900	1.0%
42	Maine	68,600	0.3%
14	Maryland	462,800	2.1%
13	Massachusetts	592,800	2.7%
11	Michigan	660,400	3.1%
20	Minnesota	374,400	1.7%
37	Mississippi	107,400	0.5%
19	Missouri	387,200	1.8%
45	Montana	44,800	0.2%
35	Nebraska	122,900	0.6%
30	Nevada	206,100	1.0%
39	New Hampshire	85,600	0.4%
10	New Jersey	674,500	3.1%
36	New Mexico	110,100	0.5%
4	New York	1,374,100	6.3%
12	North Carolina	643,900	3.0%
46	North Dakota	35,900	0.2%
8	Ohio	738,400	3.4%
31	Oklahoma	187,100	0.9%
25	Oregon	254,000	1.2%
6	Pennsylvania	817,200	3.8%
41	Rhode Island	69,500	0.3%
23	South Carolina	294,500	1.4%
47	South Dakota	33,800	0.2%
18	Tennessee	427,300	2.0%
2	Texas	1,803,400	8.3%
26	Utah	225,000	1.0%
48	Vermont	30,400	0.1%
7	Virginia	760,500	3.5%
16	Washington	443,700	2.0%
43	West Virginia	67,600	0.3%
22	Wisconsin	325,900	1.5%
50	Wyoming	18,200	0.1%

RANK	STATE	EMPLOYEES	% of USA
1	California	2,768,100	12.8%
2	Texas	1,803,400	8.3%
3	Florida	1,424,300	6.6%
4	New York	1,374,100	6.3%
5	Illinois	957,000	4.4%
6	Pennsylvania	817,200	3.8%
7	Virginia	760,500	3.5%
8	Ohio	738,400	3.4%
9	Georgia	702,000	3.2%
10	New Jersey	674,500	3.1%
11	Michigan	660,400	3.1%
12	North Carolina	643,900	3.0%
13	Massachusetts	592,800	2.7%
14	Maryland	462,800	2.1%
15	Colorado	456,700	2.1%
16	Washington	443,700	2.0%
17	Arizona	443,300	2.0%
18	Tennessee	427,300	2.0%
19	Missouri	387,200	1.8%
20	Minnesota	374,400	1.7%
21	Indiana	348,100	1.6%
22	Wisconsin	325,900	1.5%
23	South Carolina	294,500	1.4%
24	Alabama	261,000	1.2%
25	Oregon	254,000	1.2%
26	Utah	225,000	1.0%
27	Connecticut	222,800	1.0%
28	Louisiana	214,900	1.0%
29	Kentucky	214,800	1.0%
30	Nevada	206,100	1.0%
31	Oklahoma	187,100	0.9%
32	Kansas	186,300	0.9%
33	Arkansas	150,400	0.7%
34	Iowa	140,100	0.6%
35	Nebraska	122,900	0.6%
36	New Mexico	110,100	0.5%
37	Mississippi	107,400	0.5%
38	Idaho	103,100	0.5%
39	New Hampshire	85,600	0.4%
40	Hawaii	84,100	0.4%
41	Rhode Island	69,500	0.3%
42	Maine	68,600	0.3%
43	West Virginia	67,600	0.3%
44	Delaware	62,000	0.3%
45	Montana	44,800	0.2%
46	North Dakota	35,900	0.2%
47	South Dakota	33,800	0.2%
48	Vermont	30,400	0.1%
49	Alaska	27,000	0.1%
50	Wyoming	18,200	0.1%
	District of Columbia	172,300	0.8%

Source: U.S. Department of Labor, Bureau of Labor Statistics
"State Employment and Unemployment" (press release, January 24, 2020, www.bls.gov/bls/newsrels.htm)
*Seasonally adjusted preliminary data as of December 2019. National total calculated through a different formula.

Percent of Nonfarm Employees in Professional and Business Services in 2019

National Percent = 14.2% of Employees*

ALPHA ORDER				RANK ORDER		
RANK	STATE	PERCENT		RANK	STATE	PERCENT
32	Alabama	12.4		1	Virginia	18.8
47	Alaska	8.2		2	Maryland	16.6
10	Arizona	14.9		3	Colorado	16.3
35	Arkansas	11.7		4	Massachusetts	16.0
6	California	15.7		4	New Jersey	16.0
3	Colorado	16.3		6	California	15.7
25	Connecticut	13.1		7	Florida	15.6
23	Delaware	13.2		8	Illinois	15.5
7	Florida	15.6		9	Georgia	15.1
9	Georgia	15.1		10	Arizona	14.9
29	Hawaii	12.7		11	Michigan	14.8
19	Idaho	13.5		12	Nevada	14.3
8	Illinois	15.5		13	Utah	14.2
37	Indiana	11.0		14	New York	14.0
46	Iowa	8.8		14	North Carolina	14.0
27	Kansas	12.9		16	Texas	13.9
37	Kentucky	11.0		17	Rhode Island	13.7
40	Louisiana	10.8		18	Tennessee	13.6
40	Maine	10.8		19	Idaho	13.5
2	Maryland	16.6		19	Pennsylvania	13.5
4	Massachusetts	16.0		21	South Carolina	13.4
11	Michigan	14.8		22	Missouri	13.3
30	Minnesota	12.6		23	Delaware	13.2
44	Mississippi	9.2		23	Ohio	13.2
22	Missouri	13.3		25	Connecticut	13.1
44	Montana	9.2		26	Oregon	13.0
34	Nebraska	11.8		27	Kansas	12.9
12	Nevada	14.3		28	New Mexico	12.8
32	New Hampshire	12.4		29	Hawaii	12.7
4	New Jersey	16.0		30	Minnesota	12.6
28	New Mexico	12.8		30	Washington	12.6
14	New York	14.0		32	Alabama	12.4
14	North Carolina	14.0		32	New Hampshire	12.4
47	North Dakota	8.2		34	Nebraska	11.8
23	Ohio	13.2		35	Arkansas	11.7
36	Oklahoma	11.1		36	Oklahoma	11.1
26	Oregon	13.0		37	Indiana	11.0
19	Pennsylvania	13.5		37	Kentucky	11.0
17	Rhode Island	13.7		39	Wisconsin	10.9
21	South Carolina	13.4		40	Louisiana	10.8
49	South Dakota	7.5		40	Maine	10.8
18	Tennessee	13.6		42	Vermont	9.6
16	Texas	13.9		43	West Virginia	9.3
13	Utah	14.2		44	Mississippi	9.2
42	Vermont	9.6		44	Montana	9.2
1	Virginia	18.8		46	Iowa	8.8
30	Washington	12.6		47	Alaska	8.2
43	West Virginia	9.3		47	North Dakota	8.2
39	Wisconsin	10.9		49	South Dakota	7.5
50	Wyoming	6.4		50	Wyoming	6.4
					District of Columbia	21.4

Source: CQ Press using data from U.S. Department of Labor, Bureau of Labor Statistics
"State Employment and Unemployment" (press release, January 24, 2020, www.bls.gov/bls/newsrels.htm)
*Seasonally adjusted preliminary data as of December 2019. National figure calculated through a different formula.

Employees in Trade, Transportation, and Public Utilities in 2019

National Total = 27,913,000 Employees*

ALPHA ORDER					RANK ORDER			
RANK	STATE	EMPLOYEES	% of USA		RANK	STATE	EMPLOYEES	% of USA
25	Alabama	386,200	1.4%		1	California	3,058,800	10.9%
48	Alaska	65,300	0.2%		2	Texas	2,559,400	9.2%
17	Arizona	554,200	2.0%		3	Florida	1,816,500	6.5%
34	Arkansas	255,700	0.9%		4	New York	1,574,100	5.6%
1	California	3,058,800	10.9%		5	Illinois	1,218,600	4.4%
21	Colorado	479,800	1.7%		6	Pennsylvania	1,132,000	4.0%
31	Connecticut	291,600	1.0%		7	Ohio	1,024,500	3.7%
46	Delaware	81,100	0.3%		8	Georgia	963,700	3.4%
3	Florida	1,816,500	6.5%		9	New Jersey	894,700	3.2%
8	Georgia	963,700	3.4%		10	North Carolina	857,600	3.1%
42	Hawaii	119,400	0.4%		11	Michigan	797,700	2.9%
37	Idaho	145,700	0.5%		12	Virginia	654,800	2.3%
5	Illinois	1,218,600	4.4%		13	Washington	651,300	2.3%
15	Indiana	594,900	2.1%		14	Tennessee	640,900	2.3%
28	Iowa	310,700	1.1%		15	Indiana	594,900	2.1%
32	Kansas	268,100	1.0%		16	Massachusetts	581,000	2.1%
24	Kentucky	404,100	1.4%		17	Arizona	554,200	2.0%
26	Louisiana	379,100	1.4%		18	Wisconsin	548,200	2.0%
41	Maine	120,400	0.4%		19	Missouri	541,400	1.9%
22	Maryland	469,300	1.7%		20	Minnesota	539,000	1.9%
16	Massachusetts	581,000	2.1%		21	Colorado	479,800	1.7%
11	Michigan	797,700	2.9%		22	Maryland	469,300	1.7%
20	Minnesota	539,000	1.9%		23	South Carolina	417,900	1.5%
35	Mississippi	235,400	0.8%		24	Kentucky	404,100	1.4%
19	Missouri	541,400	1.9%		25	Alabama	386,200	1.4%
43	Montana	96,600	0.3%		26	Louisiana	379,100	1.4%
36	Nebraska	200,500	0.7%		27	Oregon	355,500	1.3%
33	Nevada	256,000	0.9%		28	Iowa	310,700	1.1%
38	New Hampshire	140,600	0.5%		29	Oklahoma	306,300	1.1%
9	New Jersey	894,700	3.2%		30	Utah	294,900	1.1%
39	New Mexico	138,100	0.5%		31	Connecticut	291,600	1.0%
4	New York	1,574,100	5.6%		32	Kansas	268,100	1.0%
10	North Carolina	857,600	3.1%		33	Nevada	256,000	0.9%
44	North Dakota	92,100	0.3%		34	Arkansas	255,700	0.9%
7	Ohio	1,024,500	3.7%		35	Mississippi	235,400	0.8%
29	Oklahoma	306,300	1.1%		36	Nebraska	200,500	0.7%
27	Oregon	355,500	1.3%		37	Idaho	145,700	0.5%
6	Pennsylvania	1,132,000	4.0%		38	New Hampshire	140,600	0.5%
47	Rhode Island	80,200	0.3%		39	New Mexico	138,100	0.5%
23	South Carolina	417,900	1.5%		40	West Virginia	131,500	0.5%
45	South Dakota	89,900	0.3%		41	Maine	120,400	0.4%
14	Tennessee	640,900	2.3%		42	Hawaii	119,400	0.4%
2	Texas	2,559,400	9.2%		43	Montana	96,600	0.3%
30	Utah	294,900	1.1%		44	North Dakota	92,100	0.3%
49	Vermont	54,100	0.2%		45	South Dakota	89,900	0.3%
12	Virginia	654,800	2.3%		46	Delaware	81,100	0.3%
13	Washington	651,300	2.3%		47	Rhode Island	80,200	0.3%
40	West Virginia	131,500	0.5%		48	Alaska	65,300	0.2%
18	Wisconsin	548,200	2.0%		49	Vermont	54,100	0.2%
50	Wyoming	52,700	0.2%		50	Wyoming	52,700	0.2%
						District of Columbia	33,400	0.1%

Source: U.S. Department of Labor, Bureau of Labor Statistics
   "State Employment and Unemployment" (press release, January 24, 2020, www.bls.gov/bls/newsrels.htm)
*Seasonally adjusted preliminary data as of December 2019. National total calculated through a different formula.

Percent of Nonfarm Employees in
Trade, Transportation, and Public Utilities in 2019
National Percent = 18.4% of Employees*

ALPHA ORDER

RANK	STATE	PERCENT
29	Alabama	18.4
12	Alaska	19.8
24	Arizona	18.6
10	Arkansas	19.9
40	California	17.4
42	Colorado	17.1
42	Connecticut	17.1
41	Delaware	17.2
8	Florida	20.0
3	Georgia	20.7
37	Hawaii	18.0
17	Idaho	19.1
13	Illinois	19.7
21	Indiana	18.8
15	Iowa	19.5
24	Kansas	18.6
3	Kentucky	20.7
19	Louisiana	19.0
19	Maine	19.0
45	Maryland	16.8
50	Massachusetts	15.7
38	Michigan	17.9
33	Minnesota	18.2
7	Mississippi	20.1
24	Missouri	18.6
10	Montana	19.9
16	Nebraska	19.3
39	Nevada	17.8
5	New Hampshire	20.4
1	New Jersey	21.2
47	New Mexico	16.0
47	New York	16.0
22	North Carolina	18.7
2	North Dakota	21.1
31	Ohio	18.3
35	Oklahoma	18.1
33	Oregon	18.2
22	Pennsylvania	18.7
49	Rhode Island	15.8
17	South Carolina	19.1
8	South Dakota	20.0
5	Tennessee	20.4
13	Texas	19.7
24	Utah	18.6
42	Vermont	17.1
46	Virginia	16.2
28	Washington	18.5
35	West Virginia	18.1
31	Wisconsin	18.3
29	Wyoming	18.4

RANK ORDER

RANK	STATE	PERCENT
1	New Jersey	21.2
2	North Dakota	21.1
3	Georgia	20.7
3	Kentucky	20.7
5	New Hampshire	20.4
5	Tennessee	20.4
7	Mississippi	20.1
8	Florida	20.0
8	South Dakota	20.0
10	Arkansas	19.9
10	Montana	19.9
12	Alaska	19.8
13	Illinois	19.7
13	Texas	19.7
15	Iowa	19.5
16	Nebraska	19.3
17	Idaho	19.1
17	South Carolina	19.1
19	Louisiana	19.0
19	Maine	19.0
21	Indiana	18.8
22	North Carolina	18.7
22	Pennsylvania	18.7
24	Arizona	18.6
24	Kansas	18.6
24	Missouri	18.6
24	Utah	18.6
28	Washington	18.5
29	Alabama	18.4
29	Wyoming	18.4
31	Ohio	18.3
31	Wisconsin	18.3
33	Minnesota	18.2
33	Oregon	18.2
35	Oklahoma	18.1
35	West Virginia	18.1
37	Hawaii	18.0
38	Michigan	17.9
39	Nevada	17.8
40	California	17.4
41	Delaware	17.2
42	Colorado	17.1
42	Connecticut	17.1
42	Vermont	17.1
45	Maryland	16.8
46	Virginia	16.2
47	New Mexico	16.0
47	New York	16.0
49	Rhode Island	15.8
50	Massachusetts	15.7

| | District of Columbia | 4.2 |

Source: CQ Press using data from U.S. Department of Labor, Bureau of Labor Statistics
    "State Employment and Unemployment" (press release, January 24, 2020, www.bls.gov/bls/newsrels.htm)
*Seasonally adjusted preliminary data as of December 2019. National figure calculated through a different formula.

VII. Energy and Environment

Energy Consumption in 2017

National Total = 97,621,500,000,000,000 BTUs*

ALPHA ORDER					RANK ORDER			
RANK	STATE	BTUs	% of USA		RANK	STATE	BTUs	% of USA
17	Alabama	1,900,900,000,000,000	1.9%		1	Texas	13,365,900,000,000,000	13.7%
40	Alaska	608,100,000,000,000	0.6%		2	California	7,881,300,000,000,000	8.1%
25	Arizona	1,475,400,000,000,000	1.5%		3	Louisiana	4,481,800,000,000,000	4.6%
31	Arkansas	1,057,600,000,000,000	1.1%		4	Florida	4,208,500,000,000,000	4.3%
2	California	7,881,300,000,000,000	8.1%		5	Illinois	3,871,500,000,000,000	4.0%
26	Colorado	1,462,900,000,000,000	1.5%		6	Pennsylvania	3,807,700,000,000,000	3.9%
36	Connecticut	726,400,000,000,000	0.7%		7	New York	3,684,100,000,000,000	3.8%
48	Delaware	269,800,000,000,000	0.3%		8	Ohio	3,643,700,000,000,000	3.7%
4	Florida	4,208,500,000,000,000	4.3%		9	Georgia	2,802,200,000,000,000	2.9%
9	Georgia	2,802,200,000,000,000	2.9%		10	Michigan	2,774,500,000,000,000	2.8%
47	Hawaii	283,400,000,000,000	0.3%		11	Indiana	2,700,500,000,000,000	2.8%
41	Idaho	553,900,000,000,000	0.6%		12	North Carolina	2,503,100,000,000,000	2.6%
5	Illinois	3,871,500,000,000,000	4.0%		13	Virginia	2,302,600,000,000,000	2.4%
11	Indiana	2,700,500,000,000,000	2.8%		14	Tennessee	2,166,500,000,000,000	2.2%
24	Iowa	1,559,000,000,000,000	1.6%		15	New Jersey	2,134,900,000,000,000	2.2%
30	Kansas	1,073,200,000,000,000	1.1%		16	Washington	2,096,900,000,000,000	2.1%
21	Kentucky	1,658,200,000,000,000	1.7%		17	Alabama	1,900,900,000,000,000	1.9%
3	Louisiana	4,481,800,000,000,000	4.6%		18	Minnesota	1,832,300,000,000,000	1.9%
44	Maine	392,000,000,000,000	0.4%		19	Wisconsin	1,805,800,000,000,000	1.8%
28	Maryland	1,314,700,000,000,000	1.3%		20	Missouri	1,726,100,000,000,000	1.8%
27	Massachusetts	1,424,200,000,000,000	1.5%		21	Kentucky	1,658,200,000,000,000	1.7%
10	Michigan	2,774,500,000,000,000	2.8%		22	Oklahoma	1,643,800,000,000,000	1.7%
18	Minnesota	1,832,300,000,000,000	1.9%		23	South Carolina	1,643,600,000,000,000	1.7%
29	Mississippi	1,176,400,000,000,000	1.2%		24	Iowa	1,559,000,000,000,000	1.6%
20	Missouri	1,726,100,000,000,000	1.8%		25	Arizona	1,475,400,000,000,000	1.5%
43	Montana	420,600,000,000,000	0.4%		26	Colorado	1,462,900,000,000,000	1.5%
33	Nebraska	876,000,000,000,000	0.9%		27	Massachusetts	1,424,200,000,000,000	1.5%
37	Nevada	707,200,000,000,000	0.7%		28	Maryland	1,314,700,000,000,000	1.3%
46	New Hampshire	317,500,000,000,000	0.3%		29	Mississippi	1,176,400,000,000,000	1.2%
15	New Jersey	2,134,900,000,000,000	2.2%		30	Kansas	1,073,200,000,000,000	1.1%
38	New Mexico	683,400,000,000,000	0.7%		31	Arkansas	1,057,600,000,000,000	1.1%
7	New York	3,684,100,000,000,000	3.8%		32	Oregon	1,032,200,000,000,000	1.1%
12	North Carolina	2,503,100,000,000,000	2.6%		33	Nebraska	876,000,000,000,000	0.9%
39	North Dakota	631,100,000,000,000	0.6%		34	Utah	828,700,000,000,000	0.8%
8	Ohio	3,643,700,000,000,000	3.7%		35	West Virginia	756,400,000,000,000	0.8%
22	Oklahoma	1,643,800,000,000,000	1.7%		36	Connecticut	726,400,000,000,000	0.7%
32	Oregon	1,032,200,000,000,000	1.1%		37	Nevada	707,200,000,000,000	0.7%
6	Pennsylvania	3,807,700,000,000,000	3.9%		38	New Mexico	683,400,000,000,000	0.7%
49	Rhode Island	183,900,000,000,000	0.2%		39	North Dakota	631,100,000,000,000	0.6%
23	South Carolina	1,643,600,000,000,000	1.7%		40	Alaska	608,100,000,000,000	0.6%
45	South Dakota	384,900,000,000,000	0.4%		41	Idaho	553,900,000,000,000	0.6%
14	Tennessee	2,166,500,000,000,000	2.2%		42	Wyoming	512,200,000,000,000	0.5%
1	Texas	13,365,900,000,000,000	13.7%		43	Montana	420,600,000,000,000	0.4%
34	Utah	828,700,000,000,000	0.8%		44	Maine	392,000,000,000,000	0.4%
50	Vermont	134,800,000,000,000	0.1%		45	South Dakota	384,900,000,000,000	0.4%
13	Virginia	2,302,600,000,000,000	2.4%		46	New Hampshire	317,500,000,000,000	0.3%
16	Washington	2,096,900,000,000,000	2.1%		47	Hawaii	283,400,000,000,000	0.3%
35	West Virginia	756,400,000,000,000	0.8%		48	Delaware	269,800,000,000,000	0.3%
19	Wisconsin	1,805,800,000,000,000	1.8%		49	Rhode Island	183,900,000,000,000	0.2%
42	Wyoming	512,200,000,000,000	0.5%		50	Vermont	134,800,000,000,000	0.1%
						District of Columbia	167,600,000,000,000	0.2%

Source: U.S. Department of Energy, Energy Information Administration
    "State Energy Data 2017: Consumption" (https://www.eia.gov/state/seds/)
*British Thermal Units: The amount of heat required to raise the temperature of one pound of water one degree. National total includes 19.1 trillion BTU of net imports of coal coke that are not allocated to the states.

Per Capita Energy Consumption in 2017

National Per Capita = 300,387,212 BTUs*

ALPHA ORDER				RANK ORDER		
RANK	**STATE**	**PER CAPITA**		**RANK**	**STATE**	**PER CAPITA**
14	Alabama	389,969,322		1	Louisiana	959,585,146
4	Alaska	822,090,037		2	Wyoming	884,734,105
43	Arizona	209,454,617		3	North Dakota	835,958,259
17	Arkansas	352,375,352		4	Alaska	822,090,037
47	California	200,243,927		5	Iowa	496,251,850
35	Colorado	260,678,898		6	Texas	472,372,187
45	Connecticut	203,285,649		7	Nebraska	457,215,153
30	Delaware	281,974,827		8	South Dakota	440,960,145
46	Florida	200,752,609		9	Oklahoma	418,129,705
33	Georgia	269,174,945		10	West Virginia	416,289,672
48	Hawaii	198,961,944		11	Indiana	405,597,531
22	Idaho	322,463,272		12	Montana	399,626,787
25	Illinois	302,962,056		13	Mississippi	393,640,978
11	Indiana	405,597,531		14	Alabama	389,969,322
5	Iowa	496,251,850		15	Kentucky	372,439,395
16	Kansas	368,959,796		16	Kansas	368,959,796
15	Kentucky	372,439,395		17	Arkansas	352,375,352
1	Louisiana	959,585,146		18	Minnesota	329,181,511
27	Maine	293,718,324		19	South Carolina	327,327,679
41	Maryland	218,248,474		20	New Mexico	326,706,773
44	Massachusetts	207,615,715		21	Tennessee	322,934,105
31	Michigan	278,197,963		22	Idaho	322,463,272
18	Minnesota	329,181,511		23	Ohio	312,505,092
13	Mississippi	393,640,978		24	Wisconsin	311,872,537
28	Missouri	282,658,143		25	Illinois	302,962,056
12	Montana	399,626,787		26	Pennsylvania	297,764,068
7	Nebraska	457,215,153		27	Maine	293,718,324
39	Nevada	238,122,095		28	Missouri	282,658,143
40	New Hampshire	235,396,693		29	Washington	282,473,090
38	New Jersey	240,267,176		30	Delaware	281,974,827
20	New Mexico	326,706,773		31	Michigan	278,197,963
49	New York	188,064,344		32	Virginia	272,059,589
37	North Carolina	243,771,251		33	Georgia	269,174,945
3	North Dakota	835,958,259		34	Utah	267,232,756
23	Ohio	312,505,092		35	Colorado	260,678,898
9	Oklahoma	418,129,705		36	Oregon	249,105,554
36	Oregon	249,105,554		37	North Carolina	243,771,251
26	Pennsylvania	297,764,068		38	New Jersey	240,267,176
50	Rhode Island	174,201,670		39	Nevada	238,122,095
19	South Carolina	327,327,679		40	New Hampshire	235,396,693
8	South Dakota	440,960,145		41	Maryland	218,248,474
21	Tennessee	322,934,105		42	Vermont	215,906,616
6	Texas	472,372,187		43	Arizona	209,454,617
34	Utah	267,232,756		44	Massachusetts	207,615,715
42	Vermont	215,906,616		45	Connecticut	203,285,649
32	Virginia	272,059,589		46	Florida	200,752,609
29	Washington	282,473,090		47	California	200,243,927
10	West Virginia	416,289,672		48	Hawaii	198,961,944
24	Wisconsin	311,872,537		49	New York	188,064,344
2	Wyoming	884,734,105		50	Rhode Island	174,201,670
					District of Columbia	241,183,700

Source: CQ Press using data from U.S. Department of Energy, Energy Information Administration
    "State Energy Data 2017: Consumption" (https://www.eia.gov/state/seds/)
*British Thermal Units: The amount of heat required to raise the temperature of one pound of water one degree. National figure includes 17.8 trillion BTU of net imports of coal coke that are not allocated to the states.

Energy Prices in 2017

National Rate = $17.30 per Million BTUs*

ALPHA ORDER

RANK	STATE	RATE
40	Alabama	$15.97
17	Alaska	18.74
3	Arizona	22.34
42	Arkansas	15.76
7	California	21.75
29	Colorado	17.21
2	Connecticut	23.24
11	Delaware	20.19
10	Florida	20.44
22	Georgia	17.92
1	Hawaii	27.81
35	Idaho	16.66
41	Illinois	15.89
45	Indiana	15.10
48	Iowa	13.68
28	Kansas	17.30
33	Kentucky	16.73
50	Louisiana	10.28
21	Maine	18.15
8	Maryland	21.55
6	Massachusetts	22.13
36	Michigan	16.56
38	Minnesota	16.32
39	Mississippi	16.08
16	Missouri	18.77
30	Montana	17.20
43	Nebraska	15.46
18	Nevada	18.54
4	New Hampshire	22.28
14	New Jersey	18.96
15	New Mexico	18.86
12	New York	19.78
13	North Carolina	19.00
49	North Dakota	13.36
34	Ohio	16.67
44	Oklahoma	15.37
19	Oregon	18.40
23	Pennsylvania	17.85
5	Rhode Island	22.17
20	South Carolina	18.31
37	South Dakota	16.34
27	Tennessee	17.49
47	Texas	14.04
31	Utah	16.89
9	Vermont	21.45
24	Virginia	17.82
25	Washington	17.68
26	West Virginia	17.60
32	Wisconsin	16.76
46	Wyoming	14.51

RANK ORDER

RANK	STATE	RATE
1	Hawaii	$27.81
2	Connecticut	23.24
3	Arizona	22.34
4	New Hampshire	22.28
5	Rhode Island	22.17
6	Massachusetts	22.13
7	California	21.75
8	Maryland	21.55
9	Vermont	21.45
10	Florida	20.44
11	Delaware	20.19
12	New York	19.78
13	North Carolina	19.00
14	New Jersey	18.96
15	New Mexico	18.86
16	Missouri	18.77
17	Alaska	18.74
18	Nevada	18.54
19	Oregon	18.40
20	South Carolina	18.31
21	Maine	18.15
22	Georgia	17.92
23	Pennsylvania	17.85
24	Virginia	17.82
25	Washington	17.68
26	West Virginia	17.60
27	Tennessee	17.49
28	Kansas	17.30
29	Colorado	17.21
30	Montana	17.20
31	Utah	16.89
32	Wisconsin	16.76
33	Kentucky	16.73
34	Ohio	16.67
35	Idaho	16.66
36	Michigan	16.56
37	South Dakota	16.34
38	Minnesota	16.32
39	Mississippi	16.08
40	Alabama	15.97
41	Illinois	15.89
42	Arkansas	15.76
43	Nebraska	15.46
44	Oklahoma	15.37
45	Indiana	15.10
46	Wyoming	14.51
47	Texas	14.04
48	Iowa	13.68
49	North Dakota	13.36
50	Louisiana	10.28
	District of Columbia	22.87

Source: U.S. Department of Energy, Energy Information Administration
   "State Energy Data 2017: Prices and Expenditures" (https://www.eia.gov/state/seds/)
*British Thermal Units: The amount of heat required to raise the temperature of one pound of water one degree.

Energy Expenditures in 2017

National Total = $1,136,496,000,000*

ALPHA ORDER

RANK	STATE	EXPENDITURES	% of USA
20	Alabama	$20,436,000,000	1.8%
44	Alaska	5,112,000,000	0.4%
19	Arizona	20,521,000,000	1.8%
32	Arkansas	11,305,000,000	1.0%
2	California	124,724,000,000	11.0%
26	Colorado	16,391,000,000	1.4%
31	Connecticut	12,536,000,000	1.1%
48	Delaware	3,336,000,000	0.3%
3	Florida	57,074,000,000	5.0%
8	Georgia	34,011,000,000	3.0%
41	Hawaii	5,549,000,000	0.5%
39	Idaho	6,311,000,000	0.6%
6	Illinois	40,510,000,000	3.6%
14	Indiana	27,101,000,000	2.4%
28	Iowa	13,890,000,000	1.2%
33	Kansas	11,180,000,000	1.0%
25	Kentucky	17,338,000,000	1.5%
10	Louisiana	32,041,000,000	2.8%
40	Maine	5,624,000,000	0.5%
24	Maryland	18,541,000,000	1.6%
17	Massachusetts	23,206,000,000	2.0%
9	Michigan	32,394,000,000	2.9%
22	Minnesota	20,067,000,000	1.8%
29	Mississippi	13,142,000,000	1.2%
18	Missouri	21,162,000,000	1.9%
45	Montana	4,578,000,000	0.4%
36	Nebraska	8,244,000,000	0.7%
35	Nevada	9,214,000,000	0.8%
43	New Hampshire	5,193,000,000	0.5%
12	New Jersey	29,541,000,000	2.6%
38	New Mexico	7,368,000,000	0.6%
4	New York	54,108,000,000	4.8%
11	North Carolina	30,734,000,000	2.7%
42	North Dakota	5,352,000,000	0.5%
7	Ohio	40,371,000,000	3.6%
27	Oklahoma	15,610,000,000	1.4%
30	Oregon	13,019,000,000	1.1%
5	Pennsylvania	43,927,000,000	3.9%
49	Rhode Island	3,229,000,000	0.3%
23	South Carolina	18,962,000,000	1.7%
47	South Dakota	3,836,000,000	0.3%
15	Tennessee	24,093,000,000	2.1%
1	Texas	128,571,000,000	11.3%
34	Utah	9,278,000,000	0.8%
50	Vermont	2,589,000,000	0.2%
13	Virginia	27,218,000,000	2.4%
16	Washington	23,938,000,000	2.1%
37	West Virginia	7,470,000,000	0.7%
21	Wisconsin	20,408,000,000	1.8%
46	Wyoming	4,442,000,000	0.4%

RANK ORDER

RANK	STATE	EXPENDITURES	% of USA
1	Texas	$128,571,000,000	11.3%
2	California	124,724,000,000	11.0%
3	Florida	57,074,000,000	5.0%
4	New York	54,108,000,000	4.8%
5	Pennsylvania	43,927,000,000	3.9%
6	Illinois	40,510,000,000	3.6%
7	Ohio	40,371,000,000	3.6%
8	Georgia	34,011,000,000	3.0%
9	Michigan	32,394,000,000	2.9%
10	Louisiana	32,041,000,000	2.8%
11	North Carolina	30,734,000,000	2.7%
12	New Jersey	29,541,000,000	2.6%
13	Virginia	27,218,000,000	2.4%
14	Indiana	27,101,000,000	2.4%
15	Tennessee	24,093,000,000	2.1%
16	Washington	23,938,000,000	2.1%
17	Massachusetts	23,206,000,000	2.0%
18	Missouri	21,162,000,000	1.9%
19	Arizona	20,521,000,000	1.8%
20	Alabama	20,436,000,000	1.8%
21	Wisconsin	20,408,000,000	1.8%
22	Minnesota	20,067,000,000	1.8%
23	South Carolina	18,962,000,000	1.7%
24	Maryland	18,541,000,000	1.6%
25	Kentucky	17,338,000,000	1.5%
26	Colorado	16,391,000,000	1.4%
27	Oklahoma	15,610,000,000	1.4%
28	Iowa	13,890,000,000	1.2%
29	Mississippi	13,142,000,000	1.2%
30	Oregon	13,019,000,000	1.1%
31	Connecticut	12,536,000,000	1.1%
32	Arkansas	11,305,000,000	1.0%
33	Kansas	11,180,000,000	1.0%
34	Utah	9,278,000,000	0.8%
35	Nevada	9,214,000,000	0.8%
36	Nebraska	8,244,000,000	0.7%
37	West Virginia	7,470,000,000	0.7%
38	New Mexico	7,368,000,000	0.6%
39	Idaho	6,311,000,000	0.6%
40	Maine	5,624,000,000	0.5%
41	Hawaii	5,549,000,000	0.5%
42	North Dakota	5,352,000,000	0.5%
43	New Hampshire	5,193,000,000	0.5%
44	Alaska	5,112,000,000	0.4%
45	Montana	4,578,000,000	0.4%
46	Wyoming	4,442,000,000	0.4%
47	South Dakota	3,836,000,000	0.3%
48	Delaware	3,336,000,000	0.3%
49	Rhode Island	3,229,000,000	0.3%
50	Vermont	2,589,000,000	0.2%
	District of Columbia	1,970,000,000	0.2%

Source: U.S. Department of Energy, Energy Information Administration
  "State Energy Data 2017: Prices and Expenditures" (https://www.eia.gov/state/seds/)
*The national total includes a negative $269 million for coal coke net imports, which is not allocated to the states.

Per Capita Energy Expenditures in 2017

National Per Capita = $3,497

<table>
<tr><td colspan="3">ALPHA ORDER</td><td colspan="3">RANK ORDER</td></tr>
<tr><th>RANK</th><th>STATE</th><th>PER CAPITA</th><th>RANK</th><th>STATE</th><th>PER CAPITA</th></tr>
<tr><td>12</td><td>Alabama</td><td>$4,192</td><td>1</td><td>Wyoming</td><td>$7,673</td></tr>
<tr><td>3</td><td>Alaska</td><td>6,911</td><td>2</td><td>North Dakota</td><td>7,089</td></tr>
<tr><td>48</td><td>Arizona</td><td>2,913</td><td>3</td><td>Alaska</td><td>6,911</td></tr>
<tr><td>22</td><td>Arkansas</td><td>3,767</td><td>4</td><td>Louisiana</td><td>6,860</td></tr>
<tr><td>40</td><td>California</td><td>3,169</td><td>5</td><td>Texas</td><td>4,544</td></tr>
<tr><td>47</td><td>Colorado</td><td>2,921</td><td>6</td><td>Iowa</td><td>4,421</td></tr>
<tr><td>28</td><td>Connecticut</td><td>3,508</td><td>7</td><td>Mississippi</td><td>4,398</td></tr>
<tr><td>29</td><td>Delaware</td><td>3,487</td><td>8</td><td>South Dakota</td><td>4,395</td></tr>
<tr><td>50</td><td>Florida</td><td>2,723</td><td>9</td><td>Montana</td><td>4,350</td></tr>
<tr><td>35</td><td>Georgia</td><td>3,267</td><td>10</td><td>Nebraska</td><td>4,303</td></tr>
<tr><td>17</td><td>Hawaii</td><td>3,896</td><td>11</td><td>Maine</td><td>4,214</td></tr>
<tr><td>23</td><td>Idaho</td><td>3,674</td><td>12</td><td>Alabama</td><td>4,192</td></tr>
<tr><td>39</td><td>Illinois</td><td>3,170</td><td>13</td><td>Vermont</td><td>4,147</td></tr>
<tr><td>15</td><td>Indiana</td><td>4,070</td><td>14</td><td>West Virginia</td><td>4,111</td></tr>
<tr><td>6</td><td>Iowa</td><td>4,421</td><td>15</td><td>Indiana</td><td>4,070</td></tr>
<tr><td>20</td><td>Kansas</td><td>3,844</td><td>16</td><td>Oklahoma</td><td>3,971</td></tr>
<tr><td>18</td><td>Kentucky</td><td>3,894</td><td>17</td><td>Hawaii</td><td>3,896</td></tr>
<tr><td>4</td><td>Louisiana</td><td>6,860</td><td>18</td><td>Kentucky</td><td>3,894</td></tr>
<tr><td>11</td><td>Maine</td><td>4,214</td><td>19</td><td>New Hampshire</td><td>3,850</td></tr>
<tr><td>43</td><td>Maryland</td><td>3,078</td><td>20</td><td>Kansas</td><td>3,844</td></tr>
<tr><td>33</td><td>Massachusetts</td><td>3,383</td><td>21</td><td>South Carolina</td><td>3,776</td></tr>
<tr><td>36</td><td>Michigan</td><td>3,248</td><td>22</td><td>Arkansas</td><td>3,767</td></tr>
<tr><td>24</td><td>Minnesota</td><td>3,605</td><td>23</td><td>Idaho</td><td>3,674</td></tr>
<tr><td>7</td><td>Mississippi</td><td>4,398</td><td>24</td><td>Minnesota</td><td>3,605</td></tr>
<tr><td>30</td><td>Missouri</td><td>3,465</td><td>25</td><td>Tennessee</td><td>3,591</td></tr>
<tr><td>9</td><td>Montana</td><td>4,350</td><td>26</td><td>Wisconsin</td><td>3,525</td></tr>
<tr><td>10</td><td>Nebraska</td><td>4,303</td><td>27</td><td>New Mexico</td><td>3,522</td></tr>
<tr><td>42</td><td>Nevada</td><td>3,102</td><td>28</td><td>Connecticut</td><td>3,508</td></tr>
<tr><td>19</td><td>New Hampshire</td><td>3,850</td><td>29</td><td>Delaware</td><td>3,487</td></tr>
<tr><td>34</td><td>New Jersey</td><td>3,325</td><td>30</td><td>Missouri</td><td>3,465</td></tr>
<tr><td>27</td><td>New Mexico</td><td>3,522</td><td>31</td><td>Ohio</td><td>3,462</td></tr>
<tr><td>49</td><td>New York</td><td>2,762</td><td>32</td><td>Pennsylvania</td><td>3,435</td></tr>
<tr><td>45</td><td>North Carolina</td><td>2,993</td><td>33</td><td>Massachusetts</td><td>3,383</td></tr>
<tr><td>2</td><td>North Dakota</td><td>7,089</td><td>34</td><td>New Jersey</td><td>3,325</td></tr>
<tr><td>31</td><td>Ohio</td><td>3,462</td><td>35</td><td>Georgia</td><td>3,267</td></tr>
<tr><td>16</td><td>Oklahoma</td><td>3,971</td><td>36</td><td>Michigan</td><td>3,248</td></tr>
<tr><td>41</td><td>Oregon</td><td>3,142</td><td>37</td><td>Washington</td><td>3,225</td></tr>
<tr><td>32</td><td>Pennsylvania</td><td>3,435</td><td>38</td><td>Virginia</td><td>3,216</td></tr>
<tr><td>44</td><td>Rhode Island</td><td>3,059</td><td>39</td><td>Illinois</td><td>3,170</td></tr>
<tr><td>21</td><td>South Carolina</td><td>3,776</td><td>40</td><td>California</td><td>3,169</td></tr>
<tr><td>8</td><td>South Dakota</td><td>4,395</td><td>41</td><td>Oregon</td><td>3,142</td></tr>
<tr><td>25</td><td>Tennessee</td><td>3,591</td><td>42</td><td>Nevada</td><td>3,102</td></tr>
<tr><td>5</td><td>Texas</td><td>4,544</td><td>43</td><td>Maryland</td><td>3,078</td></tr>
<tr><td>46</td><td>Utah</td><td>2,992</td><td>44</td><td>Rhode Island</td><td>3,059</td></tr>
<tr><td>13</td><td>Vermont</td><td>4,147</td><td>45</td><td>North Carolina</td><td>2,993</td></tr>
<tr><td>38</td><td>Virginia</td><td>3,216</td><td>46</td><td>Utah</td><td>2,992</td></tr>
<tr><td>37</td><td>Washington</td><td>3,225</td><td>47</td><td>Colorado</td><td>2,921</td></tr>
<tr><td>14</td><td>West Virginia</td><td>4,111</td><td>48</td><td>Arizona</td><td>2,913</td></tr>
<tr><td>26</td><td>Wisconsin</td><td>3,525</td><td>49</td><td>New York</td><td>2,762</td></tr>
<tr><td>1</td><td>Wyoming</td><td>7,673</td><td>50</td><td>Florida</td><td>2,723</td></tr>
<tr><td></td><td></td><td></td><td></td><td>District of Columbia</td><td>2,835</td></tr>
</table>

Source: CQ Press using data from U.S. Department of Energy, Energy Information Administration
"State Energy Data 2017: Prices and Expenditures" (https://www.eia.gov/state/seds/)

Average Monthly Electric Bill for Industrial Customers in 2018

National Average = $6,865 per Month

ALPHA ORDER				RANK ORDER		
RANK	STATE	MONTHLY BILL		RANK	STATE	MONTHLY BILL
10	Alabama	$23,014		1	Tennessee	$101,294
19	Alaska	13,888		2	Hawaii	96,027
22	Arizona	9,797		3	Vermont	61,432
47	Arkansas	2,320		4	Illinois	43,714
42	California	3,676		5	South Carolina	30,795
32	Colorado	6,248		6	Michigan	30,520
23	Connecticut	8,550		7	Virginia	27,368
12	Delaware	18,688		8	Wisconsin	25,777
36	Florida	5,116		9	Pennsylvania	23,855
28	Georgia	7,093		10	Alabama	23,014
2	Hawaii	96,027		11	Kentucky	20,279
49	Idaho	1,687		12	Delaware	18,688
4	Illinois	43,714		13	Nevada	18,003
16	Indiana	15,691		14	Iowa	16,329
14	Iowa	16,329		15	Ohio	15,993
44	Kansas	3,059		16	Indiana	15,691
11	Kentucky	20,279		17	Minnesota	14,986
24	Louisiana	8,532		18	North Carolina	14,402
26	Maine	7,695		19	Alaska	13,888
45	Maryland	3,015		20	New York	13,169
25	Massachusetts	7,915		21	Missouri	9,959
6	Michigan	30,520		22	Arizona	9,797
17	Minnesota	14,986		23	Connecticut	8,550
27	Mississippi	7,532		24	Louisiana	8,532
21	Missouri	9,959		25	Massachusetts	7,915
48	Montana	2,060		26	Maine	7,695
50	Nebraska	1,122		27	Mississippi	7,532
13	Nevada	18,003		28	Georgia	7,093
29	New Hampshire	6,910		29	New Hampshire	6,910
35	New Jersey	5,206		30	West Virginia	6,571
41	New Mexico	4,259		31	North Dakota	6,441
20	New York	13,169		32	Colorado	6,248
18	North Carolina	14,402		33	Rhode Island	5,314
31	North Dakota	6,441		34	Wyoming	5,293
15	Ohio	15,993		35	New Jersey	5,206
39	Oklahoma	4,578		36	Florida	5,116
46	Oregon	2,734		37	Utah	4,776
9	Pennsylvania	23,855		38	South Dakota	4,771
33	Rhode Island	5,314		39	Oklahoma	4,578
5	South Carolina	30,795		40	Texas	4,415
38	South Dakota	4,771		41	New Mexico	4,259
1	Tennessee	101,294		42	California	3,676
40	Texas	4,415		43	Washington	3,638
37	Utah	4,776		44	Kansas	3,059
3	Vermont	61,432		45	Maryland	3,015
7	Virginia	27,368		46	Oregon	2,734
43	Washington	3,638		47	Arkansas	2,320
30	West Virginia	6,571		48	Montana	2,060
8	Wisconsin	25,777		49	Idaho	1,687
34	Wyoming	5,293		50	Nebraska	1,122
					District of Columbia	1,331,850

Source: U.S. Department of Energy, Energy Information Administration
"Electric Sales, Revenue and Average Price 2018" (https://www.eia.gov/electricity/sales_revenue_price/index.cfm)

Average Monthly Electric Bill for Commercial Customers in 2018

National Average = $660 per Month

ALPHA ORDER

RANK	STATE	MONTHLY BILL
28	Alabama	$593
10	Alaska	759
9	Arizona	817
48	Arkansas	404
4	California	920
42	Colorado	467
2	Connecticut	1,124
18	Delaware	636
27	Florida	599
14	Georgia	666
1	Hawaii	1,267
49	Idaho	384
21	Illinois	626
25	Indiana	605
46	Iowa	418
24	Kansas	613
33	Kentucky	531
22	Louisiana	622
40	Maine	483
3	Maryland	1,011
5	Massachusetts	908
14	Michigan	666
13	Minnesota	684
32	Mississippi	533
19	Missouri	635
50	Montana	381
43	Nebraska	457
41	Nevada	474
31	New Hampshire	543
11	New Jersey	757
34	New Mexico	524
8	New York	838
37	North Carolina	509
12	North Dakota	689
20	Ohio	631
38	Oklahoma	505
35	Oregon	514
44	Pennsylvania	449
6	Rhode Island	850
39	South Carolina	497
30	South Dakota	545
16	Tennessee	658
23	Texas	614
17	Utah	637
45	Vermont	446
7	Virginia	840
29	Washington	556
47	West Virginia	414
26	Wisconsin	604
35	Wyoming	514

RANK ORDER

RANK	STATE	MONTHLY BILL
1	Hawaii	$1,267
2	Connecticut	1,124
3	Maryland	1,011
4	California	920
5	Massachusetts	908
6	Rhode Island	850
7	Virginia	840
8	New York	838
9	Arizona	817
10	Alaska	759
11	New Jersey	757
12	North Dakota	689
13	Minnesota	684
14	Georgia	666
14	Michigan	666
16	Tennessee	658
17	Utah	637
18	Delaware	636
19	Missouri	635
20	Ohio	631
21	Illinois	626
22	Louisiana	622
23	Texas	614
24	Kansas	613
25	Indiana	605
26	Wisconsin	604
27	Florida	599
28	Alabama	593
29	Washington	556
30	South Dakota	545
31	New Hampshire	543
32	Mississippi	533
33	Kentucky	531
34	New Mexico	524
35	Oregon	514
35	Wyoming	514
37	North Carolina	509
38	Oklahoma	505
39	South Carolina	497
40	Maine	483
41	Nevada	474
42	Colorado	467
43	Nebraska	457
44	Pennsylvania	449
45	Vermont	446
46	Iowa	418
47	West Virginia	414
48	Arkansas	404
49	Idaho	384
50	Montana	381
	District of Columbia	3,119

Source: U.S. Department of Energy, Energy Information Administration
"Electric Sales, Revenue and Average Price 2018" (https://www.eia.gov/electricity/sales_revenue_price/index.cfm)

Average Monthly Electric Bill for Residential Customers in 2018

National Average = $118 per Month

ALPHA ORDER

RANK	STATE	MONTHLY BILL
3	Alabama	$151
16	Alaska	126
10	Arizona	131
30	Arkansas	113
37	California	103
48	Colorado	84
2	Connecticut	153
22	Delaware	122
13	Florida	128
10	Georgia	131
1	Hawaii	168
42	Idaho	96
44	Illinois	95
20	Indiana	123
33	Iowa	109
17	Kansas	125
19	Kentucky	124
20	Louisiana	123
42	Maine	96
8	Maryland	134
10	Massachusetts	131
36	Michigan	104
37	Minnesota	103
5	Mississippi	139
14	Missouri	127
46	Montana	93
33	Nebraska	109
31	Nevada	112
22	New Hampshire	122
35	New Jersey	106
49	New Mexico	81
31	New York	112
17	North Carolina	125
28	North Dakota	115
28	Ohio	115
27	Oklahoma	117
40	Oregon	99
26	Pennsylvania	120
24	Rhode Island	121
4	South Carolina	144
24	South Dakota	121
6	Tennessee	137
9	Texas	132
50	Utah	77
39	Vermont	101
6	Virginia	137
46	Washington	93
14	West Virginia	127
41	Wisconsin	97
44	Wyoming	95

RANK ORDER

RANK	STATE	MONTHLY BILL
1	Hawaii	$168
2	Connecticut	153
3	Alabama	151
4	South Carolina	144
5	Mississippi	139
6	Tennessee	137
6	Virginia	137
8	Maryland	134
9	Texas	132
10	Arizona	131
10	Georgia	131
10	Massachusetts	131
13	Florida	128
14	Missouri	127
14	West Virginia	127
16	Alaska	126
17	Kansas	125
17	North Carolina	125
19	Kentucky	124
20	Indiana	123
20	Louisiana	123
22	Delaware	122
22	New Hampshire	122
24	Rhode Island	121
24	South Dakota	121
26	Pennsylvania	120
27	Oklahoma	117
28	North Dakota	115
28	Ohio	115
30	Arkansas	113
31	Nevada	112
31	New York	112
33	Iowa	109
33	Nebraska	109
35	New Jersey	106
36	Michigan	104
37	California	103
37	Minnesota	103
39	Vermont	101
40	Oregon	99
41	Wisconsin	97
42	Idaho	96
42	Maine	96
44	Illinois	95
44	Wyoming	95
46	Montana	93
46	Washington	93
48	Colorado	84
49	New Mexico	81
50	Utah	77
	District of Columbia	101

Source: U.S. Department of Energy, Energy Information Administration
"Electric Sales, Revenue and Average Price 2018" (https://www.eia.gov/electricity/sales_revenue_price/index.cfm)

Electricity Generated through Renewable Sources in 2018

National Total = 706,867,309,000 Kilowatthours*

<table>
<tr><td colspan="4">ALPHA ORDER</td><td colspan="4">RANK ORDER</td></tr>
<tr><td>RANK</td><td>STATE</td><td>KWH</td><td>% of USA</td><td>RANK</td><td>STATE</td><td>KWH</td><td>% of USA</td></tr>
<tr><td>10</td><td>Alabama</td><td>14,946,770,000</td><td>2.1%</td><td>1</td><td>Washington</td><td>90,588,345,000</td><td>12.8%</td></tr>
<tr><td>45</td><td>Alaska</td><td>1,864,714,000</td><td>0.3%</td><td>2</td><td>California</td><td>84,963,060,000</td><td>12.0%</td></tr>
<tr><td>15</td><td>Arizona</td><td>12,872,304,000</td><td>1.8%</td><td>3</td><td>Texas</td><td>81,622,541,000</td><td>11.5%</td></tr>
<tr><td>34</td><td>Arkansas</td><td>4,577,878,000</td><td>0.6%</td><td>4</td><td>Oregon</td><td>44,675,442,000</td><td>6.3%</td></tr>
<tr><td>2</td><td>California</td><td>84,963,060,000</td><td>12.0%</td><td>5</td><td>New York</td><td>36,067,537,000</td><td>5.1%</td></tr>
<tr><td>16</td><td>Colorado</td><td>12,797,342,000</td><td>1.8%</td><td>6</td><td>Oklahoma</td><td>29,763,986,000</td><td>4.2%</td></tr>
<tr><td>47</td><td>Connecticut</td><td>1,428,739,000</td><td>0.2%</td><td>7</td><td>Iowa</td><td>22,481,533,000</td><td>3.2%</td></tr>
<tr><td>50</td><td>Delaware</td><td>114,097,000</td><td>0.0%</td><td>8</td><td>Kansas</td><td>19,005,200,000</td><td>2.7%</td></tr>
<tr><td>25</td><td>Florida</td><td>7,729,109,000</td><td>1.1%</td><td>9</td><td>North Carolina</td><td>15,868,193,000</td><td>2.2%</td></tr>
<tr><td>19</td><td>Georgia</td><td>10,691,262,000</td><td>1.5%</td><td>10</td><td>Alabama</td><td>14,946,770,000</td><td>2.1%</td></tr>
<tr><td>48</td><td>Hawaii</td><td>1,298,632,000</td><td>0.2%</td><td>11</td><td>Idaho</td><td>14,809,010,000</td><td>2.1%</td></tr>
<tr><td>11</td><td>Idaho</td><td>14,809,010,000</td><td>2.1%</td><td>12</td><td>Minnesota</td><td>14,453,708,000</td><td>2.0%</td></tr>
<tr><td>17</td><td>Illinois</td><td>12,537,933,000</td><td>1.8%</td><td>13</td><td>North Dakota</td><td>13,914,105,000</td><td>2.0%</td></tr>
<tr><td>29</td><td>Indiana</td><td>6,410,420,000</td><td>0.9%</td><td>14</td><td>Montana</td><td>13,595,687,000</td><td>1.9%</td></tr>
<tr><td>7</td><td>Iowa</td><td>22,481,533,000</td><td>3.2%</td><td>15</td><td>Arizona</td><td>12,872,304,000</td><td>1.8%</td></tr>
<tr><td>8</td><td>Kansas</td><td>19,005,200,000</td><td>2.7%</td><td>16</td><td>Colorado</td><td>12,797,342,000</td><td>1.8%</td></tr>
<tr><td>33</td><td>Kentucky</td><td>4,887,823,000</td><td>0.7%</td><td>17</td><td>Illinois</td><td>12,537,933,000</td><td>1.8%</td></tr>
<tr><td>38</td><td>Louisiana</td><td>3,857,676,000</td><td>0.5%</td><td>18</td><td>Tennessee</td><td>11,483,775,000</td><td>1.6%</td></tr>
<tr><td>24</td><td>Maine</td><td>8,319,205,000</td><td>1.2%</td><td>19</td><td>Georgia</td><td>10,691,262,000</td><td>1.5%</td></tr>
<tr><td>36</td><td>Maryland</td><td>4,318,979,000</td><td>0.6%</td><td>20</td><td>Nevada</td><td>10,427,557,000</td><td>1.5%</td></tr>
<tr><td>40</td><td>Massachusetts</td><td>3,502,150,000</td><td>0.5%</td><td>21</td><td>Pennsylvania</td><td>10,156,100,000</td><td>1.4%</td></tr>
<tr><td>22</td><td>Michigan</td><td>9,675,639,000</td><td>1.4%</td><td>22</td><td>Michigan</td><td>9,675,639,000</td><td>1.4%</td></tr>
<tr><td>12</td><td>Minnesota</td><td>14,453,708,000</td><td>2.0%</td><td>23</td><td>South Dakota</td><td>9,102,944,000</td><td>1.3%</td></tr>
<tr><td>46</td><td>Mississippi</td><td>1,765,138,000</td><td>0.2%</td><td>24</td><td>Maine</td><td>8,319,205,000</td><td>1.2%</td></tr>
<tr><td>37</td><td>Missouri</td><td>3,887,245,000</td><td>0.5%</td><td>25</td><td>Florida</td><td>7,729,109,000</td><td>1.1%</td></tr>
<tr><td>14</td><td>Montana</td><td>13,595,687,000</td><td>1.9%</td><td>26</td><td>New Mexico</td><td>7,623,967,000</td><td>1.1%</td></tr>
<tr><td>27</td><td>Nebraska</td><td>7,051,604,000</td><td>1.0%</td><td>27</td><td>Nebraska</td><td>7,051,604,000</td><td>1.0%</td></tr>
<tr><td>20</td><td>Nevada</td><td>10,427,557,000</td><td>1.5%</td><td>28</td><td>Virginia</td><td>6,701,214,000</td><td>0.9%</td></tr>
<tr><td>41</td><td>New Hampshire</td><td>3,147,857,000</td><td>0.4%</td><td>29</td><td>Indiana</td><td>6,410,420,000</td><td>0.9%</td></tr>
<tr><td>44</td><td>New Jersey</td><td>1,983,485,000</td><td>0.3%</td><td>30</td><td>South Carolina</td><td>5,815,520,000</td><td>0.8%</td></tr>
<tr><td>26</td><td>New Mexico</td><td>7,623,967,000</td><td>1.1%</td><td>31</td><td>Wisconsin</td><td>5,506,504,000</td><td>0.8%</td></tr>
<tr><td>5</td><td>New York</td><td>36,067,537,000</td><td>5.1%</td><td>32</td><td>Wyoming</td><td>5,033,684,000</td><td>0.7%</td></tr>
<tr><td>9</td><td>North Carolina</td><td>15,868,193,000</td><td>2.2%</td><td>33</td><td>Kentucky</td><td>4,887,823,000</td><td>0.7%</td></tr>
<tr><td>13</td><td>North Dakota</td><td>13,914,105,000</td><td>2.0%</td><td>34</td><td>Arkansas</td><td>4,577,878,000</td><td>0.6%</td></tr>
<tr><td>42</td><td>Ohio</td><td>2,820,070,000</td><td>0.4%</td><td>35</td><td>Utah</td><td>4,470,555,000</td><td>0.6%</td></tr>
<tr><td>6</td><td>Oklahoma</td><td>29,763,986,000</td><td>4.2%</td><td>36</td><td>Maryland</td><td>4,318,979,000</td><td>0.6%</td></tr>
<tr><td>4</td><td>Oregon</td><td>44,675,442,000</td><td>6.3%</td><td>37</td><td>Missouri</td><td>3,887,245,000</td><td>0.5%</td></tr>
<tr><td>21</td><td>Pennsylvania</td><td>10,156,100,000</td><td>1.4%</td><td>38</td><td>Louisiana</td><td>3,857,676,000</td><td>0.5%</td></tr>
<tr><td>49</td><td>Rhode Island</td><td>402,603,000</td><td>0.1%</td><td>39</td><td>West Virginia</td><td>3,617,627,000</td><td>0.5%</td></tr>
<tr><td>30</td><td>South Carolina</td><td>5,815,520,000</td><td>0.8%</td><td>40</td><td>Massachusetts</td><td>3,502,150,000</td><td>0.5%</td></tr>
<tr><td>23</td><td>South Dakota</td><td>9,102,944,000</td><td>1.3%</td><td>41</td><td>New Hampshire</td><td>3,147,857,000</td><td>0.4%</td></tr>
<tr><td>18</td><td>Tennessee</td><td>11,483,775,000</td><td>1.6%</td><td>42</td><td>Ohio</td><td>2,820,070,000</td><td>0.4%</td></tr>
<tr><td>3</td><td>Texas</td><td>81,622,541,000</td><td>11.5%</td><td>43</td><td>Vermont</td><td>2,174,283,000</td><td>0.3%</td></tr>
<tr><td>35</td><td>Utah</td><td>4,470,555,000</td><td>0.6%</td><td>44</td><td>New Jersey</td><td>1,983,485,000</td><td>0.3%</td></tr>
<tr><td>43</td><td>Vermont</td><td>2,174,283,000</td><td>0.3%</td><td>45</td><td>Alaska</td><td>1,864,714,000</td><td>0.3%</td></tr>
<tr><td>28</td><td>Virginia</td><td>6,701,214,000</td><td>0.9%</td><td>46</td><td>Mississippi</td><td>1,765,138,000</td><td>0.2%</td></tr>
<tr><td>1</td><td>Washington</td><td>90,588,345,000</td><td>12.8%</td><td>47</td><td>Connecticut</td><td>1,428,739,000</td><td>0.2%</td></tr>
<tr><td>39</td><td>West Virginia</td><td>3,617,627,000</td><td>0.5%</td><td>48</td><td>Hawaii</td><td>1,298,632,000</td><td>0.2%</td></tr>
<tr><td>31</td><td>Wisconsin</td><td>5,506,504,000</td><td>0.8%</td><td>49</td><td>Rhode Island</td><td>402,603,000</td><td>0.1%</td></tr>
<tr><td>32</td><td>Wyoming</td><td>5,033,684,000</td><td>0.7%</td><td>50</td><td>Delaware</td><td>114,097,000</td><td>0.0%</td></tr>
<tr><td></td><td></td><td></td><td></td><td></td><td>District of Columbia</td><td>56,561,000</td><td>0.0%</td></tr>
</table>

Source: U.S. Department of Energy, Energy Information Administration
"Electricity" (https://www.eia.gov/electricity/data/state/)
*Includes hydroelectric, geothermal, solar thermal and photovoltaic, wind, wood and wood-derived fuels, and other biomass.

Percent of Electricity Generated through Renewable Sources in 2018

National Percent = 16.9%*

<table>
<tr><td colspan="3">ALPHA ORDER</td><td colspan="3">RANK ORDER</td></tr>
<tr><td>RANK</td><td>STATE</td><td>PERCENT</td><td>RANK</td><td>STATE</td><td>PERCENT</td></tr>
<tr><td>29</td><td>Alabama</td><td>10.3</td><td>1</td><td>Vermont</td><td>99.8</td></tr>
<tr><td>13</td><td>Alaska</td><td>29.8</td><td>2</td><td>Idaho</td><td>81.5</td></tr>
<tr><td>26</td><td>Arizona</td><td>11.5</td><td>3</td><td>Washington</td><td>77.6</td></tr>
<tr><td>35</td><td>Arkansas</td><td>6.7</td><td>4</td><td>Maine</td><td>73.7</td></tr>
<tr><td>8</td><td>California</td><td>43.5</td><td>5</td><td>South Dakota</td><td>72.2</td></tr>
<tr><td>18</td><td>Colorado</td><td>23.1</td><td>6</td><td>Oregon</td><td>69.7</td></tr>
<tr><td>45</td><td>Connecticut</td><td>3.6</td><td>7</td><td>Montana</td><td>48.2</td></tr>
<tr><td>50</td><td>Delaware</td><td>1.8</td><td>8</td><td>California</td><td>43.5</td></tr>
<tr><td>46</td><td>Florida</td><td>3.2</td><td>9</td><td>Kansas</td><td>36.8</td></tr>
<tr><td>33</td><td>Georgia</td><td>8.3</td><td>10</td><td>Iowa</td><td>35.5</td></tr>
<tr><td>23</td><td>Hawaii</td><td>13.3</td><td>11</td><td>Oklahoma</td><td>34.5</td></tr>
<tr><td>2</td><td>Idaho</td><td>81.5</td><td>12</td><td>North Dakota</td><td>32.7</td></tr>
<tr><td>35</td><td>Illinois</td><td>6.7</td><td>13</td><td>Alaska</td><td>29.8</td></tr>
<tr><td>39</td><td>Indiana</td><td>5.6</td><td>14</td><td>New York</td><td>27.2</td></tr>
<tr><td>10</td><td>Iowa</td><td>35.5</td><td>15</td><td>Nevada</td><td>26.3</td></tr>
<tr><td>9</td><td>Kansas</td><td>36.8</td><td>16</td><td>Minnesota</td><td>23.5</td></tr>
<tr><td>37</td><td>Kentucky</td><td>6.2</td><td>17</td><td>New Mexico</td><td>23.3</td></tr>
<tr><td>44</td><td>Louisiana</td><td>3.8</td><td>18</td><td>Colorado</td><td>23.1</td></tr>
<tr><td>4</td><td>Maine</td><td>73.7</td><td>19</td><td>Nebraska</td><td>19.1</td></tr>
<tr><td>30</td><td>Maryland</td><td>9.9</td><td>20</td><td>New Hampshire</td><td>18.4</td></tr>
<tr><td>24</td><td>Massachusetts</td><td>12.9</td><td>21</td><td>Texas</td><td>17.1</td></tr>
<tr><td>31</td><td>Michigan</td><td>8.4</td><td>22</td><td>Tennessee</td><td>14.1</td></tr>
<tr><td>16</td><td>Minnesota</td><td>23.5</td><td>23</td><td>Hawaii</td><td>13.3</td></tr>
<tr><td>47</td><td>Mississippi</td><td>2.8</td><td>24</td><td>Massachusetts</td><td>12.9</td></tr>
<tr><td>41</td><td>Missouri</td><td>4.8</td><td>25</td><td>North Carolina</td><td>11.8</td></tr>
<tr><td>7</td><td>Montana</td><td>48.2</td><td>26</td><td>Arizona</td><td>11.5</td></tr>
<tr><td>19</td><td>Nebraska</td><td>19.1</td><td>27</td><td>Utah</td><td>11.4</td></tr>
<tr><td>15</td><td>Nevada</td><td>26.3</td><td>28</td><td>Wyoming</td><td>10.9</td></tr>
<tr><td>20</td><td>New Hampshire</td><td>18.4</td><td>29</td><td>Alabama</td><td>10.3</td></tr>
<tr><td>48</td><td>New Jersey</td><td>2.6</td><td>30</td><td>Maryland</td><td>9.9</td></tr>
<tr><td>17</td><td>New Mexico</td><td>23.3</td><td>31</td><td>Michigan</td><td>8.4</td></tr>
<tr><td>14</td><td>New York</td><td>27.2</td><td>31</td><td>Wisconsin</td><td>8.4</td></tr>
<tr><td>25</td><td>North Carolina</td><td>11.8</td><td>33</td><td>Georgia</td><td>8.3</td></tr>
<tr><td>12</td><td>North Dakota</td><td>32.7</td><td>34</td><td>Virginia</td><td>7.0</td></tr>
<tr><td>49</td><td>Ohio</td><td>2.2</td><td>35</td><td>Arkansas</td><td>6.7</td></tr>
<tr><td>11</td><td>Oklahoma</td><td>34.5</td><td>35</td><td>Illinois</td><td>6.7</td></tr>
<tr><td>6</td><td>Oregon</td><td>69.7</td><td>37</td><td>Kentucky</td><td>6.2</td></tr>
<tr><td>43</td><td>Pennsylvania</td><td>4.7</td><td>38</td><td>South Carolina</td><td>5.9</td></tr>
<tr><td>41</td><td>Rhode Island</td><td>4.8</td><td>39</td><td>Indiana</td><td>5.6</td></tr>
<tr><td>38</td><td>South Carolina</td><td>5.9</td><td>40</td><td>West Virginia</td><td>5.4</td></tr>
<tr><td>5</td><td>South Dakota</td><td>72.2</td><td>41</td><td>Missouri</td><td>4.8</td></tr>
<tr><td>22</td><td>Tennessee</td><td>14.1</td><td>41</td><td>Rhode Island</td><td>4.8</td></tr>
<tr><td>21</td><td>Texas</td><td>17.1</td><td>43</td><td>Pennsylvania</td><td>4.7</td></tr>
<tr><td>27</td><td>Utah</td><td>11.4</td><td>44</td><td>Louisiana</td><td>3.8</td></tr>
<tr><td>1</td><td>Vermont</td><td>99.8</td><td>45</td><td>Connecticut</td><td>3.6</td></tr>
<tr><td>34</td><td>Virginia</td><td>7.0</td><td>46</td><td>Florida</td><td>3.2</td></tr>
<tr><td>3</td><td>Washington</td><td>77.6</td><td>47</td><td>Mississippi</td><td>2.8</td></tr>
<tr><td>40</td><td>West Virginia</td><td>5.4</td><td>48</td><td>New Jersey</td><td>2.6</td></tr>
<tr><td>31</td><td>Wisconsin</td><td>8.4</td><td>49</td><td>Ohio</td><td>2.2</td></tr>
<tr><td>28</td><td>Wyoming</td><td>10.9</td><td>50</td><td>Delaware</td><td>1.8</td></tr>
<tr><td></td><td></td><td></td><td></td><td>District of Columbia</td><td>71.3</td></tr>
</table>

Source: CQ Press using data from U.S. Department of Energy, Energy Information Administration
   "Electricity" (https://www.eia.gov/electricity/data/state/)
*Includes hydroelectric, geothermal, solar thermal and photovoltaic, wind, wood and wood-derived fuels, and other biomass.

Average Price of Natural Gas Delivered to Industrial Customers in 2018

National Average = $4.21 per Thousand Cubic Feet

ALPHA ORDER

RANK	STATE	RATE
42	Alabama	$4.22
23	Alaska	5.81
21	Arizona	5.98
13	Arkansas	6.78
12	California	7.12
28	Colorado	5.28
15	Connecticut	6.55
4	Delaware	10.07
18	Florida	6.38
37	Georgia	4.63
1	Hawaii	22.62
43	Idaho	3.98
24	Illinois	5.55
20	Indiana	6.10
25	Iowa	5.36
41	Kansas	4.38
40	Kentucky	4.40
47	Louisiana	3.53
6	Maine	9.26
8	Maryland	8.51
3	Massachusetts	10.31
21	Michigan	5.98
36	Minnesota	4.80
30	Mississippi	5.14
16	Missouri	6.50
17	Montana	6.42
39	Nebraska	4.48
26	Nevada	5.35
5	New Hampshire	9.81
9	New Jersey	8.03
45	New Mexico	3.72
10	New York	7.83
19	North Carolina	6.18
49	North Dakota	3.29
14	Ohio	6.65
50	Oklahoma	2.67
33	Oregon	5.01
7	Pennsylvania	8.69
2	Rhode Island	10.46
35	South Carolina	4.92
32	South Dakota	5.02
34	Tennessee	4.94
48	Texas	3.42
27	Utah	5.31
38	Vermont	4.55
31	Virginia	5.08
11	Washington	7.17
46	West Virginia	3.54
29	Wisconsin	5.20
44	Wyoming	3.92

RANK ORDER

RANK	STATE	RATE
1	Hawaii	$22.62
2	Rhode Island	10.46
3	Massachusetts	10.31
4	Delaware	10.07
5	New Hampshire	9.81
6	Maine	9.26
7	Pennsylvania	8.69
8	Maryland	8.51
9	New Jersey	8.03
10	New York	7.83
11	Washington	7.17
12	California	7.12
13	Arkansas	6.78
14	Ohio	6.65
15	Connecticut	6.55
16	Missouri	6.50
17	Montana	6.42
18	Florida	6.38
19	North Carolina	6.18
20	Indiana	6.10
21	Arizona	5.98
21	Michigan	5.98
23	Alaska	5.81
24	Illinois	5.55
25	Iowa	5.36
26	Nevada	5.35
27	Utah	5.31
28	Colorado	5.28
29	Wisconsin	5.20
30	Mississippi	5.14
31	Virginia	5.08
32	South Dakota	5.02
33	Oregon	5.01
34	Tennessee	4.94
35	South Carolina	4.92
36	Minnesota	4.80
37	Georgia	4.63
38	Vermont	4.55
39	Nebraska	4.48
40	Kentucky	4.40
41	Kansas	4.38
42	Alabama	4.22
43	Idaho	3.98
44	Wyoming	3.92
45	New Mexico	3.72
46	West Virginia	3.54
47	Louisiana	3.53
48	Texas	3.42
49	North Dakota	3.29
50	Oklahoma	2.67
	District of Columbia*	NA

Source: U.S. Department of Energy, Energy Information Administration
"Natural Gas" (https://www.eia.gov/naturalgas/annual/)
*Not applicable.

Average Price of Natural Gas Delivered to Commercial Customers in 2018

National Average = $7.78 per Thousand Cubic Feet

ALPHA ORDER

RANK	STATE	RATE
6	Alabama	$11.89
9	Alaska	9.99
16	Arizona	8.69
27	Arkansas	7.95
18	California	8.57
39	Colorado	6.83
13	Connecticut	9.23
8	Delaware	10.49
7	Florida	11.20
24	Georgia	8.17
1	Hawaii	30.96
46	Idaho	6.03
33	Illinois	7.24
30	Indiana	7.37
38	Iowa	6.84
17	Kansas	8.63
22	Kentucky	8.43
15	Louisiana	8.71
2	Maine	13.01
10	Maryland	9.57
4	Massachusetts	12.84
37	Michigan	6.91
36	Minnesota	7.08
19	Mississippi	8.50
27	Missouri	7.95
34	Montana	7.09
45	Nebraska	6.28
44	Nevada	6.34
5	New Hampshire	12.72
14	New Jersey	9.01
50	New Mexico	5.57
32	New York	7.36
20	North Carolina	8.48
49	North Dakota	5.90
47	Ohio	5.92
34	Oklahoma	7.09
20	Oregon	8.48
11	Pennsylvania	9.37
3	Rhode Island	12.98
12	South Carolina	9.35
48	South Dakota	5.91
23	Tennessee	8.41
42	Texas	6.55
30	Utah	7.37
40	Vermont	6.77
26	Virginia	8.08
29	Washington	7.90
25	West Virginia	8.11
43	Wisconsin	6.44
41	Wyoming	6.61

RANK ORDER

RANK	STATE	RATE
1	Hawaii	$30.96
2	Maine	13.01
3	Rhode Island	12.98
4	Massachusetts	12.84
5	New Hampshire	12.72
6	Alabama	11.89
7	Florida	11.20
8	Delaware	10.49
9	Alaska	9.99
10	Maryland	9.57
11	Pennsylvania	9.37
12	South Carolina	9.35
13	Connecticut	9.23
14	New Jersey	9.01
15	Louisiana	8.71
16	Arizona	8.69
17	Kansas	8.63
18	California	8.57
19	Mississippi	8.50
20	North Carolina	8.48
20	Oregon	8.48
22	Kentucky	8.43
23	Tennessee	8.41
24	Georgia	8.17
25	West Virginia	8.11
26	Virginia	8.08
27	Arkansas	7.95
27	Missouri	7.95
29	Washington	7.90
30	Indiana	7.37
30	Utah	7.37
32	New York	7.36
33	Illinois	7.24
34	Montana	7.09
34	Oklahoma	7.09
36	Minnesota	7.08
37	Michigan	6.91
38	Iowa	6.84
39	Colorado	6.83
40	Vermont	6.77
41	Wyoming	6.61
42	Texas	6.55
43	Wisconsin	6.44
44	Nevada	6.34
45	Nebraska	6.28
46	Idaho	6.03
47	Ohio	5.92
48	South Dakota	5.91
49	North Dakota	5.90
50	New Mexico	5.57
	District of Columbia	10.42

Source: U.S. Department of Energy, Energy Information Administration
"Natural Gas" (https://www.eia.gov/naturalgas/annual/)

Average Price of Natural Gas Delivered to Residential Customers in 2018

National Average = $10.50 per Thousand Cubic Feet

ALPHA ORDER

RANK	STATE	RATE
8	Alabama	$15.22
23	Alaska	10.99
6	Arizona	15.35
18	Arkansas	11.77
15	California	12.30
46	Colorado	7.72
10	Connecticut	13.92
13	Delaware	12.60
2	Florida	21.34
9	Georgia	13.98
1	Hawaii	43.48
50	Idaho	7.11
43	Illinois	8.15
38	Indiana	8.72
37	Iowa	8.94
29	Kansas	10.18
25	Kentucky	10.56
20	Louisiana	11.65
3	Maine	16.32
17	Maryland	11.79
5	Massachusetts	15.47
42	Michigan	8.19
39	Minnesota	8.69
26	Mississippi	10.38
27	Missouri	10.36
48	Montana	7.32
41	Nebraska	8.54
33	Nevada	9.24
6	New Hampshire	15.35
35	New Jersey	9.09
45	New Mexico	7.89
14	New York	12.37
16	North Carolina	12.11
49	North Dakota	7.20
34	Ohio	9.10
32	Oklahoma	9.25
24	Oregon	10.65
22	Pennsylvania	11.25
4	Rhode Island	15.65
12	South Carolina	13.53
47	South Dakota	7.66
31	Tennessee	9.47
21	Texas	11.42
36	Utah	9.04
11	Vermont	13.65
19	Virginia	11.71
28	Washington	10.28
30	West Virginia	9.84
44	Wisconsin	8.04
40	Wyoming	8.60

RANK ORDER

RANK	STATE	RATE
1	Hawaii	$43.48
2	Florida	21.34
3	Maine	16.32
4	Rhode Island	15.65
5	Massachusetts	15.47
6	Arizona	15.35
6	New Hampshire	15.35
8	Alabama	15.22
9	Georgia	13.98
10	Connecticut	13.92
11	Vermont	13.65
12	South Carolina	13.53
13	Delaware	12.60
14	New York	12.37
15	California	12.30
16	North Carolina	12.11
17	Maryland	11.79
18	Arkansas	11.77
19	Virginia	11.71
20	Louisiana	11.65
21	Texas	11.42
22	Pennsylvania	11.25
23	Alaska	10.99
24	Oregon	10.65
25	Kentucky	10.56
26	Mississippi	10.38
27	Missouri	10.36
28	Washington	10.28
29	Kansas	10.18
30	West Virginia	9.84
31	Tennessee	9.47
32	Oklahoma	9.25
33	Nevada	9.24
34	Ohio	9.10
35	New Jersey	9.09
36	Utah	9.04
37	Iowa	8.94
38	Indiana	8.72
39	Minnesota	8.69
40	Wyoming	8.60
41	Nebraska	8.54
42	Michigan	8.19
43	Illinois	8.15
44	Wisconsin	8.04
45	New Mexico	7.89
46	Colorado	7.72
47	South Dakota	7.66
48	Montana	7.32
49	North Dakota	7.20
50	Idaho	7.11
	District of Columbia	11.78

Source: U.S. Department of Energy, Energy Information Administration
"Natural Gas" (https://www.eia.gov/naturalgas/annual/)

Natural Gas Consumption in 2018

National Total = 30,075,334,000,000 Cubic Feet*

ALPHA ORDER

RANK	STATE	CUBIC FEET	% of USA
13	Alabama	749,910,000,000	2.5%
26	Alaska	355,132,000,000	1.2%
24	Arizona	384,785,000,000	1.3%
25	Arkansas	360,814,000,000	1.2%
2	California	2,136,907,000,000	7.1%
20	Colorado	487,130,000,000	1.6%
34	Connecticut	277,929,000,000	0.9%
44	Delaware	95,516,000,000	0.3%
4	Florida	1,477,100,000,000	4.9%
14	Georgia	739,110,000,000	2.5%
50	Hawaii	3,282,000,000	0.0%
42	Idaho	111,699,000,000	0.4%
8	Illinois	1,108,628,000,000	3.7%
10	Indiana	854,014,000,000	2.8%
21	Iowa	443,119,000,000	1.5%
30	Kansas	309,613,000,000	1.0%
27	Kentucky	339,922,000,000	1.1%
3	Louisiana	1,733,676,000,000	5.8%
48	Maine	46,465,000,000	0.2%
32	Maryland	300,794,000,000	1.0%
22	Massachusetts	439,098,000,000	1.5%
9	Michigan	965,419,000,000	3.2%
19	Minnesota	490,469,000,000	1.6%
17	Mississippi	576,376,000,000	1.9%
29	Missouri	322,098,000,000	1.1%
46	Montana	87,033,000,000	0.3%
39	Nebraska	185,942,000,000	0.6%
33	Nevada	299,749,000,000	1.0%
47	New Hampshire	49,923,000,000	0.2%
12	New Jersey	770,281,000,000	2.6%
35	New Mexico	271,457,000,000	0.9%
6	New York	1,350,507,000,000	4.5%
16	North Carolina	582,431,000,000	1.9%
41	North Dakota	126,719,000,000	0.4%
7	Ohio	1,139,358,000,000	3.8%
11	Oklahoma	808,689,000,000	2.7%
36	Oregon	255,713,000,000	0.9%
5	Pennsylvania	1,457,798,000,000	4.8%
43	Rhode Island	101,793,000,000	0.3%
28	South Carolina	328,289,000,000	1.1%
45	South Dakota	89,463,000,000	0.3%
23	Tennessee	391,792,000,000	1.3%
1	Texas	4,432,552,000,000	14.7%
37	Utah	243,772,000,000	0.8%
49	Vermont	13,759,000,000	0.0%
15	Virginia	634,018,000,000	2.1%
31	Washington	307,982,000,000	1.0%
38	West Virginia	204,297,000,000	0.7%
18	Wisconsin	543,015,000,000	1.8%
40	Wyoming	164,341,000,000	0.5%

RANK ORDER

RANK	STATE	CUBIC FEET	% of USA
1	Texas	4,432,552,000,000	14.7%
2	California	2,136,907,000,000	7.1%
3	Louisiana	1,733,676,000,000	5.8%
4	Florida	1,477,100,000,000	4.9%
5	Pennsylvania	1,457,798,000,000	4.8%
6	New York	1,350,507,000,000	4.5%
7	Ohio	1,139,358,000,000	3.8%
8	Illinois	1,108,628,000,000	3.7%
9	Michigan	965,419,000,000	3.2%
10	Indiana	854,014,000,000	2.8%
11	Oklahoma	808,689,000,000	2.7%
12	New Jersey	770,281,000,000	2.6%
13	Alabama	749,910,000,000	2.5%
14	Georgia	739,110,000,000	2.5%
15	Virginia	634,018,000,000	2.1%
16	North Carolina	582,431,000,000	1.9%
17	Mississippi	576,376,000,000	1.9%
18	Wisconsin	543,015,000,000	1.8%
19	Minnesota	490,469,000,000	1.6%
20	Colorado	487,130,000,000	1.6%
21	Iowa	443,119,000,000	1.5%
22	Massachusetts	439,098,000,000	1.5%
23	Tennessee	391,792,000,000	1.3%
24	Arizona	384,785,000,000	1.3%
25	Arkansas	360,814,000,000	1.2%
26	Alaska	355,132,000,000	1.2%
27	Kentucky	339,922,000,000	1.1%
28	South Carolina	328,289,000,000	1.1%
29	Missouri	322,098,000,000	1.1%
30	Kansas	309,613,000,000	1.0%
31	Washington	307,982,000,000	1.0%
32	Maryland	300,794,000,000	1.0%
33	Nevada	299,749,000,000	1.0%
34	Connecticut	277,929,000,000	0.9%
35	New Mexico	271,457,000,000	0.9%
36	Oregon	255,713,000,000	0.9%
37	Utah	243,772,000,000	0.8%
38	West Virginia	204,297,000,000	0.7%
39	Nebraska	185,942,000,000	0.6%
40	Wyoming	164,341,000,000	0.5%
41	North Dakota	126,719,000,000	0.4%
42	Idaho	111,699,000,000	0.4%
43	Rhode Island	101,793,000,000	0.3%
44	Delaware	95,516,000,000	0.3%
45	South Dakota	89,463,000,000	0.3%
46	Montana	87,033,000,000	0.3%
47	New Hampshire	49,923,000,000	0.2%
48	Maine	46,465,000,000	0.2%
49	Vermont	13,759,000,000	0.0%
50	Hawaii	3,282,000,000	0.0%
	District of Columbia	31,477,000,000	0.1%

Source: U.S. Department of Energy, Energy Information Administration
    "Natural Gas" (https://www.eia.gov/naturalgas/annual/)
*National total includes 94,178,000,000 cubic feet of consumption in the Gulf of Mexico not shown by state.

Coal Mines in 2018

National Total = 679 Mines*

ALPHA ORDER					RANK ORDER			
RANK	STATE		MINES	% of USA	RANK	STATE	MINES	% of USA
5	Alabama		30	4.4%	1	West Virginia	155	22.8%
20	Alaska		1	0.1%	2	Pennsylvania	151	22.2%
20	Arizona		1	0.1%	3	Kentucky	145	21.4%
NA	Arkansas**		NA	NA	4	Virginia	51	7.5%
NA	California**		NA	NA	5	Alabama	30	4.4%
13	Colorado		6	0.9%	6	Illinois	18	2.7%
NA	Connecticut**		NA	NA	6	Indiana	18	2.7%
NA	Delaware**		NA	NA	8	Ohio	16	2.4%
NA	Florida**		NA	NA	8	Wyoming	16	2.4%
NA	Georgia**		NA	NA	10	Maryland	14	2.1%
NA	Hawaii**		NA	NA	11	Texas	9	1.3%
NA	Idaho**		NA	NA	12	Utah	8	1.2%
6	Illinois		18	2.7%	13	Colorado	6	0.9%
6	Indiana		18	2.7%	13	Montana	6	0.9%
NA	Iowa**		NA	NA	15	North Dakota	5	0.7%
NA	Kansas**		NA	NA	15	Oklahoma	5	0.7%
3	Kentucky		145	21.4%	17	Tennessee	4	0.6%
19	Louisiana		2	0.3%	18	New Mexico	3	0.4%
NA	Maine**		NA	NA	19	Louisiana	2	0.3%
10	Maryland		14	2.1%	20	Alaska	1	0.1%
NA	Massachusetts**		NA	NA	20	Arizona	1	0.1%
NA	Michigan**		NA	NA	20	Mississippi	1	0.1%
NA	Minnesota**		NA	NA	20	Missouri	1	0.1%
20	Mississippi		1	0.1%	NA	Arkansas**	NA	NA
20	Missouri		1	0.1%	NA	California**	NA	NA
13	Montana		6	0.9%	NA	Connecticut**	NA	NA
NA	Nebraska**		NA	NA	NA	Delaware**	NA	NA
NA	Nevada**		NA	NA	NA	Florida**	NA	NA
NA	New Hampshire**		NA	NA	NA	Georgia**	NA	NA
NA	New Jersey**		NA	NA	NA	Hawaii**	NA	NA
18	New Mexico		3	0.4%	NA	Idaho**	NA	NA
NA	New York**		NA	NA	NA	Iowa**	NA	NA
NA	North Carolina**		NA	NA	NA	Kansas**	NA	NA
15	North Dakota		5	0.7%	NA	Maine**	NA	NA
8	Ohio		16	2.4%	NA	Massachusetts**	NA	NA
15	Oklahoma		5	0.7%	NA	Michigan**	NA	NA
NA	Oregon**		NA	NA	NA	Minnesota**	NA	NA
2	Pennsylvania		151	22.2%	NA	Nebraska**	NA	NA
NA	Rhode Island**		NA	NA	NA	Nevada^^	NA	NA
NA	South Carolina**		NA	NA	NA	New Hampshire**	NA	NA
NA	South Dakota**		NA	NA	NA	New Jersey**	NA	NA
17	Tennessee		4	0.6%	NA	New York**	NA	NA
11	Texas		9	1.3%	NA	North Carolina**	NA	NA
12	Utah		8	1.2%	NA	Oregon**	NA	NA
NA	Vermont**		NA	NA	NA	Rhode Island**	NA	NA
4	Virginia		51	7.5%	NA	South Carolina**	NA	NA
NA	Washington**		NA	NA	NA	South Dakota**	NA	NA
1	West Virginia		155	22.8%	NA	Vermont**	NA	NA
NA	Wisconsin**		NA	NA	NA	Washington**	NA	NA
8	Wyoming		16	2.4%	NA	Wisconsin**	NA	NA
						District of Columbia**	NA	NA

Source: U.S. Department of Energy, Energy Information Administration
"Annual Coal Report" (https://www.eia.gov/coal/annual/)
*National total includes thirteen coal mines in refuse recovery not shown by state. **Not available or no mines.

Coal Production in 2018

National Total = 756,167,000 Short Tons*

ALPHA ORDER

RANK	STATE	SHORT TONS	% of USA
10	Alabama	14,783,000	2.0%
20	Alaska	902,000	0.1%
16	Arizona	6,550,000	0.9%
NA	Arkansas**	NA	NA
NA	California**	NA	NA
11	Colorado	14,026,000	1.9%
NA	Connecticut**	NA	NA
NA	Delaware**	NA	NA
NA	Florida**	NA	NA
NA	Georgia**	NA	NA
NA	Hawaii**	NA	NA
NA	Idaho**	NA	NA
4	Illinois	49,563,000	6.6%
7	Indiana	34,598,000	4.6%
NA	Iowa**	NA	NA
NA	Kansas**	NA	NA
5	Kentucky	39,567,000	5.2%
18	Louisiana	1,483,000	0.2%
NA	Maine**	NA	NA
19	Maryland	1,298,000	0.2%
NA	Massachusetts**	NA	NA
NA	Michigan**	NA	NA
NA	Minnesota**	NA	NA
17	Mississippi	2,940,000	0.4%
22	Missouri	259,000	0.0%
6	Montana	38,610,000	5.1%
NA	Nebraska**	NA	NA
NA	Nevada**	NA	NA
NA	New Hampshire**	NA	NA
NA	New Jersey**	NA	NA
14	New Mexico	10,792,000	1.4%
NA	New York**	NA	NA
NA	North Carolina**	NA	NA
8	North Dakota	29,643,000	3.9%
15	Ohio	8,993,000	1.2%
21	Oklahoma	610,000	0.1%
NA	Oregon**	NA	NA
3	Pennsylvania	49,883,000	6.6%
NA	Rhode Island**	NA	NA
NA	South Carolina**	NA	NA
NA	South Dakota**	NA	NA
23	Tennessee	232,000	0.0%
9	Texas	24,823,000	3.3%
12	Utah	13,619,000	1.8%
NA	Vermont**	NA	NA
13	Virginia	12,715,000	1.7%
NA	Washington**	NA	NA
2	West Virginia	95,365,000	12.6%
NA	Wisconsin**	NA	NA
1	Wyoming	304,188,000	40.2%

RANK ORDER

RANK	STATE	SHORT TONS	% of USA
1	Wyoming	304,188,000	40.2%
2	West Virginia	95,365,000	12.6%
3	Pennsylvania	49,883,000	6.6%
4	Illinois	49,563,000	6.6%
5	Kentucky	39,567,000	5.2%
6	Montana	38,610,000	5.1%
7	Indiana	34,598,000	4.6%
8	North Dakota	29,643,000	3.9%
9	Texas	24,823,000	3.3%
10	Alabama	14,783,000	2.0%
11	Colorado	14,026,000	1.9%
12	Utah	13,619,000	1.8%
13	Virginia	12,715,000	1.7%
14	New Mexico	10,792,000	1.4%
15	Ohio	8,993,000	1.2%
16	Arizona	6,550,000	0.9%
17	Mississippi	2,940,000	0.4%
18	Louisiana	1,483,000	0.2%
19	Maryland	1,298,000	0.2%
20	Alaska	902,000	0.1%
21	Oklahoma	610,000	0.1%
22	Missouri	259,000	0.0%
23	Tennessee	232,000	0.0%
NA	Arkansas**	NA	NA
NA	California**	NA	NA
NA	Connecticut**	NA	NA
NA	Delaware**	NA	NA
NA	Florida**	NA	NA
NA	Georgia**	NA	NA
NA	Hawaii**	NA	NA
NA	Idaho**	NA	NA
NA	Iowa**	NA	NA
NA	Kansas**	NA	NA
NA	Maine**	NA	NA
NA	Massachusetts**	NA	NA
NA	Michigan**	NA	NA
NA	Minnesota**	NA	NA
NA	Nebraska**	NA	NA
NA	Nevada**	NA	NA
NA	New Hampshire**	NA	NA
NA	New Jersey**	NA	NA
NA	New York**	NA	NA
NA	North Carolina**	NA	NA
NA	Oregon**	NA	NA
NA	Rhode Island**	NA	NA
NA	South Carolina**	NA	NA
NA	South Dakota**	NA	NA
NA	Vermont**	NA	NA
NA	Washington**	NA	NA
NA	Wisconsin**	NA	NA
	District of Columbia**	NA	NA

Source: U.S. Department of Energy, Energy Information Administration
   "Annual Coal Report" (https://www.eia.gov/coal/annual/)
*National total includes 726,000 short tons from refuse recovery not shown by state.
**Not available or no production.

Gasoline Used in 2018

National Total = 145,235,172,000 Gallons*

RANK	STATE	GALLONS	% of USA
20	Alabama	2,737,856,000	1.9%
50	Alaska	286,129,000	0.2%
16	Arizona	3,014,859,000	2.1%
32	Arkansas	1,506,815,000	1.0%
1	California	15,528,126,000	10.7%
24	Colorado	2,391,219,000	1.6%
31	Connecticut	1,520,748,000	1.0%
43	Delaware	521,719,000	0.4%
3	Florida	9,387,461,000	6.5%
6	Georgia	5,067,266,000	3.5%
45	Hawaii	465,173,000	0.3%
39	Idaho	815,376,000	0.6%
9	Illinois	4,868,216,000	3.4%
15	Indiana	3,166,337,000	2.2%
28	Iowa	1,684,430,000	1.2%
33	Kansas	1,308,690,000	0.9%
25	Kentucky	2,253,270,000	1.6%
26	Louisiana	2,201,904,000	1.5%
41	Maine	658,457,000	0.5%
22	Maryland	2,730,974,000	1.9%
19	Massachusetts	2,820,756,000	1.9%
10	Michigan	4,867,848,000	3.4%
23	Minnesota	2,677,347,000	1.8%
29	Mississippi	1,682,011,000	1.2%
14	Missouri	3,213,117,000	2.2%
42	Montana	550,856,000	0.4%
37	Nebraska	922,934,000	0.6%
34	Nevada	1,249,965,000	0.9%
40	New Hampshire	734,864,000	0.5%
12	New Jersey	3,967,448,000	2.7%
36	New Mexico	1,022,574,000	0.7%
4	New York	5,844,464,000	4.0%
8	North Carolina	4,871,585,000	3.4%
46	North Dakota	446,320,000	0.3%
5	Ohio	5,159,762,000	3.6%
27	Oklahoma	1,990,631,000	1.4%
30	Oregon	1,649,040,000	1.1%
7	Pennsylvania	4,912,627,000	3.4%
47	Rhode Island	392,776,000	0.3%
18	South Carolina	2,855,808,000	2.0%
44	South Dakota	484,076,000	0.3%
13	Tennessee	3,421,140,000	2.4%
2	Texas	14,708,234,000	10.1%
35	Utah	1,218,571,000	0.8%
49	Vermont	289,165,000	0.2%
11	Virginia	4,136,995,000	2.8%
17	Washington	2,954,355,000	2.0%
38	West Virginia	847,699,000	0.6%
21	Wisconsin	2,737,306,000	1.9%
48	Wyoming	368,656,000	0.3%

RANK	STATE	GALLONS	% of USA
1	California	15,528,126,000	10.7%
2	Texas	14,708,234,000	10.1%
3	Florida	9,387,461,000	6.5%
4	New York	5,844,464,000	4.0%
5	Ohio	5,159,762,000	3.6%
6	Georgia	5,067,266,000	3.5%
7	Pennsylvania	4,912,627,000	3.4%
8	North Carolina	4,871,585,000	3.4%
9	Illinois	4,868,216,000	3.4%
10	Michigan	4,867,848,000	3.4%
11	Virginia	4,136,995,000	2.8%
12	New Jersey	3,967,448,000	2.7%
13	Tennessee	3,421,140,000	2.4%
14	Missouri	3,213,117,000	2.2%
15	Indiana	3,166,337,000	2.2%
16	Arizona	3,014,859,000	2.1%
17	Washington	2,954,355,000	2.0%
18	South Carolina	2,855,808,000	2.0%
19	Massachusetts	2,820,756,000	1.9%
20	Alabama	2,737,856,000	1.9%
21	Wisconsin	2,737,306,000	1.9%
22	Maryland	2,730,974,000	1.9%
23	Minnesota	2,677,347,000	1.8%
24	Colorado	2,391,219,000	1.6%
25	Kentucky	2,253,270,000	1.6%
26	Louisiana	2,201,904,000	1.5%
27	Oklahoma	1,990,631,000	1.4%
28	Iowa	1,684,430,000	1.2%
29	Mississippi	1,682,011,000	1.2%
30	Oregon	1,649,040,000	1.1%
31	Connecticut	1,520,748,000	1.0%
32	Arkansas	1,506,815,000	1.0%
33	Kansas	1,308,690,000	0.9%
34	Nevada	1,249,965,000	0.9%
35	Utah	1,218,571,000	0.8%
36	New Mexico	1,022,574,000	0.7%
37	Nebraska	922,934,000	0.6%
38	West Virginia	847,699,000	0.6%
39	Idaho	815,376,000	0.6%
40	New Hampshire	734,864,000	0.5%
41	Maine	658,457,000	0.5%
42	Montana	550,856,000	0.4%
43	Delaware	521,719,000	0.4%
44	South Dakota	484,076,000	0.3%
45	Hawaii	465,173,000	0.3%
46	North Dakota	446,320,000	0.3%
47	Rhode Island	392,776,000	0.3%
48	Wyoming	368,656,000	0.3%
49	Vermont	289,165,000	0.2%
50	Alaska	286,129,000	0.2%
	District of Columbia	121,217,000	0.1%

Source: U.S. Department of Transportation, Federal Highway Administration
   "Highway Statistics 2018" (Table MF-21, https://www.fhwa.dot.gov/policyinformation/statistics/2018/)
*Includes gasoline for highway and nonhighway uses as well as for losses allowed for evaporation and handling. "Gasoline"
includes gasohol but excludes "special fuels" such as diesel.

Per Capita Gasoline Used in 2018

National Per Capita = 445 Gallons*

ALPHA ORDER

RANK	STATE	PER CAPITA
5	Alabama	560
44	Alaska	389
37	Arizona	421
16	Arkansas	501
42	California	393
38	Colorado	420
36	Connecticut	426
8	Delaware	540
34	Florida	442
21	Georgia	482
49	Hawaii	327
29	Idaho	466
47	Illinois	383
24	Indiana	473
9	Iowa	535
32	Kansas	450
13	Kentucky	505
24	Louisiana	473
17	Maine	492
31	Maryland	452
40	Massachusetts	410
19	Michigan	488
23	Minnesota	478
3	Mississippi	564
10	Missouri	525
11	Montana	519
22	Nebraska	479
39	Nevada	413
7	New Hampshire	543
33	New Jersey	446
18	New Mexico	489
50	New York	299
28	North Carolina	469
2	North Dakota	589
34	Ohio	442
13	Oklahoma	505
41	Oregon	394
46	Pennsylvania	384
48	Rhode Island	371
4	South Carolina	562
6	South Dakota	551
13	Tennessee	505
12	Texas	514
45	Utah	386
30	Vermont	463
20	Virginia	487
42	Washington	393
27	West Virginia	470
26	Wisconsin	471
1	Wyoming	638

RANK ORDER

RANK	STATE	PER CAPITA
1	Wyoming	638
2	North Dakota	589
3	Mississippi	564
4	South Carolina	562
5	Alabama	560
6	South Dakota	551
7	New Hampshire	543
8	Delaware	540
9	Iowa	535
10	Missouri	525
11	Montana	519
12	Texas	514
13	Kentucky	505
13	Oklahoma	505
13	Tennessee	505
16	Arkansas	501
17	Maine	492
18	New Mexico	489
19	Michigan	488
20	Virginia	487
21	Georgia	482
22	Nebraska	479
23	Minnesota	478
24	Indiana	473
24	Louisiana	473
26	Wisconsin	471
27	West Virginia	470
28	North Carolina	469
29	Idaho	466
30	Vermont	463
31	Maryland	452
32	Kansas	450
33	New Jersey	446
34	Florida	442
34	Ohio	442
36	Connecticut	426
37	Arizona	421
38	Colorado	420
39	Nevada	413
40	Massachusetts	410
41	Oregon	394
42	California	393
42	Washington	393
44	Alaska	389
45	Utah	386
46	Pennsylvania	384
47	Illinois	383
48	Rhode Island	371
49	Hawaii	327
50	New York	299
	District of Columbia	173

Source: CQ Press using data from U.S. Department of Transportation, Federal Highway Administration
"Highway Statistics 2018" (Table MF-21, https://www.fhwa.dot.gov/policyinformation/statistics/2018/)
*Includes gasoline for highway and nonhighway uses as well as for losses allowed for evaporation and handling. "Gasoline" includes gasohol but excludes "special fuels" such as diesel.

Daily Production of Crude Oil in 2018

National Total = 10,990,468 Barrels a Day*

ALPHA ORDER					RANK ORDER			
RANK	STATE	BARRELS	% of USA		RANK	STATE	BARRELS	% of USA
18	Alabama	16,121	0.1%		1	Texas	4,408,425	40.1%
6	Alaska	478,904	4.4%		2	North Dakota	1,264,468	11.5%
31	Arizona	30	0.0%		3	New Mexico	682,077	6.2%
20	Arkansas	13,748	0.1%		4	Oklahoma	549,822	5.0%
7	California	463,468	4.2%		5	Colorado	487,170	4.4%
5	Colorado	487,170	4.4%		6	Alaska	478,904	4.4%
NA	Connecticut**	NA	NA		7	California	463,468	4.2%
NA	Delaware**	NA	NA		8	Wyoming	240,973	2.2%
23	Florida	5,038	0.0%		9	Louisiana	133,811	1.2%
NA	Georgia**	NA	NA		10	Utah	101,542	0.9%
NA	Hawaii**	NA	NA		11	Kansas	95,107	0.9%
30	Idaho	241	0.0%		12	Ohio	63,627	0.6%
16	Illinois	23,068	0.2%		13	Montana	59,014	0.5%
24	Indiana	4,614	0.0%		14	Mississippi	46,447	0.4%
NA	Iowa**	NA	NA		15	West Virginia	31,830	0.3%
11	Kansas	95,107	0.9%		16	Illinois	23,068	0.2%
21	Kentucky	6,205	0.1%		17	Pennsylvania	17,748	0.2%
9	Louisiana	133,811	1.2%		18	Alabama	16,121	0.1%
NA	Maine**	NA	NA		19	Michigan	14,816	0.1%
NA	Maryland**	NA	NA		20	Arkansas	13,748	0.1%
NA	Massachusetts**	NA	NA		21	Kentucky	6,205	0.1%
19	Michigan	14,816	0.1%		22	Nebraska	5,633	0.1%
NA	Minnesota**	NA	NA		23	Florida	5,038	0.0%
14	Mississippi	46,447	0.4%		24	Indiana	4,614	0.0%
29	Missouri	247	0.0%		25	South Dakota	3,488	0.0%
13	Montana	59,014	0.5%		26	Nevada	699	0.0%
22	Nebraska	5,633	0.1%		27	New York	605	0.0%
26	Nevada	699	0.0%		28	Tennessee	575	0.0%
NA	New Hampshire**	NA	NA		29	Missouri	247	0.0%
NA	New Jersey**	NA	NA		30	Idaho	241	0.0%
3	New Mexico	682,077	6.2%		31	Arizona	30	0.0%
27	New York	605	0.0%		32	Virginia	14	0.0%
NA	North Carolina**	NA	NA		NA	Connecticut**	NA	NA
2	North Dakota	1,264,468	11.5%		NA	Delaware**	NA	NA
12	Ohio	63,627	0.6%		NA	Georgia**	NA	NA
4	Oklahoma	549,822	5.0%		NA	Hawaii**	NA	NA
NA	Oregon**	NA	NA		NA	Iowa**	NA	NA
17	Pennsylvania	17,748	0.2%		NA	Maine**	NA	NA
NA	Rhode Island**	NA	NA		NA	Maryland**	NA	NA
NA	South Carolina**	NA	NA		NA	Massachusetts**	NA	NA
25	South Dakota	3,488	0.0%		NA	Minnesota**	NA	NA
28	Tennessee	575	0.0%		NA	New Hampshire**	NA	NA
1	Texas	4,408,425	40.1%		NA	New Jersey**	NA	NA
10	Utah	101,542	0.9%		NA	North Carolina**	NA	NA
NA	Vermont**	NA	NA		NA	Oregon**	NA	NA
32	Virginia	14	0.0%		NA	Rhode Island**	NA	NA
NA	Washington**	NA	NA		NA	South Carolina**	NA	NA
15	West Virginia	31,830	0.3%		NA	Vermont**	NA	NA
NA	Wisconsin**	NA	NA		NA	Washington**	NA	NA
8	Wyoming	240,973	2.2%		NA	Wisconsin**	NA	NA
						District of Columbia**	NA	NA

Source: CQ Press using data from U.S. Department of Energy, Energy Information Administration
"Petroleum Supply Annual 2018, Volume 1" (https://www.eia.gov/petroleum/supply/annual/volume1/)
*National total includes 1,770,896 barrels a day in federal offshore production. Figures for Alaska, California, Louisiana, and Texas include state offshore production.
**No reported production.

Fossil Fuel Emissions in 2017

National Total = 4,912,000,000 Metric Tons of Carbon Dioxide (CO2)*

ALPHA ORDER

RANK	STATE	TONS OF CO2	% of USA
15	Alabama	108,000,000	2.2%
40	Alaska	34,610,000	0.7%
24	Arizona	86,140,000	1.8%
30	Arkansas	64,140,000	1.3%
2	California	368,050,000	7.5%
23	Colorado	87,120,000	1.8%
41	Connecticut	33,920,000	0.7%
48	Delaware	13,090,000	0.3%
3	Florida	228,300,000	4.6%
11	Georgia	132,810,000	2.7%
44	Hawaii	18,620,000	0.4%
43	Idaho	18,690,000	0.4%
7	Illinois	203,620,000	4.1%
8	Indiana	174,970,000	3.6%
26	Iowa	76,420,000	1.6%
32	Kansas	58,650,000	1.2%
14	Kentucky	115,250,000	2.3%
5	Louisiana	216,440,000	4.4%
45	Maine	15,630,000	0.3%
34	Maryland	52,730,000	1.1%
29	Massachusetts	64,350,000	1.3%
10	Michigan	152,910,000	3.1%
22	Minnesota	88,690,000	1.8%
28	Mississippi	68,290,000	1.4%
12	Missouri	121,980,000	2.5%
42	Montana	30,890,000	0.6%
37	Nebraska	47,680,000	1.0%
39	Nevada	36,640,000	0.7%
47	New Hampshire	13,550,000	0.3%
16	New Jersey	103,210,000	2.1%
36	New Mexico	49,370,000	1.0%
9	New York	159,950,000	3.3%
13	North Carolina	115,540,000	2.4%
35	North Dakota	52,100,000	1.1%
6	Ohio	204,940,000	4.2%
20	Oklahoma	93,970,000	1.9%
38	Oregon	38,760,000	0.8%
4	Pennsylvania	216,700,000	4.4%
49	Rhode Island	10,130,000	0.2%
27	South Carolina	69,770,000	1.4%
46	South Dakota	14,560,000	0.3%
18	Tennessee	98,300,000	2.0%
1	Texas	714,550,000	14.5%
33	Utah	58,290,000	1.2%
50	Vermont	5,890,000	0.1%
17	Virginia	98,820,000	2.0%
25	Washington	80,920,000	1.6%
21	West Virginia	89,390,000	1.8%
19	Wisconsin	97,850,000	2.0%
31	Wyoming	60,950,000	1.2%

RANK ORDER

RANK	STATE	TONS OF CO2	% of USA
1	Texas	714,550,000	14.5%
2	California	368,050,000	7.5%
3	Florida	228,300,000	4.6%
4	Pennsylvania	216,700,000	4.4%
5	Louisiana	216,440,000	4.4%
6	Ohio	204,940,000	4.2%
7	Illinois	203,620,000	4.1%
8	Indiana	174,970,000	3.6%
9	New York	159,950,000	3.3%
10	Michigan	152,910,000	3.1%
11	Georgia	132,810,000	2.7%
12	Missouri	121,980,000	2.5%
13	North Carolina	115,540,000	2.4%
14	Kentucky	115,250,000	2.3%
15	Alabama	108,000,000	2.2%
16	New Jersey	103,210,000	2.1%
17	Virginia	98,820,000	2.0%
18	Tennessee	98,300,000	2.0%
19	Wisconsin	97,850,000	2.0%
20	Oklahoma	93,970,000	1.9%
21	West Virginia	89,390,000	1.8%
22	Minnesota	88,690,000	1.8%
23	Colorado	87,120,000	1.8%
24	Arizona	86,140,000	1.8%
25	Washington	80,920,000	1.6%
26	Iowa	76,420,000	1.6%
27	South Carolina	69,770,000	1.4%
28	Mississippi	68,290,000	1.4%
29	Massachusetts	64,350,000	1.3%
30	Arkansas	64,140,000	1.3%
31	Wyoming	60,950,000	1.2%
32	Kansas	58,650,000	1.2%
33	Utah	58,290,000	1.2%
34	Maryland	52,730,000	1.1%
35	North Dakota	52,100,000	1.1%
36	New Mexico	49,370,000	1.0%
37	Nebraska	47,680,000	1.0%
38	Oregon	38,760,000	0.8%
39	Nevada	36,640,000	0.7%
40	Alaska	34,610,000	0.7%
41	Connecticut	33,920,000	0.7%
42	Montana	30,890,000	0.6%
43	Idaho	18,690,000	0.4%
44	Hawaii	18,620,000	0.4%
45	Maine	15,630,000	0.3%
46	South Dakota	14,560,000	0.3%
47	New Hampshire	13,550,000	0.3%
48	Delaware	13,090,000	0.3%
49	Rhode Island	10,130,000	0.2%
50	Vermont	5,890,000	0.1%
	District of Columbia	2,640,000	0.1%

Source: U.S. Environmental Protection Agency
"Energy CO2 Emissions by State" (https://www.epa.gov/statelocalenergy/state-co2-emissions-fossil-fuel-combustion)
*Carbon dioxide (CO2) emissions from fossil fuel combustion. This represents the largest source (93%) of total CO2 emissions from all emission sources. Emissions are based on the location where fossil fuels are used. Fuels can be used in one state to generate electricity consumed in another. National figure does not include non-energy use of fuels.

Per Capita Fossil Fuel Emissions in 2017

National Per Capita = 15.1 Metric Tons of Carbon Dioxide (CO2)*

ALPHA ORDER

RANK	STATE	PER CAPITA
15	Alabama	22.2
4	Alaska	46.8
34	Arizona	12.2
16	Arkansas	21.4
45	California	9.4
26	Colorado	15.5
44	Connecticut	9.5
30	Delaware	13.7
39	Florida	10.9
32	Georgia	12.8
31	Hawaii	13.1
39	Idaho	10.9
24	Illinois	15.9
7	Indiana	26.3
11	Iowa	24.3
17	Kansas	20.2
8	Kentucky	25.9
5	Louisiana	46.3
35	Maine	11.7
49	Maryland	8.8
45	Massachusetts	9.4
27	Michigan	15.3
24	Minnesota	15.9
14	Mississippi	22.9
18	Missouri	20.0
6	Montana	29.3
10	Nebraska	24.9
33	Nevada	12.3
42	New Hampshire	10.0
37	New Jersey	11.6
13	New Mexico	23.6
50	New York	8.2
38	North Carolina	11.3
2	North Dakota	69.0
20	Ohio	17.6
12	Oklahoma	23.9
45	Oregon	9.4
21	Pennsylvania	16.9
43	Rhode Island	9.6
29	South Carolina	13.9
23	South Dakota	16.7
28	Tennessee	14.7
9	Texas	25.3
19	Utah	18.8
45	Vermont	9.4
35	Virginia	11.7
39	Washington	10.9
3	West Virginia	49.2
21	Wisconsin	16.9
1	Wyoming	105.3

RANK ORDER

RANK	STATE	PER CAPITA
1	Wyoming	105.3
2	North Dakota	69.0
3	West Virginia	49.2
4	Alaska	46.8
5	Louisiana	46.3
6	Montana	29.3
7	Indiana	26.3
8	Kentucky	25.9
9	Texas	25.3
10	Nebraska	24.9
11	Iowa	24.3
12	Oklahoma	23.9
13	New Mexico	23.6
14	Mississippi	22.9
15	Alabama	22.2
16	Arkansas	21.4
17	Kansas	20.2
18	Missouri	20.0
19	Utah	18.8
20	Ohio	17.6
21	Pennsylvania	16.9
21	Wisconsin	16.9
23	South Dakota	16.7
24	Illinois	15.9
24	Minnesota	15.9
26	Colorado	15.5
27	Michigan	15.3
28	Tennessee	14.7
29	South Carolina	13.9
30	Delaware	13.7
31	Hawaii	13.1
32	Georgia	12.8
33	Nevada	12.3
34	Arizona	12.2
35	Maine	11.7
35	Virginia	11.7
37	New Jersey	11.6
38	North Carolina	11.3
39	Florida	10.9
39	Idaho	10.9
39	Washington	10.9
42	New Hampshire	10.0
43	Rhode Island	9.6
44	Connecticut	9.5
45	California	9.4
45	Massachusetts	9.4
45	Oregon	9.4
45	Vermont	9.4
49	Maryland	8.8
50	New York	8.2
	District of Columbia	3.8

Source: CQ Press using data from U.S. Environmental Protection Agency
"Energy CO2 Emissions by State" (https://www.epa.gov/statelocalenergy/state-co2-emissions-fossil-fuel-combustion)
*Carbon dioxide (CO2) emissions from fossil fuel combustion. This represents the largest source (93%) of total CO2 emissions from all emission sources. Emissions are based on the location where fossil fuels are used. Fuels can be used in one state to generate electricity consumed in another. National figure doe not include non-energy use of fuels.

Percent Change in Fossil Fuel Emissions: 2013 to 2017

National Percent Change = 4.8% Decrease*

ALPHA ORDER				RANK ORDER		
RANK	STATE	PERCENT CHANGE		RANK	STATE	PERCENT CHANGE
40	Alabama	(9.4)		1	Mississippi	12.6
24	Alaska	(3.6)		2	Idaho	8.7
38	Arizona	(9.2)		3	Washington	8.0
33	Arkansas	(5.9)		4	Louisiana	3.4
8	California	1.9		5	Florida	3.3
25	Colorado	(3.9)		6	Texas	2.2
20	Connecticut	(3.1)		7	Vermont	2.1
26	Delaware	(4.0)		8	California	1.9
5	Florida	3.3		9	Hawaii	1.5
15	Georgia	(0.8)		10	Nevada	0.7
9	Hawaii	1.5		11	Tennessee	0.5
2	Idaho	8.7		12	Rhode Island	(0.3)
47	Illinois	(11.8)		13	South Carolina	(0.6)
45	Indiana	(11.6)		14	Oregon	(0.7)
35	Iowa	(7.3)		15	Georgia	(0.8)
49	Kansas	(15.6)		16	Minnesota	(0.9)
50	Kentucky	(15.8)		17	New York	(1.8)
4	Louisiana	3.4		18	Massachusetts	(2.1)
32	Maine	(5.8)		19	Wisconsin	(2.7)
46	Maryland	(11.7)		20	Connecticut	(3.1)
18	Massachusetts	(2.1)		21	North Dakota	(3.2)
28	Michigan	(4.9)		22	Montana	(3.3)
16	Minnesota	(0.9)		23	West Virginia	(3.4)
1	Mississippi	12.6		24	Alaska	(3.6)
36	Missouri	(7.4)		25	Colorado	(3.9)
22	Montana	(3.3)		26	Delaware	(4.0)
41	Nebraska	(10.2)		27	New Jersey	(4.4)
10	Nevada	0.7		28	Michigan	(4.9)
29	New Hampshire	(5.2)		29	New Hampshire	(5.2)
27	New Jersey	(4.4)		29	South Dakota	(5.2)
36	New Mexico	(7.4)		31	Virginia	(5.5)
17	New York	(1.8)		32	Maine	(5.8)
34	North Carolina	(6.8)		33	Arkansas	(5.9)
21	North Dakota	(3.2)		34	North Carolina	(6.8)
42	Ohio	(10.3)		35	Iowa	(7.3)
38	Oklahoma	(9.2)		36	Missouri	(7.4)
14	Oregon	(0.7)		36	New Mexico	(7.4)
44	Pennsylvania	(11.3)		38	Arizona	(9.2)
12	Rhode Island	(0.3)		38	Oklahoma	(9.2)
13	South Carolina	(0.6)		40	Alabama	(9.4)
29	South Dakota	(5.2)		41	Nebraska	(10.2)
11	Tennessee	0.5		42	Ohio	(10.3)
6	Texas	2.2		43	Wyoming	(10.7)
48	Utah	(11.9)		44	Pennsylvania	(11.3)
7	Vermont	2.1		45	Indiana	(11.6)
31	Virginia	(5.5)		46	Maryland	(11.7)
3	Washington	8.0		47	Illinois	(11.8)
23	West Virginia	(3.4)		48	Utah	(11.9)
19	Wisconsin	(2.7)		49	Kansas	(15.6)
43	Wyoming	(10.7)		50	Kentucky	(15.8)
					District of Columbia	(6.7)

Source: CQ Press using data from U.S. Environmental Protection Agency
   "Energy CO2 Emissions by State" (https://www.epa.gov/statelocalenergy/state-co2-emissions-fossil-fuel-combustion)
*Based on metric tons of carbon dioxide (CO2).

Toxic Releases: Total Pollution Released in 2018

National Total = 3,793,761,886 Pounds*

ALPHA ORDER

RANK	STATE	POUNDS	% of USA
11	Alabama	78,950,274	2.1%
1	Alaska	971,995,527	25.6%
5	Arizona	170,539,160	4.5%
23	Arkansas	36,487,460	1.0%
24	California	34,512,229	0.9%
33	Colorado	24,450,810	0.6%
47	Connecticut	2,057,672	0.1%
43	Delaware	6,457,611	0.2%
14	Florida	61,354,563	1.6%
20	Georgia	50,591,908	1.3%
46	Hawaii	2,943,091	0.1%
26	Idaho	34,369,653	0.9%
8	Illinois	121,761,454	3.2%
7	Indiana	128,636,004	3.4%
21	Iowa	39,714,667	1.0%
34	Kansas	23,985,689	0.6%
19	Kentucky	50,842,423	1.3%
6	Louisiana	146,028,476	3.8%
41	Maine	11,540,563	0.3%
44	Maryland	6,242,562	0.2%
45	Massachusetts	4,005,826	0.1%
12	Michigan	78,593,796	2.1%
32	Minnesota	27,205,942	0.7%
13	Mississippi	61,575,985	1.6%
15	Missouri	60,255,874	1.6%
18	Montana	51,395,661	1.4%
37	Nebraska	18,591,002	0.5%
2	Nevada	339,146,713	8.9%
49	New Hampshire	424,901	0.0%
40	New Jersey	12,303,337	0.3%
38	New Mexico	16,702,258	0.4%
36	New York	20,367,476	0.5%
17	North Carolina	55,013,156	1.5%
31	North Dakota	30,209,854	0.8%
9	Ohio	112,753,169	3.0%
28	Oklahoma	31,454,108	0.8%
39	Oregon	15,849,898	0.4%
16	Pennsylvania	55,157,422	1.5%
48	Rhode Island	427,844	0.0%
22	South Carolina	37,103,174	1.0%
42	South Dakota	7,526,815	0.2%
10	Tennessee	88,717,821	2.3%
4	Texas	225,215,145	5.9%
3	Utah	291,315,037	7.7%
50	Vermont	363,987	0.0%
25	Virginia	34,481,993	0.9%
30	Washington	30,232,918	0.8%
29	West Virginia	30,789,309	0.8%
27	Wisconsin	31,664,404	0.8%
35	Wyoming	21,422,761	0.6%

RANK ORDER

RANK	STATE	POUNDS	% of USA
1	Alaska	971,995,527	25.6%
2	Nevada	339,146,713	8.9%
3	Utah	291,315,037	7.7%
4	Texas	225,215,145	5.9%
5	Arizona	170,539,160	4.5%
6	Louisiana	146,028,476	3.8%
7	Indiana	128,636,004	3.4%
8	Illinois	121,761,454	3.2%
9	Ohio	112,753,169	3.0%
10	Tennessee	88,717,821	2.3%
11	Alabama	78,950,274	2.1%
12	Michigan	78,593,796	2.1%
13	Mississippi	61,575,985	1.6%
14	Florida	61,354,563	1.6%
15	Missouri	60,255,874	1.6%
16	Pennsylvania	55,157,422	1.5%
17	North Carolina	55,013,156	1.5%
18	Montana	51,395,661	1.4%
19	Kentucky	50,842,423	1.3%
20	Georgia	50,591,908	1.3%
21	Iowa	39,714,667	1.0%
22	South Carolina	37,103,174	1.0%
23	Arkansas	36,487,460	1.0%
24	California	34,512,229	0.9%
25	Virginia	34,481,993	0.9%
26	Idaho	34,369,653	0.9%
27	Wisconsin	31,664,404	0.8%
28	Oklahoma	31,454,108	0.8%
29	West Virginia	30,789,309	0.8%
30	Washington	30,232,918	0.8%
31	North Dakota	30,209,854	0.8%
32	Minnesota	27,205,942	0.7%
33	Colorado	24,450,810	0.6%
34	Kansas	23,985,689	0.6%
35	Wyoming	21,422,761	0.6%
36	New York	20,367,476	0.5%
37	Nebraska	18,591,002	0.5%
38	New Mexico	16,702,258	0.4%
39	Oregon	15,849,898	0.4%
40	New Jersey	12,303,337	0.3%
41	Maine	11,540,563	0.3%
42	South Dakota	7,526,815	0.2%
43	Delaware	6,457,611	0.2%
44	Maryland	6,242,562	0.2%
45	Massachusetts	4,005,826	0.1%
46	Hawaii	2,943,091	0.1%
47	Connecticut	2,057,672	0.1%
48	Rhode Island	427,844	0.0%
49	New Hampshire	424,901	0.0%
50	Vermont	363,987	0.0%
	District of Columbia	32,504	0.0%

Source: U.S. Environmental Protection Agency, Office of Pollution Prevention and Toxics Information Management
"2018 Toxics Release Inventory" (https://enviro.epa.gov/triexplorer/tri_release.chemical)
*National total does not include 6,798,194 pounds of toxins in U.S. territories. Includes discharges to air, surface water, underground injection, and surface land. Includes both original (or manufacturing) industries and those added by EPA since it began tracking releases.

Toxic Releases: Total Air Emissions in 2018

National Total = 600,157,519 Pounds*

ALPHA ORDER					RANK ORDER			
RANK	STATE	POUNDS	% of USA		RANK	STATE	POUNDS	% of USA
5	Alabama	28,628,036	4.8%		1	Texas	54,519,543	9.1%
47	Alaska	328,793	0.1%		2	Louisiana	53,514,993	8.9%
36	Arizona	2,310,281	0.4%		3	Ohio	36,729,021	6.1%
17	Arkansas	15,131,713	2.5%		4	Georgia	32,628,308	5.4%
26	California	7,366,934	1.2%		5	Alabama	28,628,036	4.8%
38	Colorado	2,106,247	0.4%		6	Indiana	27,523,100	4.6%
45	Connecticut	758,508	0.1%		7	Tennessee	24,018,344	4.0%
46	Delaware	739,722	0.1%		8	Illinois	23,493,791	3.9%
13	Florida	18,354,267	3.1%		9	North Carolina	22,420,564	3.7%
4	Georgia	32,628,308	5.4%		10	South Carolina	20,688,498	3.4%
40	Hawaii	1,826,598	0.3%		11	Kentucky	19,009,907	3.2%
32	Idaho	5,117,263	0.9%		12	Iowa	18,990,956	3.2%
8	Illinois	23,493,791	3.9%		13	Florida	18,354,267	3.1%
6	Indiana	27,523,100	4.6%		14	Oklahoma	17,303,828	2.9%
12	Iowa	18,990,956	3.2%		15	Virginia	16,508,012	2.8%
22	Kansas	9,776,630	1.6%		16	Mississippi	16,395,990	2.7%
11	Kentucky	19,009,907	3.2%		17	Arkansas	15,131,713	2.5%
2	Louisiana	53,514,993	8.9%		18	Pennsylvania	15,070,324	2.5%
33	Maine	3,194,318	0.5%		19	West Virginia	12,602,037	2.1%
34	Maryland	3,027,160	0.5%		20	Michigan	11,527,639	1.9%
44	Massachusetts	784,016	0.1%		21	Minnesota	9,798,757	1.6%
20	Michigan	11,527,639	1.9%		22	Kansas	9,776,630	1.6%
21	Minnesota	9,798,757	1.6%		23	Missouri	9,560,499	1.6%
16	Mississippi	16,395,990	2.7%		24	Wisconsin	9,362,108	1.6%
23	Missouri	9,560,499	1.6%		25	Utah	7,391,754	1.2%
39	Montana	2,026,538	0.3%		26	California	7,366,934	1.2%
30	Nebraska	5,878,744	1.0%		27	Washington	7,153,145	1.2%
43	Nevada	816,215	0.1%		28	North Dakota	7,032,359	1.2%
48	New Hampshire	198,581	0.0%		29	Oregon	6,032,019	1.0%
37	New Jersey	2,136,011	0.4%		30	Nebraska	5,878,744	1.0%
42	New Mexico	946,482	0.2%		31	New York	5,129,606	0.9%
31	New York	5,129,606	0.9%		32	Idaho	5,117,263	0.9%
9	North Carolina	22,420,564	3.7%		33	Maine	3,194,318	0.5%
28	North Dakota	7,032,359	1.2%		34	Maryland	3,027,160	0.5%
3	Ohio	36,729,021	6.1%		35	Wyoming	2,415,313	0.4%
14	Oklahoma	17,303,828	2.9%		36	Arizona	2,310,281	0.4%
29	Oregon	6,032,019	1.0%		37	New Jersey	2,136,011	0.4%
18	Pennsylvania	15,070,324	2.5%		38	Colorado	2,106,247	0.4%
49	Rhode Island	143,209	0.0%		39	Montana	2,026,538	0.3%
10	South Carolina	20,688,498	3.4%		40	Hawaii	1,826,598	0.3%
41	South Dakota	1,707,664	0.3%		41	South Dakota	1,707,664	0.3%
7	Tennessee	24,018,344	4.0%		42	New Mexico	946,482	0.2%
1	Texas	54,519,543	9.1%		43	Nevada	816,215	0.1%
25	Utah	7,391,754	1.2%		44	Massachusetts	784,016	0.1%
50	Vermont	32,775	0.0%		45	Connecticut	758,508	0.1%
15	Virginia	16,508,012	2.8%		46	Delaware	739,722	0.1%
27	Washington	7,153,145	1.2%		47	Alaska	328,793	0.1%
19	West Virginia	12,602,037	2.1%		48	New Hampshire	198,581	0.0%
24	Wisconsin	9,362,108	1.6%		49	Rhode Island	143,209	0.0%
35	Wyoming	2,415,313	0.4%		50	Vermont	32,775	0.0%
						District of Columbia	399	0.0%

Source: U.S. Environmental Protection Agency, Office of Pollution Prevention and Toxics Information Management
"2018 Toxics Release Inventory" (https://enviro.epa.gov/triexplorer/tri_release.chemical)
*Includes fugitive and point source air emissions. National total does not include 1,859,317 pounds of emissions in U.S. territories. Includes both original (or manufacturing) industries and those added by EPA since it began tracking releases.

Toxic Releases: Total Surface Water Discharges in 2018

National Total = 195,036,968 Pounds*

ALPHA ORDER

RANK	STATE	POUNDS	% of USA
4	Alabama	11,009,160	5.6%
37	Alaska	528,185	0.3%
50	Arizona	897	0.0%
13	Arkansas	5,807,871	3.0%
23	California	3,510,056	1.8%
35	Colorado	768,096	0.4%
44	Connecticut	33,146	0.0%
14	Delaware	5,416,033	2.8%
32	Florida	1,149,010	0.6%
10	Georgia	7,497,843	3.8%
36	Hawaii	749,919	0.4%
27	Idaho	2,837,984	1.5%
7	Illinois	7,918,692	4.1%
2	Indiana	15,242,822	7.8%
16	Iowa	5,183,654	2.7%
33	Kansas	988,894	0.5%
12	Kentucky	6,090,559	3.1%
3	Louisiana	14,368,993	7.4%
15	Maine	5,225,540	2.7%
42	Maryland	62,454	0.0%
46	Massachusetts	7,537	0.0%
22	Michigan	3,609,494	1.9%
30	Minnesota	2,288,117	1.2%
6	Mississippi	8,461,456	4.3%
28	Missouri	2,787,342	1.4%
41	Montana	74,787	0.0%
19	Nebraska	3,712,259	1.9%
45	Nevada	26,536	0.0%
49	New Hampshire	956	0.0%
18	New Jersey	3,740,529	1.9%
43	New Mexico	42,135	0.0%
17	New York	4,071,480	2.1%
8	North Carolina	7,878,937	4.0%
38	North Dakota	173,132	0.1%
11	Ohio	6,817,536	3.5%
21	Oklahoma	3,658,939	1.9%
34	Oregon	797,970	0.4%
9	Pennsylvania	7,547,793	3.9%
48	Rhode Island	1,016	0.0%
20	South Carolina	3,664,095	1.9%
25	South Dakota	2,959,692	1.5%
24	Tennessee	3,235,409	1.7%
1	Texas	17,860,978	9.2%
40	Utah	123,321	0.1%
39	Vermont	128,472	0.1%
5	Virginia	9,151,501	4.7%
26	Washington	2,949,618	1.5%
31	West Virginia	2,245,799	1.2%
29	Wisconsin	2,622,482	1.3%
47	Wyoming	5,537	0.0%

RANK ORDER

RANK	STATE	POUNDS	% of USA
1	Texas	17,860,978	9.2%
2	Indiana	15,242,822	7.8%
3	Louisiana	14,368,993	7.4%
4	Alabama	11,009,160	5.6%
5	Virginia	9,151,501	4.7%
6	Mississippi	8,461,456	4.3%
7	Illinois	7,918,692	4.1%
8	North Carolina	7,878,937	4.0%
9	Pennsylvania	7,547,793	3.9%
10	Georgia	7,497,843	3.8%
11	Ohio	6,817,536	3.5%
12	Kentucky	6,090,559	3.1%
13	Arkansas	5,807,871	3.0%
14	Delaware	5,416,033	2.8%
15	Maine	5,225,540	2.7%
16	Iowa	5,183,654	2.7%
17	New York	4,071,480	2.1%
18	New Jersey	3,740,529	1.9%
19	Nebraska	3,712,259	1.9%
20	South Carolina	3,664,095	1.9%
21	Oklahoma	3,658,939	1.9%
22	Michigan	3,609,494	1.9%
23	California	3,510,056	1.8%
24	Tennessee	3,235,409	1.7%
25	South Dakota	2,959,692	1.5%
26	Washington	2,949,618	1.5%
27	Idaho	2,837,984	1.5%
28	Missouri	2,787,342	1.4%
29	Wisconsin	2,622,482	1.3%
30	Minnesota	2,288,117	1.2%
31	West Virginia	2,245,799	1.2%
32	Florida	1,149,010	0.6%
33	Kansas	988,894	0.5%
34	Oregon	797,970	0.4%
35	Colorado	768,096	0.4%
36	Hawaii	749,919	0.4%
37	Alaska	528,185	0.3%
38	North Dakota	173,132	0.1%
39	Vermont	128,472	0.1%
40	Utah	123,321	0.1%
41	Montana	74,787	0.0%
42	Maryland	62,454	0.0%
43	New Mexico	42,135	0.0%
44	Connecticut	33,146	0.0%
45	Nevada	26,536	0.0%
46	Massachusetts	7,537	0.0%
47	Wyoming	5,537	0.0%
48	Rhode Island	1,016	0.0%
49	New Hampshire	956	0.0%
50	Arizona	897	0.0%
	District of Columbia	2,305	0.0%

Source: U.S. Environmental Protection Agency, Office of Pollution Prevention and Toxics Information Management
"2018 Toxics Release Inventory" (https://enviro.epa.gov/triexplorer/tri_release.chemical)
*National total does not include 248,108 pounds of discharges in U.S. territories. Includes both original (or manufacturing) industries and those added by EPA since it began tracking releases.

Hazardous Waste Sites on the National Priority List in 2019

National Total = 1,386 Sites*

ALPHA ORDER

RANK	STATE	SITES	% of USA
30	Alabama	14	1.0%
45	Alaska	6	0.4%
42	Arizona	9	0.6%
42	Arkansas	9	0.6%
2	California	99	7.1%
19	Colorado	21	1.5%
30	Connecticut	14	1.0%
24	Delaware	17	1.2%
7	Florida	54	3.9%
24	Georgia	17	1.2%
46	Hawaii	3	0.2%
42	Idaho	9	0.6%
8	Illinois	50	3.6%
11	Indiana	42	3.0%
35	Iowa	12	0.9%
30	Kansas	14	1.0%
34	Kentucky	13	0.9%
27	Louisiana	16	1.2%
35	Maine	12	0.9%
19	Maryland	21	1.5%
15	Massachusetts	32	2.3%
5	Michigan	67	4.8%
18	Minnesota	26	1.9%
39	Mississippi	10	0.7%
14	Missouri	34	2.5%
22	Montana	18	1.3%
24	Nebraska	17	1.2%
47	Nevada	2	0.1%
19	New Hampshire	21	1.5%
1	New Jersey	115	8.3%
27	New Mexico	16	1.2%
4	New York	86	6.2%
12	North Carolina	38	2.7%
50	North Dakota	0	0.0%
10	Ohio	43	3.1%
39	Oklahoma	10	0.7%
30	Oregon	14	1.0%
3	Pennsylvania	93	6.7%
35	Rhode Island	12	0.9%
17	South Carolina	27	1.9%
47	South Dakota	2	0.1%
22	Tennessee	18	1.3%
6	Texas	56	4.0%
29	Utah	15	1.1%
35	Vermont	12	0.9%
16	Virginia	31	2.2%
9	Washington	48	3.5%
39	West Virginia	10	0.7%
13	Wisconsin	37	2.7%
49	Wyoming	1	0.1%

RANK ORDER

RANK	STATE	SITES	% of USA
1	New Jersey	115	8.3%
2	California	99	7.1%
3	Pennsylvania	93	6.7%
4	New York	86	6.2%
5	Michigan	67	4.8%
6	Texas	56	4.0%
7	Florida	54	3.9%
8	Illinois	50	3.6%
9	Washington	48	3.5%
10	Ohio	43	3.1%
11	Indiana	42	3.0%
12	North Carolina	38	2.7%
13	Wisconsin	37	2.7%
14	Missouri	34	2.5%
15	Massachusetts	32	2.3%
16	Virginia	31	2.2%
17	South Carolina	27	1.9%
18	Minnesota	26	1.9%
19	Colorado	21	1.5%
19	Maryland	21	1.5%
19	New Hampshire	21	1.5%
22	Montana	18	1.3%
22	Tennessee	18	1.3%
24	Delaware	17	1.2%
24	Georgia	17	1.2%
24	Nebraska	17	1.2%
27	Louisiana	16	1.2%
27	New Mexico	16	1.2%
29	Utah	15	1.1%
30	Alabama	14	1.0%
30	Connecticut	14	1.0%
30	Kansas	14	1.0%
30	Oregon	14	1.0%
34	Kentucky	13	0.9%
35	Iowa	12	0.9%
35	Maine	12	0.9%
35	Rhode Island	12	0.9%
35	Vermont	12	0.9%
39	Mississippi	10	0.7%
39	Oklahoma	10	0.7%
39	West Virginia	10	0.7%
42	Arizona	9	0.6%
42	Arkansas	9	0.6%
42	Idaho	9	0.6%
45	Alaska	6	0.4%
46	Hawaii	3	0.2%
47	Nevada	2	0.1%
47	South Dakota	2	0.1%
49	Wyoming	1	0.1%
50	North Dakota	0	0.0%
	District of Columbia	1	0.1%

Source: U.S. Environmental Protection Agency
   "National Priorities List (NPL) Sites in the United States" (http://www.epa.gov/superfund/sites/npl/)
*As of November 8, 2019. Includes final and proposed General Superfund and Federal Facilities Sites. National total includes ninteen sites in Puerto Rico, two in Guam, and one in the U.S. Virgin Islands.

Hazardous Waste Sites on the National Priority List
per 10,000 Square Miles in 2019
National Rate = 3.6 Sites per 10,000 Square Miles*

ALPHA ORDER

RANK	STATE	RATE
30	Alabama	2.7
48	Alaska	0.1
45	Arizona	0.8
38	Arkansas	1.7
20	California	6.0
36	Colorado	2.0
5	Connecticut	25.3
3	Delaware	68.3
15	Florida	8.2
29	Georgia	2.9
30	Hawaii	2.7
44	Idaho	1.1
13	Illinois	8.6
11	Indiana	11.5
33	Iowa	2.1
38	Kansas	1.7
26	Kentucky	3.2
27	Louisiana	3.1
25	Maine	3.4
8	Maryland	16.9
4	Massachusetts	30.3
18	Michigan	6.9
28	Minnesota	3.0
33	Mississippi	2.1
22	Missouri	4.9
43	Montana	1.2
32	Nebraska	2.2
47	Nevada	0.2
6	New Hampshire	22.5
1	New Jersey	131.8
42	New Mexico	1.3
9	New York	15.8
17	North Carolina	7.1
50	North Dakota	0.0
12	Ohio	9.6
40	Oklahoma	1.4
40	Oregon	1.4
7	Pennsylvania	20.2
2	Rhode Island	77.7
14	South Carolina	8.4
46	South Dakota	0.3
23	Tennessee	4.3
33	Texas	2.1
37	Utah	1.8
10	Vermont	12.5
16	Virginia	7.2
19	Washington	6.7
24	West Virginia	4.1
21	Wisconsin	5.6
48	Wyoming	0.1

RANK ORDER

RANK	STATE	RATE
1	New Jersey	131.8
2	Rhode Island	77.7
3	Delaware	68.3
4	Massachusetts	30.3
5	Connecticut	25.3
6	New Hampshire	22.5
7	Pennsylvania	20.2
8	Maryland	16.9
9	New York	15.8
10	Vermont	12.5
11	Indiana	11.5
12	Ohio	9.6
13	Illinois	8.6
14	South Carolina	8.4
15	Florida	8.2
16	Virginia	7.2
17	North Carolina	7.1
18	Michigan	6.9
19	Washington	6.7
20	California	6.0
21	Wisconsin	5.6
22	Missouri	4.9
23	Tennessee	4.3
24	West Virginia	4.1
25	Maine	3.4
26	Kentucky	3.2
27	Louisiana	3.1
28	Minnesota	3.0
29	Georgia	2.9
30	Alabama	2.7
30	Hawaii	2.7
32	Nebraska	2.2
33	Iowa	2.1
33	Mississippi	2.1
33	Texas	2.1
36	Colorado	2.0
37	Utah	1.8
38	Arkansas	1.7
38	Kansas	1.7
40	Oklahoma	1.4
40	Oregon	1.4
42	New Mexico	1.3
43	Montana	1.2
44	Idaho	1.1
45	Arizona	0.8
46	South Dakota	0.3
47	Nevada	0.2
48	Alaska	0.1
48	Wyoming	0.1
50	North Dakota	0.0
	District of Columbia**	NA

Source: CQ Press using data from U.S. Environmental Protection Agency
  "National Priorities List (NPL) Sites in the United States" (http://www.epa.gov/superfund/sites/npl/)
*As of November 8, 2019. Includes final and proposed General Superfund and Federal Facilities sites. National rate excludes
sites and square miles in Puerto Rico, Guam, and the Virgin Islands. Based on land and water area of states.
**The District of Columbia has one site in its sixty-eight square miles.

Hazardous Waste Sites Deleted from the National Priorities List as of 2019

National Total = 424 Sites*

ALPHA ORDER

RANK	STATE	SITES	% of USA
35	Alabama	3	0.7%
35	Alaska	3	0.7%
35	Arizona	3	0.7%
14	Arkansas	8	1.9%
8	California	15	3.5%
35	Colorado	3	0.7%
28	Connecticut	4	0.9%
18	Delaware	7	1.7%
4	Florida	27	6.4%
24	Georgia	5	1.2%
45	Hawaii	1	0.2%
35	Idaho	3	0.7%
22	Illinois	6	1.4%
12	Indiana	10	2.4%
11	Iowa	11	2.6%
24	Kansas	5	1.2%
18	Kentucky	7	1.7%
10	Louisiana	12	2.8%
28	Maine	4	0.9%
28	Maryland	4	0.9%
14	Massachusetts	8	1.9%
6	Michigan	21	5.0%
5	Minnesota	22	5.2%
28	Mississippi	4	0.9%
24	Missouri	5	1.2%
49	Montana	0	0.0%
45	Nebraska	1	0.2%
49	Nevada	0	0.0%
45	New Hampshire	1	0.2%
1	New Jersey	35	8.3%
28	New Mexico	4	0.9%
1	New York	35	8.3%
28	North Carolina	4	0.9%
41	North Dakota	2	0.5%
14	Ohio	8	1.9%
18	Oklahoma	7	1.7%
24	Oregon	5	1.2%
3	Pennsylvania	34	8.0%
45	Rhode Island	1	0.2%
22	South Carolina	6	1.4%
41	South Dakota	2	0.5%
18	Tennessee	7	1.7%
9	Texas	13	3.1%
13	Utah	9	2.1%
41	Vermont	2	0.5%
28	Virginia	4	0.9%
7	Washington	20	4.7%
35	West Virginia	3	0.7%
14	Wisconsin	8	1.9%
41	Wyoming	2	0.5%

RANK ORDER

RANK	STATE	SITES	% of USA
1	New Jersey	35	8.3%
1	New York	35	8.3%
3	Pennsylvania	34	8.0%
4	Florida	27	6.4%
5	Minnesota	22	5.2%
6	Michigan	21	5.0%
7	Washington	20	4.7%
8	California	15	3.5%
9	Texas	13	3.1%
10	Louisiana	12	2.8%
11	Iowa	11	2.6%
12	Indiana	10	2.4%
13	Utah	9	2.1%
14	Arkansas	8	1.9%
14	Massachusetts	8	1.9%
14	Ohio	8	1.9%
14	Wisconsin	8	1.9%
18	Delaware	7	1.7%
18	Kentucky	7	1.7%
18	Oklahoma	7	1.7%
18	Tennessee	7	1.7%
22	Illinois	6	1.4%
22	South Carolina	6	1.4%
24	Georgia	5	1.2%
24	Kansas	5	1.2%
24	Missouri	5	1.2%
24	Oregon	5	1.2%
28	Connecticut	4	0.9%
28	Maine	4	0.9%
28	Maryland	4	0.9%
28	Mississippi	4	0.9%
28	New Mexico	4	0.9%
28	North Carolina	4	0.9%
28	Virginia	4	0.9%
35	Alabama	3	0.7%
35	Alaska	3	0.7%
35	Arizona	3	0.7%
35	Colorado	3	0.7%
35	Idaho	3	0.7%
35	West Virginia	3	0.7%
41	North Dakota	2	0.5%
41	South Dakota	2	0.5%
41	Vermont	2	0.5%
41	Wyoming	2	0.5%
45	Hawaii	1	0.2%
45	Nebraska	1	0.2%
45	New Hampshire	1	0.2%
45	Rhode Island	1	0.2%
49	Montana	0	0.0%
49	Nevada	0	0.0%
	District of Columbia	0	0.0%

Source: U.S. Environmental Protection Agency
 "National Priorities List (NPL) Sites in the United States" (http://www.epa.gov/superfund/sites/npl/)
*Cumulative total as of November 8, 2019. National total includes six sites in Puerto Rico and four in other U.S. territories.

VIII. Geography

Total Area of States in Square Miles in 2010

National Total = 3,796,742 Square Miles*

ALPHA ORDER

RANK	STATE	MILES	% of USA
30	Alabama	52,420	1.4%
1	Alaska	665,384	17.5%
6	Arizona	113,990	3.0%
29	Arkansas	53,179	1.4%
3	California	163,695	4.3%
8	Colorado	104,094	2.7%
48	Connecticut	5,543	0.1%
49	Delaware	2,489	0.1%
22	Florida	65,758	1.7%
24	Georgia	59,425	1.6%
43	Hawaii	10,932	0.3%
14	Idaho	83,569	2.2%
25	Illinois	57,914	1.5%
38	Indiana	36,420	1.0%
26	Iowa	56,273	1.5%
15	Kansas	82,278	2.2%
37	Kentucky	40,408	1.1%
31	Louisiana	52,378	1.4%
39	Maine	35,380	0.9%
42	Maryland	12,406	0.3%
44	Massachusetts	10,554	0.3%
11	Michigan	96,714	2.5%
12	Minnesota	86,936	2.3%
32	Mississippi	48,432	1.3%
21	Missouri	69,707	1.8%
4	Montana	147,040	3.9%
16	Nebraska	77,348	2.0%
7	Nevada	110,572	2.9%
46	New Hampshire	9,349	0.2%
47	New Jersey	8,723	0.2%
5	New Mexico	121,590	3.2%
27	New York	54,555	1.4%
28	North Carolina	53,819	1.4%
19	North Dakota	70,698	1.9%
34	Ohio	44,826	1.2%
20	Oklahoma	69,899	1.8%
9	Oregon	98,379	2.6%
33	Pennsylvania	46,054	1.2%
50	Rhode Island	1,545	0.0%
40	South Carolina	32,020	0.8%
17	South Dakota	77,116	2.0%
36	Tennessee	42,144	1.1%
2	Texas	268,596	7.1%
13	Utah	84,897	2.2%
45	Vermont	9,616	0.3%
35	Virginia	42,775	1.1%
18	Washington	71,298	1.9%
41	West Virginia	24,230	0.6%
23	Wisconsin	65,496	1.7%
10	Wyoming	97,813	2.6%

RANK ORDER

RANK	STATE	MILES	% of USA
1	Alaska	665,384	17.5%
2	Texas	268,596	7.1%
3	California	163,695	4.3%
4	Montana	147,040	3.9%
5	New Mexico	121,590	3.2%
6	Arizona	113,990	3.0%
7	Nevada	110,572	2.9%
8	Colorado	104,094	2.7%
9	Oregon	98,379	2.6%
10	Wyoming	97,813	2.6%
11	Michigan	96,714	2.5%
12	Minnesota	86,936	2.3%
13	Utah	84,897	2.2%
14	Idaho	83,569	2.2%
15	Kansas	82,278	2.2%
16	Nebraska	77,348	2.0%
17	South Dakota	77,116	2.0%
18	Washington	71,298	1.9%
19	North Dakota	70,698	1.9%
20	Oklahoma	69,899	1.8%
21	Missouri	69,707	1.8%
22	Florida	65,758	1.7%
23	Wisconsin	65,496	1.7%
24	Georgia	59,425	1.6%
25	Illinois	57,914	1.5%
26	Iowa	56,273	1.5%
27	New York	54,555	1.4%
28	North Carolina	53,819	1.4%
29	Arkansas	53,179	1.4%
30	Alabama	52,420	1.4%
31	Louisiana	52,378	1.4%
32	Mississippi	48,432	1.3%
33	Pennsylvania	46,054	1.2%
34	Ohio	44,826	1.2%
35	Virginia	42,775	1.1%
36	Tennessee	42,144	1.1%
37	Kentucky	40,408	1.1%
38	Indiana	36,420	1.0%
39	Maine	35,380	0.9%
40	South Carolina	32,020	0.8%
41	West Virginia	24,230	0.6%
42	Maryland	12,406	0.3%
43	Hawaii	10,932	0.3%
44	Massachusetts	10,554	0.3%
45	Vermont	9,616	0.3%
46	New Hampshire	9,349	0.2%
47	New Jersey	8,723	0.2%
48	Connecticut	5,543	0.1%
49	Delaware	2,489	0.1%
50	Rhode Island	1,545	0.0%
	District of Columbia	68	0.0%

Source: U.S. Bureau of the Census
  "State Area Measurements" (https://www.census.gov/geographies/reference-files/2010/geo/state-area.html)
*Total of land and water area. Revised figures as of January 1, 2010

Land Area of States in Square Miles in 2010

National Total = 3,531,905 Square Miles of Land Area*

ALPHA ORDER					RANK ORDER			
RANK	STATE		MILES	% of USA	RANK	STATE	MILES	% of USA
28	Alabama		50,645	1.4%	1	Alaska	570,641	16.2%
1	Alaska		570,641	16.2%	2	Texas	261,232	7.4%
6	Arizona		113,594	3.2%	3	California	155,779	4.4%
27	Arkansas		52,035	1.5%	4	Montana	145,546	4.1%
3	California		155,779	4.4%	5	New Mexico	121,298	3.4%
8	Colorado		103,642	2.9%	6	Arizona	113,594	3.2%
48	Connecticut		4,842	0.1%	7	Nevada	109,781	3.1%
49	Delaware		1,949	0.1%	8	Colorado	103,642	2.9%
26	Florida		53,625	1.5%	9	Wyoming	97,093	2.7%
21	Georgia		57,513	1.6%	10	Oregon	95,988	2.7%
47	Hawaii		6,423	0.2%	11	Idaho	82,643	2.3%
11	Idaho		82,643	2.3%	12	Utah	82,170	2.3%
24	Illinois		55,519	1.6%	13	Kansas	81,759	2.3%
38	Indiana		35,826	1.0%	14	Minnesota	79,627	2.3%
23	Iowa		55,857	1.6%	15	Nebraska	76,824	2.2%
13	Kansas		81,759	2.3%	16	South Dakota	75,811	2.1%
37	Kentucky		39,486	1.1%	17	North Dakota	69,001	2.0%
33	Louisiana		43,204	1.2%	18	Missouri	68,742	1.9%
39	Maine		30,843	0.9%	19	Oklahoma	68,595	1.9%
42	Maryland		9,707	0.3%	20	Washington	66,456	1.9%
45	Massachusetts		7,800	0.2%	21	Georgia	57,513	1.6%
22	Michigan		56,539	1.6%	22	Michigan	56,539	1.6%
14	Minnesota		79,627	2.3%	23	Iowa	55,857	1.6%
31	Mississippi		46,923	1.3%	24	Illinois	55,519	1.6%
18	Missouri		68,742	1.9%	25	Wisconsin	54,158	1.5%
4	Montana		145,546	4.1%	26	Florida	53,625	1.5%
15	Nebraska		76,824	2.2%	27	Arkansas	52,035	1.5%
7	Nevada		109,781	3.1%	28	Alabama	50,645	1.4%
44	New Hampshire		8,953	0.3%	29	North Carolina	48,618	1.4%
46	New Jersey		7,354	0.2%	30	New York	47,126	1.3%
5	New Mexico		121,298	3.4%	31	Mississippi	46,923	1.3%
30	New York		47,126	1.3%	32	Pennsylvania	44,743	1.3%
29	North Carolina		48,618	1.4%	33	Louisiana	43,204	1.2%
17	North Dakota		69,001	2.0%	34	Tennessee	41,235	1.2%
35	Ohio		40,861	1.2%	35	Ohio	40,861	1.2%
19	Oklahoma		68,595	1.9%	36	Virginia	39,490	1.1%
10	Oregon		95,988	2.7%	37	Kentucky	39,486	1.1%
32	Pennsylvania		44,743	1.3%	38	Indiana	35,826	1.0%
50	Rhode Island		1,034	0.0%	39	Maine	30,843	0.9%
40	South Carolina		30,061	0.9%	40	South Carolina	30,061	0.9%
16	South Dakota		75,811	2.1%	41	West Virginia	24,038	0.7%
34	Tennessee		41,235	1.2%	42	Maryland	9,707	0.3%
2	Texas		261,232	7.4%	43	Vermont	9,217	0.3%
12	Utah		82,170	2.3%	44	New Hampshire	8,953	0.3%
43	Vermont		9,217	0.3%	45	Massachusetts	7,800	0.2%
36	Virginia		39,490	1.1%	46	New Jersey	7,354	0.2%
20	Washington		66,456	1.9%	47	Hawaii	6,423	0.2%
41	West Virginia		24,038	0.7%	48	Connecticut	4,842	0.1%
25	Wisconsin		54,158	1.5%	49	Delaware	1,949	0.1%
9	Wyoming		97,093	2.7%	50	Rhode Island	1,034	0.0%
						District of Columbia	61	0.0%

Source: U.S. Bureau of the Census
"State Area Measurements" (https://www.census.gov/geographies/reference-files/2010/geo/state-area.html)
*Includes dry land temporarily or partially covered by water, such as marshland, swamps, etc.; streams and canals under one-eighth mile wide; and lakes, reservoirs, and ponds under forty acres. Revised figures as of August 2010.

Water Area of States in Square Miles in 2010

National Total = 264,837 Square Miles of Water*

ALPHA ORDER				RANK ORDER			
RANK	STATE	MILES	% of USA	RANK	STATE	MILES	% of USA
23	Alabama	1,775	0.7%	1	Alaska	94,743	35.8%
1	Alaska	94,743	35.8%	2	Michigan	40,175	15.2%
48	Arizona	396	0.1%	3	Florida	12,133	4.6%
31	Arkansas	1,143	0.4%	4	Wisconsin	11,339	4.3%
6	California	7,916	3.0%	5	Louisiana	9,174	3.5%
44	Colorado	452	0.2%	6	California	7,916	3.0%
38	Connecticut	701	0.3%	7	New York	7,429	2.8%
40	Delaware	540	0.2%	8	Texas	7,365	2.8%
3	Florida	12,133	4.6%	9	Minnesota	7,309	2.8%
22	Georgia	1,912	0.7%	10	North Carolina	5,201	2.0%
13	Hawaii	4,509	1.7%	11	Washington	4,842	1.8%
33	Idaho	926	0.3%	12	Maine	4,537	1.7%
19	Illinois	2,395	0.9%	13	Hawaii	4,509	1.7%
39	Indiana	593	0.2%	14	Ohio	3,965	1.5%
45	Iowa	416	0.2%	15	Virginia	3,285	1.2%
42	Kansas	520	0.2%	16	Massachusetts	2,754	1.0%
34	Kentucky	921	0.3%	17	Utah	2,727	1.0%
5	Louisiana	9,174	3.5%	18	Maryland	2,699	1.0%
12	Maine	4,537	1.7%	19	Illinois	2,395	0.9%
18	Maryland	2,699	1.0%	20	Oregon	2,391	0.9%
16	Massachusetts	2,754	1.0%	21	South Carolina	1,960	0.7%
2	Michigan	40,175	15.2%	22	Georgia	1,912	0.7%
9	Minnesota	7,309	2.8%	23	Alabama	1,775	0.7%
25	Mississippi	1,509	0.6%	24	North Dakota	1,698	0.6%
32	Missouri	965	0.4%	25	Mississippi	1,509	0.6%
26	Montana	1,494	0.6%	26	Montana	1,494	0.6%
41	Nebraska	524	0.2%	27	New Jersey	1,368	0.5%
36	Nevada	791	0.3%	28	Pennsylvania	1,312	0.5%
47	New Hampshire	397	0.1%	29	South Dakota	1,305	0.5%
27	New Jersey	1,368	0.5%	30	Oklahoma	1,304	0.5%
49	New Mexico	292	0.1%	31	Arkansas	1,143	0.4%
7	New York	7,429	2.8%	32	Missouri	965	0.4%
10	North Carolina	5,201	2.0%	33	Idaho	926	0.3%
24	North Dakota	1,698	0.6%	34	Kentucky	921	0.3%
14	Ohio	3,965	1.5%	35	Tennessee	909	0.3%
30	Oklahoma	1,304	0.5%	36	Nevada	791	0.3%
20	Oregon	2,391	0.9%	37	Wyoming	720	0.3%
28	Pennsylvania	1,312	0.5%	38	Connecticut	701	0.3%
43	Rhode Island	511	0.2%	39	Indiana	593	0.2%
21	South Carolina	1,960	0.7%	40	Delaware	540	0.2%
29	South Dakota	1,305	0.5%	41	Nebraska	524	0.2%
35	Tennessee	909	0.3%	42	Kansas	520	0.2%
8	Texas	7,365	2.8%	43	Rhode Island	511	0.2%
17	Utah	2,727	1.0%	44	Colorado	452	0.2%
46	Vermont	400	0.2%	45	Iowa	416	0.2%
15	Virginia	3,285	1.2%	46	Vermont	400	0.2%
11	Washington	4,842	1.8%	47	New Hampshire	397	0.1%
50	West Virginia	192	0.1%	48	Arizona	396	0.1%
4	Wisconsin	11,339	4.3%	49	New Mexico	292	0.1%
37	Wyoming	720	0.3%	50	West Virginia	192	0.1%
					District of Columbia	7	0.0%

Source: U.S. Bureau of the Census
    "State Area Measurements" (https://www.census.gov/geographies/reference-files/2010/geo/state-area.html)
*Includes permanent inland water surface, such as lakes, reservoirs, and ponds having an area of forty acres or more, canals one-eighth mile or more in width; coastal waters behind or sheltered by headlands or islands separated by less than 1 nautical mile of water, and islands under forty acres in area. Excludes areas of oceans, bays, etc., lying within U.S. jurisdiction but not defined as inland water. Revised figures as of August 2010.

Highest Point of Elevation in Feet

National High Point = 20,310 Feet Above Sea Level (Denali, Alaska)

ALPHA ORDER

RANK	STATE	HIGHEST POINT
35	Alabama	2,407
1	Alaska	20,310
12	Arizona	12,633
34	Arkansas	2,753
2	California	14,494
3	Colorado	14,433
36	Connecticut	2,380
49	Delaware	448
50	Florida	345
25	Georgia	4,784
6	Hawaii	13,796
11	Idaho	12,662
45	Illinois	1,235
44	Indiana	1,257
42	Iowa	1,670
28	Kansas	4,039
27	Kentucky	4,145
48	Louisiana	535
22	Maine	5,268
32	Maryland	3,360
31	Massachusetts	3,491
38	Michigan	1,979
37	Minnesota	2,301
47	Mississippi	806
41	Missouri	1,772
10	Montana	12,799
20	Nebraska	5,424
9	Nevada	13,140
18	New Hampshire	6,288
40	New Jersey	1,803
8	New Mexico	13,161
21	New York	5,344
16	North Carolina	6,684
30	North Dakota	3,506
43	Ohio	1,550
23	Oklahoma	4,973
13	Oregon	11,239
33	Pennsylvania	3,213
46	Rhode Island	812
29	South Carolina	3,560
15	South Dakota	7,242
17	Tennessee	6,643
14	Texas	8,749
7	Utah	13,528
26	Vermont	4,393
19	Virginia	5,729
4	Washington	14,411
24	West Virginia	4,863
39	Wisconsin	1,951
5	Wyoming	13,804

RANK ORDER

RANK	STATE	HIGHEST POINT
1	Alaska	20,310
2	California	14,494
3	Colorado	14,433
4	Washington	14,411
5	Wyoming	13,804
6	Hawaii	13,796
7	Utah	13,528
8	New Mexico	13,161
9	Nevada	13,140
10	Montana	12,799
11	Idaho	12,662
12	Arizona	12,633
13	Oregon	11,239
14	Texas	8,749
15	South Dakota	7,242
16	North Carolina	6,684
17	Tennessee	6,643
18	New Hampshire	6,288
19	Virginia	5,729
20	Nebraska	5,424
21	New York	5,344
22	Maine	5,268
23	Oklahoma	4,973
24	West Virginia	4,863
25	Georgia	4,784
26	Vermont	4,393
27	Kentucky	4,145
28	Kansas	4,039
29	South Carolina	3,560
30	North Dakota	3,506
31	Massachusetts	3,491
32	Maryland	3,360
33	Pennsylvania	3,213
34	Arkansas	2,753
35	Alabama	2,407
36	Connecticut	2,380
37	Minnesota	2,301
38	Michigan	1,979
39	Wisconsin	1,951
40	New Jersey	1,803
41	Missouri	1,772
42	Iowa	1,670
43	Ohio	1,550
44	Indiana	1,257
45	Illinois	1,235
46	Rhode Island	812
47	Mississippi	806
48	Louisiana	535
49	Delaware	448
50	Florida	345
	District of Columbia	410

Source: U.S. Department of Interior, U.S. Geological Survey

"Elevations and Distances in the United States" (https://pubs.usgs.gov/gip/Elevations-Distances/elvadist.html)

*Formerly Mt. McKinley.

Lowest Point of Elevation in Feet

National Low Point = 282 Feet Below Sea Level (Death Valley, California)*

ALPHA ORDER

RANK	STATE	LOWEST POINT
3	Alabama	0
3	Alaska	0
26	Arizona	70
25	Arkansas	55
1	California	(282)
50	Colorado	3,315
3	Connecticut	0
3	Delaware	0
3	Florida	0
3	Georgia	0
3	Hawaii	0
42	Idaho	710
32	Illinois	279
34	Indiana	320
37	Iowa	480
41	Kansas	679
31	Kentucky	257
2	Louisiana	(8)
3	Maine	0
3	Maryland	0
3	Massachusetts	0
38	Michigan	571
40	Minnesota	601
3	Mississippi	0
29	Missouri	230
46	Montana	1,800
44	Nebraska	840
36	Nevada	479
3	New Hampshire	0
3	New Jersey	0
48	New Mexico	2,842
3	New York	0
3	North Carolina	0
43	North Dakota	750
35	Ohio	455
33	Oklahoma	289
3	Oregon	0
3	Pennsylvania	0
3	Rhode Island	0
3	South Carolina	0
45	South Dakota	966
28	Tennessee	178
3	Texas	0
47	Utah	2,000
27	Vermont	95
3	Virginia	0
3	Washington	0
30	West Virginia	240
39	Wisconsin	579
49	Wyoming	3,099

RANK ORDER

RANK	STATE	LOWEST POINT
1	California	(282)
2	Louisiana	(8)
3	Alabama*	0
3	Alaska	0
3	Connecticut	0
3	Delaware	0
3	Florida	0
3	Georgia	0
3	Hawaii	0
3	Maine	0
3	Maryland	0
3	Massachusetts	0
3	Mississippi	0
3	New Hampshire	0
3	New Jersey	0
3	New York	0
3	North Carolina	0
3	Oregon	0
3	Pennsylvania	0
3	Rhode Island	0
3	South Carolina	0
3	Texas	0
3	Virginia	0
3	Washington	0
25	Arkansas	55
26	Arizona	70
27	Vermont	95
28	Tennessee	178
29	Missouri	230
30	West Virginia	240
31	Kentucky	257
32	Illinois	279
33	Oklahoma	289
34	Indiana	320
35	Ohio	455
36	Nevada	479
37	Iowa	480
38	Michigan	571
39	Wisconsin	579
40	Minnesota	601
41	Kansas	679
42	Idaho	710
43	North Dakota	750
44	Nebraska	840
45	South Dakota	966
46	Montana	1,800
47	Utah	2,000
48	New Mexico	2,842
49	Wyoming	3,099
50	Colorado	3,315
	District of Columbia	1

Source: U.S. Department of Interior, U.S. Geological Survey
 "Elevations and Distances in the United States" (https://pubs.usgs.gov/gip/Elevations-Distances/elvadist.html)
*States with "0" have sea level as lowest point.

Approximate Mean Elevation in Feet

Approximate National Mean Elevation = 2,500 Feet Above Sea Level

ALPHA ORDER

RANK	STATE	MEAN ELEVATION
40	Alabama	500
15	Alaska	1,900
7	Arizona	4,100
36	Arkansas	650
11	California	2,900
1	Colorado	6,800
40	Connecticut	500
50	Delaware	60
48	Florida	100
37	Georgia	600
10	Hawaii	3,030
6	Idaho	5,000
37	Illinois	600
34	Indiana	700
22	Iowa	1,100
14	Kansas	2,000
33	Kentucky	750
48	Louisiana	100
37	Maine	600
43	Maryland	350
40	Massachusetts	500
29	Michigan	900
21	Minnesota	1,200
45	Mississippi	300
32	Missouri	800
8	Montana	3,400
12	Nebraska	2,600
5	Nevada	5,500
25	New Hampshire	1,000
46	New Jersey	250
4	New Mexico	5,700
25	New York	1,000
34	North Carolina	700
15	North Dakota	1,900
31	Ohio	850
20	Oklahoma	1,300
9	Oregon	3,300
22	Pennsylvania	1,100
47	Rhode Island	200
43	South Carolina	350
13	South Dakota	2,200
29	Tennessee	900
17	Texas	1,700
3	Utah	6,100
25	Vermont	1,000
28	Virginia	950
17	Washington	1,700
19	West Virginia	1,500
24	Wisconsin	1,050
2	Wyoming	6,700

RANK ORDER

RANK	STATE	MEAN ELEVATION
1	Colorado	6,800
2	Wyoming	6,700
3	Utah	6,100
4	New Mexico	5,700
5	Nevada	5,500
6	Idaho	5,000
7	Arizona	4,100
8	Montana	3,400
9	Oregon	3,300
10	Hawaii	3,030
11	California	2,900
12	Nebraska	2,600
13	South Dakota	2,200
14	Kansas	2,000
15	Alaska	1,900
15	North Dakota	1,900
17	Texas	1,700
17	Washington	1,700
19	West Virginia	1,500
20	Oklahoma	1,300
21	Minnesota	1,200
22	Iowa	1,100
22	Pennsylvania	1,100
24	Wisconsin	1,050
25	New Hampshire	1,000
25	New York	1,000
25	Vermont	1,000
28	Virginia	950
29	Michigan	900
29	Tennessee	900
31	Ohio	850
32	Missouri	800
33	Kentucky	750
34	Indiana	700
34	North Carolina	700
36	Arkansas	650
37	Georgia	600
37	Illinois	600
37	Maine	600
40	Alabama	500
40	Connecticut	500
40	Massachusetts	500
43	Maryland	350
43	South Carolina	350
45	Mississippi	300
46	New Jersey	250
47	Rhode Island	200
48	Florida	100
48	Louisiana	100
50	Delaware	60
	District of Columbia	150

Source: U.S. Department of Interior, U.S. Geological Survey
"Elevations and Distances in the United States" (https://pubs.usgs.gov/gip/Elevations-Distances/)

Normal Daily Mean Temperature

National Median = 52.4 Degrees*

ALPHA ORDER

RANK	STATE	MEAN TEMPERATURE
6	Alabama	64.4
50	Alaska	32.8
8	Arizona	63.8
10	Arkansas	62.3
12	California	60.0
38	Colorado	49.1
26	Connecticut	51.8
21	Delaware**	54.8
2	Florida	72.1
5	Georgia	64.5
1	Hawaii	75.0
35	Idaho	50.6
33	Illinois	50.8
25	Indiana	52.4
39	Iowa	48.1
22	Kansas	54.4
17	Kentucky	56.8
3	Louisiana	68.0
46	Maine	43.1
19	Maryland**	55.0
37	Massachusetts	49.4
41	Michigan	46.1
47	Minnesota	42.3
9	Mississippi	63.7
18	Missouri	56.1
45	Montana	45.1
36	Nebraska	49.6
24	Nevada	52.5
49	New Hampshire	36.8
20	New Jersey	54.9
16	New Mexico	57.3
34	New York	50.7
12	North Carolina	60.0
48	North Dakota	41.6
31	Ohio	51.2
11	Oklahoma	60.7
29	Oregon	51.5
26	Pennsylvania	51.8
28	Rhode Island**	51.6
6	South Carolina	64.4
44	South Dakota	45.4
14	Tennessee	59.4
4	Texas	66.0
29	Utah	51.5
42	Vermont**	45.8
15	Virginia	57.8
32	Washington	51.0
23	West Virginia	53.3
40	Wisconsin	46.4
43	Wyoming	45.5

RANK ORDER

RANK	STATE	MEAN TEMPERATURE
1	Hawaii	75.0
2	Florida	72.1
3	Louisiana	68.0
4	Texas	66.0
5	Georgia	64.5
6	Alabama	64.4
6	South Carolina	64.4
8	Arizona	63.8
9	Mississippi	63.7
10	Arkansas	62.3
11	Oklahoma	60.7
12	California	60.0
12	North Carolina	60.0
14	Tennessee	59.4
15	Virginia	57.8
16	New Mexico	57.3
17	Kentucky	56.8
18	Missouri	56.1
19	Maryland**	55.0
20	New Jersey	54.9
21	Delaware**	54.8
22	Kansas	54.4
23	West Virginia	53.3
24	Nevada	52.5
25	Indiana	52.4
26	Connecticut	51.8
26	Pennsylvania	51.8
28	Rhode Island**	51.6
29	Oregon	51.5
29	Utah	51.5
31	Ohio	51.2
32	Washington	51.0
33	Illinois	50.8
34	New York	50.7
35	Idaho	50.6
36	Nebraska	49.6
37	Massachusetts	49.4
38	Colorado	49.1
39	Iowa	48.1
40	Wisconsin	46.4
41	Michigan	46.1
42	Vermont**	45.8
43	Wyoming	45.5
44	South Dakota	45.4
45	Montana	45.1
46	Maine	43.1
47	Minnesota	42.3
48	North Dakota	41.6
49	New Hampshire	36.8
50	Alaska	32.8

District of Columbia 56.7

Source: CQ Press using data from U.S. Department of Commerce, National Oceanic and Atmospheric Administration
   "Comparative Climatic Data" (https://www.ncdc.noaa.gov/ghcn/comparative-climatic-data)
*Based on thirty-year annual averages, 1981–2010.
**Temperatures from these states are from a single location. All other states are from two or more reporting cities within each state, which were averaged to determine each state's average.

Percent of Days That Are Sunny

National Median = 59%*

ALPHA ORDER

RANK ORDER

RANK	STATE	PERCENT OF DAYS SUNNY	RANK	STATE	PERCENT OF DAYS SUNNY
27	Alabama	58	1	Arizona	82
48	Alaska	39	2	Nevada	76
1	Arizona	82	3	New Mexico	75
8	Arkansas	65	4	California	72
4	California	72	4	Colorado	72
4	Colorado	72	6	Florida	68
27	Connecticut**	58	7	Utah**	66
NA	Delaware***	NA	8	Arkansas	65
6	Florida	68	8	Kansas	65
17	Georgia	61	8	Texas	65
12	Hawaii	63	11	Wyoming	64
12	Idaho	63	12	Hawaii	63
36	Illinois	54	12	Idaho	63
33	Indiana	56	12	Nebraska	63
23	Iowa	59	12	Oklahoma	63
8	Kansas	65	16	South Carolina	62
20	Kentucky	60	17	Georgia	61
17	Louisiana	61	17	Louisiana	61
34	Maine**	55	17	Virginia	61
34	Maryland**	55	20	Kentucky	60
27	Massachusetts**	58	20	North Carolina	60
41	Michigan	49	20	South Dakota	60
36	Minnesota	54	23	Iowa	59
23	Mississippi	59	23	Mississippi	59
23	Missouri	59	23	Missouri	59
23	Montana	59	23	Montana	59
12	Nebraska	63	27	Alabama	58
2	Nevada	76	27	Connecticut**	58
46	New Hampshire	44	27	Massachusetts**	58
38	New Jersey**	53	27	North Dakota	58
3	New Mexico	75	27	Tennessee	58
41	New York	49	32	Rhode Island**	57
20	North Carolina	60	33	Indiana	56
27	North Dakota	58	34	Maine**	55
41	Ohio	49	34	Maryland**	55
12	Oklahoma	63	36	Illinois	54
40	Oregon**	50	36	Minnesota	54
41	Pennsylvania	49	38	New Jersey**	53
32	Rhode Island**	57	38	Wisconsin	53
16	South Carolina	62	40	Oregon**	50
20	South Dakota	60	41	Michigan	49
27	Tennessee	58	41	New York	49
8	Texas	65	41	Ohio	49
7	Utah**	66	41	Pennsylvania	49
41	Vermont**	49	41	Vermont**	49
17	Virginia	61	46	New Hampshire	44
47	Washington	43	47	Washington	43
NA	West Virginia***	NA	48	Alaska	39
38	Wisconsin	53	NA	Delaware***	NA
11	Wyoming	64	NA	West Virginia***	NA
				District of Columbia**	56

Source: CQ Press using data from U.S. Department of Commerce, National Oceanic and Atmospheric Administration
   "Comparative Climatic Data" (https://www.ncdc.noaa.gov/ghcn/comparative-climatic-data)
*As a percent of possible sunshine based on annual averages updated through 2018.
**Percentages from these states are from a single location. All other states are from two or more reporting cities within each state, which were averaged to determine each state's average.
***Not available.

Average Wind Speed

National Median = 8.4 Miles per Hour*

ALPHA ORDER				RANK ORDER		
RANK	STATE	MILES PER HOUR		RANK	STATE	MILES PER HOUR
44	Alabama	6.7		1	Kansas	11.2
23	Alaska	8.6		2	Massachusetts	10.9
38	Arizona	7.0		3	Hawaii	10.8
38	Arkansas	7.0		4	South Dakota	10.5
46	California	6.4		5	Oklahoma	10.4
28	Colorado	8.2		6	Iowa	10.1
21	Connecticut	8.7		6	Nebraska	10.1
24	Delaware**	8.5		8	North Dakota	10.0
33	Florida	7.6		9	Texas	9.9
45	Georgia	6.5		10	Minnesota	9.6
3	Hawaii	10.8		10	Missouri	9.6
31	Idaho	7.7		10	New Mexico	9.6
17	Illinois	9.0		13	Wyoming	9.5
21	Indiana	8.7		14	New Jersey	9.3
6	Iowa	10.1		15	Rhode Island**	9.2
1	Kansas	11.2		16	New York	9.1
42	Kentucky	6.9		17	Illinois	9.0
35	Louisiana	7.3		18	Ohio	8.9
29	Maine	8.0		18	Wisconsin	8.9
37	Maryland**	7.2		20	Michigan	8.8
2	Massachusetts	10.9		21	Connecticut	8.7
20	Michigan	8.8		21	Indiana	8.7
10	Minnesota	9.6		23	Alaska	8.6
47	Mississippi	6.2		24	Delaware**	8.5
10	Missouri	9.6		24	Montana	8.5
24	Montana	8.5		26	Utah**	8.4
6	Nebraska	10.1		27	Vermont**	8.3
34	Nevada	7.5		28	Colorado	8.2
49	New Hampshire**	6.0		29	Maine	8.0
14	New Jersey	9.3		30	Pennsylvania	7.9
10	New Mexico	9.6		31	Idaho	7.7
16	New York	9.1		31	Virginia	7.7
35	North Carolina	7.3		33	Florida	7.6
8	North Dakota	10.0		34	Nevada	7.5
18	Ohio	8.9		35	Louisiana	7.3
5	Oklahoma	10.4		35	North Carolina	7.3
38	Oregon	7.0		37	Maryland**	7.2
30	Pennsylvania	7.9		38	Arizona	7.0
15	Rhode Island**	9.2		38	Arkansas	7.0
42	South Carolina	6.9		38	Oregon	7.0
4	South Dakota	10.5		38	Washington	7.0
48	Tennessee	6.1		42	Kentucky	6.9
9	Texas	9.9		42	South Carolina	6.9
26	Utah**	8.4		44	Alabama	6.7
27	Vermont**	8.3		45	Georgia	6.5
31	Virginia	7.7		46	California	6.4
38	Washington	7.0		47	Mississippi	6.2
50	West Virginia	5.6		48	Tennessee	6.1
18	Wisconsin	8.9		49	New Hampshire**	6.0
13	Wyoming	9.5		50	West Virginia	5.6
					District of Columbia	7.9

Source: CQ Press using data from U.S. Department of Commerce, National Oceanic and Atmospheric Administration
"Comparative Climatic Data" (https://www.ncdc.noaa.gov/ghcn/comparative-climatic-data)
*Based on annual averages updated through 2018.
**Averages from these states are from a single location. All other states are from two or more reporting cities within each state, which were averaged to determine each state's average.

Hazardous Weather Fatalities in 2018

National Total = 523 Fatalities*

ALPHA ORDER

RANK	STATE	FATALITIES	% of USA
17	Alabama	6	1.1%
47	Alaska	0	0.0%
23	Arizona	4	0.8%
26	Arkansas	3	0.6%
1	California	128	24.5%
8	Colorado	13	2.5%
26	Connecticut	3	0.6%
47	Delaware	0	0.0%
3	Florida	43	8.2%
17	Georgia	6	1.1%
26	Hawaii	3	0.6%
26	Idaho	3	0.6%
23	Illinois	4	0.8%
14	Indiana	7	1.3%
39	Iowa	1	0.2%
23	Kansas	4	0.8%
12	Kentucky	10	1.9%
17	Louisiana	6	1.1%
47	Maine	0	0.0%
5	Maryland	29	5.5%
32	Massachusetts	2	0.4%
14	Michigan	7	1.3%
32	Minnesota	2	0.4%
39	Mississippi	1	0.2%
14	Missouri	7	1.3%
39	Montana	1	0.2%
39	Nebraska	1	0.2%
2	Nevada	74	14.1%
32	New Hampshire	2	0.4%
26	New Jersey	3	0.6%
39	New Mexico	1	0.2%
8	New York	13	2.5%
6	North Carolina	28	5.4%
32	North Dakota	2	0.4%
39	Ohio	1	0.2%
17	Oklahoma	6	1.1%
11	Oregon	11	2.1%
21	Pennsylvania	5	1.0%
32	Rhode Island	2	0.4%
21	South Carolina	5	1.0%
39	South Dakota	1	0.2%
13	Tennessee	9	1.7%
4	Texas	32	6.1%
47	Utah	0	0.0%
39	Vermont	1	0.2%
7	Virginia	14	2.7%
32	Washington	2	0.4%
26	West Virginia	3	0.6%
10	Wisconsin	12	2.3%
32	Wyoming	2	0.4%

RANK ORDER

RANK	STATE	FATALITIES	% of USA
1	California	128	24.5%
2	Nevada	74	14.1%
3	Florida	43	8.2%
4	Texas	32	6.1%
5	Maryland	29	5.5%
6	North Carolina	28	5.4%
7	Virginia	14	2.7%
8	Colorado	13	2.5%
8	New York	13	2.5%
10	Wisconsin	12	2.3%
11	Oregon	11	2.1%
12	Kentucky	10	1.9%
13	Tennessee	9	1.7%
14	Indiana	7	1.3%
14	Michigan	7	1.3%
14	Missouri	7	1.3%
17	Alabama	6	1.1%
17	Georgia	6	1.1%
17	Louisiana	6	1.1%
17	Oklahoma	6	1.1%
21	Pennsylvania	5	1.0%
21	South Carolina	5	1.0%
23	Arizona	4	0.8%
23	Illinois	4	0.8%
23	Kansas	4	0.8%
26	Arkansas	3	0.6%
26	Connecticut	3	0.6%
26	Hawaii	3	0.6%
26	Idaho	3	0.6%
26	New Jersey	3	0.6%
26	West Virginia	3	0.6%
32	Massachusetts	2	0.4%
32	Minnesota	2	0.4%
32	New Hampshire	2	0.4%
32	North Dakota	2	0.4%
32	Rhode Island	2	0.4%
32	Washington	2	0.4%
32	Wyoming	2	0.4%
39	Iowa	1	0.2%
39	Mississippi	1	0.2%
39	Montana	1	0.2%
39	Nebraska	1	0.2%
39	New Mexico	1	0.2%
39	Ohio	1	0.2%
39	South Dakota	1	0.2%
39	Vermont	1	0.2%
47	Alaska	0	0.0%
47	Delaware	0	0.0%
47	Maine	0	0.0%
47	Utah	0	0.0%
	District of Columbia	0	0.0%

Source: National Weather Service, Water and Weather Services
   "2018 Summary of Hazardous Weather Fatalities" (https://www.weather.gov/hazstat/)
*Includes lightning, tornado, thunderstorm, extreme temperature, flood, coastal storm, rip current, hurricane, winter storm, fog, avalanche, and other weather events. National total does not include seven fatalities in U.S. waters or territories.

Tornadoes in 2019

National Total = 1,676 Tornadoes*

ALPHA ORDER				RANK ORDER			
RANK	STATE	TORNADOES	% of USA	RANK	STATE	TORNADOES	% of USA
7	Alabama	95	5.7%	1	Texas	188	11.2%
47	Alaska	0	0.0%	2	Mississippi	138	8.2%
30	Arizona	10	0.6%	3	Kansas	127	7.6%
19	Arkansas	31	1.8%	4	Oklahoma	99	5.9%
27	California	16	1.0%	5	Missouri	98	5.8%
12	Colorado	53	3.2%	6	Louisiana	97	5.8%
41	Connecticut	1	0.1%	7	Alabama	95	5.7%
41	Delaware	1	0.1%	8	Georgia	60	3.6%
22	Florida	25	1.5%	9	North Carolina	59	3.5%
8	Georgia	60	3.6%	9	Ohio	59	3.5%
47	Hawaii	0	0.0%	11	Minnesota	54	3.2%
35	Idaho	5	0.3%	12	Colorado	53	3.2%
16	Illinois	37	2.2%	12	Iowa	53	3.2%
15	Indiana	39	2.3%	14	Nebraska	44	2.6%
12	Iowa	53	3.2%	15	Indiana	39	2.3%
3	Kansas	127	7.6%	16	Illinois	37	2.2%
21	Kentucky	28	1.7%	17	Pennsylvania	34	2.0%
6	Louisiana	97	5.8%	18	Wisconsin	32	1.9%
41	Maine	1	0.1%	19	Arkansas	31	1.8%
32	Maryland	6	0.4%	20	Wyoming	30	1.8%
38	Massachusetts	3	0.2%	21	Kentucky	28	1.7%
32	Michigan	6	0.4%	22	Florida	25	1.5%
11	Minnesota	54	3.2%	23	Virginia	24	1.4%
2	Mississippi	138	8.2%	24	South Dakota	23	1.4%
5	Missouri	98	5.8%	25	New Mexico	21	1.3%
32	Montana	6	0.4%	26	South Carolina	18	1.1%
14	Nebraska	44	2.6%	27	California	16	1.0%
41	Nevada	1	0.1%	27	Tennessee	16	1.0%
47	New Hampshire	0	0.0%	29	North Dakota	14	0.8%
31	New Jersey	9	0.5%	30	Arizona	10	0.6%
25	New Mexico	21	1.3%	31	New Jersey	9	0.5%
36	New York	4	0.2%	32	Maryland	6	0.4%
9	North Carolina	59	3.5%	32	Michigan	6	0.4%
29	North Dakota	14	0.8%	32	Montana	6	0.4%
9	Ohio	59	3.5%	35	Idaho	5	0.3%
4	Oklahoma	99	5.9%	36	New York	4	0.2%
36	Oregon	4	0.2%	36	Oregon	4	0.2%
17	Pennsylvania	34	2.0%	38	Massachusetts	3	0.2%
41	Rhode Island	1	0.1%	38	West Virginia	3	0.2%
26	South Carolina	18	1.1%	40	Washington	2	0.1%
24	South Dakota	23	1.4%	41	Connecticut	1	0.1%
27	Tennessee	16	1.0%	41	Delaware	1	0.1%
1	Texas	188	11.2%	41	Maine	1	0.1%
47	Utah	0	0.0%	41	Nevada	1	0.1%
41	Vermont	1	0.1%	41	Rhode Island	1	0.1%
23	Virginia	24	1.4%	41	Vermont	1	0.1%
40	Washington	2	0.1%	47	Alaska	0	0.0%
38	West Virginia	3	0.2%	47	Hawaii	0	0.0%
18	Wisconsin	32	1.9%	47	New Hampshire	0	0.0%
20	Wyoming	30	1.8%	47	Utah	0	0.0%
					District of Columbia	0	0.0%

Source: National Weather Service, Storm Prediction Center
"Annual Severe Weather Report Summary - 2019" (https://www.spc.noaa.gov/climo/online/monthly/newm.html)
*Preliminary figures. Tornadoes striking more than one state are counted in each state.

Fatalities Caused by Tornadoes: 2008 to 2019

National Total = 1,055 Fatalities

ALPHA ORDER

RANK	STATE	FATALITIES	% of USA
1	Alabama	286	27.1%
32	Alaska	0	0.0%
32	Arizona	0	0.0%
6	Arkansas	64	6.1%
32	California	0	0.0%
28	Colorado	1	0.1%
32	Connecticut	0	0.0%
32	Delaware	0	0.0%
20	Florida	4	0.4%
7	Georgia	39	3.7%
32	Hawaii	0	0.0%
32	Idaho	0	0.0%
11	Illinois	23	2.2%
12	Indiana	17	1.6%
12	Iowa	17	1.6%
17	Kansas	8	0.8%
8	Kentucky	32	3.0%
14	Louisiana	13	1.2%
32	Maine	0	0.0%
23	Maryland	2	0.2%
22	Massachusetts	3	0.3%
28	Michigan	1	0.1%
19	Minnesota	5	0.5%
3	Mississippi	83	7.9%
2	Missouri	196	18.6%
23	Montana	2	0.2%
23	Nebraska	2	0.2%
32	Nevada	0	0.0%
28	New Hampshire	1	0.1%
32	New Jersey	0	0.0%
32	New Mexico	0	0.0%
18	New York	6	0.6%
10	North Carolina	30	2.8%
23	North Dakota	2	0.2%
15	Ohio	12	1.1%
4	Oklahoma	81	7.7%
32	Oregon	0	0.0%
32	Pennsylvania	0	0.0%
32	Rhode Island	0	0.0%
20	South Carolina	4	0.4%
32	South Dakota	0	0.0%
5	Tennessee	76	7.2%
9	Texas	31	2.9%
32	Utah	0	0.0%
32	Vermont	0	0.0%
16	Virginia	11	1.0%
32	Washington	0	0.0%
28	West Virginia	1	0.1%
23	Wisconsin	2	0.2%
32	Wyoming	0	0.0%

RANK ORDER

RANK	STATE	FATALITIES	% of USA
1	Alabama	286	27.1%
2	Missouri	196	18.6%
3	Mississippi	83	7.9%
4	Oklahoma	81	7.7%
5	Tennessee	76	7.2%
6	Arkansas	64	6.1%
7	Georgia	39	3.7%
8	Kentucky	32	3.0%
9	Texas	31	2.9%
10	North Carolina	30	2.8%
11	Illinois	23	2.2%
12	Indiana	17	1.6%
12	Iowa	17	1.6%
14	Louisiana	13	1.2%
15	Ohio	12	1.1%
16	Virginia	11	1.0%
17	Kansas	8	0.8%
18	New York	6	0.6%
19	Minnesota	5	0.5%
20	Florida	4	0.4%
20	South Carolina	4	0.4%
22	Massachusetts	3	0.3%
23	Maryland	2	0.2%
23	Montana	2	0.2%
23	Nebraska	2	0.2%
23	North Dakota	2	0.2%
23	Wisconsin	2	0.2%
28	Colorado	1	0.1%
28	Michigan	1	0.1%
28	New Hampshire	1	0.1%
28	West Virginia	1	0.1%
32	Alaska	0	0.0%
32	Arizona	0	0.0%
32	California	0	0.0%
32	Connecticut	0	0.0%
32	Delaware	0	0.0%
32	Hawaii	0	0.0%
32	Idaho	0	0.0%
32	Maine	0	0.0%
32	Nevada	0	0.0%
32	New Jersey	0	0.0%
32	New Mexico	0	0.0%
32	Oregon	0	0.0%
32	Pennsylvania	0	0.0%
32	Rhode Island	0	0.0%
32	South Dakota	0	0.0%
32	Utah	0	0.0%
32	Vermont	0	0.0%
32	Washington	0	0.0%
32	Wyoming	0	0.0%
	District of Columbia	0	0.0%

Source: CQ Press using data from National Weather Service, Storm Prediction Center
"Annual U.S. Killer Tornado Statistics" (https://www.spc.noaa.gov/climo/torn/fatalmap.php)

Cost of Damage from Hazardous Weather in 2018

National Total = $40,899,420,000*

ALPHA ORDER

RANK	STATE	DAMAGE	% of USA
36	Alabama	$8,340,000	0.0%
46	Alaska	3,890,000	0.0%
15	Arizona	67,450,000	0.2%
26	Arkansas	19,860,000	0.0%
1	California	19,650,670,000	48.0%
5	Colorado	669,430,000	1.6%
37	Connecticut	8,190,000	0.0%
50	Delaware	0	0.0%
2	Florida	11,409,300,000	27.9%
3	Georgia	4,433,990,000	10.8%
23	Hawaii	28,470,000	0.1%
18	Idaho	43,250,000	0.1%
10	Illinois	143,790,000	0.4%
30	Indiana	15,120,000	0.0%
6	Iowa	363,480,000	0.9%
19	Kansas	40,890,000	0.1%
21	Kentucky	30,190,000	0.1%
27	Louisiana	18,290,000	0.0%
39	Maine	7,660,000	0.0%
14	Maryland	72,340,000	0.2%
34	Massachusetts	9,570,000	0.0%
8	Michigan	201,540,000	0.5%
17	Minnesota	46,300,000	0.1%
22	Mississippi	28,710,000	0.1%
35	Missouri	9,250,000	0.0%
32	Montana	10,590,000	0.0%
12	Nebraska	123,710,000	0.3%
28	Nevada	16,760,000	0.0%
47	New Hampshire	3,450,000	0.0%
45	New Jersey	4,140,000	0.0%
38	New Mexico	8,110,000	0.0%
31	New York	14,580,000	0.0%
4	North Carolina	2,453,650,000	6.0%
24	North Dakota	26,580,000	0.1%
29	Ohio	15,940,000	0.0%
44	Oklahoma	4,680,000	0.0%
48	Oregon	1,240,000	0.0%
20	Pennsylvania	31,030,000	0.1%
49	Rhode Island	1,150,000	0.0%
41	South Carolina	5,920,000	0.0%
42	South Dakota	5,180,000	0.0%
25	Tennessee	21,260,000	0.1%
7	Texas	322,520,000	0.8%
16	Utah	55,030,000	0.1%
43	Vermont	5,050,000	0.0%
13	Virginia	93,940,000	0.2%
11	Washington	141,830,000	0.3%
40	West Virginia	6,740,000	0.0%
9	Wisconsin	186,170,000	0.5%
33	Wyoming	10,200,000	0.0%

RANK ORDER

RANK	STATE	DAMAGE	% of USA
1	California	$19,650,670,000	48.0%
2	Florida	11,409,300,000	27.9%
3	Georgia	4,433,990,000	10.8%
4	North Carolina	2,453,650,000	6.0%
5	Colorado	669,430,000	1.6%
6	Iowa	363,480,000	0.9%
7	Texas	322,520,000	0.8%
8	Michigan	201,540,000	0.5%
9	Wisconsin	186,170,000	0.5%
10	Illinois	143,790,000	0.4%
11	Washington	141,830,000	0.3%
12	Nebraska	123,710,000	0.3%
13	Virginia	93,940,000	0.2%
14	Maryland	72,340,000	0.2%
15	Arizona	67,450,000	0.2%
16	Utah	55,030,000	0.1%
17	Minnesota	46,300,000	0.1%
18	Idaho	43,250,000	0.1%
19	Kansas	40,890,000	0.1%
20	Pennsylvania	31,030,000	0.1%
21	Kentucky	30,190,000	0.1%
22	Mississippi	28,710,000	0.1%
23	Hawaii	28,470,000	0.1%
24	North Dakota	26,580,000	0.1%
25	Tennessee	21,260,000	0.1%
26	Arkansas	19,860,000	0.0%
27	Louisiana	18,290,000	0.0%
28	Nevada	16,760,000	0.0%
29	Ohio	15,940,000	0.0%
30	Indiana	15,120,000	0.0%
31	New York	14,580,000	0.0%
32	Montana	10,590,000	0.0%
33	Wyoming	10,200,000	0.0%
34	Massachusetts	9,570,000	0.0%
35	Missouri	9,250,000	0.0%
36	Alabama	8,340,000	0.0%
37	Connecticut	8,190,000	0.0%
38	New Mexico	8,110,000	0.0%
39	Maine	7,660,000	0.0%
40	West Virginia	6,740,000	0.0%
41	South Carolina	5,920,000	0.0%
42	South Dakota	5,180,000	0.0%
43	Vermont	5,050,000	0.0%
44	Oklahoma	4,680,000	0.0%
45	New Jersey	4,140,000	0.0%
46	Alaska	3,890,000	0.0%
47	New Hampshire	3,450,000	0.0%
48	Oregon	1,240,000	0.0%
49	Rhode Island	1,150,000	0.0%
50	Delaware	0	0.0%
	District of Columbia	0	0.0%

Source: National Weather Service, Water and Weather Services
"2018 Summary of Hazardous Weather Fatalities" (https://www.weather.gov/hazstat/)
*Includes property and crop damage from lightning, tornado, thunderstorm, extreme temperature, flood, coastal storm, rip current, hurricane, winter storm, fog, avalanche, and other weather events. National total does not include damage costs in U.S. territories.

National Park Service Land in 2019

National Total = 85,103,543 Acres*

ALPHA ORDER

RANK	STATE	ACRES	% of USA
41	Alabama	22,747	0.0%
1	Alaska	54,653,962	64.2%
3	Arizona	2,947,211	3.5%
26	Arkansas	104,982	0.1%
2	California	8,210,924	9.6%
12	Colorado	738,668	0.9%
46	Connecticut	7,782	0.0%
48	Delaware	904	0.0%
4	Florida	2,638,605	3.1%
34	Georgia	67,524	0.1%
18	Hawaii	371,494	0.4%
10	Idaho	806,298	0.9%
50	Illinois	115	0.0%
43	Indiana	15,575	0.0%
47	Iowa	2,713	0.0%
44	Kansas	11,628	0.0%
28	Kentucky	97,504	0.1%
39	Louisiana	27,000	0.0%
22	Maine	182,007	0.2%
32	Maryland	74,059	0.1%
36	Massachusetts	59,500	0.1%
13	Michigan	718,190	0.8%
19	Minnesota	301,352	0.4%
24	Mississippi	119,301	0.1%
31	Missouri	83,545	0.1%
8	Montana	1,274,133	1.5%
35	Nebraska	66,569	0.1%
11	Nevada	801,172	0.9%
42	New Hampshire	21,190	0.0%
27	New Jersey	99,598	0.1%
14	New Mexico	483,504	0.6%
29	New York	97,419	0.1%
15	North Carolina	410,459	0.5%
33	North Dakota	72,568	0.1%
37	Ohio	34,555	0.0%
45	Oklahoma	10,241	0.0%
21	Oregon	203,385	0.2%
25	Pennsylvania	116,509	0.1%
49	Rhode Island	331	0.0%
38	South Carolina	32,564	0.0%
20	South Dakota	296,584	0.3%
16	Tennessee	389,245	0.5%
9	Texas	1,260,150	1.5%
6	Utah	2,117,689	2.5%
40	Vermont	23,237	0.0%
17	Virginia	371,635	0.4%
7	Washington	1,967,552	2.3%
30	West Virginia	92,697	0.1%
23	Wisconsin	133,757	0.2%
5	Wyoming	2,396,431	2.8%

RANK ORDER

RANK	STATE	ACRES	% of USA
1	Alaska	54,653,962	64.2%
2	California	8,210,924	9.6%
3	Arizona	2,947,211	3.5%
4	Florida	2,638,605	3.1%
5	Wyoming	2,396,431	2.8%
6	Utah	2,117,689	2.5%
7	Washington	1,967,552	2.3%
8	Montana	1,274,133	1.5%
9	Texas	1,260,150	1.5%
10	Idaho	806,298	0.9%
11	Nevada	801,172	0.9%
12	Colorado	738,668	0.9%
13	Michigan	718,190	0.8%
14	New Mexico	483,504	0.6%
15	North Carolina	410,459	0.5%
16	Tennessee	389,245	0.5%
17	Virginia	371,635	0.4%
18	Hawaii	371,494	0.4%
19	Minnesota	301,352	0.4%
20	South Dakota	296,584	0.3%
21	Oregon	203,385	0.2%
22	Maine	182,007	0.2%
23	Wisconsin	133,757	0.2%
24	Mississippi	119,301	0.1%
25	Pennsylvania	116,509	0.1%
26	Arkansas	104,982	0.1%
27	New Jersey	99,598	0.1%
28	Kentucky	97,504	0.1%
29	New York	97,419	0.1%
30	West Virginia	92,697	0.1%
31	Missouri	83,545	0.1%
32	Maryland	74,059	0.1%
33	North Dakota	72,568	0.1%
34	Georgia	67,524	0.1%
35	Nebraska	66,569	0.1%
36	Massachusetts	59,500	0.1%
37	Ohio	34,555	0.0%
38	South Carolina	32,564	0.0%
39	Louisiana	27,000	0.0%
40	Vermont	23,237	0.0%
41	Alabama	22,747	0.0%
42	New Hampshire	21,190	0.0%
43	Indiana	15,575	0.0%
44	Kansas	11,628	0.0%
45	Oklahoma	10,241	0.0%
46	Connecticut	7,782	0.0%
47	Iowa	2,713	0.0%
48	Delaware	904	0.0%
49	Rhode Island	331	0.0%
50	Illinois	115	0.0%
	District of Columbia	8,625	0.0%

Source: National Park Service
"Listing of Acreage by State" (https://www.nps.gov/subjects/lwcf/acreagereports.htm)
*As of December 31, 2019. Includes federal and nonfederal land in national parks, monuments, historic sites, recreation areas, preserves, battlefields, grasslands, seashores, parkways, trails, and rivers. Does not include land in national forest or wildlife areas. Includes 58,155 acres in U.S. territories.

Recreation Visits to National Park Service Areas in 2018

National Total = 318,211,832 Visits*

<table>
<tr><td colspan="4">ALPHA ORDER</td><td colspan="4">RANK ORDER</td></tr>
<tr><td>RANK</td><td>STATE</td><td>VISITS</td><td>% of USA</td><td>RANK</td><td>STATE</td><td>VISITS</td><td>% of USA</td></tr>
<tr><td>37</td><td>Alabama</td><td>1,020,975</td><td>0.3%</td><td>1</td><td>California</td><td>39,908,521</td><td>12.5%</td></tr>
<tr><td>26</td><td>Alaska</td><td>2,920,249</td><td>0.9%</td><td>2</td><td>Virginia</td><td>22,171,017</td><td>7.0%</td></tr>
<tr><td>6</td><td>Arizona</td><td>12,850,196</td><td>4.0%</td><td>3</td><td>New York</td><td>19,291,389</td><td>6.1%</td></tr>
<tr><td>25</td><td>Arkansas</td><td>3,175,612</td><td>1.0%</td><td>4</td><td>North Carolina</td><td>18,121,305</td><td>5.7%</td></tr>
<tr><td>1</td><td>California</td><td>39,908,521</td><td>12.5%</td><td>5</td><td>Utah</td><td>15,125,729</td><td>4.8%</td></tr>
<tr><td>13</td><td>Colorado</td><td>7,565,055</td><td>2.4%</td><td>6</td><td>Arizona</td><td>12,850,196</td><td>4.0%</td></tr>
<tr><td>48</td><td>Connecticut</td><td>35,382</td><td>0.0%</td><td>7</td><td>Pennsylvania</td><td>9,708,439</td><td>3.1%</td></tr>
<tr><td>50</td><td>Delaware</td><td>0</td><td>0.0%</td><td>8</td><td>Florida</td><td>9,646,727</td><td>3.0%</td></tr>
<tr><td>8</td><td>Florida</td><td>9,646,727</td><td>3.0%</td><td>9</td><td>Massachusetts</td><td>9,646,316</td><td>3.0%</td></tr>
<tr><td>14</td><td>Georgia</td><td>7,519,835</td><td>2.4%</td><td>10</td><td>Tennessee</td><td>9,256,335</td><td>2.9%</td></tr>
<tr><td>20</td><td>Hawaii</td><td>4,838,838</td><td>1.5%</td><td>11</td><td>Washington</td><td>8,375,784</td><td>2.6%</td></tr>
<tr><td>39</td><td>Idaho</td><td>745,544</td><td>0.2%</td><td>12</td><td>Wyoming</td><td>7,662,402</td><td>2.4%</td></tr>
<tr><td>43</td><td>Illinois</td><td>197,717</td><td>0.1%</td><td>13</td><td>Colorado</td><td>7,565,055</td><td>2.4%</td></tr>
<tr><td>30</td><td>Indiana</td><td>2,011,116</td><td>0.6%</td><td>14</td><td>Georgia</td><td>7,519,835</td><td>2.4%</td></tr>
<tr><td>44</td><td>Iowa</td><td>193,663</td><td>0.1%</td><td>15</td><td>Mississippi</td><td>6,863,047</td><td>2.2%</td></tr>
<tr><td>45</td><td>Kansas</td><td>110,191</td><td>0.0%</td><td>16</td><td>Maryland</td><td>6,006,443</td><td>1.9%</td></tr>
<tr><td>31</td><td>Kentucky</td><td>1,742,439</td><td>0.5%</td><td>17</td><td>Nevada</td><td>5,837,312</td><td>1.8%</td></tr>
<tr><td>41</td><td>Louisiana</td><td>611,240</td><td>0.2%</td><td>18</td><td>Montana</td><td>5,547,379</td><td>1.7%</td></tr>
<tr><td>24</td><td>Maine</td><td>3,549,576</td><td>1.1%</td><td>19</td><td>Texas</td><td>5,310,767</td><td>1.7%</td></tr>
<tr><td>16</td><td>Maryland</td><td>6,006,443</td><td>1.9%</td><td>20</td><td>Hawaii</td><td>4,838,838</td><td>1.5%</td></tr>
<tr><td>9</td><td>Massachusetts</td><td>9,646,316</td><td>3.0%</td><td>21</td><td>New Jersey</td><td>4,488,754</td><td>1.4%</td></tr>
<tr><td>27</td><td>Michigan</td><td>2,745,670</td><td>0.9%</td><td>22</td><td>South Dakota</td><td>4,386,898</td><td>1.4%</td></tr>
<tr><td>36</td><td>Minnesota</td><td>1,186,406</td><td>0.4%</td><td>23</td><td>Missouri</td><td>3,622,004</td><td>1.1%</td></tr>
<tr><td>15</td><td>Mississippi</td><td>6,863,047</td><td>2.2%</td><td>24</td><td>Maine</td><td>3,549,576</td><td>1.1%</td></tr>
<tr><td>23</td><td>Missouri</td><td>3,622,004</td><td>1.1%</td><td>25</td><td>Arkansas</td><td>3,175,612</td><td>1.0%</td></tr>
<tr><td>18</td><td>Montana</td><td>5,547,379</td><td>1.7%</td><td>26</td><td>Alaska</td><td>2,920,249</td><td>0.9%</td></tr>
<tr><td>42</td><td>Nebraska</td><td>287,996</td><td>0.1%</td><td>27</td><td>Michigan</td><td>2,745,670</td><td>0.9%</td></tr>
<tr><td>17</td><td>Nevada</td><td>5,837,312</td><td>1.8%</td><td>28</td><td>Ohio</td><td>2,511,418</td><td>0.8%</td></tr>
<tr><td>49</td><td>New Hampshire</td><td>35,218</td><td>0.0%</td><td>29</td><td>New Mexico</td><td>2,113,807</td><td>0.7%</td></tr>
<tr><td>21</td><td>New Jersey</td><td>4,488,754</td><td>1.4%</td><td>30</td><td>Indiana</td><td>2,011,116</td><td>0.6%</td></tr>
<tr><td>29</td><td>New Mexico</td><td>2,113,807</td><td>0.7%</td><td>31</td><td>Kentucky</td><td>1,742,439</td><td>0.5%</td></tr>
<tr><td>3</td><td>New York</td><td>19,291,389</td><td>6.1%</td><td>32</td><td>West Virginia</td><td>1,627,458</td><td>0.5%</td></tr>
<tr><td>4</td><td>North Carolina</td><td>18,121,305</td><td>5.7%</td><td>33</td><td>South Carolina</td><td>1,612,758</td><td>0.5%</td></tr>
<tr><td>38</td><td>North Dakota</td><td>774,622</td><td>0.2%</td><td>34</td><td>Oklahoma</td><td>1,491,343</td><td>0.5%</td></tr>
<tr><td>28</td><td>Ohio</td><td>2,511,418</td><td>0.8%</td><td>35</td><td>Oregon</td><td>1,279,046</td><td>0.4%</td></tr>
<tr><td>34</td><td>Oklahoma</td><td>1,491,343</td><td>0.5%</td><td>36</td><td>Minnesota</td><td>1,186,406</td><td>0.4%</td></tr>
<tr><td>35</td><td>Oregon</td><td>1,279,046</td><td>0.4%</td><td>37</td><td>Alabama</td><td>1,020,975</td><td>0.3%</td></tr>
<tr><td>7</td><td>Pennsylvania</td><td>9,708,439</td><td>3.1%</td><td>38</td><td>North Dakota</td><td>774,622</td><td>0.2%</td></tr>
<tr><td>47</td><td>Rhode Island</td><td>60,709</td><td>0.0%</td><td>39</td><td>Idaho</td><td>745,544</td><td>0.2%</td></tr>
<tr><td>33</td><td>South Carolina</td><td>1,612,758</td><td>0.5%</td><td>40</td><td>Wisconsin</td><td>615,244</td><td>0.2%</td></tr>
<tr><td>22</td><td>South Dakota</td><td>4,386,898</td><td>1.4%</td><td>41</td><td>Louisiana</td><td>611,240</td><td>0.2%</td></tr>
<tr><td>10</td><td>Tennessee</td><td>9,256,335</td><td>2.9%</td><td>42</td><td>Nebraska</td><td>287,996</td><td>0.1%</td></tr>
<tr><td>19</td><td>Texas</td><td>5,310,767</td><td>1.7%</td><td>43</td><td>Illinois</td><td>197,717</td><td>0.1%</td></tr>
<tr><td>5</td><td>Utah</td><td>15,125,729</td><td>4.8%</td><td>44</td><td>Iowa</td><td>193,663</td><td>0.1%</td></tr>
<tr><td>46</td><td>Vermont</td><td>63,886</td><td>0.0%</td><td>45</td><td>Kansas</td><td>110,191</td><td>0.0%</td></tr>
<tr><td>2</td><td>Virginia</td><td>22,171,017</td><td>7.0%</td><td>46</td><td>Vermont</td><td>63,886</td><td>0.0%</td></tr>
<tr><td>11</td><td>Washington</td><td>8,375,784</td><td>2.6%</td><td>47</td><td>Rhode Island</td><td>60,709</td><td>0.0%</td></tr>
<tr><td>32</td><td>West Virginia</td><td>1,627,458</td><td>0.5%</td><td>48</td><td>Connecticut</td><td>35,382</td><td>0.0%</td></tr>
<tr><td>40</td><td>Wisconsin</td><td>615,244</td><td>0.2%</td><td>49</td><td>New Hampshire</td><td>35,218</td><td>0.0%</td></tr>
<tr><td>12</td><td>Wyoming</td><td>7,662,402</td><td>2.4%</td><td>50</td><td>Delaware</td><td>0</td><td>0.0%</td></tr>
<tr><td></td><td></td><td></td><td></td><td></td><td>District of Columbia</td><td>40,159,092</td><td>12.6%</td></tr>
</table>

Source: National Park Service, Public Use Statistics Office
  "National Park Service National Reports" (https://irma.nps.gov/Stats/reports/national)
*National total includes 1,326,887 visits in U.S. territories.

Percent Change in National Park Service Recreation Visits: 2017 to 2018

National Percent Change = 3.8% Decrease*

ALPHA ORDER				RANK ORDER		
RANK	STATE	PERCENT CHANGE		RANK	STATE	PERCENT CHANGE
6	Alabama	5.4		1	Vermont	37.3
7	Alaska	4.8		2	Missouri	24.0
36	Arizona	(6.7)		3	Louisiana	15.9
42	Arkansas	(9.6)		4	Idaho	7.3
21	California	(1.5)		5	North Dakota	5.7
17	Colorado	(0.7)		6	Alabama	5.4
37	Connecticut	(7.1)		7	Alaska	4.8
NA	Delaware**	NA		8	Wisconsin	4.3
33	Florida	(6.3)		9	Mississippi	3.7
12	Georgia	1.7		10	New Mexico	3.4
47	Hawaii	(19.4)		11	Wyoming	2.8
4	Idaho	7.3		12	Georgia	1.7
45	Illinois	(14.9)		13	Maine	0.8
46	Indiana	(16.9)		14	Michigan	0.1
39	Iowa	(8.5)		15	Utah	(0.2)
29	Kansas	(5.8)		16	New York	(0.3)
31	Kentucky	(6.1)		17	Colorado	(0.7)
3	Louisiana	15.9		18	Tennessee	(0.8)
13	Maine	0.8		18	Washington	(0.8)
40	Maryland	(8.6)		20	Oregon	(1.0)
38	Massachusetts	(7.9)		21	California	(1.5)
14	Michigan	0.1		22	West Virginia	(2.1)
26	Minnesota	(3.8)		23	South Dakota	(2.9)
9	Mississippi	3.7		24	Ohio	(3.0)
2	Missouri	24.0		25	Oklahoma	(3.5)
29	Montana	(5.8)		26	Minnesota	(3.8)
49	Nebraska	(25.9)		27	Nevada	(4.0)
27	Nevada	(4.0)		28	North Carolina	(4.6)
32	New Hampshire	(6.2)		29	Kansas	(5.8)
43	New Jersey	(9.8)		29	Montana	(5.8)
10	New Mexico	3.4		31	Kentucky	(6.1)
16	New York	(0.3)		32	New Hampshire	(6.2)
28	North Carolina	(4.6)		33	Florida	(6.3)
5	North Dakota	5.7		34	Pennsylvania	(6.6)
24	Ohio	(3.0)		34	South Carolina	(6.6)
25	Oklahoma	(3.5)		36	Arizona	(6.7)
20	Oregon	(1.0)		37	Connecticut	(7.1)
34	Pennsylvania	(6.6)		38	Massachusetts	(7.9)
48	Rhode Island	(25.0)		39	Iowa	(8.5)
34	South Carolina	(6.6)		40	Maryland	(8.6)
23	South Dakota	(2.9)		41	Virginia	(8.7)
18	Tennessee	(0.8)		42	Arkansas	(9.6)
44	Texas	(10.1)		43	New Jersey	(9.8)
15	Utah	(0.2)		44	Texas	(10.1)
1	Vermont	37.3		45	Illinois	(14.9)
41	Virginia	(8.7)		46	Indiana	(16.9)
18	Washington	(0.8)		47	Hawaii	(19.4)
22	West Virginia	(2.1)		48	Rhode Island	(25.0)
8	Wisconsin	4.3		49	Nebraska	(25.9)
11	Wyoming	2.8		NA	Delaware**	NA
					District of Columbia	(5.0)

Source: CQ Press using data from National Park Service, Public Use Statistics Office
   "National Park Service National Reports" (https://irma.nps.gov/Stats/reports/national)
*National percent change includes visits in U.S. territories.
**Not applicable.

IX. Government Finances: Federal

Internal Revenue Service Gross Collections in 2018

National Total = $3,465,466,627,000*

ALPHA ORDER					RANK ORDER			
RANK	STATE	COLLECTIONS	% of USA		RANK	STATE	COLLECTIONS	% of USA
30	Alabama	$26,724,809,000	0.8%		1	California	$456,555,954,000	13.2%
48	Alaska	5,287,377,000	0.2%		2	New York	281,220,376,000	8.1%
23	Arizona	46,226,885,000	1.3%		3	Texas	280,048,364,000	8.1%
27	Arkansas	32,029,540,000	0.9%		4	Florida	205,694,126,000	5.9%
1	California	456,555,954,000	13.2%		5	Illinois	161,189,282,000	4.7%
19	Colorado	58,707,795,000	1.7%		6	Ohio	140,891,209,000	4.1%
21	Connecticut	53,729,155,000	1.6%		7	New Jersey	138,976,784,000	4.0%
36	Delaware	19,038,671,000	0.5%		8	Pennsylvania	136,268,950,000	3.9%
4	Florida	205,694,126,000	5.9%		9	Massachusetts	117,998,443,000	3.4%
11	Georgia	92,804,948,000	2.7%		10	Minnesota	99,354,057,000	2.9%
41	Hawaii	9,591,724,000	0.3%		11	Georgia	92,804,948,000	2.7%
40	Idaho	10,858,404,000	0.3%		12	Washington	90,404,108,000	2.6%
5	Illinois	161,189,282,000	4.7%		13	Virginia	84,844,999,000	2.4%
20	Indiana	58,698,927,000	1.7%		14	Michigan	83,256,186,000	2.4%
33	Iowa	25,111,982,000	0.7%		15	North Carolina	82,539,491,000	2.4%
31	Kansas	25,813,743,000	0.7%		16	Maryland	72,561,209,000	2.1%
25	Kentucky	34,754,947,000	1.0%		17	Tennessee	68,888,235,000	2.0%
24	Louisiana	41,982,123,000	1.2%		18	Missouri	63,139,167,000	1.8%
44	Maine	7,925,462,000	0.2%		19	Colorado	58,707,795,000	1.7%
16	Maryland	72,561,209,000	2.1%		20	Indiana	58,698,927,000	1.7%
9	Massachusetts	117,998,443,000	3.4%		21	Connecticut	53,729,155,000	1.6%
14	Michigan	83,256,186,000	2.4%		22	Wisconsin	51,992,826,000	1.5%
10	Minnesota	99,354,057,000	2.9%		23	Arizona	46,226,885,000	1.3%
39	Mississippi	11,460,401,000	0.3%		24	Louisiana	41,982,123,000	1.2%
18	Missouri	63,139,167,000	1.8%		25	Kentucky	34,754,947,000	1.0%
47	Montana	6,229,347,000	0.2%		26	Oregon	33,802,142,000	1.0%
32	Nebraska	25,312,311,000	0.7%		27	Arkansas	32,029,540,000	0.9%
35	Nevada	23,317,912,000	0.7%		28	South Carolina	28,552,567,000	0.8%
38	New Hampshire	12,291,272,000	0.4%		29	Oklahoma	27,908,169,000	0.8%
7	New Jersey	138,976,784,000	4.0%		30	Alabama	26,724,809,000	0.8%
42	New Mexico	9,002,297,000	0.3%		31	Kansas	25,813,743,000	0.7%
2	New York	281,220,376,000	8.1%		32	Nebraska	25,312,311,000	0.7%
15	North Carolina	82,539,491,000	2.4%		33	Iowa	25,111,982,000	0.7%
46	North Dakota	6,578,855,000	0.2%		34	Utah	23,401,402,000	0.7%
6	Ohio	140,891,209,000	4.1%		35	Nevada	23,317,912,000	0.7%
29	Oklahoma	27,908,169,000	0.8%		36	Delaware	19,038,671,000	0.5%
26	Oregon	33,802,142,000	1.0%		37	Rhode Island	14,725,607,000	0.4%
8	Pennsylvania	136,268,950,000	3.9%		38	New Hampshire	12,291,272,000	0.4%
37	Rhode Island	14,725,607,000	0.4%		39	Mississippi	11,460,401,000	0.3%
28	South Carolina	28,552,567,000	0.8%		40	Idaho	10,858,404,000	0.3%
43	South Dakota	8,200,403,000	0.2%		41	Hawaii	9,591,724,000	0.3%
17	Tennessee	68,888,235,000	2.0%		42	New Mexico	9,002,297,000	0.3%
3	Texas	280,048,364,000	8.1%		43	South Dakota	8,200,403,000	0.2%
34	Utah	23,401,402,000	0.7%		44	Maine	7,925,462,000	0.2%
50	Vermont	4,417,527,000	0.1%		45	West Virginia	6,911,139,000	0.2%
13	Virginia	84,844,999,000	2.4%		46	North Dakota	6,578,855,000	0.2%
12	Washington	90,404,108,000	2.6%		47	Montana	6,229,347,000	0.2%
45	West Virginia	6,911,139,000	0.2%		48	Alaska	5,287,377,000	0.2%
22	Wisconsin	51,992,826,000	1.5%		49	Wyoming	4,930,650,000	0.1%
49	Wyoming	4,930,650,000	0.1%		50	Vermont	4,417,527,000	0.1%
						District of Columbia	28,443,717,000	0.8%

Source: U.S. Department of the Treasury, Internal Revenue Service
   "Fiscal Year 2018 IRS Data Book" (https://www.irs.gov/statistics/soi-tax-stats-irs-data-book)
*Total includes $24,870,651,000 from U.S. citizens abroad and other miscellaneous returns not shown separately.

Per Capita Internal Revenue Service Gross Collections in 2018

National Per Capita = $10,532*

ALPHA ORDER			RANK ORDER		
RANK	STATE	PER CAPITA	RANK	STATE	PER CAPITA
47	Alabama	$5,468	1	Delaware	$19,719
38	Alaska	7,192	2	Minnesota	17,722
42	Arizona	6,458	3	Massachusetts	17,144
15	Arkansas	10,642	4	New Jersey	15,640
13	California	11,570	5	Connecticut	15,044
16	Colorado	10,315	6	New York	14,399
5	Connecticut	15,044	7	Rhode Island	13,915
1	Delaware	19,719	8	Nebraska	13,145
21	Florida	9,682	9	Illinois	12,669
27	Georgia	8,829	10	Ohio	12,066
41	Hawaii	6,752	11	Maryland	12,022
43	Idaho	6,203	12	Washington	12,016
9	Illinois	12,669	13	California	11,570
28	Indiana	8,767	14	Pennsylvania	10,645
33	Iowa	7,976	15	Arkansas	10,642
26	Kansas	8,867	16	Colorado	10,315
35	Kentucky	7,791	17	Missouri	10,314
24	Louisiana	9,010	18	Tennessee	10,173
44	Maine	5,919	19	Virginia	9,980
11	Maryland	12,022	20	Texas	9,782
3	Massachusetts	17,144	21	Florida	9,682
31	Michigan	8,339	22	South Dakota	9,332
2	Minnesota	17,722	23	New Hampshire	9,081
49	Mississippi	3,844	24	Louisiana	9,010
17	Missouri	10,314	25	Wisconsin	8,953
45	Montana	5,873	26	Kansas	8,867
8	Nebraska	13,145	27	Georgia	8,829
36	Nevada	7,702	28	Indiana	8,767
23	New Hampshire	9,081	29	North Dakota	8,678
4	New Jersey	15,640	30	Wyoming	8,536
48	New Mexico	4,302	31	Michigan	8,339
6	New York	14,399	32	Oregon	8,083
34	North Carolina	7,951	33	Iowa	7,976
29	North Dakota	8,678	34	North Carolina	7,951
10	Ohio	12,066	35	Kentucky	7,791
39	Oklahoma	7,083	36	Nevada	7,702
32	Oregon	8,083	37	Utah	7,421
14	Pennsylvania	10,645	38	Alaska	7,192
7	Rhode Island	13,915	39	Oklahoma	7,083
46	South Carolina	5,616	40	Vermont	7,075
22	South Dakota	9,332	41	Hawaii	6,752
18	Tennessee	10,173	42	Arizona	6,458
20	Texas	9,782	43	Idaho	6,203
37	Utah	7,421	44	Maine	5,919
40	Vermont	7,075	45	Montana	5,873
19	Virginia	9,980	46	South Carolina	5,616
12	Washington	12,016	47	Alabama	5,468
50	West Virginia	3,830	48	New Mexico	4,302
25	Wisconsin	8,953	49	Mississippi	3,844
30	Wyoming	8,536	50	West Virginia	3,830
				District of Columbia	40,544

Source: CQ Press using data from U.S. Department of the Treasury, Internal Revenue Service
"Fiscal Year 2018 IRS Data Book" (https://www.irs.gov/statistics/soi-tax-stats-irs-data-book)
*National per capita does not include collections from U.S. citizens abroad and other miscellaneous returns not shown separately.

Federal Individual Income Tax Collections in 2018

National Total = $3,105,140,728,000*

ALPHA ORDER

RANK	STATE	COLLECTIONS	% of USA
29	Alabama	$25,133,263,000	0.8%
48	Alaska	5,100,023,000	0.2%
23	Arizona	41,753,996,000	1.3%
27	Arkansas	27,170,278,000	0.9%
1	California	400,679,339,000	12.9%
19	Colorado	54,748,985,000	1.8%
22	Connecticut	45,844,226,000	1.5%
36	Delaware	16,108,176,000	0.5%
4	Florida	191,856,807,000	6.2%
12	Georgia	79,612,457,000	2.6%
42	Hawaii	8,564,619,000	0.3%
40	Idaho	10,407,218,000	0.3%
5	Illinois	141,827,507,000	4.6%
20	Indiana	54,074,694,000	1.7%
30	Iowa	23,522,559,000	0.8%
32	Kansas	22,681,380,000	0.7%
26	Kentucky	31,441,071,000	1.0%
24	Louisiana	40,359,049,000	1.3%
44	Maine	7,676,810,000	0.2%
16	Maryland	69,039,368,000	2.2%
9	Massachusetts	108,385,087,000	3.5%
13	Michigan	78,223,049,000	2.5%
10	Minnesota	85,870,537,000	2.8%
39	Mississippi	10,789,789,000	0.3%
18	Missouri	56,792,457,000	1.8%
47	Montana	6,009,686,000	0.2%
35	Nebraska	18,992,977,000	0.6%
33	Nevada	21,963,043,000	0.7%
37	New Hampshire	11,606,329,000	0.4%
8	New Jersey	120,390,388,000	3.9%
41	New Mexico	8,715,321,000	0.3%
2	New York	254,472,758,000	8.2%
14	North Carolina	75,838,061,000	2.4%
46	North Dakota	6,263,203,000	0.2%
6	Ohio	126,652,169,000	4.1%
31	Oklahoma	23,067,396,000	0.7%
25	Oregon	32,097,454,000	1.0%
7	Pennsylvania	123,628,377,000	4.0%
38	Rhode Island	11,557,850,000	0.4%
28	South Carolina	26,683,279,000	0.9%
43	South Dakota	7,819,278,000	0.3%
17	Tennessee	61,502,290,000	2.0%
3	Texas	240,169,156,000	7.7%
34	Utah	21,637,433,000	0.7%
50	Vermont	4,286,720,000	0.1%
15	Virginia	74,465,304,000	2.4%
11	Washington	83,778,554,000	2.7%
45	West Virginia	6,624,968,000	0.2%
21	Wisconsin	47,765,785,000	1.5%
49	Wyoming	4,486,179,000	0.1%

RANK ORDER

RANK	STATE	COLLECTIONS	% of USA
1	California	$400,679,339,000	12.9%
2	New York	254,472,758,000	8.2%
3	Texas	240,169,156,000	7.7%
4	Florida	191,856,807,000	6.2%
5	Illinois	141,827,507,000	4.6%
6	Ohio	126,652,169,000	4.1%
7	Pennsylvania	123,628,377,000	4.0%
8	New Jersey	120,390,388,000	3.9%
9	Massachusetts	108,385,087,000	3.5%
10	Minnesota	85,870,537,000	2.8%
11	Washington	83,778,554,000	2.7%
12	Georgia	79,612,457,000	2.6%
13	Michigan	78,223,049,000	2.5%
14	North Carolina	75,838,061,000	2.4%
15	Virginia	74,465,304,000	2.4%
16	Maryland	69,039,368,000	2.2%
17	Tennessee	61,502,290,000	2.0%
18	Missouri	56,792,457,000	1.8%
19	Colorado	54,748,985,000	1.8%
20	Indiana	54,074,694,000	1.7%
21	Wisconsin	47,765,785,000	1.5%
22	Connecticut	45,844,226,000	1.5%
23	Arizona	41,753,996,000	1.3%
24	Louisiana	40,359,049,000	1.3%
25	Oregon	32,097,454,000	1.0%
26	Kentucky	31,441,071,000	1.0%
27	Arkansas	27,170,278,000	0.9%
28	South Carolina	26,683,279,000	0.9%
29	Alabama	25,133,263,000	0.8%
30	Iowa	23,522,559,000	0.8%
31	Oklahoma	23,067,396,000	0.7%
32	Kansas	22,681,380,000	0.7%
33	Nevada	21,963,043,000	0.7%
34	Utah	21,637,433,000	0.7%
35	Nebraska	18,992,977,000	0.6%
36	Delaware	16,108,176,000	0.5%
37	New Hampshire	11,606,329,000	0.4%
38	Rhode Island	11,557,850,000	0.4%
39	Mississippi	10,789,789,000	0.3%
40	Idaho	10,407,218,000	0.3%
41	New Mexico	8,715,321,000	0.3%
42	Hawaii	8,564,619,000	0.3%
43	South Dakota	7,819,278,000	0.3%
44	Maine	7,676,810,000	0.2%
45	West Virginia	6,624,968,000	0.2%
46	North Dakota	6,263,203,000	0.2%
47	Montana	6,009,686,000	0.2%
48	Alaska	5,100,023,000	0.2%
49	Wyoming	4,486,179,000	0.1%
50	Vermont	4,286,720,000	0.1%
	District of Columbia	25,271,452,000	0.8%

Source: U.S. Department of the Treasury, Internal Revenue Service
"Fiscal Year 2018 IRS Data Book" (https://www.irs.gov/statistics/soi-tax-stats-irs-data-book)
*Total includes $21,732,572,000 from U.S. citizens abroad and other miscellaneous returns not shown separately.

Average Revenue Collection per Federal Individual Income Tax Return in 2018

National Average = $20,303 per Return*

ALPHA ORDER				RANK ORDER		
RANK	STATE	PER RETURN		RANK	STATE	PER RETURN
44	Alabama	$12,263		1	Delaware	$34,988
38	Alaska	14,776		2	Massachusetts	31,373
40	Arizona	13,967		3	Minnesota	31,047
12	Arkansas	22,112		4	New Jersey	27,188
11	California	22,179		5	New York	26,228
17	Colorado	20,297		6	Connecticut	25,996
6	Connecticut	25,996		7	Washington	23,616
1	Delaware	34,988		8	Maryland	23,191
21	Florida	19,196		9	Illinois	23,108
24	Georgia	17,705		10	Ohio	22,546
43	Hawaii	12,346		11	California	22,179
41	Idaho	13,807		12	Arkansas	22,112
9	Illinois	23,108		13	Rhode Island	21,582
25	Indiana	17,272		14	Nebraska	20,914
36	Iowa	16,161		15	Louisiana	20,519
27	Kansas	17,002		16	Tennessee	20,376
35	Kentucky	16,379		17	Colorado	20,297
15	Louisiana	20,519		18	Missouri	20,231
47	Maine	11,712		19	Pennsylvania	19,853
8	Maryland	23,191		20	Texas	19,418
2	Massachusetts	31,373		21	Florida	19,196
33	Michigan	16,444		22	Virginia	18,840
3	Minnesota	31,047		23	South Dakota	18,640
49	Mississippi	8,763		24	Georgia	17,705
18	Missouri	20,231		25	Indiana	17,272
46	Montana	11,922		26	North Dakota	17,187
14	Nebraska	20,914		27	Kansas	17,002
37	Nevada	15,651		28	Wisconsin	16,690
32	New Hampshire	16,500		29	North Carolina	16,635
4	New Jersey	27,188		30	Oregon	16,608
48	New Mexico	9,481		31	Wyoming	16,542
5	New York	26,228		32	New Hampshire	16,500
29	North Carolina	16,635		33	Michigan	16,444
26	North Dakota	17,187		34	Utah	16,399
10	Ohio	22,546		35	Kentucky	16,379
39	Oklahoma	14,210		36	Iowa	16,161
30	Oregon	16,608		37	Nevada	15,651
19	Pennsylvania	19,853		38	Alaska	14,776
13	Rhode Island	21,582		39	Oklahoma	14,210
45	South Carolina	12,019		40	Arizona	13,967
23	South Dakota	18,640		41	Idaho	13,807
16	Tennessee	20,376		42	Vermont	13,100
20	Texas	19,418		43	Hawaii	12,346
34	Utah	16,399		44	Alabama	12,263
42	Vermont	13,100		45	South Carolina	12,019
22	Virginia	18,840		46	Montana	11,922
7	Washington	23,616		47	Maine	11,712
50	West Virginia	8,646		48	New Mexico	9,481
28	Wisconsin	16,690		49	Mississippi	8,763
31	Wyoming	16,542		50	West Virginia	8,646
					District of Columbia	72,280

Source: CQ Press using data from U.S. Department of the Treasury, Internal Revenue Service
   "Fiscal Year 2018 IRS Data Book" (https://www.irs.gov/statistics/soi-tax-stats-irs-data-book)
*National Rate includes collections and returns from U.S. citizens abroad and other miscellaneous returns not shown separately.

Adjusted Gross Income in 2017

National Total = $10,991,386,516,000*

ALPHA ORDER

RANK	STATE	A.G.I.	% of USA
26	Alabama	$118,875,683,000	1.1%
48	Alaska	23,850,805,000	0.2%
18	Arizona	193,796,597,000	1.8%
34	Arkansas	73,645,352,000	0.7%
1	California	1,521,053,498,000	13.8%
16	Colorado	209,871,043,000	1.9%
22	Connecticut	174,257,944,000	1.6%
44	Delaware	31,276,117,000	0.3%
4	Florida	726,990,316,000	6.6%
13	Georgia	298,099,458,000	2.7%
39	Hawaii	45,427,737,000	0.4%
40	Idaho	45,120,630,000	0.4%
5	Illinois	455,607,397,000	4.1%
19	Indiana	185,558,796,000	1.7%
31	Iowa	92,281,781,000	0.8%
33	Kansas	85,639,711,000	0.8%
28	Kentucky	107,719,391,000	1.0%
27	Louisiana	114,167,261,000	1.0%
42	Maine	38,803,673,000	0.4%
15	Maryland	235,433,392,000	2.1%
9	Massachusetts	327,915,769,000	3.0%
11	Michigan	299,669,273,000	2.7%
17	Minnesota	205,975,007,000	1.9%
35	Mississippi	60,763,071,000	0.6%
23	Missouri	171,469,735,000	1.6%
45	Montana	29,911,756,000	0.3%
36	Nebraska	57,727,724,000	0.5%
30	Nevada	94,288,887,000	0.9%
37	New Hampshire	54,638,447,000	0.5%
7	New Jersey	393,191,506,000	3.6%
38	New Mexico	49,150,042,000	0.4%
3	New York	836,755,149,000	7.6%
14	North Carolina	286,383,403,000	2.6%
47	North Dakota	24,151,559,000	0.2%
8	Ohio	340,321,548,000	3.1%
29	Oklahoma	97,446,059,000	0.9%
24	Oregon	132,369,515,000	1.2%
6	Pennsylvania	426,878,306,000	3.9%
43	Rhode Island	35,968,286,000	0.3%
25	South Carolina	132,261,773,000	1.2%
46	South Dakota	26,394,318,000	0.2%
21	Tennessee	183,899,122,000	1.7%
2	Texas	886,241,326,000	8.1%
32	Utah	89,567,383,000	0.8%
50	Vermont	20,318,428,000	0.2%
10	Virginia	309,803,887,000	2.8%
12	Washington	298,355,904,000	2.7%
41	West Virginia	40,035,880,000	0.4%
20	Wisconsin	184,819,205,000	1.7%
49	Wyoming	21,036,625,000	0.2%

RANK ORDER

RANK	STATE	A.G.I.	% of USA
1	California	$1,521,053,498,000	13.8%
2	Texas	886,241,326,000	8.1%
3	New York	836,755,149,000	7.6%
4	Florida	726,990,316,000	6.6%
5	Illinois	455,607,397,000	4.1%
6	Pennsylvania	426,878,306,000	3.9%
7	New Jersey	393,191,506,000	3.6%
8	Ohio	340,321,548,000	3.1%
9	Massachusetts	327,915,769,000	3.0%
10	Virginia	309,803,887,000	2.8%
11	Michigan	299,669,273,000	2.7%
12	Washington	298,355,904,000	2.7%
13	Georgia	298,099,458,000	2.7%
14	North Carolina	286,383,403,000	2.6%
15	Maryland	235,433,392,000	2.1%
16	Colorado	209,871,043,000	1.9%
17	Minnesota	205,975,007,000	1.9%
18	Arizona	193,796,597,000	1.8%
19	Indiana	185,558,796,000	1.7%
20	Wisconsin	184,819,205,000	1.7%
21	Tennessee	183,899,122,000	1.7%
22	Connecticut	174,257,944,000	1.6%
23	Missouri	171,469,735,000	1.6%
24	Oregon	132,369,515,000	1.2%
25	South Carolina	132,261,773,000	1.2%
26	Alabama	118,875,683,000	1.1%
27	Louisiana	114,167,261,000	1.0%
28	Kentucky	107,719,391,000	1.0%
29	Oklahoma	97,446,059,000	0.9%
30	Nevada	94,288,887,000	0.9%
31	Iowa	92,281,781,000	0.8%
32	Utah	89,567,383,000	0.8%
33	Kansas	85,639,711,000	0.8%
34	Arkansas	73,645,352,000	0.7%
35	Mississippi	60,763,071,000	0.6%
36	Nebraska	57,727,724,000	0.5%
37	New Hampshire	54,638,447,000	0.5%
38	New Mexico	49,150,042,000	0.4%
39	Hawaii	45,427,737,000	0.4%
40	Idaho	45,120,630,000	0.4%
41	West Virginia	40,035,880,000	0.4%
42	Maine	38,803,673,000	0.4%
43	Rhode Island	35,968,286,000	0.3%
44	Delaware	31,276,117,000	0.3%
45	Montana	29,911,756,000	0.3%
46	South Dakota	26,394,318,000	0.2%
47	North Dakota	24,151,559,000	0.2%
48	Alaska	23,850,805,000	0.2%
49	Wyoming	21,036,625,000	0.2%
50	Vermont	20,318,428,000	0.2%
	District of Columbia	34,161,870,000	0.3%

Source: U.S. Department of the Treasury, Internal Revenue Service
"Individual Tax Statistics, State Income" (https://www.irs.gov/statistics)
*Total includes $62,039,171,000 from U.S. citizens abroad and other miscellaneous returns not shown separately.

Per Capita Adjusted Gross Income in 2017

National Per Capita = $33,630*

<table>
<tr><td colspan="3">ALPHA ORDER</td><td colspan="3">RANK ORDER</td></tr>
<tr><th>RANK</th><th>STATE</th><th>PER CAPITA</th><th>RANK</th><th>STATE</th><th>PER CAPITA</th></tr>
<tr><td>46</td><td>Alabama</td><td>$24,387</td><td>1</td><td>Connecticut</td><td>$48,767</td></tr>
<tr><td>19</td><td>Alaska</td><td>32,244</td><td>2</td><td>Massachusetts</td><td>47,803</td></tr>
<tr><td>39</td><td>Arizona</td><td>27,512</td><td>3</td><td>New Jersey</td><td>44,251</td></tr>
<tr><td>44</td><td>Arkansas</td><td>24,537</td><td>4</td><td>New York</td><td>42,714</td></tr>
<tr><td>8</td><td>California</td><td>38,646</td><td>5</td><td>New Hampshire</td><td>40,509</td></tr>
<tr><td>9</td><td>Colorado</td><td>37,398</td><td>6</td><td>Washington</td><td>40,191</td></tr>
<tr><td>1</td><td>Connecticut</td><td>48,767</td><td>7</td><td>Maryland</td><td>39,083</td></tr>
<tr><td>17</td><td>Delaware</td><td>32,687</td><td>8</td><td>California</td><td>38,646</td></tr>
<tr><td>14</td><td>Florida</td><td>34,679</td><td>9</td><td>Colorado</td><td>37,398</td></tr>
<tr><td>34</td><td>Georgia</td><td>28,635</td><td>10</td><td>Minnesota</td><td>37,004</td></tr>
<tr><td>23</td><td>Hawaii</td><td>31,893</td><td>11</td><td>Virginia</td><td>36,604</td></tr>
<tr><td>42</td><td>Idaho</td><td>26,268</td><td>12</td><td>Wyoming</td><td>36,337</td></tr>
<tr><td>13</td><td>Illinois</td><td>35,653</td><td>13</td><td>Illinois</td><td>35,653</td></tr>
<tr><td>38</td><td>Indiana</td><td>27,870</td><td>14</td><td>Florida</td><td>34,679</td></tr>
<tr><td>30</td><td>Iowa</td><td>29,375</td><td>15</td><td>Rhode Island</td><td>34,071</td></tr>
<tr><td>29</td><td>Kansas</td><td>29,442</td><td>16</td><td>Pennsylvania</td><td>33,382</td></tr>
<tr><td>47</td><td>Kentucky</td><td>24,194</td><td>17</td><td>Delaware</td><td>32,687</td></tr>
<tr><td>45</td><td>Louisiana</td><td>24,444</td><td>18</td><td>Vermont</td><td>32,544</td></tr>
<tr><td>32</td><td>Maine</td><td>29,075</td><td>19</td><td>Alaska</td><td>32,244</td></tr>
<tr><td>7</td><td>Maryland</td><td>39,083</td><td>20</td><td>North Dakota</td><td>31,991</td></tr>
<tr><td>2</td><td>Massachusetts</td><td>47,803</td><td>21</td><td>Oregon</td><td>31,945</td></tr>
<tr><td>28</td><td>Michigan</td><td>30,048</td><td>22</td><td>Wisconsin</td><td>31,919</td></tr>
<tr><td>10</td><td>Minnesota</td><td>37,004</td><td>23</td><td>Hawaii</td><td>31,893</td></tr>
<tr><td>50</td><td>Mississippi</td><td>20,332</td><td>24</td><td>Nevada</td><td>31,748</td></tr>
<tr><td>36</td><td>Missouri</td><td>28,079</td><td>25</td><td>Texas</td><td>31,321</td></tr>
<tr><td>35</td><td>Montana</td><td>28,420</td><td>26</td><td>South Dakota</td><td>30,239</td></tr>
<tr><td>27</td><td>Nebraska</td><td>30,130</td><td>27</td><td>Nebraska</td><td>30,130</td></tr>
<tr><td>24</td><td>Nevada</td><td>31,748</td><td>28</td><td>Michigan</td><td>30,048</td></tr>
<tr><td>5</td><td>New Hampshire</td><td>40,509</td><td>29</td><td>Kansas</td><td>29,442</td></tr>
<tr><td>3</td><td>New Jersey</td><td>44,251</td><td>30</td><td>Iowa</td><td>29,375</td></tr>
<tr><td>48</td><td>New Mexico</td><td>23,497</td><td>31</td><td>Ohio</td><td>29,188</td></tr>
<tr><td>4</td><td>New York</td><td>42,714</td><td>32</td><td>Maine</td><td>29,075</td></tr>
<tr><td>37</td><td>North Carolina</td><td>27,890</td><td>33</td><td>Utah</td><td>28,883</td></tr>
<tr><td>20</td><td>North Dakota</td><td>31,991</td><td>34</td><td>Georgia</td><td>28,635</td></tr>
<tr><td>31</td><td>Ohio</td><td>29,188</td><td>35</td><td>Montana</td><td>28,420</td></tr>
<tr><td>43</td><td>Oklahoma</td><td>24,787</td><td>36</td><td>Missouri</td><td>28,079</td></tr>
<tr><td>21</td><td>Oregon</td><td>31,945</td><td>37</td><td>North Carolina</td><td>27,890</td></tr>
<tr><td>16</td><td>Pennsylvania</td><td>33,382</td><td>38</td><td>Indiana</td><td>27,870</td></tr>
<tr><td>15</td><td>Rhode Island</td><td>34,071</td><td>39</td><td>Arizona</td><td>27,512</td></tr>
<tr><td>41</td><td>South Carolina</td><td>26,340</td><td>40</td><td>Tennessee</td><td>27,412</td></tr>
<tr><td>26</td><td>South Dakota</td><td>30,239</td><td>41</td><td>South Carolina</td><td>26,340</td></tr>
<tr><td>40</td><td>Tennessee</td><td>27,412</td><td>42</td><td>Idaho</td><td>26,268</td></tr>
<tr><td>25</td><td>Texas</td><td>31,321</td><td>43</td><td>Oklahoma</td><td>24,787</td></tr>
<tr><td>33</td><td>Utah</td><td>28,883</td><td>44</td><td>Arkansas</td><td>24,537</td></tr>
<tr><td>18</td><td>Vermont</td><td>32,544</td><td>45</td><td>Louisiana</td><td>24,444</td></tr>
<tr><td>11</td><td>Virginia</td><td>36,604</td><td>46</td><td>Alabama</td><td>24,387</td></tr>
<tr><td>6</td><td>Washington</td><td>40,191</td><td>47</td><td>Kentucky</td><td>24,194</td></tr>
<tr><td>49</td><td>West Virginia</td><td>22,034</td><td>48</td><td>New Mexico</td><td>23,497</td></tr>
<tr><td>22</td><td>Wisconsin</td><td>31,919</td><td>49</td><td>West Virginia</td><td>22,034</td></tr>
<tr><td>12</td><td>Wyoming</td><td>36,337</td><td>50</td><td>Mississippi</td><td>20,332</td></tr>
<tr><td></td><td></td><td></td><td></td><td>District of Columbia</td><td>49,160</td></tr>
</table>

Source: CQ Press using data from U.S. Department of the Treasury, Internal Revenue Service
"Individual Tax Statistics, State Income" (https://www.irs.gov/statistics)
*National per capita does not include income from U.S. citizens abroad and other miscellaneous returns not shown separately.

Percent of Federal Individual Income Tax Returns Reporting $25,000 or Less in Adjusted Gross Income in 2017
National Percent = 35.7%*

ALPHA ORDER

RANK	STATE	PERCENT
7	Alabama	40.2
39	Alaska	32.2
20	Arizona	35.8
4	Arkansas	40.6
31	California	33.7
45	Colorado	31.0
43	Connecticut	31.5
34	Delaware	33.5
5	Florida	40.4
8	Georgia	39.5
42	Hawaii	31.8
19	Idaho	36.2
29	Illinois	34.7
18	Indiana	37.2
39	Iowa	32.2
26	Kansas	35.0
11	Kentucky	38.6
3	Louisiana	41.1
22	Maine	35.6
44	Maryland	31.1
47	Massachusetts	30.4
12	Michigan	38.5
46	Minnesota	30.8
1	Mississippi	44.0
17	Missouri	37.5
14	Montana	37.8
35	Nebraska	33.3
24	Nevada	35.5
48	New Hampshire	30.2
38	New Jersey	32.3
2	New Mexico	41.6
21	New York	35.7
13	North Carolina	38.0
49	North Dakota	30.0
22	Ohio	35.6
15	Oklahoma	37.6
33	Oregon	33.6
25	Pennsylvania	35.3
27	Rhode Island	34.9
9	South Carolina	39.1
30	South Dakota	34.2
10	Tennessee	38.7
15	Texas	37.6
36	Utah	33.1
27	Vermont	34.9
41	Virginia	32.0
50	Washington	28.5
6	West Virginia	40.3
31	Wisconsin	33.7
37	Wyoming	32.9

RANK ORDER

RANK	STATE	PERCENT
1	Mississippi	44.0
2	New Mexico	41.6
3	Louisiana	41.1
4	Arkansas	40.6
5	Florida	40.4
6	West Virginia	40.3
7	Alabama	40.2
8	Georgia	39.5
9	South Carolina	39.1
10	Tennessee	38.7
11	Kentucky	38.6
12	Michigan	38.5
13	North Carolina	38.0
14	Montana	37.8
15	Oklahoma	37.6
15	Texas	37.6
17	Missouri	37.5
18	Indiana	37.2
19	Idaho	36.2
20	Arizona	35.8
21	New York	35.7
22	Maine	35.6
22	Ohio	35.6
24	Nevada	35.5
25	Pennsylvania	35.3
26	Kansas	35.0
27	Rhode Island	34.9
27	Vermont	34.9
29	Illinois	34.7
30	South Dakota	34.2
31	California	33.7
31	Wisconsin	33.7
33	Oregon	33.6
34	Delaware	33.5
35	Nebraska	33.3
36	Utah	33.1
37	Wyoming	32.9
38	New Jersey	32.3
39	Alaska	32.2
39	Iowa	32.2
41	Virginia	32.0
42	Hawaii	31.8
43	Connecticut	31.5
44	Maryland	31.1
45	Colorado	31.0
46	Minnesota	30.8
47	Massachusetts	30.4
48	New Hampshire	30.2
49	North Dakota	30.0
50	Washington	28.5
	District of Columbia	26.8

Source: CQ Press using data from U.S. Department of the Treasury, Internal Revenue Service
"Individual Tax Statistics, State Income" (https://www.irs.gov/statistics)
*National percent includes tax returns from U.S. citizens abroad and other miscellaneous returns not shown separately.

Percent of Federal Individual Income Tax Returns Reporting $500,000 or More in Adjusted Gross Income in 2017
National Percent = 1.0%*

ALPHA ORDER				RANK ORDER		
RANK	STATE	PERCENT		RANK	STATE	PERCENT
32	Alabama	0.6		1	Connecticut	1.8
32	Alaska	0.6		2	Massachusetts	1.6
21	Arizona	0.7		3	New Jersey	1.5
45	Arkansas	0.5		4	California	1.4
4	California	1.4		4	New York	1.4
6	Colorado	1.1		6	Colorado	1.1
1	Connecticut	1.8		6	Florida	1.1
21	Delaware	0.7		6	Washington	1.1
6	Florida	1.1		9	Illinois	1.0
13	Georgia	0.9		9	Maryland	1.0
32	Hawaii	0.6		9	Texas	1.0
32	Idaho	0.6		9	Virginia	1.0
9	Illinois	1.0		13	Georgia	0.9
32	Indiana	0.6		13	Minnesota	0.9
32	Iowa	0.6		13	New Hampshire	0.9
21	Kansas	0.7		16	Nevada	0.8
45	Kentucky	0.5		16	Oregon	0.8
21	Louisiana	0.7		16	Pennsylvania	0.8
45	Maine	0.5		16	Utah	0.8
9	Maryland	1.0		16	Wyoming	0.8
2	Massachusetts	1.6		21	Arizona	0.7
21	Michigan	0.7		21	Delaware	0.7
13	Minnesota	0.9		21	Kansas	0.7
48	Mississippi	0.4		21	Louisiana	0.7
32	Missouri	0.6		21	Michigan	0.7
32	Montana	0.6		21	North Carolina	0.7
32	Nebraska	0.6		21	North Dakota	0.7
16	Nevada	0.8		21	Oklahoma	0.7
13	New Hampshire	0.9		21	Rhode Island	0.7
3	New Jersey	1.5		21	South Dakota	0.7
48	New Mexico	0.4		21	Tennessee	0.7
4	New York	1.4		32	Alabama	0.6
21	North Carolina	0.7		32	Alaska	0.6
21	North Dakota	0.7		32	Hawaii	0.6
32	Ohio	0.6		32	Idaho	0.6
21	Oklahoma	0.7		32	Indiana	0.6
16	Oregon	0.8		32	Iowa	0.6
16	Pennsylvania	0.8		32	Missouri	0.6
21	Rhode Island	0.7		32	Montana	0.6
32	South Carolina	0.6		32	Nebraska	0.6
21	South Dakota	0.7		32	Ohio	0.6
21	Tennessee	0.7		32	South Carolina	0.6
9	Texas	1.0		32	Vermont	0.6
16	Utah	0.8		32	Wisconsin	0.6
32	Vermont	0.6		45	Arkansas	0.5
9	Virginia	1.0		45	Kentucky	0.5
6	Washington	1.1		45	Maine	0.5
48	West Virginia	0.4		48	Mississippi	0.4
32	Wisconsin	0.6		48	New Mexico	0.4
16	Wyoming	0.8		48	West Virginia	0.4

District of Columbia   1.9

Source: CQ Press using data from U.S. Department of the Treasury, Internal Revenue Service
"Individual Tax Statistics, State Income" (https://www.irs.gov/statistics)
*National percent includes tax returns from U.S. citizens abroad and other miscellaneous returns not shown separately.

Federal Business Income Tax Collections in 2018

National Total = $262,742,024,000*

ALPHA ORDER

RANK	STATE	COLLECTIONS	% of USA
31	Alabama	$1,147,165,000	0.4%
47	Alaska	111,474,000	0.0%
27	Arizona	2,622,531,000	1.0%
20	Arkansas	3,950,818,000	1.5%
1	California	46,700,286,000	17.8%
25	Colorado	2,869,410,000	1.1%
13	Connecticut	7,116,335,000	2.7%
28	Delaware	2,486,794,000	0.9%
9	Florida	9,224,023,000	3.5%
11	Georgia	8,969,502,000	3.4%
38	Hawaii	683,176,000	0.3%
40	Idaho	337,959,000	0.1%
5	Illinois	13,643,665,000	5.2%
21	Indiana	3,879,084,000	1.5%
32	Iowa	1,130,801,000	0.4%
29	Kansas	1,423,611,000	0.5%
26	Kentucky	2,866,448,000	1.1%
33	Louisiana	1,063,806,000	0.4%
45	Maine	197,973,000	0.1%
24	Maryland	2,936,165,000	1.1%
12	Massachusetts	7,892,672,000	3.0%
19	Michigan	4,039,055,000	1.5%
6	Minnesota	12,141,388,000	4.6%
39	Mississippi	467,409,000	0.2%
18	Missouri	4,857,562,000	1.8%
46	Montana	157,799,000	0.1%
14	Nebraska	6,096,452,000	2.3%
34	Nevada	1,047,600,000	0.4%
44	New Hampshire	198,895,000	0.1%
4	New Jersey	14,592,522,000	5.6%
48	New Mexico	99,218,000	0.0%
2	New York	21,597,741,000	8.2%
15	North Carolina	5,748,918,000	2.2%
42	North Dakota	207,681,000	0.1%
8	Ohio	9,303,929,000	3.5%
35	Oklahoma	1,010,159,000	0.4%
36	Oregon	998,183,000	0.4%
10	Pennsylvania	9,046,083,000	3.4%
23	Rhode Island	3,024,743,000	1.2%
30	South Carolina	1,405,691,000	0.5%
41	South Dakota	296,888,000	0.1%
16	Tennessee	5,365,333,000	2.0%
3	Texas	15,756,288,000	6.0%
37	Utah	992,792,000	0.4%
49	Vermont	81,587,000	0.0%
7	Virginia	9,696,347,000	3.7%
17	Washington	4,944,899,000	1.9%
43	West Virginia	201,692,000	0.1%
22	Wisconsin	3,275,928,000	1.2%
50	Wyoming	78,787,000	0.0%

RANK ORDER

RANK	STATE	COLLECTIONS	% of USA
1	California	$46,700,286,000	17.8%
2	New York	21,597,741,000	8.2%
3	Texas	15,756,288,000	6.0%
4	New Jersey	14,592,522,000	5.6%
5	Illinois	13,643,665,000	5.2%
6	Minnesota	12,141,388,000	4.6%
7	Virginia	9,696,347,000	3.7%
8	Ohio	9,303,929,000	3.5%
9	Florida	9,224,023,000	3.5%
10	Pennsylvania	9,046,083,000	3.4%
11	Georgia	8,969,502,000	3.4%
12	Massachusetts	7,892,672,000	3.0%
13	Connecticut	7,116,335,000	2.7%
14	Nebraska	6,096,452,000	2.3%
15	North Carolina	5,748,918,000	2.2%
16	Tennessee	5,365,333,000	2.0%
17	Washington	4,944,899,000	1.9%
18	Missouri	4,857,562,000	1.8%
19	Michigan	4,039,055,000	1.5%
20	Arkansas	3,950,818,000	1.5%
21	Indiana	3,879,084,000	1.5%
22	Wisconsin	3,275,928,000	1.2%
23	Rhode Island	3,024,743,000	1.2%
24	Maryland	2,936,165,000	1.1%
25	Colorado	2,869,410,000	1.1%
26	Kentucky	2,866,448,000	1.1%
27	Arizona	2,622,531,000	1.0%
28	Delaware	2,486,794,000	0.9%
29	Kansas	1,423,611,000	0.5%
30	South Carolina	1,405,691,000	0.5%
31	Alabama	1,147,165,000	0.4%
32	Iowa	1,130,801,000	0.4%
33	Louisiana	1,063,806,000	0.4%
34	Nevada	1,047,600,000	0.4%
35	Oklahoma	1,010,159,000	0.4%
36	Oregon	998,183,000	0.4%
37	Utah	992,792,000	0.4%
38	Hawaii	683,176,000	0.3%
39	Mississippi	467,409,000	0.2%
40	Idaho	337,959,000	0.1%
41	South Dakota	296,888,000	0.1%
42	North Dakota	207,681,000	0.1%
43	West Virginia	201,692,000	0.1%
44	New Hampshire	198,895,000	0.1%
45	Maine	197,973,000	0.1%
46	Montana	157,799,000	0.1%
47	Alaska	111,474,000	0.0%
48	New Mexico	99,218,000	0.0%
49	Vermont	81,587,000	0.0%
50	Wyoming	78,787,000	0.0%
	District of Columbia	3,114,062,000	1.2%

Source: U.S. Department of the Treasury, Internal Revenue Service
  "Fiscal Year 2018 IRS Data Book" (https://www.irs.gov/statistics/soi-tax-stats-irs-data-book)
*Total includes collections and returns from international sources and others not distributed by state. Includes taxes on
corporation income (Form 1120 series) and unrelated business income from tax-exempt organizations.

Average Revenue Collection per Federal Business Income Tax Return in 2018

National Average = $36,261 per Return*

ALPHA ORDER				RANK ORDER		
RANK	**STATE**	**PER RETURN**		**RANK**	**STATE**	**PER RETURN**
31	Alabama	$16,887		1	Connecticut	$140,080
45	Alaska	8,562		2	Nebraska	134,642
28	Arizona	20,912		3	Rhode Island	130,941
8	Arkansas	73,877		4	Minnesota	96,976
12	California	52,582		5	Delaware	93,243
30	Colorado	17,575		6	Tennessee	81,730
1	Connecticut	140,080		7	New Jersey	80,050
5	Delaware	93,243		8	Arkansas	73,877
42	Florida	9,786		9	Virginia	56,556
16	Georgia	39,031		10	Ohio	54,506
25	Hawaii	25,082		11	Massachusetts	53,038
44	Idaho	8,818		12	California	52,582
17	Illinois	38,172		13	Missouri	49,246
19	Indiana	34,949		14	Kentucky	44,011
29	Iowa	18,121		15	Pennsylvania	41,508
24	Kansas	27,851		16	Georgia	39,031
14	Kentucky	44,011		17	Illinois	38,172
38	Louisiana	12,547		18	Wisconsin	35,842
46	Maine	6,574		19	Indiana	34,949
26	Maryland	22,948		20	Washington	34,027
11	Massachusetts	53,038		21	New York	32,166
27	Michigan	20,937		22	Texas	30,888
4	Minnesota	96,976		23	North Carolina	29,256
40	Mississippi	11,628		24	Kansas	27,851
13	Missouri	49,246		25	Hawaii	25,082
48	Montana	4,412		26	Maryland	22,948
2	Nebraska	134,642		27	Michigan	20,937
34	Nevada	14,662		28	Arizona	20,912
43	New Hampshire	9,473		29	Iowa	18,121
7	New Jersey	80,050		30	Colorado	17,575
50	New Mexico	3,413		31	Alabama	16,887
21	New York	32,166		32	South Carolina	16,180
23	North Carolina	29,256		33	South Dakota	15,164
36	North Dakota	12,835		34	Nevada	14,662
10	Ohio	54,506		35	Oklahoma	13,601
35	Oklahoma	13,601		36	North Dakota	12,835
37	Oregon	12,622		37	Oregon	12,622
15	Pennsylvania	41,508		38	Louisiana	12,547
3	Rhode Island	130,941		39	Utah	12,337
32	South Carolina	16,180		40	Mississippi	11,628
33	South Dakota	15,164		41	West Virginia	10,638
6	Tennessee	81,730		42	Florida	9,786
22	Texas	30,888		43	New Hampshire	9,473
39	Utah	12,337		44	Idaho	8,818
47	Vermont	5,413		45	Alaska	8,562
9	Virginia	56,556		46	Maine	6,574
20	Washington	34,027		47	Vermont	5,413
41	West Virginia	10,638		48	Montana	4,412
18	Wisconsin	35,842		49	Wyoming	3,829
49	Wyoming	3,829		50	New Mexico	3,413
					District of Columbia	165,721

Source: CQ Press using data from U.S. Department of the Treasury, Internal Revenue Service
"Fiscal Year 2018 IRS Data Book" (https://www.irs.gov/statistics/soi-tax-stats-irs-data-book)
*National average does not include income from U.S. citizens abroad and other miscellaneous returns not shown separately.
Includes taxes on corporation income (Form 1120 series) and unrelated business income from tax-exempt organizations.

Federal Tax Returns Filed in 2018

National Total = 250,321,406 Returns*

<table>
<tr><td colspan="4">ALPHA ORDER</td><td colspan="4">RANK ORDER</td></tr>
<tr><th>RANK</th><th>STATE</th><th>RETURNS</th><th>% of USA</th><th>RANK</th><th>STATE</th><th>RETURNS</th><th>% of USA</th></tr>
<tr><td>26</td><td>Alabama</td><td>3,110,306</td><td>1.2%</td><td>1</td><td>California</td><td>30,340,246</td><td>12.1%</td></tr>
<tr><td>49</td><td>Alaska</td><td>572,924</td><td>0.2%</td><td>2</td><td>Texas</td><td>19,820,986</td><td>7.9%</td></tr>
<tr><td>16</td><td>Arizona</td><td>4,783,615</td><td>1.9%</td><td>3</td><td>Florida</td><td>17,880,739</td><td>7.1%</td></tr>
<tr><td>34</td><td>Arkansas</td><td>1,968,508</td><td>0.8%</td><td>4</td><td>New York</td><td>16,294,894</td><td>6.5%</td></tr>
<tr><td>1</td><td>California</td><td>30,340,246</td><td>12.1%</td><td>5</td><td>Illinois</td><td>10,103,609</td><td>4.0%</td></tr>
<tr><td>15</td><td>Colorado</td><td>4,786,258</td><td>1.9%</td><td>6</td><td>Pennsylvania</td><td>9,862,860</td><td>3.9%</td></tr>
<tr><td>27</td><td>Connecticut</td><td>2,953,592</td><td>1.2%</td><td>7</td><td>Ohio</td><td>8,593,482</td><td>3.4%</td></tr>
<tr><td>45</td><td>Delaware</td><td>809,486</td><td>0.3%</td><td>8</td><td>New Jersey</td><td>7,491,893</td><td>3.0%</td></tr>
<tr><td>3</td><td>Florida</td><td>17,880,739</td><td>7.1%</td><td>9</td><td>Michigan</td><td>7,421,119</td><td>3.0%</td></tr>
<tr><td>10</td><td>Georgia</td><td>7,197,127</td><td>2.9%</td><td>10</td><td>Georgia</td><td>7,197,127</td><td>2.9%</td></tr>
<tr><td>40</td><td>Hawaii</td><td>1,140,767</td><td>0.5%</td><td>11</td><td>North Carolina</td><td>7,142,173</td><td>2.9%</td></tr>
<tr><td>38</td><td>Idaho</td><td>1,304,822</td><td>0.5%</td><td>12</td><td>Virginia</td><td>6,322,926</td><td>2.5%</td></tr>
<tr><td>5</td><td>Illinois</td><td>10,103,609</td><td>4.0%</td><td>13</td><td>Washington</td><td>5,914,768</td><td>2.4%</td></tr>
<tr><td>18</td><td>Indiana</td><td>4,716,950</td><td>1.9%</td><td>14</td><td>Massachusetts</td><td>5,750,512</td><td>2.3%</td></tr>
<tr><td>30</td><td>Iowa</td><td>2,424,667</td><td>1.0%</td><td>15</td><td>Colorado</td><td>4,786,258</td><td>1.9%</td></tr>
<tr><td>33</td><td>Kansas</td><td>2,215,530</td><td>0.9%</td><td>16</td><td>Arizona</td><td>4,783,615</td><td>1.9%</td></tr>
<tr><td>28</td><td>Kentucky</td><td>2,921,016</td><td>1.2%</td><td>17</td><td>Maryland</td><td>4,757,309</td><td>1.9%</td></tr>
<tr><td>25</td><td>Louisiana</td><td>3,180,658</td><td>1.3%</td><td>18</td><td>Indiana</td><td>4,716,950</td><td>1.9%</td></tr>
<tr><td>41</td><td>Maine</td><td>1,127,808</td><td>0.5%</td><td>19</td><td>Missouri</td><td>4,627,178</td><td>1.8%</td></tr>
<tr><td>17</td><td>Maryland</td><td>4,757,309</td><td>1.9%</td><td>20</td><td>Minnesota</td><td>4,548,091</td><td>1.8%</td></tr>
<tr><td>14</td><td>Massachusetts</td><td>5,750,512</td><td>2.3%</td><td>21</td><td>Wisconsin</td><td>4,524,302</td><td>1.8%</td></tr>
<tr><td>9</td><td>Michigan</td><td>7,421,119</td><td>3.0%</td><td>22</td><td>Tennessee</td><td>4,477,111</td><td>1.8%</td></tr>
<tr><td>20</td><td>Minnesota</td><td>4,548,091</td><td>1.8%</td><td>23</td><td>South Carolina</td><td>3,436,312</td><td>1.4%</td></tr>
<tr><td>35</td><td>Mississippi</td><td>1,841,166</td><td>0.7%</td><td>24</td><td>Oregon</td><td>3,356,232</td><td>1.3%</td></tr>
<tr><td>19</td><td>Missouri</td><td>4,627,178</td><td>1.8%</td><td>25</td><td>Louisiana</td><td>3,180,658</td><td>1.3%</td></tr>
<tr><td>43</td><td>Montana</td><td>983,108</td><td>0.4%</td><td>26</td><td>Alabama</td><td>3,110,306</td><td>1.2%</td></tr>
<tr><td>36</td><td>Nebraska</td><td>1,532,211</td><td>0.6%</td><td>27</td><td>Connecticut</td><td>2,953,592</td><td>1.2%</td></tr>
<tr><td>32</td><td>Nevada</td><td>2,266,197</td><td>0.9%</td><td>28</td><td>Kentucky</td><td>2,921,016</td><td>1.2%</td></tr>
<tr><td>39</td><td>New Hampshire</td><td>1,142,708</td><td>0.5%</td><td>29</td><td>Oklahoma</td><td>2,720,615</td><td>1.1%</td></tr>
<tr><td>8</td><td>New Jersey</td><td>7,491,893</td><td>3.0%</td><td>30</td><td>Iowa</td><td>2,424,667</td><td>1.0%</td></tr>
<tr><td>37</td><td>New Mexico</td><td>1,422,909</td><td>0.6%</td><td>31</td><td>Utah</td><td>2,291,197</td><td>0.9%</td></tr>
<tr><td>4</td><td>New York</td><td>16,294,894</td><td>6.5%</td><td>32</td><td>Nevada</td><td>2,266,197</td><td>0.9%</td></tr>
<tr><td>11</td><td>North Carolina</td><td>7,142,173</td><td>2.9%</td><td>33</td><td>Kansas</td><td>2,215,530</td><td>0.9%</td></tr>
<tr><td>47</td><td>North Dakota</td><td>666,380</td><td>0.3%</td><td>34</td><td>Arkansas</td><td>1,968,508</td><td>0.8%</td></tr>
<tr><td>7</td><td>Ohio</td><td>8,593,482</td><td>3.4%</td><td>35</td><td>Mississippi</td><td>1,841,166</td><td>0.7%</td></tr>
<tr><td>29</td><td>Oklahoma</td><td>2,720,615</td><td>1.1%</td><td>36</td><td>Nebraska</td><td>1,532,211</td><td>0.6%</td></tr>
<tr><td>24</td><td>Oregon</td><td>3,356,232</td><td>1.3%</td><td>37</td><td>New Mexico</td><td>1,422,909</td><td>0.6%</td></tr>
<tr><td>6</td><td>Pennsylvania</td><td>9,862,860</td><td>3.9%</td><td>38</td><td>Idaho</td><td>1,304,822</td><td>0.5%</td></tr>
<tr><td>44</td><td>Rhode Island</td><td>870,827</td><td>0.3%</td><td>39</td><td>New Hampshire</td><td>1,142,708</td><td>0.5%</td></tr>
<tr><td>23</td><td>South Carolina</td><td>3,436,312</td><td>1.4%</td><td>40</td><td>Hawaii</td><td>1,140,767</td><td>0.5%</td></tr>
<tr><td>46</td><td>South Dakota</td><td>765,091</td><td>0.3%</td><td>41</td><td>Maine</td><td>1,127,808</td><td>0.5%</td></tr>
<tr><td>22</td><td>Tennessee</td><td>4,477,111</td><td>1.8%</td><td>42</td><td>West Virginia</td><td>1,121,494</td><td>0.4%</td></tr>
<tr><td>2</td><td>Texas</td><td>19,820,986</td><td>7.9%</td><td>43</td><td>Montana</td><td>983,108</td><td>0.4%</td></tr>
<tr><td>31</td><td>Utah</td><td>2,291,197</td><td>0.9%</td><td>44</td><td>Rhode Island</td><td>870,827</td><td>0.3%</td></tr>
<tr><td>48</td><td>Vermont</td><td>578,208</td><td>0.2%</td><td>45</td><td>Delaware</td><td>809,486</td><td>0.3%</td></tr>
<tr><td>12</td><td>Virginia</td><td>6,322,926</td><td>2.5%</td><td>46</td><td>South Dakota</td><td>765,091</td><td>0.3%</td></tr>
<tr><td>13</td><td>Washington</td><td>5,914,768</td><td>2.4%</td><td>47</td><td>North Dakota</td><td>666,380</td><td>0.3%</td></tr>
<tr><td>42</td><td>West Virginia</td><td>1,121,494</td><td>0.4%</td><td>48</td><td>Vermont</td><td>578,208</td><td>0.2%</td></tr>
<tr><td>21</td><td>Wisconsin</td><td>4,524,302</td><td>1.8%</td><td>49</td><td>Alaska</td><td>572,924</td><td>0.2%</td></tr>
<tr><td>50</td><td>Wyoming</td><td>528,706</td><td>0.2%</td><td>50</td><td>Wyoming</td><td>528,706</td><td>0.2%</td></tr>
<tr><td></td><td></td><td></td><td></td><td></td><td>District of Columbia</td><td>612,290</td><td>0.2%</td></tr>
</table>

Source: U.S. Department of the Treasury, Internal Revenue Service
   "Fiscal Year 2018 IRS Data Book" (https://www.irs.gov/statistics/soi-tax-stats-irs-data-book)
*Total includes returns from international sources and other miscellaneous returns not shown separately.

Percent of Federal Returns Filed Electronically in 2018

National Percent = 71.5%*

ALPHA ORDER			RANK ORDER		
RANK	STATE	PERCENT	RANK	STATE	PERCENT
8	Alabama	73.5	1	New York	76.7
44	Alaska	68.2	2	Georgia	74.9
21	Arizona	71.7	3	Rhode Island	74.7
16	Arkansas	72.4	4	Utah	74.6
18	California	72.3	5	Nevada	74.0
41	Colorado	68.8	6	Mississippi	73.7
27	Connecticut	71.2	6	Tennessee	73.7
28	Delaware	70.9	8	Alabama	73.5
30	Florida	70.5	8	Massachusetts	73.5
2	Georgia	74.9	10	Indiana	73.2
50	Hawaii	63.3	10	New Jersey	73.2
43	Idaho	68.5	12	South Carolina	73.1
28	Illinois	70.9	13	Ohio	72.9
10	Indiana	73.2	13	Texas	72.9
37	Iowa	69.5	15	Kentucky	72.8
23	Kansas	71.4	16	Arkansas	72.4
15	Kentucky	72.8	16	Louisiana	72.4
16	Louisiana	72.4	18	California	72.3
41	Maine	68.8	19	North Carolina	71.9
36	Maryland	69.7	20	Michigan	71.8
8	Massachusetts	73.5	21	Arizona	71.7
20	Michigan	71.8	22	Minnesota	71.5
22	Minnesota	71.5	23	Kansas	71.4
6	Mississippi	73.7	23	Oklahoma	71.4
32	Missouri	70.4	23	Wisconsin	71.4
48	Montana	65.7	26	Virginia	71.3
32	Nebraska	70.4	27	Connecticut	71.2
5	Nevada	74.0	28	Delaware	70.9
38	New Hampshire	69.3	28	Illinois	70.9
10	New Jersey	73.2	30	Florida	70.5
34	New Mexico	70.3	30	Pennsylvania	70.5
1	New York	76.7	32	Missouri	70.4
19	North Carolina	71.9	32	Nebraska	70.4
49	North Dakota	64.5	34	New Mexico	70.3
13	Ohio	72.9	35	West Virginia	69.9
23	Oklahoma	71.4	36	Maryland	69.7
39	Oregon	69.2	37	Iowa	69.5
30	Pennsylvania	70.5	38	New Hampshire	69.3
3	Rhode Island	74.7	39	Oregon	69.2
12	South Carolina	73.1	39	Washington	69.2
45	South Dakota	66.1	41	Colorado	68.8
6	Tennessee	73.7	41	Maine	68.8
13	Texas	72.9	43	Idaho	68.5
4	Utah	74.6	44	Alaska	68.2
47	Vermont	65.9	45	South Dakota	66.1
26	Virginia	71.3	46	Wyoming	66.0
39	Washington	69.2	47	Vermont	65.9
35	West Virginia	69.9	48	Montana	65.7
23	Wisconsin	71.4	49	North Dakota	64.5
46	Wyoming	66.0	50	Hawaii	63.3
				District of Columbia	70.5

Source: CQ Press using data from U.S. Department of the Treasury, Internal Revenue Service
   "Fiscal Year 2018 IRS Data Book" (https://www.irs.gov/statistics/soi-tax-stats-irs-data-book)
*Total includes returns from international sources and other miscellaneous returns. Includes corporate, individual, partnership, estate, employment, and other returns. Excludes returns that cannot be filed electronically including informational returns.

Federal Individual Income Tax Returns Filed in 2018

National Total = 152,937,949 Returns*

RANK	STATE	RETURNS	% of USA	RANK	STATE	RETURNS	% of USA
24	Alabama	2,049,479	1.3%	1	California	18,065,740	11.8%
48	Alaska	345,148	0.2%	2	Texas	12,368,620	8.1%
17	Arizona	2,989,430	2.0%	3	Florida	9,994,795	6.5%
35	Arkansas	1,228,760	0.8%	4	New York	9,702,190	6.3%
1	California	18,065,740	11.8%	5	Pennsylvania	6,227,309	4.1%
22	Colorado	2,697,388	1.8%	6	Illinois	6,137,583	4.0%
28	Connecticut	1,763,529	1.2%	7	Ohio	5,617,549	3.7%
45	Delaware	460,394	0.3%	8	Michigan	4,756,819	3.1%
3	Florida	9,994,795	6.5%	9	North Carolina	4,558,998	3.0%
10	Georgia	4,496,668	2.9%	10	Georgia	4,496,668	2.9%
41	Hawaii	693,732	0.5%	11	New Jersey	4,428,107	2.9%
39	Idaho	753,748	0.5%	12	Virginia	3,952,575	2.6%
6	Illinois	6,137,583	4.0%	13	Washington	3,547,517	2.3%
15	Indiana	3,130,735	2.0%	14	Massachusetts	3,454,691	2.3%
30	Iowa	1,455,526	1.0%	15	Indiana	3,130,735	2.0%
32	Kansas	1,334,020	0.9%	16	Tennessee	3,018,332	2.0%
27	Kentucky	1,919,580	1.3%	17	Arizona	2,989,430	2.0%
25	Louisiana	1,966,875	1.3%	18	Maryland	2,976,987	1.9%
42	Maine	655,459	0.4%	19	Wisconsin	2,861,996	1.9%
18	Maryland	2,976,987	1.9%	20	Missouri	2,807,167	1.8%
14	Massachusetts	3,454,691	2.3%	21	Minnesota	2,765,790	1.8%
8	Michigan	4,756,819	3.1%	22	Colorado	2,697,388	1.8%
21	Minnesota	2,765,790	1.8%	23	South Carolina	2,220,145	1.5%
34	Mississippi	1,231,326	0.8%	24	Alabama	2,049,479	1.3%
20	Missouri	2,807,167	1.8%	25	Louisiana	1,966,875	1.3%
44	Montana	504,081	0.3%	26	Oregon	1,932,612	1.3%
37	Nebraska	908,145	0.6%	27	Kentucky	1,919,580	1.3%
31	Nevada	1,403,306	0.9%	28	Connecticut	1,763,529	1.2%
40	New Hampshire	703,427	0.5%	29	Oklahoma	1,623,300	1.1%
11	New Jersey	4,428,107	2.9%	30	Iowa	1,455,526	1.0%
36	New Mexico	919,275	0.6%	31	Nevada	1,403,306	0.9%
4	New York	9,702,190	6.3%	32	Kansas	1,334,020	0.9%
9	North Carolina	4,558,998	3.0%	33	Utah	1,319,410	0.9%
47	North Dakota	364,406	0.2%	34	Mississippi	1,231,326	0.8%
7	Ohio	5,617,549	3.7%	35	Arkansas	1,228,760	0.8%
29	Oklahoma	1,623,300	1.1%	36	New Mexico	919,275	0.6%
26	Oregon	1,932,612	1.3%	37	Nebraska	908,145	0.6%
5	Pennsylvania	6,227,309	4.1%	38	West Virginia	766,240	0.5%
43	Rhode Island	535,538	0.4%	39	Idaho	753,748	0.5%
23	South Carolina	2,220,145	1.5%	40	New Hampshire	703,427	0.5%
46	South Dakota	419,478	0.3%	41	Hawaii	693,732	0.5%
16	Tennessee	3,018,332	2.0%	42	Maine	655,459	0.4%
2	Texas	12,368,620	8.1%	43	Rhode Island	535,538	0.4%
33	Utah	1,319,410	0.9%	44	Montana	504,081	0.3%
49	Vermont	327,227	0.2%	45	Delaware	460,394	0.3%
12	Virginia	3,952,575	2.6%	46	South Dakota	419,478	0.3%
13	Washington	3,547,517	2.3%	47	North Dakota	364,406	0.2%
38	West Virginia	766,240	0.5%	48	Alaska	345,148	0.2%
19	Wisconsin	2,861,996	1.9%	49	Vermont	327,227	0.2%
50	Wyoming	271,200	0.2%	50	Wyoming	271,200	0.2%
					District of Columbia	349,635	0.2%

Source: U.S. Department of the Treasury, Internal Revenue Service
   "Fiscal Year 2018 IRS Data Book" (https://www.irs.gov/statistics/soi-tax-stats-irs-data-book)
*Total includes returns from international sources and other miscellaneous returns not shown separately.

Percent of Federal Individual Income Tax Returns Filed Electronically in 2018

National Percent = 87.8%*

ALPHA ORDER

RANK	STATE	PERCENT
20	Alabama	89.6
47	Alaska	86.5
40	Arizona	87.6
9	Arkansas	90.3
43	California	87.5
40	Colorado	87.6
28	Connecticut	88.5
36	Delaware	87.8
48	Florida	86.2
24	Georgia	89.2
50	Hawaii	83.5
15	Idaho	89.9
34	Illinois	88.0
8	Indiana	90.6
1	Iowa	93.1
4	Kansas	91.8
6	Kentucky	91.2
30	Louisiana	88.4
45	Maine	87.0
49	Maryland	84.6
28	Massachusetts	88.5
26	Michigan	88.9
11	Minnesota	90.2
14	Mississippi	90.0
22	Missouri	89.3
9	Montana	90.3
2	Nebraska	92.3
39	Nevada	87.7
43	New Hampshire	87.5
27	New Jersey	88.7
36	New Mexico	87.8
3	New York	92.1
25	North Carolina	89.0
7	North Dakota	91.0
22	Ohio	89.3
12	Oklahoma	90.1
33	Oregon	88.3
40	Pennsylvania	87.6
16	Rhode Island	89.8
16	South Carolina	89.8
5	South Dakota	91.3
20	Tennessee	89.6
46	Texas	86.8
19	Utah	89.7
30	Vermont	88.4
34	Virginia	88.0
36	Washington	87.8
30	West Virginia	88.4
12	Wisconsin	90.1
16	Wyoming	89.8

RANK ORDER

RANK	STATE	PERCENT
1	Iowa	93.1
2	Nebraska	92.3
3	New York	92.1
4	Kansas	91.8
5	South Dakota	91.3
6	Kentucky	91.2
7	North Dakota	91.0
8	Indiana	90.6
9	Arkansas	90.3
9	Montana	90.3
11	Minnesota	90.2
12	Oklahoma	90.1
12	Wisconsin	90.1
14	Mississippi	90.0
15	Idaho	89.9
16	Rhode Island	89.8
16	South Carolina	89.8
16	Wyoming	89.8
19	Utah	89.7
20	Alabama	89.6
20	Tennessee	89.6
22	Missouri	89.3
22	Ohio	89.3
24	Georgia	89.2
25	North Carolina	89.0
26	Michigan	88.9
27	New Jersey	88.7
28	Connecticut	88.5
28	Massachusetts	88.5
30	Louisiana	88.4
30	Vermont	88.4
30	West Virginia	88.4
33	Oregon	88.3
34	Illinois	88.0
34	Virginia	88.0
36	Delaware	87.8
36	New Mexico	87.8
36	Washington	87.8
39	Nevada	87.7
40	Arizona	87.6
40	Colorado	87.6
40	Pennsylvania	87.6
43	California	87.5
43	New Hampshire	87.5
45	Maine	87.0
46	Texas	86.8
47	Alaska	86.5
48	Florida	86.2
49	Maryland	84.6
50	Hawaii	83.5

	District of Columbia	85.7

Source: CQ Press using data from U.S. Department of the Treasury, Internal Revenue Service
"Fiscal Year 2018 IRS Data Book" (https://www.irs.gov/statistics/soi-tax-stats-irs-data-book)
*Total includes returns from international sources and other miscellaneous returns. Includes returns filed electronically by practitioners.

Federal Business Income Tax Returns Filed in 2018

National Total = 7,255,731 Returns*

ALPHA ORDER				RANK ORDER			
RANK	STATE	RETURNS	% of USA	RANK	STATE	RETURNS	% of USA
28	Alabama	67,932	0.9%	1	Florida	942,552	13.0%
50	Alaska	13,019	0.2%	2	California	888,134	12.2%
17	Arizona	125,405	1.7%	3	New York	671,453	9.3%
32	Arkansas	53,478	0.7%	4	Texas	510,107	7.0%
2	California	888,134	12.2%	5	Illinois	357,423	4.9%
13	Colorado	163,268	2.3%	6	Georgia	229,803	3.2%
34	Connecticut	50,802	0.7%	7	Pennsylvania	217,936	3.0%
42	Delaware	26,670	0.4%	8	North Carolina	196,503	2.7%
1	Florida	942,552	13.0%	9	Michigan	192,912	2.7%
6	Georgia	229,803	3.2%	10	New Jersey	182,292	2.5%
41	Hawaii	27,238	0.4%	11	Virginia	171,447	2.4%
37	Idaho	38,326	0.5%	12	Ohio	170,695	2.4%
5	Illinois	357,423	4.9%	13	Colorado	163,268	2.3%
19	Indiana	110,993	1.5%	14	Massachusetts	148,812	2.1%
31	Iowa	62,402	0.9%	15	Washington	145,321	2.0%
33	Kansas	51,115	0.7%	16	Maryland	127,947	1.8%
30	Kentucky	65,130	0.9%	17	Arizona	125,405	1.7%
23	Louisiana	84,787	1.2%	18	Minnesota	125,200	1.7%
39	Maine	30,115	0.4%	19	Indiana	110,993	1.5%
16	Maryland	127,947	1.8%	20	Missouri	98,638	1.4%
14	Massachusetts	148,812	2.1%	21	Wisconsin	91,400	1.3%
9	Michigan	192,912	2.7%	22	South Carolina	86,877	1.2%
18	Minnesota	125,200	1.7%	23	Louisiana	84,787	1.2%
36	Mississippi	40,198	0.6%	24	Utah	80,470	1.1%
20	Missouri	98,638	1.4%	25	Oregon	79,084	1.1%
38	Montana	35,764	0.5%	26	Oklahoma	74,272	1.0%
35	Nebraska	45,279	0.6%	27	Nevada	71,451	1.0%
27	Nevada	71,451	1.0%	28	Alabama	67,932	0.9%
44	New Hampshire	20,995	0.3%	29	Tennessee	65,647	0.9%
10	New Jersey	182,292	2.5%	30	Kentucky	65,130	0.9%
40	New Mexico	29,072	0.4%	31	Iowa	62,402	0.9%
3	New York	671,453	9.3%	32	Arkansas	53,478	0.7%
8	North Carolina	196,503	2.7%	33	Kansas	51,115	0.7%
48	North Dakota	16,181	0.2%	34	Connecticut	50,802	0.7%
12	Ohio	170,695	2.4%	35	Nebraska	45,279	0.6%
26	Oklahoma	74,272	1.0%	36	Mississippi	40,198	0.6%
25	Oregon	79,084	1.1%	37	Idaho	38,326	0.5%
7	Pennsylvania	217,936	3.0%	38	Montana	35,764	0.5%
43	Rhode Island	23,100	0.3%	39	Maine	30,115	0.4%
22	South Carolina	86,877	1.2%	40	New Mexico	29,072	0.4%
46	South Dakota	19,578	0.3%	41	Hawaii	27,238	0.4%
29	Tennessee	65,647	0.9%	42	Delaware	26,670	0.4%
4	Texas	510,107	7.0%	43	Rhode Island	23,100	0.3%
24	Utah	80,470	1.1%	44	New Hampshire	20,995	0.3%
49	Vermont	15,072	0.2%	45	Wyoming	20,575	0.3%
11	Virginia	171,447	2.4%	46	South Dakota	19,578	0.3%
15	Washington	145,321	2.0%	47	West Virginia	18,959	0.3%
47	West Virginia	18,959	0.3%	48	North Dakota	16,181	0.2%
21	Wisconsin	91,400	1.3%	49	Vermont	15,072	0.2%
45	Wyoming	20,575	0.3%	50	Alaska	13,019	0.2%
					District of Columbia	18,791	0.3%

Source: U.S. Department of the Treasury, Internal Revenue Service
  "Fiscal Year 2018 IRS Data Book" (https://www.irs.gov/statistics/soi-tax-stats-irs-data-book)
*Total includes returns from international sources and other miscellaneous returns not shown separately.

Federal Tax Refunds in 2018

National Total = 122,209,230 Refunds*

ALPHA ORDER

RANK	STATE	REFUNDS	% of USA
24	Alabama	1,664,884	1.4%
48	Alaska	278,359	0.2%
18	Arizona	2,303,811	1.9%
35	Arkansas	1,005,911	0.8%
1	California	13,936,286	11.4%
22	Colorado	2,074,066	1.7%
28	Connecticut	1,414,083	1.2%
45	Delaware	375,728	0.3%
3	Florida	8,104,382	6.6%
9	Georgia	3,686,183	3.0%
41	Hawaii	547,216	0.4%
39	Idaho	582,253	0.5%
6	Illinois	5,043,802	4.1%
15	Indiana	2,617,287	2.1%
30	Iowa	1,160,047	0.9%
33	Kansas	1,058,432	0.9%
26	Kentucky	1,606,711	1.3%
25	Louisiana	1,624,138	1.3%
42	Maine	520,986	0.4%
17	Maryland	2,350,149	1.9%
14	Massachusetts	2,751,647	2.3%
8	Michigan	3,831,167	3.1%
21	Minnesota	2,148,192	1.8%
34	Mississippi	1,027,917	0.8%
20	Missouri	2,261,721	1.9%
44	Montana	383,357	0.3%
37	Nebraska	726,066	0.6%
31	Nevada	1,149,506	0.9%
40	New Hampshire	568,291	0.5%
11	New Jersey	3,542,268	2.9%
36	New Mexico	732,976	0.6%
4	New York	7,845,925	6.4%
10	North Carolina	3,640,388	3.0%
47	North Dakota	283,621	0.2%
7	Ohio	4,622,875	3.8%
29	Oklahoma	1,314,243	1.1%
27	Oregon	1,482,650	1.2%
5	Pennsylvania	5,108,017	4.2%
43	Rhode Island	442,781	0.4%
23	South Carolina	1,745,870	1.4%
46	South Dakota	329,987	0.3%
16	Tennessee	2,503,538	2.0%
2	Texas	10,383,571	8.5%
32	Utah	1,073,228	0.9%
49	Vermont	258,687	0.2%
12	Virginia	3,163,095	2.6%
13	Washington	2,829,200	2.3%
38	West Virginia	648,880	0.5%
19	Wisconsin	2,269,359	1.9%
50	Wyoming	219,336	0.2%

RANK ORDER

RANK	STATE	REFUNDS	% of USA
1	California	13,936,286	11.4%
2	Texas	10,383,571	8.5%
3	Florida	8,104,382	6.6%
4	New York	7,845,925	6.4%
5	Pennsylvania	5,108,017	4.2%
6	Illinois	5,043,802	4.1%
7	Ohio	4,622,875	3.8%
8	Michigan	3,831,167	3.1%
9	Georgia	3,686,183	3.0%
10	North Carolina	3,640,388	3.0%
11	New Jersey	3,542,268	2.9%
12	Virginia	3,163,095	2.6%
13	Washington	2,829,200	2.3%
14	Massachusetts	2,751,647	2.3%
15	Indiana	2,617,287	2.1%
16	Tennessee	2,503,538	2.0%
17	Maryland	2,350,149	1.9%
18	Arizona	2,303,811	1.9%
19	Wisconsin	2,269,359	1.9%
20	Missouri	2,261,721	1.9%
21	Minnesota	2,148,192	1.8%
22	Colorado	2,074,066	1.7%
23	South Carolina	1,745,870	1.4%
24	Alabama	1,664,884	1.4%
25	Louisiana	1,624,138	1.3%
26	Kentucky	1,606,711	1.3%
27	Oregon	1,482,650	1.2%
28	Connecticut	1,414,083	1.2%
29	Oklahoma	1,314,243	1.1%
30	Iowa	1,160,047	0.9%
31	Nevada	1,149,506	0.9%
32	Utah	1,073,228	0.9%
33	Kansas	1,058,432	0.9%
34	Mississippi	1,027,917	0.8%
35	Arkansas	1,005,911	0.8%
36	New Mexico	732,976	0.6%
37	Nebraska	726,066	0.6%
38	West Virginia	648,880	0.5%
39	Idaho	582,253	0.5%
40	New Hampshire	568,291	0.5%
41	Hawaii	547,216	0.4%
42	Maine	520,986	0.4%
43	Rhode Island	442,781	0.4%
44	Montana	383,357	0.3%
45	Delaware	375,728	0.3%
46	South Dakota	329,987	0.3%
47	North Dakota	283,621	0.2%
48	Alaska	278,359	0.2%
49	Vermont	258,687	0.2%
50	Wyoming	219,336	0.2%
	District of Columbia	281,791	0.2%

Source: U.S. Department of the Treasury, Internal Revenue Service
   "Fiscal Year 2018 IRS Data Book" (https://www.irs.gov/statistics/soi-tax-stats-irs-data-book)
*Total includes refunds to international sources and other miscellaneous refunds not shown separately.

Value of Federal Tax Refunds in 2018

National Total = $463,884,727,000*

ALPHA ORDER

RANK	STATE	REFUNDS	% of USA
25	Alabama	$5,096,863,000	1.1%
48	Alaska	848,250,000	0.2%
22	Arizona	6,705,688,000	1.4%
35	Arkansas	2,930,577,000	0.6%
1	California	45,411,962,000	9.8%
23	Colorado	6,144,533,000	1.3%
19	Connecticut	7,716,066,000	1.7%
36	Delaware	2,259,258,000	0.5%
4	Florida	26,170,994,000	5.6%
8	Georgia	12,843,439,000	2.8%
43	Hawaii	1,475,394,000	0.3%
42	Idaho	1,504,676,000	0.3%
5	Illinois	18,719,368,000	4.0%
20	Indiana	7,262,688,000	1.6%
29	Iowa	3,888,977,000	0.8%
34	Kansas	3,065,228,000	0.7%
27	Kentucky	4,495,635,000	1.0%
24	Louisiana	5,833,844,000	1.3%
44	Maine	1,351,562,000	0.3%
18	Maryland	8,013,105,000	1.7%
13	Massachusetts	9,248,791,000	2.0%
10	Michigan	11,756,843,000	2.5%
14	Minnesota	9,053,049,000	2.0%
32	Mississippi	3,146,800,000	0.7%
16	Missouri	8,571,949,000	1.8%
46	Montana	930,997,000	0.2%
37	Nebraska	2,151,103,000	0.5%
31	Nevada	3,423,667,000	0.7%
41	New Hampshire	1,527,262,000	0.3%
7	New Jersey	14,081,384,000	3.0%
38	New Mexico	1,962,189,000	0.4%
3	New York	31,540,869,000	6.8%
11	North Carolina	10,843,239,000	2.3%
47	North Dakota	866,858,000	0.2%
9	Ohio	12,833,939,000	2.8%
28	Oklahoma	4,463,946,000	1.0%
30	Oregon	3,756,855,000	0.8%
6	Pennsylvania	16,375,053,000	3.5%
40	Rhode Island	1,733,940,000	0.4%
26	South Carolina	5,022,130,000	1.1%
45	South Dakota	960,518,000	0.2%
17	Tennessee	8,044,011,000	1.7%
2	Texas	39,044,742,000	8.4%
33	Utah	3,111,403,000	0.7%
50	Vermont	637,462,000	0.1%
12	Virginia	9,711,381,000	2.1%
15	Washington	8,624,096,000	1.9%
39	West Virginia	1,753,468,000	0.4%
21	Wisconsin	6,760,379,000	1.5%
49	Wyoming	690,631,000	0.1%

RANK ORDER

RANK	STATE	REFUNDS	% of USA
1	California	$45,411,962,000	9.8%
2	Texas	39,044,742,000	8.4%
3	New York	31,540,869,000	6.8%
4	Florida	26,170,994,000	5.6%
5	Illinois	18,719,368,000	4.0%
6	Pennsylvania	16,375,053,000	3.5%
7	New Jersey	14,081,384,000	3.0%
8	Georgia	12,843,439,000	2.8%
9	Ohio	12,833,939,000	2.8%
10	Michigan	11,756,843,000	2.5%
11	North Carolina	10,843,239,000	2.3%
12	Virginia	9,711,381,000	2.1%
13	Massachusetts	9,248,791,000	2.0%
14	Minnesota	9,053,049,000	2.0%
15	Washington	8,624,096,000	1.9%
16	Missouri	8,571,949,000	1.8%
17	Tennessee	8,044,011,000	1.7%
18	Maryland	8,013,105,000	1.7%
19	Connecticut	7,716,066,000	1.7%
20	Indiana	7,262,688,000	1.6%
21	Wisconsin	6,760,379,000	1.5%
22	Arizona	6,705,688,000	1.4%
23	Colorado	6,144,533,000	1.3%
24	Louisiana	5,833,844,000	1.3%
25	Alabama	5,096,863,000	1.1%
26	South Carolina	5,022,130,000	1.1%
27	Kentucky	4,495,635,000	1.0%
28	Oklahoma	4,463,946,000	1.0%
29	Iowa	3,888,977,000	0.8%
30	Oregon	3,756,855,000	0.8%
31	Nevada	3,423,667,000	0.7%
32	Mississippi	3,146,800,000	0.7%
33	Utah	3,111,403,000	0.7%
34	Kansas	3,065,228,000	0.7%
35	Arkansas	2,930,577,000	0.6%
36	Delaware	2,259,258,000	0.5%
37	Nebraska	2,151,103,000	0.5%
38	New Mexico	1,962,189,000	0.4%
39	West Virginia	1,753,468,000	0.4%
40	Rhode Island	1,733,940,000	0.4%
41	New Hampshire	1,527,262,000	0.3%
42	Idaho	1,504,676,000	0.3%
43	Hawaii	1,475,394,000	0.3%
44	Maine	1,351,562,000	0.3%
45	South Dakota	960,518,000	0.2%
46	Montana	930,997,000	0.2%
47	North Dakota	866,858,000	0.2%
48	Alaska	848,250,000	0.2%
49	Wyoming	690,631,000	0.1%
50	Vermont	637,462,000	0.1%
	District of Columbia	2,510,406,000	0.5%

Source: U.S. Department of the Treasury, Internal Revenue Service
"Fiscal Year 2018 IRS Data Book" (https://www.irs.gov/statistics/soi-tax-stats-irs-data-book)
*Total includes refunds to international sources and other miscellaneous refunds not shown separately.

Average Value of Federal Tax Refunds in 2018

National Average = $3,796*

ALPHA ORDER				RANK ORDER		
RANK	STATE	AVERAGE REFUND		RANK	STATE	AVERAGE REFUND
23	Alabama	$3,061		1	Delaware	$6,013
27	Alaska	3,047		2	Connecticut	5,457
34	Arizona	2,911		3	Minnesota	4,214
33	Arkansas	2,913		4	New York	4,020
16	California	3,259		5	New Jersey	3,975
31	Colorado	2,963		6	Rhode Island	3,916
2	Connecticut	5,457		7	Missouri	3,790
1	Delaware	6,013		8	Texas	3,760
17	Florida	3,229		9	Illinois	3,711
11	Georgia	3,484		10	Louisiana	3,592
43	Hawaii	2,696		11	Georgia	3,484
47	Idaho	2,584		12	Maryland	3,410
9	Illinois	3,711		13	Oklahoma	3,397
41	Indiana	2,775		14	Massachusetts	3,361
15	Iowa	3,352		15	Iowa	3,352
37	Kansas	2,896		16	California	3,259
39	Kentucky	2,798		17	Florida	3,229
10	Louisiana	3,592		18	Tennessee	3,213
46	Maine	2,594		19	Pennsylvania	3,206
12	Maryland	3,410		20	Wyoming	3,149
14	Massachusetts	3,361		21	Virginia	3,070
22	Michigan	3,069		22	Michigan	3,069
3	Minnesota	4,214		23	Alabama	3,061
23	Mississippi	3,061		23	Mississippi	3,061
7	Missouri	3,790		25	North Dakota	3,056
50	Montana	2,429		26	Washington	3,048
31	Nebraska	2,963		27	Alaska	3,047
30	Nevada	2,978		28	North Carolina	2,979
44	New Hampshire	2,687		28	Wisconsin	2,979
5	New Jersey	3,975		30	Nevada	2,978
45	New Mexico	2,677		31	Colorado	2,963
4	New York	4,020		31	Nebraska	2,963
28	North Carolina	2,979		33	Arkansas	2,913
25	North Dakota	3,056		34	Arizona	2,911
40	Ohio	2,776		34	South Dakota	2,911
13	Oklahoma	3,397		36	Utah	2,899
48	Oregon	2,534		37	Kansas	2,896
19	Pennsylvania	3,206		38	South Carolina	2,877
6	Rhode Island	3,916		39	Kentucky	2,798
38	South Carolina	2,877		40	Ohio	2,776
34	South Dakota	2,911		41	Indiana	2,775
18	Tennessee	3,213		42	West Virginia	2,702
8	Texas	3,760		43	Hawaii	2,696
36	Utah	2,899		44	New Hampshire	2,687
49	Vermont	2,464		45	New Mexico	2,677
21	Virginia	3,070		46	Maine	2,594
26	Washington	3,048		47	Idaho	2,584
42	West Virginia	2,702		48	Oregon	2,534
28	Wisconsin	2,979		49	Vermont	2,464
20	Wyoming	3,149		50	Montana	2,429
					District of Columbia	8,909

Source: CQ Press using data from U.S. Department of the Treasury, Internal Revenue Service
   "Fiscal Year 2018 IRS Data Book" (https://www.irs.gov/statistics/soi-tax-stats-irs-data-book)
*National average includes refunds to international sources and other miscellaneous refunds not shown separately.

Value of Federal Individual Income Tax Refunds in 2018

National Total = $394,886,856,000*

<table>
<tr><td colspan="4">ALPHA ORDER</td><td colspan="4">RANK ORDER</td></tr>
<tr><td>RANK</td><td>STATE</td><td>REFUNDS</td><td>% of USA</td><td>RANK</td><td>STATE</td><td>REFUNDS</td><td>% of USA</td></tr>
<tr><td>24</td><td>Alabama</td><td>$4,633,485,000</td><td>1.2%</td><td>1</td><td>California</td><td>$40,348,389,000</td><td>10.2%</td></tr>
<tr><td>48</td><td>Alaska</td><td>776,438,000</td><td>0.2%</td><td>2</td><td>Texas</td><td>32,669,264,000</td><td>8.3%</td></tr>
<tr><td>18</td><td>Arizona</td><td>6,142,458,000</td><td>1.6%</td><td>3</td><td>New York</td><td>23,874,409,000</td><td>6.0%</td></tr>
<tr><td>35</td><td>Arkansas</td><td>2,725,007,000</td><td>0.7%</td><td>4</td><td>Florida</td><td>23,828,418,000</td><td>6.0%</td></tr>
<tr><td>1</td><td>California</td><td>40,348,389,000</td><td>10.2%</td><td>5</td><td>Illinois</td><td>14,466,521,000</td><td>3.7%</td></tr>
<tr><td>21</td><td>Colorado</td><td>5,377,954,000</td><td>1.4%</td><td>6</td><td>Pennsylvania</td><td>13,386,804,000</td><td>3.4%</td></tr>
<tr><td>26</td><td>Connecticut</td><td>4,301,259,000</td><td>1.1%</td><td>7</td><td>Ohio</td><td>11,588,921,000</td><td>2.9%</td></tr>
<tr><td>44</td><td>Delaware</td><td>976,995,000</td><td>0.2%</td><td>8</td><td>New Jersey</td><td>10,635,676,000</td><td>2.7%</td></tr>
<tr><td>4</td><td>Florida</td><td>23,828,418,000</td><td>6.0%</td><td>9</td><td>Georgia</td><td>10,440,728,000</td><td>2.6%</td></tr>
<tr><td>9</td><td>Georgia</td><td>10,440,728,000</td><td>2.6%</td><td>10</td><td>Michigan</td><td>9,774,253,000</td><td>2.5%</td></tr>
<tr><td>41</td><td>Hawaii</td><td>1,386,278,000</td><td>0.4%</td><td>11</td><td>North Carolina</td><td>9,471,867,000</td><td>2.4%</td></tr>
<tr><td>40</td><td>Idaho</td><td>1,406,003,000</td><td>0.4%</td><td>12</td><td>Virginia</td><td>8,691,434,000</td><td>2.2%</td></tr>
<tr><td>5</td><td>Illinois</td><td>14,466,521,000</td><td>3.7%</td><td>13</td><td>Massachusetts</td><td>7,792,593,000</td><td>2.0%</td></tr>
<tr><td>16</td><td>Indiana</td><td>6,771,931,000</td><td>1.7%</td><td>14</td><td>Washington</td><td>7,540,784,000</td><td>1.9%</td></tr>
<tr><td>31</td><td>Iowa</td><td>3,020,797,000</td><td>0.8%</td><td>15</td><td>Tennessee</td><td>6,776,512,000</td><td>1.7%</td></tr>
<tr><td>34</td><td>Kansas</td><td>2,783,456,000</td><td>0.7%</td><td>16</td><td>Indiana</td><td>6,771,931,000</td><td>1.7%</td></tr>
<tr><td>27</td><td>Kentucky</td><td>4,216,532,000</td><td>1.1%</td><td>17</td><td>Maryland</td><td>6,627,475,000</td><td>1.7%</td></tr>
<tr><td>23</td><td>Louisiana</td><td>4,886,395,000</td><td>1.2%</td><td>18</td><td>Arizona</td><td>6,142,458,000</td><td>1.6%</td></tr>
<tr><td>42</td><td>Maine</td><td>1,211,020,000</td><td>0.3%</td><td>19</td><td>Missouri</td><td>5,800,039,000</td><td>1.5%</td></tr>
<tr><td>17</td><td>Maryland</td><td>6,627,475,000</td><td>1.7%</td><td>20</td><td>Wisconsin</td><td>5,448,085,000</td><td>1.4%</td></tr>
<tr><td>13</td><td>Massachusetts</td><td>7,792,593,000</td><td>2.0%</td><td>21</td><td>Colorado</td><td>5,377,954,000</td><td>1.4%</td></tr>
<tr><td>10</td><td>Michigan</td><td>9,774,253,000</td><td>2.5%</td><td>22</td><td>Minnesota</td><td>5,348,949,000</td><td>1.4%</td></tr>
<tr><td>22</td><td>Minnesota</td><td>5,348,949,000</td><td>1.4%</td><td>23</td><td>Louisiana</td><td>4,886,395,000</td><td>1.2%</td></tr>
<tr><td>32</td><td>Mississippi</td><td>2,977,777,000</td><td>0.8%</td><td>24</td><td>Alabama</td><td>4,633,485,000</td><td>1.2%</td></tr>
<tr><td>19</td><td>Missouri</td><td>5,800,039,000</td><td>1.5%</td><td>25</td><td>South Carolina</td><td>4,441,597,000</td><td>1.1%</td></tr>
<tr><td>45</td><td>Montana</td><td>893,359,000</td><td>0.2%</td><td>26</td><td>Connecticut</td><td>4,301,259,000</td><td>1.1%</td></tr>
<tr><td>37</td><td>Nebraska</td><td>1,870,779,000</td><td>0.5%</td><td>27</td><td>Kentucky</td><td>4,216,532,000</td><td>1.1%</td></tr>
<tr><td>30</td><td>Nevada</td><td>3,174,669,000</td><td>0.8%</td><td>28</td><td>Oklahoma</td><td>3,828,268,000</td><td>1.0%</td></tr>
<tr><td>39</td><td>New Hampshire</td><td>1,463,905,000</td><td>0.4%</td><td>29</td><td>Oregon</td><td>3,531,173,000</td><td>0.9%</td></tr>
<tr><td>8</td><td>New Jersey</td><td>10,635,676,000</td><td>2.7%</td><td>30</td><td>Nevada</td><td>3,174,669,000</td><td>0.8%</td></tr>
<tr><td>36</td><td>New Mexico</td><td>1,911,211,000</td><td>0.5%</td><td>31</td><td>Iowa</td><td>3,020,797,000</td><td>0.8%</td></tr>
<tr><td>3</td><td>New York</td><td>23,874,409,000</td><td>6.0%</td><td>32</td><td>Mississippi</td><td>2,977,777,000</td><td>0.8%</td></tr>
<tr><td>11</td><td>North Carolina</td><td>9,471,867,000</td><td>2.4%</td><td>33</td><td>Utah</td><td>2,833,970,000</td><td>0.7%</td></tr>
<tr><td>47</td><td>North Dakota</td><td>784,077,000</td><td>0.2%</td><td>34</td><td>Kansas</td><td>2,783,456,000</td><td>0.7%</td></tr>
<tr><td>7</td><td>Ohio</td><td>11,588,921,000</td><td>2.9%</td><td>35</td><td>Arkansas</td><td>2,725,007,000</td><td>0.7%</td></tr>
<tr><td>28</td><td>Oklahoma</td><td>3,828,268,000</td><td>1.0%</td><td>36</td><td>New Mexico</td><td>1,911,211,000</td><td>0.5%</td></tr>
<tr><td>29</td><td>Oregon</td><td>3,531,173,000</td><td>0.9%</td><td>37</td><td>Nebraska</td><td>1,870,779,000</td><td>0.5%</td></tr>
<tr><td>6</td><td>Pennsylvania</td><td>13,386,804,000</td><td>3.4%</td><td>38</td><td>West Virginia</td><td>1,696,996,000</td><td>0.4%</td></tr>
<tr><td>43</td><td>Rhode Island</td><td>1,151,716,000</td><td>0.3%</td><td>39</td><td>New Hampshire</td><td>1,463,905,000</td><td>0.4%</td></tr>
<tr><td>25</td><td>South Carolina</td><td>4,441,597,000</td><td>1.1%</td><td>40</td><td>Idaho</td><td>1,406,003,000</td><td>0.4%</td></tr>
<tr><td>46</td><td>South Dakota</td><td>843,273,000</td><td>0.2%</td><td>41</td><td>Hawaii</td><td>1,386,278,000</td><td>0.4%</td></tr>
<tr><td>15</td><td>Tennessee</td><td>6,776,512,000</td><td>1.7%</td><td>42</td><td>Maine</td><td>1,211,020,000</td><td>0.3%</td></tr>
<tr><td>2</td><td>Texas</td><td>32,669,264,000</td><td>8.3%</td><td>43</td><td>Rhode Island</td><td>1,151,716,000</td><td>0.3%</td></tr>
<tr><td>33</td><td>Utah</td><td>2,833,970,000</td><td>0.7%</td><td>44</td><td>Delaware</td><td>976,995,000</td><td>0.2%</td></tr>
<tr><td>50</td><td>Vermont</td><td>613,054,000</td><td>0.2%</td><td>45</td><td>Montana</td><td>893,359,000</td><td>0.2%</td></tr>
<tr><td>12</td><td>Virginia</td><td>8,691,434,000</td><td>2.2%</td><td>46</td><td>South Dakota</td><td>843,273,000</td><td>0.2%</td></tr>
<tr><td>14</td><td>Washington</td><td>7,540,784,000</td><td>1.9%</td><td>47</td><td>North Dakota</td><td>784,077,000</td><td>0.2%</td></tr>
<tr><td>38</td><td>West Virginia</td><td>1,696,996,000</td><td>0.4%</td><td>48</td><td>Alaska</td><td>776,438,000</td><td>0.2%</td></tr>
<tr><td>20</td><td>Wisconsin</td><td>5,448,085,000</td><td>1.4%</td><td>49</td><td>Wyoming</td><td>637,856,000</td><td>0.2%</td></tr>
<tr><td>49</td><td>Wyoming</td><td>637,856,000</td><td>0.2%</td><td>50</td><td>Vermont</td><td>613,054,000</td><td>0.2%</td></tr>
<tr><td></td><td></td><td></td><td></td><td></td><td>District of Columbia</td><td>809,948,000</td><td>0.2%</td></tr>
</table>

Source: U.S. Department of the Treasury, Internal Revenue Service
"Fiscal Year 2018 IRS Data Book" (https://www.irs.gov/statistics/soi-tax-stats-irs-data-book)
*Total includes refunds to international sources and other miscellaneous refunds not shown separately.

Average Value of Federal Individual Income Tax Refunds in 2018

National Average = $3,285*

RANK	STATE	AVERAGE REFUND
17	Alabama	$2,823
15	Alaska	2,852
23	Arizona	2,702
20	Arkansas	2,755
9	California	2,946
32	Colorado	2,638
3	Connecticut	3,091
26	Delaware	2,672
7	Florida	2,989
13	Georgia	2,872
42	Hawaii	2,576
45	Idaho	2,465
11	Illinois	2,916
37	Indiana	2,619
29	Iowa	2,650
25	Kansas	2,677
27	Kentucky	2,658
4	Louisiana	3,060
50	Maine	2,362
14	Maryland	2,860
12	Massachusetts	2,877
40	Michigan	2,591
44	Minnesota	2,530
10	Mississippi	2,943
39	Missouri	2,613
49	Montana	2,394
35	Nebraska	2,626
18	Nevada	2,807
38	New Hampshire	2,618
5	New Jersey	3,052
31	New Mexico	2,647
2	New York	3,099
32	North Carolina	2,638
16	North Dakota	2,831
43	Ohio	2,540
8	Oklahoma	2,964
47	Oregon	2,426
28	Pennsylvania	2,655
34	Rhode Island	2,636
41	South Carolina	2,578
36	South Dakota	2,620
21	Tennessee	2,749
1	Texas	3,203
24	Utah	2,685
48	Vermont	2,417
19	Virginia	2,789
22	Washington	2,718
29	West Virginia	2,650
46	Wisconsin	2,438
6	Wyoming	2,997

RANK	STATE	AVERAGE REFUND
1	Texas	$3,203
2	New York	3,099
3	Connecticut	3,091
4	Louisiana	3,060
5	New Jersey	3,052
6	Wyoming	2,997
7	Florida	2,989
8	Oklahoma	2,964
9	California	2,946
10	Mississippi	2,943
11	Illinois	2,916
12	Massachusetts	2,877
13	Georgia	2,872
14	Maryland	2,860
15	Alaska	2,852
16	North Dakota	2,831
17	Alabama	2,823
18	Nevada	2,807
19	Virginia	2,789
20	Arkansas	2,755
21	Tennessee	2,749
22	Washington	2,718
23	Arizona	2,702
24	Utah	2,685
25	Kansas	2,677
26	Delaware	2,672
27	Kentucky	2,658
28	Pennsylvania	2,655
29	Iowa	2,650
29	West Virginia	2,650
31	New Mexico	2,647
32	Colorado	2,638
32	North Carolina	2,638
34	Rhode Island	2,636
35	Nebraska	2,626
36	South Dakota	2,620
37	Indiana	2,619
38	New Hampshire	2,618
39	Missouri	2,613
40	Michigan	2,591
41	South Carolina	2,578
42	Hawaii	2,576
43	Ohio	2,540
44	Minnesota	2,530
45	Idaho	2,465
46	Wisconsin	2,438
47	Oregon	2,426
48	Vermont	2,417
49	Montana	2,394
50	Maine	2,362

| | District of Columbia | 2,933 |

Source: CQ Press using data from U.S. Department of the Treasury, Internal Revenue Service
   "Fiscal Year 2018 IRS Data Book" (https://www.irs.gov/statistics/soi-tax-stats-irs-data-book)
*National average includes refunds to international sources and other miscellaneous refunds not shown separately.

Value of Federal Business Income Tax Refunds in 2018

National Total = $60,089,066,000*

ALPHA ORDER

RANK	STATE	REFUNDS	% of USA
28	Alabama	$413,377,000	0.7%
43	Alaska	58,022,000	0.1%
29	Arizona	389,462,000	0.6%
36	Arkansas	153,920,000	0.3%
4	California	3,732,387,000	6.2%
24	Colorado	603,946,000	1.0%
6	Connecticut	3,252,481,000	5.4%
17	Delaware	1,135,002,000	1.9%
11	Florida	1,760,425,000	2.9%
10	Georgia	2,225,655,000	3.7%
41	Hawaii	60,660,000	0.1%
40	Idaho	65,989,000	0.1%
3	Illinois	3,743,303,000	6.2%
30	Indiana	383,515,000	0.6%
23	Iowa	831,064,000	1.4%
32	Kansas	248,578,000	0.4%
34	Kentucky	227,221,000	0.4%
22	Louisiana	887,038,000	1.5%
39	Maine	121,474,000	0.2%
13	Maryland	1,268,963,000	2.1%
16	Massachusetts	1,154,257,000	1.9%
12	Michigan	1,746,220,000	2.9%
5	Minnesota	3,556,506,000	5.9%
38	Mississippi	144,091,000	0.2%
9	Missouri	2,607,490,000	4.3%
48	Montana	26,038,000	0.0%
31	Nebraska	251,305,000	0.4%
35	Nevada	155,887,000	0.3%
46	New Hampshire	33,499,000	0.1%
7	New Jersey	3,142,270,000	5.2%
47	New Mexico	26,408,000	0.0%
1	New York	6,783,078,000	11.3%
14	North Carolina	1,203,686,000	2.0%
42	North Dakota	58,423,000	0.1%
19	Ohio	1,001,625,000	1.7%
27	Oklahoma	487,090,000	0.8%
37	Oregon	145,924,000	0.2%
8	Pennsylvania	2,693,479,000	4.5%
25	Rhode Island	554,006,000	0.9%
26	South Carolina	541,388,000	0.9%
45	South Dakota	33,614,000	0.1%
18	Tennessee	1,116,238,000	1.9%
2	Texas	5,537,533,000	9.2%
33	Utah	234,219,000	0.4%
50	Vermont	17,657,000	0.0%
20	Virginia	895,010,000	1.5%
21	Washington	888,180,000	1.5%
44	West Virginia	43,660,000	0.1%
15	Wisconsin	1,201,397,000	2.0%
49	Wyoming	21,289,000	0.0%

RANK ORDER

RANK	STATE	REFUNDS	% of USA
1	New York	$6,783,078,000	11.3%
2	Texas	5,537,533,000	9.2%
3	Illinois	3,743,303,000	6.2%
4	California	3,732,387,000	6.2%
5	Minnesota	3,556,506,000	5.9%
6	Connecticut	3,252,481,000	5.4%
7	New Jersey	3,142,270,000	5.2%
8	Pennsylvania	2,693,479,000	4.5%
9	Missouri	2,607,490,000	4.3%
10	Georgia	2,225,655,000	3.7%
11	Florida	1,760,425,000	2.9%
12	Michigan	1,746,220,000	2.9%
13	Maryland	1,268,963,000	2.1%
14	North Carolina	1,203,686,000	2.0%
15	Wisconsin	1,201,397,000	2.0%
16	Massachusetts	1,154,257,000	1.9%
17	Delaware	1,135,002,000	1.9%
18	Tennessee	1,116,238,000	1.9%
19	Ohio	1,001,625,000	1.7%
20	Virginia	895,010,000	1.5%
21	Washington	888,180,000	1.5%
22	Louisiana	887,038,000	1.5%
23	Iowa	831,064,000	1.4%
24	Colorado	603,946,000	1.0%
25	Rhode Island	554,006,000	0.9%
26	South Carolina	541,388,000	0.9%
27	Oklahoma	487,090,000	0.8%
28	Alabama	413,377,000	0.7%
29	Arizona	389,462,000	0.6%
30	Indiana	383,515,000	0.6%
31	Nebraska	251,305,000	0.4%
32	Kansas	248,578,000	0.4%
33	Utah	234,219,000	0.4%
34	Kentucky	227,221,000	0.4%
35	Nevada	155,887,000	0.3%
36	Arkansas	153,920,000	0.3%
37	Oregon	145,924,000	0.2%
38	Mississippi	144,091,000	0.2%
39	Maine	121,474,000	0.2%
40	Idaho	65,989,000	0.1%
41	Hawaii	60,660,000	0.1%
42	North Dakota	58,423,000	0.1%
43	Alaska	58,022,000	0.1%
44	West Virginia	43,660,000	0.1%
45	South Dakota	33,614,000	0.1%
46	New Hampshire	33,499,000	0.1%
47	New Mexico	26,408,000	0.0%
48	Montana	26,038,000	0.0%
49	Wyoming	21,289,000	0.0%
50	Vermont	17,657,000	0.0%
	District of Columbia	1,657,418,000	2.8%

Source: U.S. Department of the Treasury, Internal Revenue Service
"Fiscal Year 2018 IRS Data Book" (https://www.irs.gov/statistics/soi-tax-stats-irs-data-book)
*Total includes refunds to international sources and other miscellaneous refunds not shown separately. Includes taxes on corporation income (Form 1120 series) and unrelated business income from tax-exempt organizations.

Average Value of Federal Business Income Tax Refunds in 2018

National Average = $178,271*

<table>
<tr><th colspan="3">ALPHA ORDER</th><th colspan="3">RANK ORDER</th></tr>
<tr><th>RANK</th><th>STATE</th><th>AVERAGE REFUND</th><th>RANK</th><th>STATE</th><th>AVERAGE REFUND</th></tr>
<tr><td>22</td><td>Alabama</td><td>$129,545</td><td>1</td><td>Connecticut</td><td>$988,596</td></tr>
<tr><td>33</td><td>Alaska</td><td>76,749</td><td>2</td><td>Delaware</td><td>680,049</td></tr>
<tr><td>30</td><td>Arizona</td><td>82,408</td><td>3</td><td>Rhode Island</td><td>642,698</td></tr>
<tr><td>35</td><td>Arkansas</td><td>67,657</td><td>4</td><td>Minnesota</td><td>465,999</td></tr>
<tr><td>29</td><td>California</td><td>84,137</td><td>5</td><td>New Jersey</td><td>348,599</td></tr>
<tr><td>25</td><td>Colorado</td><td>113,120</td><td>6</td><td>Missouri</td><td>346,602</td></tr>
<tr><td>1</td><td>Connecticut</td><td>988,596</td><td>7</td><td>New York</td><td>280,154</td></tr>
<tr><td>2</td><td>Delaware</td><td>680,049</td><td>8</td><td>Illinois</td><td>279,810</td></tr>
<tr><td>32</td><td>Florida</td><td>76,905</td><td>9</td><td>Georgia</td><td>274,332</td></tr>
<tr><td>9</td><td>Georgia</td><td>274,332</td><td>10</td><td>Pennsylvania</td><td>266,233</td></tr>
<tr><td>44</td><td>Hawaii</td><td>30,792</td><td>11</td><td>Tennessee</td><td>235,295</td></tr>
<tr><td>41</td><td>Idaho</td><td>42,906</td><td>12</td><td>Maryland</td><td>223,095</td></tr>
<tr><td>8</td><td>Illinois</td><td>279,810</td><td>13</td><td>Louisiana</td><td>221,815</td></tr>
<tr><td>34</td><td>Indiana</td><td>75,898</td><td>14</td><td>Texas</td><td>203,264</td></tr>
<tr><td>19</td><td>Iowa</td><td>151,903</td><td>15</td><td>Massachusetts</td><td>171,331</td></tr>
<tr><td>37</td><td>Kansas</td><td>62,788</td><td>16</td><td>Wisconsin</td><td>169,881</td></tr>
<tr><td>28</td><td>Kentucky</td><td>84,658</td><td>17</td><td>Michigan</td><td>160,927</td></tr>
<tr><td>13</td><td>Louisiana</td><td>221,815</td><td>18</td><td>South Carolina</td><td>152,504</td></tr>
<tr><td>36</td><td>Maine</td><td>67,187</td><td>19</td><td>Iowa</td><td>151,903</td></tr>
<tr><td>12</td><td>Maryland</td><td>223,095</td><td>20</td><td>North Carolina</td><td>147,492</td></tr>
<tr><td>15</td><td>Massachusetts</td><td>171,331</td><td>21</td><td>Oklahoma</td><td>135,303</td></tr>
<tr><td>17</td><td>Michigan</td><td>160,927</td><td>22</td><td>Alabama</td><td>129,545</td></tr>
<tr><td>4</td><td>Minnesota</td><td>465,999</td><td>23</td><td>Washington</td><td>121,869</td></tr>
<tr><td>38</td><td>Mississippi</td><td>61,683</td><td>24</td><td>Virginia</td><td>113,666</td></tr>
<tr><td>6</td><td>Missouri</td><td>346,602</td><td>25</td><td>Colorado</td><td>113,120</td></tr>
<tr><td>50</td><td>Montana</td><td>9,662</td><td>26</td><td>Ohio</td><td>93,496</td></tr>
<tr><td>31</td><td>Nebraska</td><td>82,180</td><td>27</td><td>Utah</td><td>87,986</td></tr>
<tr><td>39</td><td>Nevada</td><td>47,425</td><td>28</td><td>Kentucky</td><td>84,658</td></tr>
<tr><td>45</td><td>New Hampshire</td><td>22,068</td><td>29</td><td>California</td><td>84,137</td></tr>
<tr><td>5</td><td>New Jersey</td><td>348,599</td><td>30</td><td>Arizona</td><td>82,408</td></tr>
<tr><td>48</td><td>New Mexico</td><td>17,238</td><td>31</td><td>Nebraska</td><td>82,180</td></tr>
<tr><td>7</td><td>New York</td><td>280,154</td><td>32</td><td>Florida</td><td>76,905</td></tr>
<tr><td>20</td><td>North Carolina</td><td>147,492</td><td>33</td><td>Alaska</td><td>76,749</td></tr>
<tr><td>40</td><td>North Dakota</td><td>46,851</td><td>34</td><td>Indiana</td><td>75,898</td></tr>
<tr><td>26</td><td>Ohio</td><td>93,496</td><td>35</td><td>Arkansas</td><td>67,657</td></tr>
<tr><td>21</td><td>Oklahoma</td><td>135,303</td><td>36</td><td>Maine</td><td>67,187</td></tr>
<tr><td>43</td><td>Oregon</td><td>31,565</td><td>37</td><td>Kansas</td><td>62,788</td></tr>
<tr><td>10</td><td>Pennsylvania</td><td>266,233</td><td>38</td><td>Mississippi</td><td>61,683</td></tr>
<tr><td>3</td><td>Rhode Island</td><td>642,698</td><td>39</td><td>Nevada</td><td>47,425</td></tr>
<tr><td>18</td><td>South Carolina</td><td>152,504</td><td>40</td><td>North Dakota</td><td>46,851</td></tr>
<tr><td>46</td><td>South Dakota</td><td>20,360</td><td>41</td><td>Idaho</td><td>42,906</td></tr>
<tr><td>11</td><td>Tennessee</td><td>235,295</td><td>42</td><td>West Virginia</td><td>38,774</td></tr>
<tr><td>14</td><td>Texas</td><td>203,264</td><td>43</td><td>Oregon</td><td>31,565</td></tr>
<tr><td>27</td><td>Utah</td><td>87,986</td><td>44</td><td>Hawaii</td><td>30,792</td></tr>
<tr><td>47</td><td>Vermont</td><td>18,966</td><td>45</td><td>New Hampshire</td><td>22,068</td></tr>
<tr><td>24</td><td>Virginia</td><td>113,666</td><td>46</td><td>South Dakota</td><td>20,360</td></tr>
<tr><td>23</td><td>Washington</td><td>121,869</td><td>47</td><td>Vermont</td><td>18,966</td></tr>
<tr><td>42</td><td>West Virginia</td><td>38,774</td><td>48</td><td>New Mexico</td><td>17,238</td></tr>
<tr><td>16</td><td>Wisconsin</td><td>169,881</td><td>49</td><td>Wyoming</td><td>16,593</td></tr>
<tr><td>49</td><td>Wyoming</td><td>16,593</td><td>50</td><td>Montana</td><td>9,662</td></tr>
<tr><td></td><td></td><td></td><td></td><td>District of Columbia</td><td>1,534,646</td></tr>
</table>

Source: CQ Press using data from U.S. Department of the Treasury, Internal Revenue Service
   "Fiscal Year 2018 IRS Data Book" (https://www.irs.gov/statistics/soi-tax-stats-irs-data-book)
*National average includes refunds to international sources and other miscellaneous refunds not shown separately.

Federal Government Expenditures in 2018

National Total = $3,408,131,000,000*

ALPHA ORDER

RANK	STATE	EXPENDITURES	% of USA
26	Alabama	$57,598,000,000	1.7%
44	Alaska	9,880,000,000	0.3%
16	Arizona	78,926,000,000	2.3%
34	Arkansas	24,118,000,000	0.7%
1	California	313,854,000,000	9.2%
27	Colorado	41,744,000,000	1.2%
20	Connecticut	68,692,000,000	2.0%
47	Delaware	7,517,000,000	0.2%
4	Florida	192,740,000,000	5.7%
22	Georgia	68,444,000,000	2.0%
41	Hawaii	12,630,000,000	0.4%
40	Idaho	13,004,000,000	0.4%
12	Illinois	89,137,000,000	2.6%
6	Indiana	137,852,000,000	4.0%
33	Iowa	24,173,000,000	0.7%
36	Kansas	18,789,000,000	0.6%
10	Kentucky	90,017,000,000	2.6%
28	Louisiana	37,723,000,000	1.1%
42	Maine	12,122,000,000	0.4%
17	Maryland	72,833,000,000	2.1%
21	Massachusetts	68,610,000,000	2.0%
15	Michigan	82,399,000,000	2.4%
8	Minnesota	101,774,000,000	3.0%
31	Mississippi	30,072,000,000	0.9%
24	Missouri	62,183,000,000	1.8%
46	Montana	9,449,000,000	0.3%
39	Nebraska	15,247,000,000	0.4%
35	Nevada	20,374,000,000	0.6%
43	New Hampshire	11,288,000,000	0.3%
23	New Jersey	66,673,000,000	2.0%
32	New Mexico	26,086,000,000	0.8%
5	New York	175,221,000,000	5.1%
18	North Carolina	71,866,000,000	2.1%
19	North Dakota	68,821,000,000	2.0%
13	Ohio	86,084,000,000	2.5%
30	Oklahoma	30,421,000,000	0.9%
29	Oregon	35,209,000,000	1.0%
2	Pennsylvania	210,817,000,000	6.2%
45	Rhode Island	9,847,000,000	0.3%
9	South Carolina	98,993,000,000	2.9%
48	South Dakota	7,190,000,000	0.2%
14	Tennessee	82,686,000,000	2.4%
3	Texas	209,251,000,000	6.1%
38	Utah	16,310,000,000	0.5%
49	Vermont	5,633,000,000	0.2%
7	Virginia	110,273,000,000	3.2%
25	Washington	61,346,000,000	1.8%
37	West Virginia	16,939,000,000	0.5%
11	Wisconsin	89,614,000,000	2.6%
50	Wyoming	4,407,000,000	0.1%

RANK ORDER

RANK	STATE	EXPENDITURES	% of USA
1	California	$313,854,000,000	9.2%
2	Pennsylvania	210,817,000,000	6.2%
3	Texas	209,251,000,000	6.1%
4	Florida	192,740,000,000	5.7%
5	New York	175,221,000,000	5.1%
6	Indiana	137,852,000,000	4.0%
7	Virginia	110,273,000,000	3.2%
8	Minnesota	101,774,000,000	3.0%
9	South Carolina	98,993,000,000	2.9%
10	Kentucky	90,017,000,000	2.6%
11	Wisconsin	89,614,000,000	2.6%
12	Illinois	89,137,000,000	2.6%
13	Ohio	86,084,000,000	2.5%
14	Tennessee	82,686,000,000	2.4%
15	Michigan	82,399,000,000	2.4%
16	Arizona	78,926,000,000	2.3%
17	Maryland	72,833,000,000	2.1%
18	North Carolina	71,866,000,000	2.1%
19	North Dakota	68,821,000,000	2.0%
20	Connecticut	68,692,000,000	2.0%
21	Massachusetts	68,610,000,000	2.0%
22	Georgia	68,444,000,000	2.0%
23	New Jersey	66,673,000,000	2.0%
24	Missouri	62,183,000,000	1.8%
25	Washington	61,346,000,000	1.8%
26	Alabama	57,598,000,000	1.7%
27	Colorado	41,744,000,000	1.2%
28	Louisiana	37,723,000,000	1.1%
29	Oregon	35,209,000,000	1.0%
30	Oklahoma	30,421,000,000	0.9%
31	Mississippi	30,072,000,000	0.9%
32	New Mexico	26,086,000,000	0.8%
33	Iowa	24,173,000,000	0.7%
34	Arkansas	24,118,000,000	0.7%
35	Nevada	20,374,000,000	0.6%
36	Kansas	18,789,000,000	0.6%
37	West Virginia	16,939,000,000	0.5%
38	Utah	16,310,000,000	0.5%
39	Nebraska	15,247,000,000	0.4%
40	Idaho	13,004,000,000	0.4%
41	Hawaii	12,630,000,000	0.4%
42	Maine	12,122,000,000	0.4%
43	New Hampshire	11,288,000,000	0.3%
44	Alaska	9,880,000,000	0.3%
45	Rhode Island	9,847,000,000	0.3%
46	Montana	9,449,000,000	0.3%
47	Delaware	7,517,000,000	0.2%
48	South Dakota	7,190,000,000	0.2%
49	Vermont	5,633,000,000	0.2%
50	Wyoming	4,407,000,000	0.1%
	District of Columbia	35,125,000,000	1.0%

Source: U.S. Department of the Treasury, USAspending.gov
"Award Data Archive" (https://www.usaspending.gov/, as of January 10, 2020)

*For fiscal year 2018. Total includes $116,129,000,000 in U.S. territories and internationally as well as expenditures not distributed by state. Expenditures allocated based on place of performance of a contract. Includes contracts, direct payments, grants, loans, insurance, and "other." The Treasury Department reports total federal spending of $4,100,000,000,000. This means an additional estimated $691,869,000,000 in expenditures are not reported through USAspending.gov.

Per Capita Federal Government Expenditures in 2018

National Per Capita = $10,077*

ALPHA ORDER

RANK	STATE	PER CAPITA		RANK	STATE	PER CAPITA
14	Alabama	$11,784		1	North Dakota	$90,783
9	Alaska	13,440		2	Indiana	20,589
15	Arizona	11,026		3	Kentucky	20,178
33	Arkansas	8,013		4	South Carolina	19,471
34	California	7,953		5	Connecticut	19,233
43	Colorado	7,335		6	Minnesota	18,154
5	Connecticut	19,233		7	Pennsylvania	16,469
36	Delaware	7,785		8	Wisconsin	15,431
21	Florida	9,073		9	Alaska	13,440
48	Georgia	6,512		10	Virginia	12,971
26	Hawaii	8,891		11	New Mexico	12,465
41	Idaho	7,428		12	Tennessee	12,211
45	Illinois	7,006		13	Maryland	12,067
2	Indiana	20,589		14	Alabama	11,784
38	Iowa	7,677		15	Arizona	11,026
49	Kansas	6,454		16	Missouri	10,158
3	Kentucky	20,178		17	Mississippi	10,088
32	Louisiana	8,096		18	Massachusetts	9,969
22	Maine	9,052		19	West Virginia	9,388
13	Maryland	12,067		20	Rhode Island	9,305
18	Massachusetts	9,969		21	Florida	9,073
29	Michigan	8,253		22	Maine	9,052
6	Minnesota	18,154		23	Vermont	9,023
17	Mississippi	10,088		24	New York	8,972
16	Missouri	10,158		25	Montana	8,908
25	Montana	8,908		26	Hawaii	8,891
35	Nebraska	7,918		27	Oregon	8,420
47	Nevada	6,730		28	New Hampshire	8,340
28	New Hampshire	8,340		29	Michigan	8,253
40	New Jersey	7,503		30	South Dakota	8,183
11	New Mexico	12,465		31	Washington	8,154
24	New York	8,972		32	Louisiana	8,096
46	North Carolina	6,922		33	Arkansas	8,013
1	North Dakota	90,783		34	California	7,953
42	Ohio	7,373		35	Nebraska	7,918
37	Oklahoma	7,721		36	Delaware	7,785
27	Oregon	8,420		37	Oklahoma	7,721
7	Pennsylvania	16,469		38	Iowa	7,677
20	Rhode Island	9,305		39	Wyoming	7,630
4	South Carolina	19,471		40	New Jersey	7,503
30	South Dakota	8,183		41	Idaho	7,428
12	Tennessee	12,211		42	Ohio	7,373
44	Texas	7,309		43	Colorado	7,335
50	Utah	5,172		44	Texas	7,309
23	Vermont	9,023		45	Illinois	7,006
10	Virginia	12,971		46	North Carolina	6,922
31	Washington	8,154		47	Nevada	6,730
19	West Virginia	9,388		48	Georgia	6,512
8	Wisconsin	15,431		49	Kansas	6,454
39	Wyoming	7,630		50	Utah	5,172

District of Columbia   50,068

Source: CQ Press using data from U.S. Department of the Treasury, USAspending.gov
"Award Data Archive" (https://www.usaspending.gov/, as of January 10, 2020)
*For fiscal year 2018. National per capita excludes expenditures and population for territories and undistributed amounts.
Expenditures allocated based on place of performance of a contract. Includes contracts, direct payments, grants, loans, insurance, and "other."

Federal Government Contract Awards in 2018

National Total = $581,320,000,000*

ALPHA ORDER

RANK	STATE	EXPENDITURES	% of USA
12	Alabama	$14,139,000,000	2.4%
36	Alaska	2,321,000,000	0.4%
7	Arizona	16,851,000,000	2.9%
43	Arkansas	968,000,000	0.2%
2	California	59,935,000,000	10.3%
15	Colorado	10,590,000,000	1.8%
10	Connecticut	15,781,000,000	2.7%
50	Delaware	321,000,000	0.1%
5	Florida	22,598,000,000	3.9%
16	Georgia	10,427,000,000	1.8%
32	Hawaii	2,544,000,000	0.4%
35	Idaho	2,389,000,000	0.4%
14	Illinois	11,409,000,000	2.0%
26	Indiana	4,390,000,000	0.8%
37	Iowa	2,285,000,000	0.4%
38	Kansas	1,874,000,000	0.3%
17	Kentucky	9,166,000,000	1.6%
30	Louisiana	3,142,000,000	0.5%
41	Maine	1,361,000,000	0.2%
4	Maryland	34,696,000,000	6.0%
9	Massachusetts	16,343,000,000	2.8%
23	Michigan	6,961,000,000	1.2%
29	Minnesota	3,365,000,000	0.6%
20	Mississippi	8,331,000,000	1.4%
8	Missouri	16,842,000,000	2.9%
46	Montana	637,000,000	0.1%
42	Nebraska	1,078,000,000	0.2%
31	Nevada	3,118,000,000	0.5%
34	New Hampshire	2,403,000,000	0.4%
21	New Jersey	7,914,000,000	1.4%
18	New Mexico	8,976,000,000	1.5%
13	New York	12,038,000,000	2.1%
25	North Carolina	6,412,000,000	1.1%
48	North Dakota	550,000,000	0.1%
22	Ohio	7,887,000,000	1.4%
27	Oklahoma	4,280,000,000	0.7%
39	Oregon	1,563,000,000	0.3%
6	Pennsylvania	18,573,000,000	3.2%
45	Rhode Island	778,000,000	0.1%
24	South Carolina	6,903,000,000	1.2%
44	South Dakota	815,000,000	0.1%
19	Tennessee	8,799,000,000	1.5%
3	Texas	49,603,000,000	8.5%
33	Utah	2,525,000,000	0.4%
47	Vermont	581,000,000	0.1%
1	Virginia	60,955,000,000	10.5%
11	Washington	14,626,000,000	2.5%
40	West Virginia	1,377,000,000	0.2%
28	Wisconsin	4,120,000,000	0.7%
49	Wyoming	478,000,000	0.1%

RANK ORDER

RANK	STATE	EXPENDITURES	% of USA
1	Virginia	$60,955,000,000	10.5%
2	California	59,935,000,000	10.3%
3	Texas	49,603,000,000	8.5%
4	Maryland	34,696,000,000	6.0%
5	Florida	22,598,000,000	3.9%
6	Pennsylvania	18,573,000,000	3.2%
7	Arizona	16,851,000,000	2.9%
8	Missouri	16,842,000,000	2.9%
9	Massachusetts	16,343,000,000	2.8%
10	Connecticut	15,781,000,000	2.7%
11	Washington	14,626,000,000	2.5%
12	Alabama	14,139,000,000	2.4%
13	New York	12,038,000,000	2.1%
14	Illinois	11,409,000,000	2.0%
15	Colorado	10,590,000,000	1.8%
16	Georgia	10,427,000,000	1.8%
17	Kentucky	9,166,000,000	1.6%
18	New Mexico	8,976,000,000	1.5%
19	Tennessee	8,799,000,000	1.5%
20	Mississippi	8,331,000,000	1.4%
21	New Jersey	7,914,000,000	1.4%
22	Ohio	7,887,000,000	1.4%
23	Michigan	6,961,000,000	1.2%
24	South Carolina	6,903,000,000	1.2%
25	North Carolina	6,412,000,000	1.1%
26	Indiana	4,390,000,000	0.8%
27	Oklahoma	4,280,000,000	0.7%
28	Wisconsin	4,120,000,000	0.7%
29	Minnesota	3,365,000,000	0.6%
30	Louisiana	3,142,000,000	0.5%
31	Nevada	3,118,000,000	0.5%
32	Hawaii	2,544,000,000	0.4%
33	Utah	2,525,000,000	0.4%
34	New Hampshire	2,403,000,000	0.4%
35	Idaho	2,389,000,000	0.4%
36	Alaska	2,321,000,000	0.4%
37	Iowa	2,285,000,000	0.4%
38	Kansas	1,874,000,000	0.3%
39	Oregon	1,563,000,000	0.3%
40	West Virginia	1,377,000,000	0.2%
41	Maine	1,361,000,000	0.2%
42	Nebraska	1,078,000,000	0.2%
43	Arkansas	968,000,000	0.2%
44	South Dakota	815,000,000	0.1%
45	Rhode Island	778,000,000	0.1%
46	Montana	637,000,000	0.1%
47	Vermont	581,000,000	0.1%
48	North Dakota	550,000,000	0.1%
49	Wyoming	478,000,000	0.1%
50	Delaware	321,000,000	0.1%
	District of Columbia	23,694,000,000	4.1%

Source: U.S. Department of the Treasury, USAspending.gov
"Award Data Archive" (https://www.usaspending.gov/, as of January 10, 2020)
*For fiscal year 2018. Total includes $51,603,000,000 in U.S. territories and internationally as well as expenditures not distributed by state. Expenditures allocated based on place of performance of a contract.

Per Capita Expenditures for Federal Government Contract Awards in 2018
National Per Capita = $1,621*

<table>
<tr><td colspan="3">ALPHA ORDER</td><td colspan="3">RANK ORDER</td></tr>
<tr><td>RANK</td><td>STATE</td><td>PER CAPITA</td><td>RANK</td><td>STATE</td><td>PER CAPITA</td></tr>
<tr><td>6</td><td>Alabama</td><td>$2,893</td><td>1</td><td>Virginia</td><td>$7,170</td></tr>
<tr><td>5</td><td>Alaska</td><td>3,158</td><td>2</td><td>Maryland</td><td>5,748</td></tr>
<tr><td>10</td><td>Arizona</td><td>2,354</td><td>3</td><td>Connecticut</td><td>4,419</td></tr>
<tr><td>50</td><td>Arkansas</td><td>322</td><td>4</td><td>New Mexico</td><td>4,289</td></tr>
<tr><td>17</td><td>California</td><td>1,519</td><td>5</td><td>Alaska</td><td>3,158</td></tr>
<tr><td>13</td><td>Colorado</td><td>1,861</td><td>6</td><td>Alabama</td><td>2,893</td></tr>
<tr><td>3</td><td>Connecticut</td><td>4,419</td><td>7</td><td>Mississippi</td><td>2,795</td></tr>
<tr><td>49</td><td>Delaware</td><td>333</td><td>8</td><td>Missouri</td><td>2,751</td></tr>
<tr><td>23</td><td>Florida</td><td>1,064</td><td>9</td><td>Massachusetts</td><td>2,375</td></tr>
<tr><td>26</td><td>Georgia</td><td>992</td><td>10</td><td>Arizona</td><td>2,354</td></tr>
<tr><td>14</td><td>Hawaii</td><td>1,791</td><td>11</td><td>Kentucky</td><td>2,055</td></tr>
<tr><td>19</td><td>Idaho</td><td>1,365</td><td>12</td><td>Washington</td><td>1,944</td></tr>
<tr><td>29</td><td>Illinois</td><td>897</td><td>13</td><td>Colorado</td><td>1,861</td></tr>
<tr><td>41</td><td>Indiana</td><td>656</td><td>14</td><td>Hawaii</td><td>1,791</td></tr>
<tr><td>35</td><td>Iowa</td><td>726</td><td>15</td><td>New Hampshire</td><td>1,775</td></tr>
<tr><td>42</td><td>Kansas</td><td>644</td><td>16</td><td>Texas</td><td>1,733</td></tr>
<tr><td>11</td><td>Kentucky</td><td>2,055</td><td>17</td><td>California</td><td>1,519</td></tr>
<tr><td>40</td><td>Louisiana</td><td>674</td><td>18</td><td>Pennsylvania</td><td>1,451</td></tr>
<tr><td>25</td><td>Maine</td><td>1,017</td><td>19</td><td>Idaho</td><td>1,365</td></tr>
<tr><td>2</td><td>Maryland</td><td>5,748</td><td>20</td><td>South Carolina</td><td>1,358</td></tr>
<tr><td>9</td><td>Massachusetts</td><td>2,375</td><td>21</td><td>Tennessee</td><td>1,299</td></tr>
<tr><td>38</td><td>Michigan</td><td>697</td><td>22</td><td>Oklahoma</td><td>1,086</td></tr>
<tr><td>46</td><td>Minnesota</td><td>600</td><td>23</td><td>Florida</td><td>1,064</td></tr>
<tr><td>7</td><td>Mississippi</td><td>2,795</td><td>24</td><td>Nevada</td><td>1,030</td></tr>
<tr><td>8</td><td>Missouri</td><td>2,751</td><td>25</td><td>Maine</td><td>1,017</td></tr>
<tr><td>45</td><td>Montana</td><td>601</td><td>26</td><td>Georgia</td><td>992</td></tr>
<tr><td>47</td><td>Nebraska</td><td>560</td><td>27</td><td>Vermont</td><td>930</td></tr>
<tr><td>24</td><td>Nevada</td><td>1,030</td><td>28</td><td>South Dakota</td><td>928</td></tr>
<tr><td>15</td><td>New Hampshire</td><td>1,775</td><td>29</td><td>Illinois</td><td>897</td></tr>
<tr><td>30</td><td>New Jersey</td><td>891</td><td>30</td><td>New Jersey</td><td>891</td></tr>
<tr><td>4</td><td>New Mexico</td><td>4,289</td><td>31</td><td>Wyoming</td><td>828</td></tr>
<tr><td>44</td><td>New York</td><td>616</td><td>32</td><td>Utah</td><td>801</td></tr>
<tr><td>43</td><td>North Carolina</td><td>618</td><td>33</td><td>West Virginia</td><td>763</td></tr>
<tr><td>35</td><td>North Dakota</td><td>726</td><td>34</td><td>Rhode Island</td><td>736</td></tr>
<tr><td>39</td><td>Ohio</td><td>675</td><td>35</td><td>Iowa</td><td>726</td></tr>
<tr><td>22</td><td>Oklahoma</td><td>1,086</td><td>35</td><td>North Dakota</td><td>726</td></tr>
<tr><td>48</td><td>Oregon</td><td>374</td><td>37</td><td>Wisconsin</td><td>709</td></tr>
<tr><td>18</td><td>Pennsylvania</td><td>1,451</td><td>38</td><td>Michigan</td><td>697</td></tr>
<tr><td>34</td><td>Rhode Island</td><td>736</td><td>39</td><td>Ohio</td><td>675</td></tr>
<tr><td>20</td><td>South Carolina</td><td>1,358</td><td>40</td><td>Louisiana</td><td>674</td></tr>
<tr><td>28</td><td>South Dakota</td><td>928</td><td>41</td><td>Indiana</td><td>656</td></tr>
<tr><td>21</td><td>Tennessee</td><td>1,299</td><td>42</td><td>Kansas</td><td>644</td></tr>
<tr><td>16</td><td>Texas</td><td>1,733</td><td>43</td><td>North Carolina</td><td>618</td></tr>
<tr><td>32</td><td>Utah</td><td>801</td><td>44</td><td>New York</td><td>616</td></tr>
<tr><td>27</td><td>Vermont</td><td>930</td><td>45</td><td>Montana</td><td>601</td></tr>
<tr><td>1</td><td>Virginia</td><td>7,170</td><td>46</td><td>Minnesota</td><td>600</td></tr>
<tr><td>12</td><td>Washington</td><td>1,944</td><td>47</td><td>Nebraska</td><td>560</td></tr>
<tr><td>33</td><td>West Virginia</td><td>763</td><td>48</td><td>Oregon</td><td>374</td></tr>
<tr><td>37</td><td>Wisconsin</td><td>709</td><td>49</td><td>Delaware</td><td>333</td></tr>
<tr><td>31</td><td>Wyoming</td><td>828</td><td>50</td><td>Arkansas</td><td>322</td></tr>
<tr><td></td><td></td><td></td><td></td><td>District of Columbia</td><td>33,775</td></tr>
</table>

Source: CQ Press using data from U.S. Department of the Treasury, USAspending.gov
"Award Data Archive" (https://www.usaspending.gov/, as of January 10, 2020)
*For fiscal year 2018. National per capita excludes expenditures and population for territories and undistributed amounts.
Expenditures allocated based on place of performance of a contract.

Federal Government Direct Payments in 2018

National Total = $1,984,043,000,000*

ALPHA ORDER				RANK ORDER			
RANK	STATE	EXPENDITURES	% of USA	RANK	STATE	EXPENDITURES	% of USA
22	Alabama	$33,265,000,000	1.7%	1	Pennsylvania	$158,311,000,000	8.0%
48	Alaska	3,145,000,000	0.2%	2	California	146,116,000,000	7.4%
16	Arizona	44,319,000,000	2.2%	3	Florida	132,881,000,000	6.7%
32	Arkansas	14,175,000,000	0.7%	4	Indiana	117,192,000,000	5.9%
2	California	146,116,000,000	7.4%	5	Texas	94,910,000,000	4.8%
28	Colorado	19,886,000,000	1.0%	6	New York	87,405,000,000	4.4%
18	Connecticut	43,778,000,000	2.2%	7	Minnesota	83,506,000,000	4.2%
46	Delaware	4,433,000,000	0.2%	8	South Carolina	82,015,000,000	4.1%
3	Florida	132,881,000,000	6.7%	9	Wisconsin	73,627,000,000	3.7%
20	Georgia	39,263,000,000	2.0%	10	Kentucky	68,170,000,000	3.4%
42	Hawaii	6,518,000,000	0.3%	11	North Dakota	65,901,000,000	3.3%
40	Idaho	7,103,000,000	0.4%	12	Tennessee	60,244,000,000	3.0%
14	Illinois	50,431,000,000	2.5%	13	Michigan	52,909,000,000	2.7%
4	Indiana	117,192,000,000	5.9%	14	Illinois	50,431,000,000	2.5%
31	Iowa	14,840,000,000	0.7%	15	Ohio	49,641,000,000	2.5%
34	Kansas	11,735,000,000	0.6%	16	Arizona	44,319,000,000	2.2%
10	Kentucky	68,170,000,000	3.4%	17	North Carolina	44,084,000,000	2.2%
29	Louisiana	19,595,000,000	1.0%	18	Connecticut	43,778,000,000	2.2%
41	Maine	6,985,000,000	0.4%	19	New Jersey	39,706,000,000	2.0%
26	Maryland	22,871,000,000	1.2%	20	Georgia	39,263,000,000	2.0%
25	Massachusetts	29,974,000,000	1.5%	21	Virginia	35,429,000,000	1.8%
13	Michigan	52,909,000,000	2.7%	22	Alabama	33,265,000,000	1.7%
7	Minnesota	83,506,000,000	4.2%	23	Missouri	31,123,000,000	1.6%
33	Mississippi	13,316,000,000	0.7%	24	Washington	30,785,000,000	1.6%
23	Missouri	31,123,000,000	1.6%	25	Massachusetts	29,974,000,000	1.5%
45	Montana	5,061,000,000	0.3%	26	Maryland	22,871,000,000	1.2%
36	Nebraska	10,589,000,000	0.5%	27	Oregon	21,243,000,000	1.1%
35	Nevada	11,232,000,000	0.6%	28	Colorado	19,886,000,000	1.0%
43	New Hampshire	6,076,000,000	0.3%	29	Louisiana	19,595,000,000	1.0%
19	New Jersey	39,706,000,000	2.0%	30	Oklahoma	17,680,000,000	0.9%
38	New Mexico	9,511,000,000	0.5%	31	Iowa	14,840,000,000	0.7%
6	New York	87,405,000,000	4.4%	32	Arkansas	14,175,000,000	0.7%
17	North Carolina	44,084,000,000	2.2%	33	Mississippi	13,316,000,000	0.7%
11	North Dakota	65,901,000,000	3.3%	34	Kansas	11,735,000,000	0.6%
15	Ohio	49,641,000,000	2.5%	35	Nevada	11,232,000,000	0.6%
30	Oklahoma	17,680,000,000	0.9%	36	Nebraska	10,589,000,000	0.5%
27	Oregon	21,243,000,000	1.1%	37	West Virginia	9,544,000,000	0.5%
1	Pennsylvania	158,311,000,000	8.0%	38	New Mexico	9,511,000,000	0.5%
44	Rhode Island	5,505,000,000	0.3%	39	Utah	8,874,000,000	0.4%
8	South Carolina	82,015,000,000	4.1%	40	Idaho	7,103,000,000	0.4%
47	South Dakota	4,083,000,000	0.2%	41	Maine	6,985,000,000	0.4%
12	Tennessee	60,244,000,000	3.0%	42	Hawaii	6,518,000,000	0.3%
5	Texas	94,910,000,000	4.8%	43	New Hampshire	6,076,000,000	0.3%
39	Utah	8,874,000,000	0.4%	44	Rhode Island	5,505,000,000	0.3%
49	Vermont	2,885,000,000	0.1%	45	Montana	5,061,000,000	0.3%
21	Virginia	35,429,000,000	1.8%	46	Delaware	4,433,000,000	0.2%
24	Washington	30,785,000,000	1.6%	47	South Dakota	4,083,000,000	0.2%
37	West Virginia	9,544,000,000	0.5%	48	Alaska	3,145,000,000	0.2%
9	Wisconsin	73,627,000,000	3.7%	49	Vermont	2,885,000,000	0.1%
50	Wyoming	2,321,000,000	0.1%	50	Wyoming	2,321,000,000	0.1%
					District of Columbia	3,131,000,000	0.2%

Source: U.S. Department of the Treasury, USAspending.gov
"Award Data Archive" (https://www.usaspending.gov/, as of January 10, 2020)
*For fiscal year 2018. Total includes $26,719,000,000 in U.S. territories and internationally as well as expenditures not distributed by state. Expenditures allocated based on place of performance of a contract. These are cash payments made by the federal government to an individual, a private firm, or another private institution.

Per Capita Federal Government Direct Payments in 2018

National Per Capita = $5,991*

ALPHA ORDER

RANK	STATE	PER CAPITA
10	Alabama	$6,806
34	Alaska	4,278
12	Arizona	6,192
22	Arkansas	4,710
47	California	3,703
48	Colorado	3,494
8	Connecticut	12,257
25	Delaware	4,592
11	Florida	6,255
45	Georgia	3,735
26	Hawaii	4,588
40	Idaho	4,058
43	Illinois	3,964
2	Indiana	17,503
21	Iowa	4,713
41	Kansas	4,031
4	Kentucky	15,281
37	Louisiana	4,205
16	Maine	5,217
44	Maryland	3,789
33	Massachusetts	4,355
14	Michigan	5,299
5	Minnesota	14,895
32	Mississippi	4,467
18	Missouri	5,084
20	Montana	4,772
13	Nebraska	5,499
46	Nevada	3,710
28	New Hampshire	4,490
31	New Jersey	4,468
27	New Mexico	4,545
30	New York	4,475
36	North Carolina	4,246
1	North Dakota	86,932
35	Ohio	4,251
29	Oklahoma	4,487
19	Oregon	5,080
7	Pennsylvania	12,367
17	Rhode Island	5,201
3	South Carolina	16,132
23	South Dakota	4,646
9	Tennessee	8,897
49	Texas	3,315
50	Utah	2,814
24	Vermont	4,620
38	Virginia	4,168
39	Washington	4,092
15	West Virginia	5,290
6	Wisconsin	12,678
42	Wyoming	4,019

RANK ORDER

RANK	STATE	PER CAPITA
1	North Dakota	$86,932
2	Indiana	17,503
3	South Carolina	16,132
4	Kentucky	15,281
5	Minnesota	14,895
6	Wisconsin	12,678
7	Pennsylvania	12,367
8	Connecticut	12,257
9	Tennessee	8,897
10	Alabama	6,806
11	Florida	6,255
12	Arizona	6,192
13	Nebraska	5,499
14	Michigan	5,299
15	West Virginia	5,290
16	Maine	5,217
17	Rhode Island	5,201
18	Missouri	5,084
19	Oregon	5,080
20	Montana	4,772
21	Iowa	4,713
22	Arkansas	4,710
23	South Dakota	4,646
24	Vermont	4,620
25	Delaware	4,592
26	Hawaii	4,588
27	New Mexico	4,545
28	New Hampshire	4,490
29	Oklahoma	4,487
30	New York	4,475
31	New Jersey	4,468
32	Mississippi	4,467
33	Massachusetts	4,355
34	Alaska	4,278
35	Ohio	4,251
36	North Carolina	4,246
37	Louisiana	4,205
38	Virginia	4,168
39	Washington	4,092
40	Idaho	4,058
41	Kansas	4,031
42	Wyoming	4,019
43	Illinois	3,964
44	Maryland	3,789
45	Georgia	3,735
46	Nevada	3,710
47	California	3,703
48	Colorado	3,494
49	Texas	3,315
50	Utah	2,814

	District of Columbia	4,463

Source: CQ Press using data from U.S. Department of the Treasury, USAspending.gov
"Award Data Archive" (https://www.usaspending.gov/, as of January 10, 2020)
*For fiscal year 2018. National per capita excludes expenditures and population for territories and undistributed amounts. Expenditures allocated based on place of performance of a contract. This includes cash payments made by the federal government to an individual, a private firm, or another private institution.

Federal Government Grants in 2018

National Total = $755,450,000,000*

ALPHA ORDER

RANK	STATE	EXPENDITURES	% of USA
26	Alabama	$9,122,000,000	1.2%
38	Alaska	4,375,000,000	0.6%
13	Arizona	16,165,000,000	2.1%
29	Arkansas	7,900,000,000	1.0%
1	California	101,584,000,000	13.4%
25	Colorado	10,181,000,000	1.3%
28	Connecticut	8,537,000,000	1.1%
45	Delaware	2,587,000,000	0.3%
5	Florida	31,318,000,000	4.1%
12	Georgia	16,677,000,000	2.2%
42	Hawaii	3,300,000,000	0.4%
43	Idaho	3,086,000,000	0.4%
7	Illinois	24,881,000,000	3.3%
14	Indiana	15,035,000,000	2.0%
33	Iowa	6,342,000,000	0.8%
36	Kansas	4,494,000,000	0.6%
22	Kentucky	11,674,000,000	1.5%
17	Louisiana	13,853,000,000	1.8%
39	Maine	3,421,000,000	0.5%
16	Maryland	14,165,000,000	1.9%
8	Massachusetts	20,976,000,000	2.8%
9	Michigan	20,895,000,000	2.8%
18	Minnesota	13,113,000,000	1.7%
30	Mississippi	7,592,000,000	1.0%
19	Missouri	12,757,000,000	1.7%
41	Montana	3,305,000,000	0.4%
44	Nebraska	3,068,000,000	0.4%
35	Nevada	5,251,000,000	0.7%
46	New Hampshire	2,535,000,000	0.3%
11	New Jersey	18,156,000,000	2.4%
32	New Mexico	7,007,000,000	0.9%
2	New York	67,634,000,000	9.0%
10	North Carolina	19,054,000,000	2.5%
47	North Dakota	2,055,000,000	0.3%
6	Ohio	25,921,000,000	3.4%
31	Oklahoma	7,474,000,000	1.0%
23	Oregon	11,271,000,000	1.5%
4	Pennsylvania	31,613,000,000	4.2%
40	Rhode Island	3,341,000,000	0.4%
27	South Carolina	8,869,000,000	1.2%
49	South Dakota	1,847,000,000	0.2%
21	Tennessee	12,094,000,000	1.6%
3	Texas	51,945,000,000	6.9%
37	Utah	4,446,000,000	0.6%
48	Vermont	2,032,000,000	0.3%
20	Virginia	12,159,000,000	1.6%
15	Washington	14,655,000,000	1.9%
34	West Virginia	5,313,000,000	0.7%
24	Wisconsin	10,446,000,000	1.4%
50	Wyoming	1,390,000,000	0.2%

RANK ORDER

RANK	STATE	EXPENDITURES	% of USA
1	California	$101,584,000,000	13.4%
2	New York	67,634,000,000	9.0%
3	Texas	51,945,000,000	6.9%
4	Pennsylvania	31,613,000,000	4.2%
5	Florida	31,318,000,000	4.1%
6	Ohio	25,921,000,000	3.4%
7	Illinois	24,881,000,000	3.3%
8	Massachusetts	20,976,000,000	2.8%
9	Michigan	20,895,000,000	2.8%
10	North Carolina	19,054,000,000	2.5%
11	New Jersey	18,156,000,000	2.4%
12	Georgia	16,677,000,000	2.2%
13	Arizona	16,165,000,000	2.1%
14	Indiana	15,035,000,000	2.0%
15	Washington	14,655,000,000	1.9%
16	Maryland	14,165,000,000	1.9%
17	Louisiana	13,853,000,000	1.8%
18	Minnesota	13,113,000,000	1.7%
19	Missouri	12,757,000,000	1.7%
20	Virginia	12,159,000,000	1.6%
21	Tennessee	12,094,000,000	1.6%
22	Kentucky	11,674,000,000	1.5%
23	Oregon	11,271,000,000	1.5%
24	Wisconsin	10,446,000,000	1.4%
25	Colorado	10,181,000,000	1.3%
26	Alabama	9,122,000,000	1.2%
27	South Carolina	8,869,000,000	1.2%
28	Connecticut	8,537,000,000	1.1%
29	Arkansas	7,900,000,000	1.0%
30	Mississippi	7,592,000,000	1.0%
31	Oklahoma	7,474,000,000	1.0%
32	New Mexico	7,007,000,000	0.9%
33	Iowa	6,342,000,000	0.8%
34	West Virginia	5,313,000,000	0.7%
35	Nevada	5,251,000,000	0.7%
36	Kansas	4,494,000,000	0.6%
37	Utah	4,446,000,000	0.6%
38	Alaska	4,375,000,000	0.6%
39	Maine	3,421,000,000	0.5%
40	Rhode Island	3,341,000,000	0.4%
41	Montana	3,305,000,000	0.4%
42	Hawaii	3,300,000,000	0.4%
43	Idaho	3,086,000,000	0.4%
44	Nebraska	3,068,000,000	0.4%
45	Delaware	2,587,000,000	0.3%
46	New Hampshire	2,535,000,000	0.3%
47	North Dakota	2,055,000,000	0.3%
48	Vermont	2,032,000,000	0.3%
49	South Dakota	1,847,000,000	0.2%
50	Wyoming	1,390,000,000	0.2%
	District of Columbia	7,975,000,000	1.1%

Source: U.S. Department of the Treasury, USAspending.gov
"Award Data Archive" (https://www.usaspending.gov/, as of January 10, 2020)
*For fiscal year 2018. Total includes $30,562,000,000 in U.S. territories and internationally as well as expenditures not distributed by state. Expenditures allocated based on place of performance of a contract. Includes funds awarded to a non-federal entity for a defined public project or purpose. Most grants are awarded to state and local governments.

Per Capita Expenditures for Federal Government Grants in 2018

National Per Capita = $2,219*

ALPHA ORDER

RANK	STATE	PER CAPITA
36	Alabama	$1,866
1	Alaska	5,951
24	Arizona	2,258
13	Arkansas	2,625
15	California	2,574
40	Colorado	1,789
20	Connecticut	2,390
12	Delaware	2,679
48	Florida	1,474
46	Georgia	1,587
23	Hawaii	2,323
42	Idaho	1,763
32	Illinois	1,956
25	Indiana	2,246
31	Iowa	2,014
47	Kansas	1,544
14	Kentucky	2,617
8	Louisiana	2,973
16	Maine	2,555
21	Maryland	2,347
7	Massachusetts	3,048
28	Michigan	2,093
22	Minnesota	2,339
17	Mississippi	2,547
29	Missouri	2,084
6	Montana	3,116
45	Nebraska	1,593
44	Nevada	1,735
35	New Hampshire	1,873
30	New Jersey	2,043
3	New Mexico	3,348
2	New York	3,463
37	North Carolina	1,835
10	North Dakota	2,711
26	Ohio	2,220
34	Oklahoma	1,897
11	Oregon	2,695
18	Pennsylvania	2,470
5	Rhode Island	3,157
43	South Carolina	1,745
27	South Dakota	2,102
41	Tennessee	1,786
38	Texas	1,814
50	Utah	1,410
4	Vermont	3,255
49	Virginia	1,430
33	Washington	1,948
9	West Virginia	2,945
39	Wisconsin	1,799
19	Wyoming	2,407

RANK ORDER

RANK	STATE	PER CAPITA
1	Alaska	$5,951
2	New York	3,463
3	New Mexico	3,348
4	Vermont	3,255
5	Rhode Island	3,157
6	Montana	3,116
7	Massachusetts	3,048
8	Louisiana	2,973
9	West Virginia	2,945
10	North Dakota	2,711
11	Oregon	2,695
12	Delaware	2,679
13	Arkansas	2,625
14	Kentucky	2,617
15	California	2,574
16	Maine	2,555
17	Mississippi	2,547
18	Pennsylvania	2,470
19	Wyoming	2,407
20	Connecticut	2,390
21	Maryland	2,347
22	Minnesota	2,339
23	Hawaii	2,323
24	Arizona	2,258
25	Indiana	2,246
26	Ohio	2,220
27	South Dakota	2,102
28	Michigan	2,093
29	Missouri	2,084
30	New Jersey	2,043
31	Iowa	2,014
32	Illinois	1,956
33	Washington	1,948
34	Oklahoma	1,897
35	New Hampshire	1,873
36	Alabama	1,866
37	North Carolina	1,835
38	Texas	1,814
39	Wisconsin	1,799
40	Colorado	1,789
41	Tennessee	1,786
42	Idaho	1,763
43	South Carolina	1,745
44	Nevada	1,735
45	Nebraska	1,593
46	Georgia	1,587
47	Kansas	1,544
48	Florida	1,474
49	Virginia	1,430
50	Utah	1,410
	District of Columbia	11,368

Source: CQ Press using data from U.S. Department of the Treasury, USAspending.gov
"Award Data Archive" (https://www.usaspending.gov/, as of January 10, 2020)
*For fiscal year 2018. National per capita excludes expenditures and population for territories and undistributed amounts.
Expenditures allocated based on place of performance of a contract. Includes funds awarded to a non-federal entity for a defined public project or purpose. Most grants are awarded to state and local governments.

Federal Government Other Expenditures in 2018

National Total = $87,319,000,000*

ALPHA ORDER

RANK	STATE	EXPENDITURES	% of USA
26	Alabama	$1,072,000,000	1.2%
50	Alaska	39,000,000	0.0%
13	Arizona	1,591,000,000	1.8%
25	Arkansas	1,074,000,000	1.2%
3	California	6,219,000,000	7.1%
24	Colorado	1,088,000,000	1.2%
35	Connecticut	597,000,000	0.7%
48	Delaware	175,000,000	0.2%
4	Florida	5,943,000,000	6.8%
9	Georgia	2,077,000,000	2.4%
45	Hawaii	267,000,000	0.3%
41	Idaho	426,000,000	0.5%
6	Illinois	2,416,000,000	2.8%
19	Indiana	1,235,000,000	1.4%
32	Iowa	705,000,000	0.8%
34	Kansas	686,000,000	0.8%
27	Kentucky	1,007,000,000	1.2%
21	Louisiana	1,134,000,000	1.3%
42	Maine	354,000,000	0.4%
23	Maryland	1,102,000,000	1.3%
17	Massachusetts	1,316,000,000	1.5%
12	Michigan	1,635,000,000	1.9%
10	Minnesota	1,790,000,000	2.0%
30	Mississippi	833,000,000	1.0%
15	Missouri	1,461,000,000	1.7%
39	Montana	445,000,000	0.5%
37	Nebraska	512,000,000	0.6%
31	Nevada	772,000,000	0.9%
44	New Hampshire	274,000,000	0.3%
29	New Jersey	897,000,000	1.0%
36	New Mexico	593,000,000	0.7%
2	New York	8,144,000,000	9.3%
8	North Carolina	2,316,000,000	2.7%
43	North Dakota	315,000,000	0.4%
5	Ohio	2,635,000,000	3.0%
28	Oklahoma	986,000,000	1.1%
22	Oregon	1,132,000,000	1.3%
7	Pennsylvania	2,321,000,000	2.7%
46	Rhode Island	223,000,000	0.3%
20	South Carolina	1,204,000,000	1.4%
39	South Dakota	445,000,000	0.5%
14	Tennessee	1,549,000,000	1.8%
1	Texas	12,793,000,000	14.7%
38	Utah	465,000,000	0.5%
49	Vermont	136,000,000	0.2%
11	Virginia	1,729,000,000	2.0%
18	Washington	1,280,000,000	1.5%
32	West Virginia	705,000,000	0.8%
16	Wisconsin	1,420,000,000	1.6%
47	Wyoming	217,000,000	0.2%

RANK ORDER

RANK	STATE	EXPENDITURES	% of USA
1	Texas	$12,793,000,000	14.7%
2	New York	8,144,000,000	9.3%
3	California	6,219,000,000	7.1%
4	Florida	5,943,000,000	6.8%
5	Ohio	2,635,000,000	3.0%
6	Illinois	2,416,000,000	2.8%
7	Pennsylvania	2,321,000,000	2.7%
8	North Carolina	2,316,000,000	2.7%
9	Georgia	2,077,000,000	2.4%
10	Minnesota	1,790,000,000	2.0%
11	Virginia	1,729,000,000	2.0%
12	Michigan	1,635,000,000	1.9%
13	Arizona	1,591,000,000	1.8%
14	Tennessee	1,549,000,000	1.8%
15	Missouri	1,461,000,000	1.7%
16	Wisconsin	1,420,000,000	1.6%
17	Massachusetts	1,316,000,000	1.5%
18	Washington	1,280,000,000	1.5%
19	Indiana	1,235,000,000	1.4%
20	South Carolina	1,204,000,000	1.4%
21	Louisiana	1,134,000,000	1.3%
22	Oregon	1,132,000,000	1.3%
23	Maryland	1,102,000,000	1.3%
24	Colorado	1,088,000,000	1.2%
25	Arkansas	1,074,000,000	1.2%
26	Alabama	1,072,000,000	1.2%
27	Kentucky	1,007,000,000	1.2%
28	Oklahoma	986,000,000	1.1%
29	New Jersey	897,000,000	1.0%
30	Mississippi	833,000,000	1.0%
31	Nevada	772,000,000	0.9%
32	Iowa	705,000,000	0.8%
32	West Virginia	705,000,000	0.8%
34	Kansas	686,000,000	0.8%
35	Connecticut	597,000,000	0.7%
36	New Mexico	593,000,000	0.7%
37	Nebraska	512,000,000	0.6%
38	Utah	465,000,000	0.5%
39	Montana	445,000,000	0.5%
39	South Dakota	445,000,000	0.5%
41	Idaho	426,000,000	0.5%
42	Maine	354,000,000	0.4%
43	North Dakota	315,000,000	0.4%
44	New Hampshire	274,000,000	0.3%
45	Hawaii	267,000,000	0.3%
46	Rhode Island	223,000,000	0.3%
47	Wyoming	217,000,000	0.2%
48	Delaware	175,000,000	0.2%
49	Vermont	136,000,000	0.2%
50	Alaska	39,000,000	0.0%
	District of Columbia	325,000,000	0.4%

Source: U.S. Department of the Treasury, USAspending.gov
"Award Data Archive" (https://www.usaspending.gov/, as of January 10, 2020)
*For fiscal year 2018. Total includes $7,244,000,000 in U.S. territories and internationally as well as expenditures not distributed by state. Expenditures allocated based on place of performance of a contract. Includes loans, insurance, and "other."

Per Capita Federal Government Other Expenditures in 2018

National Per Capita = $245*

ALPHA ORDER

RANK ORDER

RANK	STATE	PER CAPITA		RANK	STATE	PER CAPITA
30	Alabama	$219		1	South Dakota	$506
50	Alaska	53		2	Texas	447
29	Arizona	222		3	Montana	420
8	Arkansas	357		4	New York	417
47	California	158		5	North Dakota	415
36	Colorado	191		6	West Virginia	391
45	Connecticut	167		7	Wyoming	376
42	Delaware	181		8	Arkansas	357
11	Florida	280		9	Minnesota	319
35	Georgia	198		10	New Mexico	283
39	Hawaii	188		11	Florida	280
19	Idaho	243		11	Mississippi	280
38	Illinois	190		13	Oregon	271
40	Indiana	184		14	Nebraska	266
27	Iowa	224		15	Maine	264
23	Kansas	236		16	Nevada	255
25	Kentucky	226		17	Oklahoma	250
19	Louisiana	243		18	Wisconsin	245
15	Maine	264		19	Idaho	243
41	Maryland	183		19	Louisiana	243
36	Massachusetts	191		21	Missouri	239
46	Michigan	164		22	South Carolina	237
9	Minnesota	319		23	Kansas	236
11	Mississippi	280		24	Tennessee	229
21	Missouri	239		25	Kentucky	226
3	Montana	420		25	Ohio	226
14	Nebraska	266		27	Iowa	224
16	Nevada	255		28	North Carolina	223
34	New Hampshire	202		29	Arizona	222
49	New Jersey	101		30	Alabama	219
10	New Mexico	283		31	Vermont	217
4	New York	417		32	Rhode Island	211
28	North Carolina	223		33	Virginia	203
5	North Dakota	415		34	New Hampshire	202
25	Ohio	226		35	Georgia	198
17	Oklahoma	250		36	Colorado	191
13	Oregon	271		36	Massachusetts	191
42	Pennsylvania	181		38	Illinois	190
32	Rhode Island	211		39	Hawaii	188
22	South Carolina	237		40	Indiana	184
1	South Dakota	506		41	Maryland	183
24	Tennessee	229		42	Delaware	181
2	Texas	447		42	Pennsylvania	181
48	Utah	148		44	Washington	170
31	Vermont	217		45	Connecticut	167
33	Virginia	203		46	Michigan	164
44	Washington	170		47	California	158
6	West Virginia	391		48	Utah	148
18	Wisconsin	245		49	New Jersey	101
7	Wyoming	376		50	Alaska	53
					District of Columbia	463

Source: CQ Press using data from U.S. Department of the Treasury, USAspending.gov
   "Award Data Archive" (https://www.usaspending.gov/, as of January 10, 2020)
*For fiscal year 2018. National per capita excludes expenditures and population for territories and undistributed amounts.
Expenditures allocated based on place of performance of a contract. Includes funds awarded to a non-federal entity for a defined
public project or purpose. Most grants are awarded to state and local governments. Includes loans, insurance, and "other."

Federal Civilian Employees in 2017

National Total = 1,869,986 Employees*

ALPHA ORDER

RANK	STATE	EMPLOYEES	% of USA
15	Alabama	37,386	2.0%
39	Alaska	10,398	0.6%
13	Arizona	38,087	2.0%
35	Arkansas	12,557	0.7%
1	California	152,466	8.2%
16	Colorado	36,848	2.0%
42	Connecticut	7,998	0.4%
50	Delaware	3,039	0.2%
5	Florida	89,504	4.8%
6	Georgia	71,739	3.8%
23	Hawaii	23,453	1.3%
43	Idaho	7,731	0.4%
11	Illinois	44,760	2.4%
24	Indiana	22,610	1.2%
41	Iowa	8,042	0.4%
33	Kansas	15,672	0.8%
25	Kentucky	22,181	1.2%
28	Louisiana	19,537	1.0%
37	Maine	11,285	0.6%
4	Maryland	120,705	6.5%
21	Massachusetts	25,063	1.3%
18	Michigan	27,405	1.5%
32	Minnesota	16,795	0.9%
30	Mississippi	17,295	0.9%
17	Missouri	33,377	1.8%
40	Montana	8,589	0.5%
38	Nebraska	10,468	0.6%
36	Nevada	12,186	0.7%
49	New Hampshire	4,331	0.2%
22	New Jersey	24,758	1.3%
26	New Mexico	21,954	1.2%
8	New York	60,727	3.2%
12	North Carolina	42,772	2.3%
46	North Dakota	5,460	0.3%
10	Ohio	49,450	2.6%
14	Oklahoma	37,486	2.0%
31	Oregon	17,252	0.9%
7	Pennsylvania	62,366	3.3%
45	Rhode Island	6,864	0.4%
27	South Carolina	21,050	1.1%
44	South Dakota	7,547	0.4%
20	Tennessee	25,099	1.3%
3	Texas	132,952	7.1%
19	Utah	26,109	1.4%
48	Vermont	4,845	0.3%
2	Virginia	144,295	7.7%
9	Washington	53,211	2.8%
29	West Virginia	18,656	1.0%
34	Wisconsin	14,045	0.8%
47	Wyoming	4,977	0.3%

RANK ORDER

RANK	STATE	EMPLOYEES	% of USA
1	California	152,466	8.2%
2	Virginia	144,295	7.7%
3	Texas	132,952	7.1%
4	Maryland	120,705	6.5%
5	Florida	89,504	4.8%
6	Georgia	71,739	3.8%
7	Pennsylvania	62,366	3.3%
8	New York	60,727	3.2%
9	Washington	53,211	2.8%
10	Ohio	49,450	2.6%
11	Illinois	44,760	2.4%
12	North Carolina	42,772	2.3%
13	Arizona	38,087	2.0%
14	Oklahoma	37,486	2.0%
15	Alabama	37,386	2.0%
16	Colorado	36,848	2.0%
17	Missouri	33,377	1.8%
18	Michigan	27,405	1.5%
19	Utah	26,109	1.4%
20	Tennessee	25,099	1.3%
21	Massachusetts	25,063	1.3%
22	New Jersey	24,758	1.3%
23	Hawaii	23,453	1.3%
24	Indiana	22,610	1.2%
25	Kentucky	22,181	1.2%
26	New Mexico	21,954	1.2%
27	South Carolina	21,050	1.1%
28	Louisiana	19,537	1.0%
29	West Virginia	18,656	1.0%
30	Mississippi	17,295	0.9%
31	Oregon	17,252	0.9%
32	Minnesota	16,795	0.9%
33	Kansas	15,672	0.8%
34	Wisconsin	14,045	0.8%
35	Arkansas	12,557	0.7%
36	Nevada	12,186	0.7%
37	Maine	11,285	0.6%
38	Nebraska	10,468	0.6%
39	Alaska	10,398	0.6%
40	Montana	8,589	0.5%
41	Iowa	8,042	0.4%
42	Connecticut	7,998	0.4%
43	Idaho	7,731	0.4%
44	South Dakota	7,547	0.4%
45	Rhode Island	6,864	0.4%
46	North Dakota	5,460	0.3%
47	Wyoming	4,977	0.3%
48	Vermont	4,845	0.3%
49	New Hampshire	4,331	0.2%
50	Delaware	3,039	0.2%
	District of Columbia	141,367	7.6%

Source: U.S. Office of Personnel Management
"Common Characteristics of the Government" (https://www.opm.gov/feddata/)
*Non-seasonal, full-time, permanent employees as of September. Head count based on place of employment. There were an estimated 2,087,747 federal civilian employees including seasonal and non-permanent employees. Total includes 35,237 employees either outside the United States or unspecified. Excludes Central Intelligence Agency, Defense Intelligence Agency, and National Security Agency.

Rate of Federal Civilian Employees in 2017

National Rate = 56 Employees per 10,000 Population*

ALPHA ORDER

RANK	STATE	RATE
14	Alabama	77
4	Alaska	141
23	Arizona	54
30	Arkansas	42
37	California	39
18	Colorado	66
50	Connecticut	22
42	Delaware	32
29	Florida	43
17	Georgia	69
3	Hawaii	165
28	Idaho	45
40	Illinois	35
41	Indiana	34
48	Iowa	26
23	Kansas	54
25	Kentucky	50
30	Louisiana	42
10	Maine	85
1	Maryland	200
38	Massachusetts	37
47	Michigan	27
45	Minnesota	30
20	Mississippi	58
21	Missouri	55
12	Montana	82
21	Nebraska	55
36	Nevada	41
42	New Hampshire	32
46	New Jersey	28
5	New Mexico	105
44	New York	31
30	North Carolina	42
15	North Dakota	72
30	Ohio	42
7	Oklahoma	95
30	Oregon	42
26	Pennsylvania	49
19	Rhode Island	65
30	South Carolina	42
8	South Dakota	86
38	Tennessee	37
27	Texas	47
11	Utah	84
13	Vermont	78
2	Virginia	170
15	Washington	72
6	West Virginia	103
49	Wisconsin	24
8	Wyoming	86

RANK ORDER

RANK	STATE	RATE
1	Maryland	200
2	Virginia	170
3	Hawaii	165
4	Alaska	141
5	New Mexico	105
6	West Virginia	103
7	Oklahoma	95
8	South Dakota	86
8	Wyoming	86
10	Maine	85
11	Utah	84
12	Montana	82
13	Vermont	78
14	Alabama	77
15	North Dakota	72
15	Washington	72
17	Georgia	69
18	Colorado	66
19	Rhode Island	65
20	Mississippi	58
21	Missouri	55
21	Nebraska	55
23	Arizona	54
23	Kansas	54
25	Kentucky	50
26	Pennsylvania	49
27	Texas	47
28	Idaho	45
29	Florida	43
30	Arkansas	42
30	Louisiana	42
30	North Carolina	42
30	Ohio	42
30	Oregon	42
30	South Carolina	42
36	Nevada	41
37	California	39
38	Massachusetts	37
38	Tennessee	37
40	Illinois	35
41	Indiana	34
42	Delaware	32
42	New Hampshire	32
44	New York	31
45	Minnesota	30
46	New Jersey	28
47	Michigan	27
48	Iowa	26
49	Wisconsin	24
50	Connecticut	22
	District of Columbia	2,032

Source: CQ Press using data from U.S. Office of Personnel Management
   "Common Characteristics of the Government" (https://www.opm.gov/feddata/)
*Non-seasonal, full-time, permanent employees as of September. Head count based on place of employment. There were an estimated 2,087,747 federal civilian employees including seasonal and non-permanent employees. National rate excludes employees either outside the United States or unspecified. Excludes Central Intelligence Agency, Defense Intelligence Agency, and National Security Agency.

X. Government Finances: State and Local

(Continued)

(Continued)

State and Local Government Total Revenue in 2017

National Total = $3,935,880,900,000*

ALPHA ORDER

RANK	STATE	REVENUE	% of USA
26	Alabama	$49,941,680,000	1.3%
42	Alaska	14,283,536,000	0.4%
17	Arizona	65,885,427,000	1.7%
35	Arkansas	31,487,816,000	0.8%
1	California	621,633,158,000	15.8%
21	Colorado	61,936,052,000	1.6%
27	Connecticut	49,583,578,000	1.3%
45	Delaware	11,874,237,000	0.3%
4	Florida	192,419,439,000	4.9%
14	Georgia	91,611,712,000	2.3%
38	Hawaii	20,347,678,000	0.5%
40	Idaho	15,677,660,000	0.4%
6	Illinois	149,195,172,000	3.8%
19	Indiana	63,507,225,000	1.6%
29	Iowa	39,111,834,000	1.0%
33	Kansas	32,264,957,000	0.8%
28	Kentucky	44,525,376,000	1.1%
24	Louisiana	52,460,488,000	1.3%
41	Maine	14,426,263,000	0.4%
16	Maryland	72,903,723,000	1.9%
12	Massachusetts	95,424,970,000	2.4%
9	Michigan	109,921,261,000	2.8%
15	Minnesota	73,719,742,000	1.9%
32	Mississippi	32,510,369,000	0.8%
22	Missouri	61,497,472,000	1.6%
46	Montana	11,792,456,000	0.3%
37	Nebraska	24,532,065,000	0.6%
34	Nevada	32,114,231,000	0.8%
43	New Hampshire	14,042,208,000	0.4%
8	New Jersey	116,923,362,000	3.0%
36	New Mexico	26,563,220,000	0.7%
2	New York	382,542,995,000	9.7%
10	North Carolina	102,947,062,000	2.6%
47	North Dakota	10,874,440,000	0.3%
7	Ohio	141,446,336,000	3.6%
30	Oklahoma	37,859,994,000	1.0%
23	Oregon	58,145,617,000	1.5%
5	Pennsylvania	149,730,269,000	3.8%
44	Rhode Island	12,832,521,000	0.3%
25	South Carolina	52,187,280,000	1.3%
49	South Dakota	9,218,862,000	0.2%
20	Tennessee	62,808,805,000	1.6%
3	Texas	276,993,805,000	7.0%
31	Utah	32,850,285,000	0.8%
50	Vermont	8,224,640,000	0.2%
13	Virginia	91,894,050,000	2.3%
11	Washington	100,336,599,000	2.5%
39	West Virginia	20,243,802,000	0.5%
18	Wisconsin	65,076,128,000	1.7%
48	Wyoming	9,757,640,000	0.2%

RANK ORDER

RANK	STATE	REVENUE	% of USA
1	California	$621,633,158,000	15.8%
2	New York	382,542,995,000	9.7%
3	Texas	276,993,805,000	7.0%
4	Florida	192,419,439,000	4.9%
5	Pennsylvania	149,730,269,000	3.8%
6	Illinois	149,195,172,000	3.8%
7	Ohio	141,446,336,000	3.6%
8	New Jersey	116,923,362,000	3.0%
9	Michigan	109,921,261,000	2.8%
10	North Carolina	102,947,062,000	2.6%
11	Washington	100,336,599,000	2.5%
12	Massachusetts	95,424,970,000	2.4%
13	Virginia	91,894,050,000	2.3%
14	Georgia	91,611,712,000	2.3%
15	Minnesota	73,719,742,000	1.9%
16	Maryland	72,903,723,000	1.9%
17	Arizona	65,885,427,000	1.7%
18	Wisconsin	65,076,128,000	1.7%
19	Indiana	63,507,225,000	1.6%
20	Tennessee	62,808,805,000	1.6%
21	Colorado	61,936,052,000	1.6%
22	Missouri	61,497,472,000	1.6%
23	Oregon	58,145,617,000	1.5%
24	Louisiana	52,460,488,000	1.3%
25	South Carolina	52,187,280,000	1.3%
26	Alabama	49,941,680,000	1.3%
27	Connecticut	49,583,578,000	1.3%
28	Kentucky	44,525,376,000	1.1%
29	Iowa	39,111,834,000	1.0%
30	Oklahoma	37,859,994,000	1.0%
31	Utah	32,850,285,000	0.8%
32	Mississippi	32,510,369,000	0.8%
33	Kansas	32,264,957,000	0.8%
34	Nevada	32,114,231,000	0.8%
35	Arkansas	31,487,816,000	0.8%
36	New Mexico	26,563,220,000	0.7%
37	Nebraska	24,532,065,000	0.6%
38	Hawaii	20,347,678,000	0.5%
39	West Virginia	20,243,802,000	0.5%
40	Idaho	15,677,660,000	0.4%
41	Maine	14,426,263,000	0.4%
42	Alaska	14,283,536,000	0.4%
43	New Hampshire	14,042,208,000	0.4%
44	Rhode Island	12,832,521,000	0.3%
45	Delaware	11,874,237,000	0.3%
46	Montana	11,792,456,000	0.3%
47	North Dakota	10,874,440,000	0.3%
48	Wyoming	9,757,640,000	0.2%
49	South Dakota	9,218,862,000	0.2%
50	Vermont	8,224,640,000	0.2%
	District of Columbia	15,791,403,000	0.4%

Source: U.S. Bureau of the Census, Governments Division
  "2017 State and Local Government Finances" (https://www.census.gov/programs-surveys/gov-finances.html)
*Total revenue includes all money received from external sources. This includes taxes, intergovernmental transfers and insurance trust revenue, and revenue from government-owned utilities and other commercial or auxiliary enterprise.

Per Capita State and Local Government Revenue in 2017

National Per Capita = $12,105*

ALPHA ORDER

RANK	STATE	PER CAPITA
39	Alabama	$10,244
2	Alaska	19,308
47	Arizona	9,347
36	Arkansas	10,485
4	California	15,778
28	Colorado	11,029
9	Connecticut	13,874
17	Delaware	12,407
48	Florida	9,173
50	Georgia	8,798
6	Hawaii	14,287
49	Idaho	9,121
22	Illinois	11,668
45	Indiana	9,536
16	Iowa	12,442
27	Kansas	11,085
42	Kentucky	9,997
24	Louisiana	11,232
32	Maine	10,806
20	Maryland	12,100
8	Massachusetts	13,904
29	Michigan	11,018
11	Minnesota	13,240
30	Mississippi	10,874
40	Missouri	10,067
25	Montana	11,198
14	Nebraska	12,793
33	Nevada	10,804
37	New Hampshire	10,403
13	New Jersey	13,154
15	New Mexico	12,689
1	New York	19,527
41	North Carolina	10,023
5	North Dakota	14,400
19	Ohio	12,127
44	Oklahoma	9,627
7	Oregon	14,023
21	Pennsylvania	11,706
18	Rhode Island	12,146
38	South Carolina	10,393
35	South Dakota	10,557
46	Tennessee	9,362
43	Texas	9,780
34	Utah	10,586
12	Vermont	13,169
31	Virginia	10,855
10	Washington	13,513
26	West Virginia	11,141
23	Wisconsin	11,235
3	Wyoming	16,854

RANK ORDER

RANK	STATE	PER CAPITA
1	New York	$19,527
2	Alaska	19,308
3	Wyoming	16,854
4	California	15,778
5	North Dakota	14,400
6	Hawaii	14,287
7	Oregon	14,023
8	Massachusetts	13,904
9	Connecticut	13,874
10	Washington	13,513
11	Minnesota	13,240
12	Vermont	13,169
13	New Jersey	13,154
14	Nebraska	12,793
15	New Mexico	12,689
16	Iowa	12,442
17	Delaware	12,407
18	Rhode Island	12,146
19	Ohio	12,127
20	Maryland	12,100
21	Pennsylvania	11,706
22	Illinois	11,668
23	Wisconsin	11,235
24	Louisiana	11,232
25	Montana	11,198
26	West Virginia	11,141
27	Kansas	11,085
28	Colorado	11,029
29	Michigan	11,018
30	Mississippi	10,874
31	Virginia	10,855
32	Maine	10,806
33	Nevada	10,804
34	Utah	10,586
35	South Dakota	10,557
36	Arkansas	10,485
37	New Hampshire	10,403
38	South Carolina	10,393
39	Alabama	10,244
40	Missouri	10,067
41	North Carolina	10,023
42	Kentucky	9,997
43	Texas	9,780
44	Oklahoma	9,627
45	Indiana	9,536
46	Tennessee	9,362
47	Arizona	9,347
48	Florida	9,173
49	Idaho	9,121
50	Georgia	8,798

District of Columbia	22,699

Source: CQ Press using data from U.S. Bureau of the Census, Governments Division
"2017 State and Local Government Finances" (https://www.census.gov/programs-surveys/gov-finances.html)
*Total revenue includes all money received from external sources. This includes taxes, intergovernmental transfers and insurance trust revenue, and revenue from government-owned utilities and other commercial or auxiliary enterprise.

State and Local Government Revenue from the Federal Government in 2017

National Total = $707,710,461,000

RANK	STATE	REVENUE	% of USA
23	Alabama	$10,969,518,000	1.6%
38	Alaska	3,518,456,000	0.5%
13	Arizona	15,910,972,000	2.2%
29	Arkansas	8,161,223,000	1.2%
1	California	100,798,584,000	14.2%
26	Colorado	9,494,699,000	1.3%
30	Connecticut	8,097,491,000	1.1%
46	Delaware	2,441,548,000	0.3%
5	Florida	31,295,519,000	4.4%
12	Georgia	16,327,312,000	2.3%
41	Hawaii	3,098,783,000	0.4%
43	Idaho	2,755,533,000	0.4%
7	Illinois	22,856,730,000	3.2%
15	Indiana	15,103,357,000	2.1%
33	Iowa	6,671,636,000	0.9%
37	Kansas	4,412,654,000	0.6%
22	Kentucky	11,316,586,000	1.6%
17	Louisiana	13,006,478,000	1.8%
42	Maine	3,056,685,000	0.4%
16	Maryland	14,046,316,000	2.0%
11	Massachusetts	17,168,497,000	2.4%
8	Michigan	22,837,161,000	3.2%
21	Minnesota	11,697,546,000	1.7%
28	Mississippi	8,535,836,000	1.2%
18	Missouri	11,963,895,000	1.7%
40	Montana	3,277,702,000	0.5%
39	Nebraska	3,455,531,000	0.5%
34	Nevada	5,576,924,000	0.8%
47	New Hampshire	2,433,993,000	0.3%
9	New Jersey	18,878,450,000	2.7%
32	New Mexico	7,409,475,000	1.0%
2	New York	66,318,556,000	9.4%
10	North Carolina	18,428,019,000	2.6%
49	North Dakota	2,034,815,000	0.3%
6	Ohio	25,935,748,000	3.7%
31	Oklahoma	7,655,571,000	1.1%
24	Oregon	10,778,699,000	1.5%
4	Pennsylvania	32,155,432,000	4.5%
44	Rhode Island	2,623,884,000	0.4%
27	South Carolina	8,782,678,000	1.2%
50	South Dakota	1,696,361,000	0.2%
20	Tennessee	11,790,165,000	1.7%
3	Texas	45,875,975,000	6.5%
36	Utah	5,015,153,000	0.7%
48	Vermont	2,058,797,000	0.3%
19	Virginia	11,792,532,000	1.7%
14	Washington	15,675,008,000	2.2%
35	West Virginia	5,218,541,000	0.7%
25	Wisconsin	9,939,321,000	1.4%
45	Wyoming	2,593,619,000	0.4%

RANK	STATE	REVENUE	% of USA
1	California	$100,798,584,000	14.2%
2	New York	66,318,556,000	9.4%
3	Texas	45,875,975,000	6.5%
4	Pennsylvania	32,155,432,000	4.5%
5	Florida	31,295,519,000	4.4%
6	Ohio	25,935,748,000	3.7%
7	Illinois	22,856,730,000	3.2%
8	Michigan	22,837,161,000	3.2%
9	New Jersey	18,878,450,000	2.7%
10	North Carolina	18,428,019,000	2.6%
11	Massachusetts	17,168,497,000	2.4%
12	Georgia	16,327,312,000	2.3%
13	Arizona	15,910,972,000	2.2%
14	Washington	15,675,008,000	2.2%
15	Indiana	15,103,357,000	2.1%
16	Maryland	14,046,316,000	2.0%
17	Louisiana	13,006,478,000	1.8%
18	Missouri	11,963,895,000	1.7%
19	Virginia	11,792,532,000	1.7%
20	Tennessee	11,790,165,000	1.7%
21	Minnesota	11,697,546,000	1.7%
22	Kentucky	11,316,586,000	1.6%
23	Alabama	10,969,518,000	1.6%
24	Oregon	10,778,699,000	1.5%
25	Wisconsin	9,939,321,000	1.4%
26	Colorado	9,494,699,000	1.3%
27	South Carolina	8,782,678,000	1.2%
28	Mississippi	8,535,836,000	1.2%
29	Arkansas	8,161,223,000	1.2%
30	Connecticut	8,097,491,000	1.1%
31	Oklahoma	7,655,571,000	1.1%
32	New Mexico	7,409,475,000	1.0%
33	Iowa	6,671,636,000	0.9%
34	Nevada	5,576,924,000	0.8%
35	West Virginia	5,218,541,000	0.7%
36	Utah	5,015,153,000	0.7%
37	Kansas	4,412,654,000	0.6%
38	Alaska	3,518,456,000	0.5%
39	Nebraska	3,455,531,000	0.5%
40	Montana	3,277,702,000	0.5%
41	Hawaii	3,098,783,000	0.4%
42	Maine	3,056,685,000	0.4%
43	Idaho	2,755,533,000	0.4%
44	Rhode Island	2,623,884,000	0.4%
45	Wyoming	2,593,619,000	0.4%
46	Delaware	2,441,548,000	0.3%
47	New Hampshire	2,433,993,000	0.3%
48	Vermont	2,058,797,000	0.3%
49	North Dakota	2,034,815,000	0.3%
50	South Dakota	1,696,361,000	0.2%
	District of Columbia	4,766,497,000	0.7%

Source: U.S. Bureau of the Census, Governments Division
"2017 State and Local Government Finances" (https://www.census.gov/programs-surveys/gov-finances.html)

Per Capita State and Local Government Revenue from the Federal Government in 2017
National Per Capita = $2,177

ALPHA ORDER

RANK	STATE	PER CAPITA
25	Alabama	$2,250
1	Alaska	4,756
24	Arizona	2,257
10	Arkansas	2,718
13	California	2,558
43	Colorado	1,691
23	Connecticut	2,266
14	Delaware	2,551
49	Florida	1,492
47	Georgia	1,568
27	Hawaii	2,176
46	Idaho	1,603
39	Illinois	1,788
22	Indiana	2,268
29	Iowa	2,122
48	Kansas	1,516
15	Kentucky	2,541
9	Louisiana	2,785
20	Maine	2,290
19	Maryland	2,331
17	Massachusetts	2,502
21	Michigan	2,289
31	Minnesota	2,101
8	Mississippi	2,855
32	Missouri	1,959
6	Montana	3,112
37	Nebraska	1,802
35	Nevada	1,876
36	New Hampshire	1,803
28	New Jersey	2,124
3	New Mexico	3,539
4	New York	3,385
38	North Carolina	1,794
11	North Dakota	2,694
26	Ohio	2,224
33	Oklahoma	1,947
12	Oregon	2,599
16	Pennsylvania	2,514
18	Rhode Island	2,484
41	South Carolina	1,749
34	South Dakota	1,943
40	Tennessee	1,757
44	Texas	1,620
45	Utah	1,616
5	Vermont	3,297
50	Virginia	1,393
30	Washington	2,111
7	West Virginia	2,872
42	Wisconsin	1,716
2	Wyoming	4,480

RANK ORDER

RANK	STATE	PER CAPITA
1	Alaska	$4,756
2	Wyoming	4,480
3	New Mexico	3,539
4	New York	3,385
5	Vermont	3,297
6	Montana	3,112
7	West Virginia	2,872
8	Mississippi	2,855
9	Louisiana	2,785
10	Arkansas	2,718
11	North Dakota	2,694
12	Oregon	2,599
13	California	2,558
14	Delaware	2,551
15	Kentucky	2,541
16	Pennsylvania	2,514
17	Massachusetts	2,502
18	Rhode Island	2,484
19	Maryland	2,331
20	Maine	2,290
21	Michigan	2,289
22	Indiana	2,268
23	Connecticut	2,266
24	Arizona	2,257
25	Alabama	2,250
26	Ohio	2,224
27	Hawaii	2,176
28	New Jersey	2,124
29	Iowa	2,122
30	Washington	2,111
31	Minnesota	2,101
32	Missouri	1,959
33	Oklahoma	1,947
34	South Dakota	1,943
35	Nevada	1,876
36	New Hampshire	1,803
37	Nebraska	1,802
38	North Carolina	1,794
39	Illinois	1,788
40	Tennessee	1,757
41	South Carolina	1,749
42	Wisconsin	1,716
43	Colorado	1,691
44	Texas	1,620
45	Utah	1,616
46	Idaho	1,603
47	Georgia	1,568
48	Kansas	1,516
49	Florida	1,492
50	Virginia	1,393

| | District of Columbia | 6,851 |

Source: CQ Press using data from U.S. Bureau of the Census, Governments Division
"2017 State and Local Government Finances" (https://www.census.gov/programs-surveys/gov-finances.html)

Percent of State and Local Government Revenue
from the Federal Government in 2017
National Percent = 18.0%*

ALPHA ORDER

RANK	STATE	PERCENT
13	Alabama	22.0
10	Alaska	24.6
11	Arizona	24.1
5	Arkansas	25.9
39	California	16.2
43	Colorado	15.3
37	Connecticut	16.3
17	Delaware	20.6
37	Florida	16.3
29	Georgia	17.8
47	Hawaii	15.2
30	Idaho	17.6
43	Illinois	15.3
12	Indiana	23.8
34	Iowa	17.1
49	Kansas	13.7
7	Kentucky	25.4
9	Louisiana	24.8
15	Maine	21.2
21	Maryland	19.3
27	Massachusetts	18.0
16	Michigan	20.8
41	Minnesota	15.9
4	Mississippi	26.3
20	Missouri	19.5
2	Montana	27.8
48	Nebraska	14.1
31	Nevada	17.4
32	New Hampshire	17.3
40	New Jersey	16.1
1	New Mexico	27.9
32	New York	17.3
28	North Carolina	17.9
23	North Dakota	18.7
26	Ohio	18.3
19	Oklahoma	20.2
24	Oregon	18.5
14	Pennsylvania	21.5
18	Rhode Island	20.4
35	South Carolina	16.8
25	South Dakota	18.4
22	Tennessee	18.8
36	Texas	16.6
43	Utah	15.3
8	Vermont	25.0
50	Virginia	12.8
42	Washington	15.6
6	West Virginia	25.8
43	Wisconsin	15.3
3	Wyoming	26.6

RANK ORDER

RANK	STATE	PERCENT
1	New Mexico	27.9
2	Montana	27.8
3	Wyoming	26.6
4	Mississippi	26.3
5	Arkansas	25.9
6	West Virginia	25.8
7	Kentucky	25.4
8	Vermont	25.0
9	Louisiana	24.8
10	Alaska	24.6
11	Arizona	24.1
12	Indiana	23.8
13	Alabama	22.0
14	Pennsylvania	21.5
15	Maine	21.2
16	Michigan	20.8
17	Delaware	20.6
18	Rhode Island	20.4
19	Oklahoma	20.2
20	Missouri	19.5
21	Maryland	19.3
22	Tennessee	18.8
23	North Dakota	18.7
24	Oregon	18.5
25	South Dakota	18.4
26	Ohio	18.3
27	Massachusetts	18.0
28	North Carolina	17.9
29	Georgia	17.8
30	Idaho	17.6
31	Nevada	17.4
32	New Hampshire	17.3
32	New York	17.3
34	Iowa	17.1
35	South Carolina	16.8
36	Texas	16.6
37	Connecticut	16.3
37	Florida	16.3
39	California	16.2
40	New Jersey	16.1
41	Minnesota	15.9
42	Washington	15.6
43	Colorado	15.3
43	Illinois	15.3
43	Utah	15.3
43	Wisconsin	15.3
47	Hawaii	15.2
48	Nebraska	14.1
49	Kansas	13.7
50	Virginia	12.8
	District of Columbia	30.2

Source: CQ Press using data from U.S. Bureau of the Census, Governments Division
"2017 State and Local Government Finances" (https://www.census.gov/programs-surveys/gov-finances.html)
*As a percent of total revenue.

State and Local Government Own Source Revenue in 2017

National Total = $2,404,941,027,000*

<table>
<tr><td colspan="4">ALPHA ORDER</td><td colspan="4">RANK ORDER</td></tr>
<tr><th>RANK</th><th>STATE</th><th>REVENUE</th><th>% of USA</th><th>RANK</th><th>STATE</th><th>REVENUE</th><th>% of USA</th></tr>
<tr><td>27</td><td>Alabama</td><td>$29,039,047,000</td><td>1.2%</td><td>1</td><td>California</td><td>$353,127,424,000</td><td>14.7%</td></tr>
<tr><td>44</td><td>Alaska</td><td>8,113,023,000</td><td>0.3%</td><td>2</td><td>New York</td><td>232,195,846,000</td><td>9.7%</td></tr>
<tr><td>21</td><td>Arizona</td><td>35,336,712,000</td><td>1.5%</td><td>3</td><td>Texas</td><td>177,193,538,000</td><td>7.4%</td></tr>
<tr><td>35</td><td>Arkansas</td><td>17,478,588,000</td><td>0.7%</td><td>4</td><td>Florida</td><td>124,218,849,000</td><td>5.2%</td></tr>
<tr><td>1</td><td>California</td><td>353,127,424,000</td><td>14.7%</td><td>5</td><td>Illinois</td><td>95,787,218,000</td><td>4.0%</td></tr>
<tr><td>17</td><td>Colorado</td><td>42,017,516,000</td><td>1.7%</td><td>6</td><td>Pennsylvania</td><td>92,790,724,000</td><td>3.9%</td></tr>
<tr><td>25</td><td>Connecticut</td><td>32,793,902,000</td><td>1.4%</td><td>7</td><td>Ohio</td><td>81,397,506,000</td><td>3.4%</td></tr>
<tr><td>45</td><td>Delaware</td><td>7,640,306,000</td><td>0.3%</td><td>8</td><td>New Jersey</td><td>80,765,342,000</td><td>3.4%</td></tr>
<tr><td>4</td><td>Florida</td><td>124,218,849,000</td><td>5.2%</td><td>9</td><td>Michigan</td><td>65,987,194,000</td><td>2.7%</td></tr>
<tr><td>14</td><td>Georgia</td><td>56,562,247,000</td><td>2.4%</td><td>10</td><td>North Carolina</td><td>64,888,433,000</td><td>2.7%</td></tr>
<tr><td>38</td><td>Hawaii</td><td>14,133,052,000</td><td>0.6%</td><td>11</td><td>Virginia</td><td>62,106,895,000</td><td>2.6%</td></tr>
<tr><td>40</td><td>Idaho</td><td>9,393,448,000</td><td>0.4%</td><td>12</td><td>Washington</td><td>61,241,149,000</td><td>2.5%</td></tr>
<tr><td>5</td><td>Illinois</td><td>95,787,218,000</td><td>4.0%</td><td>13</td><td>Massachusetts</td><td>60,321,499,000</td><td>2.5%</td></tr>
<tr><td>19</td><td>Indiana</td><td>40,207,976,000</td><td>1.7%</td><td>14</td><td>Georgia</td><td>56,562,247,000</td><td>2.4%</td></tr>
<tr><td>28</td><td>Iowa</td><td>25,581,681,000</td><td>1.1%</td><td>15</td><td>Maryland</td><td>48,734,525,000</td><td>2.0%</td></tr>
<tr><td>31</td><td>Kansas</td><td>22,343,668,000</td><td>0.9%</td><td>16</td><td>Minnesota</td><td>46,757,207,000</td><td>1.9%</td></tr>
<tr><td>29</td><td>Kentucky</td><td>25,191,205,000</td><td>1.0%</td><td>17</td><td>Colorado</td><td>42,017,516,000</td><td>1.7%</td></tr>
<tr><td>26</td><td>Louisiana</td><td>29,301,991,000</td><td>1.2%</td><td>18</td><td>Wisconsin</td><td>40,967,489,000</td><td>1.7%</td></tr>
<tr><td>41</td><td>Maine</td><td>9,171,817,000</td><td>0.4%</td><td>19</td><td>Indiana</td><td>40,207,976,000</td><td>1.7%</td></tr>
<tr><td>15</td><td>Maryland</td><td>48,734,525,000</td><td>2.0%</td><td>20</td><td>Missouri</td><td>35,593,974,000</td><td>1.5%</td></tr>
<tr><td>13</td><td>Massachusetts</td><td>60,321,499,000</td><td>2.5%</td><td>21</td><td>Arizona</td><td>35,336,712,000</td><td>1.5%</td></tr>
<tr><td>9</td><td>Michigan</td><td>65,987,194,000</td><td>2.7%</td><td>22</td><td>Tennessee</td><td>34,618,998,000</td><td>1.4%</td></tr>
<tr><td>16</td><td>Minnesota</td><td>46,757,207,000</td><td>1.9%</td><td>23</td><td>South Carolina</td><td>33,037,507,000</td><td>1.4%</td></tr>
<tr><td>34</td><td>Mississippi</td><td>17,835,733,000</td><td>0.7%</td><td>24</td><td>Oregon</td><td>32,924,081,000</td><td>1.4%</td></tr>
<tr><td>20</td><td>Missouri</td><td>35,593,974,000</td><td>1.5%</td><td>25</td><td>Connecticut</td><td>32,793,902,000</td><td>1.4%</td></tr>
<tr><td>47</td><td>Montana</td><td>5,913,858,000</td><td>0.2%</td><td>26</td><td>Louisiana</td><td>29,301,991,000</td><td>1.2%</td></tr>
<tr><td>37</td><td>Nebraska</td><td>14,225,751,000</td><td>0.6%</td><td>27</td><td>Alabama</td><td>29,039,047,000</td><td>1.2%</td></tr>
<tr><td>33</td><td>Nevada</td><td>18,208,004,000</td><td>0.8%</td><td>28</td><td>Iowa</td><td>25,581,681,000</td><td>1.1%</td></tr>
<tr><td>42</td><td>New Hampshire</td><td>9,133,190,000</td><td>0.4%</td><td>29</td><td>Kentucky</td><td>25,191,205,000</td><td>1.0%</td></tr>
<tr><td>8</td><td>New Jersey</td><td>80,765,342,000</td><td>3.4%</td><td>30</td><td>Oklahoma</td><td>22,579,222,000</td><td>0.9%</td></tr>
<tr><td>36</td><td>New Mexico</td><td>14,230,961,000</td><td>0.6%</td><td>31</td><td>Kansas</td><td>22,343,668,000</td><td>0.9%</td></tr>
<tr><td>2</td><td>New York</td><td>232,195,846,000</td><td>9.7%</td><td>32</td><td>Utah</td><td>21,868,097,000</td><td>0.9%</td></tr>
<tr><td>10</td><td>North Carolina</td><td>64,888,433,000</td><td>2.7%</td><td>33</td><td>Nevada</td><td>18,208,004,000</td><td>0.8%</td></tr>
<tr><td>46</td><td>North Dakota</td><td>7,238,268,000</td><td>0.3%</td><td>34</td><td>Mississippi</td><td>17,835,733,000</td><td>0.7%</td></tr>
<tr><td>7</td><td>Ohio</td><td>81,397,506,000</td><td>3.4%</td><td>35</td><td>Arkansas</td><td>17,478,588,000</td><td>0.7%</td></tr>
<tr><td>30</td><td>Oklahoma</td><td>22,579,222,000</td><td>0.9%</td><td>36</td><td>New Mexico</td><td>14,230,961,000</td><td>0.6%</td></tr>
<tr><td>24</td><td>Oregon</td><td>32,924,081,000</td><td>1.4%</td><td>37</td><td>Nebraska</td><td>14,225,751,000</td><td>0.6%</td></tr>
<tr><td>6</td><td>Pennsylvania</td><td>92,790,724,000</td><td>3.9%</td><td>38</td><td>Hawaii</td><td>14,133,052,000</td><td>0.6%</td></tr>
<tr><td>43</td><td>Rhode Island</td><td>8,160,248,000</td><td>0.3%</td><td>39</td><td>West Virginia</td><td>11,514,844,000</td><td>0.5%</td></tr>
<tr><td>23</td><td>South Carolina</td><td>33,037,507,000</td><td>1.4%</td><td>40</td><td>Idaho</td><td>9,393,448,000</td><td>0.4%</td></tr>
<tr><td>49</td><td>South Dakota</td><td>5,398,019,000</td><td>0.2%</td><td>41</td><td>Maine</td><td>9,171,817,000</td><td>0.4%</td></tr>
<tr><td>22</td><td>Tennessee</td><td>34,618,998,000</td><td>1.4%</td><td>42</td><td>New Hampshire</td><td>9,133,190,000</td><td>0.4%</td></tr>
<tr><td>3</td><td>Texas</td><td>177,193,538,000</td><td>7.4%</td><td>43</td><td>Rhode Island</td><td>8,160,248,000</td><td>0.3%</td></tr>
<tr><td>32</td><td>Utah</td><td>21,868,097,000</td><td>0.9%</td><td>44</td><td>Alaska</td><td>8,113,023,000</td><td>0.3%</td></tr>
<tr><td>50</td><td>Vermont</td><td>5,016,529,000</td><td>0.2%</td><td>45</td><td>Delaware</td><td>7,640,306,000</td><td>0.3%</td></tr>
<tr><td>11</td><td>Virginia</td><td>62,106,895,000</td><td>2.6%</td><td>46</td><td>North Dakota</td><td>7,238,268,000</td><td>0.3%</td></tr>
<tr><td>12</td><td>Washington</td><td>61,241,149,000</td><td>2.5%</td><td>47</td><td>Montana</td><td>5,913,858,000</td><td>0.2%</td></tr>
<tr><td>39</td><td>West Virginia</td><td>11,514,844,000</td><td>0.5%</td><td>48</td><td>Wyoming</td><td>5,639,920,000</td><td>0.2%</td></tr>
<tr><td>18</td><td>Wisconsin</td><td>40,967,489,000</td><td>1.7%</td><td>49</td><td>South Dakota</td><td>5,398,019,000</td><td>0.2%</td></tr>
<tr><td>48</td><td>Wyoming</td><td>5,639,920,000</td><td>0.2%</td><td>50</td><td>Vermont</td><td>5,016,529,000</td><td>0.2%</td></tr>
<tr><td></td><td></td><td></td><td></td><td></td><td>District of Columbia</td><td>9,016,806,000</td><td>0.4%</td></tr>
</table>

Source: U.S. Bureau of the Census, Governments Division
"2017 State and Local Government Finances" (https://www.census.gov/programs-surveys/gov-finances.html)
*Own source revenue includes taxes, current charges, and miscellaneous general revenue. Excluded are intergovernmental transfers, insurance trust revenue, and revenue from government-owned utilities and other commercial or auxiliary enterprise.

Per Capita State and Local Government Own Source Revenue in 2017

National Per Capita = $7,396*

ALPHA ORDER

RANK	STATE	PER CAPITA
40	Alabama	$5,957
2	Alaska	10,967
50	Arizona	5,013
43	Arkansas	5,820
8	California	8,963
20	Colorado	7,482
6	Connecticut	9,176
15	Delaware	7,983
41	Florida	5,922
48	Georgia	5,432
3	Hawaii	9,923
47	Idaho	5,465
19	Illinois	7,491
38	Indiana	6,037
12	Iowa	8,138
18	Kansas	7,676
45	Kentucky	5,656
34	Louisiana	6,273
27	Maine	6,870
13	Maryland	8,089
9	Massachusetts	8,789
30	Michigan	6,614
10	Minnesota	8,397
39	Mississippi	5,966
42	Missouri	5,827
46	Montana	5,616
21	Nebraska	7,419
37	Nevada	6,126
29	New Hampshire	6,766
7	New Jersey	9,086
28	New Mexico	6,798
1	New York	11,852
33	North Carolina	6,318
5	North Dakota	9,585
26	Ohio	6,978
44	Oklahoma	5,741
16	Oregon	7,940
23	Pennsylvania	7,255
17	Rhode Island	7,724
31	South Carolina	6,580
36	South Dakota	6,181
49	Tennessee	5,160
35	Texas	6,256
25	Utah	7,047
14	Vermont	8,033
22	Virginia	7,337
11	Washington	8,247
32	West Virginia	6,337
24	Wisconsin	7,073
4	Wyoming	9,742

RANK ORDER

RANK	STATE	PER CAPITA
1	New York	$11,852
2	Alaska	10,967
3	Hawaii	9,923
4	Wyoming	9,742
5	North Dakota	9,585
6	Connecticut	9,176
7	New Jersey	9,086
8	California	8,963
9	Massachusetts	8,789
10	Minnesota	8,397
11	Washington	8,247
12	Iowa	8,138
13	Maryland	8,089
14	Vermont	8,033
15	Delaware	7,983
16	Oregon	7,940
17	Rhode Island	7,724
18	Kansas	7,676
19	Illinois	7,491
20	Colorado	7,482
21	Nebraska	7,419
22	Virginia	7,337
23	Pennsylvania	7,255
24	Wisconsin	7,073
25	Utah	7,047
26	Ohio	6,978
27	Maine	6,870
28	New Mexico	6,798
29	New Hampshire	6,766
30	Michigan	6,614
31	South Carolina	6,580
32	West Virginia	6,337
33	North Carolina	6,318
34	Louisiana	6,273
35	Texas	6,256
36	South Dakota	6,181
37	Nevada	6,126
38	Indiana	6,037
39	Mississippi	5,966
40	Alabama	5,957
41	Florida	5,922
42	Missouri	5,827
43	Arkansas	5,820
44	Oklahoma	5,741
45	Kentucky	5,656
46	Montana	5,616
47	Idaho	5,465
48	Georgia	5,432
49	Tennessee	5,160
50	Arizona	5,013
	District of Columbia	12,961

Source: CQ Press using data from U.S. Bureau of the Census, Governments Division
"2017 State and Local Government Finances" (https://www.census.gov/programs-surveys/gov-finances.html)
*Own source revenue includes taxes, current charges, and miscellaneous general revenue. Excluded are intergovernmental transfers, insurance trust revenue, and revenue from government-owned utilities and other commercial or auxiliary enterprise.

State and Local Government Tax Revenue in 2017

National Total = $1,649,348,024,000

ALPHA ORDER

RANK	STATE	REVENUE	% of USA
28	Alabama	$16,428,775,000	1.0%
49	Alaska	3,030,264,000	0.2%
21	Arizona	24,471,902,000	1.5%
34	Arkansas	12,016,756,000	0.7%
1	California	243,082,136,000	14.7%
18	Colorado	27,408,795,000	1.7%
19	Connecticut	27,297,173,000	1.7%
45	Delaware	4,676,218,000	0.3%
4	Florida	76,619,990,000	4.6%
14	Georgia	38,939,535,000	2.4%
37	Hawaii	9,457,287,000	0.6%
42	Idaho	6,379,821,000	0.4%
5	Illinois	73,702,097,000	4.5%
20	Indiana	25,929,309,000	1.6%
29	Iowa	15,693,169,000	1.0%
31	Kansas	13,515,301,000	0.8%
27	Kentucky	17,342,836,000	1.1%
24	Louisiana	20,216,960,000	1.2%
40	Maine	7,078,870,000	0.4%
15	Maryland	37,964,460,000	2.3%
9	Massachusetts	45,052,511,000	2.7%
10	Michigan	41,786,620,000	2.5%
16	Minnesota	34,390,945,000	2.1%
35	Mississippi	10,995,444,000	0.7%
22	Missouri	23,338,813,000	1.4%
46	Montana	4,084,047,000	0.2%
36	Nebraska	9,814,666,000	0.6%
32	Nevada	13,361,940,000	0.8%
41	New Hampshire	6,607,235,000	0.4%
7	New Jersey	62,026,500,000	3.8%
38	New Mexico	8,619,186,000	0.5%
2	New York	177,750,542,000	10.8%
11	North Carolina	40,677,241,000	2.5%
44	North Dakota	5,033,003,000	0.3%
8	Ohio	54,607,766,000	3.3%
30	Oklahoma	13,935,394,000	0.8%
25	Oregon	19,617,772,000	1.2%
6	Pennsylvania	66,070,277,000	4.0%
43	Rhode Island	5,876,351,000	0.4%
26	South Carolina	17,685,205,000	1.1%
48	South Dakota	3,720,441,000	0.2%
23	Tennessee	22,846,510,000	1.4%
3	Texas	117,851,727,000	7.1%
33	Utah	12,608,667,000	0.8%
47	Vermont	3,774,716,000	0.2%
12	Virginia	40,610,163,000	2.5%
13	Washington	39,663,423,000	2.4%
39	West Virginia	7,184,533,000	0.4%
17	Wisconsin	28,328,777,000	1.7%
50	Wyoming	2,720,087,000	0.2%

RANK ORDER

RANK	STATE	REVENUE	% of USA
1	California	$243,082,136,000	14.7%
2	New York	177,750,542,000	10.8%
3	Texas	117,851,727,000	7.1%
4	Florida	76,619,990,000	4.6%
5	Illinois	73,702,097,000	4.5%
6	Pennsylvania	66,070,277,000	4.0%
7	New Jersey	62,026,500,000	3.8%
8	Ohio	54,607,766,000	3.3%
9	Massachusetts	45,052,511,000	2.7%
10	Michigan	41,786,620,000	2.5%
11	North Carolina	40,677,241,000	2.5%
12	Virginia	40,610,163,000	2.5%
13	Washington	39,663,423,000	2.4%
14	Georgia	38,939,535,000	2.4%
15	Maryland	37,964,460,000	2.3%
16	Minnesota	34,390,945,000	2.1%
17	Wisconsin	28,328,777,000	1.7%
18	Colorado	27,408,795,000	1.7%
19	Connecticut	27,297,173,000	1.7%
20	Indiana	25,929,309,000	1.6%
21	Arizona	24,471,902,000	1.5%
22	Missouri	23,338,813,000	1.4%
23	Tennessee	22,846,510,000	1.4%
24	Louisiana	20,216,960,000	1.2%
25	Oregon	19,617,772,000	1.2%
26	South Carolina	17,685,205,000	1.1%
27	Kentucky	17,342,836,000	1.1%
28	Alabama	16,428,775,000	1.0%
29	Iowa	15,693,169,000	1.0%
30	Oklahoma	13,935,394,000	0.8%
31	Kansas	13,515,301,000	0.8%
32	Nevada	13,361,940,000	0.8%
33	Utah	12,608,667,000	0.8%
34	Arkansas	12,016,756,000	0.7%
35	Mississippi	10,995,444,000	0.7%
36	Nebraska	9,814,666,000	0.6%
37	Hawaii	9,457,287,000	0.6%
38	New Mexico	8,619,186,000	0.5%
39	West Virginia	7,184,533,000	0.4%
40	Maine	7,078,870,000	0.4%
41	New Hampshire	6,607,235,000	0.4%
42	Idaho	6,379,821,000	0.4%
43	Rhode Island	5,876,351,000	0.4%
44	North Dakota	5,033,003,000	0.3%
45	Delaware	4,676,218,000	0.3%
46	Montana	4,084,047,000	0.2%
47	Vermont	3,774,716,000	0.2%
48	South Dakota	3,720,441,000	0.2%
49	Alaska	3,030,264,000	0.2%
50	Wyoming	2,720,087,000	0.2%
	District of Columbia	7,455,868,000	0.5%

Source: U.S. Bureau of the Census, Governments Division
"2017 State and Local Government Finances" (https://www.census.gov/programs-surveys/gov-finances.html)

Per Capita State and Local Government Tax Revenue in 2017

National Per Capita = $5,073

ALPHA ORDER				RANK ORDER		
RANK	STATE	PER CAPITA		RANK	STATE	PER CAPITA
50	Alabama	$3,370		1	New York	$9,073
33	Alaska	4,096		2	Connecticut	7,638
48	Arizona	3,472		3	New Jersey	6,978
35	Arkansas	4,002		4	North Dakota	6,665
9	California	6,170		5	Hawaii	6,640
21	Colorado	4,881		6	Massachusetts	6,564
2	Connecticut	7,638		7	Maryland	6,301
20	Delaware	4,886		8	Minnesota	6,176
45	Florida	3,653		9	California	6,170
42	Georgia	3,739		10	Vermont	6,044
5	Hawaii	6,640		11	Illinois	5,764
43	Idaho	3,712		12	Rhode Island	5,562
11	Illinois	5,764		13	Washington	5,342
39	Indiana	3,893		14	Maine	5,302
17	Iowa	4,992		15	Pennsylvania	5,166
26	Kansas	4,643		16	Nebraska	5,118
38	Kentucky	3,894		17	Iowa	4,992
28	Louisiana	4,328		18	New Hampshire	4,895
14	Maine	5,302		19	Wisconsin	4,891
7	Maryland	6,301		20	Delaware	4,886
6	Massachusetts	6,564		21	Colorado	4,881
30	Michigan	4,189		22	Virginia	4,797
8	Minnesota	6,176		23	Oregon	4,731
44	Mississippi	3,678		24	Wyoming	4,698
41	Missouri	3,821		25	Ohio	4,682
40	Montana	3,878		26	Kansas	4,643
16	Nebraska	5,118		27	Nevada	4,495
27	Nevada	4,495		28	Louisiana	4,328
18	New Hampshire	4,895		29	South Dakota	4,260
3	New Jersey	6,978		30	Michigan	4,189
32	New Mexico	4,117		31	Texas	4,161
1	New York	9,073		32	New Mexico	4,117
36	North Carolina	3,960		33	Alaska	4,096
4	North Dakota	6,665		34	Utah	4,063
25	Ohio	4,682		35	Arkansas	4,002
46	Oklahoma	3,544		36	North Carolina	3,960
23	Oregon	4,731		37	West Virginia	3,954
15	Pennsylvania	5,166		38	Kentucky	3,894
12	Rhode Island	5,562		39	Indiana	3,893
47	South Carolina	3,522		40	Montana	3,878
29	South Dakota	4,260		41	Missouri	3,821
49	Tennessee	3,405		42	Georgia	3,739
31	Texas	4,161		43	Idaho	3,712
34	Utah	4,063		44	Mississippi	3,678
10	Vermont	6,044		45	Florida	3,653
22	Virginia	4,797		46	Oklahoma	3,544
13	Washington	5,342		47	South Carolina	3,522
37	West Virginia	3,954		48	Arizona	3,472
19	Wisconsin	4,891		49	Tennessee	3,405
24	Wyoming	4,698		50	Alabama	3,370
					District of Columbia	10,717

Source: CQ Press using data from U.S. Bureau of the Census, Governments Division
"2017 State and Local Government Finances" (https://www.census.gov/programs-surveys/gov-finances.html)

Percent of State and Local Government Revenue from Taxes in 2017

National Percent = 41.9%

ALPHA ORDER				RANK ORDER		
RANK	STATE	PERCENT		RANK	STATE	PERCENT
47	Alabama	32.9		1	Connecticut	55.1
50	Alaska	21.2		2	New Jersey	53.0
39	Arizona	37.1		3	Maryland	52.1
36	Arkansas	38.2		4	Illinois	49.4
31	California	39.1		5	Maine	49.1
14	Colorado	44.3		6	Massachusetts	47.2
1	Connecticut	55.1		7	New Hampshire	47.1
30	Delaware	39.4		8	Minnesota	46.7
27	Florida	39.8		9	Hawaii	46.5
18	Georgia	42.5		9	New York	46.5
9	Hawaii	46.5		11	North Dakota	46.3
23	Idaho	40.7		12	Vermont	45.9
4	Illinois	49.4		13	Rhode Island	45.8
22	Indiana	40.8		14	Colorado	44.3
25	Iowa	40.1		15	Virginia	44.2
20	Kansas	41.9		16	Pennsylvania	44.1
32	Kentucky	39.0		17	Wisconsin	43.5
34	Louisiana	38.5		18	Georgia	42.5
5	Maine	49.1		18	Texas	42.5
3	Maryland	52.1		20	Kansas	41.9
6	Massachusetts	47.2		21	Nevada	41.6
37	Michigan	38.0		22	Indiana	40.8
8	Minnesota	46.7		23	Idaho	40.7
45	Mississippi	33.8		24	South Dakota	40.4
37	Missouri	38.0		25	Iowa	40.1
43	Montana	34.6		26	Nebraska	40.0
26	Nebraska	40.0		27	Florida	39.8
21	Nevada	41.6		28	North Carolina	39.5
7	New Hampshire	47.1		28	Washington	39.5
2	New Jersey	53.0		30	Delaware	39.4
48	New Mexico	32.4		31	California	39.1
9	New York	46.5		32	Kentucky	39.0
28	North Carolina	39.5		33	Ohio	38.6
11	North Dakota	46.3		34	Louisiana	38.5
33	Ohio	38.6		35	Utah	38.4
40	Oklahoma	36.8		36	Arkansas	38.2
46	Oregon	33.7		37	Michigan	38.0
16	Pennsylvania	44.1		37	Missouri	38.0
13	Rhode Island	45.8		39	Arizona	37.1
44	South Carolina	33.9		40	Oklahoma	36.8
24	South Dakota	40.4		41	Tennessee	36.4
41	Tennessee	36.4		42	West Virginia	35.5
18	Texas	42.5		43	Montana	34.6
35	Utah	38.4		44	South Carolina	33.9
12	Vermont	45.9		45	Mississippi	33.8
15	Virginia	44.2		46	Oregon	33.7
28	Washington	39.5		47	Alabama	32.9
42	West Virginia	35.5		48	New Mexico	32.4
17	Wisconsin	43.5		49	Wyoming	27.9
49	Wyoming	27.9		50	Alaska	21.2
					District of Columbia	47.2

Source: CQ Press using data from U.S. Bureau of the Census, Governments Division
"2017 State and Local Government Finances" (https://www.census.gov/programs-surveys/gov-finances.html)

State and Local Government Tax Revenue
as a Percent of Personal Income in 2017
National Percent = 9.8% of Personal Income*

RANK	STATE	PERCENT
44	Alabama	8.3
50	Alaska	7.2
46	Arizona	8.2
24	Arkansas	9.6
14	California	10.3
33	Colorado	8.8
9	Connecticut	10.6
22	Delaware	9.7
48	Florida	7.6
40	Georgia	8.4
3	Hawaii	12.5
33	Idaho	8.8
7	Illinois	10.7
37	Indiana	8.6
11	Iowa	10.5
27	Kansas	9.5
27	Kentucky	9.5
19	Louisiana	9.9
5	Maine	11.4
12	Maryland	10.4
24	Massachusetts	9.6
30	Michigan	9.1
6	Minnesota	11.2
16	Mississippi	10.1
40	Missouri	8.4
37	Montana	8.6
16	Nebraska	10.1
24	Nevada	9.6
40	New Hampshire	8.4
7	New Jersey	10.7
12	New Mexico	10.4
1	New York	13.8
32	North Carolina	9.0
2	North Dakota	12.7
18	Ohio	10.0
47	Oklahoma	8.1
21	Oregon	9.8
22	Pennsylvania	9.7
9	Rhode Island	10.6
40	South Carolina	8.4
37	South Dakota	8.6
48	Tennessee	7.6
35	Texas	8.7
29	Utah	9.2
4	Vermont	11.6
35	Virginia	8.7
30	Washington	9.1
15	West Virginia	10.2
19	Wisconsin	9.9
44	Wyoming	8.3

RANK	STATE	PERCENT
1	New York	13.8
2	North Dakota	12.7
3	Hawaii	12.5
4	Vermont	11.6
5	Maine	11.4
6	Minnesota	11.2
7	Illinois	10.7
7	New Jersey	10.7
9	Connecticut	10.6
9	Rhode Island	10.6
11	Iowa	10.5
12	Maryland	10.4
12	New Mexico	10.4
14	California	10.3
15	West Virginia	10.2
16	Mississippi	10.1
16	Nebraska	10.1
18	Ohio	10.0
19	Louisiana	9.9
19	Wisconsin	9.9
21	Oregon	9.8
22	Delaware	9.7
22	Pennsylvania	9.7
24	Arkansas	9.6
24	Massachusetts	9.6
24	Nevada	9.6
27	Kansas	9.5
27	Kentucky	9.5
29	Utah	9.2
30	Michigan	9.1
30	Washington	9.1
32	North Carolina	9.0
33	Colorado	8.8
33	Idaho	8.8
35	Texas	8.7
35	Virginia	8.7
37	Indiana	8.6
37	Montana	8.6
37	South Dakota	8.6
40	Georgia	8.4
40	Missouri	8.4
40	New Hampshire	8.4
40	South Carolina	8.4
44	Alabama	8.3
44	Wyoming	8.3
46	Arizona	8.2
47	Oklahoma	8.1
48	Florida	7.6
48	Tennessee	7.6
50	Alaska	7.2

District of Columbia	13.6

Source: CQ Press using data from U.S. Bureau of the Census, Governments Division
"Annual State Personal Income" (https://apps.bea.gov/iTable/index_regional.cfm) and
"2017 State and Local Government Finances" (https://www.census.gov/programs-surveys/gov-finances.html)
*The personal income total used for this table is the sum of state estimates. This total differs from the national income and product accounts (NIPA) estimate of personal income because it omits the earnings of federal civilian and military personnel stationed abroad and of U.S. residents employed abroad temporarily by private U.S. firms.

State and Local Government General Sales Tax Revenue in 2017

National Total = $388,935,695,000*

ALPHA ORDER					RANK ORDER			
RANK	STATE	REVENUE	% of USA		RANK	STATE	REVENUE	% of USA
24	Alabama	$5,065,832,000	1.3%		1	California	$49,075,211,000	12.6%
46	Alaska	233,830,000	0.1%		2	Texas	40,392,999,000	10.4%
10	Arizona	9,663,184,000	2.5%		3	New York	30,391,564,000	7.8%
27	Arkansas	4,538,759,000	1.2%		4	Florida	27,760,897,000	7.1%
1	California	49,075,211,000	12.6%		5	Washington	18,386,514,000	4.7%
17	Colorado	7,517,416,000	1.9%		6	Ohio	15,599,802,000	4.0%
29	Connecticut	4,236,619,000	1.1%		7	Illinois	14,411,303,000	3.7%
47	Delaware	0	0.0%		8	Pennsylvania	11,430,195,000	2.9%
4	Florida	27,760,897,000	7.1%		9	North Carolina	10,538,371,000	2.7%
13	Georgia	9,287,472,000	2.4%		10	Arizona	9,663,184,000	2.5%
34	Hawaii	3,462,574,000	0.9%		11	New Jersey	9,591,881,000	2.5%
38	Idaho	1,655,240,000	0.4%		12	Tennessee	9,347,316,000	2.4%
7	Illinois	14,411,303,000	3.7%		13	Georgia	9,287,472,000	2.4%
16	Indiana	7,556,509,000	1.9%		14	Michigan	9,223,737,000	2.4%
31	Iowa	3,546,697,000	0.9%		15	Louisiana	8,647,008,000	2.2%
28	Kansas	4,298,463,000	1.1%		16	Indiana	7,556,509,000	1.9%
33	Kentucky	3,490,639,000	0.9%		17	Colorado	7,517,416,000	1.9%
15	Louisiana	8,647,008,000	2.2%		18	Missouri	6,401,636,000	1.6%
39	Maine	1,441,884,000	0.4%		19	Massachusetts	6,240,822,000	1.6%
26	Maryland	4,609,538,000	1.2%		20	Minnesota	6,106,081,000	1.6%
19	Massachusetts	6,240,822,000	1.6%		21	Wisconsin	5,610,211,000	1.4%
14	Michigan	9,223,737,000	2.4%		22	Nevada	5,487,528,000	1.4%
20	Minnesota	6,106,081,000	1.6%		23	Virginia	5,431,016,000	1.4%
32	Mississippi	3,526,913,000	0.9%		24	Alabama	5,065,832,000	1.3%
18	Missouri	6,401,636,000	1.6%		25	Oklahoma	4,661,910,000	1.2%
47	Montana	0	0.0%		26	Maryland	4,609,538,000	1.2%
37	Nebraska	2,238,300,000	0.6%		27	Arkansas	4,538,759,000	1.2%
22	Nevada	5,487,528,000	1.4%		28	Kansas	4,298,463,000	1.1%
47	New Hampshire	0	0.0%		29	Connecticut	4,236,619,000	1.1%
11	New Jersey	9,591,881,000	2.5%		30	South Carolina	3,817,158,000	1.0%
35	New Mexico	3,357,550,000	0.9%		31	Iowa	3,546,697,000	0.9%
3	New York	30,391,564,000	7.8%		32	Mississippi	3,526,913,000	0.9%
9	North Carolina	10,538,371,000	2.7%		33	Kentucky	3,490,639,000	0.9%
42	North Dakota	1,114,636,000	0.3%		34	Hawaii	3,462,574,000	0.9%
6	Ohio	15,599,802,000	4.0%		35	New Mexico	3,357,550,000	0.9%
25	Oklahoma	4,661,910,000	1.2%		36	Utah	3,322,399,000	0.9%
47	Oregon	0	0.0%		37	Nebraska	2,238,300,000	0.6%
8	Pennsylvania	11,430,195,000	2.9%		38	Idaho	1,655,240,000	0.4%
43	Rhode Island	996,390,000	0.3%		39	Maine	1,441,884,000	0.4%
30	South Carolina	3,817,158,000	1.0%		40	South Dakota	1,438,749,000	0.4%
40	South Dakota	1,438,749,000	0.4%		41	West Virginia	1,376,680,000	0.4%
12	Tennessee	9,347,316,000	2.4%		42	North Dakota	1,114,636,000	0.3%
2	Texas	40,392,999,000	10.4%		43	Rhode Island	996,390,000	0.3%
36	Utah	3,322,399,000	0.9%		44	Wyoming	646,277,000	0.2%
45	Vermont	391,489,000	0.1%		45	Vermont	391,489,000	0.1%
23	Virginia	5,431,016,000	1.4%		46	Alaska	233,830,000	0.1%
5	Washington	18,386,514,000	4.7%		47	Delaware	0	0.0%
41	West Virginia	1,376,680,000	0.4%		47	Montana	0	0.0%
21	Wisconsin	5,610,211,000	1.4%		47	New Hampshire	0	0.0%
44	Wyoming	646,277,000	0.2%		47	Oregon	0	0.0%
						District of Columbia	1,368,496,000	0.4%

Source: U.S. Bureau of the Census, Governments Division
    "2017 State and Local Government Finances" (https://www.census.gov/programs-surveys/gov-finances.html)
*Does not include special sales taxes such as those on sale of alcohol, gasoline, or tobacco.

Per Capita State and Local Government General Sales Tax Revenue in 2017

National Per Capita = $1,196*

ALPHA ORDER

RANK	STATE	PER CAPITA
31	Alabama	$1,039
46	Alaska	316
13	Arizona	1,371
8	Arkansas	1,511
17	California	1,246
14	Colorado	1,339
18	Connecticut	1,185
47	Delaware	0
16	Florida	1,323
39	Georgia	892
2	Hawaii	2,431
34	Idaho	963
24	Illinois	1,127
22	Indiana	1,135
23	Iowa	1,128
9	Kansas	1,477
40	Kentucky	784
3	Louisiana	1,851
27	Maine	1,080
41	Maryland	765
37	Massachusetts	909
36	Michigan	925
26	Minnesota	1,097
20	Mississippi	1,180
30	Missouri	1,048
47	Montana	0
21	Nebraska	1,167
4	Nevada	1,846
47	New Hampshire	0
28	New Jersey	1,079
6	New Mexico	1,604
7	New York	1,551
32	North Carolina	1,026
10	North Dakota	1,476
15	Ohio	1,337
18	Oklahoma	1,185
47	Oregon	0
38	Pennsylvania	894
35	Rhode Island	943
42	South Carolina	760
5	South Dakota	1,648
12	Tennessee	1,393
11	Texas	1,426
29	Utah	1,071
45	Vermont	627
44	Virginia	642
1	Washington	2,476
43	West Virginia	758
33	Wisconsin	969
25	Wyoming	1,116

RANK ORDER

RANK	STATE	PER CAPITA
1	Washington	$2,476
2	Hawaii	2,431
3	Louisiana	1,851
4	Nevada	1,846
5	South Dakota	1,648
6	New Mexico	1,604
7	New York	1,551
8	Arkansas	1,511
9	Kansas	1,477
10	North Dakota	1,476
11	Texas	1,426
12	Tennessee	1,393
13	Arizona	1,371
14	Colorado	1,339
15	Ohio	1,337
16	Florida	1,323
17	California	1,246
18	Connecticut	1,185
18	Oklahoma	1,185
20	Mississippi	1,180
21	Nebraska	1,167
22	Indiana	1,135
23	Iowa	1,128
24	Illinois	1,127
25	Wyoming	1,116
26	Minnesota	1,097
27	Maine	1,080
28	New Jersey	1,079
29	Utah	1,071
30	Missouri	1,048
31	Alabama	1,039
32	North Carolina	1,026
33	Wisconsin	969
34	Idaho	963
35	Rhode Island	943
36	Michigan	925
37	Massachusetts	909
38	Pennsylvania	894
39	Georgia	892
40	Kentucky	784
41	Maryland	765
42	South Carolina	760
43	West Virginia	758
44	Virginia	642
45	Vermont	627
46	Alaska	316
47	Delaware	0
47	Montana	0
47	New Hampshire	0
47	Oregon	0

District of Columbia 1,967

Source: CQ Press using data from U.S. Bureau of the Census, Governments Division
"2017 State and Local Government Finances" (https://www.census.gov/programs-surveys/gov-finances.html)
*Does not include special sales taxes such as those on sale of alcohol, gasoline, or tobacco.

State and Local Government General Retail Sales Tax Rates in 2019

National Median = 6.94 Percent*

ALPHA ORDER

RANK	STATE	PERCENT
5	Alabama	9.14
46	Alaska	1.43
11	Arizona	8.37
3	Arkansas	9.43
9	California	8.56
16	Colorado	7.63
33	Connecticut	6.35
47	Delaware	0.00
22	Florida	7.05
19	Georgia	7.29
45	Hawaii	4.41
37	Idaho	6.03
7	Illinois	8.74
23	Indiana	7.00
29	Iowa	6.82
8	Kansas	8.67
38	Kentucky	6.00
2	Louisiana	9.45
42	Maine	5.50
38	Maryland	6.00
35	Massachusetts	6.25
38	Michigan	6.00
17	Minnesota	7.43
21	Mississippi	7.07
14	Missouri	8.13
47	Montana	0.00
27	Nebraska	6.85
13	Nevada	8.14
47	New Hampshire	0.00
30	New Jersey	6.60
15	New Mexico	7.82
10	New York	8.49
25	North Carolina	6.97
27	North Dakota	6.85
20	Ohio	7.17
6	Oklahoma	8.92
47	Oregon	0.00
34	Pennsylvania	6.34
23	Rhode Island	7.00
17	South Carolina	7.43
31	South Dakota	6.40
1	Tennessee	9.47
12	Texas	8.19
26	Utah	6.94
36	Vermont	6.18
41	Virginia	5.65
4	Washington	9.17
32	West Virginia	6.39
43	Wisconsin	5.44
44	Wyoming	5.36

RANK ORDER

RANK	STATE	PERCENT
1	Tennessee	9.47
2	Louisiana	9.45
3	Arkansas	9.43
4	Washington	9.17
5	Alabama	9.14
6	Oklahoma	8.92
7	Illinois	8.74
8	Kansas	8.67
9	California	8.56
10	New York	8.49
11	Arizona	8.37
12	Texas	8.19
13	Nevada	8.14
14	Missouri	8.13
15	New Mexico	7.82
16	Colorado	7.63
17	Minnesota	7.43
17	South Carolina	7.43
19	Georgia	7.29
20	Ohio	7.17
21	Mississippi	7.07
22	Florida	7.05
23	Indiana	7.00
23	Rhode Island	7.00
25	North Carolina	6.97
26	Utah	6.94
27	Nebraska	6.85
27	North Dakota	6.85
29	Iowa	6.82
30	New Jersey	6.60
31	South Dakota	6.40
32	West Virginia	6.39
33	Connecticut	6.35
34	Pennsylvania	6.34
35	Massachusetts	6.25
36	Vermont	6.18
37	Idaho	6.03
38	Kentucky	6.00
38	Maryland	6.00
38	Michigan	6.00
41	Virginia	5.65
42	Maine	5.50
43	Wisconsin	5.44
44	Wyoming	5.36
45	Hawaii	4.41
46	Alaska	1.43
47	Delaware	0.00
47	Montana	0.00
47	New Hampshire	0.00
47	Oregon	0.00
	District of Columbia	6.00

Source: The Tax Foundation
    "State and Local Sales Tax Rates in 2019" (https://taxfoundation.org/sales-tax-rates-2019/)
*As of January 1, 2019. There are great differences on what states exempt from sales taxes. These rates are based on average local rates where local governments can set different tax rates.

State and Local Government Property Tax Revenue in 2017

National Total = $525,897,408,000

ALPHA ORDER

RANK	STATE	REVENUE	% of USA
37	Alabama	$2,836,712,000	0.5%
46	Alaska	1,568,497,000	0.3%
20	Arizona	7,748,009,000	1.5%
39	Arkansas	2,223,002,000	0.4%
1	California	63,305,785,000	12.0%
19	Colorado	8,660,564,000	1.6%
14	Connecticut	10,791,807,000	2.1%
50	Delaware	883,217,000	0.2%
6	Florida	27,898,256,000	5.3%
12	Georgia	12,089,659,000	2.3%
40	Hawaii	1,759,711,000	0.3%
41	Idaho	1,749,307,000	0.3%
5	Illinois	28,624,697,000	5.4%
21	Indiana	6,934,506,000	1.3%
26	Iowa	5,131,855,000	1.0%
27	Kansas	4,518,277,000	0.9%
31	Kentucky	3,701,559,000	0.7%
29	Louisiana	4,206,775,000	0.8%
36	Maine	2,854,444,000	0.5%
16	Maryland	9,778,344,000	1.9%
8	Massachusetts	16,703,135,000	3.2%
10	Michigan	14,121,953,000	2.7%
18	Minnesota	8,901,677,000	1.7%
33	Mississippi	3,040,524,000	0.6%
22	Missouri	6,348,472,000	1.2%
45	Montana	1,650,586,000	0.3%
30	Nebraska	3,752,183,000	0.7%
34	Nevada	3,007,466,000	0.6%
28	New Hampshire	4,464,178,000	0.8%
4	New Jersey	29,117,995,000	5.5%
44	New Mexico	1,657,728,000	0.3%
2	New York	56,853,460,000	10.8%
15	North Carolina	10,004,705,000	1.9%
48	North Dakota	1,249,091,000	0.2%
9	Ohio	15,345,259,000	2.9%
35	Oklahoma	2,872,432,000	0.5%
23	Oregon	6,165,880,000	1.2%
7	Pennsylvania	19,546,347,000	3.7%
38	Rhode Island	2,543,029,000	0.5%
24	South Carolina	6,031,636,000	1.1%
47	South Dakota	1,415,251,000	0.3%
25	Tennessee	5,876,313,000	1.1%
3	Texas	53,017,451,000	10.1%
32	Utah	3,219,441,000	0.6%
43	Vermont	1,667,338,000	0.3%
11	Virginia	13,987,458,000	2.7%
13	Washington	11,122,068,000	2.1%
42	West Virginia	1,721,936,000	0.3%
17	Wisconsin	9,586,292,000	1.8%
49	Wyoming	1,209,170,000	0.2%

RANK ORDER

RANK	STATE	REVENUE	% of USA
1	California	$63,305,785,000	12.0%
2	New York	56,853,460,000	10.8%
3	Texas	53,017,451,000	10.1%
4	New Jersey	29,117,995,000	5.5%
5	Illinois	28,624,697,000	5.4%
6	Florida	27,898,256,000	5.3%
7	Pennsylvania	19,546,347,000	3.7%
8	Massachusetts	16,703,135,000	3.2%
9	Ohio	15,345,259,000	2.9%
10	Michigan	14,121,953,000	2.7%
11	Virginia	13,987,458,000	2.7%
12	Georgia	12,089,659,000	2.3%
13	Washington	11,122,068,000	2.1%
14	Connecticut	10,791,807,000	2.1%
15	North Carolina	10,004,705,000	1.9%
16	Maryland	9,778,344,000	1.9%
17	Wisconsin	9,586,292,000	1.8%
18	Minnesota	8,901,677,000	1.7%
19	Colorado	8,660,564,000	1.6%
20	Arizona	7,748,009,000	1.5%
21	Indiana	6,934,506,000	1.3%
22	Missouri	6,348,472,000	1.2%
23	Oregon	6,165,880,000	1.2%
24	South Carolina	6,031,636,000	1.1%
25	Tennessee	5,876,313,000	1.1%
26	Iowa	5,131,855,000	1.0%
27	Kansas	4,518,277,000	0.9%
28	New Hampshire	4,464,178,000	0.8%
29	Louisiana	4,206,775,000	0.8%
30	Nebraska	3,752,183,000	0.7%
31	Kentucky	3,701,559,000	0.7%
32	Utah	3,219,441,000	0.6%
33	Mississippi	3,040,524,000	0.6%
34	Nevada	3,007,466,000	0.6%
35	Oklahoma	2,872,432,000	0.5%
36	Maine	2,854,444,000	0.5%
37	Alabama	2,836,712,000	0.5%
38	Rhode Island	2,543,029,000	0.5%
39	Arkansas	2,223,002,000	0.4%
40	Hawaii	1,759,711,000	0.3%
41	Idaho	1,749,307,000	0.3%
42	West Virginia	1,721,936,000	0.3%
43	Vermont	1,667,338,000	0.3%
44	New Mexico	1,657,728,000	0.3%
45	Montana	1,650,586,000	0.3%
46	Alaska	1,568,497,000	0.3%
47	South Dakota	1,415,251,000	0.3%
48	North Dakota	1,249,091,000	0.2%
49	Wyoming	1,209,170,000	0.2%
50	Delaware	883,217,000	0.2%
	District of Columbia	2,431,971,000	0.5%

Source: U.S. Bureau of the Census, Governments Division
"2017 State and Local Government Finances" (https://www.census.gov/programs-surveys/gov-finances.html)

Per Capita State and Local Government Property Tax Revenue in 2017

National Per Capita = $1,617

ALPHA ORDER

RANK	STATE	PER CAPITA
50	Alabama	$582
10	Alaska	2,120
34	Arizona	1,099
48	Arkansas	740
20	California	1,607
24	Colorado	1,542
3	Connecticut	3,020
43	Delaware	923
29	Florida	1,330
33	Georgia	1,161
31	Hawaii	1,236
38	Idaho	1,018
8	Illinois	2,239
35	Indiana	1,041
17	Iowa	1,632
23	Kansas	1,552
46	Kentucky	831
44	Louisiana	901
9	Maine	2,138
18	Maryland	1,623
6	Massachusetts	2,434
28	Michigan	1,416
21	Minnesota	1,599
39	Mississippi	1,017
36	Missouri	1,039
22	Montana	1,567
12	Nebraska	1,957
40	Nevada	1,012
1	New Hampshire	3,307
2	New Jersey	3,276
47	New Mexico	792
4	New York	2,902
41	North Carolina	974
15	North Dakota	1,654
30	Ohio	1,316
49	Oklahoma	730
27	Oregon	1,487
25	Pennsylvania	1,528
7	Rhode Island	2,407
32	South Carolina	1,201
19	South Dakota	1,621
45	Tennessee	876
13	Texas	1,872
37	Utah	1,037
5	Vermont	2,670
16	Virginia	1,652
26	Washington	1,498
42	West Virginia	948
14	Wisconsin	1,655
11	Wyoming	2,089

RANK ORDER

RANK	STATE	PER CAPITA
1	New Hampshire	$3,307
2	New Jersey	3,276
3	Connecticut	3,020
4	New York	2,902
5	Vermont	2,670
6	Massachusetts	2,434
7	Rhode Island	2,407
8	Illinois	2,239
9	Maine	2,138
10	Alaska	2,120
11	Wyoming	2,089
12	Nebraska	1,957
13	Texas	1,872
14	Wisconsin	1,655
15	North Dakota	1,654
16	Virginia	1,652
17	Iowa	1,632
18	Maryland	1,623
19	South Dakota	1,621
20	California	1,607
21	Minnesota	1,599
22	Montana	1,567
23	Kansas	1,552
24	Colorado	1,542
25	Pennsylvania	1,528
26	Washington	1,498
27	Oregon	1,487
28	Michigan	1,416
29	Florida	1,330
30	Ohio	1,316
31	Hawaii	1,236
32	South Carolina	1,201
33	Georgia	1,161
34	Arizona	1,099
35	Indiana	1,041
36	Missouri	1,039
37	Utah	1,037
38	Idaho	1,018
39	Mississippi	1,017
40	Nevada	1,012
41	North Carolina	974
42	West Virginia	948
43	Delaware	923
44	Louisiana	901
45	Tennessee	876
46	Kentucky	831
47	New Mexico	792
48	Arkansas	740
49	Oklahoma	730
50	Alabama	582
	District of Columbia	3,496

Source: CQ Press using data from U.S. Bureau of the Census, Governments Division
"2017 State and Local Government Finances" (https://www.census.gov/programs-surveys/gov-finances.html)

State and Local Government Property Tax as a Percent of State and Local Government Total Revenue in 2017
National Percent = 13.4%

<table>
<tr><td colspan="3">ALPHA ORDER</td><td colspan="3">RANK ORDER</td></tr>
<tr><td>RANK</td><td>STATE</td><td>PERCENT</td><td>RANK</td><td>STATE</td><td>PERCENT</td></tr>
<tr><td>50</td><td>Alabama</td><td>5.7</td><td>1</td><td>New Hampshire</td><td>31.8</td></tr>
<tr><td>31</td><td>Alaska</td><td>11.0</td><td>2</td><td>New Jersey</td><td>24.9</td></tr>
<tr><td>26</td><td>Arizona</td><td>11.8</td><td>3</td><td>Connecticut</td><td>21.8</td></tr>
<tr><td>48</td><td>Arkansas</td><td>7.1</td><td>4</td><td>Vermont</td><td>20.3</td></tr>
<tr><td>36</td><td>California</td><td>10.2</td><td>5</td><td>Maine</td><td>19.8</td></tr>
<tr><td>16</td><td>Colorado</td><td>14.0</td><td>5</td><td>Rhode Island</td><td>19.8</td></tr>
<tr><td>3</td><td>Connecticut</td><td>21.8</td><td>7</td><td>Illinois</td><td>19.2</td></tr>
<tr><td>47</td><td>Delaware</td><td>7.4</td><td>8</td><td>Texas</td><td>19.1</td></tr>
<tr><td>15</td><td>Florida</td><td>14.5</td><td>9</td><td>Massachusetts</td><td>17.5</td></tr>
<tr><td>20</td><td>Georgia</td><td>13.2</td><td>10</td><td>South Dakota</td><td>15.4</td></tr>
<tr><td>42</td><td>Hawaii</td><td>8.6</td><td>11</td><td>Nebraska</td><td>15.3</td></tr>
<tr><td>29</td><td>Idaho</td><td>11.2</td><td>12</td><td>Virginia</td><td>15.2</td></tr>
<tr><td>7</td><td>Illinois</td><td>19.2</td><td>13</td><td>New York</td><td>14.9</td></tr>
<tr><td>32</td><td>Indiana</td><td>10.9</td><td>14</td><td>Wisconsin</td><td>14.7</td></tr>
<tr><td>21</td><td>Iowa</td><td>13.1</td><td>15</td><td>Florida</td><td>14.5</td></tr>
<tr><td>16</td><td>Kansas</td><td>14.0</td><td>16</td><td>Colorado</td><td>14.0</td></tr>
<tr><td>44</td><td>Kentucky</td><td>8.3</td><td>16</td><td>Kansas</td><td>14.0</td></tr>
<tr><td>45</td><td>Louisiana</td><td>8.0</td><td>16</td><td>Montana</td><td>14.0</td></tr>
<tr><td>5</td><td>Maine</td><td>19.8</td><td>19</td><td>Maryland</td><td>13.4</td></tr>
<tr><td>19</td><td>Maryland</td><td>13.4</td><td>20</td><td>Georgia</td><td>13.2</td></tr>
<tr><td>9</td><td>Massachusetts</td><td>17.5</td><td>21</td><td>Iowa</td><td>13.1</td></tr>
<tr><td>23</td><td>Michigan</td><td>12.8</td><td>21</td><td>Pennsylvania</td><td>13.1</td></tr>
<tr><td>25</td><td>Minnesota</td><td>12.1</td><td>23</td><td>Michigan</td><td>12.8</td></tr>
<tr><td>39</td><td>Mississippi</td><td>9.4</td><td>24</td><td>Wyoming</td><td>12.4</td></tr>
<tr><td>35</td><td>Missouri</td><td>10.3</td><td>25</td><td>Minnesota</td><td>12.1</td></tr>
<tr><td>16</td><td>Montana</td><td>14.0</td><td>26</td><td>Arizona</td><td>11.8</td></tr>
<tr><td>11</td><td>Nebraska</td><td>15.3</td><td>27</td><td>South Carolina</td><td>11.6</td></tr>
<tr><td>39</td><td>Nevada</td><td>9.4</td><td>28</td><td>North Dakota</td><td>11.5</td></tr>
<tr><td>1</td><td>New Hampshire</td><td>31.8</td><td>29</td><td>Idaho</td><td>11.2</td></tr>
<tr><td>2</td><td>New Jersey</td><td>24.9</td><td>30</td><td>Washington</td><td>11.1</td></tr>
<tr><td>49</td><td>New Mexico</td><td>6.2</td><td>31</td><td>Alaska</td><td>11.0</td></tr>
<tr><td>13</td><td>New York</td><td>14.9</td><td>32</td><td>Indiana</td><td>10.9</td></tr>
<tr><td>38</td><td>North Carolina</td><td>9.7</td><td>33</td><td>Ohio</td><td>10.8</td></tr>
<tr><td>28</td><td>North Dakota</td><td>11.5</td><td>34</td><td>Oregon</td><td>10.6</td></tr>
<tr><td>33</td><td>Ohio</td><td>10.8</td><td>35</td><td>Missouri</td><td>10.3</td></tr>
<tr><td>46</td><td>Oklahoma</td><td>7.6</td><td>36</td><td>California</td><td>10.2</td></tr>
<tr><td>34</td><td>Oregon</td><td>10.6</td><td>37</td><td>Utah</td><td>9.8</td></tr>
<tr><td>21</td><td>Pennsylvania</td><td>13.1</td><td>38</td><td>North Carolina</td><td>9.7</td></tr>
<tr><td>5</td><td>Rhode Island</td><td>19.8</td><td>39</td><td>Mississippi</td><td>9.4</td></tr>
<tr><td>27</td><td>South Carolina</td><td>11.6</td><td>39</td><td>Nevada</td><td>9.4</td></tr>
<tr><td>10</td><td>South Dakota</td><td>15.4</td><td>39</td><td>Tennessee</td><td>9.4</td></tr>
<tr><td>39</td><td>Tennessee</td><td>9.4</td><td>42</td><td>Hawaii</td><td>8.6</td></tr>
<tr><td>8</td><td>Texas</td><td>19.1</td><td>43</td><td>West Virginia</td><td>8.5</td></tr>
<tr><td>37</td><td>Utah</td><td>9.8</td><td>44</td><td>Kentucky</td><td>8.3</td></tr>
<tr><td>4</td><td>Vermont</td><td>20.3</td><td>45</td><td>Louisiana</td><td>8.0</td></tr>
<tr><td>12</td><td>Virginia</td><td>15.2</td><td>46</td><td>Oklahoma</td><td>7.6</td></tr>
<tr><td>30</td><td>Washington</td><td>11.1</td><td>47</td><td>Delaware</td><td>7.4</td></tr>
<tr><td>43</td><td>West Virginia</td><td>8.5</td><td>48</td><td>Arkansas</td><td>7.1</td></tr>
<tr><td>14</td><td>Wisconsin</td><td>14.7</td><td>49</td><td>New Mexico</td><td>6.2</td></tr>
<tr><td>24</td><td>Wyoming</td><td>12.4</td><td>50</td><td>Alabama</td><td>5.7</td></tr>
<tr><td></td><td></td><td></td><td></td><td>District of Columbia</td><td>15.4</td></tr>
</table>

Source: CQ Press using data from U.S. Bureau of the Census, Governments Division
   "2017 State and Local Government Finances" (https://www.census.gov/programs-surveys/gov-finances.html)

State and Local Government Property Tax Revenue as a Percent of State and Local Government Own Source Revenue in 2017
National Percent = 21.9%*

ALPHA ORDER

RANK	STATE	PERCENT
50	Alabama	9.8
26	Alaska	19.3
17	Arizona	21.9
45	Arkansas	12.7
33	California	17.9
22	Colorado	20.6
4	Connecticut	32.9
48	Delaware	11.6
15	Florida	22.5
18	Georgia	21.4
47	Hawaii	12.5
30	Idaho	18.6
7	Illinois	29.9
36	Indiana	17.2
24	Iowa	20.1
23	Kansas	20.2
42	Kentucky	14.7
44	Louisiana	14.4
6	Maine	31.1
24	Maryland	20.1
10	Massachusetts	27.7
18	Michigan	21.4
27	Minnesota	19.0
37	Mississippi	17.0
34	Missouri	17.8
9	Montana	27.9
11	Nebraska	26.4
39	Nevada	16.5
1	New Hampshire	48.9
2	New Jersey	36.1
48	New Mexico	11.6
13	New York	24.5
40	North Carolina	15.4
35	North Dakota	17.3
28	Ohio	18.9
45	Oklahoma	12.7
29	Oregon	18.7
21	Pennsylvania	21.1
5	Rhode Island	31.2
31	South Carolina	18.3
12	South Dakota	26.2
37	Tennessee	17.0
7	Texas	29.9
42	Utah	14.7
3	Vermont	33.2
15	Virginia	22.5
32	Washington	18.2
41	West Virginia	15.0
14	Wisconsin	23.4
18	Wyoming	21.4

RANK ORDER

RANK	STATE	PERCENT
1	New Hampshire	48.9
2	New Jersey	36.1
3	Vermont	33.2
4	Connecticut	32.9
5	Rhode Island	31.2
6	Maine	31.1
7	Illinois	29.9
7	Texas	29.9
9	Montana	27.9
10	Massachusetts	27.7
11	Nebraska	26.4
12	South Dakota	26.2
13	New York	24.5
14	Wisconsin	23.4
15	Florida	22.5
15	Virginia	22.5
17	Arizona	21.9
18	Georgia	21.4
18	Michigan	21.4
18	Wyoming	21.4
21	Pennsylvania	21.1
22	Colorado	20.6
23	Kansas	20.2
24	Iowa	20.1
24	Maryland	20.1
26	Alaska	19.3
27	Minnesota	19.0
28	Ohio	18.9
29	Oregon	18.7
30	Idaho	18.6
31	South Carolina	18.3
32	Washington	18.2
33	California	17.9
34	Missouri	17.8
35	North Dakota	17.3
36	Indiana	17.2
37	Mississippi	17.0
37	Tennessee	17.0
39	Nevada	16.5
40	North Carolina	15.4
41	West Virginia	15.0
42	Kentucky	14.7
42	Utah	14.7
44	Louisiana	14.4
45	Arkansas	12.7
45	Oklahoma	12.7
47	Hawaii	12.5
48	Delaware	11.6
48	New Mexico	11.6
50	Alabama	9.8
	District of Columbia	27.0

Source: CQ Press using data from U.S. Bureau of the Census, Governments Division
"2017 State and Local Government Finances" (https://www.census.gov/programs-surveys/gov-finances.html)
*Own source revenue includes taxes, current charges, and miscellaneous general revenue. Excluded are intergovernmental transfers, insurance trust revenue, and revenue from government-owned utilities and other commercial or auxiliary enterprise.

State and Local Tax Burden as a Percent of Income in 2017

National Percent = 8.8% of Income*

<table>
<tr><td colspan="3">ALPHA ORDER</td><td colspan="3">RANK ORDER</td></tr>
<tr><td>RANK</td><td>STATE</td><td>PERCENT</td><td>RANK</td><td>STATE</td><td>PERCENT</td></tr>
<tr><td>42</td><td>Alabama</td><td>7.4</td><td>1</td><td>New York</td><td>12.2</td></tr>
<tr><td>50</td><td>Alaska</td><td>5.2</td><td>2</td><td>Hawaii</td><td>11.4</td></tr>
<tr><td>38</td><td>Arizona</td><td>7.8</td><td>3</td><td>Vermont</td><td>10.7</td></tr>
<tr><td>19</td><td>Arkansas</td><td>8.9</td><td>4</td><td>Maine</td><td>10.6</td></tr>
<tr><td>13</td><td>California</td><td>9.2</td><td>5</td><td>Minnesota</td><td>10.1</td></tr>
<tr><td>27</td><td>Colorado</td><td>8.3</td><td>6</td><td>Connecticut</td><td>9.9</td></tr>
<tr><td>6</td><td>Connecticut</td><td>9.9</td><td>6</td><td>Rhode Island</td><td>9.9</td></tr>
<tr><td>49</td><td>Delaware</td><td>5.6</td><td>8</td><td>New Jersey</td><td>9.8</td></tr>
<tr><td>46</td><td>Florida</td><td>6.7</td><td>9</td><td>Illinois</td><td>9.7</td></tr>
<tr><td>33</td><td>Georgia</td><td>8.0</td><td>10</td><td>Maryland</td><td>9.5</td></tr>
<tr><td>2</td><td>Hawaii</td><td>11.4</td><td>10</td><td>Ohio</td><td>9.5</td></tr>
<tr><td>36</td><td>Idaho</td><td>7.9</td><td>12</td><td>Iowa</td><td>9.4</td></tr>
<tr><td>9</td><td>Illinois</td><td>9.7</td><td>13</td><td>California</td><td>9.2</td></tr>
<tr><td>33</td><td>Indiana</td><td>8.0</td><td>13</td><td>Mississippi</td><td>9.2</td></tr>
<tr><td>12</td><td>Iowa</td><td>9.4</td><td>13</td><td>Nebraska</td><td>9.2</td></tr>
<tr><td>20</td><td>Kansas</td><td>8.8</td><td>16</td><td>Louisiana</td><td>9.1</td></tr>
<tr><td>22</td><td>Kentucky</td><td>8.7</td><td>16</td><td>West Virginia</td><td>9.1</td></tr>
<tr><td>16</td><td>Louisiana</td><td>9.1</td><td>16</td><td>Wisconsin</td><td>9.1</td></tr>
<tr><td>4</td><td>Maine</td><td>10.6</td><td>19</td><td>Arkansas</td><td>8.9</td></tr>
<tr><td>10</td><td>Maryland</td><td>9.5</td><td>20</td><td>Kansas</td><td>8.8</td></tr>
<tr><td>22</td><td>Massachusetts</td><td>8.7</td><td>20</td><td>New Mexico</td><td>8.8</td></tr>
<tr><td>27</td><td>Michigan</td><td>8.3</td><td>22</td><td>Kentucky</td><td>8.7</td></tr>
<tr><td>5</td><td>Minnesota</td><td>10.1</td><td>22</td><td>Massachusetts</td><td>8.7</td></tr>
<tr><td>13</td><td>Mississippi</td><td>9.2</td><td>22</td><td>Utah</td><td>8.7</td></tr>
<tr><td>38</td><td>Missouri</td><td>7.8</td><td>25</td><td>Pennsylvania</td><td>8.5</td></tr>
<tr><td>43</td><td>Montana</td><td>7.2</td><td>26</td><td>Oregon</td><td>8.4</td></tr>
<tr><td>13</td><td>Nebraska</td><td>9.2</td><td>27</td><td>Colorado</td><td>8.3</td></tr>
<tr><td>27</td><td>Nevada</td><td>8.3</td><td>27</td><td>Michigan</td><td>8.3</td></tr>
<tr><td>45</td><td>New Hampshire</td><td>7.0</td><td>27</td><td>Nevada</td><td>8.3</td></tr>
<tr><td>8</td><td>New Jersey</td><td>9.8</td><td>27</td><td>Washington</td><td>8.3</td></tr>
<tr><td>20</td><td>New Mexico</td><td>8.8</td><td>31</td><td>North Carolina</td><td>8.2</td></tr>
<tr><td>1</td><td>New York</td><td>12.2</td><td>32</td><td>Texas</td><td>8.1</td></tr>
<tr><td>31</td><td>North Carolina</td><td>8.2</td><td>33</td><td>Georgia</td><td>8.0</td></tr>
<tr><td>33</td><td>North Dakota</td><td>8.0</td><td>33</td><td>Indiana</td><td>8.0</td></tr>
<tr><td>10</td><td>Ohio</td><td>9.5</td><td>33</td><td>North Dakota</td><td>8.0</td></tr>
<tr><td>44</td><td>Oklahoma</td><td>7.1</td><td>36</td><td>Idaho</td><td>7.9</td></tr>
<tr><td>26</td><td>Oregon</td><td>8.4</td><td>36</td><td>Virginia</td><td>7.9</td></tr>
<tr><td>25</td><td>Pennsylvania</td><td>8.5</td><td>38</td><td>Arizona</td><td>7.8</td></tr>
<tr><td>6</td><td>Rhode Island</td><td>9.9</td><td>38</td><td>Missouri</td><td>7.8</td></tr>
<tr><td>41</td><td>South Carolina</td><td>7.5</td><td>40</td><td>South Dakota</td><td>7.7</td></tr>
<tr><td>40</td><td>South Dakota</td><td>7.7</td><td>41</td><td>South Carolina</td><td>7.5</td></tr>
<tr><td>48</td><td>Tennessee</td><td>6.2</td><td>42</td><td>Alabama</td><td>7.4</td></tr>
<tr><td>32</td><td>Texas</td><td>8.1</td><td>43</td><td>Montana</td><td>7.2</td></tr>
<tr><td>22</td><td>Utah</td><td>8.7</td><td>44</td><td>Oklahoma</td><td>7.1</td></tr>
<tr><td>3</td><td>Vermont</td><td>10.7</td><td>45</td><td>New Hampshire</td><td>7.0</td></tr>
<tr><td>36</td><td>Virginia</td><td>7.9</td><td>46</td><td>Florida</td><td>6.7</td></tr>
<tr><td>27</td><td>Washington</td><td>8.3</td><td>47</td><td>Wyoming</td><td>6.3</td></tr>
<tr><td>16</td><td>West Virginia</td><td>9.1</td><td>48</td><td>Tennessee</td><td>6.2</td></tr>
<tr><td>16</td><td>Wisconsin</td><td>9.1</td><td>49</td><td>Delaware</td><td>5.6</td></tr>
<tr><td>47</td><td>Wyoming</td><td>6.3</td><td>50</td><td>Alaska</td><td>5.2</td></tr>
<tr><td></td><td></td><td></td><td></td><td>District of Columbia</td><td>11.3</td></tr>
</table>

Source: CQ Press using data from U.S. Bureau of the Census, Governments Division
"Annual State Personal Income" (http://www.bea.gov/iTable/index_regional.cfm) and
"2017 State and Local Government Finances" (https://www.census.gov/programs-surveys/gov-finances.html)
*Calculated using property taxes, personal income taxes, and sales and gross receipts taxes.

State and Local Government Total Expenditures in 2017

National Total = $3,663,325,116,000*

ALPHA ORDER

RANK	STATE	EXPENDITURES	% of USA
26	Alabama	$48,692,526,000	1.3%
40	Alaska	14,928,952,000	0.4%
19	Arizona	60,174,093,000	1.6%
34	Arkansas	28,105,838,000	0.8%
1	California	567,343,727,000	15.5%
18	Colorado	60,531,135,000	1.7%
28	Connecticut	40,976,426,000	1.1%
45	Delaware	12,109,134,000	0.3%
4	Florida	176,598,452,000	4.8%
13	Georgia	85,066,181,000	2.3%
39	Hawaii	16,781,210,000	0.5%
41	Idaho	13,177,791,000	0.4%
6	Illinois	146,789,851,000	4.0%
21	Indiana	58,878,776,000	1.6%
29	Iowa	35,455,963,000	1.0%
31	Kansas	30,533,889,000	0.8%
27	Kentucky	46,111,714,000	1.3%
25	Louisiana	48,863,935,000	1.3%
42	Maine	12,814,776,000	0.3%
15	Maryland	69,565,402,000	1.9%
10	Massachusetts	93,242,336,000	2.5%
9	Michigan	98,285,404,000	2.7%
16	Minnesota	68,638,086,000	1.9%
33	Mississippi	30,079,872,000	0.8%
22	Missouri	55,153,612,000	1.5%
46	Montana	10,864,883,000	0.3%
37	Nebraska	23,154,831,000	0.6%
35	Nevada	26,115,984,000	0.7%
43	New Hampshire	12,624,760,000	0.3%
8	New Jersey	109,629,964,000	3.0%
36	New Mexico	24,759,625,000	0.7%
2	New York	348,338,956,000	9.5%
12	North Carolina	90,356,387,000	2.5%
47	North Dakota	10,807,047,000	0.3%
7	Ohio	129,747,826,000	3.5%
30	Oklahoma	34,808,426,000	1.0%
23	Oregon	53,552,014,000	1.5%
5	Pennsylvania	151,238,591,000	4.1%
44	Rhode Island	12,501,578,000	0.3%
24	South Carolina	50,527,476,000	1.4%
49	South Dakota	8,154,847,000	0.2%
20	Tennessee	59,618,172,000	1.6%
3	Texas	265,101,203,000	7.2%
32	Utah	30,316,925,000	0.8%
50	Vermont	8,113,644,000	0.2%
14	Virginia	84,098,159,000	2.3%
11	Washington	91,749,601,000	2.5%
38	West Virginia	18,192,840,000	0.5%
17	Wisconsin	62,264,296,000	1.7%
48	Wyoming	10,231,244,000	0.3%

RANK ORDER

RANK	STATE	EXPENDITURES	% of USA
1	California	$567,343,727,000	15.5%
2	New York	348,338,956,000	9.5%
3	Texas	265,101,203,000	7.2%
4	Florida	176,598,452,000	4.8%
5	Pennsylvania	151,238,591,000	4.1%
6	Illinois	146,789,851,000	4.0%
7	Ohio	129,747,826,000	3.5%
8	New Jersey	109,629,964,000	3.0%
9	Michigan	98,285,404,000	2.7%
10	Massachusetts	93,242,336,000	2.5%
11	Washington	91,749,601,000	2.5%
12	North Carolina	90,356,387,000	2.5%
13	Georgia	85,066,181,000	2.3%
14	Virginia	84,098,159,000	2.3%
15	Maryland	69,565,402,000	1.9%
16	Minnesota	68,638,086,000	1.9%
17	Wisconsin	62,264,296,000	1.7%
18	Colorado	60,531,135,000	1.7%
19	Arizona	60,174,093,000	1.6%
20	Tennessee	59,618,172,000	1.6%
21	Indiana	58,878,776,000	1.6%
22	Missouri	55,153,612,000	1.5%
23	Oregon	53,552,014,000	1.5%
24	South Carolina	50,527,476,000	1.4%
25	Louisiana	48,863,935,000	1.3%
26	Alabama	48,692,526,000	1.3%
27	Kentucky	46,111,714,000	1.3%
28	Connecticut	40,976,426,000	1.1%
29	Iowa	35,455,963,000	1.0%
30	Oklahoma	34,808,426,000	1.0%
31	Kansas	30,533,889,000	0.8%
32	Utah	30,316,925,000	0.8%
33	Mississippi	30,079,872,000	0.8%
34	Arkansas	28,105,838,000	0.8%
35	Nevada	26,115,984,000	0.7%
36	New Mexico	24,759,625,000	0.7%
37	Nebraska	23,154,831,000	0.6%
38	West Virginia	18,192,840,000	0.5%
39	Hawaii	16,781,210,000	0.5%
40	Alaska	14,928,952,000	0.4%
41	Idaho	13,177,791,000	0.4%
42	Maine	12,814,776,000	0.3%
43	New Hampshire	12,624,760,000	0.3%
44	Rhode Island	12,501,578,000	0.3%
45	Delaware	12,109,134,000	0.3%
46	Montana	10,864,883,000	0.3%
47	North Dakota	10,807,047,000	0.3%
48	Wyoming	10,231,244,000	0.3%
49	South Dakota	8,154,847,000	0.2%
50	Vermont	8,113,644,000	0.2%
	District of Columbia	17,556,756,000	0.5%

Source: U.S. Bureau of the Census, Governments Division
   "2017 State and Local Government Finances" (https://www.census.gov/programs-surveys/gov-finances.html)
*Total expenditures includes all money paid other than for retirement of debt and extension of loans. Includes payments from all sources of funds including current revenues and proceeds from borrowing and prior year fund balances. Includes intergovernmental transfers and expenditures for government-owned utilities and other commercial or auxiliary enterprise, and insurance trust expenditures.

Per Capita State and Local Government Total Expenditures in 2017

National Per Capita = $11,267*

ALPHA ORDER

RANK	STATE	PER CAPITA
32	Alabama	$9,988
1	Alaska	20,180
47	Arizona	8,537
38	Arkansas	9,359
4	California	14,400
23	Colorado	10,779
20	Connecticut	11,466
9	Delaware	12,652
48	Florida	8,419
49	Georgia	8,169
17	Hawaii	11,783
50	Idaho	7,666
19	Illinois	11,480
44	Indiana	8,841
21	Iowa	11,279
25	Kansas	10,490
27	Kentucky	10,353
26	Louisiana	10,462
36	Maine	9,599
18	Maryland	11,546
6	Massachusetts	13,586
34	Michigan	9,852
12	Minnesota	12,327
30	Mississippi	10,061
41	Missouri	9,029
28	Montana	10,317
13	Nebraska	12,075
46	Nevada	8,786
39	New Hampshire	9,353
11	New Jersey	12,334
15	New Mexico	11,827
2	New York	17,781
45	North Carolina	8,797
5	North Dakota	14,311
22	Ohio	11,124
43	Oklahoma	8,851
8	Oregon	12,915
16	Pennsylvania	11,824
14	Rhode Island	11,833
29	South Carolina	10,063
40	South Dakota	9,338
42	Tennessee	8,887
37	Texas	9,360
35	Utah	9,770
7	Vermont	12,992
33	Virginia	9,935
10	Washington	12,356
31	West Virginia	10,012
24	Wisconsin	10,750
3	Wyoming	17,673

RANK ORDER

RANK	STATE	PER CAPITA
1	Alaska	$20,180
2	New York	17,781
3	Wyoming	17,673
4	California	14,400
5	North Dakota	14,311
6	Massachusetts	13,586
7	Vermont	12,992
8	Oregon	12,915
9	Delaware	12,652
10	Washington	12,356
11	New Jersey	12,334
12	Minnesota	12,327
13	Nebraska	12,075
14	Rhode Island	11,833
15	New Mexico	11,827
16	Pennsylvania	11,824
17	Hawaii	11,783
18	Maryland	11,546
19	Illinois	11,480
20	Connecticut	11,466
21	Iowa	11,279
22	Ohio	11,124
23	Colorado	10,779
24	Wisconsin	10,750
25	Kansas	10,490
26	Louisiana	10,462
27	Kentucky	10,353
28	Montana	10,317
29	South Carolina	10,063
30	Mississippi	10,061
31	West Virginia	10,012
32	Alabama	9,988
33	Virginia	9,935
34	Michigan	9,852
35	Utah	9,770
36	Maine	9,599
37	Texas	9,360
38	Arkansas	9,359
39	New Hampshire	9,353
40	South Dakota	9,338
41	Missouri	9,029
42	Tennessee	8,887
43	Oklahoma	8,851
44	Indiana	8,841
45	North Carolina	8,797
46	Nevada	8,786
47	Arizona	8,537
48	Florida	8,419
49	Georgia	8,169
50	Idaho	7,666

District of Columbia 25,236

Source: CQ Press using data from U.S. Bureau of the Census, Governments Division
"2017 State and Local Government Finances" (https://www.census.gov/programs-surveys/gov-finances.html)
*Total expenditures includes all money paid other than for retirement of debt and extension of loans. Includes payments from all sources of funds including current revenues and proceeds from borrowing and prior year fund balances. Includes intergovernmental transfers and expenditures for government-owned utilities and other commercial or auxiliary enterprise, and insurance trust expenditures.

State and Local Government Direct General Expenditures in 2017

National Total = $3,072,175,501,000*

ALPHA ORDER

RANK	STATE	EXPENDITURES	% of USA
26	Alabama	$41,514,553,000	1.4%
40	Alaska	12,724,374,000	0.4%
20	Arizona	49,838,117,000	1.6%
34	Arkansas	25,094,715,000	0.8%
1	California	455,532,277,000	14.8%
19	Colorado	50,019,941,000	1.6%
28	Connecticut	33,915,839,000	1.1%
44	Delaware	10,794,468,000	0.4%
4	Florida	153,537,929,000	5.0%
14	Georgia	71,489,147,000	2.3%
39	Hawaii	14,003,915,000	0.5%
41	Idaho	11,629,994,000	0.4%
6	Illinois	117,171,254,000	3.8%
18	Indiana	53,244,348,000	1.7%
29	Iowa	31,323,136,000	1.0%
31	Kansas	26,908,423,000	0.9%
27	Kentucky	39,402,165,000	1.3%
25	Louisiana	42,601,795,000	1.4%
42	Maine	11,607,029,000	0.4%
15	Maryland	60,454,952,000	2.0%
11	Massachusetts	77,985,102,000	2.5%
9	Michigan	84,594,013,000	2.8%
16	Minnesota	59,331,515,000	1.9%
32	Mississippi	26,196,420,000	0.9%
21	Missouri	46,786,258,000	1.5%
47	Montana	9,479,994,000	0.3%
37	Nebraska	17,595,636,000	0.6%
35	Nevada	21,965,647,000	0.7%
43	New Hampshire	11,073,023,000	0.4%
8	New Jersey	91,943,861,000	3.0%
36	New Mexico	21,507,245,000	0.7%
2	New York	282,775,814,000	9.2%
10	North Carolina	78,557,628,000	2.6%
46	North Dakota	9,655,584,000	0.3%
7	Ohio	107,900,984,000	3.5%
30	Oklahoma	29,273,829,000	1.0%
23	Oregon	44,875,473,000	1.5%
5	Pennsylvania	129,186,398,000	4.2%
45	Rhode Island	10,492,167,000	0.3%
24	South Carolina	43,360,492,000	1.4%
50	South Dakota	7,193,791,000	0.2%
22	Tennessee	46,661,808,000	1.5%
3	Texas	227,414,209,000	7.4%
33	Utah	26,018,405,000	0.8%
49	Vermont	7,351,242,000	0.2%
13	Virginia	73,731,720,000	2.4%
12	Washington	74,535,514,000	2.4%
38	West Virginia	16,110,014,000	0.5%
17	Wisconsin	53,678,263,000	1.7%
48	Wyoming	8,879,995,000	0.3%

RANK ORDER

RANK	STATE	EXPENDITURES	% of USA
1	California	$455,532,277,000	14.8%
2	New York	282,775,814,000	9.2%
3	Texas	227,414,209,000	7.4%
4	Florida	153,537,929,000	5.0%
5	Pennsylvania	129,186,398,000	4.2%
6	Illinois	117,171,254,000	3.8%
7	Ohio	107,900,984,000	3.5%
8	New Jersey	91,943,861,000	3.0%
9	Michigan	84,594,013,000	2.8%
10	North Carolina	78,557,628,000	2.6%
11	Massachusetts	77,985,102,000	2.5%
12	Washington	74,535,514,000	2.4%
13	Virginia	73,731,720,000	2.4%
14	Georgia	71,489,147,000	2.3%
15	Maryland	60,454,952,000	2.0%
16	Minnesota	59,331,515,000	1.9%
17	Wisconsin	53,678,263,000	1.7%
18	Indiana	53,244,348,000	1.7%
19	Colorado	50,019,941,000	1.6%
20	Arizona	49,838,117,000	1.6%
21	Missouri	46,786,258,000	1.5%
22	Tennessee	46,661,808,000	1.5%
23	Oregon	44,875,473,000	1.5%
24	South Carolina	43,360,492,000	1.4%
25	Louisiana	42,601,795,000	1.4%
26	Alabama	41,514,553,000	1.4%
27	Kentucky	39,402,165,000	1.3%
28	Connecticut	33,915,839,000	1.1%
29	Iowa	31,323,136,000	1.0%
30	Oklahoma	29,273,829,000	1.0%
31	Kansas	26,908,423,000	0.9%
32	Mississippi	26,196,420,000	0.9%
33	Utah	26,018,405,000	0.8%
34	Arkansas	25,094,715,000	0.8%
35	Nevada	21,965,647,000	0.7%
36	New Mexico	21,507,245,000	0.7%
37	Nebraska	17,595,636,000	0.6%
38	West Virginia	16,110,014,000	0.5%
39	Hawaii	14,003,915,000	0.5%
40	Alaska	12,724,374,000	0.4%
41	Idaho	11,629,994,000	0.4%
42	Maine	11,607,029,000	0.4%
43	New Hampshire	11,073,023,000	0.4%
44	Delaware	10,794,468,000	0.4%
45	Rhode Island	10,492,167,000	0.3%
46	North Dakota	9,655,584,000	0.3%
47	Montana	9,479,994,000	0.3%
48	Wyoming	8,879,995,000	0.3%
49	Vermont	7,351,242,000	0.2%
50	South Dakota	7,193,791,000	0.2%
	District of Columbia	13,255,086,000	0.4%

Source: U.S. Bureau of the Census, Governments Division
"2017 State and Local Government Finances" (https://www.census.gov/programs-surveys/gov-finances.html)
*Direct general expenditures include expenditures for current operations, assistance and subsidies, interest on debt, and capital outlay. Excludes intergovernmental transfers, expenditures for government-owned utilities and other commercial or auxiliary enterprise, and insurance trust expenditures.

Per Capita State and Local Government Direct General Expenditures in 2017

National Per Capita = $9,449*

ALPHA ORDER

RANK	STATE	PER CAPITA
34	Alabama	$8,516
1	Alaska	17,200
47	Arizona	7,070
37	Arkansas	8,357
6	California	11,562
27	Colorado	8,907
19	Connecticut	9,490
8	Delaware	11,279
46	Florida	7,319
49	Georgia	6,865
18	Hawaii	9,833
50	Idaho	6,766
24	Illinois	9,164
41	Indiana	7,995
16	Iowa	9,964
22	Kansas	9,245
29	Kentucky	8,847
25	Louisiana	9,121
32	Maine	8,694
15	Maryland	10,034
7	Massachusetts	11,363
35	Michigan	8,479
10	Minnesota	10,656
30	Mississippi	8,762
42	Missouri	7,659
26	Montana	9,002
23	Nebraska	9,176
45	Nevada	7,390
39	New Hampshire	8,204
11	New Jersey	10,344
12	New Mexico	10,274
3	New York	14,434
43	North Carolina	7,649
4	North Dakota	12,786
21	Ohio	9,251
44	Oklahoma	7,444
9	Oregon	10,822
13	Pennsylvania	10,100
17	Rhode Island	9,931
33	South Carolina	8,635
38	South Dakota	8,238
48	Tennessee	6,955
40	Texas	8,029
36	Utah	8,385
5	Vermont	11,771
31	Virginia	8,710
14	Washington	10,038
28	West Virginia	8,866
20	Wisconsin	9,268
2	Wyoming	15,339

RANK ORDER

RANK	STATE	PER CAPITA
1	Alaska	$17,200
2	Wyoming	15,339
3	New York	14,434
4	North Dakota	12,786
5	Vermont	11,771
6	California	11,562
7	Massachusetts	11,363
8	Delaware	11,279
9	Oregon	10,822
10	Minnesota	10,656
11	New Jersey	10,344
12	New Mexico	10,274
13	Pennsylvania	10,100
14	Washington	10,038
15	Maryland	10,034
16	Iowa	9,964
17	Rhode Island	9,931
18	Hawaii	9,833
19	Connecticut	9,490
20	Wisconsin	9,268
21	Ohio	9,251
22	Kansas	9,245
23	Nebraska	9,176
24	Illinois	9,164
25	Louisiana	9,121
26	Montana	9,002
27	Colorado	8,907
28	West Virginia	8,866
29	Kentucky	8,847
30	Mississippi	8,762
31	Virginia	8,710
32	Maine	8,694
33	South Carolina	8,635
34	Alabama	8,516
35	Michigan	8,479
36	Utah	8,385
37	Arkansas	8,357
38	South Dakota	8,238
39	New Hampshire	8,204
40	Texas	8,029
41	Indiana	7,995
42	Missouri	7,659
43	North Carolina	7,649
44	Oklahoma	7,444
45	Nevada	7,390
46	Florida	7,319
47	Arizona	7,070
48	Tennessee	6,955
49	Georgia	6,865
50	Idaho	6,766

District of Columbia   19,053

Source: CQ Press using data from U.S. Bureau of the Census, Governments Division
"2017 State and Local Government Finances" (https://www.census.gov/programs-surveys/gov-finances.html)
*Direct general expenditures include expenditures for current operations, assistance and subsidies, interest on debt, and capital outlay. Excludes intergovernmental transfers, expenditures for government-owned utilities and other commercial or auxiliary enterprise, and insurance trust expenditures.

State and Local Government Debt Outstanding in 2017

National Total = $3,061,321,574,000*

ALPHA ORDER

RANK	STATE	DEBT	% of USA
28	Alabama	$29,965,318,000	1.0%
42	Alaska	9,471,003,000	0.3%
21	Arizona	47,063,505,000	1.5%
34	Arkansas	16,388,275,000	0.5%
1	California	467,475,067,000	15.3%
14	Colorado	57,348,929,000	1.9%
17	Connecticut	49,997,944,000	1.6%
45	Delaware	7,066,094,000	0.2%
5	Florida	134,743,130,000	4.4%
13	Georgia	57,807,261,000	1.9%
35	Hawaii	15,999,412,000	0.5%
47	Idaho	6,052,123,000	0.2%
4	Illinois	154,922,155,000	5.1%
18	Indiana	47,706,425,000	1.6%
32	Iowa	19,373,165,000	0.6%
30	Kansas	27,171,656,000	0.9%
23	Kentucky	44,766,405,000	1.5%
26	Louisiana	36,318,464,000	1.2%
44	Maine	7,853,327,000	0.3%
15	Maryland	54,513,834,000	1.8%
7	Massachusetts	96,997,008,000	3.2%
11	Michigan	72,028,820,000	2.4%
16	Minnesota	53,015,555,000	1.7%
38	Mississippi	14,561,520,000	0.5%
20	Missouri	47,118,053,000	1.5%
48	Montana	5,323,571,000	0.2%
36	Nebraska	15,886,841,000	0.5%
29	Nevada	27,356,895,000	0.9%
41	New Hampshire	10,410,326,000	0.3%
8	New Jersey	96,990,209,000	3.2%
37	New Mexico	15,806,338,000	0.5%
2	New York	350,254,568,000	11.4%
19	North Carolina	47,295,872,000	1.5%
43	North Dakota	7,992,566,000	0.3%
10	Ohio	87,665,683,000	2.9%
33	Oklahoma	18,715,015,000	0.6%
27	Oregon	35,523,663,000	1.2%
6	Pennsylvania	122,858,890,000	4.0%
39	Rhode Island	11,615,749,000	0.4%
25	South Carolina	39,076,659,000	1.3%
46	South Dakota	6,247,113,000	0.2%
24	Tennessee	42,570,091,000	1.4%
3	Texas	289,647,724,000	9.5%
31	Utah	20,716,578,000	0.7%
49	Vermont	4,753,682,000	0.2%
12	Virginia	65,941,203,000	2.2%
9	Washington	88,568,439,000	2.9%
40	West Virginia	11,182,853,000	0.4%
22	Wisconsin	46,317,868,000	1.5%
50	Wyoming	1,977,648,000	0.1%

RANK ORDER

RANK	STATE	DEBT	% of USA
1	California	$467,475,067,000	15.3%
2	New York	350,254,568,000	11.4%
3	Texas	289,647,724,000	9.5%
4	Illinois	154,922,155,000	5.1%
5	Florida	134,743,130,000	4.4%
6	Pennsylvania	122,858,890,000	4.0%
7	Massachusetts	96,997,008,000	3.2%
8	New Jersey	96,990,209,000	3.2%
9	Washington	88,568,439,000	2.9%
10	Ohio	87,665,683,000	2.9%
11	Michigan	72,028,820,000	2.4%
12	Virginia	65,941,203,000	2.2%
13	Georgia	57,807,261,000	1.9%
14	Colorado	57,348,929,000	1.9%
15	Maryland	54,513,834,000	1.8%
16	Minnesota	53,015,555,000	1.7%
17	Connecticut	49,997,944,000	1.6%
18	Indiana	47,706,425,000	1.6%
19	North Carolina	47,295,872,000	1.5%
20	Missouri	47,118,053,000	1.5%
21	Arizona	47,063,505,000	1.5%
22	Wisconsin	46,317,868,000	1.5%
23	Kentucky	44,766,405,000	1.5%
24	Tennessee	42,570,091,000	1.4%
25	South Carolina	39,076,659,000	1.3%
26	Louisiana	36,318,464,000	1.2%
27	Oregon	35,523,663,000	1.2%
28	Alabama	29,965,318,000	1.0%
29	Nevada	27,356,895,000	0.9%
30	Kansas	27,171,656,000	0.9%
31	Utah	20,716,578,000	0.7%
32	Iowa	19,373,165,000	0.6%
33	Oklahoma	18,715,015,000	0.6%
34	Arkansas	16,388,275,000	0.5%
35	Hawaii	15,999,412,000	0.5%
36	Nebraska	15,886,841,000	0.5%
37	New Mexico	15,806,338,000	0.5%
38	Mississippi	14,561,520,000	0.5%
39	Rhode Island	11,615,749,000	0.4%
40	West Virginia	11,182,853,000	0.4%
41	New Hampshire	10,410,326,000	0.3%
42	Alaska	9,471,003,000	0.3%
43	North Dakota	7,992,566,000	0.3%
44	Maine	7,853,327,000	0.3%
45	Delaware	7,066,094,000	0.2%
46	South Dakota	6,247,113,000	0.2%
47	Idaho	6,052,123,000	0.2%
48	Montana	5,323,571,000	0.2%
49	Vermont	4,753,682,000	0.2%
50	Wyoming	1,977,648,000	0.1%
	District of Columbia	14,901,082,000	0.5%

Source: U.S. Bureau of the Census, Governments Division
"2017 State and Local Government Finances" (https://www.census.gov/programs-surveys/gov-finances.html)
*Includes short-term, long-term, full faith and credit, nonguaranteed, and public debt for private purposes.

Per Capita State and Local Government Debt Outstanding in 2017

National Per Capita = $9,415*

ALPHA ORDER

RANK	STATE	PER CAPITA
41	Alabama	$6,147
4	Alaska	12,802
35	Arizona	6,677
44	Arkansas	5,457
7	California	11,865
13	Colorado	10,212
3	Connecticut	13,990
31	Delaware	7,383
37	Florida	6,423
43	Georgia	5,551
8	Hawaii	11,234
49	Idaho	3,521
5	Illinois	12,116
33	Indiana	7,163
39	Iowa	6,163
17	Kansas	9,335
14	Kentucky	10,051
25	Louisiana	7,776
42	Maine	5,882
19	Maryland	9,048
2	Massachusetts	14,133
32	Michigan	7,220
16	Minnesota	9,521
46	Mississippi	4,871
26	Missouri	7,713
45	Montana	5,055
21	Nebraska	8,285
18	Nevada	9,204
26	New Hampshire	7,713
10	New Jersey	10,912
29	New Mexico	7,551
1	New York	17,879
48	North Carolina	4,605
11	North Dakota	10,584
30	Ohio	7,516
47	Oklahoma	4,759
20	Oregon	8,567
15	Pennsylvania	9,606
9	Rhode Island	10,995
24	South Carolina	7,782
34	South Dakota	7,154
38	Tennessee	6,345
12	Texas	10,227
36	Utah	6,676
28	Vermont	7,612
23	Virginia	7,790
6	Washington	11,928
40	West Virginia	6,154
22	Wisconsin	7,997
50	Wyoming	3,416

RANK ORDER

RANK	STATE	PER CAPITA
1	New York	$17,879
2	Massachusetts	14,133
3	Connecticut	13,990
4	Alaska	12,802
5	Illinois	12,116
6	Washington	11,928
7	California	11,865
8	Hawaii	11,234
9	Rhode Island	10,995
10	New Jersey	10,912
11	North Dakota	10,584
12	Texas	10,227
13	Colorado	10,212
14	Kentucky	10,051
15	Pennsylvania	9,606
16	Minnesota	9,521
17	Kansas	9,335
18	Nevada	9,204
19	Maryland	9,048
20	Oregon	8,567
21	Nebraska	8,285
22	Wisconsin	7,997
23	Virginia	7,790
24	South Carolina	7,782
25	Louisiana	7,776
26	Missouri	7,713
26	New Hampshire	7,713
28	Vermont	7,612
29	New Mexico	7,551
30	Ohio	7,516
31	Delaware	7,383
32	Michigan	7,220
33	Indiana	7,163
34	South Dakota	7,154
35	Arizona	6,677
36	Utah	6,676
37	Florida	6,423
38	Tennessee	6,345
39	Iowa	6,163
40	West Virginia	6,154
41	Alabama	6,147
42	Maine	5,882
43	Georgia	5,551
44	Arkansas	5,457
45	Montana	5,055
46	Mississippi	4,871
47	Oklahoma	4,759
48	North Carolina	4,605
49	Idaho	3,521
50	Wyoming	3,416
	District of Columbia	21,419

Source: CQ Press using data from U.S. Bureau of the Census, Governments Division
"2017 State and Local Government Finances" (https://www.census.gov/programs-surveys/gov-finances.html)
*Includes short-term, long-term, full faith and credit, nonguaranteed, and public debt for private purposes.

State and Local Government Full-Time Equivalent Employees in 2018

National Total = 16,650,724 FTE Employees*

ALPHA ORDER

RANK	STATE	EMPLOYEES	% of USA
22	Alabama	283,939	1.7%
44	Alaska	51,876	0.3%
23	Arizona	278,779	1.7%
33	Arkansas	169,448	1.0%
1	California	1,872,571	11.2%
20	Colorado	299,636	1.8%
32	Connecticut	184,556	1.1%
46	Delaware	49,350	0.3%
4	Florida	899,621	5.4%
9	Georgia	522,795	3.1%
40	Hawaii	74,946	0.5%
39	Idaho	85,544	0.5%
5	Illinois	616,092	3.7%
16	Indiana	331,556	2.0%
31	Iowa	186,348	1.1%
29	Kansas	202,356	1.2%
26	Kentucky	244,093	1.5%
25	Louisiana	258,038	1.5%
42	Maine	69,649	0.4%
18	Maryland	303,874	1.8%
14	Massachusetts	341,164	2.0%
12	Michigan	436,726	2.6%
19	Minnesota	302,615	1.8%
30	Mississippi	187,102	1.1%
17	Missouri	318,635	1.9%
43	Montana	57,186	0.3%
36	Nebraska	121,858	0.7%
37	Nevada	116,221	0.7%
41	New Hampshire	69,929	0.4%
10	New Jersey	473,729	2.8%
35	New Mexico	124,467	0.7%
3	New York	1,205,241	7.2%
7	North Carolina	570,987	3.4%
49	North Dakota	47,052	0.3%
6	Ohio	589,389	3.5%
27	Oklahoma	208,665	1.3%
28	Oregon	206,777	1.2%
8	Pennsylvania	559,999	3.4%
48	Rhode Island	47,904	0.3%
24	South Carolina	270,541	1.6%
47	South Dakota	48,043	0.3%
15	Tennessee	335,643	2.0%
2	Texas	1,510,225	9.1%
34	Utah	155,376	0.9%
50	Vermont	39,642	0.2%
11	Virginia	452,707	2.7%
13	Washington	380,179	2.3%
38	West Virginia	102,192	0.6%
21	Wisconsin	284,159	1.7%
45	Wyoming	50,162	0.3%

RANK ORDER

RANK	STATE	EMPLOYEES	% of USA
1	California	1,872,571	11.2%
2	Texas	1,510,225	9.1%
3	New York	1,205,241	7.2%
4	Florida	899,621	5.4%
5	Illinois	616,092	3.7%
6	Ohio	589,389	3.5%
7	North Carolina	570,987	3.4%
8	Pennsylvania	559,999	3.4%
9	Georgia	522,795	3.1%
10	New Jersey	473,729	2.8%
11	Virginia	452,707	2.7%
12	Michigan	436,726	2.6%
13	Washington	380,179	2.3%
14	Massachusetts	341,164	2.0%
15	Tennessee	335,643	2.0%
16	Indiana	331,556	2.0%
17	Missouri	318,635	1.9%
18	Maryland	303,874	1.8%
19	Minnesota	302,615	1.8%
20	Colorado	299,636	1.8%
21	Wisconsin	284,159	1.7%
22	Alabama	283,939	1.7%
23	Arizona	278,779	1.7%
24	South Carolina	270,541	1.6%
25	Louisiana	258,038	1.5%
26	Kentucky	244,093	1.5%
27	Oklahoma	208,665	1.3%
28	Oregon	206,777	1.2%
29	Kansas	202,356	1.2%
30	Mississippi	187,102	1.1%
31	Iowa	186,348	1.1%
32	Connecticut	184,556	1.1%
33	Arkansas	169,448	1.0%
34	Utah	155,376	0.9%
35	New Mexico	124,467	0.7%
36	Nebraska	121,858	0.7%
37	Nevada	116,221	0.7%
38	West Virginia	102,192	0.6%
39	Idaho	85,544	0.5%
40	Hawaii	74,946	0.5%
41	New Hampshire	69,929	0.4%
42	Maine	69,649	0.4%
43	Montana	57,186	0.3%
44	Alaska	51,876	0.3%
45	Wyoming	50,162	0.3%
46	Delaware	49,350	0.3%
47	South Dakota	48,043	0.3%
48	Rhode Island	47,904	0.3%
49	North Dakota	47,052	0.3%
50	Vermont	39,642	0.2%
	District of Columbia	51,142	0.3%

Source: U.S. Bureau of the Census, Governments Division
   "Annual Survey of Public Employment and Payroll" (https://www.census.gov/programs-surveys/apes.html)
*Full-time equivalent as of March 2018.

Rate of State and Local Government Full-Time Equivalent Employees in 2018

National Rate = 509 FTE Employees per 10,000 Population*

<table>
<tr><td colspan="3">ALPHA ORDER</td><td colspan="3">RANK ORDER</td></tr>
<tr><th>RANK</th><th>STATE</th><th>RATE</th><th>RANK</th><th>STATE</th><th>RATE</th></tr>
<tr><td>11</td><td>Alabama</td><td>581</td><td>1</td><td>Wyoming</td><td>868</td></tr>
<tr><td>2</td><td>Alaska</td><td>703</td><td>2</td><td>Alaska</td><td>703</td></tr>
<tr><td>49</td><td>Arizona</td><td>389</td><td>3</td><td>Kansas</td><td>695</td></tr>
<tr><td>13</td><td>Arkansas</td><td>562</td><td>4</td><td>Vermont</td><td>633</td></tr>
<tr><td>44</td><td>California</td><td>473</td><td>5</td><td>Nebraska</td><td>632</td></tr>
<tr><td>25</td><td>Colorado</td><td>526</td><td>6</td><td>Mississippi</td><td>626</td></tr>
<tr><td>29</td><td>Connecticut</td><td>517</td><td>7</td><td>North Dakota</td><td>619</td></tr>
<tr><td>31</td><td>Delaware</td><td>510</td><td>8</td><td>New York</td><td>617</td></tr>
<tr><td>48</td><td>Florida</td><td>422</td><td>9</td><td>New Mexico</td><td>594</td></tr>
<tr><td>35</td><td>Georgia</td><td>497</td><td>10</td><td>Iowa</td><td>590</td></tr>
<tr><td>24</td><td>Hawaii</td><td>528</td><td>11</td><td>Alabama</td><td>581</td></tr>
<tr><td>42</td><td>Idaho</td><td>488</td><td>12</td><td>West Virginia</td><td>566</td></tr>
<tr><td>43</td><td>Illinois</td><td>484</td><td>13</td><td>Arkansas</td><td>562</td></tr>
<tr><td>37</td><td>Indiana</td><td>495</td><td>14</td><td>Louisiana</td><td>554</td></tr>
<tr><td>10</td><td>Iowa</td><td>590</td><td>15</td><td>North Carolina</td><td>550</td></tr>
<tr><td>3</td><td>Kansas</td><td>695</td><td>16</td><td>Kentucky</td><td>546</td></tr>
<tr><td>16</td><td>Kentucky</td><td>546</td><td>17</td><td>South Dakota</td><td>545</td></tr>
<tr><td>14</td><td>Louisiana</td><td>554</td><td>18</td><td>Minnesota</td><td>539</td></tr>
<tr><td>27</td><td>Maine</td><td>520</td><td>19</td><td>Montana</td><td>538</td></tr>
<tr><td>34</td><td>Maryland</td><td>503</td><td>20</td><td>New Jersey</td><td>532</td></tr>
<tr><td>38</td><td>Massachusetts</td><td>494</td><td>20</td><td>South Carolina</td><td>532</td></tr>
<tr><td>46</td><td>Michigan</td><td>437</td><td>22</td><td>Virginia</td><td>531</td></tr>
<tr><td>18</td><td>Minnesota</td><td>539</td><td>23</td><td>Oklahoma</td><td>529</td></tr>
<tr><td>6</td><td>Mississippi</td><td>626</td><td>24</td><td>Hawaii</td><td>528</td></tr>
<tr><td>27</td><td>Missouri</td><td>520</td><td>25</td><td>Colorado</td><td>526</td></tr>
<tr><td>19</td><td>Montana</td><td>538</td><td>25</td><td>Texas</td><td>526</td></tr>
<tr><td>5</td><td>Nebraska</td><td>632</td><td>27</td><td>Maine</td><td>520</td></tr>
<tr><td>50</td><td>Nevada</td><td>383</td><td>27</td><td>Missouri</td><td>520</td></tr>
<tr><td>30</td><td>New Hampshire</td><td>516</td><td>29</td><td>Connecticut</td><td>517</td></tr>
<tr><td>20</td><td>New Jersey</td><td>532</td><td>30</td><td>New Hampshire</td><td>516</td></tr>
<tr><td>9</td><td>New Mexico</td><td>594</td><td>31</td><td>Delaware</td><td>510</td></tr>
<tr><td>8</td><td>New York</td><td>617</td><td>32</td><td>Washington</td><td>505</td></tr>
<tr><td>15</td><td>North Carolina</td><td>550</td><td>33</td><td>Ohio</td><td>504</td></tr>
<tr><td>7</td><td>North Dakota</td><td>619</td><td>34</td><td>Maryland</td><td>503</td></tr>
<tr><td>33</td><td>Ohio</td><td>504</td><td>35</td><td>Georgia</td><td>497</td></tr>
<tr><td>23</td><td>Oklahoma</td><td>529</td><td>36</td><td>Tennessee</td><td>496</td></tr>
<tr><td>39</td><td>Oregon</td><td>493</td><td>37</td><td>Indiana</td><td>495</td></tr>
<tr><td>46</td><td>Pennsylvania</td><td>437</td><td>38</td><td>Massachusetts</td><td>494</td></tr>
<tr><td>45</td><td>Rhode Island</td><td>453</td><td>39</td><td>Oregon</td><td>493</td></tr>
<tr><td>20</td><td>South Carolina</td><td>532</td><td>40</td><td>Utah</td><td>492</td></tr>
<tr><td>17</td><td>South Dakota</td><td>545</td><td>41</td><td>Wisconsin</td><td>489</td></tr>
<tr><td>36</td><td>Tennessee</td><td>496</td><td>42</td><td>Idaho</td><td>488</td></tr>
<tr><td>25</td><td>Texas</td><td>526</td><td>43</td><td>Illinois</td><td>484</td></tr>
<tr><td>40</td><td>Utah</td><td>492</td><td>44</td><td>California</td><td>473</td></tr>
<tr><td>4</td><td>Vermont</td><td>633</td><td>45</td><td>Rhode Island</td><td>453</td></tr>
<tr><td>22</td><td>Virginia</td><td>531</td><td>46</td><td>Michigan</td><td>437</td></tr>
<tr><td>32</td><td>Washington</td><td>505</td><td>46</td><td>Pennsylvania</td><td>437</td></tr>
<tr><td>12</td><td>West Virginia</td><td>566</td><td>48</td><td>Florida</td><td>422</td></tr>
<tr><td>41</td><td>Wisconsin</td><td>489</td><td>49</td><td>Arizona</td><td>389</td></tr>
<tr><td>1</td><td>Wyoming</td><td>868</td><td>50</td><td>Nevada</td><td>383</td></tr>
<tr><td></td><td></td><td></td><td></td><td>District of Columbia</td><td>728</td></tr>
</table>

Source: CQ Press using data from U.S. Bureau of the Census, Governments Division
   "Annual Survey of Public Employment and Payroll" (https://www.census.gov/programs-surveys/apes.html)
*Full-time equivalent as of March 2018.

Average Annual Earnings of Full-Time State and Local Government Employees in 2018
National Average = $61,901*

ALPHA ORDER

RANK	STATE	SALARY
38	Alabama	$50,032
7	Alaska	70,694
23	Arizona	58,266
48	Arkansas	44,498
1	California	84,562
14	Colorado	63,517
5	Connecticut	73,725
19	Delaware	60,099
32	Florida	53,151
36	Georgia	50,696
18	Hawaii	61,823
34	Idaho	51,787
11	Illinois	66,312
39	Indiana	49,844
17	Iowa	61,987
40	Kansas	49,496
43	Kentucky	48,666
45	Louisiana	48,279
35	Maine	51,332
9	Maryland	69,225
8	Massachusetts	70,424
16	Michigan	62,698
13	Minnesota	65,605
50	Mississippi	42,723
46	Missouri	47,336
33	Montana	52,876
29	Nebraska	56,372
12	Nevada	66,089
22	New Hampshire	59,411
3	New Jersey	76,532
37	New Mexico	50,331
4	New York	76,083
30	North Carolina	53,981
26	North Dakota	57,218
25	Ohio	57,709
47	Oklahoma	46,472
10	Oregon	66,387
15	Pennsylvania	63,480
6	Rhode Island	71,689
41	South Carolina	49,218
44	South Dakota	48,565
42	Tennessee	48,850
31	Texas	53,546
24	Utah	58,172
20	Vermont	59,781
27	Virginia	57,081
2	Washington	76,546
49	West Virginia	44,200
21	Wisconsin	59,414
28	Wyoming	56,764

RANK ORDER

RANK	STATE	SALARY
1	California	$84,562
2	Washington	76,546
3	New Jersey	76,532
4	New York	76,083
5	Connecticut	73,725
6	Rhode Island	71,689
7	Alaska	70,694
8	Massachusetts	70,424
9	Maryland	69,225
10	Oregon	66,387
11	Illinois	66,312
12	Nevada	66,089
13	Minnesota	65,605
14	Colorado	63,517
15	Pennsylvania	63,480
16	Michigan	62,698
17	Iowa	61,987
18	Hawaii	61,823
19	Delaware	60,099
20	Vermont	59,781
21	Wisconsin	59,414
22	New Hampshire	59,411
23	Arizona	58,266
24	Utah	58,172
25	Ohio	57,709
26	North Dakota	57,218
27	Virginia	57,081
28	Wyoming	56,764
29	Nebraska	56,372
30	North Carolina	53,981
31	Texas	53,546
32	Florida	53,151
33	Montana	52,876
34	Idaho	51,787
35	Maine	51,332
36	Georgia	50,696
37	New Mexico	50,331
38	Alabama	50,032
39	Indiana	49,844
40	Kansas	49,496
41	South Carolina	49,218
42	Tennessee	48,850
43	Kentucky	48,666
44	South Dakota	48,565
45	Louisiana	48,279
46	Missouri	47,336
47	Oklahoma	46,472
48	Arkansas	44,498
49	West Virginia	44,200
50	Mississippi	42,723

District of Columbia   88,845

Source: CQ Press using data from U.S. Bureau of the Census, Governments Division
"Annual Survey of Public Employment and Payroll" (https://www.census.gov/programs-surveys/apes.html)
*March 2018 full-time payroll (multiplied by 12) divided by full-time employees.

State Government Total Revenue in 2017

National Total = $2,548,571,923,000*

ALPHA ORDER

RANK	STATE	REVENUE	% of USA
28	Alabama	$33,290,590,000	1.3%
42	Alaska	10,558,860,000	0.4%
18	Arizona	43,761,646,000	1.7%
31	Arkansas	25,936,260,000	1.0%
1	California	398,692,338,000	15.6%
24	Colorado	34,765,623,000	1.4%
26	Connecticut	34,335,860,000	1.3%
43	Delaware	9,552,088,000	0.4%
4	Florida	107,022,211,000	4.2%
14	Georgia	56,818,437,000	2.2%
38	Hawaii	16,136,302,000	0.6%
40	Idaho	11,761,509,000	0.5%
7	Illinois	87,972,751,000	3.5%
19	Indiana	43,734,697,000	1.7%
30	Iowa	26,799,389,000	1.1%
36	Kansas	21,425,818,000	0.8%
27	Kentucky	33,793,193,000	1.3%
22	Louisiana	36,524,948,000	1.4%
41	Maine	10,630,716,000	0.4%
16	Maryland	47,557,235,000	1.9%
11	Massachusetts	66,876,177,000	2.6%
8	Michigan	80,348,934,000	3.2%
15	Minnesota	53,817,016,000	2.1%
32	Mississippi	24,026,565,000	0.9%
21	Missouri	39,703,012,000	1.6%
46	Montana	9,060,871,000	0.4%
39	Nebraska	12,173,777,000	0.5%
34	Nevada	22,421,170,000	0.9%
44	New Hampshire	9,328,813,000	0.4%
9	New Jersey	78,755,976,000	3.1%
35	New Mexico	21,509,359,000	0.8%
2	New York	217,164,323,000	8.5%
10	North Carolina	67,556,293,000	2.7%
47	North Dakota	7,947,031,000	0.3%
6	Ohio	100,598,782,000	3.9%
29	Oklahoma	27,148,444,000	1.1%
20	Oregon	43,033,559,000	1.7%
5	Pennsylvania	102,839,111,000	4.0%
45	Rhode Island	9,112,327,000	0.4%
25	South Carolina	34,341,416,000	1.3%
50	South Dakota	6,106,444,000	0.2%
23	Tennessee	35,445,489,000	1.4%
3	Texas	164,382,118,000	6.4%
33	Utah	22,530,196,000	0.9%
48	Vermont	6,884,054,000	0.3%
13	Virginia	61,326,057,000	2.4%
12	Washington	63,127,656,000	2.5%
37	West Virginia	16,350,326,000	0.6%
17	Wisconsin	46,800,615,000	1.8%
49	Wyoming	6,785,541,000	0.3%

RANK ORDER

RANK	STATE	REVENUE	% of USA
1	California	$398,692,338,000	15.6%
2	New York	217,164,323,000	8.5%
3	Texas	164,382,118,000	6.4%
4	Florida	107,022,211,000	4.2%
5	Pennsylvania	102,839,111,000	4.0%
6	Ohio	100,598,782,000	3.9%
7	Illinois	87,972,751,000	3.5%
8	Michigan	80,348,934,000	3.2%
9	New Jersey	78,755,976,000	3.1%
10	North Carolina	67,556,293,000	2.7%
11	Massachusetts	66,876,177,000	2.6%
12	Washington	63,127,656,000	2.5%
13	Virginia	61,326,057,000	2.4%
14	Georgia	56,818,437,000	2.2%
15	Minnesota	53,817,016,000	2.1%
16	Maryland	47,557,235,000	1.9%
17	Wisconsin	46,800,615,000	1.8%
18	Arizona	43,761,646,000	1.7%
19	Indiana	43,734,697,000	1.7%
20	Oregon	43,033,559,000	1.7%
21	Missouri	39,703,012,000	1.6%
22	Louisiana	36,524,948,000	1.4%
23	Tennessee	35,445,489,000	1.4%
24	Colorado	34,765,623,000	1.4%
25	South Carolina	34,341,416,000	1.3%
26	Connecticut	34,335,860,000	1.3%
27	Kentucky	33,793,193,000	1.3%
28	Alabama	33,290,590,000	1.3%
29	Oklahoma	27,148,444,000	1.1%
30	Iowa	26,799,389,000	1.1%
31	Arkansas	25,936,260,000	1.0%
32	Mississippi	24,026,565,000	0.9%
33	Utah	22,530,196,000	0.9%
34	Nevada	22,421,170,000	0.9%
35	New Mexico	21,509,359,000	0.8%
36	Kansas	21,425,818,000	0.8%
37	West Virginia	16,350,326,000	0.6%
38	Hawaii	16,136,302,000	0.6%
39	Nebraska	12,173,777,000	0.5%
40	Idaho	11,761,509,000	0.5%
41	Maine	10,630,716,000	0.4%
42	Alaska	10,558,860,000	0.4%
43	Delaware	9,552,088,000	0.4%
44	New Hampshire	9,328,813,000	0.4%
45	Rhode Island	9,112,327,000	0.4%
46	Montana	9,060,871,000	0.4%
47	North Dakota	7,947,031,000	0.3%
48	Vermont	6,884,054,000	0.3%
49	Wyoming	6,785,541,000	0.3%
50	South Dakota	6,106,444,000	0.2%
	District of Columbia**	NA	NA

Source: U.S. Bureau of the Census, Governments Division
"2017 State and Local Government Finances" (https://www.census.gov/programs-surveys/gov-finances.html)
*Total revenue includes all money received from external sources. This includes taxes, intergovernmental transfers and insurance trust revenue, and revenue from government-owned utilities and other commercial or auxiliary enterprise.
**Not applicable.

Per Capita State Government Total Revenue in 2017

National Per Capita = $7,855*

ALPHA ORDER

RANK	STATE	PER CAPITA
40	Alabama	$6,829
1	Alaska	14,273
45	Arizona	6,208
16	Arkansas	8,637
9	California	10,119
46	Colorado	6,191
13	Connecticut	9,607
10	Delaware	9,980
50	Florida	5,102
48	Georgia	5,456
3	Hawaii	11,330
38	Idaho	6,842
37	Illinois	6,880
42	Indiana	6,567
20	Iowa	8,525
31	Kansas	7,361
29	Kentucky	7,587
28	Louisiana	7,820
26	Maine	7,963
27	Maryland	7,893
11	Massachusetts	9,744
23	Michigan	8,054
12	Minnesota	9,665
25	Mississippi	8,037
43	Missouri	6,500
19	Montana	8,604
44	Nebraska	6,349
30	Nevada	7,543
35	New Hampshire	6,911
15	New Jersey	8,860
8	New Mexico	10,275
4	New York	11,085
41	North Carolina	6,578
6	North Dakota	10,523
17	Ohio	8,625
36	Oklahoma	6,903
7	Oregon	10,378
24	Pennsylvania	8,040
17	Rhode Island	8,625
39	South Carolina	6,839
34	South Dakota	6,992
49	Tennessee	5,283
47	Texas	5,804
32	Utah	7,261
5	Vermont	11,023
33	Virginia	7,244
21	Washington	8,502
14	West Virginia	8,998
22	Wisconsin	8,080
2	Wyoming	11,721

RANK ORDER

RANK	STATE	PER CAPITA
1	Alaska	$14,273
2	Wyoming	11,721
3	Hawaii	11,330
4	New York	11,085
5	Vermont	11,023
6	North Dakota	10,523
7	Oregon	10,378
8	New Mexico	10,275
9	California	10,119
10	Delaware	9,980
11	Massachusetts	9,744
12	Minnesota	9,665
13	Connecticut	9,607
14	West Virginia	8,998
15	New Jersey	8,860
16	Arkansas	8,637
17	Ohio	8,625
17	Rhode Island	8,625
19	Montana	8,604
20	Iowa	8,525
21	Washington	8,502
22	Wisconsin	8,080
23	Michigan	8,054
24	Pennsylvania	8,040
25	Mississippi	8,037
26	Maine	7,963
27	Maryland	7,893
28	Louisiana	7,820
29	Kentucky	7,587
30	Nevada	7,543
31	Kansas	7,361
32	Utah	7,261
33	Virginia	7,244
34	South Dakota	6,992
35	New Hampshire	6,911
36	Oklahoma	6,903
37	Illinois	6,880
38	Idaho	6,842
39	South Carolina	6,839
40	Alabama	6,829
41	North Carolina	6,578
42	Indiana	6,567
43	Missouri	6,500
44	Nebraska	6,349
45	Arizona	6,208
46	Colorado	6,191
47	Texas	5,804
48	Georgia	5,456
49	Tennessee	5,283
50	Florida	5,102

District of Columbia**   NA

Source: CQ Press using data from U.S. Bureau of the Census, Governments Division
"2017 State and Local Government Finances" (https://www.census.gov/programs-surveys/gov-finances.html)
*Total revenue includes all money received from external sources. This includes taxes, intergovernmental transfers and insurance trust revenue, and revenue from government-owned utilities and other commercial or auxiliary enterprise.
**Not applicable.

State Government Intergovernmental Revenue in 2017

National Total = $656,283,270,000*

ALPHA ORDER

RANK	STATE	REVENUE	% of USA
24	Alabama	$9,949,247,000	1.5%
38	Alaska	3,286,785,000	0.5%
12	Arizona	15,247,776,000	2.3%
29	Arkansas	7,916,365,000	1.2%
1	California	93,013,830,000	14.2%
27	Colorado	8,463,350,000	1.3%
30	Connecticut	7,535,049,000	1.1%
47	Delaware	2,415,919,000	0.4%
5	Florida	27,852,122,000	4.2%
13	Georgia	15,183,797,000	2.3%
42	Hawaii	2,787,412,000	0.4%
44	Idaho	2,622,679,000	0.4%
8	Illinois	19,736,635,000	3.0%
14	Indiana	14,712,679,000	2.2%
33	Iowa	6,245,956,000	1.0%
37	Kansas	4,160,844,000	0.6%
21	Kentucky	10,829,538,000	1.7%
17	Louisiana	12,636,842,000	1.9%
41	Maine	3,020,597,000	0.5%
16	Maryland	13,203,944,000	2.0%
11	Massachusetts	16,331,054,000	2.5%
7	Michigan	21,350,680,000	3.3%
20	Minnesota	10,939,218,000	1.7%
28	Mississippi	8,211,496,000	1.3%
18	Missouri	11,322,122,000	1.7%
40	Montana	3,054,845,000	0.5%
39	Nebraska	3,179,745,000	0.5%
34	Nevada	5,234,577,000	0.8%
43	New Hampshire	2,720,430,000	0.4%
9	New Jersey	18,615,719,000	2.8%
32	New Mexico	7,226,565,000	1.1%
2	New York	60,371,092,000	9.2%
10	North Carolina	16,412,180,000	2.5%
49	North Dakota	1,825,979,000	0.3%
6	Ohio	24,305,702,000	3.7%
31	Oklahoma	7,280,359,000	1.1%
23	Oregon	9,988,321,000	1.5%
4	Pennsylvania	29,475,131,000	4.5%
46	Rhode Island	2,519,225,000	0.4%
26	South Carolina	9,007,621,000	1.4%
50	South Dakota	1,567,365,000	0.2%
19	Tennessee	11,161,689,000	1.7%
3	Texas	44,657,763,000	6.8%
36	Utah	4,524,182,000	0.7%
48	Vermont	1,991,516,000	0.3%
22	Virginia	10,699,877,000	1.6%
15	Washington	14,228,084,000	2.2%
35	West Virginia	5,109,431,000	0.8%
25	Wisconsin	9,583,175,000	1.5%
45	Wyoming	2,566,761,000	0.4%

RANK ORDER

RANK	STATE	REVENUE	% of USA
1	California	$93,013,830,000	14.2%
2	New York	60,371,092,000	9.2%
3	Texas	44,657,763,000	6.8%
4	Pennsylvania	29,475,131,000	4.5%
5	Florida	27,852,122,000	4.2%
6	Ohio	24,305,702,000	3.7%
7	Michigan	21,350,680,000	3.3%
8	Illinois	19,736,635,000	3.0%
9	New Jersey	18,615,719,000	2.8%
10	North Carolina	16,412,180,000	2.5%
11	Massachusetts	16,331,054,000	2.5%
12	Arizona	15,247,776,000	2.3%
13	Georgia	15,183,797,000	2.3%
14	Indiana	14,712,679,000	2.2%
15	Washington	14,228,084,000	2.2%
16	Maryland	13,203,944,000	2.0%
17	Louisiana	12,636,842,000	1.9%
18	Missouri	11,322,122,000	1.7%
19	Tennessee	11,161,689,000	1.7%
20	Minnesota	10,939,218,000	1.7%
21	Kentucky	10,829,538,000	1.7%
22	Virginia	10,699,877,000	1.6%
23	Oregon	9,988,321,000	1.5%
24	Alabama	9,949,247,000	1.5%
25	Wisconsin	9,583,175,000	1.5%
26	South Carolina	9,007,621,000	1.4%
27	Colorado	8,463,350,000	1.3%
28	Mississippi	8,211,496,000	1.3%
29	Arkansas	7,916,365,000	1.2%
30	Connecticut	7,535,049,000	1.1%
31	Oklahoma	7,280,359,000	1.1%
32	New Mexico	7,226,565,000	1.1%
33	Iowa	6,245,956,000	1.0%
34	Nevada	5,234,577,000	0.8%
35	West Virginia	5,109,431,000	0.8%
36	Utah	4,524,182,000	0.7%
37	Kansas	4,160,844,000	0.6%
38	Alaska	3,286,785,000	0.5%
39	Nebraska	3,179,745,000	0.5%
40	Montana	3,054,845,000	0.5%
41	Maine	3,020,597,000	0.5%
42	Hawaii	2,787,412,000	0.4%
43	New Hampshire	2,720,430,000	0.4%
44	Idaho	2,622,679,000	0.4%
45	Wyoming	2,566,761,000	0.4%
46	Rhode Island	2,519,225,000	0.4%
47	Delaware	2,415,919,000	0.4%
48	Vermont	1,991,516,000	0.3%
49	North Dakota	1,825,979,000	0.3%
50	South Dakota	1,567,365,000	0.2%

District of Columbia**   NA   NA

Source: U.S. Bureau of the Census, Governments Division
"2017 State and Local Government Finances" (https://www.census.gov/programs-surveys/gov-finances.html)
*Includes revenue from federal and local government sources.
**Not applicable.

Per Capita State Government Intergovernmental Revenue in 2017

National Per Capita = $2,023*

<table>
<tr><td colspan="3">ALPHA ORDER</td><td colspan="3">RANK ORDER</td></tr>
<tr><th>RANK</th><th>STATE</th><th>PER CAPITA</th><th>RANK</th><th>STATE</th><th>PER CAPITA</th></tr>
<tr><td>27</td><td>Alabama</td><td>$2,041</td><td>1</td><td>Alaska</td><td>$4,443</td></tr>
<tr><td>1</td><td>Alaska</td><td>4,443</td><td>2</td><td>Wyoming</td><td>4,434</td></tr>
<tr><td>22</td><td>Arizona</td><td>2,163</td><td>3</td><td>New Mexico</td><td>3,452</td></tr>
<tr><td>10</td><td>Arkansas</td><td>2,636</td><td>4</td><td>Vermont</td><td>3,189</td></tr>
<tr><td>17</td><td>California</td><td>2,361</td><td>5</td><td>New York</td><td>3,082</td></tr>
<tr><td>45</td><td>Colorado</td><td>1,507</td><td>6</td><td>Montana</td><td>2,901</td></tr>
<tr><td>24</td><td>Connecticut</td><td>2,108</td><td>7</td><td>West Virginia</td><td>2,812</td></tr>
<tr><td>11</td><td>Delaware</td><td>2,524</td><td>8</td><td>Mississippi</td><td>2,747</td></tr>
<tr><td>49</td><td>Florida</td><td>1,328</td><td>9</td><td>Louisiana</td><td>2,705</td></tr>
<tr><td>46</td><td>Georgia</td><td>1,458</td><td>10</td><td>Arkansas</td><td>2,636</td></tr>
<tr><td>31</td><td>Hawaii</td><td>1,957</td><td>11</td><td>Delaware</td><td>2,524</td></tr>
<tr><td>44</td><td>Idaho</td><td>1,526</td><td>12</td><td>Kentucky</td><td>2,431</td></tr>
<tr><td>43</td><td>Illinois</td><td>1,544</td><td>13</td><td>North Dakota</td><td>2,418</td></tr>
<tr><td>20</td><td>Indiana</td><td>2,209</td><td>14</td><td>Oregon</td><td>2,409</td></tr>
<tr><td>29</td><td>Iowa</td><td>1,987</td><td>15</td><td>Rhode Island</td><td>2,385</td></tr>
<tr><td>48</td><td>Kansas</td><td>1,430</td><td>16</td><td>Massachusetts</td><td>2,379</td></tr>
<tr><td>12</td><td>Kentucky</td><td>2,431</td><td>17</td><td>California</td><td>2,361</td></tr>
<tr><td>9</td><td>Louisiana</td><td>2,705</td><td>18</td><td>Pennsylvania</td><td>2,304</td></tr>
<tr><td>19</td><td>Maine</td><td>2,263</td><td>19</td><td>Maine</td><td>2,263</td></tr>
<tr><td>21</td><td>Maryland</td><td>2,192</td><td>20</td><td>Indiana</td><td>2,209</td></tr>
<tr><td>16</td><td>Massachusetts</td><td>2,379</td><td>21</td><td>Maryland</td><td>2,192</td></tr>
<tr><td>23</td><td>Michigan</td><td>2,140</td><td>22</td><td>Arizona</td><td>2,163</td></tr>
<tr><td>30</td><td>Minnesota</td><td>1,965</td><td>23</td><td>Michigan</td><td>2,140</td></tr>
<tr><td>8</td><td>Mississippi</td><td>2,747</td><td>24</td><td>Connecticut</td><td>2,108</td></tr>
<tr><td>33</td><td>Missouri</td><td>1,853</td><td>25</td><td>New Jersey</td><td>2,094</td></tr>
<tr><td>6</td><td>Montana</td><td>2,901</td><td>26</td><td>Ohio</td><td>2,084</td></tr>
<tr><td>39</td><td>Nebraska</td><td>1,658</td><td>27</td><td>Alabama</td><td>2,041</td></tr>
<tr><td>37</td><td>Nevada</td><td>1,761</td><td>28</td><td>New Hampshire</td><td>2,015</td></tr>
<tr><td>28</td><td>New Hampshire</td><td>2,015</td><td>29</td><td>Iowa</td><td>1,987</td></tr>
<tr><td>25</td><td>New Jersey</td><td>2,094</td><td>30</td><td>Minnesota</td><td>1,965</td></tr>
<tr><td>3</td><td>New Mexico</td><td>3,452</td><td>31</td><td>Hawaii</td><td>1,957</td></tr>
<tr><td>5</td><td>New York</td><td>3,082</td><td>32</td><td>Washington</td><td>1,916</td></tr>
<tr><td>41</td><td>North Carolina</td><td>1,598</td><td>33</td><td>Missouri</td><td>1,853</td></tr>
<tr><td>13</td><td>North Dakota</td><td>2,418</td><td>34</td><td>Oklahoma</td><td>1,851</td></tr>
<tr><td>26</td><td>Ohio</td><td>2,084</td><td>35</td><td>South Dakota</td><td>1,795</td></tr>
<tr><td>34</td><td>Oklahoma</td><td>1,851</td><td>36</td><td>South Carolina</td><td>1,794</td></tr>
<tr><td>14</td><td>Oregon</td><td>2,409</td><td>37</td><td>Nevada</td><td>1,761</td></tr>
<tr><td>18</td><td>Pennsylvania</td><td>2,304</td><td>38</td><td>Tennessee</td><td>1,664</td></tr>
<tr><td>15</td><td>Rhode Island</td><td>2,385</td><td>39</td><td>Nebraska</td><td>1,658</td></tr>
<tr><td>36</td><td>South Carolina</td><td>1,794</td><td>40</td><td>Wisconsin</td><td>1,655</td></tr>
<tr><td>35</td><td>South Dakota</td><td>1,795</td><td>41</td><td>North Carolina</td><td>1,598</td></tr>
<tr><td>38</td><td>Tennessee</td><td>1,664</td><td>42</td><td>Texas</td><td>1,577</td></tr>
<tr><td>42</td><td>Texas</td><td>1,577</td><td>43</td><td>Illinois</td><td>1,544</td></tr>
<tr><td>46</td><td>Utah</td><td>1,458</td><td>44</td><td>Idaho</td><td>1,526</td></tr>
<tr><td>4</td><td>Vermont</td><td>3,189</td><td>45</td><td>Colorado</td><td>1,507</td></tr>
<tr><td>50</td><td>Virginia</td><td>1,264</td><td>46</td><td>Georgia</td><td>1,458</td></tr>
<tr><td>32</td><td>Washington</td><td>1,916</td><td>46</td><td>Utah</td><td>1,458</td></tr>
<tr><td>7</td><td>West Virginia</td><td>2,812</td><td>48</td><td>Kansas</td><td>1,430</td></tr>
<tr><td>40</td><td>Wisconsin</td><td>1,655</td><td>49</td><td>Florida</td><td>1,328</td></tr>
<tr><td>2</td><td>Wyoming</td><td>4,434</td><td>50</td><td>Virginia</td><td>1,264</td></tr>
</table>

District of Columbia**   NA

Source: CQ Press using data from U.S. Bureau of the Census, Governments Division
"2017 State and Local Government Finances" (https://www.census.gov/programs-surveys/gov-finances.html)
*Includes revenue from federal and local government sources.
**Not applicable.

State Government Own Source Revenue in 2017

National Total = $1,313,805,927,000*

ALPHA ORDER

RANK	STATE	REVENUE	% of USA
27	Alabama	$16,822,850,000	1.3%
43	Alaska	5,058,528,000	0.4%
21	Arizona	19,482,769,000	1.5%
33	Arkansas	13,232,671,000	1.0%
1	California	195,569,881,000	14.9%
22	Colorado	19,406,670,000	1.5%
20	Connecticut	20,262,870,000	1.5%
40	Delaware	5,924,509,000	0.5%
4	Florida	56,158,246,000	4.3%
15	Georgia	28,882,254,000	2.2%
34	Hawaii	10,664,224,000	0.8%
41	Idaho	5,853,974,000	0.4%
6	Illinois	48,255,626,000	3.7%
18	Indiana	23,778,836,000	1.8%
29	Iowa	14,888,387,000	1.1%
32	Kansas	13,524,708,000	1.0%
26	Kentucky	16,884,063,000	1.3%
28	Louisiana	15,158,666,000	1.2%
42	Maine	5,558,846,000	0.4%
16	Maryland	27,817,519,000	2.1%
10	Massachusetts	38,455,695,000	2.9%
9	Michigan	42,647,999,000	3.2%
14	Minnesota	30,414,777,000	2.3%
35	Mississippi	10,505,315,000	0.8%
24	Missouri	18,208,192,000	1.4%
48	Montana	3,563,234,000	0.3%
39	Nebraska	6,845,781,000	0.5%
36	Nevada	10,107,580,000	0.8%
46	New Hampshire	4,291,814,000	0.3%
8	New Jersey	44,008,401,000	3.3%
37	New Mexico	9,988,182,000	0.8%
2	New York	104,223,148,000	7.9%
11	North Carolina	36,786,989,000	2.8%
45	North Dakota	4,822,067,000	0.4%
7	Ohio	45,470,057,000	3.5%
31	Oklahoma	13,822,030,000	1.1%
19	Oregon	20,362,710,000	1.5%
5	Pennsylvania	54,094,855,000	4.1%
44	Rhode Island	4,987,180,000	0.4%
25	South Carolina	17,180,662,000	1.3%
50	South Dakota	2,832,741,000	0.2%
23	Tennessee	18,244,035,000	1.4%
3	Texas	84,099,040,000	6.4%
30	Utah	14,175,556,000	1.1%
47	Vermont	4,034,218,000	0.3%
12	Virginia	36,486,487,000	2.8%
13	Washington	32,973,197,000	2.5%
38	West Virginia	8,073,261,000	0.6%
17	Wisconsin	25,962,345,000	2.0%
49	Wyoming	2,952,282,000	0.2%

RANK ORDER

RANK	STATE	REVENUE	% of USA
1	California	$195,569,881,000	14.9%
2	New York	104,223,148,000	7.9%
3	Texas	84,099,040,000	6.4%
4	Florida	56,158,246,000	4.3%
5	Pennsylvania	54,094,855,000	4.1%
6	Illinois	48,255,626,000	3.7%
7	Ohio	45,470,057,000	3.5%
8	New Jersey	44,008,401,000	3.3%
9	Michigan	42,647,999,000	3.2%
10	Massachusetts	38,455,695,000	2.9%
11	North Carolina	36,786,989,000	2.8%
12	Virginia	36,486,487,000	2.8%
13	Washington	32,973,197,000	2.5%
14	Minnesota	30,414,777,000	2.3%
15	Georgia	28,882,254,000	2.2%
16	Maryland	27,817,519,000	2.1%
17	Wisconsin	25,962,345,000	2.0%
18	Indiana	23,778,836,000	1.8%
19	Oregon	20,362,710,000	1.5%
20	Connecticut	20,262,870,000	1.5%
21	Arizona	19,482,769,000	1.5%
22	Colorado	19,406,670,000	1.5%
23	Tennessee	18,244,035,000	1.4%
24	Missouri	18,208,192,000	1.4%
25	South Carolina	17,180,662,000	1.3%
26	Kentucky	16,884,063,000	1.3%
27	Alabama	16,822,850,000	1.3%
28	Louisiana	15,158,666,000	1.2%
29	Iowa	14,888,387,000	1.1%
30	Utah	14,175,556,000	1.1%
31	Oklahoma	13,822,030,000	1.1%
32	Kansas	13,524,708,000	1.0%
33	Arkansas	13,232,671,000	1.0%
34	Hawaii	10,664,224,000	0.8%
35	Mississippi	10,505,315,000	0.8%
36	Nevada	10,107,580,000	0.8%
37	New Mexico	9,988,182,000	0.8%
38	West Virginia	8,073,261,000	0.6%
39	Nebraska	6,845,781,000	0.5%
40	Delaware	5,924,509,000	0.5%
41	Idaho	5,853,974,000	0.4%
42	Maine	5,558,846,000	0.4%
43	Alaska	5,058,528,000	0.4%
44	Rhode Island	4,987,180,000	0.4%
45	North Dakota	4,822,067,000	0.4%
46	New Hampshire	4,291,814,000	0.3%
47	Vermont	4,034,218,000	0.3%
48	Montana	3,563,234,000	0.3%
49	Wyoming	2,952,282,000	0.2%
50	South Dakota	2,832,741,000	0.2%
	District of Columbia**	NA	NA

Source: U.S. Bureau of the Census, Governments Division
   "2017 State and Local Government Finances" (https://www.census.gov/programs-surveys/gov-finances.html)
*Own source revenue includes taxes, current charges, and miscellaneous general revenue. Excluded are intergovernmental transfers, insurance trust revenue, and revenue from government-owned utilities and other commercial or auxiliary enterprise.
**Not applicable.

Per Capita State Government Own Source Revenue in 2017

National Per Capita = $4,049*

RANK	STATE	PER CAPITA
37	Alabama	$3,451
2	Alaska	6,838
48	Arizona	2,764
23	Arkansas	4,406
11	California	4,964
36	Colorado	3,456
6	Connecticut	5,670
5	Delaware	6,190
50	Florida	2,677
47	Georgia	2,774
1	Hawaii	7,488
39	Idaho	3,406
30	Illinois	3,774
32	Indiana	3,570
15	Iowa	4,736
17	Kansas	4,647
29	Kentucky	3,791
42	Louisiana	3,245
27	Maine	4,164
18	Maryland	4,617
7	Massachusetts	5,603
25	Michigan	4,275
8	Minnesota	5,462
35	Mississippi	3,514
45	Missouri	2,981
41	Montana	3,384
32	Nebraska	3,570
40	Nevada	3,400
44	New Hampshire	3,180
12	New Jersey	4,951
14	New Mexico	4,771
9	New York	5,320
31	North Carolina	3,582
4	North Dakota	6,385
28	Ohio	3,898
34	Oklahoma	3,515
13	Oregon	4,911
26	Pennsylvania	4,229
16	Rhode Island	4,721
38	South Carolina	3,422
43	South Dakota	3,244
49	Tennessee	2,719
46	Texas	2,969
19	Utah	4,568
3	Vermont	6,460
24	Virginia	4,310
22	Washington	4,441
21	West Virginia	4,443
20	Wisconsin	4,482
10	Wyoming	5,100

RANK	STATE	PER CAPITA
1	Hawaii	$7,488
2	Alaska	6,838
3	Vermont	6,460
4	North Dakota	6,385
5	Delaware	6,190
6	Connecticut	5,670
7	Massachusetts	5,603
8	Minnesota	5,462
9	New York	5,320
10	Wyoming	5,100
11	California	4,964
12	New Jersey	4,951
13	Oregon	4,911
14	New Mexico	4,771
15	Iowa	4,736
16	Rhode Island	4,721
17	Kansas	4,647
18	Maryland	4,617
19	Utah	4,568
20	Wisconsin	4,482
21	West Virginia	4,443
22	Washington	4,441
23	Arkansas	4,406
24	Virginia	4,310
25	Michigan	4,275
26	Pennsylvania	4,229
27	Maine	4,164
28	Ohio	3,898
29	Kentucky	3,791
30	Illinois	3,774
31	North Carolina	3,582
32	Indiana	3,570
32	Nebraska	3,570
34	Oklahoma	3,515
35	Mississippi	3,514
36	Colorado	3,456
37	Alabama	3,451
38	South Carolina	3,422
39	Idaho	3,406
40	Nevada	3,400
41	Montana	3,384
42	Louisiana	3,245
43	South Dakota	3,244
44	New Hampshire	3,180
45	Missouri	2,981
46	Texas	2,969
47	Georgia	2,774
48	Arizona	2,764
49	Tennessee	2,719
50	Florida	2,677

District of Columbia**   NA

Source: CQ Press using data from U.S. Bureau of the Census, Governments Division
"2017 State and Local Government Finances" (https://www.census.gov/programs-surveys/gov-finances.html)
*Own source revenue includes taxes, current charges, and miscellaneous general revenue. Excluded are intergovernmental transfers, insurance trust revenue, and revenue from government-owned utilities and other commercial or auxiliary enterprise.
**Not applicable.

Projected vs. Actual State Tax Collections in 2019

National Percent = 102.8% of Projected Taxes*

ALPHA ORDER

RANK	STATE	PERCENT
6	Alabama	108.1
50	Alaska	82.8
7	Arizona	107.7
33	Arkansas	102.4
29	California	103.2
9	Colorado	107.0
36	Connecticut	101.7
12	Delaware	106.1
24	Florida	103.9
42	Georgia	100.5
38	Hawaii	101.1
38	Idaho	101.1
13	Illinois	106.0
44	Indiana	100.4
46	Iowa	100.3
31	Kansas	102.8
46	Kentucky	100.3
42	Louisiana	100.5
17	Maine	105.0
27	Maryland	103.6
20	Massachusetts	104.7
19	Michigan	104.8
37	Minnesota	101.2
16	Mississippi	105.2
41	Missouri	101.0
5	Montana	108.8
26	Nebraska	103.7
35	Nevada	101.8
1	New Hampshire	118.8
30	New Jersey	102.9
21	New Mexico	104.4
49	New York	96.6
28	North Carolina	103.4
2	North Dakota	117.8
34	Ohio	102.2
15	Oklahoma	105.7
3	Oregon	113.7
32	Pennsylvania	102.7
44	Rhode Island	100.4
10	South Carolina	106.5
48	South Dakota	99.6
21	Tennessee	104.4
38	Texas	101.1
18	Utah	104.9
7	Vermont	107.7
14	Virginia	105.9
24	Washington	103.9
11	West Virginia	106.2
23	Wisconsin	104.2
4	Wyoming	112.4

RANK ORDER

RANK	STATE	PERCENT
1	New Hampshire	118.8
2	North Dakota	117.8
3	Oregon	113.7
4	Wyoming	112.4
5	Montana	108.8
6	Alabama	108.1
7	Arizona	107.7
7	Vermont	107.7
9	Colorado	107.0
10	South Carolina	106.5
11	West Virginia	106.2
12	Delaware	106.1
13	Illinois	106.0
14	Virginia	105.9
15	Oklahoma	105.7
16	Mississippi	105.2
17	Maine	105.0
18	Utah	104.9
19	Michigan	104.8
20	Massachusetts	104.7
21	New Mexico	104.4
21	Tennessee	104.4
23	Wisconsin	104.2
24	Florida	103.9
24	Washington	103.9
26	Nebraska	103.7
27	Maryland	103.6
28	North Carolina	103.4
29	California	103.2
30	New Jersey	102.9
31	Kansas	102.8
32	Pennsylvania	102.7
33	Arkansas	102.4
34	Ohio	102.2
35	Nevada	101.8
36	Connecticut	101.7
37	Minnesota	101.2
38	Hawaii	101.1
38	Idaho	101.1
38	Texas	101.1
41	Missouri	101.0
42	Georgia	100.5
42	Louisiana	100.5
44	Indiana	100.4
44	Rhode Island	100.4
46	Iowa	100.3
46	Kentucky	100.3
48	South Dakota	99.6
49	New York	96.6
50	Alaska	82.8
	District of Columbia**	NA

Source: CQ Press using data from National Association of State Budget Officers
"The Fiscal Survey of States" (Fall 2019, https://www.nasbo.org)
*For fiscal year 2019. This table compares sales, personal, and corporate income tax collections projected in adopting budgets with the amount collected.
**Not available.

State Government Tax Revenue in 2018

National Total = $1,031,001,198,000

RANK	STATE	REVENUE	% of USA
27	Alabama	$11,055,577,000	1.1%
50	Alaska	1,641,733,000	0.2%
20	Arizona	16,293,917,000	1.6%
30	Arkansas	9,843,173,000	1.0%
1	California	175,016,884,000	17.0%
21	Colorado	14,802,263,000	1.4%
18	Connecticut	19,081,475,000	1.9%
42	Delaware	4,219,706,000	0.4%
4	Florida	45,961,204,000	4.5%
14	Georgia	23,602,510,000	2.3%
36	Hawaii	7,714,451,000	0.7%
40	Idaho	4,848,359,000	0.5%
6	Illinois	39,857,069,000	3.9%
17	Indiana	19,397,879,000	1.9%
29	Iowa	10,088,480,000	1.0%
32	Kansas	9,546,790,000	0.9%
25	Kentucky	12,059,970,000	1.2%
26	Louisiana	11,357,686,000	1.1%
41	Maine	4,410,632,000	0.4%
16	Maryland	22,427,037,000	2.2%
9	Massachusetts	29,654,803,000	2.9%
8	Michigan	30,508,361,000	3.0%
12	Minnesota	26,697,469,000	2.6%
35	Mississippi	7,890,571,000	0.8%
23	Missouri	13,027,504,000	1.3%
46	Montana	2,944,827,000	0.3%
39	Nebraska	5,393,093,000	0.5%
33	Nevada	9,157,036,000	0.9%
47	New Hampshire	2,920,888,000	0.3%
7	New Jersey	35,365,046,000	3.4%
37	New Mexico	5,671,904,000	0.6%
2	New York	88,541,099,000	8.6%
11	North Carolina	27,855,070,000	2.7%
43	North Dakota	4,205,184,000	0.4%
10	Ohio	29,130,040,000	2.8%
31	Oklahoma	9,563,830,000	0.9%
24	Oregon	12,644,869,000	1.2%
5	Pennsylvania	40,709,545,000	3.9%
44	Rhode Island	3,483,100,000	0.3%
28	South Carolina	10,550,096,000	1.0%
48	South Dakota	1,917,548,000	0.2%
22	Tennessee	14,269,061,000	1.4%
3	Texas	60,328,843,000	5.9%
34	Utah	8,038,709,000	0.8%
45	Vermont	3,284,231,000	0.3%
15	Virginia	23,489,398,000	2.3%
13	Washington	26,574,889,000	2.6%
38	West Virginia	5,417,673,000	0.5%
19	Wisconsin	18,742,929,000	1.8%
49	Wyoming	1,837,401,000	0.2%

RANK	STATE	REVENUE	% of USA
1	California	$175,016,884,000	17.0%
2	New York	88,541,099,000	8.6%
3	Texas	60,328,843,000	5.9%
4	Florida	45,961,204,000	4.5%
5	Pennsylvania	40,709,545,000	3.9%
6	Illinois	39,857,069,000	3.9%
7	New Jersey	35,365,046,000	3.4%
8	Michigan	30,508,361,000	3.0%
9	Massachusetts	29,654,803,000	2.9%
10	Ohio	29,130,040,000	2.8%
11	North Carolina	27,855,070,000	2.7%
12	Minnesota	26,697,469,000	2.6%
13	Washington	26,574,889,000	2.6%
14	Georgia	23,602,510,000	2.3%
15	Virginia	23,489,398,000	2.3%
16	Maryland	22,427,037,000	2.2%
17	Indiana	19,397,879,000	1.9%
18	Connecticut	19,081,475,000	1.9%
19	Wisconsin	18,742,929,000	1.8%
20	Arizona	16,293,917,000	1.6%
21	Colorado	14,802,263,000	1.4%
22	Tennessee	14,269,061,000	1.4%
23	Missouri	13,027,504,000	1.3%
24	Oregon	12,644,869,000	1.2%
25	Kentucky	12,059,970,000	1.2%
26	Louisiana	11,357,686,000	1.1%
27	Alabama	11,055,577,000	1.1%
28	South Carolina	10,550,096,000	1.0%
29	Iowa	10,088,480,000	1.0%
30	Arkansas	9,843,173,000	1.0%
31	Oklahoma	9,563,830,000	0.9%
32	Kansas	9,546,790,000	0.9%
33	Nevada	9,157,036,000	0.9%
34	Utah	8,038,709,000	0.8%
35	Mississippi	7,890,571,000	0.8%
36	Hawaii	7,714,451,000	0.7%
37	New Mexico	5,671,904,000	0.6%
38	West Virginia	5,417,673,000	0.5%
39	Nebraska	5,393,093,000	0.5%
40	Idaho	4,848,359,000	0.5%
41	Maine	4,410,632,000	0.4%
42	Delaware	4,219,706,000	0.4%
43	North Dakota	4,205,184,000	0.4%
44	Rhode Island	3,483,100,000	0.3%
45	Vermont	3,284,231,000	0.3%
46	Montana	2,944,827,000	0.3%
47	New Hampshire	2,920,888,000	0.3%
48	South Dakota	1,917,548,000	0.2%
49	Wyoming	1,837,401,000	0.2%
50	Alaska	1,641,733,000	0.2%
	District of Columbia	7,959,386,000	0.8%

Source: U.S. Bureau of the Census, Governments Division
"2018 State Government Tax Collections" (https://www.census.gov/programs-surveys/stc.html)

Per Capita State Government Tax Revenue in 2018

National Per Capita = $3,151

ALPHA ORDER

RANK	STATE	PER CAPITA
41	Alabama	$2,262
43	Alaska	2,226
40	Arizona	2,272
16	Arkansas	3,266
7	California	4,424
35	Colorado	2,599
3	Connecticut	5,341
8	Delaware	4,363
45	Florida	2,158
42	Georgia	2,244
2	Hawaii	5,431
29	Idaho	2,764
21	Illinois	3,128
26	Indiana	2,899
18	Iowa	3,196
15	Kansas	3,279
32	Kentucky	2,699
38	Louisiana	2,437
13	Maine	3,295
11	Maryland	3,711
9	Massachusetts	4,296
22	Michigan	3,052
5	Minnesota	4,758
34	Mississippi	2,642
47	Missouri	2,126
28	Montana	2,772
27	Nebraska	2,795
23	Nevada	3,018
46	New Hampshire	2,153
10	New Jersey	3,970
31	New Mexico	2,707
6	New York	4,531
33	North Carolina	2,683
1	North Dakota	5,533
37	Ohio	2,492
39	Oklahoma	2,425
24	Oregon	3,017
20	Pennsylvania	3,179
14	Rhode Island	3,294
50	South Carolina	2,075
44	South Dakota	2,174
48	Tennessee	2,108
49	Texas	2,102
36	Utah	2,543
4	Vermont	5,244
30	Virginia	2,758
12	Washington	3,527
25	West Virginia	3,000
17	Wisconsin	3,224
19	Wyoming	3,180

RANK ORDER

RANK	STATE	PER CAPITA
1	North Dakota	$5,533
2	Hawaii	5,431
3	Connecticut	5,341
4	Vermont	5,244
5	Minnesota	4,758
6	New York	4,531
7	California	4,424
8	Delaware	4,363
9	Massachusetts	4,296
10	New Jersey	3,970
11	Maryland	3,711
12	Washington	3,527
13	Maine	3,295
14	Rhode Island	3,294
15	Kansas	3,279
16	Arkansas	3,266
17	Wisconsin	3,224
18	Iowa	3,196
19	Wyoming	3,180
20	Pennsylvania	3,179
21	Illinois	3,128
22	Michigan	3,052
23	Nevada	3,018
24	Oregon	3,017
25	West Virginia	3,000
26	Indiana	2,899
27	Nebraska	2,795
28	Montana	2,772
29	Idaho	2,764
30	Virginia	2,758
31	New Mexico	2,707
32	Kentucky	2,699
33	North Carolina	2,683
34	Mississippi	2,642
35	Colorado	2,599
36	Utah	2,543
37	Ohio	2,492
38	Louisiana	2,437
39	Oklahoma	2,425
40	Arizona	2,272
41	Alabama	2,262
42	Georgia	2,244
43	Alaska	2,226
44	South Dakota	2,174
45	Florida	2,158
46	New Hampshire	2,153
47	Missouri	2,126
48	Tennessee	2,108
49	Texas	2,102
50	South Carolina	2,075
	District of Columbia	11,331

Source: CQ Press using data from U.S. Bureau of the Census, Governments Division
"2018 State Government Tax Collections" (https://www.census.gov/programs-surveys/stc.html)

State Government Tax Revenue as a Percent of Personal Income in 2018

National Percent = 5.8% of Personal Income

ALPHA ORDER

RANK	STATE	PERCENT
33	Alabama	5.4
49	Alaska	3.7
38	Arizona	5.1
6	Arkansas	7.6
8	California	7.0
45	Colorado	4.4
8	Connecticut	7.0
4	Delaware	8.3
46	Florida	4.3
40	Georgia	4.8
2	Hawaii	9.8
17	Idaho	6.3
31	Illinois	5.5
20	Indiana	6.1
14	Iowa	6.4
14	Kansas	6.4
14	Kentucky	6.4
34	Louisiana	5.3
11	Maine	6.7
24	Maryland	5.9
22	Massachusetts	6.0
17	Michigan	6.3
4	Minnesota	8.3
8	Mississippi	7.0
43	Missouri	4.5
26	Montana	5.8
36	Nebraska	5.2
20	Nevada	6.1
50	New Hampshire	3.5
26	New Jersey	5.8
13	New Mexico	6.5
12	New York	6.6
26	North Carolina	5.8
1	North Dakota	10.0
38	Ohio	5.1
36	Oklahoma	5.2
24	Oregon	5.9
29	Pennsylvania	5.7
22	Rhode Island	6.0
42	South Carolina	4.7
47	South Dakota	4.2
43	Tennessee	4.5
47	Texas	4.2
31	Utah	5.5
3	Vermont	9.7
40	Virginia	4.8
29	Washington	5.7
7	West Virginia	7.3
19	Wisconsin	6.2
34	Wyoming	5.3

RANK ORDER

RANK	STATE	PERCENT
1	North Dakota	10.0
2	Hawaii	9.8
3	Vermont	9.7
4	Delaware	8.3
4	Minnesota	8.3
6	Arkansas	7.6
7	West Virginia	7.3
8	California	7.0
8	Connecticut	7.0
8	Mississippi	7.0
11	Maine	6.7
12	New York	6.6
13	New Mexico	6.5
14	Iowa	6.4
14	Kansas	6.4
14	Kentucky	6.4
17	Idaho	6.3
17	Michigan	6.3
19	Wisconsin	6.2
20	Indiana	6.1
20	Nevada	6.1
22	Massachusetts	6.0
22	Rhode Island	6.0
24	Maryland	5.9
24	Oregon	5.9
26	Montana	5.8
26	New Jersey	5.8
26	North Carolina	5.8
29	Pennsylvania	5.7
29	Washington	5.7
31	Illinois	5.5
31	Utah	5.5
33	Alabama	5.4
34	Louisiana	5.3
34	Wyoming	5.3
36	Nebraska	5.2
36	Oklahoma	5.2
38	Arizona	5.1
38	Ohio	5.1
40	Georgia	4.8
40	Virginia	4.8
42	South Carolina	4.7
43	Missouri	4.5
43	Tennessee	4.5
45	Colorado	4.4
46	Florida	4.3
47	South Dakota	4.2
47	Texas	4.2
49	Alaska	3.7
50	New Hampshire	3.5

	District of Columbia	13.8

Source: CQ Press using data from U.S. Bureau of the Census, Governments Division
"2018 State Government Tax Collections" (https://www.census.gov/programs-surveys/stc.html) and
U.S. Department of Commerce, Bureau of Economic Analysis
"Annual State Personal Income" (https://apps.bea.gov/iTable/index_regional.cfm)

State Government Individual Income Tax Revenue in 2018

National Total = $392,069,791,000

<table>
<tr><td colspan="4">ALPHA ORDER</td><td colspan="4">RANK ORDER</td></tr>
<tr><td>RANK</td><td>STATE</td><td>REVENUE</td><td>% of USA</td><td>RANK</td><td>STATE</td><td>REVENUE</td><td>% of USA</td></tr>
<tr><td>24</td><td>Alabama</td><td>$3,912,800,000</td><td>1.0%</td><td>1</td><td>California</td><td>$95,152,230,000</td><td>24.3%</td></tr>
<tr><td>44</td><td>Alaska</td><td>0</td><td>0.0%</td><td>2</td><td>New York</td><td>52,738,515,000</td><td>13.5%</td></tr>
<tr><td>20</td><td>Arizona</td><td>4,545,242,000</td><td>1.2%</td><td>3</td><td>Massachusetts</td><td>16,280,331,000</td><td>4.2%</td></tr>
<tr><td>29</td><td>Arkansas</td><td>2,866,175,000</td><td>0.7%</td><td>4</td><td>Illinois</td><td>15,296,693,000</td><td>3.9%</td></tr>
<tr><td>1</td><td>California</td><td>95,152,230,000</td><td>24.3%</td><td>5</td><td>New Jersey</td><td>15,037,845,000</td><td>3.8%</td></tr>
<tr><td>17</td><td>Colorado</td><td>7,510,366,000</td><td>1.9%</td><td>6</td><td>Virginia</td><td>14,105,766,000</td><td>3.6%</td></tr>
<tr><td>12</td><td>Connecticut</td><td>9,733,258,000</td><td>2.5%</td><td>7</td><td>Pennsylvania</td><td>12,800,890,000</td><td>3.3%</td></tr>
<tr><td>35</td><td>Delaware</td><td>1,652,335,000</td><td>0.4%</td><td>8</td><td>North Carolina</td><td>12,609,608,000</td><td>3.2%</td></tr>
<tr><td>44</td><td>Florida</td><td>0</td><td>0.0%</td><td>9</td><td>Minnesota</td><td>11,882,330,000</td><td>3.0%</td></tr>
<tr><td>10</td><td>Georgia</td><td>11,643,781,000</td><td>3.0%</td><td>10</td><td>Georgia</td><td>11,643,781,000</td><td>3.0%</td></tr>
<tr><td>30</td><td>Hawaii</td><td>2,430,032,000</td><td>0.6%</td><td>11</td><td>Michigan</td><td>10,238,864,000</td><td>2.6%</td></tr>
<tr><td>34</td><td>Idaho</td><td>1,835,864,000</td><td>0.5%</td><td>12</td><td>Connecticut</td><td>9,733,258,000</td><td>2.5%</td></tr>
<tr><td>4</td><td>Illinois</td><td>15,296,693,000</td><td>3.9%</td><td>13</td><td>Maryland</td><td>9,507,776,000</td><td>2.4%</td></tr>
<tr><td>19</td><td>Indiana</td><td>5,816,072,000</td><td>1.5%</td><td>14</td><td>Oregon</td><td>8,879,552,000</td><td>2.3%</td></tr>
<tr><td>25</td><td>Iowa</td><td>3,897,236,000</td><td>1.0%</td><td>15</td><td>Ohio</td><td>8,698,901,000</td><td>2.2%</td></tr>
<tr><td>27</td><td>Kansas</td><td>3,413,677,000</td><td>0.9%</td><td>16</td><td>Wisconsin</td><td>8,151,462,000</td><td>2.1%</td></tr>
<tr><td>21</td><td>Kentucky</td><td>4,499,086,000</td><td>1.1%</td><td>17</td><td>Colorado</td><td>7,510,366,000</td><td>1.9%</td></tr>
<tr><td>28</td><td>Louisiana</td><td>3,246,226,000</td><td>0.8%</td><td>18</td><td>Missouri</td><td>6,510,224,000</td><td>1.7%</td></tr>
<tr><td>36</td><td>Maine</td><td>1,605,096,000</td><td>0.4%</td><td>19</td><td>Indiana</td><td>5,816,072,000</td><td>1.5%</td></tr>
<tr><td>13</td><td>Maryland</td><td>9,507,776,000</td><td>2.4%</td><td>20</td><td>Arizona</td><td>4,545,242,000</td><td>1.2%</td></tr>
<tr><td>3</td><td>Massachusetts</td><td>16,280,331,000</td><td>4.2%</td><td>21</td><td>Kentucky</td><td>4,499,086,000</td><td>1.1%</td></tr>
<tr><td>11</td><td>Michigan</td><td>10,238,864,000</td><td>2.6%</td><td>22</td><td>South Carolina</td><td>4,432,104,000</td><td>1.1%</td></tr>
<tr><td>9</td><td>Minnesota</td><td>11,882,330,000</td><td>3.0%</td><td>23</td><td>Utah</td><td>3,991,400,000</td><td>1.0%</td></tr>
<tr><td>33</td><td>Mississippi</td><td>1,852,937,000</td><td>0.5%</td><td>24</td><td>Alabama</td><td>3,912,800,000</td><td>1.0%</td></tr>
<tr><td>18</td><td>Missouri</td><td>6,510,224,000</td><td>1.7%</td><td>25</td><td>Iowa</td><td>3,897,236,000</td><td>1.0%</td></tr>
<tr><td>38</td><td>Montana</td><td>1,300,809,000</td><td>0.3%</td><td>26</td><td>Oklahoma</td><td>3,495,264,000</td><td>0.9%</td></tr>
<tr><td>31</td><td>Nebraska</td><td>2,360,596,000</td><td>0.6%</td><td>27</td><td>Kansas</td><td>3,413,677,000</td><td>0.9%</td></tr>
<tr><td>44</td><td>Nevada</td><td>0</td><td>0.0%</td><td>28</td><td>Louisiana</td><td>3,246,226,000</td><td>0.8%</td></tr>
<tr><td>43</td><td>New Hampshire</td><td>105,759,000</td><td>0.0%</td><td>29</td><td>Arkansas</td><td>2,866,175,000</td><td>0.7%</td></tr>
<tr><td>5</td><td>New Jersey</td><td>15,037,845,000</td><td>3.8%</td><td>30</td><td>Hawaii</td><td>2,430,032,000</td><td>0.6%</td></tr>
<tr><td>39</td><td>New Mexico</td><td>1,252,651,000</td><td>0.3%</td><td>31</td><td>Nebraska</td><td>2,360,596,000</td><td>0.6%</td></tr>
<tr><td>2</td><td>New York</td><td>52,738,515,000</td><td>13.5%</td><td>32</td><td>West Virginia</td><td>1,950,571,000</td><td>0.5%</td></tr>
<tr><td>8</td><td>North Carolina</td><td>12,609,608,000</td><td>3.2%</td><td>33</td><td>Mississippi</td><td>1,852,937,000</td><td>0.5%</td></tr>
<tr><td>41</td><td>North Dakota</td><td>367,635,000</td><td>0.1%</td><td>34</td><td>Idaho</td><td>1,835,864,000</td><td>0.5%</td></tr>
<tr><td>15</td><td>Ohio</td><td>8,698,901,000</td><td>2.2%</td><td>35</td><td>Delaware</td><td>1,652,335,000</td><td>0.4%</td></tr>
<tr><td>26</td><td>Oklahoma</td><td>3,495,264,000</td><td>0.9%</td><td>36</td><td>Maine</td><td>1,605,096,000</td><td>0.4%</td></tr>
<tr><td>14</td><td>Oregon</td><td>8,879,552,000</td><td>2.3%</td><td>37</td><td>Rhode Island</td><td>1,329,152,000</td><td>0.3%</td></tr>
<tr><td>7</td><td>Pennsylvania</td><td>12,800,890,000</td><td>3.3%</td><td>38</td><td>Montana</td><td>1,300,809,000</td><td>0.3%</td></tr>
<tr><td>37</td><td>Rhode Island</td><td>1,329,152,000</td><td>0.3%</td><td>39</td><td>New Mexico</td><td>1,252,651,000</td><td>0.3%</td></tr>
<tr><td>22</td><td>South Carolina</td><td>4,432,104,000</td><td>1.1%</td><td>40</td><td>Vermont</td><td>819,330,000</td><td>0.2%</td></tr>
<tr><td>44</td><td>South Dakota</td><td>0</td><td>0.0%</td><td>41</td><td>North Dakota</td><td>367,635,000</td><td>0.1%</td></tr>
<tr><td>42</td><td>Tennessee</td><td>246,508,000</td><td>0.1%</td><td>42</td><td>Tennessee</td><td>246,508,000</td><td>0.1%</td></tr>
<tr><td>44</td><td>Texas</td><td>0</td><td>0.0%</td><td>43</td><td>New Hampshire</td><td>105,759,000</td><td>0.0%</td></tr>
<tr><td>23</td><td>Utah</td><td>3,991,400,000</td><td>1.0%</td><td>44</td><td>Alaska</td><td>0</td><td>0.0%</td></tr>
<tr><td>40</td><td>Vermont</td><td>819,330,000</td><td>0.2%</td><td>44</td><td>Florida</td><td>0</td><td>0.0%</td></tr>
<tr><td>6</td><td>Virginia</td><td>14,105,766,000</td><td>3.6%</td><td>44</td><td>Nevada</td><td>0</td><td>0.0%</td></tr>
<tr><td>44</td><td>Washington</td><td>0</td><td>0.0%</td><td>44</td><td>South Dakota</td><td>0</td><td>0.0%</td></tr>
<tr><td>32</td><td>West Virginia</td><td>1,950,571,000</td><td>0.5%</td><td>44</td><td>Texas</td><td>0</td><td>0.0%</td></tr>
<tr><td>16</td><td>Wisconsin</td><td>8,151,462,000</td><td>2.1%</td><td>44</td><td>Washington</td><td>0</td><td>0.0%</td></tr>
<tr><td>44</td><td>Wyoming</td><td>0</td><td>0.0%</td><td>44</td><td>Wyoming</td><td>0</td><td>0.0%</td></tr>
<tr><td></td><td></td><td></td><td></td><td></td><td>District of Columbia</td><td>2,066,842,000</td><td>0.5%</td></tr>
</table>

Source: U.S. Bureau of the Census, Governments Division
"2018 State Government Tax Collections" (https://www.census.gov/programs-surveys/stc.html)

Per Capita State Government Individual Income Tax Revenue in 2018

National Per Capita = $1,198

<table>
<tr><td colspan="3">ALPHA ORDER</td><td colspan="3">RANK ORDER</td></tr>
<tr><td>RANK</td><td>STATE</td><td>PER CAPITA</td><td>RANK</td><td>STATE</td><td>PER CAPITA</td></tr>
<tr><td>35</td><td>Alabama</td><td>$801</td><td>1</td><td>Connecticut</td><td>$2,724</td></tr>
<tr><td>44</td><td>Alaska</td><td>0</td><td>2</td><td>New York</td><td>2,699</td></tr>
<tr><td>38</td><td>Arizona</td><td>634</td><td>3</td><td>California</td><td>2,405</td></tr>
<tr><td>31</td><td>Arkansas</td><td>951</td><td>4</td><td>Massachusetts</td><td>2,359</td></tr>
<tr><td>3</td><td>California</td><td>2,405</td><td>5</td><td>Oregon</td><td>2,119</td></tr>
<tr><td>13</td><td>Colorado</td><td>1,319</td><td>6</td><td>Minnesota</td><td>2,118</td></tr>
<tr><td>1</td><td>Connecticut</td><td>2,724</td><td>7</td><td>Hawaii</td><td>1,711</td></tr>
<tr><td>8</td><td>Delaware</td><td>1,708</td><td>8</td><td>Delaware</td><td>1,708</td></tr>
<tr><td>44</td><td>Florida</td><td>0</td><td>9</td><td>New Jersey</td><td>1,688</td></tr>
<tr><td>24</td><td>Georgia</td><td>1,107</td><td>10</td><td>Virginia</td><td>1,656</td></tr>
<tr><td>7</td><td>Hawaii</td><td>1,711</td><td>11</td><td>Maryland</td><td>1,573</td></tr>
<tr><td>27</td><td>Idaho</td><td>1,047</td><td>12</td><td>Wisconsin</td><td>1,402</td></tr>
<tr><td>21</td><td>Illinois</td><td>1,201</td><td>13</td><td>Colorado</td><td>1,319</td></tr>
<tr><td>34</td><td>Indiana</td><td>869</td><td>14</td><td>Vermont</td><td>1,308</td></tr>
<tr><td>17</td><td>Iowa</td><td>1,235</td><td>15</td><td>Utah</td><td>1,263</td></tr>
<tr><td>23</td><td>Kansas</td><td>1,172</td><td>16</td><td>Rhode Island</td><td>1,257</td></tr>
<tr><td>29</td><td>Kentucky</td><td>1,007</td><td>17</td><td>Iowa</td><td>1,235</td></tr>
<tr><td>37</td><td>Louisiana</td><td>697</td><td>18</td><td>Montana</td><td>1,225</td></tr>
<tr><td>22</td><td>Maine</td><td>1,199</td><td>19</td><td>Nebraska</td><td>1,224</td></tr>
<tr><td>11</td><td>Maryland</td><td>1,573</td><td>20</td><td>North Carolina</td><td>1,214</td></tr>
<tr><td>4</td><td>Massachusetts</td><td>2,359</td><td>21</td><td>Illinois</td><td>1,201</td></tr>
<tr><td>28</td><td>Michigan</td><td>1,024</td><td>22</td><td>Maine</td><td>1,199</td></tr>
<tr><td>6</td><td>Minnesota</td><td>2,118</td><td>23</td><td>Kansas</td><td>1,172</td></tr>
<tr><td>39</td><td>Mississippi</td><td>620</td><td>24</td><td>Georgia</td><td>1,107</td></tr>
<tr><td>26</td><td>Missouri</td><td>1,063</td><td>25</td><td>West Virginia</td><td>1,080</td></tr>
<tr><td>18</td><td>Montana</td><td>1,225</td><td>26</td><td>Missouri</td><td>1,063</td></tr>
<tr><td>19</td><td>Nebraska</td><td>1,224</td><td>27</td><td>Idaho</td><td>1,047</td></tr>
<tr><td>44</td><td>Nevada</td><td>0</td><td>28</td><td>Michigan</td><td>1,024</td></tr>
<tr><td>42</td><td>New Hampshire</td><td>78</td><td>29</td><td>Kentucky</td><td>1,007</td></tr>
<tr><td>9</td><td>New Jersey</td><td>1,688</td><td>30</td><td>Pennsylvania</td><td>1,000</td></tr>
<tr><td>40</td><td>New Mexico</td><td>598</td><td>31</td><td>Arkansas</td><td>951</td></tr>
<tr><td>2</td><td>New York</td><td>2,699</td><td>32</td><td>Oklahoma</td><td>886</td></tr>
<tr><td>20</td><td>North Carolina</td><td>1,214</td><td>33</td><td>South Carolina</td><td>872</td></tr>
<tr><td>41</td><td>North Dakota</td><td>484</td><td>34</td><td>Indiana</td><td>869</td></tr>
<tr><td>36</td><td>Ohio</td><td>744</td><td>35</td><td>Alabama</td><td>801</td></tr>
<tr><td>32</td><td>Oklahoma</td><td>886</td><td>36</td><td>Ohio</td><td>744</td></tr>
<tr><td>5</td><td>Oregon</td><td>2,119</td><td>37</td><td>Louisiana</td><td>697</td></tr>
<tr><td>30</td><td>Pennsylvania</td><td>1,000</td><td>38</td><td>Arizona</td><td>634</td></tr>
<tr><td>16</td><td>Rhode Island</td><td>1,257</td><td>39</td><td>Mississippi</td><td>620</td></tr>
<tr><td>33</td><td>South Carolina</td><td>872</td><td>40</td><td>New Mexico</td><td>598</td></tr>
<tr><td>44</td><td>South Dakota</td><td>0</td><td>41</td><td>North Dakota</td><td>484</td></tr>
<tr><td>43</td><td>Tennessee</td><td>36</td><td>42</td><td>New Hampshire</td><td>78</td></tr>
<tr><td>44</td><td>Texas</td><td>0</td><td>43</td><td>Tennessee</td><td>36</td></tr>
<tr><td>15</td><td>Utah</td><td>1,263</td><td>44</td><td>Alaska</td><td>0</td></tr>
<tr><td>14</td><td>Vermont</td><td>1,308</td><td>44</td><td>Florida</td><td>0</td></tr>
<tr><td>10</td><td>Virginia</td><td>1,656</td><td>44</td><td>Nevada</td><td>0</td></tr>
<tr><td>44</td><td>Washington</td><td>0</td><td>44</td><td>South Dakota</td><td>0</td></tr>
<tr><td>25</td><td>West Virginia</td><td>1,080</td><td>44</td><td>Texas</td><td>0</td></tr>
<tr><td>12</td><td>Wisconsin</td><td>1,402</td><td>44</td><td>Washington</td><td>0</td></tr>
<tr><td>44</td><td>Wyoming</td><td>0</td><td>44</td><td>Wyoming</td><td>0</td></tr>
<tr><td></td><td></td><td></td><td></td><td>District of Columbia</td><td>2,942</td></tr>
</table>

Source: CQ Press using data from U.S. Bureau of the Census, Governments Division
"2018 State Government Tax Collections" (https://www.census.gov/programs-surveys/stc.html)

State Government Corporation Net Income Tax Revenue in 2018

National Total = $48,222,543,000

ALPHA ORDER

RANK	STATE	REVENUE	% of USA
21	Alabama	$577,516,000	1.2%
36	Alaska	196,321,000	0.4%
29	Arizona	373,076,000	0.8%
28	Arkansas	390,756,000	0.8%
1	California	12,488,304,000	25.9%
20	Colorado	660,100,000	1.4%
17	Connecticut	778,232,000	1.6%
33	Delaware	254,802,000	0.5%
5	Florida	2,426,900,000	5.0%
12	Georgia	1,004,298,000	2.1%
39	Hawaii	146,831,000	0.3%
34	Idaho	240,809,000	0.5%
3	Illinois	2,587,141,000	5.4%
19	Indiana	698,725,000	1.4%
23	Iowa	443,187,000	0.9%
24	Kansas	437,967,000	0.9%
22	Kentucky	511,353,000	1.1%
30	Louisiana	358,208,000	0.7%
37	Maine	185,737,000	0.4%
11	Maryland	1,033,175,000	2.1%
6	Massachusetts	2,408,947,000	5.0%
10	Michigan	1,095,023,000	2.3%
9	Minnesota	1,357,004,000	2.8%
25	Mississippi	437,407,000	0.9%
31	Missouri	333,724,000	0.7%
38	Montana	176,132,000	0.4%
32	Nebraska	313,690,000	0.7%
47	Nevada	0	0.0%
16	New Hampshire	790,011,000	1.6%
7	New Jersey	2,235,653,000	4.6%
44	New Mexico	91,488,000	0.2%
2	New York	3,617,910,000	7.5%
18	North Carolina	742,512,000	1.5%
43	North Dakota	107,277,000	0.2%
46	Ohio	9,046,000	0.0%
35	Oklahoma	234,868,000	0.5%
15	Oregon	804,453,000	1.7%
4	Pennsylvania	2,486,379,000	5.2%
40	Rhode Island	118,118,000	0.2%
26	South Carolina	424,048,000	0.9%
45	South Dakota	32,376,000	0.1%
8	Tennessee	1,644,159,000	3.4%
47	Texas	0	0.0%
27	Utah	400,885,000	0.8%
41	Vermont	110,819,000	0.2%
14	Virginia	861,897,000	1.8%
47	Washington	0	0.0%
42	West Virginia	110,068,000	0.2%
13	Wisconsin	910,466,000	1.9%
47	Wyoming	0	0.0%

RANK ORDER

RANK	STATE	REVENUE	% of USA
1	California	$12,488,304,000	25.9%
2	New York	3,617,910,000	7.5%
3	Illinois	2,587,141,000	5.4%
4	Pennsylvania	2,486,379,000	5.2%
5	Florida	2,426,900,000	5.0%
6	Massachusetts	2,408,947,000	5.0%
7	New Jersey	2,235,653,000	4.6%
8	Tennessee	1,644,159,000	3.4%
9	Minnesota	1,357,004,000	2.8%
10	Michigan	1,095,023,000	2.3%
11	Maryland	1,033,175,000	2.1%
12	Georgia	1,004,298,000	2.1%
13	Wisconsin	910,466,000	1.9%
14	Virginia	861,897,000	1.8%
15	Oregon	804,453,000	1.7%
16	New Hampshire	790,011,000	1.6%
17	Connecticut	778,232,000	1.6%
18	North Carolina	742,512,000	1.5%
19	Indiana	698,725,000	1.4%
20	Colorado	660,100,000	1.4%
21	Alabama	577,516,000	1.2%
22	Kentucky	511,353,000	1.1%
23	Iowa	443,187,000	0.9%
24	Kansas	437,967,000	0.9%
25	Mississippi	437,407,000	0.9%
26	South Carolina	424,048,000	0.9%
27	Utah	400,885,000	0.8%
28	Arkansas	390,756,000	0.8%
29	Arizona	373,076,000	0.8%
30	Louisiana	358,208,000	0.7%
31	Missouri	333,724,000	0.7%
32	Nebraska	313,690,000	0.7%
33	Delaware	254,802,000	0.5%
34	Idaho	240,809,000	0.5%
35	Oklahoma	234,868,000	0.5%
36	Alaska	196,321,000	0.4%
37	Maine	185,737,000	0.4%
38	Montana	176,132,000	0.4%
39	Hawaii	146,831,000	0.3%
40	Rhode Island	118,118,000	0.2%
41	Vermont	110,819,000	0.2%
42	West Virginia	110,068,000	0.2%
43	North Dakota	107,277,000	0.2%
44	New Mexico	91,488,000	0.2%
45	South Dakota	32,376,000	0.1%
46	Ohio	9,046,000	0.0%
47	Nevada	0	0.0%
47	Texas	0	0.0%
47	Washington	0	0.0%
47	Wyoming	0	0.0%
	District of Columbia	574,745,000	1.2%

Source: U.S. Bureau of the Census, Governments Division
"2018 State Government Tax Collections" (https://www.census.gov/programs-surveys/stc.html)

Per Capita State Government Corporation Net Income Tax Revenue in 2018

National Per Capita = $147

ALPHA ORDER				RANK ORDER		
RANK	**STATE**	**PER CAPITA**		**RANK**	**STATE**	**PER CAPITA**
27	Alabama	$118		1	New Hampshire	$582
4	Alaska	266		2	Massachusetts	349
43	Arizona	52		3	California	316
25	Arkansas	130		4	Alaska	266
3	California	316		5	Delaware	263
28	Colorado	116		6	New Jersey	251
9	Connecticut	218		7	Tennessee	243
5	Delaware	263		8	Minnesota	242
29	Florida	114		9	Connecticut	218
36	Georgia	95		10	Illinois	203
34	Hawaii	103		11	Pennsylvania	194
24	Idaho	137		12	Oregon	192
10	Illinois	203		13	New York	185
33	Indiana	104		14	Vermont	177
22	Iowa	140		15	Maryland	171
19	Kansas	150		16	Montana	166
29	Kentucky	114		17	Nebraska	163
38	Louisiana	77		18	Wisconsin	157
23	Maine	139		19	Kansas	150
15	Maryland	171		20	Mississippi	146
2	Massachusetts	349		21	North Dakota	141
32	Michigan	110		22	Iowa	140
8	Minnesota	242		23	Maine	139
20	Mississippi	146		24	Idaho	137
42	Missouri	54		25	Arkansas	130
16	Montana	166		26	Utah	127
17	Nebraska	163		27	Alabama	118
47	Nevada	0		28	Colorado	116
1	New Hampshire	582		29	Florida	114
6	New Jersey	251		29	Kentucky	114
44	New Mexico	44		31	Rhode Island	112
13	New York	185		32	Michigan	110
39	North Carolina	72		33	Indiana	104
21	North Dakota	141		34	Hawaii	103
46	Ohio	1		35	Virginia	101
41	Oklahoma	60		36	Georgia	95
12	Oregon	192		37	South Carolina	83
11	Pennsylvania	194		38	Louisiana	77
31	Rhode Island	112		39	North Carolina	72
37	South Carolina	83		40	West Virginia	61
45	South Dakota	37		41	Oklahoma	60
7	Tennessee	243		42	Missouri	54
47	Texas	0		43	Arizona	52
26	Utah	127		44	New Mexico	44
14	Vermont	177		45	South Dakota	37
35	Virginia	101		46	Ohio	1
47	Washington	0		47	Nevada	0
40	West Virginia	61		47	Texas	0
18	Wisconsin	157		47	Washington	0
47	Wyoming	0		47	Wyoming	0
					District of Columbia	818

Source: CQ Press using data from U.S. Bureau of the Census, Governments Division
"2018 State Government Tax Collections" (https://www.census.gov/programs-surveys/stc.html)

State Government General Sales Tax Revenue in 2018

National Total = $317,422,936,000*

ALPHA ORDER

RANK	STATE	REVENUE	% of USA
33	Alabama	$2,786,833,000	0.9%
46	Alaska	0	0.0%
13	Arizona	7,687,992,000	2.4%
28	Arkansas	3,498,073,000	1.1%
1	California	36,188,907,000	11.4%
32	Colorado	3,211,909,000	1.0%
21	Connecticut	4,530,509,000	1.4%
46	Delaware	0	0.0%
3	Florida	29,562,900,000	9.3%
16	Georgia	5,938,448,000	1.9%
27	Hawaii	3,529,065,000	1.1%
38	Idaho	1,790,830,000	0.6%
7	Illinois	11,336,866,000	3.6%
12	Indiana	7,795,091,000	2.5%
31	Iowa	3,279,789,000	1.0%
29	Kansas	3,304,091,000	1.0%
25	Kentucky	3,600,598,000	1.1%
22	Louisiana	4,252,693,000	1.3%
39	Maine	1,529,113,000	0.5%
20	Maryland	4,716,179,000	1.5%
15	Massachusetts	6,490,305,000	2.0%
10	Michigan	9,854,016,000	3.1%
17	Minnesota	5,830,256,000	1.8%
26	Mississippi	3,557,752,000	1.1%
24	Missouri	3,686,274,000	1.2%
46	Montana	0	0.0%
37	Nebraska	1,900,037,000	0.6%
19	Nevada	5,095,689,000	1.6%
46	New Hampshire	0	0.0%
9	New Jersey	10,459,419,000	3.3%
36	New Mexico	2,073,118,000	0.7%
5	New York	14,820,163,000	4.7%
11	North Carolina	8,009,850,000	2.5%
43	North Dakota	912,532,000	0.3%
6	Ohio	12,148,485,000	3.8%
34	Oklahoma	2,724,367,000	0.9%
46	Oregon	0	0.0%
8	Pennsylvania	10,920,832,000	3.4%
42	Rhode Island	1,048,957,000	0.3%
30	South Carolina	3,303,220,000	1.0%
41	South Dakota	1,103,624,000	0.3%
14	Tennessee	7,469,547,000	2.4%
2	Texas	36,129,876,000	11.4%
35	Utah	2,248,774,000	0.7%
45	Vermont	397,691,000	0.1%
23	Virginia	4,076,636,000	1.3%
4	Washington	15,643,017,000	4.9%
40	West Virginia	1,311,930,000	0.4%
18	Wisconsin	5,484,375,000	1.7%
44	Wyoming	689,207,000	0.2%

RANK ORDER

RANK	STATE	REVENUE	% of USA
1	California	$36,188,907,000	11.4%
2	Texas	36,129,876,000	11.4%
3	Florida	29,562,900,000	9.3%
4	Washington	15,643,017,000	4.9%
5	New York	14,820,163,000	4.7%
6	Ohio	12,148,485,000	3.8%
7	Illinois	11,336,866,000	3.6%
8	Pennsylvania	10,920,832,000	3.4%
9	New Jersey	10,459,419,000	3.3%
10	Michigan	9,854,016,000	3.1%
11	North Carolina	8,009,850,000	2.5%
12	Indiana	7,795,091,000	2.5%
13	Arizona	7,687,992,000	2.4%
14	Tennessee	7,469,547,000	2.4%
15	Massachusetts	6,490,305,000	2.0%
16	Georgia	5,938,448,000	1.9%
17	Minnesota	5,830,256,000	1.8%
18	Wisconsin	5,484,375,000	1.7%
19	Nevada	5,095,689,000	1.6%
20	Maryland	4,716,179,000	1.5%
21	Connecticut	4,530,509,000	1.4%
22	Louisiana	4,252,693,000	1.3%
23	Virginia	4,076,636,000	1.3%
24	Missouri	3,686,274,000	1.2%
25	Kentucky	3,600,598,000	1.1%
26	Mississippi	3,557,752,000	1.1%
27	Hawaii	3,529,065,000	1.1%
28	Arkansas	3,498,073,000	1.1%
29	Kansas	3,304,091,000	1.0%
30	South Carolina	3,303,220,000	1.0%
31	Iowa	3,279,789,000	1.0%
32	Colorado	3,211,909,000	1.0%
33	Alabama	2,786,833,000	0.9%
34	Oklahoma	2,724,367,000	0.9%
35	Utah	2,248,774,000	0.7%
36	New Mexico	2,073,118,000	0.7%
37	Nebraska	1,900,037,000	0.6%
38	Idaho	1,790,830,000	0.6%
39	Malne	1,529,113,000	0.5%
40	West Virginia	1,311,930,000	0.4%
41	South Dakota	1,103,624,000	0.3%
42	Rhode Island	1,048,957,000	0.3%
43	North Dakota	912,532,000	0.3%
44	Wyoming	689,207,000	0.2%
45	Vermont	397,691,000	0.1%
46	Alaska	0	0.0%
46	Delaware	0	0.0%
46	Montana	0	0.0%
46	New Hampshire	0	0.0%
46	Oregon	0	0.0%
	District of Columbia	1,493,101,000	0.5%

Source: U.S. Bureau of the Census, Governments Division
   "2018 State Government Tax Collections" (https://www.census.gov/programs-surveys/stc.html)
*Does not include special sales taxes such as those on sale of alcohol, gasoline, or tobacco.

Per Capita State Government General Sales Tax Revenue in 2018

National Per Capita = $970*

ALPHA ORDER

RANK	STATE	PER CAPITA
42	Alabama	$570
46	Alaska	0
17	Arizona	1,072
13	Arkansas	1,161
28	California	915
44	Colorado	564
5	Connecticut	1,268
46	Delaware	0
4	Florida	1,388
43	Georgia	565
1	Hawaii	2,484
21	Idaho	1,021
30	Illinois	890
12	Indiana	1,165
18	Iowa	1,039
15	Kansas	1,135
32	Kentucky	806
29	Louisiana	913
14	Maine	1,142
33	Maryland	780
27	Massachusetts	940
24	Michigan	986
18	Minnesota	1,039
10	Mississippi	1,191
41	Missouri	602
46	Montana	0
25	Nebraska	985
3	Nevada	1,679
46	New Hampshire	0
11	New Jersey	1,174
23	New Mexico	989
35	New York	758
34	North Carolina	771
8	North Dakota	1,201
18	Ohio	1,039
38	Oklahoma	691
46	Oregon	0
31	Pennsylvania	853
22	Rhode Island	992
39	South Carolina	650
7	South Dakota	1,251
16	Tennessee	1,103
6	Texas	1,259
37	Utah	711
40	Vermont	635
45	Virginia	479
2	Washington	2,076
36	West Virginia	726
26	Wisconsin	943
9	Wyoming	1,193

RANK ORDER

RANK	STATE	PER CAPITA
1	Hawaii	$2,484
2	Washington	2,076
3	Nevada	1,679
4	Florida	1,388
5	Connecticut	1,268
6	Texas	1,259
7	South Dakota	1,251
8	North Dakota	1,201
9	Wyoming	1,193
10	Mississippi	1,191
11	New Jersey	1,174
12	Indiana	1,165
13	Arkansas	1,161
14	Maine	1,142
15	Kansas	1,135
16	Tennessee	1,103
17	Arizona	1,072
18	Iowa	1,039
18	Minnesota	1,039
18	Ohio	1,039
21	Idaho	1,021
22	Rhode Island	992
23	New Mexico	989
24	Michigan	986
25	Nebraska	985
26	Wisconsin	943
27	Massachusetts	940
28	California	915
29	Louisiana	913
30	Illinois	890
31	Pennsylvania	853
32	Kentucky	806
33	Maryland	780
34	North Carolina	771
35	New York	758
36	West Virginia	726
37	Utah	711
38	Oklahoma	691
39	South Carolina	650
40	Vermont	635
41	Missouri	602
42	Alabama	570
43	Georgia	565
44	Colorado	564
45	Virginia	479
46	Alaska	0
46	Delaware	0
46	Montana	0
46	New Hampshire	0
46	Oregon	0

District of Columbia	2,126

Source: CQ Press using data from U.S. Bureau of the Census, Governments Division
"2018 State Government Tax Collections" (https://www.census.gov/programs-surveys/stc.html)
*Does not include special sales taxes such as those on sale of alcohol, gasoline, or tobacco.

State Government Motor Fuels Sales Tax Revenue in 2018

National Total = $48,262,883,000

<table>
<tr><td colspan="4">ALPHA ORDER</td><td colspan="4">RANK ORDER</td></tr>
<tr><td>RANK</td><td>STATE</td><td>REVENUE</td><td>% of USA</td><td>RANK</td><td>STATE</td><td>REVENUE</td><td>% of USA</td></tr>
<tr><td>24</td><td>Alabama</td><td>$648,639,000</td><td>1.3%</td><td>1</td><td>California</td><td>$6,351,756,000</td><td>13.2%</td></tr>
<tr><td>50</td><td>Alaska</td><td>47,149,000</td><td>0.1%</td><td>2</td><td>Texas</td><td>3,710,307,000</td><td>7.7%</td></tr>
<tr><td>18</td><td>Arizona</td><td>869,183,000</td><td>1.8%</td><td>3</td><td>Pennsylvania</td><td>3,375,429,000</td><td>7.0%</td></tr>
<tr><td>29</td><td>Arkansas</td><td>492,945,000</td><td>1.0%</td><td>4</td><td>Florida</td><td>2,799,610,000</td><td>5.8%</td></tr>
<tr><td>1</td><td>California</td><td>6,351,756,000</td><td>13.2%</td><td>5</td><td>North Carolina</td><td>1,974,782,000</td><td>4.1%</td></tr>
<tr><td>22</td><td>Colorado</td><td>675,962,000</td><td>1.4%</td><td>6</td><td>Ohio</td><td>1,912,191,000</td><td>4.0%</td></tr>
<tr><td>30</td><td>Connecticut</td><td>487,327,000</td><td>1.0%</td><td>7</td><td>Georgia</td><td>1,801,798,000</td><td>3.7%</td></tr>
<tr><td>45</td><td>Delaware</td><td>131,864,000</td><td>0.3%</td><td>8</td><td>Washington</td><td>1,713,782,000</td><td>3.6%</td></tr>
<tr><td>4</td><td>Florida</td><td>2,799,610,000</td><td>5.8%</td><td>9</td><td>New York</td><td>1,636,749,000</td><td>3.4%</td></tr>
<tr><td>7</td><td>Georgia</td><td>1,801,798,000</td><td>3.7%</td><td>10</td><td>Michigan</td><td>1,445,786,000</td><td>3.0%</td></tr>
<tr><td>47</td><td>Hawaii</td><td>88,377,000</td><td>0.2%</td><td>11</td><td>Indiana</td><td>1,420,135,000</td><td>2.9%</td></tr>
<tr><td>37</td><td>Idaho</td><td>362,234,000</td><td>0.8%</td><td>12</td><td>Illinois</td><td>1,367,939,000</td><td>2.8%</td></tr>
<tr><td>12</td><td>Illinois</td><td>1,367,939,000</td><td>2.8%</td><td>13</td><td>Tennessee</td><td>1,086,693,000</td><td>2.3%</td></tr>
<tr><td>11</td><td>Indiana</td><td>1,420,135,000</td><td>2.9%</td><td>14</td><td>Maryland</td><td>1,084,195,000</td><td>2.2%</td></tr>
<tr><td>23</td><td>Iowa</td><td>671,937,000</td><td>1.4%</td><td>15</td><td>Wisconsin</td><td>1,051,479,000</td><td>2.2%</td></tr>
<tr><td>32</td><td>Kansas</td><td>461,075,000</td><td>1.0%</td><td>16</td><td>Virginia</td><td>1,031,034,000</td><td>2.1%</td></tr>
<tr><td>21</td><td>Kentucky</td><td>702,651,000</td><td>1.5%</td><td>17</td><td>Minnesota</td><td>936,893,000</td><td>1.9%</td></tr>
<tr><td>26</td><td>Louisiana</td><td>631,641,000</td><td>1.3%</td><td>18</td><td>Arizona</td><td>869,183,000</td><td>1.8%</td></tr>
<tr><td>40</td><td>Maine</td><td>250,468,000</td><td>0.5%</td><td>19</td><td>Massachusetts</td><td>769,144,000</td><td>1.6%</td></tr>
<tr><td>14</td><td>Maryland</td><td>1,084,195,000</td><td>2.2%</td><td>20</td><td>Missouri</td><td>717,894,000</td><td>1.5%</td></tr>
<tr><td>19</td><td>Massachusetts</td><td>769,144,000</td><td>1.6%</td><td>21</td><td>Kentucky</td><td>702,651,000</td><td>1.5%</td></tr>
<tr><td>10</td><td>Michigan</td><td>1,445,786,000</td><td>3.0%</td><td>22</td><td>Colorado</td><td>675,962,000</td><td>1.4%</td></tr>
<tr><td>17</td><td>Minnesota</td><td>936,893,000</td><td>1.9%</td><td>23</td><td>Iowa</td><td>671,937,000</td><td>1.4%</td></tr>
<tr><td>34</td><td>Mississippi</td><td>436,245,000</td><td>0.9%</td><td>24</td><td>Alabama</td><td>648,639,000</td><td>1.3%</td></tr>
<tr><td>20</td><td>Missouri</td><td>717,894,000</td><td>1.5%</td><td>25</td><td>South Carolina</td><td>646,581,000</td><td>1.3%</td></tr>
<tr><td>39</td><td>Montana</td><td>254,167,000</td><td>0.5%</td><td>26</td><td>Louisiana</td><td>631,641,000</td><td>1.3%</td></tr>
<tr><td>36</td><td>Nebraska</td><td>373,889,000</td><td>0.8%</td><td>27</td><td>Oregon</td><td>538,539,000</td><td>1.1%</td></tr>
<tr><td>38</td><td>Nevada</td><td>343,386,000</td><td>0.7%</td><td>28</td><td>Utah</td><td>496,789,000</td><td>1.0%</td></tr>
<tr><td>44</td><td>New Hampshire</td><td>183,366,000</td><td>0.4%</td><td>29</td><td>Arkansas</td><td>492,945,000</td><td>1.0%</td></tr>
<tr><td>33</td><td>New Jersey</td><td>458,892,000</td><td>1.0%</td><td>30</td><td>Connecticut</td><td>487,327,000</td><td>1.0%</td></tr>
<tr><td>41</td><td>New Mexico</td><td>230,303,000</td><td>0.5%</td><td>31</td><td>Oklahoma</td><td>485,376,000</td><td>1.0%</td></tr>
<tr><td>9</td><td>New York</td><td>1,636,749,000</td><td>3.4%</td><td>32</td><td>Kansas</td><td>461,075,000</td><td>1.0%</td></tr>
<tr><td>5</td><td>North Carolina</td><td>1,974,782,000</td><td>4.1%</td><td>33</td><td>New Jersey</td><td>458,892,000</td><td>1.0%</td></tr>
<tr><td>42</td><td>North Dakota</td><td>196,649,000</td><td>0.4%</td><td>34</td><td>Mississippi</td><td>436,245,000</td><td>0.9%</td></tr>
<tr><td>6</td><td>Ohio</td><td>1,912,191,000</td><td>4.0%</td><td>35</td><td>West Virginia</td><td>419,528,000</td><td>0.9%</td></tr>
<tr><td>31</td><td>Oklahoma</td><td>485,376,000</td><td>1.0%</td><td>36</td><td>Nebraska</td><td>373,889,000</td><td>0.8%</td></tr>
<tr><td>27</td><td>Oregon</td><td>538,539,000</td><td>1.1%</td><td>37</td><td>Idaho</td><td>362,234,000</td><td>0.8%</td></tr>
<tr><td>3</td><td>Pennsylvania</td><td>3,375,429,000</td><td>7.0%</td><td>38</td><td>Nevada</td><td>343,386,000</td><td>0.7%</td></tr>
<tr><td>49</td><td>Rhode Island</td><td>79,858,000</td><td>0.2%</td><td>39</td><td>Montana</td><td>254,167,000</td><td>0.5%</td></tr>
<tr><td>25</td><td>South Carolina</td><td>646,581,000</td><td>1.3%</td><td>40</td><td>Maine</td><td>250,468,000</td><td>0.5%</td></tr>
<tr><td>43</td><td>South Dakota</td><td>187,424,000</td><td>0.4%</td><td>41</td><td>New Mexico</td><td>230,303,000</td><td>0.5%</td></tr>
<tr><td>13</td><td>Tennessee</td><td>1,086,693,000</td><td>2.3%</td><td>42</td><td>North Dakota</td><td>196,649,000</td><td>0.4%</td></tr>
<tr><td>2</td><td>Texas</td><td>3,710,307,000</td><td>7.7%</td><td>43</td><td>South Dakota</td><td>187,424,000</td><td>0.4%</td></tr>
<tr><td>28</td><td>Utah</td><td>496,789,000</td><td>1.0%</td><td>44</td><td>New Hampshire</td><td>183,366,000</td><td>0.4%</td></tr>
<tr><td>48</td><td>Vermont</td><td>82,953,000</td><td>0.2%</td><td>45</td><td>Delaware</td><td>131,864,000</td><td>0.3%</td></tr>
<tr><td>16</td><td>Virginia</td><td>1,031,034,000</td><td>2.1%</td><td>46</td><td>Wyoming</td><td>113,622,000</td><td>0.2%</td></tr>
<tr><td>8</td><td>Washington</td><td>1,713,782,000</td><td>3.6%</td><td>47</td><td>Hawaii</td><td>88,377,000</td><td>0.2%</td></tr>
<tr><td>35</td><td>West Virginia</td><td>419,528,000</td><td>0.9%</td><td>48</td><td>Vermont</td><td>82,953,000</td><td>0.2%</td></tr>
<tr><td>15</td><td>Wisconsin</td><td>1,051,479,000</td><td>2.2%</td><td>49</td><td>Rhode Island</td><td>79,858,000</td><td>0.2%</td></tr>
<tr><td>46</td><td>Wyoming</td><td>113,622,000</td><td>0.2%</td><td>50</td><td>Alaska</td><td>47,149,000</td><td>0.1%</td></tr>
<tr><td></td><td></td><td></td><td></td><td></td><td>District of Columbia</td><td>26,268,000</td><td>0.1%</td></tr>
</table>

Source: U.S. Bureau of the Census, Governments Division
"2018 State Government Tax Collections" (https://www.census.gov/programs-surveys/stc.html)

Per Capita State Government Motor Fuel Sales Tax Revenue in 2018

National Per Capita = $148

RANK	STATE	PER CAPITA
31	Alabama	$133
48	Alaska	64
38	Arizona	121
18	Arkansas	164
20	California	161
40	Colorado	119
27	Connecticut	136
27	Delaware	136
33	Florida	131
16	Georgia	171
49	Hawaii	62
9	Idaho	206
45	Illinois	107
7	Indiana	212
6	Iowa	213
22	Kansas	158
23	Kentucky	157
27	Louisiana	136
13	Maine	187
15	Maryland	179
43	Massachusetts	111
26	Michigan	145
17	Minnesota	167
25	Mississippi	146
41	Missouri	117
3	Montana	239
11	Nebraska	194
42	Nevada	113
30	New Hampshire	135
50	New Jersey	52
44	New Mexico	110
46	New York	84
12	North Carolina	190
2	North Dakota	259
18	Ohio	164
37	Oklahoma	123
34	Oregon	129
1	Pennsylvania	264
47	Rhode Island	76
36	South Carolina	127
7	South Dakota	212
20	Tennessee	161
34	Texas	129
23	Utah	157
32	Vermont	132
38	Virginia	121
5	Washington	227
4	West Virginia	232
14	Wisconsin	181
10	Wyoming	197

RANK	STATE	PER CAPITA
1	Pennsylvania	$264
2	North Dakota	259
3	Montana	239
4	West Virginia	232
5	Washington	227
6	Iowa	213
7	Indiana	212
7	South Dakota	212
9	Idaho	206
10	Wyoming	197
11	Nebraska	194
12	North Carolina	190
13	Maine	187
14	Wisconsin	181
15	Maryland	179
16	Georgia	171
17	Minnesota	167
18	Arkansas	164
18	Ohio	164
20	California	161
20	Tennessee	161
22	Kansas	158
23	Kentucky	157
23	Utah	157
25	Mississippi	146
26	Michigan	145
27	Connecticut	136
27	Delaware	136
27	Louisiana	136
30	New Hampshire	135
31	Alabama	133
32	Vermont	132
33	Florida	131
34	Oregon	129
34	Texas	129
36	South Carolina	127
37	Oklahoma	123
38	Arizona	121
38	Virginia	121
40	Colorado	119
41	Missouri	117
42	Nevada	113
43	Massachusetts	111
44	New Mexico	110
45	Illinois	107
46	New York	84
47	Rhode Island	76
48	Alaska	64
49	Hawaii	62
50	New Jersey	52
	District of Columbia	37

Source: CQ Press using data from U.S. Bureau of the Census, Governments Division
"2018 State Government Tax Collections" (https://www.census.gov/programs-surveys/stc.html)

State Tax Rates on Gasoline in 2020

National Median = 26.30 Cents per Gallon*

ALPHA ORDER				RANK ORDER		
RANK	STATE	CENTS PER GALLON		RANK	STATE	CENTS PER GALLON
32	Alabama	24.00		1	Pennsylvania	57.60
50	Alaska	8.95		2	California	53.30
44	Arizona	19.00		3	Washington	49.40
30	Arkansas	24.80		4	New Jersey	41.40
2	California	53.30		5	Illinois	39.10
40	Colorado	22.00		6	Ohio	38.50
29	Connecticut	25.00		7	Maryland	36.70
37	Delaware	23.00		8	North Carolina	36.35
12	Florida	34.40		9	Oregon	36.00
24	Georgia	27.90		10	West Virginia	35.70
49	Hawaii	16.00		11	Rhode Island	35.00
13	Idaho	33.00		12	Florida	34.40
5	Illinois	39.10		13	Idaho	33.00
20	Indiana	30.00		14	Wisconsin	32.90
18	Iowa	30.50		15	Montana	32.00
31	Kansas	24.03		16	Utah	31.10
27	Kentucky	26.00		17	Vermont	30.81
41	Louisiana	20.00		18	Iowa	30.50
20	Maine	30.00		19	Nebraska	30.20
7	Maryland	36.70		20	Indiana	30.00
32	Massachusetts	24.00		20	Maine	30.00
26	Michigan	26.30		20	South Dakota	30.00
23	Minnesota	28.60		23	Minnesota	28.60
46	Mississippi	18.40		24	Georgia	27.90
47	Missouri	17.40		25	Tennessee	27.40
15	Montana	32.00		26	Michigan	26.30
19	Nebraska	30.20		27	Kentucky	26.00
36	Nevada	23.81		28	New York	25.45
35	New Hampshire	23.83		29	Connecticut	25.00
4	New Jersey	41.40		30	Arkansas	24.80
45	New Mexico	18.88		31	Kansas	24.03
28	New York	25.45		32	Alabama	24.00
8	North Carolina	36.35		32	Massachusetts	24.00
37	North Dakota	23.00		32	Wyoming	24.00
6	Ohio	38.50		35	New Hampshire	23.83
42	Oklahoma	20.00		36	Nevada	23.81
9	Oregon	36.00		37	Delaware	23.00
1	Pennsylvania	57.60		37	North Dakota	23.00
11	Rhode Island	35.00		39	South Carolina	22.75
39	South Carolina	22.75		40	Colorado	22.00
20	South Dakota	30.00		41	Louisiana	20.00
25	Tennessee	27.40		42	Oklahoma	20.00
42	Texas	20.00		42	Texas	20.00
16	Utah	31.10		44	Arizona	19.00
17	Vermont	30.81		45	New Mexico	18.88
48	Virginia	16.20		46	Mississippi	18.40
3	Washington	49.40		47	Missouri	17.40
10	West Virginia	35.70		48	Virginia	16.20
14	Wisconsin	32.90		49	Hawaii	16.00
32	Wyoming	24.00		50	Alaska	8.95
					District of Columbia	23.50

Source: Federation of Tax Administrators
   "Motor Fuel Excise Tax Rates" (https://www.taxadmin.org/current-tax-rates)
*As of January 1, 2020. Federal gasoline tax rate is an additional 18.4 cents per gallon. Many states also allow additional local option taxes on gasoline.

State Government Motor Vehicle and Operators' License Tax Revenue in 2018

National Total = $30,575,490,000

ALPHA ORDER

RANK	STATE	REVENUE	% of USA
29	Alabama	$253,908,000	0.8%
49	Alaska	36,258,000	0.1%
27	Arizona	260,017,000	0.9%
36	Arkansas	187,248,000	0.6%
1	California	4,916,085,000	16.1%
15	Colorado	638,891,000	2.1%
25	Connecticut	281,167,000	0.9%
48	Delaware	64,807,000	0.2%
4	Florida	1,614,936,000	5.3%
22	Georgia	510,055,000	1.7%
35	Hawaii	192,063,000	0.6%
33	Idaho	205,772,000	0.7%
3	Illinois	1,734,868,000	5.7%
17	Indiana	573,088,000	1.9%
14	Iowa	686,011,000	2.2%
28	Kansas	254,859,000	0.8%
31	Kentucky	228,441,000	0.7%
44	Louisiana	94,761,000	0.3%
41	Maine	123,373,000	0.4%
21	Maryland	529,346,000	1.7%
19	Massachusetts	546,259,000	1.8%
6	Michigan	1,380,858,000	4.5%
11	Minnesota	846,777,000	2.8%
37	Mississippi	172,645,000	0.6%
24	Missouri	314,445,000	1.0%
39	Montana	163,804,000	0.5%
40	Nebraska	125,271,000	0.4%
32	Nevada	226,362,000	0.7%
45	New Hampshire	90,778,000	0.3%
13	New Jersey	715,170,000	2.3%
34	New Mexico	205,731,000	0.7%
5	New York	1,504,995,000	4.9%
9	North Carolina	974,911,000	3.2%
42	North Dakota	123,129,000	0.4%
10	Ohio	867,503,000	2.8%
12	Oklahoma	800,445,000	2.6%
16	Oregon	579,232,000	1.9%
8	Pennsylvania	1,256,860,000	4.1%
50	Rhode Island	25,620,000	0.1%
26	South Carolina	278,579,000	0.9%
46	South Dakota	89,045,000	0.3%
23	Tennessee	417,340,000	1.4%
2	Texas	2,500,140,000	8.2%
30	Utah	235,158,000	0.8%
47	Vermont	84,929,000	0.3%
20	Virginia	534,113,000	1.7%
7	Washington	1,264,941,000	4.1%
38	West Virginia	164,574,000	0.5%
18	Wisconsin	558,513,000	1.8%
43	Wyoming	95,821,000	0.3%

RANK ORDER

RANK	STATE	REVENUE	% of USA
1	California	$4,916,085,000	16.1%
2	Texas	2,500,140,000	8.2%
3	Illinois	1,734,868,000	5.7%
4	Florida	1,614,936,000	5.3%
5	New York	1,504,995,000	4.9%
6	Michigan	1,380,858,000	4.5%
7	Washington	1,264,941,000	4.1%
8	Pennsylvania	1,256,860,000	4.1%
9	North Carolina	974,911,000	3.2%
10	Ohio	867,503,000	2.8%
11	Minnesota	846,777,000	2.8%
12	Oklahoma	800,445,000	2.6%
13	New Jersey	715,170,000	2.3%
14	Iowa	686,011,000	2.2%
15	Colorado	638,891,000	2.1%
16	Oregon	579,232,000	1.9%
17	Indiana	573,088,000	1.9%
18	Wisconsin	558,513,000	1.8%
19	Massachusetts	546,259,000	1.8%
20	Virginia	534,113,000	1.7%
21	Maryland	529,346,000	1.7%
22	Georgia	510,055,000	1.7%
23	Tennessee	417,340,000	1.4%
24	Missouri	314,445,000	1.0%
25	Connecticut	281,167,000	0.9%
26	South Carolina	278,579,000	0.9%
27	Arizona	260,017,000	0.9%
28	Kansas	254,859,000	0.8%
29	Alabama	253,908,000	0.8%
30	Utah	235,158,000	0.8%
31	Kentucky	228,441,000	0.7%
32	Nevada	226,362,000	0.7%
33	Idaho	205,772,000	0.7%
34	New Mexico	205,731,000	0.7%
35	Hawaii	192,063,000	0.6%
36	Arkansas	187,248,000	0.6%
37	Mississippi	172,645,000	0.6%
38	West Virginia	164,574,000	0.5%
39	Montana	163,804,000	0.5%
40	Nebraska	125,271,000	0.4%
41	Maine	123,373,000	0.4%
42	North Dakota	123,129,000	0.4%
43	Wyoming	95,821,000	0.3%
44	Louisiana	94,761,000	0.3%
45	New Hampshire	90,778,000	0.3%
46	South Dakota	89,045,000	0.3%
47	Vermont	84,929,000	0.3%
48	Delaware	64,807,000	0.2%
49	Alaska	36,258,000	0.1%
50	Rhode Island	25,620,000	0.1%
	District of Columbia	45,588,000	0.1%

Source: U.S. Bureau of the Census, Governments Division
"2018 State Government Tax Collections" (https://www.census.gov/programs-surveys/stc.html)

Per Capita State Government Motor Vehicle and Operators' License Tax Revenue in 2018
National Per Capita = $93

ALPHA ORDER

RANK	STATE	PER CAPITA
43	Alabama	$52
46	Alaska	49
48	Arizona	36
39	Arkansas	62
13	California	124
15	Colorado	112
28	Connecticut	79
35	Delaware	67
31	Florida	76
47	Georgia	48
12	Hawaii	135
14	Idaho	117
10	Illinois	136
26	Indiana	86
1	Iowa	217
23	Kansas	88
44	Kentucky	51
50	Louisiana	20
21	Maine	92
23	Maryland	88
28	Massachusetts	79
8	Michigan	138
7	Minnesota	151
41	Mississippi	58
44	Missouri	51
6	Montana	154
37	Nebraska	65
32	Nevada	75
35	New Hampshire	67
27	New Jersey	80
17	New Mexico	98
30	New York	77
20	North Carolina	94
5	North Dakota	162
33	Ohio	74
2	Oklahoma	203
8	Oregon	138
17	Pennsylvania	98
49	Rhode Island	24
42	South Carolina	55
16	South Dakota	101
39	Tennessee	62
25	Texas	87
33	Utah	74
10	Vermont	136
38	Virginia	63
3	Washington	168
22	West Virginia	91
19	Wisconsin	96
4	Wyoming	166

RANK ORDER

RANK	STATE	PER CAPITA
1	Iowa	$217
2	Oklahoma	203
3	Washington	168
4	Wyoming	166
5	North Dakota	162
6	Montana	154
7	Minnesota	151
8	Michigan	138
8	Oregon	138
10	Illinois	136
10	Vermont	136
12	Hawaii	135
13	California	124
14	Idaho	117
15	Colorado	112
16	South Dakota	101
17	New Mexico	98
17	Pennsylvania	98
19	Wisconsin	96
20	North Carolina	94
21	Maine	92
22	West Virginia	91
23	Kansas	88
23	Maryland	88
25	Texas	87
26	Indiana	86
27	New Jersey	80
28	Connecticut	79
28	Massachusetts	79
30	New York	77
31	Florida	76
32	Nevada	75
33	Ohio	74
33	Utah	74
35	Delaware	67
35	New Hampshire	67
37	Nebraska	65
38	Virginia	63
39	Arkansas	62
39	Tennessee	62
41	Mississippi	58
42	South Carolina	55
43	Alabama	52
44	Kentucky	51
44	Missouri	51
46	Alaska	49
47	Georgia	48
48	Arizona	36
49	Rhode Island	24
50	Louisiana	20
	District of Columbia	65

Source: CQ Press using data from U.S. Bureau of the Census, Governments Division
"2018 State Government Tax Collections" (https://www.census.gov/programs-surveys/stc.html)

State Government Tobacco Product Sales Tax Revenue in 2018

National Total = $19,502,424,000

ALPHA ORDER

RANK	STATE	REVENUE	% of USA
28	Alabama	$179,929,000	0.9%
46	Alaska	55,500,000	0.3%
18	Arizona	312,808,000	1.6%
23	Arkansas	226,728,000	1.2%
1	California	2,428,121,000	12.5%
27	Colorado	193,881,000	1.0%
15	Connecticut	376,814,000	1.9%
37	Delaware	123,026,000	0.6%
4	Florida	1,172,492,000	6.0%
24	Georgia	224,910,000	1.2%
38	Hawaii	120,386,000	0.6%
47	Idaho	51,141,000	0.3%
8	Illinois	764,296,000	3.9%
14	Indiana	418,810,000	2.1%
26	Iowa	212,469,000	1.1%
36	Kansas	130,247,000	0.7%
22	Kentucky	228,749,000	1.2%
31	Louisiana	163,770,000	0.8%
35	Maine	132,950,000	0.7%
16	Maryland	372,724,000	1.9%
11	Massachusetts	594,173,000	3.0%
6	Michigan	1,007,822,000	5.2%
12	Minnesota	593,410,000	3.0%
34	Mississippi	139,733,000	0.7%
40	Missouri	97,408,000	0.5%
42	Montana	80,532,000	0.4%
45	Nebraska	57,123,000	0.3%
30	Nevada	177,161,000	0.9%
25	New Hampshire	212,698,000	1.1%
9	New Jersey	660,315,000	3.4%
41	New Mexico	93,862,000	0.5%
5	New York	1,151,660,000	5.9%
19	North Carolina	292,143,000	1.5%
48	North Dakota	28,001,000	0.1%
7	Ohio	941,105,000	4.8%
17	Oklahoma	313,411,000	1.6%
20	Oregon	263,860,000	1.4%
3	Pennsylvania	1,372,695,000	7.0%
33	Rhode Island	146,691,000	0.8%
49	South Carolina	27,199,000	0.1%
44	South Dakota	59,158,000	0.3%
21	Tennessee	248,673,000	1.3%
2	Texas	1,440,336,000	7.4%
39	Utah	114,492,000	0.6%
43	Vermont	71,078,000	0.4%
32	Virginia	160,383,000	0.8%
13	Washington	422,264,000	2.2%
29	West Virginia	177,840,000	0.9%
10	Wisconsin	617,415,000	3.2%
50	Wyoming	22,076,000	0.1%

RANK ORDER

RANK	STATE	REVENUE	% of USA
1	California	$2,428,121,000	12.5%
2	Texas	1,440,336,000	7.4%
3	Pennsylvania	1,372,695,000	7.0%
4	Florida	1,172,492,000	6.0%
5	New York	1,151,660,000	5.9%
6	Michigan	1,007,822,000	5.2%
7	Ohio	941,105,000	4.8%
8	Illinois	764,296,000	3.9%
9	New Jersey	660,315,000	3.4%
10	Wisconsin	617,415,000	3.2%
11	Massachusetts	594,173,000	3.0%
12	Minnesota	593,410,000	3.0%
13	Washington	422,264,000	2.2%
14	Indiana	418,810,000	2.1%
15	Connecticut	376,814,000	1.9%
16	Maryland	372,724,000	1.9%
17	Oklahoma	313,411,000	1.6%
18	Arizona	312,808,000	1.6%
19	North Carolina	292,143,000	1.5%
20	Oregon	263,860,000	1.4%
21	Tennessee	248,673,000	1.3%
22	Kentucky	228,749,000	1.2%
23	Arkansas	226,728,000	1.2%
24	Georgia	224,910,000	1.2%
25	New Hampshire	212,698,000	1.1%
26	Iowa	212,469,000	1.1%
27	Colorado	193,881,000	1.0%
28	Alabama	179,929,000	0.9%
29	West Virginia	177,840,000	0.9%
30	Nevada	177,161,000	0.9%
31	Louisiana	163,770,000	0.8%
32	Virginia	160,383,000	0.8%
33	Rhode Island	146,691,000	0.8%
34	Mississippi	139,733,000	0.7%
35	Maine	132,950,000	0.7%
36	Kansas	130,247,000	0.7%
37	Delaware	123,026,000	0.6%
38	Hawaii	120,386,000	0.6%
39	Utah	114,492,000	0.6%
40	Missouri	97,408,000	0.5%
41	New Mexico	93,862,000	0.5%
42	Montana	80,532,000	0.4%
43	Vermont	71,078,000	0.4%
44	South Dakota	59,158,000	0.3%
45	Nebraska	57,123,000	0.3%
46	Alaska	55,500,000	0.3%
47	Idaho	51,141,000	0.3%
48	North Dakota	28,001,000	0.1%
49	South Carolina	27,199,000	0.1%
50	Wyoming	22,076,000	0.1%
	District of Columbia	27,956,000	0.1%

Source: U.S. Bureau of the Census, Governments Division
"2018 State Government Tax Collections" (https://www.census.gov/programs-surveys/stc.html)

Per Capita State Government Tobacco Sales Tax Revenue in 2018

National Per Capita = $60

RANK	STATE	PER CAPITA
38	Alabama	$37
17	Alaska	75
36	Arizona	44
17	Arkansas	75
25	California	61
43	Colorado	34
8	Connecticut	105
3	Delaware	127
30	Florida	55
47	Georgia	21
13	Hawaii	85
45	Idaho	29
26	Illinois	60
22	Indiana	63
20	Iowa	67
34	Kansas	45
31	Kentucky	51
42	Louisiana	35
10	Maine	99
24	Maryland	62
12	Massachusetts	86
9	Michigan	101
6	Minnesota	106
33	Mississippi	47
49	Missouri	16
16	Montana	76
44	Nebraska	30
28	Nevada	58
1	New Hampshire	157
19	New Jersey	74
34	New Mexico	45
27	New York	59
46	North Carolina	28
38	North Dakota	37
14	Ohio	81
15	Oklahoma	79
22	Oregon	63
5	Pennsylvania	107
2	Rhode Island	139
50	South Carolina	5
20	South Dakota	67
38	Tennessee	37
32	Texas	50
41	Utah	36
4	Vermont	113
48	Virginia	19
29	Washington	56
11	West Virginia	98
6	Wisconsin	106
37	Wyoming	38

RANK	STATE	PER CAPITA
1	New Hampshire	$157
2	Rhode Island	139
3	Delaware	127
4	Vermont	113
5	Pennsylvania	107
6	Minnesota	106
6	Wisconsin	106
8	Connecticut	105
9	Michigan	101
10	Maine	99
11	West Virginia	98
12	Massachusetts	86
13	Hawaii	85
14	Ohio	81
15	Oklahoma	79
16	Montana	76
17	Alaska	75
17	Arkansas	75
19	New Jersey	74
20	Iowa	67
20	South Dakota	67
22	Indiana	63
22	Oregon	63
24	Maryland	62
25	California	61
26	Illinois	60
27	New York	59
28	Nevada	58
29	Washington	56
30	Florida	55
31	Kentucky	51
32	Texas	50
33	Mississippi	47
34	Kansas	45
34	New Mexico	45
36	Arizona	44
37	Wyoming	38
38	Alabama	37
38	North Dakota	37
38	Tennessee	37
41	Utah	36
42	Louisiana	35
43	Colorado	34
44	Nebraska	30
45	Idaho	29
46	North Carolina	28
47	Georgia	21
48	Virginia	19
49	Missouri	16
50	South Carolina	5

	District of Columbia	40

Source: CQ Press using data from U.S. Bureau of the Census, Governments Division
"2018 State Government Tax Collections" (https://www.census.gov/programs-surveys/stc.html)

State Tax on a Pack of Cigarettes in 2020

National Median = $1.70 per Pack*

<table>
<tr><th colspan="3">ALPHA ORDER</th><th colspan="3">RANK ORDER</th></tr>
<tr><th>RANK</th><th>STATE</th><th>TAX PER PACK</th><th>RANK</th><th>STATE</th><th>TAX PER PACK</th></tr>
<tr><td>40</td><td>Alabama</td><td>$0.68</td><td>1</td><td>Connecticut</td><td>$4.35</td></tr>
<tr><td>16</td><td>Alaska</td><td>2.00</td><td>1</td><td>New York</td><td>4.35</td></tr>
<tr><td>16</td><td>Arizona</td><td>2.00</td><td>3</td><td>Rhode Island</td><td>4.25</td></tr>
<tr><td>34</td><td>Arkansas</td><td>1.15</td><td>4</td><td>Massachusetts</td><td>3.51</td></tr>
<tr><td>10</td><td>California</td><td>2.87</td><td>5</td><td>Hawaii</td><td>3.20</td></tr>
<tr><td>38</td><td>Colorado</td><td>0.84</td><td>6</td><td>Vermont</td><td>3.08</td></tr>
<tr><td>1</td><td>Connecticut</td><td>4.35</td><td>7</td><td>Minnesota</td><td>3.04</td></tr>
<tr><td>14</td><td>Delaware</td><td>2.10</td><td>8</td><td>Washington</td><td>3.03</td></tr>
<tr><td>30</td><td>Florida</td><td>1.34</td><td>9</td><td>Illinois</td><td>2.98</td></tr>
<tr><td>48</td><td>Georgia</td><td>0.37</td><td>10</td><td>California</td><td>2.87</td></tr>
<tr><td>5</td><td>Hawaii</td><td>3.20</td><td>11</td><td>New Jersey</td><td>2.70</td></tr>
<tr><td>44</td><td>Idaho</td><td>0.57</td><td>12</td><td>Pennsylvania</td><td>2.60</td></tr>
<tr><td>9</td><td>Illinois</td><td>2.98</td><td>13</td><td>Wisconsin</td><td>2.52</td></tr>
<tr><td>37</td><td>Indiana</td><td>1.00</td><td>14</td><td>Delaware</td><td>2.10</td></tr>
<tr><td>29</td><td>Iowa</td><td>1.36</td><td>15</td><td>Oklahoma</td><td>2.03</td></tr>
<tr><td>32</td><td>Kansas</td><td>1.29</td><td>16</td><td>Alaska</td><td>2.00</td></tr>
<tr><td>35</td><td>Kentucky</td><td>1.10</td><td>16</td><td>Arizona</td><td>2.00</td></tr>
<tr><td>36</td><td>Louisiana</td><td>1.08</td><td>16</td><td>Maine</td><td>2.00</td></tr>
<tr><td>16</td><td>Maine</td><td>2.00</td><td>16</td><td>Maryland</td><td>2.00</td></tr>
<tr><td>16</td><td>Maryland</td><td>2.00</td><td>16</td><td>Michigan</td><td>2.00</td></tr>
<tr><td>4</td><td>Massachusetts</td><td>3.51</td><td>16</td><td>New Mexico</td><td>2.00</td></tr>
<tr><td>16</td><td>Michigan</td><td>2.00</td><td>22</td><td>Nevada</td><td>1.80</td></tr>
<tr><td>7</td><td>Minnesota</td><td>3.04</td><td>23</td><td>New Hampshire</td><td>1.78</td></tr>
<tr><td>39</td><td>Mississippi</td><td>0.68</td><td>24</td><td>Montana</td><td>1.70</td></tr>
<tr><td>50</td><td>Missouri</td><td>0.17</td><td>24</td><td>Utah</td><td>1.70</td></tr>
<tr><td>24</td><td>Montana</td><td>1.70</td><td>26</td><td>Ohio</td><td>1.60</td></tr>
<tr><td>41</td><td>Nebraska</td><td>0.64</td><td>27</td><td>South Dakota</td><td>1.53</td></tr>
<tr><td>22</td><td>Nevada</td><td>1.80</td><td>28</td><td>Texas</td><td>1.41</td></tr>
<tr><td>23</td><td>New Hampshire</td><td>1.78</td><td>29</td><td>Iowa</td><td>1.36</td></tr>
<tr><td>11</td><td>New Jersey</td><td>2.70</td><td>30</td><td>Florida</td><td>1.34</td></tr>
<tr><td>16</td><td>New Mexico</td><td>2.00</td><td>31</td><td>Oregon</td><td>1.33</td></tr>
<tr><td>1</td><td>New York</td><td>4.35</td><td>32</td><td>Kansas</td><td>1.29</td></tr>
<tr><td>46</td><td>North Carolina</td><td>0.45</td><td>33</td><td>West Virginia</td><td>1.20</td></tr>
<tr><td>47</td><td>North Dakota</td><td>0.44</td><td>34</td><td>Arkansas</td><td>1.15</td></tr>
<tr><td>26</td><td>Ohio</td><td>1.60</td><td>35</td><td>Kentucky</td><td>1.10</td></tr>
<tr><td>15</td><td>Oklahoma</td><td>2.03</td><td>36</td><td>Louisiana</td><td>1.08</td></tr>
<tr><td>31</td><td>Oregon</td><td>1.33</td><td>37</td><td>Indiana</td><td>1.00</td></tr>
<tr><td>12</td><td>Pennsylvania</td><td>2.60</td><td>38</td><td>Colorado</td><td>0.84</td></tr>
<tr><td>3</td><td>Rhode Island</td><td>4.25</td><td>39</td><td>Mississippi</td><td>0.68</td></tr>
<tr><td>44</td><td>South Carolina</td><td>0.57</td><td>40</td><td>Alabama</td><td>0.68</td></tr>
<tr><td>27</td><td>South Dakota</td><td>1.53</td><td>41</td><td>Nebraska</td><td>0.64</td></tr>
<tr><td>42</td><td>Tennessee</td><td>0.62</td><td>42</td><td>Tennessee</td><td>0.62</td></tr>
<tr><td>28</td><td>Texas</td><td>1.41</td><td>43</td><td>Wyoming</td><td>0.60</td></tr>
<tr><td>24</td><td>Utah</td><td>1.70</td><td>44</td><td>Idaho</td><td>0.57</td></tr>
<tr><td>6</td><td>Vermont</td><td>3.08</td><td>44</td><td>South Carolina</td><td>0.57</td></tr>
<tr><td>49</td><td>Virginia</td><td>0.30</td><td>46</td><td>North Carolina</td><td>0.45</td></tr>
<tr><td>8</td><td>Washington</td><td>3.03</td><td>47</td><td>North Dakota</td><td>0.44</td></tr>
<tr><td>33</td><td>West Virginia</td><td>1.20</td><td>48</td><td>Georgia</td><td>0.37</td></tr>
<tr><td>13</td><td>Wisconsin</td><td>2.52</td><td>49</td><td>Virginia</td><td>0.30</td></tr>
<tr><td>43</td><td>Wyoming</td><td>0.60</td><td>50</td><td>Missouri</td><td>0.17</td></tr>
<tr><td></td><td></td><td></td><td></td><td>District of Columbia</td><td>4.50</td></tr>
</table>

Source: Federation of Tax Administrators
   "State Excise Tax Rates on Cigarettes" (https://www.taxadmin.org/current-tax-rates)
*As of January 1, 2020. Many states also allow additional local option taxes on cigarettes.

State Government Alcoholic Beverage Sales Tax Revenue in 2018

National Total = $6,795,036,000

ALPHA ORDER

RANK	STATE	REVENUE	% of USA
10	Alabama	$214,615,000	3.2%
34	Alaska	39,217,000	0.6%
22	Arizona	76,378,000	1.1%
26	Arkansas	58,036,000	0.9%
4	California	376,735,000	5.5%
30	Colorado	46,989,000	0.7%
24	Connecticut	63,211,000	0.9%
40	Delaware	26,556,000	0.4%
7	Florida	293,098,000	4.3%
12	Georgia	195,696,000	2.9%
29	Hawaii	51,383,000	0.8%
48	Idaho	9,710,000	0.1%
6	Illinois	296,162,000	4.4%
27	Indiana	51,578,000	0.8%
41	Iowa	22,183,000	0.3%
17	Kansas	142,126,000	2.1%
15	Kentucky	145,648,000	2.1%
23	Louisiana	75,774,000	1.1%
43	Maine	19,647,000	0.3%
37	Maryland	31,682,000	0.5%
21	Massachusetts	85,843,000	1.3%
14	Michigan	157,335,000	2.3%
20	Minnesota	91,745,000	1.4%
33	Mississippi	40,883,000	0.6%
35	Missouri	38,932,000	0.6%
36	Montana	33,816,000	0.5%
38	Nebraska	31,230,000	0.5%
32	Nevada	45,340,000	0.7%
47	New Hampshire	12,828,000	0.2%
16	New Jersey	142,459,000	2.1%
31	New Mexico	45,497,000	0.7%
8	New York	258,327,000	3.8%
2	North Carolina	411,971,000	6.1%
49	North Dakota	8,819,000	0.1%
19	Ohio	104,977,000	1.5%
18	Oklahoma	122,247,000	1.8%
44	Oregon	19,216,000	0.3%
3	Pennsylvania	397,092,000	5.8%
42	Rhode Island	19,918,000	0.3%
13	South Carolina	179,115,000	2.6%
45	South Dakota	18,939,000	0.3%
11	Tennessee	201,713,000	3.0%
1	Texas	1,321,516,000	19.4%
28	Utah	51,420,000	0.8%
39	Vermont	26,892,000	0.4%
9	Virginia	231,250,000	3.4%
5	Washington	370,738,000	5.5%
46	West Virginia	17,576,000	0.3%
25	Wisconsin	62,498,000	0.9%
50	Wyoming	1,920,000	0.0%

RANK ORDER

RANK	STATE	REVENUE	% of USA
1	Texas	$1,321,516,000	19.4%
2	North Carolina	411,971,000	6.1%
3	Pennsylvania	397,092,000	5.8%
4	California	376,735,000	5.5%
5	Washington	370,738,000	5.5%
6	Illinois	296,162,000	4.4%
7	Florida	293,098,000	4.3%
8	New York	258,327,000	3.8%
9	Virginia	231,250,000	3.4%
10	Alabama	214,615,000	3.2%
11	Tennessee	201,713,000	3.0%
12	Georgia	195,696,000	2.9%
13	South Carolina	179,115,000	2.6%
14	Michigan	157,335,000	2.3%
15	Kentucky	145,648,000	2.1%
16	New Jersey	142,459,000	2.1%
17	Kansas	142,126,000	2.1%
18	Oklahoma	122,247,000	1.8%
19	Ohio	104,977,000	1.5%
20	Minnesota	91,745,000	1.4%
21	Massachusetts	85,843,000	1.3%
22	Arizona	76,378,000	1.1%
23	Louisiana	75,774,000	1.1%
24	Connecticut	63,211,000	0.9%
25	Wisconsin	62,498,000	0.9%
26	Arkansas	58,036,000	0.9%
27	Indiana	51,578,000	0.8%
28	Utah	51,420,000	0.8%
29	Hawaii	51,383,000	0.8%
30	Colorado	46,989,000	0.7%
31	New Mexico	45,497,000	0.7%
32	Nevada	45,340,000	0.7%
33	Mississippi	40,883,000	0.6%
34	Alaska	39,217,000	0.6%
35	Missouri	38,932,000	0.6%
36	Montana	33,816,000	0.5%
37	Maryland	31,682,000	0.5%
38	Nebraska	31,230,000	0.5%
39	Vermont	26,892,000	0.4%
40	Delaware	26,556,000	0.4%
41	Iowa	22,183,000	0.3%
42	Rhode Island	19,918,000	0.3%
43	Maine	19,647,000	0.3%
44	Oregon	19,216,000	0.3%
45	South Dakota	18,939,000	0.3%
46	West Virginia	17,576,000	0.3%
47	New Hampshire	12,828,000	0.2%
48	Idaho	9,710,000	0.1%
49	North Dakota	8,819,000	0.1%
50	Wyoming	1,920,000	0.0%
	District of Columbia	6,560,000	0.1%

Source: U.S. Bureau of the Census, Governments Division
"2018 State Government Tax Collections" (https://www.census.gov/programs-surveys/stc.html)

Per Capita State Government Alcoholic Beverage Sales Tax Revenue in 2018

National Per Capita = $21

ALPHA ORDER				RANK ORDER		
RANK	STATE	PER CAPITA		RANK	STATE	PER CAPITA
5	Alabama	$44		1	Alaska	$53
1	Alaska	53		2	Kansas	49
37	Arizona	11		2	Washington	49
20	Arkansas	19		4	Texas	46
39	California	10		5	Alabama	44
43	Colorado	8		6	Vermont	43
23	Connecticut	18		7	North Carolina	40
15	Delaware	27		8	Hawaii	36
32	Florida	14		9	South Carolina	35
20	Georgia	19		10	Kentucky	33
8	Hawaii	36		11	Montana	32
46	Idaho	6		12	Oklahoma	31
17	Illinois	23		12	Pennsylvania	31
43	Indiana	8		14	Tennessee	30
45	Iowa	7		15	Delaware	27
2	Kansas	49		15	Virginia	27
10	Kentucky	33		17	Illinois	23
24	Louisiana	16		18	New Mexico	22
30	Maine	15		19	South Dakota	21
48	Maryland	5		20	Arkansas	19
35	Massachusetts	12		20	Georgia	19
24	Michigan	16		20	Rhode Island	19
24	Minnesota	16		23	Connecticut	18
32	Mississippi	14		24	Louisiana	16
46	Missouri	6		24	Michigan	16
11	Montana	32		24	Minnesota	16
24	Nebraska	16		24	Nebraska	16
30	Nevada	15		24	New Jersey	16
41	New Hampshire	9		24	Utah	16
24	New Jersey	16		30	Maine	15
18	New Mexico	22		30	Nevada	15
34	New York	13		32	Florida	14
7	North Carolina	40		32	Mississippi	14
35	North Dakota	12		34	New York	13
41	Ohio	9		35	Massachusetts	12
12	Oklahoma	31		35	North Dakota	12
48	Oregon	5		37	Arizona	11
12	Pennsylvania	31		37	Wisconsin	11
20	Rhode Island	19		39	California	10
9	South Carolina	35		39	West Virginia	10
19	South Dakota	21		41	New Hampshire	9
14	Tennessee	30		41	Ohio	9
4	Texas	46		43	Colorado	8
24	Utah	16		43	Indiana	8
6	Vermont	43		45	Iowa	7
15	Virginia	27		46	Idaho	6
2	Washington	49		46	Missouri	6
39	West Virginia	10		48	Maryland	5
37	Wisconsin	11		48	Oregon	5
50	Wyoming	3		50	Wyoming	3
					District of Columbia	9

Source: CQ Press using data from U.S. Bureau of the Census, Governments Division
"2018 State Government Tax Collections" (https://www.census.gov/programs-surveys/stc.html)

State Government Total Expenditures in 2017

National Total = $2,314,789,560,000*

ALPHA ORDER

RANK	STATE	EXPENDITURES	% of USA
27	Alabama	$32,492,413,000	1.4%
39	Alaska	11,292,990,000	0.5%
19	Arizona	39,231,709,000	1.7%
31	Arkansas	23,058,499,000	1.0%
1	California	350,451,763,000	15.1%
22	Colorado	34,959,394,000	1.5%
28	Connecticut	31,485,085,000	1.4%
42	Delaware	10,009,281,000	0.4%
5	Florida	92,696,645,000	4.0%
14	Georgia	49,539,797,000	2.1%
38	Hawaii	12,680,681,000	0.5%
43	Idaho	9,577,387,000	0.4%
7	Illinois	85,515,250,000	3.7%
17	Indiana	40,796,778,000	1.8%
30	Iowa	23,251,841,000	1.0%
35	Kansas	19,597,970,000	0.8%
21	Kentucky	36,332,393,000	1.6%
24	Louisiana	33,791,337,000	1.5%
41	Maine	10,145,529,000	0.4%
16	Maryland	45,313,683,000	2.0%
10	Massachusetts	65,778,247,000	2.8%
9	Michigan	72,118,000,000	3.1%
15	Minnesota	47,314,264,000	2.0%
32	Mississippi	21,631,786,000	0.9%
25	Missouri	33,728,168,000	1.5%
47	Montana	7,757,132,000	0.3%
40	Nebraska	10,618,168,000	0.5%
36	Nevada	16,221,586,000	0.7%
46	New Hampshire	7,882,386,000	0.3%
8	New Jersey	72,390,316,000	3.1%
33	New Mexico	20,776,680,000	0.9%
2	New York	201,211,293,000	8.7%
11	North Carolina	55,574,192,000	2.4%
48	North Dakota	7,538,488,000	0.3%
6	Ohio	88,232,183,000	3.8%
29	Oklahoma	25,253,912,000	1.1%
20	Oregon	36,975,575,000	1.6%
4	Pennsylvania	103,525,140,000	4.5%
44	Rhode Island	8,780,320,000	0.4%
23	South Carolina	33,882,788,000	1.5%
50	South Dakota	5,265,167,000	0.2%
26	Tennessee	33,218,749,000	1.4%
3	Texas	147,926,984,000	6.4%
34	Utah	20,596,542,000	0.9%
49	Vermont	7,007,462,000	0.3%
13	Virginia	53,436,952,000	2.3%
12	Washington	55,159,390,000	2.4%
37	West Virginia	14,688,180,000	0.6%
18	Wisconsin	39,873,101,000	1.7%
45	Wyoming	8,205,984,000	0.4%

RANK ORDER

RANK	STATE	EXPENDITURES	% of USA
1	California	$350,451,763,000	15.1%
2	New York	201,211,293,000	8.7%
3	Texas	147,926,984,000	6.4%
4	Pennsylvania	103,525,140,000	4.5%
5	Florida	92,696,645,000	4.0%
6	Ohio	88,232,183,000	3.8%
7	Illinois	85,515,250,000	3.7%
8	New Jersey	72,390,316,000	3.1%
9	Michigan	72,118,000,000	3.1%
10	Massachusetts	65,778,247,000	2.8%
11	North Carolina	55,574,192,000	2.4%
12	Washington	55,159,390,000	2.4%
13	Virginia	53,436,952,000	2.3%
14	Georgia	49,539,797,000	2.1%
15	Minnesota	47,314,264,000	2.0%
16	Maryland	45,313,683,000	2.0%
17	Indiana	40,796,778,000	1.8%
18	Wisconsin	39,873,101,000	1.7%
19	Arizona	39,231,709,000	1.7%
20	Oregon	36,975,575,000	1.6%
21	Kentucky	36,332,393,000	1.6%
22	Colorado	34,959,394,000	1.5%
23	South Carolina	33,882,788,000	1.5%
24	Louisiana	33,791,337,000	1.5%
25	Missouri	33,728,168,000	1.5%
26	Tennessee	33,218,749,000	1.4%
27	Alabama	32,492,413,000	1.4%
28	Connecticut	31,485,085,000	1.4%
29	Oklahoma	25,253,912,000	1.1%
30	Iowa	23,251,841,000	1.0%
31	Arkansas	23,058,499,000	1.0%
32	Mississippi	21,631,786,000	0.9%
33	New Mexico	20,776,680,000	0.9%
34	Utah	20,596,542,000	0.9%
35	Kansas	19,597,970,000	0.8%
36	Nevada	16,221,586,000	0.7%
37	West Virginia	14,688,180,000	0.6%
38	Hawaii	12,680,681,000	0.5%
39	Alaska	11,292,990,000	0.5%
40	Nebraska	10,618,168,000	0.5%
41	Maine	10,145,529,000	0.4%
42	Delaware	10,009,281,000	0.4%
43	Idaho	9,577,387,000	0.4%
44	Rhode Island	8,780,320,000	0.4%
45	Wyoming	8,205,984,000	0.4%
46	New Hampshire	7,882,386,000	0.3%
47	Montana	7,757,132,000	0.3%
48	North Dakota	7,538,488,000	0.3%
49	Vermont	7,007,462,000	0.3%
50	South Dakota	5,265,167,000	0.2%
	District of Columbia**	NA	NA

Source: U.S. Bureau of the Census, Governments Division
"2017 State and Local Government Finances" (https://www.census.gov/programs-surveys/gov-finances.html)
*Total expenditures includes all money paid other than for retirement of debt and extension of loans. Includes payments from all sources of funds including current revenues and proceeds from borrowing and prior year fund balances. Includes intergovernmental transfers and expenditures for government-owned utilities and other commercial or auxiliary enterprise, and insurance trust expenditures. **Not applicable.

Per Capita State Government Total Expenditures in 2017

National Per Capita = $7,134*

<table>
<tr><td colspan="3">ALPHA ORDER</td><td colspan="3">RANK ORDER</td></tr>
<tr><th>RANK</th><th>STATE</th><th>PER CAPITA</th><th>RANK</th><th>STATE</th><th>PER CAPITA</th></tr>
<tr><td>33</td><td>Alabama</td><td>$6,665</td><td>1</td><td>Alaska</td><td>$15,265</td></tr>
<tr><td>1</td><td>Alaska</td><td>15,265</td><td>2</td><td>Wyoming</td><td>14,174</td></tr>
<tr><td>42</td><td>Arizona</td><td>5,566</td><td>3</td><td>Vermont</td><td>11,220</td></tr>
<tr><td>19</td><td>Arkansas</td><td>7,678</td><td>4</td><td>Delaware</td><td>10,458</td></tr>
<tr><td>11</td><td>California</td><td>8,895</td><td>5</td><td>New York</td><td>10,271</td></tr>
<tr><td>37</td><td>Colorado</td><td>6,225</td><td>6</td><td>North Dakota</td><td>9,982</td></tr>
<tr><td>12</td><td>Connecticut</td><td>8,810</td><td>7</td><td>New Mexico</td><td>9,925</td></tr>
<tr><td>4</td><td>Delaware</td><td>10,458</td><td>8</td><td>Massachusetts</td><td>9,584</td></tr>
<tr><td>50</td><td>Florida</td><td>4,419</td><td>9</td><td>Oregon</td><td>8,917</td></tr>
<tr><td>49</td><td>Georgia</td><td>4,757</td><td>10</td><td>Hawaii</td><td>8,904</td></tr>
<tr><td>10</td><td>Hawaii</td><td>8,904</td><td>11</td><td>California</td><td>8,895</td></tr>
<tr><td>41</td><td>Idaho</td><td>5,572</td><td>12</td><td>Connecticut</td><td>8,810</td></tr>
<tr><td>32</td><td>Illinois</td><td>6,688</td><td>13</td><td>Minnesota</td><td>8,497</td></tr>
<tr><td>38</td><td>Indiana</td><td>6,126</td><td>14</td><td>Rhode Island</td><td>8,311</td></tr>
<tr><td>24</td><td>Iowa</td><td>7,396</td><td>15</td><td>Kentucky</td><td>8,157</td></tr>
<tr><td>31</td><td>Kansas</td><td>6,733</td><td>16</td><td>New Jersey</td><td>8,144</td></tr>
<tr><td>15</td><td>Kentucky</td><td>8,157</td><td>17</td><td>Pennsylvania</td><td>8,094</td></tr>
<tr><td>27</td><td>Louisiana</td><td>7,235</td><td>18</td><td>West Virginia</td><td>8,084</td></tr>
<tr><td>20</td><td>Maine</td><td>7,599</td><td>19</td><td>Arkansas</td><td>7,678</td></tr>
<tr><td>22</td><td>Maryland</td><td>7,521</td><td>20</td><td>Maine</td><td>7,599</td></tr>
<tr><td>8</td><td>Massachusetts</td><td>9,584</td><td>21</td><td>Ohio</td><td>7,564</td></tr>
<tr><td>28</td><td>Michigan</td><td>7,229</td><td>22</td><td>Maryland</td><td>7,521</td></tr>
<tr><td>13</td><td>Minnesota</td><td>8,497</td><td>23</td><td>Washington</td><td>7,428</td></tr>
<tr><td>26</td><td>Mississippi</td><td>7,236</td><td>24</td><td>Iowa</td><td>7,396</td></tr>
<tr><td>44</td><td>Missouri</td><td>5,521</td><td>25</td><td>Montana</td><td>7,366</td></tr>
<tr><td>25</td><td>Montana</td><td>7,366</td><td>26</td><td>Mississippi</td><td>7,236</td></tr>
<tr><td>43</td><td>Nebraska</td><td>5,537</td><td>27</td><td>Louisiana</td><td>7,235</td></tr>
<tr><td>45</td><td>Nevada</td><td>5,457</td><td>28</td><td>Michigan</td><td>7,229</td></tr>
<tr><td>40</td><td>New Hampshire</td><td>5,840</td><td>29</td><td>Wisconsin</td><td>6,884</td></tr>
<tr><td>16</td><td>New Jersey</td><td>8,144</td><td>30</td><td>South Carolina</td><td>6,748</td></tr>
<tr><td>7</td><td>New Mexico</td><td>9,925</td><td>31</td><td>Kansas</td><td>6,733</td></tr>
<tr><td>5</td><td>New York</td><td>10,271</td><td>32</td><td>Illinois</td><td>6,688</td></tr>
<tr><td>46</td><td>North Carolina</td><td>5,411</td><td>33</td><td>Alabama</td><td>6,665</td></tr>
<tr><td>6</td><td>North Dakota</td><td>9,982</td><td>34</td><td>Utah</td><td>6,637</td></tr>
<tr><td>21</td><td>Ohio</td><td>7,564</td><td>35</td><td>Oklahoma</td><td>6,422</td></tr>
<tr><td>35</td><td>Oklahoma</td><td>6,422</td><td>36</td><td>Virginia</td><td>6,313</td></tr>
<tr><td>9</td><td>Oregon</td><td>8,917</td><td>37</td><td>Colorado</td><td>6,225</td></tr>
<tr><td>17</td><td>Pennsylvania</td><td>8,094</td><td>38</td><td>Indiana</td><td>6,126</td></tr>
<tr><td>14</td><td>Rhode Island</td><td>8,311</td><td>39</td><td>South Dakota</td><td>6,029</td></tr>
<tr><td>30</td><td>South Carolina</td><td>6,748</td><td>40</td><td>New Hampshire</td><td>5,840</td></tr>
<tr><td>39</td><td>South Dakota</td><td>6,029</td><td>41</td><td>Idaho</td><td>5,572</td></tr>
<tr><td>48</td><td>Tennessee</td><td>4,952</td><td>42</td><td>Arizona</td><td>5,566</td></tr>
<tr><td>47</td><td>Texas</td><td>5,223</td><td>43</td><td>Nebraska</td><td>5,537</td></tr>
<tr><td>34</td><td>Utah</td><td>6,637</td><td>44</td><td>Missouri</td><td>5,521</td></tr>
<tr><td>3</td><td>Vermont</td><td>11,220</td><td>45</td><td>Nevada</td><td>5,457</td></tr>
<tr><td>36</td><td>Virginia</td><td>6,313</td><td>46</td><td>North Carolina</td><td>5,411</td></tr>
<tr><td>23</td><td>Washington</td><td>7,428</td><td>47</td><td>Texas</td><td>5,223</td></tr>
<tr><td>18</td><td>West Virginia</td><td>8,084</td><td>48</td><td>Tennessee</td><td>4,952</td></tr>
<tr><td>29</td><td>Wisconsin</td><td>6,884</td><td>49</td><td>Georgia</td><td>4,757</td></tr>
<tr><td>2</td><td>Wyoming</td><td>14,174</td><td>50</td><td>Florida</td><td>4,419</td></tr>
<tr><td></td><td></td><td></td><td></td><td>District of Columbia**</td><td>NA</td></tr>
</table>

Source: CQ Press using data from U.S. Bureau of the Census, Governments Division
"2017 State and Local Government Finances" (https://www.census.gov/programs-surveys/gov-finances.html)
*Total expenditures includes all money paid other than for retirement of debt and extension of loans. Includes payments from all sources of funds including current revenues and proceeds from borrowing and prior year fund balances. Includes intergovernmental transfers and expenditures for government-owned utilities total and other commercial or auxiliary enterprise, and insurance trust expenditures. **Not applicable.

State Government Direct General Expenditures in 2017

National Total = $1,434,346,550,000*

ALPHA ORDER

RANK	STATE	EXPENDITURES	% of USA
26	Alabama	$21,748,505,000	1.5%
39	Alaska	7,949,326,000	0.6%
18	Arizona	26,793,322,000	1.9%
30	Arkansas	15,705,697,000	1.1%
1	California	188,902,437,000	13.2%
27	Colorado	21,727,986,000	1.5%
28	Connecticut	17,026,896,000	1.2%
40	Delaware	7,575,650,000	0.5%
5	Florida	61,556,858,000	4.3%
14	Georgia	30,598,753,000	2.1%
36	Hawaii	10,863,715,000	0.8%
44	Idaho	5,889,492,000	0.4%
7	Illinois	51,029,772,000	3.6%
16	Indiana	27,927,303,000	1.9%
31	Iowa	14,903,702,000	1.0%
35	Kansas	12,824,964,000	0.9%
19	Kentucky	25,994,163,000	1.8%
22	Louisiana	22,728,447,000	1.6%
42	Maine	6,667,873,000	0.5%
15	Maryland	30,060,884,000	2.1%
8	Massachusetts	46,572,438,000	3.2%
10	Michigan	41,908,302,000	2.9%
17	Minnesota	27,756,647,000	1.9%
33	Mississippi	14,071,011,000	1.0%
24	Missouri	22,666,066,000	1.6%
46	Montana	5,452,746,000	0.4%
41	Nebraska	7,392,036,000	0.5%
38	Nevada	8,798,403,000	0.6%
45	New Hampshire	5,698,524,000	0.4%
9	New Jersey	44,076,279,000	3.1%
34	New Mexico	13,501,207,000	0.9%
2	New York	103,437,832,000	7.2%
11	North Carolina	35,815,505,000	2.5%
47	North Dakota	4,812,737,000	0.3%
6	Ohio	51,298,656,000	3.6%
29	Oklahoma	16,895,839,000	1.2%
21	Oregon	25,239,467,000	1.8%
4	Pennsylvania	66,612,221,000	4.6%
43	Rhode Island	6,041,741,000	0.4%
25	South Carolina	21,844,774,000	1.5%
50	South Dakota	3,829,764,000	0.3%
23	Tennessee	22,679,997,000	1.6%
3	Texas	99,074,014,000	6.9%
32	Utah	14,681,423,000	1.0%
48	Vermont	4,749,703,000	0.3%
12	Virginia	35,726,273,000	2.5%
13	Washington	35,027,141,000	2.4%
37	West Virginia	10,571,658,000	0.7%
20	Wisconsin	25,506,865,000	1.8%
49	Wyoming	4,131,536,000	0.3%

RANK ORDER

RANK	STATE	EXPENDITURES	% of USA
1	California	$188,902,437,000	13.2%
2	New York	103,437,832,000	7.2%
3	Texas	99,074,014,000	6.9%
4	Pennsylvania	66,612,221,000	4.6%
5	Florida	61,556,858,000	4.3%
6	Ohio	51,298,656,000	3.6%
7	Illinois	51,029,772,000	3.6%
8	Massachusetts	46,572,438,000	3.2%
9	New Jersey	44,076,279,000	3.1%
10	Michigan	41,908,302,000	2.9%
11	North Carolina	35,815,505,000	2.5%
12	Virginia	35,726,273,000	2.5%
13	Washington	35,027,141,000	2.4%
14	Georgia	30,598,753,000	2.1%
15	Maryland	30,060,884,000	2.1%
16	Indiana	27,927,303,000	1.9%
17	Minnesota	27,756,647,000	1.9%
18	Arizona	26,793,322,000	1.9%
19	Kentucky	25,994,163,000	1.8%
20	Wisconsin	25,506,865,000	1.8%
21	Oregon	25,239,467,000	1.8%
22	Louisiana	22,728,447,000	1.6%
23	Tennessee	22,679,997,000	1.6%
24	Missouri	22,666,066,000	1.6%
25	South Carolina	21,844,774,000	1.5%
26	Alabama	21,748,505,000	1.5%
27	Colorado	21,727,986,000	1.5%
28	Connecticut	17,026,896,000	1.2%
29	Oklahoma	16,895,839,000	1.2%
30	Arkansas	15,705,697,000	1.1%
31	Iowa	14,903,702,000	1.0%
32	Utah	14,681,423,000	1.0%
33	Mississippi	14,071,011,000	1.0%
34	New Mexico	13,501,207,000	0.9%
35	Kansas	12,824,964,000	0.9%
36	Hawaii	10,863,715,000	0.8%
37	West Virginia	10,571,658,000	0.7%
38	Nevada	8,798,403,000	0.6%
39	Alaska	7,949,326,000	0.6%
40	Delaware	7,575,650,000	0.5%
41	Nebraska	7,392,036,000	0.5%
42	Maine	6,667,873,000	0.5%
43	Rhode Island	6,041,741,000	0.4%
44	Idaho	5,889,492,000	0.4%
45	New Hampshire	5,698,524,000	0.4%
46	Montana	5,452,746,000	0.4%
47	North Dakota	4,812,737,000	0.3%
48	Vermont	4,749,703,000	0.3%
49	Wyoming	4,131,536,000	0.3%
50	South Dakota	3,829,764,000	0.3%

District of Columbia** — NA — NA

Source: U.S. Bureau of the Census, Governments Division
   "2017 State and Local Government Finances" (https://www.census.gov/programs-surveys/gov-finances.html)
*Direct general expenditures include expenditures for current operations, assistance and subsidies, interest on debt, and capital outlay. Excludes intergovernmental transfers, expenditures for government-owned utilities and other commercial or auxiliary enterprise, and insurance trust expenditures.
**Not applicable.

Per Capita State Government Direct General Expenditures in 2017

National Per Capita = $4,421*

RANK	STATE	PER CAPITA
28	Alabama	$4,461
1	Alaska	10,745
42	Arizona	3,801
14	Arkansas	5,230
22	California	4,795
40	Colorado	3,869
23	Connecticut	4,764
2	Delaware	7,915
50	Florida	2,935
49	Georgia	2,938
3	Hawaii	7,628
46	Idaho	3,426
39	Illinois	3,991
38	Indiana	4,193
24	Iowa	4,741
29	Kansas	4,406
10	Kentucky	5,836
21	Louisiana	4,866
17	Maine	4,994
18	Maryland	4,989
6	Massachusetts	6,786
37	Michigan	4,201
19	Minnesota	4,985
27	Mississippi	4,707
43	Missouri	3,711
16	Montana	5,178
41	Nebraska	3,855
48	Nevada	2,960
35	New Hampshire	4,222
20	New Jersey	4,959
7	New Mexico	6,449
13	New York	5,280
45	North Carolina	3,487
8	North Dakota	6,373
31	Ohio	4,398
34	Oklahoma	4,296
9	Oregon	6,087
15	Pennsylvania	5,208
12	Rhode Island	5,719
33	South Carolina	4,350
32	South Dakota	4,385
47	Tennessee	3,381
44	Texas	3,498
25	Utah	4,731
4	Vermont	7,605
36	Virginia	4,220
26	Washington	4,717
11	West Virginia	5,818
30	Wisconsin	4,404
5	Wyoming	7,136

RANK	STATE	PER CAPITA
1	Alaska	$10,745
2	Delaware	7,915
3	Hawaii	7,628
4	Vermont	7,605
5	Wyoming	7,136
6	Massachusetts	6,786
7	New Mexico	6,449
8	North Dakota	6,373
9	Oregon	6,087
10	Kentucky	5,836
11	West Virginia	5,818
12	Rhode Island	5,719
13	New York	5,280
14	Arkansas	5,230
15	Pennsylvania	5,208
16	Montana	5,178
17	Maine	4,994
18	Maryland	4,989
19	Minnesota	4,985
20	New Jersey	4,959
21	Louisiana	4,866
22	California	4,795
23	Connecticut	4,764
24	Iowa	4,741
25	Utah	4,731
26	Washington	4,717
27	Mississippi	4,707
28	Alabama	4,461
29	Kansas	4,406
30	Wisconsin	4,404
31	Ohio	4,398
32	South Dakota	4,385
33	South Carolina	4,350
34	Oklahoma	4,296
35	New Hampshire	4,222
36	Virginia	4,220
37	Michigan	4,201
38	Indiana	4,193
39	Illinois	3,991
40	Colorado	3,869
41	Nebraska	3,855
42	Arizona	3,801
43	Missouri	3,711
44	Texas	3,498
45	North Carolina	3,487
46	Idaho	3,426
47	Tennessee	3,381
48	Nevada	2,960
49	Georgia	2,938
50	Florida	2,935

District of Columbia** NA

Source: CQ Press using data from U.S. Bureau of the Census, Governments Division
   "2017 State and Local Government Finances" (https://www.census.gov/programs-surveys/gov-finances.html)
*Direct general expenditures include expenditures for current operations, assistance and subsidies, interest on debt, and capital outlay. Excludes intergovernmental transfers, expenditures for government-owned utilities and other commercial or auxiliary enterprise, and insurance trust expenditures.
**Not applicable.

State Government Debt Outstanding in 2017

National Total = $1,155,507,028,000*

ALPHA ORDER

RANK	STATE	DEBT	% of USA
29	Alabama	$8,772,871,000	0.8%
39	Alaska	5,921,713,000	0.5%
24	Arizona	14,291,349,000	1.2%
40	Arkansas	4,801,939,000	0.4%
1	California	152,772,292,000	13.2%
19	Colorado	16,980,689,000	1.5%
8	Connecticut	38,756,156,000	3.4%
42	Delaware	4,561,576,000	0.4%
12	Florida	28,823,847,000	2.5%
25	Georgia	13,050,862,000	1.1%
27	Hawaii	9,656,278,000	0.8%
45	Idaho	3,369,178,000	0.3%
5	Illinois	61,821,319,000	5.4%
16	Indiana	21,842,716,000	1.9%
37	Iowa	6,149,694,000	0.5%
33	Kansas	7,538,475,000	0.7%
23	Kentucky	14,403,514,000	1.2%
18	Louisiana	18,092,508,000	1.6%
41	Maine	4,750,384,000	0.4%
13	Maryland	28,027,363,000	2.4%
3	Massachusetts	77,043,165,000	6.7%
10	Michigan	33,463,604,000	2.9%
20	Minnesota	16,363,418,000	1.4%
34	Mississippi	7,470,178,000	0.6%
17	Missouri	18,419,751,000	1.6%
48	Montana	2,795,614,000	0.2%
49	Nebraska	2,014,523,000	0.2%
46	Nevada	3,248,814,000	0.3%
31	New Hampshire	7,739,447,000	0.7%
4	New Jersey	65,874,095,000	5.7%
36	New Mexico	7,057,656,000	0.6%
2	New York	139,234,923,000	12.0%
21	North Carolina	16,310,177,000	1.4%
47	North Dakota	2,885,664,000	0.2%
9	Ohio	33,493,235,000	2.9%
30	Oklahoma	8,457,322,000	0.7%
26	Oregon	12,656,643,000	1.1%
7	Pennsylvania	47,519,575,000	4.1%
28	Rhode Island	8,932,377,000	0.8%
22	South Carolina	15,744,638,000	1.4%
43	South Dakota	3,527,703,000	0.3%
38	Tennessee	6,127,422,000	0.5%
6	Texas	50,963,262,000	4.4%
35	Utah	7,453,346,000	0.6%
44	Vermont	3,502,960,000	0.3%
14	Virginia	27,825,929,000	2.4%
11	Washington	33,427,752,000	2.9%
32	West Virginia	7,547,010,000	0.7%
15	Wisconsin	23,252,381,000	2.0%
50	Wyoming	769,721,000	0.1%

RANK ORDER

RANK	STATE	DEBT	% of USA
1	California	$152,772,292,000	13.2%
2	New York	139,234,923,000	12.0%
3	Massachusetts	77,043,165,000	6.7%
4	New Jersey	65,874,095,000	5.7%
5	Illinois	61,821,319,000	5.4%
6	Texas	50,963,262,000	4.4%
7	Pennsylvania	47,519,575,000	4.1%
8	Connecticut	38,756,156,000	3.4%
9	Ohio	33,493,235,000	2.9%
10	Michigan	33,463,604,000	2.9%
11	Washington	33,427,752,000	2.9%
12	Florida	28,823,847,000	2.5%
13	Maryland	28,027,363,000	2.4%
14	Virginia	27,825,929,000	2.4%
15	Wisconsin	23,252,381,000	2.0%
16	Indiana	21,842,716,000	1.9%
17	Missouri	18,419,751,000	1.6%
18	Louisiana	18,092,508,000	1.6%
19	Colorado	16,980,689,000	1.5%
20	Minnesota	16,363,418,000	1.4%
21	North Carolina	16,310,177,000	1.4%
22	South Carolina	15,744,638,000	1.4%
23	Kentucky	14,403,514,000	1.2%
24	Arizona	14,291,349,000	1.2%
25	Georgia	13,050,862,000	1.1%
26	Oregon	12,656,643,000	1.1%
27	Hawaii	9,656,278,000	0.8%
28	Rhode Island	8,932,377,000	0.8%
29	Alabama	8,772,871,000	0.8%
30	Oklahoma	8,457,322,000	0.7%
31	New Hampshire	7,739,447,000	0.7%
32	West Virginia	7,547,010,000	0.7%
33	Kansas	7,538,475,000	0.7%
34	Mississippi	7,470,178,000	0.6%
35	Utah	7,453,346,000	0.6%
36	New Mexico	7,057,656,000	0.6%
37	Iowa	6,149,694,000	0.5%
38	Tennessee	6,127,422,000	0.5%
39	Alaska	5,921,713,000	0.5%
40	Arkansas	4,801,939,000	0.4%
41	Maine	4,750,384,000	0.4%
42	Delaware	4,561,576,000	0.4%
43	South Dakota	3,527,703,000	0.3%
44	Vermont	3,502,960,000	0.3%
45	Idaho	3,369,178,000	0.3%
46	Nevada	3,248,814,000	0.3%
47	North Dakota	2,885,664,000	0.2%
48	Montana	2,795,614,000	0.2%
49	Nebraska	2,014,523,000	0.2%
50	Wyoming	769,721,000	0.1%
	District of Columbia**	NA	NA

Source: U.S. Bureau of the Census, Governments Division
   "2017 State and Local Government Finances" (https://www.census.gov/programs-surveys/gov-finances.html)
*Includes short-term, long-term, full faith and credit, nonguaranteed, and public debt for private purposes.
**Not applicable.

Per Capita State Government Debt Outstanding in 2017

National Per Capita = $3,561*

<table>
<tr><td colspan="3">ALPHA ORDER</td><td colspan="3">RANK ORDER</td></tr>
<tr><th>RANK</th><th>STATE</th><th>PER CAPITA</th><th>RANK</th><th>STATE</th><th>PER CAPITA</th></tr>
<tr><td>41</td><td>Alabama</td><td>$1,800</td><td>1</td><td>Massachusetts</td><td>$11,225</td></tr>
<tr><td>4</td><td>Alaska</td><td>8,005</td><td>2</td><td>Connecticut</td><td>10,844</td></tr>
<tr><td>38</td><td>Arizona</td><td>2,027</td><td>3</td><td>Rhode Island</td><td>8,455</td></tr>
<tr><td>43</td><td>Arkansas</td><td>1,599</td><td>4</td><td>Alaska</td><td>8,005</td></tr>
<tr><td>17</td><td>California</td><td>3,878</td><td>5</td><td>New Jersey</td><td>7,411</td></tr>
<tr><td>29</td><td>Colorado</td><td>3,024</td><td>6</td><td>New York</td><td>7,107</td></tr>
<tr><td>2</td><td>Connecticut</td><td>10,844</td><td>7</td><td>Hawaii</td><td>6,780</td></tr>
<tr><td>11</td><td>Delaware</td><td>4,766</td><td>8</td><td>New Hampshire</td><td>5,734</td></tr>
<tr><td>45</td><td>Florida</td><td>1,374</td><td>9</td><td>Vermont</td><td>5,609</td></tr>
<tr><td>47</td><td>Georgia</td><td>1,253</td><td>10</td><td>Illinois</td><td>4,835</td></tr>
<tr><td>7</td><td>Hawaii</td><td>6,780</td><td>11</td><td>Delaware</td><td>4,766</td></tr>
<tr><td>39</td><td>Idaho</td><td>1,960</td><td>12</td><td>Maryland</td><td>4,652</td></tr>
<tr><td>10</td><td>Illinois</td><td>4,835</td><td>13</td><td>Washington</td><td>4,502</td></tr>
<tr><td>25</td><td>Indiana</td><td>3,280</td><td>14</td><td>West Virginia</td><td>4,153</td></tr>
<tr><td>40</td><td>Iowa</td><td>1,956</td><td>15</td><td>South Dakota</td><td>4,040</td></tr>
<tr><td>34</td><td>Kansas</td><td>2,590</td><td>16</td><td>Wisconsin</td><td>4,015</td></tr>
<tr><td>26</td><td>Kentucky</td><td>3,234</td><td>17</td><td>California</td><td>3,878</td></tr>
<tr><td>18</td><td>Louisiana</td><td>3,874</td><td>18</td><td>Louisiana</td><td>3,874</td></tr>
<tr><td>21</td><td>Maine</td><td>3,558</td><td>19</td><td>North Dakota</td><td>3,821</td></tr>
<tr><td>12</td><td>Maryland</td><td>4,652</td><td>20</td><td>Pennsylvania</td><td>3,715</td></tr>
<tr><td>1</td><td>Massachusetts</td><td>11,225</td><td>21</td><td>Maine</td><td>3,558</td></tr>
<tr><td>23</td><td>Michigan</td><td>3,354</td><td>22</td><td>New Mexico</td><td>3,371</td></tr>
<tr><td>31</td><td>Minnesota</td><td>2,939</td><td>23</td><td>Michigan</td><td>3,354</td></tr>
<tr><td>35</td><td>Mississippi</td><td>2,499</td><td>24</td><td>Virginia</td><td>3,287</td></tr>
<tr><td>30</td><td>Missouri</td><td>3,015</td><td>25</td><td>Indiana</td><td>3,280</td></tr>
<tr><td>33</td><td>Montana</td><td>2,655</td><td>26</td><td>Kentucky</td><td>3,234</td></tr>
<tr><td>49</td><td>Nebraska</td><td>1,051</td><td>27</td><td>South Carolina</td><td>3,136</td></tr>
<tr><td>48</td><td>Nevada</td><td>1,093</td><td>28</td><td>Oregon</td><td>3,052</td></tr>
<tr><td>8</td><td>New Hampshire</td><td>5,734</td><td>29</td><td>Colorado</td><td>3,024</td></tr>
<tr><td>5</td><td>New Jersey</td><td>7,411</td><td>30</td><td>Missouri</td><td>3,015</td></tr>
<tr><td>22</td><td>New Mexico</td><td>3,371</td><td>31</td><td>Minnesota</td><td>2,939</td></tr>
<tr><td>6</td><td>New York</td><td>7,107</td><td>32</td><td>Ohio</td><td>2,871</td></tr>
<tr><td>44</td><td>North Carolina</td><td>1,588</td><td>33</td><td>Montana</td><td>2,655</td></tr>
<tr><td>19</td><td>North Dakota</td><td>3,821</td><td>34</td><td>Kansas</td><td>2,590</td></tr>
<tr><td>32</td><td>Ohio</td><td>2,871</td><td>35</td><td>Mississippi</td><td>2,499</td></tr>
<tr><td>37</td><td>Oklahoma</td><td>2,151</td><td>36</td><td>Utah</td><td>2,402</td></tr>
<tr><td>28</td><td>Oregon</td><td>3,052</td><td>37</td><td>Oklahoma</td><td>2,151</td></tr>
<tr><td>20</td><td>Pennsylvania</td><td>3,715</td><td>38</td><td>Arizona</td><td>2,027</td></tr>
<tr><td>3</td><td>Rhode Island</td><td>8,455</td><td>39</td><td>Idaho</td><td>1,960</td></tr>
<tr><td>27</td><td>South Carolina</td><td>3,136</td><td>40</td><td>Iowa</td><td>1,956</td></tr>
<tr><td>15</td><td>South Dakota</td><td>4,040</td><td>41</td><td>Alabama</td><td>1,800</td></tr>
<tr><td>50</td><td>Tennessee</td><td>913</td><td>42</td><td>Texas</td><td>1,799</td></tr>
<tr><td>42</td><td>Texas</td><td>1,799</td><td>43</td><td>Arkansas</td><td>1,599</td></tr>
<tr><td>36</td><td>Utah</td><td>2,402</td><td>44</td><td>North Carolina</td><td>1,588</td></tr>
<tr><td>9</td><td>Vermont</td><td>5,609</td><td>45</td><td>Florida</td><td>1,374</td></tr>
<tr><td>24</td><td>Virginia</td><td>3,287</td><td>46</td><td>Wyoming</td><td>1,330</td></tr>
<tr><td>13</td><td>Washington</td><td>4,502</td><td>47</td><td>Georgia</td><td>1,253</td></tr>
<tr><td>14</td><td>West Virginia</td><td>4,153</td><td>48</td><td>Nevada</td><td>1,093</td></tr>
<tr><td>16</td><td>Wisconsin</td><td>4,015</td><td>49</td><td>Nebraska</td><td>1,051</td></tr>
<tr><td>46</td><td>Wyoming</td><td>1,330</td><td>50</td><td>Tennessee</td><td>913</td></tr>
<tr><td></td><td></td><td></td><td></td><td>District of Columbia**</td><td>NA</td></tr>
</table>

Source: CQ Press using data from U.S. Bureau of the Census, Governments Division
    "2017 State and Local Government Finances" (https://www.census.gov/programs-surveys/gov-finances.html)
*Includes short-term, long-term, full faith and credit, nonguaranteed, and public debt for private purposes.
**Not applicable.

State Government Full-Time Equivalent Employees in 2018

National Total = 4,386,219 FTE Employees*

ALPHA ORDER					RANK ORDER			
RANK	STATE	EMPLOYEES	% of USA		RANK	STATE	EMPLOYEES	% of USA
16	Alabama	91,993	2.1%		1	California	427,272	9.7%
42	Alaska	24,464	0.6%		2	Texas	308,058	7.0%
25	Arizona	72,829	1.7%		3	New York	247,537	5.6%
29	Arkansas	62,434	1.4%		4	Florida	181,059	4.1%
1	California	427,272	9.7%		5	Pennsylvania	160,402	3.7%
17	Colorado	88,669	2.0%		6	Michigan	147,886	3.4%
31	Connecticut	58,988	1.3%		7	North Carolina	140,019	3.2%
40	Delaware	25,416	0.6%		8	New Jersey	139,102	3.2%
4	Florida	181,059	4.1%		9	Ohio	135,359	3.1%
10	Georgia	131,756	3.0%		10	Georgia	131,756	3.0%
32	Hawaii	58,058	1.3%		11	Washington	127,864	2.9%
41	Idaho	24,907	0.6%		12	Virginia	125,819	2.9%
13	Illinois	121,646	2.8%		13	Illinois	121,646	2.8%
15	Indiana	96,586	2.2%		14	Massachusetts	104,092	2.4%
35	Iowa	50,939	1.2%		15	Indiana	96,586	2.2%
34	Kansas	53,667	1.2%		16	Alabama	91,993	2.1%
18	Kentucky	85,167	1.9%		17	Colorado	88,669	2.0%
24	Louisiana	74,116	1.7%		18	Kentucky	85,167	1.9%
44	Maine	19,881	0.5%		19	Missouri	84,877	1.9%
20	Maryland	84,443	1.9%		20	Maryland	84,443	1.9%
14	Massachusetts	104,092	2.4%		21	Minnesota	84,274	1.9%
6	Michigan	147,886	3.4%		22	Tennessee	80,266	1.8%
21	Minnesota	84,274	1.9%		23	South Carolina	79,601	1.8%
33	Mississippi	54,637	1.2%		24	Louisiana	74,116	1.7%
19	Missouri	84,877	1.9%		25	Arizona	72,829	1.7%
43	Montana	19,887	0.5%		26	Oregon	72,657	1.7%
38	Nebraska	31,969	0.7%		27	Wisconsin	71,254	1.6%
39	Nevada	29,819	0.7%		28	Oklahoma	63,040	1.4%
45	New Hampshire	19,104	0.4%		29	Arkansas	62,434	1.4%
8	New Jersey	139,102	3.2%		30	Utah	62,104	1.4%
36 ·	New Mexico	45,332	1.0%		31	Connecticut	58,988	1.3%
3	New York	247,537	5.6%		32	Hawaii	58,058	1.3%
7	North Carolina	140,019	3.2%		33	Mississippi	54,637	1.2%
47	North Dakota	18,010	0.4%		34	Kansas	53,667	1.2%
9	Ohio	135,359	3.1%		35	Iowa	50,939	1.2%
28	Oklahoma	63,040	1.4%		36	New Mexico	45,332	1.0%
26	Oregon	72,657	1.7%		37	West Virginia	39,757	0.9%
5	Pennsylvania	160,402	3.7%		38	Nebraska	31,969	0.7%
46	Rhode Island	18,368	0.4%		39	Nevada	29,819	0.7%
23	South Carolina	79,601	1.8%		40	Delaware	25,416	0.6%
49	South Dakota	14,174	0.3%		41	Idaho	24,907	0.6%
22	Tennessee	80,266	1.8%		42	Alaska	24,464	0.6%
2	Texas	308,058	7.0%		43	Montana	19,887	0.5%
30	Utah	62,104	1.4%		44	Maine	19,881	0.5%
48	Vermont	14,296	0.3%		45	New Hampshire	19,104	0.4%
12	Virginia	125,819	2.9%		46	Rhode Island	18,368	0.4%
11	Washington	127,864	2.9%		47	North Dakota	18,010	0.4%
37	West Virginia	39,757	0.9%		48	Vermont	14,296	0.3%
27	Wisconsin	71,254	1.6%		49	South Dakota	14,174	0.3%
50	Wyoming	12,365	0.3%		50	Wyoming	12,365	0.3%
						District of Columbia**	NA	NA

Source: U.S. Bureau of the Census, Governments Division
   "Annual Survey of Public Employment and Payroll" (https://www.census.gov/programs-surveys/apes.html)
*Full-time equivalent as of March 2018.
**Not applicable.

Rate of State Government Full-Time Equivalent Employees in 2018

National Rate = 134 FTE Employees per 10,000 Population*

ALPHA ORDER

RANK	STATE	RATE
12	Alabama	188
2	Alaska	332
47	Arizona	102
9	Arkansas	207
45	California	108
26	Colorado	156
20	Connecticut	165
3	Delaware	263
50	Florida	85
40	Georgia	125
1	Hawaii	409
34	Idaho	142
49	Illinois	95
33	Indiana	144
21	Iowa	161
14	Kansas	184
11	Kentucky	191
24	Louisiana	159
30	Maine	149
36	Maryland	140
28	Massachusetts	151
31	Michigan	148
29	Minnesota	150
15	Mississippi	183
37	Missouri	139
13	Montana	187
19	Nebraska	166
48	Nevada	98
35	New Hampshire	141
26	New Jersey	156
7	New Mexico	216
39	New York	127
38	North Carolina	135
4	North Dakota	237
44	Ohio	116
23	Oklahoma	160
17	Oregon	173
40	Pennsylvania	125
16	Rhode Island	174
25	South Carolina	157
21	South Dakota	161
43	Tennessee	119
46	Texas	107
10	Utah	196
5	Vermont	228
31	Virginia	148
18	Washington	170
6	West Virginia	220
42	Wisconsin	123
8	Wyoming	214

RANK ORDER

RANK	STATE	RATE
1	Hawaii	409
2	Alaska	332
3	Delaware	263
4	North Dakota	237
5	Vermont	228
6	West Virginia	220
7	New Mexico	216
8	Wyoming	214
9	Arkansas	207
10	Utah	196
11	Kentucky	191
12	Alabama	188
13	Montana	187
14	Kansas	184
15	Mississippi	183
16	Rhode Island	174
17	Oregon	173
18	Washington	170
19	Nebraska	166
20	Connecticut	165
21	Iowa	161
21	South Dakota	161
23	Oklahoma	160
24	Louisiana	159
25	South Carolina	157
26	Colorado	156
26	New Jersey	156
28	Massachusetts	151
29	Minnesota	150
30	Maine	149
31	Michigan	148
31	Virginia	148
33	Indiana	144
34	Idaho	142
35	New Hampshire	141
36	Maryland	140
37	Missouri	139
38	North Carolina	135
39	New York	127
40	Georgia	125
40	Pennsylvania	125
42	Wisconsin	123
43	Tennessee	119
44	Ohio	116
45	California	108
46	Texas	107
47	Arizona	102
48	Nevada	98
49	Illinois	95
50	Florida	85

District of Columbia**	NA

Source: CQ Press using data from U.S. Bureau of the Census, Governments Division
   "Annual Survey of Public Employment and Payroll" (https://www.census.gov/programs-surveys/apes.html)
*Full-time equivalent as of March 2018.
**Not applicable.

Average Annual Earnings of Full-Time State Government Employees in 2018

National Average = $67,115*

ALPHA ORDER				RANK ORDER		
RANK	STATE	SALARY		RANK	STATE	SALARY
33	Alabama	$58,217		1	California	$90,703
10	Alaska	72,977		2	Connecticut	81,708
26	Arizona	62,031		3	Iowa	80,503
47	Arkansas	51,569		4	New Jersey	78,799
1	California	90,703		5	New York	78,642
11	Colorado	72,567		6	Massachusetts	75,732
2	Connecticut	81,708		7	Rhode Island	75,397
31	Delaware	58,818		8	Minnesota	74,402
42	Florida	55,470		9	Michigan	73,797
43	Georgia	55,422		10	Alaska	72,977
29	Hawaii	59,888		11	Colorado	72,567
17	Idaho	67,005		12	Oregon	70,586
14	Illinois	70,287		13	Washington	70,488
45	Indiana	54,316		14	Illinois	70,287
3	Iowa	80,503		15	Vermont	68,858
34	Kansas	57,822		16	Ohio	68,132
38	Kentucky	56,577		17	Idaho	67,005
30	Louisiana	58,837		18	New Hampshire	66,858
37	Maine	56,737		19	Pennsylvania	66,158
21	Maryland	65,499		20	Wisconsin	65,841
6	Massachusetts	75,732		21	Maryland	65,499
9	Michigan	73,797		22	Virginia	64,946
8	Minnesota	74,402		23	Nevada	64,922
50	Mississippi	48,599		24	Utah	64,218
49	Missouri	48,944		25	Texas	64,178
32	Montana	58,378		26	Arizona	62,031
39	Nebraska	56,574		27	North Dakota	61,723
23	Nevada	64,922		28	North Carolina	61,262
18	New Hampshire	66,858		29	Hawaii	59,888
4	New Jersey	78,799		30	Louisiana	58,837
35	New Mexico	57,490		31	Delaware	58,818
5	New York	78,642		32	Montana	58,378
28	North Carolina	61,262		33	Alabama	58,217
27	North Dakota	61,723		34	Kansas	57,822
16	Ohio	68,132		35	New Mexico	57,490
44	Oklahoma	54,837		35	South Dakota	57,490
12	Oregon	70,586		37	Maine	56,737
19	Pennsylvania	66,158		38	Kentucky	56,577
7	Rhode Island	75,397		39	Nebraska	56,574
46	South Carolina	53,114		40	Wyoming	56,269
35	South Dakota	57,490		41	Tennessee	55,722
41	Tennessee	55,722		42	Florida	55,470
25	Texas	64,178		43	Georgia	55,422
24	Utah	64,218		44	Oklahoma	54,837
15	Vermont	68,858		45	Indiana	54,316
22	Virginia	64,946		46	South Carolina	53,114
13	Washington	70,488		47	Arkansas	51,569
48	West Virginia	49,289		48	West Virginia	49,289
20	Wisconsin	65,841		49	Missouri	48,944
40	Wyoming	56,269		50	Mississippi	48,599
					District of Columbia**	NA

Source: CQ Press using data from U.S. Bureau of the Census, Governments Division
    "Annual Survey of Public Employment and Payroll" (https://www.census.gov/programs-surveys/apes.html)
*March 2018 full-time payroll (multiplied by 12) divided by full-time employees.
**Not applicable.

Local Government Total Revenue in 2017

National Total = $1,938,248,381,000*

ALPHA ORDER

ALPHA ORDER

RANK	STATE	REVENUE	% of USA
24	Alabama	$22,815,241,000	1.2%
41	Alaska	5,477,253,000	0.3%
19	Arizona	30,656,574,000	1.6%
36	Arkansas	10,614,963,000	0.5%
1	California	335,477,407,000	17.3%
16	Colorado	34,214,379,000	1.8%
27	Connecticut	20,185,149,000	1.0%
49	Delaware	3,897,389,000	0.2%
4	Florida	106,834,686,000	5.5%
12	Georgia	46,830,391,000	2.4%
46	Hawaii	4,522,265,000	0.2%
39	Idaho	6,288,408,000	0.3%
5	Illinois	80,938,747,000	4.2%
20	Indiana	30,299,193,000	1.6%
28	Iowa	17,966,397,000	0.9%
29	Kansas	15,921,276,000	0.8%
30	Kentucky	15,427,485,000	0.8%
25	Louisiana	22,003,409,000	1.1%
42	Maine	5,219,450,000	0.3%
17	Maryland	33,681,766,000	1.7%
14	Massachusetts	38,153,171,000	2.0%
11	Michigan	48,728,318,000	2.5%
18	Minnesota	32,198,814,000	1.7%
35	Mississippi	13,064,135,000	0.7%
22	Missouri	28,517,381,000	1.5%
47	Montana	4,060,646,000	0.2%
32	Nebraska	14,863,979,000	0.8%
31	Nevada	15,244,551,000	0.8%
38	New Hampshire	6,534,414,000	0.3%
9	New Jersey	50,429,684,000	2.6%
37	New Mexico	9,123,797,000	0.5%
2	New York	223,728,936,000	11.5%
10	North Carolina	49,755,739,000	2.6%
44	North Dakota	5,004,302,000	0.3%
7	Ohio	58,340,839,000	3.0%
33	Oklahoma	14,666,218,000	0.8%
26	Oregon	21,901,724,000	1.1%
6	Pennsylvania	70,277,095,000	3.6%
43	Rhode Island	5,023,245,000	0.3%
23	South Carolina	24,401,743,000	1.3%
48	South Dakota	3,988,012,000	0.2%
15	Tennessee	34,797,046,000	1.8%
3	Texas	147,614,132,000	7.6%
34	Utah	13,781,089,000	0.7%
50	Vermont	3,105,945,000	0.2%
13	Virginia	43,511,312,000	2.2%
8	Washington	51,367,280,000	2.7%
40	West Virginia	5,691,870,000	0.3%
21	Wisconsin	30,123,929,000	1.6%
45	Wyoming	4,962,509,000	0.3%

RANK ORDER

RANK	STATE	REVENUE	% of USA
1	California	$335,477,407,000	17.3%
2	New York	223,728,936,000	11.5%
3	Texas	147,614,132,000	7.6%
4	Florida	106,834,686,000	5.5%
5	Illinois	80,938,747,000	4.2%
6	Pennsylvania	70,277,095,000	3.6%
7	Ohio	58,340,839,000	3.0%
8	Washington	51,367,280,000	2.7%
9	New Jersey	50,429,684,000	2.6%
10	North Carolina	49,755,739,000	2.6%
11	Michigan	48,728,318,000	2.5%
12	Georgia	46,830,391,000	2.4%
13	Virginia	43,511,312,000	2.2%
14	Massachusetts	38,153,171,000	2.0%
15	Tennessee	34,797,046,000	1.8%
16	Colorado	34,214,379,000	1.8%
17	Maryland	33,681,766,000	1.7%
18	Minnesota	32,198,814,000	1.7%
19	Arizona	30,656,574,000	1.6%
20	Indiana	30,299,193,000	1.6%
21	Wisconsin	30,123,929,000	1.6%
22	Missouri	28,517,381,000	1.5%
23	South Carolina	24,401,743,000	1.3%
24	Alabama	22,815,241,000	1.2%
25	Louisiana	22,003,409,000	1.1%
26	Oregon	21,901,724,000	1.1%
27	Connecticut	20,185,149,000	1.0%
28	Iowa	17,966,397,000	0.9%
29	Kansas	15,921,276,000	0.8%
30	Kentucky	15,427,485,000	0.8%
31	Nevada	15,244,551,000	0.8%
32	Nebraska	14,863,979,000	0.8%
33	Oklahoma	14,666,218,000	0.8%
34	Utah	13,781,089,000	0.7%
35	Mississippi	13,064,135,000	0.7%
36	Arkansas	10,614,963,000	0.5%
37	New Mexico	9,123,797,000	0.5%
38	New Hampshire	6,534,414,000	0.3%
39	Idaho	6,288,408,000	0.3%
40	West Virginia	5,691,870,000	0.3%
41	Alaska	5,477,253,000	0.3%
42	Maine	5,219,450,000	0.3%
43	Rhode Island	5,023,245,000	0.3%
44	North Dakota	5,004,302,000	0.3%
45	Wyoming	4,962,509,000	0.3%
46	Hawaii	4,522,265,000	0.2%
47	Montana	4,060,646,000	0.2%
48	South Dakota	3,988,012,000	0.2%
49	Delaware	3,897,389,000	0.2%
50	Vermont	3,105,945,000	0.2%
	District of Columbia	16,014,698,000	0.8%

Source: U.S. Bureau of the Census, Governments Division
"2017 State and Local Government Finances" (https://www.census.gov/programs-surveys/gov-finances.html)
*Total revenue includes all money received from external sources. This includes taxes, intergovernmental transfers and insurance trust revenue, and revenue from government-owned utilities and other commercial or auxiliary enterprise.

Per Capita Local Government Total Revenue in 2017

National Per Capita = $5,961*

ALPHA ORDER

RANK	STATE	PER CAPITA
33	Alabama	$4,680
5	Alaska	7,404
41	Arizona	4,349
47	Arkansas	3,535
3	California	8,515
9	Colorado	6,092
13	Connecticut	5,648
42	Delaware	4,072
24	Florida	5,093
37	Georgia	4,497
49	Hawaii	3,175
46	Idaho	3,658
8	Illinois	6,330
36	Indiana	4,549
11	Iowa	5,715
17	Kansas	5,470
48	Kentucky	3,464
32	Louisiana	4,711
43	Maine	3,910
14	Maryland	5,590
15	Massachusetts	5,559
27	Michigan	4,884
10	Minnesota	5,783
39	Mississippi	4,370
34	Missouri	4,668
44	Montana	3,856
4	Nebraska	7,751
23	Nevada	5,129
30	New Hampshire	4,841
12	New Jersey	5,674
40	New Mexico	4,358
1	New York	11,420
29	North Carolina	4,844
7	North Dakota	6,627
25	Ohio	5,002
45	Oklahoma	3,729
18	Oregon	5,282
16	Pennsylvania	5,494
31	Rhode Island	4,755
28	South Carolina	4,860
35	South Dakota	4,567
21	Tennessee	5,187
19	Texas	5,212
38	Utah	4,441
26	Vermont	4,973
22	Virginia	5,140
6	Washington	6,918
50	West Virginia	3,132
20	Wisconsin	5,201
2	Wyoming	8,572

RANK ORDER

RANK	STATE	PER CAPITA
1	New York	$11,420
2	Wyoming	8,572
3	California	8,515
4	Nebraska	7,751
5	Alaska	7,404
6	Washington	6,918
7	North Dakota	6,627
8	Illinois	6,330
9	Colorado	6,092
10	Minnesota	5,783
11	Iowa	5,715
12	New Jersey	5,674
13	Connecticut	5,648
14	Maryland	5,590
15	Massachusetts	5,559
16	Pennsylvania	5,494
17	Kansas	5,470
18	Oregon	5,282
19	Texas	5,212
20	Wisconsin	5,201
21	Tennessee	5,187
22	Virginia	5,140
23	Nevada	5,129
24	Florida	5,093
25	Ohio	5,002
26	Vermont	4,973
27	Michigan	4,884
28	South Carolina	4,860
29	North Carolina	4,844
30	New Hampshire	4,841
31	Rhode Island	4,755
32	Louisiana	4,711
33	Alabama	4,680
34	Missouri	4,668
35	South Dakota	4,567
36	Indiana	4,549
37	Georgia	4,497
38	Utah	4,441
39	Mississippi	4,370
40	New Mexico	4,358
41	Arizona	4,349
42	Delaware	4,072
43	Maine	3,910
44	Montana	3,856
45	Oklahoma	3,729
46	Idaho	3,658
47	Arkansas	3,535
48	Kentucky	3,464
49	Hawaii	3,175
50	West Virginia	3,132

District of Columbia   23,020

Source: CQ Press using data from U.S. Bureau of the Census, Governments Division
  "2017 State and Local Government Finances" (https://www.census.gov/programs-surveys/gov-finances.html)
*Total revenue includes all money received from external sources. This includes taxes, intergovernmental transfers and insurance trust revenue, and revenue from government-owned utilities and other commercial or auxiliary enterprise.

Local Government Revenue from the Federal Government in 2017

National Total = $69,034,154,000

ALPHA ORDER

RANK	STATE	REVENUE	% of USA
16	Alabama	$1,112,489,000	1.6%
40	Alaska	239,709,000	0.3%
18	Arizona	925,526,000	1.3%
38	Arkansas	295,553,000	0.4%
1	California	12,328,532,000	17.9%
15	Colorado	1,122,226,000	1.6%
24	Connecticut	579,598,000	0.8%
49	Delaware	95,568,000	0.1%
4	Florida	3,752,147,000	5.4%
14	Georgia	1,206,910,000	1.7%
36	Hawaii	319,152,000	0.5%
45	Idaho	149,746,000	0.2%
5	Illinois	3,512,527,000	5.1%
30	Indiana	473,590,000	0.7%
31	Iowa	457,456,000	0.7%
37	Kansas	299,728,000	0.4%
27	Kentucky	528,628,000	0.8%
20	Louisiana	859,914,000	1.2%
47	Maine	113,639,000	0.2%
13	Maryland	1,245,477,000	1.8%
12	Massachusetts	1,428,229,000	2.1%
11	Michigan	1,660,901,000	2.4%
17	Minnesota	952,950,000	1.4%
32	Mississippi	439,560,000	0.6%
21	Missouri	833,255,000	1.2%
41	Montana	228,642,000	0.3%
35	Nebraska	353,795,000	0.5%
26	Nevada	578,016,000	0.8%
48	New Hampshire	103,811,000	0.2%
19	New Jersey	904,675,000	1.3%
34	New Mexico	411,820,000	0.6%
2	New York	7,177,197,000	10.4%
8	North Carolina	2,208,069,000	3.2%
39	North Dakota	251,312,000	0.4%
7	Ohio	2,269,942,000	3.3%
28	Oklahoma	520,263,000	0.8%
22	Oregon	820,803,000	1.2%
6	Pennsylvania	2,911,586,000	4.2%
44	Rhode Island	160,547,000	0.2%
33	South Carolina	435,279,000	0.6%
43	South Dakota	166,728,000	0.2%
23	Tennessee	705,283,000	1.0%
3	Texas	3,913,108,000	5.7%
29	Utah	493,906,000	0.7%
50	Vermont	69,563,000	0.1%
10	Virginia	1,826,048,000	2.6%
9	Washington	1,910,810,000	2.8%
42	West Virginia	195,134,000	0.3%
25	Wisconsin	578,309,000	0.8%
46	Wyoming	140,001,000	0.2%

RANK ORDER

RANK	STATE	REVENUE	% of USA
1	California	$12,328,532,000	17.9%
2	New York	7,177,197,000	10.4%
3	Texas	3,913,108,000	5.7%
4	Florida	3,752,147,000	5.4%
5	Illinois	3,512,527,000	5.1%
6	Pennsylvania	2,911,586,000	4.2%
7	Ohio	2,269,942,000	3.3%
8	North Carolina	2,208,069,000	3.2%
9	Washington	1,910,810,000	2.8%
10	Virginia	1,826,048,000	2.6%
11	Michigan	1,660,901,000	2.4%
12	Massachusetts	1,428,229,000	2.1%
13	Maryland	1,245,477,000	1.8%
14	Georgia	1,206,910,000	1.7%
15	Colorado	1,122,226,000	1.6%
16	Alabama	1,112,489,000	1.6%
17	Minnesota	952,950,000	1.4%
18	Arizona	925,526,000	1.3%
19	New Jersey	904,675,000	1.3%
20	Louisiana	859,914,000	1.2%
21	Missouri	833,255,000	1.2%
22	Oregon	820,803,000	1.2%
23	Tennessee	705,283,000	1.0%
24	Connecticut	579,598,000	0.8%
25	Wisconsin	578,309,000	0.8%
26	Nevada	578,016,000	0.8%
27	Kentucky	528,628,000	0.8%
28	Oklahoma	520,263,000	0.8%
29	Utah	493,906,000	0.7%
30	Indiana	473,590,000	0.7%
31	Iowa	457,456,000	0.7%
32	Mississippi	439,560,000	0.6%
33	South Carolina	435,279,000	0.6%
34	New Mexico	411,820,000	0.6%
35	Nebraska	353,795,000	0.5%
36	Hawaii	319,152,000	0.5%
37	Kansas	299,728,000	0.4%
38	Arkansas	295,553,000	0.4%
39	North Dakota	251,312,000	0.4%
40	Alaska	239,709,000	0.3%
41	Montana	228,642,000	0.3%
42	West Virginia	195,134,000	0.3%
43	South Dakota	166,728,000	0.2%
44	Rhode Island	160,547,000	0.2%
45	Idaho	149,746,000	0.2%
46	Wyoming	140,001,000	0.2%
47	Maine	113,639,000	0.2%
48	New Hampshire	103,811,000	0.2%
49	Delaware	95,568,000	0.1%
50	Vermont	69,563,000	0.1%
	District of Columbia	4,766,497,000	6.9%

Source: U.S. Bureau of the Census, Governments Division
"2017 State and Local Government Finances" (https://www.census.gov/programs-surveys/gov-finances.html)

Per Capita Local Government Revenue from the Federal Government in 2017

National Per Capita = $212

ALPHA ORDER

RANK	STATE	PER CAPITA
8	Alabama	$228
3	Alaska	324
35	Arizona	131
45	Arkansas	98
4	California	313
16	Colorado	200
27	Connecticut	162
43	Delaware	100
24	Florida	179
37	Georgia	116
10	Hawaii	224
46	Idaho	87
5	Illinois	275
50	Indiana	71
31	Iowa	146
41	Kansas	103
36	Kentucky	119
23	Louisiana	184
48	Maine	85
15	Maryland	207
14	Massachusetts	208
26	Michigan	166
25	Minnesota	171
30	Mississippi	147
33	Missouri	136
11	Montana	217
22	Nebraska	185
20	Nevada	194
49	New Hampshire	77
42	New Jersey	102
18	New Mexico	197
1	New York	366
13	North Carolina	215
2	North Dakota	333
19	Ohio	195
34	Oklahoma	132
17	Oregon	198
8	Pennsylvania	228
29	Rhode Island	152
46	South Carolina	87
21	South Dakota	191
40	Tennessee	105
32	Texas	138
28	Utah	159
38	Vermont	111
12	Virginia	216
6	Washington	257
39	West Virginia	107
43	Wisconsin	100
7	Wyoming	242

RANK ORDER

RANK	STATE	PER CAPITA
1	New York	$366
2	North Dakota	333
3	Alaska	324
4	California	313
5	Illinois	275
6	Washington	257
7	Wyoming	242
8	Alabama	228
8	Pennsylvania	228
10	Hawaii	224
11	Montana	217
12	Virginia	216
13	North Carolina	215
14	Massachusetts	208
15	Maryland	207
16	Colorado	200
17	Oregon	198
18	New Mexico	197
19	Ohio	195
20	Nevada	194
21	South Dakota	191
22	Nebraska	185
23	Louisiana	184
24	Florida	179
25	Minnesota	171
26	Michigan	166
27	Connecticut	162
28	Utah	159
29	Rhode Island	152
30	Mississippi	147
31	Iowa	146
32	Texas	138
33	Missouri	136
34	Oklahoma	132
35	Arizona	131
36	Kentucky	119
37	Georgia	116
38	Vermont	111
39	West Virginia	107
40	Tennessee	105
41	Kansas	103
42	New Jersey	102
43	Delaware	100
43	Wisconsin	100
45	Arkansas	98
46	Idaho	87
46	South Carolina	87
48	Maine	85
49	New Hampshire	77
50	Indiana	71

| | District of Columbia | 6,851 |

Source: CQ Press using data from U.S. Bureau of the Census, Governments Division
"2017 State and Local Government Finances" (https://www.census.gov/programs-surveys/gov-finances.html)

Local Government Own Source Revenue in 2017

National Total = $1,091,135,100,000*

ALPHA ORDER

RANK	STATE	REVENUE	% of USA
27	Alabama	$12,216,197,000	1.1%
44	Alaska	3,054,495,000	0.3%
22	Arizona	15,853,943,000	1.5%
37	Arkansas	4,245,917,000	0.4%
1	California	157,557,543,000	14.4%
14	Colorado	22,610,846,000	2.1%
26	Connecticut	12,531,032,000	1.1%
49	Delaware	1,715,797,000	0.2%
4	Florida	68,060,603,000	6.2%
11	Georgia	27,679,993,000	2.5%
41	Hawaii	3,468,828,000	0.3%
40	Idaho	3,539,474,000	0.3%
5	Illinois	47,531,592,000	4.4%
18	Indiana	16,429,140,000	1.5%
28	Iowa	10,693,294,000	1.0%
29	Kansas	8,818,960,000	0.8%
31	Kentucky	8,307,142,000	0.8%
24	Louisiana	14,143,325,000	1.3%
39	Maine	3,612,971,000	0.3%
16	Maryland	20,917,006,000	1.9%
15	Massachusetts	21,865,804,000	2.0%
13	Michigan	23,339,195,000	2.1%
20	Minnesota	16,342,430,000	1.5%
35	Mississippi	7,330,418,000	0.7%
17	Missouri	17,385,782,000	1.6%
48	Montana	2,350,624,000	0.2%
34	Nebraska	7,379,970,000	0.7%
32	Nevada	8,100,424,000	0.7%
36	New Hampshire	4,841,376,000	0.4%
7	New Jersey	36,756,941,000	3.4%
38	New Mexico	4,242,779,000	0.4%
2	New York	127,972,698,000	11.7%
10	North Carolina	28,101,444,000	2.6%
47	North Dakota	2,416,201,000	0.2%
8	Ohio	35,927,449,000	3.3%
30	Oklahoma	8,757,192,000	0.8%
25	Oregon	12,561,371,000	1.2%
6	Pennsylvania	38,695,869,000	3.5%
43	Rhode Island	3,173,068,000	0.3%
21	South Carolina	15,856,845,000	1.5%
46	South Dakota	2,565,278,000	0.2%
19	Tennessee	16,374,963,000	1.5%
3	Texas	93,094,498,000	8.5%
33	Utah	7,692,541,000	0.7%
50	Vermont	982,311,000	0.1%
12	Virginia	25,620,408,000	2.3%
9	Washington	28,267,952,000	2.6%
42	West Virginia	3,441,583,000	0.3%
23	Wisconsin	15,005,144,000	1.4%
45	Wyoming	2,687,638,000	0.2%

RANK ORDER

RANK	STATE	REVENUE	% of USA
1	California	$157,557,543,000	14.4%
2	New York	127,972,698,000	11.7%
3	Texas	93,094,498,000	8.5%
4	Florida	68,060,603,000	6.2%
5	Illinois	47,531,592,000	4.4%
6	Pennsylvania	38,695,869,000	3.5%
7	New Jersey	36,756,941,000	3.4%
8	Ohio	35,927,449,000	3.3%
9	Washington	28,267,952,000	2.6%
10	North Carolina	28,101,444,000	2.6%
11	Georgia	27,679,993,000	2.5%
12	Virginia	25,620,408,000	2.3%
13	Michigan	23,339,195,000	2.1%
14	Colorado	22,610,846,000	2.1%
15	Massachusetts	21,865,804,000	2.0%
16	Maryland	20,917,006,000	1.9%
17	Missouri	17,385,782,000	1.6%
18	Indiana	16,429,140,000	1.5%
19	Tennessee	16,374,963,000	1.5%
20	Minnesota	16,342,430,000	1.5%
21	South Carolina	15,856,845,000	1.5%
22	Arizona	15,853,943,000	1.5%
23	Wisconsin	15,005,144,000	1.4%
24	Louisiana	14,143,325,000	1.3%
25	Oregon	12,561,371,000	1.2%
26	Connecticut	12,531,032,000	1.1%
27	Alabama	12,216,197,000	1.1%
28	Iowa	10,693,294,000	1.0%
29	Kansas	8,818,960,000	0.8%
30	Oklahoma	8,757,192,000	0.8%
31	Kentucky	8,307,142,000	0.8%
32	Nevada	8,100,424,000	0.7%
33	Utah	7,692,541,000	0.7%
34	Nebraska	7,379,970,000	0.7%
35	Mississippi	7,330,418,000	0.7%
36	New Hampshire	4,841,376,000	0.4%
37	Arkansas	4,245,917,000	0.4%
38	New Mexico	4,242,779,000	0.4%
39	Maine	3,612,971,000	0.3%
40	Idaho	3,539,474,000	0.3%
41	Hawaii	3,468,828,000	0.3%
42	West Virginia	3,441,583,000	0.3%
43	Rhode Island	3,173,068,000	0.3%
44	Alaska	3,054,495,000	0.3%
45	Wyoming	2,687,638,000	0.2%
46	South Dakota	2,565,278,000	0.2%
47	North Dakota	2,416,201,000	0.2%
48	Montana	2,350,624,000	0.2%
49	Delaware	1,715,797,000	0.2%
50	Vermont	982,311,000	0.1%
	District of Columbia	9,016,806,000	0.8%

Source: U.S. Bureau of the Census, Governments Division
   "2017 State and Local Government Finances" (https://www.census.gov/programs-surveys/gov-finances.html)
*Own source revenue includes taxes, current charges, and miscellaneous general revenue. Excluded are intergovernmental transfers, insurance trust revenue, and revenue from government-owned utilities and other commercial or auxiliary enterprise.

Per Capita Local Government Own Source Revenue in 2017

National Per Capita = $3,356*

ALPHA ORDER				RANK ORDER		
RANK	STATE	PER CAPITA		RANK	STATE	PER CAPITA
34	Alabama	$2,506		1	New York	$6,532
4	Alaska	4,129		2	Wyoming	4,642
41	Arizona	2,249		3	New Jersey	4,135
50	Arkansas	1,414		4	Alaska	4,129
6	California	3,999		5	Colorado	4,026
5	Colorado	4,026		6	California	3,999
11	Connecticut	3,506		7	Nebraska	3,849
48	Delaware	1,793		8	Washington	3,807
15	Florida	3,245		9	Illinois	3,717
32	Georgia	2,658		10	New Hampshire	3,587
39	Hawaii	2,436		11	Connecticut	3,506
44	Idaho	2,059		12	Maryland	3,472
9	Illinois	3,717		13	Iowa	3,402
36	Indiana	2,467		14	Texas	3,287
13	Iowa	3,402		15	Florida	3,245
20	Kansas	3,030		16	North Dakota	3,200
47	Kentucky	1,865		17	Massachusetts	3,186
22	Louisiana	3,028		18	South Carolina	3,158
31	Maine	2,706		19	Ohio	3,080
12	Maryland	3,472		20	Kansas	3,030
17	Massachusetts	3,186		21	Oregon	3,029
40	Michigan	2,339		22	Louisiana	3,028
27	Minnesota	2,935		23	Virginia	3,027
37	Mississippi	2,452		24	Pennsylvania	3,025
28	Missouri	2,846		25	Rhode Island	3,003
42	Montana	2,232		26	South Dakota	2,938
7	Nebraska	3,849		27	Minnesota	2,935
30	Nevada	2,725		28	Missouri	2,846
10	New Hampshire	3,587		29	North Carolina	2,736
3	New Jersey	4,135		30	Nevada	2,725
45	New Mexico	2,027		31	Maine	2,706
1	New York	6,532		32	Georgia	2,658
29	North Carolina	2,736		33	Wisconsin	2,591
16	North Dakota	3,200		34	Alabama	2,506
19	Ohio	3,080		35	Utah	2,479
43	Oklahoma	2,227		36	Indiana	2,467
21	Oregon	3,029		37	Mississippi	2,452
24	Pennsylvania	3,025		38	Tennessee	2,441
25	Rhode Island	3,003		39	Hawaii	2,436
18	South Carolina	3,158		40	Michigan	2,339
26	South Dakota	2,938		41	Arizona	2,249
38	Tennessee	2,441		42	Montana	2,232
14	Texas	3,287		43	Oklahoma	2,227
35	Utah	2,479		44	Idaho	2,059
49	Vermont	1,573		45	New Mexico	2,027
23	Virginia	3,027		46	West Virginia	1,894
8	Washington	3,807		47	Kentucky	1,865
46	West Virginia	1,894		48	Delaware	1,793
33	Wisconsin	2,591		49	Vermont	1,573
2	Wyoming	4,642		50	Arkansas	1,414
					District of Columbia	12,961

Source: CQ Press using data from U.S. Bureau of the Census, Governments Division
"2017 State and Local Government Finances" (https://www.census.gov/programs-surveys/gov-finances.html)
*Own source revenue includes taxes, current charges, and miscellaneous general revenue. Excluded are intergovernmental transfers, insurance trust revenue, and revenue from government-owned utilities and other commercial or auxiliary enterprise.

Local Government Tax Revenue in 2017

National Total = $706,468,257,000

ALPHA ORDER

RANK	STATE	REVENUE	% of USA
27	Alabama	$6,010,623,000	0.9%
45	Alaska	1,840,478,000	0.3%
19	Arizona	10,583,291,000	1.5%
40	Arkansas	2,500,475,000	0.4%
2	California	87,450,048,000	12.4%
14	Colorado	14,211,189,000	2.0%
17	Connecticut	10,951,648,000	1.6%
48	Delaware	1,087,313,000	0.2%
4	Florida	36,401,625,000	5.2%
11	Georgia	16,520,095,000	2.3%
41	Hawaii	2,428,261,000	0.3%
44	Idaho	1,868,613,000	0.3%
5	Illinois	35,723,174,000	5.1%
24	Indiana	7,877,711,000	1.1%
28	Iowa	5,937,739,000	0.8%
31	Kansas	5,341,480,000	0.8%
29	Kentucky	5,435,077,000	0.8%
21	Louisiana	9,112,240,000	1.3%
37	Maine	2,846,314,000	0.4%
12	Maryland	16,364,665,000	2.3%
10	Massachusetts	17,534,151,000	2.5%
16	Michigan	13,158,103,000	1.9%
23	Minnesota	8,796,423,000	1.2%
36	Mississippi	3,212,413,000	0.5%
18	Missouri	10,843,308,000	1.5%
47	Montana	1,429,603,000	0.2%
34	Nebraska	4,711,561,000	0.7%
33	Nevada	4,737,322,000	0.7%
35	New Hampshire	4,110,516,000	0.6%
6	New Jersey	29,700,650,000	4.2%
38	New Mexico	2,842,915,000	0.4%
1	New York	98,072,505,000	13.9%
15	North Carolina	13,821,937,000	2.0%
46	North Dakota	1,567,677,000	0.2%
8	Ohio	24,301,298,000	3.4%
30	Oklahoma	5,365,992,000	0.8%
26	Oregon	7,703,205,000	1.1%
7	Pennsylvania	28,217,186,000	4.0%
39	Rhode Island	2,609,688,000	0.4%
25	South Carolina	7,856,380,000	1.1%
43	South Dakota	1,891,898,000	0.3%
22	Tennessee	8,952,782,000	1.3%
3	Texas	64,238,801,000	9.1%
32	Utah	4,775,778,000	0.7%
50	Vermont	647,193,000	0.1%
9	Virginia	18,397,138,000	2.6%
13	Washington	15,665,831,000	2.2%
42	West Virginia	2,092,258,000	0.3%
20	Wisconsin	10,195,281,000	1.4%
49	Wyoming	1,070,537,000	0.2%

RANK ORDER

RANK	STATE	REVENUE	% of USA
1	New York	$98,072,505,000	13.9%
2	California	87,450,048,000	12.4%
3	Texas	64,238,801,000	9.1%
4	Florida	36,401,625,000	5.2%
5	Illinois	35,723,174,000	5.1%
6	New Jersey	29,700,650,000	4.2%
7	Pennsylvania	28,217,186,000	4.0%
8	Ohio	24,301,298,000	3.4%
9	Virginia	18,397,138,000	2.6%
10	Massachusetts	17,534,151,000	2.5%
11	Georgia	16,520,095,000	2.3%
12	Maryland	16,364,665,000	2.3%
13	Washington	15,665,831,000	2.2%
14	Colorado	14,211,189,000	2.0%
15	North Carolina	13,821,937,000	2.0%
16	Michigan	13,158,103,000	1.9%
17	Connecticut	10,951,648,000	1.6%
18	Missouri	10,843,308,000	1.5%
19	Arizona	10,583,291,000	1.5%
20	Wisconsin	10,195,281,000	1.4%
21	Louisiana	9,112,240,000	1.3%
22	Tennessee	8,952,782,000	1.3%
23	Minnesota	8,796,423,000	1.2%
24	Indiana	7,877,711,000	1.1%
25	South Carolina	7,856,380,000	1.1%
26	Oregon	7,703,205,000	1.1%
27	Alabama	6,010,623,000	0.9%
28	Iowa	5,937,739,000	0.8%
29	Kentucky	5,435,077,000	0.8%
30	Oklahoma	5,365,992,000	0.8%
31	Kansas	5,341,480,000	0.8%
32	Utah	4,775,778,000	0.7%
33	Nevada	4,737,322,000	0.7%
34	Nebraska	4,711,561,000	0.7%
35	New Hampshire	4,110,516,000	0.6%
36	Mississippi	3,212,413,000	0.5%
37	Maine	2,846,314,000	0.4%
38	New Mexico	2,842,915,000	0.4%
39	Rhode Island	2,609,688,000	0.4%
40	Arkansas	2,500,475,000	0.4%
41	Hawaii	2,428,261,000	0.3%
42	West Virginia	2,092,258,000	0.3%
43	South Dakota	1,891,898,000	0.3%
44	Idaho	1,868,613,000	0.3%
45	Alaska	1,840,478,000	0.3%
46	North Dakota	1,567,677,000	0.2%
47	Montana	1,429,603,000	0.2%
48	Delaware	1,087,313,000	0.2%
49	Wyoming	1,070,537,000	0.2%
50	Vermont	647,193,000	0.1%
	District of Columbia	7,455,868,000	1.1%

Source: U.S. Bureau of the Census, Governments Division
"2017 State and Local Government Finances" (https://www.census.gov/programs-surveys/gov-finances.html)

Per Capita Local Government Tax Revenue in 2017

National Per Capita = $2,173

ALPHA ORDER				RANK ORDER		
RANK	STATE	PER CAPITA		RANK	STATE	PER CAPITA
42	Alabama	$1,233		1	New York	$5,006
9	Alaska	2,488		2	New Jersey	3,341
35	Arizona	1,501		3	Connecticut	3,064
50	Arkansas	833		4	New Hampshire	3,045
13	California	2,220		5	Illinois	2,794
8	Colorado	2,531		6	Maryland	2,716
3	Connecticut	3,064		7	Massachusetts	2,555
46	Delaware	1,136		8	Colorado	2,531
28	Florida	1,735		9	Alaska	2,488
31	Georgia	1,586		10	Rhode Island	2,470
29	Hawaii	1,705		11	Nebraska	2,457
47	Idaho	1,087		12	Texas	2,268
5	Illinois	2,794		13	California	2,220
44	Indiana	1,183		14	Pennsylvania	2,206
22	Iowa	1,889		15	Virginia	2,173
25	Kansas	1,835		16	South Dakota	2,166
43	Kentucky	1,220		17	Maine	2,132
21	Louisiana	1,951		18	Washington	2,110
17	Maine	2,132		19	Ohio	2,083
6	Maryland	2,716		20	North Dakota	2,076
7	Massachusetts	2,555		21	Louisiana	1,951
41	Michigan	1,319		22	Iowa	1,889
32	Minnesota	1,580		23	Oregon	1,858
48	Mississippi	1,075		24	Wyoming	1,849
26	Missouri	1,775		25	Kansas	1,835
37	Montana	1,358		26	Missouri	1,775
11	Nebraska	2,457		27	Wisconsin	1,760
30	Nevada	1,594		28	Florida	1,735
4	New Hampshire	3,045		29	Hawaii	1,705
2	New Jersey	3,341		30	Nevada	1,594
37	New Mexico	1,358		31	Georgia	1,586
1	New York	5,006		32	Minnesota	1,580
39	North Carolina	1,346		33	South Carolina	1,565
20	North Dakota	2,076		34	Utah	1,539
19	Ohio	2,083		35	Arizona	1,501
36	Oklahoma	1,364		36	Oklahoma	1,364
23	Oregon	1,858		37	Montana	1,358
14	Pennsylvania	2,206		37	New Mexico	1,358
10	Rhode Island	2,470		39	North Carolina	1,346
33	South Carolina	1,565		40	Tennessee	1,334
16	South Dakota	2,166		41	Michigan	1,319
40	Tennessee	1,334		42	Alabama	1,233
12	Texas	2,268		43	Kentucky	1,220
34	Utah	1,539		44	Indiana	1,183
49	Vermont	1,036		45	West Virginia	1,151
15	Virginia	2,173		46	Delaware	1,136
18	Washington	2,110		47	Idaho	1,087
45	West Virginia	1,151		48	Mississippi	1,075
27	Wisconsin	1,760		49	Vermont	1,036
24	Wyoming	1,849		50	Arkansas	833
					District of Columbia	10,717

Source: CQ Press using data from U.S. Bureau of the Census, Governments Division
"2017 State and Local Government Finances" (https://www.census.gov/programs-surveys/gov-finances.html)

Local Government Total Expenditures in 2017

National Total = $1,912,109,747,000*

ALPHA ORDER

RANK	STATE	EXPENDITURES	% of USA
24	Alabama	$23,167,484,000	1.2%
41	Alaska	5,465,826,000	0.3%
20	Arizona	29,435,631,000	1.5%
36	Arkansas	10,439,459,000	0.5%
1	California	322,776,383,000	16.9%
18	Colorado	33,209,074,000	1.7%
27	Connecticut	18,685,524,000	1.0%
49	Delaware	3,683,514,000	0.2%
4	Florida	105,692,019,000	5.5%
11	Georgia	47,873,137,000	2.5%
46	Hawaii	4,428,167,000	0.2%
38	Idaho	6,012,311,000	0.3%
5	Illinois	80,461,331,000	4.2%
21	Indiana	28,082,712,000	1.5%
28	Iowa	17,737,394,000	0.9%
29	Kansas	15,801,468,000	0.8%
30	Kentucky	15,518,125,000	0.8%
26	Louisiana	21,513,566,000	1.1%
43	Maine	5,100,185,000	0.3%
17	Maryland	33,883,541,000	1.8%
14	Massachusetts	37,004,357,000	1.9%
12	Michigan	47,740,952,000	2.5%
15	Minnesota	34,958,734,000	1.8%
35	Mississippi	12,976,666,000	0.7%
22	Missouri	27,694,853,000	1.4%
47	Montana	4,236,756,000	0.2%
31	Nebraska	14,944,857,000	0.8%
32	Nevada	14,699,259,000	0.8%
40	New Hampshire	5,643,035,000	0.3%
9	New Jersey	49,356,508,000	2.6%
37	New Mexico	8,865,365,000	0.5%
2	New York	220,022,358,000	11.5%
10	North Carolina	48,337,253,000	2.5%
42	North Dakota	5,260,655,000	0.3%
7	Ohio	60,806,467,000	3.2%
33	Oklahoma	13,963,843,000	0.7%
25	Oregon	22,313,484,000	1.2%
6	Pennsylvania	69,859,317,000	3.7%
45	Rhode Island	4,979,801,000	0.3%
23	South Carolina	23,425,049,000	1.2%
48	South Dakota	3,753,586,000	0.2%
16	Tennessee	34,283,189,000	1.8%
3	Texas	149,600,874,000	7.8%
34	Utah	13,495,299,000	0.7%
50	Vermont	2,908,100,000	0.2%
13	Virginia	42,623,691,000	2.2%
8	Washington	49,506,405,000	2.6%
39	West Virginia	5,966,406,000	0.3%
19	Wisconsin	31,273,362,000	1.6%
44	Wyoming	5,085,659,000	0.3%

RANK ORDER

RANK	STATE	EXPENDITURES	% of USA
1	California	$322,776,383,000	16.9%
2	New York	220,022,358,000	11.5%
3	Texas	149,600,874,000	7.8%
4	Florida	105,692,019,000	5.5%
5	Illinois	80,461,331,000	4.2%
6	Pennsylvania	69,859,317,000	3.7%
7	Ohio	60,806,467,000	3.2%
8	Washington	49,506,405,000	2.6%
9	New Jersey	49,356,508,000	2.6%
10	North Carolina	48,337,253,000	2.5%
11	Georgia	47,873,137,000	2.5%
12	Michigan	47,740,952,000	2.5%
13	Virginia	42,623,691,000	2.2%
14	Massachusetts	37,004,357,000	1.9%
15	Minnesota	34,958,734,000	1.8%
16	Tennessee	34,283,189,000	1.8%
17	Maryland	33,883,541,000	1.8%
18	Colorado	33,209,074,000	1.7%
19	Wisconsin	31,273,362,000	1.6%
20	Arizona	29,435,631,000	1.5%
21	Indiana	28,082,712,000	1.5%
22	Missouri	27,694,853,000	1.4%
23	South Carolina	23,425,049,000	1.2%
24	Alabama	23,167,484,000	1.2%
25	Oregon	22,313,484,000	1.2%
26	Louisiana	21,513,566,000	1.1%
27	Connecticut	18,685,524,000	1.0%
28	Iowa	17,737,394,000	0.9%
29	Kansas	15,801,468,000	0.8%
30	Kentucky	15,518,125,000	0.8%
31	Nebraska	14,944,857,000	0.8%
32	Nevada	14,699,259,000	0.8%
33	Oklahoma	13,963,843,000	0.7%
34	Utah	13,495,299,000	0.7%
35	Mississippi	12,976,666,000	0.7%
36	Arkansas	10,439,459,000	0.5%
37	New Mexico	8,865,365,000	0.5%
38	Idaho	6,012,311,000	0.3%
39	West Virginia	5,966,406,000	0.3%
40	New Hampshire	5,643,035,000	0.3%
41	Alaska	5,465,826,000	0.3%
42	North Dakota	5,260,655,000	0.3%
43	Maine	5,100,185,000	0.3%
44	Wyoming	5,085,659,000	0.3%
45	Rhode Island	4,979,801,000	0.3%
46	Hawaii	4,428,167,000	0.2%
47	Montana	4,236,756,000	0.2%
48	South Dakota	3,753,586,000	0.2%
49	Delaware	3,683,514,000	0.2%
50	Vermont	2,908,100,000	0.2%
	District of Columbia	17,556,756,000	0.9%

Source: U.S. Bureau of the Census, Governments Division
"2017 State and Local Government Finances" (https://www.census.gov/programs-surveys/gov-finances.html)
*Total expenditures includes all money paid other than for retirement of debt and extension of loans. Includes payments from all sources of funds including current revenues and proceeds from borrowing and prior year fund balances. Includes intergovernmental transfers and expenditures for government-owned utilities and other commercial or auxiliary enterprise and insurance trust expenditures.

Per Capita Local Government Total Expenditures in 2017

National Per Capita = $5,881*

ALPHA ORDER

RANK ORDER

RANK	STATE	PER CAPITA		RANK	STATE	PER CAPITA
27	Alabama	$4,752		1	New York	$11,231
5	Alaska	7,388		2	Wyoming	8,785
41	Arizona	4,176		3	California	8,192
48	Arkansas	3,476		4	Nebraska	7,794
3	California	8,192		5	Alaska	7,388
10	Colorado	5,913		6	North Dakota	6,966
20	Connecticut	5,228		7	Washington	6,667
43	Delaware	3,849		8	Illinois	6,293
23	Florida	5,039		9	Minnesota	6,278
33	Georgia	4,597		10	Colorado	5,913
50	Hawaii	3,109		11	Iowa	5,642
46	Idaho	3,498		12	Maryland	5,624
8	Illinois	6,293		13	New Jersey	5,553
39	Indiana	4,217		14	Pennsylvania	5,462
11	Iowa	5,642		15	Kansas	5,429
15	Kansas	5,429		16	Wisconsin	5,399
47	Kentucky	3,484		17	Massachusetts	5,392
32	Louisiana	4,606		18	Oregon	5,381
44	Maine	3,820		19	Texas	5,282
12	Maryland	5,624		20	Connecticut	5,228
17	Massachusetts	5,392		21	Ohio	5,213
26	Michigan	4,785		22	Tennessee	5,110
9	Minnesota	6,278		23	Florida	5,039
36	Mississippi	4,341		24	Virginia	5,035
34	Missouri	4,534		25	Nevada	4,945
42	Montana	4,023		26	Michigan	4,785
4	Nebraska	7,794		27	Alabama	4,752
25	Nevada	4,945		28	Rhode Island	4,714
40	New Hampshire	4,181		29	North Carolina	4,706
13	New Jersey	5,553		30	South Carolina	4,665
38	New Mexico	4,235		31	Vermont	4,656
1	New York	11,231		32	Louisiana	4,606
29	North Carolina	4,706		33	Georgia	4,597
6	North Dakota	6,966		34	Missouri	4,534
21	Ohio	5,213		35	Utah	4,349
45	Oklahoma	3,551		36	Mississippi	4,341
18	Oregon	5,381		37	South Dakota	4,298
14	Pennsylvania	5,462		38	New Mexico	4,235
28	Rhode Island	4,714		39	Indiana	4,217
30	South Carolina	4,665		40	New Hampshire	4,181
37	South Dakota	4,298		41	Arizona	4,176
22	Tennessee	5,110		42	Montana	4,023
19	Texas	5,282		43	Delaware	3,849
35	Utah	4,349		44	Maine	3,820
31	Vermont	4,656		45	Oklahoma	3,551
24	Virginia	5,035		46	Idaho	3,498
7	Washington	6,667		47	Kentucky	3,484
49	West Virginia	3,284		48	Arkansas	3,476
16	Wisconsin	5,399		49	West Virginia	3,284
2	Wyoming	8,785		50	Hawaii	3,109

District of Columbia   25,236

Source: CQ Press using data from U.S. Bureau of the Census, Governments Division
   "2017 State and Local Government Finances" (https://www.census.gov/programs-surveys/gov-finances.html)
*Total expenditures includes all money paid other than for retirement of debt and extension of loans. Includes payments from all sources of funds including current revenues and proceeds from borrowing and prior year fund balances. Includes intergovernmental transfers and expenditures for government-owned utilities and other commercial or auxiliary enterprise and insurance trust expenditures.

Local Government Direct General Expenditures in 2017

National Total = $1,637,828,951,000*

ALPHA ORDER

RANK	STATE	EXPENDITURES	% of USA
25	Alabama	$19,766,048,000	1.2%
43	Alaska	4,775,048,000	0.3%
22	Arizona	23,044,795,000	1.4%
36	Arkansas	9,389,018,000	0.6%
1	California	266,629,840,000	16.3%
17	Colorado	28,291,955,000	1.7%
27	Connecticut	16,888,943,000	1.0%
48	Delaware	3,218,818,000	0.2%
4	Florida	91,981,071,000	5.6%
11	Georgia	40,890,394,000	2.5%
49	Hawaii	3,140,200,000	0.2%
38	Idaho	5,740,502,000	0.4%
5	Illinois	66,141,482,000	4.0%
19	Indiana	25,317,045,000	1.5%
28	Iowa	16,419,434,000	1.0%
29	Kansas	14,083,459,000	0.9%
30	Kentucky	13,408,002,000	0.8%
24	Louisiana	19,873,348,000	1.2%
41	Maine	4,939,156,000	0.3%
16	Maryland	30,394,068,000	1.9%
15	Massachusetts	31,412,664,000	1.9%
10	Michigan	42,685,711,000	2.6%
14	Minnesota	31,574,868,000	1.9%
33	Mississippi	12,125,409,000	0.7%
20	Missouri	24,120,192,000	1.5%
46	Montana	4,027,248,000	0.2%
35	Nebraska	10,203,600,000	0.6%
31	Nevada	13,167,244,000	0.8%
40	New Hampshire	5,374,499,000	0.3%
8	New Jersey	47,867,582,000	2.9%
37	New Mexico	8,006,038,000	0.5%
2	New York	179,337,982,000	10.9%
9	North Carolina	42,742,123,000	2.6%
42	North Dakota	4,842,847,000	0.3%
7	Ohio	56,602,328,000	3.5%
32	Oklahoma	12,377,990,000	0.8%
26	Oregon	19,636,006,000	1.2%
6	Pennsylvania	62,574,177,000	3.8%
45	Rhode Island	4,450,426,000	0.3%
23	South Carolina	21,515,718,000	1.3%
47	South Dakota	3,364,027,000	0.2%
21	Tennessee	23,981,811,000	1.5%
3	Texas	128,340,195,000	7.8%
34	Utah	11,336,982,000	0.7%
50	Vermont	2,601,539,000	0.2%
13	Virginia	38,005,447,000	2.3%
12	Washington	39,508,373,000	2.4%
39	West Virginia	5,538,356,000	0.3%
18	Wisconsin	28,171,398,000	1.7%
44	Wyoming	4,748,459,000	0.3%

RANK ORDER

RANK	STATE	EXPENDITURES	% of USA
1	California	$266,629,840,000	16.3%
2	New York	179,337,982,000	10.9%
3	Texas	128,340,195,000	7.8%
4	Florida	91,981,071,000	5.6%
5	Illinois	66,141,482,000	4.0%
6	Pennsylvania	62,574,177,000	3.8%
7	Ohio	56,602,328,000	3.5%
8	New Jersey	47,867,582,000	2.9%
9	North Carolina	42,742,123,000	2.6%
10	Michigan	42,685,711,000	2.6%
11	Georgia	40,890,394,000	2.5%
12	Washington	39,508,373,000	2.4%
13	Virginia	38,005,447,000	2.3%
14	Minnesota	31,574,868,000	1.9%
15	Massachusetts	31,412,664,000	1.9%
16	Maryland	30,394,068,000	1.9%
17	Colorado	28,291,955,000	1.7%
18	Wisconsin	28,171,398,000	1.7%
19	Indiana	25,317,045,000	1.5%
20	Missouri	24,120,192,000	1.5%
21	Tennessee	23,981,811,000	1.5%
22	Arizona	23,044,795,000	1.4%
23	South Carolina	21,515,718,000	1.3%
24	Louisiana	19,873,348,000	1.2%
25	Alabama	19,766,048,000	1.2%
26	Oregon	19,636,006,000	1.2%
27	Connecticut	16,888,943,000	1.0%
28	Iowa	16,419,434,000	1.0%
29	Kansas	14,083,459,000	0.9%
30	Kentucky	13,408,002,000	0.8%
31	Nevada	13,167,244,000	0.8%
32	Oklahoma	12,377,990,000	0.8%
33	Mississippi	12,125,409,000	0.7%
34	Utah	11,336,982,000	0.7%
35	Nebraska	10,203,600,000	0.6%
36	Arkansas	9,389,018,000	0.6%
37	New Mexico	8,006,038,000	0.5%
38	Idaho	5,740,502,000	0.4%
39	West Virginia	5,538,356,000	0.3%
40	New Hampshire	5,374,499,000	0.3%
41	Maine	4,939,156,000	0.3%
42	North Dakota	4,842,847,000	0.3%
43	Alaska	4,775,048,000	0.3%
44	Wyoming	4,748,459,000	0.3%
45	Rhode Island	4,450,426,000	0.3%
46	Montana	4,027,248,000	0.2%
47	South Dakota	3,364,027,000	0.2%
48	Delaware	3,218,818,000	0.2%
49	Hawaii	3,140,200,000	0.2%
50	Vermont	2,601,539,000	0.2%
	District of Columbia	13,255,086,000	0.8%

Source: U.S. Bureau of the Census, Governments Division
"2017 State and Local Government Finances" (https://www.census.gov/programs-surveys/gov-finances.html)
*Direct general expenditures include expenditures for current operations, assistance and subsidies, interest on debt, and capital outlay. Excludes intergovernmental transfers, expenditures for government-owned utilities and other commercial or auxiliary enterprise, and insurance trust expenditures.

Per Capita Local Government Direct General Expenditures in 2017

National Per Capita = $5,037*

ALPHA ORDER				RANK ORDER		
RANK	STATE	PER CAPITA		RANK	STATE	PER CAPITA
32	Alabama	$4,054		1	New York	$9,154
4	Alaska	6,455		2	Wyoming	8,202
45	Arizona	3,269		3	California	6,767
47	Arkansas	3,127		4	Alaska	6,455
3	California	6,767		5	North Dakota	6,413
13	Colorado	5,038		6	Minnesota	5,671
19	Connecticut	4,726		7	New Jersey	5,385
43	Delaware	3,363		8	Nebraska	5,321
24	Florida	4,385		8	Washington	5,321
35	Georgia	3,927		10	Iowa	5,223
50	Hawaii	2,205		11	Illinois	5,173
44	Idaho	3,340		12	Maryland	5,045
11	Illinois	5,173		13	Colorado	5,038
39	Indiana	3,801		14	Pennsylvania	4,892
10	Iowa	5,223		15	Wisconsin	4,864
17	Kansas	4,839		16	Ohio	4,853
49	Kentucky	3,010		17	Kansas	4,839
27	Louisiana	4,255		18	Oregon	4,735
40	Maine	3,700		19	Connecticut	4,726
12	Maryland	5,045		20	Massachusetts	4,577
20	Massachusetts	4,577		21	Texas	4,531
26	Michigan	4,279		22	Virginia	4,490
6	Minnesota	5,671		23	Nevada	4,430
31	Mississippi	4,056		24	Florida	4,385
34	Missouri	3,949		25	South Carolina	4,285
37	Montana	3,824		26	Michigan	4,279
8	Nebraska	5,321		27	Louisiana	4,255
23	Nevada	4,430		28	Rhode Island	4,212
33	New Hampshire	3,982		29	Vermont	4,166
7	New Jersey	5,385		30	North Carolina	4,162
37	New Mexico	3,824		31	Mississippi	4,056
1	New York	9,154		32	Alabama	4,054
30	North Carolina	4,162		33	New Hampshire	3,982
5	North Dakota	6,413		34	Missouri	3,949
16	Ohio	4,853		35	Georgia	3,927
46	Oklahoma	3,148		36	South Dakota	3,852
18	Oregon	4,735		37	Montana	3,824
14	Pennsylvania	4,892		37	New Mexico	3,824
28	Rhode Island	4,212		39	Indiana	3,801
25	South Carolina	4,285		40	Maine	3,700
36	South Dakota	3,852		41	Utah	3,653
42	Tennessee	3,575		42	Tennessee	3,575
21	Texas	4,531		43	Delaware	3,363
41	Utah	3,653		44	Idaho	3,340
29	Vermont	4,166		45	Arizona	3,269
22	Virginia	4,490		46	Oklahoma	3,148
8	Washington	5,321		47	Arkansas	3,127
48	West Virginia	3,048		48	West Virginia	3,048
15	Wisconsin	4,864		49	Kentucky	3,010
2	Wyoming	8,202		50	Hawaii	2,205
					District of Columbia	19,053

Source: CQ Press using data from U.S. Bureau of the Census, Governments Division
   "2017 State and Local Government Finances" (https://www.census.gov/programs-surveys/gov-finances.html)
*Direct general expenditures include expenditures for current operations, assistance and subsidies, interest on debt, and capital outlay. Excludes intergovernmental transfers, expenditures for government-owned utilities and other commercial or auxiliary enterprise, and insurance trust expenditures.

Local Government Debt Outstanding in 2017

National Total = $1,905,814,546,000*

ALPHA ORDER

RANK	STATE	DEBT	% of USA
26	Alabama	$21,192,447,000	1.1%
41	Alaska	3,549,290,000	0.2%
15	Arizona	32,772,156,000	1.7%
33	Arkansas	11,586,336,000	0.6%
1	California	314,702,775,000	16.5%
10	Colorado	40,368,240,000	2.1%
34	Connecticut	11,241,788,000	0.6%
48	Delaware	2,504,518,000	0.1%
4	Florida	105,919,283,000	5.6%
9	Georgia	44,756,399,000	2.3%
38	Hawaii	6,343,134,000	0.3%
45	Idaho	2,682,945,000	0.1%
5	Illinois	93,100,836,000	4.9%
21	Indiana	25,863,709,000	1.4%
32	Iowa	13,223,471,000	0.7%
28	Kansas	19,633,181,000	1.0%
18	Kentucky	30,362,891,000	1.6%
29	Louisiana	18,225,956,000	1.0%
42	Maine	3,102,943,000	0.2%
20	Maryland	26,486,471,000	1.4%
27	Massachusetts	19,953,843,000	1.0%
11	Michigan	38,565,216,000	2.0%
13	Minnesota	36,652,137,000	1.9%
37	Mississippi	7,091,342,000	0.4%
19	Missouri	28,698,302,000	1.5%
47	Montana	2,527,957,000	0.1%
30	Nebraska	13,872,318,000	0.7%
22	Nevada	24,108,081,000	1.3%
46	New Hampshire	2,670,879,000	0.1%
16	New Jersey	31,116,114,000	1.6%
36	New Mexico	8,748,682,000	0.5%
3	New York	211,019,645,000	11.1%
17	North Carolina	30,985,695,000	1.6%
39	North Dakota	5,106,902,000	0.3%
8	Ohio	54,172,448,000	2.8%
35	Oklahoma	10,257,693,000	0.5%
25	Oregon	22,867,020,000	1.2%
6	Pennsylvania	75,339,315,000	4.0%
44	Rhode Island	2,683,372,000	0.1%
23	South Carolina	23,332,021,000	1.2%
43	South Dakota	2,719,410,000	0.1%
14	Tennessee	36,442,669,000	1.9%
2	Texas	238,684,462,000	12.5%
31	Utah	13,263,232,000	0.7%
49	Vermont	1,250,722,000	0.1%
12	Virginia	38,115,274,000	2.0%
7	Washington	55,140,687,000	2.9%
40	West Virginia	3,635,843,000	0.2%
24	Wisconsin	23,065,487,000	1.2%
50	Wyoming	1,207,927,000	0.1%

RANK ORDER

RANK	STATE	DEBT	% of USA
1	California	$314,702,775,000	16.5%
2	Texas	238,684,462,000	12.5%
3	New York	211,019,645,000	11.1%
4	Florida	105,919,283,000	5.6%
5	Illinois	93,100,836,000	4.9%
6	Pennsylvania	75,339,315,000	4.0%
7	Washington	55,140,687,000	2.9%
8	Ohio	54,172,448,000	2.8%
9	Georgia	44,756,399,000	2.3%
10	Colorado	40,368,240,000	2.1%
11	Michigan	38,565,216,000	2.0%
12	Virginia	38,115,274,000	2.0%
13	Minnesota	36,652,137,000	1.9%
14	Tennessee	36,442,669,000	1.9%
15	Arizona	32,772,156,000	1.7%
16	New Jersey	31,116,114,000	1.6%
17	North Carolina	30,985,695,000	1.6%
18	Kentucky	30,362,891,000	1.6%
19	Missouri	28,698,302,000	1.5%
20	Maryland	26,486,471,000	1.4%
21	Indiana	25,863,709,000	1.4%
22	Nevada	24,108,081,000	1.3%
23	South Carolina	23,332,021,000	1.2%
24	Wisconsin	23,065,487,000	1.2%
25	Oregon	22,867,020,000	1.2%
26	Alabama	21,192,447,000	1.1%
27	Massachusetts	19,953,843,000	1.0%
28	Kansas	19,633,181,000	1.0%
29	Louisiana	18,225,956,000	1.0%
30	Nebraska	13,872,318,000	0.7%
31	Utah	13,263,232,000	0.7%
32	Iowa	13,223,471,000	0.7%
33	Arkansas	11,586,336,000	0.6%
34	Connecticut	11,241,788,000	0.6%
35	Oklahoma	10,257,693,000	0.5%
36	New Mexico	8,748,682,000	0.5%
37	Mississippi	7,091,342,000	0.4%
38	Hawaii	6,343,134,000	0.3%
39	North Dakota	5,106,902,000	0.3%
40	West Virginia	3,635,843,000	0.2%
41	Alaska	3,549,290,000	0.2%
42	Maine	3,102,943,000	0.2%
43	South Dakota	2,719,410,000	0.1%
44	Rhode Island	2,683,372,000	0.1%
45	Idaho	2,682,945,000	0.1%
46	New Hampshire	2,670,879,000	0.1%
47	Montana	2,527,957,000	0.1%
48	Delaware	2,504,518,000	0.1%
49	Vermont	1,250,722,000	0.1%
50	Wyoming	1,207,927,000	0.1%
	District of Columbia	14,901,082,000	0.8%

Source: U.S. Bureau of the Census, Governments Division
"2017 State and Local Government Finances" (https://www.census.gov/programs-surveys/gov-finances.html)
*Includes short-term, long-term, full faith and credit, nonguaranteed, and public debt for private purposes.

Per Capita Local Government Debt Outstanding in 2017

National Per Capita = $5,861*

<table>
<tr><td colspan="3">ALPHA ORDER</td><td colspan="3">RANK ORDER</td></tr>
<tr><td>RANK</td><td>STATE</td><td>PER CAPITA</td><td>RANK</td><td>STATE</td><td>PER CAPITA</td></tr>
<tr><td>25</td><td>Alabama</td><td>$4,347</td><td>1</td><td>New York</td><td>$10,771</td></tr>
<tr><td>17</td><td>Alaska</td><td>4,798</td><td>2</td><td>Texas</td><td>8,427</td></tr>
<tr><td>19</td><td>Arizona</td><td>4,649</td><td>3</td><td>Nevada</td><td>8,111</td></tr>
<tr><td>34</td><td>Arkansas</td><td>3,858</td><td>4</td><td>California</td><td>7,988</td></tr>
<tr><td>4</td><td>California</td><td>7,988</td><td>5</td><td>Washington</td><td>7,426</td></tr>
<tr><td>8</td><td>Colorado</td><td>7,188</td><td>6</td><td>Illinois</td><td>7,281</td></tr>
<tr><td>36</td><td>Connecticut</td><td>3,146</td><td>7</td><td>Nebraska</td><td>7,234</td></tr>
<tr><td>40</td><td>Delaware</td><td>2,617</td><td>8</td><td>Colorado</td><td>7,188</td></tr>
<tr><td>16</td><td>Florida</td><td>5,049</td><td>9</td><td>Kentucky</td><td>6,817</td></tr>
<tr><td>26</td><td>Georgia</td><td>4,298</td><td>10</td><td>North Dakota</td><td>6,763</td></tr>
<tr><td>23</td><td>Hawaii</td><td>4,454</td><td>11</td><td>Kansas</td><td>6,745</td></tr>
<tr><td>50</td><td>Idaho</td><td>1,561</td><td>12</td><td>Minnesota</td><td>6,582</td></tr>
<tr><td>6</td><td>Illinois</td><td>7,281</td><td>13</td><td>Pennsylvania</td><td>5,890</td></tr>
<tr><td>32</td><td>Indiana</td><td>3,883</td><td>14</td><td>Oregon</td><td>5,515</td></tr>
<tr><td>28</td><td>Iowa</td><td>4,206</td><td>15</td><td>Tennessee</td><td>5,432</td></tr>
<tr><td>11</td><td>Kansas</td><td>6,745</td><td>16</td><td>Florida</td><td>5,049</td></tr>
<tr><td>9</td><td>Kentucky</td><td>6,817</td><td>17</td><td>Alaska</td><td>4,798</td></tr>
<tr><td>31</td><td>Louisiana</td><td>3,902</td><td>18</td><td>Missouri</td><td>4,698</td></tr>
<tr><td>45</td><td>Maine</td><td>2,324</td><td>19</td><td>Arizona</td><td>4,649</td></tr>
<tr><td>24</td><td>Maryland</td><td>4,396</td><td>20</td><td>South Carolina</td><td>4,647</td></tr>
<tr><td>39</td><td>Massachusetts</td><td>2,907</td><td>21</td><td>Ohio</td><td>4,644</td></tr>
<tr><td>33</td><td>Michigan</td><td>3,866</td><td>22</td><td>Virginia</td><td>4,503</td></tr>
<tr><td>12</td><td>Minnesota</td><td>6,582</td><td>23</td><td>Hawaii</td><td>4,454</td></tr>
<tr><td>44</td><td>Mississippi</td><td>2,372</td><td>24</td><td>Maryland</td><td>4,396</td></tr>
<tr><td>18</td><td>Missouri</td><td>4,698</td><td>25</td><td>Alabama</td><td>4,347</td></tr>
<tr><td>43</td><td>Montana</td><td>2,401</td><td>26</td><td>Georgia</td><td>4,298</td></tr>
<tr><td>7</td><td>Nebraska</td><td>7,234</td><td>27</td><td>Utah</td><td>4,274</td></tr>
<tr><td>3</td><td>Nevada</td><td>8,111</td><td>28</td><td>Iowa</td><td>4,206</td></tr>
<tr><td>49</td><td>New Hampshire</td><td>1,979</td><td>29</td><td>New Mexico</td><td>4,179</td></tr>
<tr><td>35</td><td>New Jersey</td><td>3,501</td><td>30</td><td>Wisconsin</td><td>3,982</td></tr>
<tr><td>29</td><td>New Mexico</td><td>4,179</td><td>31</td><td>Louisiana</td><td>3,902</td></tr>
<tr><td>1</td><td>New York</td><td>10,771</td><td>32</td><td>Indiana</td><td>3,883</td></tr>
<tr><td>38</td><td>North Carolina</td><td>3,017</td><td>33</td><td>Michigan</td><td>3,866</td></tr>
<tr><td>10</td><td>North Dakota</td><td>6,763</td><td>34</td><td>Arkansas</td><td>3,858</td></tr>
<tr><td>21</td><td>Ohio</td><td>4,644</td><td>35</td><td>New Jersey</td><td>3,501</td></tr>
<tr><td>41</td><td>Oklahoma</td><td>2,608</td><td>36</td><td>Connecticut</td><td>3,146</td></tr>
<tr><td>14</td><td>Oregon</td><td>5,515</td><td>37</td><td>South Dakota</td><td>3,114</td></tr>
<tr><td>13</td><td>Pennsylvania</td><td>5,890</td><td>38</td><td>North Carolina</td><td>3,017</td></tr>
<tr><td>42</td><td>Rhode Island</td><td>2,540</td><td>39</td><td>Massachusetts</td><td>2,907</td></tr>
<tr><td>20</td><td>South Carolina</td><td>4,647</td><td>40</td><td>Delaware</td><td>2,617</td></tr>
<tr><td>37</td><td>South Dakota</td><td>3,114</td><td>41</td><td>Oklahoma</td><td>2,608</td></tr>
<tr><td>15</td><td>Tennessee</td><td>5,432</td><td>42</td><td>Rhode Island</td><td>2,540</td></tr>
<tr><td>2</td><td>Texas</td><td>8,427</td><td>43</td><td>Montana</td><td>2,401</td></tr>
<tr><td>27</td><td>Utah</td><td>4,274</td><td>44</td><td>Mississippi</td><td>2,372</td></tr>
<tr><td>47</td><td>Vermont</td><td>2,003</td><td>45</td><td>Maine</td><td>2,324</td></tr>
<tr><td>22</td><td>Virginia</td><td>4,503</td><td>46</td><td>Wyoming</td><td>2,086</td></tr>
<tr><td>5</td><td>Washington</td><td>7,426</td><td>47</td><td>Vermont</td><td>2,003</td></tr>
<tr><td>48</td><td>West Virginia</td><td>2,001</td><td>48</td><td>West Virginia</td><td>2,001</td></tr>
<tr><td>30</td><td>Wisconsin</td><td>3,982</td><td>49</td><td>New Hampshire</td><td>1,979</td></tr>
<tr><td>46</td><td>Wyoming</td><td>2,086</td><td>50</td><td>Idaho</td><td>1,561</td></tr>
<tr><td></td><td></td><td></td><td></td><td>District of Columbia</td><td>21,419</td></tr>
</table>

Source: CQ Press using data from U.S. Bureau of the Census, Governments Division
"2017 State and Local Government Finances" (https://www.census.gov/programs-surveys/gov-finances.html)
*Includes short-term, long-term, full faith and credit, nonguaranteed, and public debt for private purposes.

Local Government Full-Time Equivalent Employees in 2018

National Total = 12,264,505 FTE Employees*

RANK	STATE	EMPLOYEES	% of USA	RANK	STATE	EMPLOYEES	% of USA
23	Alabama	191,946	1.6%	1	California	1,445,299	11.8%
47	Alaska	27,412	0.2%	2	Texas	1,202,167	9.8%
22	Arizona	205,950	1.7%	3	New York	957,704	7.8%
33	Arkansas	107,014	0.9%	4	Florida	718,562	5.9%
1	California	1,445,299	11.8%	5	Illinois	494,446	4.0%
21	Colorado	210,967	1.7%	6	Ohio	454,030	3.7%
32	Connecticut	125,568	1.0%	7	North Carolina	430,968	3.5%
49	Delaware	23,934	0.2%	8	Pennsylvania	399,597	3.3%
4	Florida	718,562	5.9%	9	Georgia	391,039	3.2%
9	Georgia	391,039	3.2%	10	New Jersey	334,627	2.7%
50	Hawaii	16,888	0.1%	11	Virginia	326,888	2.7%
39	Idaho	60,637	0.5%	12	Michigan	288,840	2.4%
5	Illinois	494,446	4.0%	13	Tennessee	255,377	2.1%
16	Indiana	234,970	1.9%	14	Washington	252,315	2.1%
29	Iowa	135,409	1.1%	15	Massachusetts	237,072	1.9%
27	Kansas	148,689	1.2%	16	Indiana	234,970	1.9%
26	Kentucky	158,926	1.3%	17	Missouri	233,758	1.9%
25	Louisiana	183,922	1.5%	18	Maryland	219,431	1.8%
41	Maine	49,768	0.4%	19	Minnesota	218,341	1.8%
18	Maryland	219,431	1.8%	20	Wisconsin	212,905	1.7%
15	Massachusetts	237,072	1.9%	21	Colorado	210,967	1.7%
12	Michigan	288,840	2.4%	22	Arizona	205,950	1.7%
19	Minnesota	218,341	1.8%	23	Alabama	191,946	1.6%
31	Mississippi	132,465	1.1%	24	South Carolina	190,940	1.6%
17	Missouri	233,758	1.9%	25	Louisiana	183,922	1.5%
43	Montana	37,299	0.3%	26	Kentucky	158,926	1.3%
35	Nebraska	89,889	0.7%	27	Kansas	148,689	1.2%
36	Nevada	86,402	0.7%	28	Oklahoma	145,625	1.2%
40	New Hampshire	50,825	0.4%	29	Iowa	135,409	1.1%
10	New Jersey	334,627	2.7%	30	Oregon	134,120	1.1%
37	New Mexico	79,135	0.6%	31	Mississippi	132,465	1.1%
3	New York	957,704	7.8%	32	Connecticut	125,568	1.0%
7	North Carolina	430,968	3.5%	33	Arkansas	107,014	0.9%
46	North Dakota	29,042	0.2%	34	Utah	93,272	0.8%
6	Ohio	454,030	3.7%	35	Nebraska	89,889	0.7%
28	Oklahoma	145,625	1.2%	36	Nevada	86,402	0.7%
30	Oregon	134,120	1.1%	37	New Mexico	79,135	0.6%
8	Pennsylvania	399,597	3.3%	38	West Virginia	62,435	0.5%
45	Rhode Island	29,536	0.2%	39	Idaho	60,637	0.5%
24	South Carolina	190,940	1.6%	40	New Hampshire	50,825	0.4%
44	South Dakota	33,869	0.3%	41	Maine	49,768	0.4%
13	Tennessee	255,377	2.1%	42	Wyoming	37,797	0.3%
2	Texas	1,202,167	9.8%	43	Montana	37,299	0.3%
34	Utah	93,272	0.8%	44	South Dakota	33,869	0.3%
48	Vermont	25,346	0.2%	45	Rhode Island	29,536	0.2%
11	Virginia	326,888	2.7%	46	North Dakota	29,042	0.2%
14	Washington	252,315	2.1%	47	Alaska	27,412	0.2%
38	West Virginia	62,435	0.5%	48	Vermont	25,346	0.2%
20	Wisconsin	212,905	1.7%	49	Delaware	23,934	0.2%
42	Wyoming	37,797	0.3%	50	Hawaii	16,888	0.1%
					District of Columbia	51,142	0.4%

ALPHA ORDER

RANK ORDER

Source: U.S. Bureau of the Census, Governments Division
   "Annual Survey of Public Employment and Payroll" (https://www.census.gov/programs-surveys/apes.html)
*As of March 2018.

Rate of Local Government Full-Time Equivalent Employees in 2018

National Rate = 375 FTE Employees per 10,000 Population*

ALPHA ORDER			RANK ORDER		
RANK	STATE	RATE	RANK	STATE	RATE
11	Alabama	393	1	Wyoming	654
24	Alaska	372	2	Kansas	511
46	Arizona	287	3	New York	490
33	Arkansas	355	4	Nebraska	466
30	California	365	5	Mississippi	444
27	Colorado	370	6	Iowa	429
34	Connecticut	351	7	Texas	419
49	Delaware	247	8	North Carolina	415
40	Florida	337	9	Vermont	405
24	Georgia	372	10	Louisiana	395
50	Hawaii	119	11	Alabama	393
37	Idaho	346	12	Minnesota	389
13	Illinois	388	13	Illinois	388
34	Indiana	351	13	Ohio	388
6	Iowa	429	15	South Dakota	384
2	Kansas	511	15	Virginia	384
32	Kentucky	356	17	Missouri	382
10	Louisiana	395	17	North Dakota	382
24	Maine	372	19	New Mexico	378
31	Maryland	363	20	Tennessee	377
39	Massachusetts	343	21	New Jersey	376
45	Michigan	289	21	South Carolina	376
12	Minnesota	389	23	New Hampshire	375
5	Mississippi	444	24	Alaska	372
17	Missouri	382	24	Georgia	372
34	Montana	351	24	Maine	372
4	Nebraska	466	27	Colorado	370
47	Nevada	285	28	Oklahoma	369
23	New Hampshire	375	29	Wisconsin	366
21	New Jersey	376	30	California	365
19	New Mexico	378	31	Maryland	363
3	New York	490	32	Kentucky	356
8	North Carolina	415	33	Arkansas	355
17	North Dakota	382	34	Connecticut	351
13	Ohio	388	34	Indiana	351
28	Oklahoma	369	34	Montana	351
42	Oregon	320	37	Idaho	346
43	Pennsylvania	312	37	West Virginia	346
48	Rhode Island	279	39	Massachusetts	343
21	South Carolina	376	40	Florida	337
15	South Dakota	384	41	Washington	335
20	Tennessee	377	42	Oregon	320
7	Texas	419	43	Pennsylvania	312
44	Utah	295	44	Utah	295
9	Vermont	405	45	Michigan	289
15	Virginia	384	46	Arizona	287
41	Washington	335	47	Nevada	285
37	West Virginia	346	48	Rhode Island	279
29	Wisconsin	366	49	Delaware	247
1	Wyoming	654	50	Hawaii	119
				District of Columbia	728

Source: CQ Press using data from U.S. Bureau of the Census, Governments Division
"Annual Survey of Public Employment and Payroll" (https://www.census.gov/programs-surveys/apes.html)
*Full-time equivalent as of March 2018.

Average Annual Earnings of Full-Time Local Government Employees in 2018

National Average = $60,090*

ALPHA ORDER				RANK ORDER		
RANK	STATE	SALARY		RANK	STATE	SALARY
41	Alabama	$46,372		1	California	$82,739
8	Alaska	68,649		2	Washington	79,656
20	Arizona	57,025		3	New Jersey	75,580
49	Arkansas	40,552		4	New York	75,412
1	California	82,739		5	Maryland	70,710
17	Colorado	60,409		6	Connecticut	70,135
6	Connecticut	70,135		7	Rhode Island	69,355
16	Delaware	61,432		8	Alaska	68,649
30	Florida	52,590		9	Massachusetts	68,087
34	Georgia	49,209		10	Hawaii	67,829
10	Hawaii	67,829		11	Nevada	66,500
43	Idaho	45,816		12	Illinois	65,381
12	Illinois	65,381		13	Oregon	64,024
36	Indiana	48,045		14	Pennsylvania	62,405
24	Iowa	55,401		15	Minnesota	62,204
40	Kansas	46,492		16	Delaware	61,432
45	Kentucky	44,722		17	Colorado	60,409
46	Louisiana	44,144		18	Wisconsin	57,342
35	Maine	49,154		19	Michigan	57,215
5	Maryland	70,710		20	Arizona	57,025
9	Massachusetts	68,087		21	Wyoming	56,933
19	Michigan	57,215		22	New Hampshire	56,678
15	Minnesota	62,204		23	Nebraska	56,304
50	Mississippi	40,371		24	Iowa	55,401
38	Missouri	46,764		25	Ohio	54,906
33	Montana	49,976		26	North Dakota	54,401
23	Nebraska	56,304		27	Vermont	54,371
11	Nevada	66,500		28	Virginia	54,260
22	New Hampshire	56,678		29	Utah	53,973
3	New Jersey	75,580		30	Florida	52,590
42	New Mexico	46,370		31	North Carolina	51,604
4	New York	75,412		32	Texas	50,985
31	North Carolina	51,604		33	Montana	49,976
26	North Dakota	54,401		34	Georgia	49,209
25	Ohio	54,906		35	Maine	49,154
47	Oklahoma	42,973		36	Indiana	48,045
13	Oregon	64,024		37	South Carolina	47,629
14	Pennsylvania	62,405		38	Missouri	46,764
7	Rhode Island	69,355		39	Tennessee	46,753
37	South Carolina	47,629		40	Kansas	46,492
44	South Dakota	44,869		41	Alabama	46,372
39	Tennessee	46,753		42	New Mexico	46,370
32	Texas	50,985		43	Idaho	45,816
29	Utah	53,973		44	South Dakota	44,869
27	Vermont	54,371		45	Kentucky	44,722
28	Virginia	54,260		46	Louisiana	44,144
2	Washington	79,656		47	Oklahoma	42,973
48	West Virginia	41,005		48	West Virginia	41,005
18	Wisconsin	57,342		49	Arkansas	40,552
21	Wyoming	56,933		50	Mississippi	40,371
					District of Columbia	88,845

Source: CQ Press using data from U.S. Bureau of the Census, Governments Division
   "Annual Survey of Public Employment and Payroll" (https://www.census.gov/programs-surveys/apes.html)
*March 2018 full-time payroll (multiplied by 12) divided by full-time employees.

XI. Health

Average Annual Single Coverage Health Insurance Premium per Enrolled Employee in 2018
National Average = $6,715*

ALPHA ORDER				RANK ORDER		
RANK	STATE	PREMIUM		RANK	STATE	PREMIUM
46	Alabama	$6,089		1	Alaska	$8,432
1	Alaska	8,432		2	New York	7,741
43	Arizona	6,229		3	New Jersey	7,507
49	Arkansas	5,974		4	Massachusetts	7,443
35	California	6,542		5	New Hampshire	7,405
42	Colorado	6,255		6	Connecticut	7,264
6	Connecticut	7,264		7	Illinois	7,123
15	Delaware	6,848		8	Rhode Island	7,018
27	Florida	6,674		9	South Dakota	6,931
18	Georgia	6,799		10	Vermont	6,919
37	Hawaii	6,475		11	West Virginia	6,898
44	Idaho	6,175		12	Maine	6,866
7	Illinois	7,123		13	Montana	6,862
22	Indiana	6,778		14	Nebraska	6,851
19	Iowa	6,796		15	Delaware	6,848
41	Kansas	6,262		16	Wisconsin	6,816
26	Kentucky	6,690		17	Ohio	6,804
36	Louisiana	6,537		18	Georgia	6,799
12	Maine	6,866		19	Iowa	6,796
25	Maryland	6,695		20	Minnesota	6,781
4	Massachusetts	7,443		21	Wyoming	6,779
40	Michigan	6,322		22	Indiana	6,778
20	Minnesota	6,781		23	Pennsylvania	6,769
48	Mississippi	5,993		24	South Carolina	6,708
28	Missouri	6,664		25	Maryland	6,695
13	Montana	6,862		26	Kentucky	6,690
14	Nebraska	6,851		27	Florida	6,674
47	Nevada	6,032		28	Missouri	6,664
5	New Hampshire	7,405		29	Washington	6,646
3	New Jersey	7,507		30	North Dakota	6,643
33	New Mexico	6,624		31	Virginia	6,635
2	New York	7,741		32	Oklahoma	6,630
39	North Carolina	6,339		33	New Mexico	6,624
30	North Dakota	6,643		34	Texas	6,589
17	Ohio	6,804		35	California	6,542
32	Oklahoma	6,630		36	Louisiana	6,537
38	Oregon	6,441		37	Hawaii	6,475
23	Pennsylvania	6,769		38	Oregon	6,441
8	Rhode Island	7,018		39	North Carolina	6,339
24	South Carolina	6,708		40	Michigan	6,322
9	South Dakota	6,931		41	Kansas	6,262
50	Tennessee	5,971		42	Colorado	6,255
34	Texas	6,589		43	Arizona	6,229
45	Utah	6,125		44	Idaho	6,175
10	Vermont	6,919		45	Utah	6,125
31	Virginia	6,635		46	Alabama	6,089
29	Washington	6,646		47	Nevada	6,032
11	West Virginia	6,898		48	Mississippi	5,993
16	Wisconsin	6,816		49	Arkansas	5,974
21	Wyoming	6,779		50	Tennessee	5,971
					District of Columbia	7,230

Source: U.S. Department of Health and Human Services, Agency for Healthcare Research and Quality
"Private-Sector Data by Firm Size and State" (Table II Series, Medical Expenditures Panel Survey)
(https://www.meps.ahrq.gov/mepsweb/survey_comp/Insurance.jsp)
*Enrolled employees at private-sector establishments that offer health insurance coverage.

Average Annual Family Coverage Health Insurance Premium per Enrolled Employee in 2018
National Average = $19,565*

ALPHA ORDER			RANK ORDER		
RANK	STATE	PREMIUM	RANK	STATE	PREMIUM
43	Alabama	$18,001	1	New Jersey	$22,294
4	Alaska	21,648	2	New York	21,904
31	Arizona	18,875	3	Massachusetts	21,801
44	Arkansas	17,995	4	Alaska	21,648
15	California	19,567	5	Connecticut	20,735
38	Colorado	18,314	6	West Virginia	20,709
5	Connecticut	20,735	7	New Hampshire	20,538
11	Delaware	20,098	8	Illinois	20,407
30	Florida	18,934	9	Pennsylvania	20,255
36	Georgia	18,575	10	Vermont	20,129
45	Hawaii	17,919	11	Delaware	20,098
48	Idaho	17,579	12	South Dakota	19,730
8	Illinois	20,407	13	Ohio	19,640
18	Indiana	19,551	14	Montana	19,610
41	Iowa	18,192	15	California	19,567
32	Kansas	18,825	16	Maine	19,555
25	Kentucky	19,277	16	Wisconsin	19,555
23	Louisiana	19,294	18	Indiana	19,551
16	Maine	19,555	19	Virginia	19,512
27	Maryland	19,237	20	Texas	19,460
3	Massachusetts	21,801	21	Wyoming	19,374
39	Michigan	18,242	22	Minnesota	19,327
22	Minnesota	19,327	23	Louisiana	19,294
49	Mississippi	17,384	24	South Carolina	19,284
26	Missouri	19,249	25	Kentucky	19,277
14	Montana	19,610	26	Missouri	19,249
28	Nebraska	19,015	27	Maryland	19,237
37	Nevada	18,357	28	Nebraska	19,015
7	New Hampshire	20,538	29	Oregon	18,977
1	New Jersey	22,294	30	Florida	18,934
46	New Mexico	17,861	31	Arizona	18,875
2	New York	21,904	32	Kansas	18,825
40	North Carolina	18,211	33	Washington	18,783
50	North Dakota	17,337	34	Oklahoma	18,745
13	Ohio	19,640	35	Rhode Island	18,623
34	Oklahoma	18,745	36	Georgia	18,575
29	Oregon	18,977	37	Nevada	18,357
9	Pennsylvania	20,255	38	Colorado	18,314
35	Rhode Island	18,623	39	Michigan	18,242
24	South Carolina	19,284	40	North Carolina	18,211
12	South Dakota	19,730	41	Iowa	18,192
47	Tennessee	17,663	42	Utah	18,052
20	Texas	19,460	43	Alabama	18,001
42	Utah	18,052	44	Arkansas	17,995
10	Vermont	20,129	45	Hawaii	17,919
19	Virginia	19,512	46	New Mexico	17,861
33	Washington	18,783	47	Tennessee	17,663
6	West Virginia	20,709	48	Idaho	17,579
16	Wisconsin	19,555	49	Mississippi	17,384
21	Wyoming	19,374	50	North Dakota	17,337
				District of Columbia	21,810

Source: U.S. Department of Health and Human Services, Agency for Healthcare Research and Quality
"Private-Sector Data by Firm Size and State" (Table II Series, Medical Expenditures Panel Survey)
(https://www.meps.ahrq.gov/mepsweb/survey_comp/Insurance.jsp)
*Enrolled employees at private-sector establishments that offer health insurance coverage.

Percent of Private-Sector Establishments That Offer Health Insurance: 2018

National Percent = 46.8%

ALPHA ORDER				RANK ORDER		
RANK	STATE	PERCENT		RANK	STATE	PERCENT
7	Alabama	50.3		1	Hawaii	81.9
46	Alaska	38.1		2	Maryland	56.4
28	Arizona	46.5		3	New Hampshire	54.9
39	Arkansas	42.4		4	Tennessee	51.7
26	California	47.2		5	Connecticut	51.3
36	Colorado	43.5		6	Ohio	50.8
5	Connecticut	51.3		7	Alabama	50.3
30	Delaware	45.7		8	Kansas	50.2
42	Florida	41.7		9	New Jersey	49.8
39	Georgia	42.4		10	Kentucky	49.5
1	Hawaii	81.9		11	Louisiana	49.4
48	Idaho	37.7		11	Rhode Island	49.4
33	Illinois	44.1		11	Texas	49.4
27	Indiana	46.8		14	Iowa	49.1
14	Iowa	49.1		15	Mississippi	49.0
8	Kansas	50.2		16	Michigan	48.9
10	Kentucky	49.5		16	Virginia	48.9
11	Louisiana	49.4		18	Missouri	48.8
33	Maine	44.1		18	Oklahoma	48.8
2	Maryland	56.4		20	North Dakota	48.7
22	Massachusetts	48.3		21	Pennsylvania	48.6
16	Michigan	48.9		22	Massachusetts	48.3
29	Minnesota	46.1		23	Nevada	47.8
15	Mississippi	49.0		24	New York	47.6
18	Missouri	48.8		24	West Virginia	47.6
50	Montana	34.7		26	California	47.2
47	Nebraska	38.0		27	Indiana	46.8
23	Nevada	47.8		28	Arizona	46.5
3	New Hampshire	54.9		29	Minnesota	46.1
9	New Jersey	49.8		30	Delaware	45.7
39	New Mexico	42.4		31	Wisconsin	45.5
24	New York	47.6		32	Washington	45.2
43	North Carolina	41.2		33	Illinois	44.1
20	North Dakota	48.7		33	Maine	44.1
6	Ohio	50.8		35	Oregon	43.8
18	Oklahoma	48.8		36	Colorado	43.5
35	Oregon	43.8		37	South Dakota	43.1
21	Pennsylvania	48.6		37	Vermont	43.1
11	Rhode Island	49.4		39	Arkansas	42.4
44	South Carolina	40.7		39	Georgia	42.4
37	South Dakota	43.1		39	New Mexico	42.4
4	Tennessee	51.7		42	Florida	41.7
11	Texas	49.4		43	North Carolina	41.2
49	Utah	35.3		44	South Carolina	40.7
37	Vermont	43.1		45	Wyoming	38.4
16	Virginia	48.9		46	Alaska	38.1
32	Washington	45.2		47	Nebraska	38.0
24	West Virginia	47.6		48	Idaho	37.7
31	Wisconsin	45.5		49	Utah	35.3
45	Wyoming	38.4		50	Montana	34.7
					District of Columbia	69.2

Source: U.S. Department of Health and Human Services, Agency for Healthcare Research and Quality
"Private-Sector Data by Firm Size and State" (Table II Series, Medical Expenditures Panel Survey)
(https://www.meps.ahrq.gov/mepsweb/survey_comp/Insurance.jsp)

Persons Not Covered by Health Insurance in 2018

National Total = 28,565,542 Uninsured

ALPHA ORDER

RANK	STATE	UNINSURED	% of USA
19	Alabama	481,259	1.7%
41	Alaska	90,128	0.3%
8	Arizona	749,977	2.6%
32	Arkansas	243,585	0.9%
2	California	2,825,620	9.9%
21	Colorado	421,644	1.5%
36	Connecticut	186,923	0.7%
47	Delaware	53,962	0.2%
3	Florida	2,728,485	9.6%
4	Georgia	1,411,183	4.9%
46	Hawaii	55,799	0.2%
34	Idaho	192,620	0.7%
7	Illinois	874,608	3.1%
16	Indiana	545,123	1.9%
38	Iowa	147,039	0.5%
29	Kansas	250,355	0.9%
30	Kentucky	247,641	0.9%
22	Louisiana	363,362	1.3%
40	Maine	106,187	0.4%
23	Maryland	356,708	1.2%
35	Massachusetts	188,907	0.7%
17	Michigan	534,551	1.9%
31	Minnesota	244,379	0.9%
24	Mississippi	354,151	1.2%
14	Missouri	566,327	2.0%
42	Montana	86,029	0.3%
37	Nebraska	157,612	0.6%
25	Nevada	336,191	1.2%
44	New Hampshire	77,011	0.3%
13	New Jersey	655,000	2.3%
33	New Mexico	196,250	0.7%
6	New York	1,041,233	3.6%
5	North Carolina	1,092,046	3.8%
48	North Dakota	53,935	0.2%
9	Ohio	743,905	2.6%
15	Oklahoma	548,316	1.9%
28	Oregon	293,107	1.0%
11	Pennsylvania	699,376	2.4%
49	Rhode Island	42,481	0.1%
18	South Carolina	522,459	1.8%
43	South Dakota	84,707	0.3%
12	Tennessee	674,865	2.4%
1	Texas	5,002,893	17.5%
27	Utah	295,364	1.0%
50	Vermont	24,988	0.1%
10	Virginia	731,469	2.6%
20	Washington	477,284	1.7%
39	West Virginia	114,106	0.4%
26	Wisconsin	313,158	1.1%
45	Wyoming	59,337	0.2%

RANK ORDER

RANK	STATE	UNINSURED	% of USA
1	Texas	5,002,893	17.5%
2	California	2,825,620	9.9%
3	Florida	2,728,485	9.6%
4	Georgia	1,411,183	4.9%
5	North Carolina	1,092,046	3.8%
6	New York	1,041,233	3.6%
7	Illinois	874,608	3.1%
8	Arizona	749,977	2.6%
9	Ohio	743,905	2.6%
10	Virginia	731,469	2.6%
11	Pennsylvania	699,376	2.4%
12	Tennessee	674,865	2.4%
13	New Jersey	655,000	2.3%
14	Missouri	566,327	2.0%
15	Oklahoma	548,316	1.9%
16	Indiana	545,123	1.9%
17	Michigan	534,551	1.9%
18	South Carolina	522,459	1.8%
19	Alabama	481,259	1.7%
20	Washington	477,284	1.7%
21	Colorado	421,644	1.5%
22	Louisiana	363,362	1.3%
23	Maryland	356,708	1.2%
24	Mississippi	354,151	1.2%
25	Nevada	336,191	1.2%
26	Wisconsin	313,158	1.1%
27	Utah	295,364	1.0%
28	Oregon	293,107	1.0%
29	Kansas	250,355	0.9%
30	Kentucky	247,641	0.9%
31	Minnesota	244,379	0.9%
32	Arkansas	243,585	0.9%
33	New Mexico	196,250	0.7%
34	Idaho	192,620	0.7%
35	Massachusetts	188,907	0.7%
36	Connecticut	186,923	0.7%
37	Nebraska	157,612	0.6%
38	Iowa	147,039	0.5%
39	West Virginia	114,106	0.4%
40	Maine	106,187	0.4%
41	Alaska	90,128	0.3%
42	Montana	86,029	0.3%
43	South Dakota	84,707	0.3%
44	New Hampshire	77,011	0.3%
45	Wyoming	59,337	0.2%
46	Hawaii	55,799	0.2%
47	Delaware	53,962	0.2%
48	North Dakota	53,935	0.2%
49	Rhode Island	42,481	0.1%
50	Vermont	24,988	0.1%
	District of Columbia	21,897	0.1%

Source: U.S. Bureau of the Census
"2018 American Community Survey-Table DP03" (https://data.census.gov/cedsci/)

Percent of Population Not Covered by Health Insurance in 2018

National Percent = 8.9% of Population*

ALPHA ORDER				RANK ORDER		
RANK	STATE	PERCENT		RANK	STATE	PERCENT
14	Alabama	10.0		1	Texas	17.7
5	Alaska	12.6		2	Oklahoma	14.2
10	Arizona	10.6		3	Georgia	13.7
23	Arkansas	8.2		4	Florida	13.0
30	California	7.2		5	Alaska	12.6
27	Colorado	7.5		6	Mississippi	12.1
44	Connecticut	5.3		7	Nevada	11.2
37	Delaware	5.7		8	Idaho	11.1
4	Florida	13.0		9	North Carolina	10.7
3	Georgia	13.7		10	Arizona	10.6
47	Hawaii	4.1		11	South Carolina	10.5
8	Idaho	11.1		11	Wyoming	10.5
32	Illinois	7.0		13	Tennessee	10.1
21	Indiana	8.3		14	Alabama	10.0
45	Iowa	4.7		15	South Dakota	9.8
19	Kansas	8.8		16	New Mexico	9.5
39	Kentucky	5.6		17	Missouri	9.4
25	Louisiana	8.0		17	Utah	9.4
25	Maine	8.0		19	Kansas	8.8
36	Maryland	6.0		19	Virginia	8.8
50	Massachusetts	2.8		21	Indiana	8.3
42	Michigan	5.4		21	Nebraska	8.3
46	Minnesota	4.4		23	Arkansas	8.2
6	Mississippi	12.1		23	Montana	8.2
17	Missouri	9.4		25	Louisiana	8.0
23	Montana	8.2		25	Maine	8.0
21	Nebraska	8.3		27	Colorado	7.5
7	Nevada	11.2		28	New Jersey	7.4
37	New Hampshire	5.7		29	North Dakota	7.3
28	New Jersey	7.4		30	California	7.2
16	New Mexico	9.5		31	Oregon	7.1
42	New York	5.4		32	Illinois	7.0
9	North Carolina	10.7		33	Ohio	6.5
29	North Dakota	7.3		34	Washington	6.4
33	Ohio	6.5		34	West Virginia	6.4
2	Oklahoma	14.2		36	Maryland	6.0
31	Oregon	7.1		37	Delaware	5.7
40	Pennsylvania	5.5		37	New Hampshire	5.7
47	Rhode Island	4.1		39	Kentucky	5.6
11	South Carolina	10.5		40	Pennsylvania	5.5
15	South Dakota	9.8		40	Wisconsin	5.5
13	Tennessee	10.1		42	Michigan	5.4
1	Texas	17.7		42	New York	5.4
17	Utah	9.4		44	Connecticut	5.3
49	Vermont	4.0		45	Iowa	4.7
19	Virginia	8.8		46	Minnesota	4.4
34	Washington	6.4		47	Hawaii	4.1
34	West Virginia	6.4		47	Rhode Island	4.1
40	Wisconsin	5.5		49	Vermont	4.0
11	Wyoming	10.5		50	Massachusetts	2.8
					District of Columbia	3.2

Source: U.S. Bureau of the Census
"2018 American Community Survey-Table DP03" (https://data.census.gov/cedsci/)
*This is a one-year figure. Census has discontinued three-year averages that had been used previously.

Percent of Population Lacking Access to Primary Care in 2019

National Percent = 13.0% of Population*

ALPHA ORDER

RANK	STATE	PERCENT		RANK	STATE	PERCENT
9	Alabama	21.6		1	New Mexico	38.5
31	Alaska	10.5		2	Mississippi	34.4
5	Arizona	24.2		3	Montana	25.1
36	Arkansas	8.3		4	Missouri	24.9
28	California	11.1		5	Arizona	24.2
22	Colorado	12.8		6	Florida	22.4
23	Connecticut	12.4		7	New York	21.9
15	Delaware	16.6		7	Washington	21.9
6	Florida	22.4		9	Alabama	21.6
13	Georgia	17.5		10	Michigan	19.5
45	Hawaii	3.5		11	West Virginia	19.3
20	Idaho	14.2		12	Kansas	18.9
26	Illinois	11.6		13	Georgia	17.5
38	Indiana	7.4		14	Louisiana	16.8
34	Iowa	9.2		15	Delaware	16.6
12	Kansas	18.9		16	North Dakota	16.4
24	Kentucky	12.1		17	Nevada	16.3
14	Louisiana	16.8		18	South Dakota	15.8
44	Maine	3.7		19	Wyoming	15.0
29	Maryland	10.7		20	Idaho	14.2
42	Massachusetts	4.6		21	Oklahoma	13.9
10	Michigan	19.5		22	Colorado	12.8
43	Minnesota	4.3		23	Connecticut	12.4
2	Mississippi	34.4		24	Kentucky	12.1
4	Missouri	24.9		25	South Carolina	11.9
3	Montana	25.1		26	Illinois	11.6
49	Nebraska	0.6		27	Tennessee	11.3
17	Nevada	16.3		28	California	11.1
46	New Hampshire	2.8		29	Maryland	10.7
50	New Jersey	0.1		30	Oregon	10.6
1	New Mexico	38.5		31	Alaska	10.5
7	New York	21.9		32	North Carolina	10.1
32	North Carolina	10.1		33	Utah	9.5
16	North Dakota	16.4		34	Iowa	9.2
40	Ohio	5.5		35	Texas	8.7
21	Oklahoma	13.9		36	Arkansas	8.3
30	Oregon	10.6		37	Wisconsin	8.1
47	Pennsylvania	2.4		38	Indiana	7.4
41	Rhode Island	5.4		39	Virginia	7.2
25	South Carolina	11.9		40	Ohio	5.5
18	South Dakota	15.8		41	Rhode Island	5.4
27	Tennessee	11.3		42	Massachusetts	4.6
35	Texas	8.7		43	Minnesota	4.3
33	Utah	9.5		44	Maine	3.7
48	Vermont	1.2		45	Hawaii	3.5
39	Virginia	7.2		46	New Hampshire	2.8
7	Washington	21.9		47	Pennsylvania	2.4
11	West Virginia	19.3		48	Vermont	1.2
37	Wisconsin	8.1		49	Nebraska	0.6
19	Wyoming	15.0		50	New Jersey	0.1

District of Columbia   25.4

Source: CQ Press using data from U.S. Department of Health and Human Services, Division of Shortage Designation
"State Population and HPSA Designation Population Statistics" (as of January 15, 2019)
(https://datawarehouse.hrsa.gov/tools/hdwreports/Reports.aspx)
*Percent of population considered under-served by primary medical practitioners (family and general practice doctors, internists, ob/gyns, and pediatricians). An under-served population does not have primary medical care within reasonable economic and geographic bounds.

Professionally Active Physicians in 2019

National Total = 1,005,295 Physicians*

ALPHA ORDER

RANK	STATE	PHYSICIANS	% of USA
26	Alabama	12,205	1.2%
49	Alaska	1,900	0.2%
19	Arizona	17,806	1.8%
32	Arkansas	7,150	0.7%
1	California	112,906	11.2%
23	Colorado	14,509	1.4%
22	Connecticut	15,605	1.6%
43	Delaware	3,148	0.3%
4	Florida	56,499	5.6%
12	Georgia	25,312	2.5%
42	Hawaii	3,660	0.4%
44	Idaho	3,012	0.3%
6	Illinois	43,377	4.3%
21	Indiana	16,816	1.7%
30	Iowa	8,511	0.8%
31	Kansas	7,926	0.8%
28	Kentucky	11,937	1.2%
24	Louisiana	13,821	1.4%
40	Maine	4,721	0.5%
13	Maryland	24,676	2.5%
9	Massachusetts	36,506	3.6%
8	Michigan	38,819	3.9%
18	Minnesota	18,171	1.8%
34	Mississippi	6,597	0.7%
16	Missouri	20,275	2.0%
46	Montana	2,326	0.2%
38	Nebraska	5,627	0.6%
35	Nevada	6,151	0.6%
41	New Hampshire	4,240	0.4%
10	New Jersey	30,502	3.0%
36	New Mexico	5,830	0.6%
2	New York	89,500	8.9%
11	North Carolina	28,379	2.8%
48	North Dakota	2,015	0.2%
7	Ohio	42,373	4.2%
29	Oklahoma	9,472	0.9%
27	Oregon	12,149	1.2%
5	Pennsylvania	51,069	5.1%
39	Rhode Island	4,988	0.5%
25	South Carolina	12,847	1.3%
47	South Dakota	2,041	0.2%
17	Tennessee	18,979	1.9%
3	Texas	64,602	6.4%
33	Utah	6,761	0.7%
45	Vermont	2,338	0.2%
14	Virginia	23,307	2.3%
15	Washington	22,036	2.2%
37	West Virginia	5,685	0.6%
20	Wisconsin	17,695	1.8%
50	Wyoming	1,172	0.1%

RANK ORDER

RANK	STATE	PHYSICIANS	% of USA
1	California	112,906	11.2%
2	New York	89,500	8.9%
3	Texas	64,602	6.4%
4	Florida	56,499	5.6%
5	Pennsylvania	51,069	5.1%
6	Illinois	43,377	4.3%
7	Ohio	42,373	4.2%
8	Michigan	38,819	3.9%
9	Massachusetts	36,506	3.6%
10	New Jersey	30,502	3.0%
11	North Carolina	28,379	2.8%
12	Georgia	25,312	2.5%
13	Maryland	24,676	2.5%
14	Virginia	23,307	2.3%
15	Washington	22,036	2.2%
16	Missouri	20,275	2.0%
17	Tennessee	18,979	1.9%
18	Minnesota	18,171	1.8%
19	Arizona	17,806	1.8%
20	Wisconsin	17,695	1.8%
21	Indiana	16,816	1.7%
22	Connecticut	15,605	1.6%
23	Colorado	14,509	1.4%
24	Louisiana	13,821	1.4%
25	South Carolina	12,847	1.3%
26	Alabama	12,205	1.2%
27	Oregon	12,149	1.2%
28	Kentucky	11,937	1.2%
29	Oklahoma	9,472	0.9%
30	Iowa	8,511	0.8%
31	Kansas	7,926	0.8%
32	Arkansas	7,150	0.7%
33	Utah	6,761	0.7%
34	Mississippi	6,597	0.7%
35	Nevada	6,151	0.6%
36	New Mexico	5,830	0.6%
37	West Virginia	5,685	0.6%
38	Nebraska	5,627	0.6%
39	Rhode Island	4,988	0.5%
40	Maine	4,721	0.5%
41	New Hampshire	4,240	0.4%
42	Hawaii	3,660	0.4%
43	Delaware	3,148	0.3%
44	Idaho	3,012	0.3%
45	Vermont	2,338	0.2%
46	Montana	2,326	0.2%
47	South Dakota	2,041	0.2%
48	North Dakota	2,015	0.2%
49	Alaska	1,900	0.2%
50	Wyoming	1,172	0.1%
	District of Columbia	7,346	0.7%

Source: The Henry J. Kaiser Family Foundation
"Professionally Active Dentists" (https://www.kff.org/state-category/providers-service-use/physicians/)
*Includes MDs (medical doctors) and DOs (osteopathic physicians). Includes primary care physicians and specialist physicians.

Rate of Professionally Active Physicians in 2019

National Rate = 306 Physicians per 100,000 Population*

RANK	STATE	RATE
38	Alabama	249
33	Alaska	260
39	Arizona	245
42	Arkansas	237
23	California	286
35	Colorado	252
4	Connecticut	438
14	Delaware	323
32	Florida	263
41	Georgia	238
34	Hawaii	258
50	Idaho	169
12	Illinois	342
36	Indiana	250
29	Iowa	270
27	Kansas	272
30	Kentucky	267
19	Louisiana	297
10	Maine	351
5	Maryland	408
1	Massachusetts	530
7	Michigan	389
15	Minnesota	322
45	Mississippi	222
13	Missouri	330
46	Montana	218
20	Nebraska	291
49	Nevada	200
17	New Hampshire	312
11	New Jersey	343
24	New Mexico	278
3	New York	460
28	North Carolina	271
31	North Dakota	264
9	Ohio	363
40	Oklahoma	239
22	Oregon	288
6	Pennsylvania	399
2	Rhode Island	471
36	South Carolina	250
43	South Dakota	231
24	Tennessee	278
44	Texas	223
47	Utah	211
8	Vermont	375
26	Virginia	273
21	Washington	289
16	West Virginia	317
18	Wisconsin	304
48	Wyoming	203

RANK	STATE	RATE
1	Massachusetts	530
2	Rhode Island	471
3	New York	460
4	Connecticut	438
5	Maryland	408
6	Pennsylvania	399
7	Michigan	389
8	Vermont	375
9	Ohio	363
10	Maine	351
11	New Jersey	343
12	Illinois	342
13	Missouri	330
14	Delaware	323
15	Minnesota	322
16	West Virginia	317
17	New Hampshire	312
18	Wisconsin	304
19	Louisiana	297
20	Nebraska	291
21	Washington	289
22	Oregon	288
23	California	286
24	New Mexico	278
24	Tennessee	278
26	Virginia	273
27	Kansas	272
28	North Carolina	271
29	Iowa	270
30	Kentucky	267
31	North Dakota	264
32	Florida	263
33	Alaska	260
34	Hawaii	258
35	Colorado	252
36	Indiana	250
36	South Carolina	250
38	Alabama	249
39	Arizona	245
40	Oklahoma	239
41	Georgia	238
42	Arkansas	237
43	South Dakota	231
44	Texas	223
45	Mississippi	222
46	Montana	218
47	Utah	211
48	Wyoming	203
49	Nevada	200
50	Idaho	169

| | District of Columbia | 1,041 |

Source: CQ Press using data from The Henry J. Kaiser Family Foundation
"Professionally Active Dentists" (https://www.kff.org/state-category/providers-service-use/physicians/)
*Includes MDs (medical doctors) and DOs (osteopathic physicians). Includes primary care physicians and specialist physicians.

Rate of Registered Nurses in 2018

National Rate = 902 Nurses per 100,000 Population*

ALPHA ORDER			RANK ORDER		
RANK	STATE	RATE	RANK	STATE	RATE
19	Alabama	1,013	1	South Dakota	1,446
41	Alaska	777	2	Minnesota	1,230
42	Arizona	763	3	Delaware	1,224
36	Arkansas	842	4	Rhode Island	1,195
45	California	745	5	Nebraska	1,191
28	Colorado	909	6	Missouri	1,171
32	Connecticut	879	7	Massachusetts	1,168
3	Delaware	1,224	8	Pennsylvania	1,160
37	Florida	834	9	North Dakota	1,154
49	Georgia	729	10	West Virginia	1,104
39	Hawaii	796	11	Maine	1,080
40	Idaho	786	12	Ohio	1,073
16	Illinois	1,016	13	Iowa	1,070
18	Indiana	1,014	14	Kentucky	1,032
13	Iowa	1,070	15	Vermont	1,031
24	Kansas	955	16	Illinois	1,016
14	Kentucky	1,032	17	Wisconsin	1,015
27	Louisiana	925	18	Indiana	1,014
11	Maine	1,080	19	Alabama	1,013
29	Maryland	895	20	New Hampshire	1,005
7	Massachusetts	1,168	21	Mississippi	1,000
23	Michigan	967	22	North Carolina	987
2	Minnesota	1,230	23	Michigan	967
21	Mississippi	1,000	24	Kansas	955
6	Missouri	1,171	25	Montana	951
25	Montana	951	26	New York	934
5	Nebraska	1,191	27	Louisiana	925
47	Nevada	743	28	Colorado	909
20	New Hampshire	1,005	29	Maryland	895
30	New Jersey	893	30	New Jersey	893
38	New Mexico	798	31	Tennessee	892
26	New York	934	32	Connecticut	879
22	North Carolina	987	33	South Carolina	872
9	North Dakota	1,154	34	Wyoming	867
12	Ohio	1,073	35	Oregon	860
46	Oklahoma	744	36	Arkansas	842
35	Oregon	860	37	Florida	834
8	Pennsylvania	1,160	38	New Mexico	798
4	Rhode Island	1,195	39	Hawaii	796
33	South Carolina	872	40	Idaho	786
1	South Dakota	1,446	41	Alaska	777
31	Tennessee	892	42	Arizona	763
48	Texas	733	43	Virginia	760
50	Utah	686	44	Washington	747
15	Vermont	1,031	45	California	745
43	Virginia	760	46	Oklahoma	744
44	Washington	747	47	Nevada	743
10	West Virginia	1,104	48	Texas	733
17	Wisconsin	1,015	49	Georgia	729
34	Wyoming	867	50	Utah	686
				District of Columbia	1,582

Source: CQ Press using data from U.S. Department of Labor, Bureau of Labor Statistics
   "Occupational Employment and Wages, 2018" (https://www.bls.gov/oes/)
*Does not include self-employed.

Rate of Dentists in 2019

National Rate = 57 Dentists per 100,000 Population*

<table>
<tr><td colspan="3">ALPHA ORDER</td><td colspan="3">RANK ORDER</td></tr>
<tr><th>RANK</th><th>STATE</th><th>RATE</th><th>RANK</th><th>STATE</th><th>RATE</th></tr>
<tr><td>48</td><td>Alabama</td><td>39</td><td>1</td><td>Massachusetts</td><td>79</td></tr>
<tr><td>5</td><td>Alaska</td><td>69</td><td>2</td><td>New Jersey</td><td>78</td></tr>
<tr><td>23</td><td>Arizona</td><td>51</td><td>3</td><td>California</td><td>75</td></tr>
<tr><td>50</td><td>Arkansas</td><td>38</td><td>4</td><td>New York</td><td>74</td></tr>
<tr><td>3</td><td>California</td><td>75</td><td>5</td><td>Alaska</td><td>69</td></tr>
<tr><td>9</td><td>Colorado</td><td>65</td><td>6</td><td>Connecticut</td><td>68</td></tr>
<tr><td>6</td><td>Connecticut</td><td>68</td><td>6</td><td>Hawaii</td><td>68</td></tr>
<tr><td>47</td><td>Delaware</td><td>41</td><td>6</td><td>Maryland</td><td>68</td></tr>
<tr><td>26</td><td>Florida</td><td>49</td><td>9</td><td>Colorado</td><td>65</td></tr>
<tr><td>46</td><td>Georgia</td><td>43</td><td>9</td><td>Washington</td><td>65</td></tr>
<tr><td>6</td><td>Hawaii</td><td>68</td><td>11</td><td>Illinois</td><td>63</td></tr>
<tr><td>29</td><td>Idaho</td><td>48</td><td>12</td><td>Nebraska</td><td>60</td></tr>
<tr><td>11</td><td>Illinois</td><td>63</td><td>12</td><td>Virginia</td><td>60</td></tr>
<tr><td>42</td><td>Indiana</td><td>45</td><td>14</td><td>Pennsylvania</td><td>58</td></tr>
<tr><td>29</td><td>Iowa</td><td>48</td><td>15</td><td>New Hampshire</td><td>57</td></tr>
<tr><td>29</td><td>Kansas</td><td>48</td><td>15</td><td>Utah</td><td>57</td></tr>
<tr><td>17</td><td>Kentucky</td><td>55</td><td>17</td><td>Kentucky</td><td>55</td></tr>
<tr><td>39</td><td>Louisiana</td><td>46</td><td>17</td><td>Michigan</td><td>55</td></tr>
<tr><td>34</td><td>Maine</td><td>47</td><td>17</td><td>Vermont</td><td>55</td></tr>
<tr><td>6</td><td>Maryland</td><td>68</td><td>20</td><td>Montana</td><td>54</td></tr>
<tr><td>1</td><td>Massachusetts</td><td>79</td><td>21</td><td>Minnesota</td><td>53</td></tr>
<tr><td>17</td><td>Michigan</td><td>55</td><td>22</td><td>Wisconsin</td><td>52</td></tr>
<tr><td>21</td><td>Minnesota</td><td>53</td><td>23</td><td>Arizona</td><td>51</td></tr>
<tr><td>48</td><td>Mississippi</td><td>39</td><td>23</td><td>Nevada</td><td>51</td></tr>
<tr><td>34</td><td>Missouri</td><td>47</td><td>25</td><td>Texas</td><td>50</td></tr>
<tr><td>20</td><td>Montana</td><td>54</td><td>26</td><td>Florida</td><td>49</td></tr>
<tr><td>12</td><td>Nebraska</td><td>60</td><td>26</td><td>North Carolina</td><td>49</td></tr>
<tr><td>23</td><td>Nevada</td><td>51</td><td>26</td><td>Ohio</td><td>49</td></tr>
<tr><td>15</td><td>New Hampshire</td><td>57</td><td>29</td><td>Idaho</td><td>48</td></tr>
<tr><td>2</td><td>New Jersey</td><td>78</td><td>29</td><td>Iowa</td><td>48</td></tr>
<tr><td>34</td><td>New Mexico</td><td>47</td><td>29</td><td>Kansas</td><td>48</td></tr>
<tr><td>4</td><td>New York</td><td>74</td><td>29</td><td>North Dakota</td><td>48</td></tr>
<tr><td>26</td><td>North Carolina</td><td>49</td><td>29</td><td>Rhode Island</td><td>48</td></tr>
<tr><td>29</td><td>North Dakota</td><td>48</td><td>34</td><td>Maine</td><td>47</td></tr>
<tr><td>26</td><td>Ohio</td><td>49</td><td>34</td><td>Missouri</td><td>47</td></tr>
<tr><td>39</td><td>Oklahoma</td><td>46</td><td>34</td><td>New Mexico</td><td>47</td></tr>
<tr><td>42</td><td>Oregon</td><td>45</td><td>34</td><td>Tennessee</td><td>47</td></tr>
<tr><td>14</td><td>Pennsylvania</td><td>58</td><td>34</td><td>Wyoming</td><td>47</td></tr>
<tr><td>29</td><td>Rhode Island</td><td>48</td><td>39</td><td>Louisiana</td><td>46</td></tr>
<tr><td>45</td><td>South Carolina</td><td>44</td><td>39</td><td>Oklahoma</td><td>46</td></tr>
<tr><td>39</td><td>South Dakota</td><td>46</td><td>39</td><td>South Dakota</td><td>46</td></tr>
<tr><td>34</td><td>Tennessee</td><td>47</td><td>42</td><td>Indiana</td><td>45</td></tr>
<tr><td>25</td><td>Texas</td><td>50</td><td>42</td><td>Oregon</td><td>45</td></tr>
<tr><td>15</td><td>Utah</td><td>57</td><td>42</td><td>West Virginia</td><td>45</td></tr>
<tr><td>17</td><td>Vermont</td><td>55</td><td>45</td><td>South Carolina</td><td>44</td></tr>
<tr><td>12</td><td>Virginia</td><td>60</td><td>46</td><td>Georgia</td><td>43</td></tr>
<tr><td>9</td><td>Washington</td><td>65</td><td>47</td><td>Delaware</td><td>41</td></tr>
<tr><td>42</td><td>West Virginia</td><td>45</td><td>48</td><td>Alabama</td><td>39</td></tr>
<tr><td>22</td><td>Wisconsin</td><td>52</td><td>48</td><td>Mississippi</td><td>39</td></tr>
<tr><td>34</td><td>Wyoming</td><td>47</td><td>50</td><td>Arkansas</td><td>38</td></tr>
<tr><td></td><td></td><td></td><td></td><td>District of Columbia</td><td>86</td></tr>
</table>

Source: CQ Press using data from American Dental Association as reported by The Henry J. Kaiser Family Foundation
"Professionally Active Dentists" (https://www.kff.org/state-category/providers-service-use/dentists/)
*Professionally active dentists. Rates calculated using 2019 Census population estimates.

Community Hospitals in 2017

National Total = 5,261 Hospitals*

ALPHA ORDER					RANK ORDER			
RANK	STATE	HOSPITALS	% of USA		RANK	STATE	HOSPITALS	% of USA
21	Alabama	102	1.9%		1	Texas	528	10.0%
47	Alaska	21	0.4%		2	California	362	6.9%
28	Arizona	83	1.6%		3	Florida	220	4.2%
27	Arkansas	88	1.7%		4	Pennsylvania	201	3.8%
2	California	362	6.9%		5	Ohio	198	3.8%
26	Colorado	89	1.7%		6	Illinois	189	3.6%
42	Connecticut	32	0.6%		7	New York	168	3.2%
50	Delaware	8	0.2%		8	Louisiana	163	3.1%
3	Florida	220	4.2%		9	Georgia	147	2.8%
9	Georgia	147	2.8%		10	Michigan	145	2.8%
46	Hawaii	25	0.5%		11	Kansas	144	2.7%
38	Idaho	46	0.9%		12	Wisconsin	134	2.5%
6	Illinois	189	3.6%		13	Indiana	132	2.5%
13	Indiana	132	2.5%		14	Minnesota	129	2.5%
18	Iowa	117	2.2%		14	Oklahoma	129	2.5%
11	Kansas	144	2.7%		16	Missouri	126	2.4%
20	Kentucky	109	2.1%		17	Tennessee	122	2.3%
8	Louisiana	163	3.1%		18	Iowa	117	2.2%
42	Maine	32	0.6%		19	North Carolina	114	2.2%
37	Maryland	51	1.0%		20	Kentucky	109	2.1%
30	Massachusetts	75	1.4%		21	Alabama	102	1.9%
10	Michigan	145	2.8%		22	Mississippi	100	1.9%
14	Minnesota	129	2.5%		23	Virginia	95	1.8%
22	Mississippi	100	1.9%		24	Nebraska	94	1.8%
16	Missouri	126	2.4%		25	Washington	92	1.7%
35	Montana	55	1.0%		26	Colorado	89	1.7%
24	Nebraska	94	1.8%		27	Arkansas	88	1.7%
39	Nevada	44	0.8%		28	Arizona	83	1.6%
45	New Hampshire	28	0.5%		29	New Jersey	82	1.6%
29	New Jersey	82	1.6%		30	Massachusetts	75	1.4%
40	New Mexico	41	0.8%		31	South Carolina	70	1.3%
7	New York	168	3.2%		32	Oregon	61	1.2%
19	North Carolina	114	2.2%		33	South Dakota	57	1.1%
41	North Dakota	39	0.7%		34	West Virginia	56	1.1%
5	Ohio	198	3.8%		35	Montana	55	1.0%
14	Oklahoma	129	2.5%		36	Utah	53	1.0%
32	Oregon	61	1.2%		37	Maryland	51	1.0%
4	Pennsylvania	201	3.8%		38	Idaho	46	0.9%
49	Rhode Island	11	0.2%		39	Nevada	44	0.8%
31	South Carolina	70	1.3%		40	New Mexico	41	0.8%
33	South Dakota	57	1.1%		41	North Dakota	39	0.7%
17	Tennessee	122	2.3%		42	Connecticut	32	0.6%
1	Texas	528	10.0%		42	Maine	32	0.6%
36	Utah	53	1.0%		44	Wyoming	29	0.6%
48	Vermont	14	0.3%		45	New Hampshire	28	0.5%
23	Virginia	95	1.8%		46	Hawaii	25	0.5%
25	Washington	92	1.7%		47	Alaska	21	0.4%
34	West Virginia	56	1.1%		48	Vermont	14	0.3%
12	Wisconsin	134	2.5%		49	Rhode Island	11	0.2%
44	Wyoming	29	0.6%		50	Delaware	8	0.2%
						District of Columbia	11	0.2%

Source: American Hospital Association (Chicago, IL) as reported by The Henry J. Kaiser Family Foundation
"Total Hospitals" (https://www.kff.org/other/state-indicator/total-hospitals/)
*Community hospitals are all nonfederal, short-term general, and special hospitals whose facilities and services are available to the public.

Rate of Community Hospitals in 2017

National Rate = 1.6 Community Hospitals per 100,000 Population*

ALPHA ORDER				RANK ORDER		
RANK	STATE	RATE		RANK	STATE	RATE
20	Alabama	2.1		1	South Dakota	6.5
13	Alaska	2.8		2	Montana	5.2
38	Arizona	1.2		2	North Dakota	5.2
12	Arkansas	2.9		4	Kansas	5.0
45	California	0.9		4	Wyoming	5.0
30	Colorado	1.6		6	Nebraska	4.9
45	Connecticut	0.9		7	Iowa	3.7
49	Delaware	0.8		8	Louisiana	3.5
43	Florida	1.0		9	Mississippi	3.3
36	Georgia	1.4		9	Oklahoma	3.3
26	Hawaii	1.8		11	West Virginia	3.1
14	Idaho	2.7		12	Arkansas	2.9
32	Illinois	1.5		13	Alaska	2.8
23	Indiana	2.0		14	Idaho	2.7
7	Iowa	3.7		15	Kentucky	2.4
4	Kansas	5.0		15	Maine	2.4
15	Kentucky	2.4		17	Minnesota	2.3
8	Louisiana	3.5		17	Wisconsin	2.3
15	Maine	2.4		19	Vermont	2.2
49	Maryland	0.8		20	Alabama	2.1
40	Massachusetts	1.1		20	Missouri	2.1
32	Michigan	1.5		20	New Hampshire	2.1
17	Minnesota	2.3		23	Indiana	2.0
9	Mississippi	3.3		23	New Mexico	2.0
20	Missouri	2.1		25	Texas	1.9
2	Montana	5.2		26	Hawaii	1.8
6	Nebraska	4.9		26	Tennessee	1.8
32	Nevada	1.5		28	Ohio	1.7
20	New Hampshire	2.1		28	Utah	1.7
45	New Jersey	0.9		30	Colorado	1.6
23	New Mexico	2.0		30	Pennsylvania	1.6
45	New York	0.9		32	Illinois	1.5
40	North Carolina	1.1		32	Michigan	1.5
2	North Dakota	5.2		32	Nevada	1.5
28	Ohio	1.7		32	Oregon	1.5
9	Oklahoma	3.3		36	Georgia	1.4
32	Oregon	1.5		36	South Carolina	1.4
30	Pennsylvania	1.6		38	Arizona	1.2
43	Rhode Island	1.0		38	Washington	1.2
36	South Carolina	1.4		40	Massachusetts	1.1
1	South Dakota	6.5		40	North Carolina	1.1
26	Tennessee	1.8		40	Virginia	1.1
25	Texas	1.9		43	Florida	1.0
28	Utah	1.7		43	Rhode Island	1.0
19	Vermont	2.2		45	California	0.9
40	Virginia	1.1		45	Connecticut	0.9
38	Washington	1.2		45	New Jersey	0.9
11	West Virginia	3.1		45	New York	0.9
17	Wisconsin	2.3		49	Delaware	0.8
4	Wyoming	5.0		49	Maryland	0.8

District of Columbia 1.6

Source: CQ Press using data from American Hospital Association (Chicago, IL) as reported by The Henry J. Kaiser Family Foundation "Total Hospitals" (https://www.kff.org/other/state-indicator/total-hospitals/
*Community hospitals are all nonfederal, short-term general, and special hospitals whose facilities and services are available to the public.

Births in 2018

National Total = 3,791,712 Live Births*

ALPHA ORDER

RANK	STATE	BIRTHS	% of USA
24	Alabama	57,761	1.5%
48	Alaska	10,086	0.3%
16	Arizona	80,723	2.1%
31	Arkansas	37,018	1.0%
1	California	454,920	12.0%
22	Colorado	62,885	1.7%
35	Connecticut	34,725	0.9%
46	Delaware	10,621	0.3%
4	Florida	221,542	5.8%
8	Georgia	126,172	3.3%
40	Hawaii	16,972	0.4%
38	Idaho	21,403	0.6%
5	Illinois	144,815	3.8%
14	Indiana	81,646	2.2%
30	Iowa	37,785	1.0%
33	Kansas	36,261	1.0%
26	Kentucky	53,922	1.4%
23	Louisiana	59,615	1.6%
41	Maine	12,311	0.3%
18	Maryland	71,080	1.9%
19	Massachusetts	69,109	1.8%
10	Michigan	110,032	2.9%
20	Minnesota	67,344	1.8%
32	Mississippi	37,000	1.0%
17	Missouri	73,269	1.9%
44	Montana	11,513	0.3%
36	Nebraska	25,488	0.7%
34	Nevada	35,682	0.9%
42	New Hampshire	11,995	0.3%
11	New Jersey	101,223	2.7%
37	New Mexico	23,039	0.6%
3	New York	226,238	6.0%
9	North Carolina	118,954	3.1%
45	North Dakota	10,636	0.3%
7	Ohio	135,134	3.6%
27	Oklahoma	49,800	1.3%
29	Oregon	42,188	1.1%
6	Pennsylvania	135,673	3.6%
47	Rhode Island	10,506	0.3%
25	South Carolina	56,669	1.5%
43	South Dakota	11,893	0.3%
15	Tennessee	80,751	2.1%
2	Texas	378,624	10.0%
28	Utah	47,209	1.2%
50	Vermont	5,432	0.1%
12	Virginia	99,843	2.6%
13	Washington	86,085	2.3%
39	West Virginia	18,248	0.5%
21	Wisconsin	64,098	1.7%
49	Wyoming	6,562	0.2%

RANK ORDER

RANK	STATE	BIRTHS	% of USA
1	California	454,920	12.0%
2	Texas	378,624	10.0%
3	New York	226,238	6.0%
4	Florida	221,542	5.8%
5	Illinois	144,815	3.8%
6	Pennsylvania	135,673	3.6%
7	Ohio	135,134	3.6%
8	Georgia	126,172	3.3%
9	North Carolina	118,954	3.1%
10	Michigan	110,032	2.9%
11	New Jersey	101,223	2.7%
12	Virginia	99,843	2.6%
13	Washington	86,085	2.3%
14	Indiana	81,646	2.2%
15	Tennessee	80,751	2.1%
16	Arizona	80,723	2.1%
17	Missouri	73,269	1.9%
18	Maryland	71,080	1.9%
19	Massachusetts	69,109	1.8%
20	Minnesota	67,344	1.8%
21	Wisconsin	64,098	1.7%
22	Colorado	62,885	1.7%
23	Louisiana	59,615	1.6%
24	Alabama	57,761	1.5%
25	South Carolina	56,669	1.5%
26	Kentucky	53,922	1.4%
27	Oklahoma	49,800	1.3%
28	Utah	47,209	1.2%
29	Oregon	42,188	1.1%
30	Iowa	37,785	1.0%
31	Arkansas	37,018	1.0%
32	Mississippi	37,000	1.0%
33	Kansas	36,261	1.0%
34	Nevada	35,682	0.9%
35	Connecticut	34,725	0.9%
36	Nebraska	25,488	0.7%
37	New Mexico	23,039	0.6%
38	Idaho	21,403	0.6%
39	West Virginia	18,248	0.5%
40	Hawaii	16,972	0.4%
41	Maine	12,311	0.3%
42	New Hampshire	11,995	0.3%
43	South Dakota	11,893	0.3%
44	Montana	11,513	0.3%
45	North Dakota	10,636	0.3%
46	Delaware	10,621	0.3%
47	Rhode Island	10,506	0.3%
48	Alaska	10,086	0.3%
49	Wyoming	6,562	0.2%
50	Vermont	5,432	0.1%
	District of Columbia	9,212	0.2%

Source: U.S. Department of Health and Human Services, National Center for Health Statistics
"National Vital Statistics Reports" (Vol. 68, No. 13, November 27, 2019, https://www.cdc.gov/nchs/nvss/births.htm)
*Final data by state of residence.

Birth Rate in 2018

National Rate = 11.6 Live Births per 1,000 Population*

ALPHA ORDER

RANK	STATE	RATE
21	Alabama	11.8
3	Alaska	13.7
33	Arizona	11.3
11	Arkansas	12.3
27	California	11.5
35	Colorado	11.0
47	Connecticut	9.7
35	Delaware	11.0
42	Florida	10.4
15	Georgia	12.0
19	Hawaii	11.9
12	Idaho	12.2
29	Illinois	11.4
12	Indiana	12.2
15	Iowa	12.0
9	Kansas	12.5
14	Kentucky	12.1
7	Louisiana	12.8
48	Maine	9.2
21	Maryland	11.8
45	Massachusetts	10.0
35	Michigan	11.0
15	Minnesota	12.0
10	Mississippi	12.4
15	Missouri	12.0
40	Montana	10.8
5	Nebraska	13.2
21	Nevada	11.8
49	New Hampshire	8.8
29	New Jersey	11.4
35	New Mexico	11.0
25	New York	11.6
27	North Carolina	11.5
2	North Dakota	14.0
25	Ohio	11.6
8	Oklahoma	12.6
43	Oregon	10.1
41	Pennsylvania	10.6
46	Rhode Island	9.9
34	South Carolina	11.1
4	South Dakota	13.5
19	Tennessee	11.9
5	Texas	13.2
1	Utah	14.9
50	Vermont	8.7
24	Virginia	11.7
29	Washington	11.4
43	West Virginia	10.1
35	Wisconsin	11.0
29	Wyoming	11.4

RANK ORDER

RANK	STATE	RATE
1	Utah	14.9
2	North Dakota	14.0
3	Alaska	13.7
4	South Dakota	13.5
5	Nebraska	13.2
5	Texas	13.2
7	Louisiana	12.8
8	Oklahoma	12.6
9	Kansas	12.5
10	Mississippi	12.4
11	Arkansas	12.3
12	Idaho	12.2
12	Indiana	12.2
14	Kentucky	12.1
15	Georgia	12.0
15	Iowa	12.0
15	Minnesota	12.0
15	Missouri	12.0
19	Hawaii	11.9
19	Tennessee	11.9
21	Alabama	11.8
21	Maryland	11.8
21	Nevada	11.8
24	Virginia	11.7
25	New York	11.6
25	Ohio	11.6
27	California	11.5
27	North Carolina	11.5
29	Illinois	11.4
29	New Jersey	11.4
29	Washington	11.4
29	Wyoming	11.4
33	Arizona	11.3
34	South Carolina	11.1
35	Colorado	11.0
35	Delaware	11.0
35	Michigan	11.0
35	New Mexico	11.0
35	Wisconsin	11.0
40	Montana	10.8
41	Pennsylvania	10.6
42	Florida	10.4
43	Oregon	10.1
43	West Virginia	10.1
45	Massachusetts	10.0
46	Rhode Island	9.9
47	Connecticut	9.7
48	Maine	9.2
49	New Hampshire	8.8
50	Vermont	8.7

District of Columbia	13.1

Source: U.S. Department of Health and Human Services, National Center for Health Statistics
   "National Vital Statistics Reports" (Vol. 68, No. 13, November 27, 2019, https://www.cdc.gov/nchs/nvss/births.htm)
*Final data by state of residence.

Births of Low Birthweight as a Percent of All Births in 2018

National Percent = 8.3% of Live Births*

RANK	STATE	PERCENT
3	Alabama	10.7
50	Alaska	5.9
31	Arizona	7.6
6	Arkansas	9.4
41	California	7.0
6	Colorado	9.4
31	Connecticut	7.6
13	Delaware	8.9
16	Florida	8.7
4	Georgia	10.1
23	Hawaii	8.3
38	Idaho	7.3
19	Illinois	8.5
27	Indiana	8.1
43	Iowa	6.9
36	Kansas	7.4
13	Kentucky	8.9
2	Louisiana	10.8
39	Maine	7.2
15	Maryland	8.8
31	Massachusetts	7.6
19	Michigan	8.5
43	Minnesota	6.9
1	Mississippi	12.1
16	Missouri	8.7
36	Montana	7.4
31	Nebraska	7.6
16	Nevada	8.7
45	New Hampshire	6.8
29	New Jersey	7.9
12	New Mexico	9.0
27	New York	8.1
11	North Carolina	9.2
47	North Dakota	6.6
19	Ohio	8.5
23	Oklahoma	8.3
46	Oregon	6.7
23	Pennsylvania	8.3
31	Rhode Island	7.6
5	South Carolina	9.6
47	South Dakota	6.6
10	Tennessee	9.3
19	Texas	8.5
39	Utah	7.2
41	Vermont	7.0
26	Virginia	8.2
47	Washington	6.6
6	West Virginia	9.4
30	Wisconsin	7.7
6	Wyoming	9.4

RANK	STATE	PERCENT
1	Mississippi	12.1
2	Louisiana	10.8
3	Alabama	10.7
4	Georgia	10.1
5	South Carolina	9.6
6	Arkansas	9.4
6	Colorado	9.4
6	West Virginia	9.4
6	Wyoming	9.4
10	Tennessee	9.3
11	North Carolina	9.2
12	New Mexico	9.0
13	Delaware	8.9
13	Kentucky	8.9
15	Maryland	8.8
16	Florida	8.7
16	Missouri	8.7
16	Nevada	8.7
19	Illinois	8.5
19	Michigan	8.5
19	Ohio	8.5
19	Texas	8.5
23	Hawaii	8.3
23	Oklahoma	8.3
23	Pennsylvania	8.3
26	Virginia	8.2
27	Indiana	8.1
27	New York	8.1
29	New Jersey	7.9
30	Wisconsin	7.7
31	Arizona	7.6
31	Connecticut	7.6
31	Massachusetts	7.6
31	Nebraska	7.6
31	Rhode Island	7.6
36	Kansas	7.4
36	Montana	7.4
38	Idaho	7.3
39	Maine	7.2
39	Utah	7.2
41	California	7.0
41	Vermont	7.0
43	Iowa	6.9
43	Minnesota	6.9
45	New Hampshire	6.8
46	Oregon	6.7
47	North Dakota	6.6
47	South Dakota	6.6
47	Washington	6.6
50	Alaska	5.9
	District of Columbia	10.0

Source: U.S. Department of Health and Human Services, National Center for Health Statistics
"National Vital Statistics Reports" (Vol. 68, No. 13, November 27, 2019, https://www.cdc.gov/nchs/nvss/births.htm)
*Final data by state of residence. Births of less than 2,500 grams (5 pounds 8 ounces).

Births to Teenage Mothers as a Percent of All Births in 2018

National Percent = 4.7% of Live Births*

ALPHA ORDER				RANK ORDER		
RANK	STATE	PERCENT		RANK	STATE	PERCENT
7	Alabama	6.8		1	Arkansas	7.9
28	Alaska	4.2		2	Mississippi	7.6
14	Arizona	5.8		3	New Mexico	7.5
1	Arkansas	7.9		4	West Virginia	7.2
38	California	3.7		5	Kentucky	7.1
32	Colorado	4.0		6	Oklahoma	7.0
46	Connecticut	2.8		7	Alabama	6.8
22	Delaware	4.7		8	Louisiana	6.7
26	Florida	4.4		9	Texas	6.6
12	Georgia	5.9		10	Tennessee	6.5
34	Hawaii	3.8		11	South Carolina	6.1
25	Idaho	4.5		12	Georgia	5.9
26	Illinois	4.4		12	Indiana	5.9
12	Indiana	5.9		14	Arizona	5.8
28	Iowa	4.2		15	Missouri	5.6
17	Kansas	5.3		16	Wyoming	5.5
5	Kentucky	7.1		17	Kansas	5.3
8	Louisiana	6.7		17	North Carolina	5.3
41	Maine	3.4		19	Ohio	5.2
38	Maryland	3.7		20	Nevada	5.0
50	Massachusetts	2.4		21	South Dakota	4.8
23	Michigan	4.6		22	Delaware	4.7
49	Minnesota	2.7		23	Michigan	4.6
2	Mississippi	7.6		23	Montana	4.6
15	Missouri	5.6		25	Idaho	4.5
23	Montana	4.6		26	Florida	4.4
28	Nebraska	4.2		26	Illinois	4.4
20	Nevada	5.0		28	Alaska	4.2
46	New Hampshire	2.8		28	Iowa	4.2
46	New Jersey	2.8		28	Nebraska	4.2
3	New Mexico	7.5		31	Pennsylvania	4.1
45	New York	3.0		32	Colorado	4.0
17	North Carolina	5.3		33	Rhode Island	3.9
40	North Dakota	3.5		34	Hawaii	3.8
19	Ohio	5.2		34	Oregon	3.8
6	Oklahoma	7.0		34	Virginia	3.8
34	Oregon	3.8		34	Wisconsin	3.8
31	Pennsylvania	4.1		38	California	3.7
33	Rhode Island	3.9		38	Maryland	3.7
11	South Carolina	6.1		40	North Dakota	3.5
21	South Dakota	4.8		41	Maine	3.4
10	Tennessee	6.5		41	Utah	3.4
9	Texas	6.6		41	Vermont	3.4
41	Utah	3.4		44	Washington	3.2
41	Vermont	3.4		45	New York	3.0
34	Virginia	3.8		46	Connecticut	2.8
44	Washington	3.2		46	New Hampshire	2.8
4	West Virginia	7.2		46	New Jersey	2.8
34	Wisconsin	3.8		49	Minnesota	2.7
16	Wyoming	5.5		50	Massachusetts	2.4
					District of Columbia	4.0

Source: CQ Press using data from U.S. Department of Health and Human Services, Centers for Disease Control and Prevention "CDC Wonder" (https://wonder.cdc.gov)

*Final data. Live births to women fifteen to nineteen years old by state of residence.

Births to Unmarried Women as a Percent of All Births in 2018

National Percent = 39.6% of Live Births*

ALPHA ORDER				RANK ORDER		
RANK	STATE	PERCENT		RANK	STATE	PERCENT
6	Alabama	46.8		1	Mississippi	54.1
36	Alaska	35.3		2	Louisiana	53.3
12	Arizona	44.9		3	New Mexico	51.2
10	Arkansas	45.4		4	Nevada	48.3
31	California	37.1		5	Delaware	47.0
49	Colorado	23.2		6	Alabama	46.8
31	Connecticut	37.1		7	Florida	46.4
5	Delaware	47.0		8	South Carolina	46.2
7	Florida	46.4		9	West Virginia	45.7
11	Georgia	45.1		10	Arkansas	45.4
28	Hawaii	38.1		11	Georgia	45.1
48	Idaho	27.0		12	Arizona	44.9
24	Illinois	39.3		13	Rhode Island	43.6
15	Indiana	43.2		14	Tennessee	43.5
37	Iowa	34.9		15	Indiana	43.2
33	Kansas	36.4		15	Ohio	43.2
18	Kentucky	41.9		17	Oklahoma	42.2
2	Louisiana	53.3		18	Kentucky	41.9
26	Maine	38.8		19	North Carolina	40.9
25	Maryland	39.2		20	Michigan	40.8
43	Massachusetts	32.5		20	Pennsylvania	40.8
20	Michigan	40.8		20	Texas	40.8
45	Minnesota	31.9		23	Missouri	40.3
1	Mississippi	54.1		24	Illinois	39.3
23	Missouri	40.3		25	Maryland	39.2
37	Montana	34.9		26	Maine	38.8
43	Nebraska	32.5		27	Vermont	38.5
4	Nevada	48.3		28	Hawaii	38.1
42	New Hampshire	32.9		29	New York	37.5
40	New Jersey	33.8		30	Wisconsin	37.4
3	New Mexico	51.2		31	California	37.1
29	New York	37.5		31	Connecticut	37.1
19	North Carolina	40.9		33	Kansas	36.4
45	North Dakota	31.9		34	Oregon	36.3
15	Ohio	43.2		35	South Dakota	36.1
17	Oklahoma	42.2		36	Alaska	35.3
34	Oregon	36.3		37	Iowa	34.9
20	Pennsylvania	40.8		37	Montana	34.9
13	Rhode Island	43.6		39	Virginia	34.7
8	South Carolina	46.2		40	New Jersey	33.8
35	South Dakota	36.1		41	Wyoming	33.3
14	Tennessee	43.5		42	New Hampshire	32.9
20	Texas	40.8		43	Massachusetts	32.5
50	Utah	19.2		43	Nebraska	32.5
27	Vermont	38.5		45	Minnesota	31.9
39	Virginia	34.7		45	North Dakota	31.9
47	Washington	31.1		47	Washington	31.1
9	West Virginia	45.7		48	Idaho	27.0
30	Wisconsin	37.4		49	Colorado	23.2
41	Wyoming	33.3		50	Utah	19.2
					District of Columbia	46.5

Source: U.S. Department of Health and Human Services, National Center for Health Statistics
   "National Vital Statistics Reports" (Vol. 68, No. 13, November 27, 2019, https://www.cdc.gov/nchs/nvss/births.htm)
*Final data by state of residence.

Percent of Women Receiving Late or No Prenatal Care in 2017

National Percent = 6.3% of Women*

ALPHA ORDER				RANK ORDER		
RANK	**STATE**	**PERCENT**		**RANK**	**STATE**	**PERCENT**
9	Alabama	7.5		1	New Mexico	11.5
27	Alaska	5.8		2	Texas	10.2
4	Arizona	9.0		3	Arkansas	10.0
3	Arkansas	10.0		4	Arizona	9.0
42	California	3.8		5	Nevada	8.9
24	Colorado	6.0		6	Georgia	8.5
48	Connecticut	3.3		7	Tennessee	7.7
13	Delaware	6.7		8	Florida	7.6
8	Florida	7.6		9	Alabama	7.5
6	Georgia	8.5		10	Hawaii	7.0
10	Hawaii	7.0		10	Oklahoma	7.0
40	Idaho	4.2		12	Maryland	6.9
24	Illinois	6.0		13	Delaware	6.7
18	Indiana	6.3		13	West Virginia	6.7
39	Iowa	4.4		15	Pennsylvania	6.6
42	Kansas	3.8		15	South Carolina	6.6
31	Kentucky	5.5		17	North Carolina	6.5
20	Louisiana	6.1		18	Indiana	6.3
46	Maine	3.6		18	Ohio	6.3
12	Maryland	6.9		20	Louisiana	6.1
33	Massachusetts	5.0		20	South Dakota	6.1
35	Michigan	4.9		20	Washington	6.1
42	Minnesota	3.8		20	Wyoming	6.1
36	Mississippi	4.8		24	Colorado	6.0
29	Missouri	5.6		24	Illinois	6.0
24	Montana	6.0		24	Montana	6.0
32	Nebraska	5.4		27	Alaska	5.8
5	Nevada	8.9		27	New Jersey	5.8
45	New Hampshire	3.7		29	Missouri	5.6
27	New Jersey	5.8		29	North Dakota	5.6
1	New Mexico	11.5		31	Kentucky	5.5
33	New York	5.0		32	Nebraska	5.4
17	North Carolina	6.5		33	Massachusetts	5.0
29	North Dakota	5.6		33	New York	5.0
18	Ohio	6.3		35	Michigan	4.9
10	Oklahoma	7.0		36	Mississippi	4.8
38	Oregon	4.5		36	Virginia	4.8
15	Pennsylvania	6.6		38	Oregon	4.5
49	Rhode Island	2.0		39	Iowa	4.4
15	South Carolina	6.6		40	Idaho	4.2
20	South Dakota	6.1		41	Wisconsin	4.1
7	Tennessee	7.7		42	California	3.8
2	Texas	10.2		42	Kansas	3.8
46	Utah	3.6		42	Minnesota	3.8
50	Vermont	1.7		45	New Hampshire	3.7
36	Virginia	4.8		46	Maine	3.6
20	Washington	6.1		46	Utah	3.6
13	West Virginia	6.7		48	Connecticut	3.3
41	Wisconsin	4.1		49	Rhode Island	2.0
20	Wyoming	6.1		50	Vermont	1.7
					District of Columbia	9.1

Source: CQ Press using data from U.S. Department of Health and Human Services, Centers for Disease Control and Prevention "CDC Wonder" (https://wonder.cdc.gov)

*Final data by state of residence. "Late" means care begun in third trimester.

Reported Legal Abortions in 2016

Reporting States' Total = 623,471 Abortions*

ALPHA ORDER

RANK	STATE	ABORTIONS	% of USA
24	Alabama	6,642	1.1%
44	Alaska	1,260	0.2%
14	Arizona	13,332	2.1%
32	Arkansas	3,207	0.5%
NA	California**	NA	NA
20	Colorado	8,333	1.3%
16	Connecticut	10,031	1.6%
37	Delaware	2,170	0.3%
2	Florida	69,770	11.2%
5	Georgia	33,811	5.4%
35	Hawaii	2,554	0.4%
43	Idaho	1,289	0.2%
4	Illinois	38,382	6.2%
22	Indiana	7,277	1.2%
30	Iowa	3,722	0.6%
23	Kansas	6,790	1.1%
31	Kentucky	3,312	0.5%
18	Louisiana	8,973	1.4%
38	Maine	2,021	0.3%
NA	Maryland**	NA	NA
11	Massachusetts	17,901	2.9%
8	Michigan	26,395	4.2%
17	Minnesota	10,017	1.6%
34	Mississippi	2,569	0.4%
28	Missouri	4,562	0.7%
40	Montana	1,618	0.3%
39	Nebraska	1,907	0.3%
21	Nevada	7,284	1.2%
NA	New Hampshire**	NA	NA
9	New Jersey	24,470	3.9%
27	New Mexico	4,573	0.7%
1	New York	87,325	14.0%
7	North Carolina	27,138	4.4%
45	North Dakota	1,160	0.2%
10	Ohio	20,672	3.3%
29	Oklahoma	4,294	0.7%
19	Oregon	8,942	1.4%
6	Pennsylvania	30,881	5.0%
36	Rhode Island	2,479	0.4%
25	South Carolina	5,736	0.9%
46	South Dakota	472	0.1%
15	Tennessee	11,235	1.8%
3	Texas	53,481	8.6%
33	Utah	3,008	0.5%
42	Vermont	1,298	0.2%
13	Virginia	17,058	2.7%
12	Washington	17,080	2.7%
41	West Virginia	1,428	0.2%
26	Wisconsin	5,612	0.9%
NA	Wyoming**	NA	NA

RANK ORDER

RANK	STATE	ABORTIONS	% of USA
1	New York	87,325	14.0%
2	Florida	69,770	11.2%
3	Texas	53,481	8.6%
4	Illinois	38,382	6.2%
5	Georgia	33,811	5.4%
6	Pennsylvania	30,881	5.0%
7	North Carolina	27,138	4.4%
8	Michigan	26,395	4.2%
9	New Jersey	24,470	3.9%
10	Ohio	20,672	3.3%
11	Massachusetts	17,901	2.9%
12	Washington	17,080	2.7%
13	Virginia	17,058	2.7%
14	Arizona	13,332	2.1%
15	Tennessee	11,235	1.8%
16	Connecticut	10,031	1.6%
17	Minnesota	10,017	1.6%
18	Louisiana	8,973	1.4%
19	Oregon	8,942	1.4%
20	Colorado	8,333	1.3%
21	Nevada	7,284	1.2%
22	Indiana	7,277	1.2%
23	Kansas	6,790	1.1%
24	Alabama	6,642	1.1%
25	South Carolina	5,736	0.9%
26	Wisconsin	5,612	0.9%
27	New Mexico	4,573	0.7%
28	Missouri	4,562	0.7%
29	Oklahoma	4,294	0.7%
30	Iowa	3,722	0.6%
31	Kentucky	3,312	0.5%
32	Arkansas	3,207	0.5%
33	Utah	3,008	0.5%
34	Mississippi	2,569	0.4%
35	Hawaii	2,554	0.4%
36	Rhode Island	2,479	0.4%
37	Delaware	2,170	0.3%
38	Maine	2,021	0.3%
39	Nebraska	1,907	0.3%
40	Montana	1,618	0.3%
41	West Virginia	1,428	0.2%
42	Vermont	1,298	0.2%
43	Idaho	1,289	0.2%
44	Alaska	1,260	0.2%
45	North Dakota	1,160	0.2%
46	South Dakota	472	0.1%
NA	California**	NA	NA
NA	Maryland**	NA	NA
NA	New Hampshire**	NA	NA
NA	Wyoming**	NA	NA
	District of Columbia**	NA	NA

Source: U.S. Department of Health and Human Services, Centers for Disease Control and Prevention
   "Abortion Surveillance-United States, 2016" (MMWR, Vol. 68, No. SS-11, 11/29/19, www.cdc.gov/mmwr/mmwr_ss/ss_pvol.html)
*By state of occurrence. Total is for reporting states only.
**Not reported.

Reported Legal Abortions per 1,000 Live Births in 2016

Reporting States' Ratio = 186 Abortions per 1,000 Live Births*

ALPHA ORDER				RANK ORDER		
RANK	STATE	RATIO		RANK	STATE	RATIO
30	Alabama	112		1	New York	373
30	Alaska	112		2	Florida	310
21	Arizona	158		3	Connecticut	279
36	Arkansas	84		4	Georgia	260
NA	California**	NA		5	Massachusetts	251
29	Colorado	125		6	Illinois	249
3	Connecticut	279		7	New Jersey	238
14	Delaware	197		8	Michigan	233
2	Florida	310		9	Rhode Island	230
4	Georgia	260		10	Vermont	226
25	Hawaii	141		11	North Carolina	225
45	Idaho	57		12	Pennsylvania	222
6	Illinois	249		13	Nevada	201
35	Indiana	88		14	Delaware	197
34	Iowa	94		15	Oregon	196
18	Kansas	178		16	Washington	189
43	Kentucky	60		17	New Mexico	185
24	Louisiana	142		18	Kansas	178
20	Maine	159		19	Virginia	166
NA	Maryland**	NA		20	Maine	159
5	Massachusetts	251		21	Arizona	158
8	Michigan	233		22	Ohio	150
23	Minnesota	144		23	Minnesota	144
41	Mississippi	68		24	Louisiana	142
42	Missouri	61		25	Hawaii	141
28	Montana	132		26	Tennessee	139
40	Nebraska	72		27	Texas	134
13	Nevada	201		28	Montana	132
NA	New Hampshire**	NA		29	Colorado	125
7	New Jersey	238		30	Alabama	112
17	New Mexico	185		30	Alaska	112
1	New York	373		32	North Dakota	102
11	North Carolina	225		33	South Carolina	100
32	North Dakota	102		34	Iowa	94
22	Ohio	150		35	Indiana	88
38	Oklahoma	82		36	Arkansas	84
15	Oregon	196		36	Wisconsin	84
12	Pennsylvania	222		38	Oklahoma	82
9	Rhode Island	230		39	West Virginia	75
33	South Carolina	100		40	Nebraska	72
46	South Dakota	38		41	Mississippi	68
26	Tennessee	139		42	Missouri	61
27	Texas	134		43	Kentucky	60
43	Utah	60		43	Utah	60
10	Vermont	226		45	Idaho	57
19	Virginia	166		46	South Dakota	38
16	Washington	189		NA	California**	NA
39	West Virginia	75		NA	Maryland**	NA
36	Wisconsin	84		NA	New Hampshire**	NA
NA	Wyoming**	NA		NA	Wyoming**	NA
					District of Columbia**	NA

Source: U.S. Department of Health and Human Services, Centers for Disease Control and Prevention
   "Abortion Surveillance-United States, 2016" (MMWR, Vol. 68, No. SS-11, 11/29/19, www.cdc.gov/mmwr/mmwr_ss/ss_pvol.html)
*By state of occurrence. National figure is for reporting states only.
**Not reported.

Infant Deaths in 2017

National Total = 22,335 Infant Deaths*

ALPHA ORDER				RANK ORDER			
RANK	STATE	DEATHS	% of USA	RANK	STATE	DEATHS	% of USA
18	Alabama	434	1.9%	1	Texas	2,237	10.0%
46	Alaska	59	0.3%	2	California	1,973	8.8%
14	Arizona	469	2.1%	3	Florida	1,358	6.1%
27	Arkansas	307	1.4%	4	New York	1,047	4.7%
2	California	1,973	8.8%	5	Ohio	983	4.4%
28	Colorado	291	1.3%	6	Georgia	932	4.2%
35	Connecticut	160	0.7%	7	Illinois	912	4.1%
42	Delaware	72	0.3%	8	North Carolina	847	3.8%
3	Florida	1,358	6.1%	9	Pennsylvania	841	3.8%
6	Georgia	932	4.2%	10	Michigan	755	3.4%
41	Hawaii	92	0.4%	11	Indiana	600	2.7%
39	Idaho	102	0.5%	12	Tennessee	597	2.7%
7	Illinois	912	4.1%	13	Virginia	592	2.7%
11	Indiana	600	2.7%	14	Arizona	469	2.1%
34	Iowa	203	0.9%	15	Maryland	460	2.1%
32	Kansas	221	1.0%	16	Missouri	456	2.0%
23	Kentucky	355	1.6%	17	New Jersey	453	2.0%
19	Louisiana	431	1.9%	18	Alabama	434	1.9%
43	Maine	70	0.3%	19	Louisiana	431	1.9%
15	Maryland	460	2.1%	20	Wisconsin	414	1.9%
30	Massachusetts	262	1.2%	21	Oklahoma	387	1.7%
10	Michigan	755	3.4%	22	South Carolina	371	1.7%
25	Minnesota	328	1.5%	23	Kentucky	355	1.6%
26	Mississippi	322	1.4%	24	Washington	341	1.5%
16	Missouri	456	2.0%	25	Minnesota	328	1.5%
45	Montana	64	0.3%	26	Mississippi	322	1.4%
36	Nebraska	144	0.6%	27	Arkansas	307	1.4%
33	Nevada	208	0.9%	28	Colorado	291	1.3%
47	New Hampshire	51	0.2%	29	Utah	285	1.3%
17	New Jersey	453	2.0%	30	Massachusetts	262	1.2%
37	New Mexico	140	0.6%	31	Oregon	236	1.1%
4	New York	1,047	4.7%	32	Kansas	221	1.0%
8	North Carolina	847	3.8%	33	Nevada	208	0.9%
48	North Dakota	46	0.2%	34	Iowa	203	0.9%
5	Ohio	983	4.4%	35	Connecticut	160	0.7%
21	Oklahoma	387	1.7%	36	Nebraska	144	0.6%
31	Oregon	236	1.1%	37	New Mexico	140	0.6%
9	Pennsylvania	841	3.8%	38	West Virginia	131	0.6%
44	Rhode Island	66	0.3%	39	Idaho	102	0.5%
22	South Carolina	371	1.7%	40	South Dakota	94	0.4%
40	South Dakota	94	0.4%	41	Hawaii	92	0.4%
12	Tennessee	597	2.7%	42	Delaware	72	0.3%
1	Texas	2,237	10.0%	43	Maine	70	0.3%
29	Utah	285	1.3%	44	Rhode Island	66	0.3%
50	Vermont	27	0.1%	45	Montana	64	0.3%
13	Virginia	592	2.7%	46	Alaska	59	0.3%
24	Washington	341	1.5%	47	New Hampshire	51	0.2%
38	West Virginia	131	0.6%	48	North Dakota	46	0.2%
20	Wisconsin	414	1.9%	49	Wyoming	32	0.1%
49	Wyoming	32	0.1%	50	Vermont	27	0.1%
					District of Columbia	77	0.3%

Source: U.S. Department of Health and Human Services, National Center for Health Statistics
"National Vital Statistics Reports" (Vol. 68, No. 9, 2019, https://www.cdc.gov/nchs/nvss/deaths.htm)
*Final data. Deaths of infants under one year old by state of residence.

Infant Mortality Rate in 2017

National Rate = 5.8 Infant Deaths per 1,000 Live Births*

ALPHA ORDER

RANK ORDER

RANK	STATE	RATE	RANK	STATE	RATE
5	Alabama	7.4	1	Mississippi	8.6
30	Alaska	5.7	2	Arkansas	8.2
30	Arizona	5.7	3	South Dakota	7.8
2	Arkansas	8.2	4	Oklahoma	7.7
47	California	4.2	5	Alabama	7.4
43	Colorado	4.5	5	Tennessee	7.4
43	Connecticut	4.5	7	Indiana	7.3
14	Delaware	6.6	8	Georgia	7.2
21	Florida	6.1	8	Ohio	7.2
8	Georgia	7.2	10	Louisiana	7.1
36	Hawaii	5.3	10	North Carolina	7.1
40	Idaho	4.6	12	West Virginia	7.0
21	Illinois	6.1	13	Michigan	6.8
7	Indiana	7.3	14	Delaware	6.6
36	Iowa	5.3	15	Kentucky	6.5
21	Kansas	6.1	15	South Carolina	6.5
15	Kentucky	6.5	17	Maryland	6.4
10	Louisiana	7.1	17	Wisconsin	6.4
30	Maine	5.7	19	Missouri	6.2
17	Maryland	6.4	19	Rhode Island	6.2
50	Massachusetts	3.7	21	Florida	6.1
13	Michigan	6.8	21	Illinois	6.1
38	Minnesota	4.8	21	Kansas	6.1
1	Mississippi	8.6	21	Pennsylvania	6.1
19	Missouri	6.2	25	New Mexico	5.9
34	Montana	5.4	25	Texas	5.9
33	Nebraska	5.6	25	Utah	5.9
29	Nevada	5.8	25	Virginia	5.9
47	New Hampshire	4.2	29	Nevada	5.8
43	New Jersey	4.5	30	Alaska	5.7
25	New Mexico	5.9	30	Arizona	5.7
40	New York	4.6	30	Maine	5.7
10	North Carolina	7.1	33	Nebraska	5.6
46	North Dakota	4.3	34	Montana	5.4
8	Ohio	7.2	34	Oregon	5.4
4	Oklahoma	7.7	36	Hawaii	5.3
34	Oregon	5.4	36	Iowa	5.3
21	Pennsylvania	6.1	38	Minnesota	4.8
19	Rhode Island	6.2	38	Vermont	4.8
15	South Carolina	6.5	40	Idaho	4.6
3	South Dakota	7.8	40	New York	4.6
5	Tennessee	7.4	40	Wyoming	4.6
25	Texas	5.9	43	Colorado	4.5
25	Utah	5.9	43	Connecticut	4.5
38	Vermont	4.8	43	New Jersey	4.5
25	Virginia	5.9	46	North Dakota	4.3
49	Washington	3.9	47	California	4.2
12	West Virginia	7.0	47	New Hampshire	4.2
17	Wisconsin	6.4	49	Washington	3.9
40	Wyoming	4.6	50	Massachusetts	3.7
				District of Columbia	8.1

Source: U.S. Department of Health and Human Services, National Center for Health Statistics
  "National Vital Statistics Reports" (Vol. 68, No. 9, 2019, https://www.cdc.gov/nchs/nvss/deaths.htm)
*Final data. Deaths of infants under one year old by state of residence.

Deaths in 2017

National Total = 2,813,503 Deaths*

ALPHA ORDER

ALPHA ORDER

RANK	STATE	DEATHS	% of USA
19	Alabama	53,238	1.9%
50	Alaska	4,411	0.2%
17	Arizona	57,758	2.1%
29	Arkansas	32,588	1.2%
1	California	268,189	9.5%
27	Colorado	38,063	1.4%
31	Connecticut	31,312	1.1%
45	Delaware	9,178	0.3%
2	Florida	203,636	7.2%
10	Georgia	83,098	3.0%
42	Hawaii	11,390	0.4%
40	Idaho	14,011	0.5%
7	Illinois	109,721	3.9%
14	Indiana	65,597	2.3%
32	Iowa	30,530	1.1%
33	Kansas	27,063	1.0%
23	Kentucky	48,212	1.7%
24	Louisiana	45,804	1.6%
39	Maine	14,676	0.5%
21	Maryland	49,926	1.8%
16	Massachusetts	58,803	2.1%
8	Michigan	97,602	3.5%
25	Minnesota	44,371	1.6%
30	Mississippi	32,280	1.1%
15	Missouri	61,876	2.2%
43	Montana	10,200	0.4%
38	Nebraska	16,878	0.6%
34	Nevada	24,657	0.9%
41	New Hampshire	12,504	0.4%
11	New Jersey	74,846	2.7%
36	New Mexico	18,673	0.7%
4	New York	155,358	5.5%
9	North Carolina	93,157	3.3%
47	North Dakota	6,415	0.2%
6	Ohio	123,648	4.4%
26	Oklahoma	40,452	1.4%
28	Oregon	36,624	1.3%
5	Pennsylvania	135,656	4.8%
44	Rhode Island	10,157	0.4%
22	South Carolina	49,441	1.8%
46	South Dakota	7,996	0.3%
12	Tennessee	70,096	2.5%
3	Texas	198,106	7.0%
37	Utah	18,035	0.6%
48	Vermont	6,007	0.2%
13	Virginia	68,579	2.4%
18	Washington	56,995	2.0%
35	West Virginia	23,276	0.8%
20	Wisconsin	52,681	1.9%
49	Wyoming	4,768	0.2%

RANK ORDER

RANK	STATE	DEATHS	% of USA
1	California	268,189	9.5%
2	Florida	203,636	7.2%
3	Texas	198,106	7.0%
4	New York	155,358	5.5%
5	Pennsylvania	135,656	4.8%
6	Ohio	123,648	4.4%
7	Illinois	109,721	3.9%
8	Michigan	97,602	3.5%
9	North Carolina	93,157	3.3%
10	Georgia	83,098	3.0%
11	New Jersey	74,846	2.7%
12	Tennessee	70,096	2.5%
13	Virginia	68,579	2.4%
14	Indiana	65,597	2.3%
15	Missouri	61,876	2.2%
16	Massachusetts	58,803	2.1%
17	Arizona	57,758	2.1%
18	Washington	56,995	2.0%
19	Alabama	53,238	1.9%
20	Wisconsin	52,681	1.9%
21	Maryland	49,926	1.8%
22	South Carolina	49,441	1.8%
23	Kentucky	48,212	1.7%
24	Louisiana	45,804	1.6%
25	Minnesota	44,371	1.6%
26	Oklahoma	40,452	1.4%
27	Colorado	38,063	1.4%
28	Oregon	36,624	1.3%
29	Arkansas	32,588	1.2%
30	Mississippi	32,280	1.1%
31	Connecticut	31,312	1.1%
32	Iowa	30,530	1.1%
33	Kansas	27,063	1.0%
34	Nevada	24,657	0.9%
35	West Virginia	23,276	0.8%
36	New Mexico	18,673	0.7%
37	Utah	18,035	0.6%
38	Nebraska	16,878	0.6%
39	Maine	14,676	0.5%
40	Idaho	14,011	0.5%
41	New Hampshire	12,504	0.4%
42	Hawaii	11,390	0.4%
43	Montana	10,200	0.4%
44	Rhode Island	10,157	0.4%
45	Delaware	9,178	0.3%
46	South Dakota	7,996	0.3%
47	North Dakota	6,415	0.2%
48	Vermont	6,007	0.2%
49	Wyoming	4,768	0.2%
50	Alaska	4,411	0.2%
	District of Columbia	4,965	0.2%

Source: U.S. Department of Health and Human Services, National Center for Health Statistics
"National Vital Statistics Reports" (Vol. 68, No. 9, 2019, https://www.cdc.gov/nchs/nvss/deaths.htm)
*Final data by state of residence.

Age-Adjusted Death Rate in 2017

National Rate = 731.9 Deaths per 100,000 Population*

ALPHA ORDER			RANK ORDER		
RANK	STATE	RATE	RANK	STATE	RATE
4	Alabama	917.7	1	West Virginia	957.1
37	Alaska	708.8	2	Mississippi	951.3
41	Arizona	678.5	3	Kentucky	929.9
6	Arkansas	900.1	4	Alabama	917.7
49	California	618.7	5	Oklahoma	902.4
45	Colorado	663.4	6	Arkansas	900.1
47	Connecticut	651.2	7	Tennessee	897.1
22	Delaware	749.6	8	Louisiana	881.1
43	Florida	672.1	9	Ohio	849.7
13	Georgia	793.7	10	Indiana	848.6
50	Hawaii	584.9	11	South Carolina	828.0
23	Idaho	741.8	12	Missouri	820.1
28	Illinois	724.2	13	Georgia	793.7
10	Indiana	848.6	14	North Carolina	785.6
24	Iowa	737.0	15	Michigan	783.5
18	Kansas	771.2	16	Pennsylvania	777.3
3	Kentucky	929.9	17	Maine	771.6
8	Louisiana	881.1	18	Kansas	771.2
17	Maine	771.6	19	Nevada	765.5
31	Maryland	718.1	20	Montana	757.5
42	Massachusetts	677.1	21	New Mexico	754.7
15	Michigan	783.5	22	Delaware	749.6
46	Minnesota	656.4	23	Idaho	741.8
2	Mississippi	951.3	24	Iowa	737.0
12	Missouri	820.1	25	South Dakota	736.6
20	Montana	757.5	26	Texas	735.7
27	Nebraska	726.0	27	Nebraska	726.0
19	Nevada	765.5	28	Illinois	724.2
32	New Hampshire	717.2	29	Wisconsin	722.0
44	New Jersey	667.5	30	Virginia	719.4
21	New Mexico	754.7	31	Maryland	718.1
48	New York	623.6	32	New Hampshire	717.2
14	North Carolina	785.6	32	Oregon	717.2
39	North Dakota	692.7	34	Vermont	714.9
9	Ohio	849.7	35	Wyoming	714.5
5	Oklahoma	902.4	36	Rhode Island	713.4
32	Oregon	717.2	37	Alaska	708.8
16	Pennsylvania	777.3	38	Utah	700.1
36	Rhode Island	713.4	39	North Dakota	692.7
11	South Carolina	828.0	40	Washington	688.6
25	South Dakota	736.6	41	Arizona	678.5
7	Tennessee	897.1	42	Massachusetts	677.1
26	Texas	735.7	43	Florida	672.1
38	Utah	700.1	44	New Jersey	667.5
34	Vermont	714.9	45	Colorado	663.4
30	Virginia	719.4	46	Minnesota	656.4
40	Washington	688.6	47	Connecticut	651.2
1	West Virginia	957.1	48	New York	623.6
29	Wisconsin	722.0	49	California	618.7
35	Wyoming	714.5	50	Hawaii	584.9
				District of Columbia	725.4

Source: U.S. Department of Health and Human Services, National Center for Health Statistics
"National Vital Statistics Reports" (Vol. 68, No. 9, 2019, https://www.cdc.gov/nchs/nvss/deaths.htm)
*Final data by state of residence. Age-adjusted rates eliminate the distorting effects of the aging of the population. Rates based on the year 2000 standard population.

Estimated Deaths by Cancer in 2020

National Estimated Total = 606,520 Deaths

ALPHA ORDER

RANK	STATE	DEATHS	% of USA
23	Alabama	10,530	1.7%
49	Alaska	1,090	0.2%
17	Arizona	12,580	2.1%
29	Arkansas	6,730	1.1%
1	California	60,660	10.0%
28	Colorado	8,220	1.4%
32	Connecticut	6,390	1.1%
44	Delaware	2,130	0.4%
2	Florida	45,300	7.5%
10	Georgia	17,990	3.0%
42	Hawaii	2,540	0.4%
40	Idaho	3,100	0.5%
7	Illinois	24,220	4.0%
14	Indiana	13,630	2.2%
31	Iowa	6,440	1.1%
33	Kansas	5,520	0.9%
22	Kentucky	10,540	1.7%
25	Louisiana	9,300	1.5%
38	Maine	3,350	0.6%
20	Maryland	10,790	1.8%
18	Massachusetts	12,430	2.0%
8	Michigan	21,000	3.5%
24	Minnesota	10,040	1.7%
30	Mississippi	6,700	1.1%
16	Missouri	13,010	2.1%
43	Montana	2,140	0.4%
37	Nebraska	3,520	0.6%
34	Nevada	5,460	0.9%
41	New Hampshire	2,830	0.5%
11	New Jersey	15,710	2.6%
36	New Mexico	3,730	0.6%
4	New York	34,710	5.7%
9	North Carolina	20,410	3.4%
48	North Dakota	1,260	0.2%
6	Ohio	25,380	4.2%
26	Oklahoma	8,430	1.4%
27	Oregon	8,280	1.4%
5	Pennsylvania	27,860	4.6%
45	Rhode Island	2,120	0.3%
21	South Carolina	10,780	1.8%
46	South Dakota	1,690	0.3%
13	Tennessee	14,780	2.4%
3	Texas	41,810	6.9%
38	Utah	3,350	0.6%
47	Vermont	1,450	0.2%
12	Virginia	15,220	2.5%
15	Washington	13,020	2.1%
35	West Virginia	4,750	0.8%
19	Wisconsin	11,610	1.9%
50	Wyoming	960	0.2%

RANK ORDER

RANK	STATE	DEATHS	% of USA
1	California	60,660	10.0%
2	Florida	45,300	7.5%
3	Texas	41,810	6.9%
4	New York	34,710	5.7%
5	Pennsylvania	27,860	4.6%
6	Ohio	25,380	4.2%
7	Illinois	24,220	4.0%
8	Michigan	21,000	3.5%
9	North Carolina	20,410	3.4%
10	Georgia	17,990	3.0%
11	New Jersey	15,710	2.6%
12	Virginia	15,220	2.5%
13	Tennessee	14,780	2.4%
14	Indiana	13,630	2.2%
15	Washington	13,020	2.1%
16	Missouri	13,010	2.1%
17	Arizona	12,580	2.1%
18	Massachusetts	12,430	2.0%
19	Wisconsin	11,610	1.9%
20	Maryland	10,790	1.8%
21	South Carolina	10,780	1.8%
22	Kentucky	10,540	1.7%
23	Alabama	10,530	1.7%
24	Minnesota	10,040	1.7%
25	Louisiana	9,300	1.5%
26	Oklahoma	8,430	1.4%
27	Oregon	8,280	1.4%
28	Colorado	8,220	1.4%
29	Arkansas	6,730	1.1%
30	Mississippi	6,700	1.1%
31	Iowa	6,440	1.1%
32	Connecticut	6,390	1.1%
33	Kansas	5,520	0.9%
34	Nevada	5,460	0.9%
35	West Virginia	4,750	0.8%
36	New Mexico	3,730	0.6%
37	Nebraska	3,520	0.6%
38	Maine	3,350	0.6%
38	Utah	3,350	0.6%
40	Idaho	3,100	0.5%
41	New Hampshire	2,830	0.5%
42	Hawaii	2,540	0.4%
43	Montana	2,140	0.4%
44	Delaware	2,130	0.4%
45	Rhode Island	2,120	0.3%
46	South Dakota	1,690	0.3%
47	Vermont	1,450	0.2%
48	North Dakota	1,260	0.2%
49	Alaska	1,090	0.2%
50	Wyoming	960	0.2%
	District of Columbia	1,020	0.2%

Source: American Cancer Society
"Cancer Facts & Figures 2020" (Copyright 2020, American Cancer Society, www.cancer.org/research/cancer-facts-statistics.html)

Estimated Death Rate by Cancer in 2020

National Estimated Rate = 184.8 Deaths per 100,000 Population*

ALPHA ORDER

RANK ORDER

RANK	STATE	RATE
11	Alabama	214.8
47	Alaska	149.0
41	Arizona	172.8
6	Arkansas	223.0
46	California	153.5
49	Colorado	142.7
32	Connecticut	179.2
7	Delaware	218.7
14	Florida	210.9
43	Georgia	169.4
31	Hawaii	179.4
40	Idaho	173.5
26	Illinois	191.1
19	Indiana	202.5
18	Iowa	204.1
28	Kansas	189.5
3	Kentucky	235.9
21	Louisiana	200.1
2	Maine	249.2
33	Maryland	178.5
30	Massachusetts	180.3
15	Michigan	210.3
36	Minnesota	178.0
5	Mississippi	225.1
13	Missouri	212.0
20	Montana	200.2
29	Nebraska	182.0
38	Nevada	177.3
17	New Hampshire	208.1
39	New Jersey	176.9
37	New Mexico	177.9
34	New York	178.4
25	North Carolina	194.6
45	North Dakota	165.3
9	Ohio	217.1
12	Oklahoma	213.0
24	Oregon	196.3
8	Pennsylvania	217.6
21	Rhode Island	200.1
16	South Carolina	209.4
27	South Dakota	191.0
10	Tennessee	216.4
48	Texas	144.2
50	Utah	104.5
4	Vermont	232.4
35	Virginia	178.3
42	Washington	171.0
1	West Virginia	265.0
23	Wisconsin	199.4
44	Wyoming	165.9

RANK	STATE	RATE
1	West Virginia	265.0
2	Maine	249.2
3	Kentucky	235.9
4	Vermont	232.4
5	Mississippi	225.1
6	Arkansas	223.0
7	Delaware	218.7
8	Pennsylvania	217.6
9	Ohio	217.1
10	Tennessee	216.4
11	Alabama	214.8
12	Oklahoma	213.0
13	Missouri	212.0
14	Florida	210.9
15	Michigan	210.3
16	South Carolina	209.4
17	New Hampshire	208.1
18	Iowa	204.1
19	Indiana	202.5
20	Montana	200.2
21	Louisiana	200.1
21	Rhode Island	200.1
23	Wisconsin	199.4
24	Oregon	196.3
25	North Carolina	194.6
26	Illinois	191.1
27	South Dakota	191.0
28	Kansas	189.5
29	Nebraska	182.0
30	Massachusetts	180.3
31	Hawaii	179.4
32	Connecticut	179.2
33	Maryland	178.5
34	New York	178.4
35	Virginia	178.3
36	Minnesota	178.0
37	New Mexico	177.9
38	Nevada	177.3
39	New Jersey	176.9
40	Idaho	173.5
41	Arizona	172.8
42	Washington	171.0
43	Georgia	169.4
44	Wyoming	165.9
45	North Dakota	165.3
46	California	153.5
47	Alaska	149.0
48	Texas	144.2
49	Colorado	142.7
50	Utah	104.5

	District of Columbia	144.5

Source: CQ Press using data from American Cancer Society
  "Cancer Facts & Figures 2020" (Copyright 2020, American Cancer Society, www.cancer.org/research/cancer-facts-statistics.html)
*Rates calculated using 2019 Census resident population estimates. Not age-adjusted.

Estimated New Cancer Cases in 2020

National Estimated Total = 1,806,590 New Cases*

ALPHA ORDER

RANK	STATE	CASES	% of USA
23	Alabama	28,570	1.6%
49	Alaska	2,960	0.2%
17	Arizona	36,730	2.0%
31	Arkansas	17,200	1.0%
1	California	172,040	9.5%
24	Colorado	27,290	1.5%
29	Connecticut	20,300	1.1%
43	Delaware	6,660	0.4%
2	Florida	150,500	8.3%
10	Georgia	55,190	3.1%
42	Hawaii	6,800	0.4%
39	Idaho	8,540	0.5%
6	Illinois	71,990	4.0%
14	Indiana	37,940	2.1%
30	Iowa	18,460	1.0%
34	Kansas	16,170	0.9%
25	Kentucky	26,500	1.5%
26	Louisiana	26,480	1.5%
40	Maine	8,180	0.5%
20	Maryland	34,710	1.9%
16	Massachusetts	36,990	2.0%
8	Michigan	61,770	3.4%
21	Minnesota	33,210	1.8%
32	Mississippi	17,190	1.0%
15	Missouri	37,540	2.1%
45	Montana	5,850	0.3%
37	Nebraska	10,560	0.6%
33	Nevada	16,540	0.9%
41	New Hampshire	8,060	0.4%
11	New Jersey	53,340	3.0%
38	New Mexico	9,800	0.5%
4	New York	117,910	6.5%
9	North Carolina	59,620	3.3%
47	North Dakota	4,060	0.2%
7	Ohio	71,850	4.0%
28	Oklahoma	20,530	1.1%
27	Oregon	23,330	1.3%
5	Pennsylvania	80,240	4.4%
44	Rhode Island	5,930	0.3%
22	South Carolina	31,710	1.8%
46	South Dakota	4,960	0.3%
13	Tennessee	39,360	2.2%
3	Texas	129,770	7.2%
36	Utah	11,900	0.7%
48	Vermont	3,740	0.2%
12	Virginia	47,550	2.6%
18	Washington	36,290	2.0%
35	West Virginia	12,380	0.7%
19	Wisconsin	35,280	2.0%
50	Wyoming	2,880	0.2%

RANK ORDER

RANK	STATE	CASES	% of USA
1	California	172,040	9.5%
2	Florida	150,500	8.3%
3	Texas	129,770	7.2%
4	New York	117,910	6.5%
5	Pennsylvania	80,240	4.4%
6	Illinois	71,990	4.0%
7	Ohio	71,850	4.0%
8	Michigan	61,770	3.4%
9	North Carolina	59,620	3.3%
10	Georgia	55,190	3.1%
11	New Jersey	53,340	3.0%
12	Virginia	47,550	2.6%
13	Tennessee	39,360	2.2%
14	Indiana	37,940	2.1%
15	Missouri	37,540	2.1%
16	Massachusetts	36,990	2.0%
17	Arizona	36,730	2.0%
18	Washington	36,290	2.0%
19	Wisconsin	35,280	2.0%
20	Maryland	34,710	1.9%
21	Minnesota	33,210	1.8%
22	South Carolina	31,710	1.8%
23	Alabama	28,570	1.6%
24	Colorado	27,290	1.5%
25	Kentucky	26,500	1.5%
26	Louisiana	26,480	1.5%
27	Oregon	23,330	1.3%
28	Oklahoma	20,530	1.1%
29	Connecticut	20,300	1.1%
30	Iowa	18,460	1.0%
31	Arkansas	17,200	1.0%
32	Mississippi	17,190	1.0%
33	Nevada	16,540	0.9%
34	Kansas	16,170	0.9%
35	West Virginia	12,380	0.7%
36	Utah	11,900	0.7%
37	Nebraska	10,560	0.6%
38	New Mexico	9,800	0.5%
39	Idaho	8,540	0.5%
40	Maine	8,180	0.5%
41	New Hampshire	8,060	0.4%
42	Hawaii	6,800	0.4%
43	Delaware	6,660	0.4%
44	Rhode Island	5,930	0.3%
45	Montana	5,850	0.3%
46	South Dakota	4,960	0.3%
47	North Dakota	4,060	0.2%
48	Vermont	3,740	0.2%
49	Alaska	2,960	0.2%
50	Wyoming	2,880	0.2%
	District of Columbia	3,600	0.2%

Source: American Cancer Society
"Cancer Facts & Figures 2020" (Copyright 2020, American Cancer Society, www.cancer.org/research/cancer-facts-statistics.html)
*These estimates are offered as a rough guide and should not be regarded as definitive. They are calculated by the American Cancer Society using a model based on 2002–2016 incidence data. Totals do not include basal and squamous cell skin cancers or in situ carcinomas except urinary bladder.

Estimated Rate of New Cancer Cases in 2020

National Estimated Rate = 550.4 New Cases per 100,000 Population*

ALPHA ORDER

RANK	STATE	RATE
18	Alabama	582.7
49	Alaska	404.6
40	Arizona	504.6
22	Arkansas	570.0
48	California	435.4
45	Colorado	473.9
24	Connecticut	569.4
3	Delaware	683.9
1	Florida	700.7
38	Georgia	519.8
42	Hawaii	480.3
43	Idaho	477.9
26	Illinois	568.1
27	Indiana	563.6
17	Iowa	585.1
31	Kansas	555.0
14	Kentucky	593.1
23	Louisiana	569.6
9	Maine	608.5
21	Maryland	574.1
36	Massachusetts	536.7
5	Michigan	618.5
16	Minnesota	588.9
19	Mississippi	577.6
8	Missouri	611.7
33	Montana	547.4
34	Nebraska	545.9
35	Nevada	537.0
15	New Hampshire	592.8
12	New Jersey	600.5
46	New Mexico	467.4
10	New York	606.1
25	North Carolina	568.5
37	North Dakota	532.8
7	Ohio	614.7
39	Oklahoma	518.8
32	Oregon	553.1
4	Pennsylvania	626.8
29	Rhode Island	559.8
6	South Carolina	615.9
28	South Dakota	560.7
20	Tennessee	576.4
47	Texas	447.5
50	Utah	371.2
13	Vermont	599.4
30	Virginia	557.1
44	Washington	476.6
2	West Virginia	690.8
11	Wisconsin	605.9
41	Wyoming	497.6

RANK ORDER

RANK	STATE	RATE
1	Florida	700.7
2	West Virginia	690.8
3	Delaware	683.9
4	Pennsylvania	626.8
5	Michigan	618.5
6	South Carolina	615.9
7	Ohio	614.7
8	Missouri	611.7
9	Maine	608.5
10	New York	606.1
11	Wisconsin	605.9
12	New Jersey	600.5
13	Vermont	599.4
14	Kentucky	593.1
15	New Hampshire	592.8
16	Minnesota	588.9
17	Iowa	585.1
18	Alabama	582.7
19	Mississippi	577.6
20	Tennessee	576.4
21	Maryland	574.1
22	Arkansas	570.0
23	Louisiana	569.6
24	Connecticut	569.4
25	North Carolina	568.5
26	Illinois	568.1
27	Indiana	563.6
28	South Dakota	560.7
29	Rhode Island	559.8
30	Virginia	557.1
31	Kansas	555.0
32	Oregon	553.1
33	Montana	547.4
34	Nebraska	545.9
35	Nevada	537.0
36	Massachusetts	536.7
37	North Dakota	532.8
38	Georgia	519.8
39	Oklahoma	518.8
40	Arizona	504.6
41	Wyoming	497.6
42	Hawaii	480.3
43	Idaho	477.9
44	Washington	476.6
45	Colorado	473.9
46	New Mexico	467.4
47	Texas	447.5
48	California	435.4
49	Alaska	404.6
50	Utah	371.2
	District of Columbia	510.1

Source: CQ Press using data from American Cancer Society
"Cancer Facts & Figures 2020" (Copyright 2020, American Cancer Society, www.cancer.org/research/cancer-facts-statistics.html)
*These estimates are offered as a rough guide and should not be regarded as definitive. They are calculated by the American Cancer Society using a model based on 2002–2016 incidence data. Totals do not include basal and squamous cell skin cancers or in situ carcinomas except urinary bladder. Rates calculated using 2019 Census resident population estimates.

Deaths by Accidents in 2017

National Total = 169,936 Deaths*

ALPHA ORDER

RANK	STATE	DEATHS	% of USA
25	Alabama	2,703	1.6%
47	Alaska	436	0.3%
13	Arizona	4,184	2.5%
32	Arkansas	1,625	1.0%
1	California	13,840	8.1%
22	Colorado	3,037	1.8%
28	Connecticut	2,078	1.2%
43	Delaware	608	0.4%
2	Florida	13,059	7.7%
10	Georgia	4,712	2.8%
44	Hawaii	585	0.3%
40	Idaho	876	0.5%
7	Illinois	6,019	3.5%
14	Indiana	3,978	2.3%
34	Iowa	1,536	0.9%
33	Kansas	1,567	0.9%
20	Kentucky	3,264	1.9%
24	Louisiana	2,780	1.6%
38	Maine	990	0.6%
27	Maryland	2,408	1.4%
16	Massachusetts	3,821	2.2%
9	Michigan	5,623	3.3%
23	Minnesota	2,788	1.6%
31	Mississippi	1,738	1.0%
17	Missouri	3,776	2.2%
45	Montana	579	0.3%
41	Nebraska	811	0.5%
35	Nevada	1,496	0.9%
39	New Hampshire	907	0.5%
11	New Jersey	4,482	2.6%
36	New Mexico	1,460	0.9%
6	New York	7,687	4.5%
8	North Carolina	5,985	3.5%
50	North Dakota	339	0.2%
5	Ohio	8,971	5.3%
26	Oklahoma	2,563	1.5%
29	Oregon	2,076	1.2%
4	Pennsylvania	9,527	5.6%
42	Rhode Island	718	0.4%
21	South Carolina	3,147	1.9%
46	South Dakota	537	0.3%
12	Tennessee	4,435	2.6%
3	Texas	10,763	6.3%
37	Utah	1,238	0.7%
48	Vermont	394	0.2%
15	Virginia	3,922	2.3%
19	Washington	3,455	2.0%
30	West Virginia	1,892	1.1%
18	Wisconsin	3,746	2.2%
49	Wyoming	348	0.2%

RANK ORDER

RANK	STATE	DEATHS	% of USA
1	California	13,840	8.1%
2	Florida	13,059	7.7%
3	Texas	10,763	6.3%
4	Pennsylvania	9,527	5.6%
5	Ohio	8,971	5.3%
6	New York	7,687	4.5%
7	Illinois	6,019	3.5%
8	North Carolina	5,985	3.5%
9	Michigan	5,623	3.3%
10	Georgia	4,712	2.8%
11	New Jersey	4,482	2.6%
12	Tennessee	4,435	2.6%
13	Arizona	4,184	2.5%
14	Indiana	3,978	2.3%
15	Virginia	3,922	2.3%
16	Massachusetts	3,821	2.2%
17	Missouri	3,776	2.2%
18	Wisconsin	3,746	2.2%
19	Washington	3,455	2.0%
20	Kentucky	3,264	1.9%
21	South Carolina	3,147	1.9%
22	Colorado	3,037	1.8%
23	Minnesota	2,788	1.6%
24	Louisiana	2,780	1.6%
25	Alabama	2,703	1.6%
26	Oklahoma	2,563	1.5%
27	Maryland	2,408	1.4%
28	Connecticut	2,078	1.2%
29	Oregon	2,076	1.2%
30	West Virginia	1,892	1.1%
31	Mississippi	1,738	1.0%
32	Arkansas	1,625	1.0%
33	Kansas	1,567	0.9%
34	Iowa	1,536	0.9%
35	Nevada	1,496	0.9%
36	New Mexico	1,460	0.9%
37	Utah	1,238	0.7%
38	Maine	990	0.6%
39	New Hampshire	907	0.5%
40	Idaho	876	0.5%
41	Nebraska	811	0.5%
42	Rhode Island	718	0.4%
43	Delaware	608	0.4%
44	Hawaii	585	0.3%
45	Montana	579	0.3%
46	South Dakota	537	0.3%
47	Alaska	436	0.3%
48	Vermont	394	0.2%
49	Wyoming	348	0.2%
50	North Dakota	339	0.2%
	District of Columbia	427	0.3%

Source: U.S. Department of Health and Human Services, National Center for Health Statistics
  "National Vital Statistics Reports" (Vol. 68, No. 9, 2019, https://www.cdc.gov/nchs/nvss/deaths.htm)
*Final data by state of residence. Includes motor vehicle deaths, poisoning, falls, drowning, and other accidents.

Age-Adjusted Death Rate by Accidents in 2017

National Rate = 49.4 Deaths per 100,000 Population*

ALPHA ORDER

RANK	STATE	RATE
25	Alabama	53.8
7	Alaska	63.7
22	Arizona	56.2
29	Arkansas	51.8
50	California	33.1
26	Colorado	53.6
27	Connecticut	53.2
11	Delaware	61.9
23	Florida	56.1
36	Georgia	45.2
48	Hawaii	35.7
32	Idaho	49.8
39	Illinois	44.4
16	Indiana	58.7
43	Iowa	42.7
33	Kansas	49.4
3	Kentucky	72.9
14	Louisiana	58.8
6	Maine	68.0
47	Maryland	36.9
30	Massachusetts	51.5
28	Michigan	53.0
38	Minnesota	44.6
20	Mississippi	56.3
14	Missouri	58.8
31	Montana	50.2
46	Nebraska	38.5
34	Nevada	47.8
9	New Hampshire	62.9
35	New Jersey	47.3
5	New Mexico	68.2
49	New York	35.5
20	North Carolina	56.3
44	North Dakota	41.3
2	Ohio	75.1
10	Oklahoma	62.5
37	Oregon	44.7
4	Pennsylvania	70.2
13	Rhode Island	60.0
12	South Carolina	60.2
23	South Dakota	56.1
8	Tennessee	63.0
45	Texas	38.8
40	Utah	44.2
18	Vermont	56.9
41	Virginia	44.0
41	Washington	44.0
1	West Virginia	100.3
17	Wisconsin	58.3
18	Wyoming	56.9

RANK ORDER

RANK	STATE	RATE
1	West Virginia	100.3
2	Ohio	75.1
3	Kentucky	72.9
4	Pennsylvania	70.2
5	New Mexico	68.2
6	Maine	68.0
7	Alaska	63.7
8	Tennessee	63.0
9	New Hampshire	62.9
10	Oklahoma	62.5
11	Delaware	61.9
12	South Carolina	60.2
13	Rhode Island	60.0
14	Louisiana	58.8
14	Missouri	58.8
16	Indiana	58.7
17	Wisconsin	58.3
18	Vermont	56.9
18	Wyoming	56.9
20	Mississippi	56.3
20	North Carolina	56.3
22	Arizona	56.2
23	Florida	56.1
23	South Dakota	56.1
25	Alabama	53.8
26	Colorado	53.6
27	Connecticut	53.2
28	Michigan	53.0
29	Arkansas	51.8
30	Massachusetts	51.5
31	Montana	50.2
32	Idaho	49.8
33	Kansas	49.4
34	Nevada	47.8
35	New Jersey	47.3
36	Georgia	45.2
37	Oregon	44.7
38	Minnesota	44.6
39	Illinois	44.4
40	Utah	44.2
41	Virginia	44.0
41	Washington	44.0
43	Iowa	42.7
44	North Dakota	41.3
45	Texas	38.8
46	Nebraska	38.5
47	Maryland	36.9
48	Hawaii	35.7
49	New York	35.5
50	California	33.1
	District of Columbia	61.0

Source: U.S. Department of Health and Human Services, National Center for Health Statistics
"National Vital Statistics Reports" (Vol. 68, No. 9, 2019, https://www.cdc.gov/nchs/nvss/deaths.htm)
*Final data by state of residence. Includes motor vehicle deaths, poisoning, falls, drowning, and other accidents. Age-adjusted rates based on the year 2000 standard population.

Deaths by Cerebrovascular Diseases in 2017

National Total = 146,383 Deaths*

ALPHA ORDER

RANK	STATE	DEATHS	% of USA
17	Alabama	2,931	2.0%
49	Alaska	190	0.1%
20	Arizona	2,681	1.8%
30	Arkansas	1,612	1.1%
1	California	16,355	11.2%
27	Colorado	1,988	1.4%
32	Connecticut	1,403	1.0%
42	Delaware	571	0.4%
2	Florida	12,602	8.6%
10	Georgia	4,399	3.0%
38	Hawaii	764	0.5%
41	Idaho	726	0.5%
7	Illinois	6,020	4.1%
15	Indiana	3,150	2.2%
31	Iowa	1,416	1.0%
33	Kansas	1,355	0.9%
26	Kentucky	2,050	1.4%
22	Louisiana	2,460	1.7%
40	Maine	736	0.5%
18	Maryland	2,820	1.9%
23	Massachusetts	2,367	1.6%
9	Michigan	5,002	3.4%
24	Minnesota	2,250	1.5%
29	Mississippi	1,723	1.2%
14	Missouri	3,159	2.2%
44	Montana	487	0.3%
39	Nebraska	760	0.5%
34	Nevada	1,137	0.8%
43	New Hampshire	514	0.4%
13	New Jersey	3,474	2.4%
37	New Mexico	878	0.6%
6	New York	6,264	4.3%
8	North Carolina	5,098	3.5%
47	North Dakota	337	0.2%
5	Ohio	6,425	4.4%
28	Oklahoma	1,947	1.3%
25	Oregon	2,066	1.4%
4	Pennsylvania	6,700	4.6%
45	Rhode Island	425	0.3%
19	South Carolina	2,691	1.8%
46	South Dakota	414	0.3%
12	Tennessee	3,519	2.4%
3	Texas	10,790	7.4%
36	Utah	888	0.6%
48	Vermont	249	0.2%
11	Virginia	3,555	2.4%
16	Washington	3,028	2.1%
35	West Virginia	1,058	0.7%
21	Wisconsin	2,513	1.7%
49	Wyoming	190	0.1%

RANK ORDER

RANK	STATE	DEATHS	% of USA
1	California	16,355	11.2%
2	Florida	12,602	8.6%
3	Texas	10,790	7.4%
4	Pennsylvania	6,700	4.6%
5	Ohio	6,425	4.4%
6	New York	6,264	4.3%
7	Illinois	6,020	4.1%
8	North Carolina	5,098	3.5%
9	Michigan	5,002	3.4%
10	Georgia	4,399	3.0%
11	Virginia	3,555	2.4%
12	Tennessee	3,519	2.4%
13	New Jersey	3,474	2.4%
14	Missouri	3,159	2.2%
15	Indiana	3,150	2.2%
16	Washington	3,028	2.1%
17	Alabama	2,931	2.0%
18	Maryland	2,820	1.9%
19	South Carolina	2,691	1.8%
20	Arizona	2,681	1.8%
21	Wisconsin	2,513	1.7%
22	Louisiana	2,460	1.7%
23	Massachusetts	2,367	1.6%
24	Minnesota	2,250	1.5%
25	Oregon	2,066	1.4%
26	Kentucky	2,050	1.4%
27	Colorado	1,988	1.4%
28	Oklahoma	1,947	1.3%
29	Mississippi	1,723	1.2%
30	Arkansas	1,612	1.1%
31	Iowa	1,416	1.0%
32	Connecticut	1,403	1.0%
33	Kansas	1,355	0.9%
34	Nevada	1,137	0.8%
35	West Virginia	1,058	0.7%
36	Utah	888	0.6%
37	New Mexico	878	0.6%
38	Hawaii	764	0.5%
39	Nebraska	760	0.5%
40	Maine	736	0.5%
41	Idaho	726	0.5%
42	Delaware	571	0.4%
43	New Hampshire	514	0.4%
44	Montana	487	0.3%
45	Rhode Island	425	0.3%
46	South Dakota	414	0.3%
47	North Dakota	337	0.2%
48	Vermont	249	0.2%
49	Alaska	190	0.1%
49	Wyoming	190	0.1%
	District of Columbia	246	0.2%

Source: U.S. Department of Health and Human Services, National Center for Health Statistics
   "National Vital Statistics Reports" (Vol. 68, No. 9, 2019, https://www.cdc.gov/nchs/nvss/deaths.htm)
*Final data by state of residence. Cerebrovascular diseases include stroke and other disorders of the blood vessels of the brain.

Age-Adjusted Death Rate by Cerebrovascular Diseases in 2017

National Rate = 37.6 Deaths per 100,000 Population*

ALPHA ORDER

RANK	STATE	RATE
2	Alabama	50.0
36	Alaska	35.1
42	Arizona	30.8
7	Arkansas	43.8
24	California	37.6
33	Colorado	35.8
48	Connecticut	27.8
4	Delaware	46.2
20	Florida	38.9
8	Georgia	43.5
25	Hawaii	37.5
22	Idaho	38.5
20	Illinois	38.9
15	Indiana	40.2
39	Iowa	32.8
23	Kansas	37.7
18	Kentucky	39.4
3	Louisiana	47.4
25	Maine	37.5
15	Maryland	40.2
49	Massachusetts	26.5
19	Michigan	39.3
40	Minnesota	32.6
1	Mississippi	51.1
14	Missouri	41.0
34	Montana	35.6
41	Nebraska	31.5
32	Nevada	35.9
45	New Hampshire	28.9
43	New Jersey	30.2
37	New Mexico	34.7
50	New York	24.6
10	North Carolina	43.0
35	North Dakota	35.4
11	Ohio	42.8
9	Oklahoma	43.3
17	Oregon	39.9
30	Pennsylvania	36.5
44	Rhode Island	29.4
6	South Carolina	44.9
29	South Dakota	36.7
5	Tennessee	45.0
13	Texas	41.3
31	Utah	36.2
46	Vermont	28.8
25	Virginia	37.5
28	Washington	36.9
12	West Virginia	41.8
38	Wisconsin	33.5
47	Wyoming	28.4

RANK ORDER

RANK	STATE	RATE
1	Mississippi	51.1
2	Alabama	50.0
3	Louisiana	47.4
4	Delaware	46.2
5	Tennessee	45.0
6	South Carolina	44.9
7	Arkansas	43.8
8	Georgia	43.5
9	Oklahoma	43.3
10	North Carolina	43.0
11	Ohio	42.8
12	West Virginia	41.8
13	Texas	41.3
14	Missouri	41.0
15	Indiana	40.2
15	Maryland	40.2
17	Oregon	39.9
18	Kentucky	39.4
19	Michigan	39.3
20	Florida	38.9
20	Illinois	38.9
22	Idaho	38.5
23	Kansas	37.7
24	California	37.6
25	Hawaii	37.5
25	Maine	37.5
25	Virginia	37.5
28	Washington	36.9
29	South Dakota	36.7
30	Pennsylvania	36.5
31	Utah	36.2
32	Nevada	35.9
33	Colorado	35.8
34	Montana	35.6
35	North Dakota	35.4
36	Alaska	35.1
37	New Mexico	34.7
38	Wisconsin	33.5
39	Iowa	32.8
40	Minnesota	32.6
41	Nebraska	31.5
42	Arizona	30.8
43	New Jersey	30.2
44	Rhode Island	29.4
45	New Hampshire	28.9
46	Vermont	28.8
47	Wyoming	28.4
48	Connecticut	27.8
49	Massachusetts	26.5
50	New York	24.6
	District of Columbia	35.9

Source: U.S. Department of Health and Human Services, National Center for Health Statistics
  "National Vital Statistics Reports" (Vol. 68, No. 9, 2019, https://www.cdc.gov/nchs/nvss/deaths.htm)
*Final data by state of residence. Cerebrovascular diseases include stroke and other disorders of the blood vessels of the brain. Age-adjusted rates based on the year 2000 standard population.

Deaths by Diseases of the Heart in 2017

National Total = 647,457 Deaths*

ALPHA ORDER				RANK ORDER			
RANK	STATE	DEATHS	% of USA	RANK	STATE	DEATHS	% of USA
16	Alabama	13,110	2.0%	1	California	62,797	9.7%
50	Alaska	814	0.1%	2	Florida	46,440	7.2%
17	Arizona	12,398	1.9%	3	Texas	45,346	7.0%
26	Arkansas	8,270	1.3%	4	New York	44,092	6.8%
1	California	62,797	9.7%	5	Pennsylvania	32,312	5.0%
31	Colorado	7,060	1.1%	6	Ohio	28,008	4.3%
30	Connecticut	7,138	1.1%	7	Illinois	25,394	3.9%
45	Delaware	1,990	0.3%	8	Michigan	25,187	3.9%
2	Florida	46,440	7.2%	9	New Jersey	18,840	2.9%
11	Georgia	18,389	2.8%	10	North Carolina	18,808	2.9%
42	Hawaii	2,575	0.4%	11	Georgia	18,389	2.8%
39	Idaho	3,084	0.5%	12	Tennessee	16,019	2.5%
7	Illinois	25,394	3.9%	13	Virginia	14,861	2.3%
15	Indiana	14,445	2.2%	14	Missouri	14,820	2.3%
29	Iowa	7,180	1.1%	15	Indiana	14,445	2.2%
34	Kansas	5,723	0.9%	16	Alabama	13,110	2.0%
25	Kentucky	10,343	1.6%	17	Arizona	12,398	1.9%
22	Louisiana	11,260	1.7%	18	Massachusetts	12,140	1.9%
40	Maine	2,844	0.4%	19	Wisconsin	11,860	1.8%
20	Maryland	11,653	1.8%	20	Maryland	11,653	1.8%
18	Massachusetts	12,140	1.9%	21	Washington	11,582	1.8%
8	Michigan	25,187	3.9%	22	Louisiana	11,260	1.7%
27	Minnesota	8,230	1.3%	23	Oklahoma	10,772	1.7%
28	Mississippi	7,944	1.2%	24	South Carolina	10,418	1.6%
14	Missouri	14,820	2.3%	25	Kentucky	10,343	1.6%
44	Montana	2,164	0.3%	26	Arkansas	8,270	1.3%
38	Nebraska	3,581	0.6%	27	Minnesota	8,230	1.3%
33	Nevada	6,417	1.0%	28	Mississippi	7,944	1.2%
41	New Hampshire	2,721	0.4%	29	Iowa	7,180	1.1%
9	New Jersey	18,840	2.9%	30	Connecticut	7,138	1.1%
36	New Mexico	3,896	0.6%	31	Colorado	7,060	1.1%
4	New York	44,092	6.8%	32	Oregon	6,942	1.1%
10	North Carolina	18,808	2.9%	33	Nevada	6,417	1.0%
48	North Dakota	1,326	0.2%	34	Kansas	5,723	0.9%
6	Ohio	28,008	4.3%	35	West Virginia	4,849	0.7%
23	Oklahoma	10,772	1.7%	36	New Mexico	3,896	0.6%
32	Oregon	6,942	1.1%	37	Utah	3,749	0.6%
5	Pennsylvania	32,312	5.0%	38	Nebraska	3,581	0.6%
43	Rhode Island	2,339	0.4%	39	Idaho	3,084	0.5%
24	South Carolina	10,418	1.6%	40	Maine	2,844	0.4%
46	South Dakota	1,710	0.3%	41	New Hampshire	2,721	0.4%
12	Tennessee	16,019	2.5%	42	Hawaii	2,575	0.4%
3	Texas	45,346	7.0%	43	Rhode Island	2,339	0.4%
37	Utah	3,749	0.6%	44	Montana	2,164	0.3%
47	Vermont	1,332	0.2%	45	Delaware	1,990	0.3%
13	Virginia	14,861	2.3%	46	South Dakota	1,710	0.3%
21	Washington	11,582	1.8%	47	Vermont	1,332	0.2%
35	West Virginia	4,849	0.7%	48	North Dakota	1,326	0.2%
19	Wisconsin	11,860	1.8%	49	Wyoming	1,001	0.2%
49	Wyoming	1,001	0.2%	50	Alaska	814	0.1%
					District of Columbia	1,284	0.2%

Source: U.S. Department of Health and Human Services, National Center for Health Statistics
"National Vital Statistics Reports" (Vol. 68, No. 9, 2019, https://www.cdc.gov/nchs/nvss/deaths.htm)
*Final data by state of residence.

Age-Adjusted Death Rate by Diseases of the Heart in 2017

National Rate = 165.0 Deaths per 100,000 Population*

RANK	STATE	RATE
4	Alabama	223.2
45	Alaska	135.0
41	Arizona	141.9
3	Arkansas	223.8
40	California	142.9
49	Colorado	122.7
42	Connecticut	141.6
24	Delaware	158.4
38	Florida	145.8
15	Georgia	175.8
48	Hawaii	129.8
22	Idaho	162.4
21	Illinois	163.3
13	Indiana	183.2
19	Iowa	167.4
25	Kansas	157.9
9	Kentucky	195.9
5	Louisiana	214.4
39	Maine	143.5
20	Maryland	164.5
46	Massachusetts	134.6
8	Michigan	196.1
50	Minnesota	119.1
2	Mississippi	231.6
11	Missouri	191.1
29	Montana	155.0
36	Nebraska	149.3
7	Nevada	199.3
35	New Hampshire	149.7
23	New Jersey	162.3
32	New Mexico	151.4
17	New York	171.2
27	North Carolina	156.5
44	North Dakota	137.8
12	Ohio	186.2
1	Oklahoma	237.2
47	Oregon	134.0
14	Pennsylvania	176.0
28	Rhode Island	155.7
16	South Carolina	172.0
34	South Dakota	150.1
6	Tennessee	202.2
18	Texas	169.2
33	Utah	150.2
31	Vermont	152.5
30	Virginia	154.5
43	Washington	138.8
10	West Virginia	192.0
26	Wisconsin	157.6
37	Wyoming	148.9

RANK	STATE	RATE
1	Oklahoma	237.2
2	Mississippi	231.6
3	Arkansas	223.8
4	Alabama	223.2
5	Louisiana	214.4
6	Tennessee	202.2
7	Nevada	199.3
8	Michigan	196.1
9	Kentucky	195.9
10	West Virginia	192.0
11	Missouri	191.1
12	Ohio	186.2
13	Indiana	183.2
14	Pennsylvania	176.0
15	Georgia	175.8
16	South Carolina	172.0
17	New York	171.2
18	Texas	169.2
19	Iowa	167.4
20	Maryland	164.5
21	Illinois	163.3
22	Idaho	162.4
23	New Jersey	162.3
24	Delaware	158.4
25	Kansas	157.9
26	Wisconsin	157.6
27	North Carolina	156.5
28	Rhode Island	155.7
29	Montana	155.0
30	Virginia	154.5
31	Vermont	152.5
32	New Mexico	151.4
33	Utah	150.2
34	South Dakota	150.1
35	New Hampshire	149.7
36	Nebraska	149.3
37	Wyoming	148.9
38	Florida	145.8
39	Maine	143.5
40	California	142.9
41	Arizona	141.9
42	Connecticut	141.6
43	Washington	138.8
44	North Dakota	137.8
45	Alaska	135.0
46	Massachusetts	134.6
47	Oregon	134.0
48	Hawaii	129.8
49	Colorado	122.7
50	Minnesota	119.1

	District of Columbia	189.8

Source: U.S. Department of Health and Human Services, National Center for Health Statistics
  "National Vital Statistics Reports" (Vol. 68, No. 9, 2019, https://www.cdc.gov/nchs/nvss/deaths.htm)
*Final data by state of residence. Age-adjusted rates based on the year 2000 standard population.

Deaths by Suicide in 2017

National Total = 47,173 Suicides*

RANK	STATE	DEATHS	% of USA
20	Alabama	836	1.8%
44	Alaska	200	0.4%
11	Arizona	1,327	2.8%
29	Arkansas	631	1.3%
1	California	4,312	9.1%
13	Colorado	1,181	2.5%
36	Connecticut	405	0.9%
49	Delaware	112	0.2%
3	Florida	3,227	6.8%
10	Georgia	1,451	3.1%
43	Hawaii	227	0.5%
38	Idaho	392	0.8%
8	Illinois	1,474	3.1%
17	Indiana	1,092	2.3%
34	Iowa	479	1.0%
32	Kansas	553	1.2%
24	Kentucky	770	1.6%
26	Louisiana	720	1.5%
41	Maine	274	0.6%
30	Maryland	630	1.3%
27	Massachusetts	682	1.4%
9	Michigan	1,457	3.1%
23	Minnesota	783	1.7%
35	Mississippi	445	0.9%
16	Missouri	1,151	2.4%
39	Montana	311	0.7%
40	Nebraska	275	0.6%
31	Nevada	627	1.3%
42	New Hampshire	265	0.6%
22	New Jersey	795	1.7%
33	New Mexico	491	1.0%
6	New York	1,696	3.6%
7	North Carolina	1,521	3.2%
47	North Dakota	154	0.3%
5	Ohio	1,740	3.7%
25	Oklahoma	756	1.6%
21	Oregon	825	1.7%
4	Pennsylvania	2,030	4.3%
48	Rhode Island	129	0.3%
19	South Carolina	838	1.8%
45	South Dakota	191	0.4%
15	Tennessee	1,166	2.5%
2	Texas	3,778	8.0%
28	Utah	663	1.4%
49	Vermont	112	0.2%
14	Virginia	1,179	2.5%
12	Washington	1,297	2.7%
37	West Virginia	393	0.8%
18	Wisconsin	926	2.0%
46	Wyoming	157	0.3%

RANK	STATE	DEATHS	% of USA
1	California	4,312	9.1%
2	Texas	3,778	8.0%
3	Florida	3,227	6.8%
4	Pennsylvania	2,030	4.3%
5	Ohio	1,740	3.7%
6	New York	1,696	3.6%
7	North Carolina	1,521	3.2%
8	Illinois	1,474	3.1%
9	Michigan	1,457	3.1%
10	Georgia	1,451	3.1%
11	Arizona	1,327	2.8%
12	Washington	1,297	2.7%
13	Colorado	1,181	2.5%
14	Virginia	1,179	2.5%
15	Tennessee	1,166	2.5%
16	Missouri	1,151	2.4%
17	Indiana	1,092	2.3%
18	Wisconsin	926	2.0%
19	South Carolina	838	1.8%
20	Alabama	836	1.8%
21	Oregon	825	1.7%
22	New Jersey	795	1.7%
23	Minnesota	783	1.7%
24	Kentucky	770	1.6%
25	Oklahoma	756	1.6%
26	Louisiana	720	1.5%
27	Massachusetts	682	1.4%
28	Utah	663	1.4%
29	Arkansas	631	1.3%
30	Maryland	630	1.3%
31	Nevada	627	1.3%
32	Kansas	553	1.2%
33	New Mexico	491	1.0%
34	Iowa	479	1.0%
35	Mississippi	445	0.9%
36	Connecticut	405	0.9%
37	West Virginia	393	0.8%
38	Idaho	392	0.8%
39	Montana	311	0.7%
40	Nebraska	275	0.6%
41	Maine	274	0.6%
42	New Hampshire	265	0.6%
43	Hawaii	227	0.5%
44	Alaska	200	0.4%
45	South Dakota	191	0.4%
46	Wyoming	157	0.3%
47	North Dakota	154	0.3%
48	Rhode Island	129	0.3%
49	Delaware	112	0.2%
49	Vermont	112	0.2%
	District of Columbia	47	0.1%

Source: U.S. Department of Health and Human Services, National Center for Health Statistics
  "National Vital Statistics Reports" (Vol. 68, No. 9, 2019, https://www.cdc.gov/nchs/nvss/deaths.htm)
*Final data by state of residence. Also referred to as "intentional self-harm."

Age-Adjusted Death Rate by Suicide in 2017

National Rate = 14.0 Deaths per 100,000 Population*

ALPHA ORDER

RANK	STATE	RATE
24	Alabama	16.6
2	Alaska	27.0
20	Arizona	18.2
9	Arkansas	20.8
45	California	10.5
10	Colorado	20.3
45	Connecticut	10.5
43	Delaware	11.6
37	Florida	14.0
39	Georgia	13.6
28	Hawaii	15.2
5	Idaho	23.2
44	Illinois	11.2
25	Indiana	16.3
30	Iowa	15.0
13	Kansas	19.1
21	Kentucky	16.9
28	Louisiana	15.2
16	Maine	18.9
47	Maryland	9.8
48	Massachusetts	9.5
36	Michigan	14.1
38	Minnesota	13.8
30	Mississippi	15.0
18	Missouri	18.5
1	Montana	28.9
34	Nebraska	14.7
10	Nevada	20.3
16	New Hampshire	18.9
49	New Jersey	8.3
4	New Mexico	23.3
50	New York	8.1
35	North Carolina	14.3
12	North Dakota	20.1
33	Ohio	14.8
13	Oklahoma	19.1
15	Oregon	19.0
30	Pennsylvania	15.0
42	Rhode Island	11.8
25	South Carolina	16.3
7	South Dakota	22.5
23	Tennessee	16.8
40	Texas	13.4
6	Utah	22.7
19	Vermont	18.3
40	Virginia	13.4
21	Washington	16.9
8	West Virginia	21.1
27	Wisconsin	15.4
3	Wyoming	26.9

RANK ORDER

RANK	STATE	RATE
1	Montana	28.9
2	Alaska	27.0
3	Wyoming	26.9
4	New Mexico	23.3
5	Idaho	23.2
6	Utah	22.7
7	South Dakota	22.5
8	West Virginia	21.1
9	Arkansas	20.8
10	Colorado	20.3
10	Nevada	20.3
12	North Dakota	20.1
13	Kansas	19.1
13	Oklahoma	19.1
15	Oregon	19.0
16	Maine	18.9
16	New Hampshire	18.9
18	Missouri	18.5
19	Vermont	18.3
20	Arizona	18.2
21	Kentucky	16.9
21	Washington	16.9
23	Tennessee	16.8
24	Alabama	16.6
25	Indiana	16.3
25	South Carolina	16.3
27	Wisconsin	15.4
28	Hawaii	15.2
28	Louisiana	15.2
30	Iowa	15.0
30	Mississippi	15.0
30	Pennsylvania	15.0
33	Ohio	14.8
34	Nebraska	14.7
35	North Carolina	14.3
36	Michigan	14.1
37	Florida	14.0
38	Minnesota	13.8
39	Georgia	13.6
40	Texas	13.4
40	Virginia	13.4
42	Rhode Island	11.8
43	Delaware	11.6
44	Illinois	11.2
45	California	10.5
45	Connecticut	10.5
47	Maryland	9.8
48	Massachusetts	9.5
49	New Jersey	8.3
50	New York	8.1
	District of Columbia	6.6

Source: U.S. Department of Health and Human Services, National Center for Health Statistics
"National Vital Statistics Reports" (Vol. 68, No. 9, 2019, https://www.cdc.gov/nchs/nvss/deaths.htm)
*Final data by state of residence. Also referred to as "intentional self-harm." Age-adjusted rates based on the year 2000 standard population.

Deaths by AIDS in 2017

National Total = 5,698 Deaths*

ALPHA ORDER

RANK	STATE	DEATHS	% of USA
17	Alabama	95	1.7%
47	Alaska	3	0.1%
18	Arizona	90	1.6%
28	Arkansas	45	0.8%
2	California	635	11.1%
24	Colorado	55	1.0%
25	Connecticut	52	0.9%
35	Delaware	16	0.3%
1	Florida	754	13.2%
5	Georgia	337	5.9%
37	Hawaii	12	0.2%
42	Idaho	8	0.1%
12	Illinois	140	2.5%
21	Indiana	75	1.3%
34	Iowa	18	0.3%
33	Kansas	24	0.4%
27	Kentucky	51	0.9%
9	Louisiana	164	2.9%
42	Maine	8	0.1%
7	Maryland	199	3.5%
20	Massachusetts	78	1.4%
19	Michigan	84	1.5%
31	Minnesota	37	0.6%
15	Mississippi	112	2.0%
22	Missouri	71	1.2%
47	Montana	3	0.1%
39	Nebraska	10	0.2%
23	Nevada	58	1.0%
44	New Hampshire	6	0.1%
8	New Jersey	196	3.4%
36	New Mexico	13	0.2%
4	New York	461	8.1%
6	North Carolina	210	3.7%
50	North Dakota	2	0.0%
14	Ohio	128	2.2%
29	Oklahoma	44	0.8%
30	Oregon	42	0.7%
10	Pennsylvania	154	2.7%
37	Rhode Island	12	0.2%
11	South Carolina	151	2.7%
47	South Dakota	3	0.1%
13	Tennessee	139	2.4%
3	Texas	622	10.9%
40	Utah	9	0.2%
46	Vermont	4	0.1%
16	Virginia	106	1.9%
25	Washington	52	0.9%
40	West Virginia	9	0.2%
32	Wisconsin	28	0.5%
45	Wyoming	5	0.1%

RANK ORDER

RANK	STATE	DEATHS	% of USA
1	Florida	754	13.2%
2	California	635	11.1%
3	Texas	622	10.9%
4	New York	461	8.1%
5	Georgia	337	5.9%
6	North Carolina	210	3.7%
7	Maryland	199	3.5%
8	New Jersey	196	3.4%
9	Louisiana	164	2.9%
10	Pennsylvania	154	2.7%
11	South Carolina	151	2.7%
12	Illinois	140	2.5%
13	Tennessee	139	2.4%
14	Ohio	128	2.2%
15	Mississippi	112	2.0%
16	Virginia	106	1.9%
17	Alabama	95	1.7%
18	Arizona	90	1.6%
19	Michigan	84	1.5%
20	Massachusetts	78	1.4%
21	Indiana	75	1.3%
22	Missouri	71	1.2%
23	Nevada	58	1.0%
24	Colorado	55	1.0%
25	Connecticut	52	0.9%
25	Washington	52	0.9%
27	Kentucky	51	0.9%
28	Arkansas	45	0.8%
29	Oklahoma	44	0.8%
30	Oregon	42	0.7%
31	Minnesota	37	0.6%
32	Wisconsin	28	0.5%
33	Kansas	24	0.4%
34	Iowa	18	0.3%
35	Delaware	16	0.3%
36	New Mexico	13	0.2%
37	Hawaii	12	0.2%
37	Rhode Island	12	0.2%
39	Nebraska	10	0.2%
40	Utah	9	0.2%
40	West Virginia	9	0.2%
42	Idaho	8	0.1%
42	Maine	8	0.1%
44	New Hampshire	6	0.1%
45	Wyoming	5	0.1%
46	Vermont	4	0.1%
47	Alaska	3	0.1%
47	Montana	3	0.1%
47	South Dakota	3	0.1%
50	North Dakota	2	0.0%
	District of Columbia	68	1.2%

Source: U.S. Department of Health and Human Services, National Center for Health Statistics
   "National Vital Statistics Reports" (Vol. 68, No. 9, 2019, https://www.cdc.gov/nchs/nvss/deaths.htm)
*Final data by state of residence. AIDS is Acquired Immunodeficiency Syndrome. It is a specific group of diseases or conditions
that are indicative of severe immunosuppression related to infection with the Human Immunodeficiency Virus (HIV).

Age-Adjusted Death Rate by AIDS in 2017

National Rate = 1.6 Deaths per 100,000 Population*

ALPHA ORDER

RANK	STATE	RATE
9	Alabama	2.0
NA	Alaska**	NA
16	Arizona	1.2
15	Arkansas	1.4
14	California	1.5
26	Colorado	0.9
18	Connecticut	1.1
NA	Delaware**	NA
3	Florida	3.2
4	Georgia	3.1
NA	Hawaii**	NA
NA	Idaho**	NA
23	Illinois	1.0
23	Indiana	1.0
NA	Iowa**	NA
29	Kansas	0.8
18	Kentucky	1.1
2	Louisiana	3.4
NA	Maine**	NA
5	Maryland	2.8
26	Massachusetts	0.9
29	Michigan	0.8
31	Minnesota	0.6
1	Mississippi	3.7
18	Missouri	1.1
NA	Montana**	NA
NA	Nebraska**	NA
11	Nevada	1.8
NA	New Hampshire**	NA
11	New Jersey	1.8
NA	New Mexico**	NA
8	New York	2.1
11	North Carolina	1.8
NA	North Dakota**	NA
23	Ohio	1.0
16	Oklahoma	1.2
26	Oregon	0.9
18	Pennsylvania	1.1
NA	Rhode Island**	NA
6	South Carolina	2.7
NA	South Dakota**	NA
10	Tennessee	1.9
7	Texas	2.2
NA	Utah**	NA
NA	Vermont**	NA
18	Virginia	1.1
31	Washington	0.6
NA	West Virginia**	NA
33	Wisconsin	0.4
NA	Wyoming**	NA

RANK ORDER

RANK	STATE	RATE
1	Mississippi	3.7
2	Louisiana	3.4
3	Florida	3.2
4	Georgia	3.1
5	Maryland	2.8
6	South Carolina	2.7
7	Texas	2.2
8	New York	2.1
9	Alabama	2.0
10	Tennessee	1.9
11	Nevada	1.8
11	New Jersey	1.8
11	North Carolina	1.8
14	California	1.5
15	Arkansas	1.4
16	Arizona	1.2
16	Oklahoma	1.2
18	Connecticut	1.1
18	Kentucky	1.1
18	Missouri	1.1
18	Pennsylvania	1.1
18	Virginia	1.1
23	Illinois	1.0
23	Indiana	1.0
23	Ohio	1.0
26	Colorado	0.9
26	Massachusetts	0.9
26	Oregon	0.9
29	Kansas	0.8
29	Michigan	0.8
31	Minnesota	0.6
31	Washington	0.6
33	Wisconsin	0.4
NA	Alaska**	NA
NA	Delaware**	NA
NA	Hawaii**	NA
NA	Idaho**	NA
NA	Iowa**	NA
NA	Maine**	NA
NA	Montana**	NA
NA	Nebraska**	NA
NA	New Hampshire**	NA
NA	New Mexico**	NA
NA	North Dakota**	NA
NA	Rhode Island**	NA
NA	South Dakota**	NA
NA	Utah**	NA
NA	Vermont**	NA
NA	West Virginia**	NA
NA	Wyoming**	NA

District of Columbia   9.3

Source: U.S. Department of Health and Human Services, National Center for Health Statistics
"National Vital Statistics Reports" (Vol. 68, No. 9, 2019, https://www.cdc.gov/nchs/nvss/deaths.htm)
*Final data by state of residence. AIDS is Acquired Immunodeficiency Syndrome. It is a specific group of diseases or conditions that are indicative of severe immunosuppression related to infection with the Human Immunodeficiency Virus (HIV). Age-adjusted rates based on the year 2000 standard population.
**Insufficient data to determine a reliable rate.

Adult Per Capita Alcohol Consumption in 2017

National Per Capita = 2.6 Gallons Consumed per Adult 21 Years and Older*

ALPHA ORDER

RANK	STATE	PER CAPITA
43	Alabama	2.2
9	Alaska	3.2
26	Arizona	2.6
48	Arkansas	2.0
26	California	2.6
9	Colorado	3.2
22	Connecticut	2.7
2	Delaware	4.0
16	Florida	2.9
43	Georgia	2.2
16	Hawaii	2.9
8	Idaho	3.3
22	Illinois	2.7
36	Indiana	2.4
22	Iowa	2.7
43	Kansas	2.2
43	Kentucky	2.2
16	Louisiana	2.9
12	Maine	3.1
36	Maryland	2.4
16	Massachusetts	2.9
26	Michigan	2.6
12	Minnesota	3.1
31	Mississippi	2.5
21	Missouri	2.8
4	Montana	3.5
31	Nebraska	2.5
3	Nevada	3.8
1	New Hampshire	5.3
26	New Jersey	2.6
36	New Mexico	2.4
31	New York	2.5
36	North Carolina	2.4
4	North Dakota	3.5
42	Ohio	2.3
47	Oklahoma	2.1
12	Oregon	3.1
26	Pennsylvania	2.6
16	Rhode Island	2.9
31	South Carolina	2.5
9	South Dakota	3.2
36	Tennessee	2.4
22	Texas	2.7
50	Utah	1.6
4	Vermont	3.5
36	Virginia	2.4
31	Washington	2.5
49	West Virginia	1.9
7	Wisconsin	3.4
15	Wyoming	3.0

RANK ORDER

RANK	STATE	PER CAPITA
1	New Hampshire	5.3
2	Delaware	4.0
3	Nevada	3.8
4	Montana	3.5
4	North Dakota	3.5
4	Vermont	3.5
7	Wisconsin	3.4
8	Idaho	3.3
9	Alaska	3.2
9	Colorado	3.2
9	South Dakota	3.2
12	Maine	3.1
12	Minnesota	3.1
12	Oregon	3.1
15	Wyoming	3.0
16	Florida	2.9
16	Hawaii	2.9
16	Louisiana	2.9
16	Massachusetts	2.9
16	Rhode Island	2.9
21	Missouri	2.8
22	Connecticut	2.7
22	Illinois	2.7
22	Iowa	2.7
22	Texas	2.7
26	Arizona	2.6
26	California	2.6
26	Michigan	2.6
26	New Jersey	2.6
26	Pennsylvania	2.6
31	Mississippi	2.5
31	Nebraska	2.5
31	New York	2.5
31	South Carolina	2.5
31	Washington	2.5
36	Indiana	2.4
36	Maryland	2.4
36	New Mexico	2.4
36	North Carolina	2.4
36	Tennessee	2.4
36	Virginia	2.4
42	Ohio	2.3
43	Alabama	2.2
43	Georgia	2.2
43	Kansas	2.2
43	Kentucky	2.2
47	Oklahoma	2.1
48	Arkansas	2.0
49	West Virginia	1.9
50	Utah	1.6

District of Columbia 4.2

Source: CQ Press using data from U.S. Dept of Health and Human Services, National Institute on Alcohol Abuse and Alcoholism "Apparent Per Capita Alcohol Consumption, 1977-2017" (https://pubs.niaaa.nih.gov/publications/surveillance.htm)
*This is apparent consumption of actual alcohol, not entire volume of an alcoholic beverage (for example, wine is roughly 11% absolute alcohol content). Apparent consumption is based on several sources that together approximate sales but do not actually measure consumption. Accordingly, figures for some states may be skewed by purchases by nonresidents.

Percent of Adults Who Smoke: 2018

National Median = 16.1% of Adults*

<table>
<tr><td colspan="3">ALPHA ORDER</td><td colspan="3">RANK ORDER</td></tr>
<tr><th>RANK</th><th>STATE</th><th>PERCENT</th><th>RANK</th><th>STATE</th><th>PERCENT</th></tr>
<tr><td>11</td><td>Alabama</td><td>19.2</td><td>1</td><td>West Virginia</td><td>25.3</td></tr>
<tr><td>12</td><td>Alaska</td><td>19.1</td><td>2</td><td>Kentucky</td><td>23.4</td></tr>
<tr><td>40</td><td>Arizona</td><td>14.0</td><td>3</td><td>Arkansas</td><td>22.7</td></tr>
<tr><td>3</td><td>Arkansas</td><td>22.7</td><td>4</td><td>Indiana</td><td>21.1</td></tr>
<tr><td>49</td><td>California</td><td>11.2</td><td>5</td><td>Tennessee</td><td>20.7</td></tr>
<tr><td>37</td><td>Colorado</td><td>14.5</td><td>6</td><td>Louisiana</td><td>20.5</td></tr>
<tr><td>47</td><td>Connecticut</td><td>12.2</td><td>6</td><td>Mississippi</td><td>20.5</td></tr>
<tr><td>24</td><td>Delaware</td><td>16.5</td><td>6</td><td>Ohio</td><td>20.5</td></tr>
<tr><td>37</td><td>Florida</td><td>14.5</td><td>9</td><td>Oklahoma</td><td>19.7</td></tr>
<tr><td>26</td><td>Georgia</td><td>16.1</td><td>10</td><td>Missouri</td><td>19.4</td></tr>
<tr><td>42</td><td>Hawaii</td><td>13.4</td><td>11</td><td>Alabama</td><td>19.2</td></tr>
<tr><td>35</td><td>Idaho</td><td>14.7</td><td>12</td><td>Alaska</td><td>19.1</td></tr>
<tr><td>31</td><td>Illinois</td><td>15.5</td><td>12</td><td>North Dakota</td><td>19.1</td></tr>
<tr><td>4</td><td>Indiana</td><td>21.1</td><td>14</td><td>South Dakota</td><td>19.0</td></tr>
<tr><td>23</td><td>Iowa</td><td>16.6</td><td>15</td><td>Michigan</td><td>18.9</td></tr>
<tr><td>21</td><td>Kansas</td><td>17.3</td><td>16</td><td>Wyoming</td><td>18.8</td></tr>
<tr><td>2</td><td>Kentucky</td><td>23.4</td><td>17</td><td>Montana</td><td>18.0</td></tr>
<tr><td>6</td><td>Louisiana</td><td>20.5</td><td>17</td><td>South Carolina</td><td>18.0</td></tr>
<tr><td>19</td><td>Maine</td><td>17.8</td><td>19</td><td>Maine</td><td>17.8</td></tr>
<tr><td>46</td><td>Maryland</td><td>12.6</td><td>20</td><td>North Carolina</td><td>17.4</td></tr>
<tr><td>42</td><td>Massachusetts</td><td>13.4</td><td>21</td><td>Kansas</td><td>17.3</td></tr>
<tr><td>15</td><td>Michigan</td><td>18.9</td><td>22</td><td>Pennsylvania</td><td>17.0</td></tr>
<tr><td>33</td><td>Minnesota</td><td>15.1</td><td>23</td><td>Iowa</td><td>16.6</td></tr>
<tr><td>6</td><td>Mississippi</td><td>20.5</td><td>24</td><td>Delaware</td><td>16.5</td></tr>
<tr><td>10</td><td>Missouri</td><td>19.4</td><td>25</td><td>Wisconsin</td><td>16.4</td></tr>
<tr><td>17</td><td>Montana</td><td>18.0</td><td>26</td><td>Georgia</td><td>16.1</td></tr>
<tr><td>27</td><td>Nebraska</td><td>16.0</td><td>27</td><td>Nebraska</td><td>16.0</td></tr>
<tr><td>28</td><td>Nevada</td><td>15.7</td><td>28</td><td>Nevada</td><td>15.7</td></tr>
<tr><td>29</td><td>New Hampshire</td><td>15.6</td><td>29</td><td>New Hampshire</td><td>15.6</td></tr>
<tr><td>44</td><td>New Jersey</td><td>13.1</td><td>29</td><td>Oregon</td><td>15.6</td></tr>
<tr><td>32</td><td>New Mexico</td><td>15.2</td><td>31</td><td>Illinois</td><td>15.5</td></tr>
<tr><td>45</td><td>New York</td><td>12.8</td><td>32</td><td>New Mexico</td><td>15.2</td></tr>
<tr><td>20</td><td>North Carolina</td><td>17.4</td><td>33</td><td>Minnesota</td><td>15.1</td></tr>
<tr><td>12</td><td>North Dakota</td><td>19.1</td><td>34</td><td>Virginia</td><td>15.0</td></tr>
<tr><td>6</td><td>Ohio</td><td>20.5</td><td>35</td><td>Idaho</td><td>14.7</td></tr>
<tr><td>9</td><td>Oklahoma</td><td>19.7</td><td>36</td><td>Rhode Island</td><td>14.6</td></tr>
<tr><td>29</td><td>Oregon</td><td>15.6</td><td>37</td><td>Colorado</td><td>14.5</td></tr>
<tr><td>22</td><td>Pennsylvania</td><td>17.0</td><td>37</td><td>Florida</td><td>14.5</td></tr>
<tr><td>36</td><td>Rhode Island</td><td>14.6</td><td>39</td><td>Texas</td><td>14.4</td></tr>
<tr><td>17</td><td>South Carolina</td><td>18.0</td><td>40</td><td>Arizona</td><td>14.0</td></tr>
<tr><td>14</td><td>South Dakota</td><td>19.0</td><td>41</td><td>Vermont</td><td>13.7</td></tr>
<tr><td>5</td><td>Tennessee</td><td>20.7</td><td>42</td><td>Hawaii</td><td>13.4</td></tr>
<tr><td>39</td><td>Texas</td><td>14.4</td><td>42</td><td>Massachusetts</td><td>13.4</td></tr>
<tr><td>50</td><td>Utah</td><td>9.0</td><td>44</td><td>New Jersey</td><td>13.1</td></tr>
<tr><td>41</td><td>Vermont</td><td>13.7</td><td>45</td><td>New York</td><td>12.8</td></tr>
<tr><td>34</td><td>Virginia</td><td>15.0</td><td>46</td><td>Maryland</td><td>12.6</td></tr>
<tr><td>48</td><td>Washington</td><td>12.0</td><td>47</td><td>Connecticut</td><td>12.2</td></tr>
<tr><td>1</td><td>West Virginia</td><td>25.3</td><td>48</td><td>Washington</td><td>12.0</td></tr>
<tr><td>25</td><td>Wisconsin</td><td>16.4</td><td>49</td><td>California</td><td>11.2</td></tr>
<tr><td>16</td><td>Wyoming</td><td>18.8</td><td>50</td><td>Utah</td><td>9.0</td></tr>
<tr><td></td><td></td><td></td><td></td><td>District of Columbia</td><td>13.8</td></tr>
</table>

Source: U.S. Department of Health and Human Services, Centers for Disease Control and Prevention
"Behavioral Risk Factor Surveillance Summary Prevalence Data" (https://www.cdc.gov/brfss/brfssprevalence/index.html)
*Persons 18 and older who have smoked more than 100 cigarettes during their lifetime and who currently smoke every day or some days.

Percent of Adults Overweight or Obese: 2018

National Median = 65.8% of Adults*

ALPHA ORDER			RANK ORDER		
RANK	STATE	PERCENT	RANK	STATE	PERCENT
5	Alabama	69.7	1	Mississippi	73.3
38	Alaska	64.2	2	West Virginia	72.0
34	Arizona	64.7	3	North Dakota	71.0
4	Arkansas	70.5	4	Arkansas	70.5
45	California	62.2	5	Alabama	69.7
50	Colorado	58.9	5	South Carolina	69.7
36	Connecticut	64.4	7	Oklahoma	69.6
18	Delaware	67.8	7	Texas	69.6
29	Florida	65.9	9	Iowa	69.5
22	Georgia	67.2	10	Louisiana	69.4
49	Hawaii	59.5	11	Nebraska	68.9
39	Idaho	64.1	12	Kansas	68.7
25	Illinois	66.6	13	Kentucky	68.5
27	Indiana	66.4	14	Ohio	68.4
9	Iowa	69.5	15	Wisconsin	68.1
12	Kansas	68.7	16	North Carolina	68.0
13	Kentucky	68.5	17	Tennessee	67.9
10	Louisiana	69.4	18	Delaware	67.8
32	Maine	65.7	18	South Dakota	67.8
26	Maryland	66.5	20	Nevada	67.6
47	Massachusetts	61.7	21	Michigan	67.5
21	Michigan	67.5	22	Georgia	67.2
31	Minnesota	65.8	22	New Mexico	67.2
1	Mississippi	73.3	24	Missouri	66.9
24	Missouri	66.9	25	Illinois	66.6
42	Montana	63.2	26	Maryland	66.5
11	Nebraska	68.9	27	Indiana	66.4
20	Nevada	67.6	28	Virginia	66.3
33	New Hampshire	65.0	29	Florida	65.9
44	New Jersey	62.3	29	Pennsylvania	65.9
22	New Mexico	67.2	31	Minnesota	65.8
43	New York	62.7	32	Maine	65.7
16	North Carolina	68.0	33	New Hampshire	65.0
3	North Dakota	71.0	34	Arizona	64.7
14	Ohio	68.4	35	Rhode Island	64.6
7	Oklahoma	69.6	36	Connecticut	64.4
39	Oregon	64.1	36	Wyoming	64.4
29	Pennsylvania	65.9	38	Alaska	64.2
35	Rhode Island	64.6	39	Idaho	64.1
5	South Carolina	69.7	39	Oregon	64.1
18	South Dakota	67.8	41	Washington	63.4
17	Tennessee	67.9	42	Montana	63.2
7	Texas	69.6	43	New York	62.7
46	Utah	62.1	44	New Jersey	62.3
48	Vermont	61.1	45	California	62.2
28	Virginia	66.3	46	Utah	62.1
41	Washington	63.4	47	Massachusetts	61.7
2	West Virginia	72.0	48	Vermont	61.1
15	Wisconsin	68.1	49	Hawaii	59.5
36	Wyoming	64.4	50	Colorado	58.9
				District of Columbia	55.8

Source: CQ Press using data from U.S. Department of Health and Human Services, Centers for Disease Control and Prevention "Behavioral Risk Factor Surveillance Summary Prevalence Data" (https://www.cdc.gov/brfss/brfssprevalence/index.html)
*Persons 18 and older. Overweight is defined as a Body Mass Index (BMI) of 25.0 to 29.9 regardless of sex. Obese is a BMI of 30.0 or greater. BMI is a ratio of height to weight. As an example, a person 5' 8" and weighing 165 pounds has a BMI of 25. The same height at 197 pounds has a BMI of 30.

Percent of Children Aged 19 to 35 Months Fully Immunized in 2017

National Percent = 70.4%*

ALPHA ORDER				RANK ORDER		
RANK	STATE	PERCENT		RANK	STATE	PERCENT
21	Alabama	71.2		1	Massachusetts	82.1
32	Alaska	69.5		2	Tennessee	79.3
44	Arizona	66.5		3	New Hampshire	78.9
34	Arkansas	69.4		4	North Dakota	78.8
39	California	68.6		5	Nebraska	77.9
23	Colorado	71.0		6	Delaware	77.1
10	Connecticut	75.3		6	Virginia	77.1
6	Delaware	77.1		8	Florida	76.2
8	Florida	76.2		9	Illinois	75.4
50	Georgia	65.6		10	Connecticut	75.3
31	Hawaii	69.8		11	Maryland	75.2
36	Idaho	69.2		12	South Dakota	74.7
9	Illinois	75.4		12	West Virginia	74.7
46	Indiana	66.3		14	Rhode Island	74.4
16	Iowa	72.8		15	Vermont	74.0
32	Kansas	69.5		16	Iowa	72.8
23	Kentucky	71.0		17	Maine	72.7
28	Louisiana	70.0		18	Wyoming	72.0
17	Maine	72.7		19	New Mexico	71.9
11	Maryland	75.2		20	Nevada	71.3
1	Massachusetts	82.1		21	Alabama	71.2
29	Michigan	69.9		21	Missouri	71.2
48	Minnesota	66.1		23	Colorado	71.0
38	Mississippi	68.7		23	Kentucky	71.0
21	Missouri	71.2		25	North Carolina	70.9
47	Montana	66.2		26	Pennsylvania	70.4
5	Nebraska	77.9		27	Oregon	70.3
20	Nevada	71.3		28	Louisiana	70.0
3	New Hampshire	78.9		29	Michigan	69.9
35	New Jersey	69.3		29	Washington	69.9
19	New Mexico	71.9		31	Hawaii	69.8
42	New York	67.5		32	Alaska	69.5
25	North Carolina	70.9		32	Kansas	69.5
4	North Dakota	78.8		34	Arkansas	69.4
45	Ohio	66.4		35	New Jersey	69.3
43	Oklahoma	67.3		36	Idaho	69.2
27	Oregon	70.3		36	Wisconsin	69.2
26	Pennsylvania	70.4		38	Mississippi	68.7
14	Rhode Island	74.4		39	California	68.6
49	South Carolina	66.0		40	Utah	67.9
12	South Dakota	74.7		41	Texas	67.8
2	Tennessee	79.3		42	New York	67.5
41	Texas	67.8		43	Oklahoma	67.3
40	Utah	67.9		44	Arizona	66.5
15	Vermont	74.0		45	Ohio	66.4
6	Virginia	77.1		46	Indiana	66.3
29	Washington	69.9		47	Montana	66.2
12	West Virginia	74.7		48	Minnesota	66.1
36	Wisconsin	69.2		49	South Carolina	66.0
18	Wyoming	72.0		50	Georgia	65.6

District of Columbia   74.0

Source: U.S. Department of Health and Human Services, Centers for Disease Control and Prevention
   "Vaccination Coverage Among Children" (MMWR, Vol. 67, No. 40, October 12, 2018, https://www.cdc.gov/mmwr/)
*Fully immunized (4:3:1:3:3:1:4 series) children received four doses of DTaP (Diphtheria, Tetanus Toxoids, Pertussis [Whooping Cough]), three doses of Poliovirus Vaccine, one dose of MCV (Measles-Containing Vaccine), full series (three or four doses depending on product type) of Hib (Haemophilus influenzae type b), three doses of Hepatitis B vaccine, one dose of Varicella (chickenpox) vaccine, and four doses of PCV (pneumococcal conjugate vaccine).

XII. Households and Housing

Households in 2018

National Total = 121,520,180 Households*

ALPHA ORDER

RANK	STATE	HOUSEHOLDS	% of USA
24	Alabama	1,855,184	1.5%
49	Alaska	254,551	0.2%
15	Arizona	2,614,298	2.2%
31	Arkansas	1,156,347	1.0%
1	California	13,072,122	10.8%
22	Colorado	2,176,757	1.8%
29	Connecticut	1,378,091	1.1%
45	Delaware	367,671	0.3%
3	Florida	7,809,358	6.4%
10	Georgia	3,803,012	3.1%
42	Hawaii	455,309	0.4%
39	Idaho	640,270	0.5%
6	Illinois	4,864,864	4.0%
17	Indiana	2,599,169	2.1%
30	Iowa	1,267,873	1.0%
32	Kansas	1,133,408	0.9%
26	Kentucky	1,732,713	1.4%
25	Louisiana	1,737,220	1.4%
40	Maine	570,307	0.5%
20	Maryland	2,215,935	1.8%
14	Massachusetts	2,624,294	2.2%
9	Michigan	3,957,466	3.3%
21	Minnesota	2,194,452	1.8%
34	Mississippi	1,108,630	0.9%
18	Missouri	2,434,806	2.0%
43	Montana	431,421	0.4%
37	Nebraska	765,490	0.6%
33	Nevada	1,129,810	0.9%
41	New Hampshire	531,212	0.4%
11	New Jersey	3,249,567	2.7%
36	New Mexico	794,093	0.7%
4	New York	7,367,015	6.1%
8	North Carolina	4,011,462	3.3%
47	North Dakota	319,355	0.3%
7	Ohio	4,685,447	3.9%
28	Oklahoma	1,485,310	1.2%
27	Oregon	1,639,970	1.3%
5	Pennsylvania	5,070,931	4.2%
44	Rhode Island	406,573	0.3%
23	South Carolina	1,927,991	1.6%
46	South Dakota	345,449	0.3%
16	Tennessee	2,603,140	2.1%
2	Texas	9,776,083	8.0%
35	Utah	998,891	0.8%
48	Vermont	261,373	0.2%
12	Virginia	3,175,524	2.6%
13	Washington	2,895,575	2.4%
38	West Virginia	734,703	0.6%
19	Wisconsin	2,371,960	2.0%
50	Wyoming	230,252	0.2%

RANK ORDER

RANK	STATE	HOUSEHOLDS	% of USA
1	California	13,072,122	10.8%
2	Texas	9,776,083	8.0%
3	Florida	7,809,358	6.4%
4	New York	7,367,015	6.1%
5	Pennsylvania	5,070,931	4.2%
6	Illinois	4,864,864	4.0%
7	Ohio	4,685,447	3.9%
8	North Carolina	4,011,462	3.3%
9	Michigan	3,957,466	3.3%
10	Georgia	3,803,012	3.1%
11	New Jersey	3,249,567	2.7%
12	Virginia	3,175,524	2.6%
13	Washington	2,895,575	2.4%
14	Massachusetts	2,624,294	2.2%
15	Arizona	2,614,298	2.2%
16	Tennessee	2,603,140	2.1%
17	Indiana	2,599,169	2.1%
18	Missouri	2,434,806	2.0%
19	Wisconsin	2,371,960	2.0%
20	Maryland	2,215,935	1.8%
21	Minnesota	2,194,452	1.8%
22	Colorado	2,176,757	1.8%
23	South Carolina	1,927,991	1.6%
24	Alabama	1,855,184	1.5%
25	Louisiana	1,737,220	1.4%
26	Kentucky	1,732,713	1.4%
27	Oregon	1,639,970	1.3%
28	Oklahoma	1,485,310	1.2%
29	Connecticut	1,378,091	1.1%
30	Iowa	1,267,873	1.0%
31	Arkansas	1,156,347	1.0%
32	Kansas	1,133,408	0.9%
33	Nevada	1,129,810	0.9%
34	Mississippi	1,108,630	0.9%
35	Utah	998,891	0.8%
36	New Mexico	794,093	0.7%
37	Nebraska	765,490	0.6%
38	West Virginia	734,703	0.6%
39	Idaho	640,270	0.5%
40	Maine	570,307	0.5%
41	New Hampshire	531,212	0.4%
42	Hawaii	455,309	0.4%
43	Montana	431,421	0.4%
44	Rhode Island	406,573	0.3%
45	Delaware	367,671	0.3%
46	South Dakota	345,449	0.3%
47	North Dakota	319,355	0.3%
48	Vermont	261,373	0.2%
49	Alaska	254,551	0.2%
50	Wyoming	230,252	0.2%
	District of Columbia	287,476	0.2%

Source: U.S. Bureau of the Census
   "2018 American Community Survey-Table CP02" (https://data.census.gov/cedsci/)
*A household includes all persons who occupy a housing unit. A household consists of a single family, one person living alone,
two or more families living together, or any other group of related or unrelated persons who share living arrangements.

Persons per Household in 2018

National Rate = 2.63 Persons per Household*

ALPHA ORDER				RANK ORDER		
RANK	STATE	PERSONS		RANK	STATE	PERSONS
18	Alabama	2.57		1	Utah	3.12
5	Alaska	2.79		2	Hawaii	3.02
9	Arizona	2.68		3	California	2.96
27	Arkansas	2.53		4	Texas	2.87
3	California	2.96		5	Alaska	2.79
21	Colorado	2.56		6	Georgia	2.70
29	Connecticut	2.51		7	Idaho	2.69
21	Delaware	2.56		7	New Jersey	2.69
10	Florida	2.67		9	Arizona	2.68
6	Georgia	2.70		10	Florida	2.67
2	Hawaii	3.02		11	Maryland	2.66
7	Idaho	2.69		12	Nevada	2.65
21	Illinois	2.56		13	Louisiana	2.61
30	Indiana	2.50		13	Mississippi	2.61
44	Iowa	2.41		13	Virginia	2.61
30	Kansas	2.50		16	New Mexico	2.58
30	Kentucky	2.50		16	Oklahoma	2.58
13	Louisiana	2.61		18	Alabama	2.57
50	Maine	2.28		18	New York	2.57
11	Maryland	2.66		18	South Carolina	2.57
25	Massachusetts	2.54		21	Colorado	2.56
36	Michigan	2.47		21	Delaware	2.56
30	Minnesota	2.50		21	Illinois	2.56
13	Mississippi	2.61		24	Washington	2.55
41	Missouri	2.44		25	Massachusetts	2.54
45	Montana	2.40		25	Tennessee	2.54
39	Nebraska	2.45		27	Arkansas	2.53
12	Nevada	2.65		28	North Carolina	2.52
36	New Hampshire	2.47		29	Connecticut	2.51
7	New Jersey	2.69		30	Indiana	2.50
16	New Mexico	2.58		30	Kansas	2.50
18	New York	2.57		30	Kentucky	2.50
28	North Carolina	2.52		30	Minnesota	2.50
48	North Dakota	2.30		30	Oregon	2.50
43	Ohio	2.43		30	Rhode Island	2.50
16	Oklahoma	2.58		36	Michigan	2.47
30	Oregon	2.50		36	New Hampshire	2.47
41	Pennsylvania	2.44		38	South Dakota	2.46
30	Rhode Island	2.50		39	Nebraska	2.45
18	South Carolina	2.57		39	Wyoming	2.45
38	South Dakota	2.46		41	Missouri	2.44
25	Tennessee	2.54		41	Pennsylvania	2.44
4	Texas	2.87		43	Ohio	2.43
1	Utah	3.12		44	Iowa	2.41
48	Vermont	2.30		45	Montana	2.40
13	Virginia	2.61		46	West Virginia	2.39
24	Washington	2.55		46	Wisconsin	2.39
46	West Virginia	2.39		48	North Dakota	2.30
46	Wisconsin	2.39		48	Vermont	2.30
39	Wyoming	2.45		50	Maine	2.28
					District of Columbia	2.31

Source: U.S. Bureau of the Census
  "2018 American Community Survey-Table CP02" (https://data.census.gov/cedsci/)
*A household includes all persons who occupy a housing unit. A household consists of a single family, one person living alone, two or more families living together, or any other group of related or unrelated persons who share living arrangements.

Percent of Households with One Person in 2018

National Percent = 28.0% of Households*

<table>
<tr><td colspan="3">ALPHA ORDER</td><td colspan="3">RANK ORDER</td></tr>
<tr><th>RANK</th><th>STATE</th><th>PERCENT</th><th>RANK</th><th>STATE</th><th>PERCENT</th></tr>
<tr><td>10</td><td>Alabama</td><td>29.9</td><td>1</td><td>North Dakota</td><td>32.0</td></tr>
<tr><td>44</td><td>Alaska</td><td>26.0</td><td>2</td><td>Rhode Island</td><td>31.5</td></tr>
<tr><td>42</td><td>Arizona</td><td>27.0</td><td>3</td><td>Vermont</td><td>31.3</td></tr>
<tr><td>32</td><td>Arkansas</td><td>28.2</td><td>4</td><td>New Mexico</td><td>31.1</td></tr>
<tr><td>49</td><td>California</td><td>24.0</td><td>4</td><td>Ohio</td><td>31.1</td></tr>
<tr><td>33</td><td>Colorado</td><td>28.1</td><td>4</td><td>West Virginia</td><td>31.1</td></tr>
<tr><td>23</td><td>Connecticut</td><td>29.1</td><td>7</td><td>Maine</td><td>30.8</td></tr>
<tr><td>28</td><td>Delaware</td><td>28.9</td><td>8</td><td>Louisiana</td><td>30.6</td></tr>
<tr><td>25</td><td>Florida</td><td>29.0</td><td>9</td><td>Montana</td><td>30.0</td></tr>
<tr><td>38</td><td>Georgia</td><td>27.5</td><td>10</td><td>Alabama</td><td>29.9</td></tr>
<tr><td>48</td><td>Hawaii</td><td>24.5</td><td>10</td><td>New York</td><td>29.9</td></tr>
<tr><td>47</td><td>Idaho</td><td>25.4</td><td>10</td><td>Pennsylvania</td><td>29.9</td></tr>
<tr><td>14</td><td>Illinois</td><td>29.6</td><td>13</td><td>Missouri</td><td>29.7</td></tr>
<tr><td>28</td><td>Indiana</td><td>28.9</td><td>14</td><td>Illinois</td><td>29.6</td></tr>
<tr><td>14</td><td>Iowa</td><td>29.6</td><td>14</td><td>Iowa</td><td>29.6</td></tr>
<tr><td>21</td><td>Kansas</td><td>29.2</td><td>14</td><td>Michigan</td><td>29.6</td></tr>
<tr><td>33</td><td>Kentucky</td><td>28.1</td><td>14</td><td>Mississippi</td><td>29.6</td></tr>
<tr><td>8</td><td>Louisiana</td><td>30.6</td><td>14</td><td>Nebraska</td><td>29.6</td></tr>
<tr><td>7</td><td>Maine</td><td>30.8</td><td>19</td><td>Wisconsin</td><td>29.5</td></tr>
<tr><td>40</td><td>Maryland</td><td>27.3</td><td>20</td><td>Nevada</td><td>29.4</td></tr>
<tr><td>25</td><td>Massachusetts</td><td>29.0</td><td>21</td><td>Kansas</td><td>29.2</td></tr>
<tr><td>14</td><td>Michigan</td><td>29.6</td><td>21</td><td>South Dakota</td><td>29.2</td></tr>
<tr><td>30</td><td>Minnesota</td><td>28.7</td><td>23</td><td>Connecticut</td><td>29.1</td></tr>
<tr><td>14</td><td>Mississippi</td><td>29.6</td><td>23</td><td>Wyoming</td><td>29.1</td></tr>
<tr><td>13</td><td>Missouri</td><td>29.7</td><td>25</td><td>Florida</td><td>29.0</td></tr>
<tr><td>9</td><td>Montana</td><td>30.0</td><td>25</td><td>Massachusetts</td><td>29.0</td></tr>
<tr><td>14</td><td>Nebraska</td><td>29.6</td><td>25</td><td>South Carolina</td><td>29.0</td></tr>
<tr><td>20</td><td>Nevada</td><td>29.4</td><td>28</td><td>Delaware</td><td>28.9</td></tr>
<tr><td>37</td><td>New Hampshire</td><td>27.6</td><td>28</td><td>Indiana</td><td>28.9</td></tr>
<tr><td>44</td><td>New Jersey</td><td>26.0</td><td>30</td><td>Minnesota</td><td>28.7</td></tr>
<tr><td>4</td><td>New Mexico</td><td>31.1</td><td>31</td><td>North Carolina</td><td>28.5</td></tr>
<tr><td>10</td><td>New York</td><td>29.9</td><td>32</td><td>Arkansas</td><td>28.2</td></tr>
<tr><td>31</td><td>North Carolina</td><td>28.5</td><td>33</td><td>Colorado</td><td>28.1</td></tr>
<tr><td>1</td><td>North Dakota</td><td>32.0</td><td>33</td><td>Kentucky</td><td>28.1</td></tr>
<tr><td>4</td><td>Ohio</td><td>31.1</td><td>35</td><td>Oklahoma</td><td>28.0</td></tr>
<tr><td>35</td><td>Oklahoma</td><td>28.0</td><td>35</td><td>Tennessee</td><td>28.0</td></tr>
<tr><td>40</td><td>Oregon</td><td>27.3</td><td>37</td><td>New Hampshire</td><td>27.6</td></tr>
<tr><td>10</td><td>Pennsylvania</td><td>29.9</td><td>38</td><td>Georgia</td><td>27.5</td></tr>
<tr><td>2</td><td>Rhode Island</td><td>31.5</td><td>38</td><td>Virginia</td><td>27.5</td></tr>
<tr><td>25</td><td>South Carolina</td><td>29.0</td><td>40</td><td>Maryland</td><td>27.3</td></tr>
<tr><td>21</td><td>South Dakota</td><td>29.2</td><td>40</td><td>Oregon</td><td>27.3</td></tr>
<tr><td>35</td><td>Tennessee</td><td>28.0</td><td>42</td><td>Arizona</td><td>27.0</td></tr>
<tr><td>46</td><td>Texas</td><td>25.5</td><td>43</td><td>Washington</td><td>26.2</td></tr>
<tr><td>50</td><td>Utah</td><td>19.4</td><td>44</td><td>Alaska</td><td>26.0</td></tr>
<tr><td>3</td><td>Vermont</td><td>31.3</td><td>44</td><td>New Jersey</td><td>26.0</td></tr>
<tr><td>38</td><td>Virginia</td><td>27.5</td><td>46</td><td>Texas</td><td>25.5</td></tr>
<tr><td>43</td><td>Washington</td><td>26.2</td><td>47</td><td>Idaho</td><td>25.4</td></tr>
<tr><td>4</td><td>West Virginia</td><td>31.1</td><td>48</td><td>Hawaii</td><td>24.5</td></tr>
<tr><td>19</td><td>Wisconsin</td><td>29.5</td><td>49</td><td>California</td><td>24.0</td></tr>
<tr><td>23</td><td>Wyoming</td><td>29.1</td><td>50</td><td>Utah</td><td>19.4</td></tr>
<tr><td></td><td></td><td></td><td></td><td>District of Columbia</td><td>45.6</td></tr>
</table>

Source: U.S. Bureau of the Census
   "2018 American Community Survey-Table CP02" (https://data.census.gov/cedsci/)
*A household includes all persons who occupy a housing unit. A household consists of a single family, one person living alone, two or more families living together, or any other group of related or unrelated persons who share living arrangements.

Percent of Households Headed by Married Couples in 2018

National Percent = 47.9% of Households*

ALPHA ORDER				RANK ORDER		
RANK	STATE	PERCENT		RANK	STATE	PERCENT
31	Alabama	47.4		1	Utah	60.9
9	Alaska	50.2		2	Idaho	54.5
28	Arizona	47.7		3	Hawaii	51.6
25	Arkansas	47.9		3	New Hampshire	51.6
15	California	49.4		5	New Jersey	51.2
17	Colorado	49.1		6	Wyoming	50.7
34	Connecticut	47.2		7	Kansas	50.4
32	Delaware	47.3		8	Minnesota	50.3
42	Florida	46.6		9	Alaska	50.2
37	Georgia	46.9		9	Washington	50.2
3	Hawaii	51.6		11	South Dakota	49.8
2	Idaho	54.5		11	Texas	49.8
35	Illinois	47.1		13	Virginia	49.7
24	Indiana	48.0		14	Nebraska	49.6
17	Iowa	49.1		15	California	49.4
7	Kansas	50.4		15	Montana	49.4
20	Kentucky	48.4		17	Colorado	49.1
49	Louisiana	43.1		17	Iowa	49.1
38	Maine	46.8		19	Wisconsin	48.5
22	Maryland	48.3		20	Kentucky	48.4
40	Massachusetts	46.7		20	Oregon	48.4
40	Michigan	46.7		22	Maryland	48.3
8	Minnesota	50.3		23	Oklahoma	48.2
45	Mississippi	44.4		24	Indiana	48.0
29	Missouri	47.6		25	Arkansas	47.9
15	Montana	49.4		25	North Carolina	47.9
14	Nebraska	49.6		25	Tennessee	47.9
48	Nevada	43.3		28	Arizona	47.7
3	New Hampshire	51.6		29	Missouri	47.6
5	New Jersey	51.2		29	Pennsylvania	47.6
47	New Mexico	43.4		31	Alabama	47.4
46	New York	44.0		32	Delaware	47.3
25	North Carolina	47.9		32	West Virginia	47.3
38	North Dakota	46.8		34	Connecticut	47.2
44	Ohio	45.1		35	Illinois	47.1
23	Oklahoma	48.2		36	Vermont	47.0
20	Oregon	48.4		37	Georgia	46.9
29	Pennsylvania	47.6		38	Maine	46.8
50	Rhode Island	43.0		38	North Dakota	46.8
43	South Carolina	46.5		40	Massachusetts	46.7
11	South Dakota	49.8		40	Michigan	46.7
25	Tennessee	47.9		42	Florida	46.6
11	Texas	49.8		43	South Carolina	46.5
1	Utah	60.9		44	Ohio	45.1
36	Vermont	47.0		45	Mississippi	44.4
13	Virginia	49.7		46	New York	44.0
9	Washington	50.2		47	New Mexico	43.4
32	West Virginia	47.3		48	Nevada	43.3
19	Wisconsin	48.5		49	Louisiana	43.1
6	Wyoming	50.7		50	Rhode Island	43.0
					District of Columbia	25.4

Source: U.S. Bureau of the Census
  "2018 American Community Survey-Table CP02" (https://data.census.gov/cedsci/)
*A household includes all persons who occupy a housing unit. A household consists of a single family, one person living alone, two or more families living together, or any other group of related or unrelated persons who share living arrangements. Includes married same-sex couple households.

Percent of Households Headed by Single Mothers in 2018

National Percent = 6.4% of Households*

ALPHA ORDER				RANK ORDER		
RANK	STATE	PERCENT		RANK	STATE	PERCENT
9	Alabama	6.9		1	Mississippi	8.9
37	Alaska	5.4		2	Louisiana	8.3
24	Arizona	6.2		3	Georgia	7.9
4	Arkansas	7.7		4	Arkansas	7.7
28	California	6.0		5	Texas	7.6
44	Colorado	5.1		6	Oklahoma	7.3
14	Connecticut	6.6		7	South Carolina	7.1
18	Delaware	6.4		8	Ohio	7.0
24	Florida	6.2		9	Alabama	6.9
3	Georgia	7.9		9	North Carolina	6.9
46	Hawaii	5.0		11	New Mexico	6.8
40	Idaho	5.3		11	Rhode Island	6.8
18	Illinois	6.4		13	Tennessee	6.7
14	Indiana	6.6		14	Connecticut	6.6
27	Iowa	6.1		14	Indiana	6.6
32	Kansas	5.8		14	Kentucky	6.6
14	Kentucky	6.6		17	Maryland	6.5
2	Louisiana	8.3		18	Delaware	6.4
44	Maine	5.1		18	Illinois	6.4
17	Maryland	6.5		18	Nevada	6.4
28	Massachusetts	6.0		18	New York	6.4
22	Michigan	6.3		22	Michigan	6.3
37	Minnesota	5.4		22	Missouri	6.3
1	Mississippi	8.9		24	Arizona	6.2
22	Missouri	6.3		24	Florida	6.2
48	Montana	4.7		24	South Dakota	6.2
28	Nebraska	6.0		27	Iowa	6.1
18	Nevada	6.4		28	California	6.0
49	New Hampshire	4.6		28	Massachusetts	6.0
34	New Jersey	5.7		28	Nebraska	6.0
11	New Mexico	6.8		31	Pennsylvania	5.9
18	New York	6.4		32	Kansas	5.8
9	North Carolina	6.9		32	Virginia	5.8
40	North Dakota	5.3		34	New Jersey	5.7
8	Ohio	7.0		35	West Virginia	5.6
6	Oklahoma	7.3		35	Wisconsin	5.6
40	Oregon	5.3		37	Alaska	5.4
31	Pennsylvania	5.9		37	Minnesota	5.4
11	Rhode Island	6.8		37	Washington	5.4
7	South Carolina	7.1		40	Idaho	5.3
24	South Dakota	6.2		40	North Dakota	5.3
13	Tennessee	6.7		40	Oregon	5.3
5	Texas	7.6		43	Wyoming	5.2
47	Utah	4.9		44	Colorado	5.1
50	Vermont	4.5		44	Maine	5.1
32	Virginia	5.8		46	Hawaii	5.0
37	Washington	5.4		47	Utah	4.9
35	West Virginia	5.6		48	Montana	4.7
35	Wisconsin	5.6		49	New Hampshire	4.6
43	Wyoming	5.2		50	Vermont	4.5
					District of Columbia	6.8

Source: U.S. Bureau of the Census
   "2018 American Community Survey-Table CP02" (https://data.census.gov/cedsci/)
*No spouse present in household with children under eighteen years old. A household includes all persons who occupy a housing unit. A household consists of a single family, one person living alone, two or more families living together, or any other group of related or unrelated persons who share living arrangements.

Percent of Households Headed by Single Fathers in 2018

National Percent = 2.3% of Households*

ALPHA ORDER

RANK	STATE	PERCENT
45	Alabama	1.9
2	Alaska	3.0
2	Arizona	3.0
13	Arkansas	2.4
9	California	2.5
29	Colorado	2.2
19	Connecticut	2.3
13	Delaware	2.4
41	Florida	2.0
32	Georgia	2.1
48	Hawaii	1.6
19	Idaho	2.3
32	Illinois	2.1
6	Indiana	2.7
7	Iowa	2.6
19	Kansas	2.3
19	Kentucky	2.3
13	Louisiana	2.4
32	Maine	2.1
32	Maryland	2.1
48	Massachusetts	1.6
13	Michigan	2.4
19	Minnesota	2.3
48	Mississippi	1.6
19	Missouri	2.3
9	Montana	2.5
9	Nebraska	2.5
1	Nevada	3.2
32	New Hampshire	2.1
45	New Jersey	1.9
4	New Mexico	2.8
45	New York	1.9
32	North Carolina	2.1
13	North Dakota	2.4
9	Ohio	2.5
4	Oklahoma	2.8
29	Oregon	2.2
19	Pennsylvania	2.3
32	Rhode Island	2.1
32	South Carolina	2.1
19	South Dakota	2.3
19	Tennessee	2.3
19	Texas	2.3
32	Utah	2.1
29	Vermont	2.2
41	Virginia	2.0
13	Washington	2.4
41	West Virginia	2.0
7	Wisconsin	2.6
41	Wyoming	2.0

RANK ORDER

RANK	STATE	PERCENT
1	Nevada	3.2
2	Alaska	3.0
2	Arizona	3.0
4	New Mexico	2.8
4	Oklahoma	2.8
6	Indiana	2.7
7	Iowa	2.6
7	Wisconsin	2.6
9	California	2.5
9	Montana	2.5
9	Nebraska	2.5
9	Ohio	2.5
13	Arkansas	2.4
13	Delaware	2.4
13	Louisiana	2.4
13	Michigan	2.4
13	North Dakota	2.4
13	Washington	2.4
19	Connecticut	2.3
19	Idaho	2.3
19	Kansas	2.3
19	Kentucky	2.3
19	Minnesota	2.3
19	Missouri	2.3
19	Pennsylvania	2.3
19	South Dakota	2.3
19	Tennessee	2.3
19	Texas	2.3
29	Colorado	2.2
29	Oregon	2.2
29	Vermont	2.2
32	Georgia	2.1
32	Illinois	2.1
32	Maine	2.1
32	Maryland	2.1
32	New Hampshire	2.1
32	North Carolina	2.1
32	Rhode Island	2.1
32	South Carolina	2.1
32	Utah	2.1
41	Florida	2.0
41	Virginia	2.0
41	West Virginia	2.0
41	Wyoming	2.0
45	Alabama	1.9
45	New Jersey	1.9
45	New York	1.9
48	Hawaii	1.6
48	Massachusetts	1.6
48	Mississippi	1.6

	District of Columbia	1.6

Source: U.S. Bureau of the Census
   "2018 American Community Survey-Table CP02" (https://data.census.gov/cedsci/)
*No spouse present in household with children under eighteen years old. A household includes all persons who occupy a housing unit. A household consists of a single family, one person living alone, two or more families living together, or any other group of related or unrelated persons who share living arrangements.

Same-Sex Couple Households in 2018

National Total = 995,420 Households*

ALPHA ORDER					RANK ORDER			
RANK	STATE	HOUSEHOLDS	% of USA		RANK	STATE	HOUSEHOLDS	% of USA
30	Alabama	9,121	0.9%		1	California	135,274	13.6%
49	Alaska	1,468	0.1%		2	Florida	79,144	8.0%
13	Arizona	26,097	2.6%		3	Texas	73,579	7.4%
35	Arkansas	6,156	0.6%		4	New York	70,531	7.1%
1	California	135,274	13.6%		5	Illinois	36,619	3.7%
17	Colorado	18,801	1.9%		6	Pennsylvania	34,016	3.4%
25	Connecticut	11,729	1.2%		7	Ohio	32,863	3.3%
38	Delaware	5,772	0.6%		8	Washington	32,565	3.3%
2	Florida	79,144	8.0%		9	Georgia	31,866	3.2%
9	Georgia	31,866	3.2%		10	North Carolina	28,376	2.9%
43	Hawaii	3,746	0.4%		11	Massachusetts	27,395	2.8%
44	Idaho	3,178	0.3%		12	Michigan	26,924	2.7%
5	Illinois	36,619	3.7%		13	Arizona	26,097	2.6%
21	Indiana	17,832	1.8%		14	Virginia	23,299	2.3%
33	Iowa	7,194	0.7%		15	New Jersey	22,418	2.3%
32	Kansas	8,141	0.8%		16	Oregon	19,022	1.9%
24	Kentucky	11,952	1.2%		17	Colorado	18,801	1.9%
27	Louisiana	11,181	1.1%		18	Maryland	18,794	1.9%
34	Maine	6,812	0.7%		19	Missouri	18,746	1.9%
18	Maryland	18,794	1.9%		20	Tennessee	18,125	1.8%
11	Massachusetts	27,395	2.8%		21	Indiana	17,832	1.8%
12	Michigan	26,924	2.7%		22	Wisconsin	16,436	1.7%
23	Minnesota	15,938	1.6%		23	Minnesota	15,938	1.6%
39	Mississippi	4,454	0.4%		24	Kentucky	11,952	1.2%
19	Missouri	18,746	1.9%		25	Connecticut	11,729	1.2%
46	Montana	2,021	0.2%		26	South Carolina	11,259	1.1%
40	Nebraska	4,375	0.4%		27	Louisiana	11,181	1.1%
29	Nevada	9,836	1.0%		28	Oklahoma	10,149	1.0%
37	New Hampshire	5,908	0.6%		29	Nevada	9,836	1.0%
15	New Jersey	22,418	2.3%		30	Alabama	9,121	0.9%
31	New Mexico	8,237	0.8%		31	New Mexico	8,237	0.8%
4	New York	70,531	7.1%		32	Kansas	8,141	0.8%
10	North Carolina	28,376	2.9%		33	Iowa	7,194	0.7%
47	North Dakota	1,610	0.2%		34	Maine	6,812	0.7%
7	Ohio	32,863	3.3%		35	Arkansas	6,156	0.6%
28	Oklahoma	10,149	1.0%		36	Utah	6,017	0.6%
16	Oregon	19,022	1.9%		37	New Hampshire	5,908	0.6%
6	Pennsylvania	34,016	3.4%		38	Delaware	5,772	0.6%
42	Rhode Island	4,051	0.4%		39	Mississippi	4,454	0.4%
26	South Carolina	11,259	1.1%		40	Nebraska	4,375	0.4%
48	South Dakota	1,525	0.2%		41	West Virginia	4,072	0.4%
20	Tennessee	18,125	1.8%		42	Rhode Island	4,051	0.4%
3	Texas	73,579	7.4%		43	Hawaii	3,746	0.4%
36	Utah	6,017	0.6%		44	Idaho	3,178	0.3%
45	Vermont	2,955	0.3%		45	Vermont	2,955	0.3%
14	Virginia	23,299	2.3%		46	Montana	2,021	0.2%
8	Washington	32,565	3.3%		47	North Dakota	1,610	0.2%
41	West Virginia	4,072	0.4%		48	South Dakota	1,525	0.2%
22	Wisconsin	16,436	1.7%		49	Alaska	1,468	0.1%
50	Wyoming	878	0.1%		50	Wyoming	878	0.1%
						District of Columbia	6,963	0.7%

Source: U.S. Bureau of the Census
 "Same Sex Couples Main" (https://www.census.gov/topics/families/same-sex-couples.html)
*The total is comprised of 592,561 married households and 402,859 unmarried households. Male couples are 485,065 of the households. Female couples are 510,355 of the households.

Percent of Same-Sex Household Couples Who Are Married: 2018

National Percent = 59.5% of Same-Sex Households*

ALPHA ORDER

RANK	STATE	PERCENT
23	Alabama	61.0
39	Alaska	54.8
38	Arizona	55.3
31	Arkansas	58.8
27	California	59.7
14	Colorado	62.9
4	Connecticut	70.7
43	Delaware	54.2
17	Florida	61.7
29	Georgia	59.6
11	Hawaii	65.2
26	Idaho	60.3
20	Illinois	61.4
45	Indiana	54.0
27	Iowa	59.7
43	Kansas	54.2
16	Kentucky	61.9
41	Louisiana	54.7
37	Maine	55.9
10	Maryland	66.1
22	Massachusetts	61.3
25	Michigan	60.4
18	Minnesota	61.6
7	Mississippi	67.8
13	Missouri	63.3
24	Montana	60.6
9	Nebraska	67.1
49	Nevada	48.4
30	New Hampshire	59.4
20	New Jersey	61.4
31	New Mexico	58.8
33	New York	57.6
36	North Carolina	56.4
50	North Dakota	37.6
42	Ohio	54.4
8	Oklahoma	67.5
18	Oregon	61.6
35	Pennsylvania	57.4
39	Rhode Island	54.8
46	South Carolina	52.9
3	South Dakota	77.8
48	Tennessee	52.3
34	Texas	57.5
5	Utah	69.5
2	Vermont	79.3
12	Virginia	63.8
15	Washington	62.7
6	West Virginia	68.4
47	Wisconsin	52.5
1	Wyoming	92.4

RANK ORDER

RANK	STATE	PERCENT
1	Wyoming	92.4
2	Vermont	79.3
3	South Dakota	77.8
4	Connecticut	70.7
5	Utah	69.5
6	West Virginia	68.4
7	Mississippi	67.8
8	Oklahoma	67.5
9	Nebraska	67.1
10	Maryland	66.1
11	Hawaii	65.2
12	Virginia	63.8
13	Missouri	63.3
14	Colorado	62.9
15	Washington	62.7
16	Kentucky	61.9
17	Florida	61.7
18	Minnesota	61.6
18	Oregon	61.6
20	Illinois	61.4
20	New Jersey	61.4
22	Massachusetts	61.3
23	Alabama	61.0
24	Montana	60.6
25	Michigan	60.4
26	Idaho	60.3
27	California	59.7
27	Iowa	59.7
29	Georgia	59.6
30	New Hampshire	59.4
31	Arkansas	58.8
31	New Mexico	58.8
33	New York	57.6
34	Texas	57.5
35	Pennsylvania	57.4
36	North Carolina	56.4
37	Maine	55.9
38	Arizona	55.3
39	Alaska	54.8
39	Rhode Island	54.8
41	Louisiana	54.7
42	Ohio	54.4
43	Delaware	54.2
43	Kansas	54.2
45	Indiana	54.0
46	South Carolina	52.9
47	Wisconsin	52.5
48	Tennessee	52.3
49	Nevada	48.4
50	North Dakota	37.6
	District of Columbia	61.0

Source: U.S. Bureau of the Census
   "Same Sex Couples Main" (https://www.census.gov/topics/families/same-sex-couples.html)
*Male-couple households are 59 percent married. Female-couple households are 60 percent married.

Housing Units in 2018

National Total = 138,539,906 Housing Units*

ALPHA ORDER

RANK	STATE	HOUSING UNITS	% of USA
24	Alabama	2,274,711	1.6%
49	Alaska	318,352	0.2%
14	Arizona	3,035,902	2.2%
31	Arkansas	1,380,521	1.0%
1	California	14,277,867	10.3%
22	Colorado	2,424,128	1.7%
29	Connecticut	1,521,123	1.1%
45	Delaware	438,659	0.3%
3	Florida	9,547,762	6.9%
10	Georgia	4,326,266	3.1%
42	Hawaii	546,261	0.4%
40	Idaho	735,703	0.5%
6	Illinois	5,376,176	3.9%
17	Indiana	2,903,576	2.1%
30	Iowa	1,409,568	1.0%
33	Kansas	1,280,553	0.9%
26	Kentucky	1,995,187	1.4%
25	Louisiana	2,076,136	1.5%
39	Maine	746,592	0.5%
20	Maryland	2,458,779	1.8%
16	Massachusetts	2,915,043	2.1%
9	Michigan	4,614,552	3.3%
21	Minnesota	2,455,637	1.8%
32	Mississippi	1,332,631	1.0%
18	Missouri	2,806,296	2.0%
43	Montana	515,161	0.4%
38	Nebraska	845,011	0.6%
34	Nevada	1,268,717	0.9%
41	New Hampshire	638,112	0.5%
11	New Jersey	3,628,198	2.6%
36	New Mexico	943,232	0.7%
4	New York	8,363,847	6.0%
8	North Carolina	4,684,962	3.4%
47	North Dakota	377,661	0.3%
7	Ohio	5,217,617	3.8%
28	Oklahoma	1,743,073	1.3%
27	Oregon	1,788,743	1.3%
5	Pennsylvania	5,713,136	4.1%
44	Rhode Island	469,153	0.3%
23	South Carolina	2,318,291	1.7%
46	South Dakota	397,506	0.3%
15	Tennessee	2,992,412	2.2%
2	Texas	11,101,498	8.0%
35	Utah	1,108,739	0.8%
48	Vermont	337,133	0.2%
12	Virginia	3,538,985	2.6%
13	Washington	3,148,084	2.3%
37	West Virginia	893,742	0.6%
19	Wisconsin	2,710,718	2.0%
50	Wyoming	278,615	0.2%

RANK ORDER

RANK	STATE	HOUSING UNITS	% of USA
1	California	14,277,867	10.3%
2	Texas	11,101,498	8.0%
3	Florida	9,547,762	6.9%
4	New York	8,363,847	6.0%
5	Pennsylvania	5,713,136	4.1%
6	Illinois	5,376,176	3.9%
7	Ohio	5,217,617	3.8%
8	North Carolina	4,684,962	3.4%
9	Michigan	4,614,552	3.3%
10	Georgia	4,326,266	3.1%
11	New Jersey	3,628,198	2.6%
12	Virginia	3,538,985	2.6%
13	Washington	3,148,084	2.3%
14	Arizona	3,035,902	2.2%
15	Tennessee	2,992,412	2.2%
16	Massachusetts	2,915,043	2.1%
17	Indiana	2,903,576	2.1%
18	Missouri	2,806,296	2.0%
19	Wisconsin	2,710,718	2.0%
20	Maryland	2,458,779	1.8%
21	Minnesota	2,455,637	1.8%
22	Colorado	2,424,128	1.7%
23	South Carolina	2,318,291	1.7%
24	Alabama	2,274,711	1.6%
25	Louisiana	2,076,136	1.5%
26	Kentucky	1,995,187	1.4%
27	Oregon	1,788,743	1.3%
28	Oklahoma	1,743,073	1.3%
29	Connecticut	1,521,123	1.1%
30	Iowa	1,409,568	1.0%
31	Arkansas	1,380,521	1.0%
32	Mississippi	1,332,631	1.0%
33	Kansas	1,280,553	0.9%
34	Nevada	1,268,717	0.9%
35	Utah	1,108,739	0.8%
36	New Mexico	943,232	0.7%
37	West Virginia	893,742	0.6%
38	Nebraska	845,011	0.6%
39	Maine	746,592	0.5%
40	Idaho	735,703	0.5%
41	New Hampshire	638,112	0.5%
42	Hawaii	546,261	0.4%
43	Montana	515,161	0.4%
44	Rhode Island	469,153	0.3%
45	Delaware	438,659	0.3%
46	South Dakota	397,506	0.3%
47	North Dakota	377,661	0.3%
48	Vermont	337,133	0.2%
49	Alaska	318,352	0.2%
50	Wyoming	278,615	0.2%
	District of Columbia	319,579	0.2%

Source: U.S. Bureau of the Census
  "2018 American Community Survey-Table CP04" (https://data.census.gov/cedsci/)
*A housing unit is a house, an apartment, a mobile home, a group of rooms, or a single room that is occupied (or if vacant, is intended for occupancy) as separate living quarters. Separate living quarters are those in which the occupants live and eat separately from any other persons in the building and which have direct access from the outside of the building or through a common hall.

Housing Units per Square Mile in 2018

National Average = 39.2 Housing Units*

ALPHA ORDER			RANK ORDER		
RANK	STATE	RATE	RANK	STATE	RATE
26	Alabama	44.8	1	New Jersey	489.2
50	Alaska	0.6	2	Rhode Island	449.0
33	Arizona	26.7	3	Massachusetts	371.8
34	Arkansas	26.5	4	Connecticut	314.0
13	California	91.5	5	Maryland	251.6
38	Colorado	23.4	6	Delaware	224.5
4	Connecticut	314.0	7	New York	177.1
6	Delaware	224.5	8	Florida	177.0
8	Florida	177.0	9	Pennsylvania	127.5
19	Georgia	74.7	10	Ohio	127.4
15	Hawaii	85.0	11	Illinois	96.7
44	Idaho	8.9	12	North Carolina	96.2
11	Illinois	96.7	13	California	91.5
17	Indiana	81.0	14	Virginia	89.4
36	Iowa	25.2	15	Hawaii	85.0
40	Kansas	15.7	16	Michigan	81.2
22	Kentucky	50.2	17	Indiana	81.0
24	Louisiana	47.7	18	South Carolina	77.0
37	Maine	24.2	19	Georgia	74.7
5	Maryland	251.6	20	Tennessee	72.6
3	Massachusetts	371.8	21	New Hampshire	71.2
16	Michigan	81.2	22	Kentucky	50.2
31	Minnesota	30.8	23	Wisconsin	49.9
32	Mississippi	28.4	24	Louisiana	47.7
28	Missouri	40.7	25	Washington	47.3
48	Montana	3.5	26	Alabama	44.8
43	Nebraska	11.0	27	Texas	42.4
42	Nevada	11.6	28	Missouri	40.7
21	New Hampshire	71.2	29	West Virginia	37.1
1	New Jersey	489.2	30	Vermont	36.4
45	New Mexico	7.8	31	Minnesota	30.8
7	New York	177.1	32	Mississippi	28.4
12	North Carolina	96.2	33	Arizona	26.7
46	North Dakota	5.5	34	Arkansas	26.5
10	Ohio	127.4	35	Oklahoma	25.4
35	Oklahoma	25.4	36	Iowa	25.2
39	Oregon	18.6	37	Maine	24.2
9	Pennsylvania	127.5	38	Colorado	23.4
2	Rhode Island	449.0	39	Oregon	18.6
18	South Carolina	77.0	40	Kansas	15.7
47	South Dakota	5.2	41	Utah	13.5
20	Tennessee	72.6	42	Nevada	11.6
27	Texas	42.4	43	Nebraska	11.0
41	Utah	13.5	44	Idaho	8.9
30	Vermont	36.4	45	New Mexico	7.8
14	Virginia	89.4	46	North Dakota	5.5
25	Washington	47.3	47	South Dakota	5.2
29	West Virginia	37.1	48	Montana	3.5
23	Wisconsin	49.9	49	Wyoming	2.9
49	Wyoming	2.9	50	Alaska	0.6

District of Columbia 5,239.0

Source: CQ Press using data from U.S. Bureau of the Census
   "2018 American Community Survey-Table CP04" (https://data.census.gov/cedsci/)
*Based on land area. A housing unit is a house, an apartment, a mobile home, a group of rooms, or a single room that is occupied (or if vacant, is intended for occupancy) as separate living quarters. Separate living quarters are those in which the occupants live and eat separately from any other persons in the building and which have direct access from the outside of the building or through a common hall.

Percent of Housing Units That Are Owner-Occupied in 2018

National Percent = 63.9% of Housing Units*

ALPHA ORDER

RANK	STATE	PERCENT
16	Alabama	68.0
33	Alaska	65.6
38	Arizona	64.8
31	Arkansas	65.8
49	California	54.8
36	Colorado	65.1
31	Connecticut	65.8
8	Delaware	71.0
28	Florida	65.9
40	Georgia	63.8
47	Hawaii	58.3
9	Idaho	70.7
27	Illinois	66.0
13	Indiana	68.9
4	Iowa	71.3
23	Kansas	66.2
19	Kentucky	67.4
34	Louisiana	65.5
6	Maine	71.2
21	Maryland	66.9
44	Massachusetts	61.8
6	Michigan	71.2
3	Minnesota	71.5
15	Mississippi	68.2
22	Missouri	66.8
18	Montana	67.5
26	Nebraska	66.1
48	Nevada	56.8
4	New Hampshire	71.3
39	New Jersey	64.0
23	New Mexico	66.2
50	New York	53.7
36	North Carolina	65.1
42	North Dakota	62.5
28	Ohio	65.9
35	Oklahoma	65.4
42	Oregon	62.5
14	Pennsylvania	68.6
44	Rhode Island	61.8
12	South Carolina	69.3
17	South Dakota	67.9
23	Tennessee	66.2
46	Texas	61.7
10	Utah	70.5
2	Vermont	72.2
28	Virginia	65.9
41	Washington	62.8
1	West Virginia	72.5
20	Wisconsin	67.1
11	Wyoming	70.3

RANK ORDER

RANK	STATE	PERCENT
1	West Virginia	72.5
2	Vermont	72.2
3	Minnesota	71.5
4	Iowa	71.3
4	New Hampshire	71.3
6	Maine	71.2
6	Michigan	71.2
8	Delaware	71.0
9	Idaho	70.7
10	Utah	70.5
11	Wyoming	70.3
12	South Carolina	69.3
13	Indiana	68.9
14	Pennsylvania	68.6
15	Mississippi	68.2
16	Alabama	68.0
17	South Dakota	67.9
18	Montana	67.5
19	Kentucky	67.4
20	Wisconsin	67.1
21	Maryland	66.9
22	Missouri	66.8
23	Kansas	66.2
23	New Mexico	66.2
23	Tennessee	66.2
26	Nebraska	66.1
27	Illinois	66.0
28	Florida	65.9
28	Ohio	65.9
28	Virginia	65.9
31	Arkansas	65.8
31	Connecticut	65.8
33	Alaska	65.6
34	Louisiana	65.5
35	Oklahoma	65.4
36	Colorado	65.1
36	North Carolina	65.1
38	Arizona	64.8
39	New Jersey	64.0
40	Georgia	63.8
41	Washington	62.8
42	North Dakota	62.5
42	Oregon	62.5
44	Massachusetts	61.8
44	Rhode Island	61.8
46	Texas	61.7
47	Hawaii	58.3
48	Nevada	56.8
49	California	54.8
50	New York	53.7
	District of Columbia	42.3

Source: U.S. Bureau of the Census
   "2018 American Community Survey-Table CP04" (https://data.census.gov/cedsci/)
*For occupied housing units.

New Housing Units Authorized in 2018

National Total = 1,328,827 Units*

ALPHA ORDER				RANK ORDER			
RANK	STATE	UNITS	% of USA	RANK	STATE	UNITS	% of USA
29	Alabama	14,824	1.1%	1	Texas	192,878	14.5%
49	Alaska	1,677	0.1%	2	Florida	144,427	10.9%
8	Arizona	41,664	3.1%	3	California	113,502	8.5%
33	Arkansas	10,179	0.8%	4	North Carolina	71,691	5.4%
3	California	113,502	8.5%	5	Georgia	59,315	4.5%
7	Colorado	42,627	3.2%	6	Washington	47,746	3.6%
40	Connecticut	4,815	0.4%	7	Colorado	42,627	3.2%
37	Delaware	6,003	0.5%	8	Arizona	41,664	3.1%
2	Florida	144,427	10.9%	9	New York	37,778	2.8%
5	Georgia	59,315	4.5%	10	Tennessee	37,169	2.8%
43	Hawaii	4,659	0.4%	11	South Carolina	35,487	2.7%
28	Idaho	15,824	1.2%	12	Virginia	31,977	2.4%
18	Illinois	21,510	1.6%	13	New Jersey	27,942	2.1%
19	Indiana	21,480	1.6%	14	Minnesota	25,673	1.9%
31	Iowa	11,518	0.9%	15	Utah	25,574	1.9%
34	Kansas	9,478	0.7%	16	Ohio	24,221	1.8%
30	Kentucky	13,826	1.0%	17	Pennsylvania	23,325	1.8%
27	Louisiana	15,835	1.2%	18	Illinois	21,510	1.6%
42	Maine	4,697	0.4%	19	Indiana	21,480	1.6%
23	Maryland	18,647	1.4%	20	Oregon	20,132	1.5%
25	Massachusetts	17,044	1.3%	21	Michigan	19,580	1.5%
21	Michigan	19,580	1.5%	22	Wisconsin	19,113	1.4%
14	Minnesota	25,673	1.9%	23	Maryland	18,647	1.4%
36	Mississippi	6,883	0.5%	24	Nevada	17,645	1.3%
26	Missouri	16,875	1.3%	25	Massachusetts	17,044	1.3%
38	Montana	5,099	0.4%	26	Missouri	16,875	1.3%
35	Nebraska	7,866	0.6%	27	Louisiana	15,835	1.2%
24	Nevada	17,645	1.3%	28	Idaho	15,824	1.2%
44	New Hampshire	4,445	0.3%	29	Alabama	14,824	1.1%
13	New Jersey	27,942	2.1%	30	Kentucky	13,826	1.0%
41	New Mexico	4,813	0.4%	31	Iowa	11,518	0.9%
9	New York	37,778	2.8%	32	Oklahoma	10,502	0.8%
4	North Carolina	71,691	5.4%	33	Arkansas	10,179	0.8%
45	North Dakota	3,211	0.2%	34	Kansas	9,478	0.7%
16	Ohio	24,221	1.8%	35	Nebraska	7,866	0.6%
32	Oklahoma	10,502	0.8%	36	Mississippi	6,883	0.5%
20	Oregon	20,132	1.5%	37	Delaware	6,003	0.5%
17	Pennsylvania	23,325	1.8%	38	Montana	5,099	0.4%
50	Rhode Island	1,294	0.1%	39	South Dakota	4,963	0.4%
11	South Carolina	35,487	2.7%	40	Connecticut	4,815	0.4%
39	South Dakota	4,963	0.4%	41	New Mexico	4,813	0.4%
10	Tennessee	37,169	2.8%	42	Maine	4,697	0.4%
1	Texas	192,878	14.5%	43	Hawaii	4,659	0.4%
15	Utah	25,574	1.9%	44	New Hampshire	4,445	0.3%
47	Vermont	2,080	0.2%	45	North Dakota	3,211	0.2%
12	Virginia	31,977	2.4%	46	West Virginia	2,887	0.2%
6	Washington	47,746	3.6%	47	Vermont	2,080	0.2%
46	West Virginia	2,887	0.2%	48	Wyoming	1,812	0.1%
22	Wisconsin	19,113	1.4%	49	Alaska	1,677	0.1%
48	Wyoming	1,812	0.1%	50	Rhode Island	1,294	0.1%
					District of Columbia	4,615	0.3%

Source: U.S. Bureau of the Census
   "Building Permits Survey" (https://www.census.gov/construction/bps/stateannual.html)
*Final data. Includes single and multifamily privately owned units. All places issuing building permits for privately owned
residential structures. More than 98 percent of all privately owned residential buildings constructed are in permit-issuing places.

Value of New Housing Units Authorized in 2018

National Total = $271,119,545,000*

ALPHA ORDER						RANK ORDER			

RANK	STATE	VALUE	% of USA			RANK	STATE	VALUE	% of USA
29	Alabama	$3,046,657,000	1.1%			1	Texas	$34,689,871,000	12.8%
48	Alaska	429,020,000	0.2%			2	Florida	31,543,714,000	11.6%
8	Arizona	9,727,722,000	3.6%			3	California	27,844,627,000	10.3%
34	Arkansas	1,829,441,000	0.7%			4	North Carolina	13,581,958,000	5.0%
3	California	27,844,627,000	10.3%			5	Georgia	11,146,199,000	4.1%
6	Colorado	10,230,540,000	3.8%			6	Colorado	10,230,540,000	3.8%
38	Connecticut	1,112,212,000	0.4%			7	Washington	9,807,980,000	3.6%
44	Delaware	788,602,000	0.3%			8	Arizona	9,727,722,000	3.6%
2	Florida	31,543,714,000	11.6%			9	South Carolina	8,143,578,000	3.0%
5	Georgia	11,146,199,000	4.1%			10	Tennessee	7,048,088,000	2.6%
35	Hawaii	1,359,881,000	0.5%			11	New York	6,692,382,000	2.5%
28	Idaho	3,099,095,000	1.1%			12	Virginia	5,830,512,000	2.2%
22	Illinois	4,036,281,000	1.5%			13	Minnesota	5,720,813,000	2.1%
16	Indiana	4,879,857,000	1.8%			14	Utah	5,610,557,000	2.1%
31	Iowa	2,249,100,000	0.8%			15	Ohio	5,189,339,000	1.9%
33	Kansas	1,888,570,000	0.7%			16	Indiana	4,879,857,000	1.8%
30	Kentucky	2,267,765,000	0.8%			17	Pennsylvania	4,684,321,000	1.7%
27	Louisiana	3,108,408,000	1.1%			18	Michigan	4,569,368,000	1.7%
40	Maine	959,299,000	0.4%			19	New Jersey	4,220,431,000	1.6%
24	Maryland	3,701,849,000	1.4%			20	Oregon	4,180,894,000	1.5%
21	Massachusetts	4,157,964,000	1.5%			21	Massachusetts	4,157,964,000	1.5%
18	Michigan	4,569,368,000	1.7%			22	Illinois	4,036,281,000	1.5%
13	Minnesota	5,720,813,000	2.1%			23	Wisconsin	4,008,219,000	1.5%
37	Mississippi	1,193,505,000	0.4%			24	Maryland	3,701,849,000	1.4%
26	Missouri	3,167,067,000	1.2%			25	Nevada	3,400,610,000	1.3%
42	Montana	869,896,000	0.3%			26	Missouri	3,167,067,000	1.2%
36	Nebraska	1,309,845,000	0.5%			27	Louisiana	3,108,408,000	1.1%
25	Nevada	3,400,610,000	1.3%			28	Idaho	3,099,095,000	1.1%
41	New Hampshire	875,243,000	0.3%			29	Alabama	3,046,657,000	1.1%
19	New Jersey	4,220,431,000	1.6%			30	Kentucky	2,267,765,000	0.8%
39	New Mexico	1,037,554,000	0.4%			31	Iowa	2,249,100,000	0.8%
11	New York	6,692,382,000	2.5%			32	Oklahoma	2,181,297,000	0.8%
4	North Carolina	13,581,958,000	5.0%			33	Kansas	1,888,570,000	0.7%
45	North Dakota	607,898,000	0.2%			34	Arkansas	1,829,441,000	0.7%
15	Ohio	5,189,339,000	1.9%			35	Hawaii	1,359,881,000	0.5%
32	Oklahoma	2,181,297,000	0.8%			36	Nebraska	1,309,845,000	0.5%
20	Oregon	4,180,894,000	1.5%			37	Mississippi	1,193,505,000	0.4%
17	Pennsylvania	4,684,321,000	1.7%			38	Connecticut	1,112,212,000	0.4%
50	Rhode Island	260,274,000	0.1%			39	New Mexico	1,037,554,000	0.4%
9	South Carolina	8,143,578,000	3.0%			40	Maine	959,299,000	0.4%
43	South Dakota	854,338,000	0.3%			41	New Hampshire	875,243,000	0.3%
10	Tennessee	7,048,088,000	2.6%			42	Montana	869,896,000	0.3%
1	Texas	34,689,871,000	12.8%			43	South Dakota	854,338,000	0.3%
14	Utah	5,610,557,000	2.1%			44	Delaware	788,602,000	0.3%
49	Vermont	365,383,000	0.1%			45	North Dakota	607,898,000	0.2%
12	Virginia	5,830,512,000	2.2%			46	Wyoming	593,197,000	0.2%
7	Washington	9,807,980,000	3.6%			47	West Virginia	500,078,000	0.2%
47	West Virginia	500,078,000	0.2%			48	Alaska	429,020,000	0.2%
23	Wisconsin	4,008,219,000	1.5%			49	Vermont	365,383,000	0.1%
46	Wyoming	593,197,000	0.2%			50	Rhode Island	260,274,000	0.1%
							District of Columbia	518,239,000	0.2%

Source: U.S. Bureau of the Census
"Building Permits Survey" (https://www.census.gov/construction/bps/stateannual.html)
*Final data. Includes single and multifamily privately owned units. All places issuing building permits for privately owned
residential structures. More than 98 percent of all privately owned residential buildings constructed are in permit-issuing places.

Average Value of New Housing Units in 2018

National Average = $204,029 per Unit*

ALPHA ORDER				RANK ORDER		
RANK	STATE	VALUE		RANK	STATE	VALUE
20	Alabama	$205,522		1	Wyoming	$327,371
3	Alaska	255,826		2	Hawaii	291,883
7	Arizona	233,480		3	Alaska	255,826
40	Arkansas	179,727		4	California	245,323
4	California	245,323		5	Massachusetts	243,955
6	Colorado	240,001		6	Colorado	240,001
9	Connecticut	230,989		7	Arizona	233,480
50	Delaware	131,368		8	Michigan	233,369
14	Florida	218,406		9	Connecticut	230,989
35	Georgia	187,915		10	South Carolina	229,481
2	Hawaii	291,883		11	Indiana	227,181
29	Idaho	195,848		12	Minnesota	222,834
37	Illinois	187,647		13	Utah	219,385
11	Indiana	227,181		14	Florida	218,406
30	Iowa	195,268		15	New Mexico	215,573
25	Kansas	199,258		16	Ohio	214,250
48	Kentucky	164,022		17	Wisconsin	209,712
28	Louisiana	196,300		18	Oklahoma	207,703
22	Maine	204,237		19	Oregon	207,674
26	Maryland	198,522		20	Alabama	205,522
5	Massachusetts	243,955		21	Washington	205,420
8	Michigan	233,369		22	Maine	204,237
12	Minnesota	222,834		23	Rhode Island	201,139
43	Mississippi	173,399		24	Pennsylvania	200,828
36	Missouri	187,678		25	Kansas	199,258
46	Montana	170,601		26	Maryland	198,522
47	Nebraska	166,520		27	New Hampshire	196,905
31	Nevada	192,724		28	Louisiana	196,300
27	New Hampshire	196,905		29	Idaho	195,848
49	New Jersey	151,043		30	Iowa	195,268
15	New Mexico	215,573		31	Nevada	192,724
41	New York	177,150		32	Tennessee	189,623
33	North Carolina	189,451		33	North Carolina	189,451
34	North Dakota	189,317		34	North Dakota	189,317
16	Ohio	214,250		35	Georgia	187,915
18	Oklahoma	207,703		36	Missouri	187,678
19	Oregon	207,674		37	Illinois	187,647
24	Pennsylvania	200,828		38	Virginia	182,335
23	Rhode Island	201,139		39	Texas	179,854
10	South Carolina	229,481		40	Arkansas	179,727
45	South Dakota	172,141		41	New York	177,150
32	Tennessee	189,623		42	Vermont	175,665
39	Texas	179,854		43	Mississippi	173,399
13	Utah	219,385		44	West Virginia	173,217
42	Vermont	175,665		45	South Dakota	172,141
38	Virginia	182,335		46	Montana	170,601
21	Washington	205,420		47	Nebraska	166,520
44	West Virginia	173,217		48	Kentucky	164,022
17	Wisconsin	209,712		49	New Jersey	151,043
1	Wyoming	327,371		50	Delaware	131,368

District of Columbia 112,294

Source: CQ Press using data from U.S. Bureau of the Census
"Building Permits Survey" (https://www.census.gov/construction/bps/stateannual.html)
*Final data. Includes single and multifamily privately owned units. All places issuing building permits for privately owned
residential structures. More than 98 percent of all privately owned residential buildings constructed are in permit-issuing places.

Median Value of Owner-Occupied Housing in 2018

National Median = $229,700*

ALPHA ORDER

ALPHA ORDER

RANK	STATE	MEDIAN
45	Alabama	$147,900
14	Alaska	276,100
19	Arizona	241,100
48	Arkansas	133,100
2	California	546,800
4	Colorado	373,300
13	Connecticut	277,400
17	Delaware	255,300
23	Florida	230,600
28	Georgia	189,900
1	Hawaii	631,700
21	Idaho	233,100
25	Illinois	203,400
46	Indiana	147,300
42	Iowa	152,000
41	Kansas	159,400
44	Kentucky	148,100
37	Louisiana	167,300
27	Maine	197,500
9	Maryland	324,800
3	Massachusetts	400,700
39	Michigan	162,500
20	Minnesota	235,400
49	Mississippi	123,300
38	Missouri	162,600
18	Montana	249,200
40	Nebraska	161,800
11	Nevada	292,200
16	New Hampshire	270,000
6	New Jersey	344,000
34	New Mexico	174,700
8	New York	325,500
32	North Carolina	180,600
26	North Dakota	198,700
43	Ohio	151,100
47	Oklahoma	140,000
7	Oregon	341,800
30	Pennsylvania	186,000
15	Rhode Island	273,800
36	South Carolina	170,800
35	South Dakota	171,500
33	Tennessee	177,500
30	Texas	186,000
10	Utah	303,300
21	Vermont	233,100
12	Virginia	281,700
5	Washington	373,100
50	West Virginia	121,300
29	Wisconsin	188,500
24	Wyoming	230,500

RANK ORDER

RANK	STATE	MEDIAN
1	Hawaii	$631,700
2	California	546,800
3	Massachusetts	400,700
4	Colorado	373,300
5	Washington	373,100
6	New Jersey	344,000
7	Oregon	341,800
8	New York	325,500
9	Maryland	324,800
10	Utah	303,300
11	Nevada	292,200
12	Virginia	281,700
13	Connecticut	277,400
14	Alaska	276,100
15	Rhode Island	273,800
16	New Hampshire	270,000
17	Delaware	255,300
18	Montana	249,200
19	Arizona	241,100
20	Minnesota	235,400
21	Idaho	233,100
21	Vermont	233,100
23	Florida	230,600
24	Wyoming	230,500
25	Illinois	203,400
26	North Dakota	198,700
27	Maine	197,500
28	Georgia	189,900
29	Wisconsin	188,500
30	Pennsylvania	186,000
30	Texas	186,000
32	North Carolina	180,600
33	Tennessee	177,500
34	New Mexico	174,700
35	South Dakota	171,500
36	South Carolina	170,800
37	Louisiana	167,300
38	Missouri	162,600
39	Michigan	162,500
40	Nebraska	161,800
41	Kansas	159,400
42	Iowa	152,000
43	Ohio	151,100
44	Kentucky	148,100
45	Alabama	147,900
46	Indiana	147,300
47	Oklahoma	140,000
48	Arkansas	133,100
49	Mississippi	123,300
50	West Virginia	121,300
	District of Columbia	617,900

Source: U.S. Bureau of the Census
  "2018 American Community Survey-Table CP04" (https://data.census.gov/cedsci/)
*Housing units with a mortgage.

Percent Change in House Prices: 2018 to 2019

National Percent Change = 4.9% Increase*

ALPHA ORDER			RANK ORDER		
RANK	STATE	PERCENT CHANGE	RANK	STATE	PERCENT CHANGE
20	Alabama	5.4	1	Idaho	11.6
33	Alaska	4.7	2	Arizona	7.9
2	Arizona	7.9	2	Maine	7.9
24	Arkansas	5.1	4	Utah	7.8
39	California	4.1	5	Indiana	7.4
24	Colorado	5.1	6	Vermont	7.1
49	Connecticut	2.2	7	Kansas	6.8
33	Delaware	4.7	8	New Mexico	6.4
26	Florida	5.0	8	Wisconsin	6.4
32	Georgia	4.8	10	Tennessee	6.3
11	Hawaii	6.2	11	Hawaii	6.2
1	Idaho	11.6	12	Montana	6.1
50	Illinois	1.9	12	Nebraska	6.1
5	Indiana	7.4	14	New Hampshire	6.0
44	Iowa	3.2	15	Michigan	5.8
7	Kansas	6.8	15	South Carolina	5.8
26	Kentucky	5.0	17	North Carolina	5.7
44	Louisiana	3.2	18	Ohio	5.6
2	Maine	7.9	18	Washington	5.6
48	Maryland	2.4	20	Alabama	5.4
38	Massachusetts	4.3	20	Virginia	5.4
15	Michigan	5.8	22	Pennsylvania	5.2
37	Minnesota	4.5	22	Wyoming	5.2
44	Mississippi	3.2	24	Arkansas	5.1
29	Missouri	4.9	24	Colorado	5.1
12	Montana	6.1	26	Florida	5.0
12	Nebraska	6.1	26	Kentucky	5.0
26	Nevada	5.0	26	Nevada	5.0
14	New Hampshire	6.0	29	Missouri	4.9
43	New Jersey	3.3	29	Oregon	4.9
8	New Mexico	6.4	29	Texas	4.9
42	New York	3.4	32	Georgia	4.8
17	North Carolina	5.7	33	Alaska	4.7
41	North Dakota	3.6	33	Delaware	4.7
18	Ohio	5.6	33	Rhode Island	4.7
36	Oklahoma	4.6	36	Oklahoma	4.6
29	Oregon	4.9	37	Minnesota	4.5
22	Pennsylvania	5.2	38	Massachusetts	4.3
33	Rhode Island	4.7	39	California	4.1
15	South Carolina	5.8	40	West Virginia	3.7
47	South Dakota	2.7	41	North Dakota	3.6
10	Tennessee	6.3	42	New York	3.4
29	Texas	4.9	43	New Jersey	3.3
4	Utah	7.8	44	Iowa	3.2
6	Vermont	7.1	44	Louisiana	3.2
20	Virginia	5.4	44	Mississippi	3.2
18	Washington	5.6	47	South Dakota	2.7
40	West Virginia	3.7	48	Maryland	2.4
8	Wisconsin	6.4	49	Connecticut	2.2
22	Wyoming	5.2	50	Illinois	1.9
				District of Columbia	5.6

Source: Federal Housing Finance Agency
  "State HPI Summary" (www.fhfa.gov/DataTools/Tools/Pages/House-Price-Index-%28HPI%29.aspx)
*Single-family house prices. As of September 30, 2019.

Percent Change in House Prices: 2015 to 2019

National Percent Change = 32.9% Increase*

ALPHA ORDER				RANK ORDER		
RANK	STATE	PERCENT CHANGE		RANK	STATE	PERCENT CHANGE
31	Alabama	25.9		1	Idaho	62.9
48	Alaska	12.8		2	Nevada	59.9
8	Arizona	45.7		3	Washington	57.7
37	Arkansas	21.7		4	Colorado	54.6
12	California	37.5		5	Utah	51.3
4	Colorado	54.6		6	Florida	49.1
50	Connecticut	9.5		7	Oregon	47.7
39	Delaware	19.6		8	Arizona	45.7
6	Florida	49.1		9	Georgia	40.7
9	Georgia	40.7		10	Tennessee	39.5
21	Hawaii	31.9		11	Michigan	38.7
1	Idaho	62.9		12	California	37.5
43	Illinois	17.2		13	North Carolina	36.7
16	Indiana	33.8		14	Texas	36.6
36	Iowa	22.0		15	South Carolina	36.3
29	Kansas	28.2		16	Indiana	33.8
28	Kentucky	28.3		17	Wisconsin	32.8
46	Louisiana	16.5		18	Minnesota	32.4
24	Maine	30.1		19	Nebraska	32.2
42	Maryland	17.7		20	Rhode Island	32.0
26	Massachusetts	29.7		21	Hawaii	31.9
11	Michigan	38.7		22	Ohio	31.4
18	Minnesota	32.4		23	New Hampshire	30.5
45	Mississippi	17.0		24	Maine	30.1
25	Missouri	29.9		25	Missouri	29.9
27	Montana	29.2		26	Massachusetts	29.7
19	Nebraska	32.2		27	Montana	29.2
2	Nevada	59.9		28	Kentucky	28.3
23	New Hampshire	30.5		29	Kansas	28.2
44	New Jersey	17.1		30	South Dakota	27.7
35	New Mexico	22.8		31	Alabama	25.9
32	New York	24.4		32	New York	24.4
13	North Carolina	36.7		33	Virginia	23.7
47	North Dakota	12.9		34	Pennsylvania	23.1
22	Ohio	31.4		35	New Mexico	22.8
38	Oklahoma	21.6		36	Iowa	22.0
7	Oregon	47.7		37	Arkansas	21.7
34	Pennsylvania	23.1		38	Oklahoma	21.6
20	Rhode Island	32.0		39	Delaware	19.6
15	South Carolina	36.3		40	Vermont	19.1
30	South Dakota	27.7		41	Wyoming	18.2
10	Tennessee	39.5		42	Maryland	17.7
14	Texas	36.6		43	Illinois	17.2
5	Utah	51.3		44	New Jersey	17.1
40	Vermont	19.1		45	Mississippi	17.0
33	Virginia	23.7		46	Louisiana	16.5
3	Washington	57.7		47	North Dakota	12.9
49	West Virginia	11.3		48	Alaska	12.8
17	Wisconsin	32.8		49	West Virginia	11.3
41	Wyoming	18.2		50	Connecticut	9.5
					District of Columbia	36.1

Source: Federal Housing Finance Agency
  "State HPI Summary" (www.fhfa.gov/DataTools/Tools/Pages/House-Price-Index-%28HPI%29.aspx)
*Single-family house prices. As of September 30, 2019.

Percent of Owner-Occupied Housing Units with a Mortgage in 2018

National Percent = 61.9% with Mortgages

ALPHA ORDER

RANK	STATE	PERCENT
43	Alabama	55.0
26	Alaska	61.5
19	Arizona	63.3
44	Arkansas	53.9
4	California	69.6
2	Colorado	70.1
10	Connecticut	67.2
19	Delaware	63.3
41	Florida	56.2
15	Georgia	64.6
16	Hawaii	64.4
17	Idaho	64.1
22	Illinois	62.4
14	Indiana	65.1
29	Iowa	60.1
34	Kansas	59.0
38	Kentucky	56.7
48	Louisiana	52.2
27	Maine	60.9
1	Maryland	72.4
5	Massachusetts	68.2
33	Michigan	59.3
12	Minnesota	65.4
49	Mississippi	48.3
28	Missouri	60.7
40	Montana	56.4
32	Nebraska	59.4
7	Nevada	67.8
18	New Hampshire	63.9
11	New Jersey	66.3
47	New Mexico	53.3
30	New York	59.9
24	North Carolina	62.1
46	North Dakota	53.4
22	Ohio	62.4
45	Oklahoma	53.7
13	Oregon	65.2
31	Pennsylvania	59.7
5	Rhode Island	68.2
37	South Carolina	58.5
42	South Dakota	55.2
35	Tennessee	58.6
39	Texas	56.5
3	Utah	69.9
25	Vermont	61.8
7	Virginia	67.8
7	Washington	67.8
50	West Virginia	46.0
21	Wisconsin	63.0
35	Wyoming	58.6

RANK ORDER

RANK	STATE	PERCENT
1	Maryland	72.4
2	Colorado	70.1
3	Utah	69.9
4	California	69.6
5	Massachusetts	68.2
5	Rhode Island	68.2
7	Nevada	67.8
7	Virginia	67.8
7	Washington	67.8
10	Connecticut	67.2
11	New Jersey	66.3
12	Minnesota	65.4
13	Oregon	65.2
14	Indiana	65.1
15	Georgia	64.6
16	Hawaii	64.4
17	Idaho	64.1
18	New Hampshire	63.9
19	Arizona	63.3
19	Delaware	63.3
21	Wisconsin	63.0
22	Illinois	62.4
22	Ohio	62.4
24	North Carolina	62.1
25	Vermont	61.8
26	Alaska	61.5
27	Maine	60.9
28	Missouri	60.7
29	Iowa	60.1
30	New York	59.9
31	Pennsylvania	59.7
32	Nebraska	59.4
33	Michigan	59.3
34	Kansas	59.0
35	Tennessee	58.6
35	Wyoming	58.6
37	South Carolina	58.5
38	Kentucky	56.7
39	Texas	56.5
40	Montana	56.4
41	Florida	56.2
42	South Dakota	55.2
43	Alabama	55.0
44	Arkansas	53.9
45	Oklahoma	53.7
46	North Dakota	53.4
47	New Mexico	53.3
48	Louisiana	52.2
49	Mississippi	48.3
50	West Virginia	46.0
	District of Columbia	75.0

Source: U.S. Bureau of the Census
   "2018 American Community Survey-Table CP04" (https://data.census.gov/cedsci/)

Median Monthly Mortgage Payment in 2018

National Median = $1,566*

ALPHA ORDER

RANK	STATE	MEDIAN
45	Alabama	$1,164
8	Alaska	1,895
26	Arizona	1,417
49	Arkansas	1,071
3	California	2,345
13	Colorado	1,741
6	Connecticut	2,056
17	Delaware	1,566
22	Florida	1,471
28	Georgia	1,395
2	Hawaii	2,354
37	Idaho	1,249
15	Illinois	1,665
48	Indiana	1,118
40	Iowa	1,234
30	Kansas	1,364
45	Kentucky	1,164
36	Louisiana	1,254
32	Maine	1,349
7	Maryland	1,955
4	Massachusetts	2,207
35	Michigan	1,270
19	Minnesota	1,559
47	Mississippi	1,132
37	Missouri	1,249
27	Montana	1,413
31	Nebraska	1,353
21	Nevada	1,528
9	New Hampshire	1,892
1	New Jersey	2,398
40	New Mexico	1,234
5	New York	2,098
34	North Carolina	1,284
25	North Dakota	1,425
39	Ohio	1,248
44	Oklahoma	1,214
14	Oregon	1,690
23	Pennsylvania	1,451
11	Rhode Island	1,830
43	South Carolina	1,225
33	South Dakota	1,301
42	Tennessee	1,228
16	Texas	1,603
20	Utah	1,531
18	Vermont	1,560
12	Virginia	1,752
10	Washington	1,883
50	West Virginia	1,001
29	Wisconsin	1,387
24	Wyoming	1,440

RANK ORDER

RANK	STATE	MEDIAN
1	New Jersey	$2,398
2	Hawaii	2,354
3	California	2,345
4	Massachusetts	2,207
5	New York	2,098
6	Connecticut	2,056
7	Maryland	1,955
8	Alaska	1,895
9	New Hampshire	1,892
10	Washington	1,883
11	Rhode Island	1,830
12	Virginia	1,752
13	Colorado	1,741
14	Oregon	1,690
15	Illinois	1,665
16	Texas	1,603
17	Delaware	1,566
18	Vermont	1,560
19	Minnesota	1,559
20	Utah	1,531
21	Nevada	1,528
22	Florida	1,471
23	Pennsylvania	1,451
24	Wyoming	1,440
25	North Dakota	1,425
26	Arizona	1,417
27	Montana	1,413
28	Georgia	1,395
29	Wisconsin	1,387
30	Kansas	1,364
31	Nebraska	1,353
32	Maine	1,349
33	South Dakota	1,301
34	North Carolina	1,284
35	Michigan	1,270
36	Louisiana	1,254
37	Idaho	1,249
37	Missouri	1,249
39	Ohio	1,248
40	Iowa	1,234
40	New Mexico	1,234
42	Tennessee	1,228
43	South Carolina	1,225
44	Oklahoma	1,214
45	Alabama	1,164
45	Kentucky	1,164
47	Mississippi	1,132
48	Indiana	1,118
49	Arkansas	1,071
50	West Virginia	1,001
	District of Columbia	2,506

Source: U.S. Bureau of the Census
  "2018 American Community Survey-Table CP04" (https://data.census.gov/cedsci/)
*Monthly housing costs for owner-occupied housing. Includes mortgages, equity loans, real estate taxes, and utilities.

Percent of Home Owners Spending 30% or More of Household Income on Housing Costs in 2018
National Percent = 27.7% of Home Owners*

ALPHA ORDER

ALPHA ORDER | RANK ORDER

RANK	STATE	PERCENT	RANK	STATE	PERCENT
34	Alabama	23.6	1	Hawaii	38.8
17	Alaska	28.6	2	California	38.2
22	Arizona	26.9	3	New Jersey	34.1
38	Arkansas	22.8	4	Florida	33.0
2	California	38.2	5	New York	32.8
19	Colorado	27.2	5	Rhode Island	32.8
9	Connecticut	30.5	7	Delaware	30.9
7	Delaware	30.9	7	Oregon	30.9
4	Florida	33.0	9	Connecticut	30.5
28	Georgia	25.1	10	Nevada	30.2
1	Hawaii	38.8	11	Massachusetts	30.1
25	Idaho	25.7	11	Vermont	30.1
19	Illinois	27.2	13	Montana	29.5
48	Indiana	19.9	13	New Mexico	29.5
48	Iowa	19.9	15	New Hampshire	29.1
43	Kansas	21.6	15	Washington	29.1
36	Kentucky	23.1	17	Alaska	28.6
24	Louisiana	25.9	18	Texas	27.4
23	Maine	26.0	19	Colorado	27.2
21	Maryland	27.1	19	Illinois	27.2
11	Massachusetts	30.1	21	Maryland	27.1
39	Michigan	22.7	22	Arizona	26.9
45	Minnesota	21.4	23	Maine	26.0
28	Mississippi	25.1	24	Louisiana	25.9
46	Missouri	21.3	25	Idaho	25.7
13	Montana	29.5	26	South Carolina	25.6
47	Nebraska	20.3	27	Virginia	25.5
10	Nevada	30.2	28	Georgia	25.1
15	New Hampshire	29.1	28	Mississippi	25.1
3	New Jersey	34.1	30	North Carolina	24.9
13	New Mexico	29.5	31	Pennsylvania	24.7
5	New York	32.8	32	Tennessee	24.3
30	North Carolina	24.9	33	Wyoming	23.8
50	North Dakota	17.4	34	Alabama	23.6
43	Ohio	21.6	35	Utah	23.2
40	Oklahoma	22.6	36	Kentucky	23.1
7	Oregon	30.9	37	West Virginia	22.9
31	Pennsylvania	24.7	38	Arkansas	22.8
5	Rhode Island	32.8	39	Michigan	22.7
26	South Carolina	25.6	40	Oklahoma	22.6
42	South Dakota	22.1	41	Wisconsin	22.5
32	Tennessee	24.3	42	South Dakota	22.1
18	Texas	27.4	43	Kansas	21.6
35	Utah	23.2	43	Ohio	21.6
11	Vermont	30.1	45	Minnesota	21.4
27	Virginia	25.5	46	Missouri	21.3
15	Washington	29.1	47	Nebraska	20.3
37	West Virginia	22.9	48	Indiana	19.9
41	Wisconsin	22.5	48	Iowa	19.9
33	Wyoming	23.8	50	North Dakota	17.4
				District of Columbia	26.0

Source: U.S. Bureau of the Census
  "2018 American Community Survey-Table CP04" (https://data.census.gov/cedsci/)
*For owner-occupied housing units with a mortgage. Monthly housing costs include mortgages, equity loans, real estate taxes, and utilities.

Median Annual Real Estate Taxes in 2018

National Median = $2,514*

ALPHA ORDER RANK	STATE	MEDIAN		RANK ORDER RANK	STATE	MEDIAN
50	Alabama	$591		1	New Jersey	$8,353
13	Alaska	3,250		2	Connecticut	5,889
35	Arizona	1,517		3	New Hampshire	5,641
48	Arkansas	815		4	New York	5,525
9	California	3,963		5	Massachusetts	4,790
29	Colorado	1,808		6	Illinois	4,480
2	Connecticut	5,889		7	Vermont	4,297
37	Delaware	1,472		8	Rhode Island	4,288
28	Florida	1,938		9	California	3,963
32	Georgia	1,712		10	Washington	3,579
31	Hawaii	1,730		11	Maryland	3,456
36	Idaho	1,478		12	Wisconsin	3,267
6	Illinois	4,480		13	Alaska	3,250
43	Indiana	1,214		14	Texas	3,216
21	Iowa	2,354		15	Oregon	3,140
24	Kansas	2,203		16	Pennsylvania	2,871
41	Kentucky	1,239		17	Nebraska	2,689
47	Louisiana	912		18	Maine	2,579
18	Maine	2,579		19	Minnesota	2,542
11	Maryland	3,456		20	Michigan	2,387
5	Massachusetts	4,790		21	Iowa	2,354
20	Michigan	2,387		22	Ohio	2,296
19	Minnesota	2,542		23	Virginia	2,261
45	Mississippi	960		24	Kansas	2,203
34	Missouri	1,546		25	South Dakota	2,159
26	Montana	2,014		26	Montana	2,014
17	Nebraska	2,689		27	North Dakota	1,971
33	Nevada	1,640		28	Florida	1,938
3	New Hampshire	5,641		29	Colorado	1,808
1	New Jersey	8,353		30	Utah	1,778
40	New Mexico	1,354		31	Hawaii	1,730
4	New York	5,525		32	Georgia	1,712
38	North Carolina	1,453		33	Nevada	1,640
27	North Dakota	1,971		34	Missouri	1,546
22	Ohio	2,296		35	Arizona	1,517
42	Oklahoma	1,237		36	Idaho	1,478
15	Oregon	3,140		37	Delaware	1,472
16	Pennsylvania	2,871		38	North Carolina	1,453
8	Rhode Island	4,288		39	Wyoming	1,372
46	South Carolina	939		40	New Mexico	1,354
25	South Dakota	2,159		41	Kentucky	1,239
44	Tennessee	1,205		42	Oklahoma	1,237
14	Texas	3,216		43	Indiana	1,214
30	Utah	1,778		44	Tennessee	1,205
7	Vermont	4,297		45	Mississippi	960
23	Virginia	2,261		46	South Carolina	939
10	Washington	3,579		47	Louisiana	912
49	West Virginia	727		48	Arkansas	815
12	Wisconsin	3,267		49	West Virginia	727
39	Wyoming	1,372		50	Alabama	591
					District of Columbia	3,539

Source: U.S. Bureau of the Census
"2018 American Community Survey-Table CP04" (https://data.census.gov/cedsci/)
*For owner-occupied housing units with or without mortgages.

Homeownership Rate in 2018

National Rate = 64.4%*

ALPHA ORDER				RANK ORDER		
RANK	STATE	RATE		RANK	STATE	RATE
11	Alabama	70.3		1	West Virginia	74.7
41	Alaska	63.7		2	New Hampshire	73.4
31	Arizona	65.7		3	Michigan	73.0
38	Arkansas	64.7		4	Mississippi	72.5
49	California	55.1		5	Utah	72.2
39	Colorado	64.4		6	South Carolina	72.0
34	Connecticut	65.3		7	Vermont	71.4
10	Delaware	70.8		8	Maine	71.2
33	Florida	65.5		9	Wyoming	71.1
40	Georgia	63.8		10	Delaware	70.8
47	Hawaii	59.5		11	Alabama	70.3
18	Idaho	69.2		12	Pennsylvania	69.9
29	Illinois	66.0		13	Indiana	69.8
13	Indiana	69.8		13	Kentucky	69.8
20	Iowa	68.9		13	Minnesota	69.8
25	Kansas	67.3		16	Missouri	69.7
13	Kentucky	69.8		17	Oklahoma	69.5
31	Louisiana	65.7		18	Idaho	69.2
8	Maine	71.2		19	South Dakota	69.1
27	Maryland	66.6		20	Iowa	68.9
45	Massachusetts	61.5		21	New Mexico	68.0
3	Michigan	73.0		21	Tennessee	68.0
13	Minnesota	69.8		23	Wisconsin	67.9
4	Mississippi	72.5		24	Montana	67.4
16	Missouri	69.7		25	Kansas	67.3
24	Montana	67.4		25	Ohio	67.3
28	Nebraska	66.4		27	Maryland	66.6
48	Nevada	57.8		28	Nebraska	66.4
2	New Hampshire	73.4		29	Illinois	66.0
36	New Jersey	65.0		29	Virginia	66.0
21	New Mexico	68.0		31	Arizona	65.7
50	New York	51.0		31	Louisiana	65.7
35	North Carolina	65.2		33	Florida	65.5
44	North Dakota	61.9		34	Connecticut	65.3
25	Ohio	67.3		35	North Carolina	65.2
17	Oklahoma	69.5		36	New Jersey	65.0
43	Oregon	62.0		37	Washington	64.9
12	Pennsylvania	69.9		38	Arkansas	64.7
46	Rhode Island	60.7		39	Colorado	64.4
6	South Carolina	72.0		40	Georgia	63.8
19	South Dakota	69.1		41	Alaska	63.7
21	Tennessee	68.0		42	Texas	62.7
42	Texas	62.7		43	Oregon	62.0
5	Utah	72.2		44	North Dakota	61.9
7	Vermont	71.4		45	Massachusetts	61.5
29	Virginia	66.0		46	Rhode Island	60.7
37	Washington	64.9		47	Hawaii	59.5
1	West Virginia	74.7		48	Nevada	57.8
23	Wisconsin	67.9		49	California	55.1
9	Wyoming	71.1		50	New York	51.0
					District of Columbia	39.9

Source: U.S. Bureau of the Census
"Housing Vacancies and Homeownership, Annual Statistics: 2018" (https://www.census.gov/housing/hvs/index.html)
*Percent of households occupied by the owner.

Percent of Housing Units That Are Renter-Occupied in 2018

National Percent = 36.1% of Housing Units*

<table>
<tr><td colspan="3">ALPHA ORDER</td><td colspan="3">RANK ORDER</td></tr>
<tr><td>RANK</td><td>STATE</td><td>PERCENT</td><td>RANK</td><td>STATE</td><td>PERCENT</td></tr>
<tr><td>35</td><td>Alabama</td><td>32.0</td><td>1</td><td>New York</td><td>46.3</td></tr>
<tr><td>18</td><td>Alaska</td><td>34.4</td><td>2</td><td>California</td><td>45.2</td></tr>
<tr><td>13</td><td>Arizona</td><td>35.2</td><td>3</td><td>Nevada</td><td>43.2</td></tr>
<tr><td>19</td><td>Arkansas</td><td>34.2</td><td>4</td><td>Hawaii</td><td>41.7</td></tr>
<tr><td>2</td><td>California</td><td>45.2</td><td>5</td><td>Texas</td><td>38.3</td></tr>
<tr><td>14</td><td>Colorado</td><td>34.9</td><td>6</td><td>Massachusetts</td><td>38.2</td></tr>
<tr><td>19</td><td>Connecticut</td><td>34.2</td><td>6</td><td>Rhode Island</td><td>38.2</td></tr>
<tr><td>43</td><td>Delaware</td><td>29.0</td><td>8</td><td>North Dakota</td><td>37.5</td></tr>
<tr><td>21</td><td>Florida</td><td>34.1</td><td>8</td><td>Oregon</td><td>37.5</td></tr>
<tr><td>11</td><td>Georgia</td><td>36.2</td><td>10</td><td>Washington</td><td>37.2</td></tr>
<tr><td>4</td><td>Hawaii</td><td>41.7</td><td>11</td><td>Georgia</td><td>36.2</td></tr>
<tr><td>42</td><td>Idaho</td><td>29.3</td><td>12</td><td>New Jersey</td><td>36.0</td></tr>
<tr><td>24</td><td>Illinois</td><td>34.0</td><td>13</td><td>Arizona</td><td>35.2</td></tr>
<tr><td>38</td><td>Indiana</td><td>31.1</td><td>14</td><td>Colorado</td><td>34.9</td></tr>
<tr><td>46</td><td>Iowa</td><td>28.7</td><td>14</td><td>North Carolina</td><td>34.9</td></tr>
<tr><td>26</td><td>Kansas</td><td>33.8</td><td>16</td><td>Oklahoma</td><td>34.6</td></tr>
<tr><td>32</td><td>Kentucky</td><td>32.6</td><td>17</td><td>Louisiana</td><td>34.5</td></tr>
<tr><td>17</td><td>Louisiana</td><td>34.5</td><td>18</td><td>Alaska</td><td>34.4</td></tr>
<tr><td>44</td><td>Maine</td><td>28.8</td><td>19</td><td>Arkansas</td><td>34.2</td></tr>
<tr><td>30</td><td>Maryland</td><td>33.1</td><td>19</td><td>Connecticut</td><td>34.2</td></tr>
<tr><td>6</td><td>Massachusetts</td><td>38.2</td><td>21</td><td>Florida</td><td>34.1</td></tr>
<tr><td>44</td><td>Michigan</td><td>28.8</td><td>21</td><td>Ohio</td><td>34.1</td></tr>
<tr><td>48</td><td>Minnesota</td><td>28.5</td><td>21</td><td>Virginia</td><td>34.1</td></tr>
<tr><td>36</td><td>Mississippi</td><td>31.8</td><td>24</td><td>Illinois</td><td>34.0</td></tr>
<tr><td>29</td><td>Missouri</td><td>33.2</td><td>25</td><td>Nebraska</td><td>33.9</td></tr>
<tr><td>33</td><td>Montana</td><td>32.5</td><td>26</td><td>Kansas</td><td>33.8</td></tr>
<tr><td>25</td><td>Nebraska</td><td>33.9</td><td>26</td><td>New Mexico</td><td>33.8</td></tr>
<tr><td>3</td><td>Nevada</td><td>43.2</td><td>26</td><td>Tennessee</td><td>33.8</td></tr>
<tr><td>46</td><td>New Hampshire</td><td>28.7</td><td>29</td><td>Missouri</td><td>33.2</td></tr>
<tr><td>12</td><td>New Jersey</td><td>36.0</td><td>30</td><td>Maryland</td><td>33.1</td></tr>
<tr><td>26</td><td>New Mexico</td><td>33.8</td><td>31</td><td>Wisconsin</td><td>32.9</td></tr>
<tr><td>1</td><td>New York</td><td>46.3</td><td>32</td><td>Kentucky</td><td>32.6</td></tr>
<tr><td>14</td><td>North Carolina</td><td>34.9</td><td>33</td><td>Montana</td><td>32.5</td></tr>
<tr><td>8</td><td>North Dakota</td><td>37.5</td><td>34</td><td>South Dakota</td><td>32.1</td></tr>
<tr><td>21</td><td>Ohio</td><td>34.1</td><td>35</td><td>Alabama</td><td>32.0</td></tr>
<tr><td>16</td><td>Oklahoma</td><td>34.6</td><td>36</td><td>Mississippi</td><td>31.8</td></tr>
<tr><td>8</td><td>Oregon</td><td>37.5</td><td>37</td><td>Pennsylvania</td><td>31.4</td></tr>
<tr><td>37</td><td>Pennsylvania</td><td>31.4</td><td>38</td><td>Indiana</td><td>31.1</td></tr>
<tr><td>6</td><td>Rhode Island</td><td>38.2</td><td>39</td><td>South Carolina</td><td>30.7</td></tr>
<tr><td>39</td><td>South Carolina</td><td>30.7</td><td>40</td><td>Wyoming</td><td>29.7</td></tr>
<tr><td>34</td><td>South Dakota</td><td>32.1</td><td>41</td><td>Utah</td><td>29.5</td></tr>
<tr><td>26</td><td>Tennessee</td><td>33.8</td><td>42</td><td>Idaho</td><td>29.3</td></tr>
<tr><td>5</td><td>Texas</td><td>38.3</td><td>43</td><td>Delaware</td><td>29.0</td></tr>
<tr><td>41</td><td>Utah</td><td>29.5</td><td>44</td><td>Maine</td><td>28.8</td></tr>
<tr><td>49</td><td>Vermont</td><td>27.8</td><td>44</td><td>Michigan</td><td>28.8</td></tr>
<tr><td>21</td><td>Virginia</td><td>34.1</td><td>46</td><td>Iowa</td><td>28.7</td></tr>
<tr><td>10</td><td>Washington</td><td>37.2</td><td>46</td><td>New Hampshire</td><td>28.7</td></tr>
<tr><td>50</td><td>West Virginia</td><td>27.5</td><td>48</td><td>Minnesota</td><td>28.5</td></tr>
<tr><td>31</td><td>Wisconsin</td><td>32.9</td><td>49</td><td>Vermont</td><td>27.8</td></tr>
<tr><td>40</td><td>Wyoming</td><td>29.7</td><td>50</td><td>West Virginia</td><td>27.5</td></tr>
<tr><td></td><td></td><td></td><td></td><td>District of Columbia</td><td>57.7</td></tr>
</table>

Source: U.S. Bureau of the Census
   "2018 American Community Survey-Table CP04" (https://data.census.gov/cedsci/)
*For occupied housing units.

Median Monthly Rental Payment in 2018

National Median = $1,058*

RANK	STATE	MEDIAN
44	Alabama	$788
11	Alaska	1,177
19	Arizona	1,036
50	Arkansas	731
2	California	1,520
7	Colorado	1,289
12	Connecticut	1,171
14	Delaware	1,108
10	Florida	1,182
20	Georgia	1,008
1	Hawaii	1,613
31	Idaho	848
22	Illinois	995
38	Indiana	820
46	Iowa	777
33	Kansas	840
45	Kentucky	779
30	Louisiana	854
34	Maine	839
3	Maryland	1,371
6	Massachusetts	1,295
28	Michigan	861
23	Minnesota	969
46	Mississippi	777
35	Missouri	830
40	Montana	811
35	Nebraska	830
14	Nevada	1,108
16	New Hampshire	1,090
4	New Jersey	1,336
35	New Mexico	830
8	New York	1,274
26	North Carolina	900
41	North Dakota	808
43	Ohio	797
41	Oklahoma	808
13	Oregon	1,130
25	Pennsylvania	927
21	Rhode Island	998
27	South Carolina	892
49	South Dakota	734
28	Tennessee	861
17	Texas	1,046
18	Utah	1,043
23	Vermont	969
9	Virginia	1,215
5	Washington	1,316
48	West Virginia	735
32	Wisconsin	847
39	Wyoming	818

RANK	STATE	MEDIAN
1	Hawaii	$1,613
2	California	1,520
3	Maryland	1,371
4	New Jersey	1,336
5	Washington	1,316
6	Massachusetts	1,295
7	Colorado	1,289
8	New York	1,274
9	Virginia	1,215
10	Florida	1,182
11	Alaska	1,177
12	Connecticut	1,171
13	Oregon	1,130
14	Delaware	1,108
14	Nevada	1,108
16	New Hampshire	1,090
17	Texas	1,046
18	Utah	1,043
19	Arizona	1,036
20	Georgia	1,008
21	Rhode Island	998
22	Illinois	995
23	Minnesota	969
23	Vermont	969
25	Pennsylvania	927
26	North Carolina	900
27	South Carolina	892
28	Michigan	861
28	Tennessee	861
30	Louisiana	854
31	Idaho	848
32	Wisconsin	847
33	Kansas	840
34	Maine	839
35	Missouri	830
35	Nebraska	830
35	New Mexico	830
38	Indiana	820
39	Wyoming	818
40	Montana	811
41	North Dakota	808
41	Oklahoma	808
43	Ohio	797
44	Alabama	788
45	Kentucky	779
46	Iowa	777
46	Mississippi	777
48	West Virginia	735
49	South Dakota	734
50	Arkansas	731
	District of Columbia	1,516

Source: U.S. Bureau of the Census
"2018 American Community Survey-Table CP04" (https://data.census.gov/cedsci/)
*Monthly housing costs for renter-occupied housing. Includes rent and utilities paid by the renter.

Percent of Renters Spending 30% or More of Household Income on Rent and Utilities in 2018
National Percent = 49.7% of Renters

ALPHA ORDER

RANK	STATE	PERCENT
25	Alabama	47.9
45	Alaska	43.2
30	Arizona	47.1
36	Arkansas	45.8
3	California	54.6
8	Colorado	51.3
6	Connecticut	52.5
5	Delaware	52.6
1	Florida	56.5
14	Georgia	49.7
4	Hawaii	52.9
35	Idaho	46.1
29	Illinois	47.4
33	Indiana	46.6
46	Iowa	42.4
38	Kansas	45.3
39	Kentucky	44.4
2	Louisiana	55.8
23	Maine	48.2
12	Maryland	49.8
12	Massachusetts	49.8
22	Michigan	48.3
34	Minnesota	46.2
11	Mississippi	50.0
36	Missouri	45.8
39	Montana	44.4
48	Nebraska	41.3
9	Nevada	51.1
27	New Hampshire	47.7
10	New Jersey	50.9
16	New Mexico	49.4
7	New York	52.0
26	North Carolina	47.8
50	North Dakota	38.5
39	Ohio	44.4
43	Oklahoma	43.6
15	Oregon	49.5
24	Pennsylvania	48.0
30	Rhode Island	47.1
18	South Carolina	48.7
49	South Dakota	41.0
18	Tennessee	48.7
18	Texas	48.7
42	Utah	44.3
32	Vermont	46.7
21	Virginia	48.5
27	Washington	47.7
17	West Virginia	49.3
43	Wisconsin	43.6
47	Wyoming	41.5

RANK ORDER

RANK	STATE	PERCENT
1	Florida	56.5
2	Louisiana	55.8
3	California	54.6
4	Hawaii	52.9
5	Delaware	52.6
6	Connecticut	52.5
7	New York	52.0
8	Colorado	51.3
9	Nevada	51.1
10	New Jersey	50.9
11	Mississippi	50.0
12	Maryland	49.8
12	Massachusetts	49.8
14	Georgia	49.7
15	Oregon	49.5
16	New Mexico	49.4
17	West Virginia	49.3
18	South Carolina	48.7
18	Tennessee	48.7
18	Texas	48.7
21	Virginia	48.5
22	Michigan	48.3
23	Maine	48.2
24	Pennsylvania	48.0
25	Alabama	47.9
26	North Carolina	47.8
27	New Hampshire	47.7
27	Washington	47.7
29	Illinois	47.4
30	Arizona	47.1
30	Rhode Island	47.1
32	Vermont	46.7
33	Indiana	46.6
34	Minnesota	46.2
35	Idaho	46.1
36	Arkansas	45.8
36	Missouri	45.8
38	Kansas	45.3
39	Kentucky	44.4
39	Montana	44.4
39	Ohio	44.4
42	Utah	44.3
43	Oklahoma	43.6
43	Wisconsin	43.6
45	Alaska	43.2
46	Iowa	42.4
47	Wyoming	41.5
48	Nebraska	41.3
49	South Dakota	41.0
50	North Dakota	38.5
	District of Columbia	46.5

Source: U.S. Bureau of the Census
  "2018 American Community Survey-Table CP04" (https://data.census.gov/cedsci/)

State and Local Government Expenditures
for Housing and Community Development in 2017
National Total = $52,330,460,000*

ALPHA ORDER

RANK ORDER

RANK	STATE	EXPENDITURES	% of USA		RANK	STATE	EXPENDITURES	% of USA
24	Alabama	$566,151,000	1.1%		1	California	$8,670,742,000	16.6%
32	Alaska	298,266,000	0.6%		2	New York	6,589,654,000	12.6%
28	Arizona	452,844,000	0.9%		3	Massachusetts	2,704,076,000	5.2%
40	Arkansas	200,278,000	0.4%		4	Florida	2,304,282,000	4.4%
1	California	8,670,742,000	16.6%		5	Ohio	2,163,696,000	4.1%
14	Colorado	1,110,573,000	2.1%		6	Illinois	2,090,586,000	4.0%
20	Connecticut	788,106,000	1.5%		7	Pennsylvania	2,043,008,000	3.9%
43	Delaware	159,013,000	0.3%		8	Texas	1,994,689,000	3.8%
4	Florida	2,304,282,000	4.4%		9	North Carolina	1,597,317,000	3.1%
13	Georgia	1,135,304,000	2.2%		10	Maryland	1,533,557,000	2.9%
36	Hawaii	264,274,000	0.5%		11	Washington	1,470,992,000	2.8%
44	Idaho	157,067,000	0.3%		12	New Jersey	1,382,240,000	2.6%
6	Illinois	2,090,586,000	4.0%		13	Georgia	1,135,304,000	2.2%
19	Indiana	815,531,000	1.6%		14	Colorado	1,110,573,000	2.1%
41	Iowa	170,891,000	0.3%		15	Minnesota	1,089,286,000	2.1%
35	Kansas	267,927,000	0.5%		16	Virginia	1,082,079,000	2.1%
27	Kentucky	458,897,000	0.9%		17	Michigan	1,063,165,000	2.0%
23	Louisiana	653,466,000	1.2%		18	Tennessee	827,670,000	1.6%
34	Maine	285,892,000	0.5%		19	Indiana	815,531,000	1.6%
10	Maryland	1,533,557,000	2.9%		20	Connecticut	788,106,000	1.5%
3	Massachusetts	2,704,076,000	5.2%		21	Oregon	706,877,000	1.4%
17	Michigan	1,063,165,000	2.0%		22	Missouri	702,507,000	1.3%
15	Minnesota	1,089,286,000	2.1%		23	Louisiana	653,466,000	1.2%
31	Mississippi	301,940,000	0.6%		24	Alabama	566,151,000	1.1%
22	Missouri	702,507,000	1.3%		25	Oklahoma	512,665,000	1.0%
49	Montana	89,210,000	0.2%		26	South Carolina	483,927,000	0.9%
38	Nebraska	232,232,000	0.4%		27	Kentucky	458,897,000	0.9%
33	Nevada	288,613,000	0.6%		28	Arizona	452,844,000	0.9%
39	New Hampshire	216,534,000	0.4%		29	Utah	373,585,000	0.7%
12	New Jersey	1,382,240,000	2.6%		30	Wisconsin	363,467,000	0.7%
45	New Mexico	132,263,000	0.3%		31	Mississippi	301,940,000	0.6%
2	New York	6,589,654,000	12.6%		32	Alaska	298,266,000	0.6%
9	North Carolina	1,597,317,000	3.1%		33	Nevada	288,613,000	0.6%
48	North Dakota	97,763,000	0.2%		34	Maine	285,892,000	0.5%
5	Ohio	2,163,696,000	4.1%		35	Kansas	267,927,000	0.5%
25	Oklahoma	512,665,000	1.0%		36	Hawaii	264,274,000	0.5%
21	Oregon	706,877,000	1.4%		37	Rhode Island	259,721,000	0.5%
7	Pennsylvania	2,043,008,000	3.9%		38	Nebraska	232,232,000	0.4%
37	Rhode Island	259,721,000	0.5%		39	New Hampshire	216,534,000	0.4%
26	South Carolina	483,927,000	0.9%		40	Arkansas	200,278,000	0.4%
47	South Dakota	104,715,000	0.2%		41	Iowa	170,891,000	0.3%
18	Tennessee	827,670,000	1.6%		42	Vermont	159,441,000	0.3%
8	Texas	1,994,689,000	3.8%		43	Delaware	159,013,000	0.3%
29	Utah	373,585,000	0.7%		44	Idaho	157,067,000	0.3%
42	Vermont	159,441,000	0.3%		45	New Mexico	132,263,000	0.3%
16	Virginia	1,082,079,000	2.1%		46	West Virginia	128,439,000	0.2%
11	Washington	1,470,992,000	2.8%		47	South Dakota	104,715,000	0.2%
46	West Virginia	128,439,000	0.2%		48	North Dakota	97,763,000	0.2%
30	Wisconsin	363,467,000	0.7%		49	Montana	89,210,000	0.2%
50	Wyoming	18,413,000	0.0%		50	Wyoming	18,413,000	0.0%
						District of Columbia	766,629,000	1.5%

Source: U.S. Bureau of the Census, Governments Division
   "2017 State and Local Government Finances" (https://www.census.gov/programs-surveys/gov-finances.html)
*Direct general expenditures.

Per Capita State and Local Government Expenditures for Housing and Community Development in 2017
National Per Capita = $161*

ALPHA ORDER

RANK	STATE	PER CAPITA
31	Alabama	$116
1	Alaska	403
46	Arizona	64
45	Arkansas	67
8	California	220
10	Colorado	198
7	Connecticut	221
16	Delaware	166
33	Florida	110
34	Georgia	109
13	Hawaii	186
41	Idaho	91
17	Illinois	164
27	Indiana	122
49	Iowa	54
40	Kansas	92
36	Kentucky	103
22	Louisiana	140
9	Maine	214
4	Maryland	255
2	Massachusetts	394
35	Michigan	107
12	Minnesota	196
37	Mississippi	101
32	Missouri	115
42	Montana	85
28	Nebraska	121
38	Nevada	97
18	New Hampshire	160
20	New Jersey	156
47	New Mexico	63
3	New York	336
20	North Carolina	156
24	North Dakota	129
13	Ohio	186
23	Oklahoma	130
15	Oregon	170
18	Pennsylvania	160
6	Rhode Island	246
39	South Carolina	96
29	South Dakota	120
26	Tennessee	123
44	Texas	70
29	Utah	120
4	Vermont	255
25	Virginia	128
10	Washington	198
43	West Virginia	71
47	Wisconsin	63
50	Wyoming	32

RANK ORDER

RANK	STATE	PER CAPITA
1	Alaska	$403
2	Massachusetts	394
3	New York	336
4	Maryland	255
4	Vermont	255
6	Rhode Island	246
7	Connecticut	221
8	California	220
9	Maine	214
10	Colorado	198
10	Washington	198
12	Minnesota	196
13	Hawaii	186
13	Ohio	186
15	Oregon	170
16	Delaware	166
17	Illinois	164
18	New Hampshire	160
18	Pennsylvania	160
20	New Jersey	156
20	North Carolina	156
22	Louisiana	140
23	Oklahoma	130
24	North Dakota	129
25	Virginia	128
26	Tennessee	123
27	Indiana	122
28	Nebraska	121
29	South Dakota	120
29	Utah	120
31	Alabama	116
32	Missouri	115
33	Florida	110
34	Georgia	109
35	Michigan	107
36	Kentucky	103
37	Mississippi	101
38	Nevada	97
39	South Carolina	96
40	Kansas	92
41	Idaho	91
42	Montana	85
43	West Virginia	71
44	Texas	70
45	Arkansas	67
46	Arizona	64
47	New Mexico	63
47	Wisconsin	63
49	Iowa	54
50	Wyoming	32

District of Columbia 1,102

Source: CQ Press using data from U.S. Bureau of the Census, Governments Division
    "2017 State and Local Government Finances" (https://www.census.gov/programs-surveys/gov-finances.html)
*Direct general expenditures.

State and Local Government Spending for Housing and Community Development as a Percent of All State and Local Government Expenditures in 2017 National Percent = 1.7%*

ALPHA ORDER

RANK	STATE	PERCENT
31	Alabama	1.4
5	Alaska	2.3
42	Arizona	0.9
45	Arkansas	0.8
14	California	1.9
8	Colorado	2.2
5	Connecticut	2.3
23	Delaware	1.5
23	Florida	1.5
20	Georgia	1.6
14	Hawaii	1.9
31	Idaho	1.4
16	Illinois	1.8
23	Indiana	1.5
49	Iowa	0.5
40	Kansas	1.0
37	Kentucky	1.2
23	Louisiana	1.5
2	Maine	2.5
2	Maryland	2.5
1	Massachusetts	3.5
34	Michigan	1.3
16	Minnesota	1.8
37	Mississippi	1.2
23	Missouri	1.5
42	Montana	0.9
34	Nebraska	1.3
34	Nevada	1.3
10	New Hampshire	2.0
23	New Jersey	1.5
48	New Mexico	0.6
5	New York	2.3
10	North Carolina	2.0
40	North Dakota	1.0
10	Ohio	2.0
16	Oklahoma	1.8
20	Oregon	1.6
20	Pennsylvania	1.6
2	Rhode Island	2.5
39	South Carolina	1.1
23	South Dakota	1.5
16	Tennessee	1.8
42	Texas	0.9
31	Utah	1.4
8	Vermont	2.2
23	Virginia	1.5
10	Washington	2.0
45	West Virginia	0.8
47	Wisconsin	0.7
50	Wyoming	0.2

RANK ORDER

RANK	STATE	PERCENT
1	Massachusetts	3.5
2	Maine	2.5
2	Maryland	2.5
2	Rhode Island	2.5
5	Alaska	2.3
5	Connecticut	2.3
5	New York	2.3
8	Colorado	2.2
8	Vermont	2.2
10	New Hampshire	2.0
10	North Carolina	2.0
10	Ohio	2.0
10	Washington	2.0
14	California	1.9
14	Hawaii	1.9
16	Illinois	1.8
16	Minnesota	1.8
16	Oklahoma	1.8
16	Tennessee	1.8
20	Georgia	1.6
20	Oregon	1.6
20	Pennsylvania	1.6
23	Delaware	1.5
23	Florida	1.5
23	Indiana	1.5
23	Louisiana	1.5
23	Missouri	1.5
23	New Jersey	1.5
23	South Dakota	1.5
23	Virginia	1.5
31	Alabama	1.4
31	Idaho	1.4
31	Utah	1.4
34	Michigan	1.3
34	Nebraska	1.3
34	Nevada	1.3
37	Kentucky	1.2
37	Mississippi	1.2
39	South Carolina	1.1
40	Kansas	1.0
40	North Dakota	1.0
42	Arizona	0.9
42	Montana	0.9
42	Texas	0.9
45	Arkansas	0.8
45	West Virginia	0.8
47	Wisconsin	0.7
48	New Mexico	0.6
49	Iowa	0.5
50	Wyoming	0.2

District of Columbia	5.8

Source: CQ Press using data from U.S. Bureau of the Census, Governments Division
"2017 State and Local Government Finances" (https://www.census.gov/programs-surveys/gov-finances.html)
*As a percent of direct general expenditures.

XIII. Population

Population in 2019

National Total = 328,239,523*

RANK	STATE	POPULATION	% of USA
24	Alabama	4,903,185	1.5%
48	Alaska	731,545	0.2%
14	Arizona	7,278,717	2.2%
33	Arkansas	3,017,804	0.9%
1	California	39,512,223	12.0%
21	Colorado	5,758,736	1.8%
29	Connecticut	3,565,287	1.1%
45	Delaware	973,764	0.3%
3	Florida	21,477,737	6.5%
8	Georgia	10,617,423	3.2%
40	Hawaii	1,415,872	0.4%
39	Idaho	1,787,065	0.5%
6	Illinois	12,671,821	3.9%
17	Indiana	6,732,219	2.1%
31	Iowa	3,155,070	1.0%
35	Kansas	2,913,314	0.9%
26	Kentucky	4,467,673	1.4%
25	Louisiana	4,648,794	1.4%
42	Maine	1,344,212	0.4%
19	Maryland	6,045,680	1.8%
15	Massachusetts	6,892,503	2.1%
10	Michigan	9,986,857	3.0%
22	Minnesota	5,639,632	1.7%
34	Mississippi	2,976,149	0.9%
18	Missouri	6,137,428	1.9%
43	Montana	1,068,778	0.3%
37	Nebraska	1,934,408	0.6%
32	Nevada	3,080,156	0.9%
41	New Hampshire	1,359,711	0.4%
11	New Jersey	8,882,190	2.7%
36	New Mexico	2,096,829	0.6%
4	New York	19,453,561	5.9%
9	North Carolina	10,488,084	3.2%
47	North Dakota	762,062	0.2%
7	Ohio	11,689,100	3.6%
28	Oklahoma	3,956,971	1.2%
27	Oregon	4,217,737	1.3%
5	Pennsylvania	12,801,989	3.9%
44	Rhode Island	1,059,361	0.3%
23	South Carolina	5,148,714	1.6%
46	South Dakota	884,659	0.3%
16	Tennessee	6,829,174	2.1%
2	Texas	28,995,881	8.8%
30	Utah	3,205,958	1.0%
49	Vermont	623,989	0.2%
12	Virginia	8,535,519	2.6%
13	Washington	7,614,893	2.3%
38	West Virginia	1,792,147	0.5%
20	Wisconsin	5,822,434	1.8%
50	Wyoming	578,759	0.2%

RANK	STATE	POPULATION	% of USA
1	California	39,512,223	12.0%
2	Texas	28,995,881	8.8%
3	Florida	21,477,737	6.5%
4	New York	19,453,561	5.9%
5	Pennsylvania	12,801,989	3.9%
6	Illinois	12,671,821	3.9%
7	Ohio	11,689,100	3.6%
8	Georgia	10,617,423	3.2%
9	North Carolina	10,488,084	3.2%
10	Michigan	9,986,857	3.0%
11	New Jersey	8,882,190	2.7%
12	Virginia	8,535,519	2.6%
13	Washington	7,614,893	2.3%
14	Arizona	7,278,717	2.2%
15	Massachusetts	6,892,503	2.1%
16	Tennessee	6,829,174	2.1%
17	Indiana	6,732,219	2.1%
18	Missouri	6,137,428	1.9%
19	Maryland	6,045,680	1.8%
20	Wisconsin	5,822,434	1.8%
21	Colorado	5,758,736	1.8%
22	Minnesota	5,639,632	1.7%
23	South Carolina	5,148,714	1.6%
24	Alabama	4,903,185	1.5%
25	Louisiana	4,648,794	1.4%
26	Kentucky	4,467,673	1.4%
27	Oregon	4,217,737	1.3%
28	Oklahoma	3,956,971	1.2%
29	Connecticut	3,565,287	1.1%
30	Utah	3,205,958	1.0%
31	Iowa	3,155,070	1.0%
32	Nevada	3,080,156	0.9%
33	Arkansas	3,017,804	0.9%
34	Mississippi	2,976,149	0.9%
35	Kansas	2,913,314	0.9%
36	New Mexico	2,096,829	0.6%
37	Nebraska	1,934,408	0.6%
38	West Virginia	1,792,147	0.5%
39	Idaho	1,787,065	0.5%
40	Hawaii	1,415,872	0.4%
41	New Hampshire	1,359,711	0.4%
42	Maine	1,344,212	0.4%
43	Montana	1,068,778	0.3%
44	Rhode Island	1,059,361	0.3%
45	Delaware	973,764	0.3%
46	South Dakota	884,659	0.3%
47	North Dakota	762,062	0.2%
48	Alaska	731,545	0.2%
49	Vermont	623,989	0.2%
50	Wyoming	578,759	0.2%
	District of Columbia	705,749	0.2%

Source: U.S. Bureau of the Census
"Population Estimates" (December 2019, https://www.census.gov/programs-surveys/popest.html)
*Resident population estimate as of July 1, 2019.

Population in 2018

National Total = 326,687,501*

ALPHA ORDER

ALPHA ORDER

RANK	STATE	POPULATION	% of USA
24	Alabama	4,887,681	1.5%
48	Alaska	735,139	0.2%
14	Arizona	7,158,024	2.2%
33	Arkansas	3,009,733	0.9%
1	California	39,461,588	12.1%
21	Colorado	5,691,287	1.7%
29	Connecticut	3,571,520	1.1%
45	Delaware	965,479	0.3%
3	Florida	21,244,317	6.5%
8	Georgia	10,511,131	3.2%
40	Hawaii	1,420,593	0.4%
39	Idaho	1,750,536	0.5%
6	Illinois	12,723,071	3.9%
17	Indiana	6,695,497	2.0%
31	Iowa	3,148,618	1.0%
35	Kansas	2,911,359	0.9%
26	Kentucky	4,461,153	1.4%
25	Louisiana	4,659,690	1.4%
42	Maine	1,339,057	0.4%
19	Maryland	6,035,802	1.8%
15	Massachusetts	6,882,635	2.1%
10	Michigan	9,984,072	3.1%
22	Minnesota	5,606,249	1.7%
34	Mississippi	2,981,020	0.9%
18	Missouri	6,121,623	1.9%
43	Montana	1,060,665	0.3%
37	Nebraska	1,925,614	0.6%
32	Nevada	3,027,341	0.9%
41	New Hampshire	1,353,465	0.4%
11	New Jersey	8,886,025	2.7%
36	New Mexico	2,092,741	0.6%
4	New York	19,530,351	6.0%
9	North Carolina	10,381,615	3.2%
47	North Dakota	758,080	0.2%
7	Ohio	11,676,341	3.6%
28	Oklahoma	3,940,235	1.2%
27	Oregon	4,181,886	1.3%
5	Pennsylvania	12,800,922	3.9%
44	Rhode Island	1,058,287	0.3%
23	South Carolina	5,084,156	1.6%
46	South Dakota	878,698	0.3%
16	Tennessee	6,771,631	2.1%
2	Texas	28,628,666	8.8%
30	Utah	3,153,550	1.0%
49	Vermont	624,358	0.2%
12	Virginia	8,501,286	2.6%
13	Washington	7,523,869	2.3%
38	West Virginia	1,804,291	0.6%
20	Wisconsin	5,807,406	1.8%
50	Wyoming	577,601	0.2%

RANK ORDER

RANK	STATE	POPULATION	% of USA
1	California	39,461,588	12.1%
2	Texas	28,628,666	8.8%
3	Florida	21,244,317	6.5%
4	New York	19,530,351	6.0%
5	Pennsylvania	12,800,922	3.9%
6	Illinois	12,723,071	3.9%
7	Ohio	11,676,341	3.6%
8	Georgia	10,511,131	3.2%
9	North Carolina	10,381,615	3.2%
10	Michigan	9,984,072	3.1%
11	New Jersey	8,886,025	2.7%
12	Virginia	8,501,286	2.6%
13	Washington	7,523,869	2.3%
14	Arizona	7,158,024	2.2%
15	Massachusetts	6,882,635	2.1%
16	Tennessee	6,771,631	2.1%
17	Indiana	6,695,497	2.0%
18	Missouri	6,121,623	1.9%
19	Maryland	6,035,802	1.8%
20	Wisconsin	5,807,406	1.8%
21	Colorado	5,691,287	1.7%
22	Minnesota	5,606,249	1.7%
23	South Carolina	5,084,156	1.6%
24	Alabama	4,887,681	1.5%
25	Louisiana	4,659,690	1.4%
26	Kentucky	4,461,153	1.4%
27	Oregon	4,181,886	1.3%
28	Oklahoma	3,940,235	1.2%
29	Connecticut	3,571,520	1.1%
30	Utah	3,153,550	1.0%
31	Iowa	3,148,618	1.0%
32	Nevada	3,027,341	0.9%
33	Arkansas	3,009,733	0.9%
34	Mississippi	2,981,020	0.9%
35	Kansas	2,911,359	0.9%
36	New Mexico	2,092,741	0.6%
37	Nebraska	1,925,614	0.6%
38	West Virginia	1,804,291	0.6%
39	Idaho	1,750,536	0.5%
40	Hawaii	1,420,593	0.4%
41	New Hampshire	1,353,465	0.4%
42	Maine	1,339,057	0.4%
43	Montana	1,060,665	0.3%
44	Rhode Island	1,058,287	0.3%
45	Delaware	965,479	0.3%
46	South Dakota	878,698	0.3%
47	North Dakota	758,080	0.2%
48	Alaska	735,139	0.2%
49	Vermont	624,358	0.2%
50	Wyoming	577,601	0.2%
	District of Columbia	701,547	0.2%

Source: U.S. Bureau of the Census
"Population Estimates" (December 2019, https://www.census.gov/programs-surveys/popest.html)
*Resident population. Revised estimates of July 1, 2019.

Numerical Population Change: 2018 to 2019

National Total = 1,552,022 Increase*

ALPHA ORDER

RANK	STATE	GAIN/LOSS
20	Alabama	15,504
42	Alaska	(3,594)
3	Arizona	120,693
28	Arkansas	8,071
12	California	50,635
7	Colorado	67,449
46	Connecticut	(6,233)
26	Delaware	8,285
2	Florida	233,420
5	Georgia	106,292
44	Hawaii	(4,721)
14	Idaho	36,529
49	Illinois	(51,250)
13	Indiana	36,722
30	Iowa	6,452
37	Kansas	1,955
29	Kentucky	6,520
47	Louisiana	(10,896)
33	Maine	5,155
23	Maryland	9,878
24	Massachusetts	9,868
36	Michigan	2,785
17	Minnesota	33,383
45	Mississippi	(4,871)
19	Missouri	15,805
27	Montana	8,113
25	Nebraska	8,794
10	Nevada	52,815
31	New Hampshire	6,246
43	New Jersey	(3,835)
34	New Mexico	4,088
50	New York	(76,790)
4	North Carolina	106,469
35	North Dakota	3,982
22	Ohio	12,759
18	Oklahoma	16,736
15	Oregon	35,851
40	Pennsylvania	1,067
39	Rhode Island	1,074
8	South Carolina	64,558
32	South Dakota	5,961
9	Tennessee	57,543
1	Texas	367,215
11	Utah	52,408
41	Vermont	(369)
16	Virginia	34,233
6	Washington	91,024
48	West Virginia	(12,144)
21	Wisconsin	15,028
38	Wyoming	1,158

RANK ORDER

RANK	STATE	GAIN/LOSS
1	Texas	367,215
2	Florida	233,420
3	Arizona	120,693
4	North Carolina	106,469
5	Georgia	106,292
6	Washington	91,024
7	Colorado	67,449
8	South Carolina	64,558
9	Tennessee	57,543
10	Nevada	52,815
11	Utah	52,408
12	California	50,635
13	Indiana	36,722
14	Idaho	36,529
15	Oregon	35,851
16	Virginia	34,233
17	Minnesota	33,383
18	Oklahoma	16,736
19	Missouri	15,805
20	Alabama	15,504
21	Wisconsin	15,028
22	Ohio	12,759
23	Maryland	9,878
24	Massachusetts	9,868
25	Nebraska	8,794
26	Delaware	8,285
27	Montana	8,113
28	Arkansas	8,071
29	Kentucky	6,520
30	Iowa	6,452
31	New Hampshire	6,246
32	South Dakota	5,961
33	Maine	5,155
34	New Mexico	4,088
35	North Dakota	3,982
36	Michigan	2,785
37	Kansas	1,955
38	Wyoming	1,158
39	Rhode Island	1,074
40	Pennsylvania	1,067
41	Vermont	(369)
42	Alaska	(3,594)
43	New Jersey	(3,835)
44	Hawaii	(4,721)
45	Mississippi	(4,871)
46	Connecticut	(6,233)
47	Louisiana	(10,896)
48	West Virginia	(12,144)
49	Illinois	(51,250)
50	New York	(76,790)
	District of Columbia	4,202

Source: CQ Press using data from U.S. Bureau of the Census
   "Population Estimates" (December 2019, https://www.census.gov/programs-surveys/popest.html)
*Resident population from July 1, 2018, to July 1, 2019.

Percent Change in Population: 2018 to 2019

National Percent Change = 0.5% Increase*

ALPHA ORDER				RANK ORDER		
RANK	STATE	PERCENT CHANGE		RANK	STATE	PERCENT CHANGE
25	Alabama	0.3		1	Idaho	2.1
49	Alaska	(0.5)		2	Arizona	1.7
2	Arizona	1.7		2	Nevada	1.7
25	Arkansas	0.3		2	Utah	1.7
33	California	0.1		5	South Carolina	1.3
7	Colorado	1.2		5	Texas	1.3
43	Connecticut	(0.2)		7	Colorado	1.2
12	Delaware	0.9		7	Washington	1.2
9	Florida	1.1		9	Florida	1.1
10	Georgia	1.0		10	Georgia	1.0
46	Hawaii	(0.3)		10	North Carolina	1.0
1	Idaho	2.1		12	Delaware	0.9
47	Illinois	(0.4)		12	Oregon	0.9
18	Indiana	0.5		14	Montana	0.8
29	Iowa	0.2		14	Tennessee	0.8
33	Kansas	0.1		16	South Dakota	0.7
33	Kentucky	0.1		17	Minnesota	0.6
43	Louisiana	(0.2)		18	Indiana	0.5
22	Maine	0.4		18	Nebraska	0.5
29	Maryland	0.2		18	New Hampshire	0.5
33	Massachusetts	0.1		18	North Dakota	0.5
39	Michigan	0.0		22	Maine	0.4
17	Minnesota	0.6		22	Oklahoma	0.4
43	Mississippi	(0.2)		22	Virginia	0.4
25	Missouri	0.3		25	Alabama	0.3
14	Montana	0.8		25	Arkansas	0.3
18	Nebraska	0.5		25	Missouri	0.3
2	Nevada	1.7		25	Wisconsin	0.3
18	New Hampshire	0.5		29	Iowa	0.2
39	New Jersey	0.0		29	Maryland	0.2
29	New Mexico	0.2		29	New Mexico	0.2
47	New York	(0.4)		29	Wyoming	0.2
10	North Carolina	1.0		33	California	0.1
18	North Dakota	0.5		33	Kansas	0.1
33	Ohio	0.1		33	Kentucky	0.1
22	Oklahoma	0.4		33	Massachusetts	0.1
12	Oregon	0.9		33	Ohio	0.1
39	Pennsylvania	0.0		33	Rhode Island	0.1
33	Rhode Island	0.1		39	Michigan	0.0
5	South Carolina	1.3		39	New Jersey	0.0
16	South Dakota	0.7		39	Pennsylvania	0.0
14	Tennessee	0.8		42	Vermont	(0.1)
5	Texas	1.3		43	Connecticut	(0.2)
2	Utah	1.7		43	Louisiana	(0.2)
42	Vermont	(0.1)		43	Mississippi	(0.2)
22	Virginia	0.4		46	Hawaii	(0.3)
7	Washington	1.2		47	Illinois	(0.4)
50	West Virginia	(0.7)		47	New York	(0.4)
25	Wisconsin	0.3		49	Alaska	(0.5)
29	Wyoming	0.2		50	West Virginia	(0.7)
					District of Columbia	0.6

Source: CQ Press using data from U.S. Bureau of the Census
"Population Estimates" (December 2019, https://www.census.gov/programs-surveys/popest.html)
*Resident population from July 1, 2018, to July 1, 2019.

Population per Square Mile in 2019

National Rate = 92.9 Persons per Square Mile*

<table>
<tr><td colspan="3">ALPHA ORDER</td><td colspan="3">RANK ORDER</td></tr>
<tr><td>RANK</td><td>STATE</td><td>RATE</td><td>RANK</td><td>STATE</td><td>RATE</td></tr>
<tr><td>27</td><td>Alabama</td><td>96.8</td><td>1</td><td>New Jersey</td><td>1,207.8</td></tr>
<tr><td>50</td><td>Alaska</td><td>1.3</td><td>2</td><td>Rhode Island</td><td>1,024.5</td></tr>
<tr><td>32</td><td>Arizona</td><td>64.1</td><td>3</td><td>Massachusetts</td><td>883.7</td></tr>
<tr><td>34</td><td>Arkansas</td><td>58.0</td><td>4</td><td>Connecticut</td><td>736.3</td></tr>
<tr><td>11</td><td>California</td><td>253.6</td><td>5</td><td>Maryland</td><td>622.8</td></tr>
<tr><td>37</td><td>Colorado</td><td>55.6</td><td>6</td><td>Delaware</td><td>499.6</td></tr>
<tr><td>4</td><td>Connecticut</td><td>736.3</td><td>7</td><td>New York</td><td>412.8</td></tr>
<tr><td>6</td><td>Delaware</td><td>499.6</td><td>8</td><td>Florida</td><td>400.5</td></tr>
<tr><td>8</td><td>Florida</td><td>400.5</td><td>9</td><td>Ohio</td><td>286.1</td></tr>
<tr><td>17</td><td>Georgia</td><td>184.6</td><td>9</td><td>Pennsylvania</td><td>286.1</td></tr>
<tr><td>13</td><td>Hawaii</td><td>220.4</td><td>11</td><td>California</td><td>253.6</td></tr>
<tr><td>44</td><td>Idaho</td><td>21.6</td><td>12</td><td>Illinois</td><td>228.2</td></tr>
<tr><td>12</td><td>Illinois</td><td>228.2</td><td>13</td><td>Hawaii</td><td>220.4</td></tr>
<tr><td>16</td><td>Indiana</td><td>187.9</td><td>14</td><td>Virginia</td><td>216.1</td></tr>
<tr><td>36</td><td>Iowa</td><td>56.5</td><td>15</td><td>North Carolina</td><td>215.7</td></tr>
<tr><td>41</td><td>Kansas</td><td>35.6</td><td>16</td><td>Indiana</td><td>187.9</td></tr>
<tr><td>23</td><td>Kentucky</td><td>113.1</td><td>17</td><td>Georgia</td><td>184.6</td></tr>
<tr><td>25</td><td>Louisiana</td><td>107.6</td><td>18</td><td>Michigan</td><td>176.6</td></tr>
<tr><td>39</td><td>Maine</td><td>43.6</td><td>19</td><td>South Carolina</td><td>171.3</td></tr>
<tr><td>5</td><td>Maryland</td><td>622.8</td><td>20</td><td>Tennessee</td><td>165.6</td></tr>
<tr><td>3</td><td>Massachusetts</td><td>883.7</td><td>21</td><td>New Hampshire</td><td>151.9</td></tr>
<tr><td>18</td><td>Michigan</td><td>176.6</td><td>22</td><td>Washington</td><td>114.6</td></tr>
<tr><td>30</td><td>Minnesota</td><td>70.8</td><td>23</td><td>Kentucky</td><td>113.1</td></tr>
<tr><td>33</td><td>Mississippi</td><td>63.4</td><td>24</td><td>Texas</td><td>111.0</td></tr>
<tr><td>28</td><td>Missouri</td><td>89.3</td><td>25</td><td>Louisiana</td><td>107.6</td></tr>
<tr><td>48</td><td>Montana</td><td>7.3</td><td>26</td><td>Wisconsin</td><td>107.5</td></tr>
<tr><td>43</td><td>Nebraska</td><td>25.2</td><td>27</td><td>Alabama</td><td>96.8</td></tr>
<tr><td>42</td><td>Nevada</td><td>28.1</td><td>28</td><td>Missouri</td><td>89.3</td></tr>
<tr><td>21</td><td>New Hampshire</td><td>151.9</td><td>29</td><td>West Virginia</td><td>74.6</td></tr>
<tr><td>1</td><td>New Jersey</td><td>1,207.8</td><td>30</td><td>Minnesota</td><td>70.8</td></tr>
<tr><td>45</td><td>New Mexico</td><td>17.3</td><td>31</td><td>Vermont</td><td>67.7</td></tr>
<tr><td>7</td><td>New York</td><td>412.8</td><td>32</td><td>Arizona</td><td>64.1</td></tr>
<tr><td>15</td><td>North Carolina</td><td>215.7</td><td>33</td><td>Mississippi</td><td>63.4</td></tr>
<tr><td>47</td><td>North Dakota</td><td>11.0</td><td>34</td><td>Arkansas</td><td>58.0</td></tr>
<tr><td>9</td><td>Ohio</td><td>286.1</td><td>35</td><td>Oklahoma</td><td>57.7</td></tr>
<tr><td>35</td><td>Oklahoma</td><td>57.7</td><td>36</td><td>Iowa</td><td>56.5</td></tr>
<tr><td>38</td><td>Oregon</td><td>43.9</td><td>37</td><td>Colorado</td><td>55.6</td></tr>
<tr><td>9</td><td>Pennsylvania</td><td>286.1</td><td>38</td><td>Oregon</td><td>43.9</td></tr>
<tr><td>2</td><td>Rhode Island</td><td>1,024.5</td><td>39</td><td>Maine</td><td>43.6</td></tr>
<tr><td>19</td><td>South Carolina</td><td>171.3</td><td>40</td><td>Utah</td><td>39.0</td></tr>
<tr><td>46</td><td>South Dakota</td><td>11.7</td><td>41</td><td>Kansas</td><td>35.6</td></tr>
<tr><td>20</td><td>Tennessee</td><td>165.6</td><td>42</td><td>Nevada</td><td>28.1</td></tr>
<tr><td>24</td><td>Texas</td><td>111.0</td><td>43</td><td>Nebraska</td><td>25.2</td></tr>
<tr><td>40</td><td>Utah</td><td>39.0</td><td>44</td><td>Idaho</td><td>21.6</td></tr>
<tr><td>31</td><td>Vermont</td><td>67.7</td><td>45</td><td>New Mexico</td><td>17.3</td></tr>
<tr><td>14</td><td>Virginia</td><td>216.1</td><td>46</td><td>South Dakota</td><td>11.7</td></tr>
<tr><td>22</td><td>Washington</td><td>114.6</td><td>47</td><td>North Dakota</td><td>11.0</td></tr>
<tr><td>29</td><td>West Virginia</td><td>74.6</td><td>48</td><td>Montana</td><td>7.3</td></tr>
<tr><td>26</td><td>Wisconsin</td><td>107.5</td><td>49</td><td>Wyoming</td><td>6.0</td></tr>
<tr><td>49</td><td>Wyoming</td><td>6.0</td><td>50</td><td>Alaska</td><td>1.3</td></tr>
<tr><td></td><td></td><td></td><td></td><td>District of Columbia</td><td>11,569.7</td></tr>
</table>

Source: CQ Press using data from U.S. Bureau of the Census
   "Population Estimates" (December 2019, https://www.census.gov/programs-surveys/popest.html)
*Resident population. Based on land area of states.

Male Population in 2018

National Total = 161,128,679 Males

RANK	STATE	MALES	% of USA
24	Alabama	2,364,115	1.5%
48	Alaska	384,573	0.2%
14	Arizona	3,565,339	2.2%
33	Arkansas	1,480,143	0.9%
1	California	19,663,577	12.2%
21	Colorado	2,867,868	1.8%
29	Connecticut	1,743,395	1.1%
45	Delaware	467,927	0.3%
3	Florida	10,411,777	6.5%
8	Georgia	5,115,416	3.2%
40	Hawaii	711,002	0.4%
39	Idaho	879,077	0.5%
6	Illinois	6,260,901	3.9%
17	Indiana	3,300,302	2.0%
31	Iowa	1,570,807	1.0%
34	Kansas	1,450,406	0.9%
26	Kentucky	2,201,511	1.4%
25	Louisiana	2,274,759	1.4%
42	Maine	655,373	0.4%
19	Maryland	2,928,921	1.8%
15	Massachusetts	3,350,528	2.1%
10	Michigan	4,922,143	3.1%
22	Minnesota	2,794,801	1.7%
35	Mississippi	1,447,735	0.9%
18	Missouri	3,007,563	1.9%
43	Montana	534,852	0.3%
37	Nebraska	963,382	0.6%
32	Nevada	1,521,555	0.9%
41	New Hampshire	672,266	0.4%
11	New Jersey	4,352,194	2.7%
36	New Mexico	1,037,285	0.6%
4	New York	9,488,430	5.9%
9	North Carolina	5,050,861	3.1%
47	North Dakota	389,350	0.2%
7	Ohio	5,730,718	3.6%
28	Oklahoma	1,953,046	1.2%
27	Oregon	2,077,494	1.3%
5	Pennsylvania	6,274,660	3.9%
44	Rhode Island	514,332	0.3%
23	South Carolina	2,463,326	1.5%
46	South Dakota	445,531	0.3%
16	Tennessee	3,302,924	2.0%
2	Texas	14,260,106	8.9%
30	Utah	1,592,143	1.0%
49	Vermont	309,252	0.2%
12	Virginia	4,190,648	2.6%
13	Washington	3,769,911	2.3%
38	West Virginia	894,340	0.6%
20	Wisconsin	2,892,273	1.8%
50	Wyoming	294,534	0.2%

RANK	STATE	MALES	% of USA
1	California	19,663,577	12.2%
2	Texas	14,260,106	8.9%
3	Florida	10,411,777	6.5%
4	New York	9,488,430	5.9%
5	Pennsylvania	6,274,660	3.9%
6	Illinois	6,260,901	3.9%
7	Ohio	5,730,718	3.6%
8	Georgia	5,115,416	3.2%
9	North Carolina	5,050,861	3.1%
10	Michigan	4,922,143	3.1%
11	New Jersey	4,352,194	2.7%
12	Virginia	4,190,648	2.6%
13	Washington	3,769,911	2.3%
14	Arizona	3,565,339	2.2%
15	Massachusetts	3,350,528	2.1%
16	Tennessee	3,302,924	2.0%
17	Indiana	3,300,302	2.0%
18	Missouri	3,007,563	1.9%
19	Maryland	2,928,921	1.8%
20	Wisconsin	2,892,273	1.8%
21	Colorado	2,867,868	1.8%
22	Minnesota	2,794,801	1.7%
23	South Carolina	2,463,326	1.5%
24	Alabama	2,364,115	1.5%
25	Louisiana	2,274,759	1.4%
26	Kentucky	2,201,511	1.4%
27	Oregon	2,077,494	1.3%
28	Oklahoma	1,953,046	1.2%
29	Connecticut	1,743,395	1.1%
30	Utah	1,592,143	1.0%
31	Iowa	1,570,807	1.0%
32	Nevada	1,521,555	0.9%
33	Arkansas	1,480,143	0.9%
34	Kansas	1,450,406	0.9%
35	Mississippi	1,447,735	0.9%
36	New Mexico	1,037,285	0.6%
37	Nebraska	963,382	0.6%
38	West Virginia	894,340	0.6%
39	Idaho	879,077	0.5%
40	Hawaii	711,002	0.4%
41	New Hampshire	672,266	0.4%
42	Maine	655,373	0.4%
43	Montana	534,852	0.3%
44	Rhode Island	514,332	0.3%
45	Delaware	467,927	0.3%
46	South Dakota	445,531	0.3%
47	North Dakota	389,350	0.2%
48	Alaska	384,573	0.2%
49	Vermont	309,252	0.2%
50	Wyoming	294,534	0.2%
	District of Columbia	333,307	0.2%

Source: U.S. Bureau of the Census
"State Characteristics: Vintage 2018" (https://www.census.gov/programs-surveys/popest/data/data-sets.html)

Female Population in 2018

National Total = 166,038,755 Females

ALPHA ORDER

RANK	STATE	FEMALES	% of USA
24	Alabama	2,523,756	1.6%
48	Alaska	352,865	0.2%
14	Arizona	3,606,307	2.3%
33	Arkansas	1,533,682	1.0%
1	California	19,893,468	12.4%
21	Colorado	2,827,696	1.8%
29	Connecticut	1,829,270	1.1%
45	Delaware	499,244	0.3%
3	Florida	10,887,548	6.8%
8	Georgia	5,404,059	3.4%
40	Hawaii	709,489	0.4%
39	Idaho	875,131	0.5%
6	Illinois	6,480,179	4.0%
17	Indiana	3,391,576	2.1%
30	Iowa	1,585,338	1.0%
35	Kansas	1,461,099	0.9%
26	Kentucky	2,266,891	1.4%
25	Louisiana	2,385,219	1.5%
42	Maine	683,031	0.4%
19	Maryland	3,113,797	1.9%
15	Massachusetts	3,551,621	2.2%
10	Michigan	5,073,772	3.2%
22	Minnesota	2,816,378	1.8%
32	Mississippi	1,538,795	1.0%
18	Missouri	3,118,889	1.9%
44	Montana	527,453	0.3%
37	Nebraska	965,886	0.6%
34	Nevada	1,512,837	0.9%
41	New Hampshire	684,192	0.4%
11	New Jersey	4,556,326	2.8%
36	New Mexico	1,058,143	0.7%
4	New York	10,053,779	6.3%
9	North Carolina	5,332,759	3.3%
47	North Dakota	370,727	0.2%
7	Ohio	5,958,724	3.7%
28	Oklahoma	1,990,033	1.2%
27	Oregon	2,113,219	1.3%
5	Pennsylvania	6,532,400	4.1%
43	Rhode Island	542,983	0.3%
23	South Carolina	2,620,801	1.6%
46	South Dakota	436,704	0.3%
16	Tennessee	3,467,086	2.2%
2	Texas	14,441,739	9.0%
31	Utah	1,568,962	1.0%
49	Vermont	317,047	0.2%
12	Virginia	4,327,037	2.7%
13	Washington	3,765,680	2.4%
38	West Virginia	911,492	0.6%
20	Wisconsin	2,921,295	1.8%
50	Wyoming	283,203	0.2%

RANK ORDER

RANK	STATE	FEMALES	% of USA
1	California	19,893,468	12.4%
2	Texas	14,441,739	9.0%
3	Florida	10,887,548	6.8%
4	New York	10,053,779	6.3%
5	Pennsylvania	6,532,400	4.1%
6	Illinois	6,480,179	4.0%
7	Ohio	5,958,724	3.7%
8	Georgia	5,404,059	3.4%
9	North Carolina	5,332,759	3.3%
10	Michigan	5,073,772	3.2%
11	New Jersey	4,556,326	2.8%
12	Virginia	4,327,037	2.7%
13	Washington	3,765,680	2.4%
14	Arizona	3,606,307	2.3%
15	Massachusetts	3,551,621	2.2%
16	Tennessee	3,467,086	2.2%
17	Indiana	3,391,576	2.1%
18	Missouri	3,118,889	1.9%
19	Maryland	3,113,797	1.9%
20	Wisconsin	2,921,295	1.8%
21	Colorado	2,827,696	1.8%
22	Minnesota	2,816,378	1.8%
23	South Carolina	2,620,801	1.6%
24	Alabama	2,523,756	1.6%
25	Louisiana	2,385,219	1.5%
26	Kentucky	2,266,891	1.4%
27	Oregon	2,113,219	1.3%
28	Oklahoma	1,990,033	1.2%
29	Connecticut	1,829,270	1.1%
30	Iowa	1,585,338	1.0%
31	Utah	1,568,962	1.0%
32	Mississippi	1,538,795	1.0%
33	Arkansas	1,533,682	1.0%
34	Nevada	1,512,837	0.9%
35	Kansas	1,461,099	0.9%
36	New Mexico	1,058,143	0.7%
37	Nebraska	965,886	0.6%
38	West Virginia	911,492	0.6%
39	Idaho	875,131	0.5%
40	Hawaii	709,489	0.4%
41	New Hampshire	684,192	0.4%
42	Maine	683,031	0.4%
43	Rhode Island	542,983	0.3%
44	Montana	527,453	0.3%
45	Delaware	499,244	0.3%
46	South Dakota	436,704	0.3%
47	North Dakota	370,727	0.2%
48	Alaska	352,865	0.2%
49	Vermont	317,047	0.2%
50	Wyoming	283,203	0.2%
	District of Columbia	369,148	0.2%

Source: U.S. Bureau of the Census
"State Characteristics: Vintage 2018" (https://www.census.gov/programs-surveys/popest/data/data-sets.html)

Male to Female Ratio in 2018

National Ratio = 97.0 Males per 100 Females

RANK	STATE	RATIO
49	Alabama	93.7
1	Alaska	109.0
17	Arizona	98.9
31	Arkansas	96.5
18	California	98.8
6	Colorado	101.4
39	Connecticut	95.3
49	Delaware	93.7
36	Florida	95.6
41	Georgia	94.7
10	Hawaii	100.2
9	Idaho	100.5
30	Illinois	96.6
26	Indiana	97.3
15	Iowa	99.1
13	Kansas	99.3
27	Kentucky	97.1
38	Louisiana	95.4
35	Maine	96.0
46	Maryland	94.1
45	Massachusetts	94.3
28	Michigan	97.0
14	Minnesota	99.2
46	Mississippi	94.1
32	Missouri	96.4
6	Montana	101.4
12	Nebraska	99.7
8	Nevada	100.6
20	New Hampshire	98.3
37	New Jersey	95.5
24	New Mexico	98.0
44	New York	94.4
41	North Carolina	94.7
2	North Dakota	105.0
33	Ohio	96.2
22	Oklahoma	98.1
20	Oregon	98.3
34	Pennsylvania	96.1
41	Rhode Island	94.7
48	South Carolina	94.0
4	South Dakota	102.0
39	Tennessee	95.3
19	Texas	98.7
5	Utah	101.5
25	Vermont	97.5
29	Virginia	96.8
11	Washington	100.1
22	West Virginia	98.1
16	Wisconsin	99.0
3	Wyoming	104.0

RANK	STATE	RATIO
1	Alaska	109.0
2	North Dakota	105.0
3	Wyoming	104.0
4	South Dakota	102.0
5	Utah	101.5
6	Colorado	101.4
6	Montana	101.4
8	Nevada	100.6
9	Idaho	100.5
10	Hawaii	100.2
11	Washington	100.1
12	Nebraska	99.7
13	Kansas	99.3
14	Minnesota	99.2
15	Iowa	99.1
16	Wisconsin	99.0
17	Arizona	98.9
18	California	98.8
19	Texas	98.7
20	New Hampshire	98.3
20	Oregon	98.3
22	Oklahoma	98.1
22	West Virginia	98.1
24	New Mexico	98.0
25	Vermont	97.5
26	Indiana	97.3
27	Kentucky	97.1
28	Michigan	97.0
29	Virginia	96.8
30	Illinois	96.6
31	Arkansas	96.5
32	Missouri	96.4
33	Ohio	96.2
34	Pennsylvania	96.1
35	Maine	96.0
36	Florida	95.6
37	New Jersey	95.5
38	Louisiana	95.4
39	Connecticut	95.3
39	Tennessee	95.3
41	Georgia	94.7
41	North Carolina	94.7
41	Rhode Island	94.7
44	New York	94.4
45	Massachusetts	94.3
46	Maryland	94.1
46	Mississippi	94.1
48	South Carolina	94.0
49	Alabama	93.7
49	Delaware	93.7
	District of Columbia	90.3

Source: CQ Press using data from U.S. Bureau of the Census
"State Characteristics: Vintage 2018" (https://www.census.gov/programs-surveys/popest/data/data-sets.html)

Median Age in 2018

National Median = 38.2 Years Old

<table>
<tr><td colspan="3">ALPHA ORDER</td><td colspan="3">RANK ORDER</td></tr>
<tr><td>RANK</td><td>STATE</td><td>MEDIAN AGE</td><td>RANK</td><td>STATE</td><td>MEDIAN AGE</td></tr>
<tr><td>18</td><td>Alabama</td><td>39.2</td><td>1</td><td>Maine</td><td>44.9</td></tr>
<tr><td>49</td><td>Alaska</td><td>34.6</td><td>2</td><td>New Hampshire</td><td>43.0</td></tr>
<tr><td>34</td><td>Arizona</td><td>37.9</td><td>3</td><td>Vermont</td><td>42.8</td></tr>
<tr><td>27</td><td>Arkansas</td><td>38.3</td><td>4</td><td>West Virginia</td><td>42.7</td></tr>
<tr><td>43</td><td>California</td><td>36.8</td><td>5</td><td>Florida</td><td>42.2</td></tr>
<tr><td>40</td><td>Colorado</td><td>36.9</td><td>6</td><td>Connecticut</td><td>41.0</td></tr>
<tr><td>6</td><td>Connecticut</td><td>41.0</td><td>7</td><td>Pennsylvania</td><td>40.8</td></tr>
<tr><td>8</td><td>Delaware</td><td>40.7</td><td>8</td><td>Delaware</td><td>40.7</td></tr>
<tr><td>5</td><td>Florida</td><td>42.2</td><td>9</td><td>Rhode Island</td><td>40.1</td></tr>
<tr><td>40</td><td>Georgia</td><td>36.9</td><td>10</td><td>New Jersey</td><td>40.0</td></tr>
<tr><td>18</td><td>Hawaii</td><td>39.2</td><td>11</td><td>Montana</td><td>39.9</td></tr>
<tr><td>45</td><td>Idaho</td><td>36.6</td><td>12</td><td>Michigan</td><td>39.8</td></tr>
<tr><td>27</td><td>Illinois</td><td>38.3</td><td>13</td><td>South Carolina</td><td>39.6</td></tr>
<tr><td>34</td><td>Indiana</td><td>37.9</td><td>13</td><td>Wisconsin</td><td>39.6</td></tr>
<tr><td>29</td><td>Iowa</td><td>38.2</td><td>15</td><td>Massachusetts</td><td>39.4</td></tr>
<tr><td>40</td><td>Kansas</td><td>36.9</td><td>15</td><td>Ohio</td><td>39.4</td></tr>
<tr><td>21</td><td>Kentucky</td><td>38.9</td><td>15</td><td>Oregon</td><td>39.4</td></tr>
<tr><td>38</td><td>Louisiana</td><td>37.2</td><td>18</td><td>Alabama</td><td>39.2</td></tr>
<tr><td>1</td><td>Maine</td><td>44.9</td><td>18</td><td>Hawaii</td><td>39.2</td></tr>
<tr><td>23</td><td>Maryland</td><td>38.8</td><td>20</td><td>New York</td><td>39.0</td></tr>
<tr><td>15</td><td>Massachusetts</td><td>39.4</td><td>21</td><td>Kentucky</td><td>38.9</td></tr>
<tr><td>12</td><td>Michigan</td><td>39.8</td><td>21</td><td>North Carolina</td><td>38.9</td></tr>
<tr><td>30</td><td>Minnesota</td><td>38.1</td><td>23</td><td>Maryland</td><td>38.8</td></tr>
<tr><td>36</td><td>Mississippi</td><td>37.7</td><td>23</td><td>Tennessee</td><td>38.8</td></tr>
<tr><td>25</td><td>Missouri</td><td>38.7</td><td>25</td><td>Missouri</td><td>38.7</td></tr>
<tr><td>11</td><td>Montana</td><td>39.9</td><td>26</td><td>Virginia</td><td>38.4</td></tr>
<tr><td>45</td><td>Nebraska</td><td>36.6</td><td>27</td><td>Arkansas</td><td>38.3</td></tr>
<tr><td>30</td><td>Nevada</td><td>38.1</td><td>27</td><td>Illinois</td><td>38.3</td></tr>
<tr><td>2</td><td>New Hampshire</td><td>43.0</td><td>29</td><td>Iowa</td><td>38.2</td></tr>
<tr><td>10</td><td>New Jersey</td><td>40.0</td><td>30</td><td>Minnesota</td><td>38.1</td></tr>
<tr><td>30</td><td>New Mexico</td><td>38.1</td><td>30</td><td>Nevada</td><td>38.1</td></tr>
<tr><td>20</td><td>New York</td><td>39.0</td><td>30</td><td>New Mexico</td><td>38.1</td></tr>
<tr><td>21</td><td>North Carolina</td><td>38.9</td><td>33</td><td>Wyoming</td><td>38.0</td></tr>
<tr><td>47</td><td>North Dakota</td><td>35.2</td><td>34</td><td>Arizona</td><td>37.9</td></tr>
<tr><td>15</td><td>Ohio</td><td>39.4</td><td>34</td><td>Indiana</td><td>37.9</td></tr>
<tr><td>44</td><td>Oklahoma</td><td>36.7</td><td>36</td><td>Mississippi</td><td>37.7</td></tr>
<tr><td>15</td><td>Oregon</td><td>39.4</td><td>36</td><td>Washington</td><td>37.7</td></tr>
<tr><td>7</td><td>Pennsylvania</td><td>40.8</td><td>38</td><td>Louisiana</td><td>37.2</td></tr>
<tr><td>9</td><td>Rhode Island</td><td>40.1</td><td>39</td><td>South Dakota</td><td>37.1</td></tr>
<tr><td>13</td><td>South Carolina</td><td>39.6</td><td>40</td><td>Colorado</td><td>36.9</td></tr>
<tr><td>39</td><td>South Dakota</td><td>37.1</td><td>40</td><td>Georgia</td><td>36.9</td></tr>
<tr><td>23</td><td>Tennessee</td><td>38.8</td><td>40</td><td>Kansas</td><td>36.9</td></tr>
<tr><td>48</td><td>Texas</td><td>34.8</td><td>43</td><td>California</td><td>36.8</td></tr>
<tr><td>50</td><td>Utah</td><td>31.0</td><td>44</td><td>Oklahoma</td><td>36.7</td></tr>
<tr><td>3</td><td>Vermont</td><td>42.8</td><td>45</td><td>Idaho</td><td>36.6</td></tr>
<tr><td>26</td><td>Virginia</td><td>38.4</td><td>45</td><td>Nebraska</td><td>36.6</td></tr>
<tr><td>36</td><td>Washington</td><td>37.7</td><td>47</td><td>North Dakota</td><td>35.2</td></tr>
<tr><td>4</td><td>West Virginia</td><td>42.7</td><td>48</td><td>Texas</td><td>34.8</td></tr>
<tr><td>13</td><td>Wisconsin</td><td>39.6</td><td>49</td><td>Alaska</td><td>34.6</td></tr>
<tr><td>33</td><td>Wyoming</td><td>38.0</td><td>50</td><td>Utah</td><td>31.0</td></tr>
<tr><td></td><td></td><td></td><td></td><td>District of Columbia</td><td>34.0</td></tr>
</table>

Source: U.S. Bureau of the Census
  "State Characteristics: Vintage 2018" (https://www.census.gov/programs-surveys/popest/data/data-sets.html)

Male Median Age in 2018

National Median = 36.9 Years Old

ALPHA ORDER

RANK	STATE	MEDIAN AGE
18	Alabama	37.8
48	Alaska	34.1
35	Arizona	36.6
32	Arkansas	37.0
42	California	35.7
39	Colorado	36.0
6	Connecticut	39.2
7	Delaware	39.1
5	Florida	40.6
45	Georgia	35.5
18	Hawaii	37.8
41	Idaho	35.8
29	Illinois	37.1
35	Indiana	36.6
29	Iowa	37.1
42	Kansas	35.7
20	Kentucky	37.5
40	Louisiana	35.9
1	Maine	43.4
26	Maryland	37.3
16	Massachusetts	38.0
11	Michigan	38.4
28	Minnesota	37.2
37	Mississippi	36.1
24	Missouri	37.4
9	Montana	38.8
44	Nebraska	35.6
20	Nevada	37.5
2	New Hampshire	41.6
11	New Jersey	38.4
33	New Mexico	36.7
20	New York	37.5
24	North Carolina	37.4
47	North Dakota	34.3
16	Ohio	38.0
45	Oklahoma	35.5
11	Oregon	38.4
7	Pennsylvania	39.1
11	Rhode Island	38.4
15	South Carolina	38.1
37	South Dakota	36.1
20	Tennessee	37.5
49	Texas	33.8
50	Utah	30.4
3	Vermont	41.3
29	Virginia	37.1
33	Washington	36.7
4	West Virginia	41.2
10	Wisconsin	38.6
26	Wyoming	37.3

RANK ORDER

RANK	STATE	MEDIAN AGE
1	Maine	43.4
2	New Hampshire	41.6
3	Vermont	41.3
4	West Virginia	41.2
5	Florida	40.6
6	Connecticut	39.2
7	Delaware	39.1
7	Pennsylvania	39.1
9	Montana	38.8
10	Wisconsin	38.6
11	Michigan	38.4
11	New Jersey	38.4
11	Oregon	38.4
11	Rhode Island	38.4
15	South Carolina	38.1
16	Massachusetts	38.0
16	Ohio	38.0
18	Alabama	37.8
18	Hawaii	37.8
20	Kentucky	37.5
20	Nevada	37.5
20	New York	37.5
20	Tennessee	37.5
24	Missouri	37.4
24	North Carolina	37.4
26	Maryland	37.3
26	Wyoming	37.3
28	Minnesota	37.2
29	Illinois	37.1
29	Iowa	37.1
29	Virginia	37.1
32	Arkansas	37.0
33	New Mexico	36.7
33	Washington	36.7
35	Arizona	36.6
35	Indiana	36.6
37	Mississippi	36.1
37	South Dakota	36.1
39	Colorado	36.0
40	Louisiana	35.9
41	Idaho	35.8
42	California	35.7
42	Kansas	35.7
44	Nebraska	35.6
45	Georgia	35.5
45	Oklahoma	35.5
47	North Dakota	34.3
48	Alaska	34.1
49	Texas	33.8
50	Utah	30.4
	District of Columbia	33.8

Source: U.S. Bureau of the Census
"State Characteristics: Vintage 2018" (https://www.census.gov/programs-surveys/popest/data/data-sets.html)

Female Median Age in 2018

National Median = 39.5 Years Old

<table>
<tr><th colspan="3">ALPHA ORDER</th><th colspan="3">RANK ORDER</th></tr>
<tr><th>RANK</th><th>STATE</th><th>MEDIAN AGE</th><th>RANK</th><th>STATE</th><th>MEDIAN AGE</th></tr>
<tr><td>17</td><td>Alabama</td><td>40.7</td><td>1</td><td>Maine</td><td>46.3</td></tr>
<tr><td>49</td><td>Alaska</td><td>35.1</td><td>2</td><td>New Hampshire</td><td>44.4</td></tr>
<tr><td>31</td><td>Arizona</td><td>39.3</td><td>3</td><td>Vermont</td><td>44.3</td></tr>
<tr><td>27</td><td>Arkansas</td><td>39.6</td><td>4</td><td>West Virginia</td><td>44.1</td></tr>
<tr><td>42</td><td>California</td><td>37.9</td><td>5</td><td>Florida</td><td>43.8</td></tr>
<tr><td>42</td><td>Colorado</td><td>37.9</td><td>6</td><td>Connecticut</td><td>42.7</td></tr>
<tr><td>6</td><td>Connecticut</td><td>42.7</td><td>7</td><td>Delaware</td><td>42.4</td></tr>
<tr><td>7</td><td>Delaware</td><td>42.4</td><td>7</td><td>Pennsylvania</td><td>42.4</td></tr>
<tr><td>5</td><td>Florida</td><td>43.8</td><td>9</td><td>Rhode Island</td><td>41.9</td></tr>
<tr><td>39</td><td>Georgia</td><td>38.2</td><td>10</td><td>New Jersey</td><td>41.5</td></tr>
<tr><td>15</td><td>Hawaii</td><td>40.8</td><td>11</td><td>Michigan</td><td>41.2</td></tr>
<tr><td>46</td><td>Idaho</td><td>37.4</td><td>11</td><td>South Carolina</td><td>41.2</td></tr>
<tr><td>27</td><td>Illinois</td><td>39.6</td><td>13</td><td>Montana</td><td>41.0</td></tr>
<tr><td>32</td><td>Indiana</td><td>39.1</td><td>14</td><td>Massachusetts</td><td>40.9</td></tr>
<tr><td>30</td><td>Iowa</td><td>39.4</td><td>15</td><td>Hawaii</td><td>40.8</td></tr>
<tr><td>41</td><td>Kansas</td><td>38.1</td><td>15</td><td>Ohio</td><td>40.8</td></tr>
<tr><td>21</td><td>Kentucky</td><td>40.4</td><td>17</td><td>Alabama</td><td>40.7</td></tr>
<tr><td>38</td><td>Louisiana</td><td>38.5</td><td>17</td><td>Wisconsin</td><td>40.7</td></tr>
<tr><td>1</td><td>Maine</td><td>46.3</td><td>19</td><td>New York</td><td>40.5</td></tr>
<tr><td>23</td><td>Maryland</td><td>40.3</td><td>19</td><td>Oregon</td><td>40.5</td></tr>
<tr><td>14</td><td>Massachusetts</td><td>40.9</td><td>21</td><td>Kentucky</td><td>40.4</td></tr>
<tr><td>11</td><td>Michigan</td><td>41.2</td><td>21</td><td>North Carolina</td><td>40.4</td></tr>
<tr><td>34</td><td>Minnesota</td><td>39.0</td><td>23</td><td>Maryland</td><td>40.3</td></tr>
<tr><td>32</td><td>Mississippi</td><td>39.1</td><td>24</td><td>Tennessee</td><td>40.2</td></tr>
<tr><td>25</td><td>Missouri</td><td>40.1</td><td>25</td><td>Missouri</td><td>40.1</td></tr>
<tr><td>13</td><td>Montana</td><td>41.0</td><td>26</td><td>Virginia</td><td>39.7</td></tr>
<tr><td>45</td><td>Nebraska</td><td>37.6</td><td>27</td><td>Arkansas</td><td>39.6</td></tr>
<tr><td>35</td><td>Nevada</td><td>38.8</td><td>27</td><td>Illinois</td><td>39.6</td></tr>
<tr><td>2</td><td>New Hampshire</td><td>44.4</td><td>27</td><td>New Mexico</td><td>39.6</td></tr>
<tr><td>10</td><td>New Jersey</td><td>41.5</td><td>30</td><td>Iowa</td><td>39.4</td></tr>
<tr><td>27</td><td>New Mexico</td><td>39.6</td><td>31</td><td>Arizona</td><td>39.3</td></tr>
<tr><td>19</td><td>New York</td><td>40.5</td><td>32</td><td>Indiana</td><td>39.1</td></tr>
<tr><td>21</td><td>North Carolina</td><td>40.4</td><td>32</td><td>Mississippi</td><td>39.1</td></tr>
<tr><td>47</td><td>North Dakota</td><td>36.2</td><td>34</td><td>Minnesota</td><td>39.0</td></tr>
<tr><td>15</td><td>Ohio</td><td>40.8</td><td>35</td><td>Nevada</td><td>38.8</td></tr>
<tr><td>42</td><td>Oklahoma</td><td>37.9</td><td>36</td><td>Washington</td><td>38.7</td></tr>
<tr><td>19</td><td>Oregon</td><td>40.5</td><td>36</td><td>Wyoming</td><td>38.7</td></tr>
<tr><td>7</td><td>Pennsylvania</td><td>42.4</td><td>38</td><td>Louisiana</td><td>38.5</td></tr>
<tr><td>9</td><td>Rhode Island</td><td>41.9</td><td>39</td><td>Georgia</td><td>38.2</td></tr>
<tr><td>11</td><td>South Carolina</td><td>41.2</td><td>39</td><td>South Dakota</td><td>38.2</td></tr>
<tr><td>39</td><td>South Dakota</td><td>38.2</td><td>41</td><td>Kansas</td><td>38.1</td></tr>
<tr><td>24</td><td>Tennessee</td><td>40.2</td><td>42</td><td>California</td><td>37.9</td></tr>
<tr><td>48</td><td>Texas</td><td>35.8</td><td>42</td><td>Colorado</td><td>37.9</td></tr>
<tr><td>50</td><td>Utah</td><td>31.7</td><td>42</td><td>Oklahoma</td><td>37.9</td></tr>
<tr><td>3</td><td>Vermont</td><td>44.3</td><td>45</td><td>Nebraska</td><td>37.6</td></tr>
<tr><td>26</td><td>Virginia</td><td>39.7</td><td>46</td><td>Idaho</td><td>37.4</td></tr>
<tr><td>36</td><td>Washington</td><td>38.7</td><td>47</td><td>North Dakota</td><td>36.2</td></tr>
<tr><td>4</td><td>West Virginia</td><td>44.1</td><td>48</td><td>Texas</td><td>35.8</td></tr>
<tr><td>17</td><td>Wisconsin</td><td>40.7</td><td>49</td><td>Alaska</td><td>35.1</td></tr>
<tr><td>36</td><td>Wyoming</td><td>38.7</td><td>50</td><td>Utah</td><td>31.7</td></tr>
<tr><td></td><td></td><td></td><td></td><td>District of Columbia</td><td>34.2</td></tr>
</table>

Source: U.S. Bureau of the Census
  "State Characteristics: Vintage 2018" (https://www.census.gov/programs-surveys/popest/data/data-sets.html)

White Population in 2018

National Total = 250,139,096*

RANK	STATE	POPULATION	% of USA
26	Alabama	3,379,955	1.4%
49	Alaska	481,879	0.2%
13	Arizona	5,937,806	2.4%
33	Arkansas	2,385,213	1.0%
1	California	28,531,740	11.4%
20	Colorado	4,959,310	2.0%
31	Connecticut	2,859,280	1.1%
45	Delaware	672,019	0.3%
3	Florida	16,472,125	6.6%
11	Georgia	6,360,528	2.5%
50	Hawaii	363,549	0.1%
39	Idaho	1,632,188	0.7%
6	Illinois	9,791,840	3.9%
15	Indiana	5,694,468	2.3%
30	Iowa	2,864,126	1.1%
32	Kansas	2,515,351	1.0%
22	Kentucky	3,913,936	1.6%
27	Louisiana	2,930,432	1.2%
40	Maine	1,265,648	0.5%
24	Maryland	3,552,355	1.4%
16	Massachusetts	5,577,194	2.2%
8	Michigan	7,923,927	3.2%
21	Minnesota	4,718,176	1.9%
35	Mississippi	1,766,301	0.7%
18	Missouri	5,082,571	2.0%
42	Montana	945,132	0.4%
37	Nebraska	1,703,446	0.7%
34	Nevada	2,253,711	0.9%
41	New Hampshire	1,264,217	0.5%
10	New Jersey	6,416,347	2.6%
36	New Mexico	1,718,901	0.7%
4	New York	13,619,931	5.4%
9	North Carolina	7,334,411	2.9%
46	North Dakota	661,549	0.3%
7	Ohio	9,571,522	3.8%
28	Oklahoma	2,924,365	1.2%
23	Oregon	3,635,926	1.5%
5	Pennsylvania	10,476,085	4.2%
43	Rhode Island	887,259	0.4%
25	South Carolina	3,483,455	1.4%
44	South Dakota	744,733	0.3%
17	Tennessee	5,315,272	2.1%
2	Texas	22,624,867	9.0%
29	Utah	2,865,634	1.1%
47	Vermont	589,986	0.2%
14	Virginia	5,918,670	2.4%
12	Washington	5,944,924	2.4%
38	West Virginia	1,687,993	0.7%
19	Wisconsin	5,063,526	2.0%
48	Wyoming	534,943	0.2%

RANK	STATE	POPULATION	% of USA
1	California	28,531,740	11.4%
2	Texas	22,624,867	9.0%
3	Florida	16,472,125	6.6%
4	New York	13,619,931	5.4%
5	Pennsylvania	10,476,085	4.2%
6	Illinois	9,791,840	3.9%
7	Ohio	9,571,522	3.8%
8	Michigan	7,923,927	3.2%
9	North Carolina	7,334,411	2.9%
10	New Jersey	6,416,347	2.6%
11	Georgia	6,360,528	2.5%
12	Washington	5,944,924	2.4%
13	Arizona	5,937,806	2.4%
14	Virginia	5,918,670	2.4%
15	Indiana	5,694,468	2.3%
16	Massachusetts	5,577,194	2.2%
17	Tennessee	5,315,272	2.1%
18	Missouri	5,082,571	2.0%
19	Wisconsin	5,063,526	2.0%
20	Colorado	4,959,310	2.0%
21	Minnesota	4,718,176	1.9%
22	Kentucky	3,913,936	1.6%
23	Oregon	3,635,926	1.5%
24	Maryland	3,552,355	1.4%
25	South Carolina	3,483,455	1.4%
26	Alabama	3,379,955	1.4%
27	Louisiana	2,930,432	1.2%
28	Oklahoma	2,924,365	1.2%
29	Utah	2,865,634	1.1%
30	Iowa	2,864,126	1.1%
31	Connecticut	2,859,280	1.1%
32	Kansas	2,515,351	1.0%
33	Arkansas	2,385,213	1.0%
34	Nevada	2,253,711	0.9%
35	Mississippi	1,766,301	0.7%
36	New Mexico	1,718,901	0.7%
37	Nebraska	1,703,446	0.7%
38	West Virginia	1,687,993	0.7%
39	Idaho	1,632,188	0.7%
40	Maine	1,265,648	0.5%
41	New Hampshire	1,264,217	0.5%
42	Montana	945,132	0.4%
43	Rhode Island	887,259	0.4%
44	South Dakota	744,733	0.3%
45	Delaware	672,019	0.3%
46	North Dakota	661,549	0.3%
47	Vermont	589,986	0.2%
48	Wyoming	534,943	0.2%
49	Alaska	481,879	0.2%
50	Hawaii	363,549	0.1%
	District of Columbia	320,374	0.1%

Source: U.S. Bureau of the Census
"State Characteristics: Vintage 2018" (https://www.census.gov/programs-surveys/popest/data/data-sets.html)
*Those who identified themselves as one race. "White" is defined by Census as a person having origins in any of the original peoples of Europe, North Africa, or the Middle East. There are 197,546,407 non-Hispanic whites. Census states, "Race is a self-identification data item in which respondents choose the race or races with which they most closely identify."

Percent of Population White in 2018

National Percent = 76.5%*

<table>
<tr><td colspan="3">ALPHA ORDER</td><td colspan="3">RANK ORDER</td></tr>
<tr><td>RANK</td><td>STATE</td><td>PERCENT</td><td>RANK</td><td>STATE</td><td>PERCENT</td></tr>
<tr><td>43</td><td>Alabama</td><td>69.1</td><td>1</td><td>Maine</td><td>94.6</td></tr>
<tr><td>45</td><td>Alaska</td><td>65.3</td><td>2</td><td>Vermont</td><td>94.2</td></tr>
<tr><td>22</td><td>Arizona</td><td>82.8</td><td>3</td><td>West Virginia</td><td>93.5</td></tr>
<tr><td>29</td><td>Arkansas</td><td>79.1</td><td>4</td><td>New Hampshire</td><td>93.2</td></tr>
<tr><td>37</td><td>California</td><td>72.1</td><td>5</td><td>Idaho</td><td>93.0</td></tr>
<tr><td>12</td><td>Colorado</td><td>87.1</td><td>6</td><td>Wyoming</td><td>92.6</td></tr>
<tr><td>27</td><td>Connecticut</td><td>80.0</td><td>7</td><td>Iowa</td><td>90.7</td></tr>
<tr><td>41</td><td>Delaware</td><td>69.5</td><td>7</td><td>Utah</td><td>90.7</td></tr>
<tr><td>33</td><td>Florida</td><td>77.3</td><td>9</td><td>Montana</td><td>89.0</td></tr>
<tr><td>47</td><td>Georgia</td><td>60.5</td><td>10</td><td>Nebraska</td><td>88.3</td></tr>
<tr><td>50</td><td>Hawaii</td><td>25.6</td><td>11</td><td>Kentucky</td><td>87.6</td></tr>
<tr><td>5</td><td>Idaho</td><td>93.0</td><td>12</td><td>Colorado</td><td>87.1</td></tr>
<tr><td>34</td><td>Illinois</td><td>76.9</td><td>12</td><td>Wisconsin</td><td>87.1</td></tr>
<tr><td>17</td><td>Indiana</td><td>85.1</td><td>14</td><td>North Dakota</td><td>87.0</td></tr>
<tr><td>7</td><td>Iowa</td><td>90.7</td><td>15</td><td>Oregon</td><td>86.8</td></tr>
<tr><td>16</td><td>Kansas</td><td>86.4</td><td>16</td><td>Kansas</td><td>86.4</td></tr>
<tr><td>11</td><td>Kentucky</td><td>87.6</td><td>17</td><td>Indiana</td><td>85.1</td></tr>
<tr><td>46</td><td>Louisiana</td><td>62.9</td><td>18</td><td>South Dakota</td><td>84.4</td></tr>
<tr><td>1</td><td>Maine</td><td>94.6</td><td>19</td><td>Minnesota</td><td>84.1</td></tr>
<tr><td>49</td><td>Maryland</td><td>58.8</td><td>20</td><td>Rhode Island</td><td>83.9</td></tr>
<tr><td>26</td><td>Massachusetts</td><td>80.8</td><td>21</td><td>Missouri</td><td>83.0</td></tr>
<tr><td>28</td><td>Michigan</td><td>79.3</td><td>22</td><td>Arizona</td><td>82.8</td></tr>
<tr><td>19</td><td>Minnesota</td><td>84.1</td><td>23</td><td>New Mexico</td><td>82.0</td></tr>
<tr><td>48</td><td>Mississippi</td><td>59.1</td><td>24</td><td>Ohio</td><td>81.9</td></tr>
<tr><td>21</td><td>Missouri</td><td>83.0</td><td>25</td><td>Pennsylvania</td><td>81.8</td></tr>
<tr><td>9</td><td>Montana</td><td>89.0</td><td>26</td><td>Massachusetts</td><td>80.8</td></tr>
<tr><td>10</td><td>Nebraska</td><td>88.3</td><td>27</td><td>Connecticut</td><td>80.0</td></tr>
<tr><td>35</td><td>Nevada</td><td>74.3</td><td>28</td><td>Michigan</td><td>79.3</td></tr>
<tr><td>4</td><td>New Hampshire</td><td>93.2</td><td>29</td><td>Arkansas</td><td>79.1</td></tr>
<tr><td>38</td><td>New Jersey</td><td>72.0</td><td>30</td><td>Washington</td><td>78.9</td></tr>
<tr><td>23</td><td>New Mexico</td><td>82.0</td><td>31</td><td>Texas</td><td>78.8</td></tr>
<tr><td>40</td><td>New York</td><td>69.7</td><td>32</td><td>Tennessee</td><td>78.5</td></tr>
<tr><td>39</td><td>North Carolina</td><td>70.6</td><td>33</td><td>Florida</td><td>77.3</td></tr>
<tr><td>14</td><td>North Dakota</td><td>87.0</td><td>34</td><td>Illinois</td><td>76.9</td></tr>
<tr><td>24</td><td>Ohio</td><td>81.9</td><td>35</td><td>Nevada</td><td>74.3</td></tr>
<tr><td>36</td><td>Oklahoma</td><td>74.2</td><td>36</td><td>Oklahoma</td><td>74.2</td></tr>
<tr><td>15</td><td>Oregon</td><td>86.8</td><td>37</td><td>California</td><td>72.1</td></tr>
<tr><td>25</td><td>Pennsylvania</td><td>81.8</td><td>38</td><td>New Jersey</td><td>72.0</td></tr>
<tr><td>20</td><td>Rhode Island</td><td>83.9</td><td>39</td><td>North Carolina</td><td>70.6</td></tr>
<tr><td>44</td><td>South Carolina</td><td>68.5</td><td>40</td><td>New York</td><td>69.7</td></tr>
<tr><td>18</td><td>South Dakota</td><td>84.4</td><td>41</td><td>Delaware</td><td>69.5</td></tr>
<tr><td>32</td><td>Tennessee</td><td>78.5</td><td>41</td><td>Virginia</td><td>69.5</td></tr>
<tr><td>31</td><td>Texas</td><td>78.8</td><td>43</td><td>Alabama</td><td>69.1</td></tr>
<tr><td>7</td><td>Utah</td><td>90.7</td><td>44</td><td>South Carolina</td><td>68.5</td></tr>
<tr><td>2</td><td>Vermont</td><td>94.2</td><td>45</td><td>Alaska</td><td>65.3</td></tr>
<tr><td>41</td><td>Virginia</td><td>69.5</td><td>46</td><td>Louisiana</td><td>62.9</td></tr>
<tr><td>30</td><td>Washington</td><td>78.9</td><td>47</td><td>Georgia</td><td>60.5</td></tr>
<tr><td>3</td><td>West Virginia</td><td>93.5</td><td>48</td><td>Mississippi</td><td>59.1</td></tr>
<tr><td>12</td><td>Wisconsin</td><td>87.1</td><td>49</td><td>Maryland</td><td>58.8</td></tr>
<tr><td>6</td><td>Wyoming</td><td>92.6</td><td>50</td><td>Hawaii</td><td>25.6</td></tr>
<tr><td></td><td></td><td></td><td></td><td>District of Columbia</td><td>45.6</td></tr>
</table>

Source: CQ Press using data from U.S. Bureau of the Census
 "State Characteristics: Vintage 2018" (https://www.census.gov/programs-surveys/popest/data/data-sets.html)
*Those who identified themselves as one race. "White" is defined by Census as a person having origins in any of the original peoples of Europe, North Africa, or the Middle East. Non-Hispanic whites comprise 60.4% of the total population. Census states, "Race is a self-identification data item in which respondents choose the race or races with which they most closely identify."

Black Population in 2018

National Total = 43,804,319*

RANK	STATE	POPULATION	% of USA
16	Alabama	1,310,802	3.0%
42	Alaska	27,942	0.1%
27	Arizona	364,280	0.8%
22	Arkansas	472,287	1.1%
5	California	2,556,000	5.8%
31	Colorado	259,711	0.6%
23	Connecticut	429,298	1.0%
32	Delaware	222,070	0.5%
2	Florida	3,600,121	8.2%
4	Georgia	3,411,145	7.8%
41	Hawaii	31,138	0.1%
47	Idaho	15,775	0.0%
8	Illinois	1,860,190	4.2%
20	Indiana	658,729	1.5%
34	Iowa	124,819	0.3%
33	Kansas	178,618	0.4%
26	Kentucky	375,972	0.9%
11	Louisiana	1,526,090	3.5%
45	Maine	21,877	0.0%
7	Maryland	1,867,592	4.3%
21	Massachusetts	617,097	1.4%
13	Michigan	1,408,392	3.2%
25	Minnesota	380,414	0.9%
18	Mississippi	1,128,912	2.6%
19	Missouri	724,529	1.7%
50	Montana	6,237	0.0%
35	Nebraska	98,757	0.2%
30	Nevada	305,848	0.7%
44	New Hampshire	23,293	0.1%
15	New Jersey	1,337,754	3.1%
39	New Mexico	53,576	0.1%
3	New York	3,447,729	7.9%
6	North Carolina	2,306,797	5.3%
43	North Dakota	25,620	0.1%
12	Ohio	1,517,999	3.5%
29	Oklahoma	306,890	0.7%
36	Oregon	92,958	0.2%
10	Pennsylvania	1,531,457	3.5%
37	Rhode Island	88,411	0.2%
14	South Carolina	1,380,145	3.2%
46	South Dakota	21,000	0.0%
17	Tennessee	1,155,631	2.6%
1	Texas	3,673,855	8.4%
40	Utah	45,700	0.1%
48	Vermont	8,753	0.0%
9	Virginia	1,691,267	3.9%
28	Washington	322,826	0.7%
38	West Virginia	65,231	0.1%
24	Wisconsin	389,047	0.9%
49	Wyoming	7,557	0.0%

RANK	STATE	POPULATION	% of USA
1	Texas	3,673,855	8.4%
2	Florida	3,600,121	8.2%
3	New York	3,447,729	7.9%
4	Georgia	3,411,145	7.8%
5	California	2,556,000	5.8%
6	North Carolina	2,306,797	5.3%
7	Maryland	1,867,592	4.3%
8	Illinois	1,860,190	4.2%
9	Virginia	1,691,267	3.9%
10	Pennsylvania	1,531,457	3.5%
11	Louisiana	1,526,090	3.5%
12	Ohio	1,517,999	3.5%
13	Michigan	1,408,392	3.2%
14	South Carolina	1,380,145	3.2%
15	New Jersey	1,337,754	3.1%
16	Alabama	1,310,802	3.0%
17	Tennessee	1,155,631	2.6%
18	Mississippi	1,128,912	2.6%
19	Missouri	724,529	1.7%
20	Indiana	658,729	1.5%
21	Massachusetts	617,097	1.4%
22	Arkansas	472,287	1.1%
23	Connecticut	429,298	1.0%
24	Wisconsin	389,047	0.9%
25	Minnesota	380,414	0.9%
26	Kentucky	375,972	0.9%
27	Arizona	364,280	0.8%
28	Washington	322,826	0.7%
29	Oklahoma	306,890	0.7%
30	Nevada	305,848	0.7%
31	Colorado	259,711	0.6%
32	Delaware	222,070	0.5%
33	Kansas	178,618	0.4%
34	Iowa	124,819	0.3%
35	Nebraska	98,757	0.2%
36	Oregon	92,958	0.2%
37	Rhode Island	88,411	0.2%
38	West Virginia	65,231	0.1%
39	New Mexico	53,576	0.1%
40	Utah	45,700	0.1%
41	Hawaii	31,138	0.1%
42	Alaska	27,942	0.1%
43	North Dakota	25,620	0.1%
44	New Hampshire	23,293	0.1%
45	Maine	21,877	0.0%
46	South Dakota	21,000	0.0%
47	Idaho	15,775	0.0%
48	Vermont	8,753	0.0%
49	Wyoming	7,557	0.0%
50	Montana	6,237	0.0%
	District of Columbia	326,181	0.7%

Source: U.S. Bureau of the Census
   "State Characteristics: Vintage 2018" (https://www.census.gov/programs-surveys/popest/data/data-sets.html)
*Those who identified themselves as one race. "Black" is defined by Census as a person having origins in any of the Black racial groups of Africa. Census states, "Race is a self-identification data item in which respondents choose the race or races with which they most closely identify."

Percent of Population Black in 2018

National Percent = 13.4%*

RANK	STATE	PERCENT
6	Alabama	26.8
37	Alaska	3.8
32	Arizona	5.1
13	Arkansas	15.7
30	California	6.5
34	Colorado	4.6
19	Connecticut	12.0
7	Delaware	23.0
12	Florida	16.9
3	Georgia	32.4
42	Hawaii	2.2
49	Idaho	0.9
15	Illinois	14.6
23	Indiana	9.8
36	Iowa	4.0
31	Kansas	6.1
25	Kentucky	8.4
2	Louisiana	32.7
45	Maine	1.6
4	Maryland	30.9
24	Massachusetts	8.9
16	Michigan	14.1
28	Minnesota	6.8
1	Mississippi	37.8
21	Missouri	11.8
50	Montana	0.6
32	Nebraska	5.1
22	Nevada	10.1
44	New Hampshire	1.7
14	New Jersey	15.0
40	New Mexico	2.6
10	New York	17.6
8	North Carolina	22.2
39	North Dakota	3.4
17	Ohio	13.0
27	Oklahoma	7.8
42	Oregon	2.2
19	Pennsylvania	12.0
25	Rhode Island	8.4
5	South Carolina	27.1
41	South Dakota	2.4
11	Tennessee	17.1
18	Texas	12.8
46	Utah	1.4
46	Vermont	1.4
9	Virginia	19.9
35	Washington	4.3
38	West Virginia	3.6
29	Wisconsin	6.7
48	Wyoming	1.3

RANK	STATE	PERCENT
1	Mississippi	37.8
2	Louisiana	32.7
3	Georgia	32.4
4	Maryland	30.9
5	South Carolina	27.1
6	Alabama	26.8
7	Delaware	23.0
8	North Carolina	22.2
9	Virginia	19.9
10	New York	17.6
11	Tennessee	17.1
12	Florida	16.9
13	Arkansas	15.7
14	New Jersey	15.0
15	Illinois	14.6
16	Michigan	14.1
17	Ohio	13.0
18	Texas	12.8
19	Connecticut	12.0
19	Pennsylvania	12.0
21	Missouri	11.8
22	Nevada	10.1
23	Indiana	9.8
24	Massachusetts	8.9
25	Kentucky	8.4
25	Rhode Island	8.4
27	Oklahoma	7.8
28	Minnesota	6.8
29	Wisconsin	6.7
30	California	6.5
31	Kansas	6.1
32	Arizona	5.1
32	Nebraska	5.1
34	Colorado	4.6
35	Washington	4.3
36	Iowa	4.0
37	Alaska	3.8
38	West Virginia	3.6
39	North Dakota	3.4
40	New Mexico	2.6
41	South Dakota	2.4
42	Hawaii	2.2
42	Oregon	2.2
44	New Hampshire	1.7
45	Maine	1.6
46	Utah	1.4
46	Vermont	1.4
48	Wyoming	1.3
49	Idaho	0.9
50	Montana	0.6
	District of Columbia	46.4

Source: CQ Press using data from U.S. Bureau of the Census
"State Characteristics: Vintage 2018" (https://www.census.gov/programs-surveys/popest/data/data-sets.html)
*Those who identified themselves as one race. "Black" is defined by Census as a person having origins in any of the Black racial groups of Africa. Census states, "Race is a self-identification data item in which respondents choose the race or races with which they most closely identify."

Hispanic Population in 2018

National Total = 59,871,746*

ALPHA ORDER				RANK ORDER			
RANK	STATE	POPULATION	% of USA	RANK	STATE	POPULATION	% of USA
34	Alabama	217,181	0.4%	1	California	15,540,142	26.0%
43	Alaska	53,288	0.1%	2	Texas	11,368,849	19.0%
5	Arizona	2,266,343	3.8%	3	Florida	5,562,417	9.3%
32	Arkansas	233,187	0.4%	4	New York	3,754,130	6.3%
1	California	15,540,142	26.0%	5	Arizona	2,266,343	3.8%
8	Colorado	1,235,117	2.1%	6	Illinois	2,214,142	3.7%
18	Connecticut	589,809	1.0%	7	New Jersey	1,839,359	3.1%
41	Delaware	91,974	0.2%	8	Colorado	1,235,117	2.1%
3	Florida	5,562,417	9.3%	9	New Mexico	1,029,233	1.7%
10	Georgia	1,026,737	1.7%	10	Georgia	1,026,737	1.7%
39	Hawaii	151,357	0.3%	11	North Carolina	997,349	1.7%
33	Idaho	222,908	0.4%	12	Pennsylvania	976,143	1.6%
6	Illinois	2,214,142	3.7%	13	Washington	970,358	1.6%
21	Indiana	475,237	0.8%	14	Nevada	881,148	1.5%
36	Iowa	194,432	0.3%	15	Massachusetts	847,223	1.4%
27	Kansas	351,180	0.6%	16	Virginia	820,874	1.4%
37	Kentucky	171,933	0.3%	17	Maryland	628,433	1.0%
31	Louisiana	243,811	0.4%	18	Connecticut	589,809	1.0%
49	Maine	22,850	0.0%	19	Oregon	556,396	0.9%
17	Maryland	628,433	1.0%	20	Michigan	519,022	0.9%
15	Massachusetts	847,223	1.4%	21	Indiana	475,237	0.8%
20	Michigan	519,022	0.9%	22	Ohio	460,877	0.8%
28	Minnesota	309,283	0.5%	23	Utah	450,218	0.8%
40	Mississippi	100,168	0.2%	24	Oklahoma	429,078	0.7%
30	Missouri	263,265	0.4%	25	Wisconsin	403,955	0.7%
45	Montana	42,503	0.1%	26	Tennessee	380,772	0.6%
35	Nebraska	215,872	0.4%	27	Kansas	351,180	0.6%
14	Nevada	881,148	1.5%	28	Minnesota	309,283	0.5%
44	New Hampshire	52,663	0.1%	29	South Carolina	296,046	0.5%
7	New Jersey	1,839,359	3.1%	30	Missouri	263,265	0.4%
9	New Mexico	1,029,233	1.7%	31	Louisiana	243,811	0.4%
4	New York	3,754,130	6.3%	32	Arkansas	233,187	0.4%
11	North Carolina	997,349	1.7%	33	Idaho	222,908	0.4%
48	North Dakota	29,529	0.0%	34	Alabama	217,181	0.4%
22	Ohio	460,877	0.8%	35	Nebraska	215,872	0.4%
24	Oklahoma	429,078	0.7%	36	Iowa	194,432	0.3%
19	Oregon	556,396	0.9%	37	Kentucky	171,933	0.3%
12	Pennsylvania	976,143	1.6%	38	Rhode Island	168,342	0.3%
38	Rhode Island	168,342	0.3%	39	Hawaii	151,357	0.3%
29	South Carolina	296,046	0.5%	40	Mississippi	100,168	0.2%
46	South Dakota	36,402	0.1%	41	Delaware	91,974	0.2%
26	Tennessee	380,772	0.6%	42	Wyoming	58,227	0.1%
2	Texas	11,368,849	19.0%	43	Alaska	53,288	0.1%
23	Utah	450,218	0.8%	44	New Hampshire	52,663	0.1%
50	Vermont	12,534	0.0%	45	Montana	42,503	0.1%
16	Virginia	820,874	1.4%	46	South Dakota	36,402	0.1%
13	Washington	970,358	1.6%	47	West Virginia	30,201	0.1%
47	West Virginia	30,201	0.1%	48	North Dakota	29,529	0.0%
25	Wisconsin	403,955	0.7%	49	Maine	22,850	0.0%
42	Wyoming	58,227	0.1%	50	Vermont	12,534	0.0%
					District of Columbia	79,249	0.1%

Source: U.S. Bureau of the Census
  "State Characteristics: Vintage 2018" (https://www.census.gov/programs-surveys/popest/data/data-sets.html)
*Persons of Hispanic origin may be of any race. Census states, "Race is a self-identification data item in which respondents choose the race or races with which they most closely identify."

Percent of Population Hispanic in 2018

National Percent = 18.3%*

ALPHA ORDER

RANK	STATE	PERCENT
39	Alabama	4.4
30	Alaska	7.2
4	Arizona	31.6
28	Arkansas	7.7
3	California	39.3
7	Colorado	21.7
11	Connecticut	16.5
27	Delaware	9.5
6	Florida	26.1
24	Georgia	9.8
21	Hawaii	10.7
16	Idaho	12.7
10	Illinois	17.4
31	Indiana	7.1
33	Iowa	6.2
18	Kansas	12.1
46	Kentucky	3.8
37	Louisiana	5.2
49	Maine	1.7
22	Maryland	10.4
17	Massachusetts	12.3
37	Michigan	5.2
36	Minnesota	5.5
47	Mississippi	3.4
40	Missouri	4.3
42	Montana	4.0
19	Nebraska	11.2
5	Nevada	29.0
43	New Hampshire	3.9
8	New Jersey	20.6
1	New Mexico	49.1
9	New York	19.2
25	North Carolina	9.6
43	North Dakota	3.9
43	Ohio	3.9
20	Oklahoma	10.9
14	Oregon	13.3
29	Pennsylvania	7.6
12	Rhode Island	15.9
34	South Carolina	5.8
41	South Dakota	4.1
35	Tennessee	5.6
2	Texas	39.6
13	Utah	14.2
48	Vermont	2.0
25	Virginia	9.6
15	Washington	12.9
49	West Virginia	1.7
32	Wisconsin	6.9
23	Wyoming	10.1

RANK ORDER

RANK	STATE	PERCENT
1	New Mexico	49.1
2	Texas	39.6
3	California	39.3
4	Arizona	31.6
5	Nevada	29.0
6	Florida	26.1
7	Colorado	21.7
8	New Jersey	20.6
9	New York	19.2
10	Illinois	17.4
11	Connecticut	16.5
12	Rhode Island	15.9
13	Utah	14.2
14	Oregon	13.3
15	Washington	12.9
16	Idaho	12.7
17	Massachusetts	12.3
18	Kansas	12.1
19	Nebraska	11.2
20	Oklahoma	10.9
21	Hawaii	10.7
22	Maryland	10.4
23	Wyoming	10.1
24	Georgia	9.8
25	North Carolina	9.6
25	Virginia	9.6
27	Delaware	9.5
28	Arkansas	7.7
29	Pennsylvania	7.6
30	Alaska	7.2
31	Indiana	7.1
32	Wisconsin	6.9
33	Iowa	6.2
34	South Carolina	5.8
35	Tennessee	5.6
36	Minnesota	5.5
37	Louisiana	5.2
37	Michigan	5.2
39	Alabama	4.4
40	Missouri	4.3
41	South Dakota	4.1
42	Montana	4.0
43	New Hampshire	3.9
43	North Dakota	3.9
43	Ohio	3.9
46	Kentucky	3.8
47	Mississippi	3.4
48	Vermont	2.0
49	Maine	1.7
49	West Virginia	1.7

District of Columbia — 11.3

Source: CQ Press using data from U.S. Bureau of the Census
"State Characteristics: Vintage 2018" (https://www.census.gov/programs-surveys/popest/data/data-sets.html)
*Persons of Hispanic origin may be of any race. Census states, "Race is a self-identification data item in which respondents choose the race or races with which they most closely identify."

Asian Population in 2018

National Total = 19,330,600*

ALPHA ORDER

RANK	STATE	POPULATION	% of USA
33	Alabama	73,167	0.4%
37	Alaska	49,025	0.3%
19	Arizona	263,696	1.4%
36	Arkansas	50,301	0.3%
1	California	6,063,600	31.4%
21	Colorado	197,634	1.0%
23	Connecticut	173,799	0.9%
39	Delaware	39,584	0.2%
7	Florida	631,737	3.3%
12	Georgia	453,488	2.3%
9	Hawaii	534,651	2.8%
43	Idaho	27,819	0.1%
5	Illinois	748,722	3.9%
24	Indiana	165,368	0.9%
30	Iowa	85,708	0.4%
28	Kansas	91,229	0.5%
34	Kentucky	72,806	0.4%
32	Louisiana	84,271	0.4%
44	Maine	16,674	0.1%
13	Maryland	405,682	2.1%
10	Massachusetts	492,508	2.5%
14	Michigan	337,336	1.7%
16	Minnesota	288,975	1.5%
42	Mississippi	32,152	0.2%
25	Missouri	131,046	0.7%
49	Montana	9,852	0.1%
35	Nebraska	52,343	0.3%
18	Nevada	264,411	1.4%
38	New Hampshire	40,460	0.2%
4	New Jersey	889,251	4.6%
41	New Mexico	37,256	0.2%
2	New York	1,750,013	9.1%
15	North Carolina	329,284	1.7%
47	North Dakota	13,426	0.1%
17	Ohio	287,222	1.5%
27	Oklahoma	92,179	0.5%
20	Oregon	202,394	1.0%
11	Pennsylvania	474,071	2.5%
40	Rhode Island	38,419	0.2%
29	South Carolina	89,962	0.5%
46	South Dakota	15,093	0.1%
26	Tennessee	128,526	0.7%
3	Texas	1,486,266	7.7%
31	Utah	85,389	0.4%
48	Vermont	12,581	0.1%
8	Virginia	589,046	3.0%
6	Washington	703,455	3.6%
45	West Virginia	15,338	0.1%
22	Wisconsin	176,147	0.9%
50	Wyoming	6,213	0.0%

RANK ORDER

RANK	STATE	POPULATION	% of USA
1	California	6,063,600	31.4%
2	New York	1,750,013	9.1%
3	Texas	1,486,266	7.7%
4	New Jersey	889,251	4.6%
5	Illinois	748,722	3.9%
6	Washington	703,455	3.6%
7	Florida	631,737	3.3%
8	Virginia	589,046	3.0%
9	Hawaii	534,651	2.8%
10	Massachusetts	492,508	2.5%
11	Pennsylvania	474,071	2.5%
12	Georgia	453,488	2.3%
13	Maryland	405,682	2.1%
14	Michigan	337,336	1.7%
15	North Carolina	329,284	1.7%
16	Minnesota	288,975	1.5%
17	Ohio	287,222	1.5%
18	Nevada	264,411	1.4%
19	Arizona	263,696	1.4%
20	Oregon	202,394	1.0%
21	Colorado	197,634	1.0%
22	Wisconsin	176,147	0.9%
23	Connecticut	173,799	0.9%
24	Indiana	165,368	0.9%
25	Missouri	131,046	0.7%
26	Tennessee	128,526	0.7%
27	Oklahoma	92,179	0.5%
28	Kansas	91,229	0.5%
29	South Carolina	89,962	0.5%
30	Iowa	85,708	0.4%
31	Utah	85,389	0.4%
32	Louisiana	84,271	0.4%
33	Alabama	73,167	0.4%
34	Kentucky	72,806	0.4%
35	Nebraska	52,343	0.3%
36	Arkansas	50,301	0.3%
37	Alaska	49,025	0.3%
38	New Hampshire	40,460	0.2%
39	Delaware	39,584	0.2%
40	Rhode Island	38,419	0.2%
41	New Mexico	37,256	0.2%
42	Mississippi	32,152	0.2%
43	Idaho	27,819	0.1%
44	Maine	16,674	0.1%
45	West Virginia	15,338	0.1%
46	South Dakota	15,093	0.1%
47	North Dakota	13,426	0.1%
48	Vermont	12,581	0.1%
49	Montana	9,852	0.1%
50	Wyoming	6,213	0.0%
	District of Columbia	31,025	0.2%

Source: U.S. Bureau of the Census
    "State Characteristics: Vintage 2018" (https://www.census.gov/programs-surveys/popest/data/data-sets.html)
*Those who identified themselves as one race. Census states, "Race is a self-identification data item in which respondents choose the race or races with which they most closely identify."

Percent of Population Asian in 2018

National Percent = 5.9%*

<table>
<tr><td colspan="3">ALPHA ORDER</td><td colspan="3">RANK ORDER</td></tr>
<tr><td>RANK</td><td>STATE</td><td>PERCENT</td><td>RANK</td><td>STATE</td><td>PERCENT</td></tr>
<tr><td>45</td><td>Alabama</td><td>1.5</td><td>1</td><td>Hawaii</td><td>37.6</td></tr>
<tr><td>10</td><td>Alaska</td><td>6.6</td><td>2</td><td>California</td><td>15.3</td></tr>
<tr><td>18</td><td>Arizona</td><td>3.7</td><td>3</td><td>New Jersey</td><td>10.0</td></tr>
<tr><td>41</td><td>Arkansas</td><td>1.7</td><td>4</td><td>Washington</td><td>9.3</td></tr>
<tr><td>2</td><td>California</td><td>15.3</td><td>5</td><td>New York</td><td>9.0</td></tr>
<tr><td>21</td><td>Colorado</td><td>3.5</td><td>6</td><td>Nevada</td><td>8.7</td></tr>
<tr><td>14</td><td>Connecticut</td><td>4.9</td><td>7</td><td>Massachusetts</td><td>7.1</td></tr>
<tr><td>17</td><td>Delaware</td><td>4.1</td><td>8</td><td>Virginia</td><td>6.9</td></tr>
<tr><td>25</td><td>Florida</td><td>3.0</td><td>9</td><td>Maryland</td><td>6.7</td></tr>
<tr><td>16</td><td>Georgia</td><td>4.3</td><td>10</td><td>Alaska</td><td>6.6</td></tr>
<tr><td>1</td><td>Hawaii</td><td>37.6</td><td>11</td><td>Illinois</td><td>5.9</td></tr>
<tr><td>43</td><td>Idaho</td><td>1.6</td><td>12</td><td>Texas</td><td>5.2</td></tr>
<tr><td>11</td><td>Illinois</td><td>5.9</td><td>13</td><td>Minnesota</td><td>5.1</td></tr>
<tr><td>31</td><td>Indiana</td><td>2.5</td><td>14</td><td>Connecticut</td><td>4.9</td></tr>
<tr><td>28</td><td>Iowa</td><td>2.7</td><td>15</td><td>Oregon</td><td>4.8</td></tr>
<tr><td>24</td><td>Kansas</td><td>3.1</td><td>16</td><td>Georgia</td><td>4.3</td></tr>
<tr><td>43</td><td>Kentucky</td><td>1.6</td><td>17</td><td>Delaware</td><td>4.1</td></tr>
<tr><td>37</td><td>Louisiana</td><td>1.8</td><td>18</td><td>Arizona</td><td>3.7</td></tr>
<tr><td>46</td><td>Maine</td><td>1.2</td><td>18</td><td>Pennsylvania</td><td>3.7</td></tr>
<tr><td>9</td><td>Maryland</td><td>6.7</td><td>20</td><td>Rhode Island</td><td>3.6</td></tr>
<tr><td>7</td><td>Massachusetts</td><td>7.1</td><td>21</td><td>Colorado</td><td>3.5</td></tr>
<tr><td>22</td><td>Michigan</td><td>3.4</td><td>22</td><td>Michigan</td><td>3.4</td></tr>
<tr><td>13</td><td>Minnesota</td><td>5.1</td><td>23</td><td>North Carolina</td><td>3.2</td></tr>
<tr><td>47</td><td>Mississippi</td><td>1.1</td><td>24</td><td>Kansas</td><td>3.1</td></tr>
<tr><td>34</td><td>Missouri</td><td>2.1</td><td>25</td><td>Florida</td><td>3.0</td></tr>
<tr><td>49</td><td>Montana</td><td>0.9</td><td>25</td><td>New Hampshire</td><td>3.0</td></tr>
<tr><td>28</td><td>Nebraska</td><td>2.7</td><td>25</td><td>Wisconsin</td><td>3.0</td></tr>
<tr><td>6</td><td>Nevada</td><td>8.7</td><td>28</td><td>Iowa</td><td>2.7</td></tr>
<tr><td>25</td><td>New Hampshire</td><td>3.0</td><td>28</td><td>Nebraska</td><td>2.7</td></tr>
<tr><td>3</td><td>New Jersey</td><td>10.0</td><td>28</td><td>Utah</td><td>2.7</td></tr>
<tr><td>37</td><td>New Mexico</td><td>1.8</td><td>31</td><td>Indiana</td><td>2.5</td></tr>
<tr><td>5</td><td>New York</td><td>9.0</td><td>31</td><td>Ohio</td><td>2.5</td></tr>
<tr><td>23</td><td>North Carolina</td><td>3.2</td><td>33</td><td>Oklahoma</td><td>2.3</td></tr>
<tr><td>37</td><td>North Dakota</td><td>1.8</td><td>34</td><td>Missouri</td><td>2.1</td></tr>
<tr><td>31</td><td>Ohio</td><td>2.5</td><td>35</td><td>Vermont</td><td>2.0</td></tr>
<tr><td>33</td><td>Oklahoma</td><td>2.3</td><td>36</td><td>Tennessee</td><td>1.9</td></tr>
<tr><td>15</td><td>Oregon</td><td>4.8</td><td>37</td><td>Louisiana</td><td>1.8</td></tr>
<tr><td>18</td><td>Pennsylvania</td><td>3.7</td><td>37</td><td>New Mexico</td><td>1.8</td></tr>
<tr><td>20</td><td>Rhode Island</td><td>3.6</td><td>37</td><td>North Dakota</td><td>1.0</td></tr>
<tr><td>37</td><td>South Carolina</td><td>1.8</td><td>37</td><td>South Carolina</td><td>1.8</td></tr>
<tr><td>41</td><td>South Dakota</td><td>1.7</td><td>41</td><td>Arkansas</td><td>1.7</td></tr>
<tr><td>36</td><td>Tennessee</td><td>1.9</td><td>41</td><td>South Dakota</td><td>1.7</td></tr>
<tr><td>12</td><td>Texas</td><td>5.2</td><td>43</td><td>Idaho</td><td>1.6</td></tr>
<tr><td>28</td><td>Utah</td><td>2.7</td><td>43</td><td>Kentucky</td><td>1.6</td></tr>
<tr><td>35</td><td>Vermont</td><td>2.0</td><td>45</td><td>Alabama</td><td>1.5</td></tr>
<tr><td>8</td><td>Virginia</td><td>6.9</td><td>46</td><td>Maine</td><td>1.2</td></tr>
<tr><td>4</td><td>Washington</td><td>9.3</td><td>47</td><td>Mississippi</td><td>1.1</td></tr>
<tr><td>50</td><td>West Virginia</td><td>0.8</td><td>47</td><td>Wyoming</td><td>1.1</td></tr>
<tr><td>25</td><td>Wisconsin</td><td>3.0</td><td>49</td><td>Montana</td><td>0.9</td></tr>
<tr><td>47</td><td>Wyoming</td><td>1.1</td><td>50</td><td>West Virginia</td><td>0.8</td></tr>
<tr><td></td><td></td><td></td><td></td><td>District of Columbia</td><td>4.4</td></tr>
</table>

Source: CQ Press using data from U.S. Bureau of the Census

"State Characteristics: Vintage 2018" (https://www.census.gov/programs-surveys/popest/data/data-sets.html)

*Those who identified themselves as one race. Census states, "Race is a self-identification data item in which respondents choose the race or races with which they most closely identify."

American Indian Population in 2018

National Total = 4,147,521*

ALPHA ORDER

RANK	STATE	POPULATION	% of USA
30	Alabama	34,375	0.8%
9	Alaska	113,516	2.7%
2	Arizona	380,160	9.2%
35	Arkansas	30,225	0.7%
1	California	651,076	15.7%
11	Colorado	91,120	2.2%
39	Connecticut	19,943	0.5%
46	Delaware	6,458	0.2%
10	Florida	106,984	2.6%
19	Georgia	54,882	1.3%
47	Hawaii	5,629	0.1%
34	Idaho	30,449	0.7%
15	Illinois	75,567	1.8%
37	Indiana	27,740	0.7%
41	Iowa	16,681	0.4%
29	Kansas	34,817	0.8%
43	Kentucky	13,412	0.3%
26	Louisiana	36,500	0.9%
45	Maine	9,657	0.2%
27	Maryland	36,188	0.9%
31	Massachusetts	34,112	0.8%
16	Michigan	73,499	1.8%
13	Minnesota	76,616	1.8%
40	Mississippi	18,423	0.4%
28	Missouri	35,019	0.8%
17	Montana	70,603	1.7%
36	Nebraska	28,663	0.7%
21	Nevada	50,871	1.2%
49	New Hampshire	4,090	0.1%
20	New Jersey	54,706	1.3%
5	New Mexico	228,493	5.5%
6	New York	190,414	4.6%
7	North Carolina	163,078	3.9%
25	North Dakota	41,962	1.0%
32	Ohio	33,566	0.8%
3	Oklahoma	367,043	8.8%
14	Oregon	76,023	1.8%
22	Pennsylvania	49,563	1.2%
44	Rhode Island	11,308	0.3%
38	South Carolina	27,694	0.7%
12	South Dakota	79,412	1.9%
33	Tennessee	31,826	0.8%
4	Texas	290,961	7.0%
23	Utah	48,628	1.2%
50	Vermont	2,457	0.1%
24	Virginia	46,409	1.1%
8	Washington	144,450	3.5%
48	West Virginia	4,526	0.1%
18	Wisconsin	67,571	1.6%
42	Wyoming	15,860	0.4%

RANK ORDER

RANK	STATE	POPULATION	% of USA
1	California	651,076	15.7%
2	Arizona	380,160	9.2%
3	Oklahoma	367,043	8.8%
4	Texas	290,961	7.0%
5	New Mexico	228,493	5.5%
6	New York	190,414	4.6%
7	North Carolina	163,078	3.9%
8	Washington	144,450	3.5%
9	Alaska	113,516	2.7%
10	Florida	106,984	2.6%
11	Colorado	91,120	2.2%
12	South Dakota	79,412	1.9%
13	Minnesota	76,616	1.8%
14	Oregon	76,023	1.8%
15	Illinois	75,567	1.8%
16	Michigan	73,499	1.8%
17	Montana	70,603	1.7%
18	Wisconsin	67,571	1.6%
19	Georgia	54,882	1.3%
20	New Jersey	54,706	1.3%
21	Nevada	50,871	1.2%
22	Pennsylvania	49,563	1.2%
23	Utah	48,628	1.2%
24	Virginia	46,409	1.1%
25	North Dakota	41,962	1.0%
26	Louisiana	36,500	0.9%
27	Maryland	36,188	0.9%
28	Missouri	35,019	0.8%
29	Kansas	34,817	0.8%
30	Alabama	34,375	0.8%
31	Massachusetts	34,112	0.8%
32	Ohio	33,566	0.8%
33	Tennessee	31,826	0.8%
34	Idaho	30,449	0.7%
35	Arkansas	30,225	0.7%
36	Nebraska	28,663	0.7%
37	Indiana	27,740	0.7%
38	South Carolina	27,694	0.7%
39	Connecticut	19,943	0.5%
40	Mississippi	18,423	0.4%
41	Iowa	16,681	0.4%
42	Wyoming	15,860	0.4%
43	Kentucky	13,412	0.3%
44	Rhode Island	11,308	0.3%
45	Maine	9,657	0.2%
46	Delaware	6,458	0.2%
47	Hawaii	5,629	0.1%
48	West Virginia	4,526	0.1%
49	New Hampshire	4,090	0.1%
50	Vermont	2,457	0.1%
	District of Columbia	4,296	0.1%

Source: U.S. Bureau of the Census
   "State Characteristics: Vintage 2018" (https://www.census.gov/programs-surveys/popest/data/data-sets.html)
*Those who identified themselves as one race. Includes Alaska Native populations. Census states, "Race is a self-identification data item in which respondents choose the race or races with which they most closely identify."

Percent of Population American Indian in 2018

National Percent = 1.3%*

RANK	STATE	PERCENT		RANK	STATE	PERCENT
26	Alabama	0.7		1	Alaska	15.4
1	Alaska	15.4		2	New Mexico	10.9
7	Arizona	5.3		3	Oklahoma	9.3
22	Arkansas	1.0		4	South Dakota	9.0
13	California	1.6		5	Montana	6.6
13	Colorado	1.6		6	North Dakota	5.5
30	Connecticut	0.6		7	Arizona	5.3
26	Delaware	0.7		8	Wyoming	2.7
36	Florida	0.5		9	Washington	1.9
36	Georgia	0.5		10	Oregon	1.8
43	Hawaii	0.4		11	Idaho	1.7
11	Idaho	1.7		11	Nevada	1.7
30	Illinois	0.6		13	California	1.6
43	Indiana	0.4		13	Colorado	1.6
36	Iowa	0.5		13	North Carolina	1.6
19	Kansas	1.2		16	Nebraska	1.5
47	Kentucky	0.3		16	Utah	1.5
25	Louisiana	0.8		18	Minnesota	1.4
26	Maine	0.7		19	Kansas	1.2
30	Maryland	0.6		19	Wisconsin	1.2
36	Massachusetts	0.5		21	Rhode Island	1.1
26	Michigan	0.7		22	Arkansas	1.0
18	Minnesota	1.4		22	New York	1.0
30	Mississippi	0.6		22	Texas	1.0
30	Missouri	0.6		25	Louisiana	0.8
5	Montana	6.6		26	Alabama	0.7
16	Nebraska	1.5		26	Delaware	0.7
11	Nevada	1.7		26	Maine	0.7
47	New Hampshire	0.3		26	Michigan	0.7
30	New Jersey	0.6		30	Connecticut	0.6
2	New Mexico	10.9		30	Illinois	0.6
22	New York	1.0		30	Maryland	0.6
13	North Carolina	1.6		30	Mississippi	0.6
6	North Dakota	5.5		30	Missouri	0.6
47	Ohio	0.3		30	New Jersey	0.6
3	Oklahoma	9.3		36	Florida	0.5
10	Oregon	1.8		36	Georgia	0.5
43	Pennsylvania	0.4		36	Iowa	0.5
21	Rhode Island	1.1		36	Massachusetts	0.5
36	South Carolina	0.5		36	South Carolina	0.5
4	South Dakota	9.0		36	Tennessee	0.5
36	Tennessee	0.5		36	Virginia	0.5
22	Texas	1.0		43	Hawaii	0.4
16	Utah	1.5		43	Indiana	0.4
43	Vermont	0.4		43	Pennsylvania	0.4
36	Virginia	0.5		43	Vermont	0.4
9	Washington	1.9		47	Kentucky	0.3
47	West Virginia	0.3		47	New Hampshire	0.3
19	Wisconsin	1.2		47	Ohio	0.3
8	Wyoming	2.7		47	West Virginia	0.3
					District of Columbia	0.6

ALPHA ORDER

RANK ORDER

Source: CQ Press using data from U.S. Bureau of the Census
"State Characteristics: Vintage 2018" (https://www.census.gov/programs-surveys/popest/data/data-sets.html)
*Those who identified themselves as one race. Includes Alaska Native populations. Census states, "Race is a self-identification data item in which respondents choose the race or races with which they most closely identify."

Native Hawaiian or Other Pacific Islander Population in 2018

National Total = 799,418*

ALPHA ORDER					RANK ORDER			

RANK	STATE	POPULATION	% of USA
26	Alabama	5,207	0.7%
15	Alaska	10,221	1.3%
9	Arizona	19,789	2.5%
14	Arkansas	10,881	1.4%
1	California	199,872	25.0%
13	Colorado	10,933	1.4%
34	Connecticut	3,840	0.5%
42	Delaware	1,049	0.1%
7	Florida	24,353	3.0%
12	Georgia	12,432	1.6%
2	Hawaii	144,806	18.1%
33	Idaho	3,883	0.5%
20	Illinois	8,445	1.1%
28	Indiana	4,542	0.6%
29	Iowa	4,232	0.5%
35	Kansas	3,619	0.5%
32	Kentucky	4,058	0.5%
38	Louisiana	2,889	0.4%
49	Maine	455	0.1%
24	Maryland	6,746	0.8%
22	Massachusetts	7,417	0.9%
31	Michigan	4,142	0.5%
30	Minnesota	4,145	0.5%
41	Mississippi	1,812	0.2%
19	Missouri	9,585	1.2%
43	Montana	893	0.1%
39	Nebraska	2,338	0.3%
8	Nevada	23,962	3.0%
45	New Hampshire	637	0.1%
18	New Jersey	9,984	1.2%
36	New Mexico	3,404	0.4%
6	New York	26,745	3.3%
11	North Carolina	12,989	1.6%
46	North Dakota	573	0.1%
23	Ohio	6,994	0.9%
21	Oklahoma	7,568	0.9%
10	Oregon	18,999	2.4%
16	Pennsylvania	10,056	1.3%
40	Rhode Island	2,135	0.3%
27	South Carolina	5,153	0.6%
44	South Dakota	747	0.1%
25	Tennessee	6,496	0.8%
4	Texas	42,333	5.3%
5	Utah	33,495	4.2%
50	Vermont	247	0.0%
17	Virginia	9,998	1.3%
3	Washington	59,001	7.4%
48	West Virginia	528	0.1%
37	Wisconsin	3,243	0.4%
47	Wyoming	572	0.1%

RANK	STATE	POPULATION	% of USA
1	California	199,872	25.0%
2	Hawaii	144,806	18.1%
3	Washington	59,001	7.4%
4	Texas	42,333	5.3%
5	Utah	33,495	4.2%
6	New York	26,745	3.3%
7	Florida	24,353	3.0%
8	Nevada	23,962	3.0%
9	Arizona	19,789	2.5%
10	Oregon	18,999	2.4%
11	North Carolina	12,989	1.6%
12	Georgia	12,432	1.6%
13	Colorado	10,933	1.4%
14	Arkansas	10,881	1.4%
15	Alaska	10,221	1.3%
16	Pennsylvania	10,056	1.3%
17	Virginia	9,998	1.3%
18	New Jersey	9,984	1.2%
19	Missouri	9,585	1.2%
20	Illinois	8,445	1.1%
21	Oklahoma	7,568	0.9%
22	Massachusetts	7,417	0.9%
23	Ohio	6,994	0.9%
24	Maryland	6,746	0.8%
25	Tennessee	6,496	0.8%
26	Alabama	5,207	0.7%
27	South Carolina	5,153	0.6%
28	Indiana	4,542	0.6%
29	Iowa	4,232	0.5%
30	Minnesota	4,145	0.5%
31	Michigan	4,142	0.5%
32	Kentucky	4,058	0.5%
33	Idaho	3,883	0.5%
34	Connecticut	3,840	0.5%
35	Kansas	3,619	0.5%
36	New Mexico	3,404	0.4%
37	Wisconsin	3,243	0.4%
38	Louisiana	2,889	0.4%
39	Nebraska	2,338	0.3%
40	Rhode Island	2,135	0.3%
41	Mississippi	1,812	0.2%
42	Delaware	1,049	0.1%
43	Montana	893	0.1%
44	South Dakota	747	0.1%
45	New Hampshire	637	0.1%
46	North Dakota	573	0.1%
47	Wyoming	572	0.1%
48	West Virginia	528	0.1%
49	Maine	455	0.1%
50	Vermont	247	0.0%
	District of Columbia	975	0.1%

Source: U.S. Bureau of the Census
"State Characteristics: Vintage 2018" (https://www.census.gov/programs-surveys/popest/data/data-sets.html)
*Those who identified themselves as one race. Census states, "Race is a self-identification data item in which respondents choose the race or races with which they most closely identify."

Percent of Population Native Hawaiian or Other Pacific Islander in 2018

National Percent = 0.2%*

RANK	STATE	PERCENT		RANK	STATE	PERCENT
16	Alabama	0.1		1	Hawaii	10.2
2	Alaska	1.4		2	Alaska	1.4
9	Arizona	0.3		3	Utah	1.1
8	Arkansas	0.4		4	Nevada	0.8
6	California	0.5		4	Washington	0.8
10	Colorado	0.2		6	California	0.5
16	Connecticut	0.1		6	Oregon	0.5
16	Delaware	0.1		8	Arkansas	0.4
16	Florida	0.1		9	Arizona	0.3
16	Georgia	0.1		10	Colorado	0.2
1	Hawaii	10.2		10	Idaho	0.2
10	Idaho	0.2		10	Missouri	0.2
16	Illinois	0.1		10	New Mexico	0.2
16	Indiana	0.1		10	Oklahoma	0.2
16	Iowa	0.1		10	Rhode Island	0.2
16	Kansas	0.1		16	Alabama	0.1
16	Kentucky	0.1		16	Connecticut	0.1
16	Louisiana	0.1		16	Delaware	0.1
46	Maine	0.0		16	Florida	0.1
16	Maryland	0.1		16	Georgia	0.1
16	Massachusetts	0.1		16	Illinois	0.1
46	Michigan	0.0		16	Indiana	0.1
16	Minnesota	0.1		16	Iowa	0.1
16	Mississippi	0.1		16	Kansas	0.1
10	Missouri	0.2		16	Kentucky	0.1
16	Montana	0.1		16	Louisiana	0.1
16	Nebraska	0.1		16	Maryland	0.1
4	Nevada	0.8		16	Massachusetts	0.1
46	New Hampshire	0.0		16	Minnesota	0.1
16	New Jersey	0.1		16	Mississippi	0.1
10	New Mexico	0.2		16	Montana	0.1
16	New York	0.1		16	Nebraska	0.1
16	North Carolina	0.1		16	New Jersey	0.1
16	North Dakota	0.1		16	New York	0.1
16	Ohio	0.1		16	North Carolina	0.1
10	Oklahoma	0.2		16	North Dakota	0.1
6	Oregon	0.5		16	Ohio	0.1
16	Pennsylvania	0.1		16	Pennsylvania	0.1
10	Rhode Island	0.2		16	South Carolina	0.1
16	South Carolina	0.1		16	South Dakota	0.1
16	South Dakota	0.1		16	Tennessee	0.1
16	Tennessee	0.1		16	Texas	0.1
16	Texas	0.1		16	Virginia	0.1
3	Utah	1.1		16	Wisconsin	0.1
46	Vermont	0.0		16	Wyoming	0.1
16	Virginia	0.1		46	Maine	0.0
4	Washington	0.8		46	Michigan	0.0
46	West Virginia	0.0		46	New Hampshire	0.0
16	Wisconsin	0.1		46	Vermont	0.0
16	Wyoming	0.1		46	West Virginia	0.0
					District of Columbia	0.1

Source: CQ Press using data from U.S. Bureau of the Census
   "State Characteristics: Vintage 2018" (https://www.census.gov/programs-surveys/popest/data/data-sets.html)
*Those who identified themselves as one race. Census states, "Race is a self-identification data item in which respondents choose the race or races with which they most closely identify."

Non-Hispanic White Population in 2018

National Total = 197,546,407*

ALPHA ORDER

RANK	STATE	POPULATION	% of USA
24	Alabama	3,197,324	1.6%
49	Alaska	444,411	0.2%
20	Arizona	3,902,867	2.0%
33	Arkansas	2,176,611	1.1%
1	California	14,568,608	7.4%
21	Colorado	3,868,329	2.0%
31	Connecticut	2,376,351	1.2%
46	Delaware	599,061	0.3%
3	Florida	11,399,170	5.8%
10	Georgia	5,511,319	2.8%
50	Hawaii	309,043	0.2%
38	Idaho	1,433,895	0.7%
7	Illinois	7,773,275	3.9%
11	Indiana	5,276,640	2.7%
28	Iowa	2,691,471	1.4%
32	Kansas	2,202,954	1.1%
22	Kentucky	3,766,333	1.9%
27	Louisiana	2,729,264	1.4%
39	Maine	1,246,689	0.6%
26	Maryland	3,050,812	1.5%
15	Massachusetts	4,928,183	2.5%
8	Michigan	7,485,441	3.8%
19	Minnesota	4,459,268	2.3%
34	Mississippi	1,686,128	0.9%
17	Missouri	4,858,302	2.5%
41	Montana	912,905	0.5%
36	Nebraska	1,515,603	0.8%
37	Nevada	1,476,377	0.7%
40	New Hampshire	1,220,322	0.6%
16	New Jersey	4,892,895	2.5%
42	New Mexico	777,525	0.4%
4	New York	10,830,524	5.5%
9	North Carolina	6,525,505	3.3%
45	North Dakota	638,189	0.3%
6	Ohio	9,195,982	4.7%
29	Oklahoma	2,576,177	1.3%
25	Oregon	3,155,276	1.6%
5	Pennsylvania	9,741,631	4.9%
43	Rhode Island	761,439	0.4%
23	South Carolina	3,238,535	1.6%
44	South Dakota	718,383	0.4%
14	Tennessee	4,989,758	2.5%
2	Texas	11,912,849	6.0%
30	Utah	2,466,025	1.2%
47	Vermont	579,588	0.3%
12	Virginia	5,234,514	2.6%
13	Washington	5,124,948	2.6%
35	West Virginia	1,662,293	0.8%
18	Wisconsin	4,712,894	2.4%
48	Wyoming	484,253	0.2%

RANK ORDER

RANK	STATE	POPULATION	% of USA
1	California	14,568,608	7.4%
2	Texas	11,912,849	6.0%
3	Florida	11,399,170	5.8%
4	New York	10,830,524	5.5%
5	Pennsylvania	9,741,631	4.9%
6	Ohio	9,195,982	4.7%
7	Illinois	7,773,275	3.9%
8	Michigan	7,485,441	3.8%
9	North Carolina	6,525,505	3.3%
10	Georgia	5,511,319	2.8%
11	Indiana	5,276,640	2.7%
12	Virginia	5,234,514	2.6%
13	Washington	5,124,948	2.6%
14	Tennessee	4,989,758	2.5%
15	Massachusetts	4,928,183	2.5%
16	New Jersey	4,892,895	2.5%
17	Missouri	4,858,302	2.5%
18	Wisconsin	4,712,894	2.4%
19	Minnesota	4,459,268	2.3%
20	Arizona	3,902,867	2.0%
21	Colorado	3,868,329	2.0%
22	Kentucky	3,766,333	1.9%
23	South Carolina	3,238,535	1.6%
24	Alabama	3,197,324	1.6%
25	Oregon	3,155,276	1.6%
26	Maryland	3,050,812	1.5%
27	Louisiana	2,729,264	1.4%
28	Iowa	2,691,471	1.4%
29	Oklahoma	2,576,177	1.3%
30	Utah	2,466,025	1.2%
31	Connecticut	2,376,351	1.2%
32	Kansas	2,202,954	1.1%
33	Arkansas	2,176,611	1.1%
34	Mississippi	1,686,128	0.9%
35	West Virginia	1,662,293	0.8%
36	Nebraska	1,515,603	0.8%
37	Nevada	1,476,377	0.7%
38	Idaho	1,433,895	0.7%
39	Maine	1,246,689	0.6%
40	New Hampshire	1,220,322	0.6%
41	Montana	912,905	0.5%
42	New Mexico	777,525	0.4%
43	Rhode Island	761,439	0.4%
44	South Dakota	718,383	0.4%
45	North Dakota	638,189	0.3%
46	Delaware	599,061	0.3%
47	Vermont	579,588	0.3%
48	Wyoming	484,253	0.2%
49	Alaska	444,411	0.2%
50	Hawaii	309,043	0.2%
	District of Columbia	260,268	0.1%

Source: U.S. Bureau of the Census
"State Characteristics: Vintage 2018" (https://www.census.gov/programs-surveys/popest/data/data-sets.html)
*Those who identified themselves as one race. "White" is defined by Census as a person having origins in any of the original peoples of Europe, North Africa, or the Middle East. This is a subset of the 250,139,096 white population. Persons of Hispanic origin may be of any race. Census states, "Race is a self-identification data item in which respondents choose the race or races with which they most closely identify."

Percent of Population Non-Hispanic White in 2018

National Percent = 60.4%*

ALPHA ORDER

RANK	STATE	PERCENT
30	Alabama	65.4
37	Alaska	60.3
42	Arizona	54.4
24	Arkansas	72.2
49	California	36.8
28	Colorado	67.9
29	Connecticut	66.5
34	Delaware	61.9
43	Florida	53.5
44	Georgia	52.4
50	Hawaii	21.8
10	Idaho	81.7
36	Illinois	61.0
15	Indiana	78.9
6	Iowa	85.3
20	Kansas	75.7
7	Kentucky	84.3
38	Louisiana	58.6
1	Maine	93.1
45	Maryland	50.5
26	Massachusetts	71.4
22	Michigan	74.9
13	Minnesota	79.5
39	Mississippi	56.5
14	Missouri	79.3
5	Montana	85.9
17	Nebraska	78.6
46	Nevada	48.7
4	New Hampshire	90.0
41	New Jersey	54.9
48	New Mexico	37.1
40	New York	55.4
33	North Carolina	62.8
8	North Dakota	84.0
16	Ohio	78.7
31	Oklahoma	65.3
21	Oregon	75.3
19	Pennsylvania	76.1
25	Rhode Island	72.0
32	South Carolina	63.7
11	South Dakota	81.4
23	Tennessee	73.7
47	Texas	41.5
18	Utah	78.0
2	Vermont	92.5
35	Virginia	61.5
27	Washington	68.0
3	West Virginia	92.1
12	Wisconsin	81.1
9	Wyoming	83.8

RANK ORDER

RANK	STATE	PERCENT
1	Maine	93.1
2	Vermont	92.5
3	West Virginia	92.1
4	New Hampshire	90.0
5	Montana	85.9
6	Iowa	85.3
7	Kentucky	84.3
8	North Dakota	84.0
9	Wyoming	83.8
10	Idaho	81.7
11	South Dakota	81.4
12	Wisconsin	81.1
13	Minnesota	79.5
14	Missouri	79.3
15	Indiana	78.9
16	Ohio	78.7
17	Nebraska	78.6
18	Utah	78.0
19	Pennsylvania	76.1
20	Kansas	75.7
21	Oregon	75.3
22	Michigan	74.9
23	Tennessee	73.7
24	Arkansas	72.2
25	Rhode Island	72.0
26	Massachusetts	71.4
27	Washington	68.0
28	Colorado	67.9
29	Connecticut	66.5
30	Alabama	65.4
31	Oklahoma	65.3
32	South Carolina	63.7
33	North Carolina	62.8
34	Delaware	61.9
35	Virginia	61.5
36	Illinois	61.0
37	Alaska	60.3
38	Louisiana	58.6
39	Mississippi	56.5
40	New York	55.4
41	New Jersey	54.9
42	Arizona	54.4
43	Florida	53.5
44	Georgia	52.4
45	Maryland	50.5
46	Nevada	48.7
47	Texas	41.5
48	New Mexico	37.1
49	California	36.8
50	Hawaii	21.8
	District of Columbia	37.1

Source: CQ Press using data from U.S. Bureau of the Census
"State Characteristics: Vintage 2018" (https://www.census.gov/programs-surveys/popest/data/data-sets.html)
*Those who identified themselves as one race. "White" is defined by Census as a person having origins in any of the original peoples of Europe, North Africa, or the Middle East. This non-Hispanic white subset is 79.0% of the total white population. Persons of Hispanic origin may be of any race. Census states, "Race is a self-identification data item in which respondents choose the race or races with which they most closely identify."

Multiple Race Population in 2018

National Total = 8,946,480*

ALPHA ORDER

RANK	STATE	POPULATION	% of USA
31	Alabama	84,365	0.9%
36	Alaska	54,855	0.6%
15	Arizona	205,915	2.3%
34	Arkansas	64,918	0.7%
1	California	1,554,757	17.4%
17	Colorado	176,856	2.0%
30	Connecticut	86,505	1.0%
44	Delaware	25,991	0.3%
4	Florida	464,005	5.2%
14	Georgia	227,000	2.5%
6	Hawaii	340,718	3.8%
38	Idaho	44,094	0.5%
10	Illinois	256,316	2.9%
23	Indiana	141,031	1.6%
35	Iowa	60,579	0.7%
29	Kansas	87,871	1.0%
28	Kentucky	88,218	1.0%
33	Louisiana	79,796	0.9%
45	Maine	24,093	0.3%
18	Maryland	174,155	1.9%
19	Massachusetts	173,821	1.9%
11	Michigan	248,619	2.8%
22	Minnesota	142,853	1.6%
40	Mississippi	38,930	0.4%
21	Missouri	143,702	1.6%
43	Montana	29,588	0.3%
39	Nebraska	43,721	0.5%
24	Nevada	135,589	1.5%
46	New Hampshire	23,761	0.3%
16	New Jersey	200,478	2.2%
37	New Mexico	53,798	0.6%
3	New York	507,377	5.7%
13	North Carolina	237,061	2.6%
48	North Dakota	16,947	0.2%
7	Ohio	272,139	3.0%
12	Oklahoma	245,034	2.7%
20	Oregon	164,413	1.8%
8	Pennsylvania	265,828	3.0%
42	Rhode Island	29,783	0.3%
27	South Carolina	97,718	1.1%
47	South Dakota	21,250	0.2%
25	Tennessee	132,259	1.5%
2	Texas	583,563	6.5%
32	Utah	82,259	0.9%
50	Vermont	12,275	0.1%
9	Virginia	262,295	2.9%
5	Washington	360,935	4.0%
41	West Virginia	32,216	0.4%
26	Wisconsin	114,034	1.3%
49	Wyoming	12,592	0.1%

RANK ORDER

RANK	STATE	POPULATION	% of USA
1	California	1,554,757	17.4%
2	Texas	583,563	6.5%
3	New York	507,377	5.7%
4	Florida	464,005	5.2%
5	Washington	360,935	4.0%
6	Hawaii	340,718	3.8%
7	Ohio	272,139	3.0%
8	Pennsylvania	265,828	3.0%
9	Virginia	262,295	2.9%
10	Illinois	256,316	2.9%
11	Michigan	248,619	2.8%
12	Oklahoma	245,034	2.7%
13	North Carolina	237,061	2.6%
14	Georgia	227,000	2.5%
15	Arizona	205,915	2.3%
16	New Jersey	200,478	2.2%
17	Colorado	176,856	2.0%
18	Maryland	174,155	1.9%
19	Massachusetts	173,821	1.9%
20	Oregon	164,413	1.8%
21	Missouri	143,702	1.6%
22	Minnesota	142,853	1.6%
23	Indiana	141,031	1.6%
24	Nevada	135,589	1.5%
25	Tennessee	132,259	1.5%
26	Wisconsin	114,034	1.3%
27	South Carolina	97,718	1.1%
28	Kentucky	88,218	1.0%
29	Kansas	87,871	1.0%
30	Connecticut	86,505	1.0%
31	Alabama	84,365	0.9%
32	Utah	82,259	0.9%
33	Louisiana	79,796	0.9%
34	Arkansas	64,918	0.7%
35	Iowa	60,579	0.7%
36	Alaska	54,855	0.6%
37	New Mexico	53,798	0.6%
38	Idaho	44,094	0.5%
39	Nebraska	43,721	0.5%
40	Mississippi	38,930	0.4%
41	West Virginia	32,216	0.4%
42	Rhode Island	29,783	0.3%
43	Montana	29,588	0.3%
44	Delaware	25,991	0.3%
45	Maine	24,093	0.3%
46	New Hampshire	23,761	0.3%
47	South Dakota	21,250	0.2%
48	North Dakota	16,947	0.2%
49	Wyoming	12,592	0.1%
50	Vermont	12,275	0.1%
	District of Columbia	19,604	0.2%

Source: U.S. Bureau of the Census
  "State Characteristics: Vintage 2018" (https://www.census.gov/programs-surveys/popest/data/data-sets.html)
*This includes those who identified themselves as two or more races. This is the population who did not identify themselves as one race (White, Black, American Indian/Native Alaska Native, Asian, or Native Hawaiian or Other Pacific Islander) but as a member of multiple racial groups. Census states, "Race is a self-identification data item in which respondents choose the race or races with which they most closely identify."

Percent of Population Multiple Races in 2018

National Percent = 2.7%*

ALPHA ORDER

RANK	STATE	PERCENT
48	Alabama	1.7
2	Alaska	7.4
11	Arizona	2.9
30	Arkansas	2.2
6	California	3.9
8	Colorado	3.1
23	Connecticut	2.4
15	Delaware	2.7
30	Florida	2.2
30	Georgia	2.2
1	Hawaii	24.0
19	Idaho	2.5
37	Illinois	2.0
35	Indiana	2.1
43	Iowa	1.9
10	Kansas	3.0
37	Kentucky	2.0
48	Louisiana	1.7
45	Maine	1.8
11	Maryland	2.9
19	Massachusetts	2.5
19	Michigan	2.5
19	Minnesota	2.5
50	Mississippi	1.3
25	Missouri	2.3
13	Montana	2.8
25	Nebraska	2.3
5	Nevada	4.5
45	New Hampshire	1.8
25	New Jersey	2.3
16	New Mexico	2.6
16	New York	2.6
25	North Carolina	2.3
30	North Dakota	2.2
25	Ohio	2.3
3	Oklahoma	6.2
6	Oregon	3.9
35	Pennsylvania	2.1
13	Rhode Island	2.8
43	South Carolina	1.9
23	South Dakota	2.4
37	Tennessee	2.0
37	Texas	2.0
16	Utah	2.6
37	Vermont	2.0
8	Virginia	3.1
4	Washington	4.8
45	West Virginia	1.8
37	Wisconsin	2.0
30	Wyoming	2.2

RANK ORDER

RANK	STATE	PERCENT
1	Hawaii	24.0
2	Alaska	7.4
3	Oklahoma	6.2
4	Washington	4.8
5	Nevada	4.5
6	California	3.9
6	Oregon	3.9
8	Colorado	3.1
8	Virginia	3.1
10	Kansas	3.0
11	Arizona	2.9
11	Maryland	2.9
13	Montana	2.8
13	Rhode Island	2.8
15	Delaware	2.7
16	New Mexico	2.6
16	New York	2.6
16	Utah	2.6
19	Idaho	2.5
19	Massachusetts	2.5
19	Michigan	2.5
19	Minnesota	2.5
23	Connecticut	2.4
23	South Dakota	2.4
25	Missouri	2.3
25	Nebraska	2.3
25	New Jersey	2.3
25	North Carolina	2.3
25	Ohio	2.3
30	Arkansas	2.2
30	Florida	2.2
30	Georgia	2.2
30	North Dakota	2.2
30	Wyoming	2.2
35	Indiana	2.1
35	Pennsylvania	2.1
37	Illinois	2.0
37	Kentucky	2.0
37	Tennessee	2.0
37	Texas	2.0
37	Vermont	2.0
37	Wisconsin	2.0
43	Iowa	1.9
43	South Carolina	1.9
45	Maine	1.8
45	New Hampshire	1.8
45	West Virginia	1.8
48	Alabama	1.7
48	Louisiana	1.7
50	Mississippi	1.3

District of Columbia 2.8

Source: CQ Press using data from U.S. Bureau of the Census
"State Characteristics: Vintage 2018" (https://www.census.gov/programs-surveys/popest/data/data-sets.html)
*This includes those who identified themselves as two or more races. This is the population who did not identify themselves as one race (White, Black, American Indian/Native Alaska Native, Asian, or Native Hawaiian or Other Pacific Islander) but as a member of multiple racial groups. Census states, "Race is a self-identification data item in which respondents choose the race or races with which they most closely identify."

Population under 5 Years Old in 2018

National Total = 19,810,275

ALPHA ORDER					RANK ORDER			

RANK	STATE	POPULATION	% of USA		RANK	STATE	POPULATION	% of USA
24	Alabama	293,203	1.5%		1	California	2,441,300	12.3%
48	Alaska	53,115	0.3%		2	Texas	2,024,126	10.2%
14	Arizona	435,936	2.2%		3	Florida	1,143,183	5.8%
31	Arkansas	190,343	1.0%		4	New York	1,140,442	5.8%
1	California	2,441,300	12.3%		5	Illinois	760,619	3.8%
21	Colorado	336,854	1.7%		6	Pennsylvania	702,997	3.5%
35	Connecticut	183,134	0.9%		7	Ohio	694,789	3.5%
45	Delaware	54,811	0.3%		8	Georgia	657,414	3.3%
3	Florida	1,143,183	5.8%		9	North Carolina	610,128	3.1%
8	Georgia	657,414	3.3%		10	Michigan	572,163	2.9%
40	Hawaii	87,704	0.4%		11	New Jersey	518,628	2.6%
38	Idaho	116,339	0.6%		12	Virginia	510,924	2.6%
5	Illinois	760,619	3.8%		13	Washington	462,701	2.3%
15	Indiana	418,544	2.1%		14	Arizona	435,936	2.2%
30	Iowa	198,218	1.0%		15	Indiana	418,544	2.1%
32	Kansas	189,335	1.0%		16	Tennessee	406,574	2.1%
26	Kentucky	275,412	1.4%		17	Missouri	372,713	1.9%
23	Louisiana	307,019	1.5%		18	Maryland	364,504	1.8%
41	Maine	64,282	0.3%		19	Massachusetts	360,161	1.8%
18	Maryland	364,504	1.8%		20	Minnesota	355,291	1.8%
19	Massachusetts	360,161	1.8%		21	Colorado	336,854	1.7%
10	Michigan	572,163	2.9%		22	Wisconsin	334,382	1.7%
20	Minnesota	355,291	1.8%		23	Louisiana	307,019	1.5%
34	Mississippi	185,477	0.9%		24	Alabama	293,203	1.5%
17	Missouri	372,713	1.9%		25	South Carolina	292,391	1.5%
43	Montana	62,536	0.3%		26	Kentucky	275,412	1.4%
36	Nebraska	132,968	0.7%		27	Oklahoma	260,429	1.3%
33	Nevada	185,995	0.9%		28	Utah	253,004	1.3%
42	New Hampshire	64,020	0.3%		29	Oregon	234,214	1.2%
11	New Jersey	518,628	2.6%		30	Iowa	198,218	1.0%
37	New Mexico	124,246	0.6%		31	Arkansas	190,343	1.0%
4	New York	1,140,442	5.8%		32	Kansas	189,335	1.0%
9	North Carolina	610,128	3.1%		33	Nevada	185,995	0.9%
46	North Dakota	54,695	0.3%		34	Mississippi	185,477	0.9%
7	Ohio	694,789	3.5%		35	Connecticut	183,134	0.9%
27	Oklahoma	260,429	1.3%		36	Nebraska	132,968	0.7%
29	Oregon	234,214	1.2%		37	New Mexico	124,246	0.6%
6	Pennsylvania	702,997	3.5%		38	Idaho	116,339	0.6%
47	Rhode Island	54,413	0.3%		39	West Virginia	95,257	0.5%
25	South Carolina	292,391	1.5%		40	Hawaii	87,704	0.4%
44	South Dakota	62,132	0.3%		41	Maine	64,282	0.3%
16	Tennessee	406,574	2.1%		42	New Hampshire	64,020	0.3%
2	Texas	2,024,126	10.2%		43	Montana	62,536	0.3%
28	Utah	253,004	1.3%		44	South Dakota	62,132	0.3%
50	Vermont	29,681	0.1%		45	Delaware	54,811	0.3%
12	Virginia	510,924	2.6%		46	North Dakota	54,695	0.3%
13	Washington	462,701	2.3%		47	Rhode Island	54,413	0.3%
39	West Virginia	95,257	0.5%		48	Alaska	53,115	0.3%
22	Wisconsin	334,382	1.7%		49	Wyoming	35,912	0.2%
49	Wyoming	35,912	0.2%		50	Vermont	29,681	0.1%
						District of Columbia	45,617	0.2%

Source: U.S. Bureau of the Census
"State Characteristics: Vintage 2018" (https://www.census.gov/programs-surveys/popest/data/data-sets.html)

Percent of Population under 5 Years Old in 2018

National Percent = 6.1% of Population

ALPHA ORDER

RANK	STATE	PERCENT
25	Alabama	6.0
2	Alaska	7.2
21	Arizona	6.1
11	Arkansas	6.3
15	California	6.2
30	Colorado	5.9
46	Connecticut	5.1
39	Delaware	5.7
43	Florida	5.4
15	Georgia	6.2
15	Hawaii	6.2
7	Idaho	6.6
25	Illinois	6.0
11	Indiana	6.3
11	Iowa	6.3
10	Kansas	6.5
15	Kentucky	6.2
7	Louisiana	6.6
48	Maine	4.8
25	Maryland	6.0
45	Massachusetts	5.2
39	Michigan	5.7
11	Minnesota	6.3
15	Mississippi	6.2
21	Missouri	6.1
30	Montana	5.9
6	Nebraska	6.9
21	Nevada	6.1
49	New Hampshire	4.7
35	New Jersey	5.8
30	New Mexico	5.9
35	New York	5.8
30	North Carolina	5.9
2	North Dakota	7.2
30	Ohio	5.9
7	Oklahoma	6.6
41	Oregon	5.6
42	Pennsylvania	5.5
46	Rhode Island	5.1
35	South Carolina	5.8
5	South Dakota	7.0
25	Tennessee	6.0
4	Texas	7.1
1	Utah	8.0
49	Vermont	4.7
25	Virginia	6.0
21	Washington	6.1
44	West Virginia	5.3
35	Wisconsin	5.8
15	Wyoming	6.2

RANK ORDER

RANK	STATE	PERCENT
1	Utah	8.0
2	Alaska	7.2
2	North Dakota	7.2
4	Texas	7.1
5	South Dakota	7.0
6	Nebraska	6.9
7	Idaho	6.6
7	Louisiana	6.6
7	Oklahoma	6.6
10	Kansas	6.5
11	Arkansas	6.3
11	Indiana	6.3
11	Iowa	6.3
11	Minnesota	6.3
15	California	6.2
15	Georgia	6.2
15	Hawaii	6.2
15	Kentucky	6.2
15	Mississippi	6.2
15	Wyoming	6.2
21	Arizona	6.1
21	Missouri	6.1
21	Nevada	6.1
21	Washington	6.1
25	Alabama	6.0
25	Illinois	6.0
25	Maryland	6.0
25	Tennessee	6.0
25	Virginia	6.0
30	Colorado	5.9
30	Montana	5.9
30	New Mexico	5.9
30	North Carolina	5.9
30	Ohio	5.9
35	New Jersey	5.8
35	New York	5.8
35	South Carolina	5.8
35	Wisconsin	5.8
39	Delaware	5.7
39	Michigan	5.7
41	Oregon	5.6
42	Pennsylvania	5.5
43	Florida	5.4
44	West Virginia	5.3
45	Massachusetts	5.2
46	Connecticut	5.1
46	Rhode Island	5.1
48	Maine	4.8
49	New Hampshire	4.7
49	Vermont	4.7

District of Columbia   6.5

Source: CQ Press using data from U.S. Bureau of the Census
"State Characteristics: Vintage 2018" (https://www.census.gov/programs-surveys/popest/data/data-sets.html)

Population 5 to 17 Years Old in 2018

National Total = 53,589,067

ALPHA ORDER

RANK	STATE	POPULATION	% of USA
24	Alabama	796,637	1.5%
47	Alaska	130,701	0.2%
13	Arizona	1,206,721	2.3%
34	Arkansas	512,837	1.0%
1	California	6,548,655	12.2%
22	Colorado	928,381	1.7%
30	Connecticut	552,059	1.0%
46	Delaware	148,805	0.3%
3	Florida	3,085,898	5.8%
8	Georgia	1,848,337	3.4%
40	Hawaii	215,710	0.4%
38	Idaho	330,633	0.6%
5	Illinois	2,096,647	3.9%
15	Indiana	1,149,586	2.1%
31	Iowa	532,549	1.0%
33	Kansas	516,626	1.0%
26	Kentucky	733,417	1.4%
25	Louisiana	788,897	1.5%
42	Maine	186,122	0.3%
19	Maryland	975,644	1.8%
17	Massachusetts	1,006,697	1.9%
10	Michigan	1,592,505	3.0%
20	Minnesota	947,324	1.8%
32	Mississippi	520,664	1.0%
18	Missouri	1,004,117	1.9%
43	Montana	166,898	0.3%
37	Nebraska	343,873	0.6%
35	Nevada	503,002	0.9%
41	New Hampshire	194,150	0.4%
11	New Jersey	1,435,015	2.7%
36	New Mexico	357,907	0.7%
4	New York	2,927,660	5.5%
9	North Carolina	1,690,517	3.2%
48	North Dakota	124,003	0.2%
7	Ohio	1,898,536	3.5%
27	Oklahoma	696,057	1.3%
29	Oregon	639,353	1.2%
6	Pennsylvania	1,945,914	3.6%
45	Rhode Island	150,800	0.3%
23	South Carolina	813,554	1.5%
44	South Dakota	155,474	0.3%
16	Tennessee	1,099,646	2.1%
2	Texas	5,373,973	10.0%
28	Utah	679,458	1.3%
50	Vermont	86,292	0.2%
12	Virginia	1,358,868	2.5%
14	Washington	1,200,584	2.2%
39	West Virginia	268,903	0.5%
21	Wisconsin	941,721	1.8%
49	Wyoming	98,863	0.2%

RANK ORDER

RANK	STATE	POPULATION	% of USA
1	California	6,548,655	12.2%
2	Texas	5,373,973	10.0%
3	Florida	3,085,898	5.8%
4	New York	2,927,660	5.5%
5	Illinois	2,096,647	3.9%
6	Pennsylvania	1,945,914	3.6%
7	Ohio	1,898,536	3.5%
8	Georgia	1,848,337	3.4%
9	North Carolina	1,690,517	3.2%
10	Michigan	1,592,505	3.0%
11	New Jersey	1,435,015	2.7%
12	Virginia	1,358,868	2.5%
13	Arizona	1,206,721	2.3%
14	Washington	1,200,584	2.2%
15	Indiana	1,149,586	2.1%
16	Tennessee	1,099,646	2.1%
17	Massachusetts	1,006,697	1.9%
18	Missouri	1,004,117	1.9%
19	Maryland	975,644	1.8%
20	Minnesota	947,324	1.8%
21	Wisconsin	941,721	1.8%
22	Colorado	928,381	1.7%
23	South Carolina	813,554	1.5%
24	Alabama	796,637	1.5%
25	Louisiana	788,897	1.5%
26	Kentucky	733,417	1.4%
27	Oklahoma	696,057	1.3%
28	Utah	679,458	1.3%
29	Oregon	639,353	1.2%
30	Connecticut	552,059	1.0%
31	Iowa	532,549	1.0%
32	Mississippi	520,664	1.0%
33	Kansas	516,626	1.0%
34	Arkansas	512,837	1.0%
35	Nevada	503,002	0.9%
36	New Mexico	357,907	0.7%
37	Nebraska	343,873	0.6%
38	Idaho	330,633	0.6%
39	West Virginia	268,903	0.5%
40	Hawaii	215,710	0.4%
41	New Hampshire	194,150	0.4%
42	Maine	186,122	0.3%
43	Montana	166,898	0.3%
44	South Dakota	155,474	0.3%
45	Rhode Island	150,800	0.3%
46	Delaware	148,805	0.3%
47	Alaska	130,701	0.2%
48	North Dakota	124,003	0.2%
49	Wyoming	98,863	0.2%
50	Vermont	86,292	0.2%
	District of Columbia	81,877	0.2%

Source: CQ Press using data from U.S. Bureau of the Census
"State Characteristics: Vintage 2018" (https://www.census.gov/programs-surveys/popest/data/data-sets.html)

Percent of Population 5 to 17 Years Old in 2018

National Percent = 16.4% of Population

ALPHA ORDER

RANK	STATE	PERCENT
24	Alabama	16.3
5	Alaska	17.7
18	Arizona	16.8
14	Arkansas	17.0
19	California	16.6
24	Colorado	16.3
38	Connecticut	15.5
39	Delaware	15.4
46	Florida	14.5
8	Georgia	17.6
41	Hawaii	15.2
2	Idaho	18.8
21	Illinois	16.5
11	Indiana	17.2
15	Iowa	16.9
5	Kansas	17.7
22	Kentucky	16.4
15	Louisiana	16.9
49	Maine	13.9
31	Maryland	16.1
45	Massachusetts	14.6
35	Michigan	15.9
15	Minnesota	16.9
10	Mississippi	17.4
22	Missouri	16.4
37	Montana	15.7
4	Nebraska	17.8
19	Nevada	16.6
47	New Hampshire	14.3
31	New Jersey	16.1
12	New Mexico	17.1
43	New York	15.0
24	North Carolina	16.3
24	North Dakota	16.3
28	Ohio	16.2
5	Oklahoma	17.7
40	Oregon	15.3
41	Pennsylvania	15.2
47	Rhode Island	14.3
33	South Carolina	16.0
8	South Dakota	17.6
28	Tennessee	16.2
3	Texas	18.7
1	Utah	21.5
50	Vermont	13.8
33	Virginia	16.0
35	Washington	15.9
44	West Virginia	14.9
28	Wisconsin	16.2
12	Wyoming	17.1

RANK ORDER

RANK	STATE	PERCENT
1	Utah	21.5
2	Idaho	18.8
3	Texas	18.7
4	Nebraska	17.8
5	Alaska	17.7
5	Kansas	17.7
5	Oklahoma	17.7
8	Georgia	17.6
8	South Dakota	17.6
10	Mississippi	17.4
11	Indiana	17.2
12	New Mexico	17.1
12	Wyoming	17.1
14	Arkansas	17.0
15	Iowa	16.9
15	Louisiana	16.9
15	Minnesota	16.9
18	Arizona	16.8
19	California	16.6
19	Nevada	16.6
21	Illinois	16.5
22	Kentucky	16.4
22	Missouri	16.4
24	Alabama	16.3
24	Colorado	16.3
24	North Carolina	16.3
24	North Dakota	16.3
28	Ohio	16.2
28	Tennessee	16.2
28	Wisconsin	16.2
31	Maryland	16.1
31	New Jersey	16.1
33	South Carolina	16.0
33	Virginia	16.0
35	Michigan	15.9
35	Washington	15.9
37	Montana	15.7
38	Connecticut	15.5
39	Delaware	15.4
40	Oregon	15.3
41	Hawaii	15.2
41	Pennsylvania	15.2
43	New York	15.0
44	West Virginia	14.9
45	Massachusetts	14.6
46	Florida	14.5
47	New Hampshire	14.3
47	Rhode Island	14.3
49	Maine	13.9
50	Vermont	13.8
	District of Columbia	11.7

Source: CQ Press using data from U.S. Bureau of the Census
"State Characteristics: Vintage 2018" (https://www.census.gov/programs-surveys/popest/data/data-sets.html)

Population 18 Years Old and Older in 2018

National Total = 253,768,092

RANK	STATE	POPULATION	% of USA
24	Alabama	3,798,031	1.5%
48	Alaska	553,622	0.2%
15	Arizona	5,528,989	2.2%
32	Arkansas	2,310,645	0.9%
1	California	30,567,090	12.0%
21	Colorado	4,430,329	1.7%
29	Connecticut	2,837,472	1.1%
45	Delaware	763,555	0.3%
3	Florida	17,070,244	6.7%
9	Georgia	8,013,724	3.2%
40	Hawaii	1,117,077	0.4%
39	Idaho	1,307,236	0.5%
6	Illinois	9,883,814	3.9%
17	Indiana	5,123,748	2.0%
30	Iowa	2,425,378	1.0%
35	Kansas	2,205,544	0.9%
26	Kentucky	3,459,573	1.4%
25	Louisiana	3,564,062	1.4%
42	Maine	1,088,000	0.4%
19	Maryland	4,702,570	1.9%
14	Massachusetts	5,535,291	2.2%
10	Michigan	7,831,247	3.1%
22	Minnesota	4,308,564	1.7%
33	Mississippi	2,280,389	0.9%
18	Missouri	4,749,622	1.9%
44	Montana	832,871	0.3%
37	Nebraska	1,452,427	0.6%
31	Nevada	2,345,395	0.9%
41	New Hampshire	1,098,288	0.4%
11	New Jersey	6,954,877	2.7%
36	New Mexico	1,613,275	0.6%
4	New York	15,474,107	6.1%
8	North Carolina	8,082,975	3.2%
47	North Dakota	581,379	0.2%
7	Ohio	9,096,117	3.6%
28	Oklahoma	2,986,593	1.2%
27	Oregon	3,317,146	1.3%
5	Pennsylvania	10,158,149	4.0%
43	Rhode Island	852,102	0.3%
23	South Carolina	3,978,182	1.6%
46	South Dakota	664,629	0.3%
16	Tennessee	5,263,790	2.1%
2	Texas	21,303,746	8.4%
34	Utah	2,228,643	0.9%
49	Vermont	510,326	0.2%
12	Virginia	6,647,893	2.6%
13	Washington	5,872,306	2.3%
38	West Virginia	1,441,672	0.6%
20	Wisconsin	4,537,465	1.8%
50	Wyoming	442,962	0.2%

RANK	STATE	POPULATION	% of USA
1	California	30,567,090	12.0%
2	Texas	21,303,746	8.4%
3	Florida	17,070,244	6.7%
4	New York	15,474,107	6.1%
5	Pennsylvania	10,158,149	4.0%
6	Illinois	9,883,814	3.9%
7	Ohio	9,096,117	3.6%
8	North Carolina	8,082,975	3.2%
9	Georgia	8,013,724	3.2%
10	Michigan	7,831,247	3.1%
11	New Jersey	6,954,877	2.7%
12	Virginia	6,647,893	2.6%
13	Washington	5,872,306	2.3%
14	Massachusetts	5,535,291	2.2%
15	Arizona	5,528,989	2.2%
16	Tennessee	5,263,790	2.1%
17	Indiana	5,123,748	2.0%
18	Missouri	4,749,622	1.9%
19	Maryland	4,702,570	1.9%
20	Wisconsin	4,537,465	1.8%
21	Colorado	4,430,329	1.7%
22	Minnesota	4,308,564	1.7%
23	South Carolina	3,978,182	1.6%
24	Alabama	3,798,031	1.5%
25	Louisiana	3,564,062	1.4%
26	Kentucky	3,459,573	1.4%
27	Oregon	3,317,146	1.3%
28	Oklahoma	2,986,593	1.2%
29	Connecticut	2,837,472	1.1%
30	Iowa	2,425,378	1.0%
31	Nevada	2,345,395	0.9%
32	Arkansas	2,310,645	0.9%
33	Mississippi	2,280,389	0.9%
34	Utah	2,228,643	0.9%
35	Kansas	2,205,544	0.9%
36	New Mexico	1,613,275	0.6%
37	Nebraska	1,452,427	0.6%
38	West Virginia	1,441,672	0.6%
39	Idaho	1,307,236	0.5%
40	Hawaii	1,117,077	0.4%
41	New Hampshire	1,098,288	0.4%
42	Maine	1,088,000	0.4%
43	Rhode Island	852,102	0.3%
44	Montana	832,871	0.3%
45	Delaware	763,555	0.3%
46	South Dakota	664,629	0.3%
47	North Dakota	581,379	0.2%
48	Alaska	553,622	0.2%
49	Vermont	510,326	0.2%
50	Wyoming	442,962	0.2%
	District of Columbia	574,961	0.2%

Source: U.S. Bureau of the Census
"State Characteristics: Vintage 2018" (https://www.census.gov/programs-surveys/popest/data/data-sets.html)

Percent of Population 18 Years Old and Older in 2018

National Percent = 77.6% of Population

<table>
<tr><td colspan="3">ALPHA ORDER</td><td colspan="3">RANK ORDER</td></tr>
<tr><th>RANK</th><th>STATE</th><th>PERCENT</th><th>RANK</th><th>STATE</th><th>PERCENT</th></tr>
<tr><td>26</td><td>Alabama</td><td>77.7</td><td>1</td><td>Vermont</td><td>81.5</td></tr>
<tr><td>47</td><td>Alaska</td><td>75.1</td><td>2</td><td>Maine</td><td>81.3</td></tr>
<tr><td>32</td><td>Arizona</td><td>77.1</td><td>3</td><td>New Hampshire</td><td>81.0</td></tr>
<tr><td>36</td><td>Arkansas</td><td>76.7</td><td>4</td><td>Rhode Island</td><td>80.6</td></tr>
<tr><td>30</td><td>California</td><td>77.3</td><td>5</td><td>Massachusetts</td><td>80.2</td></tr>
<tr><td>21</td><td>Colorado</td><td>77.8</td><td>6</td><td>Florida</td><td>80.1</td></tr>
<tr><td>8</td><td>Connecticut</td><td>79.4</td><td>7</td><td>West Virginia</td><td>79.8</td></tr>
<tr><td>12</td><td>Delaware</td><td>78.9</td><td>8</td><td>Connecticut</td><td>79.4</td></tr>
<tr><td>6</td><td>Florida</td><td>80.1</td><td>9</td><td>Pennsylvania</td><td>79.3</td></tr>
<tr><td>42</td><td>Georgia</td><td>76.2</td><td>10</td><td>New York</td><td>79.2</td></tr>
<tr><td>13</td><td>Hawaii</td><td>78.6</td><td>10</td><td>Oregon</td><td>79.2</td></tr>
<tr><td>48</td><td>Idaho</td><td>74.5</td><td>12</td><td>Delaware</td><td>78.9</td></tr>
<tr><td>27</td><td>Illinois</td><td>77.6</td><td>13</td><td>Hawaii</td><td>78.6</td></tr>
<tr><td>38</td><td>Indiana</td><td>76.6</td><td>14</td><td>Montana</td><td>78.4</td></tr>
<tr><td>34</td><td>Iowa</td><td>76.8</td><td>15</td><td>Michigan</td><td>78.3</td></tr>
<tr><td>43</td><td>Kansas</td><td>75.8</td><td>16</td><td>South Carolina</td><td>78.2</td></tr>
<tr><td>29</td><td>Kentucky</td><td>77.4</td><td>17</td><td>New Jersey</td><td>78.1</td></tr>
<tr><td>39</td><td>Louisiana</td><td>76.5</td><td>18</td><td>Virginia</td><td>78.0</td></tr>
<tr><td>2</td><td>Maine</td><td>81.3</td><td>18</td><td>Wisconsin</td><td>78.0</td></tr>
<tr><td>21</td><td>Maryland</td><td>77.8</td><td>20</td><td>Washington</td><td>77.9</td></tr>
<tr><td>5</td><td>Massachusetts</td><td>80.2</td><td>21</td><td>Colorado</td><td>77.8</td></tr>
<tr><td>15</td><td>Michigan</td><td>78.3</td><td>21</td><td>Maryland</td><td>77.8</td></tr>
<tr><td>34</td><td>Minnesota</td><td>76.8</td><td>21</td><td>North Carolina</td><td>77.8</td></tr>
<tr><td>41</td><td>Mississippi</td><td>76.4</td><td>21</td><td>Ohio</td><td>77.8</td></tr>
<tr><td>28</td><td>Missouri</td><td>77.5</td><td>21</td><td>Tennessee</td><td>77.8</td></tr>
<tr><td>14</td><td>Montana</td><td>78.4</td><td>26</td><td>Alabama</td><td>77.7</td></tr>
<tr><td>45</td><td>Nebraska</td><td>75.3</td><td>27</td><td>Illinois</td><td>77.6</td></tr>
<tr><td>30</td><td>Nevada</td><td>77.3</td><td>28</td><td>Missouri</td><td>77.5</td></tr>
<tr><td>3</td><td>New Hampshire</td><td>81.0</td><td>29</td><td>Kentucky</td><td>77.4</td></tr>
<tr><td>17</td><td>New Jersey</td><td>78.1</td><td>30</td><td>California</td><td>77.3</td></tr>
<tr><td>33</td><td>New Mexico</td><td>77.0</td><td>30</td><td>Nevada</td><td>77.3</td></tr>
<tr><td>10</td><td>New York</td><td>79.2</td><td>32</td><td>Arizona</td><td>77.1</td></tr>
<tr><td>21</td><td>North Carolina</td><td>77.8</td><td>33</td><td>New Mexico</td><td>77.0</td></tr>
<tr><td>39</td><td>North Dakota</td><td>76.5</td><td>34</td><td>Iowa</td><td>76.8</td></tr>
<tr><td>21</td><td>Ohio</td><td>77.8</td><td>34</td><td>Minnesota</td><td>76.8</td></tr>
<tr><td>44</td><td>Oklahoma</td><td>75.7</td><td>36</td><td>Arkansas</td><td>76.7</td></tr>
<tr><td>10</td><td>Oregon</td><td>79.2</td><td>36</td><td>Wyoming</td><td>76.7</td></tr>
<tr><td>9</td><td>Pennsylvania</td><td>79.3</td><td>38</td><td>Indiana</td><td>76.6</td></tr>
<tr><td>4</td><td>Rhode Island</td><td>80.6</td><td>39</td><td>Louisiana</td><td>76.5</td></tr>
<tr><td>16</td><td>South Carolina</td><td>78.2</td><td>39</td><td>North Dakota</td><td>76.5</td></tr>
<tr><td>45</td><td>South Dakota</td><td>75.3</td><td>41</td><td>Mississippi</td><td>76.4</td></tr>
<tr><td>21</td><td>Tennessee</td><td>77.8</td><td>42</td><td>Georgia</td><td>76.2</td></tr>
<tr><td>49</td><td>Texas</td><td>74.2</td><td>43</td><td>Kansas</td><td>75.8</td></tr>
<tr><td>50</td><td>Utah</td><td>70.5</td><td>44</td><td>Oklahoma</td><td>75.7</td></tr>
<tr><td>1</td><td>Vermont</td><td>81.5</td><td>45</td><td>Nebraska</td><td>75.3</td></tr>
<tr><td>18</td><td>Virginia</td><td>78.0</td><td>45</td><td>South Dakota</td><td>75.3</td></tr>
<tr><td>20</td><td>Washington</td><td>77.9</td><td>47</td><td>Alaska</td><td>75.1</td></tr>
<tr><td>7</td><td>West Virginia</td><td>79.8</td><td>48</td><td>Idaho</td><td>74.5</td></tr>
<tr><td>18</td><td>Wisconsin</td><td>78.0</td><td>49</td><td>Texas</td><td>74.2</td></tr>
<tr><td>36</td><td>Wyoming</td><td>76.7</td><td>50</td><td>Utah</td><td>70.5</td></tr>
<tr><td></td><td></td><td></td><td></td><td>District of Columbia</td><td>81.9</td></tr>
</table>

Source: CQ Press using data from U.S. Bureau of the Census
"State Characteristics: Vintage 2018" (https://www.census.gov/programs-surveys/popest/data/data-sets.html)

Population 18 to 24 Years Old in 2018

National Total = 30,456,902

ALPHA ORDER

RANK	STATE	POPULATION	% of USA
24	Alabama	452,658	1.5%
48	Alaska	70,377	0.2%
14	Arizona	687,396	2.3%
34	Arkansas	280,578	0.9%
1	California	3,745,395	12.3%
21	Colorado	526,828	1.7%
30	Connecticut	346,869	1.1%
46	Delaware	83,808	0.3%
4	Florida	1,754,181	5.8%
8	Georgia	1,010,347	3.3%
41	Hawaii	121,243	0.4%
38	Idaho	162,768	0.5%
5	Illinois	1,176,310	3.9%
16	Indiana	655,977	2.2%
31	Iowa	319,030	1.0%
32	Kansas	294,735	1.0%
26	Kentucky	417,732	1.4%
25	Louisiana	425,349	1.4%
43	Maine	107,124	0.4%
20	Maryland	531,360	1.7%
13	Massachusetts	701,928	2.3%
10	Michigan	961,939	3.2%
22	Minnesota	501,636	1.6%
33	Mississippi	291,924	1.0%
18	Missouri	566,385	1.9%
44	Montana	98,445	0.3%
37	Nebraska	190,708	0.6%
35	Nevada	248,789	0.8%
40	New Hampshire	126,137	0.4%
12	New Jersey	766,006	2.5%
36	New Mexico	197,455	0.6%
3	New York	1,800,166	5.9%
9	North Carolina	983,834	3.2%
45	North Dakota	84,712	0.3%
7	Ohio	1,068,198	3.5%
27	Oklahoma	379,680	1.2%
28	Oregon	365,044	1.2%
6	Pennsylvania	1,160,282	3.8%
42	Rhode Island	110,903	0.4%
23	South Carolina	468,223	1.5%
47	South Dakota	83,429	0.3%
17	Tennessee	613,790	2.0%
2	Texas	2,796,079	9.2%
29	Utah	356,310	1.2%
49	Vermont	67,219	0.2%
11	Virginia	805,047	2.6%
15	Washington	657,446	2.2%
39	West Virginia	156,849	0.5%
19	Wisconsin	551,765	1.8%
50	Wyoming	52,367	0.2%

RANK ORDER

RANK	STATE	POPULATION	% of USA
1	California	3,745,395	12.3%
2	Texas	2,796,079	9.2%
3	New York	1,800,166	5.9%
4	Florida	1,754,181	5.8%
5	Illinois	1,176,310	3.9%
6	Pennsylvania	1,160,282	3.8%
7	Ohio	1,068,198	3.5%
8	Georgia	1,010,347	3.3%
9	North Carolina	983,834	3.2%
10	Michigan	961,939	3.2%
11	Virginia	805,047	2.6%
12	New Jersey	766,006	2.5%
13	Massachusetts	701,928	2.3%
14	Arizona	687,396	2.3%
15	Washington	657,446	2.2%
16	Indiana	655,977	2.2%
17	Tennessee	613,790	2.0%
18	Missouri	566,385	1.9%
19	Wisconsin	551,765	1.8%
20	Maryland	531,360	1.7%
21	Colorado	526,828	1.7%
22	Minnesota	501,636	1.6%
23	South Carolina	468,223	1.5%
24	Alabama	452,658	1.5%
25	Louisiana	425,349	1.4%
26	Kentucky	417,732	1.4%
27	Oklahoma	379,680	1.2%
28	Oregon	365,044	1.2%
29	Utah	356,310	1.2%
30	Connecticut	346,869	1.1%
31	Iowa	319,030	1.0%
32	Kansas	294,735	1.0%
33	Mississippi	291,924	1.0%
34	Arkansas	280,578	0.9%
35	Nevada	248,789	0.8%
36	New Mexico	197,455	0.6%
37	Nebraska	190,708	0.6%
38	Idaho	162,768	0.5%
39	West Virginia	156,849	0.5%
40	New Hampshire	126,137	0.4%
41	Hawaii	121,243	0.4%
42	Rhode Island	110,903	0.4%
43	Maine	107,124	0.4%
44	Montana	98,445	0.3%
45	North Dakota	84,712	0.3%
46	Delaware	83,808	0.3%
47	South Dakota	83,429	0.3%
48	Alaska	70,377	0.2%
49	Vermont	67,219	0.2%
50	Wyoming	52,367	0.2%
	District of Columbia	74,142	0.2%

Source: U.S. Bureau of the Census
"State Characteristics: Vintage 2018" (https://www.census.gov/programs-surveys/popest/data/data-sets.html)

Percent of Population 18 to 24 Years Old in 2018

National Percent = 9.3% of Population

RANK	STATE	PERCENT
24	Alabama	9.3
17	Alaska	9.5
13	Arizona	9.6
24	Arkansas	9.3
17	California	9.5
30	Colorado	9.2
11	Connecticut	9.7
42	Delaware	8.7
48	Florida	8.2
13	Georgia	9.6
47	Hawaii	8.5
24	Idaho	9.3
30	Illinois	9.2
9	Indiana	9.8
6	Iowa	10.1
6	Kansas	10.1
24	Kentucky	9.3
35	Louisiana	9.1
50	Maine	8.0
41	Maryland	8.8
5	Massachusetts	10.2
13	Michigan	9.6
40	Minnesota	8.9
9	Mississippi	9.8
30	Missouri	9.2
24	Montana	9.3
8	Nebraska	9.9
48	Nevada	8.2
24	New Hampshire	9.3
46	New Jersey	8.6
23	New Mexico	9.4
30	New York	9.2
17	North Carolina	9.5
2	North Dakota	11.1
35	Ohio	9.1
13	Oklahoma	9.6
42	Oregon	8.7
35	Pennsylvania	9.1
4	Rhode Island	10.5
30	South Carolina	9.2
17	South Dakota	9.5
35	Tennessee	9.1
11	Texas	9.7
1	Utah	11.3
3	Vermont	10.7
17	Virginia	9.5
42	Washington	8.7
42	West Virginia	8.7
17	Wisconsin	9.5
35	Wyoming	9.1

RANK	STATE	PERCENT
1	Utah	11.3
2	North Dakota	11.1
3	Vermont	10.7
4	Rhode Island	10.5
5	Massachusetts	10.2
6	Iowa	10.1
6	Kansas	10.1
8	Nebraska	9.9
9	Indiana	9.8
9	Mississippi	9.8
11	Connecticut	9.7
11	Texas	9.7
13	Arizona	9.6
13	Georgia	9.6
13	Michigan	9.6
13	Oklahoma	9.6
17	Alaska	9.5
17	California	9.5
17	North Carolina	9.5
17	South Dakota	9.5
17	Virginia	9.5
17	Wisconsin	9.5
23	New Mexico	9.4
24	Alabama	9.3
24	Arkansas	9.3
24	Idaho	9.3
24	Kentucky	9.3
24	Montana	9.3
24	New Hampshire	9.3
30	Colorado	9.2
30	Illinois	9.2
30	Missouri	9.2
30	New York	9.2
30	South Carolina	9.2
35	Louisiana	9.1
35	Ohio	9.1
35	Pennsylvania	9.1
35	Tennessee	9.1
35	Wyoming	9.1
40	Minnesota	8.9
41	Maryland	8.8
42	Delaware	8.7
42	Oregon	8.7
42	Washington	8.7
42	West Virginia	8.7
46	New Jersey	8.6
47	Hawaii	8.5
48	Florida	8.2
48	Nevada	8.2
50	Maine	8.0
	District of Columbia	10.6

Source: CQ Press using data from U.S. Bureau of the Census
"State Characteristics: Vintage 2018" (https://www.census.gov/programs-surveys/popest/data/data-sets.html)

Population 25 to 44 Years Old in 2018

National Total = 86,975,662

ALPHA ORDER

RANK	STATE	POPULATION	% of USA
25	Alabama	1,235,842	1.4%
47	Alaska	213,515	0.2%
14	Arizona	1,866,276	2.1%
33	Arkansas	765,106	0.9%
1	California	11,299,470	13.0%
18	Colorado	1,674,501	1.9%
30	Connecticut	868,726	1.0%
45	Delaware	240,531	0.3%
3	Florida	5,357,019	6.2%
8	Georgia	2,845,848	3.3%
40	Hawaii	383,516	0.4%
38	Idaho	451,411	0.5%
5	Illinois	3,409,506	3.9%
17	Indiana	1,699,640	2.0%
32	Iowa	777,650	0.9%
35	Kansas	739,206	0.8%
27	Kentucky	1,137,056	1.3%
24	Louisiana	1,250,708	1.4%
42	Maine	312,723	0.4%
19	Maryland	1,608,413	1.8%
15	Massachusetts	1,833,565	2.1%
10	Michigan	2,459,840	2.8%
21	Minnesota	1,471,190	1.7%
34	Mississippi	759,304	0.9%
20	Missouri	1,568,044	1.8%
44	Montana	263,859	0.3%
37	Nebraska	495,034	0.6%
31	Nevada	848,525	1.0%
41	New Hampshire	323,749	0.4%
12	New Jersey	2,295,139	2.6%
36	New Mexico	534,619	0.6%
4	New York	5,310,657	6.1%
9	North Carolina	2,689,053	3.1%
48	North Dakota	205,202	0.2%
7	Ohio	2,936,472	3.4%
28	Oklahoma	1,033,606	1.2%
26	Oregon	1,156,252	1.3%
6	Pennsylvania	3,199,651	3.7%
43	Rhode Island	270,417	0.3%
23	South Carolina	1,285,287	1.5%
46	South Dakota	220,004	0.3%
16	Tennessee	1,771,334	2.0%
2	Texas	8,118,100	9.3%
29	Utah	899,522	1.0%
50	Vermont	144,692	0.2%
11	Virginia	2,295,189	2.6%
13	Washington	2,156,226	2.5%
39	West Virginia	432,122	0.5%
22	Wisconsin	1,442,093	1.7%
49	Wyoming	150,491	0.2%

RANK ORDER

RANK	STATE	POPULATION	% of USA
1	California	11,299,470	13.0%
2	Texas	8,118,100	9.3%
3	Florida	5,357,019	6.2%
4	New York	5,310,657	6.1%
5	Illinois	3,409,506	3.9%
6	Pennsylvania	3,199,651	3.7%
7	Ohio	2,936,472	3.4%
8	Georgia	2,845,848	3.3%
9	North Carolina	2,689,053	3.1%
10	Michigan	2,459,840	2.8%
11	Virginia	2,295,189	2.6%
12	New Jersey	2,295,139	2.6%
13	Washington	2,156,226	2.5%
14	Arizona	1,866,276	2.1%
15	Massachusetts	1,833,565	2.1%
16	Tennessee	1,771,334	2.0%
17	Indiana	1,699,640	2.0%
18	Colorado	1,674,501	1.9%
19	Maryland	1,608,413	1.8%
20	Missouri	1,568,044	1.8%
21	Minnesota	1,471,190	1.7%
22	Wisconsin	1,442,093	1.7%
23	South Carolina	1,285,287	1.5%
24	Louisiana	1,250,708	1.4%
25	Alabama	1,235,842	1.4%
26	Oregon	1,156,252	1.3%
27	Kentucky	1,137,056	1.3%
28	Oklahoma	1,033,606	1.2%
29	Utah	899,522	1.0%
30	Connecticut	868,726	1.0%
31	Nevada	848,525	1.0%
32	Iowa	777,650	0.9%
33	Arkansas	765,106	0.9%
34	Mississippi	759,304	0.9%
35	Kansas	739,206	0.8%
36	New Mexico	534,619	0.6%
37	Nebraska	495,034	0.6%
38	Idaho	451,411	0.5%
39	West Virginia	432,122	0.5%
40	Hawaii	383,516	0.4%
41	New Hampshire	323,749	0.4%
42	Maine	312,723	0.4%
43	Rhode Island	270,417	0.3%
44	Montana	263,859	0.3%
45	Delaware	240,531	0.3%
46	South Dakota	220,004	0.3%
47	Alaska	213,515	0.2%
48	North Dakota	205,202	0.2%
49	Wyoming	150,491	0.2%
50	Vermont	144,692	0.2%
	District of Columbia	269,761	0.3%

Source: U.S. Bureau of the Census
"State Characteristics: Vintage 2018" (https://www.census.gov/programs-surveys/popest/data/data-sets.html)

Percent of Population 25 to 44 Years Old in 2018

National Percent = 26.6% of Population

ALPHA ORDER

RANK ORDER

RANK	STATE	PERCENT	RANK	STATE	PERCENT
35	Alabama	25.3	1	Colorado	29.4
2	Alaska	29.0	2	Alaska	29.0
21	Arizona	26.0	3	California	28.6
30	Arkansas	25.4	3	Washington	28.6
3	California	28.6	5	Utah	28.5
1	Colorado	29.4	6	Texas	28.3
46	Connecticut	24.3	7	Nevada	28.0
40	Delaware	24.9	8	Oregon	27.6
37	Florida	25.2	9	New York	27.2
10	Georgia	27.1	10	Georgia	27.1
11	Hawaii	27.0	11	Hawaii	27.0
25	Idaho	25.7	11	North Dakota	27.0
14	Illinois	26.8	13	Virginia	26.9
30	Indiana	25.4	14	Illinois	26.8
44	Iowa	24.6	14	Louisiana	26.8
30	Kansas	25.4	16	Maryland	26.6
30	Kentucky	25.4	16	Massachusetts	26.6
14	Louisiana	26.8	18	Minnesota	26.2
49	Maine	23.4	18	Oklahoma	26.2
16	Maryland	26.6	18	Tennessee	26.2
16	Massachusetts	26.6	21	Arizona	26.0
44	Michigan	24.6	21	Wyoming	26.0
18	Minnesota	26.2	23	North Carolina	25.9
30	Mississippi	25.4	24	New Jersey	25.8
27	Missouri	25.6	25	Idaho	25.7
42	Montana	24.8	25	Nebraska	25.7
25	Nebraska	25.7	27	Missouri	25.6
7	Nevada	28.0	27	Rhode Island	25.6
47	New Hampshire	23.9	29	New Mexico	25.5
24	New Jersey	25.8	30	Arkansas	25.4
29	New Mexico	25.5	30	Indiana	25.4
9	New York	27.2	30	Kansas	25.4
23	North Carolina	25.9	30	Kentucky	25.4
11	North Dakota	27.0	30	Mississippi	25.4
38	Ohio	25.1	35	Alabama	25.3
18	Oklahoma	26.2	35	South Carolina	25.3
8	Oregon	27.6	37	Florida	25.2
39	Pennsylvania	25.0	38	Ohio	25.1
27	Rhode Island	25.6	39	Pennsylvania	25.0
35	South Carolina	25.3	40	Delaware	24.9
40	South Dakota	24.9	40	South Dakota	24.9
18	Tennessee	26.2	42	Montana	24.8
6	Texas	28.3	42	Wisconsin	24.8
5	Utah	28.5	44	Iowa	24.6
50	Vermont	23.1	44	Michigan	24.6
13	Virginia	26.9	46	Connecticut	24.3
3	Washington	28.6	47	New Hampshire	23.9
47	West Virginia	23.9	47	West Virginia	23.9
42	Wisconsin	24.8	49	Maine	23.4
21	Wyoming	26.0	50	Vermont	23.1
				District of Columbia	38.4

Source: CQ Press using data from U.S. Bureau of the Census
"State Characteristics: Vintage 2018" (https://www.census.gov/programs-surveys/popest/data/data-sets.html)

Population 45 to 64 Years Old in 2018

National Total = 83,904,335

ALPHA ORDER

RANK	STATE	POPULATION	% of USA
24	Alabama	1,282,637	1.5%
47	Alaska	182,719	0.2%
16	Arizona	1,717,067	2.0%
33	Arkansas	753,134	0.9%
1	California	9,853,200	11.7%
22	Colorado	1,420,771	1.7%
28	Connecticut	1,006,756	1.2%
45	Delaware	258,130	0.3%
3	Florida	5,600,973	6.7%
9	Georgia	2,697,120	3.2%
42	Hawaii	351,351	0.4%
39	Idaho	414,775	0.5%
6	Illinois	3,305,037	3.9%
17	Indiana	1,713,110	2.0%
30	Iowa	788,868	0.9%
34	Kansas	709,362	0.8%
25	Kentucky	1,174,159	1.4%
26	Louisiana	1,169,572	1.4%
41	Maine	392,154	0.5%
18	Maryland	1,631,661	1.9%
14	Massachusetts	1,860,698	2.2%
10	Michigan	2,692,864	3.2%
21	Minnesota	1,445,936	1.7%
32	Mississippi	754,686	0.9%
19	Missouri	1,581,229	1.9%
44	Montana	271,665	0.3%
38	Nebraska	463,019	0.6%
31	Nevada	771,900	0.9%
40	New Hampshire	402,757	0.5%
11	New Jersey	2,455,205	2.9%
36	New Mexico	515,012	0.6%
4	New York	5,149,750	6.1%
8	North Carolina	2,720,823	3.2%
49	North Dakota	174,828	0.2%
7	Ohio	3,096,425	3.7%
29	Oklahoma	953,754	1.1%
27	Oregon	1,057,159	1.3%
5	Pennsylvania	3,462,586	4.1%
43	Rhode Island	288,528	0.3%
23	South Carolina	1,324,757	1.6%
46	South Dakota	214,342	0.3%
15	Tennessee	1,768,969	2.1%
2	Texas	6,787,247	8.1%
35	Utah	622,333	0.7%
48	Vermont	177,208	0.2%
12	Virginia	2,232,256	2.7%
13	Washington	1,894,402	2.3%
37	West Virginia	492,823	0.6%
20	Wisconsin	1,558,134	1.9%
50	Wyoming	144,729	0.2%

RANK ORDER

RANK	STATE	POPULATION	% of USA
1	California	9,853,200	11.7%
2	Texas	6,787,247	8.1%
3	Florida	5,600,973	6.7%
4	New York	5,149,750	6.1%
5	Pennsylvania	3,462,586	4.1%
6	Illinois	3,305,037	3.9%
7	Ohio	3,096,425	3.7%
8	North Carolina	2,720,823	3.2%
9	Georgia	2,697,120	3.2%
10	Michigan	2,692,864	3.2%
11	New Jersey	2,455,205	2.9%
12	Virginia	2,232,256	2.7%
13	Washington	1,894,402	2.3%
14	Massachusetts	1,860,698	2.2%
15	Tennessee	1,768,969	2.1%
16	Arizona	1,717,067	2.0%
17	Indiana	1,713,110	2.0%
18	Maryland	1,631,661	1.9%
19	Missouri	1,581,229	1.9%
20	Wisconsin	1,558,134	1.9%
21	Minnesota	1,445,936	1.7%
22	Colorado	1,420,771	1.7%
23	South Carolina	1,324,757	1.6%
24	Alabama	1,282,637	1.5%
25	Kentucky	1,174,159	1.4%
26	Louisiana	1,169,572	1.4%
27	Oregon	1,057,159	1.3%
28	Connecticut	1,006,756	1.2%
29	Oklahoma	953,754	1.1%
30	Iowa	788,868	0.9%
31	Nevada	771,900	0.9%
32	Mississippi	754,686	0.9%
33	Arkansas	753,134	0.9%
34	Kansas	709,362	0.8%
35	Utah	622,333	0.7%
36	New Mexico	515,012	0.6%
37	West Virginia	492,823	0.6%
38	Nebraska	463,019	0.6%
39	Idaho	414,775	0.5%
40	New Hampshire	402,757	0.5%
41	Maine	392,154	0.5%
42	Hawaii	351,351	0.4%
43	Rhode Island	288,528	0.3%
44	Montana	271,665	0.3%
45	Delaware	258,130	0.3%
46	South Dakota	214,342	0.3%
47	Alaska	182,719	0.2%
48	Vermont	177,208	0.2%
49	North Dakota	174,828	0.2%
50	Wyoming	144,729	0.2%
	District of Columbia	145,755	0.2%

Source: U.S. Bureau of the Census
"State Characteristics: Vintage 2018" (https://www.census.gov/programs-surveys/popest/data/data-sets.html)

Percent of Population 45 to 64 Years Old in 2018

National Percent = 25.6% of Population

ALPHA ORDER

RANK	STATE	PERCENT
18	Alabama	26.2
39	Alaska	24.8
46	Arizona	23.9
35	Arkansas	25.0
37	California	24.9
37	Colorado	24.9
4	Connecticut	28.2
13	Delaware	26.7
16	Florida	26.3
26	Georgia	25.6
40	Hawaii	24.7
47	Idaho	23.6
23	Illinois	25.9
26	Indiana	25.6
35	Iowa	25.0
42	Kansas	24.4
16	Kentucky	26.3
32	Louisiana	25.1
2	Maine	29.3
8	Maryland	27.0
8	Massachusetts	27.0
11	Michigan	26.9
24	Minnesota	25.8
30	Mississippi	25.3
24	Missouri	25.8
26	Montana	25.6
45	Nebraska	24.0
29	Nevada	25.4
1	New Hampshire	29.7
5	New Jersey	27.6
41	New Mexico	24.6
15	New York	26.4
18	North Carolina	26.2
49	North Dakota	23.0
14	Ohio	26.5
44	Oklahoma	24.2
31	Oregon	25.2
8	Pennsylvania	27.0
6	Rhode Island	27.3
21	South Carolina	26.1
43	South Dakota	24.3
21	Tennessee	26.1
47	Texas	23.6
50	Utah	19.7
3	Vermont	28.3
18	Virginia	26.2
32	Washington	25.1
6	West Virginia	27.3
12	Wisconsin	26.8
32	Wyoming	25.1

RANK ORDER

RANK	STATE	PERCENT
1	New Hampshire	29.7
2	Maine	29.3
3	Vermont	28.3
4	Connecticut	28.2
5	New Jersey	27.6
6	Rhode Island	27.3
6	West Virginia	27.3
8	Maryland	27.0
8	Massachusetts	27.0
8	Pennsylvania	27.0
11	Michigan	26.9
12	Wisconsin	26.8
13	Delaware	26.7
14	Ohio	26.5
15	New York	26.4
16	Florida	26.3
16	Kentucky	26.3
18	Alabama	26.2
18	North Carolina	26.2
18	Virginia	26.2
21	South Carolina	26.1
21	Tennessee	26.1
23	Illinois	25.9
24	Minnesota	25.8
24	Missouri	25.8
26	Georgia	25.6
26	Indiana	25.6
26	Montana	25.6
29	Nevada	25.4
30	Mississippi	25.3
31	Oregon	25.2
32	Louisiana	25.1
32	Washington	25.1
32	Wyoming	25.1
35	Arkansas	25.0
35	Iowa	25.0
37	California	24.9
37	Colorado	24.9
39	Alaska	24.8
40	Hawaii	24.7
41	New Mexico	24.6
42	Kansas	24.4
43	South Dakota	24.3
44	Oklahoma	24.2
45	Nebraska	24.0
46	Arizona	23.9
47	Idaho	23.6
47	Texas	23.6
49	North Dakota	23.0
50	Utah	19.7
	District of Columbia	20.7

Source: CQ Press using data from U.S. Bureau of the Census
"State Characteristics: Vintage 2018" (https://www.census.gov/programs-surveys/popest/data/data-sets.html)

Population 65 Years Old and Older in 2018

National Total = 52,431,193

ALPHA ORDER				RANK ORDER			
RANK	STATE	POPULATION	% of USA	RANK	STATE	POPULATION	% of USA
23	Alabama	826,894	1.6%	1	California	5,669,025	10.8%
50	Alaska	87,011	0.2%	2	Florida	4,358,071	8.3%
13	Arizona	1,258,250	2.4%	3	Texas	3,602,320	6.9%
31	Arkansas	511,827	1.0%	4	New York	3,213,534	6.1%
1	California	5,669,025	10.8%	5	Pennsylvania	2,335,630	4.5%
24	Colorado	808,229	1.5%	6	Ohio	1,995,022	3.8%
29	Connecticut	615,121	1.2%	7	Illinois	1,992,961	3.8%
45	Delaware	181,086	0.3%	8	Michigan	1,716,604	3.3%
2	Florida	4,358,071	8.3%	9	North Carolina	1,689,265	3.2%
10	Georgia	1,460,409	2.8%	10	Georgia	1,460,409	2.8%
41	Hawaii	260,967	0.5%	11	New Jersey	1,438,527	2.7%
39	Idaho	278,282	0.5%	12	Virginia	1,315,401	2.5%
7	Illinois	1,992,961	3.8%	13	Arizona	1,258,250	2.4%
17	Indiana	1,055,021	2.0%	14	Washington	1,164,232	2.2%
30	Iowa	539,830	1.0%	15	Massachusetts	1,139,100	2.2%
34	Kansas	462,241	0.9%	16	Tennessee	1,109,697	2.1%
26	Kentucky	730,626	1.4%	17	Indiana	1,055,021	2.0%
27	Louisiana	718,433	1.4%	18	Missouri	1,033,964	2.0%
40	Maine	275,999	0.5%	19	Wisconsin	985,473	1.9%
20	Maryland	931,136	1.8%	20	Maryland	931,136	1.8%
15	Massachusetts	1,139,100	2.2%	21	South Carolina	899,915	1.7%
8	Michigan	1,716,604	3.3%	22	Minnesota	889,802	1.7%
22	Minnesota	889,802	1.7%	23	Alabama	826,894	1.6%
33	Mississippi	474,475	0.9%	24	Colorado	808,229	1.5%
18	Missouri	1,033,964	2.0%	25	Oregon	738,691	1.4%
43	Montana	198,902	0.4%	26	Kentucky	730,626	1.4%
38	Nebraska	303,666	0.6%	27	Louisiana	718,433	1.4%
32	Nevada	476,181	0.9%	28	Oklahoma	619,553	1.2%
42	New Hampshire	245,645	0.5%	29	Connecticut	615,121	1.2%
11	New Jersey	1,438,527	2.7%	30	Iowa	539,830	1.0%
35	New Mexico	366,189	0.7%	31	Arkansas	511,827	1.0%
4	New York	3,213,534	6.1%	32	Nevada	476,181	0.9%
9	North Carolina	1,689,265	3.2%	33	Mississippi	474,475	0.9%
48	North Dakota	116,637	0.2%	34	Kansas	462,241	0.9%
6	Ohio	1,995,022	3.8%	35	New Mexico	366,189	0.7%
28	Oklahoma	619,553	1.2%	36	West Virginia	359,878	0.7%
25	Oregon	738,691	1.4%	37	Utah	350,478	0.7%
5	Pennsylvania	2,335,630	4.5%	38	Nebraska	303,666	0.6%
44	Rhode Island	182,254	0.3%	39	Idaho	278,282	0.5%
21	South Carolina	899,915	1.7%	40	Maine	275,999	0.5%
46	South Dakota	146,854	0.3%	41	Hawaii	260,967	0.5%
16	Tennessee	1,109,697	2.1%	42	New Hampshire	245,645	0.5%
3	Texas	3,602,320	6.9%	43	Montana	198,902	0.4%
37	Utah	350,478	0.7%	44	Rhode Island	182,254	0.3%
47	Vermont	121,207	0.2%	45	Delaware	181,086	0.3%
12	Virginia	1,315,401	2.5%	46	South Dakota	146,854	0.3%
14	Washington	1,164,232	2.2%	47	Vermont	121,207	0.2%
36	West Virginia	359,878	0.7%	48	North Dakota	116,637	0.2%
19	Wisconsin	985,473	1.9%	49	Wyoming	95,375	0.2%
49	Wyoming	95,375	0.2%	50	Alaska	87,011	0.2%
					District of Columbia	85,303	0.2%

Source: U.S. Bureau of the Census
"State Characteristics: Vintage 2018" (https://www.census.gov/programs-surveys/popest/data/data-sets.html)

Percent of Population 65 Years Old and Older in 2018

National Percent = 16.0% of Population

<table>
<tr><td colspan="3">ALPHA ORDER</td><td colspan="3">RANK ORDER</td></tr>
<tr><td>RANK</td><td>STATE</td><td>PERCENT</td><td>RANK</td><td>STATE</td><td>PERCENT</td></tr>
<tr><td>21</td><td>Alabama</td><td>16.9</td><td>1</td><td>Maine</td><td>20.6</td></tr>
<tr><td>49</td><td>Alaska</td><td>11.8</td><td>2</td><td>Florida</td><td>20.5</td></tr>
<tr><td>12</td><td>Arizona</td><td>17.5</td><td>3</td><td>West Virginia</td><td>19.9</td></tr>
<tr><td>19</td><td>Arkansas</td><td>17.0</td><td>4</td><td>Vermont</td><td>19.4</td></tr>
<tr><td>45</td><td>California</td><td>14.3</td><td>5</td><td>Delaware</td><td>18.7</td></tr>
<tr><td>46</td><td>Colorado</td><td>14.2</td><td>5</td><td>Montana</td><td>18.7</td></tr>
<tr><td>14</td><td>Connecticut</td><td>17.2</td><td>7</td><td>Hawaii</td><td>18.4</td></tr>
<tr><td>5</td><td>Delaware</td><td>18.7</td><td>8</td><td>Pennsylvania</td><td>18.2</td></tr>
<tr><td>2</td><td>Florida</td><td>20.5</td><td>9</td><td>New Hampshire</td><td>18.1</td></tr>
<tr><td>47</td><td>Georgia</td><td>13.9</td><td>10</td><td>South Carolina</td><td>17.7</td></tr>
<tr><td>7</td><td>Hawaii</td><td>18.4</td><td>11</td><td>Oregon</td><td>17.6</td></tr>
<tr><td>31</td><td>Idaho</td><td>15.9</td><td>12</td><td>Arizona</td><td>17.5</td></tr>
<tr><td>39</td><td>Illinois</td><td>15.6</td><td>12</td><td>New Mexico</td><td>17.5</td></tr>
<tr><td>35</td><td>Indiana</td><td>15.8</td><td>14</td><td>Connecticut</td><td>17.2</td></tr>
<tr><td>17</td><td>Iowa</td><td>17.1</td><td>14</td><td>Michigan</td><td>17.2</td></tr>
<tr><td>31</td><td>Kansas</td><td>15.9</td><td>14</td><td>Rhode Island</td><td>17.2</td></tr>
<tr><td>26</td><td>Kentucky</td><td>16.4</td><td>17</td><td>Iowa</td><td>17.1</td></tr>
<tr><td>40</td><td>Louisiana</td><td>15.4</td><td>17</td><td>Ohio</td><td>17.1</td></tr>
<tr><td>1</td><td>Maine</td><td>20.6</td><td>19</td><td>Arkansas</td><td>17.0</td></tr>
<tr><td>40</td><td>Maryland</td><td>15.4</td><td>19</td><td>Wisconsin</td><td>17.0</td></tr>
<tr><td>24</td><td>Massachusetts</td><td>16.5</td><td>21</td><td>Alabama</td><td>16.9</td></tr>
<tr><td>14</td><td>Michigan</td><td>17.2</td><td>21</td><td>Missouri</td><td>16.9</td></tr>
<tr><td>31</td><td>Minnesota</td><td>15.9</td><td>23</td><td>South Dakota</td><td>16.6</td></tr>
<tr><td>31</td><td>Mississippi</td><td>15.9</td><td>24</td><td>Massachusetts</td><td>16.5</td></tr>
<tr><td>21</td><td>Missouri</td><td>16.9</td><td>24</td><td>Wyoming</td><td>16.5</td></tr>
<tr><td>5</td><td>Montana</td><td>18.7</td><td>26</td><td>Kentucky</td><td>16.4</td></tr>
<tr><td>36</td><td>Nebraska</td><td>15.7</td><td>26</td><td>New York</td><td>16.4</td></tr>
<tr><td>36</td><td>Nevada</td><td>15.7</td><td>26</td><td>Tennessee</td><td>16.4</td></tr>
<tr><td>9</td><td>New Hampshire</td><td>18.1</td><td>29</td><td>North Carolina</td><td>16.3</td></tr>
<tr><td>30</td><td>New Jersey</td><td>16.1</td><td>30</td><td>New Jersey</td><td>16.1</td></tr>
<tr><td>12</td><td>New Mexico</td><td>17.5</td><td>31</td><td>Idaho</td><td>15.9</td></tr>
<tr><td>26</td><td>New York</td><td>16.4</td><td>31</td><td>Kansas</td><td>15.9</td></tr>
<tr><td>29</td><td>North Carolina</td><td>16.3</td><td>31</td><td>Minnesota</td><td>15.9</td></tr>
<tr><td>44</td><td>North Dakota</td><td>15.3</td><td>31</td><td>Mississippi</td><td>15.9</td></tr>
<tr><td>17</td><td>Ohio</td><td>17.1</td><td>35</td><td>Indiana</td><td>15.8</td></tr>
<tr><td>36</td><td>Oklahoma</td><td>15.7</td><td>36</td><td>Nebraska</td><td>15.7</td></tr>
<tr><td>11</td><td>Oregon</td><td>17.6</td><td>36</td><td>Nevada</td><td>15.7</td></tr>
<tr><td>8</td><td>Pennsylvania</td><td>18.2</td><td>36</td><td>Oklahoma</td><td>15.7</td></tr>
<tr><td>14</td><td>Rhode Island</td><td>17.2</td><td>39</td><td>Illnois</td><td>15.6</td></tr>
<tr><td>10</td><td>South Carolina</td><td>17.7</td><td>40</td><td>Louisiana</td><td>15.4</td></tr>
<tr><td>23</td><td>South Dakota</td><td>16.6</td><td>40</td><td>Maryland</td><td>15.4</td></tr>
<tr><td>26</td><td>Tennessee</td><td>16.4</td><td>40</td><td>Virginia</td><td>15.4</td></tr>
<tr><td>48</td><td>Texas</td><td>12.6</td><td>40</td><td>Washington</td><td>15.4</td></tr>
<tr><td>50</td><td>Utah</td><td>11.1</td><td>44</td><td>North Dakota</td><td>15.3</td></tr>
<tr><td>4</td><td>Vermont</td><td>19.4</td><td>45</td><td>California</td><td>14.3</td></tr>
<tr><td>40</td><td>Virginia</td><td>15.4</td><td>46</td><td>Colorado</td><td>14.2</td></tr>
<tr><td>40</td><td>Washington</td><td>15.4</td><td>47</td><td>Georgia</td><td>13.9</td></tr>
<tr><td>3</td><td>West Virginia</td><td>19.9</td><td>48</td><td>Texas</td><td>12.6</td></tr>
<tr><td>19</td><td>Wisconsin</td><td>17.0</td><td>49</td><td>Alaska</td><td>11.8</td></tr>
<tr><td>24</td><td>Wyoming</td><td>16.5</td><td>50</td><td>Utah</td><td>11.1</td></tr>
<tr><td></td><td></td><td></td><td></td><td>District of Columbia</td><td>12.1</td></tr>
</table>

Source: CQ Press using data from U.S. Bureau of the Census
"State Characteristics: Vintage 2018" (https://www.census.gov/programs-surveys/popest/data/data-sets.html)

Population 85 Years Old and Older in 2018

National Total = 6,544,503

ALPHA ORDER					RANK ORDER			
RANK	STATE	POPULATION	% of USA		RANK	STATE	POPULATION	% of USA
23	Alabama	89,865	1.4%		1	California	743,585	11.4%
50	Alaska	6,853	0.1%		2	Florida	571,419	8.7%
14	Arizona	142,275	2.2%		3	New York	456,319	7.0%
32	Arkansas	59,017	0.9%		4	Texas	400,499	6.1%
1	California	743,585	11.4%		5	Pennsylvania	334,243	5.1%
25	Colorado	88,364	1.4%		6	Illinois	266,674	4.1%
22	Connecticut	91,871	1.4%		7	Ohio	256,337	3.9%
46	Delaware	19,837	0.3%		8	Michigan	213,986	3.3%
2	Florida	571,419	8.7%		9	New Jersey	202,293	3.1%
13	Georgia	146,633	2.2%		10	North Carolina	185,749	2.8%
37	Hawaii	41,044	0.6%		11	Massachusetts	159,852	2.4%
42	Idaho	29,419	0.4%		12	Virginia	151,892	2.3%
6	Illinois	266,674	4.1%		13	Georgia	146,633	2.2%
17	Indiana	130,810	2.0%		14	Arizona	142,275	2.2%
29	Iowa	79,091	1.2%		15	Washington	133,383	2.0%
31	Kansas	65,536	1.0%		16	Missouri	131,884	2.0%
28	Kentucky	80,618	1.2%		17	Indiana	130,810	2.0%
27	Louisiana	81,050	1.2%		18	Wisconsin	128,636	2.0%
40	Maine	33,419	0.5%		19	Minnesota	121,684	1.9%
21	Maryland	118,403	1.8%		20	Tennessee	120,062	1.8%
11	Massachusetts	159,852	2.4%		21	Maryland	118,403	1.8%
8	Michigan	213,986	3.3%		22	Connecticut	91,871	1.4%
19	Minnesota	121,684	1.9%		23	Alabama	89,865	1.4%
33	Mississippi	52,341	0.8%		24	South Carolina	88,975	1.4%
16	Missouri	131,884	2.0%		25	Colorado	88,364	1.4%
44	Montana	22,695	0.3%		26	Oregon	84,025	1.3%
35	Nebraska	43,078	0.7%		27	Louisiana	81,050	1.2%
34	Nevada	43,362	0.7%		28	Kentucky	80,618	1.2%
41	New Hampshire	30,488	0.5%		29	Iowa	79,091	1.2%
9	New Jersey	202,293	3.1%		30	Oklahoma	73,196	1.1%
36	New Mexico	41,171	0.6%		31	Kansas	65,536	1.0%
3	New York	456,319	7.0%		32	Arkansas	59,017	0.9%
10	North Carolina	185,749	2.8%		33	Mississippi	52,341	0.8%
47	North Dakota	18,796	0.3%		34	Nevada	43,362	0.7%
7	Ohio	256,337	3.9%		35	Nebraska	43,078	0.7%
30	Oklahoma	73,196	1.1%		36	New Mexico	41,171	0.6%
26	Oregon	84,025	1.3%		37	Hawaii	41,044	0.6%
5	Pennsylvania	334,243	5.1%		38	West Virginia	39,900	0.6%
43	Rhode Island	27,852	0.4%		39	Utah	37,776	0.6%
24	South Carolina	88,975	1.4%		40	Maine	33,419	0.5%
45	South Dakota	20,991	0.3%		41	New Hampshire	30,488	0.5%
20	Tennessee	120,062	1.8%		42	Idaho	29,419	0.4%
4	Texas	400,499	6.1%		43	Rhode Island	27,852	0.4%
39	Utah	37,776	0.6%		44	Montana	22,695	0.3%
48	Vermont	14,421	0.2%		45	South Dakota	20,991	0.3%
12	Virginia	151,892	2.3%		46	Delaware	19,837	0.3%
15	Washington	133,383	2.0%		47	North Dakota	18,796	0.3%
38	West Virginia	39,900	0.6%		48	Vermont	14,421	0.2%
18	Wisconsin	128,636	2.0%		49	Wyoming	10,681	0.2%
49	Wyoming	10,681	0.2%		50	Alaska	6,853	0.1%
						District of Columbia	12,153	0.2%

Source: U.S. Bureau of the Census
   "State Characteristics: Vintage 2018" (https://www.census.gov/programs-surveys/popest/data/data-sets.html)

Percent of Population 85 Years Old and Older in 2018

National Percent = 2.0% of Population

ALPHA ORDER

RANK	STATE	PERCENT
34	Alabama	1.8
50	Alaska	0.9
26	Arizona	2.0
26	Arkansas	2.0
32	California	1.9
45	Colorado	1.6
3	Connecticut	2.6
22	Delaware	2.1
2	Florida	2.7
46	Georgia	1.4
1	Hawaii	2.9
43	Idaho	1.7
22	Illinois	2.1
26	Indiana	2.0
6	Iowa	2.5
10	Kansas	2.3
34	Kentucky	1.8
43	Louisiana	1.7
6	Maine	2.5
26	Maryland	2.0
10	Massachusetts	2.3
22	Michigan	2.1
15	Minnesota	2.2
34	Mississippi	1.8
15	Missouri	2.2
22	Montana	2.1
15	Nebraska	2.2
46	Nevada	1.4
15	New Hampshire	2.2
10	New Jersey	2.3
26	New Mexico	2.0
10	New York	2.3
34	North Carolina	1.8
6	North Dakota	2.5
15	Ohio	2.2
32	Oklahoma	1.9
26	Oregon	2.0
3	Pennsylvania	2.6
3	Rhode Island	2.6
34	South Carolina	1.8
9	South Dakota	2.4
34	Tennessee	1.8
46	Texas	1.4
49	Utah	1.2
10	Vermont	2.3
34	Virginia	1.8
34	Washington	1.8
15	West Virginia	2.2
15	Wisconsin	2.2
34	Wyoming	1.8

RANK ORDER

RANK	STATE	PERCENT
1	Hawaii	2.9
2	Florida	2.7
3	Connecticut	2.6
3	Pennsylvania	2.6
3	Rhode Island	2.6
6	Iowa	2.5
6	Maine	2.5
6	North Dakota	2.5
9	South Dakota	2.4
10	Kansas	2.3
10	Massachusetts	2.3
10	New Jersey	2.3
10	New York	2.3
10	Vermont	2.3
15	Minnesota	2.2
15	Missouri	2.2
15	Nebraska	2.2
15	New Hampshire	2.2
15	Ohio	2.2
15	West Virginia	2.2
15	Wisconsin	2.2
22	Delaware	2.1
22	Illinois	2.1
22	Michigan	2.1
22	Montana	2.1
26	Arizona	2.0
26	Arkansas	2.0
26	Indiana	2.0
26	Maryland	2.0
26	New Mexico	2.0
26	Oregon	2.0
32	California	1.9
32	Oklahoma	1.9
34	Alabama	1.8
34	Kentucky	1.8
34	Mississippi	1.8
34	North Carolina	1.8
34	South Carolina	1.8
34	Tennessee	1.8
34	Virginia	1.8
34	Washington	1.8
34	Wyoming	1.8
43	Idaho	1.7
43	Louisiana	1.7
45	Colorado	1.6
46	Georgia	1.4
46	Nevada	1.4
46	Texas	1.4
49	Utah	1.2
50	Alaska	0.9
	District of Columbia	1.7

Source: CQ Press using data from U.S. Bureau of the Census
"State Characteristics: Vintage 2018" (https://www.census.gov/programs-surveys/popest/data/data-sets.html)

Percent of Native Population Born in Their State of Residence in 2018

National Percent = 67.3%

RANK	STATE	PERCENT
14	Alabama	71.7
47	Alaska	45.1
45	Arizona	45.9
27	Arkansas	64.7
7	California	76.3
44	Colorado	46.4
30	Connecticut	64.0
42	Delaware	49.6
46	Florida	45.4
32	Georgia	61.0
25	Hawaii	65.2
43	Idaho	49.5
5	Illinois	77.9
14	Indiana	71.7
9	Iowa	74.0
29	Kansas	64.1
16	Kentucky	71.5
2	Louisiana	81.5
27	Maine	64.7
37	Maryland	55.8
12	Massachusetts	72.5
1	Michigan	81.9
10	Minnesota	73.8
11	Mississippi	73.4
18	Missouri	69.3
39	Montana	54.0
18	Nebraska	69.3
50	Nevada	33.5
49	New Hampshire	43.4
21	New Jersey	67.2
33	New Mexico	60.9
3	New York	81.1
34	North Carolina	60.6
23	North Dakota	66.2
4	Ohio	78.6
26	Oklahoma	65.0
41	Oregon	50.6
6	Pennsylvania	77.3
20	Rhode Island	67.3
35	South Carolina	58.6
24	South Dakota	65.9
31	Tennessee	62.5
13	Texas	71.8
22	Utah	67.0
40	Vermont	51.8
36	Virginia	56.6
38	Washington	54.3
17	West Virginia	69.8
8	Wisconsin	74.6
48	Wyoming	43.7

RANK	STATE	PERCENT
1	Michigan	81.9
2	Louisiana	81.5
3	New York	81.1
4	Ohio	78.6
5	Illinois	77.9
6	Pennsylvania	77.3
7	California	76.3
8	Wisconsin	74.6
9	Iowa	74.0
10	Minnesota	73.8
11	Mississippi	73.4
12	Massachusetts	72.5
13	Texas	71.8
14	Alabama	71.7
14	Indiana	71.7
16	Kentucky	71.5
17	West Virginia	69.8
18	Missouri	69.3
18	Nebraska	69.3
20	Rhode Island	67.3
21	New Jersey	67.2
22	Utah	67.0
23	North Dakota	66.2
24	South Dakota	65.9
25	Hawaii	65.2
26	Oklahoma	65.0
27	Arkansas	64.7
27	Maine	64.7
29	Kansas	64.1
30	Connecticut	64.0
31	Tennessee	62.5
32	Georgia	61.0
33	New Mexico	60.9
34	North Carolina	60.6
35	South Carolina	58.6
36	Virginia	56.6
37	Maryland	55.8
38	Washington	54.3
39	Montana	54.0
40	Vermont	51.8
41	Oregon	50.6
42	Delaware	49.6
43	Idaho	49.5
44	Colorado	46.4
45	Arizona	45.9
46	Florida	45.4
47	Alaska	45.1
48	Wyoming	43.7
49	New Hampshire	43.4
50	Nevada	33.5
	District of Columbia	43.1

Source: U.S. Bureau of the Census
"2018 American Community Survey-Table R0601" (https://data.census.gov/cedsci/)

Domestic Migration of Population: 2018 to 2019

National Net Migration = 0 People*

ALPHA ORDER

RANK	STATE	NET MIGRATION
14	Alabama	9,387
36	Alaska	(9,482)
3	Arizona	91,017
21	Arkansas	2,515
50	California	(203,414)
10	Colorado	31,335
42	Connecticut	(22,059)
15	Delaware	6,961
1	Florida	133,910
6	Georgia	49,680
40	Hawaii	(13,817)
11	Idaho	27,360
48	Illinois	(104,986)
19	Indiana	3,997
33	Iowa	(5,011)
38	Kansas	(12,357)
29	Kentucky	(1,541)
45	Louisiana	(26,045)
16	Maine	6,613
43	Maryland	(23,665)
46	Massachusetts	(30,274)
44	Michigan	(23,670)
23	Minnesota	65
37	Mississippi	(10,740)
25	Missouri	(710)
17	Montana	6,024
32	Nebraska	(4,220)
7	Nevada	43,207
18	New Hampshire	4,469
47	New Jersey	(48,946)
30	New Mexico	(2,136)
49	New York	(180,649)
4	North Carolina	67,338
27	North Dakota	(1,267)
39	Ohio	(12,916)
20	Oklahoma	3,822
12	Oregon	25,821
41	Pennsylvania	(19,588)
31	Rhode Island	(3,215)
5	South Carolina	53,034
22	South Dakota	964
9	Tennessee	36,009
2	Texas	125,660
13	Utah	15,588
24	Vermont	(682)
35	Virginia	(9,136)
8	Washington	37,476
34	West Virginia	(7,073)
28	Wisconsin	(1,438)
26	Wyoming	(1,012)

RANK ORDER

RANK	STATE	NET MIGRATION
1	Florida	133,910
2	Texas	125,660
3	Arizona	91,017
4	North Carolina	67,338
5	South Carolina	53,034
6	Georgia	49,680
7	Nevada	43,207
8	Washington	37,476
9	Tennessee	36,009
10	Colorado	31,335
11	Idaho	27,360
12	Oregon	25,821
13	Utah	15,588
14	Alabama	9,387
15	Delaware	6,961
16	Maine	6,613
17	Montana	6,024
18	New Hampshire	4,469
19	Indiana	3,997
20	Oklahoma	3,822
21	Arkansas	2,515
22	South Dakota	964
23	Minnesota	65
24	Vermont	(682)
25	Missouri	(710)
26	Wyoming	(1,012)
27	North Dakota	(1,267)
28	Wisconsin	(1,438)
29	Kentucky	(1,541)
30	New Mexico	(2,136)
31	Rhode Island	(3,215)
32	Nebraska	(4,220)
33	Iowa	(5,011)
34	West Virginia	(7,073)
35	Virginia	(9,136)
36	Alaska	(9,482)
37	Mississippi	(10,740)
38	Kansas	(12,357)
39	Ohio	(12,916)
40	Hawaii	(13,817)
41	Pennsylvania	(19,588)
42	Connecticut	(22,059)
43	Maryland	(23,665)
44	Michigan	(23,670)
45	Louisiana	(26,045)
46	Massachusetts	(30,274)
47	New Jersey	(48,946)
48	Illinois	(104,986)
49	New York	(180,649)
50	California	(203,414)

District of Columbia (2,203)

Source: U.S. Bureau of the Census
    "Population Estimates" (December 2019, https://www.census.gov/programs-surveys/popest.html)
*From July 1, 2018, to June 30, 2019. Includes armed forces residing in each state. Net domestic migration is the difference between domestic inmigration to an area and domestic outmigration from it during the period. Domestic inmigration and outmigration consist of moves where both the origins and destinations are within the United States (excluding Puerto Rico).

Net International Migration: 2018 to 2019

National Net = 595,348 Immigrants*

ALPHA ORDER					RANK ORDER			
RANK	STATE	IMMIGRANTS	% of USA		RANK	STATE	IMMIGRANTS	% of USA
33	Alabama	2,772	0.5%		1	Florida	88,678	14.9%
41	Alaska	659	0.1%		2	California	74,028	12.4%
21	Arizona	7,782	1.3%		3	Texas	65,044	10.9%
46	Arkansas	268	0.0%		4	New York	45,753	7.7%
2	California	74,028	12.4%		5	Massachusetts	28,426	4.8%
17	Colorado	10,523	1.8%		6	Washington	24,103	4.0%
16	Connecticut	12,323	2.1%		7	New Jersey	21,284	3.6%
48	Delaware	73	0.0%		8	Pennsylvania	19,532	3.3%
1	Florida	88,678	14.9%		9	Illinois	19,209	3.2%
10	Georgia	15,053	2.5%		10	Georgia	15,053	2.5%
25	Hawaii	5,014	0.8%		11	Maryland	15,011	2.5%
47	Idaho	167	0.0%		12	Virginia	14,869	2.5%
9	Illinois	19,209	3.2%		13	Indiana	14,379	2.4%
13	Indiana	14,379	2.4%		14	North Carolina	14,184	2.4%
34	Iowa	2,663	0.4%		15	Michigan	13,146	2.2%
27	Kansas	4,104	0.7%		16	Connecticut	12,323	2.1%
40	Kentucky	765	0.1%		17	Colorado	10,523	1.8%
32	Louisiana	3,040	0.5%		18	Ohio	9,553	1.6%
39	Maine	852	0.1%		19	Tennessee	9,293	1.6%
11	Maryland	15,011	2.5%		20	Minnesota	9,113	1.5%
5	Massachusetts	28,426	4.8%		21	Arizona	7,782	1.3%
15	Michigan	13,146	2.2%		22	South Carolina	5,724	1.0%
20	Minnesota	9,113	1.5%		23	Utah	5,579	0.9%
37	Mississippi	1,429	0.2%		24	Missouri	5,503	0.9%
24	Missouri	5,503	0.9%		25	Hawaii	5,014	0.8%
45	Montana	322	0.1%		26	Oklahoma	4,484	0.8%
30	Nebraska	3,295	0.6%		27	Kansas	4,104	0.7%
50	Nevada	(970)	0.0%		28	Rhode Island	3,645	0.6%
35	New Hampshire	1,947	0.3%		29	Wisconsin	3,341	0.6%
7	New Jersey	21,284	3.6%		30	Nebraska	3,295	0.6%
36	New Mexico	1,546	0.3%		30	Oregon	3,295	0.6%
4	New York	45,753	7.7%		32	Louisiana	3,040	0.5%
14	North Carolina	14,184	2.4%		33	Alabama	2,772	0.5%
38	North Dakota	951	0.2%		34	Iowa	2,663	0.4%
18	Ohio	9,553	1.6%		35	New Hampshire	1,947	0.3%
26	Oklahoma	4,484	0.8%		36	New Mexico	1,546	0.3%
30	Oregon	3,295	0.6%		37	Mississippi	1,429	0.2%
8	Pennsylvania	19,532	3.3%		38	North Dakota	951	0.2%
28	Rhode Island	3,645	0.6%		39	Maine	852	0.1%
22	South Carolina	5,724	1.0%		40	Kentucky	765	0.1%
43	South Dakota	418	0.1%		41	Alaska	659	0.1%
19	Tennessee	9,293	1.6%		42	Wyoming	538	0.1%
3	Texas	65,044	10.9%		43	South Dakota	418	0.1%
23	Utah	5,579	0.9%		44	Vermont	383	0.1%
44	Vermont	383	0.1%		45	Montana	322	0.1%
12	Virginia	14,869	2.5%		46	Arkansas	268	0.0%
6	Washington	24,103	4.0%		47	Idaho	167	0.0%
49	West Virginia	(349)	0.0%		48	Delaware	73	0.0%
29	Wisconsin	3,341	0.6%		49	West Virginia	(349)	0.0%
42	Wyoming	538	0.1%		50	Nevada	(970)	0.0%
						District of Columbia	2,604	0.4%

Source: U.S. Bureau of the Census
"Population Estimates" (December 2019, https://www.census.gov/programs-surveys/popest.html)
*From July 1, 2018, to June 30, 2019. Net international migration is the difference between migration to an area from outside the United States (immigration) and migration from the area to outside the United States (emigration) during the period. Includes legal immigration and estimates of undocumented immigration.

Percent of Population Foreign Born in 2018

National Percent = 13.7% of Population*

RANK	STATE	PERCENT
46	Alabama	3.3
23	Alaska	8.2
13	Arizona	13.4
38	Arkansas	4.8
1	California	26.9
18	Colorado	9.6
11	Connecticut	14.6
20	Delaware	9.4
4	Florida	21.0
17	Georgia	10.1
6	Hawaii	18.7
30	Idaho	6.0
12	Illinois	14.1
33	Indiana	5.3
32	Iowa	5.5
25	Kansas	7.2
44	Kentucky	3.8
41	Louisiana	4.2
45	Maine	3.5
9	Maryland	15.1
7	Massachusetts	17.4
28	Michigan	7.0
21	Minnesota	8.6
48	Mississippi	2.4
41	Missouri	4.2
49	Montana	2.2
25	Nebraska	7.2
5	Nevada	19.4
29	New Hampshire	6.1
2	New Jersey	22.8
19	New Mexico	9.5
2	New York	22.8
24	North Carolina	7.9
40	North Dakota	4.7
38	Ohio	4.8
30	Oklahoma	6.0
16	Oregon	10.3
25	Pennsylvania	7.2
14	Rhode Island	13.2
34	South Carolina	5.1
43	South Dakota	4.0
34	Tennessee	5.1
8	Texas	17.2
21	Utah	8.6
37	Vermont	4.9
15	Virginia	12.5
10	Washington	14.7
50	West Virginia	1.5
34	Wisconsin	5.1
47	Wyoming	3.0

RANK	STATE	PERCENT
1	California	26.9
2	New Jersey	22.8
2	New York	22.8
4	Florida	21.0
5	Nevada	19.4
6	Hawaii	18.7
7	Massachusetts	17.4
8	Texas	17.2
9	Maryland	15.1
10	Washington	14.7
11	Connecticut	14.6
12	Illinois	14.1
13	Arizona	13.4
14	Rhode Island	13.2
15	Virginia	12.5
16	Oregon	10.3
17	Georgia	10.1
18	Colorado	9.6
19	New Mexico	9.5
20	Delaware	9.4
21	Minnesota	8.6
21	Utah	8.6
23	Alaska	8.2
24	North Carolina	7.9
25	Kansas	7.2
25	Nebraska	7.2
25	Pennsylvania	7.2
28	Michigan	7.0
29	New Hampshire	6.1
30	Idaho	6.0
30	Oklahoma	6.0
32	Iowa	5.5
33	Indiana	5.3
34	South Carolina	5.1
34	Tennessee	5.1
34	Wisconsin	5.1
37	Vermont	4.9
38	Arkansas	4.8
38	Ohio	4.8
40	North Dakota	4.7
41	Louisiana	4.2
41	Missouri	4.2
43	South Dakota	4.0
44	Kentucky	3.8
45	Maine	3.5
46	Alabama	3.3
47	Wyoming	3.0
48	Mississippi	2.4
49	Montana	2.2
50	West Virginia	1.5
	District of Columbia	13.9

Source: U.S. Bureau of the Census
    "2018 American Community Survey-Table CP02" (https://data.census.gov/cedsci/)
*"Foreign born" are persons not born in the United States, Puerto Rico, a U.S. Island Area, or abroad of American parent or parents.

Percent of Population Speaking a Language Other Than English at Home in 2018
National Percent = 21.9%*

ALPHA ORDER

RANK	STATE	PERCENT
47	Alabama	5.3
18	Alaska	16.3
8	Arizona	27.5
35	Arkansas	7.7
1	California	44.6
16	Colorado	16.7
12	Connecticut	22.1
22	Delaware	13.1
7	Florida	29.7
21	Georgia	14.0
8	Hawaii	27.5
28	Idaho	10.9
11	Illinois	23.5
31	Indiana	8.9
32	Iowa	8.8
26	Kansas	11.8
45	Kentucky	5.6
36	Louisiana	7.6
44	Maine	6.1
15	Maryland	19.3
10	Massachusetts	24.3
30	Michigan	9.8
23	Minnesota	12.2
49	Mississippi	3.7
43	Missouri	6.3
48	Montana	4.4
27	Nebraska	11.2
5	Nevada	30.9
34	New Hampshire	7.8
4	New Jersey	31.7
3	New Mexico	34.1
6	New York	30.7
24	North Carolina	12.0
37	North Dakota	7.4
39	Ohio	7.3
29	Oklahoma	10.7
19	Oregon	15.9
25	Pennsylvania	11.9
13	Rhode Island	21.7
37	South Carolina	7.4
42	South Dakota	6.8
39	Tennessee	7.3
2	Texas	35.8
20	Utah	15.8
45	Vermont	5.6
17	Virginia	16.4
14	Washington	20.0
50	West Virginia	2.5
32	Wisconsin	8.8
41	Wyoming	7.0

RANK ORDER

RANK	STATE	PERCENT
1	California	44.6
2	Texas	35.8
3	New Mexico	34.1
4	New Jersey	31.7
5	Nevada	30.9
6	New York	30.7
7	Florida	29.7
8	Arizona	27.5
8	Hawaii	27.5
10	Massachusetts	24.3
11	Illinois	23.5
12	Connecticut	22.1
13	Rhode Island	21.7
14	Washington	20.0
15	Maryland	19.3
16	Colorado	16.7
17	Virginia	16.4
18	Alaska	16.3
19	Oregon	15.9
20	Utah	15.8
21	Georgia	14.0
22	Delaware	13.1
23	Minnesota	12.2
24	North Carolina	12.0
25	Pennsylvania	11.9
26	Kansas	11.8
27	Nebraska	11.2
28	Idaho	10.9
29	Oklahoma	10.7
30	Michigan	9.8
31	Indiana	8.9
32	Iowa	8.8
32	Wisconsin	8.8
34	New Hampshire	7.8
35	Arkansas	7.7
36	Louisiana	7.6
37	North Dakota	7.4
37	South Carolina	7.4
39	Ohio	7.3
39	Tennessee	7.3
41	Wyoming	7.0
42	South Dakota	6.8
43	Missouri	6.3
44	Maine	6.1
45	Kentucky	5.6
45	Vermont	5.6
47	Alabama	5.3
48	Montana	4.4
49	Mississippi	3.7
50	West Virginia	2.5

District of Columbia   16.9

Source: U.S. Bureau of the Census
"2018 American Community Survey-Table CP02" (https://data.census.gov/cedsci/)
*Population five years old and older.

Percent of Population Speaking Spanish at Home in 2018

National Percent = 13.5%*

ALPHA ORDER

RANK	STATE	PERCENT
37	Alabama	3.3
35	Alaska	3.8
6	Arizona	20.7
26	Arkansas	5.5
2	California	28.9
12	Colorado	11.6
11	Connecticut	11.9
24	Delaware	7.2
4	Florida	22.2
19	Georgia	8.0
40	Hawaii	2.5
18	Idaho	8.2
9	Illinois	13.7
29	Indiana	4.7
32	Iowa	4.2
20	Kansas	7.9
39	Kentucky	2.8
36	Louisiana	3.6
50	Maine	0.8
17	Maryland	8.5
14	Massachusetts	9.4
38	Michigan	3.0
34	Minnesota	4.0
44	Mississippi	2.3
40	Missouri	2.5
47	Montana	1.7
24	Nebraska	7.2
5	Nevada	21.3
42	New Hampshire	2.4
7	New Jersey	16.6
3	New Mexico	26.4
8	New York	14.9
21	North Carolina	7.8
46	North Dakota	1.9
42	Ohio	2.4
23	Oklahoma	7.4
14	Oregon	9.4
27	Pennsylvania	5.2
10	Rhode Island	12.3
31	South Carolina	4.6
45	South Dakota	2.1
32	Tennessee	4.2
1	Texas	29.4
13	Utah	10.8
48	Vermont	1.2
22	Virginia	7.5
16	Washington	8.6
49	West Virginia	1.1
28	Wisconsin	4.8
29	Wyoming	4.7

RANK ORDER

RANK	STATE	PERCENT
1	Texas	29.4
2	California	28.9
3	New Mexico	26.4
4	Florida	22.2
5	Nevada	21.3
6	Arizona	20.7
7	New Jersey	16.6
8	New York	14.9
9	Illinois	13.7
10	Rhode Island	12.3
11	Connecticut	11.9
12	Colorado	11.6
13	Utah	10.8
14	Massachusetts	9.4
14	Oregon	9.4
16	Washington	8.6
17	Maryland	8.5
18	Idaho	8.2
19	Georgia	8.0
20	Kansas	7.9
21	North Carolina	7.8
22	Virginia	7.5
23	Oklahoma	7.4
24	Delaware	7.2
24	Nebraska	7.2
26	Arkansas	5.5
27	Pennsylvania	5.2
28	Wisconsin	4.8
29	Indiana	4.7
29	Wyoming	4.7
31	South Carolina	4.6
32	Iowa	4.2
32	Tennessee	4.2
34	Minnesota	4.0
35	Alaska	3.8
36	Louisiana	3.6
37	Alabama	3.3
38	Michigan	3.0
39	Kentucky	2.8
40	Hawaii	2.5
40	Missouri	2.5
42	New Hampshire	2.4
42	Ohio	2.4
44	Mississippi	2.3
45	South Dakota	2.1
46	North Dakota	1.9
47	Montana	1.7
48	Vermont	1.2
49	West Virginia	1.1
50	Maine	0.8
	District of Columbia	8.4

Source: U.S. Bureau of the Census
   "2018 American Community Survey-Table CP02" (https://data.census.gov/cedsci/)
*Population five years old and older.

Marriage Rate for Men in 2018

National Rate = 17.6 Marriages per 1,000 Men*

ALPHA ORDER			RANK ORDER		
RANK	STATE	RATE	RANK	STATE	RATE
25	Alabama	17.8	1	Idaho	25.3
4	Alaska	20.8	2	Utah	23.0
11	Arizona	19.3	3	Oklahoma	21.0
11	Arkansas	19.3	4	Alaska	20.8
34	California	16.8	4	Hawaii	20.8
19	Colorado	18.6	6	Kansas	20.2
49	Connecticut	14.2	6	Mississippi	20.2
41	Delaware	16.0	8	Washington	19.7
29	Florida	17.2	9	North Dakota	19.5
18	Georgia	18.8	10	Virginia	19.4
4	Hawaii	20.8	11	Arizona	19.3
1	Idaho	25.3	11	Arkansas	19.3
20	Illinois	18.2	11	Missouri	19.3
24	Indiana	17.9	14	Oregon	19.1
16	Iowa	19.0	14	Texas	19.1
6	Kansas	20.2	16	Iowa	19.0
26	Kentucky	17.6	17	South Dakota	18.9
35	Louisiana	16.7	18	Georgia	18.8
50	Maine	12.3	19	Colorado	18.6
28	Maryland	17.4	20	Illinois	18.2
30	Massachusetts	17.1	20	North Carolina	18.2
40	Michigan	16.1	22	Nevada	18.0
33	Minnesota	16.9	22	Tennessee	18.0
6	Mississippi	20.2	24	Indiana	17.9
11	Missouri	19.3	25	Alabama	17.8
37	Montana	16.3	26	Kentucky	17.6
27	Nebraska	17.5	27	Nebraska	17.5
22	Nevada	18.0	28	Maryland	17.4
48	New Hampshire	14.3	29	Florida	17.2
42	New Jersey	15.9	30	Massachusetts	17.1
45	New Mexico	14.7	30	Ohio	17.1
36	New York	16.5	30	Wyoming	17.1
20	North Carolina	18.2	33	Minnesota	16.9
9	North Dakota	19.5	34	California	16.8
30	Ohio	17.1	35	Louisiana	16.7
3	Oklahoma	21.0	36	New York	16.5
14	Oregon	19.1	37	Montana	16.3
44	Pennsylvania	15.3	37	Vermont	16.3
45	Rhode Island	14.7	39	West Virginia	16.2
47	South Carolina	14.4	40	Michigan	16.1
17	South Dakota	18.9	41	Delaware	16.0
22	Tennessee	18.0	42	New Jersey	15.9
14	Texas	19.1	43	Wisconsin	15.6
2	Utah	23.0	44	Pennsylvania	15.3
37	Vermont	16.3	45	New Mexico	14.7
10	Virginia	19.4	45	Rhode Island	14.7
8	Washington	19.7	47	South Carolina	14.4
39	West Virginia	16.2	48	New Hampshire	14.3
43	Wisconsin	15.6	49	Connecticut	14.2
30	Wyoming	17.1	50	Maine	12.3
				District of Columbia	25.9

Source: U.S. Bureau of the Census
   "2018 American Community Survey-Table GCT1252" (https://data.census.gov/cedsci/)
*Men age 15 and older. Marriages in the last year.

Estimated Median Age of Men at First Marriage in 2018

National Median = 30.1 Years*

ALPHA ORDER				RANK ORDER		
RANK	STATE	YEARS		RANK	STATE	YEARS
38	Alabama	28.8		1	Rhode Island	32.4
33	Alaska	29.2		2	New Hampshire	31.2
16	Arizona	30.0		3	Florida	31.0
48	Arkansas	27.4		3	Massachusetts	31.0
6	California	30.9		3	New York	31.0
19	Colorado	29.9		6	California	30.9
6	Connecticut	30.9		6	Connecticut	30.9
12	Delaware	30.5		6	New Jersey	30.9
3	Florida	31.0		9	Illinois	30.6
16	Georgia	30.0		9	Maryland	30.6
19	Hawaii	29.9		9	Pennsylvania	30.6
49	Idaho	26.9		12	Delaware	30.5
9	Illinois	30.6		12	Vermont	30.5
38	Indiana	28.8		14	Nevada	30.2
42	Iowa	28.3		15	Michigan	30.1
43	Kansas	28.1		16	Arizona	30.0
43	Kentucky	28.1		16	Georgia	30.0
16	Louisiana	30.0		16	Louisiana	30.0
29	Maine	29.6		19	Colorado	29.9
9	Maryland	30.6		19	Hawaii	29.9
3	Massachusetts	31.0		19	Minnesota	29.9
15	Michigan	30.1		19	Ohio	29.9
19	Minnesota	29.9		19	Oregon	29.9
47	Mississippi	27.6		19	South Carolina	29.9
41	Missouri	28.6		19	Virginia	29.9
36	Montana	29.0		26	New Mexico	29.8
45	Nebraska	28.0		27	Washington	29.7
14	Nevada	30.2		27	Wisconsin	29.7
2	New Hampshire	31.2		29	Maine	29.6
6	New Jersey	30.9		30	North Carolina	29.5
26	New Mexico	29.8		31	Tennessee	29.4
3	New York	31.0		32	Wyoming	29.3
30	North Carolina	29.5		33	Alaska	29.2
37	North Dakota	28.9		33	Texas	29.2
19	Ohio	29.9		33	West Virginia	29.2
46	Oklahoma	27.8		36	Montana	29.0
19	Oregon	29.9		37	North Dakota	28.9
9	Pennsylvania	30.6		38	Alabama	28.8
1	Rhode Island	32.4		38	Indiana	28.8
19	South Carolina	29.9		38	South Dakota	28.8
38	South Dakota	28.8		41	Missouri	28.6
31	Tennessee	29.4		42	Iowa	28.3
33	Texas	29.2		43	Kansas	28.1
50	Utah	26.8		43	Kentucky	28.1
12	Vermont	30.5		45	Nebraska	28.0
19	Virginia	29.9		46	Oklahoma	27.8
27	Washington	29.7		47	Mississippi	27.6
33	West Virginia	29.2		48	Arkansas	27.4
27	Wisconsin	29.7		49	Idaho	26.9
32	Wyoming	29.3		50	Utah	26.8
					District of Columbia	31.8

Source: U.S. Bureau of the Census
"2018 American Community Survey-Table B12007" (https://data.census.gov/cedsci/)
*The median age at first marriage is calculated indirectly by estimating the proportion of young people who will marry during their lifetime, calculating one-half of this proportion, and determining the age (at the time of the survey) of people at this halfway mark. It does not represent the actual median age of the population who married during the calendar year.

Marriage Rate for Women in 2018

National Rate = 16.6 Marriages per 1,000 Women*

ALPHA ORDER				RANK ORDER		
RANK	STATE	RATE		RANK	STATE	RATE
22	Alabama	17.1		1	Utah	23.1
5	Alaska	20.8		2	Wyoming	22.9
8	Arizona	19.5		3	Idaho	22.6
19	Arkansas	17.9		4	North Dakota	21.5
33	California	15.9		5	Alaska	20.8
8	Colorado	19.5		6	Oklahoma	20.3
49	Connecticut	13.2		7	Hawaii	19.6
42	Delaware	15.0		8	Arizona	19.5
35	Florida	15.7		8	Colorado	19.5
30	Georgia	16.2		10	Missouri	19.3
7	Hawaii	19.6		11	Vermont	19.0
3	Idaho	22.6		12	Kansas	18.8
26	Illinois	16.7		13	Nevada	18.7
27	Indiana	16.6		13	Oregon	18.7
20	Iowa	17.5		13	Washington	18.7
12	Kansas	18.8		16	Texas	18.1
25	Kentucky	16.8		16	Virginia	18.1
44	Louisiana	14.8		18	South Dakota	18.0
49	Maine	13.2		19	Arkansas	17.9
23	Maryland	16.9		20	Iowa	17.5
37	Massachusetts	15.6		21	Tennessee	17.4
34	Michigan	15.8		22	Alabama	17.1
23	Minnesota	16.9		23	Maryland	16.9
28	Mississippi	16.4		23	Minnesota	16.9
10	Missouri	19.3		25	Kentucky	16.8
37	Montana	15.6		26	Illinois	16.7
31	Nebraska	16.1		27	Indiana	16.6
13	Nevada	18.7		28	Mississippi	16.4
41	New Hampshire	15.5		28	New Mexico	16.4
47	New Jersey	14.3		30	Georgia	16.2
28	New Mexico	16.4		31	Nebraska	16.1
42	New York	15.0		31	Ohio	16.1
35	North Carolina	15.7		33	California	15.9
4	North Dakota	21.5		34	Michigan	15.8
31	Ohio	16.1		35	Florida	15.7
6	Oklahoma	20.3		35	North Carolina	15.7
13	Oregon	18.7		37	Massachusetts	15.6
45	Pennsylvania	14.7		37	Montana	15.6
48	Rhode Island	14.1		37	West Virginia	15.6
46	South Carolina	14.5		37	Wisconsin	15.6
18	South Dakota	18.0		41	New Hampshire	15.5
21	Tennessee	17.4		42	Delaware	15.0
16	Texas	18.1		42	New York	15.0
1	Utah	23.1		44	Louisiana	14.8
11	Vermont	19.0		45	Pennsylvania	14.7
16	Virginia	18.1		46	South Carolina	14.5
13	Washington	18.7		47	New Jersey	14.3
37	West Virginia	15.6		48	Rhode Island	14.1
37	Wisconsin	15.6		49	Connecticut	13.2
2	Wyoming	22.9		49	Maine	13.2
					District of Columbia	22.3

Source: U.S. Bureau of the Census
   "2018 American Community Survey-Table GCT1251" (https://data.census.gov/cedsci/)
*Women age 15 and older. Marriages in the last year.

Estimated Median Age of Women at First Marriage in 2018

National Median = 28.3 Years*

RANK	STATE (ALPHA ORDER)	YEARS		RANK	STATE (RANK ORDER)	YEARS
37	Alabama	26.8		1	Massachusetts	29.9
45	Alaska	26.3		2	New York	29.8
29	Arizona	27.6		3	Connecticut	29.6
40	Arkansas	26.6		4	Delaware	29.5
6	California	29.3		4	Rhode Island	29.5
23	Colorado	27.9		6	California	29.3
3	Connecticut	29.6		6	Maryland	29.3
4	Delaware	29.5		6	New Jersey	29.3
9	Florida	29.2		9	Florida	29.2
22	Georgia	28.0		10	Illinois	29.1
14	Hawaii	28.7		10	New Hampshire	29.1
38	Idaho	26.7		12	Pennsylvania	28.9
10	Illinois	29.1		13	Maine	28.8
34	Indiana	27.1		14	Hawaii	28.7
42	Iowa	26.4		15	Vermont	28.6
48	Kansas	26.1		16	Ohio	28.4
40	Kentucky	26.6		17	Michigan	28.3
20	Louisiana	28.1		17	Nevada	28.3
13	Maine	28.8		19	South Carolina	28.2
6	Maryland	29.3		20	Louisiana	28.1
1	Massachusetts	29.9		20	North Carolina	28.1
17	Michigan	28.3		22	Georgia	28.0
28	Minnesota	27.7		23	Colorado	27.9
31	Mississippi	27.3		23	Virginia	27.9
35	Missouri	26.9		23	Washington	27.9
47	Montana	26.2		26	Oregon	27.8
42	Nebraska	26.4		26	Wisconsin	27.8
17	Nevada	28.3		28	Minnesota	27.7
10	New Hampshire	29.1		29	Arizona	27.6
6	New Jersey	29.3		30	Tennessee	27.4
33	New Mexico	27.2		31	Mississippi	27.3
2	New York	29.8		31	Texas	27.3
20	North Carolina	28.1		33	New Mexico	27.2
38	North Dakota	26.7		34	Indiana	27.1
16	Ohio	28.4		35	Missouri	26.9
42	Oklahoma	26.4		35	West Virginia	26.9
26	Oregon	27.8		37	Alabama	26.8
12	Pennsylvania	28.9		38	Idaho	26.7
4	Rhode Island	29.5		38	North Dakota	26.7
19	South Carolina	28.2		40	Arkansas	26.6
45	South Dakota	26.3		40	Kentucky	26.6
30	Tennessee	27.4		42	Iowa	26.4
31	Texas	27.3		42	Nebraska	26.4
50	Utah	24.8		42	Oklahoma	26.4
15	Vermont	28.6		45	Alaska	26.3
23	Virginia	27.9		45	South Dakota	26.3
23	Washington	27.9		47	Montana	26.2
35	West Virginia	26.9		48	Kansas	26.1
26	Wisconsin	27.8		49	Wyoming	26.0
49	Wyoming	26.0		50	Utah	24.8
					District of Columbia	31.0

Source: U.S. Bureau of the Census

   "2018 American Community Survey-Table B12007" (https://data.census.gov/cedsci/)

*The median age at first marriage is calculated indirectly by estimating the proportion of young people who will marry during their lifetime, calculating one-half of this proportion, and determining the age (at the time of the survey) of people at this halfway mark. It does not represent the actual median age of the population who married during the calendar year.

Ratio of Unmarried Men to Unmarried Women in 2018

National Ratio = 111.2 Unmarried Men for Every 100 Unmarried Women*

ALPHA ORDER

RANK ORDER

RANK	STATE	RATIO		RANK	STATE	RATIO
45	Alabama	105.8		1	North Dakota	135.8
2	Alaska	127.4		2	Alaska	127.4
13	Arizona	115.5		3	Hawaii	125.2
37	Arkansas	109.3		4	Colorado	119.7
16	California	114.7		5	Washington	117.9
4	Colorado	119.7		6	Utah	117.5
39	Connecticut	108.8		7	Kansas	117.3
48	Delaware	104.8		8	Wyoming	117.1
29	Florida	111.6		9	Idaho	116.9
49	Georgia	103.8		10	Nevada	116.3
3	Hawaii	125.2		11	Montana	116.1
9	Idaho	116.9		12	Nebraska	115.6
36	Illinois	109.9		13	Arizona	115.5
33	Indiana	110.9		14	South Dakota	115.3
18	Iowa	114.3		15	New Mexico	115.1
7	Kansas	117.3		16	California	114.7
19	Kentucky	113.9		17	Minnesota	114.6
47	Louisiana	104.9		18	Iowa	114.3
31	Maine	111.0		19	Kentucky	113.9
42	Maryland	106.6		19	New Hampshire	113.9
46	Massachusetts	105.4		19	Oklahoma	113.9
27	Michigan	111.8		22	West Virginia	113.8
17	Minnesota	114.6		23	Wisconsin	113.3
50	Mississippi	103.1		24	Oregon	113.0
31	Missouri	111.0		25	Vermont	112.2
11	Montana	116.1		26	Texas	111.9
12	Nebraska	115.6		27	Michigan	111.8
10	Nevada	116.3		28	Pennsylvania	111.7
19	New Hampshire	113.9		29	Florida	111.6
34	New Jersey	110.4		30	Virginia	111.5
15	New Mexico	115.1		31	Maine	111.0
44	New York	106.1		31	Missouri	111.0
43	North Carolina	106.5		33	Indiana	110.9
1	North Dakota	135.8		34	New Jersey	110.4
35	Ohio	110.2		35	Ohio	110.2
19	Oklahoma	113.9		36	Illinois	109.9
24	Oregon	113.0		37	Arkansas	109.3
28	Pennsylvania	111.7		38	Tennessee	108.9
40	Rhode Island	108.1		39	Connecticut	108.8
41	South Carolina	107.5		40	Rhode Island	108.1
14	South Dakota	115.3		41	South Carolina	107.5
38	Tennessee	108.9		42	Maryland	106.6
26	Texas	111.9		43	North Carolina	106.5
6	Utah	117.5		44	New York	106.1
25	Vermont	112.2		45	Alabama	105.8
30	Virginia	111.5		46	Massachusetts	105.4
5	Washington	117.9		47	Louisiana	104.9
22	West Virginia	113.8		48	Delaware	104.8
23	Wisconsin	113.3		49	Georgia	103.8
8	Wyoming	117.1		50	Mississippi	103.1
					District of Columbia	90.3

Source: U.S. Bureau of the Census
"2018 American Community Survey-Table R1203" (https://data.census.gov/cedsci/)
*Population fifteen to forty-four years old.

Divorce Rate for Men in 2018

National Rate = 7.3 Divorces per 1,000 Men*

ALPHA ORDER

RANK	STATE	RATE
4	Alabama	10.1
20	Alaska	7.7
21	Arizona	7.6
1	Arkansas	10.6
39	California	6.2
6	Colorado	9.2
42	Connecticut	6.0
NA	Delaware**	NA
27	Florida	7.4
11	Georgia	8.5
19	Hawaii	7.8
14	Idaho	8.0
40	Illinois	6.1
8	Indiana	8.7
44	Iowa	5.8
23	Kansas	7.5
1	Kentucky	10.6
14	Louisiana	8.0
8	Maine	8.7
21	Maryland	7.6
46	Massachusetts	5.3
23	Michigan	7.5
40	Minnesota	6.1
14	Mississippi	8.0
7	Missouri	8.8
31	Montana	7.3
35	Nebraska	6.9
5	Nevada	9.6
18	New Hampshire	7.9
48	New Jersey	5.0
36	New Mexico	6.7
45	New York	5.5
27	North Carolina	7.4
27	North Dakota	7.4
33	Ohio	7.1
3	Oklahoma	10.5
23	Oregon	7.5
38	Pennsylvania	6.6
47	Rhode Island	5.2
31	South Carolina	7.3
42	South Dakota	6.0
8	Tennessee	8.7
13	Texas	8.2
23	Utah	7.5
49	Vermont	4.6
14	Virginia	8.0
33	Washington	7.1
27	West Virginia	7.4
36	Wisconsin	6.7
12	Wyoming	8.3

RANK ORDER

RANK	STATE	RATE
1	Arkansas	10.6
1	Kentucky	10.6
3	Oklahoma	10.5
4	Alabama	10.1
5	Nevada	9.6
6	Colorado	9.2
7	Missouri	8.8
8	Indiana	8.7
8	Maine	8.7
8	Tennessee	8.7
11	Georgia	8.5
12	Wyoming	8.3
13	Texas	8.2
14	Idaho	8.0
14	Louisiana	8.0
14	Mississippi	8.0
14	Virginia	8.0
18	New Hampshire	7.9
19	Hawaii	7.8
20	Alaska	7.7
21	Arizona	7.6
21	Maryland	7.6
23	Kansas	7.5
23	Michigan	7.5
23	Oregon	7.5
23	Utah	7.5
27	Florida	7.4
27	North Carolina	7.4
27	North Dakota	7.4
27	West Virginia	7.4
31	Montana	7.3
31	South Carolina	7.3
33	Ohio	7.1
33	Washington	7.1
35	Nebraska	6.9
36	New Mexico	6.7
36	Wisconsin	6.7
38	Pennsylvania	6.6
39	California	6.2
40	Illinois	6.1
40	Minnesota	6.1
42	Connecticut	6.0
42	South Dakota	6.0
44	Iowa	5.8
45	New York	5.5
46	Massachusetts	5.3
47	Rhode Island	5.2
48	New Jersey	5.0
49	Vermont	4.6
NA	Delaware**	NA
	District of Columbia	4.8

Source: U.S. Bureau of the Census
   "2018 American Community Survey-Table GCT1254" (https://data.census.gov/cedsci/)
*Men age 15 and older. Divorces in the last year.
**Not available.

Divorce Rate for Women in 2018

National Rate = 7.7 Divorces per 1,000 Women*

ALPHA ORDER				RANK ORDER		
RANK	STATE	RATE		RANK	STATE	RATE
7	Alabama	9.8		1	Arkansas	13.0
28	Alaska	7.6		2	South Dakota	12.1
26	Arizona	8.0		3	Oklahoma	10.8
1	Arkansas	13.0		4	Kentucky	10.5
39	California	6.7		5	Oregon	10.1
16	Colorado	8.7		6	Indiana	9.9
38	Connecticut	6.8		7	Alabama	9.8
NA	Delaware**	NA		7	West Virginia	9.8
26	Florida	8.0		9	Nevada	9.6
24	Georgia	8.1		9	Washington	9.6
39	Hawaii	6.7		11	Wyoming	9.4
23	Idaho	8.2		12	Utah	9.3
41	Illinois	6.6		13	Missouri	9.2
6	Indiana	9.9		14	Montana	9.1
34	Iowa	7.1		14	Tennessee	9.1
18	Kansas	8.6		16	Colorado	8.7
4	Kentucky	10.5		16	Mississippi	8.7
28	Louisiana	7.6		18	Kansas	8.6
22	Maine	8.3		18	North Carolina	8.6
32	Maryland	7.4		20	New Hampshire	8.4
30	Massachusetts	7.5		20	Texas	8.4
37	Michigan	6.9		22	Maine	8.3
34	Minnesota	7.1		23	Idaho	8.2
16	Mississippi	8.7		24	Georgia	8.1
13	Missouri	9.2		24	Virginia	8.1
14	Montana	9.1		26	Arizona	8.0
36	Nebraska	7.0		26	Florida	8.0
9	Nevada	9.6		28	Alaska	7.6
20	New Hampshire	8.4		28	Louisiana	7.6
46	New Jersey	5.7		30	Massachusetts	7.5
41	New Mexico	6.6		30	South Carolina	7.5
46	New York	5.7		32	Maryland	7.4
18	North Carolina	8.6		33	Ohio	7.2
49	North Dakota	4.7		34	Iowa	7.1
33	Ohio	7.2		34	Minnesota	7.1
3	Oklahoma	10.8		36	Nebraska	7.0
5	Oregon	10.1		37	Michigan	6.9
43	Pennsylvania	6.5		38	Connecticut	6.8
48	Rhode Island	4.9		39	California	6.7
30	South Carolina	7.5		39	Hawaii	6.7
2	South Dakota	12.1		41	Illinois	6.6
14	Tennessee	9.1		41	New Mexico	6.6
20	Texas	8.4		43	Pennsylvania	6.5
12	Utah	9.3		44	Vermont	6.3
44	Vermont	6.3		45	Wisconsin	6.2
24	Virginia	8.1		46	New Jersey	5.7
9	Washington	9.6		46	New York	5.7
7	West Virginia	9.8		48	Rhode Island	4.9
45	Wisconsin	6.2		49	North Dakota	4.7
11	Wyoming	9.4		NA	Delaware**	NA
					District of Columbia	5.8

Source: U.S. Bureau of the Census
   "2017 American Community Survey-Table GCT1253" (https://www.census.gov/programs-surveys/acs/)
*Women age 15 and older. Divorces in the last year.
**Not available.

Average Family Size in 2018

National Average = 3.24 Persons per Family

Source: U.S. Bureau of the Census
"2018 American Community Survey-Table CP02" (https://data.census.gov/cedsci/)

ALPHA ORDER

RANK	STATE	PERSONS
17	Alabama	3.21
5	Alaska	3.39
10	Arizona	3.29
29	Arkansas	3.10
3	California	3.56
23	Colorado	3.16
27	Connecticut	3.12
22	Delaware	3.17
7	Florida	3.31
7	Georgia	3.31
1	Hawaii	3.61
15	Idaho	3.24
17	Illinois	3.21
31	Indiana	3.09
45	Iowa	2.99
28	Kansas	3.11
35	Kentucky	3.06
9	Louisiana	3.30
50	Maine	2.85
12	Maryland	3.27
23	Massachusetts	3.16
34	Michigan	3.07
31	Minnesota	3.09
12	Mississippi	3.27
36	Missouri	3.05
44	Montana	3.00
36	Nebraska	3.05
6	Nevada	3.33
43	New Hampshire	3.03
12	New Jersey	3.27
11	New Mexico	3.28
15	New York	3.24
29	North Carolina	3.10
48	North Dakota	2.95
36	Ohio	3.05
23	Oklahoma	3.16
36	Oregon	3.05
42	Pennsylvania	3.04
19	Rhode Island	3.19
20	South Carolina	3.18
36	South Dakota	3.05
26	Tennessee	3.13
4	Texas	3.50
1	Utah	3.61
49	Vermont	2.88
20	Virginia	3.18
31	Washington	3.09
45	West Virginia	2.99
47	Wisconsin	2.97
36	Wyoming	3.05

RANK ORDER

RANK	STATE	PERSONS
1	Hawaii	3.61
1	Utah	3.61
3	California	3.56
4	Texas	3.50
5	Alaska	3.39
6	Nevada	3.33
7	Florida	3.31
7	Georgia	3.31
9	Louisiana	3.30
10	Arizona	3.29
11	New Mexico	3.28
12	Maryland	3.27
12	Mississippi	3.27
12	New Jersey	3.27
15	Idaho	3.24
15	New York	3.24
17	Alabama	3.21
17	Illinois	3.21
19	Rhode Island	3.19
20	South Carolina	3.18
20	Virginia	3.18
22	Delaware	3.17
23	Colorado	3.16
23	Massachusetts	3.16
23	Oklahoma	3.16
26	Tennessee	3.13
27	Connecticut	3.12
28	Kansas	3.11
29	Arkansas	3.10
29	North Carolina	3.10
31	Indiana	3.09
31	Minnesota	3.09
31	Washington	3.09
34	Michigan	3.07
35	Kentucky	3.06
36	Missouri	3.05
36	Nebraska	3.05
36	Ohio	3.05
36	Oregon	3.05
36	South Dakota	3.05
36	Wyoming	3.05
42	Pennsylvania	3.04
43	New Hampshire	3.03
44	Montana	3.00
45	Iowa	2.99
45	West Virginia	2.99
47	Wisconsin	2.97
48	North Dakota	2.95
49	Vermont	2.88
50	Maine	2.85
	District of Columbia	3.38

Seats in the U.S. House of Representatives in 2020

National Total = 435 Seats*

ALPHA ORDER

RANK	STATE	SEATS	% of USA
22	Alabama	7	1.6%
44	Alaska	1	0.2%
14	Arizona	9	2.1%
30	Arkansas	4	0.9%
1	California	53	12.2%
22	Colorado	7	1.6%
27	Connecticut	5	1.1%
44	Delaware	1	0.2%
3	Florida	27	6.2%
8	Georgia	14	3.2%
39	Hawaii	2	0.5%
39	Idaho	2	0.5%
5	Illinois	18	4.1%
14	Indiana	9	2.1%
30	Iowa	4	0.9%
30	Kansas	4	0.9%
25	Kentucky	6	1.4%
25	Louisiana	6	1.4%
39	Maine	2	0.5%
18	Maryland	8	1.8%
14	Massachusetts	9	2.1%
8	Michigan	14	3.2%
18	Minnesota	8	1.8%
30	Mississippi	4	0.9%
18	Missouri	8	1.8%
44	Montana	1	0.2%
36	Nebraska	3	0.7%
30	Nevada	4	0.9%
39	New Hampshire	2	0.5%
11	New Jersey	12	2.8%
36	New Mexico	3	0.7%
3	New York	27	6.2%
10	North Carolina	13	3.0%
44	North Dakota	1	0.2%
7	Ohio	16	3.7%
27	Oklahoma	5	1.1%
27	Oregon	5	1.1%
5	Pennsylvania	18	4.1%
39	Rhode Island	2	0.5%
22	South Carolina	7	1.6%
44	South Dakota	1	0.2%
14	Tennessee	9	2.1%
2	Texas	36	8.3%
30	Utah	4	0.9%
44	Vermont	1	0.2%
12	Virginia	11	2.5%
13	Washington	10	2.3%
36	West Virginia	3	0.7%
18	Wisconsin	8	1.8%
44	Wyoming	1	0.2%

RANK ORDER

RANK	STATE	SEATS	% of USA
1	California	53	12.2%
2	Texas	36	8.3%
3	Florida	27	6.2%
3	New York	27	6.2%
5	Illinois	18	4.1%
5	Pennsylvania	18	4.1%
7	Ohio	16	3.7%
8	Georgia	14	3.2%
8	Michigan	14	3.2%
10	North Carolina	13	3.0%
11	New Jersey	12	2.8%
12	Virginia	11	2.5%
13	Washington	10	2.3%
14	Arizona	9	2.1%
14	Indiana	9	2.1%
14	Massachusetts	9	2.1%
14	Tennessee	9	2.1%
18	Maryland	8	1.8%
18	Minnesota	8	1.8%
18	Missouri	8	1.8%
18	Wisconsin	8	1.8%
22	Alabama	7	1.6%
22	Colorado	7	1.6%
22	South Carolina	7	1.6%
25	Kentucky	6	1.4%
25	Louisiana	6	1.4%
27	Connecticut	5	1.1%
27	Oklahoma	5	1.1%
27	Oregon	5	1.1%
30	Arkansas	4	0.9%
30	Iowa	4	0.9%
30	Kansas	4	0.9%
30	Mississippi	4	0.9%
30	Nevada	4	0.9%
30	Utah	4	0.9%
36	Nebraska	3	0.7%
36	New Mexico	3	0.7%
36	West Virginia	3	0.7%
39	Hawaii	2	0.5%
39	Idaho	2	0.5%
39	Maine	2	0.5%
39	New Hampshire	2	0.5%
39	Rhode Island	2	0.5%
44	Alaska	1	0.2%
44	Delaware	1	0.2%
44	Montana	1	0.2%
44	North Dakota	1	0.2%
44	South Dakota	1	0.2%
44	Vermont	1	0.2%
44	Wyoming	1	0.2%
	District of Columbia**	0	0.0%

Source: U.S. Bureau of the Census

"Congressional Apportionment" (https://www.census.gov/topics/public-sector/congressional-apportionment.html)

*This table shows the number of seats after reapportionment of the 2010 census. This apportionment became effective with the Congress elected in November 2012 and that took office in January 2013.

**The District of Columbia has one non-voting delegate. Each state has two members in the U.S. Senate.

Estimated Population per U.S. House Seat in 2020

National Rate = 752,951 Persons per House Member*

ALPHA ORDER				RANK ORDER		
RANK	STATE	RATE		RANK	STATE	RATE
42	Alabama	700,455		1	Montana	1,068,778
31	Alaska	731,545		2	Delaware	973,764
7	Arizona	808,746		3	Idaho	893,533
24	Arkansas	754,451		4	South Dakota	884,659
26	California	745,514		5	Oregon	843,547
6	Colorado	822,677		6	Colorado	822,677
37	Connecticut	713,057		7	Arizona	808,746
2	Delaware	973,764		8	North Carolina	806,776
11	Florida	795,472		9	Texas	805,441
22	Georgia	758,387		10	Utah	801,490
39	Hawaii	707,936		11	Florida	795,472
3	Idaho	893,533		12	Oklahoma	791,394
41	Illinois	703,990		13	Iowa	788,768
25	Indiana	748,024		14	Virginia	775,956
13	Iowa	788,768		15	Louisiana	774,799
33	Kansas	728,329		16	Nevada	770,039
27	Kentucky	744,612		17	Missouri	767,179
15	Louisiana	774,799		18	Massachusetts	765,834
45	Maine	672,106		19	North Dakota	762,062
23	Maryland	755,710		20	Washington	761,489
18	Massachusetts	765,834		21	Tennessee	758,797
36	Michigan	713,347		22	Georgia	758,387
40	Minnesota	704,954		23	Maryland	755,710
28	Mississippi	744,037		24	Arkansas	754,451
17	Missouri	767,179		25	Indiana	748,024
1	Montana	1,068,778		26	California	745,514
46	Nebraska	644,803		27	Kentucky	744,612
16	Nevada	770,039		28	Mississippi	744,037
44	New Hampshire	679,856		29	New Jersey	740,183
29	New Jersey	740,183		30	South Carolina	735,531
43	New Mexico	698,943		31	Alaska	731,545
35	New York	720,502		32	Ohio	730,569
8	North Carolina	806,776		33	Kansas	728,329
19	North Dakota	762,062		34	Wisconsin	727,804
32	Ohio	730,569		35	New York	720,502
12	Oklahoma	791,394		36	Michigan	713,347
5	Oregon	843,547		37	Connecticut	713,057
38	Pennsylvania	711,222		38	Pennsylvania	711,222
50	Rhode Island	529,681		39	Hawaii	707,936
30	South Carolina	735,531		40	Minnesota	704,954
4	South Dakota	884,659		41	Illinois	703,990
21	Tennessee	758,797		42	Alabama	700,455
9	Texas	805,441		43	New Mexico	698,943
10	Utah	801,490		44	New Hampshire	679,856
47	Vermont	623,989		45	Maine	672,106
14	Virginia	775,956		46	Nebraska	644,803
20	Washington	761,489		47	Vermont	623,989
48	West Virginia	597,382		48	West Virginia	597,382
34	Wisconsin	727,804		49	Wyoming	578,759
49	Wyoming	578,759		50	Rhode Island	529,681
					District of Columbia**	NA

Source: CQ Press using data from U.S. Bureau of the Census
   "Congressional Apportionment" (https://www.census.gov/topics/public-sector/congressional-apportionment.html)
*Rates calculated using 2019 population estimates and do not include population of the District of Columbia. The
District has one non-voting delegate. Each state has two members in the U.S. Senate. This table is based only on U.S.
representatives and not U.S. Senate members. This table reflects reapportionment resulting from the 2010 census and
taking effect after the 2012 election. **Not applicable.

State Legislators in 2019

National Total = 7,383 Legislators*

ALPHA ORDER

RANK	STATE	LEGISLATORS	% of USA
27	Alabama	140	1.9%
49	Alaska	60	0.8%
43	Arizona	90	1.2%
30	Arkansas	135	1.8%
35	California	120	1.6%
42	Colorado	100	1.4%
9	Connecticut	187	2.5%
48	Delaware	62	0.8%
18	Florida	160	2.2%
3	Georgia	236	3.2%
46	Hawaii	76	1.0%
39	Idaho	105	1.4%
13	Illinois	177	2.4%
19	Indiana	150	2.0%
19	Iowa	150	2.0%
17	Kansas	165	2.2%
29	Kentucky	138	1.9%
25	Louisiana	144	2.0%
10	Maine	186	2.5%
8	Maryland	188	2.5%
6	Massachusetts	200	2.7%
23	Michigan	148	2.0%
5	Minnesota	201	2.7%
14	Mississippi	174	2.4%
7	Missouri	197	2.7%
19	Montana	150	2.0%
50	Nebraska	49	0.7%
47	Nevada	63	0.9%
1	New Hampshire	424	5.7%
35	New Jersey	120	1.6%
38	New Mexico	112	1.5%
4	New York	213	2.9%
15	North Carolina	170	2.3%
26	North Dakota	141	1.9%
32	Ohio	132	1.8%
22	Oklahoma	149	2.0%
43	Oregon	90	1.2%
2	Pennsylvania	253	3.4%
37	Rhode Island	113	1.5%
15	South Carolina	170	2.3%
39	South Dakota	105	1.4%
32	Tennessee	132	1.8%
11	Texas	181	2.5%
41	Utah	104	1.4%
12	Vermont	180	2.4%
27	Virginia	140	1.9%
24	Washington	147	2.0%
31	West Virginia	134	1.8%
32	Wisconsin	132	1.8%
43	Wyoming	90	1.2%

RANK ORDER

RANK	STATE	LEGISLATORS	% of USA
1	New Hampshire	424	5.7%
2	Pennsylvania	253	3.4%
3	Georgia	236	3.2%
4	New York	213	2.9%
5	Minnesota	201	2.7%
6	Massachusetts	200	2.7%
7	Missouri	197	2.7%
8	Maryland	188	2.5%
9	Connecticut	187	2.5%
10	Maine	186	2.5%
11	Texas	181	2.5%
12	Vermont	180	2.4%
13	Illinois	177	2.4%
14	Mississippi	174	2.4%
15	North Carolina	170	2.3%
15	South Carolina	170	2.3%
17	Kansas	165	2.2%
18	Florida	160	2.2%
19	Indiana	150	2.0%
19	Iowa	150	2.0%
19	Montana	150	2.0%
22	Oklahoma	149	2.0%
23	Michigan	148	2.0%
24	Washington	147	2.0%
25	Louisiana	144	2.0%
26	North Dakota	141	1.9%
27	Alabama	140	1.9%
27	Virginia	140	1.9%
29	Kentucky	138	1.9%
30	Arkansas	135	1.8%
31	West Virginia	134	1.8%
32	Ohio	132	1.8%
32	Tennessee	132	1.8%
32	Wisconsin	132	1.8%
35	California	120	1.6%
35	New Jersey	120	1.6%
37	Rhode Island	113	1.5%
38	New Mexico	112	1.5%
39	Idaho	105	1.4%
39	South Dakota	105	1.4%
41	Utah	104	1.4%
42	Colorado	100	1.4%
43	Arizona	90	1.2%
43	Oregon	90	1.2%
43	Wyoming	90	1.2%
46	Hawaii	76	1.0%
47	Nevada	63	0.9%
48	Delaware	62	0.8%
49	Alaska	60	0.8%
50	Nebraska	49	0.7%
	District of Columbia**	NA	NA

Source: National Conference of State Legislatures (Denver, CO)
"2019 Partisan Composition" (www.ncsl.org/research/about-state-legislatures/partisan-composition.aspx)
*There are 1,972 state senators (including Nebraska's 49 unicameral seats) and 5,411 state house members.
**Not applicable.

Population per State Legislator in 2019

National Rate = 44,363 Population per Legislator*

ALPHA ORDER

RANK	STATE	RATE		RANK	STATE	RATE
22	Alabama	35,023		1	California	329,269
42	Alaska	12,192		2	Texas	160,198
6	Arizona	80,875		3	Florida	134,236
32	Arkansas	22,354		4	New York	91,331
1	California	329,269		5	Ohio	88,554
12	Colorado	57,587		6	Arizona	80,875
34	Connecticut	19,066		7	New Jersey	74,018
40	Delaware	15,706		8	Illinois	71,592
3	Florida	134,236		9	Michigan	67,479
18	Georgia	44,989		10	North Carolina	61,695
36	Hawaii	18,630		11	Virginia	60,968
39	Idaho	17,020		12	Colorado	57,587
8	Illinois	71,592		13	Washington	51,802
19	Indiana	44,881		14	Tennessee	51,736
33	Iowa	21,034		15	Pennsylvania	50,601
37	Kansas	17,656		16	Nevada	48,891
24	Kentucky	32,374		17	Oregon	46,864
25	Louisiana	32,283		18	Georgia	44,989
45	Maine	7,227		19	Indiana	44,881
26	Maryland	32,158		20	Wisconsin	44,109
23	Massachusetts	34,463		21	Nebraska	39,478
9	Michigan	67,479		22	Alabama	35,023
30	Minnesota	28,058		23	Massachusetts	34,463
38	Mississippi	17,104		24	Kentucky	32,374
27	Missouri	31,154		25	Louisiana	32,283
46	Montana	7,125		26	Maryland	32,158
21	Nebraska	39,478		27	Missouri	31,154
16	Nevada	48,891		28	Utah	30,827
50	New Hampshire	3,207		29	South Carolina	30,287
7	New Jersey	74,018		30	Minnesota	28,058
35	New Mexico	18,722		31	Oklahoma	26,557
4	New York	91,331		32	Arkansas	22,354
10	North Carolina	61,695		33	Iowa	21,034
48	North Dakota	5,405		34	Connecticut	19,066
5	Ohio	88,554		35	New Mexico	18,722
31	Oklahoma	26,557		36	Hawaii	18,630
17	Oregon	46,864		37	Kansas	17,656
15	Pennsylvania	50,601		38	Mississippi	17,104
43	Rhode Island	9,375		39	Idaho	17,020
29	South Carolina	30,287		40	Delaware	15,706
44	South Dakota	8,425		41	West Virginia	13,374
14	Tennessee	51,736		42	Alaska	12,192
2	Texas	160,198		43	Rhode Island	9,375
28	Utah	30,827		44	South Dakota	8,425
49	Vermont	3,467		45	Maine	7,227
11	Virginia	60,968		46	Montana	7,125
13	Washington	51,802		47	Wyoming	6,431
41	West Virginia	13,374		48	North Dakota	5,405
20	Wisconsin	44,109		49	Vermont	3,467
47	Wyoming	6,431		50	New Hampshire	3,207

RANK ORDER

District of Columbia**		NA

Source: CQ Press using data from National Conference of State Legislatures (Denver, CO)
    "2019 Partisan Composition" (www.ncsl.org/research/about-state-legislatures/partisan-composition.aspx)
*There are 1,972 state senators (including Nebraska's 49 unicameral seats) and 5,411 state house members. National rate does not include population for the District of Columbia. Calculated using 2019 population estimates.
**Not applicable.

Registered Voters in 2018

National Total = 153,066,000

ALPHA ORDER

RANK	STATE	REGISTERED	% of USA
23	Alabama	2,490,000	1.6%
49	Alaska	337,000	0.2%
16	Arizona	3,262,000	2.1%
35	Arkansas	1,262,000	0.8%
1	California	15,690,000	10.3%
22	Colorado	2,645,000	1.7%
29	Connecticut	1,726,000	1.1%
45	Delaware	472,000	0.3%
3	Florida	9,435,000	6.2%
10	Georgia	4,840,000	3.2%
44	Hawaii	523,000	0.3%
40	Idaho	743,000	0.5%
6	Illinois	6,068,000	4.0%
18	Indiana	3,131,000	2.0%
30	Iowa	1,658,000	1.1%
32	Kansas	1,449,000	0.9%
25	Kentucky	2,389,000	1.6%
27	Louisiana	2,263,000	1.5%
39	Maine	828,000	0.5%
20	Maryland	3,095,000	2.0%
14	Massachusetts	3,345,000	2.2%
8	Michigan	5,453,000	3.6%
21	Minnesota	3,000,000	2.0%
31	Mississippi	1,599,000	1.0%
15	Missouri	3,299,000	2.2%
42	Montana	579,000	0.4%
38	Nebraska	883,000	0.6%
34	Nevada	1,277,000	0.8%
41	New Hampshire	726,000	0.5%
11	New Jersey	4,297,000	2.8%
36	New Mexico	916,000	0.6%
4	New York	8,553,000	5.6%
9	North Carolina	5,160,000	3.4%
47	North Dakota	397,000	0.3%
7	Ohio	6,062,000	4.0%
28	Oklahoma	1,777,000	1.2%
26	Oregon	2,274,000	1.5%
5	Pennsylvania	6,469,000	4.2%
43	Rhode Island	532,000	0.3%
24	South Carolina	2,430,000	1.6%
46	South Dakota	429,000	0.3%
17	Tennessee	3,183,000	2.1%
2	Texas	11,634,000	7.6%
33	Utah	1,443,000	0.9%
48	Vermont	343,000	0.2%
12	Virginia	4,159,000	2.7%
13	Washington	3,852,000	2.5%
37	West Virginia	892,000	0.6%
19	Wisconsin	3,129,000	2.0%
50	Wyoming	268,000	0.2%

RANK ORDER

RANK	STATE	REGISTERED	% of USA
1	California	15,690,000	10.3%
2	Texas	11,634,000	7.6%
3	Florida	9,435,000	6.2%
4	New York	8,553,000	5.6%
5	Pennsylvania	6,469,000	4.2%
6	Illinois	6,068,000	4.0%
7	Ohio	6,062,000	4.0%
8	Michigan	5,453,000	3.6%
9	North Carolina	5,160,000	3.4%
10	Georgia	4,840,000	3.2%
11	New Jersey	4,297,000	2.8%
12	Virginia	4,159,000	2.7%
13	Washington	3,852,000	2.5%
14	Massachusetts	3,345,000	2.2%
15	Missouri	3,299,000	2.2%
16	Arizona	3,262,000	2.1%
17	Tennessee	3,183,000	2.1%
18	Indiana	3,131,000	2.0%
19	Wisconsin	3,129,000	2.0%
20	Maryland	3,095,000	2.0%
21	Minnesota	3,000,000	2.0%
22	Colorado	2,645,000	1.7%
23	Alabama	2,490,000	1.6%
24	South Carolina	2,430,000	1.6%
25	Kentucky	2,389,000	1.6%
26	Oregon	2,274,000	1.5%
27	Louisiana	2,263,000	1.5%
28	Oklahoma	1,777,000	1.2%
29	Connecticut	1,726,000	1.1%
30	Iowa	1,658,000	1.1%
31	Mississippi	1,599,000	1.0%
32	Kansas	1,449,000	0.9%
33	Utah	1,443,000	0.9%
34	Nevada	1,277,000	0.8%
35	Arkansas	1,262,000	0.8%
36	New Mexico	916,000	0.6%
37	West Virginia	892,000	0.6%
38	Nebraska	883,000	0.6%
39	Maine	828,000	0.5%
40	Idaho	743,000	0.5%
41	New Hampshire	726,000	0.5%
42	Montana	579,000	0.4%
43	Rhode Island	532,000	0.3%
44	Hawaii	523,000	0.3%
45	Delaware	472,000	0.3%
46	South Dakota	429,000	0.3%
47	North Dakota	397,000	0.3%
48	Vermont	343,000	0.2%
49	Alaska	337,000	0.2%
50	Wyoming	268,000	0.2%
	District of Columbia	397,000	0.3%

Source: U.S. Bureau of the Census
"Voting and Registration" (Table 4a, https://www.census.gov/topics/public-sector/voting.html)

Percent of Eligible Voters Reported Registered in 2018

National Percent = 66.9%*

ALPHA ORDER				RANK ORDER		
RANK	STATE	PERCENT		RANK	STATE	PERCENT
19	Alabama	69.0		1	Maine	78.4
30	Alaska	67.7		2	Minnesota	74.9
21	Arizona	68.6		3	Iowa	74.0
49	Arkansas	58.5		4	Washington	73.7
47	California	61.5		5	Kentucky	73.5
35	Colorado	65.6		6	Michigan	73.4
25	Connecticut	68.0		6	Mississippi	73.4
32	Delaware	66.3		6	North Dakota	73.4
43	Florida	62.7		9	Wisconsin	72.8
34	Georgia	66.2		10	Oregon	72.5
50	Hawaii	53.9		11	Maryland	72.3
48	Idaho	60.6		11	Missouri	72.3
29	Illinois	67.8		13	Virginia	72.0
36	Indiana	65.3		14	Kansas	71.5
3	Iowa	74.0		15	Montana	71.3
14	Kansas	71.5		16	New Hampshire	70.8
5	Kentucky	73.5		17	Ohio	70.2
25	Louisiana	68.0		18	North Carolina	69.3
1	Maine	78.4		19	Alabama	69.0
11	Maryland	72.3		19	Vermont	69.0
25	Massachusetts	68.0		21	Arizona	68.6
6	Michigan	73.4		21	New Jersey	68.6
2	Minnesota	74.9		23	Utah	68.4
6	Mississippi	73.4		24	Pennsylvania	68.3
11	Missouri	72.3		25	Connecticut	68.0
15	Montana	71.3		25	Louisiana	68.0
32	Nebraska	66.3		25	Massachusetts	68.0
45	Nevada	61.8		25	Rhode Island	68.0
16	New Hampshire	70.8		29	Illinois	67.8
21	New Jersey	68.6		30	Alaska	67.7
46	New Mexico	61.7		31	South Dakota	67.3
44	New York	62.5		32	Delaware	66.3
18	North Carolina	69.3		32	Nebraska	66.3
6	North Dakota	73.4		34	Georgia	66.2
17	Ohio	70.2		35	Colorado	65.6
37	Oklahoma	65.1		36	Indiana	65.3
10	Oregon	72.5		37	Oklahoma	65.1
24	Pennsylvania	68.3		38	South Carolina	64.5
25	Rhode Island	68.0		38	West Virginia	64.5
38	South Carolina	64.5		40	Tennessee	63.5
31	South Dakota	67.3		40	Wyoming	63.5
40	Tennessee	63.5		42	Texas	63.3
42	Texas	63.3		43	Florida	62.7
23	Utah	68.4		44	New York	62.5
19	Vermont	69.0		45	Nevada	61.8
13	Virginia	72.0		46	New Mexico	61.7
4	Washington	73.7		47	California	61.5
38	West Virginia	64.5		48	Idaho	60.6
9	Wisconsin	72.8		49	Arkansas	58.5
40	Wyoming	63.5		50	Hawaii	53.9
				District of Columbia		77.6

Source: U.S. Bureau of the Census
    "Voting and Registration" (Table 4a, https://www.census.gov/topics/public-sector/voting.html)
*As a percent of citizen population eighteen and older.

Persons Voting in 2018

National Total = 122,281,000

RANK	STATE	VOTERS	% of USA
25	Alabama	1,830,000	1.5%
49	Alaska	263,000	0.2%
14	Arizona	2,800,000	2.3%
35	Arkansas	919,000	0.8%
1	California	13,240,000	10.8%
21	Colorado	2,342,000	1.9%
28	Connecticut	1,370,000	1.1%
45	Delaware	369,000	0.3%
3	Florida	7,918,000	6.5%
9	Georgia	4,084,000	3.3%
43	Hawaii	427,000	0.3%
40	Idaho	587,000	0.5%
6	Illinois	4,740,000	3.9%
20	Indiana	2,364,000	1.9%
30	Iowa	1,335,000	1.1%
33	Kansas	1,152,000	0.9%
26	Kentucky	1,746,000	1.4%
27	Louisiana	1,656,000	1.4%
37	Maine	693,000	0.6%
22	Maryland	2,320,000	1.9%
16	Massachusetts	2,731,000	2.2%
8	Michigan	4,418,000	3.6%
17	Minnesota	2,523,000	2.1%
32	Mississippi	1,180,000	1.0%
18	Missouri	2,509,000	2.1%
42	Montana	518,000	0.4%
38	Nebraska	676,000	0.6%
34	Nevada	1,006,000	0.8%
41	New Hampshire	576,000	0.5%
11	New Jersey	3,384,000	2.8%
36	New Mexico	715,000	0.6%
4	New York	6,775,000	5.5%
10	North Carolina	3,899,000	3.2%
46	North Dakota	335,000	0.3%
7	Ohio	4,538,000	3.7%
29	Oklahoma	1,350,000	1.1%
23	Oregon	1,918,000	1.6%
5	Pennsylvania	5,173,000	4.2%
44	Rhode Island	403,000	0.3%
24	South Carolina	1,836,000	1.5%
47	South Dakota	331,000	0.3%
19	Tennessee	2,487,000	2.0%
2	Texas	8,886,000	7.3%
31	Utah	1,214,000	1.0%
48	Vermont	273,000	0.2%
12	Virginia	3,319,000	2.7%
13	Washington	3,234,000	2.6%
39	West Virginia	610,000	0.5%
15	Wisconsin	2,776,000	2.3%
50	Wyoming	220,000	0.2%

RANK	STATE	VOTERS	% of USA
1	California	13,240,000	10.8%
2	Texas	8,886,000	7.3%
3	Florida	7,918,000	6.5%
4	New York	6,775,000	5.5%
5	Pennsylvania	5,173,000	4.2%
6	Illinois	4,740,000	3.9%
7	Ohio	4,538,000	3.7%
8	Michigan	4,418,000	3.6%
9	Georgia	4,084,000	3.3%
10	North Carolina	3,899,000	3.2%
11	New Jersey	3,384,000	2.8%
12	Virginia	3,319,000	2.7%
13	Washington	3,234,000	2.6%
14	Arizona	2,800,000	2.3%
15	Wisconsin	2,776,000	2.3%
16	Massachusetts	2,731,000	2.2%
17	Minnesota	2,523,000	2.1%
18	Missouri	2,509,000	2.1%
19	Tennessee	2,487,000	2.0%
20	Indiana	2,364,000	1.9%
21	Colorado	2,342,000	1.9%
22	Maryland	2,320,000	1.9%
23	Oregon	1,918,000	1.6%
24	South Carolina	1,836,000	1.5%
25	Alabama	1,830,000	1.5%
26	Kentucky	1,746,000	1.4%
27	Louisiana	1,656,000	1.4%
28	Connecticut	1,370,000	1.1%
29	Oklahoma	1,350,000	1.1%
30	Iowa	1,335,000	1.1%
31	Utah	1,214,000	1.0%
32	Mississippi	1,180,000	1.0%
33	Kansas	1,152,000	0.9%
34	Nevada	1,006,000	0.8%
35	Arkansas	919,000	0.8%
36	New Mexico	715,000	0.6%
37	Maine	693,000	0.6%
38	Nebraska	676,000	0.6%
39	West Virginia	610,000	0.5%
40	Idaho	587,000	0.5%
41	New Hampshire	576,000	0.5%
42	Montana	518,000	0.4%
43	Hawaii	427,000	0.3%
44	Rhode Island	403,000	0.3%
45	Delaware	369,000	0.3%
46	North Dakota	335,000	0.3%
47	South Dakota	331,000	0.3%
48	Vermont	273,000	0.2%
49	Alaska	263,000	0.2%
50	Wyoming	220,000	0.2%
	District of Columbia	313,000	0.3%

Source: U.S. Bureau of the Census
"Voting and Registration" (Table 4a, https://www.census.gov/topics/public-sector/voting.html)

Percent of Eligible Population Reported Voting in 2018

National Percent = 53.4%*

ALPHA ORDER			RANK ORDER		
RANK	STATE	PERCENT	RANK	STATE	PERCENT
37	Alabama	50.7	1	Maine	65.6
27	Alaska	52.8	2	Wisconsin	64.6
10	Arizona	58.9	3	Montana	63.8
50	Arkansas	42.6	4	Minnesota	63.0
32	California	51.9	5	North Dakota	61.9
11	Colorado	58.1	5	Washington	61.9
23	Connecticut	54.0	7	Oregon	61.1
34	Delaware	51.8	8	Iowa	59.6
28	Florida	52.6	9	Michigan	59.5
16	Georgia	55.9	10	Arizona	58.9
49	Hawaii	44.0	11	Colorado	58.1
47	Idaho	47.9	12	Utah	57.6
26	Illinois	53.0	13	Virginia	57.5
42	Indiana	49.3	14	Kansas	56.9
8	Iowa	59.6	15	New Hampshire	56.2
14	Kansas	56.9	16	Georgia	55.9
25	Kentucky	53.8	17	Massachusetts	55.5
38	Louisiana	49.8	18	Missouri	55.0
1	Maine	65.6	19	Vermont	54.9
21	Maryland	54.2	20	Pennsylvania	54.6
17	Massachusetts	55.5	21	Maryland	54.2
9	Michigan	59.5	21	Mississippi	54.2
4	Minnesota	63.0	23	Connecticut	54.0
21	Mississippi	54.2	23	New Jersey	54.0
18	Missouri	55.0	25	Kentucky	53.8
3	Montana	63.8	26	Illinois	53.0
36	Nebraska	50.8	27	Alaska	52.8
43	Nevada	48.7	28	Florida	52.6
15	New Hampshire	56.2	29	Ohio	52.5
23	New Jersey	54.0	30	North Carolina	52.4
46	New Mexico	48.1	31	Wyoming	52.1
40	New York	49.5	32	California	51.9
30	North Carolina	52.4	32	South Dakota	51.9
5	North Dakota	61.9	34	Delaware	51.8
29	Ohio	52.5	35	Rhode Island	51.6
41	Oklahoma	49.4	36	Nebraska	50.8
7	Oregon	61.1	37	Alabama	50.7
20	Pennsylvania	54.6	38	Louisiana	49.8
35	Rhode Island	51.6	39	Tennessee	49.6
43	South Carolina	48.7	40	New York	49.5
32	South Dakota	51.9	41	Oklahoma	49.4
39	Tennessee	49.6	42	Indiana	49.3
45	Texas	48.4	43	Nevada	48.7
12	Utah	57.6	43	South Carolina	48.7
19	Vermont	54.9	45	Texas	48.4
13	Virginia	57.5	46	New Mexico	48.1
5	Washington	61.9	47	Idaho	47.9
48	West Virginia	44.1	48	West Virginia	44.1
2	Wisconsin	64.6	49	Hawaii	44.0
31	Wyoming	52.1	50	Arkansas	42.6
				District of Columbia	61.1

Source: U.S. Bureau of the Census
    "Voting and Registration" (Table 4a, https://www.census.gov/topics/public-sector/voting.html)
*As a percent of citizen population eighteen and older.

Percent of Registered Population Reported Voting in 2018

National Percent = 79.9%*

ALPHA ORDER

RANK	STATE	PERCENT
46	Alabama	73.5
33	Alaska	78.0
4	Arizona	85.8
49	Arkansas	72.8
5	California	84.4
3	Colorado	88.5
23	Connecticut	79.4
29	Delaware	78.2
12	Florida	83.9
5	Georgia	84.4
15	Hawaii	81.6
26	Idaho	79.0
30	Illinois	78.1
42	Indiana	75.5
18	Iowa	80.5
22	Kansas	79.5
48	Kentucky	73.1
47	Louisiana	73.2
13	Maine	83.7
43	Maryland	75.0
15	Massachusetts	81.6
17	Michigan	81.0
9	Minnesota	84.1
45	Mississippi	73.8
37	Missouri	76.1
1	Montana	89.5
35	Nebraska	76.6
27	Nevada	78.8
24	New Hampshire	79.3
27	New Jersey	78.8
30	New Mexico	78.1
25	New York	79.2
40	North Carolina	75.6
5	North Dakota	84.4
44	Ohio	74.9
38	Oklahoma	76.0
8	Oregon	84.3
19	Pennsylvania	80.0
39	Rhode Island	75.8
40	South Carolina	75.6
34	South Dakota	77.2
30	Tennessee	78.1
36	Texas	76.4
9	Utah	84.1
21	Vermont	79.6
20	Virginia	79.8
11	Washington	84.0
50	West Virginia	68.4
2	Wisconsin	88.7
14	Wyoming	82.1

RANK ORDER

RANK	STATE	PERCENT
1	Montana	89.5
2	Wisconsin	88.7
3	Colorado	88.5
4	Arizona	85.8
5	California	84.4
5	Georgia	84.4
5	North Dakota	84.4
8	Oregon	84.3
9	Minnesota	84.1
9	Utah	84.1
11	Washington	84.0
12	Florida	83.9
13	Maine	83.7
14	Wyoming	82.1
15	Hawaii	81.6
15	Massachusetts	81.6
17	Michigan	81.0
18	Iowa	80.5
19	Pennsylvania	80.0
20	Virginia	79.8
21	Vermont	79.6
22	Kansas	79.5
23	Connecticut	79.4
24	New Hampshire	79.3
25	New York	79.2
26	Idaho	79.0
27	Nevada	78.8
27	New Jersey	78.8
29	Delaware	78.2
30	Illinois	78.1
30	New Mexico	78.1
30	Tennessee	78.1
33	Alaska	78.0
34	South Dakota	77.2
35	Nebraska	76.6
36	Texas	76.4
37	Missouri	76.1
38	Oklahoma	76.0
39	Rhode Island	75.8
40	North Carolina	75.6
40	South Carolina	75.6
42	Indiana	75.5
43	Maryland	75.0
44	Ohio	74.9
45	Mississippi	73.8
46	Alabama	73.5
47	Louisiana	73.2
48	Kentucky	73.1
49	Arkansas	72.8
50	West Virginia	68.4

District of Columbia — 78.8

Source: CQ Press using data from U.S. Bureau of the Census
"Voting and Registration" (Table 4a, https://www.census.gov/topics/public-sector/voting.html)
*As a percent of citizen population eighteen and older registered to vote.

XIV. Social Welfare

Poverty Rate in 2018

National Rate = 13.1% of Population in Poverty*

ALPHA ORDER

RANK	STATE	PERCENT		RANK	STATE	PERCENT
7	Alabama	16.8		1	Mississippi	19.7
38	Alaska	10.9		2	New Mexico	19.5
14	Arizona	14.0		3	Louisiana	18.6
5	Arkansas	17.2		4	West Virginia	17.8
25	California	12.8		5	Arkansas	17.2
44	Colorado	9.6		6	Kentucky	16.9
41	Connecticut	10.4		7	Alabama	16.8
27	Delaware	12.5		8	Oklahoma	15.6
17	Florida	13.6		9	South Carolina	15.3
12	Georgia	14.3		9	Tennessee	15.3
49	Hawaii	8.8		11	Texas	14.9
31	Idaho	11.8		12	Georgia	14.3
29	Illinois	12.1		13	Michigan	14.1
20	Indiana	13.1		14	Arizona	14.0
33	Iowa	11.2		14	North Carolina	14.0
30	Kansas	12.0		16	Ohio	13.9
6	Kentucky	16.9		17	Florida	13.6
3	Louisiana	18.6		17	New York	13.6
32	Maine	11.6		19	Missouri	13.2
47	Maryland	9.0		20	Indiana	13.1
43	Massachusetts	10.0		20	South Dakota	13.1
13	Michigan	14.1		22	Montana	13.0
44	Minnesota	9.6		23	Nevada	12.9
1	Mississippi	19.7		23	Rhode Island	12.9
19	Missouri	13.2		25	California	12.8
22	Montana	13.0		26	Oregon	12.6
35	Nebraska	11.0		27	Delaware	12.5
23	Nevada	12.9		28	Pennsylvania	12.2
50	New Hampshire	7.6		29	Illinois	12.1
46	New Jersey	9.5		30	Kansas	12.0
2	New Mexico	19.5		31	Idaho	11.8
17	New York	13.6		32	Maine	11.6
14	North Carolina	14.0		33	Iowa	11.2
39	North Dakota	10.7		34	Wyoming	11.1
16	Ohio	13.9		35	Nebraska	11.0
8	Oklahoma	15.6		35	Vermont	11.0
26	Oregon	12.6		35	Wisconsin	11.0
28	Pennsylvania	12.2		38	Alaska	10.9
23	Rhode Island	12.9		39	North Dakota	10.7
9	South Carolina	15.3		39	Virginia	10.7
20	South Dakota	13.1		41	Connecticut	10.4
9	Tennessee	15.3		42	Washington	10.3
11	Texas	14.9		43	Massachusetts	10.0
47	Utah	9.0		44	Colorado	9.6
35	Vermont	11.0		44	Minnesota	9.6
39	Virginia	10.7		46	New Jersey	9.5
42	Washington	10.3		47	Maryland	9.0
4	West Virginia	17.8		47	Utah	9.0
35	Wisconsin	11.0		49	Hawaii	8.8
34	Wyoming	11.1		50	New Hampshire	7.6
					District of Columbia	16.2

Source: U.S. Bureau of the Census
   "2018 American Community Survey-Table DP03" (https://data.census.gov/cedsci/)
*This is a one-year figure. Census has discontinued three-year averages that had been used previously. The poverty threshold
for a family of four (two children) in 2018 was $25,100.

Percent of Senior Citizens Living in Poverty in 2018

National Percent = 9.4%*

ALPHA ORDER

RANK	STATE	PERCENT
9	Alabama	10.3
46	Alaska	6.7
27	Arizona	8.6
11	Arkansas	10.2
8	California	10.5
41	Colorado	7.4
35	Connecticut	7.9
48	Delaware	6.1
7	Florida	10.6
11	Georgia	10.2
47	Hawaii	6.5
27	Idaho	8.6
24	Illinois	8.8
35	Indiana	7.9
45	Iowa	7.1
33	Kansas	8.0
11	Kentucky	10.2
2	Louisiana	12.4
20	Maine	9.1
42	Maryland	7.3
20	Massachusetts	9.1
22	Michigan	9.0
39	Minnesota	7.6
2	Mississippi	12.4
32	Missouri	8.2
17	Montana	9.4
39	Nebraska	7.6
15	Nevada	9.8
50	New Hampshire	5.5
33	New Jersey	8.0
1	New Mexico	13.3
4	New York	11.8
25	North Carolina	8.7
9	North Dakota	10.3
27	Ohio	8.6
25	Oklahoma	8.7
35	Oregon	7.9
31	Pennsylvania	8.3
5	Rhode Island	11.2
16	South Carolina	9.5
22	South Dakota	9.0
19	Tennessee	9.2
6	Texas	11.1
48	Utah	6.1
18	Vermont	9.3
30	Virginia	8.4
44	Washington	7.2
14	West Virginia	10.0
35	Wisconsin	7.9
42	Wyoming	7.3

RANK ORDER

RANK	STATE	PERCENT
1	New Mexico	13.3
2	Louisiana	12.4
2	Mississippi	12.4
4	New York	11.8
5	Rhode Island	11.2
6	Texas	11.1
7	Florida	10.6
8	California	10.5
9	Alabama	10.3
9	North Dakota	10.3
11	Arkansas	10.2
11	Georgia	10.2
11	Kentucky	10.2
14	West Virginia	10.0
15	Nevada	9.8
16	South Carolina	9.5
17	Montana	9.4
18	Vermont	9.3
19	Tennessee	9.2
20	Maine	9.1
20	Massachusetts	9.1
22	Michigan	9.0
22	South Dakota	9.0
24	Illinois	8.8
25	North Carolina	8.7
25	Oklahoma	8.7
27	Arizona	8.6
27	Idaho	8.6
27	Ohio	8.6
30	Virginia	8.4
31	Pennsylvania	8.3
32	Missouri	8.2
33	Kansas	8.0
33	New Jersey	8.0
35	Connecticut	7.9
35	Indiana	7.9
35	Oregon	7.9
35	Wisconsin	7.9
39	Minnesota	7.6
39	Nebraska	7.6
41	Colorado	7.4
42	Maryland	7.3
42	Wyoming	7.3
44	Washington	7.2
45	Iowa	7.1
46	Alaska	6.7
47	Hawaii	6.5
48	Delaware	6.1
48	Utah	6.1
50	New Hampshire	5.5
	District of Columbia	16.7

Source: U.S. Bureau of the Census
"2018 American Community Survey-Table DP03" (https://data.census.gov/cedsci/)
*People sixty-five years and older living with incomes below the poverty level.

Percent of Children Living in Poverty in 2018

National Percent = 17.7%*

<table>
<thead>
<tr><th colspan="3">ALPHA ORDER</th><th colspan="3">RANK ORDER</th></tr>
<tr><th>RANK</th><th>STATE</th><th>PERCENT</th><th>RANK</th><th>STATE</th><th>PERCENT</th></tr>
</thead>
<tbody>
<tr><td>6</td><td>Alabama</td><td>23.6</td><td>1</td><td>Mississippi</td><td>27.6</td></tr>
<tr><td>36</td><td>Alaska</td><td>13.5</td><td>2</td><td>Louisiana</td><td>26.0</td></tr>
<tr><td>13</td><td>Arizona</td><td>19.8</td><td>3</td><td>New Mexico</td><td>25.8</td></tr>
<tr><td>4</td><td>Arkansas</td><td>24.4</td><td>4</td><td>Arkansas</td><td>24.4</td></tr>
<tr><td>24</td><td>California</td><td>17.1</td><td>5</td><td>West Virginia</td><td>24.0</td></tr>
<tr><td>44</td><td>Colorado</td><td>11.5</td><td>6</td><td>Alabama</td><td>23.6</td></tr>
<tr><td>33</td><td>Connecticut</td><td>13.7</td><td>7</td><td>Kentucky</td><td>22.7</td></tr>
<tr><td>18</td><td>Delaware</td><td>18.5</td><td>8</td><td>South Carolina</td><td>22.4</td></tr>
<tr><td>15</td><td>Florida</td><td>19.3</td><td>9</td><td>Tennessee</td><td>22.1</td></tr>
<tr><td>12</td><td>Georgia</td><td>20.2</td><td>10</td><td>Oklahoma</td><td>21.3</td></tr>
<tr><td>43</td><td>Hawaii</td><td>11.6</td><td>11</td><td>Texas</td><td>20.9</td></tr>
<tr><td>31</td><td>Idaho</td><td>14.0</td><td>12</td><td>Georgia</td><td>20.2</td></tr>
<tr><td>27</td><td>Illinois</td><td>15.9</td><td>13</td><td>Arizona</td><td>19.8</td></tr>
<tr><td>21</td><td>Indiana</td><td>17.5</td><td>14</td><td>North Carolina</td><td>19.7</td></tr>
<tr><td>39</td><td>Iowa</td><td>13.1</td><td>15</td><td>Florida</td><td>19.3</td></tr>
<tr><td>30</td><td>Kansas</td><td>14.5</td><td>16</td><td>Ohio</td><td>19.2</td></tr>
<tr><td>7</td><td>Kentucky</td><td>22.7</td><td>17</td><td>Michigan</td><td>19.1</td></tr>
<tr><td>2</td><td>Louisiana</td><td>26.0</td><td>18</td><td>Delaware</td><td>18.5</td></tr>
<tr><td>32</td><td>Maine</td><td>13.8</td><td>19</td><td>New York</td><td>18.2</td></tr>
<tr><td>46</td><td>Maryland</td><td>11.2</td><td>20</td><td>Missouri</td><td>17.9</td></tr>
<tr><td>42</td><td>Massachusetts</td><td>11.8</td><td>21</td><td>Indiana</td><td>17.5</td></tr>
<tr><td>17</td><td>Michigan</td><td>19.1</td><td>21</td><td>Rhode Island</td><td>17.5</td></tr>
<tr><td>45</td><td>Minnesota</td><td>11.3</td><td>23</td><td>Nevada</td><td>17.3</td></tr>
<tr><td>1</td><td>Mississippi</td><td>27.6</td><td>24</td><td>California</td><td>17.1</td></tr>
<tr><td>20</td><td>Missouri</td><td>17.9</td><td>25</td><td>Pennsylvania</td><td>16.4</td></tr>
<tr><td>28</td><td>Montana</td><td>15.2</td><td>26</td><td>South Dakota</td><td>16.0</td></tr>
<tr><td>40</td><td>Nebraska</td><td>12.4</td><td>27</td><td>Illinois</td><td>15.9</td></tr>
<tr><td>23</td><td>Nevada</td><td>17.3</td><td>28</td><td>Montana</td><td>15.2</td></tr>
<tr><td>48</td><td>New Hampshire</td><td>10.2</td><td>29</td><td>Oregon</td><td>15.1</td></tr>
<tr><td>36</td><td>New Jersey</td><td>13.5</td><td>30</td><td>Kansas</td><td>14.5</td></tr>
<tr><td>3</td><td>New Mexico</td><td>25.8</td><td>31</td><td>Idaho</td><td>14.0</td></tr>
<tr><td>19</td><td>New York</td><td>18.2</td><td>32</td><td>Maine</td><td>13.8</td></tr>
<tr><td>14</td><td>North Carolina</td><td>19.7</td><td>33</td><td>Connecticut</td><td>13.7</td></tr>
<tr><td>49</td><td>North Dakota</td><td>9.7</td><td>34</td><td>Wisconsin</td><td>13.6</td></tr>
<tr><td>16</td><td>Ohio</td><td>19.2</td><td>34</td><td>Wyoming</td><td>13.6</td></tr>
<tr><td>10</td><td>Oklahoma</td><td>21.3</td><td>36</td><td>Alaska</td><td>13.5</td></tr>
<tr><td>29</td><td>Oregon</td><td>15.1</td><td>36</td><td>New Jersey</td><td>13.5</td></tr>
<tr><td>25</td><td>Pennsylvania</td><td>16.4</td><td>38</td><td>Virginia</td><td>13.3</td></tr>
<tr><td>21</td><td>Rhode Island</td><td>17.5</td><td>39</td><td>Iowa</td><td>13.1</td></tr>
<tr><td>8</td><td>South Carolina</td><td>22.4</td><td>40</td><td>Nebraska</td><td>12.4</td></tr>
<tr><td>26</td><td>South Dakota</td><td>16.0</td><td>41</td><td>Washington</td><td>12.1</td></tr>
<tr><td>9</td><td>Tennessee</td><td>22.1</td><td>42</td><td>Massachusetts</td><td>11.8</td></tr>
<tr><td>11</td><td>Texas</td><td>20.9</td><td>43</td><td>Hawaii</td><td>11.6</td></tr>
<tr><td>50</td><td>Utah</td><td>9.3</td><td>44</td><td>Colorado</td><td>11.5</td></tr>
<tr><td>47</td><td>Vermont</td><td>11.1</td><td>45</td><td>Minnesota</td><td>11.3</td></tr>
<tr><td>38</td><td>Virginia</td><td>13.3</td><td>46</td><td>Maryland</td><td>11.2</td></tr>
<tr><td>41</td><td>Washington</td><td>12.1</td><td>47</td><td>Vermont</td><td>11.1</td></tr>
<tr><td>5</td><td>West Virginia</td><td>24.0</td><td>48</td><td>New Hampshire</td><td>10.2</td></tr>
<tr><td>34</td><td>Wisconsin</td><td>13.6</td><td>49</td><td>North Dakota</td><td>9.7</td></tr>
<tr><td>34</td><td>Wyoming</td><td>13.6</td><td>50</td><td>Utah</td><td>9.3</td></tr>
<tr><td></td><td></td><td></td><td></td><td>District of Columbia</td><td>22.9</td></tr>
</tbody>
</table>

Source: U.S. Bureau of the Census
   "2018 American Community Survey-Table DP03" (https://data.census.gov/cedsci/)
*Children seventeen and under living in families with incomes below the poverty level.

Percent of Families Living in Poverty in 2018

National Percent = 9.3%*

ALPHA ORDER				RANK ORDER		
RANK	STATE	PERCENT		RANK	STATE	PERCENT
7	Alabama	12.2		1	New Mexico	15.1
32	Alaska	7.5		2	Mississippi	15.0
15	Arizona	9.9		3	Louisiana	13.6
5	Arkansas	12.7		4	West Virginia	13.0
20	California	9.1		5	Arkansas	12.7
43	Colorado	6.2		6	Kentucky	12.6
35	Connecticut	7.1		7	Alabama	12.2
25	Delaware	8.4		8	Oklahoma	11.4
16	Florida	9.7		8	Texas	11.4
11	Georgia	10.8		10	Tennessee	11.3
47	Hawaii	5.7		11	Georgia	10.8
26	Idaho	8.2		11	South Carolina	10.8
24	Illinois	8.5		13	North Carolina	10.2
19	Indiana	9.3		14	New York	10.0
34	Iowa	7.2		15	Arizona	9.9
28	Kansas	8.0		16	Florida	9.7
6	Kentucky	12.6		16	Ohio	9.7
3	Louisiana	13.6		18	Michigan	9.5
33	Maine	7.3		19	Indiana	9.3
46	Maryland	6.0		20	California	9.1
41	Massachusetts	6.5		20	Nevada	9.1
18	Michigan	9.5		20	Rhode Island	9.1
47	Minnesota	5.7		23	Missouri	9.0
2	Mississippi	15.0		24	Illinois	8.5
23	Missouri	9.0		25	Delaware	8.4
31	Montana	7.7		26	Idaho	8.2
35	Nebraska	7.1		27	Pennsylvania	8.1
20	Nevada	9.1		28	Kansas	8.0
50	New Hampshire	4.7		28	Oregon	8.0
40	New Jersey	6.9		28	South Dakota	8.0
1	New Mexico	15.1		31	Montana	7.7
14	New York	10.0		32	Alaska	7.5
13	North Carolina	10.2		33	Maine	7.3
47	North Dakota	5.7		34	Iowa	7.2
16	Ohio	9.7		35	Connecticut	7.1
8	Oklahoma	11.4		35	Nebraska	7.1
28	Oregon	8.0		35	Virginia	7.1
27	Pennsylvania	8.1		35	Wyoming	7.1
20	Rhode Island	9.1		39	Wisconsin	7.0
11	South Carolina	10.8		40	New Jersey	6.9
28	South Dakota	8.0		41	Massachusetts	6.5
10	Tennessee	11.3		42	Washington	6.3
8	Texas	11.4		43	Colorado	6.2
45	Utah	6.1		43	Vermont	6.2
43	Vermont	6.2		45	Utah	6.1
35	Virginia	7.1		46	Maryland	6.0
42	Washington	6.3		47	Hawaii	5.7
4	West Virginia	13.0		47	Minnesota	5.7
39	Wisconsin	7.0		47	North Dakota	5.7
35	Wyoming	7.1		50	New Hampshire	4.7
					District of Columbia	11.3

Source: U.S. Bureau of the Census
"2018 American Community Survey-Table DP03" (https://data.census.gov/cedsci/)
*Families living with incomes below the poverty level.

Percent of Female-Headed Families with Children Living in Poverty in 2018

National Percent = 35.1%*

<table>
<tr><td colspan="3">ALPHA ORDER</td><td colspan="3">RANK ORDER</td></tr>
<tr><th>RANK</th><th>STATE</th><th>PERCENT</th><th>RANK</th><th>STATE</th><th>PERCENT</th></tr>
<tr><td>2</td><td>Alabama</td><td>46.9</td><td>1</td><td>Mississippi</td><td>49.4</td></tr>
<tr><td>48</td><td>Alaska</td><td>26.5</td><td>2</td><td>Alabama</td><td>46.9</td></tr>
<tr><td>27</td><td>Arizona</td><td>33.4</td><td>3</td><td>Kentucky</td><td>45.5</td></tr>
<tr><td>6</td><td>Arkansas</td><td>44.1</td><td>4</td><td>New Mexico</td><td>45.0</td></tr>
<tr><td>33</td><td>California</td><td>31.9</td><td>5</td><td>Louisiana</td><td>44.7</td></tr>
<tr><td>45</td><td>Colorado</td><td>28.3</td><td>6</td><td>Arkansas</td><td>44.1</td></tr>
<tr><td>42</td><td>Connecticut</td><td>29.2</td><td>7</td><td>West Virginia</td><td>43.7</td></tr>
<tr><td>26</td><td>Delaware</td><td>33.5</td><td>8</td><td>Tennessee</td><td>41.7</td></tr>
<tr><td>30</td><td>Florida</td><td>32.8</td><td>9</td><td>Oklahoma</td><td>41.3</td></tr>
<tr><td>17</td><td>Georgia</td><td>35.8</td><td>10</td><td>South Carolina</td><td>40.4</td></tr>
<tr><td>46</td><td>Hawaii</td><td>27.7</td><td>11</td><td>Ohio</td><td>40.1</td></tr>
<tr><td>18</td><td>Idaho</td><td>35.6</td><td>12</td><td>North Carolina</td><td>37.5</td></tr>
<tr><td>23</td><td>Illinois</td><td>34.1</td><td>13</td><td>Michigan</td><td>37.1</td></tr>
<tr><td>16</td><td>Indiana</td><td>36.5</td><td>14</td><td>Texas</td><td>37.0</td></tr>
<tr><td>24</td><td>Iowa</td><td>33.9</td><td>15</td><td>South Dakota</td><td>36.7</td></tr>
<tr><td>25</td><td>Kansas</td><td>33.6</td><td>16</td><td>Indiana</td><td>36.5</td></tr>
<tr><td>3</td><td>Kentucky</td><td>45.5</td><td>17</td><td>Georgia</td><td>35.8</td></tr>
<tr><td>5</td><td>Louisiana</td><td>44.7</td><td>18</td><td>Idaho</td><td>35.6</td></tr>
<tr><td>19</td><td>Maine</td><td>35.5</td><td>19</td><td>Maine</td><td>35.5</td></tr>
<tr><td>50</td><td>Maryland</td><td>24.3</td><td>20</td><td>Montana</td><td>35.3</td></tr>
<tr><td>44</td><td>Massachusetts</td><td>28.9</td><td>21</td><td>Missouri</td><td>34.9</td></tr>
<tr><td>13</td><td>Michigan</td><td>37.1</td><td>22</td><td>Pennsylvania</td><td>34.6</td></tr>
<tr><td>46</td><td>Minnesota</td><td>27.7</td><td>23</td><td>Illinois</td><td>34.1</td></tr>
<tr><td>1</td><td>Mississippi</td><td>49.4</td><td>24</td><td>Iowa</td><td>33.9</td></tr>
<tr><td>21</td><td>Missouri</td><td>34.9</td><td>25</td><td>Kansas</td><td>33.6</td></tr>
<tr><td>20</td><td>Montana</td><td>35.3</td><td>26</td><td>Delaware</td><td>33.5</td></tr>
<tr><td>38</td><td>Nebraska</td><td>31.2</td><td>27</td><td>Arizona</td><td>33.4</td></tr>
<tr><td>40</td><td>Nevada</td><td>29.8</td><td>27</td><td>Wyoming</td><td>33.4</td></tr>
<tr><td>41</td><td>New Hampshire</td><td>29.5</td><td>29</td><td>New York</td><td>33.2</td></tr>
<tr><td>37</td><td>New Jersey</td><td>31.3</td><td>30</td><td>Florida</td><td>32.8</td></tr>
<tr><td>4</td><td>New Mexico</td><td>45.0</td><td>31</td><td>Rhode Island</td><td>32.6</td></tr>
<tr><td>29</td><td>New York</td><td>33.2</td><td>32</td><td>Oregon</td><td>32.5</td></tr>
<tr><td>12</td><td>North Carolina</td><td>37.5</td><td>33</td><td>California</td><td>31.9</td></tr>
<tr><td>49</td><td>North Dakota</td><td>26.4</td><td>34</td><td>Virginia</td><td>31.8</td></tr>
<tr><td>11</td><td>Ohio</td><td>40.1</td><td>34</td><td>Wisconsin</td><td>31.8</td></tr>
<tr><td>9</td><td>Oklahoma</td><td>41.3</td><td>36</td><td>Utah</td><td>31.6</td></tr>
<tr><td>32</td><td>Oregon</td><td>32.5</td><td>37</td><td>New Jersey</td><td>31.3</td></tr>
<tr><td>22</td><td>Pennsylvania</td><td>34.6</td><td>38</td><td>Nebraska</td><td>31.2</td></tr>
<tr><td>31</td><td>Rhode Island</td><td>32.6</td><td>39</td><td>Vermont</td><td>30.7</td></tr>
<tr><td>10</td><td>South Carolina</td><td>40.4</td><td>40</td><td>Nevada</td><td>29.8</td></tr>
<tr><td>15</td><td>South Dakota</td><td>36.7</td><td>41</td><td>New Hampshire</td><td>29.5</td></tr>
<tr><td>8</td><td>Tennessee</td><td>41.7</td><td>42</td><td>Connecticut</td><td>29.2</td></tr>
<tr><td>14</td><td>Texas</td><td>37.0</td><td>42</td><td>Washington</td><td>29.2</td></tr>
<tr><td>36</td><td>Utah</td><td>31.6</td><td>44</td><td>Massachusetts</td><td>28.9</td></tr>
<tr><td>39</td><td>Vermont</td><td>30.7</td><td>45</td><td>Colorado</td><td>28.3</td></tr>
<tr><td>34</td><td>Virginia</td><td>31.8</td><td>46</td><td>Hawaii</td><td>27.7</td></tr>
<tr><td>42</td><td>Washington</td><td>29.2</td><td>46</td><td>Minnesota</td><td>27.7</td></tr>
<tr><td>7</td><td>West Virginia</td><td>43.7</td><td>48</td><td>Alaska</td><td>26.5</td></tr>
<tr><td>34</td><td>Wisconsin</td><td>31.8</td><td>49</td><td>North Dakota</td><td>26.4</td></tr>
<tr><td>27</td><td>Wyoming</td><td>33.4</td><td>50</td><td>Maryland</td><td>24.3</td></tr>
<tr><td></td><td></td><td></td><td></td><td>District of Columbia</td><td>34.9</td></tr>
</table>

Source: U.S. Bureau of the Census
  "2018 American Community Survey-Table DP03" (https://data.census.gov/cedsci/)
*Households headed by females with own children under eighteen years living with them with incomes below the poverty level as a percent of all such female-headed households.

State and Local Government Expenditures for Public Welfare Programs in 2017

National Total = $673,156,029,000*

ALPHA ORDER

ALPHA ORDER

RANK	STATE	EXPENDITURES	% of USA
25	Alabama	$8,484,165,000	1.3%
42	Alaska	2,576,598,000	0.4%
12	Arizona	14,505,216,000	2.2%
28	Arkansas	7,503,934,000	1.1%
1	California	111,893,352,000	16.6%
26	Colorado	8,298,572,000	1.2%
37	Connecticut	3,818,344,000	0.6%
43	Delaware	2,543,274,000	0.4%
5	Florida	28,204,830,000	4.2%
18	Georgia	12,123,966,000	1.8%
39	Hawaii	3,083,901,000	0.5%
44	Idaho	2,522,364,000	0.4%
8	Illinois	21,498,078,000	3.2%
13	Indiana	13,940,697,000	2.1%
32	Iowa	5,964,047,000	0.9%
34	Kansas	4,138,700,000	0.6%
21	Kentucky	11,445,505,000	1.7%
22	Louisiana	11,307,304,000	1.7%
38	Maine	3,288,213,000	0.5%
15	Maryland	13,085,469,000	1.9%
7	Massachusetts	22,248,754,000	3.3%
10	Michigan	17,088,655,000	2.5%
11	Minnesota	15,254,856,000	2.3%
30	Mississippi	6,362,331,000	0.9%
24	Missouri	9,183,229,000	1.4%
46	Montana	2,233,426,000	0.3%
40	Nebraska	2,829,299,000	0.4%
35	Nevada	4,099,855,000	0.6%
45	New Hampshire	2,436,988,000	0.4%
9	New Jersey	17,804,828,000	2.6%
31	New Mexico	6,043,623,000	0.9%
2	New York	70,992,645,000	10.5%
14	North Carolina	13,386,774,000	2.0%
48	North Dakota	1,338,350,000	0.2%
6	Ohio	26,483,989,000	3.9%
29	Oklahoma	6,735,411,000	1.0%
23	Oregon	10,494,449,000	1.6%
4	Pennsylvania	33,871,007,000	5.0%
41	Rhode Island	2,691,017,000	0.4%
27	South Carolina	7,740,380,000	1.1%
49	South Dakota	1,168,162,000	0.2%
20	Tennessee	11,672,418,000	1.7%
3	Texas	38,376,668,000	5.7%
36	Utah	3,915,439,000	0.6%
47	Vermont	1,845,238,000	0.3%
19	Virginia	12,027,563,000	1.8%
17	Washington	12,490,926,000	1.9%
33	West Virginia	4,714,952,000	0.7%
16	Wisconsin	12,626,624,000	1.9%
50	Wyoming	841,817,000	0.1%

RANK ORDER

RANK	STATE	EXPENDITURES	% of USA
1	California	$111,893,352,000	16.6%
2	New York	70,992,645,000	10.5%
3	Texas	38,376,668,000	5.7%
4	Pennsylvania	33,871,007,000	5.0%
5	Florida	28,204,830,000	4.2%
6	Ohio	26,483,989,000	3.9%
7	Massachusetts	22,248,754,000	3.3%
8	Illinois	21,498,078,000	3.2%
9	New Jersey	17,804,828,000	2.6%
10	Michigan	17,088,655,000	2.5%
11	Minnesota	15,254,856,000	2.3%
12	Arizona	14,505,216,000	2.2%
13	Indiana	13,940,697,000	2.1%
14	North Carolina	13,386,774,000	2.0%
15	Maryland	13,085,469,000	1.9%
16	Wisconsin	12,626,624,000	1.9%
17	Washington	12,490,926,000	1.9%
18	Georgia	12,123,966,000	1.8%
19	Virginia	12,027,563,000	1.8%
20	Tennessee	11,672,418,000	1.7%
21	Kentucky	11,445,505,000	1.7%
22	Louisiana	11,307,304,000	1.7%
23	Oregon	10,494,449,000	1.6%
24	Missouri	9,183,229,000	1.4%
25	Alabama	8,484,165,000	1.3%
26	Colorado	8,298,572,000	1.2%
27	South Carolina	7,740,380,000	1.1%
28	Arkansas	7,503,934,000	1.1%
29	Oklahoma	6,735,411,000	1.0%
30	Mississippi	6,362,331,000	0.9%
31	New Mexico	6,043,623,000	0.9%
32	Iowa	5,964,047,000	0.9%
33	West Virginia	4,714,952,000	0.7%
34	Kansas	4,138,700,000	0.6%
35	Nevada	4,099,855,000	0.6%
36	Utah	3,915,439,000	0.6%
37	Connecticut	3,818,344,000	0.6%
38	Maine	3,288,213,000	0.5%
39	Hawaii	3,083,901,000	0.5%
40	Nebraska	2,829,299,000	0.4%
41	Rhode Island	2,691,017,000	0.4%
42	Alaska	2,576,598,000	0.4%
43	Delaware	2,543,274,000	0.4%
44	Idaho	2,522,364,000	0.4%
45	New Hampshire	2,436,988,000	0.4%
46	Montana	2,233,426,000	0.3%
47	Vermont	1,845,238,000	0.3%
48	North Dakota	1,338,350,000	0.2%
49	South Dakota	1,168,162,000	0.2%
50	Wyoming	841,817,000	0.1%
	District of Columbia	3,929,827,000	0.6%

Source: U.S. Bureau of the Census, Governments Division
"2017 State and Local Government Finances" (https://www.census.gov/programs-surveys/gov-finances.html)
*Direct general expenditures. Includes funds for cash assistance programs, medical and other vendor payments, welfare institutions, and other public welfare programs.

Per Capita State and Local Government Expenditures for Public Welfare Programs in 2017
National Per Capita = $2,070*

ALPHA ORDER

RANK	STATE	PER CAPITA
29	Alabama	$1,740
2	Alaska	3,483
24	Arizona	2,058
14	Arkansas	2,499
6	California	2,840
37	Colorado	1,478
50	Connecticut	1,068
8	Delaware	2,657
45	Florida	1,345
49	Georgia	1,164
20	Hawaii	2,165
39	Idaho	1,467
34	Illinois	1,681
23	Indiana	2,093
26	Iowa	1,897
41	Kansas	1,422
11	Kentucky	2,570
16	Louisiana	2,421
15	Maine	2,463
19	Maryland	2,172
3	Massachusetts	3,242
31	Michigan	1,713
7	Minnesota	2,740
21	Mississippi	2,128
36	Missouri	1,503
22	Montana	2,121
38	Nebraska	1,475
43	Nevada	1,379
27	New Hampshire	1,805
25	New Jersey	2,003
5	New Mexico	2,887
1	New York	3,624
47	North Carolina	1,303
28	North Dakota	1,772
17	Ohio	2,271
31	Oklahoma	1,713
13	Oregon	2,531
9	Pennsylvania	2,648
12	Rhode Island	2,547
35	South Carolina	1,542
46	South Dakota	1,338
29	Tennessee	1,740
44	Texas	1,355
48	Utah	1,262
4	Vermont	2,955
42	Virginia	1,421
33	Washington	1,682
10	West Virginia	2,595
18	Wisconsin	2,180
40	Wyoming	1,454

RANK ORDER

RANK	STATE	PER CAPITA
1	New York	$3,624
2	Alaska	3,483
3	Massachusetts	3,242
4	Vermont	2,955
5	New Mexico	2,887
6	California	2,840
7	Minnesota	2,740
8	Delaware	2,657
9	Pennsylvania	2,648
10	West Virginia	2,595
11	Kentucky	2,570
12	Rhode Island	2,547
13	Oregon	2,531
14	Arkansas	2,499
15	Maine	2,463
16	Louisiana	2,421
17	Ohio	2,271
18	Wisconsin	2,180
19	Maryland	2,172
20	Hawaii	2,165
21	Mississippi	2,128
22	Montana	2,121
23	Indiana	2,093
24	Arizona	2,058
25	New Jersey	2,003
26	Iowa	1,897
27	New Hampshire	1,805
28	North Dakota	1,772
29	Alabama	1,740
29	Tennessee	1,740
31	Michigan	1,713
31	Oklahoma	1,713
33	Washington	1,682
34	Illinois	1,681
35	South Carolina	1,542
36	Missouri	1,503
37	Colorado	1,478
38	Nebraska	1,475
39	Idaho	1,467
40	Wyoming	1,454
41	Kansas	1,422
42	Virginia	1,421
43	Nevada	1,379
44	Texas	1,355
45	Florida	1,345
46	South Dakota	1,338
47	North Carolina	1,303
48	Utah	1,262
49	Georgia	1,164
50	Connecticut	1,068
	District of Columbia	5,649

Source: CQ Press using data from U.S. Bureau of the Census, Governments Division
"2017 State and Local Government Finances" (https://www.census.gov/programs-surveys/gov-finances.html)
*Direct general expenditures. Includes funds for cash assistance programs, medical and other vendor payments, welfare institutions, and other public welfare programs.

State and Local Government Spending for Public Welfare Programs as a Percent of All State and Local Government Expenditures in 2017
National Percent = 21.9%*

ALPHA ORDER

RANK	STATE	PERCENT
28	Alabama	20.4
29	Alaska	20.2
3	Arizona	29.1
1	Arkansas	29.9
16	California	24.6
42	Colorado	16.6
49	Connecticut	11.3
19	Delaware	23.6
35	Florida	18.4
38	Georgia	17.0
24	Hawaii	22.0
26	Idaho	21.7
36	Illinois	18.3
9	Indiana	26.2
33	Iowa	19.0
46	Kansas	15.4
4	Kentucky	29.0
8	Louisiana	26.5
6	Maine	28.3
27	Maryland	21.6
5	Massachusetts	28.5
29	Michigan	20.2
11	Minnesota	25.7
18	Mississippi	24.3
31	Missouri	19.6
19	Montana	23.6
45	Nebraska	16.1
34	Nevada	18.7
24	New Hampshire	22.0
32	New Jersey	19.4
7	New Mexico	28.1
13	New York	25.1
38	North Carolina	17.0
48	North Dakota	13.9
17	Ohio	24.5
23	Oklahoma	23.0
22	Oregon	23.4
9	Pennsylvania	26.2
12	Rhode Island	25.6
37	South Carolina	17.9
44	South Dakota	16.2
15	Tennessee	25.0
40	Texas	16.9
47	Utah	15.0
13	Vermont	25.1
43	Virginia	16.3
41	Washington	16.8
2	West Virginia	29.3
21	Wisconsin	23.5
50	Wyoming	9.5

RANK ORDER

RANK	STATE	PERCENT
1	Arkansas	29.9
2	West Virginia	29.3
3	Arizona	29.1
4	Kentucky	29.0
5	Massachusetts	28.5
6	Maine	28.3
7	New Mexico	28.1
8	Louisiana	26.5
9	Indiana	26.2
9	Pennsylvania	26.2
11	Minnesota	25.7
12	Rhode Island	25.6
13	New York	25.1
13	Vermont	25.1
15	Tennessee	25.0
16	California	24.6
17	Ohio	24.5
18	Mississippi	24.3
19	Delaware	23.6
19	Montana	23.6
21	Wisconsin	23.5
22	Oregon	23.4
23	Oklahoma	23.0
24	Hawaii	22.0
24	New Hampshire	22.0
26	Idaho	21.7
27	Maryland	21.6
28	Alabama	20.4
29	Alaska	20.2
29	Michigan	20.2
31	Missouri	19.6
32	New Jersey	19.4
33	Iowa	19.0
34	Nevada	18.7
35	Florida	18.4
36	Illinois	18.3
37	South Carolina	17.9
38	Georgia	17.0
38	North Carolina	17.0
40	Texas	16.9
41	Washington	16.8
42	Colorado	16.6
43	Virginia	16.3
44	South Dakota	16.2
45	Nebraska	16.1
46	Kansas	15.4
47	Utah	15.0
48	North Dakota	13.9
49	Connecticut	11.3
50	Wyoming	9.5

| | District of Columbia | 29.6 |

Source: CQ Press using data from U.S. Bureau of the Census, Governments Division
"2017 State and Local Government Finances" (https://www.census.gov/programs-surveys/gov-finances.html)
*As a percent of direct general expenditures. Includes funds for cash assistance programs, medical and other vendor payments, welfare institutions, and other public welfare programs.

Social Security (OASDI) Payments in 2018

National Total = $988,373,000,000*

RANK	STATE	PAYMENTS	% of USA
21	Alabama	$17,537,000,000	1.8%
50	Alaska	1,518,000,000	0.2%
16	Arizona	21,622,000,000	2.2%
30	Arkansas	10,347,000,000	1.0%
1	California	92,389,000,000	9.3%
25	Colorado	13,893,000,000	1.4%
29	Connecticut	11,838,000,000	1.2%
43	Delaware	3,622,000,000	0.4%
2	Florida	72,670,000,000	7.4%
11	Georgia	28,246,000,000	2.9%
42	Hawaii	4,270,000,000	0.4%
39	Idaho	5,299,000,000	0.5%
8	Illinois	36,394,000,000	3.7%
15	Indiana	22,129,000,000	2.2%
31	Iowa	10,296,000,000	1.0%
33	Kansas	8,971,000,000	0.9%
24	Kentucky	14,841,000,000	1.5%
27	Louisiana	13,356,000,000	1.4%
40	Maine	5,078,000,000	0.5%
23	Maryland	16,695,000,000	1.7%
17	Massachusetts	20,560,000,000	2.1%
7	Michigan	36,824,000,000	3.7%
22	Minnesota	16,850,000,000	1.7%
32	Mississippi	9,815,000,000	1.0%
18	Missouri	20,117,000,000	2.0%
45	Montana	3,518,000,000	0.4%
38	Nebraska	5,464,000,000	0.6%
34	Nevada	8,364,000,000	0.8%
41	New Hampshire	5,073,000,000	0.5%
10	New Jersey	28,449,000,000	2.9%
37	New Mexico	6,420,000,000	0.6%
4	New York	59,019,000,000	6.0%
9	North Carolina	32,999,000,000	3.3%
48	North Dakota	2,041,000,000	0.2%
6	Ohio	36,880,000,000	3.7%
28	Oklahoma	12,103,000,000	1.2%
26	Oregon	13,837,000,000	1.4%
5	Pennsylvania	46,238,000,000	4.7%
44	Rhode Island	3,597,000,000	0.4%
20	South Carolina	18,073,000,000	1.8%
46	South Dakota	2,697,000,000	0.3%
13	Tennessee	22,521,000,000	2.3%
3	Texas	64,533,000,000	6.5%
36	Utah	6,488,000,000	0.7%
47	Vermont	2,360,000,000	0.2%
12	Virginia	24,705,000,000	2.5%
14	Washington	22,170,000,000	2.2%
35	West Virginia	7,385,000,000	0.7%
19	Wisconsin	19,976,000,000	2.0%
49	Wyoming	1,810,000,000	0.2%

RANK	STATE	PAYMENTS	% of USA
1	California	$92,389,000,000	9.3%
2	Florida	72,670,000,000	7.4%
3	Texas	64,533,000,000	6.5%
4	New York	59,019,000,000	6.0%
5	Pennsylvania	46,238,000,000	4.7%
6	Ohio	36,880,000,000	3.7%
7	Michigan	36,824,000,000	3.7%
8	Illinois	36,394,000,000	3.7%
9	North Carolina	32,999,000,000	3.3%
10	New Jersey	28,449,000,000	2.9%
11	Georgia	28,246,000,000	2.9%
12	Virginia	24,705,000,000	2.5%
13	Tennessee	22,521,000,000	2.3%
14	Washington	22,170,000,000	2.2%
15	Indiana	22,129,000,000	2.2%
16	Arizona	21,622,000,000	2.2%
17	Massachusetts	20,560,000,000	2.1%
18	Missouri	20,117,000,000	2.0%
19	Wisconsin	19,976,000,000	2.0%
20	South Carolina	18,073,000,000	1.8%
21	Alabama	17,537,000,000	1.8%
22	Minnesota	16,850,000,000	1.7%
23	Maryland	16,695,000,000	1.7%
24	Kentucky	14,841,000,000	1.5%
25	Colorado	13,893,000,000	1.4%
26	Oregon	13,837,000,000	1.4%
27	Louisiana	13,356,000,000	1.4%
28	Oklahoma	12,103,000,000	1.2%
29	Connecticut	11,838,000,000	1.2%
30	Arkansas	10,347,000,000	1.0%
31	Iowa	10,296,000,000	1.0%
32	Mississippi	9,815,000,000	1.0%
33	Kansas	8,971,000,000	0.9%
34	Nevada	8,364,000,000	0.8%
35	West Virginia	7,385,000,000	0.7%
36	Utah	6,488,000,000	0.7%
37	New Mexico	6,420,000,000	0.6%
38	Nebraska	5,464,000,000	0.6%
39	Idaho	5,299,000,000	0.5%
40	Maine	5,078,000,000	0.5%
41	New Hampshire	5,073,000,000	0.5%
42	Hawaii	4,270,000,000	0.4%
43	Delaware	3,622,000,000	0.4%
44	Rhode Island	3,597,000,000	0.4%
45	Montana	3,518,000,000	0.4%
46	South Dakota	2,697,000,000	0.3%
47	Vermont	2,360,000,000	0.2%
48	North Dakota	2,041,000,000	0.2%
49	Wyoming	1,810,000,000	0.2%
50	Alaska	1,518,000,000	0.2%
	District of Columbia	1,242,000,000	0.1%

Source: U.S. Department of Health and Human Services, Social Security Administration
"Social Security Bulletin, Annual Statistical Supplement 2019" (https://www.ssa.gov/policy/docs/statcomps/supplement/)
*"OASDI" is Old Age, Survivors and Disability Insurance. National total includes $15,244,000,000 in payments to recipients in U.S. territories and foreign countries.

Per Capita Social Security (OASDI) Payments in 2018

National Per Capita = $2,979*

ALPHA ORDER

RANK	STATE	PER CAPITA
8	Alabama	$3,588
49	Alaska	2,065
33	Arizona	3,021
11	Arkansas	3,438
47	California	2,341
46	Colorado	2,441
17	Connecticut	3,315
4	Delaware	3,752
12	Florida	3,421
45	Georgia	2,687
34	Hawaii	3,006
31	Idaho	3,027
40	Illinois	2,860
19	Indiana	3,305
22	Iowa	3,270
27	Kansas	3,081
14	Kentucky	3,327
39	Louisiana	2,866
2	Maine	3,792
42	Maryland	2,766
36	Massachusetts	2,987
6	Michigan	3,688
34	Minnesota	3,006
20	Mississippi	3,292
21	Missouri	3,286
16	Montana	3,317
41	Nebraska	2,838
43	Nevada	2,763
5	New Hampshire	3,748
23	New Jersey	3,202
30	New Mexico	3,068
32	New York	3,022
24	North Carolina	3,179
44	North Dakota	2,692
25	Ohio	3,159
28	Oklahoma	3,072
18	Oregon	3,309
7	Pennsylvania	3,612
13	Rhode Island	3,399
9	South Carolina	3,555
29	South Dakota	3,069
15	Tennessee	3,326
48	Texas	2,254
50	Utah	2,057
3	Vermont	3,780
38	Virginia	2,906
37	Washington	2,947
1	West Virginia	4,093
10	Wisconsin	3,440
26	Wyoming	3,134

RANK ORDER

RANK	STATE	PER CAPITA
1	West Virginia	$4,093
2	Maine	3,792
3	Vermont	3,780
4	Delaware	3,752
5	New Hampshire	3,748
6	Michigan	3,688
7	Pennsylvania	3,612
8	Alabama	3,588
9	South Carolina	3,555
10	Wisconsin	3,440
11	Arkansas	3,438
12	Florida	3,421
13	Rhode Island	3,399
14	Kentucky	3,327
15	Tennessee	3,326
16	Montana	3,317
17	Connecticut	3,315
18	Oregon	3,309
19	Indiana	3,305
20	Mississippi	3,292
21	Missouri	3,286
22	Iowa	3,270
23	New Jersey	3,202
24	North Carolina	3,179
25	Ohio	3,159
26	Wyoming	3,134
27	Kansas	3,081
28	Oklahoma	3,072
29	South Dakota	3,069
30	New Mexico	3,068
31	Idaho	3,027
32	New York	3,022
33	Arizona	3,021
34	Hawaii	3,006
34	Minnesota	3,006
36	Massachusetts	2,987
37	Washington	2,947
38	Virginia	2,906
39	Louisiana	2,866
40	Illinois	2,860
41	Nebraska	2,838
42	Maryland	2,766
43	Nevada	2,763
44	North Dakota	2,692
45	Georgia	2,687
46	Colorado	2,441
47	California	2,341
48	Texas	2,254
49	Alaska	2,065
50	Utah	2,057

| | District of Columbia | 1,770 |

Source: CQ Press using data from U.S. Department of Health and Human Services, Social Security Administration
"Social Security Bulletin, Annual Statistical Supplement 2019" (https://www.ssa.gov/policy/docs/statcomps/supplement/)
*"OASDI" is Old Age, Survivors and Disability Insurance. National per capita does not include payments or population in U.S. territories and foreign countries.

Social Security (OASDI) Monthly Payments in 2018

National Total = $84,419,840,000*

	ALPHA ORDER				RANK ORDER		
RANK	STATE	PAYMENTS	% of USA	RANK	STATE	PAYMENTS	% of USA
21	Alabama	$1,474,866,000	1.7%	1	California	$7,934,876,000	9.4%
50	Alaska	131,038,000	0.2%	2	Florida	6,265,243,000	7.4%
16	Arizona	1,874,030,000	2.2%	3	Texas	5,495,664,000	6.5%
31	Arkansas	870,892,000	1.0%	4	New York	5,045,039,000	6.0%
1	California	7,934,876,000	9.4%	5	Pennsylvania	3,934,741,000	4.7%
25	Colorado	1,202,184,000	1.4%	6	Michigan	3,124,432,000	3.7%
29	Connecticut	1,018,496,000	1.2%	7	Ohio	3,105,357,000	3.7%
43	Delaware	314,296,000	0.4%	8	Illinois	3,096,652,000	3.7%
2	Florida	6,265,243,000	7.4%	9	North Carolina	2,832,908,000	3.4%
11	Georgia	2,410,603,000	2.9%	10	New Jersey	2,436,037,000	2.9%
42	Hawaii	371,053,000	0.4%	11	Georgia	2,410,603,000	2.9%
39	Idaho	458,453,000	0.5%	12	Virginia	2,121,868,000	2.5%
8	Illinois	3,096,652,000	3.7%	13	Washington	1,913,736,000	2.3%
15	Indiana	1,877,338,000	2.2%	14	Tennessee	1,912,866,000	2.3%
30	Iowa	881,676,000	1.0%	15	Indiana	1,877,338,000	2.2%
33	Kansas	767,704,000	0.9%	16	Arizona	1,874,030,000	2.2%
24	Kentucky	1,240,569,000	1.5%	17	Massachusetts	1,759,294,000	2.1%
27	Louisiana	1,108,708,000	1.3%	18	Wisconsin	1,717,582,000	2.0%
41	Maine	434,514,000	0.5%	19	Missouri	1,705,313,000	2.0%
23	Maryland	1,435,633,000	1.7%	20	South Carolina	1,554,025,000	1.8%
17	Massachusetts	1,759,294,000	2.1%	21	Alabama	1,474,866,000	1.7%
6	Michigan	3,124,432,000	3.7%	22	Minnesota	1,457,200,000	1.7%
22	Minnesota	1,457,200,000	1.7%	23	Maryland	1,435,633,000	1.7%
32	Mississippi	823,767,000	1.0%	24	Kentucky	1,240,569,000	1.5%
19	Missouri	1,705,313,000	2.0%	25	Colorado	1,202,184,000	1.4%
45	Montana	302,993,000	0.4%	26	Oregon	1,194,143,000	1.4%
38	Nebraska	468,676,000	0.6%	27	Louisiana	1,108,708,000	1.3%
34	Nevada	723,071,000	0.9%	28	Oklahoma	1,023,523,000	1.2%
40	New Hampshire	438,065,000	0.5%	29	Connecticut	1,018,496,000	1.2%
10	New Jersey	2,436,037,000	2.9%	30	Iowa	881,676,000	1.0%
37	New Mexico	549,452,000	0.7%	31	Arkansas	870,892,000	1.0%
4	New York	5,045,039,000	6.0%	32	Mississippi	823,767,000	1.0%
9	North Carolina	2,832,908,000	3.4%	33	Kansas	767,704,000	0.9%
48	North Dakota	174,522,000	0.2%	34	Nevada	723,071,000	0.9%
7	Ohio	3,105,357,000	3.7%	35	West Virginia	613,058,000	0.7%
28	Oklahoma	1,023,523,000	1.2%	36	Utah	558,663,000	0.7%
26	Oregon	1,194,143,000	1.4%	37	New Mexico	549,452,000	0.7%
5	Pennsylvania	3,934,741,000	4.7%	38	Nebraska	468,676,000	0.6%
44	Rhode Island	308,441,000	0.4%	39	Idaho	458,453,000	0.5%
20	South Carolina	1,554,025,000	1.8%	40	New Hampshire	438,065,000	0.5%
46	South Dakota	232,719,000	0.3%	41	Maine	434,514,000	0.5%
14	Tennessee	1,912,866,000	2.3%	42	Hawaii	371,053,000	0.4%
3	Texas	5,495,664,000	6.5%	43	Delaware	314,296,000	0.4%
36	Utah	558,663,000	0.7%	44	Rhode Island	308,441,000	0.4%
47	Vermont	203,538,000	0.2%	45	Montana	302,993,000	0.4%
12	Virginia	2,121,868,000	2.5%	46	South Dakota	232,719,000	0.3%
13	Washington	1,913,736,000	2.3%	47	Vermont	203,538,000	0.2%
35	West Virginia	613,058,000	0.7%	48	North Dakota	174,522,000	0.2%
18	Wisconsin	1,717,582,000	2.0%	49	Wyoming	155,824,000	0.2%
49	Wyoming	155,824,000	0.2%	50	Alaska	131,038,000	0.2%
					District of Columbia	106,681,000	0.1%

Source: U.S. Department of Health and Human Services, Social Security Administration
"Social Security Bulletin, Annual Statistical Supplement 2019" (https://www.ssa.gov/policy/docs/statcomps/supplement/)
*For December 2018. "OASDI" is Old Age, Survivors and Disability Insurance. National total includes $1,257,813,000 in payments to recipients in U.S. territories and foreign countries.

Social Security (OASDI) Beneficiaries in 2018

National Total = 62,906,222*

ALPHA ORDER

RANK	STATE	BENEFICIARIES	% of USA
21	Alabama	1,143,125	1.8%
50	Alaska	101,402	0.2%
15	Arizona	1,349,458	2.1%
29	Arkansas	696,936	1.1%
1	California	5,962,804	9.5%
26	Colorado	874,819	1.4%
30	Connecticut	681,765	1.1%
45	Delaware	213,246	0.3%
2	Florida	4,626,156	7.4%
10	Georgia	1,830,266	2.9%
42	Hawaii	271,236	0.4%
38	Idaho	346,243	0.6%
7	Illinois	2,243,286	3.6%
14	Indiana	1,350,417	2.1%
32	Iowa	647,462	1.0%
33	Kansas	552,973	0.9%
24	Kentucky	989,575	1.6%
25	Louisiana	907,733	1.4%
40	Maine	344,482	0.5%
23	Maryland	1,001,230	1.6%
18	Massachusetts	1,273,360	2.0%
8	Michigan	2,209,084	3.5%
22	Minnesota	1,032,697	1.6%
31	Mississippi	668,877	1.1%
17	Missouri	1,293,897	2.1%
43	Montana	233,801	0.4%
39	Nebraska	345,725	0.5%
34	Nevada	536,855	0.9%
41	New Hampshire	305,855	0.5%
11	New Jersey	1,625,600	2.6%
36	New Mexico	436,551	0.7%
4	New York	3,627,340	5.8%
9	North Carolina	2,098,741	3.3%
48	North Dakota	133,773	0.2%
6	Ohio	2,356,367	3.7%
28	Oklahoma	789,288	1.3%
27	Oregon	871,988	1.4%
5	Pennsylvania	2,825,178	4.5%
44	Rhode Island	225,493	0.4%
20	South Carolina	1,143,297	1.8%
46	South Dakota	178,999	0.3%
13	Tennessee	1,452,552	2.3%
3	Texas	4,224,159	6.7%
37	Utah	406,568	0.6%
47	Vermont	150,319	0.2%
12	Virginia	1,530,417	2.4%
16	Washington	1,346,820	2.1%
35	West Virginia	475,744	0.8%
19	Wisconsin	1,233,379	2.0%
49	Wyoming	112,386	0.2%

RANK ORDER

RANK	STATE	BENEFICIARIES	% of USA
1	California	5,962,804	9.5%
2	Florida	4,626,156	7.4%
3	Texas	4,224,159	6.7%
4	New York	3,627,340	5.8%
5	Pennsylvania	2,825,178	4.5%
6	Ohio	2,356,367	3.7%
7	Illinois	2,243,286	3.6%
8	Michigan	2,209,084	3.5%
9	North Carolina	2,098,741	3.3%
10	Georgia	1,830,266	2.9%
11	New Jersey	1,625,600	2.6%
12	Virginia	1,530,417	2.4%
13	Tennessee	1,452,552	2.3%
14	Indiana	1,350,417	2.1%
15	Arizona	1,349,458	2.1%
16	Washington	1,346,820	2.1%
17	Missouri	1,293,897	2.1%
18	Massachusetts	1,273,360	2.0%
19	Wisconsin	1,233,379	2.0%
20	South Carolina	1,143,297	1.8%
21	Alabama	1,143,125	1.8%
22	Minnesota	1,032,697	1.6%
23	Maryland	1,001,230	1.6%
24	Kentucky	989,575	1.6%
25	Louisiana	907,733	1.4%
26	Colorado	874,819	1.4%
27	Oregon	871,988	1.4%
28	Oklahoma	789,288	1.3%
29	Arkansas	696,936	1.1%
30	Connecticut	681,765	1.1%
31	Mississippi	668,877	1.1%
32	Iowa	647,462	1.0%
33	Kansas	552,973	0.9%
34	Nevada	536,855	0.9%
35	West Virginia	475,744	0.8%
36	New Mexico	436,551	0.7%
37	Utah	406,568	0.6%
38	Idaho	346,243	0.6%
39	Nebraska	345,725	0.5%
40	Maine	344,482	0.5%
41	New Hampshire	305,855	0.5%
42	Hawaii	271,236	0.4%
43	Montana	233,801	0.4%
44	Rhode Island	225,493	0.4%
45	Delaware	213,246	0.3%
46	South Dakota	178,999	0.3%
47	Vermont	150,319	0.2%
48	North Dakota	133,773	0.2%
49	Wyoming	112,386	0.2%
50	Alaska	101,402	0.2%
	District of Columbia	83,059	0.1%

Source: U.S. Department of Health and Human Services, Social Security Administration
    "Social Security Bulletin, Annual Statistical Supplement 2019" (https://www.ssa.gov/policy/docs/statcomps/supplement/)
*For December 2018. "OASDI" is Old Age, Survivors and Disability Insurance. National total includes 1,543,439 beneficiaries in U.S. territories and foreign countries.

Average Monthly Social Security (OASDI) Payment in 2018

National Average = $1,355 Each Month per Beneficiary*

ALPHA ORDER

RANK	STATE	PER BENEFICIARY
43	Alabama	$1,290
42	Alaska	1,292
13	Arizona	1,389
48	Arkansas	1,250
31	California	1,331
19	Colorado	1,374
2	Connecticut	1,494
3	Delaware	1,474
27	Florida	1,354
35	Georgia	1,317
22	Hawaii	1,368
32	Idaho	1,324
18	Illinois	1,380
12	Indiana	1,390
24	Iowa	1,362
14	Kansas	1,388
47	Kentucky	1,254
50	Louisiana	1,221
45	Maine	1,261
4	Maryland	1,434
17	Massachusetts	1,382
7	Michigan	1,414
8	Minnesota	1,411
49	Mississippi	1,232
33	Missouri	1,318
41	Montana	1,296
26	Nebraska	1,356
30	Nevada	1,347
5	New Hampshire	1,432
1	New Jersey	1,499
46	New Mexico	1,259
11	New York	1,391
29	North Carolina	1,350
37	North Dakota	1,305
33	Ohio	1,318
40	Oklahoma	1,297
21	Oregon	1,369
9	Pennsylvania	1,393
22	Rhode Island	1,368
25	South Carolina	1,359
39	South Dakota	1,300
35	Tennessee	1,317
38	Texas	1,301
19	Utah	1,374
27	Vermont	1,354
16	Virginia	1,386
6	Washington	1,421
44	West Virginia	1,289
9	Wisconsin	1,393
15	Wyoming	1,387

RANK ORDER

RANK	STATE	PER BENEFICIARY
1	New Jersey	$1,499
2	Connecticut	1,494
3	Delaware	1,474
4	Maryland	1,434
5	New Hampshire	1,432
6	Washington	1,421
7	Michigan	1,414
8	Minnesota	1,411
9	Pennsylvania	1,393
9	Wisconsin	1,393
11	New York	1,391
12	Indiana	1,390
13	Arizona	1,389
14	Kansas	1,388
15	Wyoming	1,387
16	Virginia	1,386
17	Massachusetts	1,382
18	Illinois	1,380
19	Colorado	1,374
19	Utah	1,374
21	Oregon	1,369
22	Hawaii	1,368
22	Rhode Island	1,368
24	Iowa	1,362
25	South Carolina	1,359
26	Nebraska	1,356
27	Florida	1,354
27	Vermont	1,354
29	North Carolina	1,350
30	Nevada	1,347
31	California	1,331
32	Idaho	1,324
33	Missouri	1,318
33	Ohio	1,318
35	Georgia	1,317
35	Tennessee	1,317
37	North Dakota	1,305
38	Texas	1,301
39	South Dakota	1,300
40	Oklahoma	1,297
41	Montana	1,296
42	Alaska	1,292
43	Alabama	1,290
44	West Virginia	1,289
45	Maine	1,261
46	New Mexico	1,259
47	Kentucky	1,254
48	Arkansas	1,250
49	Mississippi	1,232
50	Louisiana	1,221
	District of Columbia	1,284

Source: CQ Press using data from U.S. Department of Health and Human Services, Social Security Administration
"Social Security Bulletin, Annual Statistical Supplement 2019" (https://www.ssa.gov/policy/docs/statcomps/supplement/)
*As of December 2018. "OASDI" is Old Age, Survivors and Disability Insurance. National average does not include
beneficiaries or payments in U.S. territories or foreign countries.

Social Security Supplemental Security Income Beneficiaries in 2018

National Total = 8,128,652 Beneficiaries*

ALPHA ORDER

RANK	STATE	BENEFICIARIES	% of USA
16	Alabama	161,593	2.0%
48	Alaska	12,528	0.2%
22	Arizona	118,534	1.5%
26	Arkansas	105,231	1.3%
1	California	1,239,522	15.2%
30	Colorado	72,990	0.9%
32	Connecticut	66,432	0.8%
45	Delaware	17,026	0.2%
4	Florida	576,287	7.1%
9	Georgia	259,355	3.2%
42	Hawaii	23,157	0.3%
40	Idaho	30,870	0.4%
8	Illinois	267,091	3.3%
20	Indiana	127,356	1.6%
35	Iowa	51,105	0.6%
36	Kansas	47,705	0.6%
15	Kentucky	174,203	2.1%
14	Louisiana	175,215	2.2%
37	Maine	36,875	0.5%
21	Maryland	120,975	1.5%
11	Massachusetts	183,889	2.3%
7	Michigan	271,856	3.3%
28	Minnesota	93,491	1.2%
23	Mississippi	117,106	1.4%
19	Missouri	136,317	1.7%
44	Montana	17,893	0.2%
41	Nebraska	28,262	0.3%
34	Nevada	56,441	0.7%
43	New Hampshire	18,579	0.2%
12	New Jersey	180,121	2.2%
33	New Mexico	62,929	0.8%
3	New York	629,203	7.7%
10	North Carolina	228,762	2.8%
49	North Dakota	8,411	0.1%
6	Ohio	308,223	3.8%
27	Oklahoma	96,201	1.2%
29	Oregon	88,149	1.1%
5	Pennsylvania	355,511	4.4%
38	Rhode Island	32,946	0.4%
25	South Carolina	115,152	1.4%
47	South Dakota	14,639	0.2%
13	Tennessee	176,336	2.2%
2	Texas	649,561	8.0%
39	Utah	31,489	0.4%
46	Vermont	15,237	0.2%
17	Virginia	155,879	1.9%
18	Washington	149,201	1.8%
31	West Virginia	72,326	0.9%
24	Wisconsin	116,776	1.4%
50	Wyoming	6,880	0.1%

RANK ORDER

RANK	STATE	BENEFICIARIES	% of USA
1	California	1,239,522	15.2%
2	Texas	649,561	8.0%
3	New York	629,203	7.7%
4	Florida	576,287	7.1%
5	Pennsylvania	355,511	4.4%
6	Ohio	308,223	3.8%
7	Michigan	271,856	3.3%
8	Illinois	267,091	3.3%
9	Georgia	259,355	3.2%
10	North Carolina	228,762	2.8%
11	Massachusetts	183,889	2.3%
12	New Jersey	180,121	2.2%
13	Tennessee	176,336	2.2%
14	Louisiana	175,215	2.2%
15	Kentucky	174,203	2.1%
16	Alabama	161,593	2.0%
17	Virginia	155,879	1.9%
18	Washington	149,201	1.8%
19	Missouri	136,317	1.7%
20	Indiana	127,356	1.6%
21	Maryland	120,975	1.5%
22	Arizona	118,534	1.5%
23	Mississippi	117,106	1.4%
24	Wisconsin	116,776	1.4%
25	South Carolina	115,152	1.4%
26	Arkansas	105,231	1.3%
27	Oklahoma	96,201	1.2%
28	Minnesota	93,491	1.2%
29	Oregon	88,149	1.1%
30	Colorado	72,990	0.9%
31	West Virginia	72,326	0.9%
32	Connecticut	66,432	0.8%
33	New Mexico	62,929	0.8%
34	Nevada	56,441	0.7%
35	Iowa	51,105	0.6%
36	Kansas	47,705	0.6%
37	Maine	36,875	0.5%
38	Rhode Island	32,946	0.4%
39	Utah	31,489	0.4%
40	Idaho	30,870	0.4%
41	Nebraska	28,262	0.3%
42	Hawaii	23,157	0.3%
43	New Hampshire	18,579	0.2%
44	Montana	17,893	0.2%
45	Delaware	17,026	0.2%
46	Vermont	15,237	0.2%
47	South Dakota	14,639	0.2%
48	Alaska	12,528	0.2%
49	North Dakota	8,411	0.1%
50	Wyoming	6,880	0.1%
	District of Columbia	25,816	0.3%

Source: U.S. Department of Health and Human Services, Social Security Administration
"Social Security Bulletin, Annual Statistical Supplement 2019" (https://www.ssa.gov/policy/docs/statcomps/supplement/)
*For December 2018. National total includes 1,020 beneficiaries in U.S. territories or otherwise not distributed by state. The SSI program provides income support to persons age 65 and older and blind or disabled adults and children.

Average Monthly Social Security
Supplemental Security Income Payment in 2018
National Average = $534.67 Each Month per Beneficiary*

ALPHA ORDER

RANK	STATE	AVERAGE BENEFIT
34	Alabama	$522.19
41	Alaska	516.41
15	Arizona	540.98
22	Arkansas	534.13
36	California	520.82
29	Colorado	529.49
12	Connecticut	542.61
9	Delaware	547.01
20	Florida	534.42
28	Georgia	530.44
31	Hawaii	528.04
27	Idaho	531.74
7	Illinois	553.08
10	Indiana	546.66
37	Iowa	517.97
25	Kansas	533.35
23	Kentucky	533.49
17	Louisiana	539.32
40	Maine	516.77
2	Maryland	561.29
19	Massachusetts	537.07
3	Michigan	558.14
6	Minnesota	553.89
38	Mississippi	517.05
32	Missouri	525.79
49	Montana	507.21
39	Nebraska	516.83
8	Nevada	547.11
43	New Hampshire	515.46
46	New Jersey	512.37
44	New Mexico	514.66
13	New York	542.32
35	North Carolina	522.11
50	North Dakota	497.61
5	Ohio	557.90
24	Oklahoma	533.37
14	Oregon	541.64
1	Pennsylvania	562.01
18	Rhode Island	537.58
33	South Carolina	523.13
48	South Dakota	508.11
30	Tennessee	529.36
42	Texas	516.31
21	Utah	534.18
45	Vermont	512.77
26	Virginia	533.02
4	Washington	558.11
16	West Virginia	539.74
11	Wisconsin	543.26
47	Wyoming	510.20

RANK ORDER

RANK	STATE	AVERAGE BENEFIT
1	Pennsylvania	$562.01
2	Maryland	561.29
3	Michigan	558.14
4	Washington	558.11
5	Ohio	557.90
6	Minnesota	553.89
7	Illinois	553.08
8	Nevada	547.11
9	Delaware	547.01
10	Indiana	546.66
11	Wisconsin	543.26
12	Connecticut	542.61
13	New York	542.32
14	Oregon	541.64
15	Arizona	540.98
16	West Virginia	539.74
17	Louisiana	539.32
18	Rhode Island	537.58
19	Massachusetts	537.07
20	Florida	534.42
21	Utah	534.18
22	Arkansas	534.13
23	Kentucky	533.49
24	Oklahoma	533.37
25	Kansas	533.35
26	Virginia	533.02
27	Idaho	531.74
28	Georgia	530.44
29	Colorado	529.49
30	Tennessee	529.36
31	Hawaii	528.04
32	Missouri	525.79
33	South Carolina	523.13
34	Alabama	522.19
35	North Carolina	522.11
36	California	520.82
37	Iowa	517.97
38	Mississippi	517.05
39	Nebraska	516.83
40	Maine	516.77
41	Alaska	516.41
42	Texas	516.31
43	New Hampshire	515.46
44	New Mexico	514.66
45	Vermont	512.77
46	New Jersey	512.37
47	Wyoming	510.20
48	South Dakota	508.11
49	Montana	507.21
50	North Dakota	497.61

District of Columbia	573.76

Source: U.S. Department of Health and Human Services, Social Security Administration
"Social Security Bulletin, Annual Statistical Supplement 2019" (https://www.ssa.gov/policy/docs/statcomps/supplement/)
*As of December 2018. National average includes payments to beneficiaries in U.S. territories and foreign countries. The SSI program provides income support to persons age 65 and older and blind or disabled adults and children.

Medicare Enrollees in 2018

National Total = 59,989,883 Enrollees*

ALPHA ORDER

RANK	STATE	ENROLLEES	% of USA
21	Alabama	1,027,493	1.7%
50	Alaska	96,213	0.2%
16	Arizona	1,271,312	2.1%
30	Arkansas	627,641	1.0%
1	California	6,124,095	10.2%
25	Colorado	881,044	1.5%
29	Connecticut	667,724	1.1%
45	Delaware	201,092	0.3%
2	Florida	4,412,700	7.4%
10	Georgia	1,676,019	2.8%
42	Hawaii	266,940	0.4%
40	Idaho	320,219	0.5%
7	Illinois	2,193,624	3.7%
17	Indiana	1,233,673	2.1%
31	Iowa	612,391	1.0%
33	Kansas	523,149	0.9%
24	Kentucky	912,477	1.5%
26	Louisiana	848,975	1.4%
39	Maine	331,222	0.6%
22	Maryland	1,011,531	1.7%
15	Massachusetts	1,304,654	2.2%
8	Michigan	2,024,434	3.4%
23	Minnesota	996,224	1.7%
32	Mississippi	590,989	1.0%
18	Missouri	1,204,788	2.0%
43	Montana	223,046	0.4%
38	Nebraska	338,009	0.6%
34	Nevada	511,711	0.9%
41	New Hampshire	290,178	0.5%
11	New Jersey	1,584,755	2.6%
36	New Mexico	409,851	0.7%
4	New York	3,559,173	5.9%
9	North Carolina	1,931,885	3.2%
48	North Dakota	127,675	0.2%
6	Ohio	2,295,136	3.8%
28	Oklahoma	722,454	1.2%
27	Oregon	836,937	1.4%
5	Pennsylvania	2,683,395	4.5%
44	Rhode Island	216,308	0.4%
20	South Carolina	1,040,376	1.7%
46	South Dakota	170,943	0.3%
13	Tennessee	1,325,043	2.2%
3	Texas	4,018,970	6.7%
37	Utah	386,332	0.6%
47	Vermont	143,533	0.2%
12	Virginia	1,469,980	2.5%
14	Washington	1,320,498	2.2%
35	West Virginia	433,950	0.7%
19	Wisconsin	1,142,418	1.9%
49	Wyoming	106,143	0.2%

RANK ORDER

RANK	STATE	ENROLLEES	% of USA
1	California	6,124,095	10.2%
2	Florida	4,412,700	7.4%
3	Texas	4,018,970	6.7%
4	New York	3,559,173	5.9%
5	Pennsylvania	2,683,395	4.5%
6	Ohio	2,295,136	3.8%
7	Illinois	2,193,624	3.7%
8	Michigan	2,024,434	3.4%
9	North Carolina	1,931,885	3.2%
10	Georgia	1,676,019	2.8%
11	New Jersey	1,584,755	2.6%
12	Virginia	1,469,980	2.5%
13	Tennessee	1,325,043	2.2%
14	Washington	1,320,498	2.2%
15	Massachusetts	1,304,654	2.2%
16	Arizona	1,271,312	2.1%
17	Indiana	1,233,673	2.1%
18	Missouri	1,204,788	2.0%
19	Wisconsin	1,142,418	1.9%
20	South Carolina	1,040,376	1.7%
21	Alabama	1,027,493	1.7%
22	Maryland	1,011,531	1.7%
23	Minnesota	996,224	1.7%
24	Kentucky	912,477	1.5%
25	Colorado	881,044	1.5%
26	Louisiana	848,975	1.4%
27	Oregon	836,937	1.4%
28	Oklahoma	722,454	1.2%
29	Connecticut	667,724	1.1%
30	Arkansas	627,641	1.0%
31	Iowa	612,391	1.0%
32	Mississippi	590,989	1.0%
33	Kansas	523,149	0.9%
34	Nevada	511,711	0.9%
35	West Virginia	433,950	0.7%
36	New Mexico	409,851	0.7%
37	Utah	386,332	0.6%
38	Nebraska	338,009	0.6%
39	Maine	331,222	0.6%
40	Idaho	320,219	0.5%
41	New Hampshire	290,178	0.5%
42	Hawaii	266,940	0.4%
43	Montana	223,046	0.4%
44	Rhode Island	216,308	0.4%
45	Delaware	201,092	0.3%
46	South Dakota	170,943	0.3%
47	Vermont	143,533	0.2%
48	North Dakota	127,675	0.2%
49	Wyoming	106,143	0.2%
50	Alaska	96,213	0.2%
	District of Columbia	92,528	0.2%

Source: U.S. Department of Health and Human Services, Centers for Medicare and Medicaid Services
"Medicare Enrollment Dashboard"
(https://www.cms.gov/Research-Statistics-Data-and-Systems/Statistics-Trends-and-Reports/CMSProgramStatistics/Dashboard.html)
*Includes original Medicare, Medicare Advantage, and other Medicare health plans. Includes aged and disabled enrollees. Total includes 1,246,854 enrollees in Puerto Rico and other outlying areas, foreign countries, or whose address is unknown.

Percent of Population Enrolled in Medicare in 2018

National Percent = 18.0% of Population*

ALPHA ORDER

RANK	STATE	PERCENT
5	Alabama	21.0
49	Alaska	13.1
35	Arizona	17.8
8	Arkansas	20.9
46	California	15.5
46	Colorado	15.5
26	Connecticut	18.7
9	Delaware	20.8
9	Florida	20.8
45	Georgia	15.9
25	Hawaii	18.8
30	Idaho	18.3
41	Illinois	17.2
28	Indiana	18.4
23	Iowa	19.4
34	Kansas	18.0
11	Kentucky	20.5
32	Louisiana	18.2
1	Maine	24.7
43	Maryland	16.8
24	Massachusetts	19.0
14	Michigan	20.3
35	Minnesota	17.8
16	Mississippi	19.8
17	Missouri	19.7
5	Montana	21.0
38	Nebraska	17.6
42	Nevada	16.9
4	New Hampshire	21.4
35	New Jersey	17.8
20	New Mexico	19.6
32	New York	18.2
27	North Carolina	18.6
43	North Dakota	16.8
17	Ohio	19.7
30	Oklahoma	18.3
15	Oregon	20.0
5	Pennsylvania	21.0
13	Rhode Island	20.4
11	South Carolina	20.5
22	South Dakota	19.5
20	Tennessee	19.6
48	Texas	14.0
50	Utah	12.3
3	Vermont	23.0
40	Virginia	17.3
38	Washington	17.6
2	West Virginia	24.1
17	Wisconsin	19.7
28	Wyoming	18.4

RANK ORDER

RANK	STATE	PERCENT
1	Maine	24.7
2	West Virginia	24.1
3	Vermont	23.0
4	New Hampshire	21.4
5	Alabama	21.0
5	Montana	21.0
5	Pennsylvania	21.0
8	Arkansas	20.9
9	Delaware	20.8
9	Florida	20.8
11	Kentucky	20.5
11	South Carolina	20.5
13	Rhode Island	20.4
14	Michigan	20.3
15	Oregon	20.0
16	Mississippi	19.8
17	Missouri	19.7
17	Ohio	19.7
17	Wisconsin	19.7
20	New Mexico	19.6
20	Tennessee	19.6
22	South Dakota	19.5
23	Iowa	19.4
24	Massachusetts	19.0
25	Hawaii	18.8
26	Connecticut	18.7
27	North Carolina	18.6
28	Indiana	18.4
28	Wyoming	18.4
30	Idaho	18.3
30	Oklahoma	18.3
32	Louisiana	18.2
32	New York	18.2
34	Kansas	18.0
35	Arizona	17.8
35	Minnesota	17.8
35	New Jersey	17.8
38	Nebraska	17.6
38	Washington	17.6
40	Virginia	17.3
41	Illinois	17.2
42	Nevada	16.9
43	Maryland	16.8
43	North Dakota	16.8
45	Georgia	15.9
46	California	15.5
46	Colorado	15.5
48	Texas	14.0
49	Alaska	13.1
50	Utah	12.3
	District of Columbia	13.2

Source: CQ Press using data from U.S. Department of Health and Human Services, Centers for Medicare and Medicaid Services
"Medicare Enrollment Dashboard"
(https://www.cms.gov/Research-Statistics-Data-and-Systems/Statistics-Trends-and-Reports/CMSProgramStatistics/Dashboard.html)
*Includes original Medicare, Medicare Advantage, and other Medicare health plans. Includes aged and disabled enrollees. National rate does not include enrollees or population in Puerto Rico and other outlying areas, foreign countries, or whose address is unknown.

Medicare Actual Costs in 2017

National Total = $348,396,000,000*

RANK	STATE	ACTUAL COSTS	% of USA
22	Alabama	$5,477,483,849	1.6%
50	Alaska	772,816,833	0.2%
19	Arizona	6,268,738,651	1.8%
29	Arkansas	4,000,943,849	1.1%
1	California	33,671,826,462	9.7%
28	Colorado	4,063,064,794	1.2%
26	Connecticut	4,866,220,835	1.4%
41	Delaware	1,662,857,470	0.5%
2	Florida	24,816,598,305	7.1%
14	Georgia	9,060,670,578	2.6%
47	Hawaii	868,394,554	0.2%
42	Idaho	1,584,985,596	0.5%
5	Illinois	15,400,383,814	4.4%
15	Indiana	8,053,926,279	2.3%
30	Iowa	3,984,037,399	1.1%
31	Kansas	3,780,125,182	1.1%
21	Kentucky	5,572,101,121	1.6%
23	Louisiana	5,454,323,512	1.6%
38	Maine	1,894,475,844	0.5%
13	Maryland	9,077,659,582	2.6%
11	Massachusetts	9,863,856,040	2.8%
9	Michigan	12,244,949,542	3.5%
32	Minnesota	3,286,387,434	0.9%
27	Mississippi	4,639,489,180	1.3%
16	Missouri	7,006,197,656	2.0%
43	Montana	1,282,703,061	0.4%
36	Nebraska	2,513,000,027	0.7%
34	Nevada	2,872,247,035	0.8%
37	New Hampshire	2,096,250,626	0.6%
7	New Jersey	12,800,709,100	3.7%
39	New Mexico	1,880,725,746	0.5%
4	New York	21,489,458,732	6.2%
10	North Carolina	11,070,482,681	3.2%
48	North Dakota	836,287,474	0.2%
8	Ohio	12,266,623,611	3.5%
24	Oklahoma	5,441,425,180	1.6%
33	Oregon	3,282,178,615	0.9%
6	Pennsylvania	14,137,744,194	4.1%
46	Rhode Island	978,327,954	0.3%
20	South Carolina	6,261,958,287	1.8%
44	South Dakota	1,055,054,002	0.3%
17	Tennessee	6,973,979,929	2.0%
3	Texas	24,677,807,114	7.1%
40	Utah	1,832,418,092	0.5%
45	Vermont	1,023,357,634	0.3%
12	Virginia	9,353,016,080	2.7%
18	Washington	6,864,124,646	2.0%
35	West Virginia	2,612,417,058	0.7%
25	Wisconsin	5,323,343,851	1.5%
49	Wyoming	805,612,802	0.2%

RANK ORDER

RANK	STATE	ACTUAL COSTS	% of USA
1	California	$33,671,826,462	9.7%
2	Florida	24,816,598,305	7.1%
3	Texas	24,677,807,114	7.1%
4	New York	21,489,458,732	6.2%
5	Illinois	15,400,383,814	4.4%
6	Pennsylvania	14,137,744,194	4.1%
7	New Jersey	12,800,709,100	3.7%
8	Ohio	12,266,623,611	3.5%
9	Michigan	12,244,949,542	3.5%
10	North Carolina	11,070,482,681	3.2%
11	Massachusetts	9,863,856,040	2.8%
12	Virginia	9,353,016,080	2.7%
13	Maryland	9,077,659,582	2.6%
14	Georgia	9,060,670,578	2.6%
15	Indiana	8,053,926,279	2.3%
16	Missouri	7,006,197,656	2.0%
17	Tennessee	6,973,979,929	2.0%
18	Washington	6,864,124,646	2.0%
19	Arizona	6,268,738,651	1.8%
20	South Carolina	6,261,958,287	1.8%
21	Kentucky	5,572,101,121	1.6%
22	Alabama	5,477,483,849	1.6%
23	Louisiana	5,454,323,512	1.6%
24	Oklahoma	5,441,425,180	1.6%
25	Wisconsin	5,323,343,851	1.5%
26	Connecticut	4,866,220,835	1.4%
27	Mississippi	4,639,489,180	1.3%
28	Colorado	4,063,064,794	1.2%
29	Arkansas	4,000,943,849	1.1%
30	Iowa	3,984,037,399	1.1%
31	Kansas	3,780,125,182	1.1%
32	Minnesota	3,286,387,434	0.9%
33	Oregon	3,282,178,615	0.9%
34	Nevada	2,872,247,035	0.8%
35	West Virginia	2,612,417,058	0.7%
36	Nebraska	2,513,000,027	0.7%
37	New Hampshire	2,096,250,626	0.6%
38	Maine	1,894,475,844	0.5%
39	New Mexico	1,880,725,746	0.5%
40	Utah	1,832,418,092	0.5%
41	Delaware	1,662,857,470	0.5%
42	Idaho	1,584,985,596	0.5%
43	Montana	1,282,703,061	0.4%
44	South Dakota	1,055,054,002	0.3%
45	Vermont	1,023,357,634	0.3%
46	Rhode Island	978,327,954	0.3%
47	Hawaii	868,394,554	0.2%
48	North Dakota	836,287,474	0.2%
49	Wyoming	805,612,802	0.2%
50	Alaska	772,816,833	0.2%
	District of Columbia	724,424,858	0.2%

Source: U.S. Department of Health and Human Services, Centers for Medicare and Medicaid Services
"Medicare Geographic Variation" (Public Use File)
(https://www.cms.gov/Research-Statistics-Data-and-Systems/Statistics-Trends-and-Reports/Medicare-Geographic-Variation/)
*Total actual costs not standardized for geographical variations. National figure includes payments to enrollees in Puerto Rico and other outlying areas.

Medicare Actual Costs per Beneficiary in 2017

National Rate = $6,384*

ALPHA ORDER		
RANK	STATE	PER BENEFICIARY
39	Alabama	$5,671
2	Alaska	9,372
41	Arizona	5,427
20	Arkansas	6,766
32	California	6,166
44	Colorado	5,160
11	Connecticut	8,068
4	Delaware	9,023
34	Florida	5,988
35	Georgia	5,885
49	Hawaii	3,760
42	Idaho	5,394
14	Illinois	7,697
17	Indiana	6,967
18	Iowa	6,924
13	Kansas	7,810
24	Kentucky	6,519
19	Louisiana	6,863
31	Maine	6,198
1	Maryland	10,332
5	Massachusetts	8,420
26	Michigan	6,378
50	Minnesota	3,570
7	Mississippi	8,230
30	Missouri	6,216
29	Montana	6,242
10	Nebraska	8,071
27	Nevada	6,355
9	New Hampshire	8,133
3	New Jersey	9,026
46	New Mexico	5,090
22	New York	6,720
33	North Carolina	6,088
15	North Dakota	7,111
37	Ohio	5,738
8	Oklahoma	8,150
48	Oregon	4,291
38	Pennsylvania	5,693
45	Rhode Island	5,104
25	South Carolina	6,451
23	South Dakota	6,706
40	Tennessee	5,601
21	Texas	6,748
43	Utah	5,342
12	Vermont	7,835
16	Virginia	7,075
36	Washington	5,750
28	West Virginia	6,325
47	Wisconsin	4,975
6	Wyoming	8,317

RANK ORDER		
RANK	STATE	PER BENEFICIARY
1	Maryland	$10,332
2	Alaska	9,372
3	New Jersey	9,026
4	Delaware	9,023
5	Massachusetts	8,420
6	Wyoming	8,317
7	Mississippi	8,230
8	Oklahoma	8,150
9	New Hampshire	8,133
10	Nebraska	8,071
11	Connecticut	8,068
12	Vermont	7,835
13	Kansas	7,810
14	Illinois	7,697
15	North Dakota	7,111
16	Virginia	7,075
17	Indiana	6,967
18	Iowa	6,924
19	Louisiana	6,863
20	Arkansas	6,766
21	Texas	6,748
22	New York	6,720
23	South Dakota	6,706
24	Kentucky	6,519
25	South Carolina	6,451
26	Michigan	6,378
27	Nevada	6,355
28	West Virginia	6,325
29	Montana	6,242
30	Missouri	6,216
31	Maine	6,198
32	California	6,166
33	North Carolina	6,088
34	Florida	5,988
35	Georgia	5,885
36	Washington	5,750
37	Ohio	5,738
38	Pennsylvania	5,693
39	Alabama	5,671
40	Tennessee	5,601
41	Arizona	5,427
42	Idaho	5,394
43	Utah	5,342
44	Colorado	5,160
45	Rhode Island	5,104
46	New Mexico	5,090
47	Wisconsin	4,975
48	Oregon	4,291
49	Hawaii	3,760
50	Minnesota	3,570

District of Columbia   9,556

Source: CQ Press using data from U.S. Department of Health and Human Services, Centers for Medicare and Medicaid Services "Medicare Geographic Variation" (Public Use File)
(https://www.cms.gov/Research-Statistics-Data-and-Systems/Statistics-Trends-and-Reports/Medicare-Geographic-Variation/)
*Total actual costs not standardized for geographical variations. National figure includes payments and enrollees in Puerto Rico and other outlying areas.

Medicaid Enrollment in 2017

National Total = 80,242,585 Enrollees*

ALPHA ORDER

RANK	STATE	ENROLLEES	% of USA
26	Alabama	1,037,814	1.3%
47	Alaska	155,865	0.2%
10	Arizona	1,917,183	2.4%
27	Arkansas	993,792	1.2%
1	California	13,515,168	16.8%
19	Colorado	1,381,208	1.7%
30	Connecticut	860,758	1.1%
44	Delaware	222,859	0.3%
5	Florida	3,916,490	4.9%
13	Georgia	1,813,016	2.3%
37	Hawaii	365,087	0.5%
39	Idaho	299,253	0.4%
6	Illinois	3,192,569	4.0%
17	Indiana	1,475,463	1.8%
34	Iowa	623,501	0.8%
36	Kansas	416,645	0.5%
18	Kentucky	1,403,257	1.7%
15	Louisiana	1,626,037	2.0%
41	Maine	273,451	0.3%
20	Maryland	1,326,080	1.7%
11	Massachusetts	1,874,779	2.3%
3	Michigan	4,668,815	5.8%
23	Minnesota	1,107,499	1.4%
32	Mississippi	708,992	0.9%
28	Missouri	983,835	1.2%
43	Montana	230,296	0.3%
42	Nebraska	247,894	0.3%
33	Nevada	653,968	0.8%
45	New Hampshire	204,458	0.3%
14	New Jersey	1,678,888	2.1%
29	New Mexico	898,965	1.1%
2	New York	6,105,120	7.6%
9	North Carolina	2,110,914	2.6%
49	North Dakota	92,595	0.1%
7	Ohio	3,083,411	3.8%
31	Oklahoma	808,267	1.0%
25	Oregon	1,067,322	1.3%
8	Pennsylvania	2,835,800	3.5%
38	Rhode Island	337,809	0.4%
21	South Carolina	1,217,302	1.5%
48	South Dakota	124,676	0.2%
16	Tennessee	1,522,658	1.9%
4	Texas	4,038,159	5.0%
40	Utah	284,316	0.4%
46	Vermont	183,918	0.2%
24	Virginia	1,083,750	1.4%
12	Washington	1,824,730	2.3%
35	West Virginia	521,186	0.6%
22	Wisconsin	1,197,770	1.5%
50	Wyoming	61,529	0.1%

RANK ORDER

RANK	STATE	ENROLLEES	% of USA
1	California	13,515,168	16.8%
2	New York	6,105,120	7.6%
3	Michigan	4,668,815	5.8%
4	Texas	4,038,159	5.0%
5	Florida	3,916,490	4.9%
6	Illinois	3,192,569	4.0%
7	Ohio	3,083,411	3.8%
8	Pennsylvania	2,835,800	3.5%
9	North Carolina	2,110,914	2.6%
10	Arizona	1,917,183	2.4%
11	Massachusetts	1,874,779	2.3%
12	Washington	1,824,730	2.3%
13	Georgia	1,813,016	2.3%
14	New Jersey	1,678,888	2.1%
15	Louisiana	1,626,037	2.0%
16	Tennessee	1,522,658	1.9%
17	Indiana	1,475,463	1.8%
18	Kentucky	1,403,257	1.7%
19	Colorado	1,381,208	1.7%
20	Maryland	1,326,080	1.7%
21	South Carolina	1,217,302	1.5%
22	Wisconsin	1,197,770	1.5%
23	Minnesota	1,107,499	1.4%
24	Virginia	1,083,750	1.4%
25	Oregon	1,067,322	1.3%
26	Alabama	1,037,814	1.3%
27	Arkansas	993,792	1.2%
28	Missouri	983,835	1.2%
29	New Mexico	898,965	1.1%
30	Connecticut	860,758	1.1%
31	Oklahoma	808,267	1.0%
32	Mississippi	708,992	0.9%
33	Nevada	653,968	0.8%
34	Iowa	623,501	0.8%
35	West Virginia	521,186	0.6%
36	Kansas	416,645	0.5%
37	Hawaii	365,087	0.5%
38	Rhode Island	337,809	0.4%
39	Idaho	299,253	0.4%
40	Utah	284,316	0.4%
41	Maine	273,451	0.3%
42	Nebraska	247,894	0.3%
43	Montana	230,296	0.3%
44	Delaware	222,859	0.3%
45	New Hampshire	204,458	0.3%
46	Vermont	183,918	0.2%
47	Alaska	155,865	0.2%
48	South Dakota	124,676	0.2%
49	North Dakota	92,595	0.1%
50	Wyoming	61,529	0.1%
	District of Columbia	265,547	0.3%

Source: U.S. Department of Health and Human Services, Centers for Medicare and Medicaid Services
   "2017 Medicaid Managed Care Enrollment Report" (https://www.medicaid.gov/medicaid/managed-care/enrollment/index.html)
*Unduplicated enrollment as of July 1, 2017. National total includes 1,401,921 Medicaid enrollees in Puerto Rico.

Percent of Population Enrolled in Medicaid in 2017

National Percent = 24.3% of Population*

ALPHA ORDER			RANK ORDER		
RANK	STATE	PERCENT	RANK	STATE	PERCENT
29	Alabama	21.3	1	Michigan	46.8
30	Alaska	21.1	2	New Mexico	43.0
12	Arizona	27.2	3	Louisiana	34.8
5	Arkansas	33.1	4	California	34.3
4	California	34.3	5	Arkansas	33.1
17	Colorado	24.6	6	Rhode Island	32.0
20	Connecticut	24.1	7	Kentucky	31.5
22	Delaware	23.3	8	New York	31.2
38	Florida	18.7	9	Vermont	29.5
39	Georgia	17.4	10	West Virginia	28.7
15	Hawaii	25.6	11	Massachusetts	27.3
39	Idaho	17.4	12	Arizona	27.2
16	Illinois	25.0	13	Ohio	26.4
24	Indiana	22.2	14	Oregon	25.8
36	Iowa	19.8	15	Hawaii	25.6
43	Kansas	14.3	16	Illinois	25.0
7	Kentucky	31.5	17	Colorado	24.6
3	Louisiana	34.8	17	Washington	24.6
34	Maine	20.5	19	South Carolina	24.2
26	Maryland	22.0	20	Connecticut	24.1
11	Massachusetts	27.3	21	Mississippi	23.7
1	Michigan	46.8	22	Delaware	23.3
35	Minnesota	19.9	23	Tennessee	22.7
21	Mississippi	23.7	24	Indiana	22.2
41	Missouri	16.1	24	Pennsylvania	22.2
28	Montana	21.9	26	Maryland	22.0
46	Nebraska	12.9	26	Nevada	22.0
26	Nevada	22.0	28	Montana	21.9
42	New Hampshire	15.2	29	Alabama	21.3
37	New Jersey	18.9	30	Alaska	21.1
2	New Mexico	43.0	31	Wisconsin	20.7
8	New York	31.2	32	North Carolina	20.6
32	North Carolina	20.6	32	Oklahoma	20.6
48	North Dakota	12.3	34	Maine	20.5
13	Ohio	26.4	35	Minnesota	19.9
32	Oklahoma	20.6	36	Iowa	19.8
14	Oregon	25.8	37	New Jersey	18.9
24	Pennsylvania	22.2	38	Florida	18.7
6	Rhode Island	32.0	39	Georgia	17.4
19	South Carolina	24.2	39	Idaho	17.4
43	South Dakota	14.3	41	Missouri	16.1
23	Tennessee	22.7	42	New Hampshire	15.2
43	Texas	14.3	43	Kansas	14.3
50	Utah	9.2	43	South Dakota	14.3
9	Vermont	29.5	43	Texas	14.3
47	Virginia	12.8	46	Nebraska	12.9
17	Washington	24.6	47	Virginia	12.8
10	West Virginia	28.7	48	North Dakota	12.3
31	Wisconsin	20.7	49	Wyoming	10.6
49	Wyoming	10.6	50	Utah	9.2
				District of Columbia	38.2

Source: CQ Press using data from U.S. Department of Health and Human Services, Centers for Medicare and Medicaid Services
"2017 Medicaid Managed Care Enrollment Report" (https://www.medicaid.gov/medicaid/managed-care/enrollment/index.html)
*Unduplicated enrollment as of July 1, 2017. National percent does not include recipients or population in U.S. territories.

Estimated Medicaid Expenditures in 2019

National Total = $613,095,000,000*

ALPHA ORDER

RANK	STATE	EXPENDITURES	% of USA
28	Alabama	$7,060,000,000	1.2%
41	Alaska	2,291,000,000	0.4%
12	Arizona	13,434,000,000	2.2%
27	Arkansas	7,421,000,000	1.2%
1	California	91,419,000,000	14.9%
24	Colorado	9,951,000,000	1.6%
26	Connecticut	8,100,000,000	1.3%
45	Delaware	2,181,000,000	0.4%
5	Florida	28,309,000,000	4.6%
20	Georgia	10,654,000,000	1.7%
40	Hawaii	2,327,000,000	0.4%
42	Idaho	2,285,000,000	0.4%
7	Illinois	20,952,000,000	3.4%
14	Indiana	12,482,000,000	2.0%
32	Iowa	5,535,000,000	0.9%
36	Kansas	3,760,000,000	0.6%
23	Kentucky	10,181,000,000	1.7%
18	Louisiana	11,565,000,000	1.9%
38	Maine	2,975,000,000	0.5%
17	Maryland	11,838,000,000	1.9%
9	Massachusetts	17,168,000,000	2.8%
8	Michigan	18,059,000,000	2.9%
15	Minnesota	12,452,000,000	2.0%
33	Mississippi	5,403,000,000	0.9%
22	Missouri	10,268,000,000	1.7%
46	Montana	1,805,000,000	0.3%
43	Nebraska	2,218,000,000	0.4%
35	Nevada	3,971,000,000	0.6%
44	New Hampshire	2,192,000,000	0.4%
10	New Jersey	15,345,000,000	2.5%
31	New Mexico	5,620,000,000	0.9%
2	New York	60,374,000,000	9.8%
11	North Carolina	14,287,000,000	2.3%
48	North Dakota	1,199,000,000	0.2%
6	Ohio	26,972,000,000	4.4%
30	Oklahoma	5,792,000,000	0.9%
25	Oregon	9,370,000,000	1.5%
4	Pennsylvania	32,294,000,000	5.3%
39	Rhode Island	2,772,000,000	0.5%
29	South Carolina	6,770,000,000	1.1%
49	South Dakota	917,000,000	0.1%
16	Tennessee	12,155,000,000	2.0%
3	Texas	36,493,000,000	6.0%
37	Utah	3,414,000,000	0.6%
47	Vermont	1,673,000,000	0.3%
19	Virginia	11,301,000,000	1.8%
13	Washington	12,568,000,000	2.0%
34	West Virginia	4,345,000,000	0.7%
21	Wisconsin	10,551,000,000	1.7%
50	Wyoming	627,000,000	0.1%

RANK ORDER

RANK	STATE	EXPENDITURES	% of USA
1	California	$91,419,000,000	14.9%
2	New York	60,374,000,000	9.8%
3	Texas	36,493,000,000	6.0%
4	Pennsylvania	32,294,000,000	5.3%
5	Florida	28,309,000,000	4.6%
6	Ohio	26,972,000,000	4.4%
7	Illinois	20,952,000,000	3.4%
8	Michigan	18,059,000,000	2.9%
9	Massachusetts	17,168,000,000	2.8%
10	New Jersey	15,345,000,000	2.5%
11	North Carolina	14,287,000,000	2.3%
12	Arizona	13,434,000,000	2.2%
13	Washington	12,568,000,000	2.0%
14	Indiana	12,482,000,000	2.0%
15	Minnesota	12,452,000,000	2.0%
16	Tennessee	12,155,000,000	2.0%
17	Maryland	11,838,000,000	1.9%
18	Louisiana	11,565,000,000	1.9%
19	Virginia	11,301,000,000	1.8%
20	Georgia	10,654,000,000	1.7%
21	Wisconsin	10,551,000,000	1.7%
22	Missouri	10,268,000,000	1.7%
23	Kentucky	10,181,000,000	1.7%
24	Colorado	9,951,000,000	1.6%
25	Oregon	9,370,000,000	1.5%
26	Connecticut	8,100,000,000	1.3%
27	Arkansas	7,421,000,000	1.2%
28	Alabama	7,060,000,000	1.2%
29	South Carolina	6,770,000,000	1.1%
30	Oklahoma	5,792,000,000	0.9%
31	New Mexico	5,620,000,000	0.9%
32	Iowa	5,535,000,000	0.9%
33	Mississippi	5,403,000,000	0.9%
34	West Virginia	4,345,000,000	0.7%
35	Nevada	3,971,000,000	0.6%
36	Kansas	3,760,000,000	0.6%
37	Utah	3,414,000,000	0.6%
38	Maine	2,975,000,000	0.5%
39	Rhode Island	2,772,000,000	0.5%
40	Hawaii	2,327,000,000	0.4%
41	Alaska	2,291,000,000	0.4%
42	Idaho	2,285,000,000	0.4%
43	Nebraska	2,218,000,000	0.4%
44	New Hampshire	2,192,000,000	0.4%
45	Delaware	2,181,000,000	0.4%
46	Montana	1,805,000,000	0.3%
47	Vermont	1,673,000,000	0.3%
48	North Dakota	1,199,000,000	0.2%
49	South Dakota	917,000,000	0.1%
50	Wyoming	627,000,000	0.1%
	District of Columbia**	NA	NA

Source: National Association of State Budget Officers
   "State Expenditure Report" (www.nasbo.org)
*Estimates for fiscal year 2019.
**Not available.

Percent Change in Medicaid Expenditures: 2017 to 2019

National Percent Change = 4.8% Increase*

RANK	STATE	PERCENT CHANGE		RANK	STATE	PERCENT CHANGE
	ALPHA ORDER				RANK ORDER	
14	Alabama	7.3		1	Utah	22.3
6	Alaska	11.3		2	Virginia	14.6
9	Arizona	8.1		3	West Virginia	13.5
24	Arkansas	4.5		4	Kansas	11.5
13	California	7.4		5	Florida	11.4
18	Colorado	5.8		6	Alaska	11.3
42	Connecticut	0.2		7	Indiana	10.8
49	Delaware	(4.1)		8	Hawaii	8.7
5	Florida	11.4		9	Arizona	8.1
45	Georgia	(1.6)		10	Tennessee	8.0
8	Hawaii	8.7		11	Texas	7.8
15	Idaho	6.4		12	Wisconsin	7.6
50	Illinois	(7.4)		13	California	7.4
7	Indiana	10.8		14	Alabama	7.3
30	Iowa	3.0		15	Idaho	6.4
4	Kansas	11.5		15	Oregon	6.4
44	Kentucky	(1.4)		17	Mississippi	6.3
26	Louisiana	3.8		18	Colorado	5.8
20	Maine	5.3		19	Pennsylvania	5.4
31	Maryland	2.9		20	Maine	5.3
31	Massachusetts	2.9		20	Nevada	5.3
22	Michigan	4.7		22	Michigan	4.7
48	Minnesota	(1.8)		22	Oklahoma	4.7
17	Mississippi	6.3		24	Arkansas	4.5
40	Missouri	1.1		25	Vermont	4.4
45	Montana	(1.6)		26	Louisiana	3.8
29	Nebraska	3.2		27	New Jersey	3.7
20	Nevada	5.3		28	New York	3.5
41	New Hampshire	0.6		29	Nebraska	3.2
27	New Jersey	3.7		30	Iowa	3.0
43	New Mexico	0.1		31	Maryland	2.9
28	New York	3.5		31	Massachusetts	2.9
36	North Carolina	2.4		33	South Carolina	2.5
47	North Dakota	(1.7)		33	South Dakota	2.5
39	Ohio	1.9		33	Wyoming	2.5
22	Oklahoma	4.7		36	North Carolina	2.4
15	Oregon	6.4		37	Rhode Island	2.2
19	Pennsylvania	5.4		38	Washington	2.1
37	Rhode Island	2.2		39	Ohio	1.9
33	South Carolina	2.5		40	Missouri	1.1
33	South Dakota	2.5		41	New Hampshire	0.6
10	Tennessee	8.0		42	Connecticut	0.2
11	Texas	7.8		43	New Mexico	0.1
1	Utah	22.3		44	Kentucky	(1.4)
25	Vermont	4.4		45	Georgia	(1.6)
2	Virginia	14.6		45	Montana	(1.6)
38	Washington	2.1		47	North Dakota	(1.7)
3	West Virginia	13.5		48	Minnesota	(1.8)
12	Wisconsin	7.6		49	Delaware	(4.1)
33	Wyoming	2.5		50	Illinois	(7.4)
					District of Columbia**	NA

Source: National Association of State Budget Officers
"State Expenditure Report" (www.nasbo.org)
*Estimates for fiscal year 2019.
**Not available.

Percent of Population Receiving Public Aid in 2018

National Percent = 3.1% of Population*

<table>
<tr><td colspan="3">ALPHA ORDER</td><td colspan="3">RANK ORDER</td></tr>
<tr><td>RANK</td><td>STATE</td><td>PERCENT</td><td>RANK</td><td>STATE</td><td>PERCENT</td></tr>
<tr><td>9</td><td>Alabama</td><td>3.7</td><td>1</td><td>California</td><td>5.0</td></tr>
<tr><td>25</td><td>Alaska</td><td>2.6</td><td>2</td><td>Kentucky</td><td>4.7</td></tr>
<tr><td>43</td><td>Arizona</td><td>1.9</td><td>2</td><td>West Virginia</td><td>4.7</td></tr>
<tr><td>9</td><td>Arkansas</td><td>3.7</td><td>4</td><td>Mississippi</td><td>4.2</td></tr>
<tr><td>1</td><td>California</td><td>5.0</td><td>4</td><td>New Mexico</td><td>4.2</td></tr>
<tr><td>43</td><td>Colorado</td><td>1.9</td><td>4</td><td>New York</td><td>4.2</td></tr>
<tr><td>33</td><td>Connecticut</td><td>2.4</td><td>7</td><td>Rhode Island</td><td>4.1</td></tr>
<tr><td>20</td><td>Delaware</td><td>2.8</td><td>8</td><td>Louisiana</td><td>4.0</td></tr>
<tr><td>17</td><td>Florida</td><td>3.0</td><td>9</td><td>Alabama</td><td>3.7</td></tr>
<tr><td>22</td><td>Georgia</td><td>2.7</td><td>9</td><td>Arkansas</td><td>3.7</td></tr>
<tr><td>29</td><td>Hawaii</td><td>2.5</td><td>11</td><td>Pennsylvania</td><td>3.6</td></tr>
<tr><td>43</td><td>Idaho</td><td>1.9</td><td>12</td><td>Massachusetts</td><td>3.4</td></tr>
<tr><td>36</td><td>Illinois</td><td>2.3</td><td>12</td><td>Ohio</td><td>3.4</td></tr>
<tr><td>41</td><td>Indiana</td><td>2.1</td><td>14</td><td>Maine</td><td>3.3</td></tr>
<tr><td>39</td><td>Iowa</td><td>2.2</td><td>15</td><td>Tennessee</td><td>3.2</td></tr>
<tr><td>47</td><td>Kansas</td><td>1.8</td><td>15</td><td>Vermont</td><td>3.2</td></tr>
<tr><td>2</td><td>Kentucky</td><td>4.7</td><td>17</td><td>Florida</td><td>3.0</td></tr>
<tr><td>8</td><td>Louisiana</td><td>4.0</td><td>17</td><td>Michigan</td><td>3.0</td></tr>
<tr><td>14</td><td>Maine</td><td>3.3</td><td>19</td><td>Oregon</td><td>2.9</td></tr>
<tr><td>22</td><td>Maryland</td><td>2.7</td><td>20</td><td>Delaware</td><td>2.8</td></tr>
<tr><td>12</td><td>Massachusetts</td><td>3.4</td><td>20</td><td>Oklahoma</td><td>2.8</td></tr>
<tr><td>17</td><td>Michigan</td><td>3.0</td><td>22</td><td>Georgia</td><td>2.7</td></tr>
<tr><td>33</td><td>Minnesota</td><td>2.4</td><td>22</td><td>Maryland</td><td>2.7</td></tr>
<tr><td>4</td><td>Mississippi</td><td>4.2</td><td>22</td><td>Washington</td><td>2.7</td></tr>
<tr><td>25</td><td>Missouri</td><td>2.6</td><td>25</td><td>Alaska</td><td>2.6</td></tr>
<tr><td>29</td><td>Montana</td><td>2.5</td><td>25</td><td>Missouri</td><td>2.6</td></tr>
<tr><td>42</td><td>Nebraska</td><td>2.0</td><td>25</td><td>Nevada</td><td>2.6</td></tr>
<tr><td>25</td><td>Nevada</td><td>2.6</td><td>25</td><td>South Carolina</td><td>2.6</td></tr>
<tr><td>43</td><td>New Hampshire</td><td>1.9</td><td>29</td><td>Hawaii</td><td>2.5</td></tr>
<tr><td>36</td><td>New Jersey</td><td>2.3</td><td>29</td><td>Montana</td><td>2.5</td></tr>
<tr><td>4</td><td>New Mexico</td><td>4.2</td><td>29</td><td>Texas</td><td>2.5</td></tr>
<tr><td>4</td><td>New York</td><td>4.2</td><td>29</td><td>Wisconsin</td><td>2.5</td></tr>
<tr><td>33</td><td>North Carolina</td><td>2.4</td><td>33</td><td>Connecticut</td><td>2.4</td></tr>
<tr><td>48</td><td>North Dakota</td><td>1.4</td><td>33</td><td>Minnesota</td><td>2.4</td></tr>
<tr><td>12</td><td>Ohio</td><td>3.4</td><td>33</td><td>North Carolina</td><td>2.4</td></tr>
<tr><td>20</td><td>Oklahoma</td><td>2.8</td><td>36</td><td>Illinois</td><td>2.3</td></tr>
<tr><td>19</td><td>Oregon</td><td>2.9</td><td>36</td><td>New Jersey</td><td>2.3</td></tr>
<tr><td>11</td><td>Pennsylvania</td><td>3.6</td><td>36</td><td>South Dakota</td><td>2.3</td></tr>
<tr><td>7</td><td>Rhode Island</td><td>4.1</td><td>39</td><td>Iowa</td><td>2.2</td></tr>
<tr><td>25</td><td>South Carolina</td><td>2.6</td><td>39</td><td>Virginia</td><td>2.2</td></tr>
<tr><td>36</td><td>South Dakota</td><td>2.3</td><td>41</td><td>Indiana</td><td>2.1</td></tr>
<tr><td>15</td><td>Tennessee</td><td>3.2</td><td>42</td><td>Nebraska</td><td>2.0</td></tr>
<tr><td>29</td><td>Texas</td><td>2.5</td><td>43</td><td>Arizona</td><td>1.9</td></tr>
<tr><td>50</td><td>Utah</td><td>1.2</td><td>43</td><td>Colorado</td><td>1.9</td></tr>
<tr><td>15</td><td>Vermont</td><td>3.2</td><td>43</td><td>Idaho</td><td>1.9</td></tr>
<tr><td>39</td><td>Virginia</td><td>2.2</td><td>43</td><td>New Hampshire</td><td>1.9</td></tr>
<tr><td>22</td><td>Washington</td><td>2.7</td><td>47</td><td>Kansas</td><td>1.8</td></tr>
<tr><td>2</td><td>West Virginia</td><td>4.7</td><td>48</td><td>North Dakota</td><td>1.4</td></tr>
<tr><td>29</td><td>Wisconsin</td><td>2.5</td><td>48</td><td>Wyoming</td><td>1.4</td></tr>
<tr><td>48</td><td>Wyoming</td><td>1.4</td><td>50</td><td>Utah</td><td>1.2</td></tr>
<tr><td></td><td></td><td></td><td></td><td>District of Columbia</td><td>5.9</td></tr>
</table>

Source: CQ Press using data from U.S. Department of Health and Human Services, Social Security Administration
"Social Security Bulletin, Annual Statistical Supplement 2018" (https://www.ssa.gov/policy/docs/statcomps/supplement/) and
U.S. Department of Health and Human Services, Administration for Children and Families
"TANF Caseload Data" (https://www.acf.hhs.gov/programs/ofa/programs/tanf/data-reports)
*As of December 2018. Includes recipients of Temporary Assistance to Needy Families (TANF) and/or Supplemental Security
Income payments.

Recipients of Temporary Assistance to Needy Families (TANF) Payments in 2019
National Total = 2,008,197 Monthly Recipients*

ALPHA ORDER

RANK	STATE	RECIPIENTS	% of USA
28	Alabama	16,419	0.8%
42	Alaska	6,580	0.3%
29	Arizona	13,448	0.7%
45	Arkansas	5,439	0.3%
1	California	698,524	34.8%
13	Colorado	34,046	1.7%
27	Connecticut	16,888	0.8%
35	Delaware	9,746	0.5%
5	Florida	60,816	3.0%
26	Georgia	17,580	0.9%
33	Hawaii	11,351	0.6%
48	Idaho	2,954	0.1%
20	Illinois	21,464	1.1%
34	Indiana	10,641	0.5%
24	Iowa	17,664	0.9%
47	Kansas	3,563	0.2%
12	Kentucky	34,273	1.7%
32	Louisiana	11,642	0.6%
41	Maine	7,104	0.4%
10	Maryland	39,482	2.0%
7	Massachusetts	51,954	2.6%
17	Michigan	27,233	1.4%
11	Minnesota	37,290	1.9%
43	Mississippi	6,326	0.3%
23	Missouri	18,836	0.9%
38	Montana	7,994	0.4%
37	Nebraska	8,988	0.4%
21	Nevada	20,286	1.0%
40	New Hampshire	7,177	0.4%
22	New Jersey	20,220	1.0%
18	New Mexico	23,555	1.2%
2	New York	190,283	9.5%
19	North Carolina	22,079	1.1%
49	North Dakota	2,265	0.1%
4	Ohio	91,506	4.6%
30	Oklahoma	13,118	0.7%
14	Oregon	32,600	1.6%
3	Pennsylvania	98,447	4.9%
36	Rhode Island	9,174	0.5%
25	South Carolina	17,585	0.9%
44	South Dakota	5,744	0.3%
9	Tennessee	40,674	2.0%
8	Texas	48,077	2.4%
39	Utah	7,477	0.4%
46	Vermont	4,361	0.2%
15	Virginia	31,274	1.6%
6	Washington	54,675	2.7%
31	West Virginia	12,345	0.6%
16	Wisconsin	29,569	1.5%
50	Wyoming	1,222	0.1%

RANK ORDER

RANK	STATE	RECIPIENTS	% of USA
1	California	698,524	34.8%
2	New York	190,283	9.5%
3	Pennsylvania	98,447	4.9%
4	Ohio	91,506	4.6%
5	Florida	60,816	3.0%
6	Washington	54,675	2.7%
7	Massachusetts	51,954	2.6%
8	Texas	48,077	2.4%
9	Tennessee	40,674	2.0%
10	Maryland	39,482	2.0%
11	Minnesota	37,290	1.9%
12	Kentucky	34,273	1.7%
13	Colorado	34,046	1.7%
14	Oregon	32,600	1.6%
15	Virginia	31,274	1.6%
16	Wisconsin	29,569	1.5%
17	Michigan	27,233	1.4%
18	New Mexico	23,555	1.2%
19	North Carolina	22,079	1.1%
20	Illinois	21,464	1.1%
21	Nevada	20,286	1.0%
22	New Jersey	20,220	1.0%
23	Missouri	18,836	0.9%
24	Iowa	17,664	0.9%
25	South Carolina	17,585	0.9%
26	Georgia	17,580	0.9%
27	Connecticut	16,888	0.8%
28	Alabama	16,419	0.8%
29	Arizona	13,448	0.7%
30	Oklahoma	13,118	0.7%
31	West Virginia	12,345	0.6%
32	Louisiana	11,642	0.6%
33	Hawaii	11,351	0.6%
34	Indiana	10,641	0.5%
35	Delaware	9,746	0.5%
36	Rhode Island	9,174	0.5%
37	Nebraska	8,988	0.4%
38	Montana	7,994	0.4%
39	Utah	7,477	0.4%
40	New Hampshire	7,177	0.4%
41	Maine	7,104	0.4%
42	Alaska	6,580	0.3%
43	Mississippi	6,326	0.3%
44	South Dakota	5,744	0.3%
45	Arkansas	5,439	0.3%
46	Vermont	4,361	0.2%
47	Kansas	3,563	0.2%
48	Idaho	2,954	0.1%
49	North Dakota	2,265	0.1%
50	Wyoming	1,222	0.1%
	District of Columbia	11,795	0.6%

Source: U.S. Department of Health and Human Services, Administration for Children and Families
   "TANF Caseload Data" (https://www.acf.hhs.gov/programs/ofa/programs/tanf/data-reports)
*As of March 2019. National total includes 14,444 recipients in U.S. territories (13,049 in Puerto Rico).

Percent Change in TANF Recipients: 2018 to 2019

National Percent Change = 11.6% Decrease*

	ALPHA ORDER				RANK ORDER	
RANK	STATE	PERCENT CHANGE		RANK	STATE	PERCENT CHANGE
28	Alabama	(11.3)		1	New Hampshire	9.3
40	Alaska	(15.5)		2	South Carolina	1.3
24	Arizona	(9.9)		3	Idaho	0.5
35	Arkansas	(14.3)		4	Massachusetts	(1.0)
31	California	(12.4)		5	Washington	(2.4)
18	Colorado	(8.0)		6	Oregon	(2.9)
50	Connecticut	(51.8)		7	Illinois	(5.0)
12	Delaware	(6.1)		8	West Virginia	(5.2)
26	Florida	(10.7)		9	Vermont	(5.4)
44	Georgia	(18.5)		10	South Dakota	(5.7)
22	Hawaii	(9.7)		11	Ohio	(5.8)
3	Idaho	0.5		12	Delaware	(6.1)
7	Illinois	(5.0)		13	Wyoming	(6.9)
42	Indiana	(16.6)		14	Wisconsin	(7.2)
39	Iowa	(15.3)		15	Oklahoma	(7.3)
41	Kansas	(15.9)		16	Rhode Island	(7.6)
20	Kentucky	(8.8)		17	New Mexico	(7.8)
46	Louisiana	(20.6)		18	Colorado	(8.0)
21	Maine	(9.2)		19	Maryland	(8.5)
19	Maryland	(8.5)		20	Kentucky	(8.8)
4	Massachusetts	(1.0)		21	Maine	(9.2)
29	Michigan	(11.8)		22	Hawaii	(9.7)
27	Minnesota	(10.9)		23	New York	(9.8)
49	Mississippi	(27.1)		24	Arizona	(9.9)
36	Missouri	(14.7)		25	Virginia	(10.2)
47	Montana	(22.1)		26	Florida	(10.7)
32	Nebraska	(13.0)		27	Minnesota	(10.9)
43	Nevada	(17.3)		28	Alabama	(11.3)
1	New Hampshire	9.3		29	Michigan	(11.8)
48	New Jersey	(23.6)		29	Texas	(11.8)
17	New Mexico	(7.8)		31	California	(12.4)
23	New York	(9.8)		32	Nebraska	(13.0)
37	North Carolina	(15.0)		33	Pennsylvania	(13.8)
34	North Dakota	(13.9)		34	North Dakota	(13.9)
11	Ohio	(5.8)		35	Arkansas	(14.3)
15	Oklahoma	(7.3)		36	Missouri	(14.7)
6	Oregon	(2.9)		37	North Carolina	(15.0)
33	Pennsylvania	(13.8)		38	Utah	(15.2)
16	Rhode Island	(7.6)		39	Iowa	(15.3)
2	South Carolina	1.3		40	Alaska	(15.5)
10	South Dakota	(5.7)		41	Kansas	(15.9)
44	Tennessee	(18.5)		42	Indiana	(16.6)
29	Texas	(11.8)		43	Nevada	(17.3)
38	Utah	(15.2)		44	Georgia	(18.5)
9	Vermont	(5.4)		44	Tennessee	(18.5)
25	Virginia	(10.2)		46	Louisiana	(20.6)
5	Washington	(2.4)		47	Montana	(22.1)
8	West Virginia	(5.2)		48	New Jersey	(23.6)
14	Wisconsin	(7.2)		49	Mississippi	(27.1)
13	Wyoming	(6.9)		50	Connecticut	(51.8)

District of Columbia   24.4

Source: CQ Press using data from U.S. Department of Health and Human Services, Administration for Children and Families
"TANF Caseload Data" (https://www.acf.hhs.gov/programs/ofa/programs/tanf/data-reports)
*March 2018 to March 2019. National percent includes recipients in U.S. territories.

TANF Work Participation Rates in 2018

National Rate = 52.5%*

ALPHA ORDER				RANK ORDER		
RANK	STATE	PERCENT		RANK	STATE	PERCENT
19	Alabama	53.2		1	Wyoming	85.2
17	Alaska	53.9		2	Illinois	81.8
47	Arizona	26.3		3	Idaho	79.5
34	Arkansas	38.1		4	Maine	78.4
13	California	56.9		5	Wisconsin	72.2
15	Colorado	54.7		6	Oregon	69.2
43	Connecticut	33.4		7	New Hampshire	69.0
44	Delaware	30.0		8	Massachusetts	68.4
36	Florida	36.2		9	Nebraska	61.8
50	Georgia	9.7		10	Minnesota	59.8
26	Hawaii	47.1		11	South Dakota	59.5
3	Idaho	79.5		12	Ohio	57.4
2	Illinois	81.8		13	California	56.9
42	Indiana	33.7		14	Michigan	56.6
21	Iowa	52.6		15	Colorado	54.7
29	Kansas	44.1		16	North Dakota	54.2
23	Kentucky	51.9		17	Alaska	53.9
49	Louisiana	11.7		18	West Virginia	53.3
4	Maine	78.4		19	Alabama	53.2
41	Maryland	34.6		20	Oklahoma	52.9
8	Massachusetts	68.4		21	Iowa	52.6
14	Michigan	56.6		22	South Carolina	52.5
10	Minnesota	59.8		23	Kentucky	51.9
27	Mississippi	46.7		24	Washington	51.7
46	Missouri	27.9		25	Vermont	49.2
30	Montana	44.0		26	Hawaii	47.1
9	Nebraska	61.8		27	Mississippi	46.7
28	Nevada	45.5		28	Nevada	45.5
7	New Hampshire	69.0		29	Kansas	44.1
40	New Jersey	34.8		30	Montana	44.0
31	New Mexico	42.5		31	New Mexico	42.5
33	New York	38.5		32	Utah	38.6
38	North Carolina	35.7		33	New York	38.5
16	North Dakota	54.2		34	Arkansas	38.1
12	Ohio	57.4		35	Pennsylvania	36.9
20	Oklahoma	52.9		36	Florida	36.2
6	Oregon	69.2		36	Virginia	36.2
35	Pennsylvania	36.9		38	North Carolina	35.7
45	Rhode Island	29.7		39	Tennessee	35.3
22	South Carolina	52.5		40	New Jersey	34.8
11	South Dakota	59.5		41	Maryland	34.6
39	Tennessee	35.3		42	Indiana	33.7
48	Texas	25.2		43	Connecticut	33.4
32	Utah	38.6		44	Delaware	30.0
25	Vermont	49.2		45	Rhode Island	29.7
36	Virginia	36.2		46	Missouri	27.9
24	Washington	51.7		47	Arizona	26.3
18	West Virginia	53.3		48	Texas	25.2
5	Wisconsin	72.2		49	Louisiana	11.7
1	Wyoming	85.2		50	Georgia	9.7
					District of Columbia	50.2

Source: U.S. Department of Health and Human Services, Administration for Children and Families
   "Work Participation Rates - Fiscal Year 2018" (Table 6C) (https://www.acf.hhs.gov/ofa/programs/tanf/data-reports)
*For fiscal year 2018. Work-eligible individuals with hours of participation in various work and training activities. National average includes recipients in U.S. territories.

Average Monthly TANF Assistance per Family in 2018

National Average = $423*

ALPHA ORDER				RANK ORDER		
RANK	STATE	PER FAMILY		RANK	STATE	PER FAMILY
40	Alabama	$239		1	New Hampshire	$707
2	Alaska	607		2	Alaska	607
38	Arizona	247		3	New York	601
49	Arkansas	153		4	Hawaii	590
5	California	547		5	California	547
20	Colorado	369		6	Maryland	542
9	Connecticut	464		7	Montana	498
39	Delaware	244		8	Maine	497
41	Florida	235		9	Connecticut	464
36	Georgia	253		9	Massachusetts	464
4	Hawaii	590		11	Vermont	454
30	Idaho	297		12	Wyoming	448
47	Illinois	195		13	Oregon	444
46	Indiana	198		13	South Dakota	444
26	Iowa	314		15	Rhode Island	427
34	Kansas	264		16	Washington	412
37	Kentucky	250		17	Minnesota	408
33	Louisiana	283		18	Utah	393
8	Maine	497		19	Wisconsin	370
6	Maryland	542		20	Colorado	369
9	Massachusetts	464		21	Nebraska	368
24	Michigan	328		22	Ohio	360
17	Minnesota	408		23	Nevada	329
50	Mississippi	137		24	Michigan	328
42	Missouri	218		25	New Mexico	327
7	Montana	498		26	Iowa	314
21	Nebraska	368		26	Pennsylvania	314
23	Nevada	329		28	North Dakota	310
1	New Hampshire	707		29	New Jersey	307
29	New Jersey	307		30	Idaho	297
25	New Mexico	327		30	West Virginia	297
3	New York	601		32	Virginia	285
45	North Carolina	210		33	Louisiana	283
28	North Dakota	310		34	Kansas	264
22	Ohio	360		35	Texas	260
44	Oklahoma	211		36	Georgia	253
13	Oregon	444		37	Kentucky	250
26	Pennsylvania	314		38	Arizona	247
15	Rhode Island	427		39	Delaware	244
43	South Carolina	212		40	Alabama	239
13	South Dakota	444		41	Florida	235
48	Tennessee	168		42	Missouri	218
35	Texas	260		43	South Carolina	212
18	Utah	393		44	Oklahoma	211
11	Vermont	454		45	North Carolina	210
32	Virginia	285		46	Indiana	198
16	Washington	412		47	Illinois	195
30	West Virginia	297		48	Tennessee	168
19	Wisconsin	370		49	Arkansas	153
12	Wyoming	448		50	Mississippi	137
					District of Columbia	464

Source: U.S. Department of Health and Human Services, Administration for Children and Families
"Characteristics and Financial Circumstances of TANF Recipients, Fiscal Year 2018" (Table 37)
(https://www.acf.hhs.gov/ofa/programs/tanf/data-reports)
*For fiscal year 2018. National average includes families in U.S. territories.

Percent of Households with Food Insecurity in 2018

National Percent = 11.7% of Households*

ALPHA ORDER

RANK	STATE	PERCENT
7	Alabama	14.7
31	Alaska	10.8
18	Arizona	12.4
6	Arkansas	15.1
33	California	10.6
44	Colorado	9.1
18	Connecticut	12.4
34	Delaware	10.5
22	Florida	11.7
24	Georgia	11.3
49	Hawaii	8.0
39	Idaho	9.8
32	Illinois	10.7
13	Indiana	13.5
43	Iowa	9.2
11	Kansas	13.8
7	Kentucky	14.7
3	Louisiana	15.8
12	Maine	13.6
25	Maryland	11.1
42	Massachusetts	9.3
15	Michigan	12.9
47	Minnesota	8.6
2	Mississippi	15.9
21	Missouri	12.0
36	Montana	10.3
23	Nebraska	11.4
15	Nevada	12.9
50	New Hampshire	7.8
48	New Jersey	8.5
1	New Mexico	16.8
34	New York	10.5
10	North Carolina	13.9
46	North Dakota	8.8
14	Ohio	13.2
5	Oklahoma	15.6
25	Oregon	11.1
25	Pennsylvania	11.1
28	Rhode Island	11.0
28	South Carolina	11.0
30	South Dakota	10.9
18	Tennessee	12.4
9	Texas	14.0
39	Utah	9.8
41	Vermont	9.6
38	Virginia	10.1
36	Washington	10.3
4	West Virginia	15.7
45	Wisconsin	8.9
17	Wyoming	12.6

RANK ORDER

RANK	STATE	PERCENT
1	New Mexico	16.8
2	Mississippi	15.9
3	Louisiana	15.8
4	West Virginia	15.7
5	Oklahoma	15.6
6	Arkansas	15.1
7	Alabama	14.7
7	Kentucky	14.7
9	Texas	14.0
10	North Carolina	13.9
11	Kansas	13.8
12	Maine	13.6
13	Indiana	13.5
14	Ohio	13.2
15	Michigan	12.9
15	Nevada	12.9
17	Wyoming	12.6
18	Arizona	12.4
18	Connecticut	12.4
18	Tennessee	12.4
21	Missouri	12.0
22	Florida	11.7
23	Nebraska	11.4
24	Georgia	11.3
25	Maryland	11.1
25	Oregon	11.1
25	Pennsylvania	11.1
28	Rhode Island	11.0
28	South Carolina	11.0
30	South Dakota	10.9
31	Alaska	10.8
32	Illinois	10.7
33	California	10.6
34	Delaware	10.5
34	New York	10.5
36	Montana	10.3
36	Washington	10.3
38	Virginia	10.1
39	Idaho	9.8
39	Utah	9.8
41	Vermont	9.6
42	Massachusetts	9.3
43	Iowa	9.2
44	Colorado	9.1
45	Wisconsin	8.9
46	North Dakota	8.8
47	Minnesota	8.6
48	New Jersey	8.5
49	Hawaii	8.0
50	New Hampshire	7.8
	District of Columbia	10.6

Source: U.S. Department of Agriculture, Economic Research Service
"Household Food Security in the United States, 2018" (www.ers.usda.gov/topics/food-nutrition-assistance/food-security-in-the-us/)
*Three-year average for 2016–2018. Refers to households for which access to enough food is limited by a lack of money and other resources. About one-third of food-insecure households have very low food security, meaning that at times the food intake of some household members is reduced and their normal eating patterns are disrupted.

Supplemental Nutrition Assistance Program Benefits in 2019

National Total = $53,761,253,656*

ALPHA ORDER

RANK	STATE	BENEFITS	% of USA
15	Alabama	$1,032,064,886	1.9%
43	Alaska	171,091,672	0.3%
13	Arizona	1,146,712,214	2.1%
32	Arkansas	460,333,605	0.9%
1	California	5,977,281,299	11.1%
26	Colorado	638,999,751	1.2%
30	Connecticut	584,718,600	1.1%
42	Delaware	178,138,585	0.3%
4	Florida	4,035,386,245	7.5%
7	Georgia	2,115,101,241	3.9%
33	Hawaii	448,656,306	0.8%
41	Idaho	192,918,233	0.4%
5	Illinois	2,646,035,880	4.9%
22	Indiana	819,644,875	1.5%
34	Iowa	429,315,218	0.8%
36	Kansas	265,322,548	0.5%
25	Kentucky	739,297,747	1.4%
11	Louisiana	1,214,657,938	2.3%
40	Maine	203,803,860	0.4%
20	Maryland	878,649,665	1.6%
14	Massachusetts	1,131,148,466	2.1%
9	Michigan	1,701,430,344	3.2%
31	Minnesota	509,779,277	0.9%
28	Mississippi	605,983,758	1.1%
17	Missouri	997,701,192	1.9%
44	Montana	146,944,184	0.3%
39	Nebraska	221,960,791	0.4%
29	Nevada	587,569,117	1.1%
47	New Hampshire	92,889,311	0.2%
18	New Jersey	953,558,696	1.8%
27	New Mexico	632,907,855	1.2%
3	New York	4,339,617,966	8.1%
NA	North Carolina**	NA	NA
48	North Dakota	68,523,277	0.1%
8	Ohio	2,020,497,444	3.8%
23	Oklahoma	819,546,294	1.5%
19	Oregon	884,191,064	1.6%
6	Pennsylvania	2,513,696,584	4.7%
37	Rhode Island	244,461,937	0.5%
21	South Carolina	854,652,751	1.6%
45	South Dakota	121,995,672	0.2%
10	Tennessee	1,307,247,822	2.4%
2	Texas	4,767,112,796	8.9%
38	Utah	234,552,832	0.4%
46	Vermont	100,250,504	0.2%
16	Virginia	1,002,380,166	1.9%
12	Washington	1,192,380,309	2.2%
35	West Virginia	397,899,950	0.7%
24	Wisconsin	778,699,758	1.4%
49	Wyoming	36,277,115	0.1%

RANK ORDER

RANK	STATE	BENEFITS	% of USA
1	California	$5,977,281,299	11.1%
2	Texas	4,767,112,796	8.9%
3	New York	4,339,617,966	8.1%
4	Florida	4,035,386,245	7.5%
5	Illinois	2,646,035,880	4.9%
6	Pennsylvania	2,513,696,584	4.7%
7	Georgia	2,115,101,241	3.9%
8	Ohio	2,020,497,444	3.8%
9	Michigan	1,701,430,344	3.2%
10	Tennessee	1,307,247,822	2.4%
11	Louisiana	1,214,657,938	2.3%
12	Washington	1,192,380,309	2.2%
13	Arizona	1,146,712,214	2.1%
14	Massachusetts	1,131,148,466	2.1%
15	Alabama	1,032,064,886	1.9%
16	Virginia	1,002,380,166	1.9%
17	Missouri	997,701,192	1.9%
18	New Jersey	953,558,696	1.8%
19	Oregon	884,191,064	1.6%
20	Maryland	878,649,665	1.6%
21	South Carolina	854,652,751	1.6%
22	Indiana	819,644,875	1.5%
23	Oklahoma	819,546,294	1.5%
24	Wisconsin	778,699,758	1.4%
25	Kentucky	739,297,747	1.4%
26	Colorado	638,999,751	1.2%
27	New Mexico	632,907,855	1.2%
28	Mississippi	605,983,758	1.1%
29	Nevada	587,569,117	1.1%
30	Connecticut	584,718,600	1.1%
31	Minnesota	509,779,277	0.9%
32	Arkansas	460,333,605	0.9%
33	Hawaii	448,656,306	0.8%
34	Iowa	429,315,218	0.8%
35	West Virginia	397,899,950	0.7%
36	Kansas	265,322,548	0.5%
37	Rhode Island	244,461,937	0.5%
38	Utah	234,552,832	0.4%
39	Nebraska	221,960,791	0.4%
40	Maine	203,803,860	0.4%
41	Idaho	192,918,233	0.4%
42	Delaware	178,138,585	0.3%
43	Alaska	171,091,672	0.3%
44	Montana	146,944,184	0.3%
45	South Dakota	121,995,672	0.2%
46	Vermont	100,250,504	0.2%
47	New Hampshire	92,889,311	0.2%
48	North Dakota	68,523,277	0.1%
49	Wyoming	36,277,115	0.1%
NA	North Carolina**	NA	NA
	District of Columbia	172,078,913	0.3%

Source: U.S. Department of Agriculture, Food, Nutrition and Consumer Services
    "Supplemental Nutrition Assistance Program" (https://www.fns.usda.gov/pd/supplemental-nutrition-assistance-program-snap)
*Preliminary data for fiscal year 2019. National total includes $145,187,143 to U.S. territories. Costs are for benefits only and exclude administrative expenditures. Program formerly called the Food Stamp Program.
**Not available.

Monthly Supplemental Nutrition Assistance Program Recipients in 2019

National Total = 34,474,188 Recipients*

ALPHA ORDER

RANK	STATE	RECIPIENTS	% of USA
15	Alabama	667,043	1.9%
44	Alaska	78,932	0.2%
13	Arizona	736,883	2.1%
31	Arkansas	354,917	1.0%
1	California	3,529,471	10.2%
27	Colorado	415,289	1.2%
32	Connecticut	340,447	1.0%
42	Delaware	119,787	0.3%
4	Florida	2,649,741	7.7%
7	Georgia	1,332,675	3.9%
38	Hawaii	144,922	0.4%
41	Idaho	135,922	0.4%
5	Illinois	1,639,396	4.8%
24	Indiana	530,384	1.5%
33	Iowa	295,682	0.9%
35	Kansas	185,329	0.5%
25	Kentucky	502,241	1.5%
12	Louisiana	749,560	2.2%
39	Maine	144,433	0.4%
20	Maryland	570,444	1.7%
14	Massachusetts	703,516	2.0%
9	Michigan	1,181,972	3.4%
30	Minnesota	381,779	1.1%
26	Mississippi	420,873	1.2%
18	Missouri	639,338	1.9%
43	Montana	99,368	0.3%
37	Nebraska	148,768	0.4%
29	Nevada	391,569	1.1%
46	New Hampshire	70,412	0.2%
17	New Jersey	649,128	1.9%
28	New Mexico	415,161	1.2%
3	New York	2,661,700	7.7%
NA	North Carolina**	NA	NA
48	North Dakota	45,312	0.1%
8	Ohio	1,273,257	3.7%
23	Oklahoma	531,728	1.5%
22	Oregon	554,927	1.6%
6	Pennsylvania	1,627,640	4.7%
40	Rhode Island	141,232	0.4%
21	South Carolina	558,722	1.6%
45	South Dakota	75,020	0.2%
11	Tennessee	832,130	2.4%
2	Texas	3,187,238	9.2%
36	Utah	160,829	0.5%
47	Vermont	68,277	0.2%
16	Virginia	654,882	1.9%
10	Washington	833,128	2.4%
34	West Virginia	282,662	0.8%
19	Wisconsin	572,323	1.7%
49	Wyoming	24,309	0.1%

RANK ORDER

RANK	STATE	RECIPIENTS	% of USA
1	California	3,529,471	10.2%
2	Texas	3,187,238	9.2%
3	New York	2,661,700	7.7%
4	Florida	2,649,741	7.7%
5	Illinois	1,639,396	4.8%
6	Pennsylvania	1,627,640	4.7%
7	Georgia	1,332,675	3.9%
8	Ohio	1,273,257	3.7%
9	Michigan	1,181,972	3.4%
10	Washington	833,128	2.4%
11	Tennessee	832,130	2.4%
12	Louisiana	749,560	2.2%
13	Arizona	736,883	2.1%
14	Massachusetts	703,516	2.0%
15	Alabama	667,043	1.9%
16	Virginia	654,882	1.9%
17	New Jersey	649,128	1.9%
18	Missouri	639,338	1.9%
19	Wisconsin	572,323	1.7%
20	Maryland	570,444	1.7%
21	South Carolina	558,722	1.6%
22	Oregon	554,927	1.6%
23	Oklahoma	531,728	1.5%
24	Indiana	530,384	1.5%
25	Kentucky	502,241	1.5%
26	Mississippi	420,873	1.2%
27	Colorado	415,289	1.2%
28	New Mexico	415,161	1.2%
29	Nevada	391,569	1.1%
30	Minnesota	381,779	1.1%
31	Arkansas	354,917	1.0%
32	Connecticut	340,447	1.0%
33	Iowa	295,682	0.9%
34	West Virginia	282,662	0.8%
35	Kansas	185,329	0.5%
36	Utah	160,829	0.5%
37	Nebraska	148,768	0.4%
38	Hawaii	144,922	0.4%
39	Maine	144,433	0.4%
40	Rhode Island	141,232	0.4%
41	Idaho	135,922	0.4%
42	Delaware	119,787	0.3%
43	Montana	99,368	0.3%
44	Alaska	78,932	0.2%
45	South Dakota	75,020	0.2%
46	New Hampshire	70,412	0.2%
47	Vermont	68,277	0.2%
48	North Dakota	45,312	0.1%
49	Wyoming	24,309	0.1%
NA	North Carolina**	NA	NA
	District of Columbia	101,230	0.3%

Source: U.S. Department of Agriculture, Food, Nutrition and Consumer Services
"Supplemental Nutrition Assistance Program" (https://www.fns.usda.gov/pd/supplemental-nutrition-assistance-program-snap)
*Preliminary for fiscal year 2019. National total includes 62,261 recipients in U.S. territories. Program formerly called the Food Stamp Program.
**Not available.

Average Monthly Supplemental Nutrition Assistance Program Benefit per Recipient in 2019
National Average = $129.96 per Recipient*

<u>ALPHA ORDER</u>

RANK	STATE	PER RECIPIENT
17	Alabama	$128.94
2	Alaska	180.63
16	Arizona	129.68
49	Arkansas	108.08
5	California	141.13
22	Colorado	128.22
4	Connecticut	143.13
32	Delaware	123.93
26	Florida	126.91
12	Georgia	132.26
1	Hawaii	257.99
43	Idaho	118.28
9	Illinois	134.50
18	Indiana	128.78
38	Iowa	121.00
41	Kansas	119.30
34	Kentucky	122.67
8	Louisiana	135.04
44	Maine	117.59
21	Maryland	128.36
10	Massachusetts	133.99
40	Michigan	119.96
47	Minnesota	111.27
39	Mississippi	119.99
15	Missouri	130.04
33	Montana	123.23
31	Nebraska	124.33
28	Nevada	125.05
48	New Hampshire	109.94
35	New Jersey	122.42
25	New Mexico	127.04
6	New York	135.87
NA	North Carolina**	NA
27	North Dakota	126.02
13	Ohio	132.24
20	Oklahoma	128.44
11	Oregon	132.78
19	Pennsylvania	128.70
3	Rhode Island	144.24
24	South Carolina	127.47
7	South Dakota	135.51
14	Tennessee	130.91
29	Texas	124.64
37	Utah	121.53
36	Vermont	122.36
23	Virginia	127.55
42	Washington	119.27
45	West Virginia	117.31
46	Wisconsin	113.38
30	Wyoming	124.36

<u>RANK ORDER</u>

RANK	STATE	PER RECIPIENT
1	Hawaii	$257.99
2	Alaska	180.63
3	Rhode Island	144.24
4	Connecticut	143.13
5	California	141.13
6	New York	135.87
7	South Dakota	135.51
8	Louisiana	135.04
9	Illinois	134.50
10	Massachusetts	133.99
11	Oregon	132.78
12	Georgia	132.26
13	Ohio	132.24
14	Tennessee	130.91
15	Missouri	130.04
16	Arizona	129.68
17	Alabama	128.94
18	Indiana	128.78
19	Pennsylvania	128.70
20	Oklahoma	128.44
21	Maryland	128.36
22	Colorado	128.22
23	Virginia	127.55
24	South Carolina	127.47
25	New Mexico	127.04
26	Florida	126.91
27	North Dakota	126.02
28	Nevada	125.05
29	Texas	124.64
30	Wyoming	124.36
31	Nebraska	124.33
32	Delaware	123.93
33	Montana	123.23
34	Kentucky	122.67
35	New Jersey	122.42
36	Vermont	122.36
37	Utah	121.53
38	Iowa	121.00
39	Mississippi	119.99
40	Michigan	119.96
41	Kansas	119.30
42	Washington	119.27
43	Idaho	118.28
44	Maine	117.59
45	West Virginia	117.31
46	Wisconsin	113.38
47	Minnesota	111.27
48	New Hampshire	109.94
49	Arkansas	108.08
NA	North Carolina**	NA
	District of Columbia	141.66

Source: U.S. Department of Agriculture, Food, Nutrition and Consumer Services
"Supplemental Nutrition Assistance Program" (https://www.fns.usda.gov/pd/supplemental-nutrition-assistance-program-snap)
*Preliminary for fiscal year 2019. National average includes recipients in U.S. territories. Program formerly called the Food Stamp Program.
**Not available.

Percent of Population Receiving
Supplemental Nutrition Assistance Program Benefits in 2019
National Percent = 10.5%*

ALPHA ORDER

RANK	STATE	PERCENT
6	Alabama	13.6
25	Alaska	10.8
30	Arizona	10.1
17	Arkansas	11.8
36	California	8.9
43	Colorado	7.2
32	Connecticut	9.5
14	Delaware	12.3
14	Florida	12.3
13	Georgia	12.6
28	Hawaii	10.2
41	Idaho	7.6
10	Illinois	12.9
38	Indiana	7.9
33	Iowa	9.4
45	Kansas	6.4
19	Kentucky	11.2
2	Louisiana	16.1
26	Maine	10.7
33	Maryland	9.4
28	Massachusetts	10.2
17	Michigan	11.8
44	Minnesota	6.8
4	Mississippi	14.1
27	Missouri	10.4
35	Montana	9.3
39	Nebraska	7.7
11	Nevada	12.7
47	New Hampshire	5.2
42	New Jersey	7.3
1	New Mexico	19.8
5	New York	13.7
NA	North Carolina**	NA
46	North Dakota	5.9
21	Ohio	10.9
7	Oklahoma	13.4
9	Oregon	13.2
11	Pennsylvania	12.7
8	Rhode Island	13.3
21	South Carolina	10.9
37	South Dakota	8.5
16	Tennessee	12.2
20	Texas	11.0
48	Utah	5.0
21	Vermont	10.9
39	Virginia	7.7
21	Washington	10.9
3	West Virginia	15.8
31	Wisconsin	9.8
49	Wyoming	4.2

RANK ORDER

RANK	STATE	PERCENT
1	New Mexico	19.8
2	Louisiana	16.1
3	West Virginia	15.8
4	Mississippi	14.1
5	New York	13.7
6	Alabama	13.6
7	Oklahoma	13.4
8	Rhode Island	13.3
9	Oregon	13.2
10	Illinois	12.9
11	Nevada	12.7
11	Pennsylvania	12.7
13	Georgia	12.6
14	Delaware	12.3
14	Florida	12.3
16	Tennessee	12.2
17	Arkansas	11.8
17	Michigan	11.8
19	Kentucky	11.2
20	Texas	11.0
21	Ohio	10.9
21	South Carolina	10.9
21	Vermont	10.9
21	Washington	10.9
25	Alaska	10.8
26	Maine	10.7
27	Missouri	10.4
28	Hawaii	10.2
28	Massachusetts	10.2
30	Arizona	10.1
31	Wisconsin	9.8
32	Connecticut	9.5
33	Iowa	9.4
33	Maryland	9.4
35	Montana	9.3
36	California	8.9
37	South Dakota	8.5
38	Indiana	7.9
39	Nebraska	7.7
39	Virginia	7.7
41	Idaho	7.6
42	New Jersey	7.3
43	Colorado	7.2
44	Minnesota	6.8
45	Kansas	6.4
46	North Dakota	5.9
47	New Hampshire	5.2
48	Utah	5.0
49	Wyoming	4.2
NA	North Carolina**	NA

District of Columbia 14.3

Source: CQ Press using data from U.S. Department of Agriculture, Food, Nutrition and Consumer Services
 "Supplemental Nutrition Assistance Program" (https://www.fns.usda.gov/pd/supplemental-nutrition-assistance-program-snap)
*Preliminary data for fiscal year 2019. National rate does not include recipients in U.S. territories. Program formerly called the
Food Stamp Program.
**Not available.

Percent of Households Receiving
Supplemental Nutrition Assistance Program Benefits in 2019
National Percent = 14.3% of Households*

ALPHA ORDER

RANK	STATE	PERCENT
11	Alabama	17.0
24	Alaska	13.9
31	Arizona	13.2
26	Arkansas	13.8
26	California	13.8
41	Colorado	9.5
22	Connecticut	14.4
18	Delaware	15.9
7	Florida	18.3
16	Georgia	16.2
15	Hawaii	16.4
40	Idaho	9.6
12	Illinois	16.8
42	Indiana	9.2
36	Iowa	11.2
45	Kansas	7.7
32	Kentucky	13.1
5	Louisiana	20.1
26	Maine	13.8
24	Maryland	13.9
18	Massachusetts	15.9
17	Michigan	16.0
43	Minnesota	8.8
9	Mississippi	17.7
33	Missouri	12.3
35	Montana	11.4
43	Nebraska	8.8
8	Nevada	18.2
46	New Hampshire	6.9
38	New Jersey	10.0
1	New Mexico	25.7
3	New York	20.5
NA	North Carolina**	NA
47	North Dakota	6.8
29	Ohio	13.5
13	Oklahoma	16.7
6	Oregon	19.8
10	Pennsylvania	17.2
2	Rhode Island	20.8
29	South Carolina	13.5
37	South Dakota	10.2
20	Tennessee	15.3
23	Texas	14.0
47	Utah	6.8
21	Vermont	14.7
38	Virginia	10.0
14	Washington	16.6
4	West Virginia	20.2
33	Wisconsin	12.3
49	Wyoming	4.7

RANK ORDER

RANK	STATE	PERCENT
1	New Mexico	25.7
2	Rhode Island	20.8
3	New York	20.5
4	West Virginia	20.2
5	Louisiana	20.1
6	Oregon	19.8
7	Florida	18.3
8	Nevada	18.2
9	Mississippi	17.7
10	Pennsylvania	17.2
11	Alabama	17.0
12	Illinois	16.8
13	Oklahoma	16.7
14	Washington	16.6
15	Hawaii	16.4
16	Georgia	16.2
17	Michigan	16.0
18	Delaware	15.9
18	Massachusetts	15.9
20	Tennessee	15.3
21	Vermont	14.7
22	Connecticut	14.4
23	Texas	14.0
24	Alaska	13.9
24	Maryland	13.9
26	Arkansas	13.8
26	California	13.8
26	Maine	13.8
29	Ohio	13.5
29	South Carolina	13.5
31	Arizona	13.2
32	Kentucky	13.1
33	Missouri	12.3
33	Wisconsin	12.3
35	Montana	11.4
36	Iowa	11.2
37	South Dakota	10.2
38	New Jersey	10.0
38	Virginia	10.0
40	Idaho	9.6
41	Colorado	9.5
42	Indiana	9.2
43	Minnesota	8.8
43	Nebraska	8.8
45	Kansas	7.7
46	New Hampshire	6.9
47	North Dakota	6.8
47	Utah	6.8
49	Wyoming	4.7
NA	North Carolina**	NA

District of Columbia 20.9

Source: CQ Press using data from U.S. Department of Agriculture, Food, Nutrition and Consumer Services
"Supplemental Nutrition Assistance Program" (https://www.fns.usda.gov/pd/supplemental-nutrition-assistance-program-snap)
*Preliminary data for fiscal year 2019. Percent calculated using 2018 estimated total households. National percent excludes
households in U.S. territories. Program formerly called the Food Stamp Program.
**Not available.

Average Monthly Participants in Women, Infants, and Children (WIC) Special Nutrition Program in 2019
National Total = 6,400,238 Participants*

ALPHA ORDER

RANK	STATE	PARTICIPANTS	% of USA
15	Alabama	115,410	1.8%
45	Alaska	15,978	0.2%
10	Arizona	141,959	2.2%
30	Arkansas	67,231	1.1%
1	California	929,173	14.5%
27	Colorado	81,906	1.3%
34	Connecticut	45,767	0.7%
44	Delaware	16,358	0.3%
3	Florida	429,378	6.7%
7	Georgia	202,915	3.2%
40	Hawaii	25,415	0.4%
39	Idaho	31,000	0.5%
9	Illinois	182,341	2.8%
11	Indiana	138,611	2.2%
32	Iowa	58,064	0.9%
33	Kansas	48,536	0.8%
23	Kentucky	94,296	1.5%
21	Louisiana	103,170	1.6%
42	Maine	17,475	0.3%
14	Maryland	122,569	1.9%
20	Massachusetts	103,315	1.6%
6	Michigan	205,364	3.2%
22	Minnesota	100,123	1.6%
29	Mississippi	79,106	1.2%
18	Missouri	106,733	1.7%
46	Montana	15,754	0.2%
37	Nebraska	33,989	0.5%
31	Nevada	58,744	0.9%
47	New Hampshire	12,163	0.2%
13	New Jersey	134,936	2.1%
36	New Mexico	40,487	0.6%
4	New York	378,946	5.9%
5	North Carolina	207,351	3.2%
48	North Dakota	11,405	0.2%
50	Ohio	3,087	0.0%
8	Oklahoma	192,574	3.0%
24	Oregon	91,650	1.4%
28	Pennsylvania	81,226	1.3%
19	Rhode Island	106,222	1.7%
41	South Carolina	17,962	0.3%
26	South Dakota	84,596	1.3%
43	Tennessee	16,730	0.3%
16	Texas	112,155	1.8%
2	Utah	681,555	10.6%
35	Vermont	43,646	0.7%
49	Virginia	11,321	0.2%
17	Washington	109,469	1.7%
12	West Virginia	135,297	2.1%
38	Wisconsin	32,674	0.5%
25	Wyoming	87,666	1.4%

RANK ORDER

RANK	STATE	PARTICIPANTS	% of USA
1	California	929,173	14.5%
2	Utah	681,555	10.6%
3	Florida	429,378	6.7%
4	New York	378,946	5.9%
5	North Carolina	207,351	3.2%
6	Michigan	205,364	3.2%
7	Georgia	202,915	3.2%
8	Oklahoma	192,574	3.0%
9	Illinois	182,341	2.8%
10	Arizona	141,959	2.2%
11	Indiana	138,611	2.2%
12	West Virginia	135,297	2.1%
13	New Jersey	134,936	2.1%
14	Maryland	122,569	1.9%
15	Alabama	115,410	1.8%
16	Texas	112,155	1.8%
17	Washington	109,469	1.7%
18	Missouri	106,733	1.7%
19	Rhode Island	106,222	1.7%
20	Massachusetts	103,315	1.6%
21	Louisiana	103,170	1.6%
22	Minnesota	100,123	1.6%
23	Kentucky	94,296	1.5%
24	Oregon	91,650	1.4%
25	Wyoming	87,666	1.4%
26	South Dakota	84,596	1.3%
27	Colorado	81,906	1.3%
28	Pennsylvania	81,226	1.3%
29	Mississippi	79,106	1.2%
30	Arkansas	67,231	1.1%
31	Nevada	58,744	0.9%
32	Iowa	58,064	0.9%
33	Kansas	48,536	0.8%
34	Connecticut	45,767	0.7%
35	Vermont	43,646	0.7%
36	New Mexico	40,487	0.6%
37	Nebraska	33,989	0.5%
38	Wisconsin	32,674	0.5%
39	Idaho	31,000	0.5%
40	Hawaii	25,415	0.4%
41	South Carolina	17,962	0.3%
42	Maine	17,475	0.3%
43	Tennessee	16,730	0.3%
44	Delaware	16,358	0.3%
45	Alaska	15,978	0.2%
46	Montana	15,754	0.2%
47	New Hampshire	12,163	0.2%
48	North Dakota	11,405	0.2%
49	Virginia	11,321	0.2%
50	Ohio	3,087	0.0%
	District of Columbia	11,844	0.2%

Source: U.S. Department of Agriculture, Food, Nutrition and Consumer Services
  "WIC Program" (https://www.fns.usda.gov/pd/wic-program)
*Preliminary data for fiscal year 2019. National total includes 224,599 participants in outlying areas not shown separately (Puerto Rico has 202,167 participants).

Average Monthly Benefit per Participant in Women, Infants, and Children (WIC) Special Nutrition Program in 2019
National Average = $40.91*

ALPHA ORDER				RANK ORDER		
RANK	STATE	AVERAGE BENEFIT		RANK	STATE	AVERAGE BENEFIT
16	Alabama	$44.16		1	Rhode Island	$97.91
6	Alaska	54.12		2	Ohio	60.65
37	Arizona	35.68		3	New Jersey	56.78
22	Arkansas	40.12		4	Mississippi	55.99
17	California	44.09		5	Hawaii	55.37
31	Colorado	36.75		6	Alaska	54.12
13	Connecticut	44.54		7	New York	52.36
35	Delaware	36.13		8	North Dakota	49.21
12	Florida	45.86		9	Illinois	48.73
20	Georgia	41.00		10	Louisiana	47.21
5	Hawaii	55.37		11	South Dakota	46.74
44	Idaho	32.79		12	Florida	45.86
9	Illinois	48.73		13	Connecticut	44.54
42	Indiana	33.06		14	South Carolina	44.29
47	Iowa	31.69		15	Virginia	44.20
40	Kansas	34.34		16	Alabama	44.16
23	Kentucky	39.30		17	California	44.09
10	Louisiana	47.21		18	Tennessee	41.59
21	Maine	40.75		19	Wisconsin	41.03
27	Maryland	37.27		20	Georgia	41.00
25	Massachusetts	38.90		21	Maine	40.75
28	Michigan	36.92		22	Arkansas	40.12
26	Minnesota	38.00		23	Kentucky	39.30
4	Mississippi	55.99		24	Nebraska	39.25
41	Missouri	34.17		25	Massachusetts	38.90
39	Montana	34.56		26	Minnesota	38.00
24	Nebraska	39.25		27	Maryland	37.27
32	Nevada	36.46		28	Michigan	36.92
49	New Hampshire	27.29		29	Wyoming	36.84
3	New Jersey	56.78		30	North Carolina	36.77
36	New Mexico	35.87		31	Colorado	36.75
7	New York	52.36		32	Nevada	36.46
30	North Carolina	36.77		33	Texas	36.39
8	North Dakota	49.21		34	West Virginia	36.23
2	Ohio	60.65		35	Delaware	36.13
48	Oklahoma	30.52		36	New Mexico	35.87
43	Oregon	32.81		37	Arizona	35.68
45	Pennsylvania	32.56		38	Vermont	35.29
1	Rhode Island	97.91		39	Montana	34.56
14	South Carolina	44.29		40	Kansas	34.34
11	South Dakota	46.74		41	Missouri	34.17
18	Tennessee	41.59		42	Indiana	33.06
33	Texas	36.39		43	Oregon	32.81
50	Utah	26.48		44	Idaho	32.79
38	Vermont	35.29		45	Pennsylvania	32.56
15	Virginia	44.20		46	Washington	32.42
46	Washington	32.42		47	Iowa	31.69
34	West Virginia	36.23		48	Oklahoma	30.52
19	Wisconsin	41.03		49	New Hampshire	27.29
29	Wyoming	36.84		50	Utah	26.48
					District of Columbia	43.23

Source: U.S. Department of Agriculture, Food, Nutrition and Consumer Services
   "WIC Program" (https://www.fns.usda.gov/pd/wic-program)
*Preliminary data for fiscal year 2019. National average includes outlying areas and Indian reservations not shown separately.

Percent of Public Elementary and Secondary School Students Eligible for Free or Reduced-Price Meals in 2018
National Percent = 46.5%*

ALPHA ORDER

RANK	STATE	PERCENT
14	Alabama	49.8
22	Alaska	40.1
NA	Arizona**	NA
42	Arkansas	27.1
10	California	52.4
32	Colorado	33.9
36	Connecticut	30.8
NA	Delaware**	NA
8	Florida	52.7
4	Georgia	55.5
24	Hawaii	38.1
31	Idaho	34.5
15	Illinois	47.0
19	Indiana	42.1
33	Iowa	32.5
27	Kansas	37.6
5	Kentucky	55.4
11	Louisiana	51.7
28	Maine	36.8
20	Maryland	41.1
NA	Massachusetts**	NA
17	Michigan	44.0
39	Minnesota	29.1
2	Mississippi	68.8
16	Missouri	44.3
26	Montana	37.9
30	Nebraska	35.2
9	Nevada	52.6
44	New Hampshire	22.3
35	New Jersey	32.2
1	New Mexico	69.6
13	New York	50.2
12	North Carolina	51.6
43	North Dakota	23.3
NA	Ohio**	NA
6	Oklahoma	55.1
24	Oregon	38.1
18	Pennsylvania	43.4
21	Rhode Island	40.5
3	South Carolina	62.5
37	South Dakota	30.5
NA	Tennessee**	NA
7	Texas	53.2
41	Utah	27.6
38	Vermont	29.4
23	Virginia	38.2
29	Washington	35.8
NA	West Virginia**	NA
34	Wisconsin	32.4
40	Wyoming	28.2

RANK ORDER

RANK	STATE	PERCENT
1	New Mexico	69.6
2	Mississippi	68.8
3	South Carolina	62.5
4	Georgia	55.5
5	Kentucky	55.4
6	Oklahoma	55.1
7	Texas	53.2
8	Florida	52.7
9	Nevada	52.6
10	California	52.4
11	Louisiana	51.7
12	North Carolina	51.6
13	New York	50.2
14	Alabama	49.8
15	Illinois	47.0
16	Missouri	44.3
17	Michigan	44.0
18	Pennsylvania	43.4
19	Indiana	42.1
20	Maryland	41.1
21	Rhode Island	40.5
22	Alaska	40.1
23	Virginia	38.2
24	Hawaii	38.1
24	Oregon	38.1
26	Montana	37.9
27	Kansas	37.6
28	Maine	36.8
29	Washington	35.8
30	Nebraska	35.2
31	Idaho	34.5
32	Colorado	33.9
33	Iowa	32.5
34	Wisconsin	32.4
35	New Jersey	32.2
36	Connecticut	30.8
37	South Dakota	30.5
38	Vermont	29.4
39	Minnesota	29.1
40	Wyoming	28.2
41	Utah	27.6
42	Arkansas	27.1
43	North Dakota	23.3
44	New Hampshire	22.3
NA	Arizona**	NA
NA	Delaware**	NA
NA	Massachusetts**	NA
NA	Ohio**	NA
NA	Tennessee**	NA
NA	West Virginia**	NA
	District of Columbia**	NA

Source: CQ Press using data from U.S. Department of Education, National Center for Education Statistics "ElSi Table Generator" (https://nces.ed.gov/ccd/elsi/)

*For school year 2017–2018. National rate does not include states not shown separately.

**Not available.

Child Support Collections in 2018

National Total = $28,258,093,128*

ALPHA ORDER

RANK	STATE	COLLECTIONS	% of USA
26	Alabama	$320,468,631	1.1%
44	Alaska	91,089,079	0.3%
28	Arizona	309,651,612	1.1%
32	Arkansas	226,526,488	0.8%
2	California	2,380,160,383	8.4%
27	Colorado	317,402,253	1.1%
31	Connecticut	236,288,787	0.8%
46	Delaware	73,727,914	0.3%
5	Florida	1,488,532,096	5.3%
10	Georgia	688,879,513	2.4%
42	Hawaii	95,541,812	0.3%
38	Idaho	150,628,783	0.5%
9	Illinois	766,636,244	2.7%
19	Indiana	521,988,045	1.8%
29	Iowa	304,654,109	1.1%
35	Kansas	193,295,241	0.7%
22	Kentucky	359,230,952	1.3%
21	Louisiana	411,115,194	1.5%
40	Maine	96,774,293	0.3%
20	Maryland	520,842,681	1.8%
16	Massachusetts	590,286,872	2.1%
6	Michigan	1,289,544,205	4.6%
18	Minnesota	553,660,410	2.0%
24	Mississippi	337,385,202	1.2%
17	Missouri	568,964,104	2.0%
49	Montana	61,980,050	0.2%
34	Nebraska	204,543,763	0.7%
36	Nevada	191,616,116	0.7%
45	New Hampshire	73,871,990	0.3%
8	New Jersey	1,057,922,406	3.7%
39	New Mexico	121,423,243	0.4%
3	New York	1,718,403,812	6.1%
11	North Carolina	653,822,768	2.3%
41	North Dakota	95,839,200	0.3%
4	Ohio	1,596,227,531	5.6%
25	Oklahoma	336,945,403	1.2%
23	Oregon	359,210,854	1.3%
7	Pennsylvania	1,199,364,892	4.2%
47	Rhode Island	73,322,355	0.3%
30	South Carolina	292,763,620	1.0%
43	South Dakota	93,925,896	0.3%
15	Tennessee	597,725,019	2.1%
1	Texas	4,219,325,996	14.9%
33	Utah	212,174,027	0.8%
50	Vermont	41,668,899	0.1%
14	Virginia	600,344,184	2.1%
13	Washington	631,396,686	2.2%
37	West Virginia	173,021,206	0.6%
12	Wisconsin	648,156,511	2.3%
48	Wyoming	63,098,112	0.2%

RANK ORDER

RANK	STATE	COLLECTIONS	% of USA
1	Texas	$4,219,325,996	14.9%
2	California	2,380,160,383	8.4%
3	New York	1,718,403,812	6.1%
4	Ohio	1,596,227,531	5.6%
5	Florida	1,488,532,096	5.3%
6	Michigan	1,289,544,205	4.6%
7	Pennsylvania	1,199,364,892	4.2%
8	New Jersey	1,057,922,406	3.7%
9	Illinois	766,636,244	2.7%
10	Georgia	688,879,513	2.4%
11	North Carolina	653,822,768	2.3%
12	Wisconsin	648,156,511	2.3%
13	Washington	631,396,686	2.2%
14	Virginia	600,344,184	2.1%
15	Tennessee	597,725,019	2.1%
16	Massachusetts	590,286,872	2.1%
17	Missouri	568,964,104	2.0%
18	Minnesota	553,660,410	2.0%
19	Indiana	521,988,045	1.8%
20	Maryland	520,842,681	1.8%
21	Louisiana	411,115,194	1.5%
22	Kentucky	359,230,952	1.3%
23	Oregon	359,210,854	1.3%
24	Mississippi	337,385,202	1.2%
25	Oklahoma	336,945,403	1.2%
26	Alabama	320,468,631	1.1%
27	Colorado	317,402,253	1.1%
28	Arizona	309,651,612	1.1%
29	Iowa	304,654,109	1.1%
30	South Carolina	292,763,620	1.0%
31	Connecticut	236,288,787	0.8%
32	Arkansas	226,526,488	0.8%
33	Utah	212,174,027	0.8%
34	Nebraska	204,543,763	0.7%
35	Kansas	193,295,241	0.7%
36	Nevada	191,616,116	0.7%
37	West Virginia	173,021,206	0.6%
38	Idaho	150,628,783	0.5%
39	New Mexico	121,423,243	0.4%
40	Maine	96,774,293	0.3%
41	North Dakota	95,839,200	0.3%
42	Hawaii	95,541,812	0.3%
43	South Dakota	93,925,896	0.3%
44	Alaska	91,089,079	0.3%
45	New Hampshire	73,871,990	0.3%
46	Delaware	73,727,914	0.3%
47	Rhode Island	73,322,355	0.3%
48	Wyoming	63,098,112	0.2%
49	Montana	61,980,050	0.2%
50	Vermont	41,668,899	0.1%
	District of Columbia	46,723,686	0.2%

Source: U.S. Department of Health and Human Services, Office of Child Support Enforcement
"Child Support Enforcement Annual Report to Congress" (https://www.acf.hhs.gov/css/data)
*Preliminary data for fiscal year 2018. Total does not include $326,279,466 collected in U.S. territories.

XV. Transportation

Federal Highway Funding in 2020

National Total = $43,369,794,311*

ALPHA ORDER

RANK	STATE	FUNDS	% of USA
16	Alabama	$835,773,498	1.9%
30	Alaska	552,367,435	1.3%
18	Arizona	806,010,109	1.9%
28	Arkansas	570,352,636	1.3%
1	California	4,043,264,681	9.3%
27	Colorado	589,072,823	1.4%
29	Connecticut	553,300,279	1.3%
48	Delaware	186,348,026	0.4%
3	Florida	2,087,186,638	4.8%
8	Georgia	1,422,408,300	3.3%
49	Hawaii	186,320,764	0.4%
41	Idaho	315,085,357	0.7%
6	Illinois	1,566,215,656	3.6%
13	Indiana	1,049,673,875	2.4%
32	Iowa	541,397,851	1.2%
36	Kansas	416,296,079	1.0%
22	Kentucky	731,943,941	1.7%
19	Louisiana	773,170,264	1.8%
47	Maine	203,351,344	0.5%
26	Maryland	662,000,198	1.5%
25	Massachusetts	669,060,028	1.5%
9	Michigan	1,159,861,954	2.7%
23	Minnesota	718,341,491	1.7%
33	Mississippi	532,790,130	1.2%
14	Missouri	1,042,881,411	2.4%
35	Montana	451,986,737	1.0%
40	Nebraska	318,412,580	0.7%
38	Nevada	400,017,124	0.9%
50	New Hampshire	182,012,876	0.4%
12	New Jersey	1,099,915,502	2.5%
37	New Mexico	404,542,676	0.9%
4	New York	1,849,116,555	4.3%
10	North Carolina	1,148,928,308	2.6%
44	North Dakota	273,494,740	0.6%
7	Ohio	1,476,626,048	3.4%
24	Oklahoma	698,656,538	1.6%
31	Oregon	550,618,730	1.3%
5	Pennsylvania	1,807,465,072	4.2%
45	Rhode Island	240,920,619	0.6%
21	South Carolina	737,667,142	1.7%
42	South Dakota	310,667,712	0.7%
15	Tennessee	930,899,296	2.1%
2	Texas	4,031,150,868	9.3%
39	Utah	382,525,114	0.9%
46	Vermont	223,577,785	0.5%
11	Virginia	1,121,022,241	2.6%
20	Washington	746,798,588	1.7%
34	West Virginia	481,422,307	1.1%
17	Wisconsin	828,885,848	1.9%
43	Wyoming	282,215,609	0.7%

RANK ORDER

RANK	STATE	FUNDS	% of USA
1	California	$4,043,264,681	9.3%
2	Texas	4,031,150,868	9.3%
3	Florida	2,087,186,638	4.8%
4	New York	1,849,116,555	4.3%
5	Pennsylvania	1,807,465,072	4.2%
6	Illinois	1,566,215,656	3.6%
7	Ohio	1,476,626,048	3.4%
8	Georgia	1,422,408,300	3.3%
9	Michigan	1,159,861,954	2.7%
10	North Carolina	1,148,928,308	2.6%
11	Virginia	1,121,022,241	2.6%
12	New Jersey	1,099,915,502	2.5%
13	Indiana	1,049,673,875	2.4%
14	Missouri	1,042,881,411	2.4%
15	Tennessee	930,899,296	2.1%
16	Alabama	835,773,498	1.9%
17	Wisconsin	828,885,848	1.9%
18	Arizona	806,010,109	1.9%
19	Louisiana	773,170,264	1.8%
20	Washington	746,798,588	1.7%
21	South Carolina	737,667,142	1.7%
22	Kentucky	731,943,941	1.7%
23	Minnesota	718,341,491	1.7%
24	Oklahoma	698,656,538	1.6%
25	Massachusetts	669,060,028	1.5%
26	Maryland	662,000,198	1.5%
27	Colorado	589,072,823	1.4%
28	Arkansas	570,352,636	1.3%
29	Connecticut	553,300,279	1.3%
30	Alaska	552,367,435	1.3%
31	Oregon	550,618,730	1.3%
32	Iowa	541,397,851	1.2%
33	Mississippi	532,790,130	1.2%
34	West Virginia	481,422,307	1.1%
35	Montana	451,986,737	1.0%
36	Kansas	416,296,079	1.0%
37	New Mexico	404,542,676	0.9%
38	Nevada	400,017,124	0.9%
39	Utah	382,525,114	0.9%
40	Nebraska	318,412,580	0.7%
41	Idaho	315,085,357	0.7%
42	South Dakota	310,667,712	0.7%
43	Wyoming	282,215,609	0.7%
44	North Dakota	273,494,740	0.6%
45	Rhode Island	240,920,619	0.6%
46	Vermont	223,577,785	0.5%
47	Maine	203,351,344	0.5%
48	Delaware	186,348,026	0.4%
49	Hawaii	186,320,764	0.4%
50	New Hampshire	182,012,876	0.4%
	District of Columbia	175,772,928	0.4%

Source: U.S. Department of Transportation, Federal Highway Administration
   "Highway Apportionments under the FAST Act" (https://www.fhwa.dot.gov/fastact/funding.cfm)
*Fiscal Year 2020. National total does not include federal funds for U.S. territories. Totals are before sequestration, penalties,
and post-apportionment set-asides.

Per Capita Federal Highway Funding in 2020

National Per Capita = $132*

ALPHA ORDER				RANK ORDER		
RANK	**STATE**	**PER CAPITA**		**RANK**	**STATE**	**PER CAPITA**
16	Alabama	$170		1	Alaska	$755
1	Alaska	755		2	Wyoming	488
42	Arizona	111		3	Montana	423
11	Arkansas	189		4	North Dakota	359
45	California	102		5	Vermont	358
45	Colorado	102		6	South Dakota	351
22	Connecticut	155		7	West Virginia	269
10	Delaware	191		8	Rhode Island	227
48	Florida	97		9	New Mexico	193
30	Georgia	134		10	Delaware	191
32	Hawaii	132		11	Arkansas	189
14	Idaho	176		12	Mississippi	179
38	Illinois	124		13	Oklahoma	177
21	Indiana	156		14	Idaho	176
15	Iowa	172		15	Iowa	172
24	Kansas	143		16	Alabama	170
20	Kentucky	164		16	Missouri	170
18	Louisiana	166		18	Louisiana	166
23	Maine	151		19	Nebraska	165
44	Maryland	109		20	Kentucky	164
48	Massachusetts	97		21	Indiana	156
41	Michigan	116		22	Connecticut	155
36	Minnesota	127		23	Maine	151
12	Mississippi	179		24	Kansas	143
16	Missouri	170		24	South Carolina	143
3	Montana	423		26	Wisconsin	142
19	Nebraska	165		27	Pennsylvania	141
35	Nevada	130		28	Texas	139
30	New Hampshire	134		29	Tennessee	136
38	New Jersey	124		30	Georgia	134
9	New Mexico	193		30	New Hampshire	134
50	New York	95		32	Hawaii	132
43	North Carolina	110		33	Oregon	131
4	North Dakota	359		33	Virginia	131
37	Ohio	126		35	Nevada	130
13	Oklahoma	177		36	Minnesota	127
33	Oregon	131		37	Ohio	126
27	Pennsylvania	141		38	Illinois	124
8	Rhode Island	227		38	New Jersey	124
24	South Carolina	143		40	Utah	119
6	South Dakota	351		41	Michigan	116
29	Tennessee	136		42	Arizona	111
28	Texas	139		43	North Carolina	110
40	Utah	119		44	Maryland	109
5	Vermont	358		45	California	102
33	Virginia	131		45	Colorado	102
47	Washington	98		47	Washington	98
7	West Virginia	269		48	Florida	97
26	Wisconsin	142		48	Massachusetts	97
2	Wyoming	488		50	New York	95
					District of Columbia	249

Source: CQ Press using data from U.S. Department of Transportation, Federal Highway Administration
   "Highway Apportionments under the FAST Act" (https://www.fhwa.dot.gov/fastact/funding.cfm)
*Fiscal Year 2020. National per capita does not include federal funds for U.S. territories. Totals are before sequestration, penalties, and post-apportionment set-asides. Calculated using 2019 estimated population.

Public Road and Street Mileage in 2018

National Total = 4,176,915 Miles*

ALPHA ORDER

RANK	STATE	MILES	% of USA
18	Alabama	100,962	2.4%
45	Alaska	17,050	0.4%
33	Arizona	66,782	1.6%
17	Arkansas	102,622	2.5%
2	California	175,589	4.2%
22	Colorado	88,975	2.1%
44	Connecticut	21,556	0.5%
48	Delaware	6,461	0.2%
8	Florida	123,099	2.9%
7	Georgia	128,397	3.1%
50	Hawaii	4,475	0.1%
35	Idaho	56,347	1.3%
3	Illinois	145,976	3.5%
19	Indiana	96,962	2.3%
14	Iowa	114,745	2.7%
4	Kansas	142,200	3.4%
26	Kentucky	80,180	1.9%
34	Louisiana	61,416	1.5%
43	Maine	22,815	0.5%
41	Maryland	32,269	0.8%
40	Massachusetts	36,763	0.9%
10	Michigan	122,164	2.9%
5	Minnesota	139,591	3.3%
30	Mississippi	77,477	1.9%
6	Missouri	132,094	3.2%
32	Montana	73,573	1.8%
21	Nebraska	95,262	2.3%
37	Nevada	48,458	1.2%
46	New Hampshire	16,171	0.4%
38	New Jersey	38,919	0.9%
29	New Mexico	77,605	1.9%
15	New York	113,533	2.7%
16	North Carolina	107,348	2.6%
23	North Dakota	88,050	2.1%
9	Ohio	123,014	2.9%
12	Oklahoma	116,065	2.8%
27	Oregon	79,266	1.9%
11	Pennsylvania	120,590	2.9%
49	Rhode Island	6,013	0.1%
28	South Carolina	77,992	1.9%
24	South Dakota	82,501	2.0%
20	Tennessee	96,116	2.3%
1	Texas	314,648	7.5%
36	Utah	48,913	1.2%
47	Vermont	14,253	0.3%
31	Virginia	75,369	1.8%
25	Washington	80,653	1.9%
39	West Virginia	38,850	0.9%
13	Wisconsin	115,609	2.8%
42	Wyoming	29,666	0.7%

RANK ORDER

RANK	STATE	MILES	% of USA
1	Texas	314,648	7.5%
2	California	175,589	4.2%
3	Illinois	145,976	3.5%
4	Kansas	142,200	3.4%
5	Minnesota	139,591	3.3%
6	Missouri	132,094	3.2%
7	Georgia	128,397	3.1%
8	Florida	123,099	2.9%
9	Ohio	123,014	2.9%
10	Michigan	122,164	2.9%
11	Pennsylvania	120,590	2.9%
12	Oklahoma	116,065	2.8%
13	Wisconsin	115,609	2.8%
14	Iowa	114,745	2.7%
15	New York	113,533	2.7%
16	North Carolina	107,348	2.6%
17	Arkansas	102,622	2.5%
18	Alabama	100,962	2.4%
19	Indiana	96,962	2.3%
20	Tennessee	96,116	2.3%
21	Nebraska	95,262	2.3%
22	Colorado	88,975	2.1%
23	North Dakota	88,050	2.1%
24	South Dakota	82,501	2.0%
25	Washington	80,653	1.9%
26	Kentucky	80,180	1.9%
27	Oregon	79,266	1.9%
28	South Carolina	77,992	1.9%
29	New Mexico	77,605	1.9%
30	Mississippi	77,477	1.9%
31	Virginia	75,369	1.8%
32	Montana	73,573	1.8%
33	Arizona	66,782	1.6%
34	Louisiana	61,416	1.5%
35	Idaho	56,347	1.3%
36	Utah	48,913	1.2%
37	Nevada	48,458	1.2%
38	New Jersey	38,919	0.9%
39	West Virginia	38,850	0.9%
40	Massachusetts	36,763	0.9%
41	Maryland	32,269	0.8%
42	Wyoming	29,666	0.7%
43	Maine	22,815	0.5%
44	Connecticut	21,556	0.5%
45	Alaska	17,050	0.4%
46	New Hampshire	16,171	0.4%
47	Vermont	14,253	0.3%
48	Delaware	6,461	0.2%
49	Rhode Island	6,013	0.1%
50	Hawaii	4,475	0.1%
	District of Columbia	1,514	0.0%

Source: U.S. Department of Transportation, Federal Highway Administration
  "Highway Statistics 2018" (Table HM-20, https://www.fhwa.dot.gov/policyinformation/statistics/2018/)
*Does not include 18,359 miles of roads and streets in Puerto Rico.

Percent of Public Road and Street Mileage Federally Funded in 2018

National Percent = 24.5% of Public Road and Street Mileage*

ALPHA ORDER		
RANK	STATE	PERCENT
17	Alabama	26.5
17	Alaska	26.5
43	Arizona	20.6
37	Arkansas	22.0
2	California	32.1
47	Colorado	19.8
5	Connecticut	29.4
23	Delaware	24.8
36	Florida	22.4
23	Georgia	24.8
1	Hawaii	34.9
42	Idaho	20.7
30	Illinois	23.7
19	Indiana	25.5
34	Iowa	22.9
27	Kansas	24.4
48	Kentucky	18.2
34	Louisiana	22.9
11	Maine	27.8
20	Maryland	25.4
3	Massachusetts	30.7
4	Michigan	30.0
30	Minnesota	23.7
8	Mississippi	28.4
33	Missouri	23.4
44	Montana	20.0
40	Nebraska	21.8
49	Nevada	15.9
37	New Hampshire	22.0
10	New Jersey	28.0
49	New Mexico	15.9
25	New York	24.5
37	North Carolina	22.0
41	North Dakota	21.4
25	Ohio	24.5
11	Oklahoma	27.8
32	Oregon	23.5
29	Pennsylvania	23.9
6	Rhode Island	29.3
14	South Carolina	27.3
28	South Dakota	24.1
45	Tennessee	19.9
7	Texas	28.7
45	Utah	19.9
13	Vermont	27.6
9	Virginia	28.1
21	Washington	25.3
15	West Virginia	27.1
22	Wisconsin	24.9
16	Wyoming	26.9

RANK ORDER		
RANK	STATE	PERCENT
1	Hawaii	34.9
2	California	32.1
3	Massachusetts	30.7
4	Michigan	30.0
5	Connecticut	29.4
6	Rhode Island	29.3
7	Texas	28.7
8	Mississippi	28.4
9	Virginia	28.1
10	New Jersey	28.0
11	Maine	27.8
11	Oklahoma	27.8
13	Vermont	27.6
14	South Carolina	27.3
15	West Virginia	27.1
16	Wyoming	26.9
17	Alabama	26.5
17	Alaska	26.5
19	Indiana	25.5
20	Maryland	25.4
21	Washington	25.3
22	Wisconsin	24.9
23	Delaware	24.8
23	Georgia	24.8
25	New York	24.5
25	Ohio	24.5
27	Kansas	24.4
28	South Dakota	24.1
29	Pennsylvania	23.9
30	Illinois	23.7
30	Minnesota	23.7
32	Oregon	23.5
33	Missouri	23.4
34	Iowa	22.9
34	Louisiana	22.9
36	Florida	22.4
37	Arkansas	22.0
37	New Hampshire	22.0
37	North Carolina	22.0
40	Nebraska	21.8
41	North Dakota	21.4
42	Idaho	20.7
43	Arizona	20.6
44	Montana	20.0
45	Tennessee	19.9
45	Utah	19.9
47	Colorado	19.8
48	Kentucky	18.2
49	Nevada	15.9
49	New Mexico	15.9
	District of Columbia	29.9

Source: CQ Press using data from U.S. Department of Transportation, Federal Highway Administration
"Highway Statistics 2018" (Table HM-15, http://www.fhwa.dot.gov/policyinformation/statistics/2018/)
*National percent does not include federally funded highway miles in Puerto Rico.

Average Number of Lanes Per Mile of Public Road and Street Mileage in 2018

National Average = 2.11 Lanes per Mile*

ALPHA ORDER				RANK ORDER		
RANK	STATE	LANES PER MILE		RANK	STATE	LANES PER MILE
24	Alabama	2.09		1	California	2.26
48	Alaska	2.03		2	Florida	2.23
6	Arizona	2.18		3	Maryland	2.20
39	Arkansas	2.05		4	Hawaii	2.19
1	California	2.26		4	New Jersey	2.19
30	Colorado	2.08		6	Arizona	2.18
10	Connecticut	2.13		6	Virginia	2.18
8	Delaware	2.16		8	Delaware	2.16
2	Florida	2.23		8	Texas	2.16
13	Georgia	2.12		10	Connecticut	2.13
4	Hawaii	2.19		10	North Carolina	2.13
44	Idaho	2.04		10	Ohio	2.13
20	Illinois	2.10		13	Georgia	2.12
24	Indiana	2.09		13	Louisiana	2.12
39	Iowa	2.05		13	Tennessee	2.12
44	Kansas	2.04		16	Massachusetts	2.11
24	Kentucky	2.09		16	Nevada	2.11
13	Louisiana	2.12		16	New York	2.11
39	Maine	2.05		16	Rhode Island	2.11
3	Maryland	2.20		20	Illinois	2.10
16	Massachusetts	2.11		20	Michigan	2.10
20	Michigan	2.10		20	Missouri	2.10
36	Minnesota	2.06		20	South Carolina	2.10
24	Mississippi	2.09		24	Alabama	2.09
20	Missouri	2.10		24	Indiana	2.09
44	Montana	2.04		24	Kentucky	2.09
44	Nebraska	2.04		24	Mississippi	2.09
16	Nevada	2.11		24	Pennsylvania	2.09
36	New Hampshire	2.06		24	Utah	2.09
4	New Jersey	2.19		30	Colorado	2.08
30	New Mexico	2.08		30	New Mexico	2.08
16	New York	2.11		30	Oklahoma	2.08
10	North Carolina	2.13		30	Washington	2.08
48	North Dakota	2.03		30	Wyoming	2.08
10	Ohio	2.13		35	Wisconsin	2.07
30	Oklahoma	2.08		36	Minnesota	2.06
39	Oregon	2.05		36	New Hampshire	2.06
24	Pennsylvania	2.09		36	West Virginia	2.06
16	Rhode Island	2.11		39	Arkansas	2.05
20	South Carolina	2.10		39	Iowa	2.05
48	South Dakota	2.03		39	Maine	2.05
13	Tennessee	2.12		39	Oregon	2.05
8	Texas	2.16		39	Vermont	2.05
24	Utah	2.09		44	Idaho	2.04
39	Vermont	2.05		44	Kansas	2.04
6	Virginia	2.18		44	Montana	2.04
30	Washington	2.08		44	Nebraska	2.04
36	West Virginia	2.06		48	Alaska	2.03
35	Wisconsin	2.07		48	North Dakota	2.03
30	Wyoming	2.08		48	South Dakota	2.03
					District of Columbia	2.28

Source: CQ Press using data from U.S. Department of Transportation, Federal Highway Administration
"Highway Statistics 2018" (Tables HM-20 and HM-48, https://www.fhwa.dot.gov/policyinformation/statistics/2018/)
*Lane-miles divided by public road and street mileage.

Interstate Highway Mileage in 2018

National Total = 48,440 Miles*

ALPHA ORDER

RANK	STATE	MILES	% of USA
18	Alabama	1,004	2.1%
17	Alaska	1,080	2.2%
15	Arizona	1,169	2.4%
33	Arkansas	749	1.5%
2	California	2,456	5.1%
20	Colorado	952	2.0%
45	Connecticut	346	0.7%
50	Delaware	41	0.1%
7	Florida	1,495	3.1%
11	Georgia	1,247	2.6%
49	Hawaii	55	0.1%
37	Idaho	616	1.3%
3	Illinois	2,185	4.5%
10	Indiana	1,287	2.7%
31	Iowa	789	1.6%
28	Kansas	874	1.8%
21	Kentucky	944	1.9%
22	Louisiana	943	1.9%
44	Maine	366	0.8%
42	Maryland	480	1.0%
38	Massachusetts	572	1.2%
12	Michigan	1,238	2.6%
25	Minnesota	913	1.9%
30	Mississippi	832	1.7%
8	Missouri	1,380	2.8%
14	Montana	1,192	2.5%
41	Nebraska	483	1.0%
36	Nevada	620	1.3%
47	New Hampshire	225	0.5%
43	New Jersey	432	0.9%
19	New Mexico	999	2.1%
5	New York	1,742	3.6%
9	North Carolina	1,306	2.7%
39	North Dakota	571	1.2%
6	Ohio	1,574	3.2%
24	Oklahoma	932	1.9%
34	Oregon	730	1.5%
4	Pennsylvania	1,862	3.8%
48	Rhode Island	70	0.1%
29	South Carolina	851	1.8%
35	South Dakota	679	1.4%
13	Tennessee	1,201	2.5%
1	Texas	3,459	7.1%
23	Utah	937	1.9%
46	Vermont	320	0.7%
16	Virginia	1,119	2.3%
32	Washington	764	1.6%
40	West Virginia	555	1.1%
27	Wisconsin	879	1.8%
25	Wyoming	913	1.9%

RANK ORDER

RANK	STATE	MILES	% of USA
1	Texas	3,459	7.1%
2	California	2,456	5.1%
3	Illinois	2,185	4.5%
4	Pennsylvania	1,862	3.8%
5	New York	1,742	3.6%
6	Ohio	1,574	3.2%
7	Florida	1,495	3.1%
8	Missouri	1,380	2.8%
9	North Carolina	1,306	2.7%
10	Indiana	1,287	2.7%
11	Georgia	1,247	2.6%
12	Michigan	1,238	2.6%
13	Tennessee	1,201	2.5%
14	Montana	1,192	2.5%
15	Arizona	1,169	2.4%
16	Virginia	1,119	2.3%
17	Alaska	1,080	2.2%
18	Alabama	1,004	2.1%
19	New Mexico	999	2.1%
20	Colorado	952	2.0%
21	Kentucky	944	1.9%
22	Louisiana	943	1.9%
23	Utah	937	1.9%
24	Oklahoma	932	1.9%
25	Minnesota	913	1.9%
25	Wyoming	913	1.9%
27	Wisconsin	879	1.8%
28	Kansas	874	1.8%
29	South Carolina	851	1.8%
30	Mississippi	832	1.7%
31	Iowa	789	1.6%
32	Washington	764	1.6%
33	Arkansas	749	1.5%
34	Oregon	730	1.5%
35	South Dakota	679	1.4%
36	Nevada	620	1.3%
37	Idaho	616	1.3%
38	Massachusetts	572	1.2%
39	North Dakota	571	1.2%
40	West Virginia	555	1.1%
41	Nebraska	483	1.0%
42	Maryland	480	1.0%
43	New Jersey	432	0.9%
44	Maine	366	0.8%
45	Connecticut	346	0.7%
46	Vermont	320	0.7%
47	New Hampshire	225	0.5%
48	Rhode Island	70	0.1%
49	Hawaii	55	0.1%
50	Delaware	41	0.1%
	District of Columbia	12	0.0%

Source: U.S. Department of Transportation, Federal Highway Administration
    "Highway Statistics 2018" (Table HM-15, https://www.fhwa.dot.gov/policyinformation/statistics/2018/)
*Does not include 301 miles of highway in Puerto Rico that are part of the interstate system.

Rural Road and Street Mileage in 2018

National Total = 2,951,481 Rural Miles*

ALPHA ORDER

RANK	STATE	MILES	% of USA
17	Alabama	71,923	2.4%
41	Alaska	13,735	0.5%
34	Arizona	40,400	1.4%
10	Arkansas	85,367	2.9%
18	California	71,275	2.4%
20	Colorado	68,160	2.3%
46	Connecticut	5,691	0.2%
48	Delaware	2,835	0.1%
37	Florida	36,580	1.2%
14	Georgia	76,149	2.6%
49	Hawaii	1,645	0.1%
31	Idaho	49,959	1.7%
7	Illinois	96,219	3.3%
21	Indiana	66,636	2.3%
5	Iowa	102,018	3.5%
2	Kansas	127,815	4.3%
24	Kentucky	65,027	2.2%
33	Louisiana	43,801	1.5%
40	Maine	19,599	0.7%
42	Maryland	13,561	0.5%
45	Massachusetts	6,190	0.2%
12	Michigan	84,169	2.9%
3	Minnesota	117,266	4.0%
25	Mississippi	64,413	2.2%
4	Missouri	107,598	3.6%
19	Montana	69,322	2.3%
9	Nebraska	87,239	3.0%
35	Nevada	38,170	1.3%
44	New Hampshire	11,105	0.4%
47	New Jersey	5,447	0.2%
22	New Mexico	66,428	2.3%
28	New York	63,886	2.2%
23	North Carolina	65,872	2.2%
11	North Dakota	85,152	2.9%
15	Ohio	75,519	2.6%
6	Oklahoma	97,243	3.3%
27	Oregon	64,055	2.2%
16	Pennsylvania	72,320	2.5%
50	Rhode Island	1,359	0.0%
30	South Carolina	55,129	1.9%
13	South Dakota	79,089	2.7%
26	Tennessee	64,298	2.2%
1	Texas	205,668	7.0%
36	Utah	37,543	1.3%
43	Vermont	12,751	0.4%
32	Virginia	48,754	1.7%
29	Washington	56,394	1.9%
38	West Virginia	32,191	1.1%
8	Wisconsin	91,701	3.1%
39	Wyoming	26,814	0.9%

RANK ORDER

RANK	STATE	MILES	% of USA
1	Texas	205,668	7.0%
2	Kansas	127,815	4.3%
3	Minnesota	117,266	4.0%
4	Missouri	107,598	3.6%
5	Iowa	102,018	3.5%
6	Oklahoma	97,243	3.3%
7	Illinois	96,219	3.3%
8	Wisconsin	91,701	3.1%
9	Nebraska	87,239	3.0%
10	Arkansas	85,367	2.9%
11	North Dakota	85,152	2.9%
12	Michigan	84,169	2.9%
13	South Dakota	79,089	2.7%
14	Georgia	76,149	2.6%
15	Ohio	75,519	2.6%
16	Pennsylvania	72,320	2.5%
17	Alabama	71,923	2.4%
18	California	71,275	2.4%
19	Montana	69,322	2.3%
20	Colorado	68,160	2.3%
21	Indiana	66,636	2.3%
22	New Mexico	66,428	2.3%
23	North Carolina	65,872	2.2%
24	Kentucky	65,027	2.2%
25	Mississippi	64,413	2.2%
26	Tennessee	64,298	2.2%
27	Oregon	64,055	2.2%
28	New York	63,886	2.2%
29	Washington	56,394	1.9%
30	South Carolina	55,129	1.9%
31	Idaho	49,959	1.7%
32	Virginia	48,754	1.7%
33	Louisiana	43,801	1.5%
34	Arizona	40,400	1.4%
35	Nevada	38,170	1.3%
36	Utah	37,543	1.3%
37	Florida	36,580	1.2%
38	West Virginia	32,191	1.1%
39	Wyoming	26,814	0.9%
40	Maine	19,599	0.7%
41	Alaska	13,735	0.5%
42	Maryland	13,561	0.5%
43	Vermont	12,751	0.4%
44	New Hampshire	11,105	0.4%
45	Massachusetts	6,190	0.2%
46	Connecticut	5,691	0.2%
47	New Jersey	5,447	0.2%
48	Delaware	2,835	0.1%
49	Hawaii	1,645	0.1%
50	Rhode Island	1,359	0.0%
	District of Columbia	0	0.0%

Source: U.S. Department of Transportation, Federal Highway Administration
   "Highway Statistics 2018" (Table HM-20, https://www.fhwa.dot.gov/policyinformation/statistics/2018/)
*Does not include 3,191 miles of rural roads and streets in Puerto Rico.

Urban Road and Street Mileage in 2018

National Total = 1,225,434 Urban Miles*

ALPHA ORDER

ALPHA ORDER

RANK	STATE	MILES	% of USA
15	Alabama	29,039	2.4%
45	Alaska	3,315	0.3%
17	Arizona	26,381	2.2%
27	Arkansas	17,255	1.4%
2	California	104,315	8.5%
23	Colorado	20,815	1.7%
28	Connecticut	15,865	1.3%
43	Delaware	3,626	0.3%
3	Florida	86,519	7.1%
4	Georgia	52,248	4.3%
49	Hawaii	2,831	0.2%
39	Idaho	6,388	0.5%
5	Illinois	49,756	4.1%
14	Indiana	30,326	2.5%
33	Iowa	12,727	1.0%
31	Kansas	14,385	1.2%
30	Kentucky	15,153	1.2%
26	Louisiana	17,615	1.4%
46	Maine	3,216	0.3%
25	Maryland	18,708	1.5%
13	Massachusetts	30,573	2.5%
10	Michigan	37,996	3.1%
22	Minnesota	22,325	1.8%
32	Mississippi	13,064	1.1%
18	Missouri	24,496	2.0%
42	Montana	4,251	0.3%
37	Nebraska	8,023	0.7%
36	Nevada	10,288	0.8%
40	New Hampshire	5,065	0.4%
11	New Jersey	33,473	2.7%
35	New Mexico	11,177	0.9%
6	New York	49,646	4.1%
9	North Carolina	41,477	3.4%
47	North Dakota	2,898	0.2%
8	Ohio	47,495	3.9%
24	Oklahoma	18,822	1.5%
29	Oregon	15,211	1.2%
7	Pennsylvania	48,270	3.9%
41	Rhode Island	4,654	0.4%
21	South Carolina	22,863	1.9%
44	South Dakota	3,413	0.3%
12	Tennessee	31,818	2.6%
1	Texas	108,979	8.9%
34	Utah	11,370	0.9%
50	Vermont	1,502	0.1%
16	Virginia	26,614	2.2%
19	Washington	24,258	2.0%
38	West Virginia	6,659	0.5%
20	Wisconsin	23,907	2.0%
48	Wyoming	2,851	0.2%

RANK ORDER

RANK	STATE	MILES	% of USA
1	Texas	108,979	8.9%
2	California	104,315	8.5%
3	Florida	86,519	7.1%
4	Georgia	52,248	4.3%
5	Illinois	49,756	4.1%
6	New York	49,646	4.1%
7	Pennsylvania	48,270	3.9%
8	Ohio	47,495	3.9%
9	North Carolina	41,477	3.4%
10	Michigan	37,996	3.1%
11	New Jersey	33,473	2.7%
12	Tennessee	31,818	2.6%
13	Massachusetts	30,573	2.5%
14	Indiana	30,326	2.5%
15	Alabama	29,039	2.4%
16	Virginia	26,614	2.2%
17	Arizona	26,381	2.2%
18	Missouri	24,496	2.0%
19	Washington	24,258	2.0%
20	Wisconsin	23,907	2.0%
21	South Carolina	22,863	1.9%
22	Minnesota	22,325	1.8%
23	Colorado	20,815	1.7%
24	Oklahoma	18,822	1.5%
25	Maryland	18,708	1.5%
26	Louisiana	17,615	1.4%
27	Arkansas	17,255	1.4%
28	Connecticut	15,865	1.3%
29	Oregon	15,211	1.2%
30	Kentucky	15,153	1.2%
31	Kansas	14,385	1.2%
32	Mississippi	13,064	1.1%
33	Iowa	12,727	1.0%
34	Utah	11,370	0.9%
35	New Mexico	11,177	0.9%
36	Nevada	10,288	0.8%
37	Nebraska	8,023	0.7%
38	West Virginia	6,659	0.5%
39	Idaho	6,388	0.5%
40	New Hampshire	5,065	0.4%
41	Rhode Island	4,654	0.4%
42	Montana	4,251	0.3%
43	Delaware	3,626	0.3%
44	South Dakota	3,413	0.3%
45	Alaska	3,315	0.3%
46	Maine	3,216	0.3%
47	North Dakota	2,898	0.2%
48	Wyoming	2,851	0.2%
49	Hawaii	2,831	0.2%
50	Vermont	1,502	0.1%
	District of Columbia	1,514	0.1%

Source: U.S. Department of Transportation, Federal Highway Administration
"Highway Statistics 2018" (Table HM-20, https://www.fhwa.dot.gov/policyinformation/statistics/2018/)
*Does not include 15,168 miles of urban roads and streets in Puerto Rico.

Bridges in 2018

National Total = 613,761 Bridges*

<table>
<tr><td colspan="4">ALPHA ORDER</td><td colspan="4">RANK ORDER</td></tr>
<tr><th>RANK</th><th>STATE</th><th>BRIDGES</th><th>% of USA</th><th>RANK</th><th>STATE</th><th>BRIDGES</th><th>% of USA</th></tr>
<tr><td>15</td><td>Alabama</td><td>16,130</td><td>2.6%</td><td>1</td><td>Texas</td><td>54,131</td><td>8.8%</td></tr>
<tr><td>47</td><td>Alaska</td><td>1,592</td><td>0.3%</td><td>2</td><td>Ohio</td><td>27,277</td><td>4.4%</td></tr>
<tr><td>28</td><td>Arizona</td><td>8,294</td><td>1.4%</td><td>3</td><td>Illinois</td><td>26,809</td><td>4.4%</td></tr>
<tr><td>23</td><td>Arkansas</td><td>12,892</td><td>2.1%</td><td>4</td><td>California</td><td>25,737</td><td>4.2%</td></tr>
<tr><td>4</td><td>California</td><td>25,737</td><td>4.2%</td><td>5</td><td>Kansas</td><td>24,906</td><td>4.1%</td></tr>
<tr><td>27</td><td>Colorado</td><td>8,786</td><td>1.4%</td><td>6</td><td>Missouri</td><td>24,512</td><td>4.0%</td></tr>
<tr><td>39</td><td>Connecticut</td><td>4,270</td><td>0.7%</td><td>7</td><td>Iowa</td><td>24,123</td><td>3.9%</td></tr>
<tr><td>49</td><td>Delaware</td><td>863</td><td>0.1%</td><td>8</td><td>Oklahoma</td><td>23,116</td><td>3.8%</td></tr>
<tr><td>24</td><td>Florida</td><td>12,435</td><td>2.0%</td><td>9</td><td>Pennsylvania</td><td>22,737</td><td>3.7%</td></tr>
<tr><td>17</td><td>Georgia</td><td>14,879</td><td>2.4%</td><td>10</td><td>Tennessee</td><td>20,177</td><td>3.3%</td></tr>
<tr><td>48</td><td>Hawaii</td><td>1,137</td><td>0.2%</td><td>11</td><td>Indiana</td><td>19,280</td><td>3.1%</td></tr>
<tr><td>37</td><td>Idaho</td><td>4,482</td><td>0.7%</td><td>12</td><td>North Carolina</td><td>18,377</td><td>3.0%</td></tr>
<tr><td>3</td><td>Illinois</td><td>26,809</td><td>4.4%</td><td>13</td><td>New York</td><td>17,521</td><td>2.9%</td></tr>
<tr><td>11</td><td>Indiana</td><td>19,280</td><td>3.1%</td><td>14</td><td>Mississippi</td><td>17,071</td><td>2.8%</td></tr>
<tr><td>7</td><td>Iowa</td><td>24,123</td><td>3.9%</td><td>15</td><td>Alabama</td><td>16,130</td><td>2.6%</td></tr>
<tr><td>5</td><td>Kansas</td><td>24,906</td><td>4.1%</td><td>16</td><td>Nebraska</td><td>15,349</td><td>2.5%</td></tr>
<tr><td>18</td><td>Kentucky</td><td>14,368</td><td>2.3%</td><td>17</td><td>Georgia</td><td>14,879</td><td>2.4%</td></tr>
<tr><td>22</td><td>Louisiana</td><td>12,899</td><td>2.1%</td><td>18</td><td>Kentucky</td><td>14,368</td><td>2.3%</td></tr>
<tr><td>45</td><td>Maine</td><td>2,473</td><td>0.4%</td><td>19</td><td>Wisconsin</td><td>14,275</td><td>2.3%</td></tr>
<tr><td>34</td><td>Maryland</td><td>5,357</td><td>0.9%</td><td>20</td><td>Virginia</td><td>13,931</td><td>2.3%</td></tr>
<tr><td>36</td><td>Massachusetts</td><td>5,215</td><td>0.8%</td><td>21</td><td>Minnesota</td><td>13,358</td><td>2.2%</td></tr>
<tr><td>25</td><td>Michigan</td><td>11,228</td><td>1.8%</td><td>22</td><td>Louisiana</td><td>12,899</td><td>2.1%</td></tr>
<tr><td>21</td><td>Minnesota</td><td>13,358</td><td>2.2%</td><td>23</td><td>Arkansas</td><td>12,892</td><td>2.1%</td></tr>
<tr><td>14</td><td>Mississippi</td><td>17,071</td><td>2.8%</td><td>24</td><td>Florida</td><td>12,435</td><td>2.0%</td></tr>
<tr><td>6</td><td>Missouri</td><td>24,512</td><td>4.0%</td><td>25</td><td>Michigan</td><td>11,228</td><td>1.8%</td></tr>
<tr><td>35</td><td>Montana</td><td>5,265</td><td>0.9%</td><td>26</td><td>South Carolina</td><td>9,401</td><td>1.5%</td></tr>
<tr><td>16</td><td>Nebraska</td><td>15,349</td><td>2.5%</td><td>27</td><td>Colorado</td><td>8,786</td><td>1.4%</td></tr>
<tr><td>46</td><td>Nevada</td><td>1,979</td><td>0.3%</td><td>28</td><td>Arizona</td><td>8,294</td><td>1.4%</td></tr>
<tr><td>44</td><td>New Hampshire</td><td>2,494</td><td>0.4%</td><td>29</td><td>Washington</td><td>8,278</td><td>1.3%</td></tr>
<tr><td>32</td><td>New Jersey</td><td>6,746</td><td>1.1%</td><td>30</td><td>Oregon</td><td>8,161</td><td>1.3%</td></tr>
<tr><td>40</td><td>New Mexico</td><td>4,010</td><td>0.7%</td><td>31</td><td>West Virginia</td><td>7,269</td><td>1.2%</td></tr>
<tr><td>13</td><td>New York</td><td>17,521</td><td>2.9%</td><td>32</td><td>New Jersey</td><td>6,746</td><td>1.1%</td></tr>
<tr><td>12</td><td>North Carolina</td><td>18,377</td><td>3.0%</td><td>33</td><td>South Dakota</td><td>5,824</td><td>0.9%</td></tr>
<tr><td>38</td><td>North Dakota</td><td>4,355</td><td>0.7%</td><td>34</td><td>Maryland</td><td>5,357</td><td>0.9%</td></tr>
<tr><td>2</td><td>Ohio</td><td>27,277</td><td>4.4%</td><td>35</td><td>Montana</td><td>5,265</td><td>0.9%</td></tr>
<tr><td>8</td><td>Oklahoma</td><td>23,116</td><td>3.8%</td><td>36</td><td>Massachusetts</td><td>5,215</td><td>0.8%</td></tr>
<tr><td>30</td><td>Oregon</td><td>8,161</td><td>1.3%</td><td>37</td><td>Idaho</td><td>4,482</td><td>0.7%</td></tr>
<tr><td>9</td><td>Pennsylvania</td><td>22,737</td><td>3.7%</td><td>38</td><td>North Dakota</td><td>4,355</td><td>0.7%</td></tr>
<tr><td>50</td><td>Rhode Island</td><td>780</td><td>0.1%</td><td>39</td><td>Connecticut</td><td>4,270</td><td>0.7%</td></tr>
<tr><td>26</td><td>South Carolina</td><td>9,401</td><td>1.5%</td><td>40</td><td>New Mexico</td><td>4,010</td><td>0.7%</td></tr>
<tr><td>33</td><td>South Dakota</td><td>5,824</td><td>0.9%</td><td>41</td><td>Wyoming</td><td>3,129</td><td>0.5%</td></tr>
<tr><td>10</td><td>Tennessee</td><td>20,177</td><td>3.3%</td><td>42</td><td>Utah</td><td>3,061</td><td>0.5%</td></tr>
<tr><td>1</td><td>Texas</td><td>54,131</td><td>8.8%</td><td>43</td><td>Vermont</td><td>2,778</td><td>0.5%</td></tr>
<tr><td>42</td><td>Utah</td><td>3,061</td><td>0.5%</td><td>44</td><td>New Hampshire</td><td>2,494</td><td>0.4%</td></tr>
<tr><td>43</td><td>Vermont</td><td>2,778</td><td>0.5%</td><td>45</td><td>Maine</td><td>2,473</td><td>0.4%</td></tr>
<tr><td>20</td><td>Virginia</td><td>13,931</td><td>2.3%</td><td>46</td><td>Nevada</td><td>1,979</td><td>0.3%</td></tr>
<tr><td>29</td><td>Washington</td><td>8,278</td><td>1.3%</td><td>47</td><td>Alaska</td><td>1,592</td><td>0.3%</td></tr>
<tr><td>31</td><td>West Virginia</td><td>7,269</td><td>1.2%</td><td>48</td><td>Hawaii</td><td>1,137</td><td>0.2%</td></tr>
<tr><td>19</td><td>Wisconsin</td><td>14,275</td><td>2.3%</td><td>49</td><td>Delaware</td><td>863</td><td>0.1%</td></tr>
<tr><td>41</td><td>Wyoming</td><td>3,129</td><td>0.5%</td><td>50</td><td>Rhode Island</td><td>780</td><td>0.1%</td></tr>
<tr><td></td><td></td><td></td><td></td><td></td><td>District of Columbia</td><td>244</td><td>0.0%</td></tr>
</table>

Source: U.S. Department of Transportation, Federal Highway Administration
   "Deficient Bridges by State and Highway System, 2018" (https://www.fhwa.dot.gov/bridge/nbi/condition.cfm)
*As of December 2018. Includes federal-aid and nonfederal-aid system bridges. National total does not include 2,325 bridges in Puerto Rico.

Structurally Deficient Bridges in 2018

National Total = 46,779 Structurally Deficient Bridges*

RANK	STATE	BRIDGES	% of USA		RANK	STATE	BRIDGES	% of USA
ALPHA ORDER					**RANK ORDER**			
23	Alabama	689	1.5%		1	Iowa	4,675	10.0%
44	Alaska	155	0.3%		2	Pennsylvania	3,770	8.1%
45	Arizona	150	0.3%		3	Oklahoma	2,540	5.4%
26	Arkansas	588	1.3%		4	Illinois	2,273	4.9%
7	California	1,812	3.9%		5	Missouri	2,116	4.5%
30	Colorado	473	1.0%		6	North Carolina	1,871	4.0%
38	Connecticut	308	0.7%		7	California	1,812	3.9%
49	Delaware	34	0.1%		8	New York	1,757	3.8%
35	Florida	328	0.7%		9	Louisiana	1,678	3.6%
28	Georgia	494	1.1%		10	Mississippi	1,603	3.4%
46	Hawaii	78	0.2%		11	Ohio	1,518	3.2%
37	Idaho	315	0.7%		12	West Virginia	1,444	3.1%
4	Illinois	2,273	4.9%		13	Nebraska	1,358	2.9%
15	Indiana	1,203	2.6%		14	Kansas	1,288	2.8%
1	Iowa	4,675	10.0%		15	Indiana	1,203	2.6%
14	Kansas	1,288	2.8%		16	Michigan	1,196	2.6%
18	Kentucky	1,016	2.2%		17	Wisconsin	1,054	2.3%
9	Louisiana	1,678	3.6%		18	Kentucky	1,016	2.2%
36	Maine	325	0.7%		19	South Dakota	973	2.1%
39	Maryland	274	0.6%		20	Tennessee	871	1.9%
29	Massachusetts	481	1.0%		21	South Carolina	795	1.7%
16	Michigan	1,196	2.6%		22	Texas	695	1.5%
24	Minnesota	668	1.4%		23	Alabama	689	1.5%
10	Mississippi	1,603	3.4%		24	Minnesota	668	1.4%
5	Missouri	2,116	4.5%		25	Virginia	646	1.4%
33	Montana	390	0.8%		26	Arkansas	588	1.3%
13	Nebraska	1,358	2.9%		27	New Jersey	544	1.2%
50	Nevada	27	0.1%		28	Georgia	494	1.1%
42	New Hampshire	224	0.5%		29	Massachusetts	481	1.0%
27	New Jersey	544	1.2%		30	Colorado	473	1.0%
41	New Mexico	232	0.5%		31	North Dakota	469	1.0%
8	New York	1,757	3.8%		32	Oregon	422	0.9%
6	North Carolina	1,871	4.0%		33	Montana	390	0.8%
31	North Dakota	469	1.0%		34	Washington	382	0.8%
11	Ohio	1,518	3.2%		35	Florida	328	0.7%
3	Oklahoma	2,540	5.4%		36	Maine	325	0.7%
32	Oregon	422	0.9%		37	Idaho	315	0.7%
2	Pennsylvania	3,770	8.1%		38	Connecticut	308	0.7%
43	Rhode Island	180	0.4%		39	Maryland	274	0.6%
21	South Carolina	795	1.7%		40	Wyoming	257	0.5%
19	South Dakota	973	2.1%		41	New Mexico	232	0.5%
20	Tennessee	871	1.9%		42	New Hampshire	224	0.5%
22	Texas	695	1.5%		43	Rhode Island	180	0.4%
47	Utah	66	0.1%		44	Alaska	155	0.3%
47	Vermont	66	0.1%		45	Arizona	150	0.3%
25	Virginia	646	1.4%		46	Hawaii	78	0.2%
34	Washington	382	0.8%		47	Utah	66	0.1%
12	West Virginia	1,444	3.1%		47	Vermont	66	0.1%
17	Wisconsin	1,054	2.3%		49	Delaware	34	0.1%
40	Wyoming	257	0.5%		50	Nevada	27	0.1%
						District of Columbia	8	0.0%

Source: U.S. Department of Transportation, Federal Highway Administration
"Deficient Bridges by State and Highway System, 2018" (https://www.fhwa.dot.gov/bridge/nbi/condition.cfm)
*As of December 2018. Includes federal-aid and nonfederal-aid system bridges. National total does not include structurally deficient bridges in Puerto Rico. "Structurally deficient bridges" include all bridges with any component's condition classified as "poor" or worse.

Structurally Deficient Bridges as a Percent of Total Bridges in 2018

National Percent = 7.6% of Bridges Are Structurally Deficient*

ALPHA ORDER

RANK ORDER

RANK	STATE	PERCENT		RANK	STATE	PERCENT
41	Alabama	4.3		1	Rhode Island	23.1
13	Alaska	9.7		2	West Virginia	19.9
48	Arizona	1.8		3	Iowa	19.4
38	Arkansas	4.6		4	South Dakota	16.7
27	California	7.0		5	Pennsylvania	16.6
33	Colorado	5.4		6	Maine	13.1
25	Connecticut	7.2		7	Louisiana	13.0
43	Delaware	3.9		8	Oklahoma	11.0
45	Florida	2.6		9	North Dakota	10.8
44	Georgia	3.3		10	Michigan	10.7
29	Hawaii	6.9		11	North Carolina	10.2
27	Idaho	7.0		12	New York	10.0
19	Illinois	8.5		13	Alaska	9.7
30	Indiana	6.2		14	Mississippi	9.4
3	Iowa	19.4		15	Massachusetts	9.2
34	Kansas	5.2		16	New Hampshire	9.0
26	Kentucky	7.1		17	Nebraska	8.8
7	Louisiana	13.0		18	Missouri	8.6
6	Maine	13.1		19	Illinois	8.5
36	Maryland	5.1		19	South Carolina	8.5
15	Massachusetts	9.2		21	Wyoming	8.2
10	Michigan	10.7		22	New Jersey	8.1
37	Minnesota	5.0		23	Montana	7.4
14	Mississippi	9.4		23	Wisconsin	7.4
18	Missouri	8.6		25	Connecticut	7.2
23	Montana	7.4		26	Kentucky	7.1
17	Nebraska	8.8		27	California	7.0
49	Nevada	1.4		27	Idaho	7.0
16	New Hampshire	9.0		29	Hawaii	6.9
22	New Jersey	8.1		30	Indiana	6.2
31	New Mexico	5.8		31	New Mexico	5.8
12	New York	10.0		32	Ohio	5.6
11	North Carolina	10.2		33	Colorado	5.4
9	North Dakota	10.8		34	Kansas	5.2
32	Ohio	5.6		34	Oregon	5.2
8	Oklahoma	11.0		36	Maryland	5.1
34	Oregon	5.2		37	Minnesota	5.0
5	Pennsylvania	16.6		38	Arkansas	4.6
1	Rhode Island	23.1		38	Virginia	4.6
19	South Carolina	8.5		38	Washington	4.6
4	South Dakota	16.7		41	Alabama	4.3
41	Tennessee	4.3		41	Tennessee	4.3
50	Texas	1.3		43	Delaware	3.9
47	Utah	2.2		44	Georgia	3.3
46	Vermont	2.4		45	Florida	2.6
38	Virginia	4.6		46	Vermont	2.4
38	Washington	4.6		47	Utah	2.2
2	West Virginia	19.9		48	Arizona	1.8
23	Wisconsin	7.4		49	Nevada	1.4
21	Wyoming	8.2		50	Texas	1.3
					District of Columbia	3.3

Source: CQ Press using data from U.S. Department of Transportation, Federal Highway Administration
"Deficient Bridges by State and Highway System, 2018" (https://www.fhwa.dot.gov/bridge/nbi/condition.cfm)
*As of December 2018. Includes federal-aid and nonfederal-aid system bridges. National total does not include structurally deficient bridges in Puerto Rico. "Structurally deficient bridges" include all bridges with any component's condition classified as "poor" or worse.

Vehicle-Miles of Travel in 2018

National Total = 3,240,326,543,000 Miles

RANK	STATE	MILES	% of USA
16	Alabama	71,167,207,000	2.2%
50	Alaska	5,487,320,000	0.2%
18	Arizona	66,144,511,000	2.0%
30	Arkansas	36,675,309,000	1.1%
1	California	348,795,713,000	10.8%
24	Colorado	53,953,608,000	1.7%
34	Connecticut	31,595,705,000	1.0%
45	Delaware	10,179,384,000	0.3%
3	Florida	221,815,741,000	6.8%
4	Georgia	131,455,533,000	4.1%
43	Hawaii	10,886,768,000	0.3%
39	Idaho	17,709,146,000	0.5%
8	Illinois	107,954,254,000	3.3%
12	Indiana	81,528,812,000	2.5%
31	Iowa	33,282,400,000	1.0%
32	Kansas	32,190,413,000	1.0%
26	Kentucky	49,543,606,000	1.5%
25	Louisiana	50,045,427,000	1.5%
40	Maine	14,783,555,000	0.5%
22	Maryland	59,775,435,000	1.8%
17	Massachusetts	66,771,981,000	2.1%
9	Michigan	102,397,557,000	3.2%
21	Minnesota	60,438,314,000	1.9%
28	Mississippi	40,730,439,000	1.3%
15	Missouri	76,594,999,000	2.4%
42	Montana	12,699,636,000	0.4%
37	Nebraska	20,974,735,000	0.6%
35	Nevada	28,319,012,000	0.9%
41	New Hampshire	13,776,473,000	0.4%
14	New Jersey	77,538,911,000	2.4%
36	New Mexico	27,288,307,000	0.8%
5	New York	123,510,399,000	3.8%
6	North Carolina	121,127,249,000	3.7%
46	North Dakota	9,855,664,000	0.3%
7	Ohio	114,474,441,000	3.5%
27	Oklahoma	45,433,013,000	1.4%
29	Oregon	36,848,417,000	1.1%
10	Pennsylvania	102,109,447,000	3.2%
48	Rhode Island	8,008,582,000	0.2%
23	South Carolina	56,800,683,000	1.8%
47	South Dakota	9,719,406,000	0.3%
13	Tennessee	81,321,491,000	2.5%
2	Texas	282,037,265,000	8.7%
33	Utah	32,069,288,000	1.0%
49	Vermont	7,346,350,000	0.2%
11	Virginia	85,336,102,000	2.6%
20	Washington	62,366,656,000	1.9%
38	West Virginia	19,447,323,000	0.6%
19	Wisconsin	65,885,435,000	2.0%
44	Wyoming	10,438,443,000	0.3%

RANK	STATE	MILES	% of USA
1	California	348,795,713,000	10.8%
2	Texas	282,037,265,000	8.7%
3	Florida	221,815,741,000	6.8%
4	Georgia	131,455,533,000	4.1%
5	New York	123,510,399,000	3.8%
6	North Carolina	121,127,249,000	3.7%
7	Ohio	114,474,441,000	3.5%
8	Illinois	107,954,254,000	3.3%
9	Michigan	102,397,557,000	3.2%
10	Pennsylvania	102,109,447,000	3.2%
11	Virginia	85,336,102,000	2.6%
12	Indiana	81,528,812,000	2.5%
13	Tennessee	81,321,491,000	2.5%
14	New Jersey	77,538,911,000	2.4%
15	Missouri	76,594,999,000	2.4%
16	Alabama	71,167,207,000	2.2%
17	Massachusetts	66,771,981,000	2.1%
18	Arizona	66,144,511,000	2.0%
19	Wisconsin	65,885,435,000	2.0%
20	Washington	62,366,656,000	1.9%
21	Minnesota	60,438,314,000	1.9%
22	Maryland	59,775,435,000	1.8%
23	South Carolina	56,800,683,000	1.8%
24	Colorado	53,953,608,000	1.7%
25	Louisiana	50,045,427,000	1.5%
26	Kentucky	49,543,606,000	1.5%
27	Oklahoma	45,433,013,000	1.4%
28	Mississippi	40,730,439,000	1.3%
29	Oregon	36,848,417,000	1.1%
30	Arkansas	36,675,309,000	1.1%
31	Iowa	33,282,400,000	1.0%
32	Kansas	32,190,413,000	1.0%
33	Utah	32,069,288,000	1.0%
34	Connecticut	31,595,705,000	1.0%
35	Nevada	28,319,012,000	0.9%
36	New Mexico	27,288,307,000	0.8%
37	Nebraska	20,974,735,000	0.6%
38	West Virginia	19,447,323,000	0.6%
39	Idaho	17,709,146,000	0.5%
40	Maine	14,783,555,000	0.5%
41	New Hampshire	13,776,473,000	0.4%
42	Montana	12,699,636,000	0.4%
43	Hawaii	10,886,768,000	0.3%
44	Wyoming	10,438,443,000	0.3%
45	Delaware	10,179,384,000	0.3%
46	North Dakota	9,855,664,000	0.3%
47	South Dakota	9,719,406,000	0.3%
48	Rhode Island	8,008,582,000	0.2%
49	Vermont	7,346,350,000	0.2%
50	Alaska	5,487,320,000	0.2%
	District of Columbia	3,690,678,000	0.1%

Source: U.S. Department of Transportation, Federal Highway Administration
"Highway Statistics 2018" (Table VM-2, https://www.fhwa.dot.gov/policyinformation/statistics/2018/)

Highway Fatalities in 2017

National Total = 37,133 Fatalities

ALPHA ORDER

RANK	STATE	FATALITIES	% of USA
14	Alabama	948	2.6%
49	Alaska	79	0.2%
11	Arizona	1,000	2.7%
27	Arkansas	493	1.3%
2	California	3,602	9.7%
22	Colorado	648	1.7%
36	Connecticut	278	0.7%
44	Delaware	119	0.3%
3	Florida	3,112	8.4%
4	Georgia	1,540	4.1%
46	Hawaii	107	0.3%
38	Idaho	244	0.7%
8	Illinois	1,097	3.0%
16	Indiana	914	2.5%
33	Iowa	330	0.9%
28	Kansas	461	1.2%
18	Kentucky	782	2.1%
19	Louisiana	760	2.0%
41	Maine	172	0.5%
26	Maryland	550	1.5%
32	Massachusetts	350	0.9%
10	Michigan	1,030	2.8%
31	Minnesota	357	1.0%
20	Mississippi	690	1.9%
15	Missouri	930	2.5%
40	Montana	186	0.5%
39	Nebraska	228	0.6%
34	Nevada	309	0.8%
47	New Hampshire	102	0.3%
23	New Jersey	624	1.7%
30	New Mexico	379	1.0%
12	New York	999	2.7%
5	North Carolina	1,412	3.8%
45	North Dakota	115	0.3%
6	Ohio	1,179	3.2%
21	Oklahoma	655	1.8%
29	Oregon	437	1.2%
7	Pennsylvania	1,137	3.1%
48	Rhode Island	83	0.2%
13	South Carolina	988	2.7%
42	South Dakota	129	0.3%
9	Tennessee	1,040	2.8%
1	Texas	3,722	10.0%
37	Utah	273	0.7%
50	Vermont	69	0.2%
17	Virginia	839	2.3%
25	Washington	565	1.5%
35	West Virginia	303	0.8%
24	Wisconsin	613	1.7%
43	Wyoming	123	0.3%

RANK ORDER

RANK	STATE	FATALITIES	% of USA
1	Texas	3,722	10.0%
2	California	3,602	9.7%
3	Florida	3,112	8.4%
4	Georgia	1,540	4.1%
5	North Carolina	1,412	3.8%
6	Ohio	1,179	3.2%
7	Pennsylvania	1,137	3.1%
8	Illinois	1,097	3.0%
9	Tennessee	1,040	2.8%
10	Michigan	1,030	2.8%
11	Arizona	1,000	2.7%
12	New York	999	2.7%
13	South Carolina	988	2.7%
14	Alabama	948	2.6%
15	Missouri	930	2.5%
16	Indiana	914	2.5%
17	Virginia	839	2.3%
18	Kentucky	782	2.1%
19	Louisiana	760	2.0%
20	Mississippi	690	1.9%
21	Oklahoma	655	1.8%
22	Colorado	648	1.7%
23	New Jersey	624	1.7%
24	Wisconsin	613	1.7%
25	Washington	565	1.5%
26	Maryland	550	1.5%
27	Arkansas	493	1.3%
28	Kansas	461	1.2%
29	Oregon	437	1.2%
30	New Mexico	379	1.0%
31	Minnesota	357	1.0%
32	Massachusetts	350	0.9%
33	Iowa	330	0.9%
34	Nevada	309	0.8%
35	West Virginia	303	0.8%
36	Connecticut	278	0.7%
37	Utah	273	0.7%
38	Idaho	244	0.7%
39	Nebraska	228	0.6%
40	Montana	186	0.5%
41	Maine	172	0.5%
42	South Dakota	129	0.3%
43	Wyoming	123	0.3%
44	Delaware	119	0.3%
45	North Dakota	115	0.3%
46	Hawaii	107	0.3%
47	New Hampshire	102	0.3%
48	Rhode Island	83	0.2%
49	Alaska	79	0.2%
50	Vermont	69	0.2%
	District of Columbia	31	0.1%

Source: U.S. Department of Transportation, National Highway Traffic Safety Administration
  "Traffic Safety Facts 2017" (https://crashstats.nhtsa.dot.gov/)

Highway Fatality Rate in 2017

National Rate = 1.16 Fatalities per 100 Million Vehicle-Miles of Travel

ALPHA ORDER

RANK	STATE	RATE
14	Alabama	1.34
8	Alaska	1.43
5	Arizona	1.54
13	Arkansas	1.35
32	California	1.05
22	Colorado	1.21
44	Connecticut	0.88
27	Delaware	1.14
10	Florida	1.42
20	Georgia	1.23
36	Hawaii	1.00
11	Idaho	1.41
34	Illinois	1.02
28	Indiana	1.12
37	Iowa	0.99
8	Kansas	1.43
3	Kentucky	1.59
5	Louisiana	1.54
26	Maine	1.17
42	Maryland	0.92
50	Massachusetts	0.56
35	Michigan	1.01
49	Minnesota	0.60
2	Mississippi	1.69
20	Missouri	1.23
7	Montana	1.47
31	Nebraska	1.09
28	Nevada	1.12
48	New Hampshire	0.75
46	New Jersey	0.81
17	New Mexico	1.28
46	New York	0.81
24	North Carolina	1.18
24	North Dakota	1.18
37	Ohio	0.99
16	Oklahoma	1.33
23	Oregon	1.19
28	Pennsylvania	1.12
33	Rhode Island	1.04
1	South Carolina	1.78
14	South Dakota	1.34
18	Tennessee	1.26
12	Texas	1.36
45	Utah	0.87
41	Vermont	0.93
39	Virginia	0.98
42	Washington	0.92
3	West Virginia	1.59
40	Wisconsin	0.94
18	Wyoming	1.26

RANK ORDER

RANK	STATE	RATE
1	South Carolina	1.78
2	Mississippi	1.69
3	Kentucky	1.59
3	West Virginia	1.59
5	Arizona	1.54
5	Louisiana	1.54
7	Montana	1.47
8	Alaska	1.43
8	Kansas	1.43
10	Florida	1.42
11	Idaho	1.41
12	Texas	1.36
13	Arkansas	1.35
14	Alabama	1.34
14	South Dakota	1.34
16	Oklahoma	1.33
17	New Mexico	1.28
18	Tennessee	1.26
18	Wyoming	1.26
20	Georgia	1.23
20	Missouri	1.23
22	Colorado	1.21
23	Oregon	1.19
24	North Carolina	1.18
24	North Dakota	1.18
26	Maine	1.17
27	Delaware	1.14
28	Indiana	1.12
28	Nevada	1.12
28	Pennsylvania	1.12
31	Nebraska	1.09
32	California	1.05
33	Rhode Island	1.04
34	Illinois	1.02
35	Michigan	1.01
36	Hawaii	1.00
37	Iowa	0.99
37	Ohio	0.99
39	Virginia	0.98
40	Wisconsin	0.94
41	Vermont	0.93
42	Maryland	0.92
42	Washington	0.92
44	Connecticut	0.88
45	Utah	0.87
46	New Jersey	0.81
46	New York	0.81
48	New Hampshire	0.75
49	Minnesota	0.60
50	Massachusetts	0.56
	District of Columbia	0.83

Source: U.S. Department of Transportation, National Highway Traffic Safety Administration
   "Traffic Safety Facts 2017" (https://crashstats.nhtsa.dot.gov/)

Percent of Traffic Fatalities That Were Speeding-Related in 2017

National Percent = 26.2%*

ALPHA ORDER				RANK ORDER		
RANK	STATE	PERCENT		RANK	STATE	PERCENT
30	Alabama	27.1		1	New Hampshire	56.9
11	Alaska	32.9		2	Rhode Island	49.4
19	Arizona	29.9		3	Hawaii	46.7
35	Arkansas	23.5		4	Vermont	44.9
20	California	29.7		5	Illinois	42.1
10	Colorado	35.5		5	South Carolina	42.1
12	Connecticut	31.7		7	Pennsylvania	41.2
26	Delaware	27.7		8	Missouri	37.2
49	Florida	9.6		8	New Mexico	37.2
47	Georgia	16.1		10	Colorado	35.5
3	Hawaii	46.7		11	Alaska	32.9
43	Idaho	19.7		12	Connecticut	31.7
5	Illinois	42.1		12	Montana	31.7
38	Indiana	22.8		14	New York	30.8
42	Iowa	21.2		15	Nevada	30.7
39	Kansas	22.6		16	Washington	30.4
45	Kentucky	17.6		17	Wyoming	30.1
37	Louisiana	23.3		18	North Carolina	30.0
24	Maine	28.5		19	Arizona	29.9
22	Maryland	29.1		20	California	29.7
25	Massachusetts	28.0		21	Wisconsin	29.4
36	Michigan	23.4		22	Maryland	29.1
32	Minnesota	24.9		23	Utah	28.6
50	Mississippi	8.6		24	Maine	28.5
8	Missouri	37.2		25	Massachusetts	28.0
12	Montana	31.7		26	Delaware	27.7
46	Nebraska	16.2		26	West Virginia	27.7
15	Nevada	30.7		28	Texas	27.6
1	New Hampshire	56.9		29	Oregon	27.2
44	New Jersey	19.2		30	Alabama	27.1
8	New Mexico	37.2		31	Virginia	26.1
14	New York	30.8		32	Minnesota	24.9
18	North Carolina	30.0		33	North Dakota	24.3
33	North Dakota	24.3		34	South Dakota	24.0
41	Ohio	21.4		35	Arkansas	23.5
40	Oklahoma	21.8		36	Michigan	23.4
29	Oregon	27.2		37	Louisiana	23.3
7	Pennsylvania	41.2		38	Indiana	22.8
2	Rhode Island	49.4		39	Kansas	22.6
5	South Carolina	42.1		40	Oklahoma	21.8
34	South Dakota	24.0		41	Ohio	21.4
48	Tennessee	16.0		42	Iowa	21.2
28	Texas	27.6		43	Idaho	19.7
23	Utah	28.6		44	New Jersey	19.2
4	Vermont	44.9		45	Kentucky	17.6
31	Virginia	26.1		46	Nebraska	16.2
16	Washington	30.4		47	Georgia	16.1
26	West Virginia	27.7		48	Tennessee	16.0
21	Wisconsin	29.4		49	Florida	9.6
17	Wyoming	30.1		50	Mississippi	8.6
					District of Columbia	54.8

Source: CQ Press using data from U.S. Department of Transportation, National Highway Traffic Safety Administration
"Traffic Safety Facts 2017" (https://crashstats.nhtsa.dot.gov/)

*A speeding-related crash is if the driver was charged with a speeding-related offense or if an officer indicated that racing, driving too fast for conditions, or exceeding the posted speed limit was a contributing factor in the crash.

Percent of Vehicles Involved in Fatal Crashes That Were Large Trucks in 2017

National Percent = 8.8%*

ALPHA ORDER				RANK ORDER		
RANK	STATE	PERCENT		RANK	STATE	PERCENT
36	Alabama	7.4		1	North Dakota	16.1
50	Alaska	3.9		2	Iowa	15.5
41	Arizona	6.6		3	New Mexico	14.7
8	Arkansas	12.2		4	Wyoming	14.5
40	California	6.7		5	Idaho	14.3
24	Colorado	9.2		6	Oklahoma	14.0
48	Connecticut	5.5		7	Kansas	12.3
35	Delaware	7.5		8	Arkansas	12.2
42	Florida	6.4		9	Nebraska	11.9
18	Georgia	9.8		10	Texas	11.8
49	Hawaii	4.2		10	West Virginia	11.8
5	Idaho	14.3		12	Minnesota	11.4
27	Illinois	8.8		13	Pennsylvania	10.7
16	Indiana	10.0		14	Mississippi	10.4
2	Iowa	15.5		15	South Dakota	10.1
7	Kansas	12.3		16	Indiana	10.0
39	Kentucky	7.2		16	Maine	10.0
21	Louisiana	9.6		18	Georgia	9.8
16	Maine	10.0		18	Oregon	9.8
43	Maryland	6.2		20	Washington	9.7
46	Massachusetts	5.9		21	Louisiana	9.6
46	Michigan	5.9		21	Utah	9.6
12	Minnesota	11.4		23	Ohio	9.4
14	Mississippi	10.4		24	Colorado	9.2
29	Missouri	8.5		25	Wisconsin	9.1
34	Montana	8.2		26	Tennessee	8.9
9	Nebraska	11.9		27	Illinois	8.8
33	Nevada	8.3		28	Virginia	8.7
29	New Hampshire	8.5		29	Missouri	8.5
43	New Jersey	6.2		29	New Hampshire	8.5
3	New Mexico	14.7		29	Rhode Island	8.5
32	New York	8.4		32	New York	8.4
38	North Carolina	7.3		33	Nevada	8.3
1	North Dakota	16.1		34	Montana	8.2
23	Ohio	9.4		35	Delaware	7.5
6	Oklahoma	14.0		36	Alabama	7.4
18	Oregon	9.8		36	Vermont	7.4
13	Pennsylvania	10.7		38	North Carolina	7.3
29	Rhode Island	8.5		39	Kentucky	7.2
43	South Carolina	6.2		40	California	6.7
15	South Dakota	10.1		41	Arizona	6.6
26	Tennessee	8.9		42	Florida	6.4
10	Texas	11.8		43	Maryland	6.2
21	Utah	9.6		43	New Jersey	6.2
36	Vermont	7.4		43	South Carolina	6.2
28	Virginia	8.7		46	Massachusetts	5.9
20	Washington	9.7		46	Michigan	5.9
10	West Virginia	11.8		48	Connecticut	5.5
25	Wisconsin	9.1		49	Hawaii	4.2
4	Wyoming	14.5		50	Alaska	3.9
					District of Columbia	0.0

Source: U.S. Department of Transportation, National Highway Traffic Safety Administration
   "Traffic Safety Facts: Large Trucks" (https://crashstats.nhtsa.dot.gov/)
*Large trucks are those with gross vehicle weight greater than 10,000 pounds. In 2017, 4,657 large trucks were involved in fatal crashes.

Lives Saved by Child Restraints, Seat Belts,
Air Bags, and Motorcycle Helmets in 2017
National Total = 19,942 Lives

ALPHA ORDER

RANK	STATE	LIVES	% of USA
14	Alabama	477	2.4%
47	Alaska	43	0.2%
19	Arizona	383	1.9%
28	Arkansas	280	1.4%
2	California	2,015	10.1%
26	Colorado	296	1.5%
34	Connecticut	145	0.7%
42	Delaware	56	0.3%
3	Florida	1,481	7.4%
4	Georgia	861	4.3%
46	Hawaii	45	0.2%
37	Idaho	122	0.6%
8	Illinois	613	3.1%
11	Indiana	545	2.7%
32	Iowa	179	0.9%
29	Kansas	257	1.3%
17	Kentucky	428	2.1%
18	Louisiana	398	2.0%
41	Maine	90	0.5%
27	Maryland	291	1.5%
38	Massachusetts	119	0.6%
6	Michigan	645	3.2%
30	Minnesota	234	1.2%
20	Mississippi	376	1.9%
16	Missouri	459	2.3%
40	Montana	94	0.5%
39	Nebraska	111	0.6%
35	Nevada	125	0.6%
49	New Hampshire	37	0.2%
23	New Jersey	328	1.6%
31	New Mexico	192	1.0%
10	New York	549	2.8%
5	North Carolina	856	4.3%
45	North Dakota	55	0.3%
9	Ohio	601	3.0%
25	Oklahoma	302	1.5%
24	Oregon	325	1.6%
12	Pennsylvania	512	2.6%
50	Rhode Island	34	0.2%
13	South Carolina	495	2.5%
42	South Dakota	56	0.3%
7	Tennessee	633	3.2%
1	Texas	2,192	11.0%
35	Utah	125	0.6%
48	Vermont	42	0.2%
15	Virginia	464	2.3%
21	Washington	374	1.9%
33	West Virginia	167	0.8%
22	Wisconsin	366	1.8%
42	Wyoming	56	0.3%

RANK ORDER

RANK	STATE	LIVES	% of USA
1	Texas	2,192	11.0%
2	California	2,015	10.1%
3	Florida	1,481	7.4%
4	Georgia	861	4.3%
5	North Carolina	856	4.3%
6	Michigan	645	3.2%
7	Tennessee	633	3.2%
8	Illinois	613	3.1%
9	Ohio	601	3.0%
10	New York	549	2.8%
11	Indiana	545	2.7%
12	Pennsylvania	512	2.6%
13	South Carolina	495	2.5%
14	Alabama	477	2.4%
15	Virginia	464	2.3%
16	Missouri	459	2.3%
17	Kentucky	428	2.1%
18	Louisiana	398	2.0%
19	Arizona	383	1.9%
20	Mississippi	376	1.9%
21	Washington	374	1.9%
22	Wisconsin	366	1.8%
23	New Jersey	328	1.6%
24	Oregon	325	1.6%
25	Oklahoma	302	1.5%
26	Colorado	296	1.5%
27	Maryland	291	1.5%
28	Arkansas	280	1.4%
29	Kansas	257	1.3%
30	Minnesota	234	1.2%
31	New Mexico	192	1.0%
32	Iowa	179	0.9%
33	West Virginia	167	0.8%
34	Connecticut	145	0.7%
35	Nevada	125	0.6%
35	Utah	125	0.6%
37	Idaho	122	0.6%
38	Massachusetts	119	0.6%
39	Nebraska	111	0.6%
40	Montana	94	0.5%
41	Maine	90	0.5%
42	Delaware	56	0.3%
42	South Dakota	56	0.3%
42	Wyoming	56	0.3%
45	North Dakota	55	0.3%
46	Hawaii	45	0.2%
47	Alaska	43	0.2%
48	Vermont	42	0.2%
49	New Hampshire	37	0.2%
50	Rhode Island	34	0.2%
	District of Columbia	12	0.1%

Source: CQ Press using data from U.S. Department of Transportation, National Highway Traffic Safety Administration
"Traffic Safety Facts: Lives Saved in 2017" (https://crashstats.nhtsa.dot.gov/)

Safety Belt Usage Rate in 2018

National Rate = 89.6% Use Safety Belts

ALPHA ORDER				RANK ORDER		
RANK	STATE	PERCENT		RANK	STATE	PERCENT
16	Alabama	91.8		1	Hawaii	97.8
17	Alaska	91.6		2	Georgia	96.3
38	Arizona	85.9		3	California	95.9
49	Arkansas	78.0		4	Oregon	95.8
3	California	95.9		5	Illinois	94.6
36	Colorado	86.3		6	New Jersey	94.5
14	Connecticut	92.1		7	Iowa	93.9
12	Delaware	92.4		8	Indiana	93.4
21	Florida	90.6		8	Michigan	93.4
2	Georgia	96.3		10	Washington	93.2
1	Hawaii	97.8		11	New York	92.9
41	Idaho	85.4		12	Delaware	92.4
5	Illinois	94.6		12	Minnesota	92.4
8	Indiana	93.4		14	Connecticut	92.1
7	Iowa	93.9		15	Nevada	91.9
44	Kansas	84.0		16	Alabama	91.8
25	Kentucky	89.9		17	Alaska	91.6
34	Louisiana	86.9		18	North Carolina	91.3
31	Maine	88.5		18	Texas	91.3
23	Maryland	90.3		20	Tennessee	90.9
46	Massachusetts	81.6		21	Florida	90.6
8	Michigan	93.4		22	West Virginia	90.5
12	Minnesota	92.4		23	Maryland	90.3
47	Mississippi	80.2		24	New Mexico	90.2
33	Missouri	87.1		25	Kentucky	89.9
35	Montana	86.6		26	Vermont	89.8
40	Nebraska	85.5		27	South Carolina	89.7
15	Nevada	91.9		28	Wisconsin	89.3
50	New Hampshire	76.4		29	Utah	89.0
6	New Jersey	94.5		30	Rhode Island	88.8
24	New Mexico	90.2		31	Maine	88.5
11	New York	92.9		31	Pennsylvania	88.5
18	North Carolina	91.3		33	Missouri	87.1
45	North Dakota	82.5		34	Louisiana	86.9
42	Ohio	84.9		35	Montana	86.6
39	Oklahoma	85.6		36	Colorado	86.3
4	Oregon	95.8		36	Wyoming	86.3
31	Pennsylvania	88.5		38	Arizona	85.9
30	Rhode Island	88.8		39	Oklahoma	85.6
27	South Carolina	89.7		40	Nebraska	85.5
48	South Dakota	78.9		41	Idaho	85.4
20	Tennessee	90.9		42	Ohio	84.9
18	Texas	91.3		43	Virginia	84.1
29	Utah	89.0		44	Kansas	84.0
26	Vermont	89.8		45	North Dakota	82.5
43	Virginia	84.1		46	Massachusetts	81.6
10	Washington	93.2		47	Mississippi	80.2
22	West Virginia	90.5		48	South Dakota	78.9
28	Wisconsin	89.3		49	Arkansas	78.0
36	Wyoming	86.3		50	New Hampshire	76.4
					District of Columbia	95.1

Source: U.S. Department of Transportation, National Highway Traffic Safety Administration
"Traffic Safety Facts: Seat Belt Use in 2018" (https://crashstats.nhtsa.dot.gov/)

Percent of Passenger Car Occupant Fatalities
Where Victim Used a Seat Belt in 2017
National Percent = 48% of Passenger Car Occupant Fatalities*

<table>
<tr><td colspan="3">ALPHA ORDER</td><td colspan="3">RANK ORDER</td></tr>
<tr><th>RANK</th><th>STATE</th><th>PERCENT</th><th>RANK</th><th>STATE</th><th>PERCENT</th></tr>
<tr><td>38</td><td>Alabama</td><td>37</td><td>1</td><td>California</td><td>61</td></tr>
<tr><td>12</td><td>Alaska</td><td>52</td><td>1</td><td>Oregon</td><td>61</td></tr>
<tr><td>30</td><td>Arizona</td><td>43</td><td>3</td><td>New Jersey</td><td>59</td></tr>
<tr><td>28</td><td>Arkansas</td><td>44</td><td>4</td><td>Minnesota</td><td>57</td></tr>
<tr><td>1</td><td>California</td><td>61</td><td>4</td><td>New York</td><td>57</td></tr>
<tr><td>30</td><td>Colorado</td><td>43</td><td>6</td><td>Florida</td><td>56</td></tr>
<tr><td>13</td><td>Connecticut</td><td>51</td><td>7</td><td>Texas</td><td>55</td></tr>
<tr><td>16</td><td>Delaware</td><td>49</td><td>8</td><td>Maine</td><td>54</td></tr>
<tr><td>6</td><td>Florida</td><td>56</td><td>8</td><td>Michigan</td><td>54</td></tr>
<tr><td>24</td><td>Georgia</td><td>46</td><td>10</td><td>North Carolina</td><td>53</td></tr>
<tr><td>45</td><td>Hawaii</td><td>32</td><td>10</td><td>Washington</td><td>53</td></tr>
<tr><td>40</td><td>Idaho</td><td>36</td><td>12</td><td>Alaska</td><td>52</td></tr>
<tr><td>16</td><td>Illinois</td><td>49</td><td>13</td><td>Connecticut</td><td>51</td></tr>
<tr><td>16</td><td>Indiana</td><td>49</td><td>14</td><td>Maryland</td><td>50</td></tr>
<tr><td>28</td><td>Iowa</td><td>44</td><td>14</td><td>Tennessee</td><td>50</td></tr>
<tr><td>30</td><td>Kansas</td><td>43</td><td>16</td><td>Delaware</td><td>49</td></tr>
<tr><td>16</td><td>Kentucky</td><td>49</td><td>16</td><td>Illinois</td><td>49</td></tr>
<tr><td>35</td><td>Louisiana</td><td>42</td><td>16</td><td>Indiana</td><td>49</td></tr>
<tr><td>8</td><td>Maine</td><td>54</td><td>16</td><td>Kentucky</td><td>49</td></tr>
<tr><td>14</td><td>Maryland</td><td>50</td><td>20</td><td>New Mexico</td><td>48</td></tr>
<tr><td>50</td><td>Massachusetts</td><td>20</td><td>20</td><td>Wisconsin</td><td>48</td></tr>
<tr><td>8</td><td>Michigan</td><td>54</td><td>22</td><td>South Carolina</td><td>47</td></tr>
<tr><td>4</td><td>Minnesota</td><td>57</td><td>22</td><td>Vermont</td><td>47</td></tr>
<tr><td>36</td><td>Mississippi</td><td>41</td><td>24</td><td>Georgia</td><td>46</td></tr>
<tr><td>42</td><td>Missouri</td><td>34</td><td>24</td><td>Rhode Island</td><td>46</td></tr>
<tr><td>38</td><td>Montana</td><td>37</td><td>24</td><td>Utah</td><td>46</td></tr>
<tr><td>47</td><td>Nebraska</td><td>29</td><td>24</td><td>Virginia</td><td>46</td></tr>
<tr><td>30</td><td>Nevada</td><td>43</td><td>28</td><td>Arkansas</td><td>44</td></tr>
<tr><td>48</td><td>New Hampshire</td><td>27</td><td>28</td><td>Iowa</td><td>44</td></tr>
<tr><td>3</td><td>New Jersey</td><td>59</td><td>30</td><td>Arizona</td><td>43</td></tr>
<tr><td>20</td><td>New Mexico</td><td>48</td><td>30</td><td>Colorado</td><td>43</td></tr>
<tr><td>4</td><td>New York</td><td>57</td><td>30</td><td>Kansas</td><td>43</td></tr>
<tr><td>10</td><td>North Carolina</td><td>53</td><td>30</td><td>Nevada</td><td>43</td></tr>
<tr><td>42</td><td>North Dakota</td><td>34</td><td>30</td><td>Ohio</td><td>43</td></tr>
<tr><td>30</td><td>Ohio</td><td>43</td><td>35</td><td>Louisiana</td><td>42</td></tr>
<tr><td>37</td><td>Oklahoma</td><td>38</td><td>36</td><td>Mississippi</td><td>41</td></tr>
<tr><td>1</td><td>Oregon</td><td>61</td><td>37</td><td>Oklahoma</td><td>38</td></tr>
<tr><td>42</td><td>Pennsylvania</td><td>34</td><td>38</td><td>Alabama</td><td>37</td></tr>
<tr><td>24</td><td>Rhode Island</td><td>46</td><td>38</td><td>Montana</td><td>37</td></tr>
<tr><td>22</td><td>South Carolina</td><td>47</td><td>40</td><td>Idaho</td><td>36</td></tr>
<tr><td>49</td><td>South Dakota</td><td>25</td><td>41</td><td>West Virginia</td><td>35</td></tr>
<tr><td>14</td><td>Tennessee</td><td>50</td><td>42</td><td>Missouri</td><td>34</td></tr>
<tr><td>7</td><td>Texas</td><td>55</td><td>42</td><td>North Dakota</td><td>34</td></tr>
<tr><td>24</td><td>Utah</td><td>46</td><td>42</td><td>Pennsylvania</td><td>34</td></tr>
<tr><td>22</td><td>Vermont</td><td>47</td><td>45</td><td>Hawaii</td><td>32</td></tr>
<tr><td>24</td><td>Virginia</td><td>46</td><td>45</td><td>Wyoming</td><td>32</td></tr>
<tr><td>10</td><td>Washington</td><td>53</td><td>47</td><td>Nebraska</td><td>29</td></tr>
<tr><td>41</td><td>West Virginia</td><td>35</td><td>48</td><td>New Hampshire</td><td>27</td></tr>
<tr><td>20</td><td>Wisconsin</td><td>48</td><td>49</td><td>South Dakota</td><td>25</td></tr>
<tr><td>45</td><td>Wyoming</td><td>32</td><td>50</td><td>Massachusetts</td><td>20</td></tr>
<tr><td></td><td></td><td></td><td></td><td>District of Columbia</td><td>36</td></tr>
</table>

Source: U.S. Department of Transportation, National Highway Traffic Safety Administration
"Traffic Safety Facts: Occupant Protection in Passenger Vehicles" (https://crashstats.nhtsa.dot.gov/)
*Only those fatalities where seat belts are known to have been used are counted.

Fatalities in Alcohol-Related Crashes in 2018

National Total = 12,389 Fatalities*

RANK	STATE	FATALITIES	% of USA
13	Alabama	295	2.4%
46	Alaska	36	0.3%
11	Arizona	334	2.7%
25	Arkansas	172	1.4%
2	California	1,235	10.0%
20	Colorado	219	1.8%
31	Connecticut	132	1.1%
47	Delaware	35	0.3%
3	Florida	950	7.7%
5	Georgia	447	3.6%
44	Hawaii	45	0.4%
40	Idaho	66	0.5%
7	Illinois	375	3.0%
17	Indiana	266	2.1%
34	Iowa	98	0.8%
35	Kansas	96	0.8%
26	Kentucky	169	1.4%
18	Louisiana	251	2.0%
43	Maine	49	0.4%
28	Maryland	154	1.2%
29	Massachusetts	145	1.2%
12	Michigan	323	2.6%
32	Minnesota	126	1.0%
21	Mississippi	198	1.6%
16	Missouri	279	2.3%
36	Montana	87	0.7%
37	Nebraska	78	0.6%
33	Nevada	110	0.9%
41	New Hampshire	55	0.4%
27	New Jersey	159	1.3%
30	New Mexico	138	1.1%
8	New York	361	2.9%
4	North Carolina	482	3.9%
48	North Dakota	33	0.3%
9	Ohio	340	2.7%
24	Oklahoma	179	1.4%
23	Oregon	184	1.5%
6	Pennsylvania	387	3.1%
49	Rhode Island	25	0.2%
10	South Carolina	335	2.7%
42	South Dakota	50	0.4%
14	Tennessee	289	2.3%
1	Texas	1,673	13.5%
39	Utah	70	0.6%
50	Vermont	23	0.2%
15	Virginia	285	2.3%
22	Washington	195	1.6%
38	West Virginia	71	0.6%
19	Wisconsin	235	1.9%
45	Wyoming	40	0.3%

RANK	STATE	FATALITIES	% of USA
1	Texas	1,673	13.5%
2	California	1,235	10.0%
3	Florida	950	7.7%
4	North Carolina	482	3.9%
5	Georgia	447	3.6%
6	Pennsylvania	387	3.1%
7	Illinois	375	3.0%
8	New York	361	2.9%
9	Ohio	340	2.7%
10	South Carolina	335	2.7%
11	Arizona	334	2.7%
12	Michigan	323	2.6%
13	Alabama	295	2.4%
14	Tennessee	289	2.3%
15	Virginia	285	2.3%
16	Missouri	279	2.3%
17	Indiana	266	2.1%
18	Louisiana	251	2.0%
19	Wisconsin	235	1.9%
20	Colorado	219	1.8%
21	Mississippi	198	1.6%
22	Washington	195	1.6%
23	Oregon	184	1.5%
24	Oklahoma	179	1.4%
25	Arkansas	172	1.4%
26	Kentucky	169	1.4%
27	New Jersey	159	1.3%
28	Maryland	154	1.2%
29	Massachusetts	145	1.2%
30	New Mexico	138	1.1%
31	Connecticut	132	1.1%
32	Minnesota	126	1.0%
33	Nevada	110	0.9%
34	Iowa	98	0.8%
35	Kansas	96	0.8%
36	Montana	87	0.7%
37	Nebraska	78	0.6%
38	West Virginia	71	0.6%
39	Utah	70	0.6%
40	Idaho	66	0.5%
41	New Hampshire	55	0.4%
42	South Dakota	50	0.4%
43	Maine	49	0.4%
44	Hawaii	45	0.4%
45	Wyoming	40	0.3%
46	Alaska	36	0.3%
47	Delaware	35	0.3%
48	North Dakota	33	0.3%
49	Rhode Island	25	0.2%
50	Vermont	23	0.2%
	District of Columbia	11	0.1%

Source: U.S. Department of Transportation, National Highway Traffic Safety Administration
   "Traffic Safety Facts: Alcohol-Impaired Driving" (https://crashstats.nhtsa.dot.gov/)
*Drivers with Blood Alcohol Content (BAC) of .01 or more. "Legally Drunk" BAC differs from state to state but is often .08 or higher.

Fatalities in Alcohol-Related Crashes
as a Percent of All Highway Fatalities in 2018
National Percent = 34% of Highway Fatalities*

ALPHA ORDER

RANK	STATE	PERCENT
35	Alabama	31
3	Alaska	45
24	Arizona	33
24	Arkansas	33
17	California	35
17	Colorado	35
3	Connecticut	45
31	Delaware	32
39	Florida	30
39	Georgia	30
8	Hawaii	38
43	Idaho	28
12	Illinois	36
35	Indiana	31
35	Iowa	31
48	Kansas	24
50	Kentucky	23
24	Louisiana	33
12	Maine	36
35	Maryland	31
6	Massachusetts	40
24	Michigan	33
24	Minnesota	33
39	Mississippi	30
39	Missouri	30
1	Montana	48
21	Nebraska	34
24	Nevada	33
11	New Hampshire	37
43	New Jersey	28
17	New Mexico	35
8	New York	38
21	North Carolina	34
31	North Dakota	32
31	Ohio	32
46	Oklahoma	27
12	Oregon	36
24	Pennsylvania	33
5	Rhode Island	43
31	South Carolina	32
8	South Dakota	38
43	Tennessee	28
2	Texas	46
46	Utah	27
21	Vermont	34
17	Virginia	35
12	Washington	36
48	West Virginia	24
6	Wisconsin	40
12	Wyoming	36

RANK ORDER

RANK	STATE	PERCENT
1	Montana	48
2	Texas	46
3	Alaska	45
3	Connecticut	45
5	Rhode Island	43
6	Massachusetts	40
6	Wisconsin	40
8	Hawaii	38
8	New York	38
8	South Dakota	38
11	New Hampshire	37
12	Illinois	36
12	Maine	36
12	Oregon	36
12	Washington	36
12	Wyoming	36
17	California	35
17	Colorado	35
17	New Mexico	35
17	Virginia	35
21	Nebraska	34
21	North Carolina	34
21	Vermont	34
24	Arizona	33
24	Arkansas	33
24	Louisiana	33
24	Michigan	33
24	Minnesota	33
24	Nevada	33
24	Pennsylvania	33
31	Delaware	32
31	North Dakota	32
31	Ohio	32
31	South Carolina	32
35	Alabama	31
35	Indiana	31
35	Iowa	31
35	Maryland	31
39	Florida	30
39	Georgia	30
39	Mississippi	30
39	Missouri	30
43	Idaho	28
43	New Jersey	28
43	Tennessee	28
46	Oklahoma	27
46	Utah	27
48	Kansas	24
48	West Virginia	24
50	Kentucky	23
	District of Columbia	34

Source: U.S. Department of Transportation, National Highway Traffic Safety Administration
"Traffic Safety Facts: Alcohol-Impaired Driving" (https://crashstats.nhtsa.dot.gov/)
*Drivers with Blood Alcohol Content (BAC) of .01 or more. "Legally Drunk" BAC differs from state to state but is often .08 or higher.

Percent of Fatal Traffic Accidents Involving Older Drivers in 2017

National Percent = 13.8%*

ALPHA ORDER

RANK	STATE	PERCENT
34	Alabama	13.5
27	Alaska	14.6
36	Arizona	13.4
8	Arkansas	16.9
49	California	10.0
39	Colorado	13.3
23	Connecticut	15.2
42	Delaware	12.6
20	Florida	15.4
34	Georgia	13.5
41	Hawaii	13.2
3	Idaho	19.9
36	Illinois	13.4
30	Indiana	13.8
21	Iowa	15.3
24	Kansas	15.1
12	Kentucky	16.3
48	Louisiana	10.1
1	Maine	21.1
46	Maryland	11.4
42	Massachusetts	12.6
21	Michigan	15.3
4	Minnesota	17.8
29	Mississippi	14.2
39	Missouri	13.3
17	Montana	15.8
44	Nebraska	12.3
26	Nevada	14.7
2	New Hampshire	20.4
14	New Jersey	16.0
25	New Mexico	15.0
10	New York	16.4
28	North Carolina	14.3
44	North Dakota	12.3
15	Ohio	15.9
36	Oklahoma	13.4
10	Oregon	16.4
15	Pennsylvania	15.9
32	Rhode Island	13.6
30	South Carolina	13.8
5	South Dakota	17.7
7	Tennessee	17.0
50	Texas	9.9
18	Utah	15.7
6	Vermont	17.2
9	Virginia	16.5
32	Washington	13.6
13	West Virginia	16.1
18	Wisconsin	15.7
47	Wyoming	11.0

RANK ORDER

RANK	STATE	PERCENT
1	Maine	21.1
2	New Hampshire	20.4
3	Idaho	19.9
4	Minnesota	17.8
5	South Dakota	17.7
6	Vermont	17.2
7	Tennessee	17.0
8	Arkansas	16.9
9	Virginia	16.5
10	New York	16.4
10	Oregon	16.4
12	Kentucky	16.3
13	West Virginia	16.1
14	New Jersey	16.0
15	Ohio	15.9
15	Pennsylvania	15.9
17	Montana	15.8
18	Utah	15.7
18	Wisconsin	15.7
20	Florida	15.4
21	Iowa	15.3
21	Michigan	15.3
23	Connecticut	15.2
24	Kansas	15.1
25	New Mexico	15.0
26	Nevada	14.7
27	Alaska	14.6
28	North Carolina	14.3
29	Mississippi	14.2
30	Indiana	13.8
30	South Carolina	13.8
32	Rhode Island	13.6
32	Washington	13.6
34	Alabama	13.5
34	Georgia	13.5
36	Arizona	13.4
36	Illinois	13.4
36	Oklahoma	13.4
39	Colorado	13.3
39	Missouri	13.3
41	Hawaii	13.2
42	Delaware	12.6
42	Massachusetts	12.6
44	Nebraska	12.3
44	North Dakota	12.3
46	Maryland	11.4
47	Wyoming	11.0
48	Louisiana	10.1
49	California	10.0
50	Texas	9.9
	District of Columbia	5.3

Source: U.S. Department of Transportation, National Highway Traffic Safety Administration
"Traffic Safety Facts: Older Population" (https://crashstats.nhtsa.dot.gov/)
*Drivers 65 years old and older. People 65 or older make up 16 percent of the total U.S. population.

Percent of Highway Fatalities Who Were Young Drivers in 2017

National Percent = 4.9% of Fatalities*

<table>
<tr><td colspan="3">ALPHA ORDER</td><td colspan="3">RANK ORDER</td></tr>
<tr><th>RANK</th><th>STATE</th><th>PERCENT</th><th>RANK</th><th>STATE</th><th>PERCENT</th></tr>
<tr><td>13</td><td>Alabama</td><td>6.0</td><td>1</td><td>New Hampshire</td><td>7.8</td></tr>
<tr><td>50</td><td>Alaska</td><td>1.3</td><td>2</td><td>Montana</td><td>7.5</td></tr>
<tr><td>44</td><td>Arizona</td><td>3.0</td><td>3</td><td>Mississippi</td><td>7.4</td></tr>
<tr><td>34</td><td>Arkansas</td><td>4.3</td><td>4</td><td>West Virginia</td><td>7.3</td></tr>
<tr><td>38</td><td>California</td><td>4.0</td><td>5</td><td>Wisconsin</td><td>7.2</td></tr>
<tr><td>17</td><td>Colorado</td><td>5.7</td><td>6</td><td>Maine</td><td>7.0</td></tr>
<tr><td>49</td><td>Connecticut</td><td>2.5</td><td>6</td><td>Nebraska</td><td>7.0</td></tr>
<tr><td>41</td><td>Delaware</td><td>3.4</td><td>8</td><td>Louisiana</td><td>6.4</td></tr>
<tr><td>26</td><td>Florida</td><td>4.8</td><td>9</td><td>Ohio</td><td>6.3</td></tr>
<tr><td>31</td><td>Georgia</td><td>4.6</td><td>9</td><td>Oklahoma</td><td>6.3</td></tr>
<tr><td>47</td><td>Hawaii</td><td>2.8</td><td>11</td><td>Iowa</td><td>6.1</td></tr>
<tr><td>21</td><td>Idaho</td><td>5.3</td><td>11</td><td>Kansas</td><td>6.1</td></tr>
<tr><td>18</td><td>Illinois</td><td>5.6</td><td>13</td><td>Alabama</td><td>6.0</td></tr>
<tr><td>23</td><td>Indiana</td><td>5.1</td><td>13</td><td>Rhode Island</td><td>6.0</td></tr>
<tr><td>11</td><td>Iowa</td><td>6.1</td><td>13</td><td>Washington</td><td>6.0</td></tr>
<tr><td>11</td><td>Kansas</td><td>6.1</td><td>16</td><td>Missouri</td><td>5.8</td></tr>
<tr><td>24</td><td>Kentucky</td><td>4.9</td><td>17</td><td>Colorado</td><td>5.7</td></tr>
<tr><td>8</td><td>Louisiana</td><td>6.4</td><td>18</td><td>Illinois</td><td>5.6</td></tr>
<tr><td>6</td><td>Maine</td><td>7.0</td><td>19</td><td>Massachusetts</td><td>5.4</td></tr>
<tr><td>29</td><td>Maryland</td><td>4.7</td><td>19</td><td>Texas</td><td>5.4</td></tr>
<tr><td>19</td><td>Massachusetts</td><td>5.4</td><td>21</td><td>Idaho</td><td>5.3</td></tr>
<tr><td>33</td><td>Michigan</td><td>4.4</td><td>22</td><td>North Dakota</td><td>5.2</td></tr>
<tr><td>32</td><td>Minnesota</td><td>4.5</td><td>23</td><td>Indiana</td><td>5.1</td></tr>
<tr><td>3</td><td>Mississippi</td><td>7.4</td><td>24</td><td>Kentucky</td><td>4.9</td></tr>
<tr><td>16</td><td>Missouri</td><td>5.8</td><td>24</td><td>Pennsylvania</td><td>4.9</td></tr>
<tr><td>2</td><td>Montana</td><td>7.5</td><td>26</td><td>Florida</td><td>4.8</td></tr>
<tr><td>6</td><td>Nebraska</td><td>7.0</td><td>26</td><td>Utah</td><td>4.8</td></tr>
<tr><td>48</td><td>Nevada</td><td>2.6</td><td>26</td><td>Virginia</td><td>4.8</td></tr>
<tr><td>1</td><td>New Hampshire</td><td>7.8</td><td>29</td><td>Maryland</td><td>4.7</td></tr>
<tr><td>45</td><td>New Jersey</td><td>2.9</td><td>29</td><td>New Mexico</td><td>4.7</td></tr>
<tr><td>29</td><td>New Mexico</td><td>4.7</td><td>31</td><td>Georgia</td><td>4.6</td></tr>
<tr><td>34</td><td>New York</td><td>4.3</td><td>32</td><td>Minnesota</td><td>4.5</td></tr>
<tr><td>38</td><td>North Carolina</td><td>4.0</td><td>33</td><td>Michigan</td><td>4.4</td></tr>
<tr><td>22</td><td>North Dakota</td><td>5.2</td><td>34</td><td>Arkansas</td><td>4.3</td></tr>
<tr><td>9</td><td>Ohio</td><td>6.3</td><td>34</td><td>New York</td><td>4.3</td></tr>
<tr><td>9</td><td>Oklahoma</td><td>6.3</td><td>34</td><td>Oregon</td><td>4.3</td></tr>
<tr><td>34</td><td>Oregon</td><td>4.3</td><td>34</td><td>Tennessee</td><td>4.3</td></tr>
<tr><td>24</td><td>Pennsylvania</td><td>4.9</td><td>38</td><td>California</td><td>4.0</td></tr>
<tr><td>13</td><td>Rhode Island</td><td>6.0</td><td>38</td><td>North Carolina</td><td>4.0</td></tr>
<tr><td>40</td><td>South Carolina</td><td>3.7</td><td>40</td><td>South Carolina</td><td>3.7</td></tr>
<tr><td>43</td><td>South Dakota</td><td>3.1</td><td>41</td><td>Delaware</td><td>3.4</td></tr>
<tr><td>34</td><td>Tennessee</td><td>4.3</td><td>42</td><td>Wyoming</td><td>3.3</td></tr>
<tr><td>19</td><td>Texas</td><td>5.4</td><td>43</td><td>South Dakota</td><td>3.1</td></tr>
<tr><td>26</td><td>Utah</td><td>4.8</td><td>44</td><td>Arizona</td><td>3.0</td></tr>
<tr><td>45</td><td>Vermont</td><td>2.9</td><td>45</td><td>New Jersey</td><td>2.9</td></tr>
<tr><td>26</td><td>Virginia</td><td>4.8</td><td>45</td><td>Vermont</td><td>2.9</td></tr>
<tr><td>13</td><td>Washington</td><td>6.0</td><td>47</td><td>Hawaii</td><td>2.8</td></tr>
<tr><td>4</td><td>West Virginia</td><td>7.3</td><td>48</td><td>Nevada</td><td>2.6</td></tr>
<tr><td>5</td><td>Wisconsin</td><td>7.2</td><td>49</td><td>Connecticut</td><td>2.5</td></tr>
<tr><td>42</td><td>Wyoming</td><td>3.3</td><td>50</td><td>Alaska</td><td>1.3</td></tr>
<tr><td></td><td></td><td></td><td></td><td>District of Columbia</td><td>3.2</td></tr>
</table>

Source: CQ Press using data from U.S. Department of Transportation, National Highway Traffic Safety Administration
"Traffic Safety Facts: Young Drivers" (https://crashstats.nhtsa.dot.gov/)

*Drivers fifteen to twenty years old. Based on 1,830 fatalities of young drivers. An additional 2,920 passengers, occupants in other vehicles, and nonoccupants were killed in crashes involving young drivers. Young drivers accounted for 5.4 percent of all drivers.

Licensed Drivers in 2018

National Total = 227,548,895 Licensed Drivers

RANK	STATE	DRIVERS	% of USA
22	Alabama	3,999,057	1.8%
49	Alaska	536,033	0.2%
15	Arizona	5,284,970	2.3%
32	Arkansas	2,145,334	0.9%
1	California	27,039,400	11.9%
21	Colorado	4,244,713	1.9%
28	Connecticut	2,605,612	1.1%
44	Delaware	786,504	0.3%
3	Florida	15,368,695	6.8%
9	Georgia	7,168,733	3.2%
42	Hawaii	948,417	0.4%
38	Idaho	1,252,535	0.6%
6	Illinois	8,714,788	3.8%
17	Indiana	4,589,405	2.0%
30	Iowa	2,260,271	1.0%
31	Kansas	2,149,430	0.9%
26	Kentucky	3,032,530	1.3%
24	Louisiana	3,425,435	1.5%
41	Maine	1,040,582	0.5%
18	Maryland	4,407,973	1.9%
16	Massachusetts	4,935,176	2.2%
10	Michigan	7,153,645	3.1%
25	Minnesota	3,391,057	1.5%
33	Mississippi	2,058,036	0.9%
20	Missouri	4,272,960	1.9%
43	Montana	806,204	0.4%
37	Nebraska	1,420,317	0.6%
35	Nevada	1,983,453	0.9%
39	New Hampshire	1,161,665	0.5%
11	New Jersey	6,342,876	2.8%
36	New Mexico	1,458,433	0.6%
4	New York	12,194,360	5.4%
8	North Carolina	7,509,231	3.3%
48	North Dakota	561,333	0.2%
7	Ohio	8,032,665	3.5%
29	Oklahoma	2,504,253	1.1%
27	Oregon	2,930,702	1.3%
5	Pennsylvania	8,991,370	4.0%
45	Rhode Island	756,966	0.3%
23	South Carolina	3,846,069	1.7%
46	South Dakota	638,428	0.3%
14	Tennessee	5,422,429	2.4%
2	Texas	17,370,383	7.6%
34	Utah	2,030,644	0.9%
47	Vermont	564,892	0.2%
12	Virginia	5,929,031	2.6%
13	Washington	5,909,967	2.6%
40	West Virginia	1,136,775	0.5%
19	Wisconsin	4,288,171	1.9%
50	Wyoming	419,256	0.2%

RANK	STATE	DRIVERS	% of USA
1	California	27,039,400	11.9%
2	Texas	17,370,383	7.6%
3	Florida	15,368,695	6.8%
4	New York	12,194,360	5.4%
5	Pennsylvania	8,991,370	4.0%
6	Illinois	8,714,788	3.8%
7	Ohio	8,032,665	3.5%
8	North Carolina	7,509,231	3.3%
9	Georgia	7,168,733	3.2%
10	Michigan	7,153,645	3.1%
11	New Jersey	6,342,876	2.8%
12	Virginia	5,929,031	2.6%
13	Washington	5,909,967	2.6%
14	Tennessee	5,422,429	2.4%
15	Arizona	5,284,970	2.3%
16	Massachusetts	4,935,176	2.2%
17	Indiana	4,589,405	2.0%
18	Maryland	4,407,973	1.9%
19	Wisconsin	4,288,171	1.9%
20	Missouri	4,272,960	1.9%
21	Colorado	4,244,713	1.9%
22	Alabama	3,999,057	1.8%
23	South Carolina	3,846,069	1.7%
24	Louisiana	3,425,435	1.5%
25	Minnesota	3,391,057	1.5%
26	Kentucky	3,032,530	1.3%
27	Oregon	2,930,702	1.3%
28	Connecticut	2,605,612	1.1%
29	Oklahoma	2,504,253	1.1%
30	Iowa	2,260,271	1.0%
31	Kansas	2,149,430	0.9%
32	Arkansas	2,145,334	0.9%
33	Mississippi	2,058,036	0.9%
34	Utah	2,030,644	0.9%
35	Nevada	1,983,453	0.9%
36	New Mexico	1,458,433	0.6%
37	Nebraska	1,420,317	0.6%
38	Idaho	1,252,535	0.6%
39	New Hampshire	1,161,665	0.5%
40	West Virginia	1,136,775	0.5%
41	Maine	1,040,582	0.5%
42	Hawaii	948,417	0.4%
43	Montana	806,204	0.4%
44	Delaware	786,504	0.3%
45	Rhode Island	756,966	0.3%
46	South Dakota	638,428	0.3%
47	Vermont	564,892	0.2%
48	North Dakota	561,333	0.2%
49	Alaska	536,033	0.2%
50	Wyoming	419,256	0.2%
	District of Columbia	527,731	0.2%

Source: U.S. Department of Transportation, Federal Highway Administration
"Highway Statistics 2018" (Table DL-22, https://www.fhwa.dot.gov/policyinformation/statistics/2018/)

Licensed Drivers per 1,000 Driving Age Population in 2018

National Ratio = 868 Licensed Drivers

ALPHA ORDER			RANK ORDER		
RANK	STATE	RATE	RANK	STATE	RATE
3	Alabama	1,019	1	Vermont	1,077
12	Alaska	936	2	New Hampshire	1,027
17	Arizona	925	3	Alabama	1,019
24	Arkansas	898	4	Delaware	1,000
40	California	856	5	Tennessee	998
16	Colorado	928	6	Washington	976
25	Connecticut	889	7	Nebraska	944
4	Delaware	1,000	8	Kansas	941
28	Florida	875	9	Montana	939
36	Georgia	863	10	North Dakota	938
44	Hawaii	826	11	South Carolina	937
18	Idaho	922	12	Alaska	936
42	Illinois	853	13	Louisiana	930
34	Indiana	865	13	Maine	930
22	Iowa	901	15	South Dakota	929
8	Kansas	941	16	Colorado	928
43	Kentucky	849	17	Arizona	925
13	Louisiana	930	18	Idaho	922
13	Maine	930	19	Wyoming	917
21	Maryland	908	20	Wisconsin	915
33	Massachusetts	866	21	Maryland	908
26	Michigan	884	22	Iowa	901
50	Minnesota	762	23	North Carolina	899
30	Mississippi	872	24	Arkansas	898
31	Missouri	871	25	Connecticut	889
9	Montana	939	26	Michigan	884
7	Nebraska	944	27	New Jersey	883
45	Nevada	819	28	Florida	875
2	New Hampshire	1,027	29	New Mexico	874
27	New Jersey	883	30	Mississippi	872
29	New Mexico	874	31	Missouri	871
49	New York	765	31	Utah	871
23	North Carolina	899	33	Massachusetts	866
10	North Dakota	938	34	Indiana	865
41	Ohio	855	35	Virginia	864
46	Oklahoma	810	36	Georgia	863
39	Oregon	858	36	Rhode Island	863
38	Pennsylvania	859	38	Pennsylvania	859
36	Rhode Island	863	39	Oregon	858
11	South Carolina	937	40	California	856
15	South Dakota	929	41	Ohio	855
5	Tennessee	998	42	Illinois	853
47	Texas	785	43	Kentucky	849
31	Utah	871	44	Hawaii	826
1	Vermont	1,077	45	Nevada	819
35	Virginia	864	46	Oklahoma	810
6	Washington	976	47	Texas	785
48	West Virginia	766	48	West Virginia	766
20	Wisconsin	915	49	New York	765
19	Wyoming	917	50	Minnesota	762
				District of Columbia	901

Source: CQ Press using data from U.S. Department of Transportation, Federal Highway Administration "Highway Statistics 2018" (Table DL-22, https://www.fhwa.dot.gov/policyinformation/statistics/2018/)

Motor Vehicle Registrations in 2017

National Total = 272,480,899 Motor Vehicles*

ALPHA ORDER

RANK	STATE	VEHICLES	% of USA
22	Alabama	5,056,073	1.9%
49	Alaska	804,505	0.3%
15	Arizona	5,964,434	2.2%
30	Arkansas	2,833,697	1.0%
1	California	30,795,141	11.3%
20	Colorado	5,259,960	1.9%
31	Connecticut	2,826,350	1.0%
46	Delaware	970,733	0.4%
3	Florida	16,959,269	6.2%
9	Georgia	8,442,325	3.1%
42	Hawaii	1,259,541	0.5%
38	Idaho	1,835,903	0.7%
4	Illinois	10,890,760	4.0%
13	Indiana	6,170,034	2.3%
28	Iowa	3,750,077	1.4%
32	Kansas	2,717,873	1.0%
25	Kentucky	4,293,205	1.6%
27	Louisiana	3,906,812	1.4%
44	Maine	1,094,388	0.4%
24	Maryland	4,357,598	1.6%
21	Massachusetts	5,065,221	1.9%
8	Michigan	8,518,097	3.1%
17	Minnesota	5,682,653	2.1%
35	Mississippi	2,057,476	0.8%
19	Missouri	5,568,736	2.0%
37	Montana	1,863,918	0.7%
36	Nebraska	1,965,105	0.7%
33	Nevada	2,455,442	0.9%
41	New Hampshire	1,319,117	0.5%
14	New Jersey	6,057,711	2.2%
39	New Mexico	1,740,002	0.6%
5	New York	10,857,455	4.0%
10	North Carolina	8,070,717	3.0%
45	North Dakota	1,056,758	0.4%
6	Ohio	10,809,247	4.0%
29	Oklahoma	3,744,178	1.4%
26	Oregon	4,103,451	1.5%
7	Pennsylvania	10,689,206	3.9%
47	Rhode Island	872,814	0.3%
23	South Carolina	4,404,100	1.6%
43	South Dakota	1,258,356	0.5%
16	Tennessee	5,800,489	2.1%
2	Texas	22,130,765	8.1%
34	Utah	2,355,773	0.9%
50	Vermont	621,608	0.2%
11	Virginia	7,514,484	2.8%
12	Washington	7,256,196	2.7%
40	West Virginia	1,691,237	0.6%
18	Wisconsin	5,596,635	2.1%
48	Wyoming	819,257	0.3%

RANK ORDER

RANK	STATE	VEHICLES	% of USA
1	California	30,795,141	11.3%
2	Texas	22,130,765	8.1%
3	Florida	16,959,269	6.2%
4	Illinois	10,890,760	4.0%
5	New York	10,857,455	4.0%
6	Ohio	10,809,247	4.0%
7	Pennsylvania	10,689,206	3.9%
8	Michigan	8,518,097	3.1%
9	Georgia	8,442,325	3.1%
10	North Carolina	8,070,717	3.0%
11	Virginia	7,514,484	2.8%
12	Washington	7,256,196	2.7%
13	Indiana	6,170,034	2.3%
14	New Jersey	6,057,711	2.2%
15	Arizona	5,964,434	2.2%
16	Tennessee	5,800,489	2.1%
17	Minnesota	5,682,653	2.1%
18	Wisconsin	5,596,635	2.1%
19	Missouri	5,568,736	2.0%
20	Colorado	5,259,960	1.9%
21	Massachusetts	5,065,221	1.9%
22	Alabama	5,056,073	1.9%
23	South Carolina	4,404,100	1.6%
24	Maryland	4,357,598	1.6%
25	Kentucky	4,293,205	1.6%
26	Oregon	4,103,451	1.5%
27	Louisiana	3,906,812	1.4%
28	Iowa	3,750,077	1.4%
29	Oklahoma	3,744,178	1.4%
30	Arkansas	2,833,697	1.0%
31	Connecticut	2,826,350	1.0%
32	Kansas	2,717,873	1.0%
33	Nevada	2,455,442	0.9%
34	Utah	2,355,773	0.9%
35	Mississippi	2,057,476	0.8%
36	Nebraska	1,965,105	0.7%
37	Montana	1,863,918	0.7%
38	Idaho	1,835,903	0.7%
39	New Mexico	1,740,002	0.6%
40	West Virginia	1,691,237	0.6%
41	New Hampshire	1,319,117	0.5%
42	Hawaii	1,259,541	0.5%
43	South Dakota	1,258,356	0.5%
44	Maine	1,094,388	0.4%
45	North Dakota	1,056,758	0.4%
46	Delaware	970,733	0.4%
47	Rhode Island	872,814	0.3%
48	Wyoming	819,257	0.3%
49	Alaska	804,505	0.3%
50	Vermont	621,608	0.2%
	District of Columbia	346,016	0.1%

Source: U.S. Department of Transportation, Federal Highway Administration
    "Highway Statistics 2017" (Table MV-1, https://www.fhwa.dot.gov/policyinformation/statistics/2017/)
*Includes automobiles, trucks, buses and motorcycles.

Motor Vehicles per Driving Age Population in 2017

National Rate = 1.05 Motor Vehicles*

ALPHA ORDER				RANK ORDER		
RANK	STATE	RATE		RANK	STATE	RATE
9	Alabama	1.29		1	Montana	2.20
6	Alaska	1.40		2	South Dakota	1.86
30	Arizona	1.07		3	Wyoming	1.79
17	Arkansas	1.19		4	North Dakota	1.77
41	California	0.98		5	Iowa	1.50
21	Colorado	1.17		6	Alaska	1.40
45	Connecticut	0.96		7	Idaho	1.39
11	Delaware	1.24		8	Nebraska	1.31
41	Florida	0.98		9	Alabama	1.29
36	Georgia	1.03		10	Minnesota	1.28
27	Hawaii	1.09		11	Delaware	1.24
7	Idaho	1.39		12	Oklahoma	1.22
31	Illinois	1.06		12	Oregon	1.22
21	Indiana	1.17		12	Washington	1.22
5	Iowa	1.50		15	Kentucky	1.21
17	Kansas	1.19		16	Wisconsin	1.20
15	Kentucky	1.21		17	Arkansas	1.19
31	Louisiana	1.06		17	Kansas	1.19
41	Maine	0.98		17	Vermont	1.19
46	Maryland	0.90		20	New Hampshire	1.18
46	Massachusetts	0.90		21	Colorado	1.17
31	Michigan	1.06		21	Indiana	1.17
10	Minnesota	1.28		23	Ohio	1.15
48	Mississippi	0.87		24	Missouri	1.14
24	Missouri	1.14		24	West Virginia	1.14
1	Montana	2.20		26	Virginia	1.10
8	Nebraska	1.31		27	Hawaii	1.09
36	Nevada	1.03		27	South Carolina	1.09
20	New Hampshire	1.18		29	Tennessee	1.08
49	New Jersey	0.83		30	Arizona	1.07
34	New Mexico	1.05		31	Illinois	1.06
50	New York	0.67		31	Louisiana	1.06
41	North Carolina	0.98		31	Michigan	1.06
4	North Dakota	1.77		34	New Mexico	1.05
23	Ohio	1.15		35	Utah	1.04
12	Oklahoma	1.22		36	Georgia	1.03
12	Oregon	1.22		36	Nevada	1.03
38	Pennsylvania	1.02		38	Pennsylvania	1.02
40	Rhode Island	0.99		38	Texas	1.02
27	South Carolina	1.09		40	Rhode Island	0.99
2	South Dakota	1.86		41	California	0.98
29	Tennessee	1.08		41	Florida	0.98
38	Texas	1.02		41	Maine	0.98
35	Utah	1.04		41	North Carolina	0.98
17	Vermont	1.19		45	Connecticut	0.96
26	Virginia	1.10		46	Maryland	0.90
12	Washington	1.22		46	Massachusetts	0.90
24	West Virginia	1.14		48	Mississippi	0.87
16	Wisconsin	1.20		49	New Jersey	0.83
3	Wyoming	1.79		50	New York	0.67
					District of Columbia	0.60

Source: CQ Press using data from U.S. Department of Transportation, Federal Highway Administration
"Highway Statistics 2017" (Table MV-1, https://www.fhwa.dot.gov/policyinformation/statistics/2017/)
*Persons age sixteen and older. Motor Vehicles include automobiles, trucks, buses, and motorcycles.

Average Travel Time to Work in 2018

National Average = 27.1 Minutes*

ALPHA ORDER				RANK ORDER		
RANK	STATE	MINUTES		RANK	STATE	MINUTES
22	Alabama	25.2		1	New York	34.0
45	Alaska	19.1		2	Maryland	33.3
20	Arizona	25.7		3	New Jersey	32.4
41	Arkansas	21.7		4	Massachusetts	30.5
5	California	30.2		5	California	30.2
19	Colorado	25.9		6	Illinois	29.4
14	Connecticut	26.8		7	Georgia	29.0
17	Delaware	26.4		8	Virginia	28.7
10	Florida	28.0		9	Washington	28.4
7	Georgia	29.0		10	Florida	28.0
11	Hawaii	27.6		11	Hawaii	27.6
42	Idaho	21.0		11	New Hampshire	27.6
6	Illinois	29.4		13	Pennsylvania	27.2
31	Indiana	23.9		14	Connecticut	26.8
44	Iowa	19.5		15	Texas	26.7
43	Kansas	19.7		16	West Virginia	26.5
36	Kentucky	23.5		17	Delaware	26.4
18	Louisiana	26.3		18	Louisiana	26.3
29	Maine	24.1		19	Colorado	25.9
2	Maryland	33.3		20	Arizona	25.7
4	Massachusetts	30.5		21	Tennessee	25.4
28	Michigan	24.7		22	Alabama	25.2
32	Minnesota	23.8		23	South Carolina	25.1
24	Mississippi	25.0		24	Mississippi	25.0
30	Missouri	24.0		24	Rhode Island	25.0
47	Montana	18.6		26	Nevada	24.9
46	Nebraska	18.8		27	North Carolina	24.8
26	Nevada	24.9		28	Michigan	24.7
11	New Hampshire	27.6		29	Maine	24.1
3	New Jersey	32.4		30	Missouri	24.0
37	New Mexico	23.0		31	Indiana	23.9
1	New York	34.0		32	Minnesota	23.8
27	North Carolina	24.8		32	Oregon	23.8
48	North Dakota	17.7		34	Ohio	23.6
34	Ohio	23.6		34	Vermont	23.6
38	Oklahoma	22.1		36	Kentucky	23.5
32	Oregon	23.8		37	New Mexico	23.0
13	Pennsylvania	27.2		38	Oklahoma	22.1
24	Rhode Island	25.0		39	Utah	22.0
23	South Carolina	25.1		39	Wisconsin	22.0
49	South Dakota	17.3		41	Arkansas	21.7
21	Tennessee	25.4		42	Idaho	21.0
15	Texas	26.7		43	Kansas	19.7
39	Utah	22.0		44	Iowa	19.5
34	Vermont	23.6		45	Alaska	19.1
8	Virginia	28.7		46	Nebraska	18.8
9	Washington	28.4		47	Montana	18.6
16	West Virginia	26.5		48	North Dakota	17.7
39	Wisconsin	22.0		49	South Dakota	17.3
50	Wyoming	16.2		50	Wyoming	16.2
					District of Columbia	30.9

Source: U.S. Bureau of the Census
   "2018 American Community Survey-Table DP03" (https://data.census.gov/cedsci/)
*Workers sixteen and older not working at home.

Percent of Commuters Who Drive to Work Alone in 2018

National Percent = 76.3%*

<table>
<tr><td colspan="3">ALPHA ORDER</td><td colspan="3">RANK ORDER</td></tr>
<tr><th>RANK</th><th>STATE</th><th>PERCENT</th><th>RANK</th><th>STATE</th><th>PERCENT</th></tr>
<tr><td>1</td><td>Alabama</td><td>86.3</td><td>1</td><td>Alabama</td><td>86.3</td></tr>
<tr><td>48</td><td>Alaska</td><td>68.0</td><td>2</td><td>Mississippi</td><td>85.5</td></tr>
<tr><td>34</td><td>Arizona</td><td>76.1</td><td>3</td><td>West Virginia</td><td>83.3</td></tr>
<tr><td>7</td><td>Arkansas</td><td>82.6</td><td>4</td><td>Tennessee</td><td>83.1</td></tr>
<tr><td>42</td><td>California</td><td>73.8</td><td>5</td><td>Indiana</td><td>82.9</td></tr>
<tr><td>39</td><td>Colorado</td><td>74.9</td><td>6</td><td>Louisiana</td><td>82.7</td></tr>
<tr><td>30</td><td>Connecticut</td><td>77.9</td><td>7</td><td>Arkansas</td><td>82.6</td></tr>
<tr><td>25</td><td>Delaware</td><td>79.6</td><td>8</td><td>Oklahoma</td><td>82.5</td></tr>
<tr><td>28</td><td>Florida</td><td>79.1</td><td>9</td><td>Kentucky</td><td>82.4</td></tr>
<tr><td>26</td><td>Georgia</td><td>79.4</td><td>9</td><td>Ohio</td><td>82.4</td></tr>
<tr><td>49</td><td>Hawaii</td><td>67.3</td><td>11</td><td>Missouri</td><td>82.2</td></tr>
<tr><td>24</td><td>Idaho</td><td>79.7</td><td>11</td><td>North Dakota</td><td>82.2</td></tr>
<tr><td>43</td><td>Illinois</td><td>72.7</td><td>13</td><td>Nebraska</td><td>82.1</td></tr>
<tr><td>5</td><td>Indiana</td><td>82.9</td><td>14</td><td>Kansas</td><td>82.0</td></tr>
<tr><td>17</td><td>Iowa</td><td>81.6</td><td>14</td><td>Michigan</td><td>82.0</td></tr>
<tr><td>14</td><td>Kansas</td><td>82.0</td><td>16</td><td>Wisconsin</td><td>81.7</td></tr>
<tr><td>9</td><td>Kentucky</td><td>82.4</td><td>17</td><td>Iowa</td><td>81.6</td></tr>
<tr><td>6</td><td>Louisiana</td><td>82.7</td><td>18</td><td>South Carolina</td><td>81.4</td></tr>
<tr><td>31</td><td>Maine</td><td>77.8</td><td>19</td><td>Rhode Island</td><td>81.3</td></tr>
<tr><td>41</td><td>Maryland</td><td>74.3</td><td>20</td><td>South Dakota</td><td>81.1</td></tr>
<tr><td>47</td><td>Massachusetts</td><td>69.8</td><td>21</td><td>New Hampshire</td><td>80.8</td></tr>
<tr><td>14</td><td>Michigan</td><td>82.0</td><td>22</td><td>Texas</td><td>80.7</td></tr>
<tr><td>32</td><td>Minnesota</td><td>77.7</td><td>23</td><td>North Carolina</td><td>80.6</td></tr>
<tr><td>2</td><td>Mississippi</td><td>85.5</td><td>24</td><td>Idaho</td><td>79.7</td></tr>
<tr><td>11</td><td>Missouri</td><td>82.2</td><td>25</td><td>Delaware</td><td>79.6</td></tr>
<tr><td>39</td><td>Montana</td><td>74.9</td><td>26</td><td>Georgia</td><td>79.4</td></tr>
<tr><td>13</td><td>Nebraska</td><td>82.1</td><td>27</td><td>New Mexico</td><td>79.3</td></tr>
<tr><td>29</td><td>Nevada</td><td>78.3</td><td>28</td><td>Florida</td><td>79.1</td></tr>
<tr><td>21</td><td>New Hampshire</td><td>80.8</td><td>29</td><td>Nevada</td><td>78.3</td></tr>
<tr><td>46</td><td>New Jersey</td><td>70.9</td><td>30</td><td>Connecticut</td><td>77.9</td></tr>
<tr><td>27</td><td>New Mexico</td><td>79.3</td><td>31</td><td>Maine</td><td>77.8</td></tr>
<tr><td>50</td><td>New York</td><td>53.1</td><td>32</td><td>Minnesota</td><td>77.7</td></tr>
<tr><td>23</td><td>North Carolina</td><td>80.6</td><td>33</td><td>Virginia</td><td>76.7</td></tr>
<tr><td>11</td><td>North Dakota</td><td>82.2</td><td>34</td><td>Arizona</td><td>76.1</td></tr>
<tr><td>9</td><td>Ohio</td><td>82.4</td><td>35</td><td>Wyoming</td><td>75.8</td></tr>
<tr><td>8</td><td>Oklahoma</td><td>82.5</td><td>36</td><td>Utah</td><td>75.7</td></tr>
<tr><td>44</td><td>Oregon</td><td>71.7</td><td>37</td><td>Pennsylvania</td><td>75.6</td></tr>
<tr><td>37</td><td>Pennsylvania</td><td>75.6</td><td>38</td><td>Vermont</td><td>75.4</td></tr>
<tr><td>19</td><td>Rhode Island</td><td>81.3</td><td>39</td><td>Colorado</td><td>74.9</td></tr>
<tr><td>18</td><td>South Carolina</td><td>81.4</td><td>39</td><td>Montana</td><td>74.9</td></tr>
<tr><td>20</td><td>South Dakota</td><td>81.1</td><td>41</td><td>Maryland</td><td>74.3</td></tr>
<tr><td>4</td><td>Tennessee</td><td>83.1</td><td>42</td><td>California</td><td>73.8</td></tr>
<tr><td>22</td><td>Texas</td><td>80.7</td><td>43</td><td>Illinois</td><td>72.7</td></tr>
<tr><td>36</td><td>Utah</td><td>75.7</td><td>44</td><td>Oregon</td><td>71.7</td></tr>
<tr><td>38</td><td>Vermont</td><td>75.4</td><td>45</td><td>Washington</td><td>71.0</td></tr>
<tr><td>33</td><td>Virginia</td><td>76.7</td><td>46</td><td>New Jersey</td><td>70.9</td></tr>
<tr><td>45</td><td>Washington</td><td>71.0</td><td>47</td><td>Massachusetts</td><td>69.8</td></tr>
<tr><td>3</td><td>West Virginia</td><td>83.3</td><td>48</td><td>Alaska</td><td>68.0</td></tr>
<tr><td>16</td><td>Wisconsin</td><td>81.7</td><td>49</td><td>Hawaii</td><td>67.3</td></tr>
<tr><td>35</td><td>Wyoming</td><td>75.8</td><td>50</td><td>New York</td><td>53.1</td></tr>
<tr><td></td><td></td><td></td><td></td><td>District of Columbia</td><td>34.2</td></tr>
</table>

Source: U.S. Bureau of the Census
   "2018 American Community Survey-Table DP03" (https://data.census.gov/cedsci/)
*Workers sixteen and older who traveled to work by car, truck, or van.

Percent of Commuters Who Drive to Work in Carpools in 2018

National Percent = 9.0%*

ALPHA ORDER

RANK ORDER

RANK	STATE	PERCENT		RANK	STATE	PERCENT
46	Alabama	7.9		1	Hawaii	14.7
2	Alaska	12.3		2	Alaska	12.3
5	Arizona	11.0		3	New Mexico	11.2
7	Arkansas	10.4		4	Utah	11.1
9	California	10.0		5	Arizona	11.0
35	Colorado	8.6		6	Nevada	10.5
43	Connecticut	8.1		7	Arkansas	10.4
22	Delaware	9.1		8	Wyoming	10.2
16	Florida	9.4		9	California	10.0
16	Georgia	9.4		10	Maine	9.9
1	Hawaii	14.7		11	Texas	9.8
27	Idaho	8.9		11	Washington	9.8
40	Illinois	8.3		13	Montana	9.5
27	Indiana	8.9		13	Oklahoma	9.5
43	Iowa	8.1		13	Oregon	9.5
20	Kansas	9.3		16	Florida	9.4
16	Kentucky	9.4		16	Georgia	9.4
24	Louisiana	9.0		16	Kentucky	9.4
10	Maine	9.9		16	South Carolina	9.4
31	Maryland	8.8		20	Kansas	9.3
48	Massachusetts	7.4		20	North Carolina	9.3
27	Michigan	8.9		22	Delaware	9.1
38	Minnesota	8.4		22	Virginia	9.1
27	Mississippi	8.9		24	Louisiana	9.0
38	Missouri	8.4		24	Tennessee	9.0
13	Montana	9.5		24	Vermont	9.0
33	Nebraska	8.7		27	Idaho	8.9
6	Nevada	10.5		27	Indiana	8.9
48	New Hampshire	7.4		27	Michigan	8.9
41	New Jersey	8.2		27	Mississippi	8.9
3	New Mexico	11.2		31	Maryland	8.8
50	New York	6.3		31	South Dakota	8.8
20	North Carolina	9.3		33	Nebraska	8.7
33	North Dakota	8.7		33	North Dakota	8.7
41	Ohio	8.2		35	Colorado	8.6
13	Oklahoma	9.5		35	West Virginia	8.6
13	Oregon	9.5		37	Pennsylvania	8.5
37	Pennsylvania	8.5		38	Minnesota	8.4
43	Rhode Island	8.1		38	Missouri	8.4
16	South Carolina	9.4		40	Illinois	8.3
31	South Dakota	8.8		41	New Jersey	8.2
24	Tennessee	9.0		41	Ohio	8.2
11	Texas	9.8		43	Connecticut	8.1
4	Utah	11.1		43	Iowa	8.1
24	Vermont	9.0		43	Rhode Island	8.1
22	Virginia	9.1		46	Alabama	7.9
11	Washington	9.8		47	Wisconsin	7.5
35	West Virginia	8.6		48	Massachusetts	7.4
47	Wisconsin	7.5		48	New Hampshire	7.4
8	Wyoming	10.2		50	New York	6.3

District of Columbia 5.1

Source: U.S. Bureau of the Census
"2018 American Community Survey-Table DP03" (https://data.census.gov/cedsci/)
*Workers sixteen and older who traveled to work by car, truck, or van.

Percent of Commuters Who Travel to Work by Public Transportation in 2018

National Percent = 4.9%*

ALPHA ORDER				RANK ORDER		
RANK	STATE	PERCENT		RANK	STATE	PERCENT
48	Alabama	0.3		1	New York	28.0
27	Alaska	1.2		2	New Jersey	11.7
20	Arizona	1.7		3	Massachusetts	10.2
47	Arkansas	0.4		4	Illinois	9.4
9	California	4.9		5	Maryland	7.9
15	Colorado	2.8		6	Washington	7.0
11	Connecticut	4.4		7	Pennsylvania	5.8
16	Delaware	2.2		8	Hawaii	5.7
20	Florida	1.7		9	California	4.9
19	Georgia	2.0		10	Virginia	4.5
8	Hawaii	5.7		11	Connecticut	4.4
38	Idaho	0.8		12	Oregon	4.2
4	Illinois	9.4		13	Minnesota	3.5
34	Indiana	0.9		14	Nevada	2.9
31	Iowa	1.0		15	Colorado	2.8
45	Kansas	0.5		16	Delaware	2.2
31	Kentucky	1.0		16	Rhode Island	2.2
27	Louisiana	1.2		16	Utah	2.2
41	Maine	0.6		19	Georgia	2.0
5	Maryland	7.9		20	Arizona	1.7
3	Massachusetts	10.2		20	Florida	1.7
24	Michigan	1.4		22	Ohio	1.6
13	Minnesota	3.5		23	Wisconsin	1.5
48	Mississippi	0.3		24	Michigan	1.4
25	Missouri	1.3		25	Missouri	1.3
38	Montana	0.8		25	Texas	1.3
41	Nebraska	0.6		27	Alaska	1.2
14	Nevada	2.9		27	Louisiana	1.2
34	New Hampshire	0.9		27	Wyoming	1.2
2	New Jersey	11.7		30	New Mexico	1.1
30	New Mexico	1.1		31	Iowa	1.0
1	New York	28.0		31	Kentucky	1.0
31	North Carolina	1.0		31	North Carolina	1.0
40	North Dakota	0.7		34	Indiana	0.9
22	Ohio	1.6		34	New Hampshire	0.9
45	Oklahoma	0.5		34	Vermont	0.9
12	Oregon	4.2		34	West Virginia	0.9
7	Pennsylvania	5.8		38	Idaho	0.8
16	Rhode Island	2.2		38	Montana	0.8
41	South Carolina	0.6		40	North Dakota	0.7
50	South Dakota	0.2		41	Maine	0.6
41	Tennessee	0.6		41	Nebraska	0.6
25	Texas	1.3		41	South Carolina	0.6
16	Utah	2.2		41	Tennessee	0.6
34	Vermont	0.9		45	Kansas	0.5
10	Virginia	4.5		45	Oklahoma	0.5
6	Washington	7.0		47	Arkansas	0.4
34	West Virginia	0.9		48	Alabama	0.3
23	Wisconsin	1.5		48	Mississippi	0.3
27	Wyoming	1.2		50	South Dakota	0.2
					District of Columbia	34.4

Source: U.S. Bureau of the Census
"2018 American Community Survey-Table DP03" (https://data.census.gov/cedsci/)
*Workers sixteen and older.

Annual Miles per Vehicle in 2017

National Annual Average = 11,789 Miles*

ALPHA ORDER				RANK ORDER		
RANK	STATE	MILES		RANK	STATE	MILES
6	Alabama	13,979		1	Mississippi	19,868
49	Alaska	6,860		2	New Mexico	17,058
33	Arizona	10,910		3	Georgia	14,775
14	Arkansas	12,842		4	North Carolina	14,767
30	California	11,166		5	Tennessee	14,180
38	Colorado	10,149		6	Alabama	13,979
31	Connecticut	11,145		7	Maryland	13,779
34	Delaware	10,782		8	Missouri	13,632
13	Florida	12,903		9	Maine	13,467
3	Georgia	14,775		10	Utah	13,361
46	Hawaii	8,534		11	Indiana	13,250
41	Idaho	9,423		12	Oklahoma	13,194
39	Illinois	9,918		13	Florida	12,903
11	Indiana	13,250		14	Arkansas	12,842
45	Iowa	8,928		15	New Jersey	12,795
23	Kansas	11,869		16	South Carolina	12,601
25	Kentucky	11,469		17	Louisiana	12,599
17	Louisiana	12,599		18	Massachusetts	12,371
9	Maine	13,467		19	Texas	12,335
7	Maryland	13,779		20	Michigan	11,946
18	Massachusetts	12,371		21	Vermont	11,944
20	Michigan	11,946		22	Wyoming	11,943
36	Minnesota	10,553		23	Kansas	11,869
1	Mississippi	19,868		24	Wisconsin	11,672
8	Missouri	13,632		25	Kentucky	11,469
50	Montana	6,784		26	New York	11,396
35	Nebraska	10,687		27	Virginia	11,346
29	Nevada	11,235		28	West Virginia	11,277
37	New Hampshire	10,372		29	Nevada	11,235
15	New Jersey	12,795		30	California	11,166
2	New Mexico	17,058		31	Connecticut	11,145
26	New York	11,396		32	Ohio	11,064
4	North Carolina	14,767		33	Arizona	10,910
42	North Dakota	9,195		34	Delaware	10,782
32	Ohio	11,064		35	Nebraska	10,687
12	Oklahoma	13,194		36	Minnesota	10,553
44	Oregon	8,957		37	New Hampshire	10,372
40	Pennsylvania	9,506		38	Colorado	10,149
43	Rhode Island	9,167		39	Illinois	9,918
16	South Carolina	12,601		40	Pennsylvania	9,506
48	South Dakota	7,663		41	Idaho	9,423
5	Tennessee	14,180		42	North Dakota	9,195
19	Texas	12,335		43	Rhode Island	9,167
10	Utah	13,361		44	Oregon	8,957
21	Vermont	11,944		45	Iowa	8,928
27	Virginia	11,346		46	Hawaii	8,534
47	Washington	8,464		47	Washington	8,464
28	West Virginia	11,277		48	South Dakota	7,663
24	Wisconsin	11,672		49	Alaska	6,860
22	Wyoming	11,943		50	Montana	6,784
					District of Columbia	10,739

Source: CQ Press using data from U.S. Department of Transportation, Federal Highway Administration
"Highway Statistics 2017" (Tables MV-1 and VM-2, https://www.fhwa.dot.gov/policyinformation/statistics/2017/)
*Includes automobiles, trucks, buses, and motorcycles.

Average Miles per Gallon in 2018

National Average = 18.2 Miles per Gallon*

ALPHA ORDER				RANK ORDER		
RANK	STATE	MILES PER GALLON		RANK	STATE	MILES PER GALLON
7	Alabama	20.9		1	Hawaii	22.6
43	Alaska	16.2		2	Vermont	21.6
25	Arizona	18.0		3	Florida	21.5
27	Arkansas	17.8		3	Georgia	21.5
8	California	19.6		5	Massachusetts	21.4
19	Colorado	18.7		5	North Carolina	21.4
23	Connecticut	18.3		7	Alabama	20.9
25	Delaware	18.0		8	California	19.6
3	Florida	21.5		8	Utah	19.6
3	Georgia	21.5		8	Wisconsin	19.6
1	Hawaii	22.6		11	Indiana	19.4
30	Idaho	17.7		12	Maryland	19.2
34	Illinois	17.5		12	Tennessee	19.2
11	Indiana	19.4		14	Kansas	19.1
46	Iowa	15.2		14	Maine	19.1
14	Kansas	19.1		16	Michigan	18.8
39	Kentucky	16.8		16	Missouri	18.8
21	Louisiana	18.5		16	Nevada	18.8
14	Maine	19.1		19	Colorado	18.7
12	Maryland	19.2		20	Minnesota	18.6
5	Massachusetts	21.4		21	Louisiana	18.5
16	Michigan	18.8		22	Rhode Island	18.4
20	Minnesota	18.6		23	Connecticut	18.3
30	Mississippi	17.7		24	New York	18.2
16	Missouri	18.8		25	Arizona	18.0
38	Montana	16.9		25	Delaware	18.0
45	Nebraska	15.9		27	Arkansas	17.8
16	Nevada	18.8		27	New Mexico	17.8
30	New Hampshire	17.7		27	Washington	17.8
37	New Jersey	17.0		30	Idaho	17.7
27	New Mexico	17.8		30	Mississippi	17.7
24	New York	18.2		30	New Hampshire	17.7
5	North Carolina	21.4		33	Ohio	17.6
50	North Dakota	13.5		34	Illinois	17.5
33	Ohio	17.6		35	Oregon	17.3
41	Oklahoma	16.4		36	Virginia	17.2
35	Oregon	17.3		37	New Jersey	17.0
40	Pennsylvania	16.7		38	Montana	16.9
22	Rhode Island	18.4		39	Kentucky	16.8
42	South Carolina	16.3		40	Pennsylvania	16.7
48	South Dakota	14.2		41	Oklahoma	16.4
12	Tennessee	19.2		42	South Carolina	16.3
48	Texas	14.2		43	Alaska	16.2
8	Utah	19.6		44	Wyoming	16.0
2	Vermont	21.6		45	Nebraska	15.9
36	Virginia	17.2		46	Iowa	15.2
27	Washington	17.8		47	West Virginia	15.0
47	West Virginia	15.0		48	South Dakota	14.2
8	Wisconsin	19.6		48	Texas	14.2
44	Wyoming	16.0		50	North Dakota	13.5
					District of Columbia	30.1

Source: CQ Press using data from U.S. Department of Transportation, Federal Highway Administration
"Highway Statistics 2018" (Tables MF-21 and VM-2, https://www.fhwa.dot.gov/policyinformation/statistics/2018/)
*Total vehicle-miles for 2018 divided by total highway motor-fuel use. Includes gasoline, gasohol, diesel, and other "special fuels."

Percent of Traffic Fatalities That Were Pedestrians in 2017

National Percent = 16.1%*

ALPHA ORDER

RANK	STATE	PERCENT
28	Alabama	12.6
13	Alaska	17.7
7	Arizona	21.6
43	Arkansas	8.5
6	California	23.8
22	Colorado	14.2
14	Connecticut	17.3
3	Delaware	27.7
9	Florida	21.0
15	Georgia	16.4
26	Hawaii	13.1
48	Idaho	6.6
24	Illinois	13.2
34	Indiana	11.1
47	Iowa	7.0
46	Kansas	7.2
36	Kentucky	10.6
21	Louisiana	14.6
32	Maine	11.6
10	Maryland	20.7
8	Massachusetts	21.1
20	Michigan	15.1
36	Minnesota	10.6
38	Mississippi	10.3
38	Missouri	10.3
45	Montana	7.5
41	Nebraska	8.8
1	Nevada	29.4
35	New Hampshire	10.8
2	New Jersey	29.3
11	New Mexico	19.5
5	New York	24.2
23	North Carolina	14.0
50	North Dakota	4.3
29	Ohio	12.0
30	Oklahoma	11.9
17	Oregon	15.8
27	Pennsylvania	12.9
4	Rhode Island	25.3
18	South Carolina	15.6
44	South Dakota	7.8
30	Tennessee	11.9
16	Texas	16.3
19	Utah	15.4
32	Vermont	11.6
24	Virginia	13.2
12	Washington	18.2
42	West Virginia	8.6
40	Wisconsin	9.1
49	Wyoming	4.9

RANK ORDER

RANK	STATE	PERCENT
1	Nevada	29.4
2	New Jersey	29.3
3	Delaware	27.7
4	Rhode Island	25.3
5	New York	24.2
6	California	23.8
7	Arizona	21.6
8	Massachusetts	21.1
9	Florida	21.0
10	Maryland	20.7
11	New Mexico	19.5
12	Washington	18.2
13	Alaska	17.7
14	Connecticut	17.3
15	Georgia	16.4
16	Texas	16.3
17	Oregon	15.8
18	South Carolina	15.6
19	Utah	15.4
20	Michigan	15.1
21	Louisiana	14.6
22	Colorado	14.2
23	North Carolina	14.0
24	Illinois	13.2
24	Virginia	13.2
26	Hawaii	13.1
27	Pennsylvania	12.9
28	Alabama	12.6
29	Ohio	12.0
30	Oklahoma	11.9
30	Tennessee	11.9
32	Maine	11.6
32	Vermont	11.6
34	Indiana	11.1
35	New Hampshire	10.8
36	Kentucky	10.6
36	Minnesota	10.6
38	Mississippi	10.3
38	Missouri	10.3
40	Wisconsin	9.1
41	Nebraska	8.8
42	West Virginia	8.6
43	Arkansas	8.5
44	South Dakota	7.8
45	Montana	7.5
46	Kansas	7.2
47	Iowa	7.0
48	Idaho	6.6
49	Wyoming	4.9
50	North Dakota	4.3
	District of Columbia	35.5

Source: U.S. Department of Transportation, National Highway Traffic Safety Administration
"Traffic Safety Facts: Pedestrians" (https://crashstats.nhtsa.dot.gov/)
*A pedestrian fatality is any person on foot, walking, running, jogging, hiking, sitting, or lying down who is involved in a motor vehicle traffic crash.

Percent of Traffic Fatalities That Were Bicyclists in 2017

National Percent = 2.1%*

ALPHA ORDER				RANK ORDER		
RANK	STATE	PERCENT		RANK	STATE	PERCENT
44	Alabama	0.7		1	Hawaii	5.6
30	Alaska	1.3		2	New York	4.6
6	Arizona	3.2		3	Delaware	4.2
45	Arkansas	0.6		4	Florida	4.0
5	California	3.4		5	California	3.4
11	Colorado	2.5		6	Arizona	3.2
34	Connecticut	1.1		7	Massachusetts	3.1
3	Delaware	4.2		8	Louisiana	2.9
4	Florida	4.0		8	Nevada	2.9
37	Georgia	1.0		10	New Jersey	2.7
1	Hawaii	5.6		11	Colorado	2.5
32	Idaho	1.2		11	Washington	2.5
13	Illinois	2.4		13	Illinois	2.4
28	Indiana	1.4		13	Rhode Island	2.4
27	Iowa	1.5		15	Oregon	2.3
34	Kansas	1.1		16	Utah	2.2
41	Kentucky	0.9		17	North Carolina	2.1
8	Louisiana	2.9		18	Michigan	2.0
32	Maine	1.2		18	New Hampshire	2.0
21	Maryland	1.8		20	Pennsylvania	1.9
7	Massachusetts	3.1		21	Maryland	1.8
18	Michigan	2.0		21	South Carolina	1.8
23	Minnesota	1.7		23	Minnesota	1.7
37	Mississippi	1.0		23	North Dakota	1.7
37	Missouri	1.0		25	Ohio	1.6
46	Montana	0.5		25	Texas	1.6
30	Nebraska	1.3		27	Iowa	1.5
8	Nevada	2.9		28	Indiana	1.4
18	New Hampshire	2.0		28	Virginia	1.4
10	New Jersey	2.7		30	Alaska	1.3
46	New Mexico	0.5		30	Nebraska	1.3
2	New York	4.6		32	Idaho	1.2
17	North Carolina	2.1		32	Maine	1.2
23	North Dakota	1.7		34	Connecticut	1.1
25	Ohio	1.6		34	Kansas	1.1
41	Oklahoma	0.9		34	Wisconsin	1.1
15	Oregon	2.3		37	Georgia	1.0
20	Pennsylvania	1.9		37	Mississippi	1.0
13	Rhode Island	2.4		37	Missouri	1.0
21	South Carolina	1.8		37	West Virginia	1.0
48	South Dakota	0.0		41	Kentucky	0.9
43	Tennessee	0.8		41	Oklahoma	0.9
25	Texas	1.6		43	Tennessee	0.8
16	Utah	2.2		44	Alabama	0.7
48	Vermont	0.0		45	Arkansas	0.6
28	Virginia	1.4		46	Montana	0.5
11	Washington	2.5		46	New Mexico	0.5
37	West Virginia	1.0		48	South Dakota	0.0
34	Wisconsin	1.1		48	Vermont	0.0
48	Wyoming	0.0		48	Wyoming	0.0
					District of Columbia	6.5

Source: U.S. Department of Transportation, National Highway Traffic Safety Administration
   "Traffic Safety Facts: Bicyclists and Other Cyclists" (https://crashstats.nhtsa.dot.gov/)
*A bicyclist fatality includes any person on a bicycle, tricycle, or unicycle powered solely by pedals that is involved in a vehicle traffic crash.

Percent of Recreational Boating Accidents Involving Alcohol in 2018

National Percent = 7.5% of Accidents*

ALPHA ORDER

RANK	STATE	PERCENT
9	Alabama	13.6
2	Alaska	31.8
31	Arizona	7.0
46	Arkansas	1.7
43	California	3.4
30	Colorado	7.1
37	Connecticut	5.1
42	Delaware	4.3
39	Florida	4.8
25	Georgia	7.7
48	Hawaii	0.0
32	Idaho	6.8
15	Illinois	10.4
6	Indiana	16.3
4	Iowa	19.4
41	Kansas	4.5
13	Kentucky	12.2
10	Louisiana	12.6
20	Maine	9.3
23	Maryland	8.2
24	Massachusetts	7.8
33	Michigan	6.7
15	Minnesota	10.4
7	Mississippi	16.1
8	Missouri	15.6
3	Montana	21.1
17	Nebraska	10.0
36	Nevada	5.7
25	New Hampshire	7.7
43	New Jersey	3.4
22	New Mexico	8.3
14	New York	10.5
18	North Carolina	9.9
25	North Dakota	7.7
39	Ohio	4.8
4	Oklahoma	19.4
34	Oregon	6.2
47	Pennsylvania	1.6
48	Rhode Island	0.0
45	South Carolina	3.1
1	South Dakota	33.3
29	Tennessee	7.3
35	Texas	5.9
38	Utah	4.9
48	Vermont	0.0
28	Virginia	7.5
21	Washington	8.5
11	West Virginia	12.5
19	Wisconsin	9.4
11	Wyoming	12.5

RANK ORDER

RANK	STATE	PERCENT
1	South Dakota	33.3
2	Alaska	31.8
3	Montana	21.1
4	Iowa	19.4
4	Oklahoma	19.4
6	Indiana	16.3
7	Mississippi	16.1
8	Missouri	15.6
9	Alabama	13.6
10	Louisiana	12.6
11	West Virginia	12.5
11	Wyoming	12.5
13	Kentucky	12.2
14	New York	10.5
15	Illinois	10.4
15	Minnesota	10.4
17	Nebraska	10.0
18	North Carolina	9.9
19	Wisconsin	9.4
20	Maine	9.3
21	Washington	8.5
22	New Mexico	8.3
23	Maryland	8.2
24	Massachusetts	7.8
25	Georgia	7.7
25	New Hampshire	7.7
25	North Dakota	7.7
28	Virginia	7.5
29	Tennessee	7.3
30	Colorado	7.1
31	Arizona	7.0
32	Idaho	6.8
33	Michigan	6.7
34	Oregon	6.2
35	Texas	5.9
36	Nevada	5.7
37	Connecticut	5.1
38	Utah	4.9
39	Florida	4.8
39	Ohio	4.8
41	Kansas	4.5
42	Delaware	4.3
43	California	3.4
43	New Jersey	3.4
45	South Carolina	3.1
46	Arkansas	1.7
47	Pennsylvania	1.6
48	Hawaii	0.0
48	Rhode Island	0.0
48	Vermont	0.0
	District of Columbia	0.0

Source: CQ Press using data from United States Coast Guard
   "Boating Statistics 2018" (www.uscgboating.org/statistics/accident_statistics.php)
*Alcohol involvement in a boating accident includes any accident in which alcoholic beverages are consumed in the boat and the investigating official has determined that the operator was impaired or affected while operating the boat.

Railroad Accidents and Incidents in 2018

National Total = 11,704*

ALPHA ORDER

RANK	STATE	ACCIDENTS	% of USA
15	Alabama	206	1.8%
42	Alaska	55	0.5%
35	Arizona	99	0.8%
27	Arkansas	147	1.3%
2	California	954	8.2%
22	Colorado	176	1.5%
25	Connecticut	164	1.4%
37	Delaware	79	0.7%
7	Florida	394	3.4%
9	Georgia	322	2.8%
50	Hawaii	0	0.0%
43	Idaho	45	0.4%
3	Illinois	859	7.3%
8	Indiana	355	3.0%
26	Iowa	148	1.3%
23	Kansas	172	1.5%
32	Kentucky	123	1.1%
11	Louisiana	250	2.1%
48	Maine	17	0.1%
20	Maryland	181	1.5%
12	Massachusetts	219	1.9%
24	Michigan	167	1.4%
21	Minnesota	180	1.5%
33	Mississippi	114	1.0%
14	Missouri	214	1.8%
34	Montana	105	0.9%
18	Nebraska	189	1.6%
45	Nevada	31	0.3%
49	New Hampshire	1	0.0%
5	New Jersey	744	6.4%
39	New Mexico	71	0.6%
1	New York	1,316	11.2%
18	North Carolina	189	1.6%
41	North Dakota	59	0.5%
10	Ohio	293	2.5%
29	Oklahoma	127	1.1%
29	Oregon	127	1.1%
6	Pennsylvania	649	5.5%
44	Rhode Island	33	0.3%
31	South Carolina	125	1.1%
47	South Dakota	24	0.2%
16	Tennessee	196	1.7%
3	Texas	859	7.3%
36	Utah	81	0.7%
46	Vermont	28	0.2%
17	Virginia	194	1.7%
13	Washington	217	1.9%
37	West Virginia	79	0.7%
28	Wisconsin	138	1.2%
40	Wyoming	62	0.5%

RANK ORDER

RANK	STATE	ACCIDENTS	% of USA
1	New York	1,316	11.2%
2	California	954	8.2%
3	Illinois	859	7.3%
3	Texas	859	7.3%
5	New Jersey	744	6.4%
6	Pennsylvania	649	5.5%
7	Florida	394	3.4%
8	Indiana	355	3.0%
9	Georgia	322	2.8%
10	Ohio	293	2.5%
11	Louisiana	250	2.1%
12	Massachusetts	219	1.9%
13	Washington	217	1.9%
14	Missouri	214	1.8%
15	Alabama	206	1.8%
16	Tennessee	196	1.7%
17	Virginia	194	1.7%
18	Nebraska	189	1.6%
18	North Carolina	189	1.6%
20	Maryland	181	1.5%
21	Minnesota	180	1.5%
22	Colorado	176	1.5%
23	Kansas	172	1.5%
24	Michigan	167	1.4%
25	Connecticut	164	1.4%
26	Iowa	148	1.3%
27	Arkansas	147	1.3%
28	Wisconsin	138	1.2%
29	Oklahoma	127	1.1%
29	Oregon	127	1.1%
31	South Carolina	125	1.1%
32	Kentucky	123	1.1%
33	Mississippi	114	1.0%
34	Montana	105	0.9%
35	Arizona	99	0.8%
36	Utah	81	0.7%
37	Delaware	79	0.7%
37	West Virginia	79	0.7%
39	New Mexico	71	0.6%
40	Wyoming	62	0.5%
41	North Dakota	59	0.5%
42	Alaska	55	0.5%
43	Idaho	45	0.4%
44	Rhode Island	33	0.3%
45	Nevada	31	0.3%
46	Vermont	28	0.2%
47	South Dakota	24	0.2%
48	Maine	17	0.1%
49	New Hampshire	1	0.0%
50	Hawaii	0	0.0%
	District of Columbia	127	1.1%

Source: U.S. Department of Transportation, Federal Railroad Administration, Office of Safety Analysis
"Railroad Accidents and Incidents" (Table 1.12, https://safetydata.fra.dot.gov/OfficeofSafety/Default.aspx)
*Accidents or incidents include all events reportable to the U.S. Department of Transportation. These include train accidents causing damage above an established threshold; highway-rail grade crossing incidents involving impact between railroad equipment and highway users at crossings; and all other reportable incidents that cause a fatality or injury to any person or an occupational illness to a railroad employee. There were 831 fatalities involving railroads.

Railroad Mileage Operated in 2017

National Total = 136,898 Miles of Railroad*

ALPHA ORDER

RANK	STATE	MILES	% of USA
15	Alabama	3,272	2.4%
46	Alaska	506	0.4%
36	Arizona	1,820	1.3%
26	Arkansas	2,505	1.8%
5	California	4,828	3.5%
28	Colorado	2,427	1.8%
45	Connecticut	522	0.4%
48	Delaware	243	0.2%
23	Florida	2,851	2.1%
7	Georgia	4,607	3.4%
50	Hawaii	0	0.0%
37	Idaho	1,729	1.3%
2	Illinois	7,151	5.2%
11	Indiana	3,786	2.8%
10	Iowa	3,834	2.8%
6	Kansas	4,675	3.4%
24	Kentucky	2,624	1.9%
22	Louisiana	2,940	2.1%
40	Maine	1,077	0.8%
43	Maryland	769	0.6%
41	Massachusetts	1,057	0.8%
29	Michigan	2,417	1.8%
8	Minnesota	4,258	3.1%
27	Mississippi	2,455	1.8%
9	Missouri	3,862	2.8%
12	Montana	3,719	2.7%
20	Nebraska	3,117	2.3%
39	Nevada	1,193	0.9%
47	New Hampshire	354	0.3%
42	New Jersey	952	0.7%
35	New Mexico	1,879	1.4%
14	New York	3,279	2.4%
17	North Carolina	3,161	2.3%
13	North Dakota	3,287	2.4%
3	Ohio	5,132	3.7%
18	Oklahoma	3,158	2.3%
30	Oregon	2,382	1.7%
4	Pennsylvania	5,130	3.7%
49	Rhode Island	58	0.0%
31	South Carolina	2,278	1.7%
33	South Dakota	2,029	1.5%
25	Tennessee	2,552	1.9%
1	Texas	10,506	7.7%
38	Utah	1,386	1.0%
44	Vermont	578	0.4%
19	Virginia	3,141	2.3%
21	Washington	3,032	2.2%
32	West Virginia	2,214	1.6%
16	Wisconsin	3,253	2.4%
34	Wyoming	1,890	1.4%

RANK ORDER

RANK	STATE	MILES	% of USA
1	Texas	10,506	7.7%
2	Illinois	7,151	5.2%
3	Ohio	5,132	3.7%
4	Pennsylvania	5,130	3.7%
5	California	4,828	3.5%
6	Kansas	4,675	3.4%
7	Georgia	4,607	3.4%
8	Minnesota	4,258	3.1%
9	Missouri	3,862	2.8%
10	Iowa	3,834	2.8%
11	Indiana	3,786	2.8%
12	Montana	3,719	2.7%
13	North Dakota	3,287	2.4%
14	New York	3,279	2.4%
15	Alabama	3,272	2.4%
16	Wisconsin	3,253	2.4%
17	North Carolina	3,161	2.3%
18	Oklahoma	3,158	2.3%
19	Virginia	3,141	2.3%
20	Nebraska	3,117	2.3%
21	Washington	3,032	2.2%
22	Louisiana	2,940	2.1%
23	Florida	2,851	2.1%
24	Kentucky	2,624	1.9%
25	Tennessee	2,552	1.9%
26	Arkansas	2,505	1.8%
27	Mississippi	2,455	1.8%
28	Colorado	2,427	1.8%
29	Michigan	2,417	1.8%
30	Oregon	2,382	1.7%
31	South Carolina	2,278	1.7%
32	West Virginia	2,214	1.6%
33	South Dakota	2,029	1.5%
34	Wyoming	1,890	1.4%
35	New Mexico	1,879	1.4%
36	Arizona	1,820	1.3%
37	Idaho	1,729	1.3%
38	Utah	1,386	1.0%
39	Nevada	1,193	0.9%
40	Maine	1,077	0.8%
41	Massachusetts	1,057	0.8%
42	New Jersey	952	0.7%
43	Maryland	769	0.6%
44	Vermont	578	0.4%
45	Connecticut	522	0.4%
46	Alaska	506	0.4%
47	New Hampshire	354	0.3%
48	Delaware	243	0.2%
49	Rhode Island	58	0.0%
50	Hawaii	0	0.0%
	District of Columbia	22	0.0%

Source: Association of American Railroads
   "Railroads and States" (https://www.aar.org/data-center/railroads-states)
*Includes Class I and non-Class I miles. Excludes trackage rights. Synonymous with route-miles, so that a mile of single track
is counted the same as a mile of double track.

Sources

ACT, Inc.
500 ACT Drive, P.O. Box 168
Iowa City, IA 52243-0168
319-337-1000
www.act.org

Administration for Children and Families
U.S. Department of Health and Human Services
330 C Street, SW
Washington, DC 20201
202-401-9215
www.acf.hhs.gov

American Cancer Society, Inc.
250 Williams Street, NW
Atlanta, GA 30303
800-227-2345
www.cancer.org

American Hospital Association
155 N. Wacker Drive
Chicago, IL 60606
312-422-3000
www.aha.org

Association of American Railroads
425 Third Street, SW, Suite 1000
Washington, DC 20024
202-639-2100
www.aar.org

Bureau of Economic Analysis
U.S. Department of Commerce
4600 Silver Hill Road
Washington, DC 20233
301-278-9004
www.bea.gov

Bureau of Justice Statistics
U.S. Department of Justice
810 Seventh Street, NW
Washington, DC 20531
202-307-0765
www.bjs.gov

Bureau of Labor Statistics
U.S. Department of Labor
2 Massachusetts Avenue, NE
Washington, DC 20212-0001
202-691-5200
www.bls.gov

Bureau of Transportation Statistics
U.S. Department of Transportation
1200 New Jersey Avenue, SE
Washington, DC 20590
800-853-1351
www.bts.gov

Census Bureau
4600 Silver Hill Road
Washington, DC 20233-0001
800-923-8282
www.census.gov

Centers for Disease Control and Prevention
1600 Clifton Road
Atlanta, GA 30329-4027
800-232-4636
www.cdc.gov

Centers for Medicare and Medicaid Services
7500 Security Boulevard
Baltimore, MD 21244-1850
877-267-2323
www.cms.gov

Economic Research Service
U.S. Department of Agriculture
1400 Independence Avenue, SW
Mail Stop 1800
Washington, DC 20250-0002
202-694-5139
www.ers.usda.gov

Energy Information Administration
U.S. Department of Energy
1000 Independence Avenue, SW
Washington, DC 20585
202-586-8800
www.eia.gov

Environmental Protection Agency
Ariel Rios Building
1200 Pennsylvania Avenue, NW
Washington, DC 20460
202-272-0167
www.epa.gov

Federal Bureau of Investigation
J Edgar Hoover Building
935 Pennsylvania Avenue, NW
Washington, DC 20535-0001
202-324-3000
www.fbi.gov

Federal Highway Administration
U.S. Department of Transportation
1200 New Jersey Avenue, SE
Washington, DC 20590
202-366-4000
www.fhwa.dot.gov

Federation of Tax Administrators
444 North Capitol Street, NW, Suite 348
Washington, DC 20001
202-624-5890
www.taxadmin.org

Food and Nutrition Service
U.S. Department of Agriculture
1320 Braddock Place
Alexandria, VA 22314
703-305-2062
www.fns.usda.gov

General Services Administration
1800 F Street, NW
Washington, DC 20405
844-472-4111
www.gsa.gov

Health Resources and Services Administration
5600 Fishers Lane
Rockville, MD 20857
301-443-3376
www.hrsa.gov

Institute of Museum and Library Services
955 L'Enfant Plaza North, SW, Suite 4000
Washington, DC 20024-2135
202-653-4657
www.imls.gov

Internal Revenue Service
U.S. Department of the Treasury
1111 Constitution Avenue, NW
Washington, DC 20224
202-283-1710
www.irs.gov

Medical Expenditure Panel Survey
Agency for Healthcare Research and Quality
5600 Fishers Lane
Rockville, MD 20857
301-427-1364
www.meps.ahrq.gov

National Agricultural Statistics Service
1400 Independence Avenue, SW
Washington, DC 20250
800-727-9540
www.nass.usda.gov

National Assembly of State Arts Agencies
1200 18th Street, NW, Suite 1100
Washington, DC 20036
202-347-6352
www.nasaa-arts.org

National Center for Education Statistics
U.S. Department of Education
550 12th Street, SW
Washington, DC 20202
202-403-5551
https://nces.ed.gov/

National Center for Health Statistics
U.S. Department of Health and Human Services
3311 Toledo Road
Hyattsville, MD 20782
800-232-4636
www.cdc.gov/nchs/

National Conference of State Legislatures
7700 E. First Place
Denver, CO 80230
303-364-7700
www.ncsl.org

National Education Association
1201 16th Street, NW
Washington, DC 20036-3290
202-833-4000
www.nea.org

National Highway Traffic Safety Administration
1200 New Jersey Avenue, SE
Washington, DC 20590
888-327-4236
www.nhtsa.gov

National Institute on Alcohol Abuse and Alcoholism
5635 Fishers Lane, MSC 9304
Bethesda, MD 20892-9304
301-443-3860
www.niaaa.nih.gov

National Oceanic & Atmospheric Administration
U.S. Department of Commerce
1401 Constitution Avenue, NW, Room 5128
Washington, DC 20230
202-482-2000
www.noaa.gov

Project on Student Debt
Institute for College Access and Success
1212 Broadway, Suite 1100
Oakland, CA 94612
510-318-7900
https://ticas.org/posd/home

Social Security Administration
Office of Public Inquiries
1100 West High Rise
6401 Security Boulevard
Baltimore, MD 21235
800-772-1213 (information)
www.ssa.gov

Storm Prediction Center
National Weather Service
120 David Boren Boulevard
Norman, OK 73072
405-325-3095
www.spc.noaa.gov

Tax Foundation
1325 G Street, NW, Suite 950
Washington, DC 20005
202-464-6200
www.taxfoundation.org

U.S. Department of Defense
Office of Public Affairs
1400 Defense Pentagon
Washington, DC 20301-1400
703-571-3343
www.defense.gov

U.S. Department of Veterans Affairs
810 Vermont Avenue, NW
Washington, DC 20420
800-827-1000
www.va.gov

U.S. Geological Survey
12201 Sunrise Valley Drive
Reston, VA 20192
888-275-8747
www.usgs.gov

USAspending.gov
U.S. Department of the Treasury
Bureau of Fiscal Services
3201 Pennsy Drive, Building E
Landover, MD 20785

Index